INVESTIGATION OF
THE ASSASSINATION OF PRESIDENT JOHN F. KENNEDY

HEARINGS

Before the President's Commission on the Assassination of President Kennedy

PURSUANT TO EXECUTIVE ORDER 11130, an Executive order creating a Commission to ascertain, evaluate, and report upon the facts relating to the assassination of the late President John F. Kennedy and the subsequent violent death of the man charged with the assassination and S.J. RES. 137, 88TH CONGRESS, a concurrent resolution conferring upon the Commission the power to administer oaths and affirmations, examine witnesses, receive evidence, and issue subpenas

EXHIBITS
1513 TO 1975

Volume
XXIII

UNITED STATES GOVERNMENT PRINTING OFFICE
WASHINGTON, D.C.

U.S. GOVERNMENT PRINTING OFFICE, WASHINGTON: 1964

For sale in complete sets by the Superintendent of Documents, U.S. Government Printing Office
Washington, D.C., 20402

PRESIDENT'S COMMISSION
ON THE
ASSASSINATION OF PRESIDENT KENNEDY

CHIEF JUSTICE EARL WARREN, *Chairman*

SENATOR RICHARD B. RUSSELL
SENATOR JOHN SHERMAN COOPER
REPRESENTATIVE HALE BOGGS
REPRESENTATIVE GERALD R. FORD
MR. ALLEN W. DULLES
MR. JOHN J. McCLOY

J. LEE RANKIN, *General Counsel*

Assistant Counsel

FRANCIS W. H. ADAMS
JOSEPH A. BALL
DAVID W. BELIN
WILLIAM T. COLEMAN, JR.
MELVIN ARON EISENBERG
BURT W. GRIFFIN
LEON D. HUBERT, JR.
ALBERT E. JENNER, JR.
WESLEY J. LIEBELER
NORMAN REDLICH
W. DAVID SLAWSON
ARLEN SPECTER
SAMUEL A. STERN
HOWARD P. WILLENS*

Staff Members

PHILLIP BARSON
EDWARD A. CONROY
JOHN HART ELY
ALFRED GOLDBERG
MURRAY J. LAULICHT
ARTHUR MARMOR
RICHARD M. MOSK
JOHN J. O'BRIEN
STUART POLLAK
ALFREDDA SCOBEY
CHARLES N. SHAFFER, JR.

Biographical information on the Commissioners and the staff can be found in the Commission's *Report*.

*Mr. Willens also acted as liaison between the Commission and the Department of Justice.

Contents

Commission Exhibit No. | *Page*

Commission Exhibit No. | *Page*

748-379 O—64—vol. XXIII——2

1

Date November 25, 1963

MRS. PAUL CALGROVE was interviewed at 6829 Peerless Steet, Apartment 3. MRS. CALGROVE advised that she is also known as BEATRICE CALGROVE and has the theatrical stage name of NAJADA. She stated she is presently residing at 2906 Inez Street, Pasadena, Texas; however, she is moving within two days to 6825 Peerless Street, Apartment 3, Houston. She gave her age as 23, stating she was born February 1, 1940, at El Ranchito, Texas. She advised as follows:

She went to Dallas, Texas, to the Carrousel Club as a featured exotic dancer in the winter of 1961 and worked for JACK RUBY about six months under the name of NAJADA.

She had an argument with RUBY at the bar of the Carrousel about New Years Eve, 1961, about the confused manner in which RUBY carried on his entertainment business. He slapped her and she then spoke to a Lieutenant or Captain of the Dallas Police Department Vice Squad who was in the club at the time, stating she wanted to press charges against RUBY. In the presenc of RUBY, the officer laughed at her and told her she was crazy; she then took her problem to JACK COLE, American Guild of Variety Artists (AGVA) representative and booking agent, who said the problem was not in his jurisdiction. From time to time she noticed numerous police officers enter the Carrousel Club and go to RUEY's office, after which they would be observed leaving the club with bottles of whiskey under their arm.

She recalled that one dancer, CATHY KAY, white female, about 23, blond headed, from England, was given a car by RUEY and he went with her a period of time. She stated KAY could be traced by JACK COLE of AGVA.

RUEY had a so-called mistress, who was not employed at the club but who came and went at will and frequented the club. She was described as white female, light brown hair, cut long in a pony tail, five feet five inches tall, 115 pounds, late twenties, reportedly a secretary in Dallas, Texas, that RUEY claimed he had been keeping for some five to six years. RUEY failed to ever disclose this woman's identity.

On 11/25/63 at Houston, Texas File # HO 44-939

by SA FRANK M. IVEY & CLIFTON BROWNING, JR.: mem Date dictated 11/25/63

533

COMMISSION EXHIBIT No. 1513

2

HO 44-939

She said that the husband of her former landlady, in Dallas, had been LEROY HULSE, 2515 Maple Street, and had been a uniformed patrolman on the Dallas Police Department. She said that HULSE told her several times of having bounced numerous people for the Vegas Club in Dallas, run by RUBY, and stated HULSE had possibly been employed on a part time basis by the Vegas Club as a bouncer.

534

COMMISSION EXHIBIT No. 1513—Continued

FD-302 (Rev. -25-60) FEDERAL BUREAU OF INVESTIGATION

1. Date November 26, 1963

FRANK FERRARO, 53 Parmelee Street, New Haven, Connecticut, a bus driver for Cousins Bus Sales, 500 Washington Avenue, North Haven, Connecticut, advised the following:

He was unemployed and temporarily in Dallas, Texas, about August, 1962, and recalled stopping in the Carousel Club, Dallas, Texas, operated by JACK RUBY. He had little money and RUBY offered him room and board in return for small odd jobs. He did work as handy man, and received small and irregular pay.

FERRARO described RUBY as a likeable person, but he would become angry very quick and had a violent temper. To the best of his knowledge RUBY never made any statements regarding politics, political philosophies or any politicians. He never heard RUBY express any opinion concerning any foreign governments or foreign causes.

FERRARO had never heard of OSWALD being in the Club Carousel or having any contact with RUBY.

FERRARO described the main interest of RUBY as being women. He said that RUBY was a very aggressive "wolf" but he never had a steady girl, and he never dated any of the help. To his knowledge there were no illegal activities in businesses operated by RUBY, that is in way of prostitution, narcotics, gambling, etc.

He had heard from a negro carpenter, name unknown, who was working for RUBY at that time, that RUBY, while in Chicago, Illinois, was associated with a union and had been entrusted with $50,000. RUBY allegedly skipped with the money and came to Dallas, Texas, where he started his present business.

FERRARO named the following as associates of RUBY: RALPH (LNU), operator of the Bull Pen Restaurant, Arlington, Texas; FRANK (LNU), White, male, Italian, in oil business, Dallas, Texas; HARRY (RED) LEFKOWITZ, who sold novelties in stall in the Merchandise Mart, Dallas, Texas.

On 11/25/63 at North Haven, Connecticut File # NH 44-140

by SA THOMAS L. SHEER and SA ROBERT E. ROBERTSON/bss Date dictated 11/25/63

546

2.
NH 44-140

FERRARO stated that on a Tuesday night, during September, 1962, he had become involved in an argument in the Horse Shoe Bar, Dallas, Texas, located near the Carousel Club. He returned to the Club Carousel where he changed his shirt and coat. At that time RUBY warned FERRARO not to get in any fight as the operator was his friend. FERRARO told RUBY to mind his own business.

RUBY became angry, and later followed FERRARO to the Lasso Club located near by. At the Lasso Club, RUBY walked in and told FERRARO not to threaten him or cause his friends any trouble. RUBY then struck FERRARO three or four times with brass knuckles. FERRARO received an open wound over his left eye and he had to go to the Parkland Hospital for emergency treatment.

JOHN WILSON, Attorney, Dallas, Texas, witnessed this fight and advised FERRARO to bring suit against RUBY. FERRARO decided later not to press charges concerning this matter, as RUBY gave him money to pay the hospital bill. FERRARO said he quit a few days later and left Dallas and has had no contact with RUBY since that date.

547

FD-302 (Rev. 1-25-60)

FEDERAL BUREAU OF INVESTIGATION

1

Date November 26, 1963

HERBERT CHARLES DAVID KELLY, residence 7219 Freret Street, was interviewed at his home. At the outset of the interview KELLY was advised of the identity of interviewing Agents at which time he voluntarily furnished the following information:

KELLY advised he was born April 23, 1923, in Brooklyn, New York, and he is a veteran of World War II having been in the United States Air Force. He said he was honorably discharged December 2, 1945 and his Air Force Serial Number is 32726888. KELLY said he receives a disability pension because of a severe ulcer condition which developed during his period of Air Force service.

KELLY advised that since his discharge from the service he has been in the food service field, managing restaurants, country clubs, private clubs and the like. He stated that he went to Dallas in about 1956 and worked in the Dallas area in the food service field until 1959 or 1960 when he was hospitalized in the Veterans Hospital in Dallas because of a condition of paralysis. He stated that he remained in the Veterans Hospital in Dallas for a period of about a year and around 1961 or 1962 he came to New Orleans, where he found employment as manager of the Playboy Club in New Orleans.

He stated he resided at 7000 Rawlins Street, in Dallas, and that while employed as Assistant Food Director at Titches Department Store, he met JACK LEON RUBY in 1959 through an individual known as BIG JIM, later employed as maitre d' at the Soverign Club which was then a membership supper club operated by RUBY at the site of the present Carousel Club. He advised that he was employed by RUBY as manager of the kitchen and the food service at the Soverign Club and in connection with this employment hoped to obtain a financial interest in the club. He stated that it was his impression that entertainers BRECK WALL and JOE PETERSON, an entertainment team playing at the Soverign Club, had a financial interest in the club. He advised that this team is currently playing at the Adolphus Hotel

On 11/26/63 New Orleans, Louisiana File # NO 44-2064

by SA FURMAN G. BOGGAN and SA LAWRENCE M. SHEARER :gas Date dictated 11/26/63

549

2

NO 44-2064
FGB,LMS:gas

in a show called "Bottoms Up". He advised that another individual, possibly RUBY's closest friend, an individual named PAUL, about 60 years of age, short, medium build, of Jewish extraction, and a banker possibly associated with the Republic National Bank, may have had a financial interest in the club in that RUBY occasionally obtained operating funds from this individual. This individual also counter-signed payroll checks of the club drawn on the Republic National Bank. He advised that EDWARD CASTRO, a busboy, was employed at the Soverign Club during the time and after KELLY was there and that this individual's father is chef at the Dallas City Club. He stated he belives that LEO (LNU), bartender at the Soverign Club had been an associate and acquaintance of RUBY for a number of years. He advised he belives that ABE WEINSTEIN, operator of the Colony Club, located near the Soverign Club, is well acquainted with RUBY even though a competitor in the supper club business. KELLY stated he was of the opinion that RUBY had no close friends although he associated with many individuals. He advised that RUBY was particularly friendly with law enforcement officers and went out of his way to greet officers where ever he met them. KELLY advised he was unable to identify any officer by name whom he observed in the company of RUBY. He stated that law enforcement officers, both plainclothes and uniformed police and deputy sheriffs, frequently came to the Soverign Club to converse with RUBY and on numerous occasions after receiving a telephone call RUBY would go to the police station, not too far distance from the Soverign Club.

With regard to RUBY's association with police officers in Dallas, KELLY stated that during 1959 when he was associated with RUBY, each Sunday night RUBY had what was termed "Celebrity Night" when he would endeavor to obtain name entertainers appearing in Dallas to come to the Soverign Club as his guests and hoped they would provide free entertainment. KELLY stated that each Sunday

550

night RUBY would also entertain as many as eight law enforcement officers, furnishing them gratis expensive dinners and drinks. He said he complained on several occasions to RUBY explaining that the entertainment of these law enforcement officers was very expensive and hard on the club finances. He said he pointed out that the latter did not have to cull the favor of the law enforcement officers in Dallas as he was not engaging in any illegal activities. KELLY said RUBY would reply in effect that he wanted to do this as he liked law enfofcement officers and these men did not make salarys which would enable them to have this kind of entertainment.

KELLY described RUBY as being hot tempered and very impulsive. In explaining this KELLY said that RUBY would become angered over some incident and hit another person not thinking of the consequences of his act or developments which might result from these acts. He stated that on one occasion he hit KEITH WILLIAMS, a promoter with the Williams Oil Company, because WILLIAMS had given him a $60.00 worthless check when WILLIAMS was in the club one evening with two other oil men. KELLY stated that on one occasion JOE PETERSON, one of the two entertainers who may have had an interest in the club, insisted to RUBY that he be allowed to examine the club finance records since he did not believe he was getting a fair shake. RUBY became extremely angry and hit PETERSON. He advised that RUBY was not the brooding type who would plan an act of violence against another individual, nor was he the type who would hold a grudge subsequent to such an incident.

KELLY stated that RUBY's hot temper is well known among RUBY's associates and in fact he had heard about this prior to the time he became associated with RUBY. He stated that he went so far as to purchase his own sidearm which he retained for a short time after going to work for

551

RUBY and he was guarded in his comments to RUBY during the earlier period of his association with RUBY because he did not want to incur RUBY's anger. KELLY said he since found out that he could actually argue with RUBY over differences of opinion in the operation of the business without RUBY loosing his temper.

In this regard KELLY stated that RUBY was extremely sensitive about his Jewish background and resented derogatory remarks concerning Jews. He said he felt RUBY had an extreme persecution complex and thought that everybody was against him. He stated that RUBY resented anyone using personal vulgarities when addressing RUBY.

KELLY stated that during his association with RUBY the latter had a .38 caliber snub-nose Smith & Wesson revolver which was hammerless. He said he learned this because RUBY showed it to him saying it was the very latest thing and it could actually be fired from ones coat pocket because it did not have a hammer. KELLY said he did not believe RUBY ever carried this revolver on his person but had it for protection in transporting the club's cash receipts each night.

In this regard, KELLY said that it was RUBY's habit to close up the Soverign Club and then go to the Vegas Club carrying the Soverign Club cash receipts in a small valise and usually this revolver was in the valise with the cash. He said that many times he would go with RUBY to the Vegas Club and stay with him until RUBY closed the Vegas Club each night. RUBY would then take the cash receipts of both clubs in the valise to his home and at this time RUBY was living in an apartment with his sister who lives in Dallas.

552

With regard to RUBY's personal habits, KELLY said RUBY did not use tobacco and seldom used intoxicants, however, on occasion he would have several highballs. He said that RUBY was extremely well dressed and neat and loved to eat. He said on many occasions he had fixed RUBY a steak early in the evening and RUBY would be hungry later before the club closed and would want another one. He stated there was no indication that RUBY was a gambler or associated with hoodlum type characters nor was he involved in prostitution activities. He advised that on infreqent occasions he would entertain female companions in his apartment. In this regard KELLY did not believe RUBY had any homosexual tendencies although there had been thought from time to time among people with whom KELLY was in contact that RUBY might be gay. KELLY said he did feel that RUBY was probably under sexed, but he did not think RUBY had homosexual tendencies.

With regard to the Vegas Club, KELLY said RUBY had employed a retired policeman as the bouncer at that club. KELLY did not know this individual's name.

With regard to the extent of RUBY's contacts with municipal employees associated with RUBY, KELLY said he knew of no city officials who were ever entertained by RUBY or friendly with him, claiming that RUBY was a "police buff" who had a natural likeness for police officers. He desired to be friendly with men in this profession and RUBY's associations were restricted to law enforcement officers and no other municipal officials. KELLY stated that RUBY was extremely desirious of making as much money as he could and actually "worshiped a dollar". He said that RUBY liked to hold on to his money and in many instances would not pay his employees each weekend but would sometimes wait as late as the following Wednesday before issuing weekly pay checks. KELLY could not reconcile this trait

553

on the part of RUBY with the latter's generosity in dealing with law enforcement officers. KELLY said RUBY had no interest in current affairs and never kept abreat of these through reading daily newspapers and periodicals. He said RUBY would not be capable of discussing such current affairs as United States interest in Viet Nam or the nation's missle program. He said RUBY's only interest in reading Dallas newspapers was to determine all local crime news.

KELLY stated that he did not consider RUBY to be a patriotic person yet on the other hand RUBY was not sympathetic to Communism and was in fact very much a capitolist in that he seemed interested only in financial gain. He said that as a result of RUBY's lack of interest in current affairs, RUBY had no political interest. KELLY said based on his knowledge of RUBY's thinking on current affairs it was inconceivable to him that RUBY would have shot LEE HARVEY OSWALD because the latter had assassinated the president. KELLY said that on the contrary he believed that RUBY shot OSWALD on a impulse and any motive would be that RUBY resented OSWALD having killed Dallas policeman TIPPIT.

With regard to RUBY's views concerning President KENNEDY, KELLY recalled that in 1959 when KENNEDY was campaigning in Texas, he went with RUBY as did many Dallas citizens to the Dallas airport to see President KENNEDY. KELLY recalled that RUBY commented in effect after seeing KENNEDY and listening to his speech, that KENNEDY was young and vigorous and the type of president this country needed. KELLY said this is the only comment he ever heard RUBY make about President KENNEDY.

Concerning RUBY's background, KELLY stated that in conversations with RUBY the latter mentioned he had been in Dallas about 15 years having come to Dallas from the Chicago area. From various comments made by RUBY, KELLY gathered

554

7

NO 44-2064
FGB,LMS:gas

that RUBY may have been active in union work in the Chicago area and may have had to leave Chicago because of some difficulty arising out of this union work, although KELLY could recall no specific comments made by RUBY in this regard.

With regard to RUBY's family, KELLY could recall that on one occasion RUBY remarked that he had an older brother in Chicago who was quite wealthy. Later when the club was undergoing a financial crises, KELLY sggested to RUBY that the latter could borrow money from his older brother in Chicago and RUBY replied that he could not do so as he already owed this brother too much money.

With regard to RUBY's financial condition, KELLY believed that during the period he was associated with RUBY the latter may have had some difficulty with the United States Internal Revenue Service as he believed RUBY had to go to Internal Revenue Service on two different occasions concerning his income taxes.

After coming to New Orleans KELLY advised he had no further contact with RUBY until about the middle of October, 1963, when he contacted RUBY at the Carousel Club in Dallas. He stated the purpose of this contact was to determine whether or not he could purchase restaurant fixtures and equipment from RUBY to be used in a restaurant venture KELLY was then considering in Dallas. He advised that no fixtures were available from RUBY and no restaurant was opened.

With regard to any possible association between RUB and LEE HARVEY OSWALD, KELLY said he had never heard RUBY mention this individual and he had never seen OSWALD in the Soverign Club, the Vegas Club, or in the company of RUBY. KELLY stated that because of RUBY's lack of interest in politics he did not think RUBY would have been compatable with OSWALD as KELLY has read news accounts that OSWALD was politically minded and was a Marxist and sympathetic to Communist Cuba.

555

COMMISSION EXHIBIT No. 1515—Continued

DL 44-1639
JTK:cv
1

The following investigation was conducted by SA JOHN T. KESLER:

AT HOUSTON, TEXAS

HERMAN ROSE, former porter of JACK RUBY, Silverspur Lounge, Dallas, Texas, from 1947 through 1950, was interviewed on November 25, 1963. ROSE described RUBY as a high-tempered individual and not known to be affiliated with any subversive organizations. RUBY reportedly was from Detroit or Chicago before coming to Dallas. RUBY was friendly with the local Police Department, Dallas, but no specific individuals were named.

RUBY, in addition to operating the Silverspur Lounge, Dallas, sold costume jewelry at discount rates.

556

COMMISSION EXHIBIT No. 1516

FD-302 (Rev. 3-3-59)

FEDERAL BUREAU OF INVESTIGATION

Date 11/24/63

1

BENNY H. BICKERS, 1031 Kessler Parkway, Dallas, who has owned and operated night clubs in the Dallas area for the past 20 years, advised from 1953 to 1962 he owned and operated the University Club approximately one block from the Carousel Club which is owned by JACK RUBY.

BICKERS has known RUBY for approximatly 20 years at which time RUBY came to Dallas from Chicago where RUBY had connections with several clubs. At the time RUBY came to Dallas he was known as JACK RUBENSTEIN. On several occasions RUBY came to the University Club and discussed with BICKERS about buying the University Club but BICKERS believed that RUBY was just "snooping" to see who was at the club and to see if he was doing any business. In the past BICKERS has known of numerous occasions where RUBY could not pay the girls who were stripping at the club, his master of ceremonies and his managers, and when they would ask for the pay RUBY would get mad and beat them up.

BICKERS could not recall the names of the employees who had trouble with RUBY, as most were entertainers who were only in Dallas, employed at the Carousel for one or two weeks at a time. After these occurrences BICKERS told RUBY that he was barred from the University Club and did not want him at the University Club at any time.

BICKERS stated it was common knowledge that RUBY spent time almost every day at the Dallas Police Department and was furnishing information to several Dallas policemen regarding the operations of other clubs in Dallas. For this reason when RUBY was arrested for violation in his club he was released without any conviction.

BICKERS advised his opinion of RUBY was that he was a publicity hound and attempted to be a hoodlum but did not know how and enjoyed taking advantage of girls and people employed by him when he beat them up, knowing they could do nothing about it

on 11/24/63 at Dallas, Texas File # DL 44-1639

by Special Agents WILL HAYDEN GRIFFIN & JAMES C. KENNEDY/atd Date dictated 11/23/63

5 77

COMMISSION EXHIBIT No. 1517

FD-302 (Rev. 3-3-59)

FEDERAL BUREAU OF INVESTIGATION

Date 11/25/63

1

ROGER D. TESCH, Drivers and Vehicle Records, Texas Department of Public Safety, Austin, Texas, telephonically furnished the following information regarding one JACK RUBY:

RUBY applied for Texas drivers license and passed examination on March 21, 1950, at Dallas, Texas. The Texas operators license was issued to RUBY on March 30, 1950. Presently RUBY has Texas operators license number 3098293, which license expires October 10, 1964. RUBY's current address as of February 28, 1963, was 3929 Rawlins, Dallas, Texas. The file reflects RUBY had an Illinois drivers license in 1947. RUBY is described as a white male born March 25, 1911, height 5' 9", weight 175, brown hair, brown eyes.

RUBY has had the following residences in Dallas, Texas, according to drivers license records:

1. 1950, 1717 South Ervay, Dallas, Texas;
2. April 21, 1950 - February 12, 1959, 4160 Hawthorne, Dallas, Texas;
3. June 13, 1961, 4727 Homer Street, Dallas, Texas;
4. October 8, 1962, 500 South Marsalis, Dallas, Texas;
5. February 28, 1963, 3929 Rawlins Street, Dallas, Texas.

TESCH furnished the following list of tickets issued to JACK RUBY:

on 11/24/63 at Dallas, Texas File # Dallas 44-1639

by Special Agent THOMAS M. O'MALEY/sl Date dictated 11/24/63

5 82

COMMISSION EXHIBIT No. 1518

Dallas 44-1639
2

Number	Date	Violation	Place	Disposition	Cause, Summons, or Accident No.	Receipt No.	Residence
1	4/21/50	Speeding	Dallas	$10 fine	25594	81669	4160 Hawthorne
2	9/4/50	Accident			84762		"
3	9/4/50	Negligent Collision	Dallas	$10 fine	105699	73646-4	
4	5/22/54	Ran red light	Dallas		7922		4130 Hawthorne
5	12/26/54	Illegal right turn			10446		"
6	9/26/55	Speeding			88331		"
7	1/31/56	Run red light		$3	44668	73656-C	4160 Hawthorne
8	2/13/56	Run red light		$10	49427	77269-C	"
9	2/26/56	Speeding		$10	53574	87681-C	"
10	11/26/56	Run stop sign		$3	21471	34303-C	"
11	12/17/56	Run stop sign		$3	25721	52661-C	"
	1/5/57	Illegal turn			102507		4156 Hawthorne
13	9/4/57	Run red light			267425		"
14	9/1/58	Run red light			505006		4160 Hawthorne
15	11/25/58	Speeding			568126		"
16	12/1/58	Run stop sign			562024		"
17	2/12/59	Illegal turn			599666		"

583

Number	Date	Violation	Place	Disposition	Cause, Summons, or Accident No.	Receipt No.	Residence
18	6/13/61	Negligent collision			181262		4727 Homer
19	10/8/62	Run red light			534888		500 South Marsalis
20	2/28/63	Accident with motor vehicle (MICKY ANN RHODES)			82251		3929 Rawlins

COMMISSION EXHIBIT No. 1518—Continued

DL 44-1639

4

He advised that the following Departmental and mandantory action has been taken against JACK RUBY in regard to the above-listed tickets:

5/21/59 Interviewed by Department of Public Safety, Dallas;

5/29/56 Received six months probation as a result of above interview;

8/10/59 Interview and petition filed against RUBY for being an habitual motor vehicle violator;

12/3/59 Convicted as habitual motor vehicle violator in Corporation Court, Dallas County, Dallas, Texas; put on 12 months probation and at end of probation must pass another motor vehicle examination before license reinstated;

5/16/60 Passed examination and license reinstated.

585

COMMISSION EXHIBIT No. 1518—Continued

FD-302 (Rev. 3-3-59)

FEDERAL BUREAU OF INVESTIGATION

1

Date November 29, 1963

The records of the Merchants State Bank, 5217 Ross, Dallas, reflect the following information:

An account in the name of JACK RUBY, 4727 Homer, Apartment 105, was opened June 26, 1960. RUBY's address was subsequently changed to 3929 Rawlins. This account is small and inactive, with no recent deposits or withdrawals. The only recent entries are service charges of $1.00 per month. The balance at the present time is $35.78.

An account in the name of the Carousel Club, 1312½ Commerce, Dallas, with JACK RUBY listed as the person to draw on this account, was opened on October 12, 1961. A resume of this account reflects the following information:

Date	Deposit	Withdrawal	Balance
9/30/63			$188.73
10/4/63	$ 8.82		197.55
10/10/63		$24.38	173.17
10/10/63	30.26		203.43
11/11/63	33.22		236.65
11/19/63	10.00		246.65
11/20/63		15.00	231.65
11/22/63		31.87	199.78

On July 9, 1958, an account was opened in the name of the Vegas Club, care of JACK RUBY, 3929 Rawlins, Dallas. JACK RUBY was the only person authorized to draw on this account. A resume of this account reflects the following information:

on 11/29/63 at Dallas, Texas File # DL 44-1639

by Special Agents RALPH E. RAWLINGS and EDMOND C. HARDIN/pm 607 Date dictated 11/29/63

COMMISSION EXHIBIT No. 1519

Date	Deposit	Withdrawal	Balance
9/30/63			$210.15
10/9/63		One check	160.15
10/10/63		Two checks	81.44
10/16/63		Three checks	63.91
10/22/63	A deposit minus three checks resulting in balance of		263.91
10/29/63		Four checks	134.44
11/6/63		$50.00	84.44
11/8/63		25.00	59.44
11/11/63	$200.00		259.44
11/12/63		11.65	247.79
11/20/63		25.00	222.79
11/22/63		12.82	209.97
11/25/63		50.00	159.97

Loan records reflect the following addresses for JACK RUBY from 1958 to the present time:

4160 Hawthorne
4727 Homer
11616 Jamestown Road
3508 Oak Lawn
3929 Rawlins

On June 26, 1958, JACK RUBY borrowed $1,148.00 from this bank to be repaid in 18 monthly payments. A lien on a 1956 Oldsmobile secured this loan. Final payment was made on December 8, 1959.

On December 8, 1959, JACK RUBY borrowed $704.00 to be repaid in 12 monthly payments. Final payment was made on January 2, 1961. A lien on a 1956 Oldsmobile secured this loan.

On December 29, 1960, a loan was made to S. D. RUBY, 11616 Jamestown Road, Dallas, in the amount of $3,360.00, with JACK RUBY listed as a co-signer on the note. The loan was repaid in 24 monthly payments with the final installment on March 16, 1962.

On February 14, 1961, JACK RUBY borrowed $636.00, which he repaid in 12 monthly payments, with the last installment on March 9, 1962. Security on this loan was a lien on a 1956 Oldsmobile.

608

On January 31, 1963, JACK RUBY borrowed $1,375.00, giving as security a lien on a 1960 Oldsmobile, vehicle identification No. 607T07749. He has made ten monthly payments of $76.50 each on this loan, with the last payment having been made on November 11, 1963.

On June 1, 1962, JACK RUBY borrowed $410.00 on a short-term basis, which was repaid on July 11, 1962. No security was required on this loan.

On April 27, 1959, JACK RUBY, whose address at that time was 4160 Hawthorne, rented safety deposit box No. 448. MYRTLE CHANCE, no address, was listed as his agent on the safety deposit box record, but her name was revoked as his agent on June 6, 1960. The files reflect RUBY was admitted to the safety deposit box vault on the following dates:

May 7 and 22, 1959
June 2 and 22, 1959
July 1, 9 and 20, 1959
August 21, 1959
September 4 and 21, 1959
October 28, 1959
March 18, 1960
April 12, 1960
November 14, 1960
March 21, 1961

The file reflects no entry after March 21, 1961.

RUBY has no savings account at the Merchants State Bank.

The above records are confidential and will be produced only upon the issuance of a subpoena duces tecum. V. P. SCHUMACHER, President, Merchants State Bank, 5217 Ross, Dallas, Texas, is the proper person to subpoena to produce these records.

609

HO 44-939
DL 44-1639
LAB:eah

AT HOUSTON, TEXAS

1

On November 24, 1963, information was received that JACK RUBY had been a guest of the Sheraton Lincoln Hotel, Houston, Texas, three days prior to the arrival of Governor CONNALLY, date not specified.

The following investigation was conducted by SA LEVERETTE A. BAKER on November 25, 1963:

Folio No. 54280 reflects registration on May 9, 1963, for JACK RUBY, 1312½ Commerce, Dallas, Texas, for "Day Use" only of Room 2608, and charges for unidentifiable local telephone calls. This is the only registration for RUBY located and employees of the hotel acquainted with RUBY state this was his only visit at hotel.

AL DEAN, Sheraton Lincoln, recalls JACK RUBY and stated RUBY's purpose for visit was to contact CANDY BARR, notorious stripper, to give her a dog. DEAN also stated JACK RUBY made a practice of "hustling" bell hops in hotels to get customer referrals to his clubs.

FRANK S..., Bell Captain, Sheraton Lincoln, formerly of Dallas, advised he was acquainted with name JACK RUBY in Dallas and had met him one time many months ago in Houston when he was guest of Sheraton Lincoln Hotel, but denies any knowledge of acquaintances or associates. He denied RUBY made a practice of "hustling" bell hops for customer referrals. He recalls RUBY's trip to Houston in May, 1963, was for the purpose of giving CANDY BARR a dog.

Records of the Sheraton Lincoln Hotel reflect Governor CONNALLY was a guest of the hotel on November 21-22, 1963; however, he was not a guest of the hotel at any time during May, 1963.

6.55

COMMISSION EXHIBIT No. 1520

FD-302 (Rev. 1-25-60)

FEDERAL BUREAU OF INVESTIGATION

1

Date ~~November 25, 1963~~

Mr. AL DEAN, Sheraton-Lincoln Hotel, advised that folio number 54280 reflects on May 9, 1963 one JACK RUBY, 1312½ Commerce, Dallas, Texas, had registered and obtained room number 2608 for "day use" only and charges to this account were for the room and for unidentifiable local telephone calls.

Mr. DEAN advised this is the only registration for RUBY located.

Mr. DEAN advised that Govenor CONNALLY of Texas was a guest of the hotel on November 21-22, 1963, however, he was not a guest of the hotel at any time during May, 1963.

Mr. DEAN stated that JACK RUBY had said the purpose of his visit in May, 1963 was to contact CANDY BARR, a notorious stripper, to give her a dog. He also stated that JACK RUBY made the practice of "hustling" bell hops in hotels to get customer referrals for his clubs.

Mr. DEAN has no further information or knowledge concerning JACK RUBY.

On 11-25-63 at Houston, Texas File # HO 44-939

by SA LEVERETTE A. BAKER:djw 6.56 Date dictated 11-25-63

COMMISSION EXHIBIT No. 1520—Continued

FD-302 (Rev. 1-25-60)

FEDERAL BUREAU OF INVESTIGATION

1

Date 11/26/63

LEON CORNMAN, Branch Manager, American Guild of Variety Artists (AGVA), 1107 Maison Blanch Building, New Orleans, advised that he recalled that he was contacted by a white male who identified himself as JACK RUBY, operator of the Carousel, Dallas, Texas. At this time of contact which was while on Bourbon Street, RUBY was alone and advised CORNMAN that he, RUBY was interested in obtaining the services of JADA (JEANETTE CONFORTO) who was then working at the Sho Bar on Bourbon Street. CORNMAN advised he does not specifically recall the date of contact but it was just three to five days prior to her terminating her contract with the Sho Bar and he has no way to specifically identify this date. He advised that JACK RUBY was alone at this time and he received no information as to his mode of travel to and from New Orleans or where he may have been staying at the time he was in New Orleans. RUBY indicated that in addition to being interested in hiring JADA, he was also interested in any of the show girls who may want to go to work for him in the Carousel in Dallas, Texas.

During this contact JACK RUBY presented one of his business cards for the Carousel which listed the address of the Carousel as corner of Field and Commerce, with telephone number RI 7-2362. On the reverse side of this card RUBY wrote his name in ink "JACK RUBY" with notation "WH 1-5601 home". CORNMAN advised he believed this was the home telephone of RUBY in Dallas, Texas.

Mr. CORNMAN advised he has had no further contact with RUBY nor is he able to identify any of the club owners or entertainers with whom RUBY may have had contact while in New Orleans. CORNMAN suggested that since he understands that JADA did go to work for JACK RUBY a short while after leaving the Sho Bar, he believed the date of contract with the Carousel could be obtained from the Branch Manager of the AGVA, TOM PALMER, 1500 Jackson Street, Room 510, Inter-Urban Building, Dallas, Texas, telephone number RI 2-8292. He believes that this contact would probably be able to give the approximate date that JACK RUBY was in the New Orleans area.

Mr. CORNMAN advised that at this time he has no record by which he could specifically state the date on

On 11/26/63 at New Orleans, Louisiana File # NO 44-2064

by SA JAMES E. SCHMIDT, JR. JES/bal Date dictated 11/26/63

This document contains neither recommendations nor conclusions of the FBI. It is the property of the FBI and is loaned to your agency; it and its contents are not to be distributed outside your agency.

COMMISSION EXHIBIT No. 1521

2 NO 44-2064

which he was contacted by JACK RUBY when RUBY was in New Orleans, except to say it was approximately six months ago.

JES

COMMISSION EXHIBIT No. 1521—Continued

FD-302 (Rev. 1-25-60)

FEDERAL BUREAU OF INVESTIGATION

1

Date November 27, 1963

LEON CORNMAN, Branch Manager, American Guild of Variety Artists, Maison Blanche Building, advised that the only determination he has been able to make as to date of contact by JACK RUBY was some time during the week of June 6, 1963. He advised that the way that he determined this date was from the Union Insurance Records on JADA (JEANETTE CONFORTO) explaining that the week of June 6 was the last week in which she paid these fees and that the week of June 13, 1963, another entertainer was listed in her place on these records, therefore, because of this record he believes that he was contacted by JACK RUBY on Bourbon Street during this week of June 6, 1963.

On 11/27/63 at New Orleans, Louisiana File # NO 44-2064

by SA JAMES E. SCHMIDT, JR. :sms Date dictated 11/27/63

This document contains neither recommendations nor conclusions of the FBI. It is the property of the FBI and is loaned to your agency; it and its contents are not to be distributed outside your agency.

COMMISSION EXHIBIT No. 1522

FD-302 (Rev. 1-25-60)

FEDERAL BUREAU OF INVESTIGATION

Date November 26, 1963

1

PAUL CASCIO, Manager of the Blue Angel Club, 231 Bourbon Street, New Orleans, Louisiana, advised Special Agents JAMES E. SCHMIDT, JR., and FRANK A. SASS, JR., that approximately six months ago an individual identifying himself as JACK RUBY, owner of the Carousel Lounge, Dallas, Texas, came to the Hotsy Totsy Bar, located at 232 Bourbon Street, wherehe was working as a bartender. RUBY introduced himself and claimed to be inquiring in New Orleans as to the amount of money paid to "strippers" on Bourbon Street in New Orleans. After getting a general idea of the amount of money being paid these girls and after being referred to "JADA", a dancing girl at the 500 Club on Bourbon Street, he apparently made some contact and tried to contact this "stripper".

CASCIO had no knowledge of any further contact that RUBY had with anyone in any of the other clubs on Bourbon Street.

He stated that he saw RUBY on only one occasion in the evening and at that time he was alone and no conversation ensued other than that concerning strippers.

On 11/26/63 at New Orleans, Louisiana File # NO 44-2064

by SA FRANK A. SASS, JR.
SA JAMES E. SCHMIDT, JR. /cjo Date dictated 11/26/63

This document contains neither recommendations nor conclusions of the FBI. It is the property of the FBI and is loaned to your agency; it and its contents are not to be distributed outside your agency.

COMMISSION EXHIBIT No. 1523

FD-302 (Rev. 1-25-60)

FEDERAL BUREAU OF INVESTIGATION

Date November 27, 1963

HAZEL KEMP, Cashier, Sho-Bar, 225 Bourbon Street, New Orleans, Louisiana, advised she saw an individual who she identified as JACK RUBY from the photograph, sitting at the bar in the Sho-Bar talking to JEANETTE CONFORTO (JADA). She said RUBY was not accompanied by anyone and she believes he was in the bar about five days to a week before JADA completed her engagement on June 12, 1963.

On 11/26/63 at New Orleans, Louisiana File # NO 44-2064

by SA WILLIAM J. DANIELSON & JOHN WILLIAM MILLER :dc Date dictated 11/27/63

This document contains neither recommendations nor conclusions of the FBI. It is the property of the FBI and is loaned to your agency; it and its contents are not to be distributed outside your agency.

662

COMMISSION EXHIBIT No. 1524

FD-302 (Rev. 1-25-60)

FEDERAL BUREAU OF INVESTIGATION

Date November 27, 1963

JOE HOWARD, Master of Ceremonies, Sho-Bar, 228 Bourbon Street, advised he saw JACK RUBY in the Sho-Bar about a week before JEANETTE CONFORTO (JADA) completed her engagement at the Sho-Bar. HOWARD said he did not speak to RUBY, but he did see him talking to NICK GRAFFAGNINI who at that time was night manager. He said after RUBY had gone he had asked GRAFFAGNINI who the fellow was and GRAFFAGNINI had shown him a card which stated the fellow was JACK RUBY from the Carousel Lounge, Dallas, Texas. HOWARD could furnish no information regarding RUBY as to where he stayed while in New Orleans or his mode of transportation to and from Dallas. He said at the time he saw RUBY he was alone.

On 11/26/63 at New Orleans, Louisiana File # NO 44-2064

by SA WILLIAM J. DANIELSON & JOHN WILLIAM MILLER :dc Date dictated 11/27/63

This document contains neither recommendations nor conclusions of the FBI. It is the property of the FBI and is loaned to your agency; it and its contents are not to be distributed outside your agency.

664

COMMISSION EXHIBIT No. 1525

FD-302 (Rev. 1-25-60)

FEDERAL BUREAU OF INVESTIGATION

Date November 27, 1963

NICK GRAFFAGNINI, 3562 Vincennes, New Orleans, Louisiana, advised that JACK RUBY came into the Sho-Bar a few days before JEANETTE CONFORTO (JADA) completed her engagement and wanted to know how he could go about hiring JADA for a club he had in Dallas, Texas. GRAFFAGNINI said he told him he did not handle the hiring or signing of contracts with the entertainers and he sent him to the 500 Club on Bourbon Street. He said at the time RUBY spoke to him he was alone and he had never seen him before, nor has he seen him since. GRAFFAGNINI said RUBY gave him a card with his name on it and the name Carousel Lounge, Dallas, Texas also on it. GRAFFAGNINI said he did not speak further to RUBY and he has no idea where RUBY may have stayed while in New Orleans, nor does he know how RUBY came to New Orleans and returned to Dallas.

On 11/26/63 at New Orleans, Louisiana File # NO 44-2064

by SA WILLIAM J. DANIELSON & JOHN WILLIAM MILLER :dc Date dictated 11/27/63

This document contains neither recommendations nor conclusions of the FBI. It is the property of the FBI and is loaned to your agency; it and its contents are not to be distributed outside your agency.

665

COMMISSION EXHIBIT No. 1526

FD-302 (Rev. 3-3-59)

FEDERAL BUREAU OF INVESTIGATION

Date 11/28/63

1

BILLY DON WILLIAMS, 2064 Kirby, Dallas, Texas, was interviewed at the Carousel Club, 1213½ Commerce Street, Dallas, where his wife is employed as an exotic dancer.

WILLIAMS advised that he is presently unemployed; that he met JACK RUBY during the middle of November, 1963, when he came to Dallas from Dade City, Florida. He advised that his wife answered an "ad" in the paper for exotic dancers and was given a job by RUBY.

He advised that he last saw RUBY on November 21, 1963; however, talked with him on the phone on November 23, 1963. RUBY asked him, "Don't you think it is a tragic news event and I should close the club?" RUBY was referring to the death of President KENNEDY.

WILLIAMS advised that RUBY was friendly and helpful toward he and his wife; that RUBY had offered to advance them money and was going to help WILLIAMS find a job as a musician.

on 11/27/63 at Dallas, Texas File # DL 44-1639

by Special Agent s ALVIN L. ZIMMERMAN & JOSEPH G. PEGGS/ eah Date dictated 11/28/63

This document contains neither recommendations nor conclusions of the FBI. It is the property of the FBI and is loaned to your agency; it and its contents are not to be distributed outside your agency.

681

COMMISSION EXHIBIT No. 1527

FD-302 (Rev. 3-3-59)

FEDERAL BUREAU OF INVESTIGATION

1

Date 11/24/63

GEORGE SNYDER, Records Bureau, Dallas Police Department, made available copies of nine arrests of JACK LEON RUBY, by the Dallas Police Department. The nine arrests of RUBY in chronological order are:

DATE	CHARGE	OFFENSE NO.	ADDRESS
2/4/49	Disturbing peace	99090	1717 South Ervay, Dallas, Texas
7/26/53	Investigation Carrying concealed weapon	65478	"
5/1/54	Investigation Carrying concealed weapon (pistol)	20984	1719½ South Ervay, Dallas, Texas
"	Investigation peace bond violation	21114	1717 South Ervay, Dallas, Texas
12/5/54	Investigation violation State liquor law	54814	1719½ South Ervay, Dallas, Texas
6/21/59	Permitting dancing after hours	5965906	Home address, 4727 Homer
8/21/60	Violation dance hall ordnance #1156	60-76407	4727 Homer
2/12/63	Simple assault	6330069	3929 Rawlins
3/14/63	Alias ticket 24040	63-37112	3929 Rawlins

GEORGE SNYDER, in addition to the foregoing nine arrest records of JACK LEON RUBY, made available copies of the following documents:

on 11/24/63 at Dallas, Texas File # DL 44-1639

by Special Agents WILLIAM O. JOHNSON & JOSEPH J. HANLEY/cah 697 Date dictated 11/24/63

COMMISSION EXHIBIT No. 1528

2

DL 44-1639

An arrest report, #63-30069, which furnishes the details of the "Simple Assault" arrest of JACK LEON RUBY on February 12, 1963. This report reveals a charge of simple assault made against RUBY and describes the offense as follows:

"This subject involved in fight with complainant for no apparent reason. Subject hit complainant in face several times with fists".

The disturbance described above occurred in the Burgundy Room of the Adolphus Hotel at Commerce and Akard Streets in downtown Dallas. RUBY was alleged to have assaulted DON TABON of 8546 Forest Hill in Dallas. It is noted one witness was recorded in the arrest report, namely, N. T. STINSON of 7717 North Hill in Richardson, Texas. The arresting officer was identified as J. B. TONEY, badge number 778. Disposition of this case is not recorded on the arrest report.

A Homicide Report made out by Detective J. R. LEAVELL of the Homicide Bureau, Dallas Police Department, under offense #F86056, which sets forth the details of the shooting to death of LEE HARVEY OSWALD by JACK RUBY. These details are set forth below:

"Deceased was in custody being handcuffed to Detective J. R. LEAVELLE's left wrist with Detective L. C. GRAVES holding to deceased's left arm. Deceased was marched out of the jail office into the basement to be placed in a waiting automobile for transfer to the County Jail. Deceased had been charged with the Murder of Police Officer J. D. Tippit and President John F. Kennedy. As deceased and Detectives approached the car, a white male dashed from the throng of newspaper reporters and television cameramen and fired one time with a 38 caliber revolver striking the deceased in the left side. Deceased taken to Parkland Hospital where he was undergoing emergency operation at the time he expired. Judge McBride ordered Post Morteum. Suspect was arrested at the scene".

698

COMMISSION EXHIBIT No. 1528—Continued

54441

The Homicide Report reveals the place of the offense as being the basement of Dallas City Hall, 2001 Commerce Street and the time and date of the offense as being at 11:20 a.m. on Sunday, November 24, 1963.

It is noted the copies of all the above described documents are being retained in the Dallas files.

In addition to the foregoing records of arrest, the corresponding copies of disposition records were made available which are set forth as follows:

Date	Charge	Disposition
2/4/49	Disturbing Peace	Paid $10 fine same date
7/26/53	Investigation of Carrying Concealed Weapon	Released 7/26/53; no charges filed
5/1/54	Investigation of Carrying Concealed Weapon	Released 5/1/54 no charges filed
5/1/54	Investigation violation of peace bond	Released 5/1/54 no charges filed
12/5/54	Investigation violation state liquor law	Complaint dismissed 2/8/55
6/21/59	Permitting dancing after hours	Complaint dismissed 7/8/59
8/21/60	Permitting dancing after hours	Posted $25 bond and released same date. No further disposition shown

699

Date	Charge	Disposition
2/12/63	Simple Assault	Found "not guilty" 2/27/63
3/14/63	"Alias ticket" (This arrest resulted from ignoring traffic summons)	Posted $35 bond 3/14/63. No further disposition shown.

Permanent copies, obtained from microfilm records, of the above dispositions are retained in the Dallas Office file.

700

FORM 12-39

54 Nº 54814

FIRST NAME JACK | MIDDLE NAME LEON | LAST NAME RUBY

ADDRESS 1719 1/2 S Ervay | AGE 43 | SEX M | RACE W | OCC Tavern O

ARRESTING OFFICERS E E Carlson 774, D L Blankenship 633

PLACE OF ARREST 1717 S Ervay

DATE 12-5-54 | TIME 1:30A

C V

CHG. WHEN BOOKED Inv Vio St Liq Law

---

53 Nº 65478

FIRST NAME Jack | LAST NAME Ruby

ADDRESS 1717 S. Ervay | AGE 42 | SEX M | RACE W

ARRESTING OFFICERS W. M. Wall 857 & C. W. Deloney 75I

PLACE OF ARREST 3520 Oaklawn | DATE 7-26-53

C R I 33 | DESK OFFICER Skaine

ON VIEW X

CHARGE WHEN BOOKED Inv. C. C. W.

9

Nº 99090

FIRST NAME Jack | MIDDLE NAME L. | LAST NAME Ruby

ADDRESS 1717 S. Ervay | AGE 37 | SEX M | RACE W | Cafe

BUSINESS ADDRESS 1717 S. Ervay

ARRESTING OFFICERS D N Boyd 586 L P Passons 396

DATE 2-4-49

PLACE OF ARREST 1404 Main | DESK OFFICER Wood

C R 1 40

RADIO CALL X

CHARGE WHEN BOOKED Dist. Peace

FIRST JACK | MIDDLE L. | LAST NAME RUBY | R-S-AGE WM51 | 63- 37112

HOME ADDRESS 3929 Rawlins | DATE OF BIRTH 3-25-21

ADDRESS WHERE ARRESTED 106 S. Harwood

ARRESTING OFFICERS B. J. HOLLOWAY 224

DATE 3-14-63 | TIME 10:25 | STATION N | RADIO CALL 2 | VIEW X | DISTRICT 102

CLERK nof | STATION dt

CHARGED WHEN BOOKED Alias Ticket-24040A

Relto appear 3-14-63

$35.00 21004

6

FIRST JACK | LAST NAME RUBY | EM41 | 30069

HOME ADDRESS 3929 Rawlins | DATE OF BIRTH 3-25-21

ADDRESS WHERE ARRESTED City Hall

ARRESTING OFFICERS J B Toney 773

DATE 2-12-63 | TIME 11:00 P | DIVISION R | PLATOON 3 | DISTRICT 102

DESK OFFICER Warren | CLERK re | STATION dt | VIEW X

CHARGED WHEN BOOKED Simple Assault

7

FIRST Jack | MIDDLE L. | LAST NAME Ruby | R-S-AGE WM49 | 60- 76407

HOME ADDRESS 4727 Homer | DATE OF BIRTH 3-25-11 | OCCUPATION Dance Hall

ADDRESS WHERE ARRESTED 3508 Oak Lawn

ARRESTING OFFICERS B J Gee 832 G R Johnston 1259

DATE 8-21-60 | TIME 2:20 A | DIVISION SSB | PLATOON 1 | DISTRICT 26

DESK OFFICER Gassett | CLERK rc | STATION dt | VIEW X

CHARGED WHEN BOOKED Vio. Dance Hall Ord. # 1156

BAILED TO $75 Bond

6

FIRST JACK | MIDDLE XXXX | LAST NAME RUBY | R-S-AGE WM47 | 59- 65906

HOME ADDRESS 4727 Homer | DATE OF BIRTH 3 25 12

ADDRESS WHERE ARRESTED 3508 Oak Lawn

ARRESTING OFFICERS P M PARKS 1215 V D MONAGHEN 801

DATE 6 21 59 | TIME 2:30a | DIVISION SSB

DESK OFFICER wiseman | CLERK mc | STATION dt | VIEW x

CHARGED WHEN BOOKED PERMITTING DANCING AFTER HOURS

BAILED TO 6 21 59 3a | $25 | BOND NO. 83009 Xx8x5

5

FORM 12-39

54 Nº 21114

FIRST NAME JACK | LAST NAME RUBY

ADDRESS 1717 S.Ervay | AGE 43 | SEX M | RACE W

ARRESTING OFFICERS J.R.Stephens 918 & H.M.Collins 850

PLACE OF ARREST 3508 Oak Lawn

DATE 5-1-54 | TIME 9:05 A.M.

C R. 3. 33 | DESK OFFICER Skeins

RADIO CALL X

CHG. WHEN BOOKED Inv Peace Bond Vio (Hold for Chandler)

3

FORM 12-39

54 Nº 20984

FIRST NAME JACK | LAST NAME RUBY

ADDRESS 1719 1/2 SErvay | AGE 43 | SEX M | RACE W

ARRESTING OFFICERS JF Holcomb 708, C M Barnhart 924

PLACE OF ARREST 3508 Oak Lawn

DATE 5-1-54 | TIME 12:50P

C R 2 33 | Wiseman-pdg

ON VIEW X

CHG. WHEN BOOKED Inv CCW(Pistol)

3

COMMISSION EXHIBIT No. 1528—Continued

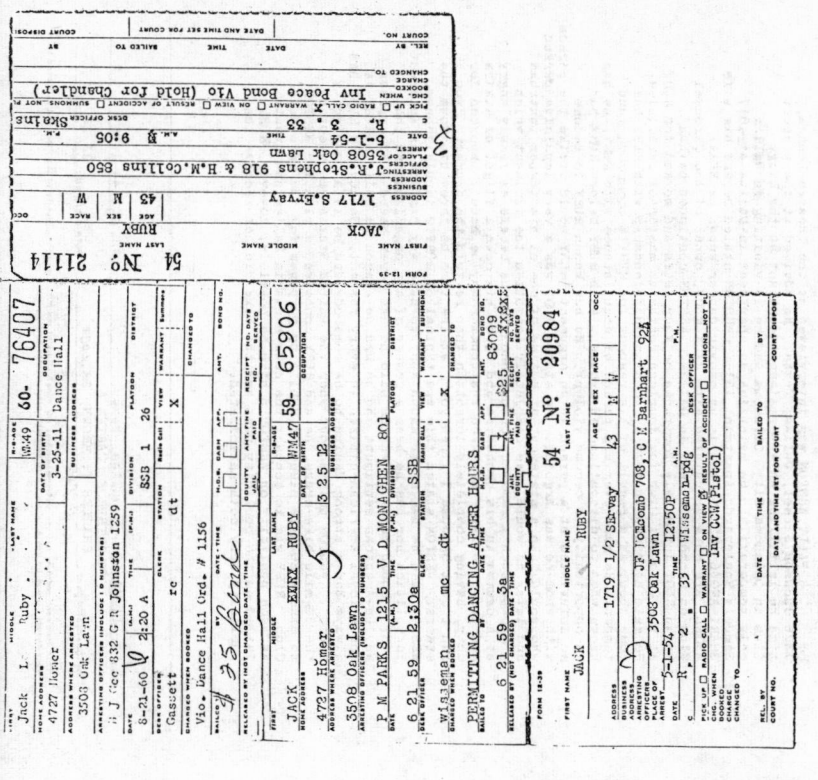

COMMISSION EXHIBIT No. 1528—Continued

Commission Exhibit No. 1529

FD-302 (Rev. 3-3-59)

FEDERAL BUREAU OF INVESTIGATION

Date 11/28/63

1

BONNIE LOUISE HETHCOAT KELLY, 3500 Armstrong, Highland Park, was interviewed at the Carousel Club, 1213½ Commerce Street, Dallas, where she is employed as a cocktail waitress.

KELLY advised she was hired by JACK RUBY in March, 1963, as she answered an "ad" in the newspaper. She stated that RUBY was good to her; that he advanced her money on occasion, and appeared to be genuinely concerned regarding her welfare and the welfare of her children. She stated she never dated him, and he never asked her to do so. She heard him make a statement at one time that the girls in the club probably would not go out with him if he asked them.

KELLY stated that everyone at the Carousel Club knows that the Master of Ceremonies, BILL DE MAR, lied when he said he had seen LEE HARVEY OSWALD at the Carousel Club. She said that if OSWALD had ever been at the club one of the waitresses would have remembered him; also, that from the Master of Ceremonies' position on the stage, one cannot see into the audience, due to the lighting arrangements in the club.

KELLY was shown a photograph of LEE HARVEY OSWALD and she advised she had never seen him at the Carousel Club or associating with JACK RUBY.

KELLY advised she knows none of the policemen by name with whom JACK was friendly by name; that JACK liked all policemen and many of them came to the club.

---

on 11/27/63 at Dallas, Texas File # DL 89-43 DL 44-1639

by Special Agents ALVIN J. ZIMMERMAN & JOSEPH G. PEGGS/eah Date dictated 11/28/63

777

This document contains neither recommendations nor conclusions of the FBI. It is the property of the FBI and is loaned to your agency; it and its contents are not to be distributed outside your agency.

Commission Exhibit No. 1530

FD-302 (Rev. 3-3-59)

FEDERAL BUREAU OF INVESTIGATION

1

Date 11/25/63

WALLY WESTON was interviewed at the Theatre Lounge, 1326 Jackson Street, Dallas, Texas. He advised at the present time he is filling an entertainment contract at the Kings Club in Oklahoma City, Oklahoma and he is visiting in Dallas only temporarily. He maintains an apartment in Dallas at 4617 Samuels Boulevard, Apartment 131. WESTON stated he and his wife SHARI ANGEL WESTON, who is an exotic dancer known as SHARI ANGEL, are both acquainted with JACK RUBY, owner of the Carousel Club on Commerce Street in Dallas. WESTON continued he has known RUBY intimately for three or four years and worked for RUBY at the Carousel Club for fourteen months as master of ceremonies. He said he presumed that his continued friendship with RUBY has come about as a result of his respect for RUBY'S eccentricities and temper. He said over his period of acquaintance with RUBY, he has known when to discontinue an argument with RUBY before RUBY had an opportunity to become violent. He has known RUBY to become so infuriated at a person in an argument, RUBY would strike the person with whom he was arguing. He stated RUBY was a very impulsive person who would make a statement at a time of one of his temper tantrums and later he would have completely forgotten the incident which provoked such a remark. On one occasion he became extremely angry at a drummer in his orchestra and threw him down a flight of stairs and two days later he asked the drummer why he hadn't reported for duty, having completely forgotten that he told the drummer, "you can't quit because I fired you", at the time he threw him down the stairs. WESTON stated this was typical of RUBY'S impulsiveness. WESTON said he has never known RUBY to have any particular interest in politics nor has he been a member of any organizations that WESTON could recall. WESTON said he has never heard RUBY express any Un-American sentiment and he had no reason to believe RUBY is not a loyal American citizen in every respect. He advised RUBY has always had a strong desire to be somebody and he is a "publicity hound". WESTON pointed out when the United States was swept by the 50-mile hike craze, he and RUBY conceived a plan for WESTON to make a 50-mile hike for publicity purposes for the Carousel Club. RUBY was to contact the news media in Dallas and create as much publicity on WESTON'S hike as possible; however, RUBY failed on the publicity part and the hike did not receive the publicity they both anticipated.

---

on 11/24/63 at Dallas, Texas File # DL 44-1639

by Special Agent ARTHUR E. CARTER & CHARLES T. BROWN, JR./cjr Date dictated 11/25/63

CTB 781

This document contains neither recommendations nor conclusions of the FBI. It is the property of the FBI and is loaned to your agency; it and its contents are not to be distributed outside your agency.

WESTON said RUBY is continuously seeking to promote business for himself at the Carousel Club and because of this he is friendly and tried to be friendly with persons he thinks will be good for his business. RUBY has spent much time around the Police Department in Dallas, the Sheriff's Office and other public places handing out business cards entitling the person receiving same to admittance to the Carousel Club and free drinks as a guest. WESTON said he knew RUBY had many friends at the Dallas Police Department as a result of promotional activities. He stated it was his personal opinion and belief that RUBY possibly murdered LEE HARVEY OSWALD for two reasons. He felt one reason could have been RUBY'S strong desire for national publicity which would result from his act or RUBY, because of his violent temper, could have become angered at the murderer of a member of the Dallas Police Department, whom he felt were his friends. WESTON said he did not believe OSWALD'S murder was connected in any way with RUBY'S political beliefs or because of RUBY'S sympathy for some foreign Government. He added he has never heard RUBY criticize the American form of Government, the leaders of this country, nor has he ever expressed any radical ideas. WESTON recalled RUBY was extremely sensitive about his being of Jewish extraction and for that reason WESTON had received specific instructions from RUBY that in his job as master of ceremonies he was to stay completely away from any jokes or comments of a racial or political nature.

WESTON said he knew RUBY did have a gun in his possession based on the following instances. About eight months ago there was an attempted burglary at the Carousel Club, which was discovered by RUBY upon his entrance into the club. RUBY ran down the back stairs of the club to his automobile, which was parked on a nearby street, secured a gun from the automobile and returned to the club, thinking the burglars still might be in the club. About six months ago two customers arriving at the club were approached by one of the club employees to pay their $2.00 fee for entrance into the club. These customers reported they had paid $2.00 to two young men who were standing at the downstairs entrance to the club as they entered. RUBY ran down the stairs just in time to see the two young boys running up the street. RUBY ran to his automobile which was nearby, got his pistol out of the trunk of the car, put it in his shirt, and began looking around for the boys. Shortly thereafter the two boys were apprehended by officers of the Dallas Police Department, at which time they were returned to the Carousel Club. When the officers took the boys to RUBY to inquire whether he wanted to file charges against the boys, RUBY hesitated and then instructed the officers to forget the whole matter because there was so little money involved.

782

RUBY instructed the police to admonish the boys for their actions and then to release them.

WESTON concluded by advising because of RUBY'S peculiar personality and violent temper, RUBY has no close personal friends. WESTON stated he felt he was possibly closer to RUBY than anyone else he knew, because over the period of three or four years, he has learned how to get along with RUBY. He added with regard to the incident when entertainer BILL DE MAR who is presently appearing at the Carousel Club reported he had seen LEE HARVEY OSWALD at the club, WESTON did not feel DE MAR could have recognized OSWALD because of the difficulty experienced in recognizing persons in the audience from the stage. WESTON pointed out a performer has a spotlight shining in his face while he is on stage and it would be very difficult for the performer to recognize anyone looking into the audience from the stage. He felt DE MAR had made the claim he saw OSWALD in the audience because of DE MAR'S desire for publicity.

Mr. WESTON said he has not seen RUBY since the President's assassination on November 22, 1963 and he is unable to account for his whereabouts since that time.

783

Commission Exhibit No. 1531

FD-302 (Rev. 3-3-59)

FEDERAL BUREAU OF INVESTIGATION

Date 11/25/63

LEON H. WORTH, 2018 South Tyler Street, was interviewed concerning his knowledge and/or association with JACK RUBY.

Mr. WORTH stated he presently operates a private club at 2707 McKinney Avenue in Dallas known as the Galaxy Club. He stated this is a private club, and he formerly operated the Top Hat Lounge located in Dallas. He stated he operated the Top Hat Lounge about ten years ago at which time JACK RUBY was operating a lounge known as the Silver Spur.

He stated he has known RUBY for approximately ten years and became acquainted with him inasmuch as he was operating the Top Hat Lounge at the same time RUBY was running the Silver Spur.

He stated at no time has he ever considered himself a personal friend of RUBY's and had never to his recollection gone to dinner with him or had drinks with him either in a coffee shop or a lounge.

Mr. WORTH stated about 1954 he divested himself of the lounge business and went in the pharmaceutical business as h... pharmacist.

He stated RUBY came to him at the time he was in the pharmaceutical business with a remedy for treating arthri... He stated RUBY wanted him to sell this arthritis remedy and would receive $100.00 a week and commissions for selling this remedy.

WORTH stated he sold this arthritis remedy for RUBY for about three months but after that time several of the checks which RUBY gave him for commission were no account checks, and so he quit doing business with RUBY and quit selling his arthritis remedy.

Mr. WORTH stated after he quit selling the arthritis remedy he had no further contact with RUBY, and up until approximately two months ago had not seen him although he had known he was in the Dallas area. He stated he saw RUBY in Phil's Delicatessen with a bunch of show people whom he believed were entertainers at the club operated by RUBY. Mr. WORTH stated he did not know any of these people and did not know of any close friends of RUBY.

He stated he never considered himself a personal friend

on 11/25/63 at Dallas, Texas File # DL 44-1639

by Special Agent SA 's WARREN A. LARSON & RAYMOND M. LESTER, JR. WAL /cv RML Date dictated 11/25/63

791

DL 44-1639
WAL:RML:cv
2

of RUBY and had never arranged for any loans nor had he loaned him any money for the purpose of operating a lounge or other business. He stated RUBY is the kind of person who is always trying to force his friendship on you, and he did not consider RUBY trustworthy or reliable and believed that RUBY would do anything for a "buck".

Mr. WORTH stated he was also of the opinion RUBY preferred "gay company" and further explained this by saying he believed RUBY preferred the company of men rather than of women. He stated he has no personal knowledge of homosexual tendencies of RUBY and that RUBY exhibited feminine tendencies in his actions and talk. He stated he did not believe that RUBY was a fighter or brawler as he had been characterized recently in newspaper clippings. He stated RUBY was a backslapper and he believed RUBY would do anything for publicity or money.

He stated he does not know of his own knowledge that RUBY is a narcotics user or that he drinks to excess.

WORTH stated that "JACK is not for anybody else but JACK RUBY". He stated he does not know anything about RUBY's politics and does not believe that RUBY is particularly patriotic or interested in politics other than in politics to promote himself.

Mr. WORTH stated that his wife and RUBY did not get along at all, and he believed that RUBY was jealous of his wife because of the husband and wife relationship.

Mr. WORTH stated he did not ever know RUBY to carry a gun and did not believe RUBY was an aggressive person.

WORTH stated he did not know any close friends that RUBY might have, and he personally did not care for RUBY in any form.

792

FD-302 (Rev. 3-3-59) FEDERAL BUREAU OF

Date 12/6/63

1

Mr. PHILIP LANCE, Apartment G, 109 10th Street, advised he is currently residing here with his wife, REBA JANE LANCE, and their two children. He advised he is currently unemployed but his wife is working at Skillern's Drugstore in Wynnewood.

LANCE advised that his last employment was at Col-Bec Restaurant in 100 block of W. Colorado Street, where he and his wife worked for approximately one week.

He stated that at approximately 7:30 p.m., Tuesday, November 26, 1963, he and his wife were working at the kitchen at Col-Bec Restaurant when a woman came through the front door right back to the kitchen. He said she advised them she was a White House reporter and that she was "trying to get information on our friend OSWALD."

LANCE stated the woman was very well dressed, in her middle 30's, black hair, stocky build, and spoke with a foreign accent.

He stated she asked them if they knew OSWALD, if he had ever been in the restaurant, or if they had ever seen him on Jefferson Street, or in the area where he last resided which was on Beckley Street.

LANCE stated the woman had a notebook and wrote in the book as she asked questions of them. He said she asked them if there were any other eating places in the area where OSWALD might possibly have gone to eat. He stated he told her to try the bowling alley which is in the 100 block of Jefferson Street.

LANCE stated when she left the restaurant he followed her out and noticed she was walking and that she walked in the direction of the bowling alley on Jefferson Street.

LANCE stated he was of the opinion she was connected with some newspaper and was attempting to obtain background information on OSWALD.

LANCE volunteered the information that his wife, REBA JANE, formerly worked for JACK RUBY at the Vegas Club and the Carousel Club as a stripper under the name of REBA. He stated she worked for approximately one year and that she quit him about a year ago.

477

on 12/5/63 at Dallas, Texas File # DL 89-43 DL 44-1639

by Special Agents WILLIAM O. JOHNSON and JOSEPH J. HANLEY/vm Date dictated 12/6/63

This document contains neither recommendations nor conclusions of the FBI. It is the property of the FBI and is loaned to your agency; it and its contents are not to be distributed outside your agency.

COMMISSION EXHIBIT NO. 1532

2
DL 89-43
DL 44-1639

He stated that he, LANCE, was acquainted with RUBY having met him through his wife. He said RUBY was continually trying to embarrass the girls who worked for him and that was one of the reasons why his wife, REBA, quit working for him. He said that one night while she was in the middle of the act before the large audience at the Carousel Club RUBY hollered out "REBA, do you shave." LANCE stated that he wanted to whip RUBY right then but he contained himself. He said his wife quit shortly thereafter.

LANCE stated he thought RUBY was an "odd character" because he never saw him in the company of girls and always had a bunch of dogs hanging around him. He said on one occasion he saw RUBY walking four "weiner dogs" on a leash and saw him kiss each dog on the nose.

LANCE advised he never saw anyone who looked like the newspaper and television pictures of OSWALD in the Col-Bec Restaurant or in JACK RUBY's clubs.

478

COMMISSION EXHIBIT NO. 1532—Continued

FD-302 (Rev. 3-3-59) FEDERAL BUREAU OF I

Date 12/6/63

1

Mrs. PHILIP LANCE, also known as Reba Jane Lance, Apartment G, 109 W. 10th Street, advised she is currently employed at Skillern's Drugstore, Wynnewood Shopping Center. She stated that during the period of the assassination of President KENNEDY she was employed at Col-Bec Restaurant on W. Colorado Street with her husband.

Mrs. LANCE stated that at approximately 7:00 p.m. on Tuesday night, November 26, 1963, she and her husband were working in the kitchen of the Col-Bec Restaurant when a woman came into the kitchen of the restaurant. This woman stated she was a White House reporter but did not exhibit any form of identification. She said this woman advised she was looking for information regarding "our friend OSWALD."

Mrs. LANCE stated the woman asked several questions about possible eating places that OSWALD might have gone to in this area. She stated the woman was very well dressed, in her early 30's, had black hair, and spoke with a foreign accent. She stated when the woman had her purse open she noticed there was a lot of money in the purse. She said this woman made notes in a small notebook. She said she was of the opinion that this woman was a reporter and was just trying to obtain information on OSWALD.

Mrs. LANCE advised she had formerly worked for JACK RUBY at both the Vegas Club and the Carousel Club. She advised she hates JACK RUBY more than any person she has ever met. She stated he had no respect for her or any of the girls who worked for him.

She stated she quit him sometime in January, 1963, after working for him for over a year because he embarrassed her before several club patrons. She said he asked her, "REBA, do you shave."

Mrs. LANCE advised RUBY tries to act big and likes to show off before a group of men. She stated RUBY is "queer for dogs" and on many occasions saw him act absolutely silly over some of his dogs.

Mrs. LANCE advised RUBY was also abnormal in other ways. She stated he hired a stripper and became fond of her just because she "had a butt that he liked."

473

on 12/5/63 at Dallas, Texas File # DL 89-43 DL 44-1639

by Special Agents WILLIAM O. JOHNSON and JOSEPH J. HANLEY:vm Date dictated 12/6/63

This document contains neither recommendations nor conclusions of the FBI. It is the property of the FBI and is loaned to your agency; it and its contents are not to be distributed outside your agency.

COMMISSION EHXIBIT NO. 1533

2
DL 89-43
DL 44-1639

Mrs. LANCE advised she had never seen RUBY in the company of women outside his place of business.

Mrs. LANCE said he always enjoyed being in the company of men but during the period she worked for him she did not see anyone resembling OSWALD in RUBY's company.

480

COMMISSION EHXIBIT NO. 1533—Continued

FD-302 (Rev. 1-25-60)

FEDERAL BUREAU OF INVESTIGATION

Date November 29, 1963

Mr. LACY C. BROOKS, Manager, Ramada Inn, Midland, Texas, advised as follows:

He was acquainted with JACK RUBY and met RUBY during the time that he, BROOKS, was the Food Manager at the Holiday Inn Central in Dallas, Texas, which was in about December, 1961. BROOKS probably did not see RUBY more than four times during 1962. On such occasions, RUBY had been hired to furnish entertainment for parties at the Holiday Inn Central, Dallas, and contacted BROOKS to advise him of this. At the time the strip tease girls arrived at the Inn, BROOKS advised them the room in which the party was to be held and the room they were to use as a dressing room. BROOKS did not make arrangements for the entertainment with RUBY, this being done by the persons sponsoring the party.

BROOKS had no business dealings with RUBY, knew nothing concerning RUBY's past or present activities other than knowing that RUBY was a well known night club operator in Dallas. BROOKS knew nothing regarding the political beliefs of RUBY and knew of no political connections of RUBY. BROOKS had no knowledge of any connection between RUBY and OSWALD.

BROOKS said RUBY had the reputation of knowing more policemen on the Dallas Police Department by their first names than did the Mayor of Dallas, this being purely hearsay as far as BROOKS was concerned. RUBY was generally known as a "good Joe".

Inasmuch as RUBY was such a well known character in Dallas, BROOKS wondered why Dallas police let a night club operator of the reputation of RUBY in the area where they were moving a person who had killed the President of the United States.

To the best of BROOK's recollection, he had approximately four contacts with RUBY during 1961 and 1962, this being his only association with RUBY.

On 11/29/63 at Midland, Texas File # EP 44-274

by SA ROY C. DAHL/st Date dictated 11/29/63

This document contains neither recommendations nor conclusions of the FBI. It is the property of the FBI and is loaned to your agency; it and its contents are not to be distributed outside your agency.

64

COMMISSION EXHIBIT No. 1534

FD-302 (Rev. 1-25-60)

FEDERAL BUREAU OF INVESTIGATION

Date November 29, 1963

ROBERT CRAVEN, residence 2977 Santa Ana Street, South Gate, California, telephone 585-4217, business address Craven Contracting Company, 407 East Pico Street, Los Angeles, California, telephone 747-5866, telephonically furnished what he knew about JACK RUBY of Dallas, Texas, as follows:

In September and October, 1963, CRAVEN and others produced a show called "How Hollywood Makes Movies" and put the show on at the Dallas State Fair, Dallas, Texas, from October 5, 1963, to October 15, 1963. The show first arrived in Dallas on Sunday, September 29, 1963, with a company of eight individuals.

Inasmuch as CRAVEN had met JACK RUBY about the year previous in November, 1962, he called upon RUBY to assist him in obtaining props and other things needed for the show. RUBY was very helpful and loaned CRAVEN's show a few props, such as a mirror and a fan, and told him where certain materials could be purchased and even furnished a few of the girls from RUBY's club, the Carousel, to participate in CRAVEN's show.

When CRAVEN first met RUBY in November, 1962, he was introduced to RUBY by a chain store manager, name not recalled. CRAVEN at the time was in Dallas only a week and had very little contact with RUBY at that time. He knew that RUBY had two clubs in Dallas and that is about all.

In October, 1963, CRAVEN had considerable contact with RUBY because RUBY came to the fair grounds and was given passes to CRAVEN's show and introduced CRAVEN to many people that RUBY knew in Dallas. He introduced CRAVEN to various news media people, police, and others.

CRAVEN described RUBY as an emotional person who was easily excited. For example, CRAVEN noted that RUBY became annoyed when his club show did not operate smoothly. He became upset with his theatrical union people in Dallas when they threatened to fine one of RUBY's girls, JOY DALE, also known as JOYCE MC DONALD, $200.00 for participating in

On 11:00 p.m. 11/27/63 at South Gate, California File # Los Angeles 44-895 ~~Dallas 44-1639~~

by SA WILLIAM W. COLBY:elc Date dictated 11/29/63

This document contains neither recommendations nor conclusions of the FBI. It is the property of the FBI and is loaned to your agency; it and its contents are not to be distributed outside your agency.

70

COMMISSION EXHIBIT No. 1535

CRAVEN's show, "How Hollywood Makes Movies." RUBY was angry with the union because RUBY was only helping out CRAVEN temporarily and did not feel it was right for the union to assess a fine.

CRAVEN does not know of any criminal connections of RUBY. RUBY told CRAVEN he was from Chicago, and CRAVEN gathered that RUBY still had friends there as on about October 9, 1963, RUBY told CRAVEN that a man from Chicago was in RUBY's club, the Carousel, and RUBY described the man as a "real swinger." RUBY did not name the man but CRAVEN thinks JOY DALE might know who this person was.

RUBY ran a clean club and was very conscientious about not violating liquor laws, such as serving drinks after closing time. CRAVEN thought this was unusual because RUBY knew every police officer in Dallas, but still he would not let even his friends have drinks on their table at closing time. RUBY told CRAVEN that there was some woman in charge of the liquor licenses in Dallas who was very strict.

RUBY did not appear to CRAVEN to have very much money. He told CRAVEN that it was a struggle for him to keep ahead because of other competition in Dallas. He loaned CRAVEN $100.00 and when CRAVEN repaid it a short time thereafter, RUBY mentioned how pleased he was to get it and said that he needed it. RUBY told CRAVEN he had a nice apartment which he rented for about $150.00 to $200.00 a month. CRAVEN was never there but was invited. He did not know with whom RUBY lived but understood he was a bachelor. He thought that RUBY had several girl friends, including JOY, but he did not know the names of the others.

CRAVEN had no political discussions with RUBY and does not believe that RUBY had radical beliefs of any kind. RUBY apparently knew that CRAVEN was a New Englander from Boston because CRAVEN has a New England accent and possibly mentioned that CRAVEN had once campaigned for President KENNEDY and had attended the inauguration ball. CRAVEN does not believe that RUBY ever discussed this nor seemed particularly interested in politics.

71

CRAVEN had no knowledge of LEE OSWALD. CRAVEN had no knowledge of any relatives of RUBY, except he knew that he had a sister in Dallas who also owned a night club.

The last contact CRAVEN had with RUBY was on about Monday, November 18, 1963, when CRAVEN telephoned RUBY in Dallas about some lumber purchases that CRAVEN had made for his show at the fair. RUBY at that time mentioned that he had problems with the theatrical union and wondered if CRAVEN could do something about it in Hollywood for RUBY.

CRAVEN had no knowledge that RUBY carried or owned a revolver. He thought of RUBY as a rough individual insofar as maintaining order in his club, but he did not see any violent actions on the part of RUBY.

72

FEDERAL BUREAU OF INVESTIGATION

Date November 27, 1963

1

BOBBY GENE MOORE, 865 43rd Street, Oakland, California, was interviewed at his home. He stated that he desired to furnish information regarding JACK RUBY, who he had known in Dallas, Texas. He stated that he had observed an interview on television with an associate of RUBY in which the associate said that RUBY had no gangster connections. MOORE furnished the following information:

He was raised in Dallas, Texas, having been born in that city on December 12, 1927. About 1951 or 1952, he was living at a rooming house at 1214 Boll Street, Dallas. This house was at the rear of Hill's Liquor Store at the corner of Ross Avenue and Boll Street. This liquor store was a front for a bookie-type operation where bets were taken on all types of athletic events and horse races. It was operated by a man named HILL, first name unknown, and his son. This gambling place was patronized by most of the gambling element in Dallas and RUBY was a frequent visitor. MOORE did not know whether or not RUBY was actually connected with the operation of the gambling place or was merely a participant.

on 11/26/63 at Oakland, California File # SF 44-494 DL 44-1639

by Special Agents DONALD F. HALLAHAN & ~~THOMAS G. MC GEE/rew/eah~~ /gl Date dictated 11/27/63

COMMISSION EXHIBIT No. 1536

Commission Exhibit No. 1537

FD-302 (Rev. 1-25-60)

FEDERAL BUREAU OF INVESTIGATION

1

Date 11/30/63

JACK PAKIS, Highway #7, Hot Springs, Arkansas, advised as follows:

He received a telephone call from JACK RUBY approximately two months ago, making inquiry about some show girl, whose name he did not recall, who had appeared at the Southern Club in the past, and whom RUBY apparently wanted to book at his club. PAKIS first became acquainted with RUBY when he, PAKIS, was in Dallas approximately six months ago to attend a PGA golf tournament. He and other associates from Hot Springs visited the club of RUBY's and became acquainted with him. Later that same evening, RUBY visited the room of PAKIS and associates to have several drinks. PAKIS advised that he had never had any other contact with RUBY and never observed RUBY in Hot Springs, Arkansas.

PAKIS advised RUBY discussed law enforcement work and his assistance to local officers on occasions, during practically the entire conversation he had with him. PAKIS is of the opinion RUBY was extremely interested in police work and considered him to be a fanatic in this regard. PAKIS recalled RUBY elaborated considerably concerning an alleged incident where he claimed he saived the lives of two Dallas Police Officers on one occasion. PAKIS was unable to recall the specific story as told by RUBY concerning his saving their lives. PAKIS was unable to furnish information of a specific nature but gained the impression that RUBY was the type that preferred to always be present where law enforcement officers were performing their duty. RUBY did not mention any names of specific officers he might have been acquainted with. PAKIS was unable to furnish the identities of other individuals acquainted with RUBY.

On 11/28/63 at Hot Springs, Arkansas File # LR 44-791

by SA CLABURN T. WHITE/mfm 104 Date dictated 11/30/63

COMMISSION EXHIBIT No. 1537

Commission Exhibit No. 1538

FD-302 (Rev. 3-3-59)

FEDERAL BUREAU OF INVESTIGATION

1

Date 12/4/63

ROSCOE R. ROBINSON, 4415 South Lamar, Dallas, Texas, was interviewed concerning his business connection and personal knowledge of JACK RUBY.

ROBINSON advised he has known RUBY since about 1950, but has had little contact with him since 1955, when ROBINSON purchased the Silver Spur from him. ROBINSON sold the Silver Spur Club about a year later and has not been in the night club business since that time. He states that as a result of leaving the club business he has lost contact with RUBY and has seen him only rarely since 1955 and then only casually.

ROBINSON states he took HOWARD MC LAUGHLIN and a woman, VIOLA (LNU), to the Carousel Club about a month ago to try to get VIOLA a job. He introduced both MC LAUGHLIN and VIOLA to RUBY and the four of them had a brief conversation. He recalls no specific conversation except the introduction and states they just talked club business and made small talk "about things in general." VIOLA did not get a job at the Carousel so far as ROBINSON knows.

A few days later, he and "SLIM" ELMO MILLER stopped at the Carousel for a drink. On this occasion, RUBY greeted them at the door, but they had no other conversation with him. ROBINSON states he has no recollection of RUBY ever stating any political views or even discussing politics.

ROBINSON had never heard of LEE HARVEY OSWALD prior to President KENNEDY's assassination and does not recall ever having seen him. He further states he knows many of the officers of the Police Department in Dallas and has never seen any of them around the Carousel Club. He was of the impression RUBY knew many of the officers but does not know how RUBY met them or what their relationship was. ROBINSON said RUBY went to Chicago sometime between 1952 and 1954 and was absent from Dallas for almost a year. He described RUBY as short-tempered and very unpredictable, but feels he shot OSWALD for some personal gain. He stated he has nothing to base this theory on, aside from his opinion of RUBY's character.

on 12/2/63 at Dallas, Texas File # DL 44-1639

by Special Agent S GARY L. WILSON & JAMES W. SWINFORD/eah 137 Date dictated 12/4/63

COMMISSION EXHIBIT No. 1538

FD-302 (Rev. 1-25-60) FEDERAL BUREAU OF INVESTIGATION

1.

Date December 2, 1963

CRAWFORD C. MARTIN, Secretary of State, State of Texas, Capitol Building, caused to be produced the corporate file of that office with respect to S & R, Inc., Dallas, Texas.

This file contains the following information:

The Corporate charter records revealed that the S & R, Inc., 1312-1/2 Commerce Street, Dallas, Texas, was granted a Corporate Charter to do business in the State of Texas under Charter No. 163178, dated February 10, 1960. The period for duration of this corporation was stated to be perpetual and the aggregate number of shares listed as 1,000 shares at par value of $1.00 each. The corporation's purpose was listed as "To manufacture, buy, sell, deal in and engage in, carry on and conduct the business of manufacturing, buying, selling and dealing in goods, wares, and merchandise of every class and description". The Post Office Address of the corporation's initial registered office was listed as 1312-1/2 Commerce Street, Dallas, Texas, and the name of its original registered agent was shown as RALPH PAUL. The number of directors constituting the initial board of directors was listed as four in number and they were to serve as directors until the first annual meeting of share holders or until their successors were elected and qualified. These individuals were listed as: RALPH PAUL, 3508 Oak Lawn, Dallas, Texas; EARL RUBY, 3508 Oak Lawn, Dallas, Texas; JOE E. SLATIN, 4819 Irwin Simmons Drive, Dallas, Texas; C. D. MERRELL, 2247 Lea Crest Drive, Dallas, Texas.

The names and addresses of the incorporators were listed as RALPH PAUL, 3508 Oak Lawn, Dallas, Texas; JOE E. SLATIN, 4819 Irwin Simmons Drive, Dallas, Texas; and C. D. MERRELL, 2247 Lea Crest Drive, Dallas, Texas. These last three incorporators were shown to have signed the articles of incorporation and their signatures were notarized on the articles of incorporation by STANLEY M. KAUFMAN, Notary Public in and for Dallas County, Texas, this notarization having been dated February 9, 1960.

The corporate charter file further revealed that

On 11/29/63 at Austin, Texas File # SA 44-748

by SA H. T. BURK/jmb Date dictated 11/29/63

139

2.

SA 44-748

Secretary of State FRANK LAKE, Secretary of State's Office, Austin, Texas, on March 6, 1962, signed a formal instrument wherein he stated that on that day he had considered the forfeiture of the charter of the S & R, Inc., charter # 163178, Ledger #114509, a corporation organized under the laws of the State of Texas, and that he had determined and finds the following facts:

1. That said corporation's right to do business in this state was previously forfeited on July 17, 1961;

2. That the comptroller of Public Accounts has duly certified to his office that said corporation has no assets from which a judgment for the franchise taxes, penalties and court costs may be satisfied;

3. That the comptroller of Public Accounts has further certified that the said corporation has failed and refused to revive its right to do business prior to the first day of January next, suceeding the day of forfeiture of its right to do business and as provided by law;

4. That the above determination and findings of fact have been approved by the Attorney General of Texas. This order signed by FRANK LAKE ordered that the charter of the above named corporation be, and the same is hereby forfeited without judicial ascertainment and made null and void, and that proper entry be made upon the permanent files and records of such corporation, to show such forfeiture as of the date hereof. Witnessed his hand and seal March 6, 1962.

This file likewise contained a copy of a letter dated February 16, 1962, from ROBERT S. CALVERT, Comptroller of the State of Texas, addressed to the Tax Assessor Collector of Dallas County, Dallas, Texas, concerning the S & R, Inc., 1312-1/2 Commerce Street, Dallas, Texas, in which CALVERT requested the Assessor Collector of Dallas County to furnish any information from the records of the Tax Assessor Collector of Dallas County concerning the assessed value of the following named property owned by the above corporation, if any, for the tax year, 1961.

On the bottom of this letter referred to above, the Tax Assessor Collector of Dallas County certified that the S. & R, Inc. had no real property on the rendered or unrendered rolls of Dallas County, Texas, and had no property on the rendered personal property rolls of that county.

140

3.

SA 44-748

This certification was signed by the Dallas County Tax Assessor Collector dated February 22, 1962.

The file further contains a letter from WILL WILSON, Attorney General of the State of Texas, dated March 6, 1962, addressed to Honorable FRANK LAKE, Secretary of State, Austin, Texas, concerning the S & R, Inc. in which the Attorney General's Office of the State of Texas approved the determination of the Office of Comptroller of Public Accounts to the effect the S & R, Inc. was without assets from which franchise taxes, penalties, and court costs may be satisfied against such corporation. This letter authorized the Secretary of State's Office that the approval of the Attorney General of the State of Texas for forfeiture of the charter was granted.

141

FD-302 (Rev. 1-25-60) FEDERAL BUREAU OF INVESTIGATION

Date 11-29-63

Miss. MILI PERELE, hostess, Hut Lounge, El Paso, Texas advised the following: She was employed by Ruby as a strip tease artist at Carousel Club in Dallas for eight months in 1961, and for two months in 1962. Ruby was quick to admonish employees for wrongdoing but was just as quick to praise them for good work. Ruby had a bad temper on occasions when employees violated contracts or when patrons got out of hand. Ruby operated a very strict burlesque show and did not allow mixing of the performers and the customers. No negroes were allowed to patronize Ruby's two clubs, not because he disliked negroes but for business reasons. Ruby had no outside relationships with his employees.

Ruby was very passionate in his beliefs; whatever he believed he believed violently and whatever he disbelieved he disbelieved just as violently. On several occasions Ruby was known to have arguments with persons who had criticized the President of the United States.

Ruby never discussed his past but had told people that he was from Chicago. He was a democrat and was very active in his synagogue. Many police officers, both in and out of uniform, patronized Ruby's clubs but were not known to have any dealings with them.

Perele had no reason to doubt Ruby's patriotism or loyalty to the United States. Ruby was never known to make any disloyal statements or to have any subversive connections.

Perele worked at Carousel Club with Kathy Kaye, Cherry Lynn, and Najada. Ralph Paul of Dallas, was known to be a business associate of Ruby. Ruby obtained his exotic dancers from Jack Cole, Talent Agency operator, Dallas, Texas. Ruby had a widowed or a divorced sister in Dallas who was much like Ruby.

On 11-29-63 at El Paso, Texas File # EP 44-274

by GEORGE E. AIKEN, JR. HAROLD LEON DAVIS /drh 159 Date dictated 11-29-63

FEDERAL BUREAU OF INVESTIGA ION

Date 12/2/63

1

Miss JULIE TAYLOR, Aka. Mrs. Julie Case, Mrs. Ricky Case, who is presently engaged in a performance as an Exotic Dancer at the Civic Theatre and who is temporarily residing at Onondaga Hotel, Syracuse, permanent residence 144-70 41st Avenue, Flushing 54, Long Island, New York, advised as follows:

She was booked by her agent, EDDIE CAPLAN, New York City, through JACK COLE, an agent at Dallas, Texas, to play at the Carousel, Dallas, Texas, for five weeks, from the middle of July, 1962, to August, 1962. She played the date as an Exotic Dancer with her husband, RICKY CASE, as Master of Ceremonies. She was the sole out-of-town talent at the club at that time, all other talent being local talent of JACK RUBY. She became acquainted with RUBY during the above run. He appeared to be very good to his employees, protective, concerned for their welfare, and his business was operated in accordance with good taste and for the protection of his employees. He did not allow people to drink with his employees since that is against the union rules.

RUBY did not run an after-hours joint at that time. All liquor was removed from the tables of customers at 12:55 AM. His customers were mainly conventioneers. None of RUBY's customers or associates with whom she saw him speaking at length impressed her as being either hoodlums or anything but businessmen. She did not note any great number of Dallas policemen in the place, at least in uniform. She did observe the Vice Squad to come to the place at intervals, as she understood they did at all the other clubs, to check to see if there were any violations of codes regarding scanty dress on stage. The policemen did not get familiar with any of the employees, to her knowledge, nor did they appear to be overly friendly with JACK RUBY.

She recalled that she never saw RUBY ever making a play for any of the employees, he did not appear to have a favorite, and she does not ever recall seeing him at any time

On 11/27/63 at Syracuse, New York File # Albany 44-267 Dallas 44-1639

by SAs ROBERT S. REA & JOHN L. KELLY:pab Date dictated 11/27/63

164

COMMISSION EXHIBIT No. 1541

2

AL 44-267

alone with any of the girls. She always saw him with a group. RUBY did have a party at his home for the employees while she was there. Only the performers and other employees were present, to her knowledge. RUBY and his bartender, name not known, did all the preparation of the food. She referred to them as "looking like 'old women'". She stated that she had never received any indication that RUBY was homosexual and had never received any such information from any of the employees. She believed him to be a gentleman at all times, even when throwing someone out of the place, not given to any temper, violent acts or any other action which was at all questioned. She never had any conversation with him or in his presence concerning politics.

Miss TAYLOR advised that she had observed an interview on television which indicated that one of the performers had observed OSWALD in the audience at the club. She stated she did not believe this because she knows from experience that any such act would have bright lights on stage. She cannot see anyone to recognize except for the first row and she works under soft lights.

165

COMMISSION EHXIBIT No. 1541—Continued

The following investigation was conducted by SA DANIEL B. FLEMING on November 26, 1963:

AT GREAT FALLS, MONTANA:

CARME PITRELLO, 4802 South Westshore Boulevard, Avenue A 20, Tampa, Florida; and PAUL SALOS, 4802 South Westshore Boulevard, Avenue B 19, Tampa, were interviewed at the Park Hotel, where they are presently engaged as entertainers at night club operated by hotel. Both readily admitted to knowing JACK LEON RUBY as the owner of a strip tease night club near the Theatre Lounge Night Club, Dallas, Texas, where they were employed for 40 weeks, beginning Labor Day, 1962. Both stated they met RUBY through the night club he operated, as their club closed an hour before RUBY's did and after quitting work they went to the club operated by RUBY.

Both PITRELLO and SALOS stated that they were fond of RUBY, but described him as emotional, quick-tempered, and an employer who was interested in his help and entertainers. Neither PITRELLO nor SALOS ever worked for RUBY, but stated they observed his treatment of his entertainers, all of whom spoke highly of RUBY's treatment of them. According to the two, RUBY would not permit any rough stuff or abusive treatment of his strippers or entertainers, would not permit prostitutes or "B" girls to work in his club, and maintained good control of the patrons and activities in his club. RUBY would not permit jokes about "Jews" and, if he liked a person, he would do anything for him. Both stated RUBY, they recall, has a terrific memory and could remember behavior of patrons who had been there before, even if a long time had elapsed between their visits.

PITRELLO and SALOS both stated that they had been to RUBY's apartment. He had invited them and their families to come and told them to bring their children, so that the children could swim in the pool nearby, none being available where PITRELLO and SALOS resided. Both stated that RUBY is a weight lifter and extremely proud of his good physical condition, which he achieves by constant exercise. According to them, RUBY does not drink, gamble, or disipate in any manner. Both described RUBY as a lonely man, fair in his dealings with the public, and employes; and they are shocked that he shot OSWALD.

CARME PITRELLO said that he remembered RUBY was an avid follower of former President KENNEDY, never missing a broadcast or TV appearance, but not given to making any public remarks about the policies or programs of KENNEDY. PITRELLO said that RUBY is well known to Dallas, knew many people, and is well known to the Dallas Police Department. PITRELLO said that he did not think this unusual, as the clubs are checked each night by the Dallas police.

In regard to TRUITT WALTON, Dallas Police Officer, PITRELLO stated that he had seen WALTON at the club on several occasions, checking the club while on duty, and said that WALTON had been there off duty with a girl. PITRELLO said he did not think any unusual relationship existed between RUBY and WALTON, and said that he knew that another Dallas Police Officer, known to him as "TEX," had been there several times. He added he knew of no privileges given RUBY by the police, not afforded other club owners.

PITRELLO said he had joked with RUBY about criminal syndicates and remembered that RUBY had remarked that he did not like them or think them funny, but never mentioned to PITRELLO that he knew anything about them. RUBY had indicated to PITRELLO and SALOS that he had been in Chicago, Illinois, in the past, but did not discuss it with them, telling them that it was a "hard life" and to "knock it off" referring to his Chicago life.

PITRELLO said that RUBY had told him that in the past, he had been heckled by a patron who called him a "Jew Boy," but he avoided trouble with this person, until by chance they met at another club, where this same person made the remark, "Look, Jew Boy with a girl." RUBY told PITRELLO that at this point he lost his temper and floored the man with his fist. PITRELLO said that he knew of no girl friend of RUBY, but RUBY frequently took the girl entertainers to dinner and was known as the type of club owner who would go out of his way to help entertainers to get a start or to make good. PITRELLO said that in his opinion, RUBY's only interests in life were his club, his help, and his dogs.

PITRELLO said he knew of no organizations that RUBY belonged to, and he never gave any indication that he was allied with any group opposed to the United States.

DL 44-1638

3

PITRELLO said that he and SALOS had put on a show one night at the Vegas Club, second club owned by RUBY, which they stated was an after-hours club, selling only beer. This club was operated by a sister of RUBY, whom PITRELLO said he knew only as "EDNA," but did not know anything about her. PITRELLO said he remembered that RUBY had told them that he had started his club with but $3,000. Both PITRELLO and SALOS said that they were shocked at remarks attributed to a business associate of RUBY's, known only to them as "ABIE," who was reported as saying RUBY had shot OSWALD because of "financial loss to his club, and his patriotism was based on the dollar." Neither knew of the true association existing between RUBY and "ABIE," but were perturbed over "ABIE's" remarks.

PAUL SALOS stated that the Dallas Police Officer named "TEX" is GLEN D. NEAL, and he could not think of any friends or associates who were close to RUBY, stating that he thought RUBY to be known to many people, but essentially a lonely man. SALOS also said that he did not know of any groups that RUBY was associated with and knew of no underworld associates or hangerson at RUBY's club.

Both PITRELLO and SALOS said they were thoroughly shocked that RUBY had shot OSWALD, and both said they did not recognize the photograph of OSWALD as that of anyone they had seen at the club operated by RUBY. Both stated they knew of no foreign element that frequented RUBY's club, and described it as a typical Dallas strip tease night club.

PITRELLO and SALOS said that they would be in Great Falls, Montana, at the Park Hotel until December 7, 1963, after which they hoped to go to Calgary, Alberta, Canada, for an engagement and thereafter go to Vancouver, British Colubmia. They have an agent who represents them, JACK COLE, 515 Interurban Boulevard, Jackson Street, Dallas, Texas. Both stated they expect their wives to join them next week and, if they could be of further assistance, they would be glad to do so.

172

COMMISSION EXHIBIT No. 1542—Continued

FD-302 (Rev. 1-25-60)

FEDERAL BUREAU OF INVESTIGA

Date November 29, 1963

IRVIN CHARLES MAZZEI, 12231 Hesby Street, North Hollywood, California, advised that until November 19, 1963, he was Western Regional Director of the Associated Guild of Variety Artists (AGVA) with an office at 6513 Hollywood Boulevard, Hollywood, California.

Mr. MAZZEI advised that he met JACK RUBY for the first time in Dallas, Texas, during March of 1958 shortly after the Dallas area had been included in the Western Region of AGVA. He was introduced to RUBY at RUBY's nightclub by JAMES DOLAN, the Branch Manager of the Dallas office of AGVA. RUBY wanted to buy drinks and dinner for MAZZEI. However, MAZZEI declined and remained in the nightclub for only about ten minutes. DOLAN said RUBY was a chronic complainer and hot-tempered. No business was transacted on this meeting.

During March of 1961 MAZZEI journeyed to Dallas to address the membership of the Dallas branch of AGVA, the Executive Committee members and to meet various nightclub operators in the Dallas area. He stayed at the Adolphous Hotel one and one-half days, during which time a cocktail party was held at the hotel in his behalf, hosted by Mr. CHARLES HOFFMAN, a national board member of AGVA, and ALTON SHARP, the branch manager of the Dallas office. At the party he again met RUBY and had a runin with him because RUBY tried to monopolize MAZZEI's time. RUBY claimed that his competitors in Dallas nightclubs were putting on amateur shows the same night as RUBY, causing too much spread in the customer potential. RUBY wanted the union to get the competitors to change nights or have the union eliminate amateur shows completely.

RUBY stated he had labor connections in Chicago, that he could pressure MAZZEI. RUBY alleged to be a personal friend of the Midwest Regional Director of AGVA at that time, one ERNIE FAST, who is presently on the Interim Committee of AGVA. RUBY said he would take care of MAZZEI if his demands were not met. MAZZEI stated he did not take the threat seriously, as he frequently receives this type of action from nightclub owners.

On November 29, 1963 at North Hollywood, California File # LA 44-895

by SA CHARLES B. SULLIVAN CBS:CM Date dictated November 29, 1963

This document contains neither recommendations nor conclusions of the FBI. It is the property of the FBI and is loaned to your agency; it and its contents are not to be distributed outside your agency.

191

COMMISSION EHXIBIT No. 1543

LA 44-895
2

RUBY showed MAZZEI an honorary Dallas Police Department membership card and displayed a small gun which he carried in his belt. RUBY claimed he was well known in Dallas, had good contacts and had "ins" with the Dallas Police Department. MAZZEI stated that in his opinion RUBY was attempting to impress him, and RUBY was advised that the matter would be looked into, and that RUBY could do whatever his competitors were doing.

At this same time RUBY insisted that MAZZEI come to his nightclub, and on that evening MAZZEI and HOFFMAN went to RUBY's nightclub. They remained at the nightclub for about twenty minutes with RUBY wanting to buy them drinks and beginning to complain about the same subject. MAZZEI told him that he preferred not to talk about it, that he had made his comments and would look into it further.

MAZZEI did not have any contact with RUBY until about October 1961, at which time he dropped into RUBY's nightclub while in Dallas. He remained about twenty minutes, during which time RUBY complained about the same thing. On this occasion RUBY made the statement, "If you don't help me, eventually I'm going to blow my top and go over and bust up the joints", referring to competitors' nightclubs. MAZZEI again told him there was nothing he could do at that time, and RUBY became quite angry.

MAZZEI had no further contact with RUBY until about October of 1962. From October 1962 until November 16, 1963, RUBY has called MAZZEI about eight times on the telephone. Two of these calls were made during the latter part of 1962 and pertained to the same complaint RUBY had previously expressed.

In February 1963 a directive was issued by AGVA ordering the elimination of amateur nights in nightclubs which maintained membership in AGVA. During the first part of March 1963 RUBY called MAZZEI on the telephone and stated he was happy with the decision and stated that he would comply by cutting out his amateur shows completely.

About this same time one ABE WEINSTEIN, a Dallas nightclub owner, flew from Dallas to Los Angeles and contacted MAZZEI. WEINSTEIN requested an extension of the deadline for stopping amateur shows due to previous commitments. MAZZEI granted a two-week extension to WEINSTEIN.

192

LA 44-895
3

On this same date MAZZEI called TOM PALMER in Dallas, who was the representative for AGVA. He advised PALMER of the extension granted to WEINSTEIN and directed PALMER to contact RUBY and advise him he would be granted the same extension.

On the next day MAZZEI received a telephone call from his boss in New York City, one BOBBY FAYE, National Administrative Secretary of AGVA. He learned from FAYE that RUBY was dissatisfied and had flown from Dallas to New York to see Mr. FAYE and was, in fact, sitting in FAYE's office when the call was made by FAYE. MAZZEI discussed the matter with FAYE and advised him that the amateur shows would be eliminated no later than the latter part of March 1963.

During April of 1963 RUBY again called MAZZEI concerning his nightclub competitors in Dallas. RUBY alleged that the other nightclub owners had influenced the amateur artists to join AGVA and were allegedly paying them at the accepted wage scale set by AGVA. RUBY claimed they were utilizing these amateur performers on the same nights and calling them auditions. RUBY alleged that, in fact, they were not paying the performers the scale set by AGVA, and that the performers were kicking back some of the money to the nightclub owners. He alleged that this action was merely a subterfuge to continue amateur nights. RUBY claimed that he had newspaper advertisements of his competitors proving this and would send them to MAZZEI. MAZZEI later learned that he had sent the advertisements to BOBBY FAYE.

In April or May of 1963 MAZZEI received a telephone call from a WILLIAM MILLER. Mr. MAZZEI knows MILLER personally as a person active in show business and promoting entertainers. MILLER stated that he was a friend of RUBY's and was calling on behalf of RUBY in an attempt to straighten out the matters of amateur nights in Dallas nightclubs. He explained the problem to MILLER, and MILLER agreed there was nothing that could be done concerning the situation.

From April 1963 to November 16, 1963, MILLER received about four telephone calls from RUBY, who always complained about the same matter, auditions and/or amateur nights in Dallas nightclubs.

On November 16, 1963, MAZZEI received a telephone call at his residence, telephone number 7661193, at about 9:00 P.M.

193

On all previous occasions RUBY had called MAZZEI at his office, telephone number HO 4-8281. MAZZEI's home telephone is unlisted, and he asked RUBY how he obtained his home telephone number. RUBY stated that he had connections, and that he hated to bother MAZZEI. RUBY claimed that he had two striptease girls who would say they did not get the AGVA approved pay scale for performing at the auditions in other Dallas nightclubs. MAZZEI told RUBY to get this information in writing; however, RUBY stated the girls would not put it in writing. RUBY then offered to pay MAZZEI's transportation expenses to Dallas so that he could talk to the girls. RUBY did not mention any names. MAZZEI told RUBY he would be unable to come to Dallas for about a week and a half.

RUBY then complained that one of his girls under contract with him was working in Abe's Theater Lounge on her off nights, and this was a breach of contract with RUBY. MAZZEI agreed the practice was unethical, improper, and he would look into it and contact him later. RUBY made the statement, "You had better, or I'll break her head."

RUBY related to MAZZEI that he had just squashed a complaint against him for beating one of his dancers. RUBY stated that his friends in the Dallas Police Department had advised him that he would get the worst end of a court hearing. He stated that he paid the girl $150.00 and got the thing squashed. MAZZEI is of the opinion that RUBY was attempting to impress him with his toughness. MAZZEI promised RUBY that he would look into all of these matters and, if necessary, take them before the union if the allegations proved true.

On this same evening MAZZEI placed a call to ABE WEINSTEIN at the Colony Club in Dallas regarding the allegations by RUBY of a girl working for WEINSTEIN who was under contract to RUBY. WEINSTEIN assured him that this was not true; that she had completed her obligations to RUBY. MAZZEI agreed that they could straighten the matter out on his next trip to Dallas.

On November 18, 1963, BOBBY FAYE called MAZZEI on the telephone regarding RUBY's making the same complaint to FAYE.

On another occasion, exact period unknown, RUBY made the statement that he needed no bouncing at his nightclubs; that

194

he took care of anybody who got out of line. He said that he always had "his baby" and patted his side to indicate a weapon.

MAZZEI stated that on November 25, 1963, a New York Times reporter called him direct from New York City requesting information about RUBY. He also received a call from a Dallas newspaper on the same date. He furnished both callers a statement that in his opinion RUBY was a very excitable, neurotic type of individual who never thinks a problem out and does things on impulse. He stated this was still his opinion, and added that he thought the only possible motive RUBY could have for shooting OSWALD was that he felt he had suffered a loss of business due to OSWALD's act and, further, RUBY might have felt he could gain some notoriety by shooting OSWALD, thereby becoming publicly known in the nightclub business.

MAZZEI stated he had no knowledge concerning any association of RUBY with OSWALD; knew nothing of his background, hoodlum or gambling connections or Police Department connections, other than those mentioned by RUBY. RUBY had mentioned that he had connections with the "Syndicate" and labor in Chicago and used to work for the "Syndicate" in Chicago. MAZZEI stated he does not recall the exact occasion this was mentioned, and RUBY did not go into any detail concerning these connections. MAZZEI has no information concerning possible subversive connections, radical or extremist views, relatives, associates or girl friends of RUBY. He has no information of his own knowledge concerning any previous violent actions by RUBY.

195

FD-302 (Rev. 1-25-60)

Commission Exhibit No. 1544

FEDERAL BUREAU OF INVESTIGAT

Date November 29, 1963

WILLIAM MILLER, 6675 Whitley Terrace, Hollywood, California, telephone HO 4-4785, advised at his residence on November 29, 1963, that he is currently unemployed, has in the past been the operator of various night clubs, and in addition, has been one to obtain entertainment for night clubs.

MILLER related that he did not know RUBY personally and to his knowledge had never seen him in person or had any contact with him except for one telephone conversation sometime in 1963. He stated that he did not know the exact date but believed it to be sometime in the spring of 1963. He stated that he had received a telephone call from Dallas, Texas, from RUBY in which RUBY had asked MILLER if he could obtain some girls to help sponsor an amateur striptease contest in his Dallas clubs. MILLER stated that he would be unable to do so. For any efforts on the part of MILLER in obtaining the girls, RUBY was to send MILLER some Wilkenson razor blades, a new type of blade made in England. This was never done.

MILLER stated that RUBY advised that he was acquainted with one MC WILLIE who had worked for MILLER as a pit boss at the Riverside Hotel in Reno, Nevada, at a time when MILLER had an interest in the hotel.

MILLER advised that RUBY stated he was having trouble with the Union in Dallas regarding amateur nights. RUBY said that the Union would not let him run the amateur strip nights, but that his competitors were doing so. RUBY asked MILLER if he could help him by virtue of his contacts with show business. MILLER stated he called IRVIN MAZZEI, Regional Director of Associated Guild of Variety Artists in Los Angeles and told MAZZEI he was calling for a friend, JACK RUBY, in Dallas concerning Union trouble and problems with RUBY's competitors in Dallas. MAZZEI told MILLER he would look into the matter further.

MILLER added that the original call came to his residence, but at the time he was at the home of TED LEFF in Beverly Hills and subsequently had the call transferred to the LEFF phone CR 1-9722.

MILLER said that he had recently talked to MC WILLIE at the Thunderbird Hotel in Las Vegas where MC WILLIE is employed,

On 11/29/63 at Hollywood, California File # Los Angeles 44-895

by SA's JEROME K. CROWE & RICHARD J. BUXTON (A):ism Date dictated 11/29/63

This document contains neither recommendations nor conclusions of the FBI. It is the property of the FBI and is loaned to your agency; it and its contents are not to be distributed outside your agency.

196

COMMISSION EXHIBIT No. 1544

LA 44-895
2

and that MC WILLIE had furnished MILLER's name and phone number to RUBY as a show business contact who might help him with his Union problems.

MILLER related that in the event that he was needed for any further information concerning any matter that he could be reached at the HO 4-4785 number.

197

COMMISSION EXHIBIT No. 1544—Continued

DL 44-1639
MM 44-1412

AT MIAMI, FLORIDA

On January 2, 1961, Inspector LOUIS JORDAN, Immigration and Naturalization Service, Miami, telephonically contacted the Miami FBI Office saying a man in his office wished to make a complaint regarding an American citizen who had been in Cuba. Subsequently, LEWIS J. McWILLIE telephonically stated he had been at the Havana Airport about two weeks previous en route to Miami and heard an unidentified white male giving an inflammatory type speech against the United States. McWILLIE was quite certain this person was an American citizen and was traveling with a group of friends and belonged to an American organization sympathetic toward Cuba. McWILLIE said he arrived in Miami on the same flight with this individual, but did not know his name.

The "Miami Herald" of January 7, 1961, reported that LEWIS McWILLIE arrived in Miami on January 2, 1961, on a flight from Havana. Among the passengers on the flight was LAVERNE KAUTT, age 54, of 2456 Estes Avenue, Chicago. KAUTT was returning with Fair Play for Cuba committee tourists who had visited Cuba in defiance of a U. S. State Department request that they stay home. The article states that on the plane "KAUTT said our Government and our President were no good and FIDEL CASTRO was a great fellow. When the plane landed, McWILLIE's fist landed on KAUTT's nose. KAUTT landed on his back on the ground."

McWILLIE received phone calls from Chicago and Miami and mail from Washington, all complimentary. The article identified KAUTT as a Chicago school teacher.

211

COMMISSION EXHIBIT No. 1545

1

Date November 27, 1963

LEWIS J. MC WILLIE, 3627 Eastern, Las Vegas, Nevada, was interviewed on November 25, 1963. MC WILLIE formerly worked for FRED BROWNING at the Top of the Hill Club between Dallas and Ft. Worth, Texas, in Tarrant County. This was an illegal gambling operation where he worked during the 1940's. He stated that he has known JACK RUBY since 1947 or 1948, and that RUBY formerly operated the Vegas Club and now also operates the Carrousel Club in Dallas. He said that he has known RUBY for somewhere between 15 and 20 years, first getting acquainted with him in Dallas, but knew him only as an operator of a night club. He stated that to his knowledge, RUBY has never been involved in any other kind of enterprise, and to his knowledge no one else was associated with him in the Vegas Club. He said that as far as he knew, RUBY operated this establishment within the law and was not known to him to be involved in gambling, prostitution, or illegal liquor sales. He said that he did know that RUBY had come to Dallas from Chicago, but did not know of any particular associates of RUBY. He said RUBY had visited the Top of the Hill, but was not a frequent visitor there. He said he would think that RUBY probably knew most of the members of the Dallas Police Department, simply because of the type of establishment that he ran, but felt that this would be the only basis of any association with the Dallas Police Department since he felt that the operation was a legal one.

MC WILLIE said that he had gone to Cuba to work at the Tropicana in Havana, Cuba, and while there sometime in 1959, RUBY had been in Cuba for about a one week's vacation and he had seen RUBY there at that time. He said he knew of no interests RUBY might have had in Cuba.

MC WILLIE said that he returned from Cuba on January 2, 1961, on the same plane which carried some other passengers, at least one of whom expressed a dislike for President EISENHOWER and America's actions in regards

On 11/25/63 at Las Vegas, Nevada File # LV 44-48

by SAs LEO A. STEVENS & WARREN E. SALISBURY :alf Date dictated 11/26/63

212

COMMISSION EXHIBIT No. 1546

to Cuba and it was his recollection that this individual was a member of the Fair Play for Cuba organization. He stated that he had become highly incensed over the remarks this individual made while waiting for the plane in Havana and during the travel to the United States, but that he had controlled his emotions concerning this man's remarks until after the plane's arrival in Miami, whereupon he had physically attacked this individual because of the remarks he had made concerning the United States. He said that this matter received local publicity in Miami press and that he was also interviewed by the Federal Bureau of Investigation in Miami concerning this situation. He stated that it would be his belief that JACK RUBY would also be very much opposed to any such organization and also pointed out that he had talked to JACK RUBY following this incident and RUBY had remarked to him that he had done the right thing in attacking this man.

He stated that he had correspondence with RUBY and maintained contact with him principally through this means and sometime in early 1963 had felt that he needed some type of protection around the house and had requested RUBY, believed by letter, to obtain a gun for him. He stated he did not specify what kind of gun he wanted but that he had subsequently learned that a COD package awaited him at the Post Office. He stated that he had discussed this matter with his wife and they had decided not to pick up the gun which had been mailed from Dallas, Texas, as they were afraid their children might find the gun. He stated he was sure that this gun was sent to him through RUBY's efforts based upon his initial request. He stated he does not know what disposition might have been made of the gun.

He said his last contacts with RUBY were about two months ago when RUBY contacted him via telephone concerning some trouble he was having with a show, as a result of which he referred RUBY to BILL MILLER, the owner of the Riverside Hotel in Reno, where MC WILLIE had formerly been Club Manager. Their discussion on this occasion had to do only with the club's act with which RUBY was concerned.

213

MC WILLIE said that since RUBY's name had first come to his attention in connection with the killing of OSWALD, he had searched his mind concerning a possible motive and had come to the conclusion in his own mind that RUBY must have been brooding over the death of the President and that this was an insane act on the part of RUBY. He stated that he is certain in his own mind that RUBY has no underworld connections, although he might be acquainted with some figures in gambling and other illegal activities and stated that the only person that he could suggest who might be on a more intimate basis with RUBY other than the members of the immediate family, was a girl he went with in Dallas, Texas, for about four years by the name of ALICE.

He stated he has never known RUBY to visit Las Vegas and is certain that if RUBY did he would have been in contact with him, as RUBY knows where he works and how to contact him. He also feels that their acquaintance is such that RUBY would not pass through Las Vegas without being in touch with him. He stated he does not know RUBY to have ever been involved in any bookie activity, or in any gambling of any nature other than as a player.

MC WILLIE advised that ELAINE MYNIER is a Dallas girl who worked at the Avis Rental in the Dallas Airport Terminal Building and is acquainted with RUBY. He recalled she visited Havana, and stayed for about two weeks. He denied having used her as a courier between RUBY and himself, explaining that there was no restriction at the time and had he wanted to get a message to RUBY, he would have telephoned him.

214

FD-302 (Rev. 3-3-59) FEDERAL BUREAU OF INVESTIGATION

1

Date 12/6/63

A. B. HAMMETT, Patrolman, Police Department, Dallas, Texas, advised that he has no specific information to the effect that numerous members of the Dallas Police Department frequented the Carousel Club on a "free-loading" basis. He has been at the Carousel Club on only one occasion. He is not sure of the date, but believes it was about 18 to 24 months ago. He was off duty and was there only long enough to observe one floor show, possibly not more than 20 to 30 minutes. Sergeant JERRY HILL of the Dallas Police Department was with him. He is not sure whether or not he met RUBY that night at the Carousel Club, but believes he may have. About the time he and Sergeant HILL were leaving, the Carousel was beginning to fill up with customers. He noticed several off-duty policeman and their wives or dates in the crowd, but does not presently recall their identities other than Lieutenant JAY FINLEY. He has no information to indicate they were being treated by RUBY at no cost.

Mr. HAMMETT has been told by JAMES UNDERWOOD and JOE SCOTT of KRLD that Sergeant JERRY HILL has boasted to them that officers could go to the Carousel Club after hours to drink and associate with the girl employees. He stated he attached no significance to this report since Sergeant HILL is commonly known to make idle boasts of this nature.

30

on 12/5/63 at Dallas, Texas DL File # 44-1639

by Special Agents RALPH E. RAWLINGS and JAMES F. GLONEK :1p Date dictated 12/5/63

This document contains neither recommendations nor conclusions of the FBI. It is the property of the FBI and is loaned to your agency; it and its contents are not to be distributed outside your agency.

COMMISSION EXHIBIT No. 1547

FD-302 (Rev. 1-25-60) FEDERAL BUREAU— Commission Exhibit No. 1548

Date 1/3/64

CHARLES EDWARD MORGAN, 5220 South University, Apartment 303, telephone 752-7091, was interviewed at his home in this matter in the presence of his wife. He advised that both he and his wife know JACK RUBY and that he had worked for him for approximately four years between 1956 and 1960 in the Dallas, Texas night club which RUBY owned. He identified the night club as the Vegas Club and stated that he worked as a pianist in a musical group headed by JOE JOHNSON.

MORGAN advised that he had always found JACK RUBY to be a nice guy who was sympathetic to people and who put himself out on occasion to make loans to members of the musical group. He said that RUBY seemed able to take care of himself and he heard that RUBY worked out a couple times a week at a health club in Dallas, Texas. He recalled that when troublesome situations arose about the night club RUBY, as the owner, would act as the peace maker and always seemed able to control any situation.

During the four years that he worked for RUBY there was only one occasion when a situation got out of hand. This was sometime in 1958 when RUBY was turned on by some brawlers he had unsuccessfully tried to separate and he had to fight his way out of this situation. He said that RUBY, with his eyes blackened and his lip cut, rushed back of the bar and got a pistol. He said that RUBY came out from behind the bar and fired one shot into the ceiling whereupon everything quieted down in a hurry. RUBY then put the brawlers out of the night club. MORGAN said that he admired the cool way that RUBY acted in this situation in that he did not fire the pistol at the brawlers but rather seemed interested in stopping the brawl. He said that he did not feel that RUBY was a violent man by nature.

In regard to other observations of RUBY he commented that RUBY did not seem to care too much about women as during the four years that he worked for him in that he never fooled around with any of the women in the night club. He said that RUBY just seemed interested in making a success of his night club business.

MORGAN advised that he is presently playing in a jazz group known as the 3 Notes currently featured at the 13 Club, Cicero Avenue and Madison Street. He advised that he can always be located through the Musicians Protective Union, 6200 South Cottage Grove, telephone MU 4-2850.

On 1/3/64 at Chicago, Illinois File # CG 44-645

by SA EDWARD J. NEAFSEY/jas Date dictated 1/3/64

This document contains neither recommendations nor conclusions of the FBI. It is the property of the FBI and is loaned to your agency; it and its contents are not to be distributed outside your agency.

81

COMMISSION EXHIBIT No. 1548

Commission Exhibit No. 1549

FD-302 (Rev. 3-3-59)

FEDERAL BUREAU OF INVESTIGATION

1

Date 12/12/63

ERICH KAMINSKI, Lieutenant, Vice Squad, Special Services Bureau, Police Department, Dallas, Texas, was advised he did not have to make any statement and any statement he made could be used against him. He was also advised he could consult an attorney of his own choice. At the outset of the interview, Lieutenant KAMINSKI was advised of the identity of the interviewing Agent. He advised as follows:

He resides at 11018 Joaquin, Dallas, Texas. He joined the Dallas Police Department in May, 1951. Prior to that, he was a member of the Milwaukee, Wisconsin Police Department for five years. Upon joining the Dallas Police Department, he was assigned to the Patrol Division until 1952. He worked with the Vice Squad for a number of months between 1952 and 1954, when he rejoined the Vice Squad on a permanent basis.

He first met JACK RUBY sometime during 1953 or 1954, while working with the Patrol Division. As he recalled, this was during the course of checking the Vegas Club as part of his regular duties. All of his dealings with JACK RUBY since that time have been during the regular course of business. In recent years, he has recalled seeing JACK RUBY a number of times at the Special Services Bureau when RUBY was filing applications for dancing and liquor licenses. During the last two years, he has checked the Carousel Club in downtown Dallas about once a week. During that time, he has also checked the Vegas Club, but he does not recall seeing RUBY there during that time.

He has never visited any of RUBY's clubs socially. He has never accepted favors of any kind from JACK RUBY. RUBY did ask him frequently during the last six years if he could buy him a steak dinner, but he always politely declined and made it clear to RUBY that as a police officer he would not accept favors.

Most of the officers in the Special Services Bureau have met JACK RUBY at one time or another during their work, as have the officers of the Patrol & Traffic Divisions who have worked the districts where RUBY's businesses are located. He does not know the identity of

35

on 12/11/63 at Dallas, Texas File # DL 44-1639

by Special Agent JOHN E. DALLMAN/eah Date dictated 12/12/63

DL 44-1639

2

any officer who is a particularly good friend of RUBY, and did not know anyone who knew RUBY better than anyone else. He never heard of any officers working for RUBY and he, personally, never worked for RUBY and was never asked to.

Lieutenant KAMINSKI recalled that the last time he saw RUBY was sometime during late October or early November, 1963. This was at the Special Services Bureau and RUBY was apparently inquiring about some type of license. He did not converse with him, but merely said, "Hello," as he recalls.

He knows very little concerning RUBY's personal life and had no idea that he was violent. RUBY always acted like a "big shot" and he had heard RUBY came from Chicago. He knows nothing concerning RUBY's background other than that and knows of no connection between RUBY and the mob element in Chicago or elsewhere.

He never heard RUBY engage in conversation concerning politics and has no idea what his political convictions or connections are. He never knew RUBY to carry a gun.

RUBY was a braggart and he recalled the last time he saw him at the Carousel Club that RUBY had told him he had the Persona Razor Blade dealership for the whole State of Texas. He stated he, naturally, did not believe this statement.

On November 22, 1963, his assignment was to handle a security detail on Main Street, in downtown Dallas. After the assassination of the President, he spent the afternoon at the Texas Book Depository Building, but arrived there after the escape of LEE HARVEY OSWALD. He was part of the security force at the Police Headquarters after OSWALD's arrest. On November 23, 1963, he was in the offices of the Special Services Bureau from 8:00 AM to 6:00 PM. He was not assigned to any security detail

36

DL 44-1639

3

detail on that day and did not know what security arrangements were made. On November 24, 1963, he was again in his office from 9:00 AM until 9:30 PM and took no part in the security arrangements. He had no knowledge of the general security arrangements taken during the entire week end and knew of no unauthorized persons that were allowed to enter the building. He, personally, did not check the identification of anyone, as he had no opportunity to.

He knew nothing concerning LEE HARVEY OSWALD prior to the President's assassination and knows of no connection between OSWALD and JACK RUBY.

Lieutenant KAMINSKI stated he was not a good friend of JACK RUBY and he had no particular respect or liking for the individual. He made it his point to have no social contact with him, including off-duty visits to his clubs, and his on-duty contacts were brief and businesslike.

37

COMMISSION EXHIBIT No. 1549—Continued

FD-302 (Rev. 3-3-59)

FEDERAL BUREAU OF INVESTIGATION

1

Date December 13, 1963

GLENN W. BYRD, 5531 Merrimac, Dallas, Texas, was interviewed inasmuch as his name was found among the personal possessions of JACK RUBY. BYRD furnished the following information:

He was a member of the University Park Police Department, a suburb of Dallas, Texas, for many years and graduated from the FBI National Academy in 1940. After completing military service and working as a Special Agent for the Office of Price Administration (OPA), he was hired in 1947 as Chief Investigator for District Attorney WILL WILSON, Dallas, Texas. It was about this time that he first heard of JACK RUBY or JACK RUBENSTEIN. He had no occasion to come into contact with this man even though he knew RUBY as a night club operator,

In October, 1951, BYRD stated he became Justice of the Peace of Precinct #1, Dallas County, Texas. He believes RUBY was brought into his courtroom on one occasion on a simple assault charge or some breach of peace charge with some entertainer who was working at RUBY's club. BYRD was of the opinion the charges were dropped without prosecution. BYRD continued that he remained a Justice of the Peace until September, 1962, when he was elected to the office of County Clerk, Dallas County, Texas.

About October, 1963, RUBY came to the County Clerk's Office and was attempting to obtain information regarding some charges concerning a peace bond brought against him by a girl entertainer at one of his clubs. RUBY was concerned that Justice of the Peace Judge RICHBERG might void his business license. RUBY's inquiries were referred to BYRD and BYRD telephonically contacted Judge RICHBERG. Judge RICHBERG told BYRD that he was of the opinion that the girl entertainer who was a strip tease dancer had brought these charges against RUBY in an effort to gain publicity and the Judge planned to dismiss these charges. BYRD related the information to RUBY and RUBY appeared to be very grateful. In fact, he said he planned to send "courtesy cards" to BYRD and other staff members in the County Clerk's Office. BYRD stated that he did not receive a card to the Carousel Club and that to his knowledge none of his staff members received such a card.

on 12/12/63 at Dallas, Texas File # Dallas 44-1639

by Special Agents ALLEN H. SMITH & TOM E. CHAPOTON:BL Date dictated 12/12/63

126

COMMISSION EXHIBIT No. 1550

DL 44-1639
2

BYRD continued that cards to various night clubs in the Dallas area are passed out rather freely and in fact he, BYRD, passes out "courtesy cards" to individuals. BYRD stated he has been giving out these "courtesy cards" since he was a Justice of the Peace in 1951. BYRD stated these "courtesy cards"are addressed to "public officials" and indicate that the bearer should be extended any courtesy that the official is empowered to extend under the laws imposed on him by his office. BYRD continued that these cards mean absolutely nothing and will get the holder nothing but the people who get these cards feel that they are "privileged" or "something special" and they are terrific for "making friends." BYRD estimated that he has given out over 50,000 of these "courtesy cards" since 1951. He continued that if one of these cards bore the name of JACK RUBY it is quite possible that RUBY could have obtained one from any member of his office or that a card could have been mailed to RUBY in a routine fashion in that RUBY's name may have appeared on one of numerous mailing lists from which cards were prepared and mailed.

BYRD continued that he has seen RUBY only on rare occasions, is acquainted with him, but does not consider him to be a friend or business associate. He has no knowledge of any business activities or business associates or friends of RUBY, nor does he know of any contacts RUBY may have had with the Dallas Police Department. BYRD stated he did not know OSWALD and had no knowledge of any connection or association between RUBY and OSWALD.

127

Commission Exhibit No. 1551

FD-302 (Rev. 3-3-59) FEDERAL BUREAU OF

1

Date December 12, 1963

A. L. DAVIS, 6304 Halifax Road, advised his telephone number at home is FE 8-6469. Mr. DAVIS stated that he recently went into bankruptcy with his grocery chain. He stated that about a month ago, after DAVIS' name had been in the papers regarding the bankruptcy, he received a call from a man who identified himself to DAVIS as JACK RUBY. RUBY told DAVIS that he had heard about DAVIS going bankrupt and that RUBY wanted someone with ability to operate a night club in Dallas. RUBY said, according to DAVIS, that he had an idea of opening a club similar to the Playboy Night Clubs and that he knew of a location. DAVIS stated that he was noncommittal and DAVIS ended the conversation that if he were interested he would get in touch with RUBY. DAVIS stated that he has never met RUBY and has never been in any of RUBY's clubs.

on 12/10/63 at Fort Worth, Texas File # DL 44-1639

by Special Agent JOSEPH M. MYERS/jn Date dictated 12/11/63

137

DL 44-1639
TEC:gj
1

The following investigation was conducted by SA TOM E. CHAPOTON, JR., at Dallas, Texas:

On December 2, 1963, RICHARD DRAKE, Ticket Agent, Greyhound Bus Station, advised that the owner of Hamburger Haven, (FNU) LEIPSEIG is acquainted with JACK RUBY.

On December 9, 1963, JOSEPH LEIPSIC, owner Hamburger Haven, 5410 Harry Hines Boulevard, Dallas, Texas, advised SAs ALLEN H. SMITH and TOM E. CHAPOTON, JR. that approximately eight years ago he purchased pizza pie crusts from JACK RUBY who sold this type merchandise to restaurants. Since that time RUBY has been operating night clubs and LEIPSIC has only seen RUBY when RUBY has come into the Hamburger Haven as a customer. LEIPSIC stated that RUBY might possibly eat at the Hamburger Haven once or twice a year. LEIPSIC continued that he is acquainted with JACK RUBY only as a customer and that he has no knowledge of RUBY's associates, business dealings or activities. LEIPSIC does not know LEE HARVEY OSWALD and has no idea whether or not there was any association between OSWALD and RUBY.

146

COMMISSION EXHIBIT No. 1552

FD-302 (Rev. 3-3-59)

FEDERAL BUREAU OF INVESTIGATION

Date 12-5-63

1

CHARLES DUARTE, 1418½ Congress, Houston, Texas, advised SA JAMES L. WILLIAMSON that he has resided in Houston for the past year but for the 14 years before, resided in Dallas and knew JACK RUBY during that time.

He stated he knew RUBY was from Chicago but knew of no connections with any hoodlum element in Chicago and stated he believed RUBY's night club operation in Dallas was not financed by any hoodlum element.

He stated he did not believe RUBY had any extreme political beliefs and stated RUBY was only interested in making money.

He stated RUBY had mentioned to him on several occasions that he was selling hot jewelry and furs but said he had never seen any of these items.

He advised he did not know OSWALD and did not know if he was known to RUBY.

He stated he knew of no girl friends of RUBY and said that R. D. MATTHEWS, who is employed at a Redman's Club in Dallas and who was a past member of the DELOIS GREEN Gang, is well acquainted with RUBY.

on 12-3-63 at Houston, Texas File # DL 44-1639 HO 44-939

147

by Special Agent JAMES L. WILLIAMSON - md. Date dictated 12-4-63

This document contains neither recommendations nor conclusions of the FBI. It is the property of the FBI and is loaned to your agency; it and its contents are not to be distributed outside your agency.

COMMISSION EXHIBIT No. 1553

Commission Exhibit No. 1554

FD-302 (Rev. 3-3-59)

FEDERAL BUREAU OF INVESTIGATION

1

Date 12/4/63

ROBERT L. GURLEY, 1260 Stevens Ridge Drive, Dallas, Texas, employed as manager at Gene's Music Bar for the past four years, advised that he has known JACK RUBY for about ten years but has never heard of LEE HARVEY OSWALD. He advised RUBY operated the Carousel Lounge on Commerce Street which lounge was backed financially by RALPH PAUL. RUBY in his estimation was the outgoing type in appearance, by that he meant he slapped people on the back, gave them a handshake and always appeared to be in a good humor. He advised, however, that RUBY was impulsive, violent, emotional and erratic and would fight anyone with the slighest provocation. He advised RUBY never came into the Music Bar that he knew of, and he never knew anyone who lived with RUBY although he recalled about a year and a half to two years ago an episode occurred that might indicate RUBY had been living with someone. He said in this regard, RUBY had chased a fellow out of the Carousel Lounge through the Adolphus Garage to the Lasso Bar. He said this male tried to call the police on the telephone, but RUBY got to him first and beat him up. He said RUBY apologized to him for beating up the individual in the Lasso Bar and made the comment that this was gratitude for setting a fellow up with a place to live or words to that effect. He said he did not bother to call police officers, and he did not know the individual's name. He said that there were rumors going around before the assassination of President KENNEDY to the effect that JACK RUBY was playing around with various males and that the rumors increased after the shooting of the President, however, he said there were no homosexual overtones. He said he heard RUBY used to put younger men up in apartments, but he did not know any of these individuals or the reason for RUBY's actions.

GURLEY advised that he did make a statement that RUBY might have killed OSWALD because they may have been "playing around together" and that RUBY might have been embarrassed if his name had been mentioned by OSWALD. He said, however, that this was merely speculation on his part, and he further advised that he had speculated that possibly JACK RUBY was known to a number of police officers since he thought a few of them had visited the Carousel

161

on 12/4/63 at Dallas, Texas File # DL 89-43, DL 44-1639

by Special Agents ROBERT E. BASHAM & JAMES J. WARD/cv Date dictated 12/4/63

This document contains neither recommendations nor conclusions of the FBI. It is the property of the FBI and is loaned to your agency; it and its contents are not to be distributed outside your agency.

DL 89-43
DL 44-1639
REB:JJW:cv
2

Lounge on and off. He added that possibly when the police officers saw RUBY in the police headquarters during the transportation of OSWALD that they did not pay any attention to RUBY. He stated that possibly if police officers had not known RUBY they would have asked him to move on as they probably did others.

GURLEY advised when he learned RUBY had shot OSWALD, he was a little surprised but knowing RUBY's violent nature he could understand same.

He stated he had talked to HENRY HENSON, a reporter for the Chicago Daily News, Sunday or Monday night about some background information concerning RUBY.

162

FD-302 (Rev. 3-3-59) FEDERAL BUREAU OF INVESTIGA..ON

1

Date 12/5/63

Mr. PRENTIS I. VAUGHN, Pilot, American Airlines, based at Dallas, Texas, advised that he flies the route between Dallas, Fort Worth, and Washington, D. C., several times a week. He was scheduled to make the return flight to Fort Worth this same date, and his residence address is Route B124A, Euless, Texas.

VAUGHN stated that approximately six years ago he had engaged in the part-time occupation of drilling water wells. In this regard, he recalled drilling a well on property owned by two partners, one named MORTON GIMPLE and the other believed to be JACK LEON RUBY. He stated that he was almost positive in his identification of the latter. Tese partners owned Log Cabin Enterprises which was a night club open only on the weekends and utilized for private parties. Log Cabin Enterprises was located adjacent to Grapevine Lake between Fort Worth and Dallas, Texas.

VAUGHN stated that in connection with this job, he had been in personal contact with GIMPLE on a number of occasions, however, had only conversed by telephone with the other partner, whom he believed to be identical with RUBY. GIMPLE lived in Chicago where he was believed to own either a night club or restaurant, and he traveled frequently to Dallas to handle his business interests. He recalled that GIMPLE, while visiting in Dallas, stayed at the apartment of his partner and both men were single at that time.

VAUGHN vaguely recalls that during a telephone conversation with the individual believed to be RUBY, it was mentioned that he also had an interest in the Vegas Club, also located in Dallas. He does not know whether Log Cabin Enterprises is still in existence or owned by the same individuals.

VAUGHN stated that he has closely examined his own correspondence and business records in an effort to locate an address for GIMPLE, however, has been unable to do so.

VAUGHN was not in Dallas at the time of the President's assassination or the subsequent murder of LEE HARVEY OSWALD.

183

on 12/4/63 at Washington, D. C. File # DL 44-1639 WFO 44-520

by Special Agent RICHARD W. KAISER/RWK:wjt/csh Date dictated 12/5/63

COMMISSION EXHIBIT No. 1555

2

DL 44-1639
WFO 44-520

He has no other information concerning this matter but felt that this business association involving the individual whom he believed to be JACK RUBY would be of possible interest to this Bureau.

184

COMMISSION EXHIBIT No. 1555—Continued

Commission Exhibit No. 1556

FD-302 (Rev. 3-3-59)

FEDERAL BUREAU OF INVESTIGATION

Date 12-8-63

1

WALTER EUGENE "GENE" LAWRENCE, Gene's Music Bar, 307 S. Akard, Dallas, furnished the following information:

LAWRENCE has known JACK RUBY for about 15 years. RUBY's sister, EVA, contacted LAWRENCE and asked if he could recommend someone to help her run the Silver Spur. LAWRENCE recommended PAT PADGETT, who at that time was a recently retired enlisted man from the service. Shortly thereafter, JACK RUBY came to Dallas and ran PADGETT off from the club. In fact, LAWRENCE saw PADGETT with a banged up head and learned RUBY had allegedly attacked PADGETT with as black jack for no reason.

LAWRENCE usually ran into RUBY whenever LAWRENCE went to the courthouse or police department on business. LAWRENCE last saw RUBY as he recalls in December, 1962, when LAWRENCE went to the Police Department to renew his dance license.

LAWRENCE, a little over a year ago, would frequently give RUBY a ride home when both would be leaving their night clubs in the early morning. At that time, RUBY lived in a house in back of the Holiday Inn Motel.

LAWRENCE never seen RUBY with a gun, but has heard he always carried one and was quick to pull it when he had trouble with a customer at his club.

RUBY and LAWRENCE always got along and the only difficulty which ever came up was when RUBY opened his Carousel Club and came to LAWRENCE's Lasso Bar and was passing out free passes for his Carousel Club opening. LAWRENCE asked RUBY not to give passes to his customers while in the Lasso Bar and RUBY slapped him on the back, saying he could not blame RUBY for trying.

LAWRENCE never heard RUBY was a homosexual and since

199

on 12-7-63 at Dallas, Texas File # DL 44-1639

by Special Agent R. NEIL QUIGLEY & JOHN E. DALLMAN - md Date dictated 12-8-63

2

DL 44-1639

most of the "gay crowd" hangs out at LAWRENCE's Music Bar, he doubts RUBY is an active homosexual. LAWRENCE never saw RUBY with anyone in particular to his knowledge and never recalls RUBY being on a date with a girl. LAWRENCE has seen RUBY in the early morning after the closing of the Carousel Club walking several dogs in front of the club.

RUBY never mentioned any out-of-town trips. However, PAPPY DOLSON, booking agent for theatrical people would have had more contact with RUBY and might be able to furnish further information.

LAWRENCE stated he did not know RUBY owned a car and never saw RUBY in a car to his knowledge. LAWRENCE advised he presently operated the following businesses:

Gene's Music Bar
307 S. Akard

Lasso Bar
215 S. Akard

Jungle Hut Lounge
415 N. Harwood

Golden Steer #2
301 S. Akard

Chiffon'e Beauty Salon
305 S. Akard

200

Commission Exhibit No. 1557

FEDERAL BUREAU OF INVESTIGATION

1

Date 12/7/63

HARMON SCHEPPS, President, Schepps Dairy, Inc., 4935 Dolphin Road, residence 7015 Currin, Dallas, Texas, was contacted at his place of business and voluntarily furnished the following information:

STANLEY KAUFMAN, his attorney, introduced him to JACK RUBY about eight years ago in RUBY's night club, which he believed was called "Cell Block 7". He believed that this was later called the Vegas Club. As he recalled, RUBY talked about getting a divorce or just having obtained a divorce.

The next time he saw RUBY was in late 1955 or early 1956 in the Congregation Shearith Israel and at this time he talked with RUBY briefly. He saw RUBY on numerous occasions after this at the Synagogue but no one ever accompanied RUBY to church to his knowledge. He has seen him numerous times on the streets of Dallas and their conversation has always been of a general nature and nothing in particular has ever been discussed. As far as he knows, RUBY has never been in any kind of trouble and has always seemed to be of very even temperament. Everyone he knows has always had kind words to say about RUBY. RUBY is a very friendly person but is a strong competitor in business. RUBY has never carried any type of firearm and to his knowledge did not have a violent nature.

He knows nothing of RUBY's background, in fact, he did not know RUBY had a sister in Dallas until he read it in the newspaper. He knew him only as the owner of the Carousel Club and the Vegas Club. About one year ago RUBY asked him if he would put a sign outside of the Carousel Club. He told RUBY the sign would cost $900.00 and he would have to pay $300.00 down, $300.00 when the sign was half completed and $300.00 when the sign was completed. This sign was installed and RUBY paid as agreed. Shortly after this sign was installed he was accompanied by DAVE, NATE and SIDNEY WEINBERG, owners of the Dallas Transit System, and they went to the Carousel Club. RUBY greeted them and was his

v35

on 12/5/63 at Dallas, Texas File # DL 44-1639

by Special Agents ALTON E. BRAMBLETT and LANSING P. LOGAN - gi Date dictated 12/7/63

COMMISSION EXHIBIT No. 1557

DL 44-1639
2

usual friendly self. About one week after this visit, he met RUBY on the street and asked him if one of his girls was available. RUBY replied he was not in that type of business.

He stated about a year ago, he asked RUBY if he knew Mr. PAUL, first name not known, who owns the "Bull Pen" in Arlington, Texas. RUBY told him he did and he asked RUBY if he would contact PAUL and attempt to obtain a contract to furnish milk products to the "Bull Pen". RUBY made a sincere effort to do this but he never obtained any milk business from PAUL. He never talked any politics with RUBY but did not believe he was a "red or even pink" in his political beliefs, as he went to church and apparently believed in God. If he ever had believed RUBY was a Communist or had any feelings along those lines, he would have had nothing to do with RUBY.

On about November 21, 1963, STANLEY KAUFMAN told him that RUBY brought a stripper, name not known, in from New Orleans to work in his Carousel Club, but someone in authority had told RUBY that he should not do this as this girl was a trouble maker. RUBY brought this girl in to work in his club but fired her after about two days. The stripper then went to Judge RICHBERG, a local justice of the peace, and made false statements against RUBY. The judge brought RUBY before him and it ended up that RUBY paid the stripper her full week's salary. He did not know any further details regarding this.

He has never known LEE HARVEY OSWALD nor does he know of any association between OSWALD and RUBY. He stated the last time he saw RUBY was about eight weeks ago and this was on the downtown streets of Dallas. At this time, he asked RUBY if he would like to have a cup of coffee and RUBY declined.

He has informed STANLEY KAUFMAN that if RUBY needs financial assistance in this matter, he is willing to help in any way he can.

v36

COMMISSION EXHIBIT No. 1557—Continued

Commission Exhibit No. 1558

FD-302 (Rev. 1-25-60) FEDERAL BUREAU OF INVESTIGATION

1

Date December 4, 1963

ROBERT STUART, aka Buddy King, Veterans Hospital, advised he worked for JACK RUBY at Dallas, Texas, for three or four months in the late summer and fall of 1961, as manager and Master of Ceremonies of the Carrousel Club. When he first went to work for RUBY, the club was known as the Sovereign Club and was a private club. RUBY obtained a liquor license and the name was changed to the Carrousel Club and became an open night club.

STUART said he knew of no criminal associates of RUBY. He said there was an individual, name unknown, who was from Chicago and dropped in to the club on occasions. He thought this individual was on the "shady side" because on one occasion this man tried to sell STUART a diamond ring for $200, and STUART believed the ring to be in excess of $500. Also, this man tried to sell STUART a watch on another occasion for a very low price. STUART described this individual as white male, age 52 to 55, height 5'6", weight 175 pounds, hair gray, receding on both sides of forehead. He said he had the impression RUBY had known this man in Chicago.

STUART knew of no communist sympathies on the part of RUBY, and said in fact RUBY hated the communists and in conversations bitterly denounced them.

He also advised he knew of no association between RUBY and LEE HARVY OSWALD.

On 12/4/63 at Reno, Nevada File # LV 44-48

by SA FORD E. HOLMES FEH:alf Date dictated 12/4/63

COMMISSION EXHIBIT NO. 1558

Commission Exhibit No. 1559

FD-302 (Rev. 3-3-59) FEDERAL BUREAU OF INVESTIGATION

1

Date December 2, 1963

CARLOS JOSEPH MALONE, also known as "Chubby" Malone, who operates Duffy's Tavern, 308 East Market Street, Louisville, Kentucky, a known hangout for prostitutes, advised as follows:

In the summer of either 1957 or 1958 he went from Louisville, Kentucky, to Ellis Park Race Track at Henderson, Kentucky, with the late Lieutenant ELLIS JOSEPH, also known as "Gyp" Joseph, who had been a member of the Louisville Police Department from 1934 until permitted to resign in 1952 as an outgrowth of charges alleging theft.

While at Ellis Park, JOSEPH introduced him to a JACK RUBY, whom he recalled is the same individual whose photograph has recently appeared in newspaper publicity in connection with the shooting of LEE HARVEY OSWALD. JOSEPH told him that RUBY was a "syndicate man out of Chicago." MALONE did not know where RUBY was living at that time. Lieutenant JOSEPH appeared to be well acquainted with RUBY and both remained together during the races at the track on that particular day.

MALONE advised that JOSEPH told him that RUBY was a "good friend", and had some "hot" horses, that is, tips on winners, allegedly on the horses that were being bet by the "syndicate" on that date. MALONE stated that RUBY had a number of winners that date. RUBY was accompanied by an unrecalled white male, age 45 to 50, of Jewish extraction. This individual remained with RUBY and JOSEPH on that occasion.

MALONE has had no contact with RUBY since that time.

MALONE was unaware of any other contacts or associates of RUBY and had no information indicating membership by RUBY in any group or association whatsoever excepting as previously referred to as the "syndicate."

on 12/2/63 at Louisville, Kentucky File # LS 44-542

by Special Agent s WILLIAM E. CORRIGAN, JR. & EDWIN H. EILERS/jaj/csh Date dictated 12/2/63

COMMISSION EXHIBIT NO. 1559

FD-302 (Rev. 3-3-59)

FEDERAL BUREAU OF INVESTIGATION

1

Date December 13, 1963

WALTER C. BROWN, 4826 Mills Place, Dallas, Texas, was interviewed at the Castaway Club, 5600 East Mockingbird Lane. BROWN was reported to have previously played at the Vegas Club in Dallas, Texas, for JACK RUBY. Mr. BROWN furnished the following information:

BROWN has been playing with JOE JOHNSON's Band for approximately 3½ years and for over 3 years of this period BROWN played at the Vegas Club in Dallas for JACK RUBY. The band left the Vegas Club on about November 3, 1963, after some disagreement between the band leader, JOE JOHNSON, and JACK RUBY. BROWN did not know RUBY on a close personal basis since his relationship with RUBY was strictly that of an employer-employee. In addition, RUBY spent the majority of his time at the Carousel Club in Dallas as the Vegas Club was managed by RUBY's sister, EVA GRANT. BROWN knows nothing concerning RUBY's personal life.

After viewing a photograph of LEE HARVEY OSWALD, BROWN indicated that OSWALD was unknown to him. BROWN indicated that although numerous police officers stopped in the Vegas Club from time to time, he knew of no officer who was particularly close to RUBY or EVA GRANT.

on 12/11/63 at Dallas, Texas File # Dallas 44-1639

by Special Agents ALVIN E. ZIMMERMAN & JOSEPH G. PEGGS:BL 294 Date dictated 12/11/63

This document contains neither recommendations nor conclusions of the FBI. It is the property of the FBI and is loaned to your agency; it and its contents are not to be distributed outside your agency.

COMMISSION EXHIBIT No. 1560

FD-302 (Rev. 1-25-60)

FEDERAL BUREAU OF INVESTIGA

Date 12/5/63

Commission Exhibit No. 1561

ASSOCIATES AND EMPLOYEES OF JACK L. RUBY

JANET ADAMS CONFORTO, nee MOLE, who dances professionally as a "strip tease" performer under the name, "JADA", was interviewed at the New York Office of the Federal Bureau of Investigation on December 4, 1963.

She furnished the following information:

She had been associated with her husband, JOSEPH CONFORTO, from whom she is now separated, in the operation of a strip tease club known as "Madame Francine's" at 440 Bourbon Street, New Orleans, Louisiana. This club closed in June, 1963.

JACK RUBY came to New Orleans by car in June, 1963. RUBY may have heard about CONFORTO through EARL NORMAN, a comedian, whom she believed had worked in some clubs in Dallas, Texas and may have worked for JACK RUBY.

While in New Orleans, RUBY went to the French Opera House, a strip tease club on Bourbon Street, operated by HAROLD TANNENBAUM. RUBY had apparently never met TANNENBAUM on any previous occasion. The purpose of RUBY's trip to New Orleans, according to RUBY, was to scout for talent for his club in Dallas, Texas. TANNENBAUM introduced CONFORTO to RUBY at the French Opera House. RUBY offered her $550 per week to perform at the Carousel Club in Dallas, Texas. CONFORTO wanted to take a vacation at that time and told RUBY she was not interested. A week or so later, RUBY sent a telegram to HAROLD TANNENBAUM requesting CONFORTO to work for him for two or three weeks at the Carousel Club. CONFORTO did not reply to this telegram.

On 12/4/63 at New York, New York File # NY 44-974

by SAS JAMES J. ROGERS and EDMUND FLANAGAN/pb 297 Date dictated 12/5/63

This document contains neither recommendations nor conclusions of the FBI. It is the property of the FBI and is loaned to your agency; it and its contents are not to be distributed outside your agency.

COMMISSION EXHIBIT No. 1561

CONFORTO drove to Dallas, Texas the end of June, 1963 for a vacation. Her recollection is that one, "PAPPY" DOLSON, who is well-known in the Dallas area, took her to the Carousel Club where she again met RUBY.

RUBY again tried to hire her asking her to work for just two weeks. At first she refused, but then consented to work at the Carousel Club and did begin performing there on July 17, 1963 under a two month contract at a salary of $300 a week. Her understanding was that if her act went over well in the club, RUBY would raise her salary to $550 per week.

She later found out that RUBY had penciled in on the contract that it was renewable only at his option and she had no right to cancel the contract on its' expiration, September 17, 1963.

She signed a new contract on September 17, 1963 for $300 per week. This contract was to last until January 1, 1964 and she, at first, thought her weekly salary was to be $350. This contract was signed through theatrical agent, JACK COLE of Dallas, Texas and was to contain a mutual cancellation option at the end of the contract term.

CONFORTO found out later that RUBY had apparently prior to the signing of the contract, changed the terms so that only he had the option to cancel at the end of the contract term.

CONFORTO explained that she would be paid each Monday, by check which she immediately had RUBY cash, and she was never able to understand the amounts deducted from her salary by RUBY. She frequently tried to discuss this matter with him, but he always told her that he was busy and she never did finally settle this matter with him. This was constantly a matter of contention between her and RUBY.

298

Near the end of October, 1963, CONFORTO was staying at a motel in Dallas, Texas and had her son, now age 3½, with her. She was ill with a bad cold and wanted to take Thursday and Friday off. RUBY was incensed because she wanted to take time off and apparently did not believe that she was ill. She was treated at the motel by a Doctor HESSER, and she did not work on Thursday, which she believed was October 24, 1963.

She did work on Friday, October 25, 1963 and she noticed that RUBY seemed very angry with her apparently because she had not worked on the previous day. At the end of her number on Friday, October 25, 1963, RUBY turned off the lights at the end of her act to humiliate her.

She worked on October 26, 1963 and told RUBY that she wanted to take Sunday and Monday off and he became very incensed at this. At about 5:15 p. m. on Tuesday, RUBY sent a telegram to CONFORTO telling her that she was fired and that he intended to sue her for two weeks pay.

The following day, Wednesday, she went to TOM PALMER of the American Guild of Variety Artists (AGVA) in Dallas, Texas and complained to PALMER about her dispute with RUBY. He told her to work until the following Sunday and then pick up all her gowns and leave. She went to work at the Carousel Club on Wednesday. After her first number, RUBY again turned off the lights on her and began screaming at her. He told her that he would not let her go on stage the rest of that evening. She went back to the club on Thursday and RUBY would not let her perform. She was afraid that he might do some damage to her gowns which were in the club and which she indicated were expensive.

299

On October 31, 1963 she went to see Judge RICHBERG. and signed a warrant against RUBY. She explained that she merely wanted a restraining order against RUBY and did not want him arrested. However, someone at the court informed her that she could not get a restraining order since she worked in the same building with RUBY. She also had explained the purpose of signing this warrant to Judge RICHBERG.

On Friday night, she went to Judge RICHBERG's court and RUBY was there after apparently having been arrested. In a loud voice, RUBY made accusations against her, accused her of being a prostitute and of entertaining men in her motel room where she was residing with her son. She does not know the exact outcome of this court action, however, she did not work at the club again and the following Sunday, she went to the club and picked up her gowns.

While she was employed at the club, she noted that RUBY frequently used obscene language in her presence and in the presence of the other female employees. He had on only one occasion asked her to go on a date with a friend of his who was in Dallas on a visit, but she refused.

On one occasion, RUBY asked her to move into his apartment indicating that their relationship would be a platonic one, but she refused. She described RUBY as emotional, nervous and the type who loved to be the center of attraction. He liked people to consider him a "colorful person and a character."

He was always hustling, trying to build up business for his club and occasionally when people were waiting in line to get into other strip tease clubs, he would talk to people on these lines and try to get them to go to his club.

300

While she was at the club, someone whose identity she does not know, complained that her act was "too strong". When RUBY heard this, he accused her of trying to ruin him and the club. She telephonically contacted some official, name unknown, in Dallas, Texas and requested that they view her act and she would make any necessary changes. She believed her act was then approved.

RUBY was the type who liked to tell people that the police let him "get away with things at his club", because of his friendship with the police, but she did not believe that this was true.

She had on several occasions, noticed a bulge on RUBY's hip and on at least one occasion he patted his clothing and indicated that he carried a gun. She saw the gun on one occasion and she believed that it was a .38 snub-nose. She saw him throw it in the trunk of his car.

Although she did not consider RUBY as cruel and vicious or the type who would intentionally harm anyone, he was always verbally abusing his employees.

WALLY WESTON, who was the Master of Ceremonies at the club, left RUBY's employ sometime in October and is now believed to be at the Merry-Go-Round in Louisville, Kentucky.

WALLY WESTON left partly because of differences with RUBY and partly because of a family problem.

She did not know of any association he had with members of the underworld, but he did frequently tell people he "knew all the boys", meaning racketeers.

301

6.

NY 44-974

He constantly fought with his sister, whom she believes had a part interest in the club and was reported to have physically abused her with his fists.

CONFORTO indicated that after her dispute with RUBY, RUBY called a number of her friends to "bum-rap her. CONFORTO said she meant he tried to run down her character. He also did the same thing to WALLY WESTON.

She expressed the opinion that the only reason RUBY shot LEE HARVY OSWALD was so he could be a hero to the people of Dallas and the country. He loved publicity and she felt that he did not care if he got 10 or 15 years in jail as long as he succeeded in getting a lot of publicity.

She pointed out that a number of things that happened in October had caused RUBY to be depressed. He had stated at that time that his friends were running out on him and no one was supporting him. He had lost his case with AGVA concerning his dispute with two other Dallas clubs regarding amateur night. Also, WALLY WESTON and CONFORTO had left his club.

CONFORTO, on November 25, 1963 was driving to New Orleans, Louisiana, and was about 100 miles outside of Dallas, Texas when she heard over the radio that RUBY had killed, LEE HARVEY OSWALD. She became so upset that she returned to Dallas and then decided to come to New York.

She stated that she has been interviewed in New York by representatives of the New York Daily News and the New World Telegram, and has appeared on local television programs.

302

7.

NY 44-974

She had no knowledge of any association between RUBY and LEE HARVEY OSWALD. She had never seen OSWALD in the Carousel Club, or at any place.

She was born February 12, 1936 at New York, New York. She was married at the age of 18, to NICK BONNEY in California. At the age of 19, she married JOSEPH CUFFARI, in Baltimore, Maryland. Her third husband was RALPH SMALLWOOD, whom she married at Bainbridge, Georgia at the age of 22. Her fourth husband is JOSEPH CONFORTO, whom she married 2½ years ago in New Orleans, Louisiana. She has one child JOSEPH JEROME ADAMS PETER CONFORTO, who was born May 14, 1959, New Orleans, Louisiana.

JOSEPH CONFORTO is the father of this child and the child is now with her ex-sister-in-law, JENNIE CANNELLA, 401 Sable Drive, Arabi, Louisiana.

303

Date 12/6/63

1.

ASSOCIATES OF RUBY

ROBERT FAYE, former National Administrative Secretary of the American Guild of Variety Artists (AGVA) was contacted on December 5, 1963, at his residence, 96 Fifth Avenue, New York. He furnished the following information:

His connection with the AGVA was terminated on November 19, 1963.

He never had any personal contact with JACK RUBY. He recalled that he had spoken via a long-distance telephone call with RUBY about 6 times during 1963.

All of these calls were made by RUBY to him at the AGVA office in New York, and they concerned the problem that RUBY was having with two other clubs in Dallas involving amateur night.

FAYE had learned that these striptease clubs in Dallas and other cities in Texas were featuring an amateur night. The clubs would allow girls with no experience to try out on the stage as "striptease" performers. When FAYE heard about this, he contacted the regional director of the AGVA, IRVING MAZZEI, and told him that the amateur nights in the striptease clubs would have to stop. MAZZEI in turn contacted TOM PALMER, the AGVA representative in Dallas, and he informed the striptease clubs in Dallas, including the Carousel Club, they would have to stop running amateur night. The AGVA maintained the girls would have to be paid. RUBY then cancelled the amateur night, but the

On 12/5/63 at New York, New York File # 44-974

by SA JAMES J. ROGERS/pm 307 Date dictated 12/6/63

2.

NY 44-974

other clubs continued to run amateur night although they paid the performers. RUBY called up AGVA headquarters in New York and told FAYE that the other two clubs in Dallas were indicating to the public that they continued to run amateur night and would have a contest in which the audience would applaud each performer based on their judgment of her act.

FAYE then contacted TOM PALMER, the AGVA representative in Dallas, and told him to have the other clubs cease running the amateur night in the nature of a contest.

FAYE's recollection was the last time RUBY called him was some time about the middle of November. He did recall RUBY compalined that since he was forced to cancel amateur night, his business had fallen off and he had on one occasion sent the register tape from the Carousel Club to prove to FAYE that his business was actually falling off. FAYE returned this tape without examining it. FAYE had no knowledge of any connection between RUBY and OSWALD and he had never seen or had any contact with OSWALD.

308

Commission Exhibit No. 1563

SI 44-383
JTH/ksw:BL
1

The following investigation was conducted by SA JACK T. HAZEN and SA J. HOMER THOMASSON at Danville, Illinois:

JOHN JOSEPH McNAUGHTON, also known as Johnny Turner, his stage name, advised on November 26, 1963, that he was a master of ceremonies presently employed at Lil's Jockey Club, Belgium, Illinois. He stated that he was presently residing on McVey Road, Tilton, Illinois; but that his permanent home address was 2921 Qualtrough Street, San Diego 6, California. He stated that he could always be located by writing to him in care of the Black Cat Cafe, 12 North Franklin Street, Danville, Illinois.

MC NAUGHTON stated that on October 30, 1963, he received a telegram from his agent, MIKE RIAFF, AGVA Union, St. Louis Missouri, advising him that he would do the show for the Carousel Club, Dallas, Texas, for one week, opening November 4, 1963. He stated that he subsequently went to Dallas, Texas, and made contact with the manager of the Carousel Club, a person known only to him as "JACK", whom he described as:

Race:	White
Sex:	Male
Nationality:	American
Age:	Late forties
Height:	5'7" - 5'8"
Weight:	160-170 pounds
Hair:	Dark, thinning

He stated that he recognized "JACK" as an individual pictured in newspapers as JACK RUBY, the individual who shot LEE HARVEY OSWALD on November 24, 1963. MC NAUGHTON stated that he thereafter worked for five hours a night between the hours of 9 PM and 2 AM as an emcee at the club and completed six days of entertainment and left one day early as he did not like the working conditions. He stated the reason he left one day early is because

329

SI 44-383
JTH/ksw
2

"JACK" was continually finding fault with his emceeing and kept him working harder than he expected to work. He stated that his only conversation with "JACK" concerned his employment and that he never engaged in conversation with "JACK" concerning his personal activities. He stated that his exact employment dates were from Monday, November 4 through Saturday night, November 9, 1963, at which time "JACK" gave him $175.00 in cash, consisting of twenties, tens and fives. He stated that approximately ten minutes later, "JACK" came around to him and demanded $25.00 back stating that he had not worked the full seven days. MC NAUGHTON stated that he handed "JACK" back the $25.00 and had no further words with him. He stated that in his opinion, "JACK" was a "screwy gangster-type character and very nervous". He stated that he never saw him with a gun nor did he ever see a gun at the club. He stated that he was never in "JACK's" office.

MC NAUGHTON stated that he did not make the acquaintance of any of the customers at the Carousel Club and stated that he seldom saw anyone in the audience with the exception of the first row of seats inasmuch as the lights on the stage more or less blinded him. He stated that to the best of his knowledge, he had never seen LEE HARVEY OSWALD at the club. He stated that there were approximately four strip-teasers working at the time he was employed but he could not recall any of their names. He stated that he stayed at the Alamo Motel on U. S. Highway #80 West on the old road. He stated that he drove a 1960 white Thunderbird with 1963 California license KUN451. He stated that he recalls there were two other emcees working in the neighborhood of the Carousel Club and one emcee was EARL NORMAN, employed by the Theater Lounge, and the other was ARTIE BROOKS, employed at a night club located on the same street as the Carousel Club. MC NAUGHTON stated that he is quite sure that "JACK" was present on every day that he was employed and never received any information that he had made any out-of-town trips. He also stated that to the best of his knowledge, he had never seen any law enforcement officers at the Carousel Club during his employment. He stated the name TAMI TRUE was familiar to him but that he could not recall where he had heard this name. He also stated that he had never played

330

SI 44-383
DL 44-1639
JTH/ksw:BL/csh

at the Carousel Club before and did not intend to emcee at this club again inasmuch as he disliked the manager named "JACK."

The following is a description of MC NAUGHTON as obtained by observation and interrogation:

Name:	JOHN JOSEPH MC NAUGHTON
Alias:	Johnny Turner (stage name)
Race:	White
Sex:	Male
Natinality:	American
Date of Birth:	August 24, 1918
Height:	5'8"
Weight:	164 pounds
Hair:	Gray
Eyes:	Blue
Marital Status:	Single
Occupation:	Emcee

331

COMMISSION EXHIBIT No. 1563—Continued

FD-302 (Rev. 3-3-59) FEDERAL BUREAU OF INVESTIGATION

Commission Exhibit No. 1564

Date December 6, 1963

JOE PETERSON, Adolphus Hotel, Dallas, Texas, advised he, and BRECK WALL, are entertainers and are presently producing and starring in a review, "Bottoms Up" at the Century Room in the Adolphus Hotel. WALL advised he first met JACK RUBY in Dallas approximately four years ago at the Vegas Club in 1960, the exact date not recalled. RUBY approached WALL and PETERSON and made a deal for WALL and PETERSON to produce and appear in a show at the Sovereign Club, Dallas, Texas. The agreement was that WALL and PETERSON would have one-half interest in the club. After producing and starring in a show for 30 days at the Sovereign Club, RUBY was approached by WALL to draw up a contract. RUBY would not discuss any contract at the time.

One day after the contract discussion, WALL and PETERSON had an offer to produce and star in a one night show at the Century Room at the Adolphus Hotel for a National Nurses Convention. They were to receive $2,500 for this show. RUBY refused to release WALL and PETERSON for the show, but instead, arranged through AGVA for WALL and PETERSON to appear under the sponsorship of JACK RUBY. WALL and PETERSON did produce and work in the show and they received information that RUBY and AGVA split the $2,500 between them and WALL and PETERSON did not receive any money at all.

on 12/6/63 at Dallas, Texas File # DL 44-1639

by Special Agents JAMES C. KENNEDY & WILL HAYDEN GRIFFIN/jn Date dictated 12/6/63

332

COMMISSION EXHIBIT No. 1564

Commission Exhibit No. 1565

FD-302 (Rev. 3-3-59)

FEDERAL BUREAU OF INVESTIGAT

1

Date 12/7/63

"Miami Herald" of November 27, 1963, carried article by JOHN MC DONALD, former employee of JACK RUBY in Dallas. MC DONALD is employed aboard the Motor Vessel Pilot One. He stated he worked for RUBY as Maitre D when RUBY opened Sovereign Club, Dallas. He quit after two months because of low pay. He describes RUBY as miserly, headstrong, and capable of any action to attain his own goals. He states RUBY once engaged in fist fight with JOE PETERSON, who was producing shows at the Sovereign. MC DONALD has no information concerning RUBY's background, associates, membership in any organization, or acquaintance with police officers. He does not know OSWALD, and never heard of him prior to November 22, 1963.

on 11/27/63 at Miami, Florida File # Miami 44-1412 Dallas 44-1639

by Special Agent ROBERT K. LEWIS :lp Date dictated 12/2/63

341

Commission Exhibit No. 1566

FD-302 (Rev. 3-3-59)

FEDERAL BUREAU OF INVESTIGA N

1

Date December 6, 1963

BRECK WALL, Adolphus Hotel, Dallas, Texas, advised he, and JOE PETERSON, are entertainers and are presently producing and starring in a review, "Bottoms Up" at the Century Room in the Adolphus Hotel. WALL advised he first met JACK RUBY in Dallas approximately four years ago at the Vegas Club in 1960, the exact date not recalled. RUBY approached WALL and PETERSON and made a deal for WALL and PETERSON to produce and appear in a show at the Sovereign Club, Dallas, Texas. The agreement was that WALL and PETERSON would have one-half interest in the club. After producing and starring in a show for 30 days at the Sovereign Club, RUBY was approached by WALL to draw up a contract. RUBY would not discuss any contract at the time.

One day after the contract discussion, WALL and PETERSON had an offer to produce and star in a one night show at the Century Room at the Adolphus Hotel for a National Nurses Convention. They were to receive $2,500 for this show. RUBY refused to release WALL and PETERSON for the show, but instead, arranged through AGVA for WALL and PETERSON to appear under the sponsorship of JACK RUBY. WALL and PETERSON did produce and work in the show and they received information that RUBY and the AGVA split the $2,500 between them and WALL and PETERSON did not receive any money at all.

On the morning after the one night show at the Century Room, WALL went to RUBY's office in the Carousel Club across from the Adolphus Hotel. WALL approached RUBY for payment of the 30 days that they had produced and starred in the show at the Sovereign Club and also for pay for the show produced and starred in at the Century Room. WALL stated that RUBY was very angry because he wanted money and hit him in the mouth, knocking out one tooth. WALL ran down the steps and back to the Adolphus Hotel. Several days later, RUBY appeared at the Adolphus and apologized to WALL and PETERSON and since then, they have all been very good friends but have not been to closely associated. WALL could furnish no information as to close associates of RUBY. WALL advised from what he had learned from newspapers and television, he did not believe that RUBY would associate with a person of OSWALD's character.

on 12/6/63 at Dallas, Texas File # DL 44-1639

by Special Agents JAMES C. KENNEDY & WILL HAYDEN GRIFFIN/jn Date dictated 12/6/63

342

FD-302 (Rev. 3-3-59) FEDERAL BUREAU OF INVESTIGATION

1

Date 12/9/63

BRYAN POWELL, owner of Graphic Studios, 1310 Main Street, advised that either on November 1 or November 4, 1963, a young man, name unknown, came into the shop with some material for JACK RUBY from the Carousel Club. The man indicated the work desired and asked that the company secure an estimate for the work and call RUBY. He made up the estimate and thereafter called RUBY at the Carousel Club. RUBY told him to go ahead and make up the merchandise.

Either on the same day that he called RUBY which would have been on November 4, 1963, or shortly thereafter, RUBY came over and personally discussed the work.

At this time, RUBY gave POWELL and POWELL's employee, JOHN LACY, permanent passes for the Carousel Club and indicated he would have plastic membership cards made and mail them to them. POWELL advised he had not gone to the Carousel Club using this pass and has never been in the establishment.

His contact with RUBY was limited to the one time when RUBY came into his shop and their discussion involved only the production of the material RUBY desired. POWELL noticed, however, that during the discussion RUBY at one time took out a large wallet containing cards and money. In getting some material out of this wallet, possibly the Carousel Club membership cards, POWELL noticed that RUBY had a number of $100 bills in his wallet. He was unable to determine the exact number of $100 bills but estimated there could have been any where from five to twenty $100 bills in the wallet. RUBY made some reference to this money indicating that it was not actually his as he "owed it to Uncle Sam".

The work was completed on November 8, 1963, and delivered by LACY to the Carousel Club. The invoice dated November 8, 1963, indicated that this work consisted of the following material: 1,000 pieces of letterhead stationery of the Carousel Club; 1,000 envelopes; 2,000 business cards from the Carousel Club; 2,000 handbills advertising the Carousel Club and 2,000 handbills advertising a product called the "Waistisizer" or some such spelling.

POWELL explained that the Waistisizer handbills

on 12/6/63 at Dallas, Texas File # DL 44-1639

by Special Agent JAMES F. GLONEK - gj Date dictated 12/9/63

343

COMMISSION EXHIBIT No. 1567

DL 44-1639
2

related to some product that RUBY had and was trying to sell.

POWELL advised he was not acquainted with LEE HARVEY OSWALD and knew of no association between OSWALD and RUBY. POWELL advised that it appeared RUBY had inadvertently furnished an extra sheet of paper in the material he had originally sent over to Graphic Studios in connection with making up the above referred to order. He explained that in the envelope with this material was a piece of paper containing a number of names, addresses and telephone numbers. He furnished this sheet of paper to SA JAMES F. GLONEK. This paper contained the following entries:

JOHN & FAYE VOUDOURIS
Austin Maintenance
HI-42771 - Auto Ph. #853

BOB KAPLAN
ED-6-1988 Contact w/ Jack Walker, [illegible]
Ft. Worth

DICK WALKER
PE 7-5553 atty, re abortion

PAT
EX 1-7392

HOUSTON NICHOLS
EM 8-2575

GEORGE MOORE
PE 80058

JENEL BAYS
Marritta, Ga. or Haizel

DONNA CARSON
DA-1-6977

JOE GLAZER
JU-2-0370
Direct Phone

344

COMMISSION EXHIBIT No. 1567—Continued

DL 44-1639
3

COBO CLEANERS
8135 Liverois
Detroit 21, Michigan

L. J. MC WILLIE
3040 Kishner Drive
Apt. 204

WILLIE EPSTEIN
63 W. 38th St.
New York
c/o BERNARD EPSTEIN

DORREL
LA-1-9879

JOHN ANDERSON
BL 4-9348

CHAPMAN MOTERS
TA48258

SHERIE ASTON
NE 1 1489
Chicago

NICK TURMAN
TA 46229

LAWRENCE V. MEYERS
ST. 28920

KWIK CLEANERS
TA4903

MARGIE
BL 5-5656

HENRY SEGAL
227 E. Ontario

MARTY died Sept. 25, 1962

CANDY
OL 7 3025

345

COMMISSION EXHIBIT No. 1567—Continued

DL 44-1639
4

MICKEY RYAN
DA 4-4378

ROBT. MOSS
TA 1-0762

DOVIE
EX 1-1594

346

Commission Exhibit No. 1568

FD-302 (Rev. 3-3-59)

FEDERAL BUREAU OF INVESTIG ON

1

Date December 8, 1963

JACK J. ROWE, 1003 Brook Hollow, Irving, Texas, was contacted at the Jack Rowe Barber Shop, 240 Village Center, Irving, Texas. He furnished the following information:

He advised that he was the leader of the Rowe Brothers Band which played at the Silver Spur Club owned by JACK RUBY for about one month during 1950. He stated as the leader of the band he had more close personal contact with RUBY than the other brothers. As far as he knew, RUBY was the sole owner of the club and his sister, whose name he did not know, apparently operated a supper club somewhere in Dallas at that time. Later the band played intermittently on radio station KSKY in Dallas and RUBY sponsored some of the programs. The last time he saw RUBY was about five years ago when he stopped at a barber shop across the street from RUBY's Vegas Club. He stopped over to see JACK RUBY and had lunch with him.

His only contact with RUBY was in regard to business arrangements and he is not a social friend. He knew nothing of RUBY's background other than that he had come to Dallas from Chicago. He knows nothing concerning his personal life or political convictions. RUBY was the type of individual who became emotionally disturbed when someone caused trouble at the club, more than a number of other club operators that he had worked for would be. He never knew RUBY to carry a gun.

He had heard that a number of years ago that a DUB DICKERSON, a musician, who apparently worked for RUBY, had been involved in a fight with him. He understood that DICKERSON had bitten off one of RUBY's fingers during the fight. The last he heard of DICKERSON he was working at a motel as a bellboy on Highway #183 in Dallas. He believed this was the Baxter Inn at that time but stated that the motel is now part of the Holiday Inn chain. The last time he saw DICKERSON was at this motel about two years ago. He does not know if he still works there or where he lives.

Prior to the assassination he had never heard of LEE HARVEY OSWALD and he knows of no connection between OSWALD and RUBY.

on 12/7/63 at Dallas, Texas File # Dallas 44-1639

by Special Agent JOHN E. DALLMAN:BL Date dictated 12/8/63

This document contains neither recommendations nor conclusions of the FBI. It is the property of the FBI and is loaned to your agency; it and its contents are not to be distributed outside your agency.

354

FD-302 (Rev. 3-3-59)

FEDERAL BUREAU OF INVESTIGATION

1

Date December 11, 1963

JOE E. SLATIN, Apartment #801, Dorchester Hotel, 911 St. Joseph, employee at Banker's Drug, 206 South Ervay, Dallas, Texas, advised he has been acquainted with the Commerce Street area of Dallas since about 1948. In the period from 1948 until about 1960 he operated a drinking establishments in that area including the Band Box, the Holiday Bar, and the "22" Club.

In the late 1940's or early 1950's he became acquainted with JACK RUBY who at that time came to Dallas from Chicago, Illinois, to help his sister, EVA, operate the Silver Spur night club. From that time through the 1950's, he became casually acquainted with RUBY as another operator of drinking establishments. He formed the impression that RUBY was an individual who constantly sought publicity and who attempted to become a successful operator of night clubs.

RUBY indicated that he had grown up in a rough area of Chicago and that it was his intention to make a success of himself in the Dallas area. RUBY got the reputation of being a quick tempered individual but a person who was always fair. RUBY kept in good condition and handled whatever trouble developed around the Silver Spur. He developed somewhat of a reputation of being good with his fists and appeared capable of handling any trouble that developed there.

In middle or late 1959, SLATIN got the idea of opening a private membership club on Commerce Street. He knew that this type of drinking club was illegal but at the time it appeared that a number of such clubs were in operation and making money. With the idea of opening such a club he approached JAMES DUNN who agreed to form such a club with him. DUNN put up about $5,000 and SLATIN rented the upstairs property at 1312½ Commerce Street and began redecorating the place and lining up help. This club had every indication of being a success as numerous memberships were being secured but at about that time there were a number of raids on such clubs by Dallas authorities resulting in unfavorable publicity and it appeared that their club would have trouble opening. By this time the money supplied by DUNN had been used up. RUBY had dropped around to see the place and SLATIN approached him regarding further financing.

on 12/10/63 at Dallas, Texas File # Dallas 44-1639

by Special Agent JAMES F. GLONEK:BL Date dictated 12/10/63

360

COMMISSION EXHIBIT No. 1569

DL 44-1639
2

RUBY agreed to put up $5,000 to form the Soveeign Club. RUBY arranged with an attorney for incorporation papers for the S & R, Inc., which was to be the corporation. In connection with raising the $5,000, RUBY made a point to explain to SLATIN that he was securing this money from a brother in Chicago. In actuality, SLATIN suspected that the $5,000 was RUBY's own money and that RUBY mentioned his brother putting up the money to forestall any attempt by the Internal Revenue Service (IRS) to attach this money. RUBY had indicated to SLATIN prior to this time that he was having difficulties with the IRS.

The club opened in either late January or early February, 1960, but business was not too good. It was obvious to SLATIN that RUBY was attempting to go "too high class" in the operation and that the business as he desired it to be conducted could never be successful. In addition, RUBY exhibited several temper tantrums, and was generally hard to get along with. Their business relationship was deteriorating but it never reached the point where in their arguments they ever came to blows. As a result of this situation and because he knew the business would never be successful, SLATIN voluntarily withdrew. At the time he withdrew he got no money but RUBY had promised him $300 which never has been paid.

Since that time, he has only seen RUBY on about three or four occasions. On these occasions RUBY dropped by the Banker's Drug to talk with him and always invited him over to the Carousel Club which he was operating on the premises of the old Sovereign Club. He never did take up RUBY's invitation to go to the Carousel Club. On one of the occasions when RUBY visited him he borrowed $100 from RUBY. RUBY gave him the money in a menner indicating that it was a loan but SLATIN actually considered it only a part of the $300 he had coming when he withdrew from the Sovereign Club.

On one occasion about six months or more ago, RUBY contacted him at his residence telephonically indicating he was having trouble with his business because he was not being allowed to operate some strip tease acts as his competitors were doing. He appeared to be upset but SLATIN told him there was not much that could be done about the situation. RUBY indicated he was glad to talk to SLATIN and that he had actually called him because SLATIN appeared to be the type of person who could calm him, RUBY, down.

361

COMMISSION EXHIBIT No. 1569—Continued

DL 44-1639
3

SLATIN advised that the last time he saw RUBY was about three or four months ago when RUBY dropped into the drugstore for a very casual visit.

SLATIN advised that throughout the period he knew RUBY he was aware that RUBY was acquainted with police officers at the Silver Spur, at the Vegas Club, and at the Carousel Club. He advised, however, that this association just appeared to be RUBY's normal desire to know all people. He could not recall the names of any particular police officers RUBY knew. He advised that from the manner in which RUBY talked with the officers at these establishments it did not appear that RUBY was granting these men any special favors.

SLATIN advised that he never knew RUBY to ever carry a gun. It was his impression that RUBY thought he could handle himself well enough with his fists that he did not need a gun.

SLATIN advised that RUBY never exhibited any interest in politics.

Although RUBY was always around downtown and made a special point of meeting people and remembering their names, he did not appear to have many close friends. The only person SLATIN recalled who could be considered a close friend of RUBY, would have been RALPH PAUL. He advised he never saw RUBY out with a woman and considered this just a little peculiar. He has heard rumors that RUBY was a homosexual but he personally never saw anything which would indicate to him that RUBY was a homosexual. SLATIN explained that when he operated the Band Box during the mid 1950's, it was a "queer joint" so that consequently he became familiar with that type of person. It got to the point that he felt he could "spot a queer" by seeing that man around a little bit. In his contacts and associations with RUBY, he never did form the opinion that RUBY was a queer.

SLATIN advised that he has thought about RUBY quite a bit since the Sunday morning when RUBY shot OSWALD in the basement of City Hall. Based on the association he has had with RUBY, in the past, it is his impression that RUBY was merely seeking publicity when he shot OSWALD. RUBY had a

362

DL 44-1639
4

strong feeling for the underdog and this probably prompted his actions. He probably had no intention of actually killing OSWALD but probably hoped to just wound him, get a lot of publicity out of the situation and thereby become a "big shot."

SLATIN advised that he was not acquainted with OSWALD and that he doubted very seriously that RUBY would have been acquainted with him. He explained throughout the period he knew RUBY, RUBY made a point of referring to all men quite a bit younger then he was as "punks" whether these individuals were customers in his place or people he came in contact with from some other situation. In view of OSWALD's age, he doubted that RUBY would ever have associated with him.

363

FD-302 (Rev. 3-3-59)

FEDERAL BUREAU OF INVESTIGATION

1

Date 12/6/63

JOE B. TURNER, Manager of Corrigan Properties, 211 North Ervay, Dallas, Texas, advised that EDWIN B. JORDAN, son-in-law of L. F. CORRIGAN, was formerly associated with Corrigan Properties, but is now an official of Mercantile National Bank, Dallas. TURNER is in possession of all contracts and agreements on properties owned by CORRIGAN.

TURNER has known JACK RUBY for the past six years and has handled the lease contracts concerning the property where JACK RUBY's Vegas Club is located.

TURNER described RUBY as "pushy." On numerous occasions when TURNER was talking on the telephone in his private office on confidential matters, he would look up to see RUBY standing in the middle of his office. Further, RUBY would want to know the details and circumstances concerning the call being made. In event L. F. CORRIGAN was in his office, RUBY would insist that he talk to CORRIGAN for no particular reason other than he just wanted to see "the boss."

TURNER advised his records reflected the property at 3508 Oaklawn was first leased from May 1, 1956 to April 30, 1957, to S. D. RUBY or EVA GRANT. This lease was the only one handled by EDWIN B. JORDAN.

This lease was cancelled and a new lease with the same dates was issued in the name of JACK RUBY alone. This lease was renewed on May 1, 1957, for a one-year period and again on May 1, 1958, at which time this lease was to run to May 31, 1960.

On June 1, 1960, the rent was raised to $600 per month and the term of the lease was for a four-year and nine-month period to expire on the last day of February, 1965.

TURNER stated that on the day before President KENNEDY was assassinated, which was November 21, 1963, RUBY had paid the rent for the month of November, 1963. RUBY has not, to date, paid the monthly rent for the month of December, 1963, which became due on December 1, 1963.

---

on 12/6/63 at Dallas, Texas File # DL 44-1639

by Special Agents WILL HAYDEN GRIFFIN & JAMES C. KENNEDY/eah Date dictated 12/6/63

368

COMMISSION EXHIBIT No. 1570

FD-302 (Rev. 3-3-59)

FEDERAL BUREAU OF INVESTIGATION

1

Date 12/5/63

WILLIAM F. ALEXANDER, Assistant District Attorney, Dallas County, Texas, advised that he was accompanied by Captain WILL FRITZ and Detective B. L. SENKLE, of the Homicide Bureau of the Dallas Police Department, with a court order to examine JACK L. RUBY's safety deposit box at the Merchants State Bank, Dallas, Texas. Mr. ALEXANDER stated this box was found to be empty and absolutely nothing in the box. This box was rented by RUBY in 1958, Box No. 448. ALEXANDER does not have the exact date of the rental. At the time it was rented it had MYRTLE CHANCE as a co-signer. CHANCE, according to ALEXANDER, was a waitress in one of RUBY's clubs.

The records of the Merchants State Bank reflected that CHANCE had opened the box once on July 1, 1959. According to ALEXANDER, RUBY canceled CHANCE off the signature card of this box on June 6, 1960. RUBY's last visit to this box was March 21, 1961. RUBY paid annual payment March 20, 1963. ALEXANDER states RUBY appears to have been in this box approximately ten times.

---

on 12/3/63 at Dallas, Texas File # DL 44-1639

by Special Agent VINCENT E. DRAIN - LAC Date dictated 12/4/63

378

COMMISSION EXHIBIT No. 1571

Commission Exhibit No. 1572

FD-302 (Rev. 3-3-59)

EDERAL BUREAU OF INVESTIGATI

Date 12/5/63

1

Captain WILL FRITZ, Homicide Bureau, Dallas Police Department, stated that he, along with Detective B. L. SHENKLE of the Dallas Police Department, Dallas, Texas, with a court order in the hands of WILLIAM F. ALEXANDER, Assistant District Attorney, Dallas County, Texas, examined the safety deposit box of one JACK RUBY in the Merchants State Bank, Dallas, Texas, on December 3, 1963. This box was found to be empty and absolutely nothing in the box. This box was rented in 1958, Box No. 448, by JACK RUBY. FRITZ does not have the exact dates of rental. At the time it was rented, according to FRITZ, it had one MYRTLE CHANCE as a co-signer. CHANCE, according to FRITZ, was a waitress in one of RUBY's clubs.

CHANCE opened the box on July 1, 1959. On June 6, 1960, RUBY canceled CHANCE off as a co-signer of this box. According to FRITZ, RUBY's last visit to this box was March 21, 1961. RUBY paid annual payment March 20, 1963, for this box. FRITZ states RUBY appears to have been in this box approximately ten times.

on 12/3/63 at Dallas, Texas File # DL 44-1639

by Special Agent VINCENT E. DRAIN - LAC Date dictated 12/4/63

379

Commission Exhibit No. 1573

FD-302 (Rev. 3-3-59)

DERAL BUREAU OF INVESTIGATIC

Date 12/5/63

1

B. L. SENKLE, Detective, Homicide Bureau, Dallas Police Department, Dallas, Texas, stated on December 3, 1963, he accompanied Dallas County, Texas, Assistant District Attorney WILLIAM F. ALEXANDER and Captain WILL FRITZ, of the Homicide Bureau of the Dallas Police Department, Dallas, Texas, to the Merchants State Bank, where they examined with a court order safety deposit box of JACK RUBY. He stated that he did not look at the records but that he did observe the box when it was opened, and it was empty.

He did examine the safety deposit box of JACK L. RUBY which he was told by Captain FRITZ and ALEXANDER was the box the records reflected as being assigned to JACK RUBY.

on 12/3/63 at Dallas, Texas File # DL 44-1639

by Special Agent VINCENT E. DRAIN - LAC Date dictated 12/4/63

380

1

Date 12/7/63

Records of the Bank of Services and Trusts, Murphy and Commerce Streets, disclose a checking account was opened at this bank on Februray 17, 1960, in the name "S & R, Inc.," Dallas, Texas, with an initial deposit of $500. The signature card maintained on this account disclosed two signatures were required on checks drawn on the account, namely "JOE E. SLATIN" and "JACK RUBY." The street address of S & R, Inc., is shown as 1312½ Commerce.

The signature card was revised on May 15, 1960, to add as an authorized signature "RALPH PAUL."

A total of 14 deposits were made to this account from February 17, 1960, to December 7, 1960, inclusively, of funds totaling $9,200; however, the average balance in the account during this same period was approximately $100.

This account as of December 4, 1963, was still carried as a current account, but reflects no activity, other than the posting of service charges, since December 7, 1960.

The balance in the account as of December 7, 1960, was $73.00; and as of October 8, 1963, (last date posted) was $64.

Records of this bank disclose no additional accounts, loans, or rental of safe deposit box since January 1, 1962, by S & R, Inc., JACK LEON RUBY, JACK RUBENSTEIN, Carousel Club, or Vegas Club.

The foregoing information is available only upon the issuance of a subpoena duces tecum, which should be directed to Mr. J. B. LINDQUIST, Cashier, Bank of Services and Trusts, Dallas, Texas.

on 12/4/63 at Dallas, Texas File # DL 44-1639

by Special Agent ALFRED C. ELLINGTON :lp Date dictated 12/5/63

381

COMMISSION EXHIBIT No. 1574

1

Date 12/7/63

On December 5, 1963, the records of the Merchants State Bank, 5217 Ross Street, Dallas, Texas, reflected the following information, contained in the following documents:

1. A bank statement relative to Carousel, 1312½ Commerce, Dallas, Texas, Account # 08 236 3, reflecting the following entries:

CHECKS	DEPOSITS	DATE	NO OF CHECKS PAID	BALANCE
Balance Brought Forward --		OCT 31 '63		$203.43
	$33.22	NOV 11 '63		236.65
	10.00	NOV 19 '63		246.65
15.00		NOV 20 '63	1	231.65
31.87		NOV 22 '63	2	199.78

2. Check dated November 19, 1963, payable to the Dallas City Water Works in the amount of $31.87, signed Carousel Club - JACK RUBY.

3. Check dated November 15, 1963, payable to the National Business and Secretarial Service, Dallas, in the amount of $15, signed Carousel Club - JACK RUBY.

4. Bank statement for the Vegas Club, care of JACK RUBY, 3929 Rawlins, Dallas, Texas, Account # 18 106, reflecting the following entries:

Balance Brought Forward --		OCT 31 '63		134.44
50.00		NOV 6 '63	1	84.44
25.00		NOV 8 '63	2	59.44
	200.00	NOV 11 '63	2	259.44
11.65		NOV 12 '63	3	247.79
25.00		NOV 20 '63	4	222.79

on 12/6/63 at Dallas, Texas File # DL 44-1639

by Special Agent EDMOND C. HARDIN :lp Date dictated 12/7/63

382

COMMISSION EXHIBIT No. 1575

DL 44-1639

2

CHECKS	DEPOSITS	DATE	NO OF CHECKS PAID	BALANCE
$12.82		NOV 22'63	5	$209.97
50.00		NOV 25'63	6	159.97

5. Check dated October 23, 1963, payable to Angeles, Inc., signed Vegas Club - JACK RUBY, in the amount of $25.

6. Check dated November 2, 1963, payable to the Dallas City Water Works for $11,65, signed Vegas Club - JACK RUBY.

7. Check dated November 4, 1963, payable to ABE KLEINMAN, signed Vegas Club - JACK RUBY.

8. Check dated November 19, 1963, payable to the Dallas City Water Works for $12.82, signed Vegas Club - JACK RUBY.

9. Check dated November 20, 1963, payable to GRAHAM COCH, for $50, signed Vegas Club - JACK RUBY.

10. Notice of charge against account dated November 20, 1963, in the amount of $25, for unpaid item as follows: Check dated October 28, 1963, for $25, drawn on the Republic National Bank of Houston, Texas, signed R. H. SHEPPARD, returned marked "Account Closed."

11. Copies of six ledger sheets for JACK RUBY, account # 77 069, reflecting the following entries:

CHECKS	DEPOSITS	DATE	NO OF CHECKS PAID	BALANCE
Balance Brought Forward --		MAY 15'63		$88.50
$ 4.40		MAY 20'63	1	84.10
1.00-SC		MAY 20'63	1	83.10
30.00		MAY 27'63	2	53.10
8.00		MAY 30'63	3	45.10
20.00		JUN 4'63	4	25.10
7.65		JUN 17'63	5	17.45
Balance Brought Forward --		JUN 18'63		17.45
1.00-SC		JUN 20'63		16.45
	$33.45	JUN 21'63		49.90
	30.00	JUN 28'63		79.90
	7.00	JUL 2'63		86.90

383

COMMISSION EXHIBIT No. 1575—Continued

DL 44-1639

3

CHECKS	DEPOSITS	DATE	NO OF CHECKS PAID	BALANCE
Balance Brought Forward --		JUL 16'63		$86.90
$ 3.50		JUL 17'63	1	83.40
1.00-SC		JUL 18'63	1	82.40
14.06		AUG 7'63	2	68.34
7.25		AUG 8'63	3	61.09
Balance Brought Forward --		AUG 15'63		61.09
1.00-SC		AUG 20'63		60.09
4.95		AUG 22'63	1	55.14
	$16,00	AUG 23'63	1	71.14
	32.30	AUG 30'63	1	103.44
5.00 15.00		SEP 10'63	3	83.44
40.00		SEP 13'63	4	43.44
Balance Brought Forward --		SEP 17'63		43.44
50.00	50,00	SEP 19'63		43.44
1.00-SC		SEP 19'63		42.44
50,00	50.00	SEP 20'63	1	42.44
3,06		OCT 4'63	2	39.38
1.60		OCT 11'63	3	37.78
Balance Brought Forward		OCT 15'63		37.78
1.00-SC		OCT 17'63		36.78

14. Copies of five ledger sheets for Carousel, Account # 08 236 3, reflecting the following entries:

CHECKS	DEPOSITS	DATE	NO OF CHECKS PAID	BALANCE
Balance Brought Forward --		MAY 31'63		134.47
14.77		JUN 3'63	1	119.70
	55.78	JUN 3'63	1	175.48
	16.04	JUN 10'63	1	191.52
Balance Brought Forward --		JUN 28'63		191.52
	350.00	JUL 5'63		541.52
46.15		JUL 10'63	1	495.37
	16.84	JUL 12'63	1	512.21
64.00		JUL 16'63	2	448.21
34.53 75.00		JUL 22'63	4	338.68
Balance Brought Forward --		JUL 31'63		338.68
7.65		AUG 5'63	1	331.03
45.00		AUG 7'63	2	286.03
87.36		AUG 8'63	3	198.67
	24.24	AUG 9'63	3	222.91
50.00		AUG 12'63	4	172.91
47.25		AUG 13'63	5	125.66
14.84		AUG 23'63	6	110.82
	151.00	AUG 30'63	6	261.82

384

COMMISSION EXHIBIT No. 1575—Continued

DL 44-1639

4

CHECKS	DEPOSITS	DATE	NO OF CHECKS PAID	BALANCE
Balance Brought Forward --		AUG 30'63		$261.82
$ 9.80		SEP 5'63	1	252.02
30.00	45.00	SEP 9'63	3	177.02
8.50		AUG 6'63	4	168.52
	$ 25.16	SEP 12'63	4	193.68
29.45		SEP 16'63	5	164.23
	24.50	SEP 30'63	5	188.73
Balance Brought Forward --		SEP 30'63		188.73
	8.82	OCT 4'63		197.55
24.38		OCT 10'63	1	173.17
	30.26	OCT 10'63	1	203.43

13. Copies of three ledger sheets for Vegas Club, care of JACK RUBY, 3929 Rawlins, Dallas 19, Texas, Account # 18 106, reflecting the following entries:

Balance Brought Forward --		MAY 31'63		245.14
95.42		JUL 3'63	1	249.72
.90-SC		JUN 7'63	1	148.82
38.15		JUN 10'63	2	110.67
85.03		JUN 12'63	3	25.64
50.00	50.00	JUN 14'63	5	25.64
50.00	200.00	JUN 18'63	4	175.64
2.75		JUN 28'63	5	172.89
Balance Brought Forward		AUG 30'63		101.31
50.00		SEP 9'63	1	51.31
13.24		SEP 10'63	2	35.07
	200.00	SEP 12'63	2	238.07
1.45		SEP 18'63	3	236.52
26.47		SEP 23'63	4	210.15
Balance Brought Forward		SEP 30'63		210.15
50.00		OCT 9'63	1	160.15
78.71		OCT 10'63	2	81.44
17.53		OCT 16'63	3	63.91
	200.00	OCT 22'63	3	263.91
129.47		OCT 29'63	4	134.44

The above records are confidential and will be produced only upon the issuance of a subpoena duces tecum. Mr. V. P. SCHUMACHER, President, Merchants State Bank, 5217 Ross, Dallas, Texas, is the proper person to subpoena to produce these records.

385

COMMISSION EXHIBIT No. 1575—Continued

PRESIDENT'S COMMISSION
ON THE
ASSASSINATION OF PRESIDENT KENNEDY
200 Maryland Ave. N.E.
Washington, D.C. 20002
Telephone 543-1400

J. LEE RANKIN, General Counsel

August 13, 1964

Mr. J. Edgar Hoover
Director
Federal Bureau of Investigation
Department of Justice
Washington, D.C., 20535

Dear Mr. Hoover:

Reference is made to pages 382-385 of the December 14, 1963, Clements Report. These materials reflect the activities of checking accounts at the Merchants State Bank, 5217 Ross Street, Dallas, Texas, of the Carousel Club, the Vegas Club, and Jack Ruby.

The Carousel Club record extends to November 22, 1963; the Vegas Club record, to November 25, 1963; and Ruby's record, to October 17, 1963. The Commission would appreciate your communicating with the Merchants State Bank to ascertain whether there has been any recent activity in any of these accounts. For the sake of completeness, the Commission would appreciate notification concerning any changes made in these accounts since the dates provided in the Clements Report.

Because the Commission plans to publish its Report in the very near future, it is extremely important that this information be conveyed to the Commission at the earliest possible time.

Sincerely,

J. Lee Rankin
General Counsel

COMMISSION EXHIBIT No. 1575—Continued

UNITED STATES DEPARTMENT OF JUSTICE

FEDERAL BUREAU OF INVESTIGATION

In Reply, Please Refer to File No.

Dallas, Texas
August 19, 1964

JACK L. RUBY;
LEE HARVEY OSWALD

The President's Commission on the Assassination of President Kennedy, in a letter dated August 13, 1964, made reference to previous examination of records of the Merchants State Bank, Dallas, Texas, relating to accounts of the Carousel Club, Vegas Club, and Jack L. Ruby. It was requested re-examination be made to determine any activity in such accounts since dates of previous examinations.

Attached are results of investigation requested.

COMMISSION EXHIBIT No. 1575—Continued

FD-302 (Rev. 3-3-59)

FEDERAL BUREAU OF INVESTIGATION

Date August 19, 1964

1

On August 18, 1964, the records of the Merchants State Bank, 5217 Ross Avenue, Dallas, Texas, were examined and revealed the following information concerning the following accounts:

JACK RUBY CHECKING ACCOUNT
NUMBER 77 069

The balance of this account brought forward as of July 15, 1964, was $36.78 and the account was closed on July 17, 1964, with a zero balance on a check drawn on the Merchants State Bank, in the amount of $35.78, dated July 17, 1964, made payable to EVA L. GRANT, signed JACK RUBY and EVA L. GRANT on the face of the check and endorsed EVA L. GRANT on the back of the check. The one dollar difference between the account balance and the check drawn to close the account was a one dollar service charge made by the bank.

VEGAS CLUB CHECKING ACCOUNT
NUMBER 18 106 (CARE OF JACK RUBY)

This account reflects a balance brought forward as of October 31, 1963, of $134.44. The following activity was noted:

CHECKS	DEPOSITS	DATE	NO. OF CHECKS PAID	BALANCE
$50.00		11/6/63	1	$84.44
25.00		11/8/63	2	59.44
	$200.00	11/11/63	2	259.44

on 8/18/64 at Dallas, Texas File # DL 44-1639

by Special Agent RAYMOND P. YELCHAK /jtf Date dictated 8/18/64

COMMISSION EXHIBIT No. 1575—Continued

CHECKS	DEPOSITS	DATE	NO. OF CHECKS PAID	BALANCE
$11.65		11/12/63	3	$247.79
25.00		11/20/63	4	222.79
12.82		11/22/63	5	210.57
50.00		11/25/63	6	159.97

The balance brought forward as of November 29, 1963, was $159.97.

The following activity was noted:

CHECKS	DEPOSITS	DATE	NO. OF CHECKS PAID	BALANCE
$35.23		12/2/63	1	$124.74
35.23 (error correction)		12/2/63		159.97
.67 (service charge)		12/5/63		159.30
.67 (error correction)		12/5/63		159.97
35.23 and 93.70		12/13/63	2	31.04

The balance brought forward as of December 31, 1963, was $31.04.

The following activity was noted:

CHECKS	DEPOSITS	DATE	NO. OF CHECKS PAID	BALANCE
$ .67 (service charge)		1/3/64		$30.37
15.50		1/8/64	1	14.87
3.89		1/14/64	2	10.98
10.98		1/28/64	3	.00

This account was closed on a zero balance on a check drawn on the Merchants State Bank, made payable to the Vegas Club in the amount of $10.98, dated January 27, 1964, signed EVA L. GRANT on the front, and endorsed EVA L. GRANT on the back.

CAROUSEL CHECKING ACCOUNT
NUMBER 08 236 3

This account reflects a balance brought forward as of October 31, 1963, of $203.43.

The following activity was noted:

CHECKS	DEPOSITS	DATE	NO. OF CHECKS PAID	BALANCE
	$33.22	11/11/63		$236.65
	10.00	11/19/63		246.65
$15.00		11/20/63	1	231.65
31.87		11/22/63	2	199.78

The balance brought forward as of November 29, 1963, was $199.78.

DL 44-1639
4

The following activity was noted:

CHECKS	DEPOSITS	DATE	NO. OF CHECKS PAID	BALANCE
$86.24		12/3/63	1	$113.54
	$ 9.90	12/11/63	1	123.44
9.90		12/13/63	2	113.54
	130.60	12/16/63	2	244.14
87.50		12/19/63	3	156.64
	20.00	12/31/63	3	176.64

The balance brought forward as of December 31, 1963, was $176.64.

The following activity was noted:

CHECKS	DEPOSITS	DATE	NO. OF CHECKS PAID	BALANCE
$20.00		1/6/64	1	$156.64
	$20.00	1/6/64	1	176.64
.54 (service charge)		1/7/64	1	176.10
20.00		1/13/64	2	156.10
	47.00	1/14/64	2	203.10
	20.00	1/24/64	2	223.10
	20.00	1/29/64	2	243.10

COMMISSION EXHIBIT No. 1575—Continued

DL 44-1639
5

The balance brought forward as of January 31, 1964, was $243.10.

The following activity was noted:

CHECKS	DEPOSITS	DATE	NO. OF CHECKS PAID	BALANCE
	$50.00	2/5/64		$293.10
$22.00 and 55.00		2/11/64	2	216.10
	13.88	2/20/64	2	229.98

The balance brought forward on February 28, 1964, was $229.98, and this account was closed on March 6, 1964, with a zero balance on a check drawn on the Merchants State Bank, dated March 6, 1964, in the amount of $229.98, made payable to EVA L. GRANT and signed on the front "Carousel by Eva L. Grant" and endorsed on the back Eva L. Grant.

The above information is confidential and will be produced only upon the issuance of a subpoena duces tecum directed to Mr. V. P. SCHUMACHER, President, Merchants State Bank, 5217 Ross Avenue, Dallas, Texas.

COMMISSION EXHIBIT No. 1575—Continued

FD-302 (Rev. 1-25-60)

FEDERAL BUREAU OF INVESTIGATION

1

Date 12/6/63

Mrs. VIRGINIA BOWMAKER, 5809 South Minnie, was interviewed, and she advised as follows:

She was formerly employed at the T-Bone Night Club, Wichita, Kansas, from August 1962, to August 1963. During her employment there she recalled hearing another employee, name unrecalled, make a statement that JACK RUBY, the owner of some night clubs in Dallas, Texas, was or had been in the T-Bone. Mrs. BOWMAKER denied that she knew this person stating that the only information she can recall is that RUBY supposedly was there to see a "stripper" called "PRECIOUS DIAMOND."

BOWMAKER denied that she was familiar with any of the entertainers who had previously appeared at the T-Bone Club other than a former "stripper" known as GAIL RAVEN, who stayed at the BOWMAKER residence on one occasion. She advised she still writes to this person and directs her letters to GAIL RAVEN, c/o Mrs. JOHN FINCH, Box 332, Woodsboro, Texas. BOWMAKER denied that she knew RUBY or could furnish any information about him.

On 12/4/63 at Wichita, Kansas File # KC 44-497

by SAs JAMES F. MILLER and ROBERT ALLEN ELKINS (lib) Date dictated 12/5/63

440

COMMISSION EXHIBIT No. 1576

FD-302 (Rev. 1-25-60)

FEDERAL BUREAU OF INVESTIGATION

1

Date 12/6/63

THELMA CORNWELL, 4635½ South Broadway, advised as follows:

She was formerly employed at the T-Bone Night Club in Wichita, Kansas, from April 1961, to November 1963. During this period of time a man was pointed out to her as being JACK RUBY, the owner or operator of some Dallas, Texas, night clubs, as being a customer of the T-Bone. She denied knowing the dates he was in the club or who pointed him out to her, but was of the opinion this happened on only one or two occasions. She did recall serving dinner to RUBY on an unrecalled evening at the club and described RUBY as a "dumpy little fat man."

CORNWELL stated that she was of the opinion the night she served RUBY he was with or waiting for an exotic dancer known as "Precious Diamond" who was then employed at the T-Bone. She stated she thought this was about Christmas-time, 1962, because it was about the time of the Christmas parties. CORNWELL also recalled that VIRGIL PEEL, who works at the Boeing Company, and who also operates the private club known as the Westair Private Club, located in the Town and Country Motel, West 54 Highway, Wichita, claimed that RUBY gave him a card for one of his clubs in Dallas at that time. PEEL was at that time also employed at the T-Bone. CORNWELL said she did not recall seeing RUBY talk to or visit anyone other than the dancer. CORNWELL denied that she could furnish any other information regarding RUBY, his associates, or his reason for being in Wichita, Kansas.

CORNWELL suggested that if anyone wanted to contact "Precious Diamond" she could probably be contacted through the agent, JACK COLE, 515 Interurban Building, Dallas, Texas.

On 12/4/63 at Wichita, Kansas File # KC 44-497

by SAs JAMES F. MILLER and ROBERT ALLEN ELKINS Date dictated 12/5/63

441

COMMISSION EXHIBIT No. 1577

Commission Exhibit No. 1578

FD-302 (Rev. 1-25-60)

FEDERAL BUREAU OF INVESTIGATION

1

Date 12/6/63

BETH HILL, 1915 West McArthur, a waitress at the T-Bone Night Club, 220 East 47th Street South, was interviewed at her place of employment and she advised as follows:

She has been a waitress at the T-Bone for a period of about six years. She recalled having seen JACK RUBY in the T-Bone on a couple of occasions, however, this was at least a year ago. She denied she knew the date he was there, but did recall he was with another man, description unknown and appeared to be interested in an exotic dancer known as "Precious Diamond", who was then appearing at the club. HILL said the only other thing she could recall was that RUBY was pointed out to her by a former T-Bone employee, THELMA CORNWELL, who seemed to know him, and who told her RUBY owned some "club" in Dallas, Texas. HILL denied having any other information regarding RUBY or any of his associates.

On 12/4/63 at Wichita, Kansas File # KC 44-497

by SAs JAMES F. MILLER and ROBERT ALLEN ELKINS (lib) Date dictated 12/5/63

442

Commission Exhibit No. 1579

FD-302 (Rev. 1-25-60)

FEDERAL BUREAU OF INVESTIGATION

Date 12/6/63

KAREN SIMMONS, 2222 West Sunnybrook Road, advised as follows:

She is a waitress at the T-Bone Night Club, 220 East 47th Street, South, and has been so employed for the past three years. She recalled that sometime in the past she waited table for a customer who someone at the T-Bone later advised her was JACK RUBY, a night club operator from Dallas, Texas. SIMMONS recalled this as being during a period when a "stripper" called GAIL RAYBURN (phonetic), an exotic dancer, was appearing at the club. SIMMONS estimated the time as about one year ago.

SIMMONS claimed that upon this occasion, RUBY was accompanied by another unknown male and a female SIMMONS could only describe as having blonde hair. SIMMONS was of the opinion someone had told her this blonde was also an exotic dancer. She recalled that RUBY was at the club all evening for all three shows and apparently was interested in GAIL RAYBURN.

SIMMONS stated that after JACK RUBY had shot and killed LEE HARVEY OSWALD in Dallas, Texas, she had heard that THELMA CORNWELL, a former waitress at the club, had telephonically contacted JEAN BOWMAKER, another former waitress at the club and reminded BOWMAKER that she, BOWMAKER, had waited on RUBY at the T-Bone Club. BOWMAKER had supposedly made the statement she did not recall RUBY. SIMMONS claimed she could furnish no additional information regarding RUBY or his associates.

On 12/4/63 at Wichita, Kansas File # KC 44-497

by SAs JAMES F. MILLER and ROBERT ALLEN ELKINS (lib) Date dictated 12/5/63

443

Commission Exhibit No. 1580

1
SL 44-496
AJR/mwf

AT ST. LOUIS, MISSOURI:

On November 26, 1963, there was received at the St. Louis Office of the FBI by Special Delivery mail an anonymous letter as follows:

"To: the F.B.I. 11/26/63

"Subject: Jack Ruby - Dallas

"I do not wish to get involved, however in the interest of national security I wish to advise that Jack Ruby was in New York on or about August 4, 1963 stayed at the New Hilton Hotel_ arrived via American Airlines I believe sometime between 9:00 & 11:00 P.M. Supposedily there to see about talent for his nightclub_ was carrying a brown briefcase & was in a very jolly mood. We believe Jack Ruby to be the type of person that would do or commit an act of this type only if there were a specific reason behind it relating to business or otherwised forced.

"From a citizen who loves his country and his President."

444

COMMISSION EXHIBIT NO. 1580

FEDERAL BUREAU OF INVESTIGATION

Date 11/29/63

Commission Exhibit No. 1581

PAUL VALENTINE, Assistant General Manager, New York Hilton Hotel at Rockefeller Center, 1335 Avenue of the Americas, advised that a check of his records reflect that JACK RUBY, 223 South Ewing, Dallas, Texas, and who is affiliated with the Carousel Club, 1312½ Commerce, Dallas, Texas, checked into the New York Hilton Hotel at 10:59 p.m., August 4, 1963, and departed 4:40 p.m., August 6, 1963. At the time RUBY registered at the hotel, he furnished the registration clerk with a business card of the Carousel Club. This card, according to Mr. VALENTINE was attached to the registration card.

While staying at the hotel, RUBY made no local New York calls, but he did make the following long distance calls:

Date	Number
August 4, 1963	Area Code 213 5230930
August 4, 1963	Area Code 213 2740043
August 5, 1963	Area Code 213 2740043
August 4, 1963	Area Code 214 7472362
August 5, 1963	Area Code 214 7472362
August 5, 1963	Area Code 214 5284775
August 5, 1963	Area Code 807 2754891

On 11/25/63 at New York, New York File # NY

by SAS EDMUND FLANAGAN AND JAMES J. ROGERS:aam Date dictated 11/27/63

445

COMMISSION EXHIBIT NO. 1581

NY

According to Mr. VALENTINE, subject's total bill of $51.62 was paid by cash at the time he departed from the hotel.

446

COMMISSION EXHIBIT NO. 1581—Continued

FD-302 (Rev. 1-25-60)

FEDERAL BUREAU OF INVESTIGATION

Date 11/29/63

Commission Exhibit No. 1582

MAL B. KOVNIT, Chief Room Clerk, New York Hilton Hotel at Rockefeller Center, 1335 Avenue of the Americas, advised that he recalls registering JACK RUBY, 223 South Ewing, Dallas, Texas, on August 4, 1963. He stated that at the time RUBY registered, he gave him a business card of the Carousel Club in Dallas, Texas. KOVNIT stated that RUBY informed that he was in New York City locking for talent for his night club. He stated that RUBY informed him that he was not going to go to any legitimate booking agents, but rather was going to look around the New York night clubs.

KOVNIT stated that he recalled that RUBY was a "flashy dresser" and seemed to be an extrovert and the type who was always saying hello and shaking hands with everyone with whom he came in contact.

On 11/25/63 at New York, New York File # NY

by SAS EDMUND FLANAGAN AND JAMES J. ROGERS:aam Date dictated 11/27/63

447

COMMISSION EXHIBIT NO. 1582

Commission Exhibit No. 1583

Date 11/29/63

VINCENT GRAVIANO, Assistant Credit Manager, New York Hilton Hotel at Rockefeller Center, 1335 Avenue of the Americas, advised that at the time JACK RUBY registered at this hotel, there was some question concerning the room rent. GRAVIANO stated he could not recall the exact circumstances, but remembered that while RUBY was registering, he gave him a business card from the Carousel Club in Dallas, Texas.

GRAVIANO stated he could recall nothing further concerning RUBY or as to the purpose of RUBY's trip to New York City.

GRAVIANO stated that it is the custom of the Hilton Hotel to make a notation of how the guest departed, if they do so by a taxi cab. He stated that a review of his records concerning RUBY's departure reflected no card as to the going out by a taxi cab.

On 11/25/63 at New York, New York File # NY

by SAS EDMUND FLANAGAN AND JAMES J. ROGERS:aam Date dictated 11/27/63

448

COMMISSION EXHIBIT No. 1583

Commission Exhibit No. 1584

1

Date December 9, 1963

MELVIN RAY, Manager, Belair Motel, 5398 East 11th Street, Tulsa, Oklahoma, advised that TAMMI TRUE frequently stays at Bel-Air Motel and was registered at the motel during period April 14, 1963 to June 6, 1963. RAY recalled that just prior to May 25, 1963, TRUE informed him that JACK RUBY would be staying at Bel-Air Motel during the night of May 25, 1963 and requested that a room be reserved for RUBY and the charge be added to her account. An individual believed to be JACK RUBY did stay at the motel during the night of May 25, 1963. This person did not execute a registration card. No telephone was available in RUBY's room but two local calls and one long distance call were made from TRUE's room on May 26, 1963 and a possibility exists that calls could have been made by RUBY but no information was available to indicate calls were made by RUBY. Local calls were made to WE 2-3510 and WE 6-5945. From information available in directories, number WE 5-3510 is listed to J. A. FOUGLEY, no address given. Number WE 6-5945 is listed to DENISE JONES, 2638 East Oklahoma Street, Tulsa, Oklahoma. Long distance call is only listed in motel records as being made to operator 135, Oklahoma City, Oklahoma. RAY pointed out that TRUE makes considerable number of local and long distance calls when she stays at the motel.

RAY recalled that on two occasions in the past, TRUE was accompanied by RALPH PAUL who gave his address as Dallas, Texas, and is described as a white male, age 30 to 35, 6', 160 pounds, thin build, black hair, neat appearance, occupation is musician. No further information is available in regard to PAUL.

on 11/26/63 at Tulsa, Oklahoma File # DL 44-1639 OC 44-430

by Special Agent THOMAS W. MC LAIN/jn Date dictated 12/4/63

450

COMMISSION EXHIBIT No. 1584

Commission Exhibit 1585

DL 44-1639
1

The following investigation was conducted by SA DANIE F. BODINE at Houston:

On December 2, 1963, Mr. PATRICK CUMMINGS, Desk Agent, Avis Rent-A-Car, 2120 Louissiana, Houston, Texas, telephonically advised that on May 8, 1963, RUBY rented a 1963 Ford from Avis with the expressed intent to drive to Edna, Texas, to take a puppy to CANDY BARR.

The Avis Rent-A-Car records were made available and they revealed the following:

A $50.00 deposit was paid at 3:48 PM on May 8, 1963, and the car was returned at 5:37 AM on May 9, 1963, to the Avis agent at Houston International Airport. The space for local contacts on contract was left blank because of the expressed intent to return it the same day, thus no contact needed. The car was rented to JACK LEON RUBY, 3929 Rawlins, Dallas, Texas.

458

FD-302 (Rev. 1-25-60)

FEDERAL BUREAU OF INVESTIGAT

Commission Exhibit No. 1586

Date December 3, 1963

1

GORDON KENT, local Las Vegas television commentator, advised that a source of his, whom he refused to identify, had told him that JACK RUBY had been in Las Vegas, the weekend of November 16 and 17, 1963, at which time he, RUBY, had played golf at the Tropicana Golf Club, and had also made out a credit application at the Stardust Hotel. KENT stated that the source had also advised him that RUBY had previously and still had a credit card at the Riviera Hotel and Casino, Las Vegas, Nevada. KENT stated thathe had included the above information in his 6:00 p.m. newscast on November 29, 1963.

On 12/3/63 at Las Vegas, Nevada File # Las Vegas 44-48

by SAS ARTHUR N. BARRETT and DONALD M. HOLLAND: DMH/nph Date dictated 12/3/63

460

1 — Commission Exhibit No. 1587 —

Date December 3, 1963

MARK MARQUESS, Golf Professional, Tropicana Country Club, advised on this date that to his knowledge, JACK RUBY, the killer of OSWALD, had never played golf at that course. He stated that it was entirely possible that RUBY could have played golf at that course without his knowledge, but that he felt reasonably certain that if RUBY had played there, it was some time ago. MARQUESS stated that he caused a review of records of that Country Club to be made with respect to RUBY being entered on said records as a player, with negative results.

He advised that he had heard rumors that RUBY had played that golf course but that he had been unable to corroborate or refute same in discussing same with personnel of that course. He further advised that he had been informed that a Las Vegas television newscaster had mentioned RUBY's presence in town at a recent date, but that he had no first hand knowledge of same. He offered the opinion that he doubted very strongly that RUBY could have played the Tropicana Golf Course in the recent past, adding that pictures of RUBY, both on television and in the newspapers, were completely unfamiliar to him.

MARQUESS advised that he was well acquainted with PRESTON FEINBERG, and that while the latter and his wife both maintained golf clubs at the Club, neither had played golf at that course in recent months.

On 12/2/63 at Las Vegas, Nevada File # LV 44-48

by SA FRANCIS J. SCHMIDT:bmr Date dictated 12/2/63

462

COMMISSION EXHIBIT No. 1587

FEDERAL BUREAU OF INVESTIGATION

1 — Commission Exhibit No. 1588 —

Date December 3, 1963

A. J. RICCI, Bell Captain Hotel Tropicana, stated that although he has heard rumors that JACK RUBY, aka Rubenstein, had been in Las Vegas recently and stayed at the hotel he could not recall having seen him. He stated that he had heard that RUBY had played golf at the Tropicana Country Club, but does not know this to be a fact. He feels sure that if RUBY had been in the hotel he, RICCI, would have known it. He recalled that about a year or so ago a JACK RUBY who he believes to be identical with JACK RUBY, Dallas, Texas, based upon newspaper photographs, did come to Las Vegas and that he had asked RICCI to make reservations for a flight to Chicago. RICCI stated the reason he recalled this was that during the time RICCI was trying to make the reservation, RUBY changed the spelling of his name several times. He recalls RUBY changed the name to RUBIN, RUBEN, and RUBENSTEIN. RICCI did not know in which name RUBY finally got the reservation.

RICCI stated that no record is kept as to who uses the hotel's Rolls Royce. However, it has been in Los Angeles since November 5, 1963 and will remain there where it was taken for repairs until December 6, 1963.

RICCI stated that to his knowledge PRESTON FEINBERG does not and never has played golf.

On 11/29/63 at Las Vegas, Nevada File # LV 44-48

by SAs ALLEN W. HANSEN; RICHARD E. RODERMUND: AWH/je Date dictated 11/29/63

463

COMMISSION EXHIBIT No. 1588

FD-302 (Rev. 1-25-60)

FEDERAL BUREAU OF INVESTIGATION

Commission Exhibit No. 1589

1

Date December 3, 1963

JOSEPH STEFAN, Caddymaster, Tropicana Golf Club, advised on this date that records of his office for the past thirty days, did not reflect a registration for golf in the name of JACK RUBY and/or JACK RUBENSTEIN. He advised that records of his office are maintained for thirty days and then destroyed. He stated that photographs of RUBY, both on television and in the newspapers, were unfamiliar to him. He advised that when the news of RUBY's killing of OSWALD first appeared on television, he had the impression that at one time RUBY might have played golf at that course, since he is sure that at some time during the past year, a player from Texas, had given him a card from the Carousel Club in Dallas and told him to look him up if he ever got to Dallas. STEFAN advised that he made a search of personal effects at the Club and also at his home with negatives results regarding said card. He stated that he could not recall how long ago it was, but that he must have thrown the card away. He advised that he also, in conjunction with MARK MARQUESS, the golf professional at the course, had a review made of the records of the Registration Desk at the Club with negative results regarding the name of JACK RUBY and/or JACK RUBENSTEIN.

STEFAN stated that to the best of knowledge PRESTON FEINBERG of the Tropicana Hotel has not played golf at that course in at least 8 months.

STEFAN advised that he was positive that FEINBERG had not played golf at that course in the past thirty days, adding that while FEINBERG and his wife maintain clubs in the locker room, FEINBERG has not played since he had a heart attack some time ago. He further described FEINBERG as a novice golfer who took up the game on only two or three occasions before being stricken with a heart attack.

STEFAN advised that he had discussed RUBY with the caddies at the Tropicana Course and none could recall RUBY as ever having played golf at that course.

On 11/30/63 at Las Vegas, Nevada File # LV 44-48

by SA FRANCIS J. SCHMIDT: bmr Date dictated 12/2/63

464

COMMISSION EXHIBIT No. 1589

FD-302 (Rev. 1-25-60)

FEDERAL BUREAU OF INVESTIGATION

Commission Exhibit No. 1590

1

Date December 3, 1963

ERNEST MUSCATELLO, Bartender, Hotel Tropicana, stated that he did not know JACK RUBY, also known as RUBENSTEIN, and knows nothing about him. He claimed that he has not been in Dallas, Texas, except for a few times when he was in the service, and that was several years ago.

On 11/29/63 at Las Vegas, Nevada File # Las Vegas 44-48

by SAS ALLAN W. HANSEN and RICHARD E. RODERMUND: RER/nph Date dictated 11/29/63

465

COMMISSION EXHIBIT No. 1590

1
LV 44-48
DL 44-1639

The following investigation was conducted by SAs ALLEN W. HANSEN and WAYNE M. DRAKE, on November 25, 1963:

AT LAS VEGAS, NEVADA

WILLIAM RICE, Pitboss, Tropicana Hotel-Casino, stated that he does not know JACK RUBY and has had no association with him, but might recognize him if shown photograph.

JACK WOMBLE, Assistant Manager, Tropicana Hotel, advised that he had checked registrations back to January 1, 1963, and records did not reflect registration of JACK RUBY, aka RUBENSTEIN.

JOHN JOHNSON, Casino Cashier, Hotel Tropicana, advised that JACK RUBY does not have a credit card established.

B. P. SAUMBY, Manager, Golf Club Motel, checked the registration records and advised that he could find no registration for JACK RUBY, aka RUBENSTEIN.

CARL LA MARCA, Bar Manager, Castaways Casino, advised he knew JACK RUBY as JACK RUBENSTEIN, only slightly, but knew nothing about his personal or professional life. He has not seen RUBY since January of 1963.

JUNE WISDOM, Reservations Manager, Castaways Hotel, checked records back to December, 1962, and there was no record that JACK RUBY has ever registered at the Castaways.

The following investigation was conducted by SAs CARL F. FREEMAN and RONALD L. MALEY, on November 25, 1963:

Mr. JAMES PHIL LONG, owner, Phil Long's Casino, Las Vegas, advised that he has never had any information relative to JACK RUBY and to his knowledge has never seen him. LONG stated he is originally from the Fort Worth-Dallas area, but came to Las Vegas in 1947. LONG stated that he gathered from news reports that RUBY had only been in the Dallas area since approximately 1950, which would have made it impossible for him to have known him there, and he has not met him since that time in the Las Vegas area.

466

COMMISSION EXHIBIT NO. 1591

2
LV 44-48

BEN GOFFSTEIN, Casino Manager, Pioneer Club, Downtown Las Vegas, advised that he does not know RUBENSTEIN and has heard no rumors to the effect that RUBENSTEIN has ever visited Las Vegas, Nevada. GOFFSTEIN stated that through his contacts in downtown Las Vegas, he would have heard if RUBENSTEIN had visited downtown Las Vegas. He further advised that he personally feels that if RUBENSTEIN had ever visited Las Vegas, he would have frequented the strip casinos at Las Vegas, Nevada, instead of the downtown areas. GOFFSTEIN stated that any information coming to his attention concerning RUBENSTEIN will be furnished by him personally to the local FBI.

The following investigation was conducted by SAs JAMES E. DOYLE and ROBERT D. LEE, on November 25, 1963:

ROBERT RYNE, 1219 Arrowhead Avenue, Casino Manager, Silver Palace, advised that he worked in Dallas, Texas, for one month in 1945 and he was not acquainted with JACK RUBY. He stated he had no friends or associates from the Dallas area, with the exception of BENNIE BINION and he did not know whether BINION was acquainted with RUBY or not. He stated he believed BINION came to Las Vegas from Dallas in about 1947.

Records of Las Vegas Police Department and Sheriff's Office, as checked by SA LEO A. STEVENS, on November 25, 1963, reflect no information concerning RUBY.

The following investigation was conducted by SAs RICHARD E. RODERMUND and ROBERT G. CASEY, on November 25, 1963:

CECIL SIMMONS, part owner, Desert Inn Hotel, Las Vegas, advised he has not been in Dallas except for two or three visits in four or five years. He recalled he had seen JACK RUBY on no more than ten occasions. The times he had seen RUBY were in the Adolphus and Baker Hotels, and he recalled RUBY went to the barber shop in the Adolphus which was the same one that he (SIMMONS) used. RUBY had a night club across the street from the Adolphus and invited SIMMONS on two or three occasions to visit it, but SIMMONS never did. SIMMONS stated he did not know RUBY other than to "say hello".

467

COMMISSION EXHIBIT NO. 1591—Continued

Commission Exhibit No. 1592

FD-302 (Rev. 3-3-59)

FEDERAL BUREAU OF INVESTIGATION

1

Date 12/10/63

JOSEPH R. CAVAGNARO, Front Office Manager of the Sheraton-Hilton Hotel, downtown Dallas, who resides at 604 Opal Lane furnished the following information:

He was transferred to Dallas approximately eight years ago and JACK RUBY was one of the first men he met after arriving in Dallas. He met RUBY at the B & B Restaurant in Dallas where they both ate occasionally. A friendship developed between him and JACK RUBY and has continued since that time. He has had JACK RUBY to his home on three or four occasions for dinner and RUBY often stops by the hotel for coffee with CAVAGNARO. After CAVAGNARO married, he did not have as close an association with RUBY as previously but they have continued to be friends. RUBY has given a Dachshund dog to CAVAGNARO for his boys and comes by CAVAGNARO's home approximately once every six months to see how the dog is getting along and to visit with CAVAGNARO and his family.

RUBY has talked politics with CAVAGNARO on occasion at CAVAGNARO's desk in the hotel. CAVAGNARO stated that he, CAVAGNARO, was an ardent KENNEDY man and JACK RUBY apparently was pro-KENNEDY himself. RUBY had made statements to CAVAGNARO that KENNEDY was doing a great job and CAVAGNARO felt that RUBY meant this sincerely. CAVAGNARO and his wife were in RUBY's night club approximately two months ago but have not made a habit of going there often.

CAVAGNARO said that he liked JACK RUBY very much and that he found RUBY to be a "square shooter". He advised that RUBY was very emotional and was very gentle, particularly to his dogs. He advised that RUBY always had two or three dogs with him and seemed to be very fond of dogs. He stated that RUBY "cried like a baby" on one occasion when one of the dogs got hurt.

CAVAGNARO stated that he had seen RUBY at the hotel most of the time and that RUBY would go out of his way to do things for him and his wife. He stated that his wife is very fond of RUBY. He characterized RUBY as being irresponsible and pointed out that he was very irresponsible as far as keeping appointments.

on 12/9/63 at Dallas, Texas File # DL 44-1639

130

by Special Agent JACK B. PEDEN gj Date dictated 12/10/63

This document contains neither recommendations nor conclusions of the FBI. It is the property of the FBI and is loaned to your agency; it and its contents are not to be distributed outside your agency.

DL 44-1639
2

RUBY did not impress CAVAGNARO as being particularly interested in current events and at no time did he notice that RUBY had any subversive tendencies. RUBY spent a great deal of time, thought and energy in connection with his business and many of his trips to the hotel were for the purpose of ascertaining what conventions were due to be held in Dallas in the near future. RUBY apparently did this so that he could plan his own night club business on the basis of the conventions expected.

RUBY according to CAVAGNARO "knew all the policemen in town". CAVAGNARO stated RUBY was well acquainted with a great number of policemen and particularly the policemen who were in or had been in the Special Service of the Police. He stated that he knew RUBY was a close friend of Lieutenant GILMORE and ERIC KAMINSKI. CAVAGNARO informed that in approximately 1957, RUBY managed a little colored boy who sang and danced. RUBY apparently thought the boy had talent and was helping the boy make a success in the entertainment world. RUBY on one occasion took the boy to Chicago to appear on television. CAVAGNARO has no information as to whether the boy was a success or not.

CAVAGNARO informed that he was certainly surprised at the news when it came to his attention that RUBY had shot OSWALD, as he had never observed anything in RUBY's character to indicate that RUBY would do such a thing. CAVAGNARO advised that he knows of no connection between JACK RUBY and LEE HARVEY OSWALD and he never heard RUBY speak of OSWALD. He further stated that he had never seen OSWALD to his knowledge.

131

[redacted]

1 — Commission Exhibit No. 1593 — Date November 27, 1963

BEN GOFFSTEIN, Casino Manager, Pioneer Club, downtown Las Vegas, Nevada, advised on November 25, 1963, he does not know JACK RUBENSTEIN and has heard no rumors to the effect that RUBENSTEIN has ever visited Las Vegas, Nevada. GOFFSTEIN stated that through his contacts in downtown Las Vegas, he would have heard if RUBENSTEIN had visited downtown Las Vegas. He further advised that he personally feels that if RUBENSTEIN had ever visited Las Vegas, he would have frequented the Strip casinos at Las Vegas, Nevada, instead of the downtown areas. GOFFSTEIN stated that any information coming to his attention concerning RUBENSTEIN will be furnished by him personally to the local Federal Bureau of Investigation.

On 11/25/63 at Las Vegas, Nevada File # LV 44-48

by SAs CARL F. FREEMAN & RONALD L. MALEY :alf Date dictated 11/26/63

468

COMMISSION EXHIBIT No. 1593

[redacted]

1 — Commission Exhibit No. 1594 — Date November 26, 1963

THOMAS JOSEPH CALLAHAN, owner of the Pioneer Club, a downtown Las Vegas gambling casino, advised this date he does not know JACK RUBY nor does he have any information concerning RUBY; however, he advised that should he learn of any information concerning this individual, he will contact the Las Vegas Office of the Federal Bureau of Investigation.

On 11/25/63 at Las Vegas, Nevada File # LV 44-48

by SA CARL F. FREEMAN CFF:alf Date dictated 11/25/63

469

COMMISSION EXHIBIT No. 1594

FD-302 (Rev. 1-25-60)

FEDERAL BUREAU OF INVESTIGATION

[redacted]

Commission Exhibit No. 1595

Date November 27, 1963

ROBERT RYNE, 1219 Arrowhead Avenue, Casino Manager, Silver Palace, Las Vegas, Nevada, was interviewed November 25, 1963. He advised that he worked in Dallas, Texas, for one month in 1945, and he was not acquainted with JACK RUBY. He stated he had no friends or associates from the Dallas area, with the exception of BENNY BINION, and he did not know whether BINION was acquainted with RUBY or not. He stated he believed BINION came to Las Vegas, from Dallas, in about 1947.

On 11/25/63 at Las Vegas, Nevada File # LV 44-48

by SAs CARL F. FREEMAN & RONALD L. MALEY :alf Date dictated 11/26/63

This document contains neither recommendations nor conclusions of the FBI. It is the property of the FBI and is loaned to your agency; it and its contents are not to be distributed outside your agency.

470

COMMISSION EXHIBIT No. 1595

FD-302 (Rev. 1-25-60)

FEDERAL BUREAU OF INVESTIGATION

[redacted]

1 — Commission Exhibit No. 1596

Date December 3, 1963

PAUL F. COE, Assistant Hotel Manager, Thunderbird Hotel, advised that a recheck of the hotel records under his supervision failed to reflect that a JACK RUBY, JACK RUBENSTEIN, or variations of that spelling, ever resided at the Thunderbird. COE advised this record check consisted of checking the registered guests, non registered guests, and the cancellation lists for 1963.

COE stated no record is maintained on calls to the Thunderbird.

On 11/29/63 at Las Vegas, Nevada File # LV 44-48

by SA WAYNE H. DRAKE:bmr Date dictated 11/29/63

This document contains neither recommendations nor conclusions of the FBI. It is the property of the FBI and is loaned to your agency; it and its contents are not to be distributed outside your agency.

473

COMMISSION EXHIBIT No. 1596

FD-302 (Rev. 1-25-60)

FEDERAL BUREAU OF —

Commission Exhibit No. 1597

1

Date December 3, 1963

JOHN BACKUS, Boxman, Horseshoe Club, Las Vegas, Nevada, advised that to the best of his knowledge he does not know JACK RUBY of Dallas, Texas. He advised that he left Dallas, Texas, either in 1947 or 1948, and came to Las Vegas, Nevada, where he has since been employed in gambling casinos.

He does recall a small Jewish fellow who during the latter forties ran a "stripper school" in Dallas, Texas; however, he does know if this individual is identical with JACK RUBY or not. He cannot recall this individual's name, nor has he seen this individual since leaving Dallas, Texas.

On 11/26/63 at Las Vegas, Nevada File # LV 44-48

by SA CARL F. FREEMAN & SA ROBERT M. JACKSON CFF/aa Date dictated 11/29/63

This document contains neither recommendations nor conclusions of the FBI. It is the property of the FBI and is loaned to your agency; it and its contents are not to be distributed outside your agency.

475

COMMISSION EXHIBIT No. 1597

FD-302 (Rev. 1-25-60)

FEDERAL BUREAU OF INVESTIGATION

Commission Exhibit No. 1598

1

Date December 3, 1963

CARL BARBALOT, General Manager of the Tropicana Country Club Golf Course, advised that he was not acquainted with JACK RUBY and/or JACK RUBENSTEIN and further that the photographs of RUBY appearing on television and in the newspapers were not familiar to him. BARBALOT stated that to his knowledge, RUBY had never played golf at the Tropicana. He advised that the extent of his knowledge of RUBY was to the effect that he had heard rumors that RUBY had visited Las Vegas, but that these rumors reached him subsequent to the killing of OSWALD by RUBY, during the time that RUBY was being mentioned extensively on television and in the newspapers. He stated that in various general discussions of the subject, he had never heard anyone advise that they knew RUBY on a personal basis nor anyone who had stated that they had seen RUBY in Las Vegas.

On 11/30/63 at Las Vegas, Nevada File # LV 44-48

by SA FRANCIS J. SCHMIDT:bmr Date dictated 12/2/63

This document contains neither recommendations nor conclusions of the FBI. It is the property of the FBI and is loaned to your agency; it and its contents are not to be distributed outside your agency.

476

COMMISSION EXHIBIT No. 1598

FD-302 (Rev. 1-25-60) FEDERAL BUREAU OF INV— Commission Exhibit No. 1599

1

Date December 3, 1963

Mr. RICHARD CHAPPELL, Manager of the Riviera Hotel, Las Vegas, Nevada, advised that he, upon hearing the broadcast of news commentator GORDON KENT on November 29, 1963, had immediately searched all the records of the Riviera Hotel, both credit and hotel registration records for the name JACK RUBY or JACK RUBENSTEIN, and that he had been unable to locate any such record.

Mr. CHAPPELL stated that he knows of no reason why any hotel in Las Vegas, would conceal the fact that RUBY had been a guest or had held a credit card. On December 3, 1963, Mr. CHAPPELL again searched the records of the Riviera Hotel with negative results.

On 12/3/63 at Las Vegas, Nevada File # Las Vegas 44-48

by SAS ARTHUR N. BARRETT and DONALD M. HOLLAND: DMH/nph Date dictated 12/3/63

477

COMMISSION EXHIBIT NO. 1599

FD-302 (Rev. 1-25-60) FEDERAL BUREAU OF INVESTIGA N

Commission Exhibit No. 1600

1

Date December 3, 1963

JOHN TIHISTA, Credit Manager, Stardust Hotel, advised that about one month ago, GILBERT COSKEY, Cashier in the hotel casino cage, came to TIHISTA with a check from a customer to determine whether or not it should be cashed. According to COSKEY, the customer wanting to cash the check had no previous credit; however, COSKEY stated that the man was from Dallas and owned a night club in that city. He believed COSKEY had stated the man's name was RUBY. TIHISTA stated that apparently this incident occurred on a weekend since they were unable to contact the customer's bank, and therefore, did not accept the check.

TIHISTA reviewed hotel registration records for the months of September, October, and November but could not locate a registration for the name RUBY or RUBINSTEIN.

TIHISTA stated there was no credit application for the name RUBY or RUBINSTEIN at the Stardust.

On 12/2/63 at Las Vegas, Nevada File # LV 44-48

by SA JAMES E. DOYLE:bmr Date dictated 12/2/63

478

COMMISSION EXHIBIT NO. 1600

FD-302 (Rev. 1-25-60) FEDERAL BUREAU OF— Commission Exhibit No. 1601

1

Date December 3, 1963

GILBERT COSKEY, Casino Cashier, Stardust Hotel, advised that about four weeks ago an individual from Dallas, Texas, believed by the name RUBY approached the casino credit department and attempted to have a check cashed. COSKEY recalled that the man talked about owning the Vegas Club and another night club in Dallas. COSKEY stated he took the check to JOHN TIHISTA, Credit Manager, for approval informing TIHISTA that the customer reportedly was from Dallas and owned night clubs in that city. COSKEY stated that if he recalls correctly, TIHISTA refused to cash this check since the customer had no previous credit with the hotel. He could recall nothing more concerning this incident, but after seeing a photo of RUBY in the paper and reading about his background, he was certain that RUBY and the person attempting to cash a check at the Stardust were one and the same.

On 12/2/63 at Las Vegas, Nevada File # LV 44-48

by SA JAMES E. DOYLE:bmr Date dictated 12/3/63

This document contains neither recommendations nor conclusions of the FBI. It is the property of the FBI and is loaned to your agency; it and its contents are not to be distributed outside your agency.

479

COMMISSION EXHIBIT No. 1601

FD-302 (Rev. 1-25-60) EDERAL BUREAU OF INVESTIGAT

Commission Exhibit No. 1602

1

Date December 3, 1963

PRESTON FEINBERG, 401 Parkway West, advised he is an owner of almost six percent of the Tropicana Hotel, Las Vegas, Nevada. He was born in Chicago, Illinois, and lived in the Chicago area all his life until coming to Las Vegas, five years ago at the request of J. K. HOUSSELS, Sr., Chairman of the Board of the Tropicana Hotel. He lived in the Chicago suburbs of Oak Park and River Forest, Illinois, just before coming to Las Vegas. He owns a scrap metal company and was a partner in Howard's, a Plymouth - De Soto dealership in Chicago.

FEINBERG stated he does not know JACK RUBY, also known as JACK RUBENSTEIN, and has, to his knowledge, never met RUBY. He advised he never heard of RUBY in Chicago, and has never been to Texas. He also stated he does not play golf and has never lent the Rolls Royce, owned by the Tropicana Hotel, to RUBY. FEINBERG stated he drove the Rolly Royce to Los Angeles, California, on November 5, 1963, for repairs and re-painting, and the car is still there and will not be ready until December 6, 1963.

On 11/29/63 at Las Vegas, Nevada File # Las Vegas 44-48

by SAC DEAN W. ELSON, and SAS ALLAN W. HANSEN and RICHARD E. RODERMUND: RER/nph Date dictated 11/29/63

This document contains neither recommendations nor conclusions of the FBI. It is the property of the FBI and is loaned to your agency; it and its contents are not to be distributed outside your agency.

480

COMMISSION EXHIBIT No. 1602

FD-302 (Rev. 1-25-60) FEDERAL BUREAU OF IN— Commission Exhibit No. 1603

1 Date December 3, 1963

RALPH J. FRANCE, also known as Frog, 914 South Second Street, employed as Shill Boss at the Castaways Casino, advised Special Agent WAYNE H. DRAKE the following on November 30, 1963: He is not acquainted with RUBY and has no friends or associates in Dallas. He has had the nick name of Frog for over thirty years and does not know of other persons in Las Vegas with the same nick name.

On 11/30/63 at Las Vegas, Nevada File # LV 44-48

by SA WAYNE H. DRAKE /je Date dictated 12/3/63

481

COMMISSION EXHIBIT NO. 1603

— Commission Exhibit No. 1604 —

LV 44-48
DMH:bmr
1

On November 29, 1963, the following individuals advised Special Agent ALLEN W. HANSEN that a check of Flight Manifests out of Dallas, Texas, to Las Vegas, for a period of November 11, 1963, through November 24, 1963, failed to identify any passengers as identical with subject RUBY:

W. R. HARWOOD, United Air Lines

WILL RIDDLE, Delta Air Lines

JOHN GLIBOWSKI, Trans World Air Lines

483

COMMISSION EXHIBIT NO. 1604

Commission Exhibit No. 1605

FD-302 (Rev. 3-3-59)
1

FEDERAL BUREAU OF I

Date November 30, 1963

JOHN D. GAUGHAN, 1131 Comstock Drive, owner, El Corte Hotel, was interviewed, at which time he stated he does not know JACK RUBY.

On November 24, 1963, he attended a rodeo in Las Vegas with BENNIE BINION and BINION's son JACK, and at that time the name of JACK RUBY came up in conversation. The BINIONs, originally from Dallas, Texas, stated they did not know RUBY with the exception that BENNIE BINION believed he had heard of RUBY before. GAUGHAN stated he talked to numerous individuals at the rodeo and an unrecalled individual mentioned that RUBY had been in Las Vegas, about a week ago, and stayed at the Sahara Hotel.

GAUGHAN, who is also an owner of record of the Flamingo Hotel, advised he had just been in telephonic contact with JERRY GORDON, Manager of the Flamingo, and GORDON stated that RUBY was unknown to individuals at the Flamingo and had never stayed there to his knowledge. GAUGHAN stated that Flamingo Hotel representative, JERRY ROSENBERG, Dallas, Texas, telephone number EM 8-6930, would certainly know RUBY and could possibly furnish information concerning him.

on 11/25/63 at Las Vegas, Nevada File # LV 44-48 DL 44-1639

by Special Agents JAMES E. DOYLE and ROBERT D. LEE/pm Date dictated 11/26/63

484

This document contains neither recommendations nor conclusions of the FBI. It is the property of the FBI and is loaned to your agency; it and its contents are not to be distributed outside your agency.

COMMISSION EXHIBIT No. 1605

FD-302 (Rev. 3-3-59)

FEDERAL BUREAU OF INVESTIGATION

Commission Exhibit No. 1606

Date December 5, 1963

(1)

JOYCE LEE McDONALD, 424½ W. 10th Street, Apartment 3, Dallas, Texas, was interviewed at the Carousel Club, 1312½ Commerce, Dallas, in an attempt to identify an unknown male who visited the Carousel Club during the first part of October, 1963, and was referred to by RUBY as a "real swinger" from Chicago. Miss McDONALD furnished the following information:

Sometime around October 10, 1963, Miss McDONALD was employed on a part-time basis by ROBERT CRAVEN who operated a show at the State Fairgrounds in Dallas. CRAVEN and his partners, BOB MILES and MARVIN GARDNER, had financial difficulty, and as a result wrote a $100 check which JACK RUBY cashed, and which was subsequently returned for lack of funds.

At about the same time that RUBY cashed this check, Miss McDONALD met LAWRENCE V. MEYERS from Chicago at the Carousel Club. During one of several evenings that McDONALD saw MEYERS at the club she had several drinks with him and was told by MEYERS that he had business interests in Chicago, Minneapolis, and Las Vegas, Nevada, and that his headquarters was in Chicago, Illinois. Miss McDONALD did not know the relationship between RUBY and MEYERS, but felt that they knew each other only casually.

One or two days after first meeting MEYERS, Miss McDONALD saw MEYERS at the fairgrounds in Dallas, and having already heard about CRAVEN's bad check for $100, MEYERS gave Miss McDONALD a check signed LAWRENCE V. MEYERS, in the amount of $200, made payable to JACK RUBY, drawn on an unknown Chicago bank. This check was to assist CRAVEN and McDONALD in operating the show at the fairgrounds. After checking with the Chicago bank and learning that the check was good, RUBY cashed the $200 check. McDONALD then reimbursed RUBY the $100 he had lost as a result of CRAVEN's check and kept the remaining $100 for her own personal use.

Miss McDONALD could not explain MEYERS' motive in giving her the $200 and indicated that MEYERS had never made any improper advances to McDONALD, but she felt that he would no doubt make some type of request of her in the future.

McDONALD next saw MEYERS on the evening of November 21, 1963, when he appeared at the Carousel Club with a girl by the

on 12/2/63 at Dallas, Texas File # DL 44-1639

by Special Agents JOSEPH PEGGS and ALVIN ZIMMERMAN:bnm Date dictated 12/4/63

527

This document contains neither recommendations nor conclusions of the FBI. It is the property of the FBI and is loaned to your agency; it and its contents are not to be distributed outside your agency.

COMMISSION EXHIBIT No. 1606

Commission Exhibit No. 1607

Date December 6, 1963

1

Captain O. T. SLAUGHTER, Chief, Record Bureau, Police Department, Dallas, Texas, advised his records reflect JACK LEON RUBY, 1719½ South Ervay Street, Dallas, age 43 in 1954, arrest #54-54814, was arrested on December 5, 1954, at 1:30 a.m., for investigation violation of State Liquor Law, transferred to county. The arresting officers were shown as E. E. CARLSON and D. L. BLANKENSHIP.

Captain SLAUGHTER stated his records reflect the above case was filed on December 8, 1954, in Dallas County Criminal Court #3, and dismissed on February 8, 1955.

His records reflected no other arrests for RUBY for violation of the State Liquor Law.

on 12/5/63 at Dallas, Texas File # Dallas 44-1639

by Special Agent JAMES E. GARRIS:BL Date dictated 12/5/63

545

FD-302 (Rev. 3-3-59)

FEDERAL BUREAU OF INVESTIGATION

Commission Exhibit No. 1608

1

Date December 6, 1963

Sergeant M. A. SOUTHERLAND, Assistant Chief in Charge of Record Bureau, Police Department, Dallas, Texas, made available the "Arresting Officer's Report" concerning the arrest of JACK LEON RUBY on December 5, 1954. The report reflects the following information:

Name of Person arrested:	JACK LEON RUBY
Date:	December 5, 1954
Address of suspect:	1719½ S. Ervay
Time:	1:30 a.m.
Sex:	Male
Race:	White
Age:	43
Occupation:	Tavern operator
Where arrested:	1717 South Ervay
Offense suspected:	Investigation violation State Liquor Law - having beern on table after hours.
Date offense committed:	December 5, 1954
Where:	1717 South Ervay
Name of complainant:	Officers E. E. CARLSON, ID # 774 and D. L. BLANKENSHIP, ID #633.
Details which prompted arrest:	This man is the owner and operator of the Silver Club located at 1717 South Ervay, was in charge tonight at the time arresting officers saw bottle partl fill with Schlitz beer on the table occupied by EUGENIA MARY O'BRIEN and MARY JANE SCHULTZ. When BLANKENSHIP attempted to get the bottle, Miss O'BRIEN tried to hold the bottle and said that it was her beer.

on 12/5/63 at Dallas, Texas File # Dallas 44-1639

by Special Agent JAMES E. GARRIS:BL Date dictated 12/5/63

546

COMMISSION EXHIBIT No. 1608

FD-302 (Rev. 3-3-59)

FEDERAL BUREAU OF INVESTIGATION

Commission Exhibit No. 1609

1

Date December 6, 1963

J. G. VICKERY, Clerk, Identification Bureau, Police Department, Dallas, Texas, made available the identification file of JACK LEON RUBY, identification number 36398, which reflects a "Case Report" filed on December 8, 1954, concerning the arrest of JACK LEON RUBY on December 5, 1954. The case report reflects RUBY was arrested at 1:30 a.m., December 5, 1954, at 1717 South Ervay by Officers E. E. CARLSON and D. L. BLANKENSHIP and charged with violation of Article II, Section 19 (16), permitting consumption during forbidden hours on Sunday.

The Case Report reflects the above arrest of RUBY was dismissed on February 8, 1955.

The Case Report reflects under "Summary of Case" that "this man is the owner and operator of the Silver Club located at 1717 South Ervay and was present and in charge at the time. He permitted EUGENIA MARY O'BRIEN and MARY JANE SCHULTZ to consume a pert of a bottle of Schlitz beer during forbidden hours on Sunday."

on 12/5/63 at Dallas, Texas File # Dallas 44-1639

by Special Agent JAMES E. GARRIS:BL Date dictated 12/5/63

547

COMMISSION EXHIBIT No. 1609

FD-302 (Rev. 3-3-59)

FEDERAL BUREAU OF INVESTIGATION

Commission Exhibit No. 1610

Date December 6, 1963

1

Mrs. PEARL SHUMATE, Chief Clerk, Dallas County Criminal Court #3, County Building, Dallas, Texas, advised that criminal file docket #1, page 45, shows entries for dockets 1788-C and 1789-C both under the name JACK LEON RUBY, both showing the offense as "Liquor Violation," and both reflecting cases dismissed on February 8, 1955.

Mrs. SHUMATE made available dockets 1788-C and 1789-C which reflect the following information:

DOCKET #1788-C:

The State of Texas, versus JACK LEON RUBY, filed December 8, 1954, capias issued December 8, 1954. Defendant's attorney was shown as TOM HOWARD, 1415 Republic Bank Building, Dallas, Texas.

An "information" filed on December 8, 1954, reflects that the defendant, JACK LEON RUBY, "on or about December 5, 1954, in the County of Dallas and State of Texas, the said date being Sunday, was then and there the holder of a Retail Dealer's on Premises License, theretofore issued by the Texas Liquor Control Board of the State of Texas fo_ the premises located at 1717 South Ervay and between the hours of 1:15 a.m. and 1:00 o'clock p.m. to-wit: 1:30 a.m. on said day, the said defendant did then and there unlawfully permit EUGENIA MARY O'BRIEN to consume an alcoholic beverage on the said licensed premises and situate."

Signed "HENRY WADE, Criminal District Attorney, Dallas County, Texas."

A "Motion of District Attorney to Dismiss Prosecution," filed on February 8, 1955, reflects that "this is a Liquor Violation case. The witnesses in this case, Officers BLANKENSHIP and CARLEON advised that they conducted the investigation, but that it was filed without their knowledge. The police report states that they observed customers consuming beer after hours. Both officers stated that this is incorrect and they did not observe the customers consuming beer. It is recommended that this case be dismissed because of insufficient evidence."

Signed "LEM BROTHERTON, Assistant District Attorney of

on 12/5/63 at Dallas, Texas File # Dallas 44-1639

by Special Agent JAMES E. GARRIS:BL Date dictated 12/5/63

548

DL 44-1639
2

Dallas County, Texas, and HENRY WADE, District Attorney of Dallas County, Texas."

DOCKET #1789-C:

The State of Texas versus JACK LEON RUBY, filed December 8, 1954, capias issued December 8, 1954. Defendant's attorney was shown as TOM HOWARD, 1415 Republic Bank Building, Dallas, Texas.

An "information" filed on December 8, 1954, reflects that the defendant, JACK LEON RUBY, "on or about December 5, 1954, in the county of Dallas and state of Texas, the said date being Sunday, was then and there the holder of a Retail Dealer's on Premises License, theretofore issued by the Texas Liquor Control Board of the State of Texas for the premises located at 1717 South Ervay, and between the hours of 1:15 a.m. and 1:00 p.m., to-wit: 1:30 a.m. of said day the said defendant did then and there unawfully permit MARY JANE SCHULTZ to consume an alcoholic beverage on the said premises, and situate."

Signed "Henry Wade, Criminal District Attorney of Dallas County, Texas."

A "Motion of District Attorney to Dismiss Prosecution," filed on February 8, 1955, reflects that "this is a Liquor Violation case. The witnesses in this case, Officers BLANKENSHIP and CARLEON advised that they conducted the investigation, but that it was filed without their knowledge. The police report states that they observed customers consuming beer after hours. Both officers stated that this is incorrect and they did not observe the customers consuming beer. It is recommended that this case be dismissed because of insufficient evidence."

Signed "LEM BROTHERTON, Assistant District Attorney of Dallas County, Texas, and HENRY WADE, District Attorney of Dallas County, Texas."

549

1 Commission Exhibit No. 1611 Date December 9, 1963

Detective D. L. BLANKENSHIP, Special Service Branch, Dallas, Texas Police Department, who resides at 2807 Province Lane, Dallas, was contacted concerning his joint arrest, with Detective E. E. CARLSON, of JACK LEON RUBY on December 5, 1954 for alleged violation by RUBY of the State Liquor Law. BLANKENSHIP was advised he did not have to make a statement, that any statement he did make could be used against him in a court of law, and that he could consult an attorney at any time he desired. BLANKENSHIP voluntarily advised as follows:

A copy of the "Arresting Officer's Report", arrest number 54814, dated December 5, 1954, reflecting JACK LEON RUBY, 1719½ South Ervay, was arrested by Dallas Police Officers D. L. BLANKENSHIP and E. E. CARLSON for "Inv. Vio. State Liquor Law - having beer on table after hours," was exhibited to BLANKENSHIP.

The report states "Give complete details as to what you know, what you saw or what you were told about suspect which prompted this arrest:" The following comments were reflected on the report in answer to the above:

"This man is the owner and operator of the Silver Club located at 1717 S Ervay, was in charge tonight at the time arresting officers saw bottle partly fill with Schlitz beer on the table occupied by Eugenia Mary O'Brien and Mary Jane Schultz. When Blankenship attempted to get the bottle Miss O'Brien tried to hold the bottle and said that it was her beer.
TLCB Number will be attached to this sheet.
The bottle of Schlitz was about half full of beer, placed in the property room."

A copy of the "Case Report" concerning the arrest of JACK LEON RUBY on December 5, 1954 by officers BLANKENSHIP and CARLSON, identification number 36398 was also exhibited to BLANKENSHIP. This report reflects RUBY was charged with "Violation Art. II, Sec. 19 (16)permitting consumption during forbidden hours on Sunday." Under "Summary of Case" it was stated that "This man is the owner and operator of the Silver Club located at 1717 South Ervay and was present and in charge at the time. He permitted Eugenia Mary O'Brien and Mary Jane

on 12/9/63 at Dallas, Texas File # DL 44-1639

by Special Agents JAMES E. GARRIS & JACK B. PEDEN/jn Date dictated 12/9/63

550

Commission Exhibit No. 1611

2
DL 44-1639

Schultz to consume a part of a bottle of Schlitz beer during forbidden hours on Sunday."

BLANKENSHIP stated that the curfew hours on Sunday morning for the sale and consumption of alcholic beverages is 1:15 A.M.

BLANKENSHIP believed either he or CARLSON prepared the "Case Report" since it was a policy during 1954 for the arresting officers to prepare case reports when persons were arrested by them.

BLANKENSHIP advised that to the best of his recollection the "Details" set out above as reflected on the "Arresting Officer's Report," and the "Summary of Case" set out above as reflected on the "Case Report", are true and correct. He does not recall at this time whether or not he actually saw the customers consuming beer after hours at the Silver Club, but he said that from previous experience he did not arrest a night club owner unless he saw the night club owner's customers actually consuming beer after hours. He added that since JACK LEON RUBY was arrested for the murder of LEE HARVEY OSWALD,he checked the identification record of RUBY and learned that the above mentioned arrest made by him and officer E. E. CARLSON had been dismissed.

BLANKENSHIP related that after he and officer CARLSON arrested RUBY in 1954 and charged him, as stated above, he heard nothing further concerning the matter and he ~~had nothing to do with~~ the dismissal. Furthermore, he stated no one ever contacted him about the charge against RUBY.

The following information appearing in a "Motion of District Attorney to Dismiss Prosecution," filed in Dallas County Criminal Court Number 3 on February 8, 1955, under Docket number 1788-C (naming EUGENIA MARY O'BRIEN as customer), in the case of the State of Texas versus JACK LEON RUBY, was read to BLANKENSHIP:

"This is a liquor violation case. The witnesses in this case officers Blankenship and Carlson advised that they conducted the investigation, but that it was filed without their knowledge. The police report stated that they observed customers consuming beer after hours. Both officers stated that this is incorrect and they did not observe the customers consuming beer. It is recommended that this case be dismissed because of insufficient evidence."

551

Commission Exhibit No. 1611—Continued

3
DL 44-1639

Signed "Lem Brotherton, Assistant District Attorney of Dallas County, Texas; Henry Wade, District Attorney of Dallas County, Texas."

A "Motion of District Attorney to Dismiss Prosecution," filed in Dallas County Criminal Court Number 3 on February 8, 1955, under Docket Number 1789-C (naming MARY JANE SCHULTZ as customer), which reflected the same information as Docket Number 1788-C, was called to CARLSON's attention.

In relation to the above, BLANKENSHIP advised it is possible, though not probable, that his report was filed without his knowledge.

Concerning the statement appearing in the above mentioned "Motion" that "The police report states that they (arresting officers) observed customers consuming beer after hours. Both officers stated that this is incorrect and they did not observe the customers consuming beer," BLANKENSHIP commented as follows:

He does not recall being contacted by anyone in the Dallas County District Attorney's Office, or by anyone else, and advising them that "this is incorrect." To the best of his recollection the statement "this is incorrect," appearing in the "Motion" is false.

BLANKENSHIP stated he had known RUBY for sometime prior to December, 1954, when he and officer E. E. CARLSON arrested RUBY but BLANKENSHIP was unable to recall the specific date he first became acquainted with him. BLANKENSHIP said he did, however, become acquainted with RUBY when he was on the Vice Squad and through a routine check of RUBY's night club. BLANKENSHIP added he has been on the Vice Squad (Special Service Bureau) for about twelve years.

BLANKENSHIP related that since he has been on the Vice Squad, he had made official visits to RUBY's night clubs on numerous occasions, since the Vice Squad has the responsibility of seeing that performances at all night clubs at Dallas are orderly and "clean". He added that outside of his official visits to RUBY's night clubs, he has been to RUBY's clubs as a customer on two or three occasions. On these occasions, he did not pay the cover charge but did pay for the beer and food served to him.

552

COMMISSION EXHIBIT No. 1611—Continued

4
DL 44-1639

The last time BLANKENSHIP visited one of RUBY's clubs was approximately the latter part of October, 1963, when BLANKENSHIP took his wife to the Vegas Club.

BLANKENSHIP said he has never been employed by RUBY and he has never had any social contacts with him.

He described RUBY as an egotistical person with a quick temper, nervous, fidgety and he never relaxes. RUBY likes to be a "big dog" and he likes to be noticed, according to BLANKENSHIP. He added that RUBY never discussed politics in his presence. He stated that he has never had any reason to question the loyalty of RUBY to the United States Government.

BLANKENSHIP advised that all police officers assigned to the Vice Squad probably know RUBY but he knew of none who is closely acquainted with RUBY or who might consider RUBY a friend. He knew of no police officer who has worked for RUBY.

BLANKENSHIP related it is his understanding that RUBY was an acquaintance of JOE BONDS, former night club owner in Dallas, who was arrested and sentenced in approximately 1955 to 15 years in the State Penitentiary, Huntsville, Texas, on the charge of sodomy.

BLANKENSHIP advised he did not know LEE HARVEY OSWALD and he knew of no association between RUBY and OSWALD. BLANKENSHIP never saw OSWALD in RUBY's night clubs.

BLANKENSHIP said he was off duty on the day OSWALD was shot by RUBY. He said he has no idea how RUBY gained entrance to the basement of the Dallas City Hall on the morning of November 24, 1963.

BLANKENSHIP stated he did not see or talk with RUBY at any time between November 22, 1963 and November 24, 1963.

557

COMMISSION EXHIBIT No. 1611—Continued

FEDERAL BUREAU OF INVESTIGA ON

Commission Exhibit No. 1612

Date December 8, 1963

(1)

Detective E. E. CARLSON, Identification Bureau, Dallas, Texas, Police Department, who resides at 5733 Penrose, Dallas, was contacted concerning his joint arrest, with Detective D. L. BLANKENSHIP, of JACK LEON RUBY on December 5, 1954, for alleged violation by RUBY of the State Liquor Law. CARLSON was advised he did not have to make a statement, that any statement he did make could be used against him in a court of law, and that he could consult an attorney at any time he desired. CARLSON voluntarily advised as follows:

A copy of the "Arresting Officer's Report," arrest no. 54814, dated December 5, 1954, reflecting JACK LEON RUBY, 1719 1/2 South Ervay, was arrested by Dallas police officers D. L. BLANKENSHIP and E. E. CARLSON, for "Inv. Vio. State Liquor Law - Having beer on table after hours," was exhibited to CARLSON.

The Report states, "Give complete details as to what you know, what you saw or what you were told about suspect which prompted this arrest:" The following comments were reflected on the Report in answer to the above:

"This man is the owner and operator of the Silver Club located at 1717 S Ervay, was in charge tonight at the time arresting officers saw bottle partly fill with Schlitz beer on the table occupied by Eugenia Mary O'Brien and Mary Jane Schultz. When Blankenship attempted to get the bottle Miss O'Brien tried to hold the bottle and said that it was her beer.
TLCB Number will be attached to this sheet.
The bottle of Schlitz was about half full of beer, placed in the property room."

CARLSON obtained from the Identification File of JACK LEON RUBY, Identification No. 36398, a copy of the "Case Report" concerning the arrest of RUBY on December 5, 1954, by Officer BLANKENSHIP and him. This report reflects RUBY was charged with "Violation Art. II, Sec. 19 (16) Permitting comsumption during forbidden hours on Sunday." Under "Summary of Case" it was stated that "This man is the owner and operator of the Silver Club located at 1717 South Ervay and was present and in charge at the time. He permitted Eugenia Mary O'Brien and Mary Jane Schultz to consume a pert of a bottle of Schlitz beer during forbidden hours on Sunday."

CARLSON believes he typed the above "Case Report" as he recognized certain wording and punctuation in the report.

on 12/6/63 at Dallas, Texas File # DL 44-1639

by Special Agent s JAMES E. GARRIS and JACK B. PEDEN:bnm Date dictated 12/7/63

554

COMMISSION EXHIBIT No. 1612

DL 44-1639
(2)

CARLSON advised that to the best of his recollection the "Details" set out above, as reflected on the "Arresting Officer's Report," and the "Summary of Case" set out above, as reflected on the "Case Report," are true and correct, although he does not recall seeing the customers actually consuming beer after hours. He added that he never withdrew the above charge. He said he observed from the "Case Report" that the charge against RUBY was dismissed. He added that after he arrested RUBY and charged him, as stated above, he heard nothing further concerning the matter and he had nothing to do with the dismissal. Furthermore, he stated no one ever contacted him about the charge against RUBY.

The following information appearing in a "Motion of District Attorney to Dismiss Prosecution," filed in Dallas County Criminal Court No. 3, on February 8, 1955, under Docket No. 1788-C (naming EUGENIA MARY O'BRIEN as customer), in the case of the State of Texas vs. JACK LEON RUBY, was read to CARLSON:

"This is a liquor violation case. The witnesses in this case Officers Blankenship and Carleon advised that they conducted the investigation, but that it was filed without their knowledge. The police report states that they observed customers consuming beer after hours. Both officers stated that this is incorrect and they did not observe the customers consuming beer. It is recommended that this case be dismissed because of insufficient evidence."

Signed: "LEM BROTHERTON, Assistant District Attorney of Dallas County, Texas; HENRY WADE, District Attorney of Dallas County, Texas."

A "Motion of District Attorney to Dismiss Prosecution," filed in Dallas County Criminal Court No. 3 on February 8, 1955, under Docket no. 1789-C (naming MARY JANE SCHULTZ as customer), which reflected the same information as Docket no. 1788-C, was called to CARLSON's attention.

In relation to the above, CARLSON advised it is possible, though not probable, that his report was filed without his knowledge. CARLSON pointed out that the "Arresting Officer's Report" reflects the offense as being "Inv. Vio. State Liquor Law - Having beer on table after hours" and under "Details" of that report it is not stated that the arresting officers observed customers consuming beer after hours, but does state that the arresting officers saw a Schlitz beer bottle, about half full of beer, on the table of customers after hours.

CARLSON checked his files and no arrest record for EUGENIA MARY O'BRIEN or MARY JANE SCHULTZ was located.

CARLSON also pointed out that the "Case Report," mentioned above, believed to have been typed by him, states the charge as "Violation Art. II,

555

COMMISSION EXHIBIT No. 1612—Continued

DL 44-1639
(3)

"Sec 19 (16) Permitting consumption during forbidden hours on Sunday" and under "Summary of Case" it was stated that RUBY permitted customers to consume a part of a bottle of Schlitz beer during forbidden hours on Sunday.

CARLSON said to the best of his recollection, as mentioned previously, he did not see the customers actually consuming the beer after hours, but did see a partly filled bottle of beer on the customers' table after hours.

Concerning the statement appearing in the above-mentioned "motion" that "the police report states that they (arresting officers) observed customers consuming beer after hours. Both officers stated that this is incorrect and they did not observe the customers consuming beer," CARLSON commented as follows:

He does not now recall being contacted by anyone in the Dallas County District Attorney's Office, or by anyone else, and advising them that "this is incorrect." To the best of his recollection the statement "this is incorrect." appearing in the "motion," is false.

CARLSON made available a copy of Vernon's Penal Code of the State of Texas Annotated, Volume 1 A, which contains Title II (concerning malt liquors), Article 667, Section 19, paragraph 16, of the Texas Liquor Control Act, which states as follows:

"Violated any provisions of this act or any rule or regulation of the board at any time during the existence of the license sought to be cancelled or within the next preceding license period of any license held by the licensee."

Paragraph 17 of this same Section reads as follows:

"Consumed or permitted the consumption of alcoholic beverages on the licensed premises during any time when such consumption is prohibited as provided in Section 4 (c) of Article I of the Texas Liquor Control Act."

CARLSON advised that the curfew hour on Sunday mornings for the sale and consumption of alcoholic beverages is 1:15 a.m.

CARLSON advised he first met JACK RUBY in early 1954 when he was assigned to the Vice Squad. He said Detective D. L. BLANKENSHIP, who was also on the Vice Squad at that time, introduced him to RUBY.

556

DL 44-1639
(4)

He said while on the Vice Squad it was his duty to check burlesque shows from time to time and for a period of about two years he checked out RUBY's Club Vegas and found his place was orderly and "clean" at all times. He said that since he left the Vice Squad he has patronized RUBY's Club Vegas and Carousel Club several times as a customer. He added that on two or three occasions, during his visits to RUBY's clubs, RUBY would not let him pay the cover charge or pay for beer.

He stated the last time he visited one of RUBY's clubs was about two or three weeks before RUBY shot LEE HARVEY OSWALD. On that occasion he invited a friend, LOUIS BONNEY, part-time instructor, North Texas State University, Denton, Texas, to accompany him to the Carousel Club. CARLSON said neither he nor BONNEY paid the cover charge or for two beers consumed by each. He said this was the first time he had been to RUBY's club in approximately one year.

CARLSON related he has never worked for JACK RUBY and he has had no social relationship with RUBY. He described RUBY as a nervous, fidgety person who always seemed interested in how a person felt about him. He has seen RUBY lose his temper a number of times, but never in a violent state. CARLSON said RUBY never mentioned former President KENNEDY to him, nor did he ever discuss politics.

CARLSON declined to answer the following questions:

1. Do you know of any Dallas Police Officers who are personal friends of JACK RUBY?
2. Do you know of any Dallas Police Officers who are personally acquainted with JACK RUBY?
3. Do you know of any Dallas Police Officers who formerly worked for JACK RUBY?

CARLSON stated he never knew LEE HARVEY OSWALD and he had never seen OSWALD in RUBY's night clubs. He knew of no association between OSWALD and RUBY.

CARLSON related he was at his home, off duty, on the morning that OSWALD was shot by JACK RUBY.

He had no opinion as to how JACK RUBY gained entrance to the basement of City Hall on the morning RUBY shot OSWALD.

557

FEDERAL BUREAU OF

1

Date 12/13/63

MATTIE (Mrs. COLUMBUS) NELSON, 2635 Forrest Avenue, telephone HA-8-7147, was interviewed with reference to information from HAL COLLINS, La Jolla, California, to the effect that in early 1950, JACK RUBY had tried to adopt a child. She was interviewed in the presence of her husband, COLUMBUS NELSON. She related the following:

Her son, BEN ESTES NELSON, stage name "LITTLE DADDY" NELSON, was born September 28, 1947, at Franklin, Texas. When about two and one-half or three years old, Mr. and Mrs. NELSON discovered that "LITTLE DADDY" had learned to dance and do jigs and was very talented. He also learned to keep time with sticks and spoons, etc. When he was about five years old, he appeared on some amateur programs which she could not remember and came to the attention of JACK RUBY, who was then operating the Silver Spur night club in Dallas. "LITTLE DADDY" was then put under contract by JACK RUBY and appeared in night clubs in Dallas, including the Silver Spur, Vegas Club and Bob Wills' Ranch House. This would have been about 1951 or 1952. JACK RUBY was so impressed with "LITTLE DADDY" that he took him to Chicago, his parents accompanying "LITTLE DADDY" and JACK RUBY got him dates in some night clubs in the Chicago area and "LITTLE DADDY" appeared on one television program in Chicago. This was about 1953 or 1954. RUBY had the child on a contract and acted as his manager and got a percentage of his earnings during the time that the child was performing. "LITTLE DADDY" last entertained for JACK RUBY about eight or nine years ago which would have been 1954 or 1955.

They have had no contact with RUBY for eight or nine years except on one occasion in November, 1962, when JACK RUBY telephoned and asked them if they needed anything and stated that if they ever did need anything, just let him know.

Mrs. NELSON was unacquainted with LEE HARVEY OSWALD by name or photograph as being anyone known to her as being a friend or associate of JACK RUBY. She

on 12/12/63 at Dallas, Texas File # DL 44-1639

by Special Agent s A. H. SMITH and TOM P. CHAPOTON, JR. - gi Date dictated 12/13/63

13

COMMISSION EXHIBIT No. 1613

DL 44-1639
2

knew of no organizations to which JACK RUBY belonged and stated that all the while they had known him they believed him to be a loyal citizen. Mrs. NELSON said that on several occasions JACK RUBY expressed his desire to adopt "LITTLE DADDY".

14

COMMISSION EXHIBIT No. 1613—Continued

Commission Exhibit No. 1614

FD-302 (Rev. 3-3-59)

FEDERAL BUREAU OF INV

1

Date 12/16/63

HENRY D. AKIN, JR., 7249 Elmridge, Dallas, Texas, furnished the following information:

AKIN is a partner in the law firm of Akin, Vial, Hamilton & Koch, Mercantile Security Building, Dallas. GRAHAM KOCH, a partner in the law firm, has handled tax matters for JACK RUBY. AKIN recalled that RUBY had appeared at his office to consult KOCH on tax matters on November 19, 1963.

AKIN advised that RUBY had intended to send members of the law firm passes to the Carousel Club, which were to have been enclosed in laminated plastic cases. AKIN advised he never received a pass from RUBY.

AKIN stated he had no close personal association with RUBY and that all business matters between his company and RUBY had been handled by GRAHAM KOCH. AKIN did not know OSWALD and he had no knowledge of any acquaintance between OSWALD and RUBY.

on 12/16/63 at Dallas, Texas File # DL 44-1639

by Special Agent JAMES S. WEIR/eah Date dictated 12/16/63

31

Commission Exhibit No. 1615

FD-302 (Rev. 3-3-59)

FEDERAL BUREAU OF

1

Date 12/16/63

Lieutenant GEORGE C. ARNETT, whose name was furnished on November 25, 1963, by REAGAN TURMAN, prize fighter, Los Angeles, California, as friend of JACK RUBY, furnished the following information:

Lieutenant ARNETT advised that he resides at 3918 Fortune Lane, Dallas, is presently stationed at the Northwest Area Substation of the Dallas Police Department and has been a member of this department continuously since 1955.

ARNETT advised that he first met JACK RUBY in 1953 when ARNETT was an agent of the Liquor Control Board in Dallas under the following circumstances:

ARNETT and his wife, together with another agent and his wife went to the Vegas Club, operated by RUBY. While there, one of the dancers deliberately indecently exposed herself and as a result, ARNETT reported this matter which resulted in three weeks suspension against RUBY relative to the operation of that club. ARNETT stated that since that time, he has been to one or more of RUBY's establishments on a more or less regular basis and since 1955 he regularly visited the Vegas Club which was on his beat. Occasionally he did continue to go there with his wife and friends. He stated that he had occasion to feel that RUBY always attempted to operate his club legally and to the best of his ability and insisted that his employees and customers obeyed the laws. ARNETT gave as an example the fact that occasionally after the curfew relative to drinking intoxicating liquors in public, RUBY would use a flashlight to play over the tables and customers in the darkened area of the club to make sure that no one had alcoholic beverages in sight and was not violating the consuming law relative to consuming liquor after hours.

Lieutenant ARNETT stated that he never associated with RUBY on a social basis but felt that he did become very well acquainted with him as an individual, although he never discussed politics with RUBY. He stated that RUBY was an unpredictable type of person who would do anything to help a friend in need and who would also be quick to

on 12/15/63 at Dallas, Texas File # DL 44-1639

by Special Agent EDMOND C. HARDIN - gj Date dictated 12/16/63

32

DL 44-1639
2

lose his temper and act against anyone whomhe felt did him wrong.

Lieutenant ARNETT stated that RUBY was well known among the members of the Dallas Police Department and was rather friendly with them., He added that by the nature of RUBY's occupation, he felt it necessary to know as many people as possible and to be on good terms with the law enforcement agencies and members of the press. He added that he does not recall to what extent RUBY may have known police officer J. D. TIPPIT (deceased) but added that he does not believe he was more friendly with TIPPIT than the average police officer. ARNETT advised that he feels that RUBY may have been motivated in his shooting of LEE HARVEY OSWALD by the fact OSWALD had shot TIPPIT but he also feels that RUBY would have resented the murder of other Dallas police officers as much.

ARNETT stated he last saw RUBY on November 15, 1963, this being at the Vegas Club. He spoke with RUBY only briefly and does not recall that the conversation was concerning anything unusual.

Lieutenant ARNETT advised he did not know OSWALD and was not present when OSWALD was shot by RUBY. He added that he does not know of any relationship which may have existed between RUBY and OSWALD and knows nothing concerning the manner in which RUBY gained access to the basement area of the Dallas Police Department prior to shooting OSWALD. He also does not know of anyone who may have conspired with RUBY in this connection.

Lieutenant ARNETT stated that he has no additional pertinent information concerning this case.

33

COMMISSION EXHIBIT NO. 1615—Continued

FD-302 (Rev. 3-3-59) FEDERAL BUREAU OF I — Commission Exhibit No. 1616

1 Date December 16, 1963

WILLIE BARKER, 1733 Union Bowers, whose name and address appear on a Carousel Club pass card, advised as follows:

BARKER stated that he is employed as doorman at the Sheraton-Dallas Hotel and through his position, met JACK RUBY a year or so ago and has seen RUBY in the lobby of this hotel on several occasions since then. He stated his acquaintance with RUBY is based entirely upon a business relationship explaining that RUBY on several occasions, while at the hotel, gave him several blank temporary pass cards to his place of business and requested BARKER to give same to guests of the hotel.

BARKER stated that about October 15, 1963, RUBY gave him a permanent pass card to the Carousel Club but he has not used same and has not been to this club or to any other club operated by RUBY.

BARKER advised that he did not know LEE HARVEY OSWALD and received no information indicating a relationship between OSWALD and RUBY. He stated that he has no information as to the shooting of OSWALD by RUBY or as to anyone who may have assisted RUBY in entering the basement of the Dallas Police Department prior to shooting OSWALD. He stated that he has no information concerning this matter and never obtained any substantial information concerning RUBY's background activities and associates.

on 12/16/63 at Dallas, Texas File # DL 44-1639

by Special Agent EDMOND C. HARDIN/jn Date dictated 12/16/63

36

COMMISSION EXHIBIT NO. 1616

Commission Exhibit No. 1617

DL 44-1639
JBP:bnm
(1)

The following investigation was conducted by SA JACK B. PEDEN on December 13, 1963:

MARGUERITE ARMSTRONG, 2409 Maple, Dallas, Texas, was interviewed for the purpose of ascertaining how her name and the address, 2417 Maple, were found in search of JACK RUBY's car.

She informed that she has lived at 2409 Maple all her life. She stated that the property at 2417 Maple has been for sale for a period of approximately two years. She advised that it is possible that JACK RUBY was considering buying that property and had in mind to buy her home which, she pointed out, is very old, in connection with his attempt to purchase property at 2417 Maple. She stated that there have been numerous real estate men who have had that property up for sale and she does not know the man who last had it for sale. She said that he had his for sale sign in front of the property until approximately one week ago.

MARGUERITE ARMSTRONG advised that she does not know JACK RUBY personally and to her knowledge has never seen him. She also said that she does not know LEE HARVEY OSWALD.

On December 14, 1963, Mr. OLEN ALEXANDER, who resides at 9963 Mixon, telephone FL 1-3630, Dallas, Texas, was interviewed as to how his name, with telephone number EM 8-8304 was found in the car of JACK RUBY when it was searched. Mr. ALEXANDER said that the telephone number EM 8-8304 is an office phone which he has occasion to use from time to time in his real estate business. He advised that he is in the real estate business in Dallas, and that he met JACK RUBY approximately October 23, 1963. Mr. ALEXANDER said that he cannot definitely give the date, but it was at approximately that time.

ALEXANDER advised as follows:

He has a building at 2417 Maple which every night club operator in Dallas wants. (It is noted that the address 2417 Maple was also written among some of RUBY's things, along with the name of MARGUERITE ARMSTRONG.) JACK RUBY contacted ALEXANDER about the property at 2417 Maple and indicated that he was interested in buying this property. RUBY indicated a real desire to purchase the building, which is priced at $75,000, but apparently did not have sufficient funds for this. ALEXANDER said that RUBY said something to the effect that he would "see some of my friends," but that he was not recontacted by RUBY about the property.

38

DL 44-1639
(2)

On the occasion when RUBY contacted ALEXANDER, ALEXANDER made an appointment with him and showed him the building. On this same occasion RUBY told ALEXANDER to come to his Carousel Club at any time he wanted, free of charge, and bring his wife. ALEXANDER said that he never took RUBY up on this offer and has not seen him since that time.

ALEXANDER said that so far as he knows he does not know LEE HARVEY OSWALD and certainly knows of no connection between RUBY and OSWALD.

A search of the Dallas telephone criss-cross directory as conducted by SA JOHN B. PEDEN on December 13, 1963, reflects that the telephone number WH 8-7101 is listed to the Admiral Alloy Steel Corporation, 2802 Rector.

It is noted that that phone number appeared among RUBY's things obtained as result of search of RUBY's car.

On December 14, 1963, JOHN H. BRECHT, 6310 Airline, Dallas, Texas, was interviewed regarding the telephone number EM 1-4174 which appeared in JACK RUBY's possessions, found in search of his car.

MR. BRECHT said he formerly lived at 3124 Westminster, and that at both addresses he had the telephone number EM 1-4174. He stated, however, that he is unable to advise how his phone number came into the possession of RUBY. Mr. BRECHT said that to his knowledge he has never seen JACK RUBY, and has no recollection of ever having any contact of any kind with him.

He also stated that he does not know LEE HARVEY OSWALD.

On December 13, 1963, Mr. LEE A. BEDFORD, 1005 Chippendale, Dallas, Texas, was interviewed as to how the telephone number DA 1-2746 was found during a search of JACK RUBY's car.

Mr. BEDFORD advised that the phone number DA 1-2746 is for the Casa Linda Catering Service, at 10800 Garland Road. He advised that the only contact he ever had with JACK RUBY was approximately five or six years ago.

BEDFORD furnished the following information:

At the one time he saw JACK RUBY, approximately five or six years ago, RUBY had a little colored boy with whom, whom BEDFORD believed was called "LITTLE DADDY." RUBY was promoting this boy and felt that the boy had

39

DL 44-1639
(3)
JDP:bnm

talent. On the occasion when BEDFORD met RUBY, RUBY had the boy at a private party at the Casa Linda Lodge where the boy sang some songs. At that particular time RUBY invited BEDFORD to come as a guest to his night club, which BEDFORD believes was the Silver Spur. BEDFORD never attended the night club and has had no additional contact with RUBY.

BEDFORD also said he knows of no relationship between RUBY and LEE HARVEY OSWALD.

40

COMMISSION EXHIBIT No. 1617—Continued

Commission Exhibit No. 1618

1

Date December 13, 1963

JOHN N. CRAWFORD, JR., 1518 16th Street, advised he is the pilot for the Texas Department of Corrections (TDC). In June, 1962 while staying overnight in Dallas, Texas, he visited the Carousel Club. During conversation with unrecalled other persons, CRAWFORD was approached by JACK RUBY, who stated he was the owner of the Carousel Club. RUBY said he understood CRAWFORD was employed by the TDC and asked CRAWFORD if he knew CANDY BARR who was then an inmate in the prison system. RUBY then inquired of CRAWFORD as to whether CRAWFORD knew any person who might help him in obtaining an early parole from prison for CANDY BARR. RUBY stated he desired to have CANDY BARR work in his club "instructing other girls". CRAWFORD stated he was unable to furnish any information to RUBY and thereafter terminated the conversation with him but not until RUBY asked for and was given a business card of CRAWFORDS, containing his name, address and telephone number in Huntsville.

CRAWFORD stated this was his only contact with RUBY and he was unable to provide further information.

On 12-13-63 at Huntsville, Texas File # HO 44-939

by SA ROBERT E. WIATT:djw Date dictated 12-13-63

This document contains neither recommendations nor conclusions of the FBI. It is the property of the FBI and is loaned to your agency; it and its contents are not to be distributed outside your agency.

72

COMMISSION EXHIBIT No. 1618

FD-302 (Rev. 3-3-59) FEDERAL BUREAU OF IN[VESTIGATION]

Commission Exhibit No. 1619

1

Date December 13, 1963

ARTHUR R. SANDERS, White Rock Terrace Club, 4875 Lawther Drive, residence 9019 Lanshire, Dallas, Texas, furnished the following information:

SANDERS has known JACK RUBY for about 12 years. SANDERS was formerly in the decorating business and he met JACK RUBY about 12 years ago at the Fair Park, Dallas, at which time RUBY was promoting some sort of gadget to be used as an attachment or sewing machine. He obtained SANDERS to build a booth for him at the fair to be used in promoting this gadget. SANDERS has had occasional contact with RUBY since that time, the last time being about one year ago when SANDERS attended a meeting of the Retail Beer Dealers Association held at Louann's in Dallas.

SANDERS has had no social contacts with RUBY and has no knowledge of RUBY's associates or recent activities. He has never patronized any of the clubs operated by RUBY and to his knowledge, has never been to SANDER's club.

SANDERS did not know LEE HARVEY OSWALD and has no knowledge of any connection between RUBY and OSWALD.

on 12/12/63 at Dallas, Texas File # DL 44-1639

by Special Agent PAUL L. SCOTT/jn Date dictated 12/12/63

This document contains neither recommendations nor conclusions of the FBI. It is the property of the FBI and is loaned to your agency; it and its contents are not to be distributed outside your agency.

148

FD-302 (Rev. 3-3-59) FEDERAL BUREAU OF INVESTIGATION

Commission Exhibit No. 1620

Date 12-16-63

1

GAYLE M. TIPPIT, Detective, Special Services Bureau, Dallas Police Department, home address 10831 Cotillion, advised that he first began working for the Dallas Police Department in 1950, and soon thereafter he met JACK RUBY, who was at that time operating the Silver Spur Night Club at 1717 S. Ervay. He was assigned to this area and it was his duty to periodically check the Silver Spur which was a combination dance hall and beer tavern. During this period of time he became very well acquainted with JACK RUBY and determined that he ran an orderly establishment and would not allow any disturbances or disorderly conduct. He acted as his own bouncer and would forcibly expell anyone who caused trouble at the club. He was very friendly and helpful to the patroling officers and requested no special favors of the officers.

In subsequent years, Mr. TIPPIT had occasion to contact RUBY while he was operating the Vegas Club and the Carousel Club, although his contacts in recent years have been infrequent. He personally has no knowledge of any illegal activities on the part of RUBY, such as gambling, narcotics, or prostitution.

Detective TIPPIT advised that he had not known LEE HARVEY OSWALD prior to the assassination of President KENNEDY and had no information indicating a connection between OSWALD and RUBY.

Detective TIPPIT stated that on November 24, 1963, he was on duty on the second floor of the Municipal Building at the time OSWALD was slain by RUBY. He was in the office of the Special Services Bureau and had no opportunity to see what was going on in the basement. He did not see RUBY on that date. He was not aware of the security plans concerning the transfer of OSWALD to the County Jail, but did note that he had to identify himself to Patrolmen on duty on the third floor when he had occasion to go to that floor on the morning of November 24, 1963.

on 12-16-63 at Dallas, Texas File # DL 44-1639

by Special Agent JAMES F. GLONEK & RALPH E. RAWLINGS - md Date dictated 12-16-63

153

This document contains neither recommendations nor conclusions of the FBI. It is the property of the FBI and is loaned to your agency; it and its contents are not to be distributed outside your agency.

FD-302 (Rev. 3-3-59)

FEDERAL BUREAU OF INV

Commission Exhibit No. 1621

1

Date 12/15/63

JOHNNY COLA, 2140 Siesta Drive, who was reported to be a close associate of RUBY furnished the following information:

During 1948, COLA was employed as a musician by JOE BONDS at the Sky Club in Dallas. Through BONDS, COLA met JACK RUBY who at that time was operating the Silver Spur Club in Dallas. Subsequent to his employment at the Sky Club, COLA later worked as a musician at the Colony Club on Commerce Street in Dallas, which is located next door to the Carousel Club. From about 1948 to 1956, COLA knew RUBY on a close personal basis. Subsequent to 1956, he has seen him only infrequently and has not associated with him socially.

COLA was shown a photograph of LEE HARVEY OSWALD at which time he advised that OSWALD was unknown to him and he knew of no association between OSWALD and RUBY. COLA knew of no policemen with whom RUBY was particularly close, however, he pointed out that RUBY at least had a speaking acquaintance with most of the policemen in the Dallas Police Department. COLA knows of no particularly strong political belief on the part of JACK RUBY but considered him to be a loyal American and knows of no subversive activities on the part of RUBY.

COLA could furnish no information concerning the reason for RUBY shooting OSWALD but pointed out that RUBY was a highly emotional individual and could have convinced himself that it was the thing to do.

on 12/13/63 at Dallas, Texas File # DL 44-1639

by Special Agents JOSEPH PEGGS and ALVIN ZIMMERMAN - gi Date dictated 12/15/63

186

This document contains neither recommendations nor conclusions of the FBI. It is the property of the FBI and is loaned to your agency; it and its contents are not to be distributed outside your agency.

COMMISSION EXHIBIT No. 1621

FD-302 (Rev. 3-3-59)

FEDERAL BUREAU OF INVESTIGATION

[redacted]

Commission Exhibit No. 1622

1

Date 12/15/63

DEWEY F. GROOM, 2631 Fonville, was interviewed at the Longhorn Ranch Club, 216 Cornith. GROOM was reported to have been formerly employed by RUBY. GROOM furnished the following information:

GROOM first worked for and became acquainted with RUBY during 1949 when GROOM's band played for RUBY at the Silver Spur Club. He continued his association with RUBY for about five years, after which GROOM went into business for himself. During the period from 1949 to about 1954, GROOM was closely associated with RUBY and knew him on a close personal basis. Subsequent to 1954, GROOM saw RUBY very infrequently and at the most two or three times a year.

GROOM was shown a photograph of LEE HARVEY OSWALD and indicated that OSWALD was unknown to him and he knew of no association between OSWALD and RUBY. GROOM could recall no police officer with whom RUBY was particularly close, however, he pointed out that RUBY knew many officers since he made it a point to cultivate their friendship. GROOM had never discussed politics with RUBY and did not feel that RUBY had any strong political beliefs. RUBY did greatly admire men who were in highly-placed positions. GROOM knew of no subversive activities on the part of RUBY and considered RUBY a loyal American citizen. GROOM was not surprised when he heard that RUBY had shot OSWALD since RUBY is a highly emotional individual who has very intense likes and dislikes.

GROOM last saw RUBY approximately three or four weeks prior to the time he shot OSWALD and as indicated above, knows very little concerning RUBY's personal life since 1953 or 1954.

on 12/13/63 at Dallas, Texas File # DL 44-1639

by Special Agents JOSEPH PEGGS and ALVIN ZIMMERMAN - gi Date dictated 12/15/63

190

This document contains neither recommendations nor conclusions of the FBI. It is the property of the FBI and is loaned to your agency; it and its contents are not to be distributed outside your agency.

COMMISSION EXHIBIT No. 1622

FD-302 (Rev. 3-3-59)

FEDERAL BUREAU OF IN.

Commission Exhibit No. 1623

Date December 15, 1963

1

ISAIAH HOWARD HAYNES, 2114 Holland, Grand Prairie, Texas, and 1917 Galveston, Grand Prairie, Texas, telephone AN 2-4855, was interviewed as an employee of S & R Incorporated, doing business as the Carousel Club during 1961-62. HAYNES advised that he is employed as a houseman-porter-chauffeur for LLOYD B. SANDS, 3821 Windsor Avenue, telephone LA 6-8166, and hal had this job for the past 9 years.

HAYNES stated he has worked for JACK RUBY at various clubs owned by RUBY since 1947. He usually works at these clubs as a porter-handyman and has worked at the Silver SPur Club, Vegas Club and Carousel Club. He works at the Sands residence during the day and usually does what maintenance and clean-up work necessary at the various clubs owned by RUBY, between the hours of 4:00 and 7:00 p.m. He receives his instructions as to what is to be done at these clubs from either JACK RUBY or EVA GRANT by telephone.

HAYNES stated that when he is working around these clubs there is seldom anyone else there and he has not been around the clubs at night for approximately 7-8 years.

He stated that he considers JACK RUBY a very nice man to work for and stated that he does not know anything about RUBY's personal life, associates, or business dealings. He did not know if RUBY had any personal connections with the Dallas Police Department. He stated that RUBY had a revolver that he carried in a money sack when he, RUBY, was carrying the receipts from the clubs which were placed in the same sack with the gun. HAYNES continued that he did not know LEE HARVEY OSWALD and had never seen OSWALD in any of the clubs and did not know whether or not RUBY ever had any association with OSWALD.

on 12/12/63 at Grand Prairie, Texas File # Dallas 44-1639

by Special Agent s ALLEN H. SMITH & TOM E. CHAPOTON:BL Date dictated 12/14/63

191

This document contains neither recommendations nor conclusions of the FBI. It is the property of the FBI and is loaned to your agency; it and its contents are not to be distributed outside your agency.

COMMISSION EXHIBIT No. 1623

FD-302 (Rev. 3-3-59)

FEDERAL BUREAU OF INVESTIGATION

Commission Exhibit No. 1624

1

Date 12/12/63

WILLIAM EARL "PAT" O'DONNELL, JR., 11009 Myrtice, was contacted at his residence and immediately advised of the official identity of the interviewing Agents. He was advised of the fact that he did not have to make any statement, but that any statement he did make could be used against him in court. He was advised of his right to consult an attorney.

O'DONNELL furnished the following information concerning his association with JACK RUBY:

He has known RUBY since late 1947 or early 1948, as he was employed by him at this time at the Silver Spur night club on South Ervay Street in Dallas as a singer. He was employed by RUBY intermittently until 1951 when he served in the Armed Forces from 1951 through 1953. His next association with RUBY was in 1956 when he was employed intermittently as doorman and also in 1959 when RUBY opened the Carousel and he and JIMMY RHODES, a photographer from Sulphur Springs, Texas, helped RUBY set up the show at the Carousel and trained the girls. He recalls that at this time owners of other night clubs in Dallas were putting pressure on RUBY to prevent him from opening the Carousel which would be in competition with them, and that RUBY was forced to seek his Mastersof Ceremonies from locations other than Dallas. He also helped RUBY by furnishing performers and other people for his show at the Carousel.

He considers RUBY a sincerely humane person but also emotionally unstable but considered RUBY's sister, EVA GRANT, more unstable than RUBY. O'DONNELL furnished the following instances concerning RUBY's behavior:

In 1959, O'DONNELL's wife was in a hospital in a serious condition and RUBY voluntarily donated blood and gave O'DONNELL $100.00 to help defray hospital expenses. RUBY also gave O'DONNELL $100.00 in 1957 when O'DONNELL travelled to the National Disc Jockey Convention in Nashville, Tennessee. Both of these gifts were entirely unsolicited by O'DONNELL.

on 12/11/63 at Dallas, Texas File # DL 44-1639

by Special Agent s EDWARD J. MABEY and KENNETH P. HUGHES - gj Date dictated 12/12/63

200

This document contains neither recommendations nor conclusions of the FBI. It is the property of the FBI and is loaned to your agency; it and its contents are not to be distributed outside your agency.

O'DONNELL furnished the following information concerning what he considers RUBY's "unreasonable side":

In 1957 or 1958, an unidentified man pulled a pistol on RUBY in the Vegas Club as RUBY was standing behind the bar. RUBY kept his pistol on a shelf underneath the bar and this pistol was within easy reach at this time. Instead of reaching for the pistol, RUBY jumped over the bar, slapped the pistol from the man's hand and almost beat the man to death with his fists, put the gun back in the man's pocket and then threw him out. Approximately three months after this, also in the Vegas Club, a man approximately 6'3", weighing about 230 pounds, was having an argument with a woman and he slapped her. JACK RUBY beat this man to the floor and then threw him out the door. He then told him "if you are that kind of man, crawl away". He then made this individual crawl down the street. On another occasion, O'DONNELL stated that RUBY threw him out of the Carousel Club approximately two or three months after it opened. O'DONNELL explained that he advised RUBY that the whole scheme of the stage was ruined because RUBY changed the lighting without consulting anyone. RUBY then told him to get out of his club and never to come back. Several days later, RUBY called O'DONNELL and asked him why he had not been around. When O'DONNELL told RUBY that he had thrown him out a few days before, RUBY said "you know I didn't mean that".

O'DONNELL stated he is still employed intermittently by RUBY as a doorman which job consists of taking the cover charge from customers as they enter the Carousel Club and arranging for a waiter. Since RUBY has been incarcerated, ANDY ANDREWS, a colored boy hired by RUBY as a bartender three or four years ago, is managing the Carousel Club.

O'DONNELL continued that he believes RUBY to be too emotional an individual to be able to plan anything in advance as he does not believe RUBY could concentrate on any one topic for more than five minutes. He stated he

201

does not know of any connection between RUBY and OSWALD and failed to identify a photograph of OSWALD as anyone he has ever seen in or around the Carousel Club. He stated he had not seen JACK RUBY for approximately one and one-half months prior to the shooting of OSWALD. He stated he knew that RUBY carried a gun when he would be carrying the night's receipts with him after closing the club. He carried this gun in a zipper coin bag and usually left it in the coin bag during the evening when he was at the club. As to RUBY's entering the basement of the Police and Courts Building on November 24, 1963, O'DONNELL stated he believes that he himself could have walked into the basement that morning because of the fact that he believes anyone who knows anyone on the police force could have gotten into the basement. He stated that RUBY is on speaking terms with about 700 out of the 1200 men on the police force and was not at all surprised to learn of RUBY's admittance to the basement.

O'DONNELL stated that his father, WILLIAM EARL O'DONNELL, SR., known as "COWBOY", is running for the post of State Representative in Dallas, Texas, and that his grandfather, WILLIAM EMITT O'DONNELL, was a U. S. Marshal at Shreveport, Louisiana.

O'DONNELL stated that as long as he has known JACK RUBY he has never heard of any affiliation of RUBY's to any group of men or organization but he added that it is impossible in the type of business in which RUBY is engaged not to associate in some degree with so-called "syndicate" men, gamblers, pimps or the like. He stated that BOB LAWRENCE, who came from Las Vegas a few years ago and tried to set up a club of his own in Dallas, Texas, was a syndicate man and that he and RUBY were in almost constant conflict. LAWRENCE finally left the Dallas area after an unsuccessful attempt to engage in business in the Dallas area.

O'DONNELL stated that Sergeant FRAZIER of the Vice Squad, Dallas Police Department, frequents the Carousel Club and also Lieutenant ROY of the Burglary and Theft Division and that on almost any night of the week there are several uniformed officers both on and off duty who drop by the club and drink coffee in the back and watch a free show.

202

DL 44-1639
4

O'DONNELL stated it is customary when known police officers, other performers or waiters from other clubs drop in to admit them without a cover charge and to buy them a round of drinks. He stated this is the custom in both the Vegas and Carousel Clubs. O'DONNELL stated he is unable to furnish the names of police officers frequenting these clubs as he knows them only by sight.

O'DONNELL stated he is a licensed talent manager for the American Federation of Musicians, license number 3683, and helps RUBY out at his club because of business connections.

203

FD-302 (Rev. 1-25-60) FEDERAL BUREAU OF IN— Commission Exhibit No. 1625

1

Date 12/11/63

Lieutenant FLOYD HANNON, (National Academy) Wichita, Kansas Police Department, advised SA ROBERT ALLEN ELKINS this date, that a THELMA CORNWELL, waitress at the Westair Club, Wichita, Kansas, called him and advised him that she had given some information to two FBI Agents. HANNON advised that CORNWELL said that some of this information was not correct, and that she wanted to correct this information. She related the following to HANNON:

GAIL RAVEN was working at the T-Bone Club in Wichita, Kansas at the time JACK RUBY came to the T-Bone Club in Wichita, Kansas, instead of exotic dancer, PRECIOUS DIAMOND. CORNWELL told HANNON that this was the later part of January 1963, and while RUBY was in town he stayed at the Cassa Siesta Motel. Lieutenant HANNON advised that he checked the records of the Cassa Siesta Motel and found that JACK RUBY made one phone call from the Cassa Siesta Motel while he stayed there in January 1963. This phone call was to number JA 4-3224, which is listed as the T-Bone Club, Wichita, Kansas.

On 12/5/63 at Wichita, Kansas File # KC 44-497

by SA ROBERT ALLEN ELKINS:aks Date dictated 12/5/63

261

1

Date 12/11/63

VIRGIL PEEL, Room 8, Cassa Siesta Motel, Wichita, Kansas, advised that he is the manager of the Westair Club, Wichita, Kansas. PEEL stated that until April 1963, he worked at the T-Bone Club, Wichita, Kansas. PEEL advised that while he was employed at the T-Bone Club, Wichita, Kansas in late January or early February 1963, an exotic dancer by the name of GAIL RAVEN introduced him to JACK LEON RUBY. PEEL advised that he only met RUBY on this one evening and did not remember who he was with or anything about hom. PEEL stated that he doubted if he could recognize RUBY again if he ever saw him in person.

On 12/5/63 at Wichita, Kansas File # KC 44-497

by SA ROBERT ALLEN ELKINS:aks Date dictated 12/5/63

This document contains neither recommendations nor conclusions of the FBI. It is the property of the FBI and is loaned to your agency; it and its contents are not to be distributed outside your agency.

262

COMMISSION EXHIBIT No. 1626

1

Date 12/11/63

JIM JONKER, 4523 South Market Street, Wichita, Kansas, advised that he is the manager of the T-Bone Club, Wichita, Kansas. JONKER stated that last February, JACK RUBY was at the T-Bone Club to visit a dancer by the name of GAIL RAVEN of Dallas, Texas. JONKER stated that RAVEN was performing as an exotic dancer at the T-Bone Club at that time. JONKER stated that there was a couple with RUBY from Dallas, whom he did not know. JONKER advised that the man with RUBY was of average size and the woman was blond, that was all he could remember concerning this couple.

JONKER stated that GAIL RAVEN had spoken of JACK RUBY several times and of the Carousel Club at Dallas, Texas, where RAVEN had performed in the past. JONKER stated that he did not know JACK RUBY and had only met him on this one occasion when he was introduced to RUBY by GAIL RAVEN. JONKER advised that in the entertainment circle he had never heard anything about RUBY in connection with subversive activities.

On 12/5/63 at Wichita, Kansas File # KC 44-497

by SA ROBERT ALLEN ELKINS:aks Date dictated 12/5/63

This document contains neither recommendations nor conclusions of the FBI. It is the property of the FBI and is loaned to your agency; it and its contents are not to be distributed outside your agency.

263

COMMISSION EXHIBIT No. 1627

Commission Exhibit No. 1628

FD-302 (Rev. 3-3-59)

FEDERAL BUREAU OF INVESTIGATION

Date 12-19-63

1

WILLIAM F. ALEXANDER, Aka., Bill Alexander, Assistant District Attorney, Dallas County, called at the FBI Office and advised that he has been assigned by District Attorney HENRY WADE to handle the prosecution of JACK L. RUBY for the shooting of LEE HARVEY OSWALD.

ALEXANDER stated it has come to his attention that EARL GOETZ, reporter for the "Milwaukee Sentinel" has information to the effect that RUBY had a roommate in 1957 - 1958 by the name of FRANK FERRARA or FRANK FERRARO who was close to RUBY until FERRARA and RUBY got into a fight and immediately thereafter FERRARO left Dallas by plane and was met at the International Airport by JOE VELACHI.

ALEXANDER stated he believes that if there was any connection between RUBY and the syndicate, Mafia, or other hoodlums, it would have come to the attention of his office through various gamblers and hoodlum informants of his office and no such information has come to his attention.

ALEXANDER stated he has never been a customer or guest in the Carousel Club and is not a member and never received a membership card to RUBY's club. He speculated if the name "William F. Alexander" or variations thereof was found in RUBY's possession, it is likely RUBY may have intended sending him a card.

ALEXANDER stated his office has employed a psychiatrist by the name of SILVANO ARIETI, 22 East 72nd Street, New York City, who is coming to Dallas, December 21, 1963, and that he plans to have ARIETI examine RUBY between 8:00 and 10:00 a.m. Sunday, December 22, 1963, without the knowledge of the defense attorneys of RUBY.

ALEXANDER discussed various potential witnesses who could place RUBY at various places during the period November 21 - 24, 1963, whom he contemplates utilizing as witnesses or utilizing th information furnished by them in cross - examination of RUBY in

on 12-19-63 at Dallas, Texas File # DL 44-1639

by Special Agent J. CALVIN RICE & MANNING C. CLEMENTS - md, Date dictated 12-19-63

2

2

DL 44-1639

order to impress the jury with the thorough investigation which has been conducted in this case.

ALEXANDER stated the jurors who will hear RUBY's case will come from a panel of 500 names and that he is hopeful that this office will search these names against the persons interviewed in connection with the investigation by the FBI of the OSWALD - RUBY matter, to insure that any "nuts" will be brought to his attention and he can exclude same from the jury.

ALEXANDER stated he has no information other than what has been in the paper concerning the source of funds for RUBY's defense.

ALEXANDER stated Detective D.L. BLANKENSHIP, Dallas Police Department has known RUBY over the years during RUBY's stay in Dallas. ALEXANDER stated he has no information or knowledge to support allegations in the press that RUBY received favors from the Dallas Police Department or that Dallas Police Officers were offered or received favors from RUBY.

3

FD-302 (Rev. 3-3-59)

FEDERAL BUREAU OF INVESTIGATION

[redacted]

Commission Exhibit No. 1629

Date December 20, 1963

(1)

H. H. (ANDY) ANDERSON, Manager, Adolphus Hotel, Dallas, Texas, advised he had Carousel Club pass no. 136. He stated he obtained this card at a press party several months ago when all club owners were in attendance. As Mr. ANDERSON books all entertainment for the Century Room at the Adolphus, he was invited to the party. During the evening, JACK RUBY gave each person in attendance a club pass card.

Mr. ANDERSON advised he knew RUBY on sight but had never been friendly with him and had never associated with him to any extent. ANDERSON advised he did not know LEE HARVEY OSWALD and did not know if RUBY had ever known OSWALD.

on 12/19/63 at Dallas, Texas File # DL 44-1639

by Special Agents JAMES C. KENNEDY and WILL HAYDEN GRIFFIN:bnm 31 Date dictated 12/19/63

This document contains neither recommendations nor conclusions of the FBI. It is the property of the FBI and is loaned to your agency; it and its contents are not to be distributed outside your agency.

COMMISSION EXHIBIT No. 1629

FD-302 (Rev. 3-3-59)

FEDERAL BUREAU OF

Commission Exhibit No. 1630

1

Date 12/18/63

B. A. BATES, JR., 2707 Bridal Wreath, Dallas, Texas, whose name and address, together with his place of employment, "Dallas Morning News", appears on Carousel Club pass card number 159, furnished the following information:

Mr. BATES stated that through his employment in the Advertising Section of the "Dallas Morning News", he had occasion to come in contact with JACK RUBY during the past one and one-half years from time to time. He stated that these contacts were always in connection with advertisements placed by RUBY in the newspaper relative to his places of amusement. He added that his acquaintance with RUBY is limited to these business contacts and that he has never associated with him socially or discussed politics with him. He stated that he last saw RUBY on about November 15, 1963, when RUBY was again at the "Dallas Morning News" building. On this occasion, RUBY gave him a pass card to the Carousel Club, which pass card he never used. BATES stated that when he last saw RUBY he noted nothing exceptional in his conversation with RUBY.

He added that he never knew LEE HARVEY OSWALD and never received information which might indicate a relationship between OSWALD and RUBY. He further stated that he has no information concerning the shooting of OSWALD by RUBY or concerning the manner in which RUBY entered the basement area of the Dallas Police Department prior to the shooting.

on 12/17/63 at Dallas, Texas File # DL 44-1639

by Special Agent EDMOND C. HARDIN - gj ECH 35 Date dictated 12/18/63

This document contains neither recommendations nor conclusions of the FBI. It is the property of the FBI and is loaned to your agency; it and its contents are not to be distributed outside your agency.

COMMISSION EXHIBIT No. 1630

FD-302 (Rev. 3-3-59) FEDERAL BUREAU OF I—

Commission Exhibit No. 1631

1

Date December 18, 1963

EDWARD B. BELLOCCHIO, Room 218, 1517 Commerce Street, Dallas, Texas, was interviewed in that Carousel Club pass card number 111 was issued in that name.

BELLOCCHIO stated that during October, 1963, he was in Colombo's Pizza Bakery, 2415 North Haskell, talking to DENNIS TOOCH, who had a group of passes to the Carousel Club and asked BELLOCCHIO if he would like to have one. As BELLOCCHIO recalled, he told him yes but he did not think anything more about it.

A week or so later, BELLOCCHIO was in Sols Turf Bar at 1515 Commerce having a sandwich when JACK RUBY came in and walked up to him and stated that he had something for him. He handed BELLOCCHIO a Carousel Club pass card number 111, made out in his, BELLOCCHIO's name. BELLOCCHIO continued that he had never seen JACK RUBY before in his life and is sure that RUBY thought he, BELLOCCHIO, was his brother, FRANK BELLOCCHIO, whom RUBY is slightly acquainted. BELLOCCHIO stated he looks very much like his brother FRANK. He thanked RUBY for the card and recalled passing the time of the day with RUBY for about five minutes. He continued that he has not used this card and has not seen RUBY since that time. He does not know anything about RUBY's business activities or whether or not RUBY had any connections with the police. He did not know the whereabouts of JACK RUBY on November 22-24, 1963, and whether or not RUBY was associated with LEE HARVEY OSWALD in any manner. BELLOCCHIO stated he did not know LEE HARVEY OSWALD.

on 12/17/63 at Dallas, Texas File # DL 44-1639

by Special Agent TOM E. CHAPOTON, JR./jn Date dictated 12/18/63

COMMISSION EXHIBIT NO. 1631

FD-302 (Rev. 1-25-60) FEDERAL BUREAU OF INVESTIGATION

Commission Exhibit No. 1632

Date December 17, 1963

1

Mr. THEODORE LOUIS FLEMING, Unit Number 7, 4 H Motel, 4777 North Broadway, telephone 442-1772, was interviewed at his place of employment, Regent Investment Company, 900 28th Street, Boulder, Colorado.

Mr. FLEMING stated that he was employed in April, 1955 as a police officer on the Dallas, Texas, Police Department and remained in that employment until March of 1963 when he resigned in order to better his financial condition. He continued that he is not married, and that he first met JACK RUBY about 1958 at the Carousel, a night club in Dallas, Texas, specializing in strip-tease shows. He continued that this night club was operated by JACK RUBY, and that from about 1958 to March of 1963 he (FLEMING) occasionally visited the club, possibly once a month, to "have a beer and see a show." He stated that during this period he, as well as many Dallas police officers, were casual acquaintances of JACK RUBY and were on a "first name basis" with RUBY. He continued that RUBY is a man who "loves policemen" and very seldom let them pay for anything in his night club. FLEMING enlarged on this statement by advising that at times RUBY let him pay for his drinks; however, he estimated that 90 per cent of the time he received no check when he visited the Carousel. He advised further that he was of the opinion that most of the other police officers who frequented the Carousel were treated in much the same manner.

He advised further that during his service on the Dallas Police Department, he was assigned at times in the down town district and does not recall ever being called to the Carousel on a complaint of any kind; however, he has visited the Carousel on an official investigation on some occasions. He added that this was usually when he was attempting to locate someone he was looking for, and that in his opinion, JACK RUBY was generally known "as a pretty damn good night club operator who had a sincere love for police officers." FLEMING explained this statement further by stating that so far as he knows, RUBY is a normal male person who has shown no indication to him to be effeminate

On 12/17/63 at Boulder, Colorado File # DN 44-387

65

by SA KENNETH BRIDENSTINE; SA RICHARD L. CAMPBELL/pgj Date dictated 12/17/63

COMMISSION EXHIBIT NO. 1632

in any manner and merely has a high regard for police officers.

FLEMING stated further that he (FLEMING) was a good friend of the late Officer J. D. TIPPET; however, he does not recalled ever having seen TIPPET frequent the Carousal and does not know if RUBY was even acquainted with him.

He advised further that while RUBY liked policement and seldom let them pay their checks at his club, RUBY at no time requested any favors of FLEMING or, to his knowledge, of any other police officer. FLEMING continued that in fact he could not recall ever having seen JACK RUBY at the Dallas Police Department. He added that he certainly did not consider him a "hanger on" at the Police Department.

FLEMING advised that there is no vice or moral squad as such at the Dallas Police Department; however, this phase of the police activities is handled by the Special Service Bureau which has a complement of 40 to 45 men. FLEMING continued that to his knowledge there is no one in this Bureau that was any closer to RUBY than the ordinary policeman.

FLEMING repeated that in his opinion RUBY killed OSWALD solely because OSWALD killed a policeman; however, that possibly part of his motive might have been publicity. He added that he does not feel that RUBY committed this murder because OSWALD killed President KENNEDY.

FLEMING advised further that no crime of this magnitude occurred in Dallas during his time in the Police Department, and so he cannot visualize the security measures that the Police Department may have used when OSWALD was in custody. He continued that he has no knowledge as to how RUBY may have gained entrance to the basement of the

Dallas Police Department unless some rookie policeman believed him to be a detective and allowed him to pass. FLEMING stated he does not believe any officer of the Dallas Police Department was involved in any conspiracy with RUBY to kill OSWALD; however, he added that there is a "good likelihood" that any officer acquainted with RUBY would have allowed him to enter the Police Building if he requested permission to do so.

FLEMING stated further that he does not recall ever having discussed any type of politics with JACK RUBY and has no information in his possession indicating that RUBY and OSWALD were acquainted.

He advised further that he does not believe that RUBY was acquainted with Chief of Police in Dallas and that he does not believe that RUBY is acquainted with Captain WILL FRITZ in charge of homicide at Dallas Police Department. He added that FRITZ in a bachelor, but that he has never seen him at the Carousel Club.

FLEMING stated that there is no information in his possession on which he could base an opinion on whether any person might have conspired with RUBY to kill OSWALD.

FLEMING advised that he is unable to furnish specific names of particular Dallas policemen with whom RUBY was acquainted, because in his opinion he was a casual acquaintance of almost every Dallas policeman. He continued that he did visit the Carousel about once a month, but that during this period he does not recall seeing any Dallas policemen present in the club habitually.

FLEMING advised further that as far as he knows, RUBY appeared to be a normal individual, and he cannot think of anything peculiar about him except that RUBY seemed to have an obsession about a furnace thermostate located in the Carousel Club. FLEMING went on to

67

DN 44-387
4

explain that he recalls kidding RUBY about the thermostat because RUBY was unable to walk past the thermostat without stopping to adjust it.

FLEMING advised further that he recalls that in about February, 1962, a Dallas detective, whose name he cannot recall, was killed while working on a prostitution case and that the master of ceremonies, several show girls, and other employees from the Carousel attended this officer's funeral. FLEMING added that he was unable to recall whether or not RUBY attended this funeral.

FLEMING concluded that he was unable to furnish any additional information concerning this matter; however, he planned to be in Dallas, Texas, over the Christmas holidays and if he learned anything additional, he would immediately notify the FBI.

COMMISSION EXHIBIT No. 1632—Continued

FD-302 (Rev. 3-3-59)

FEDERAL BUREAU OF INVESTIGATION

Commission Exhibit No. 1633

Date December 19, 1963

1

DAN ALVIN GUNN, 3005 West 27th, Apartment #23, Amarillo, Texas, advised he was currently a pilot with Central Airlines and during the period April, 1960 to July, 1960 he had lived at the Continental Apartments, Dallas, Texas. GUNN advised there were three other pilots living with him at the time - AL PIERCE and EVERETT MAYO, both of whom are pilots for Central Airlines living in Irving, Texas; and R. L. PATTERSON, who is currently in the U. S. Navy stationed at Norfolk, Virginia.

GUNN advised he and his roommates met JACK RUBY through a BILL MARCUS, now deceased, who was part-owner of the apartments and that he (GUNN) had been more or less in charge of the swimming pool area at those apartments. GUNN stated that RUBY seemed like a great promoter and was always promoting his Vegas Club and a private club that he was just starting. GUNN advised RUBY asked him to promote some business for a private club through the airline crews and employees. GUNN stated this private club was located where the Carousel Club is now located in Dallas.

In describing RUBY, GUNN stated that RUBY seemed to like people, was always promoting his interests, and seemed to be cautious about running a legitimate club and business. GUNN further stated that RUBY was always well dressed and always seemed extremely busy. GUNN advised that while they were acquainted RUBY's brother JACK or JACOB, and RUBY's sister, name unknown, lived with him in RUBY's apartment. He advised that RUBY's brother worked for a while at the Vegas Club and GUNN advised he had no reason to doubt their relationship or remember their names.

GUNN advised he had never heard RUBY mention his political beliefs and he had never known RUBY to show his temper or violence, although RUBY had once told him (GUNN) that he had lost part of his finger in a fight.

GUNN advised he was aware of no trouble RUBY had had with local law enforcement although RUBY had mentioned that he was checked often by the Liquor Control Board. GUNN advised he never heard RUBY mention the Dallas Police Department or heard him speak of employing any members of the Dallas Police Department at his clubs. He advised the only bouncer RUBY might have employed of which he was aware was an ex-boxer

82

on 12/18/63 at Amarillo, Texas File # Dallas 44-1639

by Special Agents DONALD J. CESARE & STEPHEN A. REDSHAW:BL Date dictated 12/18/63

COMMISSION EXHIBIT No. 1633

DL 44-1639
2

name unrecalled, who had visited RUBY at the apartments.

GUNN stated he had no information that indicated RUBY had known LEE HARVEY OSWALD prior to the assassination of the President.

GUNN advised the only other persons who might have known RUBY at the apartments were Mrs. BILL MARCUS, wife of the deceased owner of Continental Apartments; ROGER NAIL, pilot for Braniff Airlines who took his (GUNN's) place; or a Dallas promoter named PAUL (LNU), who had promoted the opening of the Gaslight Club, Dallas. GUNN advised this promoter had visited RUBY on many occasions at the apartments.

83

COMMISSION EXHIBIT No. 1633—Continued

1

Date 12/17/63

TRAVIS HALL, 6902 Red Bud Drive, employed as cashier at County Clerk's Office, Records Building, Record and Main Streets, advised that he formerly managed Sammy's Restaurant on Greenville Avenue. He advised he knew JACK RUBY for the past ten years, and RUBY used to come to the restaurant occasionally. He stated he went to all of RUBY's clubs: the Silver Spur, the Vegas, the Sovereign, and the Carousel, on a number of occasions with his wife. He stated he met RUBY through BILL HOWARD, who owned the Stork Club on Oaklawn, near RUBY's Vegas Club. He stated he never heard RUBY mention LEE HARVEY OSWALD and he did not know OSWALD until the Presidential assassination, and added he had no knowledge of any connection between the two. He said he considered RUBY a good-hearted individual, but was high strung and emotional. He said on a few occasions he had observed RUBY get mad at various individuals and throw them out of his clubs.

HALL advised that about three or four weeks before the Presidential assassination, RUBY came by his place of business and struck up a casual conversation and asked HALL for his address, which he provided RUBY. He said at that time he intended to give HALL a card to his club. He advised that on the Tuesday before the President was shot, RUBY stopped by his place of business again and furnished him a club pass card, which number he could not recall. He said this was the last time he saw RUBY and was quite shocked to learn that RUBY had shot OSWALD on November 24, 1963.

on 12/17/63 at Dallas, Texas File # DL 44-1639

by Special Agents JAMES J. WARD and ROBERT E. BASHAM :lp Date dictated 12/17/63

84

COMMISSION EXHIBIT No. 1634

FD-302 (Rev. 3-3-59) FEDERAL BUREAU OF

1

Date 12/19/63

EDWARD H. MC BEE, 3705 Travis, Apartment C, furnished the following information:

MC BEE, a bartender, is now in the employ of BOB NORTON, owner of three night clubs in Dallas, The Pago, The Red Garter, and The Keynote. MC BEE is subject to work assignments at any of these night clubs.

MC BEE first met RUBY in about 1954 or 1955 at a Christmas Party. MC BEE has worked in various night clubs in Dallas as a waiter and, in recent years, as a bartender. His employment over the years has repeatedly placed him in contact with JACK RUBY.

MC BEE, for many years, has frequented the Vegas Club and is acquainted with EVA GRANT, JACK RUBY's sister. The Vegas Club has always been a gathering or meeting place for night club employees, especially cocktail waitresses, as the Vegas Club remains open until 2:00 AM, whereas, most of the other night clubs close at midnight or 1:00 AM.

When JACK RUBY opened the Sovereign Club, the present location of the Carousel Club, MC BEE was a bartender at the opening of the club. He worked for RUBY for about a week and quit when RUBY would not pay him on schedule. MC BEE was never again in the employment of JACK RUBY.

During the approximate period 1960 - 1962, MC BEE and his then roommate, CHESTER MEYERS, maintained an apartment at 3939 Travis, Apartment 2. Their apartment became a place for night club employees to party after closing hours. Often times, the parties would continue until 6:00 or 7:00 AM. JACK RUBY frequently would show up at the parties and usually brought some of the girls from his club.

RUBY rarely took a drink, as he could not hold his liquor. On one occasion, in approximately 1961, RUBY and some of his showgirls appeared at an after-hour party at MC BEE's apartment. RUBY, that night, seemed to have been

on 12/19/63 at Dallas, Texas File # DL 44-1639

by Special Agent JAMES S. WEIR/eah Date dictated 12/19/63

112

DL 44-1639

2

drinking prior to his arrival. While at MC BEE's apartment, RUBY drank some wine.

During the party, one of the girls, whose exact identity MC BEE cannot now recall, did a gyrating and suggestive dance. Someone in the group suggested that RUBY join her and that he do a strip. RUBY removed his outer garments down to his undershirt and shorts. All the while the girl did her dance. RUBY then attempted to do the twist dance and worked himself into a position where he was kneeling on the floor, with the girl doing her gyrating dance only inches away from RUBY's face. She then backed off. At this point, to the best of MC BEE's recollection, RUBY, in a loud and excited voice, said, "Come on, man or woman. I'll take anyone on."

MC BEE advised that nothing became of this incident and the party continued.

Prior to the above incident, MC BEE and the roommate, CHESTER MEYERS, had, at times, wondered if RUBY might be a person who is bisexual. After the above incident, MC BEE and MEYERS concluded there is a strong possibility RUBY is bisexual.

MC BEE stated he had no concrete proof to back up his opinion, and he can cite no other instance where RUBY behaved as he did on the above cited occasion.

MC BEE advised RUBY is a bachelor and, to his knowledge, has always lived alone.

MC BEE advised RUBY is the type of person who has a lot of friends and, at the same time, there are many who do not like him. If RUBY liked a person, RUBY would stick by that person and help him in time of need. Conversely, RUBY, if he did not like someone, would not hesitate to express his dislike. RUBY liked to play the role of "big shot" and often took pride in citing prominent persons as personal friends. Although RUBY knew many, and probably most, of the officers in the Dallas Police Department, MC BEE did not know of any who were close personal friends of RUBY.

113

DL 44-1639

3

MC BEE last saw RUBY sometime in September or early October, 1963, when MC BEE stopped in at the Vegas Club. MC BEE did not know LEE HARVEY OSWALD and has no knowledge of any acquaintance between OSWALD and RUBY.

1104

COMMISSION EXHIBIT No. 1635—Continued

FD-302 (Rev. 1-25-60)

FEDERAL BUREAU OF INVESTIGATION

Commission Exhibit No. 1636

Date December 16, 1963

1

Mrs. EDWARD J. (MARY) PULLMAN was interviewed at the residence of her brother, IRV LEVA, 7061 Izard Street, Omaha, Nebraska. She furnished the following information relative to her knowledge of JACK L. RUBY:

She worked for RUBY at the Carousel Club, Dallas, Texas, as a hostess for approximately three months prior to early September, 1963. She has known RUBY as a speaking acquaintance in Dallas for approximately the past ten years, but her only social contact with him took place during the period she worked for him and consisted of eating at a restaurant with him on a few occasions after work.

She was never acquainted with LEE HARVEY OSWALD and never knew this individual to have any contact with RUBY or to frequent the Carousel Club. She saw pictures of OSWALD in the papers following the assassination of President KENNEDY and could not recall ever having seen OSWALD at the Carousel Club or any place else.

Mrs. PULLMAN was at a loss to explain why RUBY shot OSWALD, but stated she knew RUBY, based on conversations with him, to have had a very high regard for President KENNEDY. RUBY was the type person who never concealed his feelings and would always tell people exactly what he thought of them.

The Carousel Club was frequented by most of the officers of the Dallas Police Department, as were most clubs of this type in Dallas. Through these visits she felt certain that RUBY knew most of these officers on a first-name basis. She did not believe RUBY had been more friendly with Dallas police officers than the other night club owners in Dallas. The police officers visiting the Carousel Club were never given a bill in connection with their visits there, but this was the policy of practically all of the burlesque-type clubs in Dallas which strived to maintain good relations with the Dallas Police Department.

According to Mrs. PULLMAN, the only organizations to which RUBY belonged were religious organizations and she was certain he had no subversive affiliations.

On 12/14/63 at Omaha, Nebraska File # OM 44-209 DL 44-1639

by SAs GEORGE D. WATT and MASON R. MADDUX, Jr.:mrh 232 Date dictated 12/16/63

COMMISSION EXHIBIT No. 1636

OM 44-209
DL 44-1639
2

She stated RUBY on one occasion told her he had been raised in a bad neighborhood and had done practically everything before coming to Dallas from Chicago and he appeared sincere in wanting to operate a legitimate business and to be respected in Dallas. She stated he insisted on the entertainers in his club abiding by his instructions that they present a "clean" show and because of this RUBY had difficulty with some entertainers, mostly strippers.

During the period she worked for RUBY the only traveling he did was a trip to either New York or California to the American Artists Guild to discuss business. She never heard him mention other trips that he might have made. She doubted that he had done much traveling since he devoted practically all of his time in the operation of the Carousel Club.

During her contact with RUBY she knew of only one close associate of his and this was RALPH PAUL, whom she believed to possibly be RUBY's partner in the Carousel Club. She knew of no other individuals with whom he associated.

Her last contact with RUBY took place in early November, 1963, when RUBY visited her home to discuss the invention of a friend of his with her husband.

233

COMMISSION EXHIBIT No. 1636—Continued

FD-302 (Rev. 3-3-59) FEDERAL BUREAU OF INVESTIGATION

1 — Commission Exhibit No. 1637 — Date 12/18/63

Mrs. MARGARET JEAN "JEANNIE" SIMS, 1309 Huddleston, Grand Prairie, Texas, advised that her nickname JEANNIE and telephone number AN 2-4910, could logically appear on a note pad in RUBY's possession as she has worked for him in the past.

She worked at the Carousel Club as a cigarette girl, full time from August, 1960 until October, 1961 and intermittently from October, 1962 until about March, 1963. This was night work and through most of this period she also had a day-time job. In connection with her work as a cigarette girl, she received tips and a commission on sales. In about March, 1963, by her calculations JACK RUBY owed her about $50.00 on commissions but he told her by his calculations he only owed her about $25.00. They got in an argument over this and he threatened to "throw her down the stairs". She "just dared" him to touch her. RUBY did not throw her down the stairs but appeared to be very angry. She left the club, went downstairs and called the Dallas Police Department from the parking garage. A police officer, name not recalled, answered this disturbance call, told her the situation was such that it would be very difficult to determine facts in the matter and suggested that she should probably take whatever amount of money RUBY offered. She left the area and had GORDON SIMS, from whom she was then divorced, but whom she has since remarried, go to the Carousel Club later to get the money due her. GORDON SIMS evidentally saw RUBY because he brought her $42.00.

When she first went to work at the Carousel Club, other female employees told her JACK RUBY would probably try to date her but RUBY never did. She heard from other employees, names not recalled, that RUBY dated both men and women, so she assumed he was "bi-sexual". She did not know the identity of any men or women whom RUBY dated.

She advised that RUBY was very quick tempered but that the above argument regarding commissions was the only serious argument she had with him. She had heard that RUBY kept order in the Carousel Club and would throw anybody down the stairs who was creating a disturbance but she never saw him do this to any customer or employee.

on 12/18/63 at Grand Prairie, Texas File # DL 44-1639

by Special Agent JAMES F. GLONEK - gl 234 Date dictated 12/18/63

COMMISSION EXHIBIT No. 1637

DL 44-1639
2

She advised she has seen officers of the Dallas Police Department in the Carousel Club, but does not recall any of them by name. In all instances, it appeared that they were there on official business in checking the club and they did not appear to get any special favors from RUBY.

RUBY appeared very interested in making the Carousel Club a financial success and it appeared that he was doing well. His interest in making the club a success plus a very intense interest in several dogs he owned, appeared to be his main concerns in life.

She advised that for about the last year or so that she worked at the Carousel Club, GEORGE SENATOR spent quite a bit of time at the Club and was in fact there so much that it appeared to her he might have a financial interest in the place. She knew of no personal association between RUBY and SENATOR away from the Carousel Club.

She explained that after she had the argument with RUBY in about March, 1963, she secured employment as cigarette girl at the Theater Club, which was upstairs over the Theater Lounge. Business there was not going to well so she secured similar employment downstairs at the Theater Lounge proper. She considered herself a personal friend of KATHY KAY who had been working at the Carousel Club for a long time and has visited KATHY at the Carousel Club on a number of occasions since March, 1963. She last was in the Carousel Club about two weeks prior to the assassination of President KENNEDY visiting KATHY. On most of the occasions, when she has gone to the Carousel Club to visit KATHY, she also saw JACK RUBY but has talked with him only very briefly because of their previous misunderstanding.

She advised she was not acquainted with LEE HARVEY OSWALD, knew of no association between RUBY and OSWALD and knew of no other individuals as possibly involved in the shootings.

Regarding the shooting of OSWALD by RUBY, she advised that this situation surprised her when it happened as she had never seen RUBY carrying a gun. She advised, however, that the fact that RUBY shot OSWALD was understandable to her because he was a very unpredictable person.

235

COMMISSION EXHIBIT No. 1637—Continued

FD-302 (Rev. 3-3-59) FEDERAL BUREAU OF INVESTIGATION

Commission Exhibit No. 1638

1

Date 12/19/63

L. W. "TED" NEWBERRY, 4130 Hawthorne, Dallas, was interviewed concerning a cabin reportedly owned by JACK RUBY at Lake Grapevine, Grapevine, Texas. He related the following:

In about 1954, he, NEWBERRY, was handling a promotion of selling one square inch of uranium land for 25 cents in various concessions and cigar stores in the Dallas area. He said that JACK RUBY had gotten in touch with him and tried to become associated with him in this promotion, but he, NEWBERRY, had declined. At the time, RUBY gave NEWBERRY a pass to his Vegas Club located on Oak Lawn in Dallas. In 1955 or 1956, NEWBERRY, who is a part-time contractor also, conceived the idea of building some simulated log cabins at Grapevine Lake and went to JACK RUBY with the idea.

RUBY, at this time, was living at the apartment located at 4158 Hawthorne, and he would occasionally see RUBY in the neighborhood walking his dog. He talked with RUBY on several such occasions and RUBY thought that the idea of the log cabins would be profitable, so they went into sort of a partnership. The business was known as Northwest Log Cabins, and the name was registered with the Fictitious Names Division of the County Clerk in Dallas.

NEWBERRY stated that RUBY and RUBY's partner, MORTON GIMPLE, were to handle the sale of the cabins and he, NEWBERRY, was to get his cost back from the construction and share in the profits. The first cabin was built on Red Bird Lane at Lake Grapevine in the area known as Placid Peninsula and was located just across the road from the property of Mr. T. A. YATES. The first cabin took approximately nine months to construct. The reason it took so long was because NEWBERRY was involved in an automobile accident and was unable to continuously work at the project.

During the construction, JACK RUBY and MORTON GIMPLE would occasionally come down and help nail the logs up or do other manual labor, which both seemed to enjoy. The cabins cost much more to construct than was anticipated, and the project was unsuccessful from a financial standpoint. The cabin was built sometime in 1957 or 1958. At about the same time, RUBY was having difficulties with the Internal Revenue Service in Dallas and was

on 12/16/63 at Dallas, Texas File # DL 44-1639

by Special Agent ALLEN H. SMITH - LAC 241 Date dictated 12/17/63

COMMISSION EXHIBIT No. 1638

DL 44-1639
2

being represented by an attorney, STANLEY KAUFMAN. When the partnership dissolved, RUBY and GIMPLE took over the cabin and paid NEWBERRY for his expenses and costs. He does not know but assumes that KAUFMAN took over ownership of the cabin by representing RUBY in his contest with Internal Revenue Service. After the first cabin was built, NEWBERRY continued and built another cabin adjacent to the first one and subsequently built another one at Lake LaVonne.

To his knowledge, JACK RUBY never lived in the cabin and never gave any parties there or did any entertaining whatsoever. On one occasion, just after the completion of the cabin, NEWBERRY had several guests down on one occasion for a week-end, but JACK RUBY was not among them.

Since the dissolving of their partnership in the log cabin enterprise some four or five years ago, NEWBERRY has seen JACK RUBY on only one occasion, and that was in early November 1963 when they were both stopped by a traffic light in downtown Dallas and shouted greetings at each other.

NEWBERRY was unacquainted with LEE HARVEY OSWALD and had never seen him in JACK RUBY's company. He had no knowledge of any conspiracy on the part of RUBY to shoot OSWALD and stated that he knew of no associates of JACK RUBY who were members of the Dallas Police Department.

245

COMMISSION EXHIBIT No. 1638—Continued

FD-302 (Rev. 3-3-59) FEDERAL BUREAU OF INVE— Commission Exhibit No. 1639

1 Date 12/19/63

Mrs. WILEY DISMUKES, Route # 1, Box 169E, Grapevine, Texas, was interviewed concerning the cabin reportedly owned by JACK RUBY at Lake Grapevine. She related the following:

Her husband operates Wiley's Shoe Store at 3517 Oak Lawn, Dallas, Texas, which is just across the street from JACK RUBY's Club Vegas. Mr. and Mrs. DISMUKES have been casually acquainted with JACK RUBY for several years, knowing him from his ownership of the Vegas and seeing him in the neighborhood where the shoe store is located.

About four or five years ago, two log cabins were built just down the road from the DISMUKES place at Lake Grapevine, but she was unaware that JACK RUBY was one of the principals in the building of the cabins. To her knowledge, the cabin across from T. A. YATES has been owned by a Dallas attorney, STANLEY KAUFMAN, ever since it was built. She said she had never seen JACK RUBY at the cabin. Sometime after KAUFMAN bought the cabin, he gave a party and invited everyone in the neighborhood, but she and her husband did not attend.

Mrs. DISMUKES stated that she did not know LEE HARVEY OSWALD and knew of no association between RUBY and OSWALD. She had no idea why RUBY shot OSWALD. She had no knowledge of any association between RUBY and members of the Dallas Police Department.

on 12/15/63 at Grapevine, Texas File # DL 44-1639

by Special Agent S ALLEN H. SMITH and TOM E. CHAPOTON, JR. - LAC Date dictated 12/17/63

346

COMMISSION EXHIBIT No. 1639

FEDERAL BUREAU OF INVESTIGATION

Date 12/19/63

WILEY DISMUKES, Route # 1, Box 169E, Grapevine, Texas, was interviewed at his shoe store, Wiley's, 3517 Oak Lawn, concerning the cabin owned by RUBY at Lake Grapevine. He related the following:

He has known JACK RUBY as a neighboring businessman for eight or nine years. He occasionally goes into RUBY's night club at Vegas Club, for a glass of beer, but is not socially acquainted with JACK RUBY. In about 1958 or 1959, JACK RUBY and some of RUBY's associates, names unknown to DISMUKES, put up some cabins a short distance from his (DISMUKES) place at Lake Grapevine. The venture was unsuccessful and, to his knowledge, only two cabins were built. He occasionally saw JACK RUBY during the construction of the first cabin but never knew him to live at Lake Grapevine in the log cabin or at any other place at the lake.

Mr. DISMUKES was not acquainted with LEE HARVEY OSWALD and stated he did not know why RUBY had shot him. He knew of no association between RUBY and members of the Dallas Police Department. He said that he had recently seen JACK RUBY in the neighborhood on Oak Lawn, but their association is casual and his only conversation was wishing one another good morning or good afternoon.

on 12/15/63 at Dallas, Texas File # DL 44-1639

by Special Agent s ALLEN H. SMITH and TOM E. CHAPOTON, JR. - LAC Date dictated 12/17/63

247

COMMISSION EXHIBIT No. 1640

DL 44-1639
AHS:LAC
1

The following individuals at Lake Grapevine, Grapevine, Texas, were interviewed by SA ALLEN H. SMITH on December 6, 1963, concerning any knowledge they might have had relative to JACK RUBY owning property in the vicinity of the lake. None of these individuals was acquainted with JACK RUBY and stated that they knew nothing about his owning any cabins or property in the vicinity. They are as follows:

Mrs. V. L. BURGESS
Route 1, Box 152

Mrs. MILDRED CLAUSSER
Route 1, Box 155

Mrs. BERTHA WILBURN
Route 1, Box 154

Mrs. W. E. HAMILTON
Route 1, Box 148E.

248

COMMISSION EXHIBIT No. 1641

FD-302 (Rev. 3-3-59)

FEDERAL BUREAU OF INVESTIGATION

[redacted]

Commission Exhibit No. 1642

1

Date 12/19/63

T. A. YATES, Route 1, Box 148, Grapevine Lake, Grapevine, Texas, was interviewed concerning information by JACK H. BROWNE relative to a cabin owned by JACK RUBY at Grapevine Lake and also concerning information furnished by PRENTISS I. VAUGHN concerning the drilling of a water well on property of Log Cabin Enterprises. He related the following:

About four or five years ago, JACK RUBY, in association with TED NEWBERRY and MORTON GIMPLE, built two log cabins near YATES's house at Grapevine Lake. The cabins were built for resale, but apparently they were too high-priced and they were the only ones built. During the building of the first cabin, JACK RUBY would occasionally come out to Grapevine Lake to help with the construction. An airline pilot later drilled a well on the RUBY property, but he could not remember who this individual was. TED NEWBERRY, to his recollection, was the one who had the idea of building the cabins and got JACK RUBY and MORTON GIMPLE to finance the project.

JACK RUBY never lived in the cabin, which was just across the road from YATES's residence. However, during the sales promotion, there was one party given and YATES was invited. He could not recall who the other guests were. The enterprise was not profitable and went out of business and RUBY's attorney, STANLEY KAUFMAN, bought the property or acquired it in some manner unknown to YATES. KAUFMAN still uses the cabin as a week-end or summer retreat.

Mr. YATES stated that LEE HARVEY OSWALD was unknown him and he had never seen him at RUBY's cabin. He has no idea why RUBY shot OSWALD and knew of no connections RUBY might have had with the Dallas Police Department. He said he last saw RUBY about a year ago when RUBY came to Grapevine and asked him if he would board a couple of RUBY's dogs, which he declined to do.

on 12/13/63 at At Grapevine, Texas 249 File # DL 44-1639

by Special Agents ALLEN H. SMITH and TOM E. CHAPOTON, JR. - LAC Date dictated 12/17/63

This document contains neither recommendations nor conclusions of the FBI. It is the property of the FBI and is loaned to your agency; it and its contents are not to be distributed outside your agency.

COMMISSION EXHIBIT No. 1642

FD-302 (Rev. 3-3-59)

FEDERAL BUREAU OF IN—

Commission Exhibit No. 1643

Date December 18, 1963

(1)

Located in the automobile of JACK RUBY was the name of GRACE WILKINS, telephone number LA 3-4228, 6001 1/2 Tremont. Mrs. GRACE WILKINS, 6001 1/2 Tremont, Dallas, Texas, voluntarily furnished the following information:

About three weeks before the assassination of President JOHN F. KENNEDY, there appeared in the "Dallas Morning News" a classified ad which requested that someone with $5,000 invest in a private night club. This ad gave a box number at the "Dallas Morning News." She answered this ad by letter and requested more details regarding the private club. JACK RUBY telephonically contacted her about three or four days later and told her he owned a night club in Dallas, and that he had a good location for a private club.

She requested RUBY to contact her son, who is an attorney in Dallas, to discuss further details regarding this club. RUBY has not contacted her son, nor has he contacted her further. She has never met RUBY, nor does she know anything regarding RUBY's background. She has never met LEE HARVEY OSWALD, nor does she know of any connection between RUBY and OSWALD.

on 12/16/63 at Dallas, Texas File # DL 44-1639

by Special Agent ALTON E. BRAMBLETT:bnm Date dictated 12/18/63

This document contains neither recommendations nor conclusions of the FBI. It is the property of the FBI and is loaned to your agency; it and its contents are not to be distributed outside your agency.

283

COMMISSION EXHIBIT No. 1643

Commission Exhibit No. 1644

1 Date 12/18/63

Mrs. ANN WOODRUFF, 3636 Hearthstone, telephone CH. 7-6468, Dallas, Texas, was interviewed, in that her name was found in RUBY's automobile.

She advised that about two or three months ago, possibly August or September, she observed an ad in the Dallas Morning News offering a night club for sale. In that a friend of hers, who lives out of Dallas, was interested in purchasing a small night club, she wrote a letter to the newspaper box number requesting additional information regarding this night club and gave her phone number. Sometime later, she received a telephone call from a man who identified himself as "Mr. RUBY," who described the night club as a strip club, and she told him that this was not the type of night club her friend would be interested in purchasing.

She related that this is the only time she has ever talked to RUBY and she has never seen RUBY in person. She stated she could furnish absolutely no information concerning RUBY or his activities, and had no knowledge of any association between RUBY and LEE HARVEY OSWALD. She stated she did not know OSWALD.

on 12/14/63 at Dallas, Texas 28-1 File # DL 44-1639

by Special Agent TOM E. CHAPOTON, JR./eah Date dictated 12/17/63

COMMISSION EXHIBIT No. 1644

Commission Exhibit No. 1645

FD-302 (Rev. 3-3-59)

FEDERAL BUREAU OF INVESTIGATION

1 Date 12/4/63

CHESTER ARTHUR MYERS, JR., who resides at 3920 Travis, Apartment D, Dallas, Texas, furnished the following information:

MYERS is an employee of the Cabana Motel, Dallas, and he assists in the operation of the lounges and clubs at the Cabana Motel. He was born August 3, 1929, at Sherman, Texas.

He first became acquainted with JACK RUBY during the period 1950 - 1953, when RUBY was operating the Silver Spur Club in Dallas which he, MYERS, frequented. In about 1955, MYERS became acquainted with EVA RUBY GRANT, sister of JACK RUBY, who was then operating the Vegas Club, Dallas, Texas.

In 1957, MYERS returned to Dallas, Texas, from Sherman, Texas, where he had been attending Austin College. Since 1957, MYERS has been employed at various night club establishments and, through his employment, has maintained contact and association with JACK RUBY and EVA RUBY GRANT, on both a professional and social basis.

MYERS recalled that EVA GRANT once told him that she started the Silver Spur Club for the purpose of having her brother, JACK RUBY, take over the club operation when he returned from military service.

MYERS could recall only one instance when RUBY displayed a violent temper and physically ejected a patron from his club. MYERS stated that he recalled other instances when patrons became obnoxious and belligerent at RUBY's club at which time, in MYERS' opinion, RUBY would have been justified in ejecting them from the establishment; however, on these other occasions, RUBY did maintain his composure and did not eject them physically.

MYERS described RUBY as a person who, at times, is highly tempermental and excitable. He described RUBY as a person who could not be termed a big spender or a flashy dresser, or one who would try to impress people. According to MYERS, RUBY is the type of person who, upon

on 12/3/63 at Dallas, Texas File # DL 44-1639

by Special Agents JAMES S. WEIR & RICHARD E. HARRISON/eah 97 Date dictated 12/3/63

COMMISSION EXHIBIT No. 1645

DL 44-1639

2

accepting a person as his friend, will do anything for that person, conversely, if RUBY takes a disliking to a person, he will express his sentiments and will go out of his way to avoid any contact with such a person. MYERS feels that RUBY considers him as a friend.

RUBY once offered MYERS a job as floorman or manager of the Sovereign Club at the Carousel Club. RUBY advised MYERS that he, RUBY, would give him the food concession if he would take the job. MYERS felt that RUBY was, at the time of that offer, making a sincere offer to him, as RUBY stated MYERS would have the final say in the operation of the Sovereign Club. MYERS turned down the job, as he felt that RUBY subsequently would not be able to refrain from injecting his, RUBY's, ideas into the operation of the Sovereign Club. MYERS was of the opinion that RUBY, at that time, had ideas of capturing the "carriage trade" and he, RUBY, did not feel he had the personality to cope with this type of clientele.

Approximately three or four years ago, MYERS heard what he termed "gossip," from now unrecalled sources, that RUBY was a homosexual. MYERS stated he had no specific information that would substantiate this allegation. MYERS recalled that RUBY liked to have big, athletic-type men in his employ and, at the same time, liked to have young, good-looking boys in his employ.

In all the years MYERS has known RUBY, MYERS can recall only one instance when RUBY had a date with a woman. In approximately 1957, when MYERS was a waiter at the Twin Tree Club in Dallas, MYERS received a telephone call from RUBY. RUBY told MYERS of his date for that evening and he had called MYERS to ask MYERS the type of wine he should order with the dinner and for any other general information, in an apparent effort to impress his woman companion. RUBY, on many occasions, would take his female employees out to coffee or lunch but, in MYERS' opinion, RUBY had no social interest in any of them. According to MYERS, RUBY's sole interests were in his club and his dogs. RUBY did not appear to be interested

98

DL 44-1639

3

in politics nor did he appear to be a religious man; however, MYERS did recall that EVA GRANT, RUBY's sister, once mentioned that JACK was a religious man.

MYERS stated that prior to approximately six months ago RUBY, from time to time, had periods of financial stress at the Carousel Club. EVA GRANT had mentioned to MYERS that JACK RUBY, on occasions, would come to the Vegas Club, which she operated, and take money from her receipts in order to pay the salaries of his employees at the Carousel Club. Within the last six months, RUBY has indicated to MYERS that his business at the Carousel Club had improved.

MYERS is not acquainted with LEE HARVEY OSWALD, nor does he have any information which would indicate RUBY and OSWALD knew each other.

MYERS stated he was at a loss to explain why RUBY shot OSWALD as he did.

99

1 Date 12/23/63

HUGH GENE SMITH, 9841 Lanshire Drive, telephone number DI 8-3820, a former Dallas police officer, voluntarily furnished the following information:

He first met JACK RUBY in 1957 at the Vegas Club which RUBY owned. He stated that the club was recommended to him by a police officer, whose name he could not now recall. He stated when he joined the Dallas Police Department in 1958 he visited the club on numerous occasions in an official capacity. He stated that RUBY always liked police officers and that a great many attended the club socially. He stated that RUBY gave numerous policemen whiskey for Christmas. He stated he had received whiskey from RUBY on three different occasions and on one of these occasions, RUBY delivered a fifth of whiskey to his home. He could not recall the names of the policemen that received whiskey from RUBY and does not believe that any policeman did any type of favor for RUBY for receiving this whiskey.

He stated a former policeman named DENBOW, first name not recalled, was very closely associated with RUBY. He stated DENBOW was a bachelor and he believes that DENBOW used RUBY's apartment on several occasions. He does not believe that DENBOW ever did any favors for RUBY in an official capacity or that DENBOW ever took any money from RUBY. As far as he knew, the relationship between RUBY and DENBOW was strictly social. DENBOW once told him that RUBY knew a number of Chicago hoodlums but he does not recall any names that DENBOW mentioned that RUBY knew.

He stated that he understood that RUBY had a bad temper but that he never saw RUBY get violent or angry at any time. As far as he was concerned, RUBY was always friendly and he believed that RUBY would do a favor for any friend if he could. He recalled that about three years ago, RUBY asked him to fix a $3.00 parking ticket for him. He explained that any Dallas police officer could pay a $3.00 parking ticket for $1.00. He told RUBY this and RUBY said never mind that he would pay the parking ticket.

on 12/20/63 at Dallas, Texas File # DL 44-1639

by Special Agents LANSING P. LOGAN and ALTON E. BRAMBLETT - gj Date dictated 12/23/63

97

DL 44-1639
2

He stated that RUBY always liked police officers and he believed the newspapers had it wrong when they stated that RUBY killed OSWALD because of his affection for JACQUELINE KENNEDY and the KENNEDY children. He believed that the reason RUBY killed OSWALD was because OSWALD had killed Officer TIPPIT.

BOB RICH, who is a regular customer at the Vegas Club, once told him that RUBY attempted to get BUDDY TURMAN, an ex-prize fighter and also a bouncer at the Vegas Club, to go to bed with him. He stated that RICH lives on Reagan Street some place and his father owns some parking lots in Dallas and his father resides some place in Irving, Texas. He stated that he does not believe that RUBY ever paid any Dallas police officer and he believed that no officer would accept any money from RUBY as the Police Department is a very "tight outfit".

He stated that he has never worked for JACK RUBY nor does he know of any other Dallas police officer that has been so employed.

He does not know LEE HARVEY OSWALD nor does he know of any association between RUBY and OSWALD. SMITH summarized by saying that he believed RUBY was a very friendly and sincere person as far as he knew. SMITH stated that he had never seen RUBY outside of his clubs and knew nothing concerning his background or any of his close associates. He added that he had not seen RUBY in four or five months.

98

FD-302 (Rev. 3-3-59) FEDERAL BUREAU OF INVESTIGATION

[redacted]

Commission Exhibit No. 1647

1

Date December 19, 1963

J. S. BURDEN, 432 Daniel Street, advised he was in the Silver Spur Club which was operated by JACK RUBY several years ago. He does not know RUBY personally nor any of RUBY's associates and knows nothing of any connection between RUBY and OSWALD. Mr. BURDEN stated he does not know why RUBY would have his name but assumed the only way he could have gotten it would have been due to his visiting the Silver Spur Club.

on 12/18/63 at Dallas, Texas File # DL 44-1639

by Special Agent LEO L. ROBERTSON/jn Date dictated 12/19/63

119

FD-302 (Rev. 1-25-60) FEDERAL BUREAU OF INVESTIGATION Commission Exhibit No. 1648

Date 12/20/63

HEIDI LEE BALLOWE, stage name LISA LAND, advised she was employed as a dance instructor at the Holiday Dance Studio, Dallas, Texas during 1959 and she met JACK RUBY at this time at the Vegas Club, which she and other studio employees patronized.

BALLOWE advised she was employed by JACK RUBY as an exotic dancer during February or March, 1961 and was so employed until December, 1961, at which time she resigned.

BALLOWE advised members of the Dallas Police Department occasionally were guests at the Carousel Club, but she had never received any information which would indicate RUBY was "paying off" to the Dallas Police. She stated Officers GANAWAY and GILMORE of the Dallas Police Department watched the Carousel operation very closely and RUBY always cautioned the dancers to be careful in their acts when these two officers were in the Club. She stated these two officers had never been in the Club as guests and it appeared to aggravate RUBY that he could not be on good terms with these two officers.

BALLOWE advised it was rumored RUBY knew of activities concerning the strip clubs at City Hall and at the Police Department, however, she could not shed light concerning his source of information.

BALLOWE advised she had never heard RUBY discuss politics of any kind with anyone and stated his main interest appeared to be making a success of the Carousel Club.

BALLOWE advised she considered RUBY to have paranoid tendencies in that he frequently made statements to the effect that the Police Department and operators of the other strip clubs in Dallas were after him. She stated RUBY had a violent temper and continually harrassed the employees at the Club, and on many occasions would make remarks without thinking and later apologize. She

On 12/18/63 at Norman, Oklahoma File # OC 44-430

by SAs GLENN E. SILVEY & DAVID W. MC CLUGAGE/jk Date dictated 12/19/63

142.

OC 44-430
2

also described RUBY as a very enthusiastic person who was very eager to make a success of his endeavors.

BALLOWE advised she had very little contact with RUBY since December, 1961, and could furnish no information regarding his activities since that time. She was doubtful RUBY would be associated in any way with LEE HARVEY OSWALD.

BALLOWE was of the opinion RUBY shot OSWALD because of his bad temper and possibly because of the publicity angle.

BALLOWE advised she understood JACK RUBY had frequently dated and had possibly lived with MILLIE PERELLE (phonetic) an exotic dancer believed to be in El Paso, Texas at the present time. She further advised RUBY's closest friend was EARL NORMAN, Master of Ceremonies at the Carousel Club for a considerable length of time. She advised RUBY was fairly well acquainted with JIMMY LEVINE, Skyliner Club, Fort Worth, Texas.

BALLOWE advised RUBY's sister EVE had been in Dallas several years and and at the time RUBY opened the Carousel Club, EVE managed the Vegas Club. She stated RUBY had on occasion struck EVE during arguments about operation of the club.

BALLOWE advised she is currently on the Board of the A.G.V.A. in Dallas and the Board had received several complaints concerning working conditions at the Carousel Club. She stated the complaints were mainly concerning the hours, but two of the complaints had been that RUBY expected the dancers to associate with the customers.

143

COMMISSION EXHIBIT No. 1648—Continued

1 Date 12/20/63

EDWARD CASTRO, 2814 Douglas Street, advised that he was a former employee of JACK RUBY at the Sovereign club; that he was employed by RUBY during 1960 as a bus boy, porter, dishwasher and general handy man. He said that he obtained this employment through answering an ad in the newspaper and later quit as he did not want to work nights. CASTRO advised that he knew little about the private life of JACK RUBY in that he only had an employee-employer relationship with him. He said that RUBY was a good employer, was generally friendly and helpful. According to CASTRO, RUBY was friendly with all law enforcement officers and numerous officers came into the club, however, he did not know the names of any of the police officers with whom RUBY was particularly friendly.

CASTRO said that he did not know LEE HARVEY OSWALD; that he never saw him at the Sovereign Club and could furnish no information which would connect RUBY and OSWALD.

CASTRO was questioned regarding the whereabouts of DELORES CASTRO who is reported to have been a former employee of RUBY. He advised that DELORES CASTRO was employed as a waitress at the Sovereign Club approximately two and one-half years ago; that he could furnish no information as to her present whereabouts. He advised that she was of no relation to him and that CASTRO is a very common Spanish name.

on 12/19/63 at Dallas, Texas File # DL 44-1639

by Special Agent ALVIN ZIMMERMAN - gj 145 Date dictated 12/20/63

COMMISSION EXHIBIT No. 1649

FD-302 (Rev. 3-3-59) FEDERAL BUREAU OF I

Commission Exhibit No. 1650

Date 12/23/63

1

VIRGINIA DITULLIO, 2663 Millmar Drive, telephone number DA 7-0163, was interviewed at Tiny's Lounge, 7525 East Grand Avenue, and voluntarily furnished the following information:

On November 24, 1963, she sent a telegram to JACK RUBY at the Dallas City Jail. She advised she had been drinking at the time but as she recalls the telegram said something like "good shooting and glad you did it", with a P.S., "former employee".

She was formerly employed at the Vegas Club in 1960 as a waitress for approximately three months. She had met JACK RUBY, who owned the Vegas Club about three years before she became employed in the Vegas Club. She was introduced to RUBY by her former husband, TINY DITULLIO. Her relationship with RUBY was always of a casual nature and she never had any discussions with RUBY regarding any of his political beliefs.

When she was employed at the Vegas Club RUBY would take her home nearly every night. She made it clear to RUBY that it was just a ride home and nothing further. RUBY respected her wishes and never made any advances toward her. She considered RUBY "high strung" but she never saw him get violent. He would always help anyone if he could and was always a very friendly fellow.

She did not know any girls that RUBY dated but was sure that he went out with quite a number. She did not know any of RUBY's close friends or anything regarding his background except that he was originally from Chicago, Illinois. She was also very friendly with RUBY's sister EVA and on one occasion, she recalled that EVA asked her would she open and run the Vegas Club for her. As she recalled, this was a Jewish holiday and EVA did not want to work that day. She opened the Vegas Club, handled the money and so forth, and closed the club that night. She has the greatest respect for RUBY and EVA and sometimes believes that if RUBY had not shot OSWALD, she might have done it herself. She did not know LEE HARVEY OSWALD nor of any association between RUBY and OSWALD. She last saw RUBY approximately one and one-half years ago at the Vegas Club. She added that her former husband might be able to furnish additional information.

on 12/20/63 at Dallas, Texas File # DL 44-1639

by Special Agent ALTON E. BRAMBLETT - gj Date dictated 12/23/63

This document contains neither recommendations nor conclusions of the FBI. It is the property of the FBI and is loaned to your agency; it and its contents are not to be distributed outside your agency.

154

FD-302 (Rev. 3-3-59) FEDERAL BUREAU OF I

Commission Exhibit No. 1651

Date 12/23/63

1

WINNIE FAYE FLOYD, 847 Peavy Road, who formerly resided at 3359 Delhi, advised that she has known JACK RUBY for fifteen years, when he first operated the Silver Spur on South Ervay Street, Dallas. She further advised that she has been in all of his clubs, the Silver Spur, the Vegas Club and the Carousel. She advised that JOE SLAYTIN started the Sovereign Club in 1960 or 1961 and she was working for him before RUBY became a part owner with SLAYTIN. She said she worked as a hostess and manager for SLAYTIN and also with RUBY.

FLOYD advised that she got into a fight with RUBY about an altercation at the Sovereign Club when a group of people came in to the club and asked to join another party already present. She said that RUBY came over to her and told her not to give them a check, that the latter group were friends of his. She said she had already made a check out for the first party at the table and when she tried to give the check to them RUBY caught her by the arm. She said that he started to cuss her out in front of everyone and then he struck her in the face with his hand, splitting her lip. She said she took her shoe off and tried to hit him on the head.

She advised that there were numerous people in the club at the time and the show was going on. She said that she knew of other instances where RUBY had shoved a girl upstairs and had dragged another around in the garage and he was an individual with a terrible temper with customers as well as employees. She said for this reason he never used a bouncer at the club and he took care of most of that type of work when it was demanded. She advised that he never carried a gun as far as she knew and never entered into any political discussions. She said that he never heard him mention LEE HARVEY OSWALD and she herself never heard of OSWALD until the Presidential assassination. She said she never knew of any connection between the two.

She said that she worked for RUBY about a month in all before the altercation, when she left, and that later the club folded up and then became a public club prior to the present Carousel Club, where they employed strippers. She said she last saw RUBY at the Carousel about six weeks ago and that he had forgotten the incident.

on 12/19/63 at Dallas, Texas File # DL 44-1639

by Special Agent s JAMES J. WARD and ROBERT E. BASHAM - LAC Date dictated 12/19/63

157

This document contains neither recommendations nor conclusions of the FBI. It is the property of the FBI and is loaned to your agency; it and its contents are not to be distributed outside your agency.

DL 44-1639
2

FLOYD advised that she did not know anything about RUBY's personal life but knew he had dated a girl called ALICE for quite some time back in 1958 when RUBY was living at the Continental House with his sister EVA. She said as far as JOE SLAYTIN was concerned, he was presently operating a drug store at the Mercantile Bank Building and she believed he was living at the Dorchester House on Gaston Avenue.

158

COMMISSION EXHIBIT No. 1651—Continued

FD-302 (Rev. 3-3-59) FEDERAL BUREAU OF — Commission Exhibit No. 1652

1

Date Dec. 20, 1963

Mrs. JANICE NORMAN JONES, also known as NEESIE, a former waitress at the Carousel Club, furnished the following information:

She was employed by RUBY at the Carousel Club as a waitress from December 1, 1962, until July, 1963, and she obtained this job after reading an advertisement in the Dallas Morning News. She recalls that RUBY was a generous person who gave Christmas gifts to his employees and also recalls RUBY gave a Thanksgiving dinner and a Fourth of July party for his employees during the time she worked for him. RUBY also gave a fifth of whisky to each policeman who would come into his club during the Christmas season. He also would not take any money from these policemen when they visited his club at other times during the year. She is unable to identify any of these police officers by name.

She recalls RUBY took only one trip during her employment and that was to Edna, Texas, to visit a person named CANDY BARR. She understands that CANDY BARR had just been released from prison at this time. The last time she saw RUBY was at the Carousel Club on the night she quit and does not remember ever seeing LEE HARVEY OSWALD in the Carousel Club. She does not know of any connection between RUBY and OSWALD.

on 12/18/63 at Euless, Texas File # DL 44-1639

by Special Agent EDWARD J. MABEY/csh Date dictated 12/19/63

169

COMMISSION EXHIBIT No. 1652

FD-302 (Rev. 1-25-60) FEDERAL BUREAU OF INV— Commission Exhibit No. 1653

1

Date 12/20/63

Mr. VERNON ROY SMITH, 176 South Osceola Street, Denver, Colorado, no telephone, (landlord's telephone WEst 5-5859), was interviewed at May D & F Department Store.

Mr. SMITH advised that he first met JACK RUBY about October, 1960, and that he worked for him from that time until about December, 1960, as a handyman around the Sovereign Club, a private membership club operated by RUBY in Dallas, Texas. SMITH continued that he quit his job about December, 1960, because he did not care to work any longer for RUBY. He described RUBY as being "very different." He enlarged upon this by stating that RUBY "would curse you out and later apologize." He continued that hedid not care to work for RUBY because of this emotional part of his personality.

SMITH stated further that RUBY also operated a nightclub known as the Vegas Club which was a low type nightclub and SMITH was of the opinion that RUBY was trying to "upgrade himself" when he opened the Sovereign Club since it was a very plush club and the members, who SMITH does not know by name, all appear to be well off financially. SMITH continued that he had "heard" from an unrecalled source, probably another employee, that every new girl that came to work at the Sovereign Club was expected to go out with RUBY or "stay late" at the club with him after closing hours. SMITH stated that he is unable to furnish the names of any of these girls or the source of this rumor but that he recalls one night after the club closed he had to return for some reason and knocked on the door to gain entrance. He continued that RUBY finally appeared at the door to let him in and SMITH noted that RUBY's shirt was rumpled up so as to appear that he had had it off and rapidly put it back on to answer the door. SMITH continued that RUBY allowed him to enter on this occasion and as he went to some part of the club to secure whatever he came back for, he noticed one

On 12/19/63 at Denver, Colorado File # DN 44-387

by SA RAY M. HICKMAN and SA RICHARD L. CAMPBELL - nls Date dictated 12/20/63

187

DN 44-387
2

of the new girls employed by RUBY sitting in RUBY's office; however, she was fully attired. SMITH further described RUBY as a normal male so far as he knows with no effeminate actions. He stated that he has no knowledge of any close associations between RUBY and Dallas policemen and does not ever recall seeing Dallas policemen in uniform in the Sovereign Club except for one occasion when he saw a uniformed officer come to the reception desk in the club and speak to the receptionist; however, he did not enter the main part of the club. SMITH added that it is possible that plain-clothed men from the Dallas Police Department were entertained in the club without his knowledge.

SMITH advised that he has never seen LEE HARVEY OSWALD and has no information concerning any association between OSWALD or JACK RUBY. He advised further that in his opinion RUBY killed OSWALD because of his grief over the death of President KENNEDY.

SMITH added that he does not know of any close associates of JACK RUBY and would have no opinion as to whether or not RUBY conspired with any person to plot the death of OSWALD. SMITH concluded that he was unable to furnish any additional information concerning this matter but that if he learned anything additional, he would immediately notify the FBI.

188

U. S. TREASURY DEPARTMENT
INTERNAL REVENUE SERVICE
REGIONAL COMMISSIONER
DALLAS, TEXAS

IN REPLY REFER TO

January 9, 1964

Mr. Arnold Sagalyn, Director
Office Law Enforcement Coordination
Room 1462 - Main Treasury Building
Department of the Treasury
Washington 25, D. C.

Dear Mr. Sagalyn:

Mr. John D. Lathem, National Office Chief of Enforcement Branch, A&TTD, has asked me to forward to you a resume of the information which we furnished him relative to Jack Ruby, who killed President Kennedy's assassin, and Ruby's former roommate, George Senator. This information was transmitted orally by phone, and I understand was relayed orally to the Department of Justice.

Jack Ruby moved to Dallas about 1946. On April 20, 1955, he made application to the Texas Liquor Control Board for a beer license at the Vegas Club, 3508 Oak Lawn. In connection with this application, Ruby submitted a personal history statement in which he stated that he was born on March 25, 1911, in Chicago, Illinois. He listed the following persons as references.

Stanley Kaufman, Mercantile National Bank, Dallas, Texas
Alice Nichols, 5707 Redondo, Dallas, Texas
Jack Russell, Musician's Union, Dallas, Texas

In this same application Jack Ruby admitted to the following arrests.

1931 - selling copyrighted songs - 10-day jail sentence
1953 - carrying concealed weapons - no disposition shown
1954 - carrying concealed weapons - no disposition shown
1954 - peace bond violation - no disposition shown
1959 - disturbing the peace - $10.00 fine
1960 - violation of dance hall ordnance - $25.00 fine

Jack Leon Ruby also stated that he had been arrested four or five times for misdemeanors from 1947 to 1953.

COMMISSION EXHIBIT No. 1654

Mr. Arnold Sagalyn -2-

In addition to the admissions made by Ruby, booking slips at the Dallas City jail reveal the following:

59-65906, 6/21/59 - permitting dancing after hours - $25.00 fine
54-54814, 12/5/54 - investigations of violation of State liquor laws - no disposition shown
49-99090, 2/4/49 - disturbing peace - no disposition shown
63-30069, 2/12/63 - simple assault - no disposition shown
63-37112, 3/14/63 - alias ticket - cash bond $35.00

The booking slips which are attached and made a part of this report list home addresses, all in Dallas, at: 4727 Homer, 1719½ S. Ervay, 1717 S. Ervay, and 3929 Rawlins.

Records in the office of the District Director, Internal Revenue Service, Dallas, Texas, reveal that special occupational tax stamp as a retail dealer in fermented malt liquor was purchased by Jack Ruby, sole owner of the Vegas Club, 3508 Oak Lawn, Dallas, Texas, for the periods beginning on the following dates: 7/1/55, 7/1/56, 7/1/58, 7/1/59, 7/1/61, 7/1/62, and 7/1/63.

The District Director's records do not show that a special occupational tax stamp was purchased for this trade name and location for the period beginning July 1, 1957, or July 1, 1960; however, records of the Texas Liquor Control Board show that he was in business those years. The District Director's records also reflect that a special occupational tax stamp as a retail dealer in wine and beer was purchased by S&R, Inc., dba The Carousel Club, 1312½ Commerce Street, Dallas, Texas, for the period July 1, 1962, and July 1, 1963.

On March 8, 1961, S&R, Inc., made application to the Texas Liquor Control Board for a license to operate The Carousel Club at 1312½ Commerce Street, Dallas, Texas. The application listed as corporate officers: Ralph Paul, President; Sam D. Ruby, Vice President; and Jack Ruby, Vice President.

Records at the Texas Liquor Control Board also reveal that the license at the Vegas Club was suspended for a period of five days in 1953 for allowing an obscene performance and that a curfew violation occurred in 1954 for which no suspension was handed down. In 1956 the license

COMMISSION EXHIBIT No. 1654—Continued

Mr. Arnold Sagalyn -3-

of the Vegas Club was suspended for three days for a dishonored check to a wholesaler and in 1958 a ten-day suspension was given for allowing drunks on the premises. There is a strong indication that Jack Ruby is either a homosexual or a bisexual, although there is no concrete evidence to support this contention. It is also strongly hinted that he has underworld connections in the City of Chicago. This also is unverified.

George Senator who was residing with Jack Ruby at the time of his arrest is a comparative newcomer to the City of Dallas and very little is known of his past. He has no known criminal record.

Sources of information for this report are the District Director, Internal Revenue Service; Texas Liquor Control Board; and the Dallas Police Department.

Sincerely,

H. S. Caplinger
Assistant Regional Commissioner
Alcohol and Tobacco Tax

Attachments
Cpies DD records,
Police records

COMMISSION EXHIBIT No. 1654—Continued

Commission Exhibit No. 1655

JK 44-346
DL 44-1639
CHM:sla
1

The following investigation was conducted by SA CLAUDE H. MEADOW, JR. at Gainesville, Florida, on December 17, 1963:

Mrs. BLANCHE McWILLIE, whose home address is 3631 Southwest 18th Terrace, Miami, Florida, was interviewed at the residence of her daughter, NANCY A. McWILLIE, 3705 Southwest 20th Street, Gainesville. Mrs. McWILLIE advised she has known JACK LEON RUBY for about 12 or 15 years having met him through her son, LEWIS, in Dallas, Texas. She advised that her son, LEWIS, at the time she met RUBY, was operating a night club in Dallas.

Mrs. McWILLIE advised she would visit her son about twice a year staying about a month during each visit. She advised that her son was residing at that time in the Maple Terrace Apartments which is an apartment hotel. RUBY did not live in the same apartment building but would visit with her and her son practically every day. She advised RUBY had an apartment somewhere in Dallas, but that she never visited him in this apartment. She recalls that RUBY at the time, was operating the Vegas Club in Dallas which, according to Mrs. McWILLIE, was not an elaborate club but was supposed to have been a decent club. She advised that her acquaintance with RUBY was restricted to her son's apartment, and that the last time she saw RUBY was about seven years ago.

She recalls that she believes the last time she saw RUBY he was going with a girl named ALICE (Last Name Unknown) and understood this girl to be a schoolteacher. She described ALICE as being in her early 30's, a nicely dressed girl, very refined looking with brown hair and of average height.

Mrs. McWILLIE stated that she had always considered RUBY to be a well mannered individual who did not drink or smoke, and that she had never heard anything unfavorable concerning him during the time she was visiting her son in Dallas.

93

COMMISSION EXHIBIT No. 1655

JK 44-346
2

Mrs. McWILLIE advised she did not know LEE HARVEY OSWALD and had never heard his name mentioned by JACK RUBY.

94

COMMISSION EXHIBIT No. 1655—Continued

FD-302 (Rev. 1-25-60)

FEDERAL BUREAU OF —

Commission Exhibit No. 1656

Date ______

Bill Gus Komodore, 541 East Fifth Street, Apartment 8, New York City, was interviewed by Special Agents Timothy B. Lagrone and Robert J. Lawson on December 30, 1963. Komodore advised that he is an artist and actively engaged in teaching painting and art where he maintains a studio at 410 Grand Street, New York City.

Komodore stated that he does not know Jack Ruby but possibly had worked in one of his night clubs for one night only. He explained that he formerly resided in Dallas, Texas, at 3031 Congress Street for approximately a two year period during 1960 and 1961. During this time, he was employed by the Dallas Museum of Contemporary Arts in Dallas.

During his above employment he used to purchase his art supplies from the Asel Art Supply Store in Dallas and while in that store on one occasion one of the store employees, known to him as "Frenchie", told him if he was interested in working in a night club as a waiter, he could earn from $50.00 to $100.00 per night. "Frenchie" told him he, "Frenchie", and another Asel Employee worked nights as waiters at the Soverign Club, downtown Dallas, and if Komodore would contact the maitre d' at that club, Komodore would probably be employed as a waiter.

Komodore subsequently went to the Soverign Club, address not recalled, where he was interviewed by the maitre d' and hired as a night waiter at that club. When he reported for work, the maitre d' informed him he would not be paid a salary but would received 15 per cent of the amount of the checks from tables he served. He was also shown a guest list of approximately 30 or more names that would be guests of the club and would not be required to pay for their meals or drinks.

On 12/30/63 at New York, New York File # NY-44-974

by SAS TIMOTHY B. LAGRONE & ROBERT J. LAWSON:bca Date dictated 1/2/64

177

COMMISSION EXHIBIT No. 1656

NY 44-974

Komodore worked all night the first night and when he finished his work wanted to collect his pay but was told by the maitre d' he did not have any pay due him because all the customers he served were on the guest list and did not have to pay their checks. Komodore's protests were of no avail and he received no pay for the night's work. Because of this he worked at above club only that one night.

During the night he worked at above club, the maitre d' pointed out a man at one of the tables, stating that this man was the boss and Komodore was to be the waiter for that table. The individual pointed out as the boss was sitting at the table with a girl and Komodore served them. Komodore could not recall having heard the boss's name and could described him only as short and well-dressed. Komodore further related he has seen pictures of Jack Ruby on television and in newspapers; however, due to the lapse of time and the fact the interior of the club was extremely dark, he could not say whether or not the above individual described as the boss was Jack Ruby. Komodore stated it would only be an assumption on his part, since apparently someone believes that he was at one time an employee of Ruby, that the boss he served at the club would possibly have been Jack Ruby. He could think of no other possible connection he would have had with Ruby.

According to Komodore "Frenchie" had said that above club was the only place in Dallas that could serve mixed drinks to tables and this was possible only because the club had a deal with the District Attorney. "Frenchie" also told him that the District Attorney's name was on above mentioned guest list and further this list contained mostly names of city officials.

NY 44-974

Komodore described the Soverign Club as being very exclusive, stating that the silverware was apparently so expensive that the waiters were required to sign for all the silverware they used at their respective tables. He did not, however, like the atmosphere of the club and because of what "Frenchie" had told him, got the definite impression the club was being operated illegally.

In conclusion, Komodore said that unless above mentioned boss of the club was in fact Jack Ruby, or the Soverign Club was owned by Ruby, then to his knowledge he has never met nor seen Ruby nor been employed by him, and could furnish no information concerning him, his associates or friends.

1

Date 12/21/63

RICHARD WILLIAM PROEBER, 410 Westheimer, Houston, Texas, advised that he has been in Houston for about three years. Prior to his arrival in Houston, he had lived in Dallas. He had moved to Dallas in 1958 from Wisconsin, and left Dallas in 1961 for Houston. He advised he was employed at the Merchants State Bank, and, as a part-time job, had worked as a waiter in one of JACK RUBY's private clubs. He could not quite recall the name of RUBY's club, but he thinks it was the Vegas Club.

PROEBER said that he only worked for about two months at RUBY's club and left because he was afraid that his job at the club would be harmful to his position at the bank.

PROEBER said that he first went to JACK RUBY's club as a Stage Manager for an All Girl Review. This review was a stripper production run by BRECK WALL and JOE PETERSON. These two men were under a contract with RUBY for girl entertainment.

PROEBER advised that he did not personally know JACK RUBY, but had waited on him on many occasions in RUBY's club. He said that RUBY was a very rough character and was always very nervous. He said that RUBY would "fly off the handle" at the least little thing.

PROEBER advised that on one occasion JACK RUBY severely beat JOE PETERSON over a contract dispute. He said that RUBY had two of his associates hold PETERSON while RUBY beat him. It was after this incident that PROEBER quit his job as a waiter.

PROEBER advised that, to the best of his recollection, he had never seen LEE HARVEY OSWALD in JACK RUBY's club, or anywhere else. He knows of no connection between JACK RUBY and LEE HARVEY OSWALD.

PROEBER advised that he never heard JACK RUBY discuss politics in the night club or anywhere else. He

On 12/21/63 at Houston, Texas File # HO 44-939

by SA DANIEL D. DREILING/lc Date dictated 12/21/63

182

COMMISSION EXHIBIT No. 1657

2

HO 44-939

said of all the times he heard RUBY talking, it was about gambling, girls or booze. He said RUBY was a loud-mouth and liked to belittle people in public. He said that RUBY would constantly "dress down" his help.

When asked of JACK RUBY's association with Dallas Police Department, PROEBER advised that RUBY's club was frequented by Dallas Police officials. He said it was talk amongst RUBY's help that RUBY was "paying off" the Dallas Police Department for special favors. PROEBER had no idea of what these special favors consisted nor did he know the identities of any Dallas Police Officers involved.

183

COMMISSION EXHIBIT No. 1657—Continued

FD-302 (Rev. 1-25-60)

FEDERAL BUREAU OF INVESTIGATION

Commission Exhibit No. 1658

Date 12/26/63

1

HERMAN VIRDIE SMITH, 117 West 112th Street, Los Angeles, California, advised he was formerly employed as a drummer for various bands at clubs owned by JACK RUBY at Dallas, Texas. He approximated he was so employed from about 1953 until March 1961. He said he was a member of the LEO PHILLIPS Band about 1953 at the Silver Spur Bar in South Dallas. He was employed by band leader JOE JOHNSON at the Vegas Club in Dallas on several occasions between 1958 and August 1959 and November 1960 until about March 1961. He said he also was a member of Red Calhoun's Band between 1950 and 1956. SMITH pointed out that the three bandleaders are Negroes and are well known in the Dallas, Texas, area.

SMITH said that about 1955 or 1956, when he was employed by Red Calhoun, JACK RUBY had an argument with RED CALHOUN. RUBY had "brass knuckles" and hit CALHOUN in the mouth causing CALHOUN to have about 8 stitches taken in his mouth. About November 1960 JOE JOHNSON was out of the Dallas, Texas, area and SMITH attempted to get a band together to play for RUBY's bar. He said he was unsuccessful and at that time had an oral argument only with RUBY. He said that RUBY was usually nice to SMITH but that a minute later he could have a "very violent temper." He explained RUBY talks to most people as if they are "children" and "kids" people during such conversation. He said, however, that one could not talk to RUBY in the same manner or RUBY "would blow his cork."

SMITH said RUBY was a strict individual in that he would refuse admittance to a bar for such a thing as not liking ones appearance generally. He said he was a "sympathetic" man in that he financially assisted many people at various times. He added RUBY had a "belligerent attitude" but would never get into an argument with certain types of individuals unless RUBY had one or more associates present with him. He said RUBY did not allow "expressive dancing" in his clubs and that if individuals

On 12/23/63 at Los Angeles, California File # LA 44-895

by SA JAMES D. FAZIOLA/meh Date dictated 12/26/63

-188-

2
LA 44-895

did not fall in line with the thoughts of RUBY he would "run off the customers from the premises." SMITH considered that if one "crossed RUBY" they would become an enemy of RUBY. He said EVA GRANT, RUBY's sister, ran the Vegas Club about 1959. He considered EVA and her temperament and personality to be much like RUBYs.

SMITH concluded by stating he has not been in Dallas nor seen or heard from RUBY since SMITH left in early 1961. He said he did not know LEE HARVEY OSWALD or of any connection between OSWALD and RUBY.

-189-

FD-302 (Rev. 3-3-59) FEDERAL BUREAU OF ...

1

Date 12/24/63

JAMES H. (JIMMY) RHODES, presently residing at the home of his parents, 719 Brinker Street, while convalescing from recent major surgery, advised he is a photographer, producer of stage entertainment, and a bartender. He noted for the past two years he has worked mainly as a free-lance photographer, maintaining business offices at two locations, namely, 2535 Cedar Springs and 3524 Cedar Springs, both Dallas, Texas.

RHODES volunteered he served in the U. S. Army Air Corps for four and one-half years during World War II and, following discharge, moved from Sulphur Springs, Texas to Dallas, Texas. He noted subsequently, during the Korean conflict, he was recalled to active duty in the U. S. Air Force serving approximately thirteen months. Following this most recent discharge, RHODES had become employed with KRLD Radio and Television, in Dallas, and, about this time, first met JACK RUBY, who was then operating the Silver Spur Night Club located on South Ervay Street, Dallas. He said he met RUBY through one TINY GRANT, a night club Master of Ceremonies, now deceased. In 1959, upon learning RHODES was a photographer, RUBY approached him with a request RHODES do some publicity work and photographs for his night club businesses. Sometime thereafter, believed in late 1959, RHODES said he terminated his employment with KRLD and started free-lance photography work. RUDY became a client of his and would send various performers to RHODES for publicity shots.

RHODES said it was his recollection RUBY sold the Silver Spur in early 1960 and thereafter purchased the Vegas Club. At about the same time, RUBY opened a private club known as the Sovereign Club, which he later converted to a public club, changing the name to the Carousel Club. It was at this time RUBY requested RHODES to go to work for him as a "general handy man," his duties being to help RUBY book shows, train girls for dancing, [illegible]

on 12/16&20/63 at Dallas, Texas File # DL 44-1639

by Special Agent DEL D. DRAKE/eah Date dictated 12/23/63

195

COMMISSION EXHIBIT No. 1659

DL 44-1639

2

supervise writing for floor shows and, on occasion, fill in as a bartender at the Carousel. RHODES stated he worked in this capacity for about three months and then moved back to Sulphur Springs, Texas, in late Summer, 1960, where he did some free-lance lighting and photography work. He noted, however, while in Sulphur Springs, he commuted back and forth to Dallas doing photography and publicity work for performers appearing at various Dallas night clubs, including RUBY's clubs. Since that time, he has had contact with RUBY on an average of about two or three times per month, always in connection with publicity work, which RUBY employed him to perform.

RHODES related in his association with RUBY he came to know RUBY as a person who is "fanatical in his beliefs;" good to his help; one who really loved to be liked by people; an individual who wanted the police as his friends; a fierce competitor; and a man with an "uncontrollable temper," but who would get over his display of temper quickly. RHODES advised close associates to RUBY known to him were TINY GRANT, mentioned above, RALPH PAUL; JOE JOHNSON, a Negro bandleader; WALLY WESTON, a Master of Ceremonies; BRECK WALL and JOE PETERSON, theatrical producers; EARL NORMAN; BILL WILLIS, a drummer in various bands, and FRANK FISHER, a musician in various Dallas bands. Concerning PAUL, RHODES said he is of the opinion PAUL was the financial backer in most of RUBY's ventures and the person who would be financially able to pay for the defense of RUBY, regardless of the amount of money needed for attorneys' fees.

In the period he has been associated with RUBY and particularly during the time of his employment by RUBY RHODES observed RUBY was very friendly with members of the Dallas Police Department and, in particular, with members of the Vice Squad. RHODES said during his three-month employment he recalled many officers of the Dallas Police Department came in and out of the Carousel, including both uniformed

196

COMMISSION EXHIBIT No. 1659—Continued

DL 44-1639

3

patrolmen, as well as plain-clothes officers. He said RUBY always served these officers Cokes or coffee and permitted them free access to the kitchen at the Carousel, where they could help themselves to food. He said RUBY never objected to the appearance of the officers at the club and gave orders to the bartender and waitresses that the officers should never be charged for anything they received at the club. He said this was standard procedure in many of the Dallas night clubs and was not solely limited to the Carousel Club, insofar as police officers were concerned. RHODES said he recalled on occasions RUBY would take Dallas police officers out to eat at night.

When questioned, RHODES claimed an inability to recall the identity of the officers referred to above, stating although he saw the officers in the club, he was never introduced to them.

RHODES said he recalled that, approximately one month after the Carousel became a public club in 1960, a large party was held there by a group of thirty or forty police officers. He said it was his recollection it was at the time a police or sheriffs' convention was being held in Dallas and a number of the officers in attendance at the party were from out of town. RHODES claimed he did not know who made the arrangements for this party, nor could he identify any of the officers in attendance, other than to state he, RHODES, was bartender for the affair and that RUBY told him "the chief" was there. RHODES pointed out he did not actually see "the chief" and he assumed he was referring to Chief CURRY, of the Dallas Police Department. RHODES said the party in question took place during regular club hours and it was his understanding RUBY "picked up the tab." When asked, RHODES was unable to furnish the identity of any other employees of the Carousel Club who were present, or otherwise corroborate his statements with respect to the party.

197

DL 44-1639

4

In addition to the above, RHODES said he also recalled during his three-month employment at the Carousel that fourteen members of the Dallas Police Department Vice Squad also attended a party at the Carousel, which party was held after hours. RHODES claimed he was the bartender for this affair and that the officers drank "mostly Cokes." He alleged there were no waitresses present at the affair, nor could he identify any witnesses who could verify his statement concerning this party. RHODES claimed although he could remember the number of officers in attendance he could not, however, identify any of the officers, again claiming he never met any of them and only knew them by sight.

RHODES explained RUBY was "very cranky" about serving any alcohol after hours because he did not want to break the law. RHODES said RUBY "had no reason to pay off officers," as he would not tolerate law breaking in the Carousel. On many occasions rehearsals and try-outs would be held after hours because theatrical agents would bring their acts in at that time for RUBY to approve or disapprove. Sometimes there were officers, but he never saw any fraternizing between officers and members of the acts.

RHODES also stated if BOB LARKIN, former host at the Colony Club, who is now working at the Monmarte Club, were contacted, he would have no trouble identifying the names of the Vice Squad members and the other officers who were always hanging around the Carousel Club, because the same officers were also in and out of the Colony Club.

RHODES explained that there was one particular team of officers who were always coming to the Carousel Club or the Colony Club and he cannot think of their names, but they should be well known to LARKIN and ABE WEINSTEIN, owner of the Colony Club.

198

RHODES readily admitted that he had sold eight negatives of RUBY to Time Magazine, but he understood that although Time paid him, they were actually for Life Magazine. He said he had been paid $200 and that the entire matter had been handled through SHEL HERSHORN, Black Star Agency, 2936 Fondren, Dallas, Telephone EM 1-6508; or 3023 Routh, Telephone RI 7-0440. He stated they were the only photographs he had of RUBY and that they were pictures of RUBY interviewing a female entertainer, and there were some other entertainers in and out of RUBY's office. There were no pictures of customers. He said he did not know the name of the entertainer. RHODES permitted SA DRAKE to view the negatives he had prepared for mailing to HERSHORN. The negatives reflected an outline of a person resembling RUBY, and a female in shorts and a top which appeared to be a costume used by entertainers such as dancers.

There were shots of RUBY at a desk and in the other negatives there were observed what appeared to be other female entertainers. RHODES stated that these negatives were being mailed to HERSHORN. He stated that he had no other negatives, as he had searched his photography work to make sure he did not have other material which might interest some of the national publications, who, RHODES said, would buy anything picturing RUBY or his clubs.

In discussing photography, RHODES stated that at the Carousel Club there had been two amateur photographers, whose names he did not know, who more or less had the run of the place for the shooting of pictures of customers and entertainers and, if these persons were identified, he was sure that they should have some material that would depict customers in the Carousel Club. RHODES said he believed that these individuals used Polaroid cameras. He also stated that he was sure that these two amateurs could be identified by making inquiry at the Carousel Club in Dallas.

In conclusion, RHODES stated he had never seen OSWALD and did not know OSWALD ever being in the company of RUBY or so much as ever being in one of RUBY's clubs. He did say that RUBY would receive a great deal of publicity out of what he had done, and that there were probably many people in Dallas who felt that RUBY should go free. RHODES said he had never heard the name of OSWALD mentioned prior to seeing him on television the day of the assassination of President KENNEDY.

FD-302 (Rev. 3-3-59)

'EDERAL BUREAU OF

Date 12/17/63

1

Chief of Police JESSE E. CURRY, Dallas Police Department, advised that he had heard that there had been a relationship between JACK RUBY and some of the police officers, that RUBY was reported to have been a co-signer on some loans obtained at Dallas banks by Dallas police officers. CURRY advised that he had had this checked and that they had not been able to find one instance where this was true. He stated that Lieut. JACK REVILL, of the Intelligence Section, was the one who had done the checking, and he suggested that REVILL be contacted.

on 12/13/63 at Dallas, Texas File # DL 44-1639

by Special Agent LEO L. ROBERTSON - LAC Date dictated 12/16/63

222

FD-302 (Rev. 3-3-59)

FEDERAL BUREAU OF II

Date December 17, 1963

(1)

Lieutenant JACK REVILL, Dallas Police Department, Dallas, Texas, advised that he obtained a list of Dallas Police Department personnel who were on duty in the basement (or the proximity thereof) prior to or at the time LEE HARVEY OSWALD was shot November 24, 1963. He stated this list of police officers was furnished to LEE DRAIN, Vice President, Republic National Bank; DEWEY PRESLEY, Senior Vice President, First National Bank; JAMES C. TYCUS, President, Oak Cliff Bank and Trust Co.; A. B. WRIGHT, SR., Chairman of the Board and TERRY DICKINS, Vice President, American Bank and Trust Company, and H. E. CRABBE, Assistant Vice President, Merchants State Bank.

He stated officials of the above banks reported they were unable to locate any record of JACK RUBY being a co-maker on any note of a police officer in their bank at any time.

on 12/16/63 at Dallas, Texas File # DL 44-1639

by Special Agent LEO L. ROBERTSON/LAC:bnm Date dictated 12/16/63

223

DL 44-1639
RCE:gj
1

Investigation at the following Dallas, Texas banks in the period December 5, 1963, through December 10, 1963, determined no record existed at the respective institutions of a current checking account; savings account; credit file; loan folio; or safe deposit box, under the names JACK L. RUBY; JACK RUBENSTEIN; Carousel Club; Vegas Club; and S & R, Inc.:

Park Cities Bank and Trust Company;

Mercantile National Bank in Dallas;

National Bank of Commerce;

Industrial National Bank;

American Bank and Trust Company;

Greenville Avenue State Bank;

Exchange Bank and Trust Company;

South Oak Cliff State Bank;

Republic National Bank of Dallas;

Buckner State Bank;

Grove State Bank;

Northwest National Bank;

Wynnewood State Bank.

Records of the Park Cities Bank and Trust Company did disclose an account had been maintained there under the style, "JACK RUBY, 4160 Hawthorne, c/o Vegas Night Club, Dallas, Texas", but that such account which was opened in February, 1959, had been closed in August, 1960.

224

COMMISSION EXHIBIT No. 1662

DL 44-1639
lp

1

Investigation conducted at the following banks, and contacts with officials of these banks as indicated, failed to disclose checking or savings accounts, loans, or the rental of safe deposit boxes, in the names of any of the following:

JACK LEON RUBY
JACK RUBENSTEIN
CAROUSEL CLUB
VEGAS CLUB
S & R, INC.

BANK	DATE	PERSON CONTACTED
First National Bank in Dallas	12/5/63	ROY LAMBERT, Auditor
First Citizens Bank	12/5/63	JAMES WEST, Cashier
Fair Park National Bank	12/5/63	RICHARD MC CLASKEY, Assistant Cashier

225

COMMISSION EXHIBIT No. 1662—Continued

FD-302 (Rev. 3-3-59)

FEDERAL BUREAU OF INVESTIGATION

Date December 21, 1963

1

JEAN FLYNN, 2410 Connecticut Lane, Dallas, Texas, advised she worked as a cigarette girl for JACK RUBY at the Carousel Club for about five months beginning in about June, 1962. She terminated her employment because she did not like to work for RUBY. He always behaved as a gentleman and she had no arguments with him; however, he was very nervous, was always running around telling people what to do and she just did not care to work under those conditions. She last saw RUBY briefly at the Dallas State Fair in September.

She advised she never saw RUBY with a gun. She had heard that he was very quick tempered and had thrown people down the stairs at the Carousel Club for getting out of line but she never saw him do this or get involved in any violent arguments with anyone.

She explained that it was a general rumor among the employees that RUBY was sexually interested in both men and women and she assumed he was "bi-sexual." She knew of no men or women who RUBY supposedly dated and could recall the names of no individuals who claimed to actually know anything about RUBY along these lines.

RUBY was an extrovert and wanted to make friends with everybody. Although he was a very friendly type person with everybody he appeared to have very few close friends. She could recall only one person who appeared to be a close friend of RUBY, namely RALPH PAUL. Numerous police officers whose names she could not recall came around the Carousel both in uniform and plain clothes but these calls appeared business in nature. RUBY was friendly with these individuals but no more so than he was friendly with other people. She never saw RUBY give police officers any special favors other than not charging them for coming into the Carousel and possibly giving them a cup of coffee or a coke. She never saw any police officers drinking alcoholic beverages at the Carousel.

RUBY did not appear to be interested in politics. His main interests in life seemed to be several small dogs that he kept and a very strong desire to make the Carousel Club a successful business.

Regarding the Carousel Club, RUBY was very

on 12/20/63 at Dallas, Texas File # Dallas 44-1639

by Special Agent s JAMES F. GLONEK and JOHN E. DALLMAN:BL Date dictated 12/21/63

159

COMMISSION EXHIBIT NO. 1663

DL 44-1639
2

conscious that the convention trade was the backbone of his business and went out of his way to encourage trade from individuals visiting in town, particularly those staying in the downtown hotels.

She recalled RUBY mentioning that he originally came from Chicago. He spoke of being raised in a very tough neighborhood and being from a very poor family. FLYNN advised she is aware that there is an organized criminal element in Chicago, Illinois, referred to as the "syndicate" but nothing which RUBY ever said or anything she heard about him indicated that he associated with or was a part of this organization prior to the time he left Chicago for Dallas.

FLYNN advised that the shooting of LEE HARVEY OSWALD by RUBY surprised her. In thinking over this situation, it is her opinion that RUBY's motivation for the shooting developed out of his fear that OSWALD's assassination of President KENNEDY in Dallas would ruin the convention trade and ultimately ruin his business.

She was not acquainted with LEE HARVEY OSWALD, knew of no association between OSWALD and RUBY and knew of no other individuals possibly involved with either of these two men in the shootings.

160

COMMISSION NO. EXHIBIT 1663—Continued

FD-302 (Rev. 3-3-59) FEDERAL BUREAU OF Commission Exhibit No. 1664

1 Date 12/17/63

D. R. PORTER, Hillcrest State Bank, 6517 Hillcrest, University Park, Texas advised that their records contain no information as far as checking accounts, savings accounts, safety deposit boxes, credit or loan files, for JACK L. RUBY, JACK RUBENSTEIN, Vegas Club, or Carousel Club. He further advised that he checked cashier's checks issued for September 1, 1963, to November 24, 1963, but none were purchased by JACK L. RUBY or JACK RUBENSTEIN or by the Vegas Club or Carousel Club.

on 12/17/63 at University Park, Texas File # DL 44-1639

by Special Agents JAMES J. WARD and ROBERT E. BASHAM :lp Date dictated 12/17/63

This document contains neither recommendations nor conclusions of the FBI. It is the property of the FBI and is loaned to your agency; it and its contents are not to be distributed outside your agency.

226

COMMISSION EXHIBIT No. 1664

FD-302 (Rev. 3-3-59) FEDERAL BUREAU Commission Exhibit No. 1665

1 Date December 20, 1963

Mr. HARRY K. YEAGER, Vice President and Cashier, Preston State Bank, furnished the following information:

Records of that bank failed to reflect a record of a checking account; savings account; safety deposit box, credit file, or loan folio on JACK L. RUBY; JACK RUBENSTEIN; Vegas Club or Carousel Club.

He said a check of the cashier's check register from September 1, 1963 to November 24, 1963, failed to reflect any record of a cashier's check being purchased by RUBY during that period.

Mr. YEAGER further advised their bank has no record of RUBY being listed as a co-signer on any notes.

on 12/18/63 at Dallas, Texas File # DL 44-1639

by Special Agents JAMES J. WARD & ROBERT E. BASHAM/jn Date dictated 12/19/63

This document contains neither recommendations nor conclusions of the FBI. It is the property of the FBI and is loaned to your agency; it and its contents are not to be distributed outside your agency.

227

COMMISSION EXHIBIT No. 1665

FD-302 (Rev. 3-3-59)

FEDERAL BUREAU OF

Commission Exhibit No. 1666

Date December 22, 1963

(1)

Mr. GARY A. JONES, Secretary-Treasurer, Dallas Clearing House Association, Inc., Fidelity Union Life Building, Dallas, Texas, advised his association maintains an index of all makers, and a separate index for all co-makers, of loans granted to individuals by any bank which is a member of this association.

He conducted a search of the files of his office with respect to the listing of co-makers on all loans, current and closed, made by Dallas Banks which are members of his association, and advised he found no record of JACK LEON RUBY, or JACK LEON RUBENSTEIN or variations of these names, as a co-maker on any such note.

on 12/20/63 at Dallas, Texas File # DL 44-1639

by Special Agent SA ALFRED C. ELLINGTON:bnm Date dictated 12/22/63

228

FD-302 (Rev. 3-3-59)

FEDERAL BUREAU OF

Commission Exhibit No. 1667

Date 12/24/63

1

Records of the Bank of Services and Trusts, Dallas, were checked and revealed that their cashier's checks issued between September 1, 1963, and November 24, 1963, reflected on September 27, 1963, the Carousel Club purchased a Cashier's Check # 22854 in the amount of $200.00 for the Power and Light Company of Dallas, and that on November 5, 1963, the S & R, Inc. (Carousel Club) purchased a $550.00 Cashier's Check # 23517, payable to the estate of H. H. WATSON.

On December 4, 1963, the S & R, Inc. (Carousel) purchased a $550.00 Cashier's Check # 23998, which was also payable to the estate of H. H. WATSON. These cashier's checks to the estate of H. H. WATSON were deposited in the Republic National Bank, Dallas, in the account of HOWELL H. WATSON by JACK D. WATSON, of Watson & Watson Trusts Account.

In regard to the last cashier's check purchased, the colored porter from the Carousel Club, name unknown, brought the club's receipts into the bank and obtained the cashier's check.

Their records contained no loans, savings accounts, checking accounts for JACK RUBY, JACK RUBENSTEIN, Carousel or Vegas Clubs. However, they did have an account for the S & R, Inc., and for the old Sovereign Club, which account was now closed. They exhibited the signature cards for the S & R, Inc., which indicated that on February 17, 1960, JOE E. SLATIN and JACK RUBY opened the account with a $500.00 deposit. They advised that the account was revised on May 15, 1960, to add the signature RALPH PAUL, 1312-1/2 Commerce, telephone RI 7-0025.

It is noted that the only noticeable large deposit was on September 21, 1960, when there was a deposit of $3,000.00. Prior to this deposit, on August 12, 1960, the account had a balance of $76.00. On the same date of the deposit of $3,000.00, there was a check written in the amount of $2,000.00, leaving a balance of $1,076.00. On September 23, 1960, a $1,000.00 check was written, leaving a balance of $75.00 after a $1.00 service fee charge had been deducted. It was noted that at the end of December 1960 the account contained $73.00 and there has been no activity since, with the exception of the deductions of $1.00 for service charges, and the account now totals $64.00.

on 12/20/63 at Dallas, Texas File # DL 44-1639

by Special Agent S ROBERT E. BASHAM and JAMES J. WARD - LAC Date dictated 12/20/63

229

DL 44-1639
2

The microfilms for September were checked and one was located in which EARL RUBY advanced to the Carousel Club, 1312-1/2 Commerce, a check in the amount of $3,000.00 on September 21, 1960. He then located on microfilm a receipt indicating that JACK RUBY, on September 22, 1960, entered $2,000.00 in the "Sovereign Club", which was listed at the address 1312-1/2 Commerce.

The above records can be produced only upon the issuance of a subpoena duces tecum to Mr. J. B. LINDQUIST, Vice President and Cashier, Bank of Services and Trusts, Dallas, Texas.

230

COMMISSION EXHIBIT No. 1667—Continued

FD-302 (Rev. 3-3-59) FEDERAL BUREAU OF — Commission Exhibit No. 1668

Date December 19, 1963

1

Miss INGRID CARTER, Teller, Merchants State Bank, 5217 Ross Avenue, Dallas, Texas, advised she has been employed here for the past five years. She stated that during this time JACK RUBY has purchased numerous cashier's checks from her. She believed most cashier's checks purchased by RUBY were for his rental payments.

Miss CARTER said that on most occasions, when RUBY purchased cashier's checks, he was alone, although she recalls that sometime ago, a young man whose identity is unknown to her, did accompany RUBY to the bank on several occasions. She advised that about two weeks before RUBY shot LEE HARVEY OSWALD, RUBY purchased a cashier's check from her and commented to her that he had to take his "pep" pills to give him energy and make him happy. She added that RUBY was somewhat of a nervous person and at times he was friendly and jovial and at other times he seemed depressed and moody.

Miss CARTER knew nothing about RUBY's personal life and, other than her contacts with him at the bank, had no association with him. She knew none of his friends or acquaintances. She said he never mentioned the Dallas Police Department or having friends on that department.

Miss CARTER did not know LEE HARVEY OSWALD and knew of no association between RUBY and OSWALD.

on 12/16/63 at Dallas, Texas File # Dallas 44-1639

by Special Agent JAMES E. GARRIS:BL Date dictated 12/17/63

231

COMMISSION EXHIBIT No. 1668

FD-302 (Rev. 3-3-59)

FEDERAL BUREAU O— Commission Exhibit No. 1669

Date December 18, 1963

1

The records of the Merchants State Bank, 5217 Ross Avenue, Dallas, Texas, were reviewed and reflected that from September 1, 1963 to November 24, 1963, JACK RUBY or S & R, Inc., purchased the following cashier's checks from that bank:

September 4, 1963, cashier's check #126243, purchased by S & R, Inc., doing business as (DBA) Carousel, payee - Estate of H. H. WATSON, $550.

September 30, 1963, cashier's check #127757, purchased by JACK RUBY, payee - Congregation Church Sheartith Israel, $110.

September 30, 1963, cashier's check #127758, purchased by JACK RUBY, payee - American Society Composers Authors Publishers, $60.

October 25, 1963, cashier's check #129380, purchased by S & R, Inc., DBA Carousel, payee - Texas State Treasurer, $1,071.

October 25, 1963, cashier's check #129381, purchased by JACK RUBY, Vegas Club, payee - Texas State Treasurer, $390.10.

November 21, 1963, cashier's check #130930, purchased by JACK RUBY, Vegas Club, payee - L. F. CORRIGAN, $500.

The above records can be made available only upon the issuance of a subpoena duces tecum which should be directed to Mr. VICTOR P. SCHUMACHER, President, Merchants State Bank, 5217 Ross Avenue, Dallas, Texas, or his authorized representative.

on 12/16/63 at Dallas, Texas File # Dallas 44-1639

by Special Agent JAMES E. GARRIS:BL Date dictated 12/17/63

232

FD-204 (Rev. 3-3-59)

UNITED STATES DEPARTMENT OF JUSTICE
FEDERAL BUREAU OF INVESTIGATION

Commission Exhibit No. 1670

Copy to:

Report of: SA EDWARD P. GAZUR Office: Cleveland
Date: 12/31/63
Field Office File #: 105-7674 Bureau File #: 105-82555
Title: LEE HARVEY OSWALD

Character: INTERNAL SECURITY - R

Synopsis:

STELLA BRAY, nee Kalifia, a stripper known as "YUM YUM" on 12/30/63, advised she was booked into JACK RUBY's Carousel Club, Dallas, for a three month engagement during Summer, 1956. She recalls RUBY was a calm individual who was well known in Dallas. She had no information relative to RUBY's political affiliation, background and had never seen or heard of LEE HARVEY OSWALD prior to the President's assassination.

- RUC -

DETAILS:

FD 302 (Rev. 1-25-60)

FEDERAL BUREAU OF INVESTIGATION

Date December 31, 1963

(1)

STELLA BRAY, nee Kalifia, also known as Mrs. CHARLES BRAY, the Village Apartments, 1538 Payne Avenue, Cleveland, Ohio, advised that she is a stripper who dances under the name "YUM YUM."

She related that during the Summer of 1956, she was booked into the Carousel Club, Dallas, Texas, which was owned and operated by JACK RUBY, by her booking agent, LILLIAN MC CARDELL of Houston, Texas. She could not recall the specific months although she did remember that it was during the Summer, and it was her first engagement as a stripper.

She noted that at the time there were five strippers on the bill including herself and a CINDY EMBERS, who was the headliner. She could not recall the identities of the other three girls and last knew CINDY EMBERS to be engaged in stripping on the West Coast.

She advised that her relations with JACK RUBY were strictly that of an employer and employee and further that RUBY never had anything but business dealings with the strippers. She stated that during her three month engagement she casually spoke to RUBY and often saw him eating breakfast at a restaurant frequented by show people. The one thing that still stands out in her mind was the fact that everyone in Dallas seemed to know RUBY and she recalls that often people seemed to go out of their way to say hello to him. She said she had no information pertaining

On 12/30/63 at Cleveland, Ohio File # Cleveland 105-7674

by SAs EDWARD P. GAZUR and JOHN J. BARRETT:ktk Date dictated 12/31/63

This document contains neither recommendations nor conclusions of the FBI. It is the property of the FBI and is loaned to your agency; it and its contents are not to be distributed outside your agency.

2

COMMISSION EXHIBIT No. 1670—Continued

(2)

CV 105-7674

to his background.

She stated that she recalls RUBY to be very calm individual who never seemed to get excited. For this reason, she stated that she could hardly believe that RUBY killed LEE HARVEY OSWALD.

She noted that she never discussed politics with RUBY and no information ever came to her attention concerning his political affiliation. She had no reason to believe that he was other than an average American who was solely interested in making a living. She further reflected that she had never seen or heard of LEE HARVEY OSWALD prior to the President's assassination.

She concluded by saying that she can always be reached through her booking agent, LILLIAN MC CARDELL, Houston, Texas.

3*

COMMISSION EXHIBIT No. 1670—Continued

FD-302 (Rev. 3-3-59) FEDERAL BUREAU OF

Date 11/29/63

1

Mrs. LEONARD REPSKY, nee JUNE LAVERNE GRADY, 626 West 10th, first met JACK RUBY approximately 12 years ago when she was a teen-age usherette at the Tower Theater. She, in company with four companions, visited JACK RUBY's Vegas Club shortly after its opening or while in the preparation of opening. Ruby at this time closed the door and served beer to the five teenagers despite the fact they were minors.

Mrs. REPSKY later became a waitress at the B & B restaurant located two doors from the Vegas Club on Oaklawn which was frequented by JACK RUBY. She stated that he would come in in a jovial mood and 30 minutes to an hour later would return in an entirely different mood. On one occasion while she was in the Vegas Club, she was engaged in an argument with her escort. When RUBY passed the booth where they were sitting, RUBY stopped, picked up her boy friend, knocked him to the floor, cursed him, threw him out of the Vegas Club, and forbade his return.

On another occasion Mrs. REPSKY was at the Carousel Club owned by JACK RUBY and stated an elderly couple aged approximately 50, evidently got into an argument but were not making any loud disturbance, when JACK RUBY went over to the table, grabbed the woman by the arm, shook and jostled her to the head of the stairs and then gave her a shove down the stairs. RUBY then turned, knocked the gray-haired, slender, short male escort to the floor in the hallway and repeatedly kicked him.

Mrs. REPSKY stated she considered JACK RUBY to be "mean and violent tempered." She stated also in her opinion she did not feel that his shooting of OSWALD had been prompted by love of the KENNEDY family or anyone else, as she definitely felt him incapable of caring for anyone. She stated she had on occasion heard RUBY talk to his sister "like a dog."

Mrs. REPSKY also stated she had never heard JACK RUBY discuss politics in any way. She stated she did not know whether or not RUBY had known LEE OSWALD before shooting him but in her opinion, after reading of OSWALD since the assassination of the President, "they were two of a kind."

on 11/29/63 at Dallas, Texas File # Dallas 44-1639

by Special Agents LEO L. ROBERTSON and JAMES C. KENNEDY/sl Date dictated 11/29/63

329

DL 44-1639

2

Mrs. REPSKY is presently employed as a waitress at the After Glow Tavern and stated she did not want her name used or information furnished by her divulged for fear of reprisals from either JACK RUBY or her friends.

330

FD-302 (Rev. 3-3-59) FEDERAL BUREAU OF INVESTIGATION

1 Date 1/16/64

Mr. JOHN B. WILSON, JR., Attorney with offices at Room 820, Fidelity Union Life Building, 1511 Bryan, Dallas, Texas, advised that during approximately September of 1962 he was drinking beer at the Lasso Bar which was located across the street from the Baker Hotel in Dallas, Texas, when, between 7:00 and 7:30 PM, a man attired in a t-shirt entered the bar and asked a barmaid to loan him a dime to make a telephone call. She complied and the man whom he later found to be FRANK FERRARO proceeded to use the telephone which was located on the wall near where Mr. WILSON was sitting. Before the call was completed, another man whom Mr. WILSON later determined to be JACK RUBY entered the bar and proceeded to assault FERRARO. Mr. WILSON emphasized that he did not see brass knucks used by RUBY but that from the amount of blood issuing from wounds incurred by FERRARO during the fight, it was his conclusion that some device such as brass knucks had been used by RUBY. FERRARO bled profusely and Mr. WILSON, fearful that great bodily harm might result should the fight continue, stepped between RUBY and FERRARO and broke up the fight. He is unable to recall any of the conversation or remarks made by either FERRARO or RUBY during the fight and he had no knowledge or information as to the reason for the fight.

After the fight was stopped WILSON accompanied both RUBY and FERRARO outside where he looked for a policeman. Within a short time a squad car arrived. Mr. WILSON did not know whether the car's arrival was in response to a telephone call or whether it had been merely cruising in that area. He was not aware of the identities of the police officers. He noted that they apparently intended to arrest FERRARO and to do nothing to RUBY, whereupon he advised them he had witnessed the assault and since RUBY had been the aggressor they were arresting the wrong man. The officers then asked FERRARO whether or not he desired to press charges against RUBY and on WILSON's advice FERRARO answered in the affirmative. In the meantime, RUBY disappeared.

Mr. WILSON then gave FERRARO $5.00 to pay for taxi fare to Parkland Hospital as it appeared his wounds required medical attention.

on 1/15/64 at Dallas, Texas File # DL 44-1639

by Special Agent HAROLD R. DOBSON - gj Date dictated 1/15/64

63

COMMISSION EXHIBIT No. 1672

DL 44-1639
2

Mr. WILSON stated his principal impression of the attitude of the police officers was that they were quite willing to arrest FERRARO but were extremely reluctant to do anything about RUBY.

Mr. WILSON stated he had heard of RUBY prior to the above incident and that RUBY had on at least one occasion been pointed out to him but that he had not recognized RUBY until RUBY had given his name.

Mr. WILSON had no subsequent contact with RUBY.

A few days following the above incident, FERRARO appeared at Mr. WILSON's office and repaid the $5.00 loaned him. He asked Mr. WILSON to represent him in a civil suit for damages against RUBY because of the assault but Mr. WILSON advised him it would be contrary to the ethics of the legal profession for him to represent a client in a matter in which he himself would be a material witness. He expressed his willingness to FERRARO at that time to appear as a witness against RUBY if necessary. He described FERRARO's attitude toward suing RUBY as being "wishy washy" as one minute FERRARO would talk about how nice RUBY had been to him and how he would hate to cause him any trouble and next moment he would become quite angry and indicate a desire to institute suit. Several weeks later WILSON received a letter from FERRARO who was at that time in Milwaukee, Wisconsin, asking for the names of attorneys in Dallas who might be employed to institute a civil suit against RUBY based on the assault. WILSON talked of the matter to one associate who indicated no interest in representing FERRARO due to the fact that FERRARO was in Wisconsin which would make ready communication between attorney and client difficult. WILSON wrote FERRARO that he had been unable to interest any Dallas attorneys in instituting the action. WILSON stated he had destroyed the envelope which had contained FERRARO's letter and that he at this time had no way of determining FERRARO's Milwaukee address.

Mr. WILSON stated he had told the above story to a college friend, RONNIE DUGGER, who is currently the editor of a newspaper known as the "Texas Observer".

64

COMMISSION EXHIBIT No. 1672—Continued

DL 44-1639
3

Apparently DUGGER had told the story to a Milwaukee, Wisconsin reporter because since the shooting of OSWALD Mr. WILSON has received two or three telephone calls from a newspaper reporter in Milwaukee, Wisconsin, whose name he is now unable to recall requesting additional information concerning FERRARO and the assault by RUBY. It appeared from such long-distance telephone calls that the reporter had determined FERRARO had resided at Milwaukee, Wisconsin, for a period of approximately two weeks and that the reporter has been unsuccessful in determining FERRARO's subsequent whereabouts.

Mr. WILSON stated he had previously been interviewed by Special Agents of the FBI concerning the appearance of the name "JOHN WILSON, Bond" among RUBY's papers. He had advised during the previous interview that he could think of no reason why his name should have appeared as he never represented RUBY and his only personal contact with him had been during the assault above mentioned. He stated that the general shock resulting from news of KENNEDY's assassination had also caused him to forget to mention during the previous interview a matter which might or might not be of some importance.

On the evening of November 23, 1963, Mr. WILSON attended a dinner. An individual known to him as SAM B. BALLEN was also in attendance and during the course of the meal indicated that he had been acquainted with LEE HARVEY OSWALD as OSWALD had applied to him for employment. BALLEN stated that OSWALD had not impressed him as the type of person who would do such a terrible thing but that he had become almost convinced at that time that OSWALD had actually assassinated KENNEDY.

Mr. WILSON stated he had never heard of LEE HARVEY OSWALD prior to the assassination and that he knew of no connection or association between RUBY and OSWALD. Except for the apparent reticence of the police officers to arrest or otherwise detain RUBY following the assault as previously mentioned, Mr. WILSON had no knowledge or information as to the nature and extent, if any, of RUBY's contacts and association with members of the Dallas Police Department. He was aware of no reason why RUBY shot OSWALD.

65

COMMISSION EXHIBIT No. 1672—Continued

FD-302 (Rev. 3-3-59)

FEDERAL BUREAU OF INVESTIGATION

Date 1/10/64

1

HOWELL H. WATSON, Watson & Watson Realtors, Fidelity Union Life Building, Dallas, Texas, furnished the following information:

Watson & Watson Realtors handles certain properties owned by H. H. NICHOLS and CLARICE NICHOLS, individually and as trustees of the estate of L. L. NICHOLS (deceased), formerly Nichols Enterprises. Included in this property is the building located at 1312 Commerce Street, Dallas, Texas.

WATSON reviewed his file concerning the property at 1312-1/2 Commerce Street and advised this property was originally leased in December 1959 to one JOE E. SLATIN for a monthly rental of $550.00. A lease agreement dated April 1960 reflects JOE E. SLATIN as lessee.

WATSON said records of his company do not reflect all transactions relative to this piece of property; however, it was his understanding that JOE E. SLATIN originally leased the building with the intention of operating a club; however, SLATIN did not have sufficient funds and in early 1960 JACK RUBY entered into a business arrangement with SLATIN to operate the club, which was then known as the Sovereign Club.

A letter in WATSON's file dated April 20, 1963, is addressed to JACK RUBY, c/o Sovereign Club, Inc. A lease dated June 20, 1960, bears the signature Sovereign Club and JACK RUBY individually. A check of the records relative to property at 1312-1/2 Commerce made November 6, 1962, reflected JACK RUBY and JOE E. SLATIN had executed a lease on December 1, 1959, effective five years from December 1, 1959, to November 30, 1964. As of November 1962 the account was four months delinquent. A letter dated February 14, 1963, to JACK RUBY, Sovereign Club, Inc., reflected he was behind $1,650.00 in rent due.

The Watson record reflected that on March 1, 1963, a new lease was executed in the name of S & R, Inc., and JACK RUBY individually. The Watson file did not reflect the officers of S & R, Inc., and the lease was signed only by JACK RUBY for the corporation and individually. Watson records show that subsequent to March 1963 all rents on the property at 1312-1/2 Commerce

on 1/9/64 at Dallas, Texas File # DL 44-1639

by Special Agent PAUL L. SCOTT - LAC Date dictated 1/10/64

71

COMMISSION EXHIBIT No. 1673

DL 44-1639
2

Street were paid as due. These payments were made by cashier's check handed personally to ALVA F. MC KNIGHT, Watson salesman, or by mail.

At the time the new lease was executed in March 1963 salesman MC KNIGHT had suggested that the property be rented to another tenant; however, HOUSTON H. NICHOLS, owner of the property, who was personally acquainted with JACK RUBY, instructed that RUBY's lease be renewed.

HOWELL H. WATSON advised that neither he nor his brother, JACK D. WATSON, was personally acquainted with JACK RUBY or had any knowledge of his associates and activities other than operation of the Sovereign and Carousel Clubs.

HOWELL WATSON has never seen JACK RUBY and his brother, JACK WATSON, had seen him on only one occasion in connection with rental of the property at 1312-1/2 Commerce. WATSON did not know LEE HARVEY OSWALD and had no knowledge of any connection between RUBY and OSWALD.

WATSON advised he had no knowledge of persons connected with the S & R, Inc., other than JACK RUBY and that his company had had no dealings with anyone other than JACK RUBY.

WATSON advised that payment of rents by cashier's check was not the usual method of payment; however, he recalled that in early 1960 a check of JACK RUBY's in payment of rent had been returned by the bank and at that time it is possible the owner had requested him to make subsequent payments by cashier's check. He knew of no other reason why the rent would be paid by cashier's check rather than personal check or in cash.

72

COMMISSION EXHIBIT No. 1673—Continued

FD-302 (Rev. 3-3-59)

FEDERAL BUREAU OF

1

Date 1/6/64

HENRY "RED" CALHOUN (former employee of RUBY), 4906 Linnet Lane, furnished the following information:

CALHOUN is a musician by trade. During 1950 - 1954, CALHOUN had a combo which worked for JACK RUBY during this four-year period. In about 1954, CALHOUN had an argument with RUBY, at which time RUBY struck him in the mouth, which required medical treatment and sixteen stitches. After this fight with RUBY, CALHOUN quit working for RUBY and has had nothing to do with him since that time.

CALHOUN could furnish no reason for RUBY shooting LEE HARVEY OSWALD, with the exception of the fact that he has a violent temper. When RUBY loses his temper, he has no control over himself.

CALHOUN knows of no connection between LEE HARVEY OSWALD and JACK RUBY and knows of no police officers with whom RUBY was particularly close.

on 1/3/64 at Dallas, Texas File # DL 44-1639

by Special Agent JOSEPH G. PEGGS/eah Date dictated 1/6/64

78

COMMISSION EXHIBIT No. 1674

FD-302 (Rev. 3-3-59)

FEDERAL BUREAU OF INVESTIGATION

[redacted]

1 — Commission Exhibit No. 1675 — Date 1/14/64

ROBERT DAIGNEAULT, 14431 Avalon, Farmers Branch, was reinterviewed to determine if he knew of the existence of a deal between the Sovereign Club and the District Attorney's Office which permitted the Club to serve mixed drinks at tables.

Mr. DAIGNEAULT worked as a waiter at the Sovereign Club on a part-time basis during 1960 and knows of no deal between the Sovereign Club and the District Attorney's Office. He pointed out that the Sovereign Club was chartered as a private club and as such was legally permitted to serve mixed drinks at the tables at the club. DAIGNEAULT knew of no guest list of city officials being maintained at the Sovereign Club and feels sure he would have known if such a list existed. He knows of no Maitre D' who worked at the club during his employment as the waiters usually seated the people as they came in and no Maitre D' was needed.

on 1/11/64 at Farmers Branch, Texas File # DL 44-1639

by Special Agent JOSEPH G. PEGGS - gj Date dictated 1/14/64

83

COMMISSION EXHIBIT No. 1675

FD-302 (Rev. 3-3-59)

FEDERAL BUREAU OF INVESTIGATION

[redacted]

— Commission Exhibit No. 1676 — Date 1/14/64

1

WILLIS D. DICKERSON, also known as "DUB" DICKERSON, 2442 Hawthorne Street, Dallas, whose name was furnished by JACK J. ROWE as having possibly worked for RUBY in the past and at one time had a fight with RUBY, furnished the following information:

DICKERSON advised that he is presently unemployed but is a musician by trade and plays the guitar. He first met RUBY in about 1950 or 1951 when he played his guitar in a small combo for RUBY for a period of about three months. Since DICKERSON during that period had been changing from one combo to another, he does not recall the particular combo or the members of the combo in which he played for RUBY.

DICKERSON related that several months after he quit working at RUBY's club, he dropped into the club at about 12:30 or 1:00 AM sometime in about 1951 in order to be with RUBY's musicians during the after-hour period. There were still some customers in the place and DICKERSON pulled up a chair to a table of four people whom he recognized and sat down. He partially blocked the aisle and RUBY walked by and kicked DICKERSON's chair and stated, "DUB, you know you can't block the aisle like that".

DICKERSON said he replied to RUBY that "RUBY could go to hell" and if that was the way RUBY felt about it DIC..RSON said he would not return to his club any more. DICKERSON walked outside and RUBY followed him, making some derogatory remark which DICKERSON does not recall. DICKERSON repeated to RUBY that he could "go to hell" and that DICKERSON did not plan to return any more. RUBY became extremely angry and struck DICKERSON in the face with his fist, knocking him down. When DICKERSON got to his feet, RUBY pushed him against a wall and while holding him to the wall, with one hand in DICKERSON's face, RUBY began striking DICKERSON in the groin with his knee.

DICKERSON stated that during this activity one of RUBY's fingers entered DICKERSON's mouth and DICKERSON, partly gritting from the blow and partly in self-defense, bit down hard on RUBY's finger and partially severed it at the first joint. He learned

on 1/14/64 at Dallas, Texas File # DL 44-1639

by Special Agent EDMOND C. HARDIN - LAC Date dictated 1/14/64

84

COMMISSION EXHIBIT No. 1676

later that RUBY had to have the tip of this finger amputated. DICKERSON stated he saw RUBY only a few times following this incident and RUBY later told him he was not angry with him for the incident. No charges were filed by either party as a result of this fight.

DICKERSON stated he last saw RUBY in about 1958 at the Vegas Club and had a short, friendly conversation with him. He added that he never knew LEE HARVEY OSWALD and never had any reason to suspect that RUBY ever knew OSWALD or associated with him. He further stated that he has no information concerning the assassination of President KENNEDY or the shooting of OSWALD by RUBY.

85

COMMISSION EXHIBIT No. 1676—Continued

Date 1/6/64

1

Mr. LOUIS TOM LOY, 4057 Brynmawr Drive, Dallas, Texas, furnished the following information:

LOY initially met JACK RUBY when LOY, as a member of a Dixieland Combo, played at the Vegas Club on week ends for approximately a year in 1953 - 1954. During that period, LOY had no personal business dealings with RUBY, as he was only a member of the band; however, he, on occasion during that period, did talk to RUBY. In approximately 1954, the Dixieland Combo that played at the Vegas Club received a better offer and thus terminated their employment at the Vegas Club.

In approximately 1961, LOY, as a member of a musical combo known as the Cellblock Seven, accepted an offer from RUBY to play at the Sovereign Club for approximately four week ends. To the best of his recollection, the group stayed on for an extra week end, making it a total of five week ends that they played at the Sovereign Club. At that time, they left the Sovereign Club and accepted an engagement at a different night club.

LOY recalled that he last saw JACK RUBY in late October or early November, 1963, approximately three weeks prior to the assassination of President KENNEDY. At that time, RUBY appeared at the Levee Night Club, where LOY was playing as a member of a musical combo.

LOY described RUBY as a person who impressed him as being crude, uneducated, and definitely outspoken. LOY further described RUBY as a person who, when he had the Sovereign Club, had hoped to make the "big time" as a night club operator as he had planned to make the Sovereign Club into a club where he would cater to the carriage trade. It was LOY's opinion that this was

on 1/2/64 at Dallas, Texas File # DL 44-1639

by Special Agent JAMES S. WEIR/eah Date dictated 1/3/64

104

COMMISSION EXHIBIT No. 1677

DL 44-1639

2

RUBY's chief desire. LOY stated he did not know LEE HARVEY OSWALD nor did he have any information of any acquaintance between OSWALD and RUBY.

105

COMMISSION EXHIBIT No. 1677—Continued

FD-302 (Rev. 3-3-59)

FEDERAL BUREAU OF INVESTIGATION

1

Date 1/15/64

ROBERT WEAVER, 5818 Velasco, Dallas, furnished the following information:

WEAVER stated that he has known JACK RUBY since the late 1940's when RUBY was operating the Silver Spur night club. WEAVER often frequented the Silver Spur and over the period of years got to know RUBY casually and had a speaking acquaintance with him. He advised that at no time did he socialize with RUBY and he reiterated that his acquaintanceship was based on his, WEAVER, attendance at the Silver Spur and the Vegas Clubs. Sometime in 1961, WEAVER accidentally bumped into RUBY at a waffle shop late at night in the vicinity of the Carousel Club. In conversing with RUBY that night, WEAVER identified himself to RUBY as a Public Accountant and RUBY, upon learning of WEAVER's occupation, asked WEAVER to handle the quarterly reports and returns of the Vegas Club and the Carousel Club. WEAVER accepted the business offer from RUBY and did work on the books for both clubs. He stated that he did complete a Schedule C tax return for the Vegas Club for the year of 1960 or 1961. WEAVER was unable to state definitely for which year he did make out the return. WEAVER did start a corporation return for the Carousel Club but never was able to complete the return. He advised that he had problems with the Carousel Club return as RUBY kept some of his papers and bills at his apartment, some at the Vegas Club, some at the Carousel Club and some in his car. WEAVER recalled that he probably worked on the Carousel Club corporation return until late 1961 or early 1962 when he decided to give up the task as he could not get all the needed reports and bills together.

It is WEAVER's recollection that the Carousel Club is part of a corporation known as the S & R Corporation of which RUBY is an officer. WEAVER advised that he last saw RUBY in early 1962 or possibly late 1961, when he, WEAVER, was working on RUBY's books.

WEAVER advised that he could recall no information regarding any form of bills or IOU's in the possession of RUBY that would in any way reflect any acquaintance or

on 1/14/64 at Dallas, Texas File # DL 44-1639

by Special Agents JAMES S. WEIR and JOSEPH G. PEGGS - gj Date dictated 1/14/64

119

COMMISSION EXHIBIT No. 1678

DL 44-1639
2

association between OSWALD and RUBY. WEAVER was definite on this point. WEAVER advised that he did not know LEE HARVEY OSWALD and he has no information reflecting any association or acquaintanceship between OSWALD and RUBY.

120

COMMISSION EXHIBIT No. 1678—Continued

FD-302 (Rev. 3-3-59)

F.. ERAL BUREAU OF INVESTIGATION

1

Date 1/10/64

The records of the Bank of Dallas, 3708 Lemmon Avenue, Dallas, Texas, reflect a joint savings account, number 90238, in the names EVA GRANT, 3929 Rawlins, and JACK RUBY, no address listed. The account was activated in July, 1962, with a deposit of $100.00. The current balance in the account is $116.15. The account reflects no withdrawals.

The Bank of Dallas records also reflect a joint safety deposit box, number 71, in the names EVA GRANT and JACK RUBY which was opened in August, 1962.

The above information was obtained with the understanding that it would not be revealed except in a court proceeding following the issuance of a subpoena duces tecum addressed to Mr. JAMES DONNELL, Vice President, Bank of Dallas.

on 1/10/64 at Dallas, Texas File # DL 44-1639

by Special Agent JAMES S. WEIR - gj Date dictated 1/10/64

121

COMMISSION EXHIBIT No. 1679

DL 44-1639
AS:gj
1

The following investigation was conducted by SAS HAROLD R. DOBSON, EDMOND C. HARDIN, JOHN T. MC MURRER, JOSEPH G. PEGGS, PAUL L. SCOTT, JAMES J. WARD and JAMES S. WEIR:

The following people at the below listed banking and savings and loan institutions, on the dates indicated, advised that JACK L. RUBY, by his true name and known aliases, is unknown to their records:

DATE

January 8, 1964: ANN HALL, Vice President, Grand Prairie Savings Association, 114 East Main Street, Dallas, Texas;

Mrs. DOROTHY WHEELER, Secretary, Security Savings Association, 2302 West Illinois, Dallas, Texas;

Mr. R. A. LUNDAHL, President, Southwest Savings Association, Fidelity Union Tower Building, Dallas, Texas; also covers Preston Branch, 5921 Preston Road, Dallas, Texas;

HAROLD S. GREGG, President, Trinity Savings and Loan Association, 1838 South Buckner, Dallas, Texas;

RICHARD COLE, Assistant Vice President, Mesquite Savings and Loan Association, 410 West Main Street, Mesquite, Texas;

WALTER BEACH, Vice President, First National Bank, Garland, Texas;

JAMES RUSH, Senior Vice President, Garland Bank and Trust Company, Garland, Texas;

M. H. HAMPTON, Vice President, First National Bank, Grand Prairie, Texas;

122

COMMISSION EXHIBIT No. 1680

DL 44-1639
2

WANDA BEASLEY, Assistant Vice President, First National Bank, Main and Lancaster Streets, Mesquite, Texas;

W. NORMAN GILBERT, Vice President, Grand Prairie State Bank, Grand Prairie, Texas;

LYNN M. STRICKLAND, Assistant Cashier, The First National Bank of Lancaster, Lancaster, Texas;

MERRILL MATTHEWS, Vice President and Cashier, Mesquite State Bank, 917 Military Road, Mesquite, Texas;

January 9, 1964: Mrs. SALLY ENGER, Secretary, Citizens Savings and Loan Association, 715 East Main, Dallas, Texas;

W. C. H. JACKSON, Secretary-Treasurer, Dallas Federal Savings and Loan Association, Main Office, Dallas Federal Savings and Loan Association Building, Dallas, Texas; also covers Casa Linda Office, 200 Casa Linda; Oak Cliff Office, 255 Wynnewood Village; Preston Center Office, 6019 Berkshire; Richardson Office, 52 Richardson Heights Shopping Village, all of Dallas, Texas; and Farmers Branch Office, Valley Wood Shopping Village, Farmers Branch, Texas;

ARTHUR SEGELHURST, Secretary-Treasurer and Vice President, Exchange Park Savings and Loan Association, Braniff Building, Dallas, Texas;

KENNETH E. KING, Controller, First Federal Savings and Loan Association, Main Office, 1811 Commerce Street, Dallas, Texas; also covers Town North Branch, Preston Royal Shopping Village; North Lake Branch, 440 Northlake Shopping Center; Southland Center Branch, 436 Olive Street, Dallas, Texas;

123

COMMISSION EXHIBIT No. 1680—Continued

FRANK R. GARROTT, Vice President, Guardian Savings and Loan Association, Main Office, 1217 Main Street, Dallas, Texas; also covers Inwood Branch, 5501 Lovers Lane; Oak Cliff Branch, 543 West Jefferson, Dallas, Texas;

DON H. BROWN, Secretary-Treasurer, Republic Savings and Loan Association, Main Office, 3636 Lemmon, Dallas, Texas; also covers Branch Office, 4123 Abrams Road, Dallas, Texas;

MARLENE PUGH, Assistant Secretary, Metropolitan Federal Savings and Loan Association, Main Office, 1400 Main Street, Dallas, Texas; also covers Preston Forest Branch, 11611 Preston Road, Dallas, Texas;

H. E. BROWN, Special Loan Officer, Richardson Savings and Loan Association, Main Office, North Central Expressway, Dallas, Texas; also covers Loan Office, North Central Expressway; Farmers Branch Office, Farmers Branch Shopping Center, Farmers Branch, Texas;

HAROLD G. ALTON, Vice President and Cashier, Seagoville State Bank, North Kauffman and West Elm Streets, Seagoville, Texas;

MARY WILLIAMS, Vice President, The Citizens State Bank, 200 Main Street, Richardson, Texas;

JIM SCHALLENBERGER, Vice President, First Bank and Trust Company of Richardson, Richardson, Texas;

January 10, 1964: Mrs. BEATRICE MARTIN, Vice President and Secretary, Oak Cliff Savings and Loan Association, Main Office, 334 Center Street, Dallas, Texas; also covers

124

Arlington Office, 800 East Abrams, Arlington, Texas; Casa View Office, 2600 Gus Thomason, Dallas, Texas; Pleasant Grove Office, 1500 South Buckner, Dallas; Preston Branch Office, 6071 Sherry Lane, Dallas, Texas;

JOHN R. RITTENBERRY, Vice President, Duncanville Savings Association, 202 North Main Street, formerly of 110 East Orange, Dallas, Texas;

DOROTHY STANTON, Assistant Secretary, Investors Savings Association, 500A South Oak Cliff Shopping Center, Dallas, Texas;

TOBY L. PROCTOR, Vice President, Farm and Home Savings Association, 1900 Main Street, Dallas, Texas;

JOHN M. CHERRY, President, American Savings Association, 1700 Commerce, Dallas, Texas;

OTIS WHEELER, Vice President, North Dallas Bank and Trust Company, 11811 Preston Road, Dallas, Texas;

DON MONROE, Vice President, Casa Linda National Bank, 234 Casa Linda Plaza, Dallas, Texas;

HERSCHELL MASSEY, JR., Vice President, Trinity National Bank, 2519 Fort Worth Avenue, Dallas, Texas;

KENNETH HUGHES, Vice President, The Dallas County State Bank, 1101 South Josey Lane, Carrolton, Texas;

WILLIAM SPEGIN, Vice President, First National Bank of Duncanville, Duncanville, Texas;

125

DL 44-1639
5

R. W. THOMAS, Cashier, Central Bank and Trust Company, Farmers Branch, Texas;

C. G. INNERARITY, President, First National Bank of Irving, Irving, Texas;

JOHN HOPPER, Head Bookkeeper, Irving State Bank and Trust Company, Irving, Texas;

GARLAND LANINGHAM, Cashier, Southwest Bank and Trust Company, Irving, Texas;

January 13, 1964: A. A. BARNES, Vice President, Hillside National Bank, 400 Hillside Village, Dallas, Texas.

126

FD-302 (Rev. 3-3-59)

FEDERAL BUREAU OF INVESTIGATION

1

Date 1/20/64

Mrs. BOBBY BRADFORD, also known as MELBA MOORE, residence Route 4, Box 40B, Crockett, Texas, currently residing at 3101½ San Jacinto, a former employee of JACK RUBY furnished the following information:

MOORE is presently employed as a professional singer at the Mont Martre Club, South Browder Street, Dallas, Texas. In 1960 or 1961, while residing in Dallas with her grandmother, MOORE was contacted by SAMUEL PRATT, an entertainer who asked her if she wanted to work at the Vegas Club. He said that they needed a singer for one night and she might obtain additional work at this club. She went to the Vegas Club which was operated by JACK RUBY and did one night show. She had expected to be paid at least $25.00 for the night's performance, however, when the show was over RUBY paid her only $3.00. She has not worked for RUBY since that time and she has not seen him since that time. She has no knowledge of RUBY's activities or associates. She said SAMUEL PRATT, a tap dancer, formerly worked for RUBY at the Vegas Club two or three times a month for a period of about one year.

MOORE did not know LEE HARVEY OSWALD and has no knowledge of any connection between RUBY and OSWALD.

on 1/18/64 at Dallas, Texas File # DL 44-1639

by Special Agent PAUL L. SCOTT - gj Date dictated 1/20/64

70

FD-302 (Rev. 3-3-59)

FEDERAL BUREAU OF INVESTIGATION

1

Date 1/22/64

Mrs. ELVIRA BERTHA SCOTT, 3013 Mc Lean Street, advised that for approximately two weeks during the summer of 1961 she worked for JACK RUBY at the Carousel Club as a stripper. She quit because RUBY was not paying her the money as promised. Her professional name while working at the club was MONA LU and her husband is FRANK SCOTT.

Mrs. SCOTT advised that she has not seen RUBY since she quit his employment. She stated that she never at any time associated with RUBY outside the club and has never heard him express any opinions politically and definitely not regarding LEE HARVEY OSWALD. She stated that she does not know LEE HARVEY OSWALD.

She stated she has no knowledge that RUBY ever carried a gun and could not furnish any further information concerning him.

on 1/21/64 at Fort Worth, Texas File # DL 44-1639

by Special Agent MALON L. JENNINGS - gj Date dictated 1/21/64

84

COMMISSION EXHIBIT No. 1682

FD-302 (Rev. 3-3-59)

FEDERAL BUREAU OF INVESTIGATION

1

Date 1/21/64

GORDON SIMS (reported to be the husband of former employee of RUBY), 1309 Huddleston, furnished the following information:

SIMS's wife, MARGARET JEAN SIMS, worked for JACK RUBY at the Carousel Club as a cigarette girl from August, 1962, until October, 1962, and on a part-time basis from October, 1962, until March, 1963. In March, 1963, JACK RUBY owed Mrs. SIMS approximately $45.00 to $50.00 in commissions and Mrs. SIMS and RUBY became involved in an argument over this money and RUBY threatened Mrs. SIMS telling her that he would throw her down the stairs.

Mrs. SIMS quit as a result of this argument.

A few days after this argument, GORDON SIMS went to the Carousel Club in an attempt to obtain the money owed Mrs. SIMS. When he arrived at the club he found that RUBY was not there and he, SIMS, obtained the money from ANDREW ARMSTRONG who worked for RUBY at the Carousel Club.

SIMS knows RUBY on a very casual basis and knows nothing concerning his personal life or political beliefs.

LEE HARVEY OSWALD is unknown to SIMS and he could furnish no information connecting LEE HARVEY OSWALD and RUBY.

on 1/20/64 at Grand Prairie, Texas File # DL 44-1639

by Special Agent JOSEPH G. PEGGS - gj Date dictated 1/21/64

85

COMMISSION EXHIBIT No. 1683

FD-302 (Rev. 1-25-60)

FEDERAL BUREAU OF INVESTIGATION

— Commission Exhibit No. 1684 —

Date January 22, 1964

1

JOAN LEAVELLE, also known as TONI TURNER, was interviewed at the residence of her parents, 619 El Prado, West Palm Beach, Florida. She said she lived in Dallas, Texas, for a number of years where she worked as a dancer, mostly in the Colony Club. She first met JACK RUBY when he opened the Carousel next to the Colony Club about three years ago; worked for him as a dancer for about 4 weeks about 2 years ago, and has known him as a casual social acquaintance for the past three years. She said she was never closely associated with RUBY and knows nothing about his activities prior to his opening the Carousel. She believed he was also associated, along with his sister, with the Vegas Club in Dallas, and she knew nothing else of his business activities. His closest associate, insofar as LEAVELLE knew, was the small, grey haired man who ran the Carousel after RUBY went to jail and LEAVELLE knew of no close female acquaintance of RUBY's although she knew RUBY enjoyed normal relations with females.

LEAVELLE said as an employer, RUBY was quite strict and expected alot of his employees. She said she was expected to do more acts when working for RUBY than when working at other clubs and expected to do more mingling with the customers between acts. She said RUBY's main interest seemed to be making money. He had a bad temper and was nervous and high strung and he was not predictable in that one day he was real nice to his employees and the next quite gruff.

Mrs. LEAVELLE said insofar as she knows, RUBY's association with the Dallas Police Department was like that of other club owners; that is he treated all of the police officers well and did not charge them when they attended his club during off hours. She said she knew of no particularly close contact between RUBY and any particular Dallas police officer but she and others noted RUBY was allowed to run a little "rougher" show than other clubs in Dallas.

On 1/20/64 at West Palm Beach, Florida File # Miami 44-1412

by SA RICHARD B. KELLOGG:cmw Date dictated 1/20/64

89

— Commission Exhibit No. 1684 —

MM 44-1412
2

She said she was in Dallas when the late President was killed and when RUBY killed LEE OSWALD and she was surprised as everyone else. She said she knows no one who was not surprised and has heard no one say they had any idea why it happened. She said she did not have the opportunity to speak with RUBY between the time the President was shot and the time OSWALD was shot and never heard RUBY discuss the proposed trip to Dallas by the late President so had no knowledge of why RUBY did what he did. She said she knew nothing about RUBY which would indicate he is particuarly patriotic or otherwise and had no reason to associate RUBY with OSWALD or OSWALD's activities.

Mrs. LEAVELLE advised that the Dallas Detective to whom OSWALD was handcuffed when he was shot is the uncle of her estranged husband, BILL LEAVELLE. She said she is well acquainted with Detective LEAVELLE and has spoken with him since OSWALD's death and she feels certain he was as amazed as anyone by what happened.

90

FD-302 (Rev. 3-3-59)

FEDERAL BUREAU OF INVESTIGATION

Date 1/24/64

1

HELEN VINES, 9008 San Benito Way, Apartment 101, Dallas, Texas, telephone DAvis 4-4614, was interviewed at the Theatre Lounge, 1326 Jackson Street, in the presence of her booking agent, CARL (PAPPY) DOLSEN. She advised she also has as her booking agent, JACK COLE, who recently moved his offices from Dallas, Texas, to the Papas Building, Houston, Texas.

With regard to her knowledge of and acquaintance with JACK L. RUBY, she furnished the following information:

She has known RUBY for about fifteen years, having met him while he was operating the Silver Spur Club in Dallas, Texas. RUBY employed her for about two months as a waitress, and she dated him a few times during that employment. She has seen him on occasion through the years from 1948 until the present time and feels that she knows him as well as any other girl who had similar-type contacts with him. She described RUBY as a good employer and as a nice person; however, he has the human weakness of a quick and violent temper. She said that RUBY has frequent temper tantrums, and these usually last until the cause of them has passed or has been satisfied.

She, VINES, has been employed as a stripper and exotic dancer for approximately five years and uses the professional name of PRECIOUS DIAMOND. She has never worked for JACK RUBY in any capacity, with the exception of her employment for him as a waitress as mentioned above.

VINES advised that she has spent the last year working in Dallas, Texas, and was last out of town in about January 1963. She believes she returned to Dallas sometime in February 1963. She advised that she could not recall the chronology of her last out-of-town trip, however believes that during the Christmas season of 1962 she was in Lubbock, Texas, and traveled from there to Kansas City, Missouri. She may have worked for a period of time at the T Bone Club in Wichita, Kansas, while she was en route from Lubbock, Texas, to Kansas City, Missouri; however, she is not sure of this. She said she has worked at Wichita, Kansas, at the T Bone Club on two different occasions, and one of these occasions may have been in January 1963.

on 1/22/64 at Dallas, Texas File # DL 44-1639

by Special Agent ALBERT SAYERS - LAC Date dictated 1/23/64

91

COMMISSION EXHIBIT No. 1685

DL 44-1639
2

At this point in the interview, VINES consulted her Agent, CARL (PAPPY) DOLSEN, with regard to his recollection of her trip at that time, and he said he does not believe that she stopped at Wichita, Kansas, during that trip. He added that the records regarding her last trip to Wichita, Kansas, would be in the office of the American Guild of Variety Artists in Kansas City, Missouri, or in the office of JACK COLE in the Papas Building in Houston, Texas.

VINES continued by saying that during the times she was at Wichita, Kansas--whenever those times may have been--she had no contact whatever with JACK L. RUBY. She added that she has no knowledge whatever of JACK L. RUBY ever having been in Wichita, Kansas. She advised that the strippers who work at the T Bone Club in Wichita usually are there on a 2- or 3-week appointment and usually stay at the Casa Siesta Motel, which is located near the T Bone Club.

It was pointed out to her that GAIL RAVEN, whom she knows and who is also a stripper, had said that she, RAVEN, had replaced her, VINES, at the T Bone Club on January 20, 1963. VINES advised that she does not have a clear recollection of who replaced her the last time she worked at Wichita, Kansas, and therefore could not verify in good conscience what had been said by GAIL RAVEN.

VINES advised that she last saw JACK RUBY in about August 1963, when she went to the Carousel Club to visit with WALLY WESTON, a master of ceremonies who was employed there at that time. She advised that her agents and managers where she is now working do not approve of their girls' visiting or going to the Carousel Club because it is a business competitor. She said for this reason she remained at the Carousel Club for only a few minutes and just greeted RUBY and passed the time of day with him for a few minutes. Nothing specific was discussed and after visiting a short time with WALLY WESTON, she returned to her own place of employment.

VINES advised that she has read various news accounts connected with the assassination of President JOHN F. KENNEDY and other news accounts connected with the shooting of LEE HARVEY OSWALD by JACK L. RUBY. She advised that she does not know LEE HARVEY OSWALD and has never seen him in person although she has viewed news photographs of him. She advised that she has never

92

COMMISSION EXHIBIT No. 1685—Continued

DL 44-1639
3

had any information and has never heard anything which would give her the impression that there is any connection between JACK L. RUBY and LEE HARVEY OSWALD.

She added that she has no information with regard to JACK L. RUBY's associations with anyone connected with the Dallas Police Department.

93

COMMISSION EXHIBIT No 1685—Continued

FD-302 (Rev. 3-3-59)

FEDERAL BUREAU OF INVESTIGATION

[redacted]

Commission Exhibit No. 1686

1

Date 1/17/64

BILL ALEXANDER, District Attorney, Dallas County, Texas, advised as follows:

During the morning of January 16, 1964, he proceeded to the Bank of Dallas, 3708 Lemmon Avenue, together with another Assistant District Attorney, Dallas County, and ROBERT M. CRITES, Special Agent, Internal Revenue Service, Dallas. Mr. ALEXANDER had in his possession a State search warrant authorizing the opening of Safety Deposit Box #71, Bank of Dallas, which is presently rented in the names of EVA GRANT and JACK RUBY.

At the above named bank, Mr. ALEXANDER showed his search warrant to Mr. JAMES DONNELL, Vice President, Bank of Dallas. Mr. DONNELL had a copy made of same and retained this copy for his records.

Based on this search warrant, Mr. DONNELL caused Safety Deposit Box #71 to be opened at 10:22 AM on that date. When opened, this box was completely empty.

on 1/16/64 at Dallas, Texas File # DL 44-1639

by Special Agent EDMOND C. HARDIN - gl Date dictated 1/16/64

96

COMMISSION EXHIBIT No. 1686

FD-302 (Rev. 3-3-59)

FEDERAL BUREAU OF INVESTIGATION

Commission Exhibit No. 1687

Date 1/17/64

1

The records of the Bank of Dallas, 3708 Lemmon Avenue, reflected that safety deposit box No. 71 in the names of EVA GRANT and JACK RUBY, which was first opened on July 12, 1962, was entered on only one occasion, namely August 20, 1962. The identity of the person opening the box at this time is not reflected.

The above information was obtained with the understanding that it would not be revealed except in a court proceeding following the issuance of a subpoena duces tecum addressed to Mr. JAMES DONNELL, Vice President, Bank of Dallas.

on 1/15/64 at Dallas, Texas File # DL 44-1639

by Special Agent EDMOND C. HARDIN - LAC Date dictated 1/16/64

97

COMMISSION EXHIBIT NO. 1687

Commission Exhibit No. 1688

DL 44-1639
ADN:gj
1

The following investigation was conducted by SA ALFRED D. NEELEY, at Dallas, Texas:

During interview on December 21, 1963, JACK LEON RUBY advised "at a time when CASTRO was popular in the United States" he read of an individual in the vicinity of Houston, Texas, having been engaged in "gun running" to CASTRO. RUBY stated that he attempted to contact this individual by telephone as he had in mind "making a buck" by possibly acquiring some jeeps or other similar equipment which he might sell to persons interested in their importation to Cuba. RUBY claimed nothing came of this. On January 14, 1964, Assistant District Attorney WILLIAM ALEXANDER, Dallas, advised that he had learned from some source, RUBY had reportedly had contact with one DAVIS described as an ex-convict believed living in Beaumont, Texas. ALEXANDER stated he understood the FBI, Houston, had handled the investigation of this person resulting in conviction for gun-running activities.

The Houston Office advised by communication January 17, 1964, that investigation had failed to identify (FNU) DAVIS either at Houston or Beaumont, Texas. The Houston Office advised that ROBERT RAY MC KEOWN was the most logical individual to whom RUBY referred. MC KEOWN was arrested February 25, 1958, and on October 24, 1958, he was sentenced in the U. S. District Court, SDT, Houston, Texas, to sixty days to serve and $500.00 fine on a charge of conspiracy to smuggle goods to Cuba and given a two year sentence suspended for five years on his second count. The Houston Office further stated that on March 28, 1958, information obtained from the Houston Chronicle (newspaper) disclosed at a hearing regarding this matter, a partial list of arms obtained at residence of MC KEOWN was produced and entered in evidence by CHESLEY JONES, an agent of the Alcohol and Tobacco Tax Unit, Dallas, Texas.

23

COMMISSION EXHIBIT NO. 1688

DL 44-1639
2

On January 28, 1964, CHESLEY JONES, Agent, Alcohol and Tobacco Tax Unit, 1114 Commerce Street, advised that he could not recall an individual by the name of (FNU) DAVIS in the ROBERT RAY MC KEOWN case but would check his file and the indices of his office to determine if such person could be identified. Mr. JONES advised on January 29, 1964, that he was unable to identify (FNU) DAVIS through a check of the MC KEOWN file or the indices of his office.

24

1

HO 44-939
DWF/mem

The following investigation was conducted by Special Agent DANIEL W. FULTS, JR.:

AT HOUSTON, TEXAS

On January 24, 1964, at the file room of "The Houston Chronicle" newspaper the following information was noted pertaining to ROBERT RAY MC KEOWN:

On April 28, 1959, the photograph of MC KEOWN and FIDEL CASTRO appeared in "The Houston Chronicle" newspaper. CASTRO, on that occasion, briefly visited Houston, Texas. The article accompanying the photograph quoted CASTRO as saying that when MC KEOWN could come to Cuba he would be given a post in the Cuban Government or perhaps would be given some franchises.

The March 12, 1958, edition of "The Houston Chronicle" noted that a partial list of the weapons seized in the home of MC KEOWN, located in the Shady Lake section near Pasadena, Texas, was entered in evidence at a bond hearing for MC KEOWN by CHESLEY JONES, Dallas, Texas, an agent of the Alcohol, Tobacco Tax Unit of the Internal Revenue Service.

On January 27, 1964, Captain GUS GEORGE, Harris County Sheriff's Office, advised no record would be available at this time concerning an individual reportedly calling from Dallas, Texas, in early 1959 for the purpose of getting in touch with ROBERT RAY MC KEOWN.

25

Date January 28, 1964

ROBERT RAY MC KEOWN, born January 28, 1913, residence Bay Cliff, Texas, unlisted telephone number Bay Cliff 9661492, upon interview at the Houston Division of the FBI furnished the following information:

He is presently employed as a salesman for the Houston Slush Pump Company, 2112 Quitman Street, Houston, and he formerly resided with his sister, MRS. FRANK DENNY, 9138 Wayfarer Street, Houston. His wife makes her residence in Miami, Florida. On February 25, 1958, he was arrested and charged with conspiracy to smuggle guns and related equipment to Cuba for the benefit and use of FIDEL CASTRO and his forces. On October 24, 1958, in the United States District Court, Southern District of Texas, Houston, Texas, he was sentenced for these activities to 60 days to serve and fined $500 on one count, and was given a two year sentence suspended for five years on good behavior on a second count. The period of his probation expired December 11, 1963. At the time of his arrest, conviction and sentencing, considerable publicity concerning him and his activities appeared in the press. His photograph appeared in the newspapers on a number of occasions. He knows FIDEL CASTRO personally, and when CASTRO visited Houston, Texas, briefly in April, 1959, MC KEOWN went to the Houston Airport, visited with CASTRO, and had his photograph taken with CASTRO. This photograph was widely publicized. CASTRO tried to persuade him to stay on the airplane and proceed to Cuba with him (CASTRO). However, because he was then on probation, he told CASTRO it would not be possible. CASTRO was somewhat irritated at this, and suggested that MC KEOWN disregard the probation and go anyway. CASTRO stated he would give MC KEOWN a Government position in Cuba or perhaps he might give him some franchises or concessions there. MC KEOWN responded that he fully intended to comply with his probation to the letter, and stated he would come to Cuba when he could do so in a completely legal manner.

During 1958, while MC KEOWN was out on bond and prior to his sentencing, he and a MR. JARRETT entered a partnership and opened up the J and M Drive-In on Red Bluff Road near Taylor Lake and Clear Lake, in the vicinity of

On 1/24/64 at Houston, Texas File # HO 44-939

by SA DANIEL W. FULTS, JR. : mem Date dictated 1/28/64

26

Kemah and Seabrook, Texas. MC KEOWN obtained his share of the funds for this venture by borrowing from CARLOS PRIO SOCARRAS, former President of Cuba with whom he had a close friendship. About two years ago, MR. JARRETT died, and the business was sold.

FIDEL CASTRO took over the leadership of Cuba on about January 1, 1959, following the revolution which he had led. About one week after that, while he was on duty at the J and M Drive-In, Harris County, Texas, Deputy Sheriff ANTHONY "BOOTS" AYO appeared and said that some person had been frantically calling the Harris County Sheriff's Office in an effort to locate MC KEOWN. The name of the caller was not known to AYO, but he was calling from Dallas, Texas, and on the last call had said it was a life and death matter. MC KEOWN advised AYO to provide the caller with the telephone number of the J and M Drive-In. In about one hour's time, (8:00 p.m. or 8:30 p.m.) a person called MC KEOWN on the telephone and said his name was "Rubenstein". The caller said he was calling from Dallas, Texas, and indicated he was aware that MC KEOWN had influence in Cuba and particularly with CASTRO. The caller stated he wanted to get three individuals out of Cuba who were being held by CASTRO. He stated that if MC KEOWN could achieve their release he would be paid $5,000 for each person. The caller added that a person in Las Vegas, Nevada, would put up the money. MC KEOWN replied that he most certainly was interested in making some money, and assured the caller he could obtain the release of any person being detained by CASTRO; however, MC KEOWN specifically advised the caller he would do nothing toward this end until he was paid $5,000.00 in cash at the outset. The caller stated he would clear this with the man in Las Vegas, and would later recontact MC KEOWN. Nothing further was ever heard from this individual by MC KEOWN.

About three weeks following this telephone call, a man personally appeared at the J and M Drive-In and spoke with MC KEOWN. This person did not identify himself to MC KEOWN, nor did MC KEOWN ask his name. The man said he had a proposition whereby MC KEOWN could make $25,000. When he indicated genuine interest in the man's proposition, they went to the rear of the Drive-In where patrons sit to

27

drink beer and where they could talk more privately. The man stated he had an option on a great number of jeeps which were in Shreveport, Louisiana, and he desired to sell them to CASTRO at a very profitable figure. He wanted MC KEOWN to provide him with a letter of introduction to CASTRO, which letter would clearly indicate that the bearer was responsible and reliable. MC KEOWN said he would gladly provide such a letter of introduction for a fee of $25,000, but before he undertook to do anything he would have to have in hand at least $5,000.00 in cash. The man indicated he wanted the letter right away, whereupon MC KEOWN asked if he had the necessary $5,000 in his pocket. The man said that he did not, but that he would go and get the money and return. According to MC KEOWN, the man never returned nor did he ever again see him.

MC KEOWN stated that from the numerous photographs he has seen in the press and in magazines of JACK RUBY, the man with whom he talked concerning the letter of introduction to CASTRO resembles RUBY. The man gave the impression of being or trying to be a "big shot", and his manner and attitude was rather haughty. While his recollection of this man is somewhat hazy at this time, he vividly recalls the man had a small patch on his nose. MC KEOWN recalled he had asked the fellow what the patch was for, and he was advised that he had attempted to take out a blackhead and a small infection developed. To the best of his recollection, this man was probably 45 to 50 years of age, 5' 8" to 5' 10" in height, 200 pounds, stocky build, well dressed. He recalled the man had a tie clasp which matched his cuff links. He had no idea how the fellow traveled to the J and M Drive-In, and he never ascertained the man's name. MC KEOWN advised that he feels strongly that this individual was in fact JACK RUBY, the man whose photograph he has seen many times recently in the press.

MC KEOWN commented that because of the publicity accorded him in connection with his gun smuggling activities, he was literally besieged with requests for favors, requests for interceding with CASTRO, et cetera, following CASTRO's successful effort in Cuba. He stated his inability to leave the United States during his probationary period prevented him from fulfilling some of these requests which would have provided fabulous fees.

He remarked he is not certain that the above-described telephone caller from Dallas or the man who personally appeared at the J and M Drive-In was identical with the JACK RUBY who killed LEE HARVEY OSWALD. To his knowledge, he has never seen or met LEE HARVEY OSWALD.

MC KEOWN stated that he knew of no one by the name of "Davis" who was convicted for gun running activity with Cuba.

FD-302 (Rev. 1-25-60)

FEDERAL BUREAU OF INVESTIGATION

1

Date January 28, 1964

A. J. "BOOTS" AYO, residence 328 Bayshore Drive, La Porte, Texas, telephone - La Porte number GA-1-0144, upon interview at his place of employment, Jay Marks Chevrolet Company, La Porte, Texas, advised as follows:

He is well acquainted with ROBERT "DICK" MC KEOWN but has not talked to him in the past month or two. MC KEOWN formerly owned the J and M Drive-In located on Red Bluff Road near Clear Creak some two years previous. AYO was formerly employed as a Patrolman by the Harris County Sheriff's Office. AYO recalled on one occasion his office contacted him (AYO) by radio and wanted to know how to contact MC KEOWN. AYO told his office he would personally check and advise. The Harris County Sheriff's Office told AYO by radio at the time that some person from Dallas, Texas, was exceedingly intent on trying to contact MC KEOWN by telephone. AYO was not furnished the name of the individual calling nor the nature of the caller's business. AYO proceeded to the J and M Drive-In, told MC KEOWN about the telephone call, and MC KEOWN furnished AYO the telephone number of the J and M Drive-In, which AYO relayed by radio to the Harris County Sheriff's Office. This incident took place not too long after MC KEOWN had opened the J and M Drive-In because a telephone had not been installed for a very long time.

AYO stated he could recall nothing further about this matter and at the time it impressed him as just a routine matter. He commented he had always found MC KEOWN reliable, although at the present time MC KEOWN may have to watch his drinking, inasmuch as he (MC KEOWN) is now off probation.

On 1/27/64 at La Porte, Texas File # HO 44-939

by SA DANIEL W. FULTS, JR. : mem Date dictated 1/28/64

36

This document contains neither recommendations nor conclusions of the FBI. It is the property of the FBI and is loaned to your agency; it and its contents are not to be distributed outside your agency.

COMMISSION EXHIBIT No. 1689—Continued

Commission Exhibit No. 1690

UNITED STATES DEPARTMENT OF JUSTICE

FEDERAL BUREAU OF INVESTIGATION

In Reply, Please Refer to File No.

WASHINGTON 25, D. C.

March 26, 1964

JACK L. RUBY
LEE HARVEY OSWALD - VICTIM

The following information concerning Lewis Joseph McWillie was developed by the FBI in connection with another matter.

The January 3, 1961, edition of the "Chicago American," a Chicago daily newspaper, on page 5, column 2, contains an article captioned "Teacher Ducks Talk of Punch." The article states that LaVerne Kautt, a teacher at Senn High School, refused to answer questions by reporters after having promised three times to talk to the press. Kautt stated, "My advisers agree this is a private matter. I have nothing to say about it." The article reflects that Kautt was in Havana over the week end with eighty other Chicagoans who were guests of the Fair Play for Cuba Committee. Lewis McWillie, of Miami, told the "Chicago American" that he was waiting to board a plane for Miami in Cuba when Kautt started talking to Cuban newspapermen. Kautt told the reporters that everything that Castro and the Cuban Government was doing is a good thing, even taking property from the Americans. He said that the United States wasn't anything but an imperialistic government. McWillie stated Kautt also strongly denounced American newspapers quoting him as saying they constantly misinterpret and misrepresent stories that come from Cuba because imperialist advertisers dictate editorial policy to American newspapers. McWillie said he was so annoyed over what Kautt said that when their plane landed at Miami, he asked Kautt to repeat his remarks on American soil. Kautt refused and McWillie said, "He made a move like he was going to hit me so I hit him in the nose."

The January 4, 1961, edition of the "Chicago Tribune," a Chicago daily newspaper, on page 5, contained an article captioned "Teacher to be Questioned on Fidel Fracas." It mentions that Assistant Superintendent Richard C. McVey, who is in charge of school personnel, planned to talk with LaVerne Kautt concerning possible disciplinary action by school officials and the Board of Education in connection with statements made by Kautt in Cuba concerning the American Government. McVey said that if it is found that Kautt is a member of the Communist Party or any organization that advocates overthrow of the Government, he would be discharged

COMMISSION EXHIBIT No. 1690

for violating a non-Communist oath he signed in 1955. The article further reflects that Kautt, when interviewed by a "Tribune" reporter in Senn High School, denied comments attributed to him and said the situation was "ridiculous." He said, "What I said I would be willing to repeat to the Superintendent of Schools, the President or to anybody." Kautt said he is a registered Republican voter, not a Communist and just a tourist who got involved in a situation. Kautt described himself as an average school teacher, not wealthy, and said he got a circular in the mail about the trip to Cuba for $200.00. "On a teacher's salary I couldn't afford what it would normally cost. It was a tremendous opportunity to take this trip." Kautt considered the incident in Havana where McWillie took offense at something he was saying a misunderstanding.

The January 6, 1961, edition of the "Chicago Sun Times," a Chicago daily newspaper, on page 7, column 1, contained an article captioned "Teacher Who Got Punched Denies He Praised Castro." The article states that Chicago school teacher LaVerne E. Kautt denied Thursday that he praised Cuba's Fidel Castro or criticized the United States after a trip to the island. "I believe him," said Richard C. McVey, Assistant Superintendent in charge of school personnel. McVey said even if Kautt made the remarks attributed to him, he certainly could not take any action against him. He went to Cuba on a legitimate leave of absence and did not try to pass himself off falsely as a school representative. "It is not my intent to muzzle an individual's prerogative to freedom of speech." McVey said he learned that McWillie, the former manager of the Tropicana Night Club in Havana, had just had most of his assets confiscated by the Castro regime. "Under those circumstances, it is not too hard to understand why he might swing at anyone who said anything that might possibly be construed as favorable to Cuba."

- 2 -

COMMISSION EXHIBIT No. 1690—Continued

FD-302 (Rev. 1-25-60)

FEDERAL BUREAU OF [redacted]

Commission Exhibit No. 1691

Date 3/23/61

LEWIS McWILLIE, 3631 Southwest 18th Terrace, Miami, Florida, advised that he is the former manager of the Tropicana Night Club in Havana, Cuba. He stated that when returning to the United States from Cuba and waiting at the Havana International Airport for his flight to Miami, he overheard an American talking to a group of men who apparently were Cuban newspaper correspondents. He stated that the American spoke in English and was denouncing "President EISENHOWER and American imperialism." He told the Cubans that all Americans thought about was the dollar and that in his opinion, the government of FIDEL CASTRO was the right kind of government. McWILLIE advised that this American was wearing the Fair Play for Cuba Committee badge and another badge indicating he was a guest of the Cuban Government which he took off before arriving in the United States. McWILLIE advised that he and this American both traveled to the United States aboard the same airplane and that when they arrived at Miami, McWILLIE went up to this man and said, "Why don't you make remarks you made in Havana?" McWILLIE stated the man then made a sudden movement and McWILLIE hit him. McWILLIE further stated that police officers at the airport asked this American whether he wanted to prefer charges against McWILLIE and he refused. McWILLIE stated that he did not know the name of this man, LA VERNE KAUTT, until he saw it in the newspapers.

On 3/22/61 at Miami, Florida File # 100-14601

by SA JOHN E. MOONE:ush Date dictated 3/23/61

This document contains neither recommendations nor conclusions of the FBI. It is the property of the FBI and is loaned to your agency; it and its contents are not to be distributed outside your agency.

COMMISSION EXHIBIT No. 1691

Commission Exhibit No. 1692

Extract of information in the Social Security Administration files concerning Lewis J. McWillie, Account No. 410-12-9167 and Account No. 425-26-0314.

On December 3, 1937, Lewis Joseph McWillie applied for a social security account number and was issued Account No. 410-12-9167. He alleged the following:

Address:	41 N. Bellevue, Apt. 55 Memphis, Tennessee
Employer:	Miss Club Walls, Mississippi
Date of birth:	May 4, 1908, in Denver, Colorado
Parents' names:	William Compton McWillie and Blanch Chapman

On August 23, 1940, Lewis Joseph McWillie again applied for a social security account number and was issued Account No. 425-26-0314. He showed his address as 277 N. Waloran, Memphis, Tennessee, and his place of birth as Salt Lake City, Utah. He indicated that he was unemployed.

Mr. McWillie's earnings record shows no earnings reported before 1939. Beginning 1939, the earnings record shows the following:

Year	Quarter(s)	Employer
1939	1st	Little Peabody Tipton, Tennessee
	2nd	Little Peabody Tipton, Tennessee
	3rd	No earnings reported.
	4th	No earnings reported.

COMMISSION EXHIBIT No. 1692

Year	Quarter(s)	Employer
1940	1st	The Delta Club Frank Thomas Cleveland, Mississippi
	2nd	The Delta Club Frank Thomas Cleveland, Mississippi
	3rd	No earnings reported.
	4th	No earnings reported.
1941	1st	No earnings reported.
	2nd	No earnings reported.
	3rd	Uncle Bud's Cabin L. F. Varnado - Owner McComb, Mississippi
	4th	Uncle Bud's Cabin L. F. Varnado - Owner McComb, Mississippi
		J. C. Adams III - Jess Zilliox Et Al Blue Bonnett Hotel Dallas, Texas
1942	1st	J. C. Adams III Et Al c/o Blue Bonnett Hotel Dallas, Texas
		J. C. Adams III - Jess Zilliox Et Al Blue Bonnett Hotel Dallas, Texas
		Earl Dalton - I. M. Miller - R. I. Scarborough - L. B. Binion - Johnnie Avon & Bennie Bickers Southland Hotel Dallas, Texas
		Glen Lake Country Club J. C. Adams III - I. H. Miller Sr. - R. I. Scarborough & L. B. Binion 4030 Penrod Street Dallas, Texas

COMMISSION EXHIBIT No. 1692—Continued

3

Year	Quarter(s)	Employer
1942	2nd	J. C. Adams III Et Al c/o Blue Bonnett Hotel Dallas, Texas
	3rd	Earl Dalton - I. M. Miller - R. I. Scarborough - L. B. Binion - Johnnie Avon & Bennie Bickers Southland Hotel Dallas, Texas
	4th	Earl Dalton - I. M. Miller - R. I. Scarborough - L. B. Binion - Johnnie Avon & Bennie Bickers Southland Hotel Dallas, Texas
1943	1st	Earl Dalton - I. M. Miller - R. I. Scarborough - L. B. Binion - Johnnie Avon & Bennie Bickers Southland Hotel Dallas, Texas
	2nd	Earl Dalton - I. M. Miller - R. I. Scarborough - L. B. Binion - Johnnie Avon & Bennie Bickers Southland Hotel Dallas, Texas
	3rd	Earl Dalton - I. M. Miller - R. I. Scarborough - L. B. Binion - Johnnie Avon & Bennie Bickers Southland Hotel Dallas, Texas
		Fred Browning & Earl Dalton Arlington, Texas
	4th	Fred Browning & Earl Dalton Arlington, Texas
1944	1st	Fred Browning & Earl Dalton Arlington, Texas
	2nd	Fred Browning & Earl Dalton Arlington, Texas
	3rd	No earnings reported.
	4th	No earnings reported.

COMMISSION EXHIBIT No. 1692—Continued

4

Year	Quarter(s)	Employer
1945	1st	Fred Browning & Earl Dalton Arlington, Texas
	2nd	Fred Browning & Earl Dalton Arlington, Texas
	3rd	No earnings reported.
	4th	No earnings reported.
1946	1st	Fred Browning & Earl Dalton Arlington, Texas
	2nd	Fred Browning & Earl Dalton Arlington, Texas
	3rd	No earnings reported.
	4th	No earnings reported.
1947	1st	No earnings reported.
	2nd	Fred Browning & Earl Dalton Arlington, Texas
	3rd	Fred Browning & Earl Dalton Arlington, Texas
	4th	No earnings reported.
1948	All	No earnings reported.
1949	1st	Fred Browning & Earl Dalton Arlington, Texas
	2nd	Fred Browning & Earl Dalton Arlington, Texas
	3rd	No earnings reported.
	4th	No earnings reported.
1950	1st	Fred Browning & I. H. Miller B & M P. O. Box 353 Arlington, Texas

COMMISSION EXHIBIT No. 1692—Continued

Year	Quarter(s)	Employer
1950	2nd	Fred Browning & I. H. Miller B & M P. O. Box 353 Arlington, Texas
	3rd	No earnings reported.
	4th	No earnings reported.
1951	1st	Fred Browning & I. H. Miller B & M P. O. Box 353 Arlington, Texas
	2nd	No earnings reported.
	3rd	No earnings reported.
	4th	No earnings reported.
1952	All	Self-employed.
1953	1st	G. E. Trojack 7739 Lovers Lane Dallas, Texas
	2nd	G. E. Trojack 7739 Lovers Lane Dallas, Texas
	3rd	No earnings reported.
	4th	No earnings reported.
1954	All	Self-employed.
1955	All	Self-employed.
1956	All	No earnings reported.
1957	All	Self-employed.
1958	All	No earnings reported.
1959	All	No earnings reported.
1960	All	No earnings reported.

COMMISSION EXHIBIT No. 1692—Continued

Year	Quarter(s)	Employer
1961	1st	No earnings reported.
	2nd	Park Lake Enterprises Inc. Cal Neva Lodge Crystal Bay Lake Tahoe, Nevada
	3rd	Park Lake Enterprises Inc. Cal Neva Lodge Crystal Bay Lake Tahoe, Nevada Riverside Casino Corp. Riverside Hotel Reno, Nevada
	4th	Riverside Casino Corp. Riverside Hotel Reno, Nevada
1962	1st	Riverside Casino Corp. Riverside Hotel Reno, Nevada
	2nd	Riverside Casino Corp. Riverside Hotel Reno, Nevada
	3rd	No earnings reported.
	4th	No earnings reported.
1963	1st	Badger Deer Et Al Thunderbird Hotel Co. Highway 91 Las Vegas, Nevada
	2nd	Badger Deer Et Al Thunderbird Hotel Co. Highway 91 Las Vegas, Nevada
	3rd	No earnings reported.
	4th	No earnings reported.

COMMISSION EXHIBIT No. 1692—Continued

For each of the years 1952 and 1955, Mr. McWillie reported self-employment income in the business of "Gaming" and "Wagering."

For the year 1954, Mr. McWillie reported self-employment income showing as the source, "Partner in partnership - Amusement."

For the year 1957, Mr. McWillie reported self-employment income showing as the source, "Financial Transactions."

Mr. McWillie is shown in our files as the owner of a social club (no trade name) showing the business address as 210 Maple Terrace, Dallas, Texas. On his application for an employer identification number, he indicated he started the business August 6, 1956.

COMMISSION EXHIBIT No. 1692—Continued

Item 4

In connection with a survey of gambling activities in the Dallas Division, the following information wherein Jack Ruby is mentioned was obtained.

On July 9, 1959, Lieutenant Jack Revill, Criminal Intelligence Section, Dallas Police Department, furnished the following:

On April 2, 1959, the Dallas Police Department received a letter from the Oklahoma City Police Department that Sidney Siedband, FBI number 773833, a Dallas gambler, had been arrested in Oklahoma City and in his possession were a large number of telephone numbers of Dallas and Fort Worth contacts. The Oklahoma City Police Department requested the Dallas Police Department to identify the Dallas contacts. They were identified as follows:

Al Meadows, FBI number 856929, phone FL 77950, at 2438 Inwood, Dallas, gambler and ex-convict;

Oscar Colquitt Swain, also known as "Cotton," FBI number 492723, phone TA 45779, 2203 N. Carroll, Dallas, gambler and ex-convict;

Isadore "Izzy" Miller, FBI number 261801A, phone EM 82986, 8609 Beauregard, gambler;

Lewis Joseph McWillie, also known as Lewis Joseph Martin, Lewis Joseph Chapman, Lewis Olney, FBI number 4404064, RI 26748, 3207 Raleigh, Dallas, gambler and murderer;

Jessie Ray McPherson, Dallas Police Department number 29310, TA 31076, gambler;

Billy Ray Grimes, FBI number 587736A, phone FR 18538, gambler in Dallas and Arlington, Texas;

John B. Turns, also known as "J. B.", FBI number 2845377, phones EM 46232, EV 14185, AN 21060, 6135 Parkdale, Dallas, gambler;

COMMISSION EXHIBIT No. 1693

Elmer Ray Solomn, Dallas Police Department number 28438, phone RI 71796, co-owner of Turf Bar, 1515 Commerce Street, Dallas, with

Johnnie Eli Stone, FBI number 245126, both gamblers and cafe operators.

Other persons listed as contacts of Siedband but not fully identified by the Dallas Police Department are the following:

Johnny Marshall, phone LA 86331, 3625 Cole, operator of Shreveport, Louisiana, gambling house;

Jack Keller, phone DA 44574, 1001 Waterford, owner of Keller's Drive In, on Samuel's Boulevard, known associate of numerous gamblers;

Freddie Merrill, phone DA 12856, 7177 Fisher Road, operates gambling house with R. T. "Chick" Flournoy, Rockwall, Texas, gambler;

Margie Moore, resides in Y.W.C.A., known associate of Dallas gamblers;

Jack Ruby, phone LA 84243, operator of Vegas Club, 3508 Oak Lawn;

Kristian Day Kristoffersen, FBI number 329282A, phone TA 15778, 5926 Winton Street, Dallas, Dallas gambler.

There was a phone number MA 43000, Fort Worth, which was ascertained to be a gambling house at 2222 Jacksboro Highway, Fort Worth, operated by Fay Kirkwood and Lewis Joseph McWillie.

There was a notation in subject's possession showing contact with W. M. "Boston" Smith, at phone Clearview 84294, Aledo, Texas; Jim Henley at the Cipango Club, Dallas, and Dallas bail bondsmen, Smith and Stovall, 106 South Record, Dallas.

Lieutenant Revill stated all or most of the above persons are known gamblers or connected with gambling activities.

COMMISSION EXHIBIT No. 1693—Continued

FD-302 (Rev. 1-25-60)

FEDERAL BUREAU OF INVESTIGATION

1 Date 4/1/64

Mr. PRENTIS I. VAUGHN, Pilot, American Airlines, based at Dallas, Texas, stated that he was on flight layover in Washington, D.C. (WDC).

VAUGHN referred to his previous contact with the Washington Field Office, Federal Bureau of Investigation, on December 4, 1963, and desired to furnish the following additional information:

He stated that in an effort to obtain further information concerning his business dealings with JACK LEON RUBY, he had rechecked his personal business records. He located a tablet bearing notations which he had made on October 22, 1958, concerning a business transaction with RUBY and his business partner, MARTIN GIMPLE. VAUGHN noted that he had previously been in error when he stated that GIMPLE's first name was MORTON.

VAUGHN stated there was also a notation indicating GIMPLE was the partner and roommate of JACK RUBY, and that they were the owners of the Northern Log Cabin Corporation, telephone number LA 8-4243. VAUGHN stated that there was another notation under GIMPLE's name which listed the address, Chelsea Hotel, Wilson Avenue. VAUGHN believed this had been GIMPLE's address in Chicago, Illinois.

VAUGHN also exhibited a deposit slip for his account at the Hurst State Bank, Hurst, Texas, dated October 15, 1958. One item thereon listed a check in the amount of $291.25 payable to VAUGHN from MARTIN GIMPLE as payment for business services.

On 12/6/63 at Washington, D.C. 41 File # WFO 44-520

by SA RICHARD WOOD KAISER:laj Date dictated 3/27/64

COMMISSION EXHIBIT No. 1694

Commission Exhibit No. 1695

UNITED STATES DEPARTMENT OF JUSTICE

FEDERAL BUREAU OF INVESTIGATION

In Reply, Please Refer to
File No.

Dallas, Texas
May 14, 1964

JACK L. RUBY;
LEE HARVEY OSWALD (Deceased)

On May 13, 1964, MILLARD M. PANNILL, Production Manager, Plastelite Engineering Company, 920 Foch Street, Fort Worth, Texas, advised that in the fall of 1963 his company commenced production of a "Twist Board". He stated the "Twist Board" consists basically of three parts: a small fiberboard base approximately six inches by six inches; an upper board approximately one foot square; and, a "Lazy Susan" disk-type bearing plate which joins the two boards.

PANNILL stated all materials, with the exception of the "Lazy Susan bearing", were obtained from stock on hand or purchased locally from their lumber sources. PANNILL displayed an invoice from the Triangle Manufacturing Company, 700 Division Street, Oshkosh, Wisconsin, reflecting the sale of 1000 "6C Lazy Susan Bearings" to Plastelite Engineering Company at a cost of $.45 each, total bill, $450.00.

One thousand of the "Twist Boards" were manufactured by his company, PANNILL related, of which about five hundred were sold to various companies and individuals, and about five hundred are still in stock at their warehouse. PANNILL explained that production was stopped at one thousand because they were not selling well. He said they were "a fad that never caught on". The "Twist Boards" were to retail at $3.95, but, due to a number of factors, they did not find acceptance on the market and the company had taken a loss on the promotion.

PANNILL advised that in September 1963 JACK RUBY had seen the "Twist Board" demonstrated on local television

COMMISSION EXHIBIT No. 1695

Re: JACK L. RUBY;
LEE HARVEY OSWALD (Deceased)

and he contacted Mr. RICHARD ADAMS, company president, and made arrangements to purchase some of the boards. PANNILL said company invoices reflected two shipments, one dozen and six dozen boards, were sent to The Carousel Club, 1321½ Commerce Street, Dallas, Texas, on September 25, 1963, and September 27, 1963, respectively. The total bill for the boards, approximately $162.00, is still on the company books, said PANNILL, and nothing has ever been paid on it.

He stated the boards are no longer being sold anywhere, to his knowledge, and there are no plans for future promotion of it.

PANNILL made available a complimentary copy of the "Twist Board", as well as a descriptive sheet of instructions which was normally enclosed with the board when it was being sold in retail stores.

- 2 -

COMMISSION EXHIBIT No. 1695—Continued

FEDERAL BUREAU OF INVESTIGATION

Date November 26, 1963

1

JOE BONDS, Texas Department of Corrections Number 151515, upon interview at Wynne Prison Farm, advised as follows:

BONDS is serving a sentence on a sodomy charge out of Dallas, Texas.

He has known JACK RUBY from 1948 until 1954. Bonds introduced RUBY to the owner of the Silver Spur Night Club in Dallas, Texas in 1948, and RUBY subsequently bought this club. In 1952, RUBY became a partner with BONDS in the Vegas Club, Dallas, but bought BONDS out several months later for $2500. BONDS described RUBY as not interested in politics, but more interested in money and publicity in connection with business ventures. RUBY had a bad temper, would fight with night club customers, and considered himself a "tough guy". RUBY was very friendly with police officers, and this began when an officer names JOHNNY SIDES was killed. RUBY held a benefit for SIDES at his club and turned the proceeds over to the family of SIDES.

RUBY, according to BONDS, would encourage police officers to frequent his clubs, and he gave some of them off-duty paying jobs in his clubs. He would also give free dinners and drinks to officers, and made women available to officers who were both entertainers and customers. BONDS furnished no identities of police officers so favored, but indicated they were primarily members of the Dallas Police Department. BONDS further commented that during the Korean War RUBY welcomed service men at his club, and he treated them to free meals and drinks.

On 11/25/63 at Huntsville, Texas File # HO 44-939

by SA ROBERT E. WIATT:bp Date dictated 11/25/63

486

COMMISSION EXHIBIT No. 1696

Form No. 1598 (Revised) Memorandum Report (7-1-60)

UNITED STATES SECRET SERVICE
TREASURY DEPARTMENT

S.R.

ORIGIN Field OFFICE Houston, Texas FILE NO. CO-2-34,030

TYPE OF CASE	STATUS	TITLE OR CAPTION
Assassination	Closed - Houston	Lee Harvey Oswald
INVESTIGATION MADE AT: Houston, Texas	PERIOD COVERED: November 25-Dec. 3, '63	
INVESTIGATION MADE BY: SAIC Lane Bertram		

DETAILS

SYNOPSIS

Inmate of the Texas Prison System, Joe Bonds, allegedly a former business partner of Jack Rubenstein.

DETAILS OF INVESTIGATION

This case originated in the Houston Office on November 25, 1963 upon receipt of a phone call from Dr. C. A. Dwyer, Texas Prison System psychiatrist, who advised that a prisoner, Joe Bonds, presently in TDC on a charge of sodomy from Dallas, Texas about 1952, serving an eight to ten year sentence, due to be released in the near future, had advised him that he formerly owned the Vegas Club in Dallas, prior to his arrest and felt sorry for Jack Rubenstein therefore took him in as a partner, and part owner of the Vegas Club. He later received demands from Rubenstein that he get out of the partnership and was offered $2500. Since this represented a $500 profit, Bonds accepted the money and got out of the club.

Dr. Dwyer further advised that Bonds stated Ruby was friendly with the police and had refused to attempt to help him in his present case as it might affect his relationship with the police department. He alleged that Ruby's served drinks and food to the Dallas police thinking that his friendship with them would lessen their harrassment in the operation of his club. He also advised that Ruby carries a small revolver most of the time.

On December 3, Inspector Thomas Kelley in Dallas was advised briefly of the above and stated that it would not be necessary to interview inmate Joe Bonds at Wynn State Farm, Huntsville, Texas

DISPOSITION

In view of the above this inquiry is closed.

DISTRIBUTION	COPIES	REPORT MADE BY	DATE
Chief	Orig	SPECIAL AGENT	540
Dallas	1-cc	APPROVED: SPECIAL AGENT IN CHARGE	DATE 12/3/63
Houston	1-cc		
LB/mts			

(CONTINUE ON PLAIN PAPER)

COMMISSION EXHIBIT No. 1696—Continued

UNITED STATES DEPARTMENT OF JUSTICE

FEDERAL BUREAU OF INVESTIGATION

In Reply, Please Refer to
File No.

Las Vegas, Nevada

June 11, 1964

**JACK L. RUBY, ALSO KNOWN AS;
LEE HARVEY OSWALD, ALSO
KNOWN AS - VICTIM**

On June 8, 1964, Mr. Lewis J. Mc Willie was interviewed at his residence, 3627 Eastern Avenue, Las Vegas, Nevada, by Special Agents of the Federal Bureau of Investigation. Mr. Mc Willie furnished the following information.

He went to Cuba in September, 1958, and immediately went to work at the Tropicana Casino, remainin there as manager until May, 1960, after which he left and worked at the Capri Hotel-Casino from May, 1960 to January 2, 1961, as a pitboss. He stated the Tropicana was Cuban owned and that he did not know the owner of the Capri, but that he worked under one Angelo Di Christofano (Phonetic).

In 1959, date unrecalled, he wrote to Ruby and asked him if he would like to come to Havana for a week. He stated there was no ulterior motive and that he had been a close friend of Ruby's and extended this invitation as one would to a brother. He realized Ruby was working hard with his Dallas night club and felt that Ruby needed a rest. Because the cost of plane tickets in Havana could be paid for by pesos for approximately 1/5 of a cost of a ticket in the United States, he purchased a round trip ticket for Ruby at his own expense and mailed it to Ruby in Dallas, after which Ruby boarded a plane and flew to Havana for a visit.

He arranged for Ruby to stay in a small hotel, about three blocks from the Nacional Hotel, name unrecalle Ruby, during his stay in Havana, would come out to the Tropicana where Mc Willie was working from nine PM to two AM, and wait for Mc Willie to get off duty, after

COMMISSION EXHIBIT No. 1697

which they would have a few drinks together. He does not know of any contacts made by Ruby, if any, and believes that Ruby was sightseeing as any other tourist during his Cuban stay.

With regard to the relationship between Castro supporters and the Havana gambling community, Mc Willie advised that as soon as Castro came into power, all Americans had to leave and that as far as he knows, prior to this time, there was no understanding between representatives of the gambling industry and Castro's supporters. He recalled that as soon as Castro took over, the hired help, such as the waiters, rebelled against Casino management and American ownership was forced out of the gambling business. Prior to that time there had been only speculation as to the fate of gambling interests should a change in Government come about but Mc Willie knew of no arrangements or liaison between the gambling interests and Castro.

Mc Willie characterizes Ruby as being completely apolitical and to his knowledge has no connections with the Castro or Batista supporters. He never heard Ruby mention politics or any political connections except on one occasion in Dallas. Mc Willie indicated an acquaintance with Congressman Bruce Alger, either a Representative or Senator from Texas, whose wife was a patron of Ruby's night club. This acquaintance was more social and personal than political. Other than Alger, Mc Willie knows Ruby to be well acquainted with virtually every officer of the Dallas Police force and had an arrangement whereby off duty policemen were hired at Ruby's expense to maintain order in his night club. Here again Mc Willie did not feel that Ruby's acquaintance with police officers stemmed from political interests but rather that Ruby had a genuine liking for law enforcement officers. He also noted that Ruby is not a gambler and does not know the gambling business, further indicating to him that Ruby had no motive in visiting Cuba other than for a week of rest and relaxation.

Regarding prisoners of war, Mc Willie stated that he had not been imprisoned nor were any of his friends; however, he had heard that Harvey Harr, who had worked at the Nacional Casino had been imprisoned for a year after Castro took control. He has since seen Harr in Las Vegas but does not know his present whereabouts. He stated Harr was arrested after he, Mc Willie, left Havana. Mc Willie recalled that diplomatic relations between Cuba and the United States were abrogated on January 3, 1961, the day after Mc Willie left Cuba and that Harr had remained in Cuba after Mc Willie's departure. He does not know why Harr was arrested but expressed the belief that all Americans who had not heeded a warning to leave Havana faced arrest. To his knowledge, Harr and Ruby are not acquainted. Mc Willie stated that he personally left Havana to avoid arrest. He recalled a Captain Morgan whom he had known casually who had been with Castro in the mountains and whom he later understood had been arrested by Castro and put before a firing squad because he was not completely sympathetic with Castro's cause. He stated he does not know a Robert Mc Keown.

Mc Willie denied that he had had any contact with anyone concerning sale of jeeps or guns or the smuggling of refugees out of Cuba or release of any of Castro's prisoners. He stated that likewise to his knowledge Ruby had taken no action in behalf of such prisoners. He did recall that Ruby kept a couple of old guns at his residence, although he was not a gun collector. These were kept for his personal use as protection against intruders and not for any active aggressive use to the best of his knowledge. He feels certain that Ruby had no contact with anyone interested in the sale of weapons or jeeps under any circumstances.

With further regard to the air line ticket purchased by Mc Willie, he stated that as best he can recall, the peso evaluation of this ticket was about $75.00, and that he had personally absorbed the cost.

He could not be certain whether Ruby repaid him for this ticket after Ruby reached Havana, again explaining that he purchased the ticket at Havana and mailed it to Ruby at 1/5 of what it would cost Ruby to buy a comparable ticket in Dallas. He does not recall standing any other expenses for Ruby in connection with the trip and was unable to state whether Ruby had repaid him for the cost of the ticket or not.

Mc Willie did not see or hear from Ruby after Mc Willie returned to the United States except that in June, 1961, Mc Willie then in Florida, obtained employment at Lake Tahoe, Nevada, and en route from Miami to Lake Tahoe stopped in Dallas where he stayed overnight in Ruby's apartment. He saw Ruby only for about two or three hours on this occasion, during which time Ruby did not express any interest in politics or any other item of significance, conversation centering around their personal lives and Ruby's night club operation as separated from any political matters.

Concerning more recent contacts, Mc Willie stated he cannot be certain whether he wrote or called Ruby from Las Vegas to Dallas, Texas, requesting Ruby to obtain a pistol. He stated he knew Ruby could obtain a weapon in Dallas, probably more reasonably than Mc Willie could procure one in Las Vegas and that he had asked Ruby to send a weapon to him. He knows Ruby caused a weapon to be sent to him as he was notified of a parcel at the post office but that he did not want to go to the post office and pick it up and let it return to the dealer without ever seeing the weapon or taking it out of the post office.

He also believes Ruby called him at the Thunderbird Hotel-Casino where Mc Willie is employed regarding some union trouble Ruby was having in Dallas and requesting Mc Willie put him in touch with someone who could help him in this matter. Mc Willie contacted Bill Miller who formerly operated the Riverside Hotel at

Reno, Nevada, and believes he may have called Ruby back from his, Mc Willie's, residence advising Ruby to contact Miller. He believes Ruby later called him back, not recalling whether at the hotel or his residence, advising Mc Willie that he was going to meet with the American Guild of Variety Artists president in New York. He believes that Ruby later sent him a post card from New York stating that he had met the American Guild of Variety Artists president, and had ironed out all his troubles.

He stated he does not recall ever calling Ruby from the Thunderbird Hotel because of the complications of billing his personal calls through the hotel switchboard and that he definitely did not call from any of the Thunderbird pay stations. He stated that when he called Ruby, the call was on his residence phone and that he can recall no phone calls other than those mentioned above.

He stated he has had no contact with Ruby since the assassination of President Kennedy and could not have anticipated Ruby's killing of Oswald. He stated he had had no contact with Ruby's attorneys but that a reporter had called him from Dallas regarding the sale of arms and jeeps to Castro's interests. He stated that took place during the Ruby trial and that while he did not relish the thought of talking to a reporter, he very truthfully replied to this inquiry that he did not know what the reporter was talking about.

In summation, Mc Willie stated that his association with Ruby was strictly social and personal without any intertwined business interests or gambling interests, knowing that Ruby is not a gambler and does not understand the gambling business. He did not know of any political interests or activities on Ruby's part nor of any particular affinity Ruby might have for former President Kennedy. He stated he can only assume in retrospect from his knowledge of Ruby's personality that Ruby felt he would become a national hero by exterminating President Kennedy's assassin.

...concerning Eileen Rubenstein Kaminsky, Account No. 360-01-9972

On November 2, 1937, Eileen Rubenstein applied for a social security number, alleging the following:

Address:	624 S. Independence Boulevard Chicago, Illinois
Employer:	S. B. Adler Drug Stores 2035 N. Clark Street or 6800 N. Sheridan Road Chicago, Illinois
Date of birth:	July 11, 1917, in Chicago, Illinois
Parents' names:	Joseph Rubenstein and Fanny Turek

On October 22, 1948, she changed her name in our records to Eileen Kaminsky giving her address as 2146 N. Spaulding, Chicago, Illinois. She indicated that she was unemployed and that marriage was the reason for the change in name.

Mrs. Kaminsky's earnings record shows the following:

Year	Quarter(s)	Employer
1937	1st	No earnings reported.
	2nd	No earnings reported.
	3rd	No earnings reported.
	4th	S. B. Adler 6800 Sheridan Road Chicago, Illinois
1938	1st	S. B. Adler 6800 Sheridan Rd. Chicago, Illinois Adler Drug Co. 1620 E. 53rd Street Chicago, Illinois

COMMISSION EXHIBIT No. 1698

Year	Quarter(s)	Employer
1938	2nd	Adler Drug Co. 1620 E. 53rd Street Chicago, Illinois
	3rd	Adler Drug Co. 1620 E. 53rd Street Chicago, Illinois
	4th	Adler Drug Co. 1620 E. 53rd Street Chicago, Illinois
1939	1st	Adler Drug Co. 1620 E. 53rd Street Chicago, Illinois
	2nd	No earnings reported.
	3rd	No earnings reported.
	4th	Bryn Mawr Drug Co. 1039 Bryn Mawr Avenue Chicago, Illinois
1940	1st	Bryn Mawr Drug Co. 1039 Bryn Mawr Avenue Chicago, Illinois
	2nd	Bryn Mawr Drug Co. 1039 Bryn Mawr Avenue Chicago, Illinois
	3rd	Bryn Mawr Drug Co. 1039 Bryn Mawr Avenue Chicago Illinois S. B. Adler 6800 Sheridan Road Chicago, Illinois
	4th	No earnings reported.
1941	1st	No earnings reported.
	2nd	No earnings reported
	3rd	Continental Products Inc. 2036 S. Michigan Avenue Chicago, Illinois
	4th	No earnings reported.

COMMISSION EXHIBIT No. 1698—Continued

Year	Quarter(s)	Employer
1942	1st	No earnings reported.
	2nd	Hol-Mar Co. 125 W. Ohio Street Chicago, Illinois
	3rd	Hol-Mar Co. 125 W. Ohio Street Chicago, Illinois
	4th	Hol-Mar Co. 125 W. Ohio Street Chicago, Illinois
1943	All	Hol-Mar Co. 125 W. Ohio Street Chicago, Illinois
1944	All	Hol-Mar Co. 125 W. Ohio Street Chicago, Illinois
1945	All	Hol-Mar Co. 125 W. Ohio Street Chicago, Illinois
1946	1st	Jack, Sam & Earl Rubenstein Earl Products Co. 1144 S. St. Louis Avenue Chicago 24, Illinois
	2nd	Jack, Sam & Earl Rubenstein Earl Products Co. 1144 S. St. Louis Avenue Chicago 24, Illinois
	3rd	Jack, Sam & Earl Rubenstein Earl Products Co. 1144 S. St. Louis Avenue Chicago 24, Illinois Edward C. Ruttenberg Sales Inc. 222 W. North Bank Drive Chicago, Illinois
	4th	Edward C. Ruttenberg Sales Inc. 222 W. North Bank Drive Chicago, Illinois

Year	Quarter(s)	Employer
1947	1st	E. I. & George E. Pasternak Paramount Garment Co. 711 S. Dearborn Street Chicago 5, Illinois Edward C. Ruttenberg Sales Inc. 222 W. North Bank Drive Chicago 10, Illinois
	2nd	E. I. & George E. Pasternak Paramount Garment Co. 711 S. Dearborn Street Chicago 5, Illinois
	3rd	E. I. & George E. Pasternak Paramount Garment Co. 711 S. Dearborn Street Chicago 5, Illinois
	4th	E. I. & George E. Pasternak Paramount Garment Co. 711 S. Dearborn Street Chicago 5, Illinois
1948	1st	E. I. & George E. Pasternak Paramount Garment Co. 711 S. Dearborn Street Chicago 5, Illinois
	2nd	E. I. & George E. Pasternak Paramount Garment Co. 711 S. Dearborn Street Chicago 5, Illinois
	3rd	No earnings reported.
	4th	Jerome & Bernard Garber Jackie Sportswear Co. 326 W. Adams Street Chicago 6, Illinois
1949	1st	Bennie Schwartz & Joseph Lazar Bennie Schwartz Formals 318 W. Adams Street Chicago 6, Illinois Jerome & Bernard Garber Jackie Sportswear Co. 326 W. Adams Street Chicago 6, Illinois

Year	Quarter(s)	Employer
1949	2nd	Bennie Schwartz & Joseph Lazar Bennie Schwartz Formals 318 W. Adams Street Chicago 6, Illinois
	3rd	No earnings reported.
	4th	No earnings reported.
1950	1st	Sam & Earl R. Ruby Earl Products Co. 701 N. Sangamon Street Chicago 22, Illinois
	2nd	U. S. Millinery Corp. 314 S. Franklin Street Chicago 6, Illinois
	3rd	U. S. Millinery Corp. 314 S. Franklin Street Chicago 6, Illinois
	4th	U. S. Millinery Corp. 314 S. Franklin Street Chicago 6, Illinois
1951	1st	U. S. Millinery Corp. 314 S. Franklin Street Chicago 6, Illinois
		Sam & Earl R. Ruby Earl Products Co. 701 N. Sangamon Street Chicago 22, Illinois
	2nd	Sam & Earl R. Ruby Earl Products Co. 701 N. Sangamon Street Chicago 22, Illinois
	3rd	Sam & Earl R. Ruby Earl Products Co. 701 N. Sangamon Street Chicago 22, Illinois
	4th	Sam & Earl R. Ruby Earl Products Co. 701 N. Sangamon Street Chicago 22, Illinois

COMMISSION EXHIBIT No. 1698—Continued

Year	Quarter(s)	Employer
1952	1st	No earnings reported.
	2nd	No earnings reported.
	3rd	V.A. & R. Klama 9736 Lawndale Avenue Evergreen Park, Illinois
	4th	No earnings reported.
1953	All	No earnings reported.
1954	All	No earnings reported.
1955	All	No earnings reported.
1956	All	No earnings reported.
1957	All	No earnings reported.
1958	All	No earnings reported.
1959	All	No earnings reported.
1960	All	No earnings reported.
1961	All	No earnings reported.
1962	All	No earnings reported.
1963	All	No earnings reported.

COMMISSION EXHIBIT No. 1698—Continued

FD-302 (Rev. 1-25-60)

FEDERAL BUREAU OF INVESTIGATION

Commission Exhibit No. 1699

Date 7/17/64

1

EDWARD J. NERAD, Chief Administrative Officer, Family Court of Cook County, Illinois (FCCC), was interviewed in the office of MICHAEL F. HENEGHAN, Chief Probation Officer, FCCC, 2246 West Roosevelt Road. Mr. HENEGHAN was present during the interview.

NERAD advised that the notation "September 30, 1922; Blumenthal" which appears on the FCCC Master File Card for EVA RUBENSTEIN, Case No. 83383, and which does not appear anywhere in her legal file is explained as follows:

The Master File Card reflects any dates which the FCCC's procedure organization considered important. These did not necessarily reflect court appearances only; however, EVA RUBENSTEIN's FCCC Legal Files reflect only court appearances, dates on which either she or someone acting in her behalf would have appeared before the court.

With regard to the specific notation "September 30, 1922; Blumenthal," NERAD advised that this, in his considered opinion, involved the date on which a probation officer was asked to more or less supervise EVA RUBENSTEIN's dependency case. He stated the specifics concerning this as well as any of the minor details concerning EVA's connection with the court would have been contained in the Social Service File concerning her. This file he said would have been destroyed sometime ago because of age and is no longer available.

Mr. NERAD, after reviewing the EVA RUBENSTEIN FCCC Legal Files, advised that at no time had she ever had an Incorrigibility Hearing. With regard to EVA's reportedly being "released from probation April 23, 1926," NERAD advised that the court documents actually contain the wording concerning this hearing "permanent release from guardianship" and that the statement that she was released from "probation" on that date as previously set out was an error either on his part or Mr. HENEGHAN's.

Mr. NERAD at this point stated that when originally contacted by the FBI, he stated that Cook County Juvenile Court records from the period in which the RUBENSTEIN family was in contact with the court

On 7/15/64 at Chicago, Illinois File # 44-645

by SA HERBERT F. BRIICK/sbw Date dictated 7/17/64

2
CG 44-645

would be on microfilm record. He stated after searching for and locating the record, it was ascertained that they had not been microfilmed and the information obtained was from the original documents.

Mr. NERAD advised that the type of activity which might have resulted in incorrigibility proceedings concerning HYMAN and/or EVA RUBENSTEIN or any child could have been the result of a widely varied type of activity on a child's part from disobedience, truancy and simple misdemeanor to the most serious type of felony.

NERAD could make no definite statement as to whether incorrigibility proceedings were the normal concomitant of dependency hearings involving a broken or unstable home. He stated of the most often happening in his past experience which began in the 1930's was that it was more likely that a dependency hearing would be the outgrowth of an incorrigibility hearing. Once a child was declared incorrigible, an investigation into his background would indicate a broken or unstable home making dependency hearings necessary.

NERAD stated that the effect of a declaration of incorrigibility and placement on probation would vary with the probation officer assigned to the case and would depend upon the seriousness of the reason of the incorrigibility finding. Some probation officers, he stated, handled the child assigned to them on an individual basis and would only make them report if they felt it was necessary. NERAD stated that no record schedule on visits to the subject's home were set up and the probation officer used his own discretion in handling each case. He stated that if a child persisted in his incorrigibility, the ultimate punishment the court had would be to have sent him to St. Charles Training School, St. Charles, Illinois. He stated that apparently this did not happen to HYMAN RUBENSTEIN inasmuch as his Master Card File did not indicate that he had ever been sent there.

FD-302 (Rev. 3-3-59)

FEDERAL BUREAU OF INVESTIGATION

1

Date 7/20/64

EVA GRANT, 3929 Rawlins, telephone LA 6-6258, advised BERTHA MILLER, if alive, would be 80 years of age or more. She is the niece of Mrs. GRANT's mother, FANNIE RUBENSTEIN, the daughter of SARAH MOSKEWITZ (phonetic), Mrs. RUBENSTEIN's half-sister.

Mrs. GRANT said it is her understanding her mother had one brother, HARRY RUTLAND, deceased, and perhaps four sisters, SARAH being the oldest and who had a different father. BLANCHE and RACHEL LENA were full sisters of Mrs. RUBENSTEIN and there was another, first name not recalled. The only ones who came to this country, to her knowledge, were her mother, SARAH, and brother, HARRY. She said her mother corresponded with her sisters in Poland prior to World War I, but they were reportedly killed in a pogrom during World War I period.

Mrs. GRANT said she is uncertain as to brothers and sisters of her father, JOSEPH RUBENSTEIN. She said ABRAHAM RUBENSTEIN, father of Dr. HYMAN I. RUBENSTEIN, was a brother. She said there was another ABRAHAM RUBENSTEIN at one time in Chicago who was a nephew or cousin of her father.

She stated her parents were not given to joining organizations or attending meetings and she knew of no organization to which they belonged.

Mrs. GRANT stated BERTHA MILLER's husband is deceased. She was living in Chicago at an unrecalled address in 1958-59, but is understood to have moved to live with a daughter, BELLE (Mrs. HARRY) STERN in Milwaukee, Wisconsin. HARRY STERN was last known to be a distributor of automobile parts. Mrs. GRANT professed to be unable to supply addresses. Mrs. STERN has a daughter married to a doctor, name not known. Mrs. MILLER had a sister, FANNIE FINKLESTEIN, address unknown, and a brother, JACOB, deceased.

on 7/20/64 at Dallas, Texas File # DL 44-1639

by Special Agent MANNING C. CLEMENTS/ds 68 Date dictated 7/20/64

COMMISSION EXHIBIT No. 1700

2

DL 44-1639

Mrs. GRANT professed to have no information that any of her relatives have been members of the Communist Party or any subversive organization.

70

COMMISSION EXHIBIT No. 1700—Continued

FD-302 (Rev. 1-25-60) FEDERAL BUREAU OF INVESTIGATION

— Commission Exhibit No. 1701 —

Date July 23, 1964

1

Mrs. BELLE F. STERN, nee MILLER, also known as Mrs. HARRY S. STERN, 8500 West Lawrence Avenue, Milwaukee, Wisconsin, advised that she is the daughter of the late MEYER MILLER and BERTHA MILLER, nee MUSKOWITZ. Mrs. STERN stated that her mother, Mrs. BERTHA MILLER, nee MUSKOWITZ, was born in Poland about 1881 or 1882, now being approximately 82 years of age. She said that Mrs. MILLER has been ill with arteriosclerosis of several years' duration, and she consequently is senile. She said that Mrs. MILLER makes her home with her son, MORRIS MILLER (brother of Mrs. STERN) at Apartment Number 2, 2349 West Devon Avenue, Chicago, Illinois. She said that MORRIS MILLER (now approximately 50 years of age) suffered some mental upsets throughout his adult life, although he is now ambulatory and employed by his brother, SIDNEY (age approximately 56) in a delivery service business, operated from 5816 North Spaulding Avenue, telephone KE 9-9080, Chicago, Illinois.

Mrs. STERN acknowledged acquaintance with EVA GRANT of Dallas, Texas. Upon reflection, she stated it is her understanding that her maternal grandmother, the late Mrs. HYMAN MUSKOWITZ (given name unknown) was a sister of EVA GRANT's grandmother, name unknown. She stated that consequently her common ancestry with EVA GRANT consists of their great grandparents, names unknown. Mrs. STERN advised that she had no recollection of EVA GRANT's parents or siblings including JACK RUBY, nor was she able to identify the relationship of her family with any family named RUBENSTEIN or RUBY.

According to Mrs. STERN, her parents MEYER MILLER, born in Lithuania, and BERTHA MILLER, nee MUSKOWITZ, born in Poland, immigrated to the United States during the late nineteenth century and were married in New York City in the late 1890s. She recalled that BERTHA MILLER, nee MUSKOWITZ, had one brother, JACOB MUSKOWITZ, who died about 30 years ago, and two sisters, Mrs. LENA BATKIN, now deceased, and Mrs. FANNIE FINKLEMAN, age 90 plus, and presently a geriatric patient in an unknown nursing home in the Chicago, Illinois area. She said that seven other siblings of BERTHA MILLER, nee

On 7/21/64 at MILWAUKEE, WISCONSIN File # MI 44-173

by SA CHARLES F. AHERN & SA M. W. MEEKINS/sve Date dictated 7/23/64

MI 44-173
- 2 -

MUSKOWITZ died prior to attaining adulthood.

Mrs. STERN stated that she was born on October 11, 1902 and grew up in Chicago, Illinois. She said that upon her marriage 46 years ago she assumed residence in Wisconsin where she has resided continuously since. She said that consequently she has lived a considerable distance from the residence of her parents and siblings who have remained in the Chicago area. She explained that for this reason she has not maintained close contact with her more remote relatives. It is her recollection, however, that many years ago EVA GRANT, as a young girl, occasionally visited in the Chicago area.

The interview of Mrs. BELLE F. STERN took place in the presence of her husband, HARRY S. STERN whom she consulted from time to time for assistance in refreshing her recollection.

42

FD-302 (Rev. 1-25-60) FEDERAL BUREAU OF INVESTIGATION

Commission Exhibit No. 1702 Date 4/2/64

1

SAUL MOLDOFSKY, 2720 Bryn Mawr Avenue, telephone LOngbeach 1-7891, advised that he and his brother, SIDNEY, were in business as the Shelby Printing Company, 328 South Jefferson Street, Chicago, Illinois, from approximately 1938 to 1944. Prior to 1938, he was affiliated with the Globe Printing and Embossing Company, Chicago, Illinois.

He stated that in the latter part of December, 1941, or early January, 1942, he and EDWARD SCHWARTZ came upon the idea of promoting a "Remember Pearl Harbor" plaque. SCHWARTZ, according to MOLDOFSKY, said that he had the right man for the distribution and sale of the plaque, namely "SPARKY" RUBENSTEIN. Mr. MOLDOFSKY stated that RUBENSTEIN is identical with JACK RUBY, who shot and killed LEE HARVEY OSWALD.

MOLDOFSKY stated that he did not know JACK RUBY well and could recall no specific details concerning him. He stated that there were problems in getting out the "Remember Pearl Harbor" plaque because none of the proofs were acceptable to RUBY, whom SCHWARTZ described as a "perfectionist." He stated that it took anywhere from four to six weeks to develop a proof that was acceptable to RUBY and by that time, the market was flooded with the "Remember Pearl Harbor" idea and their promotion never materialized.

MOLDOFSKY stated that the entire business relationship with RUBY was handled by SCHWARTZ. This also included the filing of the copyright for the promotional idea. He said that the name Liberty Distributing Company sounded familiar to him, but he could not associate it with JACK RUBY. MOLDOFSKY stated that he, SCHWARTZ and the RUBENSTEINs lived in the same general neighborhood in Chicago around Roosevelt Road and California Avenue. He said he knew nothing of JACK RUBY's personal life and only recalls meeting JACK RUBY's brother, EARL, who also was a novelty salesman in the Chicago area. He stated that he did not know enough about EARL to offer

79

On 4/2/64 at Chicago, Illinois File # CG 44-645

by SA GEORGE HENRY BENIGNI/mav/rms Date dictated 4/2/64

COMMISSION EXHIBIT No. 1702

2

CG 44-645

any comment on him. The only associate that he knows of RUBY is SCHWARTZ.

In this regard, MOLDOFSKY offered that SCHWARTZ, who introduced him to EARL, probably could give a good insight into the background of JACK RUBY and his family. He stated that SCHWARTZ possibly lived with the RUBENSTEIN family for a period of time until he, SCHWARTZ, could get himself established in the Chicago area after arriving from Canada.

MOLDOFSKY advised that SCHWARTZ is currently in business as the Gardena Printers, Gardena, California.

MOLDOFSKY further stated that his brother, SIDNEY, is currently in business at the Howlan Printing Company, 1845 West Carroll, Chicago, Illinois. He stated that he feels certain that his brother never had any contact with JACK RUBY.

80

COMMISSION EXHIBIT No. 1702—Continued

FD-302 (Rev. 1-25-60) FEDERAL BUREAU OF INVESTIGA

Commission Exhibit No. 1703

1

Date 4/9/64

ART WAYNE, Television Producer and Director, 1970 Mandeville Canyon Road, Brentwood, California, furnished the following information:

He has recently returned from a picture making trip in Africa and was out of the country at the time of ex-President KENNEDY's death. He and JACK RUBY were childhood friends in Chicago many years ago. He resided on the West side of Chicago some four or five blocks from the apartment where the RUBINSTIEN family lived. He and JACK RUBY played sandlot baseball, basketball and a lot of handball together. At one time they were fellow members at the Medina Athletic Club in Chicago. JACK neither drank nor smoked and always kept himself in excellent physical condition.

The RUBINSTIENS were a poor family but were very repectable and to the best of his knowledge, all were very fine individuals. He does not recall how JACK made his living in Chicago as he grew into manhood. JACK had a car when he (WAYNE) was first getting into showbusiness and would drive him around to his various singing engagements at clubs and hotels in Chicago. JACK looked up to him as he became increasingly successful in showbusiness in the Chicago area and on many occasions would be in attendance at his various entertainment engagements. He left Chicago about twenty years ago and during this period has been completely out of touch with JACK RUBY. During this period, however, he has seen JACK's brother EARL on several occasions for brief visits.

He recalls JACK RUBY having a very violent temper and always seemed eager to take the part of the underdog in any altercation that confronted him. In one incident about twenty-five years ago when he and JACK were together on a downtown Chicago street, they happened to come upon a man using abusive language to an old lady. JACK took up for the lady and the two engaged in a bitter fight. Shortly thereafter JACK complained of being dizzy and after walking him around for a while, he took JACK to a hospital for treatment somewhere in the North side Chicago area, the name of the hospital not recalled. JACK spent at least several hours in the hospital and it is his recollection that he suffered a slight concussion.

On 4/8/64 at Brentwood, California File # Los Angeles 44-895

by SA PHILLIP B. DEILY/kls 16 Date dictated 4/9/64

2
LA 44-895

JACK would even engage in bitter fist fights with his brother, EARL, over matters which they disagreed upon. He feels that JACK RUBY, as well as they knew each other, would have not hesitated to punch him in the nose if he (WAYNE) had sufficiently aroused RUBY. There were other incidences, he cannot recall the specifics, where JACK would take up for the underdog and become violently aroused and in his opinion a normal individual would not react to similar situations in such a manner. He recalls that at one time, JACK's brother, EARL, took wrestling lessons and he suspects that EARL might have been motivated by reasons of self-preservation.

Because of the above conduct on the part of JACK, he seriously questions JACK's mental health since he does not feel that a normal healthy individual would have acted and reacted to certain situations as did JACK RUBY. He feels that JACK was completely loyal to his country, never knew him to carry a gun or to be involved in any trouble with law enforcement. He never knew LEE HARVEY OSWALD and has no knowledge of JACK ever associating with persons or organizations of questionable loyalty. He has always liked JACK RUBY, would never want to do or say anything that would be harmful to him, but honestly feels that JACK was not a mentally healthy person at the time of their association in Chicago.

17

SELECTIVE SERVICE SYSTEM
1724 F STREET NW.
WASHINGTON, D.C. 20435

OFFICE OF THE DIRECTOR

ADDRESS REPLY TO
THE DIRECTOR OF SELECTIVE SERVICE

August 5, 1964

Commission Exhibit No. 1704

TO : Mr. Murray Laulicht
President's Commission on the Assination of
President Kennedy
200 Maryland Avenue, N. E.
Washington, D. C.

FROM : Colonel Bernard T. Franck III
Chief, Office of Legislation, Liaison
and Public Information

SUBJECT: Class I-H

Pursuant to telephone conversation of yesterday, the following reference to Class I-H appears in a study of World War II operations, Selective Service System, Special Monograph No. 5, "The Classification Process":

Class I-H had been provided on August 31, 1941, to conform to the law as amended at that time, as the proper classification for registrants in Class I who had reached their twenty-eight birthday. This class was abolished November 19, 1942, after the law had been further amended to expunge that provision.

INSURE FREEDOM'S FUTURE—AND YOUR OWN—BUY UNITED STATES SAVINGS BONDS

COMMISSION EXHIBIT No. 1704

NATIONAL HEADQUARTERS
SELECTIVE SERVICE SYSTEM
451 INDIANA AVENUE NORTHWEST
WASHINGTON 25, D. C. 20435

OFFICE OF THE DIRECTOR

ADDRESS REPLY TO
THE DIRECTOR OF SELECTIVE SERVICE

Honorable J. Lee Rankin
Room 401, Veterans of Foreign Wars Building
200 Maryland Avenue, N. E.
Washington, D C. 20002

Subject: RUBENSTEIN, Jack
alias
RUBY, Jack

Dear Mr. Rankin:

This refers to your letter of March 6, 1964, requesting that this Headquarters forward to your office copies of all documents in the possession of Local Board No. 124, Chicago, Illinois, or elsewhere, relating to the subject registrant of the Selective Training and Service Act of 1940. Local Board No. 124 passed out of existence with the lapse of the 1940 Act on March 31, 1947.

The individual files of registrants of the Selective Training and Service Act of 1940 were destroyed in 1955, pursuant to National Archives Job No. II-NNA-1478, approved by the Joint Committee on the Disposition of Executive Papers in accordance with the Records Disposal Act of 1943, in House Report No. 198, dated March 10, 1955. The only remaining records concerning individuals registered under that Act are (1) the Registration Cards, (2) the Classification Records, a ledger showing the actions taken by the local board with respect to each individual, and (3) the files of aliens classified in Class IV-C, those who claimed exemption from military service because of their nationality. A copy of the Registration Card for Jack Rubenstein, and a transcript of the information contained in the Classification Record concerning him, all of his extant records, have previously been furnished your office.

The State Director of Selective Service for Massachusetts, in reply to my letter of March 11, 1964, has advised me that no record is found in his office of the registration of Jack Rubenstein on October 16, 1940, at Faneuil Hall, Boston, Massachusetts.

A search of the central files of this Headquarters, which have been accessioned by the Archivist of the United States, reveals no record that the case of the subject registrant was referred to

COMMISSION EXHIBIT No. 1705

Honorable Lee Rankin
Veterans of Foreign Wars Bldg. -2- 3-17-64

Washington at any time during the 1940 operation.

Should I be able to be of any further assistance in this case, I will be glad to cooperate to the best of my ability.

Sincerely yours,

Lewis B. Hershey
DIRECTOR

COMMISSION EXHIBIT No. 1705—Continued

Commission Exhibit No. 1706

RUBENSTEIN JACK

RUBENSTEIN — 36666107
(Last name) (Army serl. No.)

JACK — NONE
(First name) (Middle initial)

P.C.H. Air Corp
(Arm or service for which enlisted or inducted)

...r or race WHITE

...LACE X IN BOX INDICATING COMPONENT)

☐ Regular Army. ☐ National Guard of the United States.

...y of United States:

☐ For Regular Army units.
☐ For National Guard units.
☒ Selective Service and Training.

Regular Army Reserve—Active duty.

Enlisted Reserve Corps—Active duty.

SERVICE RECORD

covering period

...m MAY 21 1943, 19...., to ...., 19....

For instructions see AR 345-125

D., A. G. O. Form No. 24
(December 12, 1941)

16—25350-2

1

INDUCTION RECORD

(This induction record will be filled out only in case the man enters the service through induction by selective service)

Local board of origin: Chicago City-224
(Board No., city and State)

Date of arrival at induction station: MAY 21 1943

Date and place of induction: MAY 21 1943 Chicago, Ill.

By whom inducted: ... 2nd Lt. A.U.S.
(Name)
(Grade and arm or service)

Place to which sent: CAMP GRANT, ILLINOIS
(Post, camp, or reception center)

Date sent: MAY 28 1943

RECORDS OF IMMUNIZATION

(See par. 6, AR 40-215, for details relative to immunization records)

SMALLPOX VACCINATION

Date	Result [1]
7-2-43	Immune

TYPHOID VACCINATIONS

7-2-43	Comp

OTHER VACCINATIONS

Kind	Date
Tet. Tox 1st Dose	6-17-43
" " 2nd "	11 Oct 43
" " 3rd "	10 Nov 4_

DIPHTHERIA SUSCEPTIBILITY TEST—SCHICK

Date	Result [1]
	1st shot
Typhus	6-7-44
Cholera	6-7-44
Yellow Fever	6-7-44 B3354 1/2 cc

CARRIER EXAMINATIONS
(See AR 40-310)

Date	Parasite examined for	Kind of specimen [2]	Positive or negative
MAY 21 1943	X-Ray of Chest Essentially Normal		

[1] Record as vaccinia, vaccinoid, or immune reaction.
[2] Record as positive, positive combined, negative-pseudo or negative.
[3] Record as feces, urine, sputum, blood, etc.

B.T.O

2

INDUCTION ENLISTMENT RECORD

RUBENSTEIN JACK — 36 666 107
(Last name) (First name) (Middle initial) (Army serial No.)

Born: MARCH 27, 1911 CHICAGO, ILL.
(Month, day, and year) (City or town) (State or country)

Height 5 ft. 9 in. Weight 175 lb. Eyes BROWN Hair BROWN

Complexion DARK Size of gas mask Univ. Size of shoe 9 D

Married or single SINGLE Occupation SALESMAN

EDUCATIONAL QUALIFICATIONS

Years in: Grammar school 8 High school 1 College or university ....

Graduate work .... Specialized in ....

Speaks *English, ~~French, Spanish, German~~.

OCCUPATIONAL QUALIFICATIONS

SELLS NOVELTIES & PREMIUMS $ 3000.00 AR
(Main occupation) (Weekly wages)

Years .... as *apprentice, journeyman, expert.

Just what did he do? ....

.... $ ....
(Next best occupation) (Weekly wages)

Years .... as *apprentice, journeyman, expert.

Just what did he do? ....

HOME ADDRESS AND NEAREST RELATIVE

Home address: 3650 LEXINGTON
(Number and street or rural route; if none, so state)
CHICAGO, ILL.
(City, town, or post office) (State or country)

Name and address of nearest relative: ~~FANNIE RUBENSTEIN~~
(Name)
~~MOTHER 3650 LEXINGTON~~
(Relationship) (Number and street or rural route; if none, so state)
~~CHICAGO, ILL.~~
(City, town, or post office) (State or country)

Person to be notified in case of emergency: Earl ... RUBENSTEIN
(Name)
BROTHER 3650 LEXINGTON
(Relationship; if friend, so state) (Number and street or rural route; if none, so state)
CHICAGO, ILL.
(City, town, or post office) (State or country)

SEE REMARKS ...

DESIGNATION OF BENEFICIARY

(To be entered only from appropriate enlistment or induction record or W. D., A. G. O. Form No. 41)

~~1 FANNIE RUBENSTEIN MOTHER~~
(Name and degree of relationship of beneficiary)
~~3650 LEXINGTON, CHICAGO, ILL.~~
(Address)

(2) ~~HYMAN RUBENSTEIN BROTHER~~
(Name and degree of relationship of alternate beneficiary)
~~3650 LEXINGTON, CHICAGO, ILL.~~
(Address)

(3) MARIAN RUBENSTEIN SISTER
(Name and degree of relationship of alternate beneficiary)
3650 LEXINGTON, CHICAGO, ILL.
(Address)

CURRENT ~~ENLISTMENT~~ INDUCTION

(See "Remarks—Financial" (par. 3c, AR 345-125))

Age at enlistment 32 years 2 months.

†Accepted for service at ....

†Enlisted at .... on the .... day of ...., 19....

in grade of .... by ....

for ....
(Company, regiment, arm, or service)

to serve D OF W PLUS 6 MOS years.
(Words and figures)

Completed 0 years 0 months 0 days for longevity pay, at enlistment. Has over 0 years' service.

(Initials of officer)

Physical defects at enlistment ....

* Strike out words not applicable.
† No entry required for men secured through Selective Service.

16—25350-2

PRIOR SERVICE

First show prior service in the Regular Army, then insert headings to show service in the United States Army, Volunteers, Navy, Marine Corps, and National Guard or Organized Militia, in the order named.

______ from ______, 19__, to ______, 19__
(Co., regt., arm, or service)
Discharged as ______ (Grade); ______ (Character); By reason of ______
(Data required by par. 8, AR 345-125)

______ from ______, 19__, to ______, 19__
(Co., regt., arm, or service)
Discharged as ______ (Grade); ______ (Character); By reason of ______
(Data required by par. 8, AR 345-125)

______ from ______, 19__, to ______, 19__
(Co., regt., arm, or service)
Discharged as ______ (Grade); ______ (Character); By reason of ______
(Data required by par. 8, AR 345-125)

______ from ______, 19__, to ______, 19__
(Co., regt., arm, or service)
Discharged as ______ (Grade); ______ (Character); By reason of ______
(Data required by par. 8, AR 345-125)

______ from ______, 19__, to ______, 19__
(Co., regt., arm, or service)
Discharged as ______ (Grade); ______ (Character); By reason of ______
(Data required by par. 8, AR 345-125)

______ from ______, 19__, to ______, 19__
(Co., regt., arm, or service)
Discharged as ______ (Grade); ______ (Character); By reason of ______
(Data required by par. 8, AR 345-125)

______ from ______, 19__, to ______, 19__
(Co., regt., arm, or service)
Discharged as ______ (Grade); ______ (Character); By reason of ______
(Data required by par. 8, AR 345-125)

______ from ______, 19__, to ______, 19__
(Co., regt., arm, or service)
Discharged as ______ (Grade); ______ (Character); By reason of ______
(Data required by par. 8, AR 345-125)

______ from ______, 19__, to ______, 19__
(Co., regt., arm, or service)
Discharged as ______ (Grade); ______ (Character); By reason of ______
(Data required by par. 8, AR 345-125)

______ from ______, 19__, to ______, 19__
(Co., regt., arm, or service)
Discharged as ______ (Grade); ______ (Character); By reason of ______
(Data required by par. 8, AR 345-125)

______ from ______, 19__, to ______, 19__
(Co., regt., arm, or service)
Discharged as ______ (Grade); ______ (Character); By reason of ______
(Data required by par. 8, AR 345-125)

COMMISSION EXHIBIT No. 1706—Continued

MILITARY QUALIFICATIONS

Served as ______ (Highest grade held) in the United States Army in the World War
Holds commission as ______ (Grade) ______ (Station) in the Officers' Reserve Corps
Graduate of Sec Sea 13 (Noncommissioned officers' or special service school)

ARMY SPECIALTY

Specialty	*Rating, with date	*Rerating, with date
A.P. Eng Mech 747	5/sk 3/26/44	

* Ex=Excellent; VG=Very good; G=Good; F=Fair.

SPECIAL DUTY

As	At	From	To	Authority
A.M. Student	T.S.I FLD, N.C.	5 Sept 43	11 Feb 44	SO 43 F-44
Student 747 P.V.Z.	[illegible]	2/14/44	3/23/44	

ARTICLES OF WAR
(Read to soldier as required by the 110th Article of War)

Date	Initials	Date	Initials
6/6/43	[illegible]	6 JAN 1946	[illegible]
6 Sept 43	[illegible]		
[illegible]	[illegible]		

SEX MORALITY
Course completed (see AR 40-235) Sec 13 6/6/43, 19__

QUALIFICATION IN ARMS
(Special qualifications attained in the use of the various arms and additional compensation therefor)

Qualified as ______ (Grade designation), 19__
Compensation $______ per month. Aggregate or final score ______
Order publishing fact of qualification ______ (Number) (Source) (Date)

Qualified as ______ (Grade designation), 19__
Compensation $______ per month. Aggregate or final score ______
Order publishing fact of qualification ______ (Number) (Source) (Date)

Qualified as ______ (Grade designation), 19__
Compensation $______ per month. Aggregate or final score ______
Order publishing fact of qualification ______ (Number) (Source) (Date)

Qualified as ______ (Grade designation), 19__
Compensation $______ per month. Aggregate or final score ______
Order publishing fact of qualification ______ (Number) (Source) (Date)

Qualified as ______ (Grade designation), 19__
Compensation $______ per month. Aggregate or final score ______
Order publishing fact of qualification ______ (Number) (Source) (Date)

16—28260-1

COMMISSION EXHIBIT No. 1706—Continued

[M]ILITARY RECORD

AP[POINTMENT], PROMOTION, OR REDUCTION, WITH AUTHORITY THEREFOR

Grade	Date	Authority	Initials
Pvt	[illegible]	[illegible]	
Pvt	21 Mar 43	[illegible]	[illegible]
PFC (T)	12-1-44	[illegible] AAB CHATHAM FLD GA	[illegible]

SPECIALIST RATINGS

Class	Qualification	From	To	Authority	Initials

ORGANIZATIONS TO WHICH ATTACHED

Organization	From	To
Co. B, 1633 S U Camp Grant, Ill	6/4/43	6/9/43.
[illegible]	[illegible]	
Sick Eng Dp KF Miss	6-10-43	9-3-43
792 [illegible] Seymour-Johnson Field, N.C.	5 Sept 43	15 Feb 44

ORIGINAL ASSIGNMENT AND ORGANIZATIONS TO WHICH SUBSEQUENTLY ASSIGNED DURING THIS ENLISTMENT PERIOD

Assigned to company, regiment, arm, or service	Station	Date
225 Stat Crew Sec	Blumenthal Fld NC	4-26-44
114 AAF BU Sec H	C F Ga	6-9-44
Sq D 324th	B U C F Ga	[illegible] JAN 45
Sq M 324th	B U C F Ga	8 SEP 45
301st AAF BU Sq K 3AF	CAP, Drew Fld, Fla.	27 Nov 45
300 [illegible]	Tampa Fla	28 Dec 45

[illegible] added 2/16/44

COMMISSION EXHIBIT No. 1706—Continued

5

MILITARY RECORD

Appointment, Promotions Or Reduction, with Authority Therefor

Grade	Date	Authority	Initials

SPECIALIST RATINGS

Class	Qualif.	From	To	Auth	Init

ORGANIZATIONS TO WHICH ATTACHED

Organization	From	To
18TH AAFTTD	FEB 16 1944	MAR 23 1944

ORGINAL ASSIGNMENT AND ORGANIZATIONS TO WHICH SUBSEQUENTLY ASSIGNED DURING THIS ENLISTMENT PERIOD

Asgd. to Co., Regiment, arm or service	Station	Date

COMMISSION EXHIBIT No. 1706—Continued

6

FURLOUGES

From 24 Mar 44 to 11 April 44 (9 da)
Authority AR 615-275
Extended 10 (Number of days) per TWX 326 Fi GP
Rejoined 12 April 44

From 5 Nov. 1944 to 18 Nov. 1944
Authority AR 615-275
Extended (Number of days) per
Rejoined 17 Nov. 1944

From 5 MAY 1945 to 24 MAY 1945
Authority AR 615-275
Extended (Number of days) per
Rejoined 25 MAY 1945

From 15 DEC. 45 to 2 JAN. 46
Authority Par 11A (v) AR 615-275 4 days T.T.
Extended 5 (Number of days) per USCG
Rejoined 8 JAN. 1946

From .... to ....
Authority ....
Extended (Number of days) per ....
Rejoined ....

From .... to ....
Authority ....
Extended (Number of days) per ....
Rejoined ....

From .... to ....
Authority ....
Extended (Number of days) per ....
Rejoined ....

FOREIGN SERVICE

Left United States for duty in ....
From .... on ...., 19....
Arrived at .... on ...., 19....
Left .... for the United States on ...., 19....
Arrived at .... on ...., 19....
Left United States for duty in ....
From .... on ...., 19....
Arrived at .... on ...., 19....
Left .... for the United States on ...., 19....
Arrived at .... on ...., 19....

MEDALS, DECORATIONS, AND CITATIONS

Name of decoration	Authority and date
Good Conduct Medal	Ge 13, [illegible] 25 Nov 45
AM Campaign Medal	WD CIR 326, 25 Oct 45
World War II Victory Medal	

16—28250-1

COMMISSION EXHIBIT No. 1706—Continued

7

TIME LOST PRIOR TO THE NORMAL DATE OF EXPIRATION OF TERM OF ENLISTMENT TO BE MADE GOOD UNDER 107th ARTICLE OF WAR:

(a) Absence without proper authority or in desertion.

From	To	Days

(b) Time actually in confinement under sentence or while awaiting trial and disposition of case, if trial resulted in conviction.

From	To	Days

(c) Unable to perform duty through the intemperate use of drugs or alcoholic liquor or through disease or injury the result of his own misconduct.

From	To	Days

ABSENCE SUBSEQUENT TO THE NORMAL DATE OF EXPIRATION OF TERM OF ENLISTMENT

(a) Absence without proper authority or in desertion.

From	To	Days

(b) Time actually in confinement under sentence or while awaiting trial and disposition of case, if trial resulted in conviction.

From	To	Days

(c) Unable to perform duty through the intemperate use of drugs or alcoholic liquor or through disease or injury the result of his own misconduct.

From	To	Days

COMMISSION EXHIBIT No. 1706—Continued

RECORD OF TRIALS BY COURTS MARTIAL

________ C. M., ______ (No.) A. W. ______ (Date of offense) 19___ ______ (Synopsis of specifications)

Sentence announced and adjudged ______, 19___

Sentence as approved ______

______ Approved ______, 19___

I certify the above is correct.

______ (Name, grade, and organization)

Unexecuted portion of confinement and forfeiture remitted per ______

Released from confinement ______, 19___

______ (Name, grade, and organization)

________ C. M., ______ (No.) A. W. ______ (Date of offense) 19___ ______ (Synopsis of specifications)

Sentence announced and adjudged ______, 19___

Sentence as approved ______

______ Approved ______, 19___

I certify the above is correct.

______ (Name, grade, and organization)

Unexecuted portion of confinement and forfeiture remitted per ______

Released from confinement ______, 19___

______ (Name, grade, and organization)

________ C. M., ______ (No.) A. W. ______ (Date of offense) 19___ ______ (Synopsis of specifications)

Sentence announced and adjudged ______, 19___

Sentence as approved ______

______ Approved ______, 19___

I certify the above is correct.

______ (Name, grade, and organization)

Unexecuted portion of confinement and forfeiture remitted per ______

Released from confinement ______, 19___

______ (Name, grade, and organization)

________ C. M., ______ (No.) A. W. ______ (Date of offense) 19___ ______ (Synopsis of specifications)

Sentence announced and adjudged ______, 19___

Sentence as approved ______

______ Approved ______, 19___

I certify the above is correct.

______ (Name, grade, and organization)

Unexecuted portion of confinement and forfeiture remitted per ______

Released from confinement ______, 19___

______ (Name, grade, and organization) 16—25350-1

COMMISSION EXHIBIT No. 1706—Continued

INSERT TO SERVICE RECORD
ALLOTMENTS, Class A & B Continued

Class F deduction of pay authorized as follows:
$ 22.00 per month, commencing July 1 1943, and expiring with termination of service, in favor of

(Name) (Relationship)

Fannie Rutkowski Rubenstein mother

Joseph (none) Rubenstein father

Application filed June 7/43 ___

Discontinued ______ 19__

Reason ______

Discontinuance forwarded ______ 19__

By ______
(name and grade of forwarding officer

Acknowledgement received ______ 19__

COMMISSION EXHIBIT No. 1706—Continued

S______ and adjudged ______

Sentence as approved ______

______ Approved ______, 19___

I certify the above is correct.

______ (Name, grade, and organization)

Unexecuted portion of confinement and forfeiture remitted per ______

Released from confinement ______, 19___

______ (Name, grade, and organization)

________ C. M., ______ (No.) A. W. ______ (Date of offense) 19___ ______ (Synopsis of specifications)

Sentence announced and adjudged ______, 19___

Sentence as approved ______

______ Approved ______, 19___

I certify the above is correct.

______ (Name, grade, and organization)

Unexecuted portion of confinement and forfeiture remitted per ______

Released from confinement ______, 19___

______ (Name, grade, and organization)

________ C. M., ______ (No.) A. W. ______ (Date of offense) 19___ ______ (Synopsis of specifications)

Sentence announced and adjudged ______, 19___

Sentence as approved ______

______ Approved ______, 19___

I certify the above is correct.

______ (Name, grade, and organization)

Unexecuted portion of confinement and forfeiture remitted per ______

Released from confinement ______, 19___

______ (Name, grade, and organization)

CLASS E ALLOTMENTS

Class E allotments of pay authorized as follows:

$______ per month for ______ months, commencing ______, 19___

and expiring ______, 19___, in favor of ______

______ for the purpose of ______

Discontinued ______, 19___, reason ______

W. D., A. G. O. Form No. 30, mailed to Finance Officer, U. S. Army, Washington, D. C., ______, 19___, by ______ (Name and grade of forwarding officer)

Acknowledgment of discontinuance received ______, 19___

insert attached page 9 7-1-43

COMMISSION EXHIBIT No. 1706—Continued

$______ per month for ______ months, commencing ______________, 19____
and expiring ______________, 19____, in favor of ______________
______________ for the purpose of ______________
Discontinued ______________, 19____, reason ______________
W. D., A. G. O. Form No. 30, mailed to Finance Officer, U. S. Army, Washington, D. C., ______________, 19____, by ______________
(Name and grade of forwarding officer)
Acknowledgment of discontinuance received ______________, 19____

$______ per month for ______ months, commencing ______________, 19____
and expiring ______________, 19____, in favor of ______________
______________ for the purpose of ______________
Discontinued ______________, 19____, reason ______________
W. D., A. G. O. Form No. 30, mailed to Finance Officer, U. S. Army, Washington, D. C., ______________, 19____, by ______________
(Name and grade of forwarding officer)
Acknowledgment of discontinuance received ______________, 19____

NATIONAL SERVICE LIFE INSURANCE
~~GOVERNMENT INSURANCE~~

Allmt NSL
Deduction of pay for ~~Government insurance~~ authorized as follows:
Class ~~D~~ N insurance ~~deduction of~~ Allmt $ 7.30 per month for indef months,
commencing June 1/43, 19____, and expiring indef, 19____
for payment of monthly premium on $ 10,000 Discontinued ______________, 19____
reason ______________ W. D., A. G. O. Form No. 30, mailed to Veterans' Administration, Washington, D. C., on ______________, 19____
by ______________
(Name and grade of forwarding officer)

Deduction of pay for Government insurance authorized as follows:
Class D insurance deduction of $______________ per month for ______________ months,
commencing ______________, 19____, and expiring ______________, 19____
for payment of monthly premium on $______________ Discontinued ______________, 19____
reason ______________ W. D., A. G. O. Form No. 30, mailed to Veterans' Administration, Washington D. C., on ______________, 19____
by ______________
(Name and grade of forwarding officer)

Deduction of pay for Government insurance authorized as follows:
Class D insurance deduction of $______________ per month for ______________ months,
commencing ______________, 19____, and expiring ______________, 19____
for payment of monthly premium on $______________ Discontinued ______________, 19____
reason ______________ W. D., A. G. O. Form No. 30, mailed to Veterans' Administration, Washington, D. C., on ______________, 19____
by ______________
(Name and grade of forwarding officer) 16—28250-1

DEPOSITS

Date	Amount Dol.	Amount Ct.	Total amount Dol.	Total amount Ct.	Name and grade of finance officer accepting deposit	Initials
______ and ____/100 Dollars.						
______ and ____/100 Dollars.						
______ and ____/100 Dollars.						
______ and ____/100 Dollars.						
______ and ____/100 Dollars.						
______ and ____/100 Dollars.						
______ and ____/100 Dollars.						
______ and ____/100 Dollars.						
______ and ____/100 Dollars.						
______ and ____/100 Dollars.						
______ and ____/100 Dollars.						
______ and ____/100 Dollars.						
______ and ____/100 Dollars.						
______ and ____/100 Dollars.						
______ and ____/100 Dollars.						

PAY DETAINED BY COURTS MARTIAL ENTERED ON PAY ROLL

Month	Amount Dol.	Amount Ct.	Vou. No.	Name and grade of finance officer	Accounts for
______, 19____					
______, 19____					
______, 19____					
______, 19____					

CLOTHING ACCOUNT

CLOTHING DRAWN

Date of issue	Money value clothing	Initials	Date of issue	Money value clothing	Initials

GRATUITOUS ISSUE OF CLOTHING

CLOTHING SETTLEMENTS

Date	Due soldier	Due United States	Roll on which collected	Initials*
______ and ____/100 Dollars.				
______ and ____/100 Dollars.				
______ and ____/100 Dollars.				
______ and ____/100 Dollars.				
______ and ____/100 Dollars.				
______ and ____/100 Dollars.				
______ and ____/100 Dollars.				
______ and ____/100 Dollars.				
______ and ____/100 Dollars				
______ and ____/100 Dollars.				

* Initials of organization commander. 16—28250-1

Under this heading will be shown all financial matters not entered elsewhere such as stoppages for loss of or damage to Government property, amounts due on account of partial payments, overpayments, etc.

Enlistment allowance of $ ____

for the grade of ____

paid by ____

at ____ 19__

Entitled to travel pay to ____ (Place at which accepted for previous enlistment)

Received no travel pay upon discharge on ____, 19__ to reenlist.

Date	Description and amount due U. S. or soldier	Roll on which collected
WD AGO FORM 23 ISSUED		1943
	JUNE 4	1943
I desire cl f ded com July 1,1943.		
	Jack Rubenstein	
	DUE FROM GAIG	
	for ECONO	
	JUL	
	Sol Filed Appn under service men's dependents allowance act of 1942 for class F in the amount of $22.00 from 7-1-43	
	AUG 43 PAID	
14-Feb-44	Last Paid 31 Jan-44.	
14-Feb 44	DUE US QM LDRY $2.00	Feb/44
	FEB	44 PAID
15 Mar/44	Due U.S. Part. Pay 12.00 Vou 325237 Accts of C. K. Lichter, Col. F.D.	
3/23/44	Due US. Q M Ldry 0.40 Feb/44	
3/23/44	Due US. Q.M. Ldry 0.90 Mar/44	
4-26-44	Due Sol fur rats from 3/ [illegible] to 19 April incl.	
	MAR 44 PAID	
	APR 44 PAID	

COMMISSION EXHIBIT No. 1706—Continued

Date	Description and amount due U. S. or soldier	Roll on which collected
		MAR 44 PAID
7 June 44	Due US M/R Ldry $1.50	
	JUL 44 PAID	JUN 44 PAID
JUL 12	Due US M/R Ldry	
AUG 4 '44	DUE US M/R LDRY $1.50	
		AUG 44 PAID
7 SEP '44	DUE US M/R LDRY $1.50	
		SEP 44 PAID
		OCT 44 PAID
OCT '44	DUE US M/R LDRY $1.50	
17 NOV '44	DUE US M/R LDRY $1.50	
20 Nov 44	[illegible]	
		NOV 44 PAID
1 DEC '44	Cptd Pfc fr Pvt [illegible] 338 Chatham Fld, Ga	1 DEC '44
		DEC 44 PAID
18 DEC '44	DUE US M/R LDRY $1.50	JAN 45 PAID
JAN '45	DUE US M/R LDRY $1.50	
		FEB 45 PAID
23 FEB '45	DUE US M/R LDRY $1.50	MAR 45 PAID
19 MAR '45	DUE US M/R LDRY $1.50	
		APR 45 PAID
14 APR '45	DUE US M/R LDRY $1.50	
8 MAY '45	DUE US M/R LDRY $1.50	
		MAY 45 PAID
30 MAY '45	Due Sol C of R For Furlough fr 5/5/45 to 5/24/45 Incl.	
		JUN 45 PAID
	DUE US M/R LDRY $1.50	
JUL 45 PAID		
21 JUL '45	DUE US M/R LDRY $1.50	
		AUG 45 PAID
23 AUG '45	DUE US M/R LDRY $1.50	JUL '45
	SEP 4 5 1945	
13 SEP '45	DUE US M/R LDRY $1.50	AUG '45
11 OCT '45	DUE US M/R LDRY $1.50	SEP '45
10-31-45		OCT 45 PAID

1 insert added Nov 45

COMMISSION EXHIBIT No. 1706—Continued

INSERT TO SERVICE RECORD

REMARKS—FINANCIAL—Continued

Date	Description and amount due U. S. or soldier	Roll on which collected
16 NOV	DUE US M/R LDRY $1.50	
3 Nov 45	Due U.S. L'DRY $1.50	NOV
26 Nov 45	Due US P/P $20.00 pd Nov 45 incl, sig W.H. Pucell, Capt, AC	
1 JAN 1946	Last Pd to incl	31 DEC 1945
	Last Pd to incl	31 JAN 46
FEB 14 '46	Due U.S. $1.50 Ldry.	
'46	Due So. Fuel Rat. Jan	3 To Jan 7

WD AGO FORM 24-4
1 MAY 1937

1 insert

COMMISSION EXHIBIT No. 1706—Continued

REMARKS—ADMINISTRATIVE

Under this heading will be shown all administrative matter not shown elsewhere and not of a character authorizing pay. Show wounds, battles, engagements, etc., and such other entries not set forth elsewhere as may be required to make soldier's record complete.

[illegible]

Religious Preference: Jewish

[illegible]

Grant, Ill. on MAY 28 1943

[illegible]

(1) Amended NS Ins Act Explained

Major, Infantry

[illegible] 5/23/43

Dog Tags issued 5/23/43 Kees[ler] Fld Miss.

RCA 86

G.C.T 108-D

M.A.-2 90

Completed 8 weeks basic training

Keesler Field, Miss.

Qualified for Combat Crew per Med. Insp. O.

Keester Field, Miss., dated JUN 17 1943

Carbine Cal 30 Fam 45 rds 8-2-43

Sub Mach Cal 45 Fam 25 rds 8-2-43

Rifle 30 Cal Qual 70 rds Unqual 8-2-43

~~Pistol 45 Cal Qual 45 rds~~

SEX MORALITY LECT 6 Sep 43

Sex Hygiene [illegible] 6 Sept 43

Physical Fitness Test - score 47

Keesler Fld Miss 28 June 43

(2) Insert Added 12 FEB 44
3rd insert 3/18/44

(1) insert to Page 15 attached.
15 June 43

COMMISSION EXHIBIT No. 1706—Continued

INSERT TO SERVICE RECORD
REMARKS-ADMINISTRATIVE CONT'D.

Reported for active duty at [illegible] Co. Grant, Ill. on June 4, 1943

G. E. Johnson
G. E. JOHNSON
CAPT. A.G.D.
ASS'T. ADJUTANT

I certify that to the best of my knowledge I am in the same physical condition as at the time of induction.

Jack Rubenstein
(Signature of Soldier)

A physical inspection indicates that this man is in the same physical condition as at the time of induction.
Date of inspection

Martin J. Rosenthal
MARTIN J. ROSENTHAL
MAJOR MEDICAL CORPS

The benefits of National Service Life Insurance explained to soldier.

G. G. Kuns
G.G. KUNS
CAPT. INF.
ASS'T. ADJUTANT

Reordered to active duty 6/4 1943 as per SO # 35 Par # 3 dated 5/28-1943.

(1)

COMMISSION EXHIBIT No. 1706—Continued

ADMINISTRATIVE PAGE 15

Graduated; Airplane Mechanics Course; TS, AAF, ETTC, Seymour Johnson Field, N.C. Date 11-Feb-44
1st and 2nd echelon maintenance light bombardment type aircraft, and R-1820 and 2600 engines

Completed equivalent of 4 Wks., basic training at Seymour Johnson Field, N.C.
Fired Carbine M-1 30-cal., 145 Rounds. Qualification Course
Marksman Rating 163
Fired Thompson Sub-Machine Gun 45 cal., 25 Rounds Familiarization Course.
Date Fired 10 Feb 1944

Soldier ~~not~~ is recommended for Good Conduct Medal. Date 14-Feb 1944

2 (2)

COMMISSION EXHIBIT No. 1706—Continued

INSERT TO S/R (Cont'd)
REMARKS-ADMINISTRATIVE

16th AAF Tech. Tng. Det.
Republic Avn. Corp.
Farmingdale, New York
Grad. Factory Tng Course
AP.ENG. MECH. P-47
3/21/44 Total Hrs: 224
Final Wtd. Gr: 80.7
Sol Completed [illegible] at Keesler Fld Miss
Advanced First & Second
Echelon Maint. P-47

Sol Completed 1/2 prescribed Courses in Medical Training and Malaria Control. 6-7-44

Sol favorably Recommended for Good Conduct Medal on Transfer - 6-7-44

Comp lectures in Mal. Control, PERS. ADJ, ORIENTATION, FIRST AID, Fld Sanitation, Venereal presence 15 July 1944

COMP 6hrs C W TNG
CHATHAM FLD. GA. 18 AUG 1944

PPS-211111 C/FLD, GA 1-8-45

114th AAF Base Unit discontinued
30 April 1945 per G.O. #31 Hq 1AF
dtd 21 April 1945. 2114th AAF BU
d[illegible] 1945 per G.O. No.
40 [illegible] Air Force dtd 24 April
19[illegible]

(3)

(1) insert to page 15 attached.
15 June [illegible]

COMMISSION EXHIBIT No. 1706—Continued

INSERT TO SERVICE RECORD

REMARKS—ADMINISTRATIVE—Continued

AUTHORIZED [illegible] CAMPAIGN
RIBBON AND [illegible] MEDAL [illegible]
WD CIR 325, 25 OCT [illegible]

Sol. Favorably Considered for Good Conduct Award
AAB, Chatham Fld. Ga. CLAJP 26 NOV 45

NEAREST relative:
EARL RUBENSTEIN (BROTHER)
3650 LEXINGTON St,
CHICAGO, ILL.

DESIGNATION OF BENEFICIARIES:
(1) SEE PAGE 2
(2) EARL RUBENSTEIN (BROTHER)
(ADDRESS AS ABOVE)

WD AGO [illegible] #41 - 26 Nov. 45

Disch. Auth. AR 615-368 RR 1-1
A.EPMP 1841 17 JAN 46

W. D., A. G. O. Form No. 24-3
May 1, 1937

(4)

3-8655

COMMISSION EXHIBIT No. 1706—Continued

16

INDORSEMENTS

These indorsements are filled out in all cases when a soldier deserts or is transferred from one company or detachment to another company or detachment and in all changes of station except with an organization, and upon transfer to inactive status. These indorsements will not be used when a soldier is only attached to another organization for either rations or quarters or both.

1st Ind.

1633 S U Camp Grant, Ill.,
June 9, 19 43.

To Co. AAF TP RTC Keesler Fld., Miss.

This soldier was transferred to yr. comd.
per Par 3, S O 51 - HQ 1613th. SU Camp Grant, Ill
and left this organization June 9, 1943.

He was last paid to include [illegible] date, 19
by [illegible]
(Name and grade of finance officer or agent officer, if any)

Due United States; if nothing, so state nothing.

*Due soldier at date of nothing.

F ded.

This soldier †has / †has not a Class E allotment running which has been deducted from his pay to include not deducted., 19

This soldier has authorized a Class N deduction for Government insurance which has been deducted from his pay to include not deducted., 19

His character is unknown

Efficiency rating as soldier unknown.

I have personally verified all entries in this indorsement.

[signature]
(Name)
G. E. J[illegible]SON, Capt., A. G. D.
(Grade and organization)

This soldier reported 6-11, 19 43

*Here enter any amounts due soldier and not paid to date, such as monetary allowance in lieu of quarters and subsistence; if nothing, so state.
†Strike out words not applicable.
16—25259-2

COMMISSION EXHIBIT No. 1706—Continued

Initials	Authority	Date	Grade

APPOINTMENT, PROMOTION, OR REDUCTION, WITH AUTHORITY THEREFOR

MILITARY

3D

To CO, Sheppard Fld, Texas ..., 19...

This soldier was transferred to ... yr comd pp 3 SO 2 Hq ACTS

per ...

and left this organization ... AUG ... 1943

He was last paid to include ... JUL 31 1943 ..., 19...

by C. H. BURD, Major, FD
(Name and grade of finance officer or agent officer, if any)

Due United States; if nothing, so state ...

Void

Void

* Due soldier at date of ... Transfer-Accrued Pay

This soldier †has / †has not a Class E allotment running which has been deducted from his pay to include JUL 31 1943 ..., 19...

This soldier has authorized a Class D deduction for Government insurance which has been deducted from his pay to include JUL 31 1943 ..., 19...

His character is Not Observed

Efficiency rating as soldier Not Observed

I have personally verified all entries in this indorsement.

(Name)

(Grade and organization)

This soldier reported ..., 19...

*Here enter any amounts due soldier and not paid to date, such as monetary allowance in lieu of quarters and subsistence; if nothing, so state.
†Strike out words not applicable.

Jack Ruby 36666 107

INSERT TO SERVICE RECORD

2nd Ind.

51st Tr. Co.
Keesler Field, Miss. SEP 3 1943 ..., 19...

To ... 2d AAF ...

This soldier was transferred to ... yr comd pp 1 SO 24 Hq. ACTS,

per 8-31-43 ... and left this organization ..., 19...

He was last paid to include ..., 19...

by ...
(Name and grade of finance officer or agent officer, if any)

Due United States; if nothing, so state ... 1.50

D

* Due soldier at date of Transfer-Accrued Pay

This soldier †has / †has not a Class F allotment running which has been deducted from his pay to include ..., 19...

This soldier has authorized a Class D deduction for Government insurance which has been deducted from his pay to include ..., 19...

His character is Not Observed

Efficiency rating as soldier Not Observed

I have personally verified all entries in this indorsement.

James F. Moots
JAMES F. MOOTS, W. O., AC
(Name)
Asst. Personnel Adj.
(Grade and organization)

This soldier reported 3 Sept, 1943 ... (Organization to which transferred)

and was assigned to ... (see page 5).

*Here enter any amounts due soldier and not paid to date, such as monetary allowance in lieu of quarters and subsistence; if nothing, so state.
†Strike out words not applicable.

W. D., A. G. O. Form No. 24-2
May 1, 1937

Reproduced K.F., Miss. Auth: Par. 1 J, C4, AR 345-125.

18

3d Ind.

..., 19...

To C.O. ... Republic ...

This soldier was transferred to ...

per S.O. #43 P-36 This Hq

and left this organization 15 Feb, 1944

He was last paid to include 31 Jan, 1944.

by ... Maj
(Name and grade of finance officer or agent officer, if any)

Due United States; if nothing, so state
SEE REMARKS FINANCIAL

* Due soldier at date of ... ACCRUED PAY ...

This soldier †has / †has not a Class E allotment running which has been deducted from his pay to include 31 Jan, 1944

This soldier has authorized a Class D deduction for Government insurance which has been deducted from his pay to include 31 Jan, 1944.

His character is EXCELLENT

Efficiency rating as soldier EXCELLENT

I have personally verified all entries in this indorsement.

Walter S. Cowart
WALTER S. COWART
(Name)
2d Lt. ...
(Grade and organization) FEB 16 1944

This soldier reported ..., 19...

*Here enter any amounts due soldier and not paid to date, such as monetary allowance in lieu of quarters and subsistence; if nothing, so state.
†Strike out words not applicable.

4th Ind.

13th [illegible] Tech. [illegible] Det.
[illegible]
[illegible] 23 1944

To Co. I, A.F. 326th [illegible]

This soldier was transferred to [illegible] Fld, N.C.

per [illegible] 4 [illegible] 37 [illegible] 3/23/44

and left this organization [illegible] 23 1944

He was last paid to include FEB 29 1944, 19__

by [illegible] McALLISTER, Col., F.D.
(Name and grade of finance officer or agent officer, if any)

Due United States; if nothing, so state
[illegible] "Financial"

* Due soldier at date of [illegible]

This soldier has not a Class F allotment running which has been deducted from his pay to include [illegible], 19__

This soldier has authorized a Class D deduction for Government insurance which has been deducted from his pay to include [illegible], 19__

His character is Excellent [illegible]

Efficiency rating as soldier Excellent [illegible]

I have personally verified all entries in this indorsement.

Hubert J. Brich [signature]
HUBERT J. BRICH (Name), [illegible] (J.G.)
Personnel Officer
(Grade and organization)

This soldier reported D-2 Static Crew Sect 4-26-1944

*Here enter any amounts due soldier and not paid to date, such as monetary allowance in lieu of quarters and subsistence; if nothing, so state.
†Strike out words not applicable.

COMMISSION EXHIBIT No. 1706—Continued

5th Ind.

Unit Personnel Sec, 124th AAF Base Unit (?)
Bluethenthal Fld, N.C. 7 June, 1944

To CO 114th AAF Base Unit (B), Chatham Fld, Ga.

This soldier was transferred to your Comd

per Par 1, SO 141, Hq AAB Bluethenthal Fld, N.C.

and left this organization 8 June, 1944

He was last paid to include 31st May, 1944

by J.P. WARRICK, 1st Lt, FD
(Name and grade of finance officer or agent officer, if any)

Due United States; if nothing, so state Due U.S. Ldry $1.50

* Due soldier at date of Transf: A.P. + A.

Has a Cl "F" almt - ded to 31 May 44

This soldier has not a Class E allotment running which has been deducted from his pay to include nothing, 19__

This soldier has authorized a Class D deduction for Government insurance which has been deducted from his pay to include 31 May, 1944

His character is Excellent

Efficiency rating as soldier Excellent

I have personally verified all entries in this indorsement.

Aleck H. Brownstein [signature]
ALECK H. BROWNSTEIN, (Name)
Capt, AC, Unit Personnel Officer
(Grade and organization)

This soldier reported 6-9-1944

*Here enter any amounts due soldier and not paid to date, such as monetary allowance in lieu of quarters and subsistence; if nothing, so state.
†Strike out words not applicable.
16—25250-1

COMMISSION EXHIBIT No. 1706—Continued

6th Ind.

SO M 324th Base Unit CO TS
[illegible] 11-26, 1945

To CO 301 AAF BU DREW FLD, FLA

This soldier was transferred to [illegible]

per Par 3 SO 331 HQ AAF Chatham [illegible] 11-27-45

and left this organization [illegible], 1945

He was last paid to include 31 OCT 45, 19__

by W. E. WEBER, CAPT., F.D.
(Name and grade of finance officer or agent officer, if any)

Due United States; if nothing, so state [illegible] 1.50 NOV
M/C LDRY $1.50 OCT 45
P/P $30.00 Pd Nov 45 accts, D.H. Pucci, Capt. [illegible]
ALLOTMENT STATUS
CL N $7.30
CL F $22.00
DED THRU OCT 45

Total $52.30

* Due soldier at date of TRF Accrd Pay & Alws

This soldier has not a Class E allotment running which has been deducted from his pay to include __________, 19__

This soldier has authorized a Class D deduction for Government insurance which has been deducted from his pay to include __________, 19__

His character is Excellent

Efficiency rating as soldier Excellent

I have personally verified all entries in this indorsement.

Elizabeth R. Smith [signature]
ELIZABETH R. SMITH (Name)
1st Lt. [illegible] 324 AAF BU
(Grade and organization)

This soldier reported __________, 19__

*Here enter any amounts due soldier and not paid to date, such as monetary allowance in lieu of quarters and subsistence; if nothing, so state.
†Strike out words not applicable.

COMMISSION EXHIBIT No. 1706—Continued

22

7th Ind.

DEC 1 0 1945

To ...

This soldier was transferred to

per ... and left this organization DEC 1 0 1945, 19...

He was last paid to include OCT 3 1 1945, 19...

by ... (Name and grade of finance officer or agent officer, if any)

Due United States; if nothing, so state.

ALLOTMENT STATUS		
Class	Amt. Deducted	Ded. thru:
B		
D		
E		
F		OCT 3 1 1945
N	2.20	OCT 3 1 1945

*Due soldier at date of TRF: ACCRUED PAY & ALWS

†This soldier {has / has not} a Class E allotment running which has been deducted from his pay to include ..., 19...

†This soldier has authorized a Class D deduction for Government insurance which has been deducted from his pay to include ..., 19...

His character is ...

Efficiency rating as soldier ...

I have personally verified all entries in this indorsement.

Russell R Sparks

(Name)

(Grade and organization)

This soldier reported ..., 19...

*Here enter any amounts due soldier and not paid to date, such as monetary allowance in lieu of quarters and subsistence; if nothing, so state.
†Strike out words not applicable.

16—25250-1

COMMISSION EXHIBIT No. 1706—Continued

8 Inc.

300 AAF BU, HQ THIRD AF
TAMPA, FLA. 1946
To CO, WD Sep Ctr,
FT Sheridan, Ill.
This soldier was transferred to
YOUR COMMAND,
per PAR 7 SO #36 HQ 3AF 2 FEB 3...
and left this organization 17 Feb 1946
He was last paid to include ... 19
by J. C. DUDLEY, MAJ, AC
(name & grade of finance officer or agent officer, if any)
Due United States; if nothing state
Due U.S. 1.50 4 day

CL	AMT DED	DED THRU
E	22.00	JAN 31 46
N	2.20	JAN 31 46

Due Soldier at date of trfd accrued pay & alws
Due So Fuel BAL JAN 3 To JAN 7.

His character is EXCELLENT
Efficiency rating as soldier EXCELLENT
I have personally verified all entries in this indorsement.

C. L. Robbins Jr.

Capt., A. C.
Personnel Officer

300th AAF BU
Tampa, Fla.

COMMISSION EXHIBIT No. 1706—Continued

23

FINAL INDORSEMENT

(Company or detachment)

(Place)

..., 19...

To The Adjutant General:

(Last name) (First name) (Middle initial) (Army serial No.)

(Grade) (Organization)

was separated from the service by reason of ... (State specific cause. See par. 37c, AR 345-125)

... on ... (Date)

at ... (Place) ... authority ...

Retained in service ... days to make good time lost (A. W. 107).

Absent from duty ... days subsequent to normal date of expiration of term of enlistment.

Retained in service ... days for convenience of the Government on account of ...

His character is ...

Efficiency rating as soldier ...

*Final statement furnished. *Paid on final pay roll.
*Discharge certificate furnished, W. D., A. G. O. Form No. 55, 56, 57.

Due United States; if nothing, so state ...

DISCHARGED

†Due soldier at date of ...

Address furnished for future references: ... (Number and street or rural route)

(City, town, or post office) (State or country)

Receipt of Discharge Certificate is acknowledged.

Signature of Soldier: ...

I have verified the foregoing entries.

Name signed ... Lt. Air Corps

Name typed or printed ... A. A. F. BU.

(Grade and organization)

*Strike out words and figures not applicable.
†Here enter any amounts due soldier and not paid to date, such as monetary allowance in lieu of quarters and subsistence; if nothing, so state.

COMMISSION EXHIBIT No. 1706—Continued

24

Initials	Name, grade, and organization (Typewritten or printed)
	L. Tarrant 2nd
	Capt. C.A.C.
	L. E. DAVIES C.W.O., A.C. Asst. Personnel Adj.
	WALTER F. COWART 2ND LT WAC
	ROBERT J. DRISH, W.O. (jg) Personnel Officer
	ALECK H. BROWNSTEIN Capt AC 124th AAF Base Unit (?)
	CHARLES R. BROWN 1ST LT AC
	VERNARD I CARTER 2ND LT AC ASST U P C 114 AAF B U
	ELIZABETH R. SMITH 1st LT. A. C. 324 AAF BU
	JOHN E. ROQUEMORE, Capt., AC Asst. Military Personnel Officer 324 AAF BU CHATHAM FIELD, GA
	JAMES Y. WATSON Capt., A. C. 300th AAF BU Personnel Officer Tampa, Fla.

16—25250-2

COMMISSION EXHIBIT No. 1706—Continued

TAG

ALLOTMENT DISCONTINUANCE
NOTICE UPON DISCHARGE OR RELEASE FROM ACTIVE DUTY

332 338 11
No. E 6934382

NAME AND PERMANENT MAILING ADDRESS	ARMY SERIAL NUMBER	GRADE	REASON FOR SEPARATION	DATE OF SEPARATION	DATE OF BIRTH, IF AVAILABLE
RUBENSTEIN JACK 3650 LEXINGTON ST CHICAGO ILL	36 666 107	PFC	DISCH	21 FEB 46F	E 25 MAR 11

ENTER IN THE SPACE PROVIDED BELOW EACH ALLOWANCE OR ALLOTMENT NOW IN EFFECT

(No Entry Here)

	ALLOTMENT	AMOUNT (1)	EFFECTIVE DATE MONTH AND YEAR (First Deduction) (2)	FINAL DEDUCTION MADE FOR MONTH OF (3)
FAMILY ALLOWANCE APPLICATION NUMBER, IF IN SERVICE RECORD: X- / VETERANS ADMINISTRATION NUMBER (No Entry Here): N-	N	$ 7.30	JUN 43	FEB 46
ENTER NAMES OF "E" ALLOTTEES, IF IN SERVICE RECORD (1) (2) (3)	E	$		
NAME AND LOCATION OF ORGANIZATION EFFECTING DISCHARGE OR RELEASE: SEP CTR #32 1612 SCU FT SHERIDAN ILL	D	$		
TYPED NAME, GRADE, AND TITLE OF PERSONNEL OR DISBURSING OFFICER EFFECTING DISCONTINUANCE (No Signature Necessary): LELAND E RICE CAPT FD DO	F	$ 22.00	JUL 43	FEB 46

WD AGO FORM 30-S
1 SEP 1945
6 PART

TO: THE ADJUTANT GENERAL'S OFFICE, WASHINGTON 25, D. C.
(Folded and inserted in the service record in cases of enlisted personnel)

1

PREVIOUS EDITIONS MAY BE USED.

PATENTED—MOORE BUSINESS FORMS, INC., NIAGARA FALLS, N.Y.

COMMISSION EXHIBIT No. 1707

ENLISTED RECORD AND REPORT OF SEPARATION
HONORABLE DISCHARGE

1. LAST NAME - FIRST NAME - MIDDLE INITIAL: RUBENSTEIN JACK
2. ARMY SERIAL NO.: 36 666 107
3. GRADE: PFC
4. ARM OR SERVICE: AAF
5. COMPONENT: AUS
6. ORGANIZATION: 300TH AAF BU
7. DATE OF SEPARATION: 21 FEB 46
8. PLACE OF SEPARATION: SEPARATION CENTER FORT SHERIDAN ILL
9. PERMANENT ADDRESS FOR MAILING PURPOSES: 3650 LEXINGTON ST CHICAGO ILL
10. DATE OF BIRTH: 25 MAR 11
11. PLACE OF BIRTH: CHICAGO ILL
12. ADDRESS FROM WHICH EMPLOYMENT WILL BE SOUGHT: SEE 9
13. COLOR EYES: BROWN
14. COLOR HAIR: BROWN
15. HEIGHT: 5-8
16. WEIGHT: 173 LBS.
17. NO. DEPEND.: 1
18. RACE: WHITE X NEGRO OTHER (specify)
19. MARITAL STATUS: SINGLE X MARRIED OTHER (specify)
20. U.S. CITIZEN: YES X NO
21. CIVILIAN OCCUPATION AND NO.: MANAGER OWNER & SALESMAN OF EARL PRODUCTS CO 1-80010

MILITARY HISTORY

22. DATE OF INDUCTION: 21 MAY 43
23. DATE OF ENLISTMENT:
24. DATE OF ENTRY INTO ACTIVE SERVICE: 28 MAY 43
25. PLACE OF ENTRY INTO SERVICE: CP GRANT ILL
SELECTIVE SERVICE DATA: 26. REGISTERED: YES X NO; 27. LOCAL S.S. BOARD NO.: 124; 28. COUNTY AND STATE: CHICAGO ILL
29. HOME ADDRESS AT TIME OF ENTRY INTO SERVICE: SEE 9
30. MILITARY OCCUPATIONAL SPECIALTY AND NO.: AIRPLANE & ENGINE MECH 747
31. MILITARY QUALIFICATION AND DATE (i.e., infantry, aviation and marksmanship badges, etc.): SS W/CARBINE
32. BATTLES AND CAMPAIGNS: NONE
33. DECORATIONS AND CITATIONS: VICTORY MEDAL AMERICAN THEATER RIBBON GOOD CONDUCT MEDAL
34. WOUNDS RECEIVED IN ACTION: NONE
35. LATEST IMMUNIZATION DATES: SMALLPOX: JUL 43; TYPHOID: NOV 45; TETANUS: JUN 44; OTHER (specify):
36. SERVICE OUTSIDE CONTINENTAL U.S. AND RETURN: DATE OF DEPARTURE: ; DESTINATION: NONE; DATE OF ARRIVAL:
37. TOTAL LENGTH OF SERVICE: CONTINENTAL SERVICE: YEARS 2 MONTHS 8 DAYS 24; FOREIGN SERVICE: YEARS 0 MONTHS 0 DAYS 0
38. HIGHEST GRADE HELD: PFC
39. PRIOR SERVICE: NONE
40. REASON AND AUTHORITY FOR SEPARATION: CONVN OF GOVT RR 1-1 DEMOBILIZATION AR 615 365 15 DEC 44 AND AFPMP 1841 DTD 18 JAN 46 SERVICE
41. SERVICE SCHOOLS ATTENDED: AP ... 747 1944 AP & ENG MECH P-47 1944
42. EDUCATION (Years): Grammar 8; High School 2; College 0

PAY DATA VO 30779

43. LONGEVITY FOR PAY PURPOSES: YEARS 2 MONTHS 9 DAYS 1
44. MUSTERING OUT PAY: TOTAL $200; THIS PAYMENT $100
45. SOLDIER DEPOSITS:
46. TRAVEL PAY: $1.30
47. TOTAL AMOUNT, NAME OF DISBURSING OFFICER: $111.60 LELAND E RICE CAPT FD

INSURANCE NOTICE

IMPORTANT: IF PREMIUM IS NOT PAID WHEN DUE OR WITHIN THIRTY-ONE DAYS THEREAFTER, INSURANCE WILL LAPSE. MAKE CHECKS OR MONEY ORDERS PAYABLE TO THE TREASURER OF THE U. S. AND FORWARD TO COLLECTIONS SUBDIVISION, VETERANS ADMINISTRATION, WASHINGTON 25, D. C.

48. KIND OF INSURANCE: Nat. Serv. X; U.S. Govt.; None
49. HOW PAID: Allotment X; Direct to V.A.
50. Effective Date of Allotment Discontinuance: FEB 46
51. Date of Next Premium Due (One month after 50): MAR 46
52. PREMIUM DUE EACH MONTH: $7.30
53. INTENTION OF VETERAN TO: Continue X; Continue Only $; Discontinue

54. RIGHT THUMB PRINT
55. REMARKS (This space for completion of above items or entry of other items specified in W. D. Directives)
LAPEL BUTTON ISSUED
ASR SCORE (2 SEP 45) 27
INACTIVE STATUS ERC FROM 21 MAY 43 TO 27 MAY 43

56. SIGNATURE OF PERSON BEING SEPARATED: [signature]
57. PERSONNEL OFFICER (Type name, grade and organization - signature): W S RISEDORPH 1ST LT WAC [signature]

WD AGO FORM 53 - 55, 1 November 1944. This form supersedes all previous editions of WD AGO Forms 53 and 55 for enlisted persons entitled to an Honorable Discharge, which will not be used after receipt of this revision.

2. FINAL INDORSEMENT COPY (Affixed to final indorsement page of Service Record)

COMMISSION EXHIBIT No. 1707—Continued

CONSULTATION REQUEST AND REPORT

Name Grade Ward

Rubenstein, Jack, Pfc., 36666107, Sq. H, Chatham Field, Ga.

To: Date 1-24 1945

For consultation because of

Provisional diagnosis

Routine. ☐
Emergency. ☐

[signature] M. C.

Date 24 January 1945

Opinion of consultant:

This patient gives a history of an old injury of the left thumb which continues to pain. The thumb was X-Rayed January 15, 1945, at which time there was observed a small rounded bone fragment along the superior dorsal border of the first metacarpo-phalangeal joint, and most likely representing the end result of a small chip fracture at that level. There is no evidence of any posttraumatic arthritic change at the joint level. The remaining bones of the thumb are negative. This patient would be benefited by physiotherapy but no further treatment is indicated other than this.

[signature] M. C.
JOHN R. GLOVER, Captain

JCP/M-7—W. D., A. G. O. Form No. 8-40, 21 June 1944
(This form supersedes W. D., M. D. Form No. 55 E-1, 31 May 1939, which may be used until existing stocks are exhausted.)

COMMISSION EXHIBIT No. 1707—Continued

Form 55 A-1
MEDICAL DEPARTMENT, U. S. ARMY
(Authorized Dec. 31, 1942)

ABBREVIATED CLINICAL RECORD

Name Rubinstein, Jack Grade Pfc. Ward 102

(This sheet to be used in conjunction with 55A, M.D. in cases where the data hereon will suffice to conform with existing regulations.)

Pertinent history, chief complaint, and condition on admission.

For a number of years patient has had plantar warts which he states he had trimmed frequently in civilian life. Lately they have become sensitive and in addition he has developed athlete's foot.

Complete physical examination is negative except for the following:

Plantar wart on sole of right foot beneath 4 th meta tarsal phalangeal joint and another callous on rim of left sole beneath great toe.
Also small discrete blisters (vesicles) on sole of feet, worse on left.
Impr. Plantar warts
& Trychophytosis, feet, moderate

Progress:

25 Feb 45 – Under local treatment patients athlete's foot infection seems to have improved. [illegible]
26 Feb 45 – Having consultation plantar warts [illegible]
27 Feb 45 – Patient's Trychophytosis has improved. He was seen by Lt Near who advocated meta-tarsal pads, bars of feet and recommends duty.
[illegible]

(Use both sides of this sheet)

16—32780-1

4

COMMISSION EXHIBIT No. 1707—Continued

TEMPERATURE—TREATMENT—NURSE'S NOTES

DATE	A.M. T	A.M. P	A.M. R	P.M. T	P.M. P	P.M. R	ST	WT	MEDICATION AND NURSE'S NOTES
22 Feb 45	98	80	20	98	88	22	4½		New pt adm @ 8³⁰ am. Ambulatory.
									Castellani's sol to feet.
23 Feb.	98	84	20						Feet washed c soap & H2O then
									Castellani's paint between toes.
24 Feb.	98⁸	76	20	98	80	18			Feet washed c soap & H2O then Castellani's
									sol applied between toes followed by cotton.
25 Feb.	97²	84	20	98²	80	20			Both feet washed c white soap & H2O.
									Castellani's Sol applied between toes – followed by cotton.
26 Feb.	98⁶	80	18	98⁴	80	16			Feet washed c white soap & H2O. Castellani's Sol applied between toes followed by cotton
27 Feb.	96⁸	72	18						Feet washed c white soap & H2O Castellani's Sol applied between toes – followed by cotton.

LABORATORY REPORTS

(Paste third report here and succeeding ones on above lines)

(Paste second report with top at this line)

(Paste first report with top at this line)

16—32780-1 ☆ U. S. GOVERNMENT PRINTING OFFICE : 1943

COMMISSION EXHIBIT No. 1707—Continued

Form 55 G-1
Medical Department, U. S. Army
(Revised May 31, 1939)

TREATMENT

Name Rubinstein, Jack Grade Pfc. Ward 102

Date	
22 Feb	Castellani's Sol to toes of both feet. Capt Sikes / MAL

16—10819 (OVER)

COMMISSION EXHIBIT No. 1707—Continued

Form 55 E-1
Medical Department, U. S. Army
(Revised May 31, 1939)

CONSULTATION REQUEST AND REPORT

Name Rubinstein, Jack Grade ______ Ward 102

Date 26 Feb, 1945

Consultation requested because of Plantar Warts.

Provisional diagnosis athletes foot

Routine.
~~Emergency.~~

Capt. Sikes M. C.

Date 26 Feb, 1945
Office, Chief of Surgery Service.
To Chief of Orthopedics Service.
Approved.
Disapproved.
______ M. C.

Date ______, 19....
Office, Chief of ______ Service.
To ______
For consultation.
______ M. C.

Date ______, 19....

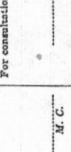

Opinion of consultant:
Has Plantar warts under
of metatarsal heads bilaterally, pigmented. Also fallen transverse arches bilaterally. Would recommend metatarsal bars (none available) and removal of warts by cautery or x-ray Rx's as soon as an opportunity for this presents itself. Will give

(OVER)

COMMISSION EXHIBIT No. 1707—Continued

him felt pads for the transverse arches.

Nee
1-25-61

Commission Exhibit No. 1707—Continued

Rubinstein, Jack H

admit to 102

(1) Epidermophytosis, infected.
(2) Callousitis

T/4 R. F. Kelly

Commission Exhibit No. 1707—Continued

Armed Forces' Original
D. S. S. Form 221
January 30, 1942

6-7-43 NOT YET ASSIGNED
RRC CAMP GRANT, ILL.

Local Board No. 124 81
Chicago City 731
124
(LOCAL BOARD DATE STAMP WITH CODE)

REPORT OF PHYSICAL EXAMINATION AND INDUCTION

First examination ☐ Second examination ☐ Third examination ☐ Fourth examination ☐
(To be filled in by local board clerk. Check number of examination made by local board)

SECTION I.—GENERAL (To be filled in by the local board clerk from the Selective Service Questionnaire, D. S. S. Form 40. Write "none" opposite the questions where no information is given. Do not leave any question blank.)

(To be filled in by Armed Forces) 36566187 (Armed Forces Serial No.)

Do Not Enter Anything in This Column: Residence — State; County; Place inducted; Date Inducted — Day; Month; Year; Source; Nativity; Year of birth; Race/citizenship; Education; Occupation; Marital

1. Name (page 1) Jack (First) (Middle) Rubenstein (Last)
2. Address (page 1) 3650 Lexington (Street or rural route) Chicago (Town or city) Cook (County) Ill (State)
3. Social Security No. (Series I, line 5) None 4. Registrant's order number (page 1) 1912
5. Physical or mental defects or diseases (Series II, line 1) None
6. Treatment at an institution, sanitarium, or asylum (Series II, line 2) no (Yes or no)
7. Education (Number years completed) (Series III): Elementary school 8 High school 1 Vocational school, college, or university
8. Occupation: (a) Title of present job (Series IV, line 2 (a), or Series V, line 1) Salesman
(b) Duties (Series IV, line 2 (b)) Sell novelties and premiums
(c) Title of last job, if unemployed (Series IV, line 3)
9. Years experience in this work (Series IV, line 2 (c), or Series V, line 2)
10. Income (Series IV, line 2 (d)): Average annual (Weekly, monthly, annual) earnings $ 3000.00
11. Employment class (Series IV, line 2 (e)): Permanent employee ☐; Temporary employee ☐; Apprentice ☐; Independent worker ☑; Unpaid family worker ☐; Employer ☐; Student (Series IV, line 4 (a)) ☐
12. Business of present employer (Series IV, line 2 (g)) Merchandising
13. Marital status (Series VII, line 1): Single ☑; Widower ☐; Divorced ☐; Married, not separated ☐; Married, separated ☐
14. Number of dependents (Series VII, line 3 (a) fifth column except N. C.'s plus line 4 (a) fifth column) 1
15. Birthplace (Series IX, line 1) Chicago (Town or city) Ill (State) U.S.A. (Country)
16. Birth date (Series IX, line 2) March (Month) 25 (Day) 1911 (Year)
17. Race (Series IX, line 3): White ☑; Negro ☐; Other (specify)
18. Citizenship: United States citizen (Series IX, line 4) yes (Yes or no); Declarant alien (Series IX, line 7) (Yes or no)
19. Previous U. S. military service (Series XII): None ☑; Army ☐; National Guard ☐; Navy ☐; Marine Corps ☐; Coast Guard ☐
20. Type of discharge (Series XII): Specify /
21. Date of registrant's affidavit (top of page 8) 14th (Day) June (Month) 1941 (Year)

INSTRUCTIONS

1. An original and three copies of this form will be prepared for each registrant called up for physical examination. The original is designated as the Armed Forces' Original; the first carbon copy, the National Headquarters' Copy; the second carbon copy, the Surgeon General's (Army)—Bureau of Medicine and Surgery (Navy)—Commandant Marine Corps (M. C.) Copy; and the third carbon copy, the Local Board's Copy. Instructions are contained on each copy.
2. Forms of men rejected by the armed forces will be marked "Rejected by the Armed Forces" in large letters at the top of page 1.
3. If the registrant is not sent to the induction station of the armed forces, or is rejected by the induction station of the armed forces, this original will be filed, along with "Local Board's Copy" (3d copy), in the registrant's Cover Sheet (Form 53).
4. For registrants accepted by the induction station of the armed forces: If inducted by the ARMY, this original accompanied by F. B. I. Military Fingerprint Card will be forwarded from induction station to The Adjutant General, Washington, D. C.; if inducted by the NAVY or COAST GUARD, this original will be forwarded through the Main Recruiting Station to the Bureau of Navigation, Washington, D. C.; if inducted by the MARINE CORPS, this original will be sent to the Commandant, Headquarters, U. S. Marine Corps, Washington, D. C.
5. Fingerprints are required only on this original and only for registrants who are inducted. If inducted by ARMY, prepare F. B. I. Military Fingerprint Card.

ORIGINAL COPY (Page 1)

COMMISSION EXHIBIT No. 1707—Continued

SECTION II.—REPORT OF LOCAL BOARD EXAMINING PHYSICIAN AND LOCAL BOARD CLASSIFICATION.

22. If registrant's answer to Item 6 above is "yes," when and for what ailment(s)
23. Is registrant now or previously an enrollee in the Civilian Conservation Corps: No ☐; Yes ☐
24. Serological test (syphilis): Date 1-27-43 Result neg
Second serological test (syphilis): Date Result
25. Examining physician's remarks
26. (a) Do you find that the above-named registrant has any of the defects set forth in Part I of the List of Defects (Form 220)? (If in doubt, answer "no," and give details.) no (Answer yes or no) If answer is "yes," describe the defects, in order of significance
(b) Do you find that the above-named registrant has any of the defects set forth in Part II of the List of Defects (Form 220) (If in doubt, answer "no," and give details.) no (Answer yes or no) If answer is "yes," describe the defects, in order of significance
(c) I have examined the above-named registrant in accordance with Selective Service Regulations.
(d) Signature of examining physician [illegible signature]
(e) Place [illegible] (Town or city) (State) (f) Date Jan. 28, 1943
27. (a) This Local Board has classified the above-named registrant in Class 1a
(b) Signature of Member of Local Board William J. Wilcox
(c) Place Chicago Ill (Town or city) (County) (State) (d) Date 2-1-43

SECTION III.—NEAREST RELATIVE, PERSON TO BE NOTIFIED IN CASE OF EMERGENCY, AND DESIGNATION OF BENEFICIARY (To be filled out at the induction station of the armed forces for only those registrants accepted for military service.)

A. Nearest relative and person to be notified in case of emergency:
28. Nearest relative Fannie Rubenstein (Other than wife or minor child. Name in full)
29. Relationship mother 30. Address 3650 Lexington, Chicago, Ill. (Number and street or rural route; if none, so state) (City, town, or post office) (State or country)
31. Person to be notified in case of emergency Hyman Rubenstein (Name in full)
32. Relationship brother (If friend, so state) 33. Address same as mother's (Number and street or rural route; if none, so state) (City, town, or post office) (State or country)
B. Designation of beneficiary:
34. The persons eligible to be my beneficiary are designated below:
(1) None (Full name of wife; if no wife, or if she is deceased or divorced, so state) (Wife's full address)
(2) None (Full name and address of each minor child and each dependent child over 21 years of age. If there are no children, so state. If the address is the same as the wife's, so state. Do not repeat address)
35. In the event of my leaving no widow or child, or their decease before payment is made, I then designate as my beneficiary the dependent relative whose name, relationship, and address are shown below:
(3) Marian Rubenstein (sister) same as mother's (If designation of beneficiary is declined, man must state in own handwriting: "I decline to designate any person as my beneficiary")
36. In the event of the death or disqualification of the last-named dependent relative before payment is made, I then designate as my beneficiary the dependent relative whose name, relationship, and address are shown below:
(4) Eileen Rubenstein (sister) same as mother's (If beneficiary is named in line 35 but naming of alternate is declined, man must state in own handwriting: "I decline to designate an alternate beneficiary")
37. Signature of registrant Jack (First name) (Middle name) Rubenstein (Last name)
38. Witnessed at Chicago, Ill. on May 21, 1943
W. Skurnik (Signature of witness attesting) N. SKURNIK, 2nd Lt., A.U.S. (Name of witness typed) (Grade and organization)

ORIGINAL COPY (PAGE 2)

COMMISSION EXHIBIT No. 1707—Continued

SECTION IV.—PHYSICAL EXAMINATION RESULTS: (All Items Must Be Filled In. Indicate Normal or None Where Applicable. To Be Filled Out by the Medical Board at the Induction Station of the Armed Forces.)

39. Eye abnormalities ..... none
40. Ear, nose, throat abnormalities ..... none
41. Mouth and gum abnormalities ..... none
42. Teeth: (a) Indicate restorable carious teeth by circling; nonrestorable carious teeth by /; missing natural teeth by X.

Right								EXAMINEE'S	Left							
8	7	6	5	4	3	2	1		1	2	3	4	5	6	7	8
16	15	14	13	12	11	10	9		9	10	11	12	13	14	15	16

(b) Remarks, including other defects ..... none
(c) Prosthetic dental appliances ..... none
(d) Remediable dental defects ..... none
43. Skin ..... normal
44. Varicose veins ..... Poplitcal bilateral, mild, N.S.
45. Hernia ..... Patent umbilicus, no impulse, no hernia.
46. Hemorrhoids ..... none
47. Genito-urinary (non-venereal) ..... normal
48. Venereal diseases ..... none
49. Feet ..... normal
50. Musculoskeletal defects ..... none
51. Abdominal viscera ..... normal
52. Cardiovascular system ..... normal
53. Lungs ..... normal
54. Chest X-ray ..... negative
55. Mental ..... normal
56. Nervous system ..... normal
57. Endocrine system ..... normal
58. Other defects and/or diseases or other remarks ..... none
59. Summary of defects in order of significance ..... ACCEPTABLE UNDER MR 1-9

Do Not Write in This Column

60. Vision, without correction:
(a) Right eye 20/40
(b) Left eye 20/30
61. Vision, with correction:
(a) Right eye .....
(b) Left eye .....
62. Color perception* .....
63. Hearing:
(a) Right ear 15/15
(b) Left ear 15/15
64. Height 68 inches.
65. Weight 177 pounds.
66. (a) Girth, at nipples; inspiration 42 inches.
(b) Girth, at nipples; expiration 40 inches.
(c) Girth, at umbilicus 36 inches.
67. Posture: Good ☒ Fair ☐ Poor ☐
68. Frame: Heavy ☐ Med. ☒ Light ☐
69. Color of hair brown
70. Color of eyes brown
71. Complexion dark
72. Pulse, sitting 78
73. Pulse, after exercise* .....
74. Pulse, 2 minutes after exercise* .....
75. Blood pressure:
(a) Systolic 120
(b) Diastolic 72
76. Urinalysis:
(a) Specific gravity 1.022
(b) Albumin NEGATIVE
(c) Sugar NEGATIVE
(d) Microscopic* .....
77. Other data:

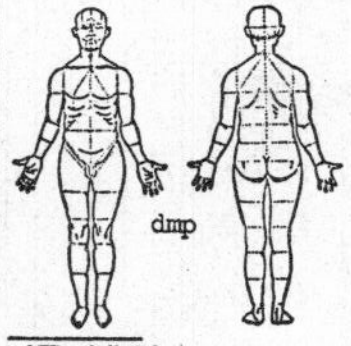

* When indicated.

ORIGINAL COPY (PAGE 3) 16—20941-2

SECTION IV.—PHYSICAL EXAMINATION RESULTS—Continued.

78. I CERTIFY that the above-named registrant was carefully examined, that the results of the examination have been correctly recorded on this form and that to the best of my knowledge and belief—

(a) ..... (Enter name of registrant if this subsection is applicable) is physically and mentally qualified for general military service.

(b) ..... (Enter name of registrant if this subsection is applicable) is physically and mentally qualified for general military service after the satisfactory correction of the following remediable defects: .....

This registrant would have been accepted for general military service had the remediable defects herein specified been remedied at the time of this examination.

(c) ..... (Enter name of registrant if this subsection is applicable) is physically qualified for limited military service only by reason of .....

(d) ..... (Enter name of registrant if this subsection is applicable) is physically qualified for limited military service after the satisfactory correction of the following remediable defects: .....

This registrant would have been acceptable for limited military service had the remediable defects herein specified been remedied at the time of this examination.

(e) ..... (Enter name of registrant if this subsection is applicable) is physically and/or mentally disqualified for military service by reason of .....

(f) ..... (Enter name of registrant if this subsection is applicable) is disqualified for military service because of .....

(g) Signature ..... Medical Examiner. (h) Title .....

(i) Name typed or stamped .....

79. (a) ..... JACK RUBENSTEIN ..... (Enter name of registrant if this subsection is applicable) was this date inducted for (general; limited) [strike out inapplicable word] military service into the (fill in appropriate Service, such as Army, Navy, Marine Corps, or Coast Guard) ARMY of the United States and ~~sent to~~ Trs'fd to ERC to report for active duty May 28, 1943 at .....

(b) ..... (Enter name of registrant if this subsection is applicable) was this date rejected for service in the (fill in appropriate service, such as Army, Navy, Marine Corps, or Coast Guard) ..... of the United States.

(c) Place CHICAGO, ILL. (d) Signature .....
(e) Date MAY 21, 1943 (f) Name typed or stamped ..... 2ND LT. AUS (Grade and organization)

SECTION V.—LOCAL BOARD CHANGE IN CLASSIFICATION AFTER EXAMINATION BY THE INDUCTION STATION OF THE ARMED FORCES.

80. (a) Based on the entries in (a), (c), (d), (e), or (f) of Item 78, above, the Local Board has changed the above-named registrant's classification to Class .....
(b) Based on the entries in (b) of Item 78, above, the Local Board has retained the above-named registrant in Class .....
(c) Place ..... (d) Date .....
(e) Signature of member of local board .....

FINGERPRINTS—RIGHT HAND

1. THUMB	2. INDEX	3. MIDDLE	4. RING	5. LITTLE

ORIGINAL COPY (PAGE 4) 16—20941-2 U. S. GOVERNMENT PRINTING OFFICE

COMMISSION EXHIBIT No. 1707—Continued

COMMISSION EXHIBIT No. 1707—Continued

LAST NAME	FIRST NAME	MIDDLE INITIAL	A.S.N.	GRADE	DATE OF BIRTH	YRS. H.S.	YRS. CLG.
QUALIFIED X (5 in Cp.) ... FIRE ... se [illegible]STEIN,	JACK		36666107	Pvt.	3/25/11	2	None

1ST O S S N	YRS. AT IT	WAGE	LIMITED SERVICE		COLLEGE MAJOR
321	12	125.00 $ PER Wk.	No		None
2ND. O S S N	**YRS AT IT**	**WAGE**	**DATE INDUCTED**	**BASIC TRAINING CENTER**	**COURSE CLASSIFIED FOR**
010	2	75.00 $ PER Wk.	5/21/43	Keesler Fld, Miss.	
1ST. CHOICE OF COURSE	**2ND CHOICE OF COURSE**		**3RD. CHOICE OF COURSE**		**COURSE ENROLLED IN**
					Airplane Mech.

TEST SCORES

FORM NO.	TYPE	ST. SCORE	FORM NO.	TYPE	ST. SCORE	FORM NO.	TYPE	ST. SCORE
Id	G. C. T.	III 108						
Ma-3	M. A	III 90						
Roal		IV 86						

ASSGD. TO CL. NO.	DATE
275-43	9-6-43
SIGNATURE OF DIRECTOR OF TRAINING	[signature]
GRADE	Colonel, Air Corps,

SYM	PHASE	HOURS	REL. WT.	PHASE GRADE	WTD. GRADE	DEMERITS		INSTRUCTOR
-1	Aircraft Mechanics' Tools	60		85				
-2	Airplane Structures	66		82				
-3	Airp. Hydr. Sys. & Misc. Equip.	48		83				
-4	Aircraft Propellers	48		80				10/20/43
E-1	Aircraft Engines	48		81				
A-5	Aircraft Instruments	54		81		1	1	
E-2	Aircraft Electrical Systems	54		84				
E-3	Eng. Induction, Fuel & Oil Sys.	54		76				
E-4	Engine Operation & Test	48		79				1/1/44
I-1	Airplane Inspection I	48		78				
I-2	Airplane Inspection II	48		77				
I-3	Airplane Inspection III	42		80				
I-4	Graduation Field Test	54		77				
	TOTAL OR AVERAGE	672		80			1	FORM 13

COMMISSION EXHIBIT No. 1707—Continued

STUDENT RECORD A. A. F. T. T. C.

FORM NO. 13

PERSONNEL RECORD

ACTION	S. O.	DATE	REASON
Entered School	248 P14	9-5-43	Student
Graduated 10 Feb 44	43 P36	2-12-44	Transferred

REMARKS

LEGEND

TESTS
- FORM NO. -- NUMBER GIVEN TEST SUCH AS Ta-7a OR 6-R-E
- TYPE ----- KIND OF TEST SUCH AS MECHANICAL MOVEMENTS
- ST. SCORE -- STANDARD SCORE OF TEST
- G. C. T. ---- GENERAL CLASSIFICATION TEST
- M. A. ----- MECHANICAL APTITUDE
- O S S N ----- OCCUPATIONAL SPECIFICATION SERIAL NUMBER

- SYM. ------ PHASE SYMBOL
- REL. WT. --- RELATIVE WEIGHT OF SUBJECT OR PHASE
- WTD. GRADE - WEIGHTED GRADE OF SUBJECT OR PHASE

COMMISSION EXHIBIT No. 1707—Continued

REPORT OF PHYSICAL EXAMINATION OF ENLISTED PERSONNEL PRIOR TO DISCHARGE, RELEASE FROM ACTIVE DUTY OR RETIREMENT

1. Last name—First name—Middle initial	2. Army Serial Number	3. Grade	4. Regiment, arm or service
RUBENSTEIN JACK	36 646 107	PFC	

5. Permanent mailing address	6. Color	7. Age in years	8. Sex	9. Syphilis Register: In S/R? Yes or No	Closed in S/R?[1] Yes or No
AAF W 5-29 330 3650 LEXINGTON ST CHICAGO ILL					

STATEMENT AND MEDICAL HISTORY OF EXAMINEE

	Yes or No			
10. At the present time do you have any wound, injury or disease which is disabling? If answer is yes, list those conditions first under Item 11.	No			
11. List all significant diseases, wounds, and injuries. State circumstances under which wounds or injuries were incurred and date of onset. Answer yes or no in Columns 1 to 4. (Continue on back if necessary)	1 EPTS 2*	2 AMS 3*	3 IMS 4*	4 PD 5*
No history of Malaria or Syphilis.				

RECORD OF PHYSICAL EXAMINATION

12. Teeth—Indicate restorable carious teeth by O, non-restorable carious teeth by /, missing natural teeth by X, teeth replaced by denture, horizontal line over X, as XXX and teeth replaced by fixed bridge, oval to include abutments, as (4 5 6)

RIGHT								EXAMINEE'S	LEFT							
8	7	6	5	4	3	2	1		1	2	3	4	5	6	7	8
16	15	14	13	12	11	10	9		9	10	11	12	13	14	15	X

Cl IV

		13. Mouth and gum abnormalities: None
		14. Dental prosthesis: Servicebility: None
15. Skin: Normal	16. Genito-Urinary (And pelvic for women): Varicocele, left non-symptomatic.	17. Venereal diseases: None
18. Varicose veins: None	19. Hernia: None	20. Anus and Rectum: Normal
21. Musculoskeletal defects: None	22. Feet: Normal	23. Abdominal Wall and Viscera: Normal
24. Cardiovascular system: Normal	25. Blood pressure: Systolic 110; Diastolic 60	26. Pulse: Sitting 64; Immediately after exercise; Two minutes after exercise
27. Lungs: Normal	28. Chest X-ray: Negative	29. Height (Shoeless): 68 In.; 30. Weight (Stripped): 170 Lbs.
31. Neurological diagnosis: Normal	32. Psychiatric diagnosis: Normal	33. Endocrine system: Normal
34. Eye abnormalities: None	35. Uncorrected — Vision — Corrected: Right eye 20/30; Left eye 20/30; Right eye 20/; Left eye 20/	36. Urinalysis: Sp. Gr.; Albumin Neg.; Sugar Neg.; Micro. 6* None
37. Ear, nose, throat, abnormalities: None	38. Hearing (Whispered voice): Right ear 15 /15; Left ear 15 /15	39. Blood serology result: Kahn test-negative.
40. In your opinion will wound, injury or disease result in: Disability? Yes or No; Untimely death? Yes or No; Condition:	41. In your opinion was wound, injury, or disease incurred in line of duty? Yes or No; Condition:	42. In your opinion does individual meet physical and mental standards for discharge? Yes or No: Yes. If not, state why
43. Remarks, special tests, or other defects (Continue on back): None		
44. Date of examination: 20 February 1946. 45. Location: 1612 SCU Sep. Ctr. #32 Ft. Sheridan, Ill	46. Typed name and grade: R. D. DWYER, 1st LT, M.C.	47. Signature: R. D. Dwyer

WD AGO FORM 38, 1 DEC 1944. This form supersedes form WD AGO 38, 15 May 1944, which may be used until existing stocks are exhausted.

1* Prior to arrival at separation center
2* Incurred or existed prior to entrance in military service
3* Aggravated by military service
4* Incurred while in military service.
5* Present physical defects.
6* When indicated.

INSTRUCTIONS:
1. Send to The Adjutant General inclosed with S/R
2. Work sheet
3. Laboratory Reports form (WD AGO ...)

16

COMMISSION EXHIBIT No. 1707—Continued

... continuation of remarks or other defects from the reverse side only.

REPORT OF BOARD OF REVIEW
(See Instruction 2)

From a careful consideration of the case and a critical examination of the enlisted person, we find that: | Yes or No

1. He meets physical and mental standards for discharge.
2. He meets physical and mental standards for discharge except as follows:
3. The defect, wound, injury, or disease is likely to result in untimely death.
4. The defect, wound, injury, or disease is likely to result in permanent disability.
5. In our opinion, the defect, wound, injury, or disease was incurred in line of duty in the military service of the United States.

Location	Typed name	Grade	Signature
		M.C.	
Date	**Typed name**	**Grade**	**Signature**
		M.C.	

INSTRUCTIONS:
1. This report will be made out for all enlisted personnel immediately preceding separation by discharge and release from active duty, unless discharged on a certificate of disability, or retirement for service.
2. If the declaration of the enlisted man under item ten (10) when yes only, and the certificate of the examining surgeon do not agree, the case will be referred to a board of review to consist of not less than two medical officers, convened in accordance with appropriate Army Regulations.
3. Report will be prepared in duplicate. Each item provided for will be completed with an appropriate notation. The original will be signed.

17

COMMISSION EXHIBIT No. 1707—Continued

CONSULTATION REQUEST AND REPORT

Name Rubenstein, Jack Grade Pfc. Ward

To: Sq. H, 114th B.U., 38366107 Date , 19

For consultation because of

Provisional diagnosis

Routine. ☐
Emergency. ☐

M. C.

Date 9 February 1945

Opinion of consultant:

Patient was seen in this clinic on the 24th of January at which time X-Ray revealed a small chip fracture of the left thumb at the distal interphalangeal joint with non-union. Physiotherapy was ordered and has been administered daily since that time with considerable improvement although thepatient states that he still experiences pain in wet weather. Patient is advised to continue his duty for a month's period and if there is still pain, he can return for further physiotherapy.

JOHN R. GLOVER, Captain M. C.

CI-7-d W. D., A. G. O. Form No. 8-40, 21 June 1944
(This form supersedes W. D., M. D. Form No. 55 E-1, 31 May 1939, which may be used until existing stocks are exhausted.)

18

COMMISSION EXHIBIT No. 1707—Continued

CONSULTATION REQUEST AND REPORT

Name Grade Ward

To: Rubenstein, Jack, Pfc., 38366107, Sq. H, Chatham Field, Ga. Date , 19

For consultation because of

Provisional diagnosis

Routine. ☐
Emergency. ☐

M. C.

Date 24 January 1945

Opinion of consultant:

This patient gives a history of an old injury of the left thumb which continues to pain. The thumb was X-Rayed January 15, 1945, at which time there was observed a small rounded bone fragment along the superior dorsal border of the first metacarpo-phalangeal joint, and most likely representing the end result of a small chip fracture at that level. There is no evidence of any posttraumatic arthritic change at the joint level. The remaining bones of the thumb are negative. This patient would be benefited by physiotherapy but no further treatment is indicated other than this.

JCP/H-7-a W. D., A. G. O. Form No. 8-40, 21 June 1944
(This form supersedes W. D., M. D. Form No. 55 E-1, 31 May 1939, which may be used until existing stocks are exhausted.)

JOHN R. GLOVER, Captain M. C.

19

COMMISSION EXHIBIT No. 1707—Continued

Commission Exhibit No. 1708

Form No. 184

COPY

MEMORANDUM REPORT
BUREAU OF NARCOTICS

CASE FILE No.	SE No.	DISTRICT NO.	GEN. FILE TITLE: Taylor Crossland, Maurice O. Melton, Paul Roland Jones
REPORT MADE AT: Chicago, Illinois DATE: October 31, 1947 BY: A. E. Aman	RELATED FILES: SE-202, Mafia, F 234 and 240		OTHER OFFICERS: Arthur R. Adams, Customs Agent Chicago, Illinois

SUBJECT OF THIS MEMORANDUM: Investigation re: Taylor Crossland, Maurice O. Melton, Paul Roland Jones

RECOMMENDATION: PENDING: CLOSE: FURTHER INVESTIGATION: 11-7-55

DETAILS (If report is over two pages in length summarize in first paragraph)

On October 29, 1947, we interviewed Jack Ruby, a permanent guest, Room 6-142, of the Congress Hotel, Chicago. He identified the photograph of Paul Roland Jones, and has known him for the past four or five months inasmuch as Paul Jones is a friend of his sister, Eva Grant, proprietress of the Singapore Supper Club, 1717 S. Ervay Street, Dallas, Texas. He was introduced to Paul Roland Jones by Eva Grant.

Jack Ruby has talked to Paul Jones on numerous occasions while visiting his sister in Dallas,Texas, but has never had any conversations with him relative to narcotic drugs nor has he ever talked to Paul Jones in the city of Chicago, either personally or via telephone. According to Jack Ruby he was visiting in Dallas, Texas, on August 2nd and 3rd, 1947, which are the dates that Paul Jones, Taylor Crossland and Maurice Melton were in Chicago.

Jack Ruby is a sales promoter, and calls himself a merchandise distributor. He is 36 years of age, 5' 9" tall, weighs about 160, wavy hair, with a high receding hair line, a large, sharp, pointed nose, a fashionable dresser, is of Jewish extraction, and was born at Chicago, Illinois. He is also a brother of Hyman Rubenstein.

Hyman Rubenstein was interviewed, and the attached statement is herewith enclosed; also two business letters, which, seemingly, substantiate his sworn statement.

The registration records of the Sherman Hotel, Chicago, indicates that Paul Jones occupied Rooms 1024 and 674 from October 10, 1947, to October 21, 1947, and the telephone calls made by him have been checked and were made to all legitimate organizations.

The files of this office and the files of the Bureau of Identification, Chicago Police Department, have been examined and there are no records involving Hyman Rubenstein, 3650 W. Lexington St., Chicago, Illinois, or Jack Ruby, his brother, who resides as a permanent guest at the Congress Hotel, Chicago.

COPY OF THIS MEMO FURNISHED TO

BUREAU: (2) 11-5-1947

DISTRICT No. SCA- Laredo, Texas (Ben White) (1)
SCA- Chicago, Ill. (2)

FILES:

SIGNATURES

/s/ A. E. Aman (NARCOTIC AGENT OR INSPECTOR)

APPROVED: /s/ Henry Carman (DISTRICT SUPERVISOR)

12-23-63 cc: Mr. Patrick Putnam, FBI

COMMISSION EXHIBIT No. 1708

COPY

UNITED STATES OF AMERICA, (
SS
DISTRICT OF ILLINOIS)

STATEMENT

I, Hyman Rubenstein, having been informed by Albert E. Aman, known to me to be an agent of the Bureau of Narcotics of the Treasury Department of the United States, and Arthur R. Adams, known to me to be an agent of the Bureau of Customs of the Treasury Department, that I may decline to answer any questions propounded to me by him on the ground that the answers thereto may tend to incriminate me; and having also been informed that this statement may be used in evidence against me in criminal or other proceedings; and no threats of any character having been made against me and no physical violence having been used against my person, and no reward nor immunity having been promised to me in consideration for my making said statement by said Aman or any other person acting for or on behalf of the United States; I do freely and voluntarily make the following statement:

My name is Hyman Rubenstein. I am 46 years of age, born in Warsaw, Poland, and I was naturalized about 1922 in the Federal Building, Chicago, Illinois. My occupation is the candy and novelty business, and I am the proprietor of the Victory Products Company, 3650 Lexington Street, Chicago, Illinois.

I reside with my father, my brother, Sammy, my sister, Marian, and a nephew named Ronnie at 3650 Lexington Street. I have lived in Chicago since I have been 2½ years of age, at which time my people migrated from Poland.

Mr. Aman: Q. I hand you three (3) photographs. Will you examine them and inform me whether or not you know these people.

A. I met Taylor Crossland and Maurice Costello Melton only once. Paul Roland Jones I have known for about a year or less.

Q. When was the first time you met Paul Jones?

A. About ten months ago. He called me at my home and said he was a friend of my sister, Eva Grant, and that he would like to see me if I wasn't too busy. We met at the Sherman Hotel in the Celtic Room, and our conversation was merely general subjects of the day. The next time I met him was on a Sunday morning after he called me at my home, and this meeting was held at the Sherman Hotel in the Celtic Room. He introduced me to Taylor Crossland and Maurice Costello Melton, and we all had breakfast together. The latter meeting held at Hotel Sherman, Celtic Room, took place during the first week of August, 1947.

During this period of time the conversation was about general subjects. We walked around the Loop for about one hour and I pointed out places of interest to the men. Later, I suggested driving them to the Airport because I wasn't busy and inasmuch as they said they were going to Wichita, Kansas. While in my automobile, Melton and Crossland asked

- 1 -

COMMISSION EXHIBIT No. 1708—Continued

me if I could get them a connection on steel pipes and I said I would let them know tomorrow, which I did, and mailed the sample (3/4 inch pipe) to Paul Jones at 3904 Junius Street, Dallas, Texas. I also wrote him a letter with specifications and prices. I never heard a word from him since.

During the period of time spent with Jones, Melton and Crossland, a discussion came up about lumber, inasmuch as Melton asked me. Melton suggested that he could get me carloads of lumber at a very good price. I believe a brother of his had a connection in a lumber mill. I suggested if he would cut off a one foot sample slab so that I could show it to some people here in Chicago, we might be able to do some business. He promised me he would, but I never got a sample.

While we were waiting for the plane, Taylor suggested something about a gold mine that he had with an engineer partner on the Pacific Coast of Mexico. I told him that it took too much money for a guy like me. He said, "Do you think you can find somebody?" I told him there was only one party that I knew who was a prospector and a miner and knows more about that business then I do, and I gave him the name of Joseph Cunningham, located at Room 428, Rowan Bldg., 458 Spring, Los Angeles, Off. Tel. Van Dyke 4044.

Crossland said he would have his engineer write to Cunningham as he knows more about the details of gold mining. No more was ever heard further on this subject. (Residence Tel. Chapman 52801)

During this conversation Paul Jones said that he would like to pick up some new cars if any contacts could be made, but I never tried to make any, and that ended that.

The next time I met Paul Jones was on or about the 15th of October, and he remained in Chicago approximately a week. He called me upon his arrival, at my home, and asked me to meet him in Room 574 at the Sherman Hotel, which I did. He introduced me to a Mr. Wagner, and the importance of my meetings with him each day that he was here was that Mr. Wagner was the inventor of a new type of rubber fabric to be used for re-capping tires. Paul Jones said that he met and talked with Jack Keeshin of the Keeshin Motor Express Corporation, and that Jack Keeshin was going to give it a trial. Paul Jones also said that he made a trip to Canada and attempted to interest either the Goodyear Rubber and the U. S. Rubber Company in this product, but was informed that he would have to take the matter up with the U. S. office in Ohio.

During this week Paul Jones asked me if I could get him 700 gallons of bulk-four-year-old whiskey. I wrote him special delivery air mail letter after he left Chicago, and told him I could get him the whiskey — to find out from his people what they would pay, and to let me know immediately. I have never heard from him on this matter, either.

- 2 -

Commission Exhibit No. 1709—Continued

During these several meetings that I had with Paul Jones, he never mentioned opium, nor any other narcotic drug to me, nor did Crossland or Maurice Melton.

For the Government's information, I want it to be known very clearly that I am a businessman; that I have never been arrested on any charge, and that I absolutely know nothing about opium, or narcotics in any shape, manner or form, nor the illicit traffic of narcotic drugs.

UNITED STATES OF AMERICA }
} SS
DISTRICT OF ILLINOIS }

HYMAN RUBENSTEIN, being first duly sworn, deposes and says that he has read the foregoing statement in question and answer form by him subscribed and knows the contents thereof, and that the same is true in substance and in fact, except as to those matters stated therein to be upon information and belief, and that as to those matters he believes it to be true.

/s/ Hyman Rubenstein

Subscribed and sworn to before me this 30th day of October, A. D. 1947.

Witnessed by:

/s/ Albert E. Aman, Narcotic Agent

- 3 -

Commission Exhibit No. 1709—Continued

UNITED STATES DEPARTMENT OF JUSTICE

FEDERAL BUREAU OF INVESTIGATION
Dallas, Texas

In Reply, Please Refer to
File No.

July 9, 1964

JACK L. RUBY;
LEE HARVEY OSWALD

The investigation reported herein was based on a request in a letter of June 4, 1964, from the President's Commission on the Assassination of President Kennedy for information concerning the existence of phonographic records and papers which former Dallas County Sheriff Steve Guthrie claims were made in connection with Dallas crime investigation, 1946 - 1948. It was also requested it be determined where they are now maintained, how extensive they are, and whether or not they are indexed to show any mention of Ruby.

Records of the Dallas Office of the Federal Bureau of Investigation include three transcripts of conferences held, at which Paul Rowland Jones, Steve Guthrie and George Butler were present, to explore the possibilities of opening Dallas up to gambling with a payoff to be made to Guthrie, who was to become Sheriff of Dallas County. These conferences were held in Dallas on November 1, 5 & 7, 1946. At the time, some of the material recorded on November 1, 1946, was inaudible and a detailed transcript could not be obtained. It was stated some of the records made on that date were summarized, but it was believed the transcript contained all pertinent material discussed at this meeting.

A review of the transcript of the meeting of November 1, 1946, disclosed it was concerned, in part, with a conversation in which Jones told Guthrie that the latter was to pick a local man which the "syndicate" would put in business, would rent a building for him and finance him, and that such a place would be located "in the county" rather than "in the city." The man to be selected would be a local man with a regular business and he would hire local men to run the place. The names of local men

16

COMMISSION EXHIBIT No. 1709

Re: JACK L. RUBY;
LEE HARVEY OSWALD

Bob Fletcher, Tom Cooley and Sherman Little were mentioned. No mention was made of Jack L. Ruby, no specific location was discussed, and there was no discussion concerning the opening of a restaurant at Industrial and Commerce Streets, Dallas.

Review of a transcript of the meeting on November 7, 1946, disclosed a conversation concerning the opening of a gambling establishment in the county, away from the city of Dallas, but no specifics were discussed in this regard, and Ruby's name was not mentioned.

Review of the three transcripts failed to disclose any mention of Ruby or that the discussion ever reached the stage where the particular gambling establishment would be located or who the individual would be to operate it. No mention was made of a restaurant or gambling establishment to be located at Commerce and Industrial Streets.

On June 11, 1964, Lieutenant George Butler, Juvenile Bureau, Dallas Police Department, advised the transcripts of all recordings made in 1946 of the conferences between Steve Guthrie, Paul Rowland Jones and others, at the time Jones was trying to bribe Guthrie to permit gambling in Dallas County were furnished to the Dallas Office of the Federal Bureau of Investigation. Butler said he does not know where the original records might be, but stated the Jones case was submitted to the Texas Supreme Court and it is possible the records were retained by that court.

Butler said Jack Ruby did not arrive in Dallas until about a year after the Jones case "was made," to the best of his recollection. After his arrival in Dallas, Ruby opened his first establishment on South Ervay Street, which was frequented by Jones, along with other Chicago friends of Ruby. Jones was free on appeal at the time and told Butler that Ruby and his sister, Eva Grant, had just come to Dallas and made a lot of money in San Francisco in the "punchboard racket."

17

COMMISSION EXHIBIT No. 1709—Continued

Re: JACK L. RUBY;
LEE HARVEY OSWALD

"The Dallas Morning News" issue of April 16, 1947, included an article concerning the playing of records in the trial of Jones and a number of local persons were mentioned in the records. The name of Jack Ruby was not mentioned in the article.

18

COMMISSION EXHIBIT No. 1709—Continued

OPTIONAL FORM NO. 10
MAY 1962 EDITION
GSA GEN. REG. NO. 27
5010-104

Commission Exhibit No. 1710

UNITED STATES GOVERNMENT

Memorandum

601.0

U. S. Secret Service

TO: SAIC Bouck - PRS

DATE: November 29, 1963

FROM: Chief

SUBJECT: Jack Ruby

Assistant to the Commissioner of Narcotics George Gaffney telephonically advised the undersigned on Tuesday, November 26, 1963, that in the course of a search of their files in a case of theirs reflected that in 1947 they were advised by Customs that Paul Roland Jones, Morris Melton and Taylor Crossland were involved in the act of smuggling opium in Mexico.

Customs asked Narcotics in Chicago to interview Hyman and Jack Ruby at the Congress Hotel to ascertain if they were involved with Jones. The meeting between Jones, Hyman and Jack Ruby was arranged by Eva Grant, 1717 South Ervay Street, who operated the Singapore Club. They met in Jack Ruby's room at the Congress Hotel, Room 6-142.

Co-defendant Melton stated that Hyman and Jack Ruby when propositioned concerning narcotics refused to any part of it.

This information was telephonically communicated to Inspector Kelley in Dallas, Texas on November 26, 1963.

[signature]

cc: SAIC Sorrels, Dallas

194

COMMISSION EXHIBIT No. 1710

FD-302 (Rev. 1-25-60)

FEDERAL BUREAU OF IN[redacted]

Commission Exhibit No. 1711

Date 11/29/63

1

Mr. HERBERT EDEN, 3846 Beverly Ridge Drive, advised that he has resided at this residence just a few days having moved from 928 Clarke Street, LosAngeles, California. He advised that his former telephone was OL 2-3849 and is presently 789-3696.

Mr. EDEN advised that he is a commedian and is presently engaged in the Body Shop located at 8250 Sunset Boulevard, Hollywood, California. During the end of October 1962 EDEN advised that he had a contract with the Colony Club in Dallas, Texas, next door to the Carousel Club owned by JACK RUBY. EDEN advised that he met RUBY on one of his first evenings in which he worked at the Colony Club. He advised that RUBY took he and EARL NORMAN, the commedian whose place he was taking at the Colony Club to breakfast. He advised that he associated on a social basis with RUBY and he would frequently go over to the Carousel when he was not entertaining to see the commedian or to visit with JACK RUBY. He advised that JACK RUBY did not get along with the owner of the Colony Club but was friendly with the employees and entertainers of the Colony Club as well as his own club, the Carousel. He advised that JACK RUBY asked him to work for him at the Carousel Club and that he originally turned RUBY's offer down because he was booked on tour and had prior committments. He also advised that RUBY within the last two weeks telephoned him at his home asking him to come to work. EDEN advised, however, that RUBY is not able to pay him enough money and for this reason turned RUBY down.

EDEN advised he associated with RUBY for about 4 weeks during his first engagement at the Colony Club and was again associated with RUBY over a three week period during the end of December 1962, and part of January, 1963, when he was again booked at the Colony Club.

MAGID advised that he knows RUBY has a sister in Dallas, Texas, who operates the Club Vegas, a rock and roll club. He stated that RUBY apparently owns the Club Vegas and his sister

On 11/28/63 at Sherman Oaks, California File # LA 44-895

by SA EUGENE I. TUGGEY, JR. SA JOSEPH P. BACKUS/meh Date dictated 11/29/63

177

COMMISSION EXHIBIT No. 1711

manages the club or possibly the two of them have some kind of partnership arrangement,

He advised that to his knowledge RUBY has no gangland connections and is not involved with any hoodlums. He stated that the Club is a legitimate business and is run "very clean." He further advised that he has no knowledge concerning any possible subversive activities or connections on the part of RUBY. He further stated that he had no knowledge of any connections RUBY might have had with the Fair Play for Cuba. EDEN further advised that the Dallas police officers whom he met through RUBY seemed very friendly to RUBY. He believed that RUBY knew everyone of importance on the Dallas Police Force. He stated this was due to the fact that RUBY is a very "outgoing guy" and because of his position as a club owner would come in contact with many police officers.

EDEN advised that prior to the President's assassination, as part of an act he did quite a bit of topical political type jokes in which he would poke fun at the present administration, the President JOHN F. KENNEDY and his wife JACQUELINE KENNEDY. He advised that JACK RUBY told him on one occasion that the jokes were funny but that only idiots would laugh at them. He stated that RUBY prohibited any of the entertainers from saying anything or using any material that would reflect adversely against "Negroes, Jews or the Kennedys." He commented to EDEN that he did not appreciate commedians "knocking the President or his wife JACQUELINE KENNEDY."

Mr. EDEN stated that from his acquaintance and knowledge of JACK RUBY he believes that his action in shooting HARVEY LEE OSWALD was the result of a "brooding sick man." He advised that RUBY was able to change moods in an instant and recalls one evening he was sitting in the back of the club with RUBY and they were having a very jovial conversation. During the conversation one of the waitresses came up to RUBY and told him that entertainer BILLY DEMARS, a ventriloquist, was getting a bad time from a customer who was calling DEMARS names. In a flash RUBY's attitude changed to a very rough gruff man and he immediately went to the customer and in very quick fashion removed him from the club. He advised that after this RUBY came back to the table

178

COMMISSION EXHIBIT No. 1711—Continued

and resumed his jovial attitude. He advised that RUBY was the type of person who could change his manner in an instant.

He further advised that he possesses no information concerning LEE HARVEY OSWALD and never heard of OSWALD until the news of the assassination was broadcast over the elevision. He advised that he knows of no connection between OSWALD or RUBY.

179

COMMISSION EXHIBIT No. 1711—Continued

FD-302 (Rev. 3-3-59)

FEDERAL BUREAU OF INVESTIGATION

Date 11/24/63

ABE L. WEINSTEIN, 11028 Westmere Circle, owner and operator of Abe's Colony Club, advised he has been in the club business for thirty years and that JACK RUBENSTEIN is a competitor of his, operating the Carousel next door for the past two or three years. WEINSTEIN stated he does not speak to RUBENSTEIN because he does not approve of RUBENSTEIN's ethics. He stated that on some occasions when he has a crowd waiting to get in his place of business, RUBENSTEIN will come over and pass out cards and offer free drinks to get the customers to come to RUBENSTEIN's club.

He stated he really knows nothing about RUBENSTEIN, but understands that he originally came from Chicago to Dallas in approximately 1950; that he is single; that he has a sister named EVA GRANT, who owns and operates the Vegas Club in Dallas.

WEINSTEIN stated that he has received long distance calls, November 24, 1963, from WALTER CRONKITE; Life Magazine, The Kansas City Star, and the Houston Post, making inquiry concerning JACK RUBENSTEIN, and he has advised each of those sources that he knows nothing about RUBENSTEIN. He stated that approximately three weeks ago RUBENSTEIN had a fight with one of the strippers working at RUBENSTEIN's and she had him put under a peace bond, and he was arrested and had her put under a peace bond. He stated he also recalls hearing that when RUBENSTEIN formerly operated the Silver Spur, he got into a fight with a man, name not now recalled, who bit RUBENSTEIN's finger off.

He stated the only persons that he can think of who may know something about RUBENSTEIN would be JACK COLE, theatrical agent, now at Houston, who formerly officed in the Interurban Building in Dallas; TOM PALMER, District Manager of AGVA, Dallas, and Lieutenant JIM GILMORE of the Dallas Police Department, who is in charge of dance halls, and is in his place of business, as well as RUBENSTEIN's every night they are open.

WEINSTEIN stated that he knows nothing about LEE HARVEY OSWALD. He stated the photograph of OSWALD, New Orleans, Louisiana No. 112723, looks almost identical with JACK RUBENSTEIN.

on 11/24/63 at Dallas, Texas File # DL 44-1639

by Special Agent JOHN CALVIN RICE and JCR ALFRED D. NEELEY ADN/HM Date dictated 11/24/63

579

COMMISSION EXHIBIT No. 1712

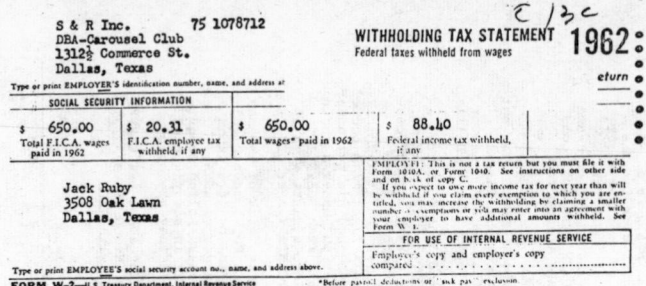

S & R Inc. 75 1078712
DBA-Carousel Club
1312½ Commerce St.
Dallas, Texas

Type or print EMPLOYER'S identification number, name, and address at

C 13c

WITHHOLDING TAX STATEMENT **1962**

Federal taxes withheld from wages

eturn

SOCIAL SECURITY INFORMATION			
$ 650.00	$ 20.31	$ 650.00	$ 88.40
Total F.I.C.A. wages paid in 1962	F.I.C.A. employee tax withheld, if any	Total wages* paid in 1962	Federal income tax withheld, if any

Jack Ruby
3508 Oak Lawn
Dallas, Texas

Type or print EMPLOYEE'S social security account no., name, and address above.

EMPLOYEE: This is not a tax return but you must file it with Form 1040A, or Form 1040. See instructions on other side and on back of copy C.

If you expect to owe more income tax for next year than will be withheld if you claim every exemption to which you are entitled, you may increase the withholding by claiming a smaller number of exemptions or you may enter into an agreement with your employer to have additional amounts withheld. See Form W-4.

FOR USE OF INTERNAL REVENUE SERVICE

Employee's copy and employer's copy compared . . . .

FORM W-2—U.S. Treasury Department, Internal Revenue Service

*Before payroll deductions or "sick pay" exclusion.

Commission Exhibit No. 1713

NOTICE TO EMPLOYEE:

1. Income Tax Wages.—This statement is important. It must be filed with your U. S. Income Tax Return for 1962. If your account number, name, or address is stated incorrectly, correct the information on copy B and notify your employer.

2. Social Security Wages.—If your wages were subject to social security taxes, but are not shown, your social security wages are the same as wages shown under "Income Tax Information," but not more than $4,800.

3. Credit For F.I.C.A. Tax.—If more than $150.00 of F.I.C.A. (social security) employee tax was withheld during 1962 because you received wages from more than one employer, the excess should be claimed as a credit against income tax. See instructions with your income tax return.

☆ U. S. GOVERNMENT PRINTING OFFICE

Commission Exhibit No. 1713—Continued

Form 1040 — U.S. Treasury Department, Internal Revenue Service

U.S. INDIVIDUAL INCOME TAX RETURN—1962

or taxable year beginning .... 1962, ending .... 19 ....

Your Social Security Number

First name and initial: Jack — Last name: Ruby — Occupation: Night Club Operator

Home address: 223 So. Ewing, Apt. 207 (Number and street or rural route)

Wife's Social Security Number

Dallas (City, town, or post office) — Texas (State) — Occupation

Check one: [X] Single; [ ] Unmarried "Head of Household"; [ ] Surviving widow or widower with dependent child; [ ] Married filing joint return (even if only one had income); [ ] Married filing separate return—If wife or husband also filing separately, give name

INCOME—(If joint return, include all income of both husband and wife)

1. Wages, salaries, tips, etc., and excess of allowances over business expenses.

Employer's name	Where employed (city and state)	(a) Wages, etc.	(b) Federal income tax withheld
S & R, Inc.	Dallas, Texas	$ 650 00	$ 88 40

If either you or your wife worked for more than one employer, see page 4 of instructions

2. Totals	650 00	88 40
3. "Sick pay" if included in line 1 (attach required statement)		
4. Subtract line 3 from total wages		650 00
5a. Dividends (Schedule B)		
b. Interest (Schedule B or other list)		
c. Rents, royalties, pensions, etc. (Schedule B)		
6. Business income (Schedule C)		5,619 65
7. Sale or exchange of property (Schedule D)		
8. Farm income (Schedule F)		
9. Total (add lines 4 through 8)		6,269 65

● Attach Copy B of Forms W-2 Here ●

FIGURE YOUR TAX BY USING EITHER 10 OR 11

10. Tax Table — If line 9 is less than $5,000 and you do not itemize deductions—Complete page 2 exemption schedule. Copy total exemptions here ...... Find your tax in table on page 10 of instructions. Do not use lines 11 a, b, c, or d. Enter tax on line 12.

11. Tax Rate Schedule

a. If you itemize deductions, enter total from page 2. If line 9 is $5,000 or more and you do not itemize, enter 10% of line 9 but not more than $1,000 ($500 if married and filing separate return).	626 97
b. Subtract line 11a from line 9	5,642 68
c. Copy total exemptions from page 2 here 1, multiply by $600	600 00
d. Subtract line 11c from line 11b	5,042 68

Figure your tax on this amount by using tax rate schedule on page 9 of instructions and enter tax on line 12.

12. Tax (from either tax table or tax rate schedule)	1,111 10
13. Self-employment tax (Schedule C-3 or F-1)	195 05
14. Total (add lines 12 and 13)	1,306 15

PAYMENTS AND CREDITS

15a. Tax withheld (line 2, col. (b) above). Attach Forms W-2	88 40	
b. Payments and credits on 1962 Declaration of Estimated Tax		
c. Dividends received credit		
d. Retirement income credit		
e. Investment credit (Form 3468)		
f. Other credits (Specify—see page 5 of instructions)		
g. Total (add lines a, b, c, d, e, and f)		88 40

District Director's office where amount on line 15b was paid

REMITTANCE SEP 18 1963 DIST. D.R. INT. REV. DALLAS MAIL UNIT

TAX DUE OR REFUND

16. If payments and credits (line 15g) are less than tax (line 14), enter Balance Due here. Pay in full with this return to "Internal Revenue Service." File with your District Director.	1,217 75
17. If payments and credits (line 15g) are larger than tax (line 14), enter Overpayment here	
18. Amount of line 17 you wish credited to 1963 Estimated Tax	
19. Subtract line 18 from line 17. Apply this balance to: [ ] U.S. Savings Bonds; or [ ] Refund	

● Attach Check or Money Order Here ●

c30—16—77172—1

★ List your exemptions and sign on other side

3

COMMISSION EXHIBIT No. 1713—Continued

Form 1040—1962 — Page 2

SCHEDULE A.—EXEMPTIONS (See page 6 of instructions)

1. Exemptions for yourself—and wife (only if all her income is included in this return, or she had no income)

Check boxes which apply:
(a) Regular $600 exemption — X Yourself / Wife
(b) Additional $600 exemption if 65 or over at end of 1962 — Yourself / Wife
(c) Additional $600 exemption if blind at end of 1962 — Yourself / Wife
Enter number of boxes checked → 1

2. Exemptions for your children and other dependents (list below)
● If an exemption is based on a multiple-support agreement of a group of persons, attach the declarations described on page 6 of instructions.

NAME (Enter figure 1 in the last column to right for each name listed; Give address if different from yours)	Relationship	Months lived in your home. If born or died during year also write "B" or "D"	Did dependent have income of $600 or more?	Amount YOU furnished for dependent's support. If 100% write "ALL"	Amount furnished by OTHERS including dependent	
				$	$	

3. Total exemptions (lines 1 and 2 above). (Enter here and on line 10 or 11c, page 1) → 1

ITEMIZED DEDUCTIONS—If you do not use tax table or standard deduction

If husband and wife not legally separated file separate returns and one itemizes deductions the other must also itemize.
If necessary, write more than one item on a line or attach additional sheets. Put name, address and Social Security number on all attachments

Contributions (If other than money, submit description of property, including cost or other basis, date of acquisition and method of valuation)
Total paid (not to exceed 20% of line 9, page 1, except as described on page 7 of instructions) → $

Interest expense
Total interest →

Taxes: Real estate taxes; State and local sales taxes; State income taxes; Other taxes (specify)
Total taxes →

Medical and dental expense (Submit itemized list. Do not enter any expense compensated by insurance or otherwise)
NOTE: If you or your wife are 65 or over, or if either has a dependent parent 65 or over, see page 8 of Instructions for possible larger deduction.
1. Total cost of medicine and drugs $
2. Enter 1% of line 9, page 1
3. Subtract line 2 from line 1
4. Other medical, dental expenses (Include hospital insurance premiums)
5. Total (add lines 3 and 4)
6. Enter 3% of line 9, page 1 (see note above) $
7. Subtract line 6 from line 5; see page 8 of instructions for maximum limitation

Other deductions (See page 8 of instructions)
Total →

Total deductions (Enter here and on line 11a, page 1) → $

EXPENSE ACCOUNT INFORMATION: Did you receive an expense allowance or reimbursement, or charge expenses to your employer? [ ] Yes [X] No. If "Yes," did you submit itemized accounting of all such expenses to your employer? [ ] Yes [ ] No. See page 4, instructions.

Did you file a return last year? [X] Yes [ ] No. If name or address on last year's returns was different from this year, enter name and address used last year.
Jack Ruby, 500 South Marsailles, Apt. 205 Dallas, Texas

I declare under penalties of perjury that I have examined this return (including accompanying schedules and statements) and to the best of my knowledge and belief it is true, correct, and complete. If prepared by a person other than taxpayer, his declaration is based on all information of which he has any knowledge.

Sign here: Jack Ruby 9/13/63 (Taxpayer's signature and date) (If joint return, BOTH HUSBAND AND WIFE MUST SIGN) (Wife's signature and date)

Sign here: [signature] (Signature of preparer other than taxpayer) — 1104 Fidelity Union Life Bldg. Dallas, Texas (Address) — 9-13-63 (Date)

c30—16—77172—1

4

COMMISSION EXHIBIT No. 1713—Continued

SCHEDULE C (Form 1040) U. S. Treasury Department Internal Revenue Service	PROFIT (OR LOSS) FROM BUSINESS OR PROFESSION (Compute social security self-employment tax on Schedule C-3 (Form 1040))	1962

Attach this schedule to your income tax return, Form 1040 — Partnerships, joint ventures, etc., must file on Form 1065

Name and address as shown on page 1, Form 1040: Jack Ruby, 223 So. Ewing, Apt. 207, Dallas, Texas — Your Social Security Number:

A. Principal business activity Night Club ; product (See separate instructions) (For example: retail—grocer, wholesale—tobacco, legal—services, manufacturing—furniture, etc.)

B. Business name Club Vegas **C.** Employer Identification Number 75-0949491

D. Business location 3508 Oak Lawn (Number and street or rural route) Dallas (City or post office) Texas (State)

E. Indicate method of accounting: ☒ cash; ☐ accrual; ☐ other.

1.	Gross receipts or gross sales $ .... Less: Returns and allowances $		48,150 00
2.	Inventory at beginning of year (If different than last year's closing inventory attach explanation)	165.00	
3.	Merchandise purchased $ ...., less cost of any items withdrawn from business for personal use $	6,697.23	
4.	Cost of labor (do not include salary paid to yourself)		
5.	Material and supplies		
6.	Other costs (explain in Schedule C-1)		
7.	Total of lines 2 through 6	6,862.23	
8.	Inventory at end of this year	175.00	
9.	**Cost of goods sold** (line 7 less line 8)		6,687 23
10.	**Gross profit** (subtract line 9 from line 1)		41,462 77

OTHER BUSINESS DEDUCTIONS

11.	Depreciation (explain in Schedule C-2)	2,502.24	
12.	Taxes on business and business property (explain in Schedule C-1)	6,000.00	
13.	Rent on business property	228.47	
14.	Repairs (explain in Schedule C-1)	22,359.88	
15.	Salaries and wages not included on line 4 (exclude any paid to yourself)		
16.	Insurance		
17.	Legal and professional fees		
18.	Commissions		
19.	Amortization (attach statement)		
20.	Interest on business indebtedness		
21.	Bad debts arising from sales or services		
22.	Losses of business property (attach statement)		
23.	Depletion of mines, oil and gas wells, timber, etc. (attach schedule)		
24.	Other business expenses (explain in Schedule C-1)	4,752.53	
25.	Total of lines 11 through 24		35,843 12
26.	**Net profit (or loss)** (subtract line 25 from line 10). Enter here; on line 1, Schedule C-3; and on line 6, page 1, Form 1040		5,619 65

SCHEDULE C-1. EXPLANATION OF LINES 6, 12, 14, AND 24

Line No.	Explanation	Amount	Line No.	Explanation	Amount
24	Advertising	$ 2,283.12	14	Repairs & Maint.	$ 228.47
24	Telep. & Teleg.	334.78			
24	Light, Heat & Water	1,141.25			
24	Ice	218.76			
24	Laundry Service	171.16			
24	Supplies	279.83			
24	Dues & Subscription	291.00			
24	Misc. Expense	32.63			

16—77170-1

5

[illegible] foreign government, or an international organization which is organized under the International Organizations Immunities Act, is subject to the social security self-employment tax. These employees should report their income from such employment on line 5(e), of this Schedule, compute their self-employment tax, and file the schedule with their Form 1040. In item B of Schedule SE, enter "Employee of foreign government, etc."

Farm income.—Farmers report farm income and net earnings from farm self-employment on separate Schedules F and F-1 (Form 1040).

EXCLUSIONS

Income (or loss) from the following sources and deductions attributable thereto are not taken into account in figuring net earnings from self-employment. Use line 4 to exclude any such amounts reported on separate Schedule C (Form 1040) that should not be taken into account in figuring your self-employment income.

Doctors of medicine.—Income from the performance of service as a doctor of medicine or income from the performance of such service by a partnership.

Christian Science practitioners.—Income from the performance of service as a Christian Science practitioner, unless such Christian Science practitioner elects by filing Form 2031 to be covered by the Social Security Act, as explained above.

Religious services.—Income from the performance of service by a duly ordained, commissioned, or licensed minister of a church in the exercise of his ministry or by a member of a religious order in the exercise of duties required by such order, unless such minister or member of a religious order elects by filing Form 2031 to be covered by the Social Security Act, as explained above.

Employees and public officials.—Income (fees, salaries, etc.) from the performance of service as:

(a) a public official, including a notary public;
(b) an employee or employee representative under the railroad retirement system; or
(c) an employee (except as indicated above).

Note.—The income of an employee over the age of 18 from the sale of newspapers or magazines to an ultimate consumer is subject to the self-employment tax if the income consists of retained profits from such sales.

Real estate rentals.—Rentals from real estate, except rentals received in the course of a trade or business as a real estate dealer. This includes cash and crop shares received from a tenant or sharefarmer. These amounts should be reported in Part IV, Schedule B (Form 1040). However, rental income from a farm is not excluded if the rental arrangement provides for material participation by the landlord and he does participate materially in the production or in the management of the production of one or more farm products on his land. Such income represents farm earnings and should be reported on separate Schedules F and F-1.

Payments for the use or occupancy of rooms or other space where services are also rendered to the occupant, such as rooms in hotels, boarding houses, apartment houses furnishing hotel services, tourist camps, or homes, or space in parking lots, warehouses, or storage garages do not constitute rentals from real estate and are included in determining net earnings from self-employment on this Schedule.

Interest and dividends.—Dividends on shares of stock, and interest on bonds, debentures, notes, certificates, or other evidences

JOINT RETURNS

Where husband and wife file a joint income tax return, Schedule C-3 (Form 1040) should show the name of the one with self-employment income. Where husband and wife each have self-employment income, separate Schedules C and C-3 must be attached for each. In such cases the total of amounts shown on line 26 of each separate Schedule C should be entered on line 6, page 1, Form 1040, and the aggregate self-employment tax (line 11) Schedule C-3 should be entered on line 13, page 1, Form 1040.

COMMUNITY INCOME

For the purpose of computing net earnings from self-employment, if any of the income from a trade or business is community income, all the income from such trade or business is considered the income of the husband unless the wife exercises substantially all the management and control of the trade or business, in which case all of such income is considered the income of the wife. (Also see instructions on partnerships below.)

If separate income tax returns are filed by husband and wife, Schedules C and C-3 should be attached to the return of the one with self-employment income. Community income included on Schedule C must be allocated between the two returns (on line 6, page 1, Form 1040) on the basis of the community property laws.

PARTNERSHIPS

In computing his combined net earnings from self-employment, a partner should include his entire share of such earnings from a partnership including any guaranteed payments. No part of that share may be allocated to the partner's wife (or husband) even though the income may, under State law, be community income. In the case of a husband and wife partnership, like other partnerships, the distributive share of each should be entered in Part V of Schedule B (Form 1040), for income tax purposes. For self-employment tax purposes the distributive share of each partner should be entered on line 5(b), of this Schedule (except that farm partnership earnings are to be reported on line 1(b), Schedule F-1 (Form 1040) rather than on line 5(b) of this schedule).

Note.—If a member of a continuing partnership dies, a portion of the deceased partner's distributive share of the partnership's ordinary income (or loss) for the taxable year of the partnership in which he died must be included in the partner's net earnings from self-employment. In such cases consult your nearest Internal Revenue Service office as to how to report.

SCHEDULE SE (Form 1040)

Schedule SE, which is the lower portion of this Schedule, provides the Social Security Administration with the information on self-employment income necessary for computing benefits.

To assure proper credit to your account, be sure to enter your name and social security account number on Schedule SE (Form 1040) exactly as they are shown on your social security card. If you do not have a social security account number, you must get one. These account numbers are obtainable from any social security district office. Your local post office will give you the address. Do not delay filing your return beyond the due date.

Regardless of whether joint or separate returns are filed by husband and wife, Schedule SE (Form 1040) must show only the name of the one with the self-employment income. However, if both had self-employment income, a separate Schedule SE must be filed by each.

U.S. GOVERNMENT PRINTING OFFICE 16—77170-1

6

SCHEDULE C-3 (Form 1040) | U. S. Treasury Department—Internal Revenue Service | **COMPUTATION OF SOCIAL SECURITY SELF-EMPLOYMENT TAX** (See instructions on page 2) | 1962

▶ If you had wages of $4,800 or more which were subject to social security taxes, do not fill in this page.
▶ Complete only one Schedule C-3; if you had more than one business, combine profits (or losses) from all of your businesses on this Schedule.
▶ Each self-employed person must file a separate schedule. See instructions, page 2, for joint returns and partnerships.

NAME AND ADDRESS (as shown on page 1 of Form 1040)
Jack Ruby, 223 So. Ewing, Apt. 207, Dallas, Texas

NAME OF SELF-EMPLOYED PERSON (as shown on social security card) — Your Social Security Number
Jack Ruby

1. Net profit (or loss) shown on line 26 Schedule C (Form 1040) (**Enter combined amount if more than one business**)	5,619 65	
2. Add to net profit (or subtract from net loss) losses of business property shown on line 22, Schedule C		
3. Total (or difference)		5,619 65
4. Net income (or loss) from excluded services or sources included on line 3 (see "Exclusions," page 2) Specify excluded services or sources		
5. Net earnings (or loss) from self-employment—		
(a) From business (line 3 less any amount on line 4)		5,619 65
(b) From partnerships, joint ventures, etc. (other than farming)		
(c) From service as a minister, member of a religious order, or a Christian Science practitioner Enter only if you have filed or are filing Form 2031 (see instructions, page 2).		
(d) From farming reported on line 2 (or line 3 if option used), separate Schedule F-1 (Form 1040)		
(e) From service with a foreign government or international organization		
6. Total net earnings (or loss) from self-employment reported on line 5. Enter here and in item F below **(If line 6 is under $400, you are not subject to self-employment tax. Do not fill in rest of page.)**		5,619 65
7. The largest amount of combined wages and self-employment earnings subject to social security tax is	$ 4,800 00	
8. Total wages, covered by social security, paid to you during the taxable year. (For "Covered" wages see "F. I. C. A. Wages" box on Form W-2.) Enter here and in item G, below	650 00	
9. Balance (line 7 less line 8)	$ 4,150 00	
10. Self-employment income—line 6 or 9, whichever is smaller. Enter here and in item H, below		4,150 00
11. Self-employment tax—If line 10 is $4,800, enter $225.60; if less, multiply the amount on line 10 by 4.7%. Enter this amount here and on line 13, page 1, Form 1040		195 05

Do not detach

7

COMMISSION EXHIBIT No. 1713—Continued

SCHEDULE C-2. EXPLANATION OF DEDUCTION FOR DEPRECIATION CLAIMED ON LINE 11

This schedule is designed for taxpayers using the new guideline lives and administrative procedures described in Revenue Procedure 62-21 as well as for those taxpayers who wish to continue using previously authorized procedures. Where double headings appear use the first heading for the new procedure and the second heading for the older procedure.

1. Group and guideline class —OR— Description of property	2. Cost or other basis at beginning of year —OR— Cost or other basis	3. Asset additions in year (amount) —OR— Date acquired	4. Asset retirements in year (amount) (applicable only to Rev. Proc. 62-21)	5. Depreciation allowed or allowable in prior years	6. Method of computing depreciation	7. Class life —OR— Rate (%) or life	8. Depreciation for this year
1. Totals							

2. Less: Amount of depreciation claimed elsewhere in Schedule C
3. Balance—Enter here and on line 11, page 1
4. Amount of additional first-year depreciation included above
5. Cost or other basis of fully depreciated assets still in use

INVENTORY QUESTIONS

1. Was inventory valued at—Cost ☒; lower of cost or market ☐; other ☐. If other, attach explanation.
2. Have write-downs been made to inventory? Yes ☐ No ☐. If "Yes," were the write-downs computed on the basis of:
   (a) ☐ Percentage reductions from parts of the inventory
   (b) ☐ Percentage reductions from the total inventory
   (c) ☐ Valuation of individual items.
   If "a" or "b" is checked, enter the percentage of write-downs ....%. For "a," "b," or "c" enter the dollar amount of write-downs $........
   (If not available, estimate and indicate that the figure is an estimate.)
3. Was the inventory verified by physical count during the year?
   Yes ☐ No ☐. If "No," attach explanation of how the closing inventory was determined.
4. Was there any substantial change in the manner of determining quantities, costs or valuations between the opening and closing inventories? Yes ☐ No ☒. If "Yes," attach explanation.

NOTE: If a direct answer cannot be given to a question, attach explanation.

EXPENSE ACCOUNT INFORMATION

Enter information with regard to yourself and your five highest paid employees. In determining the five highest paid employees, expense account allowances must be added to their salaries and wages. However, the information need not be submitted for any employee for whom the combined amount is less than $10,000, or for yourself if your expense account allowance plus line 26, page 1, is less than $10,000. See separate instructions for Schedule C, for definition of "expense account."

Name	Expense account	Salaries and Wages
Owner		XXXXXXXXXXXXX
1.		
2.		
3.		
4.		
5.		

Did you claim a deduction for expenses connected with: (If answer to any question is "YES," check applicable boxes within that question.)

F. A hunting lodge ☐, working ranch or farm ☐, fishing camp ☐, resort property ☐, pleasure boat or yacht ☐, or other similar facility ☐? (Other than where the operation of the facility was your principal business.) ☐ YES ☒ NO

G. Vacations for you or members of your family, or employees or members of their families? (Other than vacation pay reported on Form W-2.) ☐ YES ☒ NO

H. The leasing, renting, or ownership of a hotel room or suite ☐, apartment ☐, or other dwelling ☐, which was used by you, your customers, employees, or members of their families? (Other than use by yourself or employees while in business travel status.) ☐ YES ☒ NO

I. The attendance of members of your family or your employees' families at conventions or business meetings? ☐ YES ☒ NO

o80—16—77170-1

8

COMMISSION EXHIBIT No. 1713—Continued

JACK RUBY - DBA
CLUB VEGAS
3508 OAK LAWN-DALLAS, TEXAS

STATEMENT OF INCOME, PROFIT & LOSS
CALENDAR YEAR 1962

Gross Receipts			$48,150.00
Cost of Goods Sold			
Inventory 1-1-62		$ 165.00	
Purchases		6,697.23	
		$6,862.23	
Less: Inventory 12-31-62		175.00	
Total Cost of Goods Sold			$ 6,687.23
Gross Profit			$41,462.77
Less: Operating Expenses			
Salaries		$22,359.88	
Rent		6,000.00	
Advertising		2,283.12	
Telephone & Telegraph		334.78	
Light, Heat & Water		1,141.25	
Ice		218.76	
Laundry		171.16	
Supplies		279.83	
Repairs & Maintenance		228.47	
Dues		291.00	
Taxes		2,502.24	
F.I.C.A.	$ 698.86		
T.E.C.	282.70		
Fed. Unemployment Tax	161.54		
License-Beer	30.00		
State & County	64.38		
State Tax	1,264.76		
Miscellaneous Expense		32.63	
Total Expenses			$35,843.12
Net Income			$ 5,619.65

9

FORM 2688
(Rev. Nov. 1962)

U.S. Treasury Department—Internal Revenue Service

APPLICATION FOR EXTENSION OF TIME TO FILE

U.S. Individual Income Tax Return

File in duplicate with your District Director on or before the due date for filing the return.

Name JACK RUBY
Address 3508 OAKLAWN AVE. (Number and street or rural route)
DALLAS (City, town, or post office) (Postal zone number) TEXAS (State)
Your Social Security Number

(See Instructions on Reverse Side)

1. An extension of time until APRIL 30TH is hereby requested in which to file the individual income tax return (Form 1040) of the taxpayer named above for the calendar year 1962 or other taxable year beginning .... and ending ....

2. State *in detail* the reason the extension is needed (see instruction 3): INCOMPLETE RECORDS

3. Did you file an individual income tax return on time (including any authorized extension) for each of the 3 years immediately preceding the year for which this extension is requested? ☐ Yes ☐ No

If the answer is NO, list each year during the 3-year period for which a return was not timely filed, and state the reason.

4. Were you required to file a declaration of estimated tax for the year for which this extension is requested? ☐ Yes ☐ No
If the answer is YES, was each installment payment made on or before its due date? ☐ Yes ☐ No ☐ None required

.... (Date) Jack Ruby (Taxpayer's signature*)

*If signed on behalf of the taxpayer by another person, see instruction 6 on reverse side.

THE INTERNAL REVENUE SERVICE WILL INDICATE BELOW WHETHER THE EXTENSION IS GRANTED OR DENIED AND WILL RETURN THE ORIGINAL OF THIS APPLICATION TO YOU

NOTICE TO APPLICANT:

☐ Your application is approved. This form must be attached to your individual income tax return when filed as evidence that the extension was granted. Interest accrues at the rate of 6 percent per year on any tax due for the year from the regular due date of the return until paid.

☐ Your application cannot be considered since it was received in this office after the due date of the return. Your return should be filed without further delay. Please attach this form to the return to explain the delay in filing.

☑ Careful consideration has been given to the reasons and other data given in your application but it has been determined that the extension is not warranted. Your return should be filed by the regular due date or within 10 days of the date of signature of this notice. If the end of such 10-day period is later than the regular due date. Please attach this form to the return to explain the delay in filing.

☐ Other:

APR 4 1963 (Date) 10 Ellis Campbell, Jr. (District Director)

INSTRUCTIONS

1. When to file.—A taxpayer desiring an extension of time for filing an individual income tax return on Form 1040 must submit an application on or before the due date of the return. If possible the application should be submitted in sufficient time to enable the District Director to consider and to act on the application before the regular due date of the return.

2. How and where to file.—Complete this form in duplicate and file with the District Director of Internal Revenue for the district in which you live.

U.S. citizens abroad who have no legal residence or place of business in the United States should file with the Director of International Operations, Internal Revenue Service, Washington 25, D.C. If a U.S. citizen abroad is requesting an extension of time for filing because he expects to receive income which will be exempt under section 911 of the Internal Revenue Code, he should use Form 2350 rather than this form.

3. Reasons for extension.—The District Director will grant a reasonable extension of time for filing a return if the taxpayer files a timely application which establishes that he is unable to file the return by the due date because of circumstances beyond his control. Generally, an application will be considered in the light of the efforts made by the taxpayer to fulfill his own filing responsibility, rather than the convenience of anyone who assists him. However, consideration will be given to circumstances in which the taxpayer's practitioner is unable, due to reasons beyond his control, to complete the return for filing by the due date, or to other circumstances in which a taxpayer is unable to get essential professional assistance in spite of timely efforts to obtain it.

The reason for the application which is called for in Item 2 should be explained to clearly describe the circumstances beyond the taxpayer's control, which have caused the unavoidable delay in filing the return. Applications which give incomplete reasons such as "illness" or "practitioner too busy" without adequate explanations, will not be approved.

4. Blanket requests.—Blanket requests for extensions will not be granted.

5. Period of extension.—Generally, extensions of time on an initial application will be limited to a period of time not in excess of 60 days. Longer periods of time will not be granted unless sufficient need for such extended period is clearly shown. In no event will an extension be granted in excess of 6 months for taxpayers within the United States.

6. Signature.—The application must be signed by the taxpayer or a duly authorized agent. If it is signed by a person with a duly authorized power of attorney, a statement to that effect should be made below. It will not be necessary to attach a copy of the power of attorney.

If the taxpayer is unable to sign the application because of illness, absence, or other good cause, any person standing in close personal or business relationship to him may sign the application. However, the signer must state below the reasons for his signature and his relationship to the taxpayer.

U.S. GOVERNMENT PRINTING OFFICE : 1962—O—646806

(For additional information)

11

COMMISSION EXHIBIT No. 1713—Continued

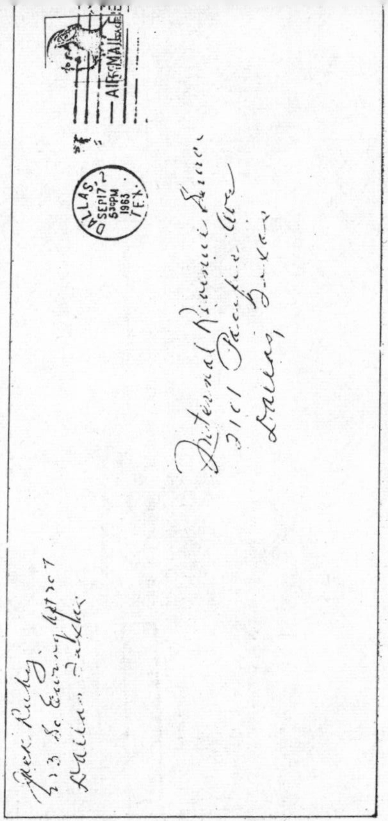

12

COMMISSION EXHIBIT No. 1713—Continued

EXTRACT FROM .H-15. 62 5-21-62 1714

21 - 49n-0586.13

FORM 1040

U.S. Treasury Department
Internal Revenue Service

U.S. INDIVIDUAL INCOME TAX RETURN—1961

or taxable year beginning .... 1961, ending 19

F 611094
Your Social Security Number

PLEASE PRINT OR TYPE

First name and initial	Last name	Occupation
Jack	Ruby	Night Club Oper

(If joint return of husband and wife, use first names and middle initials of both)

Home address: 3508 Oak Lawn (Number and street or rural route)

Wife's Social Security Number

Dallas (City, town, or post office) , (Postal zone number) Texas (State)

Occupation

Check One: [X] Single; [ ] Unmarried "Head of Household"; [ ] Surviving widow or widower with dependent child; [ ] Married filing joint return; [ ] Married filing separate return—Name of wife (husband)

● Attach Check or Money Order Here ●

● Attach Copy B of Forms W-2 Here ●

INCOME—(If joint return, include all income of both husband and wife)

1. Wages, salaries, tips, etc., and excess of allowances over business expenses.

Employer's name	Where employed (city and state)	(a) Wages, etc.	(b) Federal income tax withheld
Carousel Club	Dallas, Texas	$ 900 00	$
...e than one employer, see page 4 of instructions	Totals here →	900 00	

Assessment	Dist.
Tax $	
Pen. $ 56.82	
Int. $ 3.40	
Total $ 60.22	
IR Code Section 6651A 6601	
Initials	Assessm't Date
...ount No. 0 62 3450	

2. ...
3. ...ttach required statement) → 900 00
4. ...
5. ...pensions, e... (Schedule B—if required by instructions page 5) 6,255 29
6. ...
7. ...edule D) ...
8. ... 7,155 29
9. ...

REC'D WITH REMITTANCE 75 MAY 21 1962 DIST. DIRECTOR INT REV DALLAS ... TELLER ...

...BY USING EITHER 10 OR 11

11. Tax Rate Schedule

If line 9 is less than $5,000 and you do not itemize deductions—

a. If you itemize deductions, enter total from page 2. If line 9 is $5,000 or more and you do not itemize, enter 10% of line 9 but not more than $1,000 ($500 if married and filing separate return). 715 52

b. Subtract line 11a from line 9 ... 6,439 77

c. Copy total exemptions from page 2 here 1, multiply by $600. 600 00

d. Subtract line 11c from line 11b ... 5,839 77

Figure your tax on this amount by using tax rate schedule on page 9 of instructions and enter tax on line 12.

Over assessment	Dist. DALLAS
Tax $ 18 cc	
Pen. $	
$	
Int. $	
Total $ 18.00	
Initials ERC 11-20-62	
Sched. No. 62-C-1262	

12. ...e schedule) ... 1,318 18
13. ...or F-1) ...
14. ...

...YMENTS AND CREDITS

15. a. ...ve). Attach Forms W-2
b. ...claration of Estimated Tax ... 750 00
c. ...
d. Retirement income credit ...
e. Other credits (Specify—see page 5 of instructions) ...
f. Total (add lines a, b, c, d and e) ... 750 00

District Director's office where amount on line 15b was paid

TAX DUE OR REFUND

16. If payments and credits (line 15f) are less than tax (line 14), enter Balance Due here → 586 18

Pay in full with this return to "Internal Revenue Service."

17. If payments and credits (line 15f) are larger than tax (line 14), enter Overpayment here →

18. Line 17 to be: (a) Credited on 1962 estimated tax $........; (b) Refunded $........

I declare under penalties of perjury that I have examined this return (including accompanying schedules and statements) and to the best of my knowledge and belief it is true, correct, and complete. If prepared by a person other than taxpayer, his declaration is based on all information of which he has any knowledge.

Sign here: Jack Ruby 5 - 19 - 62 (Taxpayer's signature and date) (If joint return, BOTH HUSBAND AND WIFE MUST SIGN) (Wife's signature and date)

Sign here: Bob Weaver (Signature of preparer other than taxpayer) 1706 1/2 Forest Ave. (Address) 5 - 19 - 62 (Date)

44
51

COMMISSION EXHIBIT No. 1714

SCHEDULE A.—EXEMPTIONS (See page 6 of instructions)

1. Exemptions for yourself—and wife (only if all her income is included in this return, or she had no income)

Check blocks which apply.
(a) Regular $600 exemption ... [X] Yourself [ ] Wife
(b) Additional $600 exemption if 65 or over at end of 1961 ... [ ] Yourself [ ] Wife
(c) Additional $600 exemption if blind at end of 1961 ... [ ] Yourself [ ] Wife
Enter number of exemptions checked → 1

2. Exemptions for your children and other dependents (list below)
• If an exemption is based on a multiple-support agreement of a group of persons, attach the declarations described on page 6 of instructions.

NAME Enter figure 1 in the last column to right for each name listed (Give address if different from yours)	Relationship	ANSWER ONLY FOR DEPENDENTS OTHER THAN YOUR CHILDREN: Months lived in your home. If born or died during year also write "B" or "D"	Did dependent have income of $600 or more?	Amount YOU furnished for dependent's support. If 100% write "ALL"	Amount furnished by OTHERS including dependent	
				$	$	

3. Total exemptions. (Enter here and on line 10 or 11c, page 1) ... 1

ITEMIZED DEDUCTIONS—If you do not use tax table or standard deduction

If husband and wife (not legally separated) file separate returns and one itemizes deductions, the other must also itemize

Show to whom paid. If necessary, write more than one item on a line or attach additional sheets. Please put your name and address on any attachments

Contributions (If other than money, submit description of property and method of valuation)
Total paid (not to exceed 20% of line 9, page 1, except as described on page 7 of instructions) ... $

Interest
Total interest

Taxes
Real estate taxes ... State income taxes ...
State and local sales taxes ... Other taxes (specify) ...
Total taxes

Medical and dental expense (Submit itemized list. Do not enter any expense compensated by insurance or otherwise)

NOTE: If you or your wife are 65 or over, or if either has a dependent parent 65 or over, see page 8 of Instructions for possible larger deduction.

1. Total cost of medicine and drugs ... $
2. Enter 1% of line 9, page 1 ...
3. Subtract line 2 from line 1 ...
4. Other medical and dental expenses (Including hospital insurance premiums) ...
5. Total (add lines 3 and 4) ...
6. Enter 3% of line 9, page 1 ... $
7. Subtract line 6 from line 5; see page 8 of instructions for maximum limitation ...

Other deductions (See page 8 of instructions and attach required information)
Total

TOTAL DEDUCTIONS (Enter here and on line 11a, page 1) ... $

EXPENSE ACCOUNT INFORMATION

Did you receive an expense allowance or reimbursement, or charge expenses to your employer? ... [ ] Yes [ ] No
If "Yes," did you submit itemized accounting of expenses to your employer? ... [ ] Yes [ ] No
See page 4, instructions.

U.S. GOVERNMENT PRINTING OFFICE 1961 O—600590

COMMISSION EXHIBIT NO. 1714—Continued

SCHEDULE C (Form 1040) U. S. Treasury Department Internal Revenue Service	PROFIT (OR LOSS) FROM BUSINESS OR PROFESSION (Compute social security self-employment tax on Schedule C-3 (Form 1040))	1961

Attach this Schedule to your Income Tax Return, Form 1040 — Partnerships, Joint Ventures, Etc., Must File On Form 1065

Name and address as shown on page 1, Form 1040

Jack Ruby - 3508 Oak Lawn - Dallas , Texas

A. Principal business activity (See separate instructions) Night Club (Retail trade, wholesale trade, lawyer, etc.) (Principal product or service)

B. Business name Club Vegas **C.** Employer Identification Number 750 949 491

D. Business location 3508 Oak Lawn - Dallas , Texas (Number and street or rural route) (City or post office) (State)

1. Total receipts $ 47,555.70, less allowances, rebates, and returns $		$47,555	70
2. Inventory at beginning of year (If different than last year's closing inventory attach explanation)	150.00		
3. Merchandise purchased $ 6933.70, less any items withdrawn from business for personal use $	6,933.70		
4. Cost of labor (do not include salary paid to yourself)			
5. Material and supplies	226.00		
6. Other costs (explain in Schedule C-2)			
7. Total of lines 2 through 6	7,309.70		
8. Inventory at end of this year 165	~~40,411.00~~		
9. Cost of goods sold (line 7 less line 8)		7,144	70
10. Gross profit (subtract line 9 from line 1)		40,411	00

OTHER BUSINESS DEDUCTIONS

11. Salaries and wages not included on line 4 (exclude any paid to yourself)	21,398.00		
12. Rent on business property	6,000.00		
13. Interest on business indebtedness			
14. Taxes on business and business property	2,488.70		
15. Losses of business property (attach statement)			
16. Bad debts arising from sales or services			
17. Depreciation (explain in Schedule C-1)			
18. Repairs (explain in Schedule C-2)	513.50		
19. Depletion of mines, oil and gas wells, timber, etc. (attach schedule)			
20. Amortization (attach statement)			
21. Insurance			
22. Legal and professional fees Accounting	200.00		
23. Commissions			
24. Other business expenses (explain in Schedule C-2)	3,555.51		
25. Total of lines 11 through 24		34,155	71
26. Net profit (or loss) (subtract line 25 from line 10). Enter here; on line 1, Schedule C-3; and on line 6, page 1, Form 1040		6,255	29

INVENTORY INFORMATION

1. Method of inventory valuation—Cost [X]; lower of cost or market [ ]; other [ ]. If other, attach explanation.
2. Was the method of inventory valuation indicated above the same method used for 1960? [X] Yes [ ] No. If "No" attach explanation.
3. If inventory is valued at lower of cost or market, enter total cost $............ and total market valuation $............ of those items valued at market.
4. If closing inventory was taken by physical count, enter date inventory was taken 12 - 31 - 61. If not at end of year, attach an explanation of how the end of year count was determined.
5. If closing inventory was not taken by a physical count, attach an explanation of how inventory items were counted or measured.

16—76579-1

COMMISSION EXHIBIT No. 1714—Continued

SCHEDULE C-1. EXPLANATION OF DEDUCTION FOR DEPRECIATION CLAIMED ON LINE 17

1. Kind of property (if buildings, state material of which constructed). Exclude land and other nondepreciable property	2. Date acquired	3. Cost or other basis (exclude land)	4. Depreciation allowed (or allowable) in prior years	5. Method of computing depreciation	6. Rate (%) or life (years)	7. Depreciation for this year
		$	$			$

1. Total
2. Less: Amount of depreciation claimed elsewhere in Schedule C
3. Balance—Enter here and on line 17, page 1

Amount of additional first-year depreciation included above

SCHEDULE C-2. EXPLANATION OF LINES 6, 18, AND 24

Line No.	Explanation	Amount	Line No.	Explanation	Amount
24	Laundry 207.81	$			$
	Utilities 2,228.81				
	Signs 29.00				
	Advertising				
	1,089.89	$3,555.51			

EXPENSE ACCOUNT INFORMATION

Enter information with regard to yourself and your five highest paid employees. In determining the five highest paid employees, expense account allowances must be added to their salaries and wages. However, the information need not be submitted for any employee for whom the combined amount is less than $10,000, or for yourself if your expense account allowance plus line 26, page 1, is less than $10,000. See separate instructions for Schedule C, for definition of "expense account."

Name	Expense account	Salaries and Wages
Owner		XXXXXXXXXXXXX
1.		
2.		
3.		
4.		
5.		

Did you claim a deduction for expenses connected with: (If answer to any question is "YES," check applicable boxes within that question.)

E. A hunting lodge ☐, working ranch or farm ☐, fishing camp ☐, resort property ☐, pleasure boat or yacht ☐, or other similar facility ☐? (Other than where the operation of the facility was your principal business.) ☐ YES ☐ NO

F. Vacations for you or members of your family, or employees or members of their families? (Other than vacation pay reported on Form W-2.) ☐ YES ☐ NO

G. The leasing, renting, or ownership of a hotel room or suite ☐, apartment ☐, or other dwelling ☐, which was used by you, your customers, employees, or members of their families? (Other than use by yourself or employees while in business travel status.) ☐ YES ☐ NO

H. The attendance of members of your family or your employees' families at conventions or business meetings? ☐ YES ☐ NO

16—76679-1

Commission Exhibit No. 1714—Continued

SCHEDULE C-3 (Form 1040)	U.S. Treasury Department—Internal Revenue Service **COMPUTATION OF SOCIAL SECURITY SELF-EMPLOYMENT TAX** **(See instructions on page 2)**	1961

▶ If you had wages of $4,800 or more which were subject to the deduction for social security, do not fill in this Schedule.
▶ Complete only one Schedule C-3; if you had more than one business, combine profits (or losses) from all of your businesses on this Schedule.
▶ Each self-employed person must file a separate schedule. See instructions, page 2, for joint returns and partnerships.

NAME AND ADDRESS (as shown on page 1 of Form 1040)

NAME OF SELF-EMPLOYED PERSON (as shown on social security card)

1. Net profit (or loss) shown on line 26 Schedule C (Form 1040) **(Enter combined amount if more than one business)**..........
2. Add to net profit (or subtract from net loss) losses of business property shown on line 15, Schedule C..........
3. Total (or difference)..........
4. Net income (or loss) from excluded services or sources included on line 3 (see "Exclusions," page 2)..........
   Specify excluded services or sources ....
5. Net earnings (or loss) from self-employment—
   (a) From business (line 3 less any amount on line 4)..........
   (b) From partnerships, joint ventures, etc. (other than farming)..........
   (c) From service as a minister, member of a religious order, or a Christian Science practitioner.......... Enter only if you have filed or are filing Form 2031 (see instructions, page 2).
   (d) From farming reported on line 2 (or line 3 if option used), separate Schedule F-1 (Form 1040)..........
   (e) From service with a foreign government or international organization..........
6. Total net earnings (or loss) from self-employment reported on line 5. Enter here and on line 6 below..........
   (If line 6 is under $400, you are not subject to self-employment tax. Do not fill in rest of page.)
7. The largest amount of combined wages and self-employment earnings subject to social security tax is.......... $ 4,800 | 00
8. Total wages, covered by social security, paid to you during the taxable year. (For "Covered" wages see "F. I. C. A. Wages" box on Form W-2.) Enter here and on line 7, below..........
9. Balance (line 7 less line 8).......... $
10. Self-employment income—line 6 or 9, whichever is smaller. Enter here and on line 8, below..........
11. Self-employment tax—If line 10 is $4,800, enter $216.00; if less, multiply the amount on line 10 by 4½%.... Enter this amount here and on line 13, page 1, Form 1040..........

Important.—The amounts reported on the form below are for your social security account. This account is used in figuring any benefits, based on your earnings, payable to you, your dependents, and your survivors. Fill in each item **accurately** and **completely**, but do not detach.

SCHEDULE SE (Form 1040)
U. S. Treasury Department
Internal Revenue Service

U. S. REPORT OF SELF-EMPLOYMENT INCOME — 1961

For crediting to your social security account

1. Indicate year covered by this return (even though income was received only in part of year): Calendar year 1961 ☐; or other taxable year beginning ...., 1961, ending .... If less than 12 months, was short year due to (a) ☐ Death, or (b) ☐ Change in accounting period, or (c) ☐ Other.
2. BUSINESS ACTIVITIES SUBJECT TO SELF-EMPLOYMENT TAX (Grocery store, restaurant, etc.)
3. BUSINESS ADDRESS (number and street, city or post office, postal zone number, State)
4. SOCIAL SECURITY ACCOUNT NUMBER OF PERSON NAMED IN ITEM 5 BELOW ➡
5. PRINT OR TYPE NAME OF SELF-EMPLOYED PERSON AS SHOWN ON SOCIAL SECURITY CARD
   PRINT OR TYPE HOME ADDRESS (number and street or rural route)
   (City or post office, postal zone number, State)

PLEASE DO NOT WRITE IN THIS SPACE

6. ENTER TOTAL EARNINGS FROM SELF-EMPLOYMENT SHOWN ON LINE 6 ABOVE..
7. ENTER WAGES, IF ANY, SHOWN ON LINE 8 ABOVE......
8. ENTER AMOUNT SHOWN ON LINE 10 ABOVE..........

SE

16—76679-1 GPO

COMMISSION EXHIBIT No. 1714—Continued

In general, every individual deriving self-employment income during the taxable year of $400, or more, from a trade or business carried on by him or from a partnership of which he is a member is subject to the self-employment tax. This computation is made on lines 1 through 11. This tax must be paid regardless of age and even though the individual is receiving social security benefits.

Ministers, members of religious orders, and Christian Science practitioners.—Duly ordained, commissioned, or licensed ministers of churches, members of religious orders (who have not taken a vow of poverty), and Christian Science practitioners are not automatically covered by the Social Security Act, but may elect to be covered by filing Form 2031. Copies are available in the office of any district director of Internal Revenue. The instructions on the form set out the provisions of the law which permit these forms under certain conditions to be filed to cover ministers, and others mentioned above. Do not delay filing your income tax return beyond the due date even though you have not obtained a Form 2031. In such case, complete this Schedule, file it with Form 1040, and then file Form 2031 as promptly as possible to make your election.

Ministers and members of religious orders who desire coverage shall in addition to their other items of income include for the purpose of determining net earnings from self-employment (but not for income tax purposes) the rental value of a parsonage or allowance for the rental value of the parsonage, and the value of meals and lodging furnished them for the convenience of their employers.

U. S. Citizens employed by foreign governments or international organizations.—A U. S. citizen employed in the United States, Puerto Rico, Guam, American Samoa, or the Virgin Islands by a foreign government, an instrumentality wholly owned by a foreign government, or an international organization which is organized under the International Organizations Immunities Act, is subject to the social security self-employment tax. These employees should report their income from such employment on line 5(e), of this Schedule, compute their self-employment tax, and file the schedule with their Form 1040. On line 2 of Schedule SE, enter "Employee of foreign government, etc."

Farm income.—Farmers report farm income and net earnings from farm self-employment on separate Schedules F and F-1 (Form 1040).

EXCLUSIONS

Income (or loss) from the following sources and deductions attributable thereto are not taken into account in figuring net earnings from self-employment. Use line 4 to exclude any such amounts reported on separate Schedule C (Form 1040) that should not be taken into account in figuring your self-employment income.

Doctors of medicine.—Income from the performance of service as a doctor of medicine or income from the performance of such service by a partnership.

Christian Science practitioners.—Income from the performance of service as a Christian Science practitioner, unless such Christian Science practitioner elects by filing Form 2031 to be covered by the Social Security Act, as explained above.

Religious services.—Income from the performance of service by a duly ordained, commissioned, or licensed minister of a church in the exercise of his ministry or by a member of a religious order in the exercise of duties required by such order, unless such minister or member of a religious order elects by filing Form 2031 to be covered by the Social Security Act, as explained above.

Employees and public officials.—Income (fees, salaries, etc.) from the performance of service as:

(a) a public official, including a notary public;
(b) an employee or employee representative under the railroad retirement system; or
(c) an employee (except as indicated above).

Note.—The income of an employee over the age of 18 from the sale of newspapers or magazines to an ultimate consumer is subject to the self-employment tax if the income consists of retained profits from such sales.

Real estate rentals.—Rentals from real estate, except rentals received in the course of a trade or business as a real estate dealer. This includes cash and crop shares received from a tenant or sharefarmer. These amounts should be reported in Part IV, Schedule B (Form 1040). However, rental income from a farm is not excluded if the rental arrangement provides for material participation by the landlord and he does participate materially in the production or in the management of the production of one or more farm products on his land. Such income represents farm earnings and should be reported on separate Schedules F and F-1.

Payments for the use or occupancy of rooms or other space where services are also rendered to the occupant, such as rooms in hotels, boarding houses, apartment houses furnishing hotel services, tourist camps, or homes, or space in parking lots, warehouses, or storage garages do not constitute rentals from real estate and are included in determining net earnings from self-employment on this Schedule.

Interest and dividends.—Dividends on shares of stock, and interest on bonds, debentures, notes, certificates, or other evidences of indebtedness, issued with interest coupons or in registered form by a corporation, or by a government or political subdivision thereof, unless received in the course of a trade or business as a dealer in stocks or securities. These amounts should be reported in Parts I and II of Schedule B.

Property gains and losses.—Gain or loss: (a) from the sale or exchange of a capital asset; (b) to which sections 631 and 1231 are applicable; or (c) from the sale, exchange, involuntary conversion, or other disposition of property if such property is neither (1) stock in trade or other property of a kind which would properly be includible in inventory if on hand at the close of the taxable year, nor (2) property held primarily for sale to customers in the ordinary course of the trade or business. These amounts should be reported on separate Schedule D (Form 1040).

Net operating losses.—No deduction for net operating losses of other years shall be allowed in determining the net earnings from self-employment. Such deduction should be entered on line 3, Part V of Schedule B.

No deductions for personal exemptions.—The deductions for personal exemptions are not allowable in determining net earnings from self-employment.

MORE THAN ONE TRADE OR BUSINESS

If an individual is engaged in more than one trade or business, his net earnings from self-employment are the combined net earnings from self-employment of all his trades or businesses. Thus, the loss sustained in one trade or business will operate to reduce the income derived from another trade or business. An individual shall fill in and file only one Schedule C-3, including Schedule SE, for any one year.

JOINT RETURNS

Where husband and wife file a joint income tax return, Schedule C-3 (Form 1040) should show the name of the one with self-employment income. Where husband and wife each have self-employment income, separate Schedules C and C-3 must be attached for each. In such cases the total of amounts shown on line 26 of each separate Schedule C should be entered on line 6, page 1, Form 1040, and the aggregate self-employment tax (line 11) Schedule C-3 should be entered on line 13, page 1, Form 1040.

COMMUNITY INCOME

For the purpose of computing net earnings from self-employment, if any of the income from a trade or business is community income, all the income from such trade or business is considered the income of the husband unless the wife exercises substantially all the management and control of the trade or business, in which case all of such income is considered the income of the wife. (Also see instructions on partnerships below.)

If separate income tax returns are filed by husband and wife, Schedules C and C-3 should be attached to the return of the one with self-employment income. Community income included on Schedule C must be allocated between the two returns (on line 6, page 1, Form 1040) on the basis of the community property laws.

PARTNERSHIPS

In computing his combined net earnings from self-employment, a partner should include his entire share of such earnings from a partnership including any guaranteed payments. No part of that share may be allocated to the partner's wife (or husband) even though the income may, under State law, be community income. In the case of a husband and wife partnership, like other partnerships, the distributive share of each should be entered in Part V of Schedule B (Form 1040), for income tax purposes. For self-employment tax purposes the distributive share of each partner should be entered on line 5(b), of this Schedule (except that farm partnership earnings are to be reported on line 1(b), Schedule F-1 (Form 1040) rather than on line 5(b) of this schedule).

Note.—If a member of a continuing partnership dies, a portion of the deceased partner's distributive share of the partnership's ordinary income (or loss) for the taxable year of the partnership in which he died must be included in the partner's net earnings from self-employment. In such cases consult your nearest Internal Revenue Service office as to how to report.

SCHEDULE SE (Form 1040)

Schedule SE, which is the lower portion of this Schedule, provides the Social Security Administration with the information on self-employment income necessary for computing benefits.

To assure proper credit to your account, be sure to enter your name and social security account number on Schedule SE (Form 1040) exactly as they are shown on your social security card. If you do not have a social security account number, you must get one. These account numbers are obtainable from any social security district office. Your local post office will give you the address. Do not delay filing your return beyond the due date.

Regardless of whether joint or separate returns are filed by husband and wife, Schedule SE (Form 1040) must show only the name of the one with the self-employment income. However, if both had net earnings from self-employment, a separate Schedule SE must be filed by each.

U.S. GOVERNMENT PRINTING OFFICE 16—76670-1

COMMISSION EXHIBIT No. 1714—Continued

FORM **1040** | **U.S. INDIVIDUAL INCOME TAX RETURN—1960** | OF 4 123

COMP. 4 PROV. D

For Taxable Year Beginning ...., 1960, Ending ...., 19....

Assessment	Dist. Dallas
Tax $	
Pen. $	48.97
Int. $	
Total $	
IR Code Section	
Initials	Assessm't Date
Account No.	P 62 417

First name and initial: JACK — Last name: RUBY

(If this is a joint return of husband and wife, use first names and middle initials of both)

Home address: 4727 Homer (Number and street or rural route)

Dallas (City, town, or post office) (Postal zone number) Texas (State)

Occupation: Dance Hall Owner | Wife's Social Security Number | Occupation

...apply. ...all of her ...this return, or if she had no income.

(a) Regular $600 exemption .... ☒ Yourself ☐ Wife

(b) Additional $600 exemption if 65 or over at end of taxable year. ☐ Yourself ☐ Wife

(c) Additional $600 exemption if blind at end of taxable year..... ☐ Yourself ☐ Wife

Enter number of exemptions checked →

2 ... Enter number of children listed →

3 ...ed for other persons listed at top of page 2......

4 ...ns claimed on lines 1, 2, and 3......

Over assessment	Dist. Dallas
Tax $	120.00
Pen. $	
Int. $	1.34
Total $	121.34
Initials	
Sched. No.	62 C 227

5. ..., commissions, tips, and other compensation before payroll deductions (including ...vance paid by your employer over your ordinary and necessary business expenses. See instructions, pp. 5

Where Employed (City and State) | (a) Wages, etc. | (b) Federal Income Tax Withheld

RECEIVED MAY 22 1961 DIST. DIRECTOR INT. REV. DALLAS TELLERS #1

Enter totals here →

6. ...5 (See instructions, page 7. Attach required statement.)...

If the social security (FICA) withheld f... wages exceeded $... because you or your... had more than one employer, see instructions page 5.

7.	Balance (line 5 less line 6)......	$
8.	Profit (or loss) from business from separate Schedule C......	9703 90
9.	Profit (or loss) from farming from separate Schedule F......	
10.	Other income (or loss) from page 3 (**Dividends, Interest, Rents, Pensions, etc.**)	
11.	Adjusted Gross Income (sum of lines 7, 8, 9, and 10)......	$ 9703 90

● Check if unmarried "Head of Household" ☐, or "Surviving Widow or Widower" with dependent child ☐. (See Instructions pp. 7

12.	TAX on income on line 11. (If line 11 is under $5,000, and you do not itemize deductions, use Tax Table on page 16 of instructions to find your tax and check here ☐. If line 11 is $5,000 or more, or if you itemize deductions, compute your tax on page 2 and enter here the amount from line 9, page 2).	$ 2005
13.	(a) Dividends received credit from line 5 of Schedule J...... $ (b) Retirement income credit from line 12 of Schedule K....	
14.	Balance (line 12 less line 13)......	$ 2005
15.	Enter your self-employment tax from separate Schedule C or F......	216
16.	Sum of lines 14 and 15......	$ 2221
17.	(a) Federal tax withheld (line 5, col. (b) above). Attach Forms W-2, Copy B. $ (b) Payments and credits on 1960 Declaration of Estimated Tax (See page 8, instructions.) District Director's office where paid	$
18.	If your tax (line 12 or 16) is larger than your payments (line 17), enter the **BALANCE DUE** here → **Pay in full with this return to "Internal Revenue Service." If less than $1.00, file return without payment.**	$ 2221
19.	If your payments (line 17) are larger than your tax (line 12 or 16), enter the **OVERPAYMENT** here → **If less than $1.00, the overpayment will be refunded only upon application.**	$
20.	Amount of line 19 to be: (a) Credited on 1961 estimated tax $......; (b) Refunded $......	

(If income was all from wages, omit lines 13 through 16)

ATTACH COPY B OF FORMS W-2 HERE ● Income — Exemptions — Tax due or refund — EXTENSION GRANTED TO

Did you receive an expense allowance or reimbursement, or charge expenses to your employer?.. ☐ Yes ☐ No (See page 6, instructions.)

If "Yes," did you submit an itemized accounting of expenses to your employer?...... ☐ Yes ☐ No

County in which you live.	Is your wife (husband) filing a separate return for 1960? ☐ Yes ☒ No. If "yes," enter her (his) name and do not claim the exemption on this return.	Do you owe any Federal tax for years before 1960? ☐ Yes ☐ No. If "Yes," enter here the Internal Revenue District where the account is outstanding.
Dallas		

I declare under the penalties of perjury that this return (including any accompanying schedules and statements) has been examined by me and to the best of my knowledge and belief is a true, correct, and complete return. If the return is prepared by a person other than the taxpayer, his declaration is based on all the information relating to the matters required to be reported in the return of which he has any knowledge.

Sign here: Jack Ruby (Taxpayer's signature and date) (If this is a joint return, BOTH HUSBAND AND WIFE MUST SIGN) (Wife's signature and date)

Fred M. Hekeiner (Signature of preparer other than taxpayer) — 4515 Live Oak - Dallas, Texas (Address) — 5-18-61 (Date)

#27E

COMMISSION EXHIBIT No. 1715

Form 1040—1960 **EXEMPTIONS FOR PERSONS OTHER THAN YOUR WIFE AND CHILDREN** Page 2

Name	Relationship	Months lived in your home. If born or died during year also write "B" or "D"	Did dependent have gross income of $600 or more?	Amount YOU furnished for dependent's support. If 100% write "All"	Amount furnished by OTHERS including dependent (See instructions, p. 4)
				$	$

Enter on line 3, page 1, the number of exemptions claimed above.

→ If an exemption is based on a multiple-support agreement of a group of persons, attach the declarations described on page 5 of instructions.

ITEMIZED DEDUCTIONS—IF YOU DO NOT USE TAX TABLE OR STANDARD DEDUCTION

If Husband and Wife (Not Legally Separated) File Separate Returns and one Itemizes Deductions, the Other Must Also Itemize

State to whom paid. If necessary, write more than one item on a line or attach additional sheets. Please put your name and address on any attachments.

Contributions

Total paid but not to exceed 20% of line 11, page 1, except as described on page 8 of instructions $

Interest

Total interest

Taxes

Real estate taxes .... State income taxes ....

State and local sales taxes .... Other taxes (specify) ....

Total taxes

Medical and dental expense (Submit itemized list. Do not enter any expense compensated by insurance or otherwise)

NOTE: If you or your wife are 65 years of age or over, or if you or your wife have a dependent parent 65 or over, do not use this schedule. See page 9 of the instructions for larger deduction. Others use schedule below.

1. Total cost of medicine and drugs .... $
2. 1 percent of line 11, page 1 ....
3. Excess, if any, of line 1 over line 2 ....
4. Other medical and dental expenses ....
5. Total of lines 3 and 4 ....
6. Enter 3 percent of line 11, page 1 .... $
7. Allowable amount (excess of line 5 over line 6; see page 10 for maximum limitation) ....

Other deductions (See page 10 of instructions and attach information required)

Total

TOTAL DEDUCTIONS (Enter here and on line 2 of Tax Computation, below) .... $

TAX COMPUTATION—IF YOU DO NOT USE THE TAX TABLE

1. Enter Adjusted Gross Income from line 11, page 1	$ 9703	90
2. If deductions are itemized above, enter total of such deductions. If deductions are not itemized *and line 1, above, is $5,000 or more,* enter the smaller of 10 percent of line 1 or $1,000 ($500 if a married person filing a separate return)	970	39
3. Balance (line 1 less line 2)	8733	51
4. Multiply $600 by total number of exemptions claimed on line 4, page 1	600	00
5. Taxable Income (line 3 less line 4)	8133	51
6. Tax on amount on line 5. Use appropriate tax rate schedule on page 15 of instructions. **Do not use Tax Table on page 16**	2005	39
7. If you had capital gains and the alternative tax applies, enter the tax from separate Schedule D		
8. Tax credits. If you itemized deductions, enter: (a) Credit for income tax payments to a foreign country or U.S. possession (Attach Form 1116) .... $ (b) Tax paid at source on tax-free covenant bond interest and credit for partially tax-exempt interest .... (c) Total .... Enter here →		
9. Enter here and on line 12, page 1, the amount shown on line 6 or 7 less amount claimed on line 8(c)	$ 2005	39

c70—16—76135-1

COMMISSION EXHIBIT No. 1715—Continued

FORM T-66 REV. 10-57 U.S. TREASURY DEPARTMENT — INTERNAL REVENUE SERVICE

PAYMENT HISTORY CARD

LAST NAME	FIRST NAME	ACCOUNT NUMBER	TAX YEAR
RUBY	JACK	75 111 4000018	60

STREET ADDRESS	CITY — ZONE — STATE
3508 OAKLAWN	DALLAS TEX

ESTIMATED TAX	OVERPAYMENT CREDIT	DOCUMENT NUMBER DIST.	DOCUMENT NUMBER BLOCK	DATE MO.	DATE DAY	DATE YR.	PAYMENTS	TOTAL PAYMENTS
120 00				04	15	60	120 00	
							120 00	*

435221

Commission Exhibit No. 1715—Continued

THE CLUB VEGAS
Dallas, Texas

Year 1960

Statement of Income

INCOME		
Sales		
Bar		$ 24,508.46
Cost of Sales		
Inventory 1-1-1960	$ 250.00	
Merchandise Purchased	6,975.00	
Total available merchandise	7,225.00	
Less: Inventory 12-31-1960	145.00	
Cost of Goods Sold		7,080.00
Gross Profit - Bar sales		17,428.46
OTHER INCOME		
Admissions		26,734.85
Miscellaneous		319.10
Gross Income		44,482.41
EXPENSES		
Salaries & Wages	21,802.00	
FICA Taxes	654.06	
Supplies	724.78	
Utilities	1,163.45	
Rent	5,500.00	
Advertising	705.56	
Repairs & Maintenance	381.05	
Legal & Audit	340.00	
Sales Promotion	200.50	
Taxes & Licenses	574.72	
Linen Supply	182.84	
Depreciation	599.92	
Contract Labor	98.25	
Payroll Taxes (Unemployment)	196.55	
ASCAP & BMI	50.00	
Office Expense	138.18	
Telephone	771.16	
Exterminator	20.00	
Miscellaneous	67.95	
Automobile & Parking	607.54	34,778.51
Net Income		$ 9,703.90

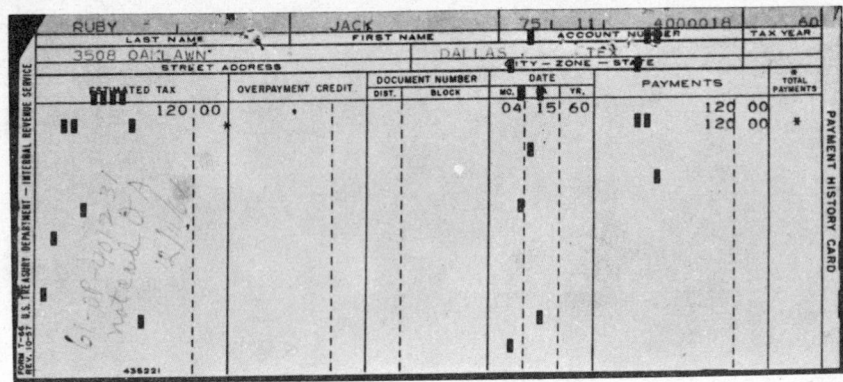

Commission Exhibit No. 1715—Continued

SCHEDULE C (Form 1040)
U. S. Treasury Department
Internal Revenue Service

PROFIT (OR LOSS) FROM BUSINESS OR PROFESSION

1960

(Compute Social Security Self-Employment Tax on Page 3)

A. Business name and location THE CLUB VEGAS 3508 Oak Lawn Dallas, Texas

B. Principal Business Activity Dance Hall (Retail trade, lawyer, etc.) (Principal product or service) (See Instructions, page 2)

C. Employer's Identification Number I 75-094 9491

1. Total receipts $........, less allowances, rebates, and returns $		$	
2. Inventory at beginning of year	$		
3. Merchandise purchased $........, less any items withdrawn from business for personal use $			
4. Cost of labor (do not include salary paid to yourself)	Schedule		
5. Material and supplies			
6. Other costs (explain in Schedule C-2)			
7. Total of lines 2 through 6	$		
8. Inventory at end of year			
9. Cost of goods sold (line 7 less line 8)			
10. Gross profit (line 1 less line 9)		$	
OTHER BUSINESS DEDUCTIONS			
11. Salaries and wages not included on line 4 (exclude any paid to yourself)	$		
12. Rent on business property			
13. Interest on business indebtedness	Schedule		
14. Taxes on business and business property			
15. Losses of business property (attach statement)			
16. Bad debts arising from sales or services			
17. Depreciation (explain in Schedule C-1)			
18. Repairs (explain in Schedule C-2)			
19. Depletion of mines, oil and gas wells, timber, etc. (attach schedule)			
20. Amortization (attach statement)			
21. Other business expenses (explain in Schedule C-2)			
22. Total of lines 11 through 21			
23. Net profit (or loss) (line 10 less line 22). Enter here; on line 24, page 3; and on line 8, page 1, Form 1040		$ 9703	90

Schedule C-1. EXPLANATION OF DEDUCTION FOR DEPRECIATION CLAIMED ON LINE 17

1. Kind of property (if buildings, state material of which constructed). Exclude land and other nondepreciable property	2. Date acquired	3. Cost or other basis (Exclude land)	4. Depreciation allowed (or allowable) in prior years	5. Method of computing depreciation	6. Rate (%) or life (years)	7. Depreciation for this year
		$	$			$
				Schedule		

Additional first year depreciation (attach statement)

EXPENSE ACCOUNT INFORMATION

Enter information with regard to yourself and your five highest paid employees. In determining the highest five paid employees, expense account allowances must be added to their salaries and wages. However, the information need not be submitted for any employee for whom the combined amount is less than $10,000, or for yourself if your expense account allowance plus line 23, above, is less than $10,000. See instructions, page 2, for definition of "expense account".

Name	Expense account	Salaries and Wages
Owner	$	XXXXXXXXXXXXX
1.		$
2.		
3.		
4.		
5.		

C

ADDITIONAL INFORMATION

Did you claim a deduction for expenses connected with: (If answer to any question is "YES," check applicable boxes within that question.)

D. A hunting lodge ☐, working ranch or farm ☐, fishing camp ☐, resort property ☐, pleasure boat or yacht ☐, or other similar facility ☐? (Other than where the operation of the facility was your principal business.) ☐ YES ☒ NO

E. Vacations for owner or employees, or members of their families? (Other than vacation pay reported on Form W-2.) ☐ YES ☒ NO

F. The leasing, renting, or ownership of a hotel room or suite ☐, apartment ☐, or other dwelling ☐, which was used by you, your customers, employees, or members of their families? (Other than use by yourself or employees while in business travel status.) ☐ YES ☒ NO

G. The attendance of members of your family or your employees' families at conventions or business meetings? ☐ YES ☒ NO

16—76072-1

COMMISSION EXHIBIT No. 1715—Continued

Schedule C-2. EXPLANATION OF LINES 6, 18, AND 21

Line No.	Explanation	Amount	Line No.	Explanation	Amount
		$			$

INSTRUCTIONS

If you owned a business, or practiced a profession, you must fill in separate Schedule C on other side and enter the net profit (or loss) on line 8, page 1, Form 1040. If you had more than one business, or husband and wife had separate businesses, a separate page 1 of Schedule C must be completed for each business.

All farmers should use separate Schedule F (Form 1040) to report their farm income whether reporting on the cash or accrual method.

Income from any trade or business is subject to the social security self-employment tax, unless specifically excluded. See page 4.

Item A—Business Name and Location.—Do not use home address as business address unless business is actually conducted from home. Enter street address rather than box numbers.

Item B—Business Activity.—State the general classification of business activity, as well as the principal product or service. For example, "Wholesale fruit," "Retail men's apparel," "Manufacture of upholstered wooden household furniture," "Transportation by truck," "Broker, real estate," "Contractor—carpenter work," etc. Do not use such terms as "partnership," "owner," "student," etc. The "principal business activity" is the one which accounts for the largest percentage of your total receipts.

Line 1—Total Receipts.—Include all income derived from your trade or business. Enter in the space provided such items as returned sales, rebates, and allowances from the sale price or service charge.

If you have dividend income from stocks held by you in the ordinary course of carrying on your trade or business, such dividends must be considered together with your dividends from stocks regularly held for investment purposes in computing your dividend exclusion and credit on pages 3 and 4, Form 1040.

Installment Sales.—If you use the installment method of reporting income from sales, you must attach to your return a schedule showing separately for the years 1957, 1958, 1959, and 1960 the following: (a) Gross sales; (b) cost of goods sold; (c) gross profits; (d) percentage of profits to gross sales; (e) amounts collected; and (f) gross profits on amounts collected.

COST OF GOODS SOLD

Lines 2–9.—If you are engaged in a trade or a business in which the production, purchase, or sale of merchandise is an income producing factor, you must take inventories of merchandise and materials on hand at the beginning and end of the taxable year in order to reflect the gross profits correctly. The usual methods of valuing inventory are (a) cost or (b) cost or market whichever is lower. The method properly adopted for the first year in which inventory is taken must be continued unless permission to change is secured from the Commissioner of Internal Revenue, Washington 25, D.C. Application for permission to change the method of valuing inventories must be made in writing and filed with the Commissioner within 90 days after the beginning of the taxable year in which it is desired to effect a change. You should enter the letters "C" or "C or M" immediately before the amount column if inventories are valued either at cost, or at cost or market whichever is lower.

OTHER BUSINESS DEDUCTIONS

Line 15—Losses of Business Property.—You may deduct losses of business property by fire, storm, or other casualty, or theft, to the extent not compensated by insurance or otherwise and not made good by repairs claimed as a deduction. Attach a statement showing a description of the property, date acquired, cost, subsequent improvements, depreciation allowed or allowable since acquisition, insurance, salvage value, and deductible loss.

Line 16—Bad Debts Arising From Sales or Services.—Include debts, or portions thereof, arising from sales or professional services that have been included in income, which have been definitely ascertained to be worthless; or such reasonable amount as has been added within the taxable year to a reserve for bad debts. A debt which is deducted as bad and which reduces your tax must, if subsequently collected, be returned as income for the year in which collected.

Line 17—Depreciation and Obsolescence.—You may deduct a reasonable allowance for exhaustion, wear and tear, and obsolescence of property used in the trade or business. For additional information regarding depreciation, especially on new property acquired or constructed after December 31, 1953, and additional first year depreciation, see depreciation section in the instructions for Form 1040. If a deduction is claimed on account of depreciation, fill in Schedule C–1. In case obsolescence is included, state separately amount claimed and basis upon which it is computed. The value or cost of land must not be included in this schedule, and where land and buildings were purchased for a lump sum, the cost of the building subject to depreciation must be established. The adjusted property accounts and the accumulated depreciation shown in the schedule should be reconciled with those accounts as reflected on your books.

Line 18—Repairs.—You may deduct the cost of incidental repairs, including labor, supplies, and other items, which do not add to the value or appreciably prolong the life of the property. Expenditures for new buildings, machinery, and equipment, or for permanent improvements or betterments which increase the value of the property are chargeable to capital accounts. Expenditures for restoring or replacing property are not deductible, since such expenditures are chargeable to capital accounts or to depreciation reserve depending on how depreciation is charged on your books.

Line 19—Depletion of Mines, Oil and Gas Wells, Timber, Etc.—If a deduction is claimed on account of depletion, procure from your District Director Form M (mines and other natural deposits), Form O (oil and gas), or Form T (timber), fill in and file with return. If complete valuation data have been filed with questionnaire in previous years, then file with your return information necessary to bring depletion schedule up to date.

Line 20—Amortization.—If you elect the deduction with respect to the amortization of the adjusted basis of (a) any emergency facility with respect to which the Government has issued a certificate of necessity, or (b) a grain storage facility, a statement of the pertinent facts should be filed with your return. (See sections 168 and 169 of the Internal Revenue Code.)

For the election to amortize research or experimental expenditures not subject to depreciation or depletion, see section 174 of the Code.

For the election to amortize trademark or trade name expenditures, see section 177 of the Code.

Line 21—Other Business Expenses.—Include all ordinary and necessary business expenses for which no space is provided in the schedule. Any deduction claimed should be explained in Schedule C–2. Do not include cost of business equipment or furniture, expenditures for replacements, or for permanent improvements to property, or personal living and family expenses.

Net Operating Loss Deduction.—Any net operating loss deduction should be entered on line 3, Schedule H, page 3, of Form 1040. See instructions for Form 1040 and submit computation.

Expense Account Information.—Expense account allowance means: (a) amounts, other than compensation, received as advances or reimbursements, and (b) amounts paid by or for you for expenses incurred by or on behalf of yourself or your employees, including all amounts charged through any type of credit card, for which a deduction is claimed in this schedule.

However, this term does not include amounts paid for: (a) the purchase of goods for resale or use in your business; (b) incidental expenses, such as the purchase of office supplies or for local transportation in connection with an errand; (c) such fringe benefits as hospitalization insurance, approved pension trust funds and unemployment insurance; and (d) in the case of persons supplying legal, accounting, engineering or other professional services, the expenses which will be billed directly to the client (however, these persons should maintain records reasonably sufficient to establish the business purpose for the expenditure).

c48—16—76072-1

COMMISSION EXHIBIT No. 1715—Continued

DEPRECIATION SCHEDULE

NAME Jack Ruby - dba - The Club Vegas

ADDRESS 3508 Oak Lawn — Dallas, Texas

YEAR ENDING 12-31-1960

FILE NO.

FOLIO

FORM

	1. KIND OF PROPERTY (If buildings, state material of which constructed). Exclude land and other nondepreciable property	2. Date acquired	3. Cost or other basis	4. Depreciation allowed (or allowable) in prior years	5. Method of computing depreciation	6. Rate (%) or life (years)	7. Depreciation for this year	
1	Cash Register	1-1-57	250 00	187 56	S/L	4 yrs.	62 44	1
2	Sign	1-1-57	500 00	299 88	✓	5 yrs	99 96	2
3	Microphone & Stand	8-31-58	56 74	38 42	✓	2 yrs.	19 22	3
4	Tape Recorder	12-1-59	95 00	3 96	✓	2 yrs.	47 50	4
5								5
6	Auto (90% Business - 90% X 1648.00)	10-31-58	1483 20	432 60	✓	4 yrs.	370 80	6
7								7
8								8
9								9
10								10
11								11
12								12
13								13
14								14
15								15
16								16
17								17
18								18
19								19
20								20
21								21
	TOTAL						599 92	

NO. 41

COMMISSION EXHIBIT No. 1715—Continued

COMPUTATION OF SOCIAL SECURITY SELF-EMPLOYMENT TAX
(See Instructions—Page 4)

▶ **If you had wages of $4,800 or more which were subject to the deduction for social security, do not fill in this page.**
▶ **Complete only one page 3; if you had more than one business, combine profits (or losses) from all of your businesses on this page.**
▶ **Each self-employed person must file a separate schedule. See instructions, page 4, for joint returns and partnerships.**

NAME OF SELF-EMPLOYED PERSON (as shown on social security card)

Jack Ruby

24. Net profit (or loss) shown on line 23, page 1 (**Enter combined amount if more than one business**)	$ 9703	90		
25. Add to net profit (or subtract from net loss) losses of business property shown on line 15, page 1		0		
26. Total (or difference)			$ 9703	90
27. Net income (or loss) from excluded services or sources included on line 26 (See "Exclusions," page 4)				
Specify excluded services or sources				
28. Net earnings (or loss) from self-employment—				
(a) From business (line 26 less any amount on line 27)			$ 9703	90
(b) From partnerships, joint ventures, etc. (other than farming)				
(c) From service as a minister, member of a religious order, or a Christian Science practitioner. Enter only if you have filed or are filing Form 2031 (See instructions, page 4).				
(d) From farming reported on line 12 (or line 13 if option used), separate Schedule F (Form 1040)				
(e) From service with a foreign government or international organization				
29. Total net earnings (or loss) from self-employment reported on line 28. Enter here and on line 6 below (**If line 29 is under $400, you are not subject to self-employment tax. Do not fill in rest of page.**)			$ 9703	90
30. The largest amount of combined wages and self-employment earnings subject to social security tax is	$ 4,800	00		
31. Total wages, covered by social security, paid to you during the taxable year. (For "Covered" wages see "F. I. C. A. Wages" box on Form W-2.) Enter here and on line 7, below		0		
32. Balance (line 30 less line 31)	$ 4,800	00		
33. Self-employment income—line 29 or 32, whichever is smaller. Enter here and on line 8, below			$ 4800	00
34. Self-employment tax—If line 33 is $4,800, enter $216.00; if less, multiply the amount on line 33 by 4½%. Enter this amount here and on line 15, page 1, Form 1040			$ 216	00

COMMISSION EXHIBIT No. 1715—Continued

international organization which is organized under the International Organizations Immunities Act, is subject to the social security self-employment tax for 1960 and subsequent years. These employees should report their income from such employment on line 28(e), page 3, compute their self-employment tax, and file this schedule with their Form 1040. On line 2 of Schedule SE, enter "Employee of foreign government, etc."

Farm income.—Farmers report farm income and net earnings from farm self-employment on separate Schedule F (Form 1040).

EXCLUSIONS

Income (or loss) from the following sources and deductions attributable thereto are not taken into account in figuring net earnings from self-employment. Use line 27 to exclude any such amounts reported on page 1 that should not be taken into account in figuring your self-employment income.

Doctors of medicine.—Income from the performance of service as a doctor of medicine or income from the performance of such service by a partnership.

Christian Science practitioners.—Income from the performance of service as a Christian Science practitioner, unless such Christian Science practitioner elects by filing Form 2031 to be covered by the Social Security Act, as explained above.

Religious services.—Income from the performance of service by a duly ordained, commissioned, or licensed minister of a church in the exercise of his ministry or by a member of a religious order in the exercise of duties required by such order, unless such minister or member of a religious order elects by filing Form 2031 to be covered by the Social Security Act, as explained above.

Employees and public officials.—Income (fees, salaries, etc.) from the performance of service as:

(a) a public official, including a notary public;
(b) an employee or employee representative under the railroad retirement system; or
(c) an employee (except as indicated above).

Note.—The income of an employee over the age of 18 from the sale of newspapers or magazines to an ultimate consumer is subject to the self-employment tax if the income consists of retained profits from such sales.

Real estate rentals.—Rentals from real estate, except rentals received in the course of a trade or business as a real estate dealer. This includes cash and crop shares received from a tenant or sharefarmer. These amounts should be reported in Schedule G of Form 1040. However, rental income from a farm is not excluded if the rental arrangement provides for material participation by the landlord and he does participate materially in the production or in the management of the production of one or more farm products on his land. Such income represents farm earnings and should be reported on separate Schedule F (Form 1040).

Payments for the use or occupancy of rooms or other space where services are also rendered to the occupant, such as rooms in hotels, boarding houses, apartment houses furnishing hotel services, tourist camps, or homes, or space in parking lots, warehouses, or storage garages do not constitute rentals from real estate and are included in determining net earnings from self-employment on Schedule C.

Interest and dividends.—Dividends on shares of stock, and interest on bonds, debentures, notes, certificates, or other evidences

Schedule C (Form 1040) should show the name of the one with self-employment income. Where husband and wife each have self-employment income, a separate Schedule C must be attached for each. In such cases the total of amounts shown on line 23 of each separate schedule should be entered on line 8, page 1, Form 1040, and the aggregate self-employment tax (line 34) should be entered on line 15, page 1, Form 1040.

COMMUNITY INCOME

For the purpose of computing net earnings from self-employment, if any of the income from a trade or business is community income, all the income from such trade or business is considered the income of the husband unless the wife exercises substantially all the management and control of the trade or business, in which case all of such income is considered the income of the wife. (Also see instructions on Partnerships below.)

If separate income tax returns are filed by husband and wife, a complete Schedule C should be attached to the return of the one with self-employment income. Community income included on such a schedule must be allocated between the two returns (on line 8, page 1, Form 1040) on the basis of the community property laws.

PARTNERSHIPS

In computing his combined net earnings from self-employment, a partner should include his entire share of such earnings from a partnership including any guaranteed payments. No part of that share may be allocated to the partner's wife (or husband) even though the income may, under State law, be community income. In the case of a husband and wife partnership, like other partnerships, the distributive share of each should be entered in Schedule H, page 3 of Form 1040, for income tax purposes. For self-employment tax purposes the distributive share of each partner should be entered on line 28(b), page 3, of this form (except that farm partnership earnings are to be reported on line 11(b), separate Schedule F (Form 1040) rather than on line 28(b) of this schedule).

Note.—If a member of a continuing partnership dies, a portion of the deceased partner's distributive share of the partnership's ordinary income (or loss) for the taxable year of the partnership in which he died must be included in the partner's net earnings from self-employment. In such cases consult your nearest Internal Revenue Service office as to how to report.

SCHEDULE SE (Form 1040)

Schedule SE, which is the lower portion of page 3 of Schedule C, provides the Social Security Administration with the information on self-employment income necessary for computing benefits.

To assure proper credit to your account, be sure to enter your name and social security account number on Schedule SE (Form 1040) exactly as they are shown on your social security card. If you do not have a social security account number, you must get one. These account numbers are obtainable from any Social Security district office. Your local post office will give you the address. Do not delay filing your return beyond the due date.

Regardless of whether joint or separate returns are filed by husband and wife, Schedule SE (Form 1040) must show only the name of the one with the self-employment income. However, if both had net earnings from self-employment, a separate Schedule SE must be filed by each.

U.S. GOVERNMENT PRINTING OFFICE 16—76072-1

COMMISSION EXHIBIT No. 1715—Continued

IF INCOME WAS ALL FROM SALARIES AND WAGES, TEAR OFF THIS PAGE AND FILE ONLY PAGES 1 AND 2

Schedule A.—INCOME FROM DIVIDENDS (Income from Savings (Building) and Loan Associations and Credit Unions should be entered as interest in Schedule B)

1. Name of qualifying corporation declaring dividend (See instructions, page 11): (Indicate by (H), (W), (J) whether stock is held by husband, wife, or jointly) — Amount $
2. Total $
3. Exclusion of $50 (If both husband and wife received dividends, each is entitled to exclude not more than $50 of his (her) own dividends)
4. Excess, if any, of line 2 over line 3. Enter here and on line 1, Schedule J $
5. Name of nonqualifying corporation declaring dividend:
6. Enter total of lines 4 and 5 $

Schedule B.—INCOME FROM INTEREST (This includes interest credited to your account)

Name of payer	Amount	Name of payer	Amount
	$		$

Enter total here→

Schedule D Summary.—GAINS AND LOSSES FROM SALES OR EXCHANGES OF PROPERTY

1. From sale or exchange of capital assets (from separate Schedule D)
2. From sale or exchange of property other than capital assets (from separate Schedule D)

Schedule E.—INCOME FROM PENSIONS AND ANNUITIES (See instructions, page 12)

Part I.—General Rule

1. Investment in contract $
2. Expected return $
3. Percentage of income to be excluded (line 1 divided by line 2) %
4. Amount received this year $
5. Amount excludable (line 4 multiplied by line 3)
6. Taxable portion (excess of line 4 over line 5)

Part II.—Where your employer has contributed all or part of the cost and your contribution will be recovered tax-free within three years. If your cost was fully recovered in prior years, enter the total amount received in line 5 omitting lines 1 through 4.

1. Cost of annuity (amounts you paid) $
2. Cost received tax-free in past years
3. Remainder of cost (line 1 less line 2) $
4. Amount received this year $
5. Taxable portion (excess, if any, of line 4 over line 3)

Schedule G.—INCOME FROM RENTS AND ROYALTIES

1. Kind and location of property (Identify whether rent or royalty)	2. Amount of rent or royalty	3. Depreciation (explain in Sch. I) or depletion	4. Repairs (attach itemized list)	5. Other expenses (attach itemized list)
	$	$	$	$
1. Totals	$	$	$	$

2. Net income (or loss) from rents and royalties (column 2 less sum of columns 3, 4, and 5)

Schedule H.—OTHER INCOME OR LOSSES

1. Partnerships (name, address, and nature of income)
2. Estates or trusts (name and address)
3. Other sources (state nature)

Total income (or loss) from above sources (Enter here and on line 10, page 1) $

o70—10—76135—1

COMMISSION EXHIBIT No. 1715—Continued

Schedule I.—EXPLANATION OF DEDUCTION FOR DEPRECIATION CLAIMED IN SCHEDULE G

1. Kind of property (if buildings, state material of which constructed). Exclude land and other nondepreciable property	2. Date acquired	3. Cost or other basis (Exclude land)	4. Depreciation allowed (or allowable) in prior years	5. Method of computing depreciation	6. Rate (%) or life (years)	7. Depreciation for this year

Additional first year depreciation (Attach statement) ....
Total ....

Schedule J.—DIVIDENDS RECEIVED CREDIT (See instructions, page 14)

1. Amount of dividends on line 4, Schedule A .... $
2. Tentative credit (4 percent of line 1) ....

LIMITATION ON CREDIT

3. Tax shown on line 12, page 1, plus amount, if any, shown on line 8(b), page 2 ....
4. 4 percent of taxable income ....

Taxable Income Means:
(a) If tax is computed on page 2, the amount shown on line 5, page 2.
(b) If Tax Table is used, the amount shown on line 11, page 1, less 10 percent thereof, and less the deduction for exemptions ($600 multiplied by the number of exemptions claimed on line 4, page 1).

5. Dividends received credit. Enter here and on line 13(a), page 1, the smallest of the amounts on line 2, 3, or 4, above .... $

Schedule K.—RETIREMENT INCOME CREDIT (See instructions, page 14)

This credit does not apply
1. If you received pensions or annuities of $1,200 or more from Social Security or Railroad Retirement;
2. If you are under 65 years of age and had "earned income" of $2,100 or more; OR
3. If you are 65 or over and under 72, and had "earned income" of $2,400 or more.

If separate return, use column B only. If joint return, use column A for wife and column B for husband →	A	B
Did you receive earned income in excess of $600 in each of any 10 calendar years before the taxable year 1960? Widow or widowers see instructions, page 14	☐ Yes ☐ No	☐ Yes ☐ No
If answer above is "Yes" in either column, furnish all information below in that column.		
1. Retirement income for taxable year:		
(a) **For taxpayers under 65 years of age:** Enter only income received from pensions and annuities under public retirement systems and included in line 11, page 1, of this return	$	$
(b) **For taxpayers 65 years of age or older:** Enter total of pensions and annuities, interest, and dividends included in line 11, page 1, and gross rents included in column 2, Schedule G, page 3, of this return ..		
LIMITATION ON RETIREMENT INCOME		
2. Maximum amount of retirement income for credit computation	$ 1,200 00	$ 1,200 00
3. Deduct:		
(a) Amounts received in taxable year as pensions or annuities under the Social Security Act, the Railroad Retirement Acts, and certain other exclusions from gross income ..		
(b) Earned income received in taxable year: (This line does not apply to persons 72 years of age or over)		
(1) Taxpayers under 65 years of age, enter amount in excess of $900		
(2) Taxpayers 65 or over and under 72, enter amount in excess of $1,200		
4. Total of lines 3(a) and 3(b)		
5. Balance (line 2 minus line 4)		
6. Line 5 or line 1, whichever is smaller		
7. Tentative credit (20 percent of line 6)		

8. Total tentative credit on this return (total of amounts on line 7, columns A and B) ....

LIMITATION ON RETIREMENT INCOME CREDIT

9. Amount of tax shown on line 12, page 1 ....
10. Less: Dividends received credits from line 5, Schedule J, above ....
11. Balance (line 9 less line 10) ....
12. Retirement income credit. Enter here and on line 13(b), page 1, the amount on line 8 or line 11, whichever is smaller .... $

U.S. GOVERNMENT PRINTING OFFICE c70—16—76135-1

COMMISSION EXHIBIT No. 1715—Continued

FORM L-39 (2-58)

U. S. TREASURY DEPARTMENT
INTERNAL REVENUE SERVICE
DISTRICT DIRECTOR
DALLAS 1, TEXAS

NO REPLY RECEIVED

January 5, 1962

IN REPLY REFER TO
1212:JLO:lg
S

Jack Ruby
4727 Homer
Dallas, Texas

Account No. OP 401231
Taxable Year 1960
Additional Charge $ 48.97

Section 6654 of the Internal Revenue Code of 1954 imposes an additional charge for underpayment of estimated tax. The rate of this charge, like interest, is 6 percent per annum on the amount of the underpayment for the period of underpayment. The charge is mandatory unless the taxpayer qualifies under one or more of four specific exceptions provided by law.

The most common of these exceptions may apply in cases where the estimate and payments were based on the tax shown on the income tax return for the preceding year. The income tax return for the preceding year must cover a period of twelve months and show a tax liability. Another of the exceptions may apply if the taxpayer has paid an amount equal to or greater than a tax computed on the basis of the facts shown on his income tax return for the preceding year, using the rates and exceptions for the year in which the underpayment of estimated tax occurred. These two exceptions, as well as two others provided by law, are explained on the enclosed Form 2210. Please read all four of them carefully to see whether any of them applies to your case.

The instructions for preparing an income tax return on Form 1040 inform the taxpayer that, if he had an underpayment of estimated tax and believes that the additional charge should not be asserted due to one or more of these relief provisions, he should attach a statement to his return explaining which of the exceptions applies in his case and showing any necessary computations.

Although it appears that you have underpaid your estimated tax for the taxable year indicated above, we do not find a statement attached to your income tax return for such year. However, we realize that these new provisions of law are not familiar to many taxpayers and we want to afford you another opportunity to furnish the necessary information. You may use the enclosed Form 2210 for this purpose or merely send us a statement in whatever form you prefer.

If you do not file a statement within 20 days from the date of this letter, it will be assumed that the additional charge shown at the top of this letter is in order.

We have also found errors in the arithmetic on your return for the above taxable year which resulted in your having decreased your income tax by $ 120.00. Any bill or refund resulting from the errors in arithmetic will take into account the additional charge for underpayment of estimated tax unless you file a statement establishing that this additional charge should not be made.

The arithmetical error adjustment was made because you claimed less estimated tax than was paid.

Your reply to this letter should be addressed to the District Director of Internal Revenue, Collection Division, at the above address, or if necessary you may call RI-8-5611, Ext. 473.

Sincerely,

Ellis Campbell, Jr.,

Ellis Campbell, Jr.
District Director

Enclosure:
Form 2210

COMMISSION EXHIBIT No. 1715—Continued

L 39 1212:C:RR:[redacted] I-[illegible] [illegible] #27 D

FORM 2328
(REV. NOV. 1957)
TRANSLUCENT

U. S. TREASURY DEPARTMENT - INTERNAL REVENUE SERVICE

COMPUTATION OF THE ADDITION FOR UNDERPAYMENT OF INDIVIDUAL ESTIMATED INCOME TAX

Under section 6654 of the Internal Revenue Code of 1954

SCHEDULE NO.

NAME OF TAXPAYER: Ruby

YEAR ENDED (OR PERIOD)

AMOUNT OF THE INSTALLMENT FOR THE PURPOSES OF COMPUTING THE ADDITION

1. Tax shown on the return .... $ 2005
2. 70% of line 1 (66 2/3% if farmer) .... $
3. Amount of the installment (line 2 divided by the number of the installments) .... $ 351

APPLICATION OF TAX WITHHELD

(This section is used only if the taxpayer has not established the dates on which all amounts were actually withheld)

4. Income tax withheld .... $
5. Amount of tax withheld applied to each installment (line 4 divided by the number of installments) .... $

COMPUTATION OF THE UNDERPAYMENT				COMPUTATION OF THE ADDITION				
DUE DATE OF INSTALLMENT (a)	AMOUNT OF INSTALLMENT (line 3) (b)	TIMELY PAYMENTS AND CREDITS (Include line 5) (c)	AMOUNT OF THE INSTALLMENT NOT TIMELY PAID (Col. (b) less Col. (c)) (d)	LATE PAYMENTS ON INSTALLMENT * (e)	DATE PAID OR DUE DATE OF RETURN, WHICHEVER IS EARLIER (f)	PERIOD OF UNDERPAYMENT (Col. (f) less Col. (a)) (g)	FACTOR (rate at 6% per annum) (h)	AMOUNT OF THE ADDITION (Col. (h) times Col. (e)) (i)
4-15-60	351	120	231		4-15-61	12 mo	06	13.86
6-15-60	"	—	351		"	10	05	17.55
9-15-60	"	—	351		"	7	035	12.29
1-15-61	"	—	351			3	015	5.27
							TOTAL	48.97

Key: *Addition not asserted due to application of (a) Section 6654(d)(1)(A); (b) Section 6654(d)(1)(B); (c) Section 6654(d)(1)(C); (d) Section 6654(d)(2).

*For purposes of computing the addition late payments on installments not made before the due date of the return are shown as having been made on that date.

GPO:1958 O-468220

COMMISSION EXHIBIT No. 1715—Continued

FORM 1040 U.S. Treasury Department Internal Revenue Service

U.S. INDIVIDUAL INCOME TAX RETURN—1959

C 13 C

or Other Taxable Year Beginning .... 1959, Ending .... 19....
(PLEASE TYPE OR PRINT)

1716

Commission Exhibit No. 1716

Name: Jack Ruby
(If this is a joint return of husband and wife, ...)

Home address: 4727 Homer
(Number and street)

Dallas (City, town, or post office) | (Postal zone number) | Texas (State)

Your Social Security Number: 359 10 589 | Occupation: Dance Hall Owner | Wife's Social Security Number | Occupation

● ATTACH CHECK OR MONEY ORDER HERE ● ATTACH COPY B OF FORMS W-2 HERE ●

Exemptions

1. Check blocks which apply. Check for wife only if all of her income is included in this return, or if she had no income.
   (a) Regular $600 exemption .... [X] Yourself [ ] Wife
   (b) Additional $600 exemption if 65 or over at end of taxable year .... [ ] Yourself [ ] Wife
   (c) Additional $600 exemption if blind at end of taxable year .... [ ] Yourself [ ] Wife
   Enter number of exemptions checked → 1
2. List first names of your children who qualify as dependents; give address if different from yours. Enter number of children listed →
3. Enter number of exemptions claimed for other persons listed at top of page 2 ....
4. Enter the total number of exemptions claimed on lines 1, 2, and 3 1

Income

5. Enter all wages, salaries, bonuses, commissions, tips, and other compensation before payroll deductions (including any excess of expense account or similar allowance paid by your employer over your ordinary and necessary business expenses. See instructions, pp. 5-6.)

Employer's Name	Where Employed (City and State)	(a) Wages, etc.	(b) Income Tax Withheld
		$	$
	Enter totals here →	$	$

6. Less: Excludable "Sick Pay" in line 5 (See instructions, page 7. Attach required statement.) ....
7. Balance (line 5 less line 6) .... $
8. Profit (or loss) from business from separate Schedule C 14,060 86
9. Profit (or loss) from farming from separate Schedule F ....
10. Other income (or loss) from page 3 (Dividends, Interest, Rents, Pensions, etc.)
11. Adjusted Gross Income (sum of lines 7, 8, 9, and 10) .... $ 14,060 86

If the social security tax (FICA) withheld from wages exceeded $120 because you or your wife had more than one employer, see instructions, page 5.

● Check if unmarried "Head of Household" [ ], or "Surviving Widow or Widower" with dependent child [ ]. (See instructions pp. 7-8)

Tax due or refund

12. TAX on income on line 11. (If line 11 is under $5,000, and you do not itemize deductions, use Tax Table on page 16 of instructions to find your tax and check here [ ]. If line 11 is $5,000 or more, or if you itemize deductions, compute your tax on page 2 and enter here the amount from line 9, page 2). $ 3,598 17

If income was all from wages, omit lines 13 through 16

13. (a) Dividends received credit from line 5 of Schedule J .... $
    (b) Retirement income credit from line 12 of Schedule K ....
14. Balance (line 12 less line 13) .... $ 3,598 17
15. Enter your self-employment tax from separate Schedule C or F 180 00
16. Sum of lines 14 and 15 .... $ 3,778 17
17. (a) Tax withheld (line 5 above). Attach Forms W-2, Copy B .... $
    (b) Payments and credits on 1959 Declaration of Estimated Tax (See page 8, instructions.) 480 00 $ 480 00
    District Director's office where paid ....
18. If your tax (line 12 or 16) is larger than your payments (line 17), enter the **BALANCE DUE** here → $ 3,298 17
    Pay in full with this return to "Internal Revenue Service." If less than $1.00, file return without payment.
19. If your payments (line 17) are larger than your tax (line 12 or 16), enter the **OVERPAYMENT** here → $ 22.99
    If less than $1.00, the overpayment will be refunded only upon application.
20. Amount of line 19 to be: (a) Credited on 1960 estimated tax $..........; (b) Refunded $..........

3321.16

Did you receive an expense allowance or reimbursement, or charge expenses to your employer? [ ] Yes [X] No (See page 6, instructions.)
If "Yes," did you submit an itemized accounting of expenses to your employer? [ ] Yes [ ] No

County in which you live: Dallas

Is your wife (husband) filing a separate return for 1959? [ ] Yes [X] No. If "yes," enter her (his) name and do not claim the exemption on this return.

If you owe any Federal tax for years before 1959, enter here the Internal Revenue District where the account is outstanding.

I declare under the penalties of perjury that this return (including any accompanying schedules and statements) has been examined by me and to the best of my knowledge and belief is a true, correct, and complete return. If the return is prepared by a person other than the taxpayer, his declaration is based on all the information relating to the matters required to be reported in the return of which he has any knowledge.

Sign here: Jack Ruby 4/18/60
(Taxpayer's signature and date) (If this is a joint return, BOTH HUSBAND AND WIFE MUST SIGN) (Wife's signature and date)

Alexander Grant & Company
(Signature of preparer other than taxpayer)

ALEXANDER GRANT & COMPANY
1220 Mercantile Securities Building
DALLAS 1, TEXAS
(Address)

APR 18 1960
(Date)

c70—16—75313-1

Commission Exhibit No. 1716

Form **2210**

U.S. Treasury Department—Internal Revenue Service

STATEMENT RELATING TO UNDERPAYMENT OF ESTIMATED INCOME TAX BY INDIVIDUALS

(To be filed with Form 1040 or Form 1040W)

1959

Name

Jack Ruby

Address (Number, street, city, postal zone, and State)

Declarations of Estimated Tax (Form 1040-ES) and payments of estimated tax are required to be made by individuals whose income taxes are not sufficiently paid throughout the year by means of withholding from wages and salaries. The law imposes an additional charge for failure to pay estimated tax in the amounts and by the installment dates specified by law.

This form is intended to help taxpayers to determine whether, on each installment date, their payments were equal to ¼ of 70 percent of the tax liability shown on their returns. If any payment was less than this amount, the form also provides for: (a) determining whether a taxpayer qualifies under any of the four statutory exceptions to the application of the additional charge, and (b) figuring the amount of such charge, if any.

The form is designed for the usual situation in which a taxpayer files his return on a calendar year basis, and is required to pay his estimated tax in four equal installments. Your computation will be different if you were not required to file a declaration until a date later than April 15, 1959, or if you amended your declaration. In this case you may obtain advice at your nearest Internal Revenue Service office.

If your return is not on a calendar year basis, change the installment dates below to correspond with your fiscal year.

PART I.—FOR ALL INDIVIDUALS EXCEPT FARMERS (Farmers Use Part II)

Computation of Underpayments

By filling in lines 1 through 4 below you can determine whether by each installment date you paid less than 17½% (¼ of 70%) of the tax liability shown on your return. If you paid at least 17½% by each installment date, it will not be necessary to file this form.

1. Income tax shown on line 14, page 1, Form 1040 for 1959 [1] $3,598.17

	Due Dates of Installments			
	Apr. 15, 1959	June 15, 1959	Sept. 15, 1959	Jan. 15, 1960
2. Enter in each column 17½ percent of amount on line 1	$ 629.68	$ 629.68	$ 629.68	$ 629.68
3. (a) Amounts paid, credited, or withheld[2] for each period	$ 120.00	$ 120.00	$ 120.00	$ 120.00
(b) Overpayment of previous installment [3]	X X X X X X X X			
(c) Total of line 3				
4. Underpayment (or overpayment) (line 2 less line 3(c))	$	$	$	$

[1] For Form 1040W use the amount on line 11, page 1, minus the amount on line 12(c) of that form.

[2] The amount of tax withheld for the year may be considered withheld in four equal installments, or you may use the amounts actually withheld for the period. If your return was filed by January 31, 1960, and the balance of tax paid in full, include such balance on line 3(a) for the January 15, 1960, installment.

[3] Any overpayment of an installment on line 4 in excess of all prior underpayments should be applied as a credit against the next installment.

There is no additional charge imposed on an underpayment shown on line 4 for any installment date if by that date you made the minimum payment determined under any one of the four following exceptions (see table at top of page 2 for summary of computations):

Exception 1.—This exception applies if the total amount paid equals or exceeds the total amount which would have been due if the estimated tax were the tax shown on your 1958 return. This exception may apply if you had a substantial increase in income over the previous year. The 1958 return must cover a taxable year of 12 months and must show a tax liability.

Exception 2.—This exception applies if the total amount paid equals or exceeds the total amount which would have been due if the estimated tax were a tax based on the facts shown on your 1958 income tax return but computed at the 1959 tax rates and with the personal exemptions for 1959. Use a Form 1040 or Form 1040W for 1959 as a guide in making this computation.

Exception 3.—This exception applies if by the installment date there was paid at least 70 percent of a tax which would have been due by the installment date, computed by placing on an annual basis the taxable income for the months ending in the taxable year before the month in which the installment was required to be paid. This exception may apply in cases in which smaller amounts of income are received in the earlier part of the year than in the later part.

To make this computation, figure your income[4] from the first of the year to the end of the month before the applicable installment date. Divide this amount by the number of months and multiply by 12. Then figure what your tax would have been if this had been your income for the year.

Exception 4.—This exception applies if the total amount paid by the installment date equals or exceeds 90 percent of a tax computed on the basis of the actual taxable income for the months ending in the taxable year before the month in which the installment was required to be paid. This exception generally applies when large amounts of income are received late in the year.

To make this computation, figure your income from the first of the year to the end of the month before the applicable installment date. Then figure what your 1959 income tax would have been if this had been your income for the year.

[4] Income for this purpose is the adjusted gross income if you used the standard deduction, or the taxable income computed without the deduction for personal exemptions if you itemized your deductions.

COMMISSION EXHIBIT No. 1716—Continued

	Apr. 15, 1959	June 15, 1959	Sept. 15, 1959	Jan. 15, 1960
5. Total amount paid or withheld as shown on line 3 (a) from Jan. 1 through the date indicated	$ 120.00	$ 120.00	$ 120.00	$ 120.00
6. Exception 1. 1958 tax $ 476.00 (Line 14, page 1, Form 1040 for 1958)	25% of 1958 tax $ 119.00	50% of 1958 tax $ 119.00	75% of 1958 tax $ 119.00	100% of 1958 tax $ 119.00
7. Exception 2. (Attach computation.) Tax based on 1958 income, 1959 rates and exemptions $	25% of this tax $	50% of this tax $	75% of this tax $	100% of this tax $
8. Exception 3. (Show computations on separate sheet and attach.)	17½% of tax on annualized income $	35% of tax on annualized income $	52½% of tax on annualized income $	X X X X X X X X
9. Exception 4. (Show computations on separate sheet and attach.)	90% of tax (Jan. 1 through Mar. 31) $	90% of tax (Jan. 1 through May 31) $	90% of tax (Jan. 1 through Aug. 31) $	X X X X X X X X

On line 5 fill in the cumulative totals of the amounts shown on line 3 (a), page 1, which were paid, credited, or withheld from January 1, 1959, up to and including the appropriate installment date.

For each date on which an underpayment is indicated on line 4, page 1, fill in the information called for on any one of the lines 6 through 9 which you believe will relieve you from the additional charge. For each installment on which an underpayment is indicated, only one exception need be shown. A different exception may be applied to each of the underpayments.

For each period compare the amount on line 5 with any amount shown on line 6, 7, 8, or 9 for the same period. If the amount on line 5 is equal to or more than the amount shown on any one of these lines, there is no additional charge for the underpayment indicated on line 4, page 1, for that date.

Computation of Additional Charge

If you show an underpayment of estimated tax on line 4, page 1, for any of the installments and one or more of the exceptions is not applicable, you should compute the additional charge by completing the portion(s) of this schedule applicable to the underpaid installment(s).

	Due Dates of Installments			
	Apr. 15, 1959	June 15, 1959	Sept. 15, 1959	Jan. 15, 1960
10. Amount of underpayment (from line 4, page 1)	$	$	$	$
11. Date of payment or April 15, 1960, whichever is earlier [1]				
12. Number of days from due date of installment to the date shown on line 11 above				
13. Additional charge (6 percent per year on the amount on line 10 for the number of days shown on line 12)	$	$	$	$

14. Total of amounts on line 13. On page 1, of your Income Tax return, show this amount in the bottom margin as "Additional Charge" and increase the amount of the "Balance Due" or decrease the amount of the "Overpayment" accordingly .... $

[1] If you made more than one payment for a given installment, attach statement showing separate computation for each payment. If you filed your return and paid the balance of tax due by January 31, 1960, such balance shall be considered paid as of January 15, 1960.

PART II.—FOR FARMERS

It is not necessary to file this form if your return is filed and tax due paid by February 15, 1960

Computation of Underpayment

1. Income tax shown on line 14, page 1, Form 1040 for 1959 .... $
2. 66⅔ percent of the amount on line 1 (the minimum amount due on Jan. 15, 1960) .... $
3. Amount paid, credited, or withheld by Jan. 15, 1960 ....
4. Underpayment of estimated tax (line 2 less line 3). (If none, do not file this form) .... $
5. **Exception 1.**—Income tax liability on line 14, page 1, Form 1040 for 1958 .... $
   (The 1958 return must cover a taxable year of 12 months and must show a tax liability.)
   If the amount on line 3, above, equals or exceeds this amount, the additional charge is not applicable.
6. **Exception 2.**—This exception applies if the total amount paid equals or exceeds the total amount which would have been due if the estimated tax were a tax based on the facts shown on your 1958 income tax return computed at the 1959 tax rates and with the personal exemptions for 1959. Use a Form 1040 for 1959 as a guide in making this computation, and enter such tax here .... $
   If the amount on line 3, above, equals or exceeds this amount, the additional charge is not applicable.

Computation of Additional Charge

7. Number of days from Jan. 15, 1960, to date of payment or Apr. 15, 1960, whichever is earlier ....
8. Additional charge (6 percent per year on the amount shown on line 4, above, for the number of days shown on line 7, above). On page 1, Form 1040, show this amount in the bottom margin as "Additional Charge" and increase line 18 or decrease line 19 accordingly .... $

U.S. GOVERNMENT PRINTING OFFICE : 1959—O-513479

COMMISSION EXHIBIT No. 1716—Continued

SCHEDULE C (Form 1040)

U. S. Treasury Department—Internal Revenue Service

PROFIT (OR LOSS) FROM BUSINESS OR PROFESSION

(Compute Social Security Self-Employment Tax on Page 3)

1959

Attach this schedule to your Income Tax Return, Form 1040 — Partnerships, Joint Ventures, Etc., Must File On Form 1065

For Calendar Year 1959, or other taxable year beginning ...., 1959, and ending ...., 19

Name as shown on page 1, Form 1040 Jack Ruby

If you had more than one business, or husband and wife had separate businesses, a separate page 1 of Schedule C must be completed for each business.

A. Principal business activity: Dance Hall (Retail trade, wholesale trade, lawyer, etc.) (Principal product or service)
(See instructions, page 2)

B. Business name: Club Vegas

C. Employer's Identification Number: I-75-0949491

D. Business location: 3508 Oak Lawn (Number and street or rural route) Dallas, Texas (City or post office) (State)

1. Total receipts $........, less allowances, rebates, and returns $		$	
2. Inventory at beginning of year	$		
3. Merchandise purchased $........, less any items withdrawn from business for personal use $			
4. Cost of labor (do not include salary paid to yourself)			
5. Material and supplies			
6. Other costs (explain in Schedule C-2)			
7. Total of lines 2 through 6	$		
8. Inventory at end of year			
9. Cost of goods sold (line 7 less line 8)		Schedule attached	
10. Gross profit (line 1 less line 9)		$	
OTHER BUSINESS DEDUCTIONS			
11. Salaries and wages not included on line 4 (exclude any paid to yourself)	$		
12. Rent on business property			
13. Interest on business indebtedness			
14. Taxes on business and business property			
15. Losses of business property (attach statement)			
16. Bad debts arising from sales or services			
17. Depreciation (explain in Schedule C-1)			
18. Repairs (explain in Schedule C-2)			
19. Depletion of mines, oil and gas wells, timber, etc. (attach schedule)			
20. Amortization (attach statement)			
21. Other business expenses (explain in Schedule C-2)			
22. Total of lines 11 through 21			
23. Net profit (or loss) (line 10 less line 22). Enter here; on line 24, page 3; and on line 8, page 1, Form 1040		$ 14,060	86

Schedule C-1. EXPLANATION OF DEDUCTION FOR DEPRECIATION CLAIMED ON LINE 17

1. Kind of property (if buildings, state material of which constructed). Exclude land and other nondepreciable property	2. Date acquired	3. Cost or other basis	4. Depreciation allowed (or allowable) in prior years	5. Method of computing depreciation	6. Rate (%) or life (years)	7. Depreciation for this year
		$	$			$
		Schedule				

Schedule C-2. EXPLANATION OF LINES 6, 18, AND 21

Line No.	Explanation	Amount	Line No.	Explanation	Amount
		$			$
		Schedule			

c48—16—75307-1

C

COMMISSION EXHIBIT NO. 1716—Continued

Page 3

COMPUTATION OF SOCIAL SECURITY SELF-EMPLOYMENT TAX
(See Instructions—Page 4)

▶ If you had wages of $4,800 or more which were subject to the deduction for social security, do not fill in this page.
▶ Complete only one page 3; if you had more than one business, combine profits (or losses) from all of your businesses on this page.
▶ Each self-employed person must file a separate schedule. See instructions, page 4, for joint returns and partnerships.

NAME OF SELF-EMPLOYED PERSON (as shown on social security card)
Jack Ruby

24. Net profit (or loss) shown on line 23, page 1 **(Enter combined amount if more than one business)**	$ 14,060	86		
25. Add to net profit (or subtract from net loss) losses of business property shown on line 15, page 1				
26. Total (or difference)			$ 14,060	86
27. Net income (or loss) from excluded services or sources included on line 26 (See "Exclusions," page 4)				
Specify excluded services or sources				
28. Net earnings (or loss) from self-employment—				
(a) From business (line 26 less any amount on line 27)			$ 14,060	86
(b) From partnerships, joint ventures, etc. (other than farming)				
(c) From service as a minister, member of a religious order, or a Christian Science practitioner. Enter only if you elect Social Security coverage by filing Form 2031 (See instructions, page 4).				
(d) From farming reported on line 12 or 13, separate Schedule F (Form 1040)				
29. Total net earnings (or loss) from self-employment reported on line 28. Enter here and on line 6 below			$ 14,060	86
(If line 29 is under $400, you are not subject to self-employment tax. Do not fill in rest of page.)				
30. The largest amount of combined wages and self-employment earnings subject to social security tax is	$ 4,800	00		
31. Total wages, covered by social security, paid to you during the taxable year. (For "Covered" wages see "F. I. C. A. Wages" box on Form W-2.) Enter here and on line 7, below				
32. Balance (line 30 less line 31)	$ 4,800	00		
33. Self-employment income—line 29 or 32, whichever is smaller. Enter here and on line 8, below			$ 4,800	00
34. Self-employment tax—take 3¾% of the amount on line 33. (You can do this by multiplying the amount on line 33 by .0375.) Enter this amount here and on line 15, page 1, Form 1040			$ 180	00

COMMISSION EXHIBIT No. 1716—Continued

JACK RUBY, DBA THE CLUB VEGAS
Dallas, Texas

Year 1959

Statement of Income

INCOME		
Sales		
Bar - net		$27,454.10
Cost of sales		
Inventory, 1-1-59	$ 245.00	
Purchases	9,257.34	
Total available merchandise	9,502.34	
Less inventory, 12-31-59	250.00	9,252.34
Gross profit - bar sales		18,201.76
OTHER INCOME		
Admissions - less taxes		30,664.85
Miscellaneous - machines		2,115.34
Gross income		50,981.95
EXPENSES		
Salaries	22,234.91	
Supplies	677.43	
Rent and utilities	6,539.07	
Laundry	117.65	
Advertising	1,673.57	
Depreciation	1,011.92	
Repairs and maintenance	587.35	
Legal and audit	800.00	
Contract labor	839.15	
Taxes and license	701.59	
Auto and parking	650.41	
Equipment rental	181.00	
Payroll taxes	686.40	
ASCAP and BMI	70.00	
Night watch service	64.00	
Miscellaneous	86.64	36,921.09
Net income		$14,060.86

COMMISSION EXHIBIT No. 1716—Continued

(TA)XPAYER'S NAME Jack Ruby, DBA, The Club Vegas

(AD)DRESS 3508 Oak Lawn

Dallas, Texas

TAXABLE YEAR 1959

SCHEDULE OF DEPRECIATION

Property	Date Acquired	Cost	Previous Depreciation	Remaining Value	Estimated Life	Remaining Life	Depreciation taken this year
Ice box	1-1-57	700 00	700 00	-0-	2 yrs		-0-
Chairs and tables, booths	1-1-57	650 00	650 00	-0-	2 yrs		-0-
Air conditioner	1-1-57	1000 00	666 72	333 28	3 yrs		333 28
1 piano	1-1-57	75 00	75 00	-0-	2 yrs		-0-
1 heater	1-1-57	150 00	150 00	-0-	2 yrs		-0-
Cash registers	1-1-57	250 00	125 04	124 96	4 yrs		62 52
Sign	1-1-57	500 00	199 92	300 08	5 yrs		99 96
Television set	1-1-57	50 00	50 00	-0-	1½ yrs		-0-
Amplifier set	1-1-57	75 00	49 92	25 08	3 yrs		25 08
small refrigerator	5-1-57	45 00	45 00	-0-	1 yr		-0-
Hi-Fi set	1-8-58	125 00	62 50	62 50	2 yrs		62 50
Speakers	1-10-58	50 00	25 00	25 00	2 yrs		25 00
Microphone and stand	8-24-58	57 64	9 60	48 04	2 yrs		28 82
tape recorder	12-1-59	95 00	-0-	95 00	2 yrs		3 96
Auto (90% Business - 90% of $1,648.00)	10-31-58	1483 20	61 80	1421 40	4 yrs		370 80
Total		5305 84	2870 50	2435 34			1011 92

Form 1040—1959 **EXEMPTIONS FOR PERSONS OTHER THAN YOUR WIFE AND CHILDREN** Page 2

Name	Relationship	Months lived in your home. If born or died during year also write "B" or "D"	Did dependent have gross income of $600 or more?	Amount YOU furnished for dependent's support. If 100% write "All"	Amount furnished by OTHERS including dependent
				$	$

Enter on line 3, page 1, the number of exemptions claimed above.
→ If an exemption is based on a multiple-support agreement of a group of persons, attach the declarations described on page 5 of instructions.

ITEMIZED DEDUCTIONS—IF YOU DO NOT USE TAX TABLE OR STANDARD DEDUCTION

If Husband and Wife (Not Legally Separated) File Separate Returns and One Itemizes Deductions, the Other Must Also Itemize
State to whom paid. If necessary write more than one item on a line or attach additional sheets. Please put your name and address on any attachments.

Contributions	Total paid but not to exceed 20% of line 11, page 1, except as described on page 8 of instructions	$	
Interest	Total interest		
Taxes	Total taxes		
Medical and dental expense (If 65 or over, see instructions, page 10)	Submit itemized list. Do not enter any expense compensated by insurance or otherwise 1. Cost of medicines and drugs IN EXCESS of 1 percent of line 11, page 1 .... $ 2. Other medical and dental expenses 3. Total .... $ 4. Enter 3 percent of line 11, page 1 5. Allowable amount (excess of line 3 over line 4). (See instructions, page 10, for limitations.)		
Other Deductions (See page 10 of instructions and attach information required)	Total		
	TOTAL DEDUCTIONS (Enter here and on line 2 of Tax Computation, below)	$	

TAX COMPUTATION—IF YOU DO NOT USE THE TAX TABLE

1. Enter Adjusted Gross Income from line 11, page 1	$ 14,060	86
2. If deductions are itemized above, enter total of such deductions. If deductions are not itemized ***and line 1, above, is $5,000 or more,*** enter the smaller of 10 percent of line 1 or $1,000 ($500 if a married person filing a separate return)	1,000	00
3. Balance (line 1 less line 2)	13,060	86
4. Multiply $600 by total number of exemptions claimed on line 4, page 1	600	00
5. Taxable Income (line 3 less line 4)	12,460	86
6. Tax on amount on line 5. Use appropriate tax rate schedule on page 15 of instructions. Do not use Tax Table on page 16	3,598	17
7. If you had capital gains and the alternative tax applies, enter the tax from separate Schedule D		
8. Tax credits. If you itemized deductions, enter: (a) Credit for income tax payments to a foreign country or U. S. possession (Attach Form 1116) ..... $ (b) Tax paid at source on tax-free covenant bond interest and credit for partially tax-exempt interest (c) Total ..... **Enter here →**		
9. Enter here and on line 12, page 1, the amount shown on line 6 or 7 less amount claimed on line 8(c)	$ 3,598	17

c70—16—75313-1 GPO

COMMISSION EXHIBIT NO. 1716—Continued

COMPUTATION PROVED F.A. 2-EWL X-2 JRD CLOSED ON SURVEY BF 1054407

FORM **1040**

U. S. Treasury Department Internal Revenue Service

U. S. INDIVIDUAL INCOME TAX RETURN

1956

For calendar year or other taxable year beginning ...., 1956, and ending ...., 195....

PLEASE TYPE OR PRINT

Name (If this is a joint return of husband and wife, use first names of both): EARL R. AND MARGIE G. RUBY

Your Social Security No. and Occupation: 326-05-2183 Self-Employed

Home Address (Number and street or rural route): 1922 WEST HOOD STREET

Wife's Social Security No. and Occupation: - housewife

(City or post office) CHICAGO (Zone) (County) COOK (State) ILLINOIS

If Income Was All From Salaries and Wages, Use Pages 1 and 2 Only. If Such Income Was Less Than $5,000, You May Need to Use Page 1 Only. See Page 3 of the Instructions.

Exemptions

1. Check blocks which apply. Check for wife if she had no income or her income is included in this return.
   - Regular $600 exemption .... [X] Yourself [X] Wife
   - Additional exemption if 65 or over at end of taxable year ... [ ] Yourself [ ] Wife
   - Additional exemption if blind at end of taxable year .... [ ] Yourself [ ] Wife
   - Enter number of blocks checked → 2
2. List names of your children who qualify as dependents; give address if different from yours. Robert F. Joyne F. Denise A. — Enter number of children listed → 3
3. Enter number of exemptions claimed for other persons listed at top of page 2 1
4. Enter the total number of exemptions claimed on lines 1, 2, and 3 6

Income

5. Enter all wages, salaries, bonuses, commissions, and other compensation received in 1956, before payroll deductions. Outside salesmen and persons claiming traveling, transportation, or reimbursed expenses, see instructions, page 6.

Employer's Name	Where Employed (City and State)	Wages, etc.	Income Tax Withheld
		$	$
Enter totals here →		$	$

6. Less: Excludable "Sick Pay" in line 5 (See instructions, page 6. Attach required explanation.) ....
7. Balance (line 5 less line 6) .... $
8. Profit (or loss) from business from separate Schedule C 11,570.91
9. Profit (or loss) from farming from separate Schedule F ....
10. Other income (or loss) from page 3 .... 75.00
11. ADJUSTED GROSS INCOME (sum of lines 7, 8, 9, and 10) .... $ 11,645.91

Special computation: Unmarried or legally separated persons qualifying as "Head of Household," see instructions, page 7, and check here [ ] Widows and widowers who are entitled to the special tax computation, see instructions, page 7, and check here [ ]

If income on line 11 is under $5,000, and you do not itemize deductions, use Tax Table on page 16 of instructions. If income is $5,000 or more, or if you itemize deductions, compute your tax on page 2.

Tax due or Refund

12. Enter tax from the Tax Table, or from line 9, page 2. Please check if you use Tax Table [ ] .. $ 1,273.31

If income was all from wages, omit lines 13 through 16

13. (a) Dividends received credit from line 5 of Schedule J .. $
    (b) Retirement income credit from line 12 of Schedule K ..
14. Balance (line 12 less line 13) .... $ 1,273.31
15. Enter your self-employment tax from separate Schedule C or F 126.00
16. Sum of lines 14 and 15 .... $ 1,399.31
17. (a) Tax withheld (line 5 above). Attach Forms W-2 (Copy B) .... $
    (b) Payments and credits on 1956 Declaration of Estimated Tax (See page 8, instructions.) 1,035.16 — $ 1,035.16
    District Director's office where paid 1st Illinois
18. If your tax (line 12 or 16) is larger than your payments (line 17), enter the balance here → $ 364.15
    Pay in full with this return; if less than $1.00, do not remit.
19. If your payments (line 17) are larger than your tax (line 12 or 16), enter the overpayment here → $
    If less than $1.00, it will be refunded only upon application. See instructions, page 8.

Enter amount of line 19 to be: Credited on 1957 estimated tax $............; Refunded $............

30 APR 15 1957 INT. REV. RECD WITH REMITTANCE

Did you pay or agree to pay anyone for assistance in the preparation of your return? [X] Yes [ ] No If "Yes," enter his name. Harold Kaminsky

Is your wife (husband) making a separate return for 1956? [ ] Yes [X] No If "Yes," enter her (his) name.

Do you owe any Federal tax for years before 1956? [ ] Yes [X] No

Taxpayer sign here

I declare under the penalties of perjury that this return (including any accompanying schedules and statements) has been examined by me and to the best of my knowledge and belief is a true, correct, and complete return.

Earl R. Ruby 4/12/57 (Your signature) (Date) Margie G. Ruby (If this is a joint return, wife's signature) APR 12 1957 (Date)

→ To assure split-income benefits, husband and wife must include all their income and, even though only one has income, BOTH MUST SIGN.

Preparer (other than taxpayer) sign here

I declare under the penalties of perjury that I prepared this return for the person(s) named herein; and that this return (including any accompanying schedules and statements) is, to the best of my knowledge and belief, a true, correct, and complete return based on all the information relating to the matters required to be reported in this return of which I have any knowledge.

Harold Kaminsky (Individual or Firm Signature) 7305 W. Palmer St (Address) 3/29/57 (Date)

COMMISSION EXHIBIT No. 1716—Continued

EXEMPTIONS FOR PERSONS OTHER THAN YOUR WIFE AND CHILDREN

Name	Relationship	Number of months dependent lived in your home. If born or died during year also write "B" or "D"	Did dependent have gross income of $600 or more?	Amount YOU spent for dependent's support. If 100% write "All"	Amount spent by OTHERS including dependent from own funds
Joseph Rubenstein 1360 West Estes Avenue Chicago, Illinois	Father	None	No	$ All	$ None

Enter on line 3, page 1, the number of exemptions claimed above.
→ If an exemption is based on a multiple-support agreement of a group of persons, attach information described on page 5 of instructions.

ITEMIZED DEDUCTIONS—IF YOU DO NOT USE TAX TABLE OR STANDARD DEDUCTION

If Husband and Wife (Not Legally Separated) File Separate Returns and One Itemizes Deductions, the Other Must Also Itemize

Describe deductions and state to whom paid. If more space is needed, attach additional sheets. Please put your name and address on any attachments.

Contributions	Schedule Attached		
	Total (not to exceed 20% of line 11, page 1, except as described on page 8 of instructions)		$ 198.50
Interest	Home Federal Savings-Mortgage	$721.56	
	Total		721.56
Taxes	Real Estate Taxes	$306.00	
	Sales Tax	200.00	
	Total		506.00
Medical and dental expense (If 65 or over, see instructions, page 9)	Submit itemized list. Do not enter any expense compensated by insurance or otherwise.		
	1. Cost of medicines and drugs, in excess of 1 percent of line 11, page 1	$	
	2. Other medical and dental expenses	817.80	
	3. Total	$ 817.80	
	4. Enter 3 percent of line 11, page 1	349.38	
	5. Allowable amount (excess of line 3 over line 4). (See instructions, page 9, for limitations.)		468.42
Child care	Expenses for care of children and certain other dependents not to exceed $600 (See page 10 of instructions and attach statement)		
Casualty losses	Total losses (not compensated by insurance or otherwise)		
Miscellaneous			
	Total		
	TOTAL DEDUCTIONS (Enter on line 2 of Tax Computation, below)		$ 1,894.48

TAX COMPUTATION—IF YOU DO NOT USE THE TAX TABLE

1.	Enter Adjusted Gross Income from line 11, page 1	$ 11,645.91
2.	If deductions are itemized above, enter total of such deductions. If deductions are not itemized *and line 1, above, is $5,000 or more:* (a) married persons filing separately enter $500; (b) all others enter 10 percent of line 1, or $1,000, whichever is smaller	1,894.48
3.	Balance (line 1 less line 2)	9,751.43
4.	Multiply $600 by total number of exemptions claimed on line 4, page 1	3,600.00
5.	TAXABLE INCOME (line 3 less line 4)	6,151.43
6.	Tax on amount on line 5. Use appropriate Tax Rate Schedule on page 11 of instructions	1,273.31
7.	If you had capital gains and the alternative tax applies, enter the tax from separate Schedule D	
8.	Tax credits. If you itemized deductions, enter: (a) Credit for income tax payments to a foreign country or U. S. possession (Attach Form 1116) $ (b) Tax paid at source on tax-free covenant bond interest and credit for partially tax-exempt interest	
9.	Enter here and on line 12, page 1, the amount shown on line 6 or 7 less amount claimed on line 8	$ 1,273.31

16—72754—1 GPO

COMMISSION EXHIBIT No. 1716—Continued

EARL R. and MARGIE G. RUBY

1922 WEST HOOD STREET

CHICAGO, COOK, ILLINOIS

FORM 1040 - 1956

PAGE 2 - CONTRIBUTIONS

Community Fund	$ 10.00
Cong. Ezeas Israel	10.00
Jewish Peoples Home	65.00
Grant Hospital	15.00
Illinois Police Benevolent Ass'n	5.00
Boy Scouts	8.00
Blind Service	5.00
General Orphan Assylum	5.00
Cancer Fund	10.00
American Red Cross	20.00
Miscellaneous Charities	20.50
Hadassah	25.00
TOTAL	$198.50

PAGE 2 - MEDICAL EXPENSES

Daniel L. Streicker, M.D.	$125.00
Marvin W. Aren, M.D.	75.00
Dr. William Semiloff	19.00
Dr. Herbert Goldt	10.00
Dr. John Kleber	9.00
Dr. Willard Kerman	5.00
Mount Sinai Hospital	209.30
Columbus Hospital	217.00
Dr. Berman	28.50
Dr. I. P. Bronstein	120.00
TOTAL	$817.80

COMMISSION EXHIBIT No. 1716—Continued

SCHEDULE C (Form 1040)	U. S. Treasury Department—Internal Revenue Service **PROFIT (OR LOSS) FROM BUSINESS OR PROFESSION** (For Computation of Self-Employment Tax, see Page 3)	1956

Attach this schedule to your Income Tax Return, Form 1040 — Partnerships, Joint Ventures, Etc. Must File On Form 1065

For Calendar Year 1956, or other taxable year beginning ...., 1956, and ending ...., 195

Name and Address as shown on page 1, Form 1040

EARL R. RUBY, 1922 WEST HOOD STREET, CHICAGO, ILLINOIS

Item (see instructions—page 2)

A. Principal business activity: Manufacturers of Novelties and Premiums
(Retail trade, wholesale trade, lawyer, etc.) (Principal product or service)

B. Business name: Earl Products Company

C. Business address: 701 North Sangamon Street, Chicago, Illinois
(Number and street or rural route) (City or post office) (County) (State)

● IMPORTANT—If you had more than one business, a separate page 1 of Schedule C must be completed for each business.

Line (see instructions—page 2)		
1. Total receipts $ 167,435.23, less allowances, rebates, and returns $ 74.42		$ 167,360.81
2. Inventory at beginning of year	$ 7,481.22	
3. Merchandise purchased $ 75,112.58, less any items withdrawn from business for personal use $	75,112.58	
4. Cost of labor (do not include salary paid to yourself)	27,097.51	
5. Material and supplies		
6. Other costs (explain in Schedule C-2)	10,924.37	
7. Total of lines 2 through 6	$ 120,615.68	
8. Inventory at end of year	9,614.40	
9. Cost of goods sold (line 7 less line 8)		111,001.28
10. Gross profit (line 1 less line 9)		$ 56,359.53
OTHER BUSINESS DEDUCTIONS		
11. Salaries and wages not included on line 4 (do not include any paid to yourself)	$ 7,706.84	
12. Rent on business property	3,345.00	
13. Interest on business indebtedness		
14. Taxes on business and business property		
15. Losses of business property (attach statement)		
16. Bad debts arising from sales or services		
17. Depreciation and obsolescence (explain in Schedule C-1)	2,035.06	
18. Repairs (explain in Schedule C-2)		
19. Depletion of mines, oil and gas wells, timber, etc. (attach schedule)		
20. Amortization (attach statement)		
21. Other business expenses (explain in Schedule C-2)	31,701.72	
22. Total of lines 11 through 21		44,788.62
23. Net profit (or loss) (line 10 less line 22). Also enter on line 24, page 3 of this schedule, and on line 8, page 1, Form 1040		$ 11,570.91

Schedule C-1. EXPLANATION OF DEDUCTION FOR DEPRECIATION CLAIMED ON LINE 17

1. Kind of property (if buildings, state material of which constructed). Exclude land and other nondepreciable property	2. Date acquired	3. Cost or other basis	4. Depreciation allowed (or allowable) in prior years	5. Method of computing depreciation	6. Rate (%) or life (years)	7. Depreciation for this year
Furniture & Fixt.	Various	$ 1848.20	$ 1091.44	St. Line	10 yrs	$ 290.07
Automobiles	Various	4246.70	733.72	St. Line	4 yrs	730.87
Machinery & Equip.	Various	11293.29	7758.08	St. Line	10 yrs	1104.12
						$ 2035.06

Schedule C-2. EXPLANATION OF LINES 6, 18, AND 21

Line No.	Explanation	Amount	Line No.	Explanation	Amount
6	Schedule Attached	$ 10924.37	21	Schedule Attached	$ 31701.72

16—72767-1

C

COMMISSION EXHIBIT No. 1716—Continued

EARL R. and MARGIE R. RUBY

1922 WEST HOOD STREET

CHICAGO, ILLINOIS

FORM 1040 - 1956
SCHEDULE C - LINE 3

MERCHANDISE PURCHASED

Merchandise purchased	$73,210.64
Freight, express	1,901.94
	$75,112.58

SCHEDULE C - LINE 6
LINE 6 - OTHER COSTS

Heat, light and power	$ 1,675.30
Manufacturers excise tax	1,038.53
Shop supplies and expense	3,538.47
Payroll taxes	1,935.16
Insurance expense	1,620.41
Repairs and maintenance	1,116.50
	$10,924.37

COMMISSION EXHIBIT No. 1716—Continued

EARL R. and MARGIE R. RUBY

1922 WEST HOOD STREET

CHICAGO, ILLINOIS

FORM 1040 - 1956

SCHEDULE C-2

OTHER BUSINESS EXPENSES

Advertising	$ 3,187.53
Auto expense	1,759.80
Bank service charges	100.22
Sales commissions	6,789.93
Credit and collection expense	57.75
Discounts allowed	847.31
Professional fees	1,389.04
Miscellaneous general expense	530.53
Office supplies and expense	1,000.66
Postage	8,487.92
Shipping expense	5,969.30
Telephone	1,476.15
Travel and Sales expense	2,126.29
Recovery of Bad Debts	(120.69)
	$31,701.72

COMMISSION EXHIBIT No. 1716—Continued

Page 3

COMPUTATION OF SELF-EMPLOYMENT TAX
(For social security)
(See Instructions—Page 4)

▶ Each self-employed person must file a separate schedule. See instructions, page 4, for joint returns and partnerships.
▶ If you had wages of $4,200 or more which were subject to the deduction for social security, do not fill in this page.
▶ If you have more than one business, a separate page 1, Schedule C, must be completed for each business. However, only one page 3 is to be completed and filed showing the combined net profit or loss from such businesses.

NAME OF SELF-EMPLOYED PERSON (as shown on social security card)

EARL R. RUBY

STATE EACH BUSINESS ACTIVITY SUBJECT TO SELF-EMPLOYMENT TAX (for example: Restaurant, Building Contractor, but not Partner or Owner)

MANUFACTURER OF NOVELTIES AND PREMIUMS

Line		
24. Net profit (or loss) shown on line 23, page 1 (Enter combined amount if more than one business)	$ 11,570.91	
25. Add to net profit (or subtract from net loss) losses of business property shown on line 15, page 1		
26. Total (or difference)		$ 11,570.91
27. Net income (or loss) from excluded services or sources included on line 26		
Specify excluded services or sources		
28. Net earnings (or loss) from self-employment—		
(a) From business (line 26 less any amount on line 27)		$ 11,570.91
(b) From partnerships, joint ventures, etc. (other than farming)		
(c) From service as a minister, member of a religious order or a Christian Science practitioner		
(d) From farming reported on line 12 or 13, separate Schedule F (Form 1040)		
29. Total net earnings (or loss) from self-employment reported on line 28		$ 11,570.91
(If line 29 is under $400, you are not subject to self-employment tax. Do not fill in rest of page.)		
30. Maximum amount subject to self-employment tax	$ 4,200.00	
31. Less: Total wages, subject to deduction for social security, paid to you during the taxable year. (For wages reported on Form W-2, see "F. I. C. A. Wages" box.)		
32. Balance (line 30 less line 31)	$ 4,200.00	
33. Self-employment income—line 29 or 32, whichever is smaller		$ 4,200.00
34. Self-employment tax—3 percent of amount on line 33. Enter here and on line 15, page 1, Form 1040		$ 126.00

FILL IN ...

Commission Exhibit No. 1716—Continued

SCHEDULE D (Form 1040)

U. S. Treasury Department—Internal Revenue Service

GAINS AND LOSSES FROM SALES OR EXCHANGES OF PROPERTY

1956

Attach this schedule to your Income Tax Return, Form 1040

For Calendar Year 1956, or other taxable year beginning ...., 1956, and ending ...., 195..

Name and Address

EARL R. AND MARGIE R. RUBY, 1922 W. HOOD ST. CHICAGO, ILLINOIS

(I) CAPITAL ASSETS

Short-Term Capital Gains and Losses—Assets Held Not More Than 6 Months

a. Kind of property (if necessary, attach statement of descriptive details not shown below)	b. Date acquired (mo., day, yr.)	c. Date sold (mo., day, yr.)	d. Gross sales price (contract price)	e. Depreciation allowed (or allowable) since acquisition or March 1, 1913 (attach schedule)	f. Cost or other basis and cost of subsequent improvements (if not purchased, attach explanation)	g. Expense of sale	h. Gain or loss (column d plus column e less sum of columns f and g)
1.			$	$	$	$	$

2. Enter your share of net short-term gain (or loss) from partnerships and fiduciaries
3. Enter unused capital loss carryover from 5 preceding taxable years (**Attach statement**)
4. Net short-term gain (or loss) from lines 1, 2, and 3 .... $

Long-Term Capital Gains and Losses—Assets Held More Than 6 Months

a. Kind of property	b. Date acquired	c. Date sold	d. Gross sales price	e. Depreciation	f. Cost or other basis	g. Expense of sale	h. Gain or loss
5. 1950 Station Wagon Plymouth	1950	Aug. 1956	$ 150.00	$ 1968.00	$ 1968.00	$ -	$ 150.00

6. Enter the full amount of your share of net long-term gain (or loss) from partnerships and fiduciaries
7. Net long-term gain (or loss) from lines 5 and 6 .... $ 150.00
8. Combine the amounts shown on lines 4 and 7, and enter the net gain (or loss) here .... $ 150.00
9. **If line 8 shows a GAIN**—Enter 50 percent of line 7 or 50 percent of line 8, whichever is smaller. **(Enter zero if there is a loss or no entry on line 7)** 75.00
10. Deduct line 9 from line 8. Enter balance here and on line 1, Schedule D Summary on page 3 of Form 1040 .... $ 75.00
11. **If line 8 shows a LOSS**—Enter here and on line 1, Schedule D Summary, Form 1040, the **smallest** of the following: (a) the amount on line 8; (b) taxable income computed without regard to capital gains and losses and the deduction for exemptions; or (c) $1,000 .... $

COMPUTATION OF ALTERNATIVE TAX

(See instructions on other side as to when the alternative tax applies)

12. Enter the amount from line 5, page 2, of Form 1040 .... $
13. Enter amount from line 9
14. Balance (line 12 less line 13) .... $
15. Enter tax on amount on line 14 (Use applicable Tax Rate Schedule on page 11 of Form 1040 Instructions) .... $
16. Enter 50 percent of line 13
17. Alternative tax (line 15 plus line 16). If smaller than amount on line 6, page 2, Form 1040, enter this alternative tax on line 7, page 2, Form 1040 .... $

(II) PROPERTY OTHER THAN CAPITAL ASSETS

a. Kind of property (if necessary, attach statement of descriptive details not shown below)	b. Date acquired (mo., day, yr.)	c. Date sold (mo., day, yr.)	d. Gross sales price (contract price)	e. Depreciation allowed (or allowable) since acquisition or March 1, 1913 (attach schedule)	f. Cost or other basis and cost of subsequent improvements (if not purchased, attach explanation)	g. Expense of sale	h. Gain or loss (column d plus column e less sum of columns f and g)
1.			$	$	$	$	$

2. Enter your share of gain (or loss) from partnerships and fiduciaries
3. Net gain (or loss) from lines 1 and 2. Enter here and on line 2, Schedule D Summary, Form 1040 .... $

cnr—16—72755-1

COMMISSION EXHIBIT No. 1716—Continued

IF INCOME WAS ALL FROM SALARIES AND WAGES, TEAR OFF THIS PAGE AND FILE ONLY PAGES 1 AND 2

Schedule A.—INCOME FROM DIVIDENDS

1. Name of qualifying corporation declaring dividend (See instructions, page 12) — Amount $
2. Total $
3. Exclusion of $50 (If both husband and wife received dividends, each is entitled to exclude not more than $50 of his (her) dividends)
4. Enter excess, if any, of line 2 over line 3 $
5. Name of nonqualifying corporation declaring dividend:
6. Enter total of lines 4 and 5 $

Schedule B.—INCOME FROM INTEREST

Name of payer	Amount	Name of payer	Amount
	$		$

Enter total here→

Schedule D Summary.—GAINS AND LOSSES FROM SALES OR EXCHANGES OF PROPERTY

1. From sale or exchange of capital assets (from separate Schedule D) 75.00
2. From sale or exchange of property other than capital assets (from separate Schedule D)

Schedule E.—INCOME FROM PENSIONS OR ANNUITIES (See instructions, page 13)

Part I.—General Rule

1. Investment in contract $
2. Expected return $
3. Percentage of income to be excluded (line 1 divided by line 2) %
4. Amount received this year $
5. Amount excludable (line 4 multiplied by line 3)
6. Taxable portion (excess, if any, of line 4 over line 5)

Part II.—Where your cost will be recovered within three years and your employer has contributed part of the cost

1. Cost of annuity (amounts paid in) $
2. Cost received tax-free in past years
3. Remainder of cost (line 1 less line 2) $
4. Amount received this year $
5. Taxable portion (excess, if any, of line 4 over line 3)

Schedule G.—INCOME FROM RENTS AND ROYALTIES

1. Kind and location of property	2. Amount of rent or royalty	3. Depreciation (explain in Sch. I) or depletion	4. Repairs (attach itemized list)	5. Other expenses (attach itemized list)
	$	$	$	$
1. Totals	$	$	$	$

2. Net income (or loss) from rents or royalties (column 2 less sum of columns 3, 4, and 5)

Schedule H.—INCOME FROM PARTNERSHIPS, ESTATES, TRUSTS, AND OTHER SOURCES

1. Partnership (name and address)
2. Estate or trust (name and address)
3. Other sources (state nature)

Total income (or loss) from above sources (Enter here and on line 10, page 1) $ 75.00

Schedule I.—EXPLANATION OF DEDUCTION FOR DEPRECIATION CLAIMED IN SCHEDULE G

1. Kind of property (if buildings, state material of which constructed). Exclude land and other nondepreciable property	2. Date acquired	3. Cost or other basis	4. Depreciation allowed (or allowable) in prior years	5. Method of computing depreciation	6. Rate (%) or life (years)	7. Depreciation for this year
		$	$			$

10—72754-1

COMMISSION EXHIBIT No. 1716—Continued

APR 15 - 73 -- 0226.52 A

Commission Exhibit No. 1717

FORM **1040**
U. S. Treasury Department
Internal Revenue Service

U. S. INDIVIDUAL INCOME TAX RETURN—1958

or Other Taxable Year Beginning .... 1958, Ending .... 195...
(PLEASE TYPE OR PRINT)

Name: **Jack Ruby**
(If this is a joint return of husband and wife, use first names and middle initials of both)

Home address: **4156 Hawthorne**
(Number and street or rural route)

Dallas (City, town, or post office) **19** (Postal zone number) **Texas** (State)

Your Social Security Number	Occupation	Wife's Social Security Number	Occupation
359 10 589	Dance Hall Owner		

If Income Was All From Salaries and Wages, Use Pages 1 and 2 Only. See Page 3 of the Instructions.

Exemptions

1. Check blocks which apply. Check for wife if she had no income or her income is included in this return.
   - (a) Regular $600 exemption .... ☒ Yourself ☐ Wife
   - (b) Additional $600 exemption if 65 or over at end of taxable year ☐ Yourself ☐ Wife
   - (c) Additional $600 exemption if blind at end of taxable year ☐ Yourself ☐ Wife
   - Enter number of exemptions checked → 1
2. List first names of your children who qualify as dependents; give address if different from yours. Enter number of children listed →
3. Enter number of exemptions claimed for other persons listed at top of page 2 .... —
4. Enter the total number of exemptions claimed on lines 1, 2, and 3 1

Income

5. Enter all wages, salaries, bonuses, commissions, tips, and other compensation before payroll deductions (including any excess of expense account or similar allowance paid by your employer over your ordinary and necessary business expenses. See instructions, pp. 5-6.)

Employer's Name	Where Employed (City and State)	(a) Wages, etc.	(b) Income Tax Withheld
		$	$
Enter totals here →		$	$

6. Less: Excludable "Sick Pay" in line 5 (See instructions, page 7. Attach required statement.) ...
7. Balance (line 5 less line 6) .... $
8. Profit (or loss) from business from separate Schedule C 3,274.64
9. Profit (or loss) from farming from separate Schedule F ....
10. Other income (or loss) from page 3 (dividends, interest, rents, pensions, etc.) ....
11. ADJUSTED GROSS INCOME (sum of lines 7, 8, 9, and 10) .... $ 3,274.64

If either you or your wife had more than one employer and the social security tax (FICA) withheld from wages exceeded $94.50, see instructions, page 5.

● ATTACH COPY B OF FORMS W-2 HERE ●

Unmarried or legally separated persons qualifying as "Head of Household," see instructions, page 7, and check here ☐

Widows and widowers with dependent child who are entitled to the special tax computation, see instructions, page 8, and check here ☐

Tax due or refund

12. Tax on income on line 11. (If line 11 is under $5,000, and you do not itemize deductions, use Tax Table on page 16 of instructions to find your tax and check here ☒. If line 11 is $5,000 or more, or if you itemize deductions, compute your tax on page 2 and enter here the amount from line 9, page 2) $ 476.00

If income was all from wages, omit lines 13 through 16

13. (a) Dividends received credit from line 5 of Schedule J .... $
    (b) Retirement income credit from line 12 of Schedule K ....
14. Balance (line 12 less line 13) .... $ 476.00
15. Enter your self-employment tax from separate Schedule C or F 110.52
16. Sum of lines 14 and 15 .... $ 586.52
17. (a) Tax withheld (line 5 above). Attach Forms W-2, Copy B .... $
    (b) Payments and credits on 1958 Declaration of Estimated Tax (See page 8, instructions.) ● 360.00 $ 360.00
    District Director's office where paid **Dallas, Texas**
18. If your tax (line 12 or 16) is larger than your payments (line 17), enter the **BALANCE DUE** here → $ 226.52
    Pay in full with this return to "Internal Revenue Service." If less than $1.00, file return without payment.
19. If your payments (line 17) are larger than your tax (line 12 or 16), enter the **OVERPAYMENT** here → $
    If less than $1.00, the overpayment will be refunded only upon application.
20. Amount of line 19 to be: (a) Credited on 1959 estimated tax $ ....; (b) Refunded $ ....

5

Did you receive an expense allowance or reimbursement, or charge expenses to your employer? ☐ Yes ☒ No (See page 6, instructions.)
If "Yes," did you submit an itemized accounting of expenses to your employer? ☐ Yes ☐ No

County in which you live. **Dallas**

Is your wife (husband) filing a separate return for 1958? ☐ Yes ☒ No If "Yes," enter her (his) name.

Do you owe any Federal tax for years before 1958? ☐ Yes ☒ No

I declare under the penalties of perjury that this return (including any accompanying schedules and statements) has been examined by me and to the best of my knowledge and belief is a true, correct, and complete return. If the return is prepared by a person other than the taxpayer, his declaration is based on all the information relating to the matters required to be reported in the return of which he has any knowledge.

Sign here: Jack Ruby 4/15/59
(Taxpayer's signature and date) (If this is a joint return, BOTH HUSBAND AND WIFE MUST SIGN) (Wife's signature and date)

W. B. Goode & Company
(Signature of preparer other than taxpayer)

W. B. GOODE & COMPANY
1220 Mercantile Securities Bldg
DALLAS, TEXAS
(Address)

APR 9 1959
(Date)

c70—16—74557-1

COMMISSION EXHIBIT No. 1717

JACK RUBY DBA CLUB VEGAS
Dallas, Texas

1958

Statement of Income

	: Twelve months : ended : December 31, 1958 :
Sales	
Bar - net	$20,978.25
Cost of sales	
Inventory - beginning	283.00
Purchases	7,870.52
Total available merchandise	$ 8,153.52
Less inventory - ending	245.00
Cost of sales	$ 7,908.52
Gross profit - bar sales	$13,069.73
Other income	
Admissions - less taxes	23,597.12
Miscellaneous - machines	1,088.80
Total income	$37,755.65
Expenses	
Salaries	18,152.00
Supplies	551.78
Rent and utilities	6,536.98
Laundry	80.56
Advertising	1,733.61
Depreciation	1,498.90
Interest	.76
Repairs and maintenance	558.35
Legal and audit	1,520.00
Contract labor	1,589.57
Taxes and license	433.52
Police department	7.00
Auto and parking	835.95
Equipment rental	309.00
Payroll tax	478.83
Miscellaneous	119.20
ASCAP & BMI	60.00
Bad debts	15.00
Total expenses	$34,481.01
NET INCOME	$ 3,274.64

COMMISSION EXHIBIT No. 1717—Continued

SCHEDULE C (Form 1040)

U. S. Treasury Department—Internal Revenue Service

PROFIT (OR LOSS) FROM BUSINESS OR PROFESSION

(Compute Social Security Self-Employment Tax on Page 3)

1958

Attach this schedule to your Income Tax Return, Form 1040 — Partnerships, Joint Ventures, Etc., Must File On Form 1065

For Calendar Year 19 58 or other taxable year beginning , 19 , and ending , 19

Name as shown on page 1, Form 1040 **Jack Ruby**

If you had more than one business, or husband and wife had separate businesses, a separate page 1 of Schedule C must be completed for each business.

A. Principal business activity: (See instructions, page 2) **Dance Hall** (Retail trade, wholesale trade, lawyer, etc.) (Principal product or service)

B. Business name: **Club Vegas**

C. Business location: **3508 Oak Lawn** (Number and street or rural route) **Dallas** (City or post office) **Dallas, Texas** (County) (State)

D. Did you file an Employer Quarterly Tax Return, Form 941, for any quarter of 1958? [X] Yes [ ] No. **E.** Employer's Identification Number, if any **I 75-0949491** **F.** Is this business within the legal boundaries of a municipality? [X] Yes [ ] No.

G. Did you own this business on December 31, 1958? [X] Yes [ ] No. **H.** How many months in 1958 did you own this business? **12 mos.**

1. Total receipts $......, less allowances, rebates, and returns $		$
2. Inventory at beginning of year	$	
3. Merchandise purchased $......, less any items withdrawn from business for personal use $		
4. Cost of labor (do not include salary paid to yourself)		
5. Material and supplies		
6. Other costs **(explain in Schedule C–2)**		
7. Total of lines 2 through 6	$	SCHEDULE ATTACHED
8. Inventory at end of year		
9. Cost of goods sold (line 7 less line 8)		
10. Gross profit (line 1 less line 9)		$
OTHER BUSINESS DEDUCTIONS		
11. Salaries and wages not included on line 4 (exclude any paid to yourself)	$	
12. Rent on business property		
13. Interest on business indebtedness		
14. Taxes on business and business property		
15. Losses of business property **(attach statement)**		
16. Bad debts arising from sales or services		
17. Depreciation **(explain in Schedule C–1)**		
18. Repairs **(explain in Schedule C–2)**		
19. Depletion of mines, oil and gas wells, timber, etc. **(attach schedule)**		
20. Amortization **(attach statement)**		
21. Other business expenses **(explain in Schedule C–2)**		
22. Total of lines 11 through 21		
23. Net profit (or loss) (line 10 less line 22). Enter here; on line 24, page 3; and on line 8, page 1, Form 1040		$ 3,274.64

Schedule C–1. EXPLANATION OF DEDUCTION FOR DEPRECIATION CLAIMED ON LINE 17

1. Kind of property (if buildings, state material of which constructed). Exclude land and other nondepreciable property	2. Date acquired	3. Cost or other basis	4. Depreciation allowed (or allowable) in prior years	5. Method of computing depreciation	6. Rate (%) or life (years)	7. Depreciation for this year
		$	$			$
		SCHEDULE ATTACHED				

Schedule C–2. EXPLANATION OF LINES 6, 18, AND 21

Line No.	Explanation	Amount	Line No.	Explanation	Amount
		$			$

e48—16—74556—1

C

COMMISSION EXHIBIT NO. 1717—Continued

TAXPAYER'S NAME Jack Ruby DBA

ADDRESS The Club Vegas
3508 Oak Lawn, Dallas, Texas

TAXABLE YEAR 1958

SCHEDULE OF DEPRECIATION

No	Property	Date Acquired	Cost	Previous Depreciation	Remaining Value	Estimated Life	Remaining Life	Depreciation taken this year
1	Ice box	1-1-57	700 00	350 04	349 96	2 yrs		349 96
2	Chairs and tables, booths	1-1-57	650 00	324 96	325 04	2 yrs		325 04
3	Air conditioner	1-1-57	1000 00	333 36	666 64	3 yrs		333 36
4	1 piano	1-1-57	75 00	37 44	37 56	2		37 56
5	1 heater	1-1-57	150 00	75 00	75 00	2		75 00
6	Cash registers	1-1-57	250 00	62 52	187 48	4		62 52
7	Signs	1-1-57	500 00	99 96	400 04	5		99 96
8	T.V. set	1-1-57	50 00	33 36	16 64	1½ yrs		16 64
9	Amplifier set	1-1-57	75 00	24 96	50 04	3		24 96
10	1 small refrigerator	3-1-57	45 00	30 00	15 00	1 yr		15 00
11	Hi-Fi set	1-8-58	125 00		125 00	2 yrs		62 50
12	Speakers	1-10-58	50 00		50 00	2		20 00
13	Microphone and stand	8-31-58	57 64		57 64	2		9 60
14								
15								
16	Auto, 90% Business - 90% of 1648 00	10 31 58	1483 20		1483 20	4 yrs		61 80
17								
18								
19								
20								
21								
22								
23								
24								
25								
26								
27								
28								
	Total		5210 84	1371 60	3839 24			1498 90

COMPUTATION OF SOCIAL SECURITY SELF-EMPLOYMENT TAX
(See Instructions—Page 4)

▶ **If you had wages of $4,200 or more which were subject to the deduction for social security, do not fill in this page.**
▶ **Complete only one page 3; if you had more than one business, combine profits (or losses) from all of your businesses on this page.**
▶ **Each self-employed person must file a separate schedule. See instructions, page 4, for joint returns and partnerships.**

NAME OF SELF-EMPLOYED PERSON (as shown on social security card)
Jack Ruby

24. Net profit (or loss) shown on line 23, page 1 **(Enter combined amount if more than one business)**	$ 3,274.64	
25. Add to net profit (or subtract from net loss) losses of business property shown on line 15, page 1		
26. Total (or difference)		$ 3,274.64
27. Net income (or loss) from excluded services or sources included on line 26 (See "Exclusions," page 4)		
Specify excluded services or sources		
28. Net earnings (or loss) from self-employment—		
(a) From business (line 26 less any amount on line 27)		$ 3,274.64
(b) From partnerships, joint ventures, etc. (other than farming)		
(c) From service as a minister, member of a religious order, or a Christian Science practitioner. Enter only if you elect Social Security coverage by filing Form 2031 (See instructions, page 4).		
(d) From farming reported on line 12 or 13, separate Schedule F (Form 1040)		
29. Total net earnings (or loss) from self-employment reported on line 28. Enter here and on line 6 below **(If line 29 is under $400, you are not subject to self-employment tax. Do not fill in rest of page.)**		$ 3,274.64
30. The largest amount subject to social security self-employment tax is ($4,800 for years ending after December 31, 1958)	$ 4,200 00	
31. Less: Total wages, subject to deduction for social security, paid to you during the taxable year. (For wages reported on Form W-2, see "F. I. C. A. Wages" box.) Enter here and on line 7, below	-0-	
32. Balance (line 30 less line 31)	$ 4,200.00	
33. Self-employment income—line 29 or 32, whichever is smaller. Enter here and on line 8, below		$ 3,274.64
34. Self-employment tax—take 3⅜% of the amount on line 33. (You can do this by multiplying the amount on line 33 by .03375.) Enter this amount here and on line 15, page 1, Form 1040		$ 110.52

COMMISSION EXHIBIT No. 1717—Continued

Commission Exhibit No. 1718

FORM **1040**
U. S. Treasury Department
Internal Revenue Service

U. S. INDIVIDUAL INCO[ME TAX RETURN 1957]

or Other Taxable Year Beginning ......, 1957, Ending ...... 1718 ...... 195..
(PLEASE TYPE OR PRINT)

C 13

Name: Jack Ruby
(If this is a joint return of husband and wife, use first names of both)

Home address: 4160 Hawthorne
(Number and street or rural route)

Dallas (City, town, or post office) 19 (Postal zone number) Texas (State)

Your Social Security Number: 359 10 589 | Occupation: Dance Hall Owner | Wife's Social Security Number | Occupation

If Income Was All From Salaries and Wages, Use Pages 1 and 2 Only. See Page 3 of the Instructions.

Exemptions

1. Check blocks which apply. Check for wife if she had no income or her income is included in this return.
   (a) Regular $600 exemption — [X] Yourself [ ] Wife
   (b) Additional $600 exemption if 65 or over at end of taxable year — [ ] Yourself [ ] Wife
   (c) Additional $600 exemption if blind at end of taxable year — [ ] Yourself [ ] Wife
   Enter number of exemptions checked → 1
2. List first names of your children who qualify as dependents; give address if different from yours. **Enter number of children listed** →
3. Enter number of exemptions claimed for other persons listed at top of page 2
4. Enter the total number of exemptions claimed on lines 1, 2, and 3 1

Income

● ATTACH COPY B OF FORMS W-2 HERE ●

5. Enter all wages, salaries, bonuses, commissions, tips, and other compensation received in 1957, before payroll deductions.

Employer's Name	Where Employed (City and State)	(a) Wages, etc.	(b) Income Tax Withheld
		$	$
	Enter totals here →	$	$

6. Less: (a) Travel, reimbursed expenses, etc. (See instructions, page 6. Attach required statements.) $
   (b) Excludable "Sick Pay" in line 5
7. Balance (line 5 less line 6) ...... $
8. Profit (or loss) from business from separate Schedule C 2,619.52
9. Profit (or loss) from farming from separate Schedule F ......
10. Other income (or loss) from page 3 (dividends, interest, rents, pensions, etc.)
11. ADJUSTED GROSS INCOME (sum of lines 7, 8, 9, and 10) ...... $ 2,619.52

If social security tax (FICA) withheld from your wages exceeded $94.50, see instructions, page 5.

Unmarried or legally separated persons qualifying as "Head of Household," see instructions, page 7, and check here [ ]

Widows and widowers who are entitled to the special tax computation, see instructions, page 7, and check here [ ]

Tax due or refund

12. Tax on income on line 11. (If line 11 is under $5,000, and you do not itemize deductions, use Tax Table on page 16 of instructions to find your tax and check here [x]. If line 11 is $5,000 or more, or if you itemize deductions, compute your tax on page 2 and enter here the amount from line 9, page 2) ...... $ 350.00

If income was all from wages, omit lines 13 through 16

13. (a) Dividends received credit from line 5 of Schedule J ...... $
    (b) Retirement income credit from line 12 of Schedule K ......
14. Balance (line 12 less line 13) ...... $ 350.00
15. Enter your self-employment tax from separate Schedule C or F 88.41
16. Sum of lines 14 and 15 ...... $ 438.41
17. (a) Tax withheld (line 5 above). Attach Forms W-2 (Copy B) ...... $
    (b) Payments and credits on 1957 Declaration of Estimated Tax (See page 8, instructions) ● 200.00 ...... $ 200.00
    District Director's office where paid: Dallas, Texas
18. If your tax (line 12 or 16) is larger than your payments (line 17), **enter the balance due here** → $ 238.41
    Pay in full with this return to "Internal Revenue Service." If less than $1.00, file return without payment.
19. If your payments (line 17) are larger than your tax (line 12 or 16), **enter the overpayment here** → $ 3.40
    If less than $1.00, the overpayment will be refunded only upon application. See instructions, page 8.
20. Amount of line 19 to be: (a) Credited on 1958 estimated tax $ ...... ; (b) Refunded $ 241.81

RECEIVED JUN 16 ... DIST. ... DALLAS

County in which you live: Dallas

Is your wife (husband) making a separate return for 1957? [ ] Yes [X] No If "Yes," enter her (his) name.

Do you owe any Federal tax for years before 1957? [ ] Yes [X] No

TAXPAYER—I declare under the penalties of perjury that this return (including any accompanying schedules and statements) has been examined by me and to the best of my knowledge and belief is a true, correct, and complete return.

Sign here: Jack Ruby (Your signature) 6/14/58 (Date) (If this is a joint return, wife's signature) (Date)

→ To assure split-income benefits, husband and wife must include all their income and, even though only one has income, BOTH MUST SIGN.

PREPARER (other than taxpayer)—I declare under the penalties of perjury that I prepared this return for the person(s) named herein; and that this return (including any accompanying schedules and statements) is, to the best of my knowledge and belief, a true, correct, and complete return based on all the information relating to the matters required to be reported in this return of which I have any knowledge.

Sign here: W. B. Goode Company (Individual or Firm Signature) W. B. GOODE & COMPANY 1220 Mercantile Securities Bldg. DALLAS, TEXAS (Address) APR 21 1958 (Date)

COMMISSION EXHIBIT NO. 1718

SCHEDULE C (Form 1040)

U. S. Treasury Department—Internal Revenue Service

PROFIT (OR LOSS) FROM BUSINESS OR PROFESSION

(For Computation of Self-Employment Tax, see Page 3)

1957

Attach this schedule to your Income Tax Return, Form 1040 — Partnerships, Joint Ventures, Etc. Must File On Form 1065

For Calendar Year 1957, or other taxable year beginning ...., 1957, and ending 195

Name and Address as shown on page 1, Form 1040

Jack Ruby, 41[illegible] Hawthorne, Dallas, Texas

A. Principal business activity: (See instructions, page 2) Dance Hall (Retail trade, wholesale trade, lawyer, etc.) .... (Principal product or service)

B. Business name: Club Vegas

C. Business address: 3508 Oak Lawn (Number and street or rural route) Dallas (City or post office) Texas (State)

● **IMPORTANT**—If you had more than one business, a separate page 1 of Schedule C must be completed for each business.

1. Total receipts $........, less allowances, rebates, and returns $........		$
2. Inventory at beginning of year	$	
3. Merchandise purchased $........, less any items withdrawn from business for personal use $........		
4. Cost of labor (do not include salary paid to yourself)		
5. Material and supplies		
6. Other costs (explain in Schedule C–2)		
7. Total of lines 2 through 6	$	
8. Inventory at end of year		
9. Cost of goods sold (line 7 less line 8)		
10. Gross profit (line 1 less line 9)		$
OTHER BUSINESS DEDUCTIONS		
11. Salaries and wages not included on line 4 (do not include any paid to yourself)	$	
12. Rent on business property		
13. Interest on business indebtedness		
14. Taxes on business and business property		
15. Losses of business property (attach statement)		
16. Bad debts arising from sales or services		
17. Depreciation (explain in Schedule C–1)		
18. Repairs (explain in Schedule C–2)		
19. Depletion of mines, oil and gas wells, timber, etc. (attach schedule)		
20. Amortization (attach statement)		Schedule attached
21. Other business expenses (explain in Schedule C–2)		
22. Total of lines 11 through 21		
23. Net profit (or loss) (line 10 less line 22). Enter here; on line 24, page 3; and on line 8, page 1, Form 1040		$ 2,619.52

Schedule C-1. EXPLANATION OF DEDUCTION FOR DEPRECIATION CLAIMED ON LINE 17

1. Kind of property (if buildings, state material of which constructed). Exclude land and other nondepreciable property	2. Date acquired	3. Cost or other basis	4. Depreciation allowed (or allowable) in prior years	5. Method of computing depreciation	6. Rate (%) or life (years)	7. Depreciation for this year
		$	$			$

Schedule C-2. EXPLANATION OF LINES 6, 18, AND 21

Line No.	Explanation	Amount	Line No.	Explanation	Amount
		$			$

16—72761-2

C

COMMISSION EXHIBIT No. 1718—Continued

Club Vegas
Dallas, Texas

STATEMENT OF INCOME

For the Twelve Months ended December 31, 1957

SALES		
Bar - net		$21,182.2
COST OF SALES		
Inventory - beginning	$ 200.00	
Purchases	8,116.87	
Total available merchandise	$ 8,316.87	
Less inventory - ending	283.00	
Cost of sales		8,033.8
Gross profit - bar sales		$13,148.4
OTHER INCOME		
Admissions - less tax		19,002.3
Machines		1,512.0
Miscellaneous		8.8
Total income		$33,671.6
EXPENSES		
Salaries	$11,783.00	
Supplies	378.94	
Rent and utilities	6,857.27	
Laundry	67.71	
Advertising	1,576.24	
Depreciation	1,371.60	
Interest	1.75	
Repairs and maintenance	1,406.80	
Legal and audit	562.50	
Contract labor	3,699.50	
Taxes and licenses	332.42	
Police department	756.00	
Auto expenses	817.34	
Equipment rental	824.75	
Cash over and short	(131.21)	
ASCAP and BMI	250.00	
Payroll taxes	403.46	
Miscellaneous	94.01	31,052.0
NET INCOME		$ 2,619.5

COMMISSION EXHIBIT No. 1718—Continued

TAXPAYER'S NAME CLUB VEGAS

ADDRESS 3508 OAK LAWN

DALLAS, TEXAS

TAXABLE YEAR 1957

SCHEDULE OF DEPRECIATION

No	Property	Date Acquired	Cost	Previous Depreciation	Remaining Value	Estimated Life	Remaining Life	Depreciation taken this year
1	Ice Box	1-57	700.00	-0-	700.00	24	24	350.34
2	Chairs, tables and booths	1-57	650.00	-0-	650.00	24	24	324.96
3	Air conditioner	1-57	1000.00	-0-	1000.00	36	36	333.36
4	Piano	1-57	75.00	-0-	75.00	24	24	37.44
5	Heater	1-57	150.00	-0-	150.00	24	24	75.00
6	2 cash registers	1-57	250.00	-0-	250.00	48	48	62.52
7	Sign	1-57	500.00	-0-	500.00	60	60	99.96
8	T.V. set	1-57	50.00	-0-	50.00	18	18	33.36
9	Amplifier system	1-57	75.00	-0-	75.00	36	36	24.96
10	Small refrigerator	5-57	45.00	-0-	45.00	12	12	30.00
11								
12								
13								
14								
15								
16								
17								
18								
19								
20								
21								
22								
23								
24								
25								
26								
27								
28								
	Total		3495.00	0	3495.00			1371.60

COMMISSION EXHIBIT No. 1718—Continued

COMPUTATION OF SELF-EMPLOYMENT TAX
(For social security)
(See Instructions—Page 4)

▶ Each self-employed person must file a separate schedule. See instructions, page 4, for joint returns and partnerships.
▶ If you had wages of $4,200 or more which were subject to the deduction for social security, do not fill in this page.
▶ If you have more than one business, a separate page 1, Schedule C, must be completed for each business. However, only one page 3 is to be completed and filed showing the combined net profit or loss from such businesses.

NAME OF SELF-EMPLOYED PERSON (as shown on social security card)
Jack Ruby

STATE EACH BUSINESS ACTIVITY SUBJECT TO SELF-EMPLOYMENT TAX (for example: Restaurant, Building Contractor, but not Partner or Owner)
Dance Hall

Line		
24. Net profit (or loss) shown on line 23, page 1 (**Enter combined amount if more than one business**)	$ 2,619.52	
25. Add to net profit (or subtract from net loss) losses of business property shown on line 15, page 1		
26. Total (or difference)		$ 2,619.52
27. Net income (or loss) from excluded services or sources included on line 26		
Specify excluded services or sources		
28. Net earnings (or loss) from self-employment—		
(a) From business (line 26 less any amount on line 27)		$ 2,619.52
(b) From partnerships, joint ventures, etc. (other than farming)		
(c) From service as a minister, member of a religious order, or a Christian Science practitioner. Enter only if you elect Social Security coverage by filing Form 2031 (See instructions, page 4).		
(d) From farming reported on line 12 or 13, separate Schedule F (Form 1040)		
29. Total net earnings (or loss) from self-employment reported on line 28		$ 2,619.52
(If line 29 is under $400, you are not subject to self-employment tax. Do not fill in rest of page.)		
30. Maximum amount subject to self-employment tax	$ 4,200 00	
31. Less: Total wages, subject to deduction for social security, paid to you during the taxable year. (For wages reported on Form W-2, see "F. I. C. A. Wages" box.)	-0-	
32. Balance (line 30 less line 31)	$ 4,200.00	
33. Self-employment income—line 29 or 32, whichever is smaller		$ 2,619.52
34. Self-employment tax—take 3⅜% of the amount on line 33. (You can do this by multiplying the amount on line 33 by .03375.) Enter this amount here and on line 15, page 1, Form 1040		$ 88.41

Commission Exhibit No. 1718—Continued

. S. TREASURY DEPARTMENT Internal Revenue Service DALLAS REGION FL-20	APPLICATION FOR EXTENSION OF TIME FOR FILING FEDERAL INCOME TAX RETURNS	To be filed with the District Director for your district

INSTRUCTIONS

his form is to be used by individuals, partnerships, and fiduciar- es to request an extension of time for filing income tax returns. t must be prepared in quadruplicate, and submitted on or before he due date of the return. If extension of time is authorized, ree copies will be returned to you properly validated, one to be ttached to the return and the others to be retained by you.

See instructions on reverse for partnerships and fiduciaries, also special instructions for additional extensions.

Separate application must be prepared for each taxpayer.

This form may be reproduced if the same general format is used and quality, weight and color of paper is similar.

xtension to be mailed to:

W. B. GOODE & COMPANY
1220 Mercantile Securities Bldg.
Dallas 1, Texas

Name and Address of Applicant:

JACK RUBY
4160 Hawthorne St.
Dallas 19, Texas

pplication is made for an extension of time to 6-15-58 (60 days from due date), within which to file the follow- g federal income tax return: Form No. 1040 ☒ 1041 ☐ 1065 ☐

Check only one:

Taxable year ending Dec. 31, 1957.

his extension is necessary for the following reasons:

Additional time is needed for our accountants to obtain and assemble the necessary information to file a complete and accurate return.

: is understood that if no return is filed, the granting of this extension will not in any way relieve the taxpayer of crim- al penalties provided by law for failure to file a tax return.

Jack Ruby — Signature of Applicant or Agent

4/14/58 — Date

n view of the reasons set forth, an extension of time is granted to the date shown. The tax due MUST BE PAID IN ULL WHEN THE RETURN IS FILED, WITH INTEREST AT THE RATE OF 6% PER ANNUM FROM DUE DATE TO ATE OF PAYMENT. Valid only if stamped APPROVED.

(DO NOT write in this space. For use of INTERNAL REVENUE SERVICE)

APPROVED
If additional time is required both copies of this extension must be returned for further validation.

Crump Ptg. Co. Dallas

COMMISSION EXHIBIT No. 1718—Continued

INSTRUCTIONS

ORIGINAL REQUESTS FOR EXTENSIONS OF TIME WILL BE GRANTED FOR A PERIOD OF ONLY SIXTY DAYS EXCEPT FOR CORPORATIONS.

REQUESTS FOR EXTENSIONS OF TIME MUST SHOW A VALID REASON. INABILITY TO PAY THE TAX DUE IS NOT A VALID REASON FOR REQUESTING AN EXTENSION. WE WILL EXPECT PAYMENT IN FULL OF THE BALANCE OF TAX AT THE TIME THE RETURN IS FILED.

SPECIAL INSTRUCTIONS FOR REQUESTS FOR FIDUCIARY, FORM 1041, AND PARTNERSHIP, FORM 1065.

An extension will be granted for a Fiduciary, Form 1041, only if a tentative return and remittance (25% of the tax for an estate or the entire tax for a trust, as disclosed by the tentative return) accompanies this application.

If you have requested an extension for a partnership, Form 1065, and you desire or need an extension for each individual partner, a separate request must be made for an extension of time for filing Forms 1040 of each partner.

REQUEST FOR AN ADDITIONAL EXTENSION OF TIME BEYOND THE ORIGINAL:

Additional extensions will not ordinarily be granted except in unusual circumstances, and then only for 30 days. In such instances, a statement setting forth the reasons for requesting an additional extension must be submitted prior to the date granted on the original extension. The statement should state clearly why an additional extension is necessary and why it was not possible to complete the return within the original extension time. Additional extensions will be granted only over the signature of the taxpayer. All copies of the original validated extension form must accompany the statement.

SPECIAL INSTRUCTIONS FOR REQUESTING EXTENSIONS ON CORPORATION INCOME TAX RETURNS, FORMS 1120:

All corporations are required to use Form 7004, U. S. Treasury Department, Internal Revenue Service for requesting extensions of time to file corporation income tax returns. Upon receipt of Form 7004, provided the requirements of this form have been met, the extension requested is to be considered as having been granted by this office and no approved copy will be mailed to you.

COMMISSION EXHIBIT No. 1718—Continued

COMMISSION EXHIBIT No. 1718–Continued

Commission Exhibit No. 1719

FORM **1040**
U. S. Treasury Department
Internal Revenue Service

U. S. INDIVIDUAL INCOME TAX RETURN 1719

1956

For calendar year or other taxable year beginning ...., 1956, and ending ...., 195....
PLEASE TYPE OR PRINT

Name (If this is a joint return of husband and wife, use first names of both)
Jack Ruby

Your Social Security No. and Occupation
359-10-589
Dance Hall Owner
Wife's Social Security No. and Occupation

Home Address (Number and street or rural route)
4156 Hawthorne
(City or post office) Dallas (Zone) 19 (County) Dallas (State) Texas

If Income Was All From Salaries and Wages, Use Pages 1 and 2 Only. If Such Income Was Less Than $5,000, You May Need to Use Page 1 Only. See Page 3 of the Instructions.

Exemptions

1. Check blocks which apply. Check for wife if she had no income or her income is included in this return.
   - Regular $600 exemption ☒ Yourself ☐ Wife
   - Additional exemption if 65 or over at end of taxable year ☐ Yourself ☐ Wife
   - Additional exemption if blind at end of taxable year ☐ Yourself ☐ Wife
   - Enter number of blocks checked → 1
2. List names of your children who qualify as dependents; give address if different from yours. Enter number of children listed →
3. Enter number of exemptions claimed for other persons listed at top of page 2
4. Enter the total number of exemptions claimed on lines 1, 2, and 3 1

Income

5. Enter all wages, salaries, bonuses, commissions, and other compensation received in 1956, before payroll deductions. Outside salesmen and persons claiming traveling, transportation, or reimbursed expenses, see instructions, page 6.

Employer's Name	Where Employed (City and State)	Wages, etc.	Income Tax Withheld
		$	$
		$	$

RECEIVED
75 JUL 15 1957
DIST. DIRECTOR INT. REV. DALLAS
TELLER = #1
NO REMITTANCE REC'D

6. Less: Excludable "Sick Pay" in line 5 (See instructions, page 6. Attach required explanation)
7. Balance (line 5 less line 6) ...... $
8. Profit (or loss) from business from separate Schedule C 7,437.01
9. Profit (or loss) from farming from separate Schedule F
10. Other income (or loss) from page 3
11. ADJUSTED GROSS INCOME (sum of lines 7, 8, 9, and 10) ...... $ 7,437.01 ✓

Special computation
Unmarried or legally separated persons qualifying as "Head of Household," see instructions, page 7, and check here ☐
Widows and widowers who are entitled to the special tax computation, see instructions, page 7, and check here ☐

If income on line 11 is under $5,000, and you do not itemize deductions, use Tax Table on page 16 of instructions. If income is $5,000 or more, or if you itemize deductions, compute your tax on page 2. 1387.

Tax due or refund

12. Enter tax from the Tax Table, or from line 9, page 2. Please check if you use Tax Table ☐ ...... $ 1,401.10
13. (a) Dividends received credit from line 5 of Schedule J ...... $
    (b) Retirement income credit from line 12 of Schedule K ...... -0-
14. Balance (line 12 less line 13) ...... 1387.99 ...... $ 1,401.10
15. Enter your self-employment tax from separate Schedule C or F 126.00
16. Sum of lines 14 and 15 ...... 1513.99 ...... $ 1,527.10

(If income was all from wages, omit lines 13 through 16)

17. (a) Tax withheld (line 5 above). Attach Form W-2 (Copy B) ...... $
    (b) Payments and credits on 1956 Declaration of Estimated Tax (See page 8, instructions.) ...... $ -0-
    District Director's office where paid 5% Pen
18. If your tax (line 12 or 16) is larger than your payments (line 17), enter the balance here ...... 1513.99 ...... $ 1,527.10
    Pay in full with this return; if less than $1.00, do not remit.
    75.70
19. If your payments (line 17) are larger than your tax (line 12 or 16), enter the overpayment here
    If less than $1.00, it will be refunded only upon application. See instructions, page 8.
    P 28.67

Enter amount of line 19 to be: Credited on 1957 estimated tax $ ...... ; Refunded $ ......

Did you pay or agree to pay anyone for assistance in the preparation of your return? ☒ Yes ☐ No If "Yes," enter his name.
W. B. Goode & Company

Is your wife (husband) making a separate return for 1956? ☐ Yes ☒ No If "Yes," enter her (his) name. 161836

Do you owe any Federal tax for years before 1956? ☐ Yes ☒ No

Taxpayer sign here
I declare under the penalties of perjury that this return (including any accompanying schedules and statements) has been examined by me and to the best of my knowledge and belief is a true, correct, and complete return.

(Your signature) (Date) (If this is a joint return, wife's signature) (Date)

➤ To assure split-income benefits, husband and wife must include all their income and, even though only one has income, BOTH MUST SIGN.

Preparer (other than taxpayer) sign here
I declare under the penalties of perjury that I prepared this return for the person(s) named herein; and that this return (including any accompanying schedules and statements) is, to the best of my knowledge and belief, a true, correct, and complete return based on all the information relating to the matters required to be reported in this return of which I have any knowledge.

W. B. Goode & Company (Individual or Firm Signature)
W. B. GOODE & COMPANY
1220 Mercantile Securities Bldg. (Address)
DALLAS, TEXAS
JUL 12 1957 (Date)

16—72754-1

14

Commission Exhibit No. 1719

EXEMPTIONS FOR PERSONS OTHER THAN YOUR WIFE AND CHILDREN

Name	Relationship	Number of months dependent lived in your home. If born or died during year also write "B" or "D"	Did dependent have gross income of $600 or more?	Amount YOU spent for dependent's support. If 100% write "All"	Amount spent by OTHERS including dependent from own funds
				$	$

Enter on line 3, page 1, the number of exemptions claimed above.
→ If an exemption is based on a multiple-support agreement of a group of persons, attach information described on page 5 of instructions.

ITEMIZED DEDUCTIONS—IF YOU DO NOT USE TAX TABLE OR STANDARD DEDUCTION

If Husband and Wife (Not Legally Separated) File Separate Returns and One Itemizes Deductions, the Other Must Also Itemize

Describe deductions and state to whom paid. If more space is needed, attach additional sheets. Please put your name and address on any attachments.

Contributions	Total (not to exceed 20% of line 11, page 1, except as described on page 8 of instructions)	$
Interest	Total	
Taxes	Total	
Medical and dental expense (If 65 or over, see instructions, page 9)	Submit itemized list. Do not enter any expense compensated by insurance or otherwise. 1. Cost of medicines and drugs, in excess of 1 percent of line 11, page 1 .... $ 2. Other medical and dental expenses .... 3. Total .... $ 4. Enter 3 percent of line 11, page 1 .... 5. Allowable amount (excess of line 3 over line 4). (See instructions, page 9, for limitations.)	
Child care	Expenses for care of children and certain other dependents not to exceed $600 (See page 10 of instructions and attach statement)	
Casualty losses	Total losses (not compensated by insurance or otherwise)	
Miscellaneous	Total	
	TOTAL DEDUCTIONS (Enter on line 2 of Tax Computation, below)	$

TAX COMPUTATION—IF YOU DO NOT USE THE TAX TABLE

1. Enter Adjusted Gross Income from line 11, page 1		$ 7,437.01 ✓
2. If deductions are itemized above, enter total of such deductions. If deductions are not itemized *and line 1, above, is $5,000 or more:* (a) married persons filing separately enter $500; (b) all others enter 10 percent of line 1, or $1,000, whichever is smaller	743.70	700.00 ✓
3. Balance (line 1 less line 2)	6693.31	6,737.01 ✗
4. Multiply $600 by total number of exemptions claimed on line 4, page 1		600.00
5. TAXABLE INCOME (line 3 less line 4)	6093.31	6,137.01
6. Tax on amount on line 5. Use appropriate Tax Rate Schedule on page 11 of instructions	1387.99	1,401.10 ✗
7. If you had capital gains and the alternative tax applies, enter the tax from separate Schedule D		
8. Tax credits. If you itemized deductions, enter: (a) Credit for income tax payments to a foreign country or U. S. possession (Attach Form 1116) .... $ (b) Tax paid at source on tax-free covenant bond interest and credit for partially tax-exempt interest		1387.99
9. Enter here and on line 12, page 1, the amount shown on line 6 or 7 less amount claimed on line 8		$ 1,401.10 ✗

COMMISSION EXHIBIT No. 1719—Continued

SCHEDULE C (Form 1040)

U. S. Treasury Department—Internal Revenue Service

PROFIT (OR LOSS) FROM BUSINESS OR PROFESSION

(For Computation of Self-Employment Tax, see Page 3)

1956

Attach this schedule to your Income Tax Return, Form 1040 — Partnerships, Joint Ventures, Etc. Must File On Form 1065

For Calendar Year 1956, or other taxable year beginning ...., 1956, and ending ...., 195

Name and Address as shown on page 1, Form 1040

Jack Ruby, 4156 Hawthorne, Dallas, Texas

Item (**see instructions—page 2**)

A. Principal business activity: Dance Hall (Retail trade, wholesale trade, lawyer, etc.) (Principal product or service)

B. Business name: Club Vegas

C. Business address: 3508 Oak Lawn (Number and street or rural route) Dallas (City or post office) Dallas (County) Texas (State)

● **IMPORTANT**—If you had more than one business, a separate page 1 of Schedule C must be completed for each business.

Line (**see instructions—page 2**)

Line			
1.	Total receipts $........, less allowances, rebates, and returns $........		$
2.	Inventory at beginning of year	$	SCHEDULE ATTACHED
3.	Merchandise purchased $........ less any items withdrawn from business for personal use $........		
4.	Cost of labor (do not include salary paid to yourself)		
5.	Material and supplies		
6.	Other costs (**explain in Schedule C-2**)		
7.	Total of lines 2 through 6	$	
8.	Inventory at end of year		
9.	**Cost of goods sold** (line 7 less line 8)		
10.	**Gross profit** (line 1 less line 9)		$

OTHER BUSINESS DEDUCTIONS

Line			
11.	Salaries and wages not included on line 4 (do not include any paid to yourself)	$	SCHEDULE ATTACHED
12.	Rent on business property		
13.	Interest on business indebtedness		
14.	Taxes on business and business property		
15.	Losses of business property (**attach statement**)		
16.	Bad debts arising from sales or services		
17.	Depreciation and obsolescence (**explain in Schedule C-1**)		
18.	Repairs (**explain in Schedule C-2**)		
19.	Depletion of mines, oil and gas wells, timber, etc. (**attach schedule**)		
20.	Amortization (**attach statement**)		
21.	Other business expenses (**explain in Schedule C-2**)		
22.	Total of lines 11 through 21		
23.	**Net profit (or loss)** (line 10 less line 22). Also enter on line 24, page 3 of this schedule, and on line 8, page 1, Form 1040		$ 7,437.01

Schedule C-1. EXPLANATION OF DEDUCTION FOR DEPRECIATION CLAIMED ON LINE 17

1. Kind of property (if buildings, state material of which constructed). Exclude land and other nondepreciable property	2. Date acquired	3. Cost or other basis	4. Depreciation allowed (or allowable) in prior years	5. Method of computing depreciation	6. Rate (%) or life (years)	7. Depreciation for this year
		$	$			$

Schedule C-2. EXPLANATION OF LINES 6, 18, AND 21

Line No.	Explanation	Amount	Line No.	Explanation	Amount
		$			$

16—72767-1

C

COMMISSION EXHIBIT No. 1719—Continued

If you owned a business, or practiced a profession, you must fill in separate Schedule C on other side and enter the net profit (or loss) on line 8, page 1, Form 1040.

Separate Schedule C should include income from (1) sale of merchandise, or products of manufacturing, mining, and construction; (2) business service; and (3) professional service. In general, you should report any income in the earning of which you have incurred expenses for material, labor, supplies, and the like.

All farmers should use separate Schedule F (Form 1040) to report their farm income whether reporting on the cash or accrual method.

Item A—Business Activity.—State the general classification of business activity, as well as the principal product or service. For example, "Wholesale food," "Retail men's apparel," "Manufacture of upholstered wooden household furniture," "Transportation by truck," "Broker, real estate," "Contractor—carpenter work," "Physician," etc. Do not use such terms as "partnership," "owner," "student," etc. The "principal business activity" is the one which accounts for the largest percentage of your total receipts. All trades and businesses except those specifically excluded are subject to self-employment tax.

Item C—Business Address.—Do not use home address as business address unless business is actually conducted from home.

Line 1—Total Receipts.—Include all income derived from your trade or business. Enter in the space provided such items as returned sales, rebates, and allowances from the sale price or service charge.

If you have dividend income from stocks held by you in the ordinary course of carrying on your trade or business, such dividends must be considered together with your dividends from stocks regularly held for investment purposes in computing your dividend exclusion and credit.

Installment Sales.—If you use the installment method of reporting income from sales, you must attach to your return a schedule showing separately for the years 1953, 1954, 1955, and 1956 the following: (a) Gross sales; (b) cost of goods sold; (c) gross profits; (d) percentage of profits to gross sales; (e) amounts collected; and (f) gross profits on amount collected.

COST OF GOODS SOLD

Lines 2–9.—If you are engaged in a trade or a business in which the production, purchase, or sale of merchandise is an income producing factor, you must take inventories of merchandise and materials on hand at the beginning and end of the taxable year in order to reflect the gross profits correctly. The usual methods of valuing inventory are (a) cost and (b) cost or market whichever is lower. The method properly adopted for the first year in which inventory is taken must be continued unless permission to change is secured from the Commissioner of Internal Revenue, Washington 25, D. C. Application for permission to change the method of valuing inventories must be made in writing and filed with the Commissioner within 90 days after the beginning of the taxable year in which it is desired to effect a change. You should enter the letters "C" or "C or M" immediately before the amount column if inventories are valued either at cost, or at cost or market whichever is lower.

Other methods of valuing inventories of material or merchandise are provided for dealers in securities, for farmers, for miners, for manufacturers who produce more than one product from a single process, and for retail merchants using the "retail method."

A special method based on cost, LIFO, is allowable only if you file an application on Form 970 with your return for the first year used. The requirements for adopting and using the LIFO method are set forth on Form 970. Thereafter, you must attach a separate schedule showing: (a) a summary of all inventories; (b) with respect to inventories computed under the LIFO method, the computation of quantities and cost by acquisition levels.

OTHER BUSINESS DEDUCTIONS

Line 11—Salaries and Wages.—Enter all salaries and wages not included as "Cost of Labor" in "Cost of Goods Sold." Do not deduct any salary or wages for your own services or services of others not performed in connection with your business.

Line 12—Rent on Business Property.—Rents paid or accrued on business property in which you have no equity are deductible. Do not include rent for a building, or any part, which you occupy solely for residential purposes.

Line 13—Interest on Business Indebtedness.—Interest on business indebtedness to others is deductible. Do not include interest to yourself on capital invested in or advanced to the business.

Line 14—Taxes on Business and Business Property.—Include taxes paid or accrued on business property or incurred in carrying on your business. Federal import duties and Federal excise and stamp taxes are deductible if paid or incurred in carrying on a trade or business. Do not include taxes assessed against local benefits of a kind tending to increase the value of the property assessed, as for paving, sewers, front foot benefits, etc.

Line 15—Losses of Business Property.—You may deduct losses of business property by fire, storm, or other casualty, or theft, not compensated by insurance or otherwise and not made good by repairs claimed as a deduction. Attach a statement showing a description of the property, date acquired, cost, subsequent improvements, depreciation allowable since acquisition, insurance, salvage value, and deductible loss.

Line 16—Bad Debts Arising From Sales or Services.—Include debts, or portions thereof, arising from sales or professional services that have been included in income, which have been definitely ascertained to be worthless; or such reasonable amount as has been added within the taxable year to a reserve for bad debts. A debt which is deducted as bad and which reduces your tax must, if subsequently collected, be returned as income for the year in which collected.

Line 17—Depreciation and Obsolescence.—You may deduct a reasonable allowance for exhaustion, wear and tear, and obsolescence of property used in the trade or business. For additional information regarding depreciation, especially on new property acquired or constructed after December 31, 1953, see depreciation section in the instructions for Form 1040.

If a deduction is claimed on account of depreciation, fill in Schedule C–1. In case obsolescence is included, state separately amount claimed and basis upon which it is computed. The value or cost of land must not be included in this schedule, and where land and buildings were purchased for a lump sum, the cost of the building subject to depreciation must be established. The adjusted property accounts and the accumulated depreciation shown in the schedule should be reconciled with those accounts as reflected on your books.

Line 18—Repairs.—You may deduct the cost of incidental repairs, including labor, supplies, and other items, which do not add to the value or appreciably prolong the life of the property. Expenditures for new buildings, machinery, and equipment, or for permanent improvements or betterments which increase the value of the property are chargeable to capital accounts. Expenditures for restoring or replacing property are not deductible, since such expenditures are chargeable to capital accounts or to depreciation reserve depending on how depreciation is charged on your books.

Line 19—Depletion of Mines, Oil and Gas Wells, Timber, Etc.—If a deduction is claimed on account of depletion, procure from your District Director Form M (mines and other natural deposits), Form O (oil and gas), or Form T (timber), fill in and file with return. If complete valuation data have been filed with questionnaire in previous years, then file with your return information necessary to bring depletion schedule up to date, setting forth in full a statement of all transactions bearing on deductions from or additions to value of physical assets during the taxable year with explanation of how depletion deduction for the taxable year has been determined. (See sections 615 and 616 of the Internal Revenue Code of 1954 for election to capitalize or deduct expenditures for exploration and development of mineral properties.)

Line 20—Amortization.—If you elect the deduction with respect to the amortization of the adjusted basis of (a) any emergency facility with respect to which the Government has issued a certificate of necessity, or (b) a grain storage facility, a statement of the pertinent facts should be filed with your return. (See sections 168 and 169 of the Internal Revenue Code of 1954.)

For the election to amortize research or experimental expenditures not subject to depreciation or depletion, see section 174 of the Code.

For the election to amortize trademark or tradename expenditures, see section 177 of the Code.

Line 21—Other Business Expenses.—Include all ordinary and necessary business expenses for which no space is provided in the schedule. Any deduction claimed should be explained in Schedule C–2. Do not include cost of business equipment or furniture, expenditures for replacements, or for permanent improvements to property, or personal living and family expenses.

Net Operating Loss Deduction.—Any net operating loss deduction should be applied as an adjustment of the amount shown on line 11, page 1, Form 1040. See instructions for Form 1040 and attach statement.

16—72767—1

COMMISSION EXHIBIT No. 1719—Continued

Jack Ruby
dba Club Vegas
Dallas, Texas

For the Year ended December 31, 1956

INCOME STATEMENT

Sales		$ 19,750.64
Cost of sales		
Purchases - beer	$ 6,810.56	
Purchases - other merchandise	1,221.47	
Total merchandise available	$ 8,032.03	
Less inventory - ending	200.00	
Cost of sales		7,832.03
Gross profit on sales		$ 11,918.61
Admissions		18,003.85
Coin machines		761.85
Miscellaneous income		10.96
Total income		$ 30,695.27
Expenses:		
Wages	$ 3,964.50	
Supplies	407.26	
Rent	4,800.00	
Utilities	1,826.80	
Laundry	167.21	
Advertising	381.22	
Repairs and maintenance	787.73	
Legal and accounting	325.00	
Contract labor	7,537.50	
Taxes and license	1,681.75	
Police Department	462.00	
Auto	326.57	
Equipment rental	15.00	
Cash short	49.00	
ASCAP and BMI	180.00	
Miscellaneous	346.72	
Total expenses		23,258.26
Net income		$ 7,437.01

COMMISSION EXHIBIT No. 1719—Continued

COMPUTATION OF SELF-EMPLOYMENT TAX
(For social security)
(See Instructions—Page 4)

▶ **Each self-employed person must file a separate schedule. See instructions, page 4, for joint returns and partnerships.**
▶ **If you had wages of $4,200 or more which were subject to the deduction for social security, do not fill in this page.**
▶ **If you have more than one business, a separate page 1, Schedule C, must be completed for each business. However, only one page 3 is to be completed and filed showing the combined net profit or loss from such businesses.**

NAME OF SELF-EMPLOYED PERSON (as shown on social security card)
Jack Ruby

STATE EACH BUSINESS ACTIVITY SUBJECT TO SELF-EMPLOYMENT TAX (for example: Restaurant, Building Contractor, but not Partner or Owner)
Dance Hall

Line		
24. Net profit (or loss) shown on line 23, page 1 (**Enter combined amount if more than one business**)	$ 7,437.01	
25. Add to net profit (or subtract from net loss) losses of business property shown on line 15, page 1		
26. Total (or difference)		$ 7,437.01
27. Net income (or loss) from excluded services or sources included on line 26		
Specify excluded services or sources		
28. Net earnings (or loss) from self-employment—		
(a) From business (line 26 less any amount on line 27)		$ 7,437.01
(b) From partnerships, joint ventures, etc. (other than farming)		
(c) From service as a minister, member of a religious order or a Christian Science practitioner		
(d) From farming reported on line 12 or 13, separate Schedule F (Form 1040)		
29. Total net earnings (or loss) from self-employment reported on line 28		$ 7,437.01
(If line 29 is under $400, you are not subject to self-employment tax. Do not fill in rest of page.)		
30. Maximum amount subject to self-employment tax	$ 4,200.00	
31. Less: Total wages, subject to deduction for social security, paid to you during the taxable year. (For wages reported on Form W-2, see "F. I. C. A. Wages" box.)	-0-	
32. Balance (line 30 less line 31)	$ 4,200.00	
33. Self-employment income—line 29 or 32, whichever is smaller		$ 4,200.00
34. Self-employment tax—3 percent of amount on line 33. Enter here and on line 15, page 1, Form 1040		$ 126.00

COMMISSION EXHIBIT No. 1719—Continued

utable thereto are not taken into account in figuring net earnings from self-employment. Use line 27 to exclude any such amounts reported on page 1 that should not be taken into account in figuring your self-employment income.

Doctors of medicine.—Income from the performance of service as a doctor of medicine or income from the performance of such service by a partnership.

Christian Science practitioners.—Income from the performance of service as a Christian Science practitioner, unless such Christian Science practitioner has elected by filing Form 2031 to be covered by the Social Security Act, as explained above.

Religious services.—Income from the performance of service by a duly ordained, commissioned, or licensed minister of a church in the exercise of his ministry or by a member of a religious order in the exercise of duties required by such order, unless such minister or member of a religious order has elected by filing Form 2031 to be covered by the Social Security Act, as explained above.

Employees and public officials.—Income from the performance of service as:

(a) a public official, including a notary public;

(b) an employee or employee representative under the railroad retirement system; or

(c) an employee.

Note.—The income of an employee over the age of 18 from the sale of newspapers or magazines to an ultimate consumer is subject to the self-employment tax if the income consists of retained profits from such sales.

Real estate rentals.—Rentals from real estate, except rentals received in the course of a trade or business as a real estate dealer. This includes cash and crop shares received from a tenant or sharefarmer. These amounts should be reported in Schedule G of Form 1040. However, rental income from a farm is not excluded if the rental arrangement provides for material participation by the landlord and he does participate materially in the production or in the management of the production of farm products on his land. Such income represents farm earnings and should be reported on separate Schedule F (Form 1040).

Payments for the use or occupancy of rooms or other space where services are also rendered to the occupant, such as rooms in hotels, boarding houses, apartment houses furnishing hotel services, tourist camps, tourist homes, or space in parking lots, warehouses, or storage garages do not constitute rentals from real estate and, therefore, are included in determining net earnings from self-employment.

Interest and dividends.—Dividends on shares of stock, and interest on bonds, debentures, notes, certificates, or other evidences of indebtedness, issued with interest coupons or in registered form by a corporation, or by a government or political subdivision thereof, unless received in the course of a trade or business as a dealer in

...ule C (Form 1040) should show the name of the one with self-employment income. Where husband and wife each have self-employment income, a separate Schedule C must be attached for each. In such cases the total of amounts shown on line 23 of each separate schedule should be entered on line 8, page 1, Form 1040, and the aggregate self-employment tax (line 34) should be entered on line 15, page 1, Form 1040.

COMMUNITY INCOME

For the purpose of computing net earnings from self-employment, if any of the income from a trade or business is community income, all the income from such trade or business is considered the income of the husband unless the wife exercises substantially all the management and control of the trade or business, in which case all of such income is considered the income of the wife.

If separate income tax returns are filed by husband and wife, a complete Schedule C should be attached to the return of the one with self-employment income. Community income included on such a schedule must, however, be allocated between the two returns (on line 8, page 1, Form 1040) on the basis of the community property laws.

Partnerships.—In computing his combined net earnings from self-employment, a partner should include his entire share of such earnings from a partnership including any guaranteed payments. No part of that share may be attributed to the partner's wife (or husband) even though the income may, under State law, be community income. In the case of a husband and wife partnership, like other partnerships, the distributive share of each should be entered in Schedule H, page 3 of Form 1040, for income tax purposes. For self-employment tax purposes the distributive share of each partner should be entered on line 28(b), page 3, of this form (except that farm partnership earnings are to be reported on line 11(b), separate Schedule F (Form 1040) rather than on line 28(b) of this schedule).

SCHEDULE SE (Form 1040)

This schedule provides the Social Security Administration with the information on self-employment income necessary for computing benefits under the social security program.

To assure proper credit to your account, be sure to enter your name and social security account number on Schedule SE (Form 1040) exactly as they are shown on your social security card. If you do not have a social security account number, you must get one. These account numbers are obtainable from any of the approximately 600 Social Security Administration offices throughout the country. The telephone directory or your local post office will give you the address. Do not delay filing your return beyond the due date.

Regardless of whether joint or separate returns, Form 1040, are filed by husband and wife, Schedule SE (Form 1040) must show only the name of the one with the self-employment income. If both had net earnings from self-employment, a separate Schedule SE must be filed by each.

U. S. GOVERNMENT PRINTING OFFICE: 1956 O - 391662 16—72767-1

Commission Exhibit No. 1719—Continued

U. S. TREASURY DEPARTMENT
Internal Revenue Service
DALLAS REGION
FL-20

APPLICATION FOR EXTENSION OF TIME FOR FILING FEDERAL INCOME TAX RETURNS

To be filed with the District Director for your district

INSTRUCTIONS

This form is to be used by individuals, partnerships, and fiduciaries to request an extension of time for filing income tax returns. It must be prepared in quadruplicate, and submitted on or before the due date of the return. If extension of time is authorized, three copies will be returned to you properly validated, one to be attached to the return and the others to be retained by you.

See instructions on reverse for partnerships and fiduciaries, also special instructions for additional extensions.

Separate application must be prepared for each taxpayer.

This form may be reproduced if the same general format is used and quality, weight and color of paper is similar.

Extension to be mailed to:

Jack Ruby,
4156 Hawthorne
Dallas, Texas.

Name and Address of Applicant:

Jack Ruby
4156 Hawthorne St.,
Dallas, Texas.

Application is made for an extension of time to June 15, 1957 (days from due date), within which to file the following federal income tax return: Form No. 1040 1041 1065

Check only one: [X] [ ] [ ] Taxable year ending 12-30-56

This extension is necessary for the following reasons:

Unable to get records together

75 RECEIVED APR 15 1957 DIST. DIR. INT. REV. DALLAS ASST. CASHIER

It is understood that if no return is filed, the granting of this extension will not in any way relieve the taxpayer of criminal penalties provided by law for failure to file a tax return.

Jack Ruby — Signature of Applicant or Agent

4-15-57 — Date

In view of the reasons set forth, an extension of time is granted to the date shown. The tax due MUST BE PAID IN FULL WHEN THE RETURN IS FILED, WITH INTEREST AT THE RATE OF 6% PER ANNUM FROM DUE DATE TO DATE OF PAYMENT. Valid only if stamped APPROVED.

(DO NOT write in this space. For use of INTERNAL REVENUE SERVICE)

APPROVED
If additional time is required both copies of this extension must be returned for further validation.

ADDITIONAL EXTENSION TO
7-15-57
APPROVED
RJ

CONNELL PTG. DALLAS

COMMISSION EXHIBIT No. 1719—Continued

Commission Exhibit No. 1720

TDA HISTORY SHEET

Taxpayer : Jack Ruby Phones:

Address :

Employer :

Occupation: Social Security Number

Telephone Directory	City Directory	Postal Records	Courthouse Records	Office Records	Social Sec. Administration	Tax Liens Filed	Other

Date	Revenue Officer	Contacts
7-29-58	RED	Talked to Mr. Orenbaum and he said to call T/P in and tell him the offer has been rejected and that it will do no good to submit another offer unless he submit an offer in the amount of his equity in his assets. If he does not submit an offer in that amount, the entire amt. of delinquency has to be collected.
8-22-58	RED	Talked to Mr. Ruby on the phone LA-8-4243 and I told him that his offer had been rejected. told him that if he submitted another offer it would have to be in the amount of the equity in his assets. He remarked that he might go out on a limb, in regard to it. (I took this statement to mean that Ruby promised to come to office 11:00 AM Monday Aug 25th, 1958.
8-25-58	RED	Mr. Ruby called & promised to be here at 1:00 AM today.

U. S. TREASURY DEPARTMENT - INTERNAL REVENUE SERVICE DIR-DAL 10 IRS-Crump Printing Co., Dallas

COMMISSION EXHIBIT No. 1720

TDA HISTORY SHEET

Taxpayer : Jack Ruby Phones: ______

Address : ______

Employer : ______

Occupation: ______ Social Security Number ______

Telephone Directory	City Directory	Postal Records	Courthouse Records	Office Records	Social Sec. Administration	Tax Liens Filed	Other

Date	Revenue Officer	Contacts
-26-58	RED	Taxpayer came to office & had joint conference with Mr. Arenbaum & myself. He promised that he was ~~goin~~ going to raise *2000.00 in Addition to the ~~500~~ 500.00 Treasury ck and apply the full 2500.00 on his liability. He asked if he could pay the balance at 250.00 per month.
-28-58	RED	Taxpayer came in & paid 1300.00. ($800.00 by Cashier Ck. & Endorsed Treasury Ck. over to District Director of Internal Revenue in Amt. of $500.00). T/P signed agreement to pay 200.00 monthly, (See Agreement) and took blank 433AB to fill out and bring back to office
-2-58	RED	T/P came in & paid 200.00 Cash
10/27/58		Reviewed - Collection procedure & agreement are OK - Close follow up needed - [initials]
-3-58	RED	Ruby came in & paid *200.00 currency

U. S. TREASURY DEPARTMENT - INTERNAL REVENUE SERVICE

DIR-DAL 10
IRS-Crump Printing Co., Dallas

COMMISSION EXHIBIT No. 1720—Continued

TDA HISTORY SHEET

Taxpayer : Jack Ruby Phones:

Address :

Employer :

Occupation: Social Security Number

Telephone Directory	City Directory	Postal Records	Courthouse Records	Office Records	Social Sec. Administration	Tax Liens Filed	Other

Date	Revenue Officer	Contacts
12-3-58	RED	T/P came in & paid $200.00 in currency
2-2-59	RED	TDA for add'l 1957 FUTA Received today
2-5-59	RED	T/P paid TDA for 1957 ADDL FUTA & also paid 200.00 on old acct. Payment was made thru OCF in my absence.
2-24-59	RED	T/P came in & pd. 200.00 in currency.
3/20/59-		Reviewed - Present agreement & Collection procedure OK - [initials]
8-6-59	RED	Ruby phoned & said he would be here tomorrow.
8-7-59	RED	Ruby came in & pd. 200.00 in currency
9-8-59	RED	Accrual Collectible Card submitted today showing accrued interest due $174.73
10-1-59	RED	Mr. Jack Ruby came in & paid 200.00 cash. Of this 200.00 cash pmt., $174.73 was applied to fully pay accrued interest due on TDA acct #55 6 75901, and the remaining portion of the pmt. $25.27 was applied ~~[illegible]~~ as partial pmt on TDA ~~#~~ acct # 55 6 75902

U. S. TREASURY DEPARTMENT - INTERNAL REVENUE SERVICE DIR-DAL 10

3

COMMISSION EXHIBIT No. 1720—Continued

TDA HISTORY SHEET

Taxpayer : ______________________ Phones: ____________

Address : ______________________ ____________

Employer : ______________________ ____________

Occupation: ______________ Social Security Number ____________

Telephone Directory	City Directory	Postal Records	Courthouse Records	Office Records	Social Sec. Administration	Tax Liens Filed	Other
		- Jack Ruby	-				

Date	Revenue Officer	Contacts
10/21/59-		Reviewed - Continue present collection procedure + follow up - Agreement OK - (initials)
2-59	RED	Ruby came in + pd. 200.00 in cash. He said he was going to owe 15,000.00 because of an audit Mr. Hill made. Said he was going to have to raise 2000.00 on it when he was billed. ~~He~~ I asked him to try to raise enough to pay this one off too when he raised the 2000.00. He shook his head in the affirmative that he would. When I saw Ruby a while back he indicated that he was going to owe some more tax + he asked me to figure up the exact amount he owed on this liability. I reminded him of this today + asked him if he intended to pay this one off + ~~at~~. I believe he said he ~~wanted~~ wanted to know total amount he owed, this liability and the other liability together. I believe

U. S. TREASURY DEPARTMENT - INTERNAL REVENUE SERVICE DIR-DAL 10

-17-59	REO	Phoned LA 8 4775, no ans. Phoned LA 8 4243, no ans.

COMMISSION EXHIBIT No. 1720—Continued

TDA HISTORY SHEET

Taxpayer : __________ Phones: __________

Address : __________

Employer : __________

Occupation: __________ Social Security Number __________

Telephone Directory	City Directory	Postal Records	Courthouse Records	Office Records	Social Sec. Administration	Tax Liens Filed	Other

Date	Revenue Officer	Contacts
11-18-59	RED	Phoned LA 8 4243, no ans. Phoned LA 8 4775, no ans. Phoned LA 8 4775 again. T/P not in. Left message for him to call me.
		Mr. Ruby returned my call. I told him we needed a 433 AB Financial Statement. He told me he could have it completed by next Monday or Tuesday. I mailed him blank copies of 433 AB & 433 D.
12-4-59	RED	Phoned LA 8 4775 (Vegas Club). T/P not in. Left message for him to call me. Phoned LA 8 4243, no answer.
		I checked with Special Procedures and a Lien was filed in July 1955 to cover the above account and three others (The last 2 digits of the other acts were 00, 01, 03. These apparently are acts I have previously collected).
12-4-59	RED	Ruby returned my call & promised that he would get the financial statement and his pmt. to me by Tuesday 12-8-59.

U. S. TREASURY DEPARTMENT - INTERNAL REVENUE SERVICE DIR-DAL 10

5

COMMISSION EXHIBIT No. 1720—Continued

TDA HISTORY SHEET

Taxpayer : ______________________ Phones: ____________

Address : ______________________ ____________

Employer : ______________________ ____________

Occupation: ____________ Social Security Number ____________

Telephone Directory	City Directory	Postal Records	Courthouse Records	Office Records	Social Sec. Administration	Tax Liens Filed	Other

Date	Revenue Officer	Contacts
[illegible]-8-59	RED	t/p came in + paid 200.00 in cash. Said he didn't have the financial statement yet, but said he would definitely have it here by this coming Friday at the latest.
[illegible]-11-59	RED	Ruby phoned said his accountant didn't have the financial statement ready. He said they would definitely have it ready next Tuesday.
[illegible]-16-59	RED	Lady from Alexander Grant Accounting Co phoned + stated that they were working on the financial statement for Jack Ruby + she talked like they would have it completed in a couple more days.
2/17/59	SH	T.L. OK. – History Sheet Documented as to efforts to obtain 433AB – OK.
[illegible]-60	RED	I phoned LA 8 4775 (Vegas Club) in attempt to talk to Jack Ruby regarding his promise to bring the ~~433AB~~ 433AB to office, but he was not in.
[illegible]-60	RED	R/O George Hightower phoned LA 8 4283 in attempt to get T/P to bring 433AB to office but no one ans. phone. Hightower phoned Grant & Co. CPA + talked to Mrs. Smoker who said they would have the financial statement in next 2 or 3 days and will mail to me.

U. S. TREASURY DEPARTMENT - INTERNAL REVENUE SERVICE DIR-DAL 10

COMMISSION EXHIBIT NO. 1720—Continued

TDA HISTORY SHEET

Taxpayer : ______________________ Phones: __________

Address : ______________________ __________

Employer : ______________________ __________

Occupation: ____________ Social Security Number ____________

Telephone Directory	City Directory	Postal Records	Courthouse Records	Office Records	Social Sec. Administration	Tax Liens Filed	Other

Date	Revenue Officer	Contacts
1-18-60	RED	TDA for Excise Tax (1st Q 56 thru 3rd Q 59) received by assignment. (I made request for Fed Tax Lien on this TDA on 1-8-60 and Notice of Lien was filed on 1-11-60
2-3-60	RED	T/P came in + Pd. 200. cash. He promised to bring the financial statement next Wednesday Feb 10th. Talked like the accounting people were holding up the financial statement because he owed them some money.
2-10-60	RED	Mr. Ruby phoned while I was out + left message that he will call back tomorrow. Said his accountant has not gotten the financial statement prepared yet.
2-18-60	RED	Phoned LA 8 4243, no ans Phoned LA 8 4775, no ans.
3-3-60	RED	Some lady who said she was friend of Jack Ruby ~~brought~~ paid 200.00 cash pmt for T/P. Said Ruby had flu. Said he had an unlisted tel # but she couldn't remember the number. Said he lived on Homer St. but she couldn't remember the number, 47 something

U. S. TREASURY DEPARTMENT - INTERNAL REVENUE SERVICE DIR-DAL 10

7

Commission Exhibit No. 1720—Continued

TDA HISTORY SHEET

Taxpayer : Phones:

Address :

Employer :

Occupation: Social Security Number

Telephone Directory	City Directory	Postal Records	Courthouse Records	Office Records	Social Sec. Administration	Tax Liens Filed	Other

Date	Revenue Officer	Contacts
-23-60	RED	TDA for 4th Q 59 WH ~~Excise~~ Tx received by assignment
-24-6	RED	Fed. Tx Lien Filed on 4th Q 59 TDA
3/25/60-		Reviewed - On next contact April 1960 - get 433 for collection analysis - ex sec payments - Get formal agreement - (initials)
-1-60	RED	Status report DIR-DAL 454 was submitted in duplicate to Group Supervisor.
-5-60	RED	Mr. Ruby came to office & Pd. 200.00 in Cash & promised faithfully to bring financial statement by or before next Tuesday April 12th.
		2 TDA's representing Excise TAX assessments for 4th Q 59 received by assignment today.
		The above 200.00 pmt. was applied as follows:
		$51.81 to fully pay TDA #602355142 4th Q 59 Excise
		$86.93 " " " #602355186 4th Q 59 Excise
		$61.26 to apply as partial pmt. on above TDA.
-12-60	RED	Ruby phoned and I believe he said he was at his accountants office

U. S. TREASURY DEPARTMENT - INTERNAL REVENUE SERVICE DIR-DAL 10

8

COMMISSION EXHIBIT No. 1720—Continued

TDA HISTORY SHEET

Taxpayer : Phones:

Address :

Employer :

Occupation: Social Security Number

Telephone Directory	City Directory	Postal Records	Courthouse Records	Office Records	Social Sec. Administration	Tax Liens Filed	Other

Date	Revenue Officer	Contacts
4-14-60	RED	Lady from Alexander Grant accounting office phoned & promised that the financial statement would be ready by noon tomorrow.
4-15-60	RED	T/P came in around 5:00 PM & brought 433AB in duplicate, however, it was not complete, I had him to leave the duplicate & he promised to complete the original and bring it back tomorrow.
4-19-60	RED	TDA for 1959 FUTA received by assignment.
4-20-60	RED	Phoned TA 79983 but it is address at 2010 Euclid & lady there said they did not know Jack Ruby. Said they ~~often~~ get calls asking for him. Went by Alexander Grant Acctg office at 1220 Mercantile Securities Bldg & inquired about financial ~~statement~~. Also procured Tel # TA 79883 which is T/P's correct number. Phoned this number when I got back to office but Ruby was out. I left message with the sister for him to contact me.

U. S. TREASURY DEPARTMENT - INTERNAL REVENUE SERVICE DIR-DAL 10

9

COMMISSION EXHIBIT No. 1720—Continued

TAX 57.55
33
57.88

57.55
32
57.87

9a

COMMISSION EXHIBIT No. 1720—Continued

TDA HISTORY SHEET

Taxpayer : ______________________ Phones: ____________

Address : ______________________ ____________

Employer : ______________________ ____________

Occupation: ______________ Social Security Number ______________

Telephone Directory	City Directory	Postal Records	Courthouse Records	Office Records	Social Sec. Administration	Tax Liens Filed	Other

Date	Revenue Officer	Contacts
4-22-60	RED	Phoned Jack Ruby & he said he had to go to his accountant office today and would be here at our office at 3:30 PM. Said he would pay off the 1959 FUTA TDA today.
		Met T/P at Mercantile Securities Bldg & he paid cash in amt of 57.87 which cleared TDA for 1959 TDA #60 3 880408
		T/P said he would bring financial statement to office next Monday
4-25-60	RED	T/P came in & left 433 AB financial statement. He did not have 433 D filled out but promised to come in at 3:00 PM on April 26th.
4-26-60	RED	Ruby called & said he was not feeling so hot, and asked if he could come in tomorrow. He promised to come in before 2:00 PM tomorrow.
4-28-60	RED	T/P came in & left Monthly income and expense Analysis, during my absence from my desk

U. S. TREASURY DEPARTMENT - INTERNAL REVENUE SERVICE DIR-DAL 10

10

COMMISSION EXHIBIT No. 1720—Continued

TDA HISTORY SHEET

Taxpayer : ______________________ Phones: ______________

Address : ______________________ ______________

Employer : ______________________ ______________

Occupation: ______________ Social Security Number ______________

Telephone Directory	City Directory	Postal Records	Courthouse Records	Office Records	Social Sec. Administration	Tax Liens Filed	Other

Date	Revenue Officer	Contacts
3-60	RED	Ruby left telephone message that he would be in Monday 6-6-60.
-60	RED	Ruby phoned & said he would be in before noon tomorrow.
7-60	RED	Phoned TA 7 9883, no ans.
7-60	RED	Mr. Ruby came in. He said his gross business had dropped off since he had left the 433 D with me. (He had not made a new formal agreement, so he took the 433D which was not fully complete and I gave him 2 other blank 433 D forms to complete & return). He said he would complete it and return it to me in a few days. I made a copy of the 433 D before I gave it back to him.

U. S. TREASURY DEPARTMENT - INTERNAL REVENUE SERVICE DIR-DAL 10

COMMISSION EXHIBIT No. 1720—Continued

TDA HISTORY SHEET

acct # 59 A 11 545077
acct # 60 2 165528
acct # 55 6 75902 (accrual collectible)

Taxpayer : Jack Ruby   Phones: ______

Address : ______

Employer : ______

Occupation: ______ Social Security Number ______

Telephone Directory	City Directory	Postal Records	Courthouse Records	Office Records	Social Sec. Administration	Tax Liens Filed	Other

Date	Revenue Officer	Contacts
7-7-60	RED	Mr Ruby phoned & said he would be in tomorrow at 3:00 PM & make his payment. He said he would get me to help him with the 433 D. I told him that he would be the one that would know the information about the 433 D and that if he couldn't get it correct he ~~had~~ might ought to get an accountant to help him with it. I asked him if he could get it correct and bring it ~~out~~ in tomorrow & he said "no" that he would have to look up the accountant. He said that he would get it correct and bring it in Tuesday July 12th 1960
7-8-60	RED	T/P came to office & I took him to OCF. T/P remitted 200.00 to Cashier Accrual Coll TDA #55 6 75902 fully paid.

U. S. TREASURY DEPARTMENT - INTERNAL REVENUE SERVICE   DIR-DAL 10

12

COMMISSION EXHIBIT No. 1720—Continued

TDA HISTORY SHEET

Taxpayer : ______________________ Phones: ____________

Address : ______________________ ____________

Employer : ______________________ ____________

Occupation: ____________ Social Security Number ____________

Telephone Directory	City Directory	Postal Records	Courthouse Records	Office Records	Social Sec. Administration	Tax Liens Filed	Other

Date	Revenue Officer	Contacts
13-60	RED	T/P came in and ~~[illegible]~~ furnished 433 D with formal agreement.
25-60	RED	TDA for 1959 IT issued by assignment
30-60	RED	TDA for 1st Q 1960 WH issued by assignment
9-60	RED	Agreement received from Mr. Ruby regarding TDA for 1st Q 1960. This was an agreement pertaining to this particular TDA and is in addition to regular partial pay agreement we already have on T/P's over-all liability. Mr. Ruby said that his 2nd Q 60 WH has been fully paid.
9-15-60	RED	Lien Filed on 1st Q 60 WH TDA
4-60	RED	Ruby phoned & said he would be in next Monday & pay 275.00. He said business had been off.
		Status report submitted to Group Sup.

U. S. TREASURY DEPARTMENT - INTERNAL REVENUE SERVICE DIR-DAL 10

3

COMMISSION EXHIBIT No. 1720—Continued

TDA HISTORY SHEET

Taxpayer : ______ Phones: ______

Address : ______

Employer : ______

Occupation: ______ Social Security Number ______

Telephone Directory	City Directory	Postal Records	Courthouse Records	Office Records	Social Sec. Administration	Tax Liens Filed	Other

Date	Revenue Officer	Contacts
10-10-60	RED	T/P came in + pd 250.00 to Cashier. T/P promised me that he would pay $25.00 next Monday. (The $250.00 remittance fully pd TDA for 4th ¼ 59 WH and made partial pmt on 1959 IT)
11-7-60	RED	Phoned TA 79883, T/P out. left message for him to call. Ruby ret. my call. He said he would bring in $50.00 next monday and that he had big party coming up on 11-18-60 and that he would pay 300.00 on November 18, 1960.
11-23-60	RED	Phoned TA 79883, no ans
11-28-60	RED	Phoned TA 79883, no ans
11-29-60	RED	Phoned TA 79883 T/P's sister seemed to think T/P was here yesterday, but I told her he was not. Said she would get in touch with him + tell him to ~~call~~ contact me

U. S. TREASURY DEPARTMENT - INTERNAL REVENUE SERVICE DIR-DAL 10

14

COMMISSION EXHIBIT No. 1720—Continued

TDA HISTORY SHEET

Taxpayer : ______________________ Phones: ____________

Address : ______________________ ____________

Employer : ______________________ ____________

Occupation: ____________ Social Security Number ____________

Telephone Directory	City Directory	Postal Records	Courthouse Records	Office Records	Social Sec. Administration	Tax Liens Filed	Other

Date	Revenue Officer	Contacts
29-60	RED	T/P came in + paid 50.00 cash. Said 50.00 was all he had. Said he had paid 32 ¢ withholding taxes. Said he hasn't drawn a penny out of Sovereign Club. Said Sovereign Club has not made any profit. I told Mr. Ruby that we needed a new income + expense statement (433 D) and he said to figure out his average net income, we would have to give him some time on it. Said he would have to refer to his records to see how he was doing. I gave him 433 D to fill out and bring back. T/P said he would try to pay 300.00 on agreement of 9-9-60 on December 7, 1960 and also try to make his regular pmt. on 12-7-60.

. S. TREASURY DEPARTMENT - INTERNAL REVENUE SERVICE DIR-DAL 10

5

COMMISSION EXHIBIT No. 1720—Continued

TDA HISTORY SHEET

Taxpayer : ______________________ Phones: ____________

Address : ______________________ ____________

Employer : ______________________ ____________

Occupation: ______________ Social Security Number ____________

Telephone Directory	City Directory	Postal Records	Courthouse Records	Office Records	Social Sec. Administration	Tax Liens Filed	Other

Date	Revenue Officer	Contacts
12/6/60		Reviewed - Collection action OK - Analyze new 433 ab for possible O.C. action on big account - Get taxpayer caught up on payments - (JMC)
12-9-60	REO	T/P came in & paid 150.00 Cash. He said business had been rough. But said the Holidays coming on there would be more activity. I gave Mr Ruby 433AB blanks in duplicate & ~~told~~ asked him to complete them or get an accountant to complete them if he was unable to do it, and bring the completed financial statement in next week. He said he would get to work on it.
12-19-60	REO	Phoned T/P's residence, TA 7 9883, no ans. " " " again. His sister answered phone. I told her to tell him that we needed some money on these accounts and to advise him to come to office by 9:00 o'clock in the morning.

U. S. TREASURY DEPARTMENT - INTERNAL REVENUE SERVICE DIR-DAL 10

16

COMMISSION EXHIBIT No. 1720—Continued

TDA HISTORY SHEET

Taxpayer : ______________________ Phones: ____________

Address : ______________________ ____________

Employer : ______________________ ____________

Occupation: ____________ Social Security Number ____________

Telephone Directory	City Directory	Postal Records	Courthouse Records	Office Records	Social Sec. Administration	Tax Liens Filed	Other

Date	Revenue Officer	Contacts
2-20-60	RED	Ruby phoned. I told him we had to have this WH acct. paid off by Thursday. He promised that he would raise the money and bring it in Thurs. morning. I told him we would like for him to bring the completed financial statement Thurs. too. Said he would do what he could. Said his accountants were busy & that he owed them some money.
2-21-60	RED	Ruby phoned & said he would bring $251.88 before 10:00 AM in the morning.
2-22-60	RED	Jack Ruby came in & made cash pmt. of $251.88 fully paying ~~[illegible]~~ remaining balance due on WH 1ST ½ 60 TDA
-3-61	RED	Drove to 4727 Homer. T/P lives in apt. # 105. He was not home. Left apt. card with his sister for T/P to come to office Monday 1:00 to 1:30

U. S. TREASURY DEPARTMENT - INTERNAL REVENUE SERVICE DIR-DAL 10

17

COMMISSION EXHIBIT No. 1720—Continued

TDA HISTORY SHEET

Taxpayer :	Jack Ruby	Phones:	TDA EXCISE
			TDA 1959 IT
Address :			
Employer :			
Occupation:		Social Security Number	

Bal on 1959 IT 2999.87

Telephone Directory	City Directory	Postal Records	Courthouse Records	Office Records	Social Sec. Administration	Tax Liens Filed	Other

Date	Revenue Officer	Contacts
2-6-60	RED	t/p came in & paid 150.00 Cash. He said he would have to refer to his records at home to fill out the financial statement. Promised to bring the statement in Next Monday
2-27-61	RED	TA11777 A Mr. Fred [illegible] Came by. Said he was going to fill out a financial statement for Mr. Ruby. I gave him 433 AB blanks and 433 D blanks. Talked like he would try to have it completed by next Monday.
3/8/61-		Reviewed - Continue efforts to get F.S. for further analysis and follow-up. Close follow up on pay dates needed - [illegible]
3-29-61	RED	Phoned Residence, T/P not home. Left word with his sister for him to come to office in the morning.

U. S. TREASURY DEPARTMENT - INTERNAL REVENUE SERVICE DIR-DAL 10

18

COMMISSION EXHIBIT NO. 1720—Continued

TDA HISTORY SHEET
(Continuation)

DATE	REVENUE OFFICER	CONTACTS
3-30-61	RED	Mr Ruby came in & Pd. 300.00 cash and promised that he would furnish a financial statement on May 1, 1961.
5-4-61	RED	Ruby called in my absence & left message that he would have all records by Monday.
5-8-61	RED	T/P failed to show up.
5-22-61	RED	Phoned T/P's residence. He said he had everything fixed up, + ready and would see me at 3:30 PM today. Mr. Ruby came in. Promised he would make a payment next Friday. He brought a statement of income (as of 1960) and balance sheet as of 12-31-60. I told him the statement was not complete and he promised to complete the 433AB & bring it to me next Monday. He said he had his bank acct at Merchants State Bank. I asked him about the 2 lots he sold up at Grapevine - He said his sister owned the lots,

RC-DAL COL - 621 (9-60)

19

COMMISSION EXHIBIT No. 1720—Continued

7-31-61 Mr Ruby came to office & paid Cash in the amt of 894.85 to Cashier, which fully paid TDA for 1st Q 61 WH.

TDA HISTORY SHEET

TAXPAYER'S NAME AND ADDRESS	HOME PHONE BUSINESS PHONE
EMPLOYER	EMPLOYER'S PHONE
OCCUPATION	SOCIAL SECURITY NUMBER

TELEPHONE DIRECTORY	CITY DIRECTORY	POSTAL RECORDS	COURTHOUSE RECORDS	OFFICE RECORDS	SOCIAL SECURITY ADMINISTRATION	OTHER

DATE	REVENUE OFFICER	CONTACTS

U. S. TREASURY DEPARTMENT - Internal Revenue Service

RC-DAL COL - 821 (9-60)

19a

Commission Exhibit No. 1720—Continued

TDA HISTORY SHEET
(Continuation)

DATE	REVENUE OFFICER	CONTACTS
5-24-61	RED	I sat in on interview with
		R/O Oscar Haslam & Jack Ruby.
		Mr Ruby paid 699.87 cash
		on 1959 IT TDA & promised again
		that he would furnish complete
		financial statement next Monday.
6-6-61	RED	Ruby came in & brought new Financial
		Statements. In addition to above 2 TDA's
		There are 2 related TDAS on
		Sovereign Club Inc. One for 3rd Q 60 WH
		& one for 4th Q 60 WH. Mr. Ruby signed
		formal agreement to pay 3rd Q 60 on
		Sovereign Club Inc on 6-12-61 and 4th Q 60
		on or before 6-23-61. Promised to come in
		on 6-12-61 regarding agreement on his
		1959 IT TDA and the outstanding
		Excise TAX TDA
6-30-61	RED	Mr. Ruby came in & signed formal
		agreement. He said he thinks he will
		start drawing some income from the
		Carousel Club in October this year.
	7/18/61-	Reviewed- Continuous contact needed.
		keep taxpayer current on P.P. and

RC-DAL COL. 821 (9-60)

continue efforts to get O.C. on big
excise tax account-
Increase part pay on review dates —
(initials)
— over —

20

COMMISSION EXHIBIT No. 1720—Continued

TDA HISTORY SHEET
(Continuation)

TAXPAYER: Jack Ruby

DATE	REVENUE OFFICER	CONTACT
9-1-61	RED	Phoned LA 8 4775, Club Vegas T/P not in. Info oper: Jack Ruby office LA 8 4775 " " THE Carousel - RI 7 2362
		Phoned Carousel Club, Ruby said he had paid the $712.08. Said he would come in next Tuesday & pay $150.00.
		Phoned accounting - Nothing has been posted to TDA for 2nd Q 61 WH
9-11-61	RED	Phoned Carousel RI 7 2362, Mr. Ruby said today was his ~~bad~~ holiday & that he would see me tomorrow.
10-4-61	RED	Phoned T/P. He promised to bring some money in the morning.
10-5-61	RED	T/P came in & pd. 150.00 cash & said he would pay the pmt. of 150.00 (that he was behind on) in 10 days.
10-23-61	RED	TDA for 1960 IT liability received by trans. from OCF
11-2-61	RED	Phoned Carousel Club, RI 7 2362. Mr Ruby was reported to be out. I left message for him to come to our office 10:00 AM in the morning.

IR-DAL COL. 821 (9-60)

11/3/61- Reviewed - Talked with T.P. and agent Sternett in re: O.C. told to either submit offer or we would begin levy + lien action - (MO)

21

COMMISSION EXHIBIT No. 1720—Continued

TDA HISTORY SHEET
(Continuation)

DATE	REVENUE OFFICER	CONTACTS
11-3-61	RED	Mr Ruby came in + paid cash in the amt of $150.00 to Cashier, applying it on Dec 1959 IT TDA.
		Mr Ruby, Mr Grenbaum, Internal Revenue Agent Glenn Stinnette + ~~myself~~ myself had conference regarding the case.
		Mr Ruby said ~~he~~ that he was going to submit Offer in Compromise by November 17th on both the Excise Tax Liability + the Income Tax Liability.
11/20/61-		Reviewed - Taxpayer not (Fred Greener called) in regards to O.C. - was given an extension to 11/27/61 - to get forms roughed up to submit to Stennett - Continue close contact and follow up to get O.C. completed - Continue close check on current liability - (JMO)
11-30-61	RED	Mr. Ruby phoned and asked for Mr. Grenbaum. He left message that he will bring papers in tomorrow.

RC-DAL COL. - 621 (9-60)

12-1-61 RED Mr. Ruby promised to bring in the offer in Compromise papers tomorrow and pay the initial pmt. of ~~$~~ 500.00

22

COMMISSION EXHIBIT No. 1720—Continued

TDA HISTORY SHEET
(Continuation)

TAXPAYER: Jack Ruby

DATE	REVENUE OFFICER	CONTACTS
12-12-61	RED	Mr. Ruby phoned in my absence & left message that he would be in 3:00 12-13-6[1]
12-15-61	RED	Mr. Ruby called & said he would have the papers ready next Tuesday.
12-20-61	RED	Regarding Question 22 on Form 433. Accountant Mr. Schriener said he could get Mr. Ruby's records for 1961 and be able to submit figures for 1961 in answer to question 22 in a week or 10 days after 1st of year. I talked to Stinnette & he said the oper statement that Mr. Ruby had with the 433 which included Jan 1, thru 9-30-61 would be sufficient. I called Mr. Schriener & he said that he would try to get the Fin Stat in by 12-22 & if not, before I get back Wed 12-27-61
12-27-61	RED	Jack Ruby came in in my absence & talked to R/O Hightower. Hightower left message for me to see him.
1-16-62	RED	I asked Mr Ruby on telephone what hold up was on O C & he said his accountant was supposed to revise some figures on the financial stat but that the accountant was in hospital, but that he was going to see him tomorrow.

821 (9-60)

23

COMMISSION EXHIBIT No. 1720—Continued

TDA HISTORY SHEET (Continuation)		TAXPAYER
DATE	REVENUE OFFICER	CONTACTS
-29-62	RED	Visited Carousel Club. Mr. Ruby said his accountant, Mr. Schreiner was still in Baylor Hosp. Said he will visit him today.
	3/7/62-	Reviewed - Continue contact with T.P. to get O.C. in. - Get info on current liabilities of Ruby. (CMO)
-13-62	RED	Phoned Carousel Club. Ruby was out. I left message that it was urgent for Mr. Ruby to come to office at 9:00 AM in the morning & see me.
-14-62	RED	Ruby came to office. Said his accountant, Fred Schreiner was still in Baylor Hospital. Said he should be out on Friday 16th. Ruby said he planned to bring OC papers in next Monday or Tuesday. Ruby said it was a good guess that he would owe \$1200.00 Income Tax for 1961, but said that he would be able to pay the 1200.00 in full on time when he filed his return. See attached notes on my inquiry of Mr. Ruby regarding other tax liabilities. (back of this sheet)

RC-DAL COL - 821 (9-60)

~~over~~

24

COMMISSION EXHIBIT No. 1720—Continued

Interview of 2-14-62

~~[illegible]~~

Carousel Club WH + SS for 4th 1/4 61 has been paid

Carousel Club

FORM 17 4th 1/4 61

Excise Tax

Assessment 1,067.28

.61

Form 17 - amt. paid 650.00

Green Receipt attached dated 2-14-62 showing 417.89 paid

4th 1/4 WH on Vegas club

Green Cashier Receipt dated 2-9-62

" amt 700.00

Bal of 35.50 due

Ret has not been filed yet however

4th 1/4 61 Excise on Vegas club has not been paid

" " " Return has been filed

Will ~~bring~~ mail completed 941 on Sovereign club to office. (2nd 1/4 61)

Total tax amt to approx 45.00

25

COMMISSION EXHIBIT No. 1720—Continued

TDA HISTORY SHEET
(Continuation)

Jack Ruby

DATE	REVENUE OFFICER	CONTACTS
2/28/62	EHH	Rec. TDA's
3/2/62	EHH	T.P. in office & Paid 4th qt exc. & W/H on Vegas Club. S&R Inc.
		DBA-Carousel - President Ralph Paul - Copeland Rd. Arlington, Texas
		Sam Ruby, VP - Rochelle St. Dallas
		Jack Ruby, V.P. & Gen Mgr.
		Leo Torti, Sec. & Treas. Employee of Club.
		4th qt exc. & W/H filed & Paid on S&R Inc.
		Ruby will be in with O.C. Tuesday at 4PM. - Warned that I would not contact him. He not filing Ex S. Told would have to come thru me as long as I have case - Claims 11 & 12 B paid on Vegas Club.
3/6/62	EHH	O.C. Received all returns with pmt in full thru me (or DARB pending) until O.C. accepted. Says he will pay [?] when due [illegible] pd. Ex S for '61 - will file E.S. for 1962. Paid AD & Beer Thru Cashier

(checked as has been paid)

RC-DAL COL. 821 (9-60)

26

COMMISSION EXHIBIT No. 1720—Continued

TDA HISTORY SHEET

TAXPAYER'S NAME AND ADDRESS	HOME PHONE
Jack Ruby Dallas, Tex	BUSINESS PHONE
EMPLOYER	EMPLOYER'S PHONE
OCCUPATION	SOCIAL SECURITY NUMBER

TELEPHONE DIRECTORY	CITY DIRECTORY	POSTAL RECORDS	COURTHOUSE RECORDS	OFFICE RECORDS	SOCIAL SECURITY ADMINISTRATION	OTHER

DATE	REVENUE OFFICER	CONTACTS
6-11-62	EL	Rec'd TDA. There is also an Offer in Compromise on this year. notified B. Collier. She will advise if this acct is to be included
6-12-62	EL	B Collier called back. This acct is not included in Offer. However, Bonnie has alerted Mr. DeLay to check on this acct before closing Offer.

U. S. TREASURY DEPARTMENT - Internal Revenue Service RC-DAL COL - 821 (9-60)

27

COMMISSION EXHIBIT No. 1720—Continued

TDA HISTORY SHEET
(Continuation)

Ruby

DATE	REVENUE OFFICER	CONTACTS
3/15/62	BH	Taxpayer to notify DIR when necessary — 1040 + ES to be filed thru DAR-Coll. — Quarterly returns to be filed with me until offer is accepted or rejected —
		Transfer to Dart — Offer submitted. ~~[illegible]~~
3/16/62	BH	Transfer to Inactive.
12/3/62	[illegible]	Changed to [illegible] 11-8-62 — no contact this date.
1-17-63	[illegible]	Reviewed — F.S. out of date.
2-25-63	V. KLEINER	Rec'd TDA.'s (4)
3/25/63	K	Rec'd WHTF 4/62 TDA, also rec'd C/A to full pay same.
3/27/63	K	rec'd two 14-C's. checked with cashier on 11B. it has not been paid
3/28/63	K	Executed RC Dal 854. - Called TP @ RI 72362 — not in, left # for him to call me by 1:30 PM.
3/28/63	K	TP called, instructed him to bring sufficient data to prepare 433AB + Receipts for past 6 months. Will come in at 2:00 PM Thurs Apr. 4 (continued)

RC-DAL-COL - 821 (9-60)

28

COMMISSION EXHIBIT No. 1720—Continued

TDA HISTORY SHEET
(Continuation)

TAXPAYER Jack Ruby

DATE	REVENUE OFFICER	CONTACTS
3/28/63	ctd	His accountant has all his books. He will secure the information requested and bring it in. Cause: Used money to operate business Cure: Advised TP to purchase D&R. Canvs: Owes no other taxes PRDA not acceptable as TP is self employed Lounge Operator Liens already filed. Address 4727 Homer Phone LA 8-4775 (Office) Banks @ Merchants SB & Empire SB.
4/4/63	K	TP called, his accountant will not be able to prepare the necessary info until after April 15. Therefore I postponed our appointment until 4/22/63 @ 1:00 P.M.
4-22-63	K	TP came in, Secured 433 AB C&D Cause: TP was advised that he did not have to pay cabaret tax due to legal suit which was later won by the U.S. Cure: TP is now making monthly deposit of Trust Fund money.

RC-DAL COL. 821 (9-60)

29

COMMISSION EXHIBIT No. 1720—Continued

TDA HISTORY SHEET
(Continuation)

TAXPAYER Jack Ruby

DATE	REVENUE OFFICER	CONTACTS
4-22-63	K	Canvis: TP has not yet filed 1040 for 1962, 1040ES for 1st 1/4 1963 and has not paid COAD Tax for FY 1963. He will pay these taxes prior to submitting an offer in compromise later this month. He has applied for an extension of time on his delinquent returns. Unable to complete 433 AB at this time, TP was in very much of a hurry to leave, had very urgent business to attend. Will secure info necessary to complete 433 AB + file it with me by 5-1-63
5-20-63	K	Rec'd 14C for W3 + W2-As 1960
5-21-63	K	Called Koch - nothing has been done on O/in Comp. as yet. will try to get it in next week.
5-23-63	K	Attorney called, all delinquent returns will be filed by 5-31-63 will go from there with offer.
	5/29/63	- Talked with T.P.s attorney - has to go to Washington D.C. on emergency case cannot complete O.C. by 5/31/63 will call when he returns and set new date.

RC-DAL COL. - 821 (9-60)

30

COMMISSION EXHIBIT No. 1720—Continued

TDA HISTORY SHEET

TAXPAYER'S NAME AND ADDRESS	HOME PHONE
	BUSINESS PHONE
EMPLOYER	EMPLOYER'S PHONE
OCCUPATION	SOCIAL SECURITY NUMBER

TELEPHONE DIRECTORY	CITY DIRECTORY	POSTAL RECORDS	COURTHOUSE RECORDS	OFFICE RECORDS	SOCIAL SECURITY ADMINISTRATION	OTHER

DATE	REVENUE OFFICER	CONTACTS
	6/6/63 -	Talked to Graham Koch - O.C. is prepared and will be submitted as soon as arrangements can be made to borrow money - All returns (1040) are to be brought to current basis at time O.C. is submitted. Will contact this office not later than 6/14/63 - (initials)
6-11-63	(initials)	TP's Attorney brought in forms 656 Offer in compromise, holding to see if current on all returns before submitting offer. Sent 2275 Atty says all returns current.
	6/14/63 -	Reviewed - Continue close follow up - Submit O.C. as soon as returns can be verified that T.P. is current (initials)

U. S. TREASURY DEPARTMENT - Internal Revenue Service RC-DAL COL - 821 (9-60)

31

COMMISSION EXHIBIT No. 1720—Continued

TDA HISTORY SHEET

TAXPAYER'S NAME AND ADDRESS	HOME PHONE
Jack Ruby Club Vigon, 3508 Oak Lawn,	BUSINESS PHONE
EMPLOYER	EMPLOYER'S PHONE
OCCUPATION	SOCIAL SECURITY NUMBER

TELEPHONE DIRECTORY	CITY DIRECTORY	POSTAL RECORDS	COURTHOUSE RECORDS	OFFICE RECORDS	SOCIAL SECURITY ADMINISTRATION	OTHER

DATE	REVENUE OFFICER	CONTACTS
9-13-63	[initials]	Recd T.D.A.
10-1-63	[initials]	Went to Carousel @ 1312½ Commerce – t.p.
		not in – left #. t.p. called 10/3/63, tax paid,
10-3-63	[initials]	Went to Accounting, found money (DR)
		$164.43 C.A. to follow
		2275 to files for all 1960 941's
		for preparation of W-3

U. S. TREASURY DEPARTMENT - Internal Revenue Service RC-DAL COL. 821 (9-60)

COMMISSION EXHIBIT No. 1720—Continued

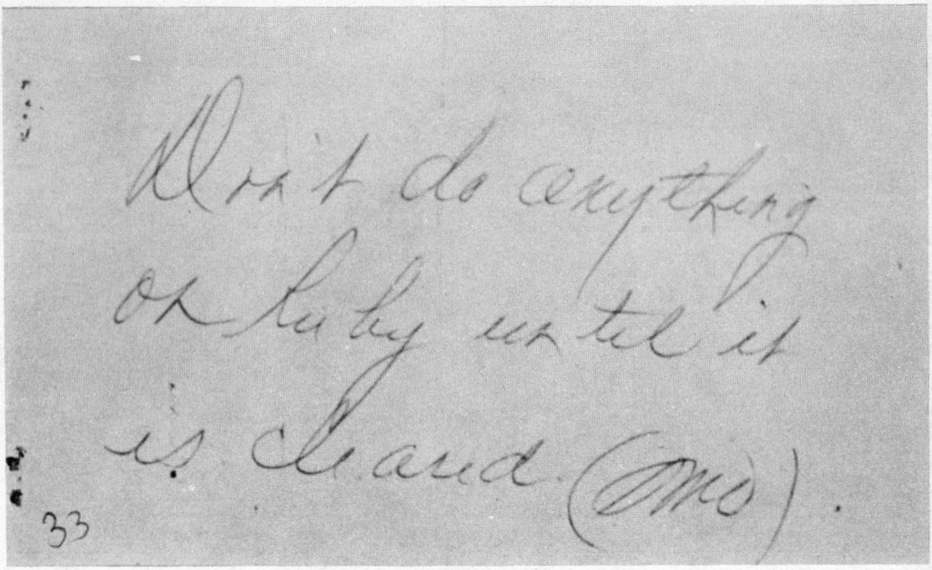

Don't do anything
on Ruby until it
is cleared.
33

Commission Exhibit No. 1720—Continued

3328

TDA HISTORY SHEET

AXPAYER'S NAME AND ADDRESS	HOME PHONE
Jack Ruby	BUSINESS PHONE
MPLOYER	EMPLOYER'S PHONE
CCUPATION	SOCIAL SECURITY NUMBER

ELEPHONE DIRECTORY	CITY DIRECTORY	POSTAL RECORDS	COURTHOUSE RECORDS	OFFICE RECORDS	SOCIAL SECURITY ADMINISTRATION	OTHER

DATE	REVENUE OFFICER	CONTACTS
-26-63	HGJ	Rec'd (4) TDA's $39,067.84
		Discussed with Gp. Supervisor & Collection Mgr. -
		Levy considered - call Phil Pierce x909,
		determine status of OIC - Pierce in conference
		will call back. Hal Pendleton called,
		talked w/ Orenbaum, file now
		in hands of Intelligence (Mr. Cooner)
-27-63	HGJ	Hold up levy action, as per Gp. Supvr. Note
-6-63	HGJ	Conference, Mr. Niel, Mr. Cooner, Mr. Pierce
		Mr. Horton & Gp. Supvr. - Mr. Cooner to
		coordinate all action here - I will
		get instructions as to how & when
		to proceed.
-9-63	HGJ	Mr. Horton advised that we can serve
		levy, Agent Bob Klein will accompany
		me.
		Levy served & picked up $3,149 - same

S. TREASURY DEPARTMENT - Internal Revenue Service RC-DAL COL - 821 (9-60)

34

COMMISSION EXHIBIT No. 1720—Continued

TDA HISTORY SHEET
(Continuation)

TAXPAYER: Jack Ruby

DATE	REVENUE OFFICER	CONTACTS
		subsequently taken to intelligence for listing of serial numbers, etc. Capt. King was questioned as to any other claims to the money and his answer was in the negative. The Police Dept. showed all funds as belonging to Jack Ruby, and separated into sacks and restored as to source from which they obtained the money. Form #809 written as follows; No. 8158225 for a/c #60BP300661, tax $1,501.80, Int $343.77, Lien $1.00, Amt. $1,846.57
		No. 8158226 for a/c #61OP401231, tax $1,322.54
		= 1,846.57
		1,322.54
		$3,169.11

RC-DAL COL. - 821 (9-60)

35

COMMISSION EXHIBIT No. 1720—Continued

TDA HISTORY SHEET

TAXPAYER'S NAME AND ADDRESS	HOME PHONE
Jack Ruby	
	BUSINESS PHONE
EMPLOYER	EMPLOYER'S PHONE
OCCUPATION	SOCIAL SECURITY NUMBER

TELEPHONE DIRECTORY	CITY DIRECTORY	POSTAL RECORDS	COURTHOUSE RECORDS	OFFICE RECORDS	SOCIAL SECURITY ADMINISTRATION	OTHER

DATE	REVENUE OFFICER	CONTACTS
[illegible]-22-63	[illegible]	Offer in Compromise resubmitted, to conform to manual requirements — amounts changed to agree with current balances unpaid etc. this was handled as (990) case.
[illegible]-9-63	[illegible]	Levy served on Capt. King at Dallas Police Station, picked up $3,169.11 I was accompanied by Robert W. Klein, Agent from Mr. [illegible]'s office. Funds taken to Mr. [illegible]'s office by Mr. Klein.

S. TREASURY DEPARTMENT - Internal Revenue Service RC-DAL COL - 821 (9-60)

Commission Exhibit No. 1720—Continued

Status Report of Accounts totaling $10,000 or more on any one Taxpayer, Partnership, or man and wife.

Date of this Report 6-30-60 (Kind(s) of Tax Excise & Withholding

Name of Taxpayer(s) Jack Ruby
dba The Club Vegas

Address 1220 Mercantile Securities Bldg., Dallas, Texas

Total Due This Date 17,542.11 Age of Oldest Acct. Less than one year

Tax Liens Filed? Yes X No ___. If No explain why below.

Financial Statement Procured? Yes X No ___. If No explain why below.

Give below current status. If on installment payment basis give details. If no action possible, explain why. Furnish all pertinent information using back of this for 200.00 monthly

Taxpayer is paying on installment basis, however, I am at present attempting to procure a xxxx new 433D and new formal agreement from him.

Approved ______________________ R. E. Davis
Group Supervisor Collection Officer or Person to whom assigned

U. S. Treasury - Internal Revenue Service DIR-DAL-454 (9-57)

Commission Exhibit No. 1721

Status Report of Accounts totaling $10,000 or more on any one Taxpayer, Partnership, or man and wife.

Date of this Report 9-30-60 (Kind(s) of Tax Excise, Withholding, & Income

Name of Taxpayer(s) Jack Ruby

Address 4727 Homer, Dallas, Texas

Total Due This Date $20,942.39 Age of Oldest Acct. Less than one year

Tax Liens Filed? Yes X No ___. If No explain why below.

Financial Statement Procured? Yes X No ___. If No explain why below.

Give below current status. If on installment payment basis give details. If no action possible, explain why. Furnish all pertinent information using back of this form if necessary. Taxpayer is paying $275.00 monthly on installment basis. Taxpayer has signed an extra agreement to make additional installment payments of $300.00 on 11-1-60, $200.00 on 12-15-60 and $184.64 plus accrued interest xx by 1-1-61 in order to fully pay 1st ½ 60 WH liability which is included in above figure.

Approved ______________________ ______________________
Group Supervisor Collection Officer or Person to whom assigned

U. S. Treasury - Internal Revenue Service DIR-DAL-454 (9-57)

Commission Exhibit No. 1721—Continued

Status Report of Accounts totaling $10,000 or more on any one Taxpayer, Partnership, or man and wife.

Date of this Report **12-22-60** (Kind(s) of Tax **Income, Excise**

Name of Taxpayer(s) **Jack Ruby, DBA Club Vegas**

Address **4727 Homer, Dallas, Texas**

Total Due This Date **20,028.92** Age of Oldest Acct. **1 to 2 yrs(23C 11-20-59)**
(Outstanding balance on excise TDA is $16,879.05)
Tax Liens Filed? Yes **X** No ____. If No explain why below.

Financial Statement Procured? Yes **X** No ____. If No explain why below.

Give below current status. If on installment payment basis give details. If no action possible, explain why. Furnish all pertinent information using back of this form if necessary.

Taxpayer has been paying on installment basis. He made final pmt. on 4/60 WH on 12-22-60. I furnished T/P with 433AB forms on 12-9-60 for him to complete and return. When I receive the new financial statement I will analyse it for possible Offer In Compromise action on the Excise acct

Approved ______________________ R. E. Davis
Group Supervisor — Collection Officer or Person to whom assigned

U. S. Treasury - Internal Revenue Service DIR-DAL-454 (9-57)

COMMISSION EXHIBIT No. 1721—Continued

Status Report of Accounts totaling $10,000 or more on any one Taxpayer, Partnership, or man and wife.

Date of this Report **3-31-61** Kind(s) of Tax **Income, Excise**

Name of Taxpayer(s) **Jack Ruby, DBA Club Vegas**

Address **4727 Homer, Dallas, Texas**

Total Due This Date **19,578.92** Age of Oldest Acct. **1 to 2 yrs(23C 11-20-59**
(Outstanding balance on excise TDA is $16,879.05)
Tax Liens Filed? Yes **X** No ____. If No, explain why below.

Financial Statement Procured? Yes **X** No ____. If No, explain why below.

Give below current status. If on installment payment basis, give details. If no action possible, explain why. Furnish all pertinent information using back of this form if necessary.

I am still in process of trying to get new financial statement from T/P. He made $300.00 partial pmt on IT TDA on 3-30-61 and promised the new financial statement on 5-1-61. I will analyse the new 433 AB for possible Offer In Compromise Action. R. E. Davis

Approved ______________________
Collection Manager or Group Supervisor — Revenue Officer

Reviewed and Approved ______________________
Assistant Chief, DAR Branch or Collection Manager

U. S. Treasury - Internal Revenue Service DIR-DAL-454 (1-61)

COMMISSION EXHIBIT No. 1721—Continued

STATUS REPORT OF ACCOUNTS

(Totaling $10,000 or more on any one taxpayer, partnership, or man and wife)

NAME AND ADDRESS OF TAXPAYER(S)

Jack Ruby DBA
Club Vegas
3508 Oak Lawn
Dallas, Texas

DATE OF REPORT: June 23, 1961

KIND(S) OF TAX: Excise, Income

TOTAL DUE THIS DATE: $ 18,879.05

AGE OF OLDEST ACCOUNT: Between 1 and 2 years

TAX LIENS FILED? [X] YES [ ] NO IF NO, EXPLAIN.

FINANCIAL STATEMENT PROCURED [X] YES [ ] NO IF NO, EXPLAIN.

CURRENT STATUS OF ACCOUNT: IF ON INSTALLMENT PAYMENT BASIS, GIVE DETAILS. IF NO ACTION POSSIBLE, EXPLAI[N]. FURNISH ALL PERTINENT INFORMATION USING BACK OF THIS FORM, IF NECESSARY.

T/P made pmt of $699.87 on above income tax account on 5-24-61 and since tha[t] date has paid $557.97 liquidating employment accounts for 3 taxpable quarter[s] on Sovereign Club, Inc. I have recently procured new financial statement and have an appointment with T/P on 6-26-61 at which time I will attempt to procure new formal agreement on above liability.

REVENUE OFFICER (Signature) R. E. Davis

APPROVED: COLLECTION MANAGER OR GROUP SUPERVISOR

REVIEWED AND APPROVED:

Asst. Chief, DAR Branch or Collection Manager

U. S. TREASURY DEPARTMENT - Internal Revenue Service RC-DAL COL - 854 (6-61)

COMMISSION EXHIBIT No. 1721—Continued

STATUS REPORT OF ACCOUNTS

(Totaling $10,000 or more on any one taxpayer, partnership, or man and wife)

NAME AND ADDRESS OF TAXPAYER(S)

Jack Ruby DBA
Club Vegas
3508 Oak Lawn
Dallas, Texas

DATE OF REPORT: August 25, 1961

KIND(S) OF TAX: Excise, Income

TOTAL DUE THIS DATE: 18,879.05

AGE OF OLDEST ACCOUNT: Between 1 and 2 yrs.

TAX LIENS FILED? [X] YES [ ] NO IF NO, EXPLAIN.

FINANCIAL STATEMENT PROCURED [X] YES [ ] NO IF NO, EXPLAIN.

CURRENT STATUS OF ACCOUNT: IF ON INSTALLMENT PAYMENT BASIS, GIVE DETAILS. IF NO ACTION POSSIBLE, EXPLAI[N]. FURNISH ALL PERTINENT INFORMATION USING BACK OF THIS FORM, IF NECESSARY.

T/P is one pmt delinquent on new formal agreement procured on 6-30-61, however, on 7-31-61 he paid $894.85 cash to Cashier which fully paid TDA for 1st ½ 61 WH.

REVENUE OFFICER (Signature) R. E. Davis

APPROVED: COLLECTION MANAGER OR GROUP SUPERVISOR

REVIEWED AND APPROVED:

Asst. Chief, DAR Branch or Collection Manager

U. S. TREASURY DEPARTMENT - Internal Revenue Service RC-DAL COL - 854 (6-61)

COMMISSION EXHIBIT No. 1721—Continued

STATUS REPORT OF ACCOUNTS

(Totaling $10,000 or more on any one taxpayer, partnership, or man and wife)

NAME AND ADDRESS OF TAXPAYER(S) Jack Ruby DBA Club Vegas 3508 Oaklawn Dallas, Texas	DATE OF REPORT 9-30-61 KIND(S) OF TAX Excise Income
TAX LIENS FILED? [X] YES [ ] NO IF NO, EXPLAIN.	TOTAL DUE THIS DATE 18,580.22 AGE OF OLDEST ACCOUNT between 1 & 2 yrs.

FINANCIAL STATEMENT PROCURED [X] YES [ ] NO IF NO, EXPLAIN.

CURRENT STATUS OF ACCOUNT: IF ON INSTALLMENT PAYMENT BASIS, GIVE DETAILS. IF NO ACTION POSSIBLE, EXPLAIN. FURNISH ALL PERTINENT INFORMATION USING BACK OF THIS FORM, IF NECESSARY.

T/P is one payment delinquent on new formal agreement procured on 6-30-61. According to this agreement the Taxpayer's financial status is due to be reviewed on 10-16-61.

REVENUE OFFICER (*Signature*) R. E. Davis — R. E. Davis APPROVED: COLLECTION MANAGER OR GROUP SUPERVISOR	REVIEWED AND APPROVED: *Asst. Chief, DAR Branch or Collection Manager*

U. S. TREASURY DEPARTMENT - Internal Revenue Service RC-DAL COL - 854 (6-61)

COMMISSION EXHIBIT No. 1721—Continued

Status Report of Accounts Totaling $10,000 or More
on any one Taxpayer, Partnership, or Man and Wife

Date of this Report 10-26-61 Kind(s) of Tax Excise; Income

Name of Taxpayer(s) Jack Ruby DBA Club Vegas

Address 3508 Oak Lawn, Dallas, Texas

Total Due This Date 20,826.73 Age of Oldest Acct. Between 1 & 2 yrs.

Tax Liens Filed? Yes X No ____. If No, explain why below.

Financial Statement Procured? Yes X No ____. If No, explain why below.

Give below current status. If on installment payment basis, give details. If no action possible, explain why. Furnish all pertinent information using back of this form if necessary.

See Back

Approved ______________________
Collection Manager or Group Supervisor

R. E. Davis
Revenue Officer

Reviewed and Approved ______________________
Assistant Chief, DAR Branch or Collection Manager

U. S. TREASURY DEPARTMENT - Internal Revenue Service DIR-DAL-454 (1-61)

T/P is one payment delinquent on formal agreement procured on 6-30-61. According to this agreement he was due to come to office on 10-16-61 for a review of his financial status, but he failed to do so. TDA showing $2246.51 due on 1960 Income tax, was assigned to on 10-23-61.

COMMISSION EXHIBIT No. 1721—Continued

STATUS REPORT OF ACCOUNTS

(Totaling $10,000 or more on any one taxpayer, partnership, or man and wife)

NAME AND ADDRESS OF TAXPAYER(S)

JACK RUBY DBA CLUB VEGAS
3508 OAK LAWN
DALLAS, TEXAS

DATE OF REPORT: 11-30-61

KIND(S) OF TAX: EXCISE; INCOME

TOTAL DUE THIS DATE: 20,676.73

AGE OF OLDEST ACCOUNT: BETWEEN 2 & 3 YR.

TAX LIENS FILED? [X] YES [ ] NO IF NO, EXPLAIN.

FINANCIAL STATEMENT PROCURED [X] YES [ ] NO IF NO, EXPLAIN.

CURRENT STATUS OF ACCOUNT: IF ON INSTALLMENT PAYMENT BASIS, GIVE DETAILS. IF NO ACTION POSSIBLE, EXPLAI
FURNISH ALL PERTINENT INFORMATION USING BACK OF THIS FORM, IF NECESSARY.

MR. RUBY HAS PROPOSED OFFER IN COMPROMISE, AND IS SUPPOSED TO HAVE THE COMPLETED OFFER IN THIS OFFICE WITH IN A FEW DAYS.

REVENUE OFFICER *(Signature)* R. E. Davis

APPROVED: COLLECTION MANAGER OR GROUP SUPERVISOR

REVIEWED AND APPROVED:

Asst. Chief, DAR Branch or Collection Manager

U. S. TREASURY DEPARTMENT - Internal Revenue Service RC-DAL COL - 854 (6-61)

Commission Exhibit No. 1721—Continued

STATUS REPORT OF ACCOUNTS

(Totaling $10,000 or more on any one taxpayer, partnership, or man and wife)

NAME AND ADDRESS OF TAXPAYER(S)

Jack Ruby DBA
Club Vegas
3508 Oak Lawn
Dallas, Texas

DATE OF REPORT: January 29, 1962

KIND(S) OF TAX: Excise Tax; Income "

TOTAL DUE THIS DATE: 20,676.73

AGE OF OLDEST ACCOUNT: Between 2 & 3 years

TAX LIENS FILED? [X] YES [ ] NO IF NO, EXPLAIN.

FINANCIAL STATEMENT PROCURED [X] YES [ ] NO IF NO, EXPLAIN.

CURRENT STATUS OF ACCOUNT: IF ON INSTALLMENT PAYMENT BASIS, GIVE DETAILS. IF NO ACTION POSSIBLE, EXPLA
FURNISH ALL PERTINENT INFORMATION USING BACK OF THIS FORM, IF NECESSARY.

Taxpayer has proposed offer in compromise. I asked Mr. Ruby by telephone on 1-16-62 what hold up on OC was and he said his accountant was supposed to revise some figures on the financial statement, but that the accountant was in hospital but that he was going to see him next day. My intentions are to attempt personal contact with Mr. Ruby this date to determine how soon he plans on getting the offer in.

REVENUE OFFICER *(Signature)* R. E. Davis

APPROVED: COLLECTION MANAGER OR GROUP SUPERVISOR

REVIEWED AND APPROVED:

Asst. Chief, DAR Branch or Collection Manager

U. S. TREASURY DEPARTMENT - Internal Revenue Service RC-DAL COL - 854 (6-6

Commission Exhibit No. 1721—Continued

STATUS REPORT OF ACCOUNTS

(Totaling $10,000 or more on any one taxpayer, partnership, or man and wife)

NAME AND ADDRESS OF TAXPAYER(S)

Jack Ruby
DBA Club Vegas
3508 Oak Lawn
Dallas, Texas

DATE OF REPORT: 3 31 62

KIND(S) OF TAX: Excise & IT

TAX LIENS FILED? [X] YES [ ] NO IF NO, EXPLAIN.

TOTAL DUE THIS DATE: $20,555.39

AGE OF OLDEST ACCOUNT: 2 yrs 4 mos 11 das

FINANCIAL STATEMENT PROCURED [X] YES [ ] NO IF NO, EXPLAIN.

CURRENT STATUS OF ACCOUNT: IF ON INSTALLMENT PAYMENT BASIS, GIVE DETAILS. IF NO ACTION POSSIBLE, EXPLAIN. FURNISH ALL PERTINENT INFORMATION USING BACK OF THIS FORM, IF NECESSARY.

Offer in Compromise pending.

REVENUE OFFICER (*Signature*): Eva Lane, Inactive Accts.

REVIEWED AND APPROVED:

APPROVED: COLLECTION MANAGER OR GROUP SUPERVISOR

Asst. Chief, DAR Branch or Collection Manager

U. S. TREASURY DEPARTMENT - Internal Revenue Service RC-DAL COL - 854 (6-61)

COMMISSION EXHIBIT No. 1721—Continued

STATUS REPORT OF ACCOUNTS

(Totaling $10,000 or more on any one taxpayer, partnership, or man and wife)

NAME AND ADDRESS OF TAXPAYER(S)

Jack Ruby
Club Vegas
3508 Oak Lawn
Dallas, Texas

DATE OF REPORT: 12/20/1962

KIND(S) OF TAX: Income & Excise

TAX LIENS FILED? [ ] YES [ ] NO IF NO, EXPLAIN.
x

TOTAL DUE THIS DATE: 20,555.39

AGE OF OLDEST ACCOUNT: 11/20/59

FINANCIAL STATEMENT PROCURED [ ] YES [ ] NO IF NO, EXPLAIN.

Current financial statement attached to O/C file

CURRENT STATUS OF ACCOUNT: IF ON INSTALLMENT PAYMENT BASIS, GIVE DETAILS. IF NO ACTION POSSIBLE, EXPLAIN. FURNISH ALL PERTINENT INFORMATION USING BACK OF THIS FORM, IF NECESSARY.

Taxpayer's Offer in Compromise rejected. Collection efforts will instituted.

REVENUE OFFICER (*Signature*): C. J. Phelps

REVIEWED AND APPROVED:

APPROVED: COLLECTION MANAGER OR GROUP SUPERVISOR

Asst. Chief, DAR Branch or Collection Manager

U. S. TREASURY DEPARTMENT - Internal Revenue Service RC-DAL COL - 854 (6-61)

COMMISSION EXHIBIT No. 1721—Continued

STATUS REPORT OF ACCOUNTS

(Totaling $10,000 or more on any one taxpayer, partnership, or man and wife)

NAME AND ADDRESS OF TAXPAYER(S)
Jack Ruby
4727 Homer
Dallas, Texas

DATE OF REPORT
3/28/63

KIND(S) OF TAX
Excise & Income Tax

TAX LIENS FILED? [X] YES [ ] NO IF NO, EXPLAIN.

TOTAL DUE THIS DATE
39,190.40

AGE OF OLDEST ACCOUNT
2½ Years (approx)

FINANCIAL STATEMENT PROCURED [X] YES [ ] NO IF NO, EXPLAIN.

CURRENT STATUS OF ACCOUNT: IF ON INSTALLMENT PAYMENT BASIS, GIVE DETAILS. IF NO ACTION POSSIBLE, EXPLA
FURNISH ALL PERTINENT INFORMATION USING BACK OF THIS FORM, IF NECESSARY.

Taxpayer's offer in compromise rejected, collection efforts will be resumed.

Accts. were assigned to me 2/25/63

REVENUE OFFICER *(Signature)*
Van D. Kleiner

REVIEWED AND APPROVED:

APPROVED: COLLECTION MANAGER OR GROUP SUPERVISOR

Asst. Chief, DAR Branch or Collection Manager

U. S. TREASURY DEPARTMENT - Internal Revenue Service

RC-DAL COL - 854 (8-61

COMMISSION EXHIBIT No. 1721—Continued

STATUS REPORT OF ACCOUNTS

(Totaling $10,000 or more on any one taxpayer, partnership, or man and wife)

NAME AND ADDRESS OF TAXPAYER(S)
Jack Ruby, dba. Club Vegas
3508 Oak Lawn
Dallas, Texas

DATE OF REPORT
6/21/63

KIND(S) OF TAX Income 1959 & P-1960, Excise 56 thru 59 & 59 thru 6/30/60

TAX LIENS FILED? [X] YES [ ] NO IF NO, EXPLAIN.

TOTAL DUE THIS DATE
39,129.13

AGE OF OLDEST ACCOUNT
3 yrs. 7 months.

FINANCIAL STATEMENT PROCURED [X] YES [ ] NO IF NO, EXPLAIN.

CURRENT STATUS OF ACCOUNT: IF ON INSTALLMENT PAYMENT BASIS, GIVE DETAILS. IF NO ACTION POSSIBLE, EXPLA
FURNISH ALL PERTINENT INFORMATION USING BACK OF THIS FORM, IF NECESSARY.

T/P has submitted an offer-in-compromise, which is being held until it can be detirmined whether the T/P is current on all classes of tax.

6/24/63, 2275's returned, returns will not be available until 7/15/63; O/C submitted.

REVENUE OFFICER *(Signature)*

REVIEWED AND APPROVED:

APPROVED: COLLECTION MANAGER OR GROUP SUPERVISOR

Asst. Chief, DAR Branch or Collection Manager

U. S. TREASURY DEPARTMENT - Internal Revenue Service

RC-DAL COL - 854 (8-6

COMMISSION EXHIBIT No. 1721—Continued

STATUS REPORT OF ACCOUNTS

(Totaling $10,000 or more on any one taxpayer, partnership, or man and wife)

NAME AND ADDRESS OF TAXPAYER(S)

Jack Ruby
4727 Homer
Dallas, Texas

DATE OF REPORT: September 23, 1963

KIND(S) OF TAX: IT & EXCISE

TAX LIENS FILED? [X] YES [ ] NO IF NO, EXPLAIN.

TOTAL DUE THIS DATE: 39,067.84

AGE OF OLDEST ACCOUNT: 3 years 10 months

FINANCIAL STATEMENT PROCURED [X] YES [ ] NO IF NO, EXPLAIN.

CURRENT STATUS OF ACCOUNT: IF ON INSTALLMENT PAYMENT BASIS, GIVE DETAILS. IF NO ACTION POSSIBLE, EXPLAIN. FURNISH ALL PERTINENT INFORMATION USING BACK OF THIS FORM, IF NECESSARY.

Offer in Compromise filed 8-14-63. Still pending.

REVENUE OFFICER *(Signature)*: R. S ouse, Inactive Accts

APPROVED: COLLECTION MANAGER OR GROUP SUPERVISOR: [signature]

REVIEWED AND APPROVED:

Asst. Chief, DAR Branch or Collection Manager

U. S. TREASURY DEPARTMENT - Internal Revenue Service RC-DAL COL - 854 (6-61)

COMMISSION EXHIBIT NO. 1721—Continued

Commission Exhibit No. 1722

PAYMENT AGREEMENT

I, the undersigned, declare that because of my present financial condition, as evidenced by my financial statement which has been submitted, I am unable at this time to pay the internal revenue taxes outstanding against me in the amount shown below, together with interest at 6% per year. I, therefore, request the privilege of paying such taxes as follows:

AMOUNT OF TAXES OWED (Plus interest at 6% per year) $17,486.59 — $ 275.00 to be paid on 1st of each month. and $ ______ to be paid on First payment of 275.00 due on August 1 1960. of each ______ thereafter until the liability is paid in full. I will contact Revenue Officer R. E. Davis on November 1, [illegible]

I agree that I will increase my payments in amounts equal to any installment payments which are liquidated during the term of this agreement and that I will timely pay all other internal revenue taxes for which I become liable during the term of this agreement. and if my income has increased, I will increase my monthly payments.

I further understand and agree that if I fail to meet any of the conditions stated herein, or if it is determined that collection of the tax is in jeopardy, the privilege of making installment payments may be withdrawn and the entire amount of my tax liability collected by levy on my income or by seizure of my property without further notification to me.

DATE	SIGNATURE OF TAXPAYER	
7-13-60	Jack Ruby	
ACCOUNT ASSIGNED TO	AGREEMENT EXAMINED AND APPROVED (Signature)	DATE APPROVED
	[illegible signature]	7/13/60

FORM 433-D (11-56)

U. S. GOVERNMENT PRINTING OFFICE: 1958 O - 48557

FORM 433-D (NOV. 1956)

U. S. TREASURY DEPARTMENT - INTERNAL REVENUE SERVICE

MONTHLY INCOME AND EXPENSE ANALYSIS

TAXPAYER'S NAME AND ADDRESS
JACK RUBY
4727 HOMER, DALLAS, TEXAS

INCOME		PERSONAL EXPENSES	
Take home pay (Husband)	$ NONE	Rent or home payment	$ 160.00
Take home pay (Wife)	NONE	Groceries	160.00
Contributions from others	NONE	Installment payments (list below)	NONE
Net income from business MONTH	700.00	Utilities	NONE
Other (specify)	NONE	Auto expenses	NONE
		Other (specify)	NONE
The above net income is		LAUNDRY + DRY CLEANING	ABOUT 30.00
all the income I have		BARBER WORK, MANICURES, TIPS	16.00
from any source.		CLOTHING	20.00
TOTAL	$ 700.00	TOTAL	$ 386.00
NET DIFFERENCE (Income minus personal expenses)			$

SCHEDULE OF INSTALLMENT PAYMENTS

PAYEE	KIND OF PROPERTY	BALANCE DUE	DATE OF FINAL PAY'T.	MONTHLY PAYMENT
		$		$
	NONE			
TOTAL MONTHLY INSTALLMENT PAYMENTS (Enter above)				$

COMMISSION EXHIBIT NO. 1722

PAYMENT AGREEMENT

I, the undersigned, declare that because of my present financial condition, as evidenced by my financial statement which has been submitted, I am unable at this time to pay the internal revenue taxes outstanding against me in the amount shown below, together with interest at 6% per year. I, therefore, request the privilege of paying such taxes as follows:

AMOUNT OF TAXES OWED (*Plus interest at 6% per year*)	
$ 17,486.54	$ 275.00 to be paid on 1st of each month and $ ______ to be paid on

First payment of 275.00 due on August 1, 1960. of each ______ thereafter until the liability is paid in full.

I will contact Revenue Officer R. E. Davis on November 1, 1960

I agree that I will increase my payments in amounts equal to any installment payments which are liquidated during the term of this agreement and that I will timely pay all other internal revenue taxes for which I become liable during the term of this agreement.

until my income has increased, I will increase my monthly payments

I further understand and agree that if I fail to meet any of the conditions stated herein, or if it is determined that collection of the tax is in jeopardy, the privilege of making installment payments may be withdrawn and the entire amount of my tax liability collected by levy on my income or by seizure of my property without further notification to me.

DATE	SIGNATURE OF TAXPAYER	
8/60	Jack Ruby	
ACCOUNT ASSIGNED TO	AGREEMENT EXAMINED AND APPROVED (*Signature*)	DATE APPROVED
	[illegible]	

FORM 433-D (11-56)

U. S. GOVERNMENT PRINTING OFFICE: 1958 O-48557

COPY

FORM 433-D (NOV. 1956)

U. S. TREASURY DEPARTMENT - INTERNAL REVENUE SERVICE

MONTHLY INCOME AND EXPENSE ANALYSIS

TAXPAYER'S NAME AND ADDRESS
JACK RUBY
4727 HOMER DALLAS, TEXAS

INCOME		PERSONAL EXPENSES	
Take home pay (Husband)	$ NONE	Rent or home payment	$ 160.00 MO
Take home pay (Wife)	NONE	Groceries	160.00 MO
Contributions from others	NONE	Installment payments (list below)	NONE
Net income from business MONTH	700.00	Utilities	NONE
Other (specify)	NONE	Auto expenses	NONE
The above net income is		Other (specify)	
all the income I have		LAUNDRY + DRY CLEANING abt	30.00 MO
from any source.		BARBER WORK, MANICURES, TIPS	16.00 MO
		CLOTHING	20.00 MO
TOTAL	$ 700.00	TOTAL	$ 386.00 MO
NET DIFFERENCE (Income minus personal expenses)			$

SCHEDULE OF INSTALLMENT PAYMENTS

PAYEE	KIND OF PROPERTY	BALANCE DUE	DATE OF FINAL PAY'T.	MONTHLY PAYMENT
		$		$
	NONE			
TOTAL MONTHLY INSTALLMENT PAYMENTS (Enter above)				$

COMMISSION EXHIBIT NO. 1722—Continued

PAYMENT AGREEMENT

I, the undersigned, declare that because of my present financial condition, as evidenced by my financial statement which has been submitted, I am unable at this time to pay the internal revenue taxes outstanding against me in the amount shown below, together with interest at 6% per year. I, therefore, request the privilege of paying such taxes as follows:

AMOUNT OF TAXES OWED (*Plus interest at 6% per year*) $ 18,879.05

$ 150.00 to be paid on Aug 1, 1961, and $ 150.00 to be paid on Sept. 1, 191, 150.00 of each on Oct. 1, 1961 thereafter until the liability is paid in full.

I will confer with R. E. Davis on 10-16-61 for review of the account and my financial status

I agree that I will increase my payments in amounts equal to any installment payments which are liquidated during the term of this agreement and that I will timely pay all other internal revenue taxes for which I become liable during the term of this agreement.

I further understand and agree that if I fail to meet any of the conditions stated herein, or if it is determined that collection of the tax is in jeopardy, the privilege of making installment payments may be withdrawn and the entire amount of my tax liability collected by levy on my income or by seizure of my property without further notification to me.

DATE	SIGNATURE OF TAXPAYER	
6-30-61	Jack Ruby	
ACCOUNT ASSIGNED TO	AGREEMENT EXAMINED AND APPROVED (*Signature*)	DATE APPROVED
	[signature]	6/30/61

★ U. S. GOVERNMENT PRINTING OFFICE : 1960 O - 536582 FORM 433-D (REV. 1-60)

FORM 433-D (REV. JAN. 1960)

U. S. TREASURY DEPARTMENT - INTERNAL REVENUE SERVICE

MONTHLY INCOME AND EXPENSE ANALYSIS

TAXPAYER'S NAME AND ADDRESS

Jack Ruby
4727 Homer Dallas, Texas

INCOME		PERSONAL EXPENSES	
Take home pay (Husband)	$ None	Rent	$ ~~160.00~~ 140.00 Mo
Take home pay (Wife)	None	~~Groceries~~ EATING OUT JR	~~160.00~~ Mo 140.00
Contributions from others	None	Encumbrances (from Form 433-C) JR	
Net income from business	500.00 mo. Approx	Utilities	None
Other (specify)	None	Auto expenses	
I am not drawing any income from any source, other than Club Vegas. JR. 6/30/61		Other (specify) Clothing	About 20.00
		Laundry & Dry Cleaning	" 30.00
		Barber, Manicure, Tips etc	" 16.00
TOTAL	$ 500.00	JR TOTAL	$ ~~386.00~~ 346.0

NET DIFFERENCE (Income minus personal expenses)

FORM 433-D (REV. 1-60)

COMMISSION EXHIBIT No. 1722—Continued

PAYMENT AGREEMENT

I, the undersigned, declare that because of my present financial condition, as evidenced by my financial statement which has been submitted, I am unable at this time to pay the internal revenue taxes outstanding against me in the amount shown below, together with interest at 6% per year. I, therefore, request the privilege of paying such taxes as follows:

AMOUNT OF TAXES OWED *(Plus interest at 6% per year)* $ 39,190.41

$ 63.00 to be paid on 5-20-63 and $ 63.00 to be paid on 20th of each Month thereafter until the liability is paid in full.

I agree that I will increase my payments in amounts equal to any installment payments which are liquidated during the term of this agreement and that I will timely pay all other internal revenue taxes for which I become liable during the term of this agreement.

I further understand and agree that if I fail to meet any of the conditions stated herein, or if it is determined that collection of the tax is in jeopardy, the privilege of making installment payments may be withdrawn and the entire amount of my tax liability collected by levy on my income or by seizure of my property without further notification to me.

DATE	SIGNATURE OF TAXPAYER	
4-22-63	Jack Ruby	
ACCOUNT ASSIGNED TO	**AGREEMENT EXAMINED AND APPROVED (Signature)**	**DATE APPROVED**
Kleiner	Dan D. Kleiner	4-22-63

U. S. GOVERNMENT PRINTING OFFICE : 1961 O - 108397 - B

FORM 433-D (REV. 1-60)

FORM 433-D (REV. JAN. 1960)

U. S. TREASURY DEPARTMENT - INTERNAL REVENUE SERVICE

MONTHLY INCOME AND EXPENSE ANALYSIS

TAXPAYER'S NAME AND ADDRESS

INCOME		PERSONAL EXPENSES	
Take home pay (Husband)	$ 537.50	Rent	$ 125.00
Take home pay (Wife)	—	Groceries	107.50
Contributions from others	—	Encumbrances (from Form 433-C)	76.00
Net income from business	—	Utilities	—
Other (specify)	—	Auto expenses	60.00
		Other (specify) Ldry & Clothes	50.00
		Parking	20.00
		YMCA Dues	6.00
		Insurance	10.00
		Maid	20.00
TOTAL	$ 537.50	TOTAL	$ 474.50
NET DIFFERENCE (Income minus personal expenses)			63.00

FORM 433-D (REV. 1-60)

COMMISSION EXHIBIT No. 1722—Continued

PAYMENT AGREEMENT

I, the undersigned, declare that because of my present financial condition, as evidenced by my financial statement which has been submitted, I am unable at this time to pay the internal revenue taxes outstanding against me in the amount shown below, together with interest at 6% per year. I, therefore, request the privilege of paying such taxes as follows:

AMOUNT OF TAXES OWED (Plus interest at 6% per year) $3,325.09 + Int. & Lien Costs $ 200.00 to be paid on the 1ST WEEK OF OCTOBER and $ ____ to be paid on 1958 and 200.00 each month following of each ____ thereafter until the liability is paid in full. until Tax and interest fully paid.

I agree that I will increase my payments in amounts equal to any installment payments which are liquidated during the term of this agreement and that I will timely pay all other internal revenue taxes for which I become liable during the term of this agreement.

I further understand and agree that if I fail to meet any of the conditions stated herein, or if it is determined that collection of the tax is in jeopardy, the privilege of making installment payments may be withdrawn and the entire amount of my tax liability collected by levy on my income or by seizure of my property without further notification to me.

DATE	SIGNATURE OF TAXPAYER	
8-28-58	Jack Ruby	
ACCOUNT ASSIGNED TO	AGREEMENT EXAMINED AND APPROVED (Signature)	DATE APPROVED
R E Davis	[illegible signature]	

FORM 433-D (11-56)

U. S. GOVERNMENT PRINTING OFFICE : 1957 O - 106088

COMMISSION EXHIBIT No. 1723

U.S. TREASURY DEPARTMENT
INTERNAL REVENUE SERVICE

TAXPAYER DELINQUENT ACCOUNT OCT 3 1957 L

	DATE	DEBIT	CREDIT	UNPAID BALANCE
PEN		2,047.08	2 JUN 24 1959	2,047.08

P JACK RUBY
1619½ S ERVAY
DALLAS TEXAS

55 6 75901 EXC 19
52 MAR ORIG 52 5 5328
100% PEN

Date of First Notice 6 23 55

Date of Second Notice

EXC

Interest

Lien Fees and Other Charges

RECEIVED 75 OCT 2 1959 DIST. DIR. DEL ACCTS. & ... DALLAS

Date Notice of Lien Filed

ACCOUNT NUMBER AND REMARKS

The taxpayer named above is liable for the Internal Revenue tax assessed against him in the amount set forth together with all additions provided by law, and neglects or refuses to pay the same after demand. The total amount due constitutes a lien in favor of the United States upon all property and rights to property belonging to this taxpayer. The law further provides for seizure and sale of any property or rights to property of the taxpayer liable as aforesaid, or for levy upon his salary, wages, or other income to satisfy payment of the account shown.

B. Davis 3/21/58

DATE	NATURE OF REMITTANCE, ETC.	PAYMENT	TDA BALANCE	INTEREST
10-2-58	Cash	126.88	1920.20	402.25
11-3-58	Cash	200.00	1720.20	10.24
12-3-58	Cash	200.00	1520.20	8.60
1-5-59	Cash	200.00	1320.20	8.36
2-5-59	✓	200.00	1120.20	6.82
2-24-59	✓	200.00	920.20	3.55

TY ITEM 69 - PART 2 (12-54)

TDA PAYMENT CONTINUATION SHEET

NAME JACK RUBY
1619½ S. ERVAY, DALLAS, TEXAS

ACCOUNT NO. 55 6 75901

DATE	NATURE OF REMITTANCE	PAYMENT	TDA BALANCE	INTEREST
	Brought Forward		920.20	439.82
4-7-59	Cash	200.00	720.20	6.44
5-5-59	Cash	200.00	520.20	3.36
6-3-59	Cash	200.00	320.20	2.51
7-6	✓	200.00	120.20	1.76
8-7-59	Cash	200.00	— 0 —	.64
			TOTAL →	454.53
	Amt. of 8-7-59 pmt. applied to Interest			79.80
				374.73
8-31-59	Cash	200.00	Int. bal. →	174.73
10-1-59	Cash	174.73		— 0 —

U.S. TREASURY DEPARTMENT - INTERNAL REVENUE SERVICE

RC-DAL FORM 425 (11-57)

COMMISSION EXHIBIT No. 1723—Continued

PAYMENT AGREEMENT

I, the undersigned, declare that because of my present financial condition, as evidenced by my financial statement which has been submitted, I am unable at this time to pay the internal revenue taxes outstanding against me in the amount shown below, together with interest at 6% per year. I, therefore, request the privilege of paying such taxes as follows:

1st ¼ 60 WH

AMOUNT OF TAXES OWED (Plus interest at 6% per year)

$ 684.64 — $ 300.00 to be paid on 11-1-60, and $ 200.00 to be paid on 12-15-60 and Balance by January 1, 1960. These payments are in addition to my regular pmts on other agreement. of each ______ thereafter until the liability is paid in full.

I agree that I will increase my payments in amounts equal to any installment payments which are liquidated during the term of this agreement and that I will timely pay all other internal revenue taxes for which I become liable during the term of this agreement.

I further understand and agree that if I fail to meet any of the conditions stated herein, or if it is determined that collection of the tax is in jeopardy, the privilege of making installment payments may be withdrawn and the entire amount of my tax liability collected by levy on my income or by seizure of my property without further notification to me.

3rd ¼ 60 WH has been fully paid R.

DATE	SIGNATURE OF TAXPAYER	
9-9-60	Jack Ruby	
ACCOUNT ASSIGNED TO	AGREEMENT EXAMINED AND APPROVED (Signature)	DATE APPROVED
REO	R. E. Davis OK [illegible]	9-9-60

U. S. GOVERNMENT PRINTING OFFICE: 1958 O-485557 — FORM 433-D (11-55)

COMMISSION EXHIBIT No. 1724

~~8 25 60~~

L-31 DATE | L-30 DATE | 2264 DATE | F.F. REQ. DATE | U | L | L | U | BATCH DESIGNATION

JACK RUBY DBA
THE CLUB VEGAS
3508 OAK LAWN
DALLAS TEX

ACCOUNT NUMBER: 60 6 165863

PAYROLL DEDUCTION | PART PMT. AGREEMENT

NOTICE OF LIEN — DATE FILED 9-15-60 — CHARGES 7.00

3 . 5 5 60

RECEIVED
DEC 23 1960
DIST. DIR. INT. REV.
DALLAS
OCF #3

Class of Tax	Period	Mo.	Day	Yr.		Debits		Form 23-C Mo.	Day	Yr.	1st Notice Date Mo.	Day	Yr.
WH	1ST ¼ 60					676 98		7	8	60	7	8	60
					IN	7 66							

UNPAID BALANCE 684 64 — ISSUED TO R. E. Davis — DATE 8/26/60
ACCRUED INTEREST FROM — TO 6 09
TOTAL 690 73

Date	Nature of Remittance	Payment	TDA Balance	Interest	Trfd. To
11-7-60	Cash	250.00	434.64	13.54	
11-29-60	Cash	50.00	384.64	1.57	
12-9-60	Cash	150.00	234.64	.63	
12-22-60	Cash	251.88	— 0 —	.50	
				16.24	Lien
				1.00	
				— 0 —	

U. S. TREASURY DEPARTMENT—INTERNAL REVENUE SERVICE
IRS FORM 69 (REV. 10-58) PART 2 — (OVER)

TAXPAYER DELINQUENT ACCOUNT

HISTORY SHEET

DATE	ACTION TAKEN	DATE	ACTION TAKEN
9-30-60	Received by [illegible] (REO)		

COMMISSION EXHIBIT No. 1724—Continued

U.S. TREASURY DEPARTMENT
INTERNAL REVENUE SERVICE

TAXPAYER DELINQUENT ACCOUNT OCT 3 1957

P JACK RUBY
1619½ S ERVAY
DALLAS TEXAS

55 6 75902 EXC 19
52 APR ORIG 52 6 5764
100% PEN

	DATE	DEBITS	CREDITS	UNPAID BALANCE
PEN		1,278.61	2 JUN 24 1955	1,278.61

Date of First Notice

6 23 55
Date of Second Notice

Interest accrued

Lien Fees and Other Charges

EXC

TOTAL

ACCOUNT NUMBER AND REMARKS 4-17-58 mcc

RECEIVED JUL 12 1960

RECEIVED OCT 3 1960

Date Notice of Lien Filed July 13 1955

The taxpayer named above is liable for the Internal Revenue tax assessed against him in the amount set forth together with additions provided by law, and neglects or refuses to pay the same after demand. The total amount due constitutes a lien in fa[vor] of the United States upon all property and rights to property belonging to this taxpayer. The law further provides for sei[zure] and sale of any property or rights to property of the taxpayer liable as aforesaid, or for levy upon his salary, wages, or other inc[ome] to satisfy payment of the account shown.

R Davis 5/21/58

DATE	NATURE OF REMITTANCE, ETC.	PAYMENT	TDA BALANCE	INTEREST
10-1-59	Cash	25.27	1,252.74	327.60
12-2-59	Cash	200.00	1,052.74	12.74
12-8-59	Cash	200.00	852.74	1.03
1-5-60	✓	200.00	652.74	3.92
2-3-60	Cash	200.00	452.74	3.11
3-3-60	Cash	200.00	252.74	2.27

TY ITEM 69 - PART 2 (12-54) over

COMMISSION EXHIBIT No. 1725

TDA PAYMENT CONTINUATION SHEET

NAME Jack Ruby
1619½ S. Ervay
Dallas, Texas

ACCOUNT NO. 55 6 75902

DATE	NATURE OF REMITTANCE	PAYMENT	TDA BALANCE	INTEREST
	BROUGHT FORWARD		252.74	350.6
4-5-60	Cash	61.26	191.48	1.3
5/6	Cash Tax 191.48 Int 8.52	200.00	-0-	.9
				353.0 / 8.5
		Interest	Balance	344.4
6/2/60	Cash (credited to tax)	200.00	200.00 CB	
7-8-60	Cash Int Only	144.48	200.00 CB	
9-19-60	D/A (9-30) int	200.00		

U.S. TREASURY DEPARTMENT - INTERNAL REVENUE SERVICE RC-DAL FORM 425 (11-5[?])

COMMISSION EXHIBIT No. 1725—Continued

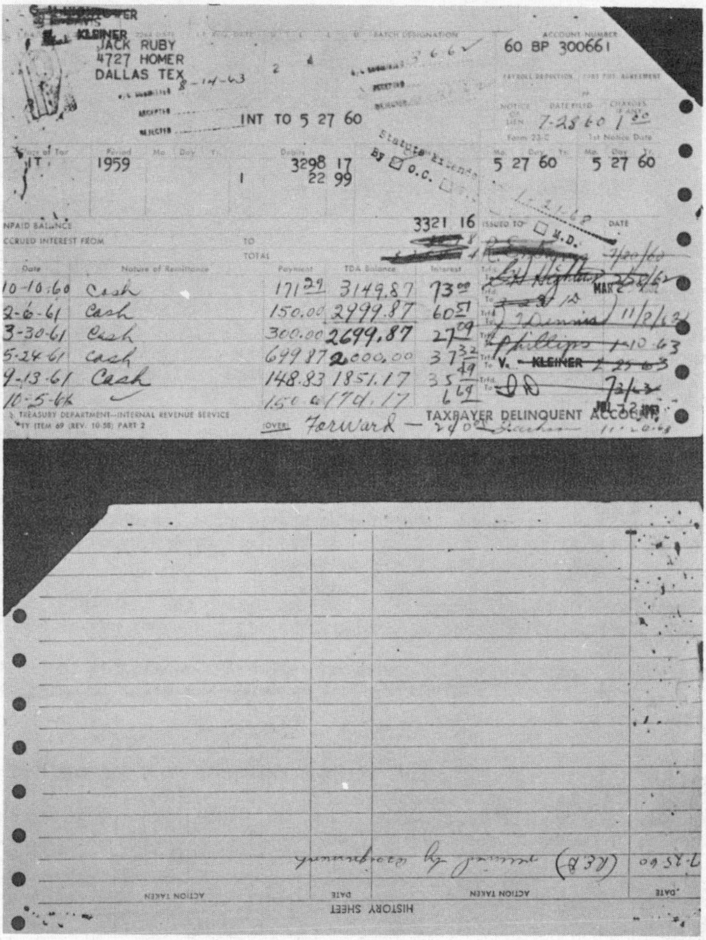

JACK RUBY
4727 HOMER
DALLAS TEX 8-14-63

ACCOUNT NUMBER: 60 BP 300661

INT TO 5 27 60

Notice date: 7-28-60

Kind of Tax	Period	Debits		
IT	1959	3298 17 / 22 99	5 27 60	5 27 60

UNPAID BALANCE 3321 16

ACCRUED INTEREST FROM / TO / TOTAL

Date	Nature of Remittance	Payment	TDA Balance	Interest
10-10-60	Cash	171.29	3149.87	73.00
2-6-61	Cash	150.00	2999.87	60.51
3-30-61	Cash	300.00	2699.87	27.09
5-24-61	Cash	699.87	2000.00	37.32
9-13-61	Cash	148.83	1851.17	35.49
10-5-61		150.00	1701.17	6.69

U.S. TREASURY DEPARTMENT—INTERNAL REVENUE SERVICE

(OVER) Forward

TAXPAYER DELINQUENT ACCOUNT

V. KLEINER

HISTORY SHEET

DATE | ACTION TAKEN | DATE | ACTION TAKEN

7-25-60 (RER) issued by assignment

Commission Exhibit No. 1726

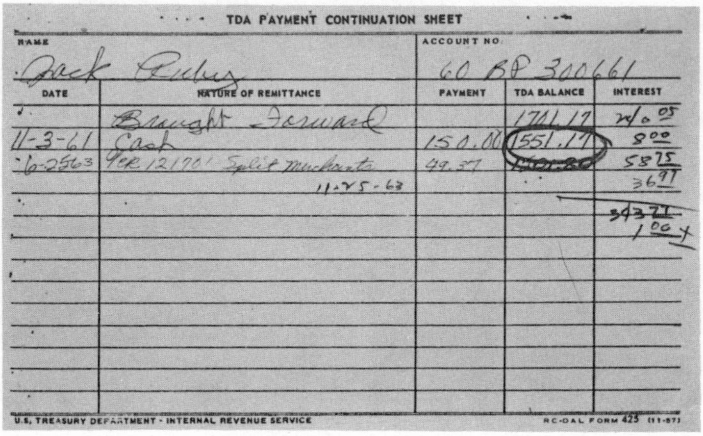

TDA PAYMENT CONTINUATION SHEET

NAME		ACCOUNT NO.		
Jack Ruby		60 BP 300661		
DATE	NATURE OF REMITTANCE	PAYMENT	TDA BALANCE	INTEREST
	Brought Forward		1701.17	240.05
11-3-61	Cash	150.00	1551.17	8.00
6-25-63	Per 12170' Split Merchants 11-25-63	49.37		58.75
				36.97
				343.77
				1.00 +

U.S. TREASURY DEPARTMENT - INTERNAL REVENUE SERVICE — RC-DAL FORM 425 (11-57)

Commission Exhibit No. 1726—Continued

S. M. Orenbaun
Group Supervisor

March 13, 1962

G. H. Hightower
Revenue Officer

Jack Ruby - Offer in Compromise

Taxpayer is offering the sum of $1,500.00 in installments to compromise his 1959 and 1960 Income Tax totaling $3,797.68 plus interest and the sum of $6,500.00 in installments to compromise excise taxes 1st qt. '56 thru 2 q '59 totaling $16,879.05 plus interest. Collateral Agreement is a part of the offers.

As evidenced by 433, taxpayer does not have assets to sell, or on which to borrow to pay the total taxes due.

Taxpayer states that the excise taxes were not collected from his customers and paid to Internal Revenue on advice from his attorney based on rulings on similar clubs that sales of food and beverages were incidental to dancing and not subject to excise tax.

In spite of the above, taxpayer is not contesting the liability, but is submitting his offer based on inability to pay the total amount due.

Taxpayer is current with his excise and withholding taxes at the present time with the exception of the account on which his offer is being made.

He has agreed to purchase depository receipts when required, and file quarterly returns with cashier's check in full payment with me as evidence of his intention to remain current from this date forward.

Taxpayer will also bring his 1961 Income Tax return to me with payment in full, and also file and pay 1040 ES for 1962.

In view of the above, and the fact that taxpayer is without funds to pay the assessments in full, I recommend that his offers in Compromise be accepted.

G. H. Hightower
G. H. Hightower
Revenue Officer

APPROVED:

S M Orenbaum
S. M. Orenbaum

COMMISSION EXHIBIT NO. 1727

Form 1271
U. S. TREASURY DEPARTMENT
Internal Revenue Service
(Rev. Nov. 1953)

REJECTION OR WITHDRAWAL MEMORANDUM

INTERNAL REVENUE SERVICE

In re: Offer to compromise liability of:

Jack Ruby
3508 Oak Lawn
Dallas, Texas

61-IT-41
Case No. 1 Date 10-16-62
Symbols
Office District Director
City
District Dallas

Liability as follows:

YEAR	DATE ASSESSED	TAX	INTEREST ASSESSED	PENALTY	TOTAL
1959	5-27-60	$1,528.18	$22.99		$1,551.17
1960	6-23-61	2,100.05	25.12		2,125.17
	Totals	$3,628.23	$48.11		$3,676.34

Kind of tax Income
Amount of offer $1,500.00
Number of pending offers 2
Date notice of lien filed 10-20-61

Recommend offer be rejected
Glen W. Stennett
C. M. DeLay, Reviewer 10-31-62
Recommendation approved for reasons stated hereinafter:
Ellis Campbell, Jr.
(District Director of Internal Revenue)

I. SUMMARY

U. S. GOVERNMENT PRINTING OFFICE : 1955 O - 362478 49-AF

COMMISSION EXHIBIT No. 1727—Continued

Form 1271
U. S. TREASURY DEPARTMENT
INTERNAL REVENUE SERVICE
(Rev. Nov. 1953)

REJECTION OR WITHDRAWAL MEMORANDUM

INTERNAL REVENUE SERVICE

61-ET-104

In re: Offer to compromise liability of:
Jack Ruby
3508 Oak Lawn
Dallas, Texas

Case No. 1 **Date** 10-16-62
Symbols
Office District Director
City
District Dallas

Liability as follows:

YEAR	DATE ASSESSED	TAX	INTEREST ASSESSED	PENALTY	TOTAL
1¼ 1956	thru				
2¼ 1959	11-20-59	$15,464.85	$1,414.20		$16,879.05
	TOTALS				$16,879.05

Kind of tax Excise, Babaret
Amount of offer $6,500.00
Number of pending offers 2
Date notice of lien filed 1-12-60

Recommend offer be rejected
Glen W. Harnett
C. M. DeLay Reviewer 10-31-62
Recommendation approved for reasons stated hereinafter:
Ellis Campbell, Jr.
(District Director of Internal Revenue)

I. SUMMARY

U. S. GOVERNMENT PRINTING OFFICE : 1955 O - 362478 49-AF

3

COMMISSION EXHIBIT No. 1727—Continued

Jack Ruby

I. SUMMARY

The taxpayer is seeking to compromise under the authority of Section 7122 of the Internal Revenue Code unpaid tax liability including interest of Excise, cabaret tax for the first quarter 1956 through the second quarter 1959 totaling $16,879.05 and of income tax for 1959 totaling $1,551.17 and 1960 totaling $2,125.17 plus accrued interest. The amounts offered are $6,500.00 on the Excise, cabaret tax liability and $1,500.00 on the income tax liability with $400.00 paid with the offer on Excise tax liability and the balance payable $300.00 quarterly beginning April 1, 1962; and with $100.00 paid on the income tax offer and the balance payable $50.00 quarterly for four quarters beginning April 1, 1962 with subsequent quarterly payments of $75.00 each, together with 6% interest, waiver of refunds, default agreement and other provisions on Form 656 (Rev. 7-57). In addition the taxpayer agrees to additional payments of 20%, 30% and 50% respectively of annual income in excess of $5,000.00, $7,500.00 and $10,000.00 for the years of 1961 to 1970.

The offers are recommended for rejection for the reason that as the offers are on the basis of doubt as to collectibility, and it is found that the taxpayer will have considerable liability in addition to the liability sought to be compromised for Excise, cabaret tax liability for the periods of third quarter 1959 through third quarter 1961 which the taxpayer would also be unable to pay.

II. FACTS AS TO LIABILITY

The income tax liability is the tax liability according to the return of the taxpayer as filed. Although the taxpayer agreed to the additional Excise, cabaret tax liability, he had the view that his business was a dance-hall and that sales were not taxable for cabaret. He says that he did not file returns for later periods in view of pending litigation on that issue until recent court decisions that for sales of a substantial portion of receipts of dance-halls are taxable for cabaret tax.

III. FACTS AS TO COLLECTIBILITY

Jack Ruby is 50 years of age and single. In view of the rejection of the offers, information is not included regarding the taxpayer's financial condition.

IV. CONCLUSION

The offers are recommended for rejection because of additional Excise, cabaret tax liabilities for which there will also be doubt as to collectibility

4

COMMISSION EXHIBIT No. 1727—Continued

TRANSFER TDA TO:

Dallas- R/O Dennis — Type A Office
(City)

Dallas, Texas — District
(City and State)

☐ Director, Office of International Operations
Washington 25, D. C.

NAME OF TAXPAYER: Jack Ruby

CURRENT ADDRESS: ~~3508 Oak Lawn~~
Dallas, Texas

TRANSFER IS: (Check one)

☒ District Office TDA
☐ ADP-TDA, Out of Region
☐ ADP-TDA, Inter District - In Region
☐ ADP-TDA, Intra District

REFERENCE NUMBER AND CLASS OF TAX

61 OP 401231 IT $2,125.17
59 A 11 545077 Exc $16,879.05
60 BP 300661 IT 1,551.17

☐ Transferee office requests transfer. Request attached.

☐ District Directors agree to transfer. Explain under remarks.

☐ Completed courtesy investigation. Transfer accepted. Form 2209 attached.

☐ Completed courtesy investigation indicates taxpayer within transferee office area. Insufficient information furnished to permit disposition of account.

☐ Foreign, APO or FPO address (To International Operations only.)

☐ No reply to courtesy investigation. Copy of Form 2209 attached.

RECEIVED
NOV 9 1962
DIST. DIR. INT. REV.
DALLAS
OCF #13

REMARKS

Offer in Compromise rejected. Form 1271 and c/c of rejection letter attached.

ORIGINATING TYPE A OFFICE	REVENUE OFFICER'S SIGNATURE	GROUP SUPERVISOR'S SIGNATURE	DATE
Dallas OCF	Eva Lane, Inactive Accts		11 8 62

U. S. TREASURY DEPARTMENT - INTERNAL REVENUE SERVICE — TDA TRANSFER — FORM 2650 (REV. 12-61)

COMMISSION EXHIBIT No. 1727—Continued

Eva Love

OCT 31 1962

A:R

Mr. Jack Ruby
3508 Oak Lawn
Dallas, Texas

Dear Mr. Ruby:

I have carefully considered the offer of $1,500 submitted to compromise your income tax liability for the years 1959 and 1960.

Your offer is hereby rejected for the reason that the tax is legally due, and you have not been filing returns for other Federal taxes and paying these taxes as they became due.

Please take up with us the matter of payment of the liability.

Sincerely yours,

(Signed) Ellis Campbell, Jr.

Ellis Campbell, Jr.
District Director

250.00 paid on Offer
~~100~~

6

COMMISSION EXHIBIT No. 1727—Continued

OCT 31 1962 A&R

Mr. Jack Ruby
3508 Oak Lawn
Dallas, Texas

Dear Mr. Ruby:

I have carefully considered the offer of $6,500 submitted to compromise your liability for excise (Cabaret) taxes for the first quarter of 1956 through the second quarter of 1959.

Your offer is hereby rejected for the reason that the tax is legally due, and you have not been filing returns for other Federal taxes and paying these taxes as they became due.

Please take up with us the matter of payment of the liability.

Sincerely yours,

(Signed) Ellis Campbell, Jr.

Ellis Campbell, Jr.
District Director

$1000 paid on Offer

7

COMMISSION EXHIBIT No. 1727—Continued

OPTIONAL FORM NO. 10
MAY 1952 EDITION
GSA GEN. REG. NO. 27
5010-106

Commission Exhibit No. 1728

UNITED STATES GOVERNMENT

Memorandum

TO : Chief, DAR Branch, Dallas District DATE: November 26, 1963

Through: S. M. Orenbaun, Group Supervisor

FROM : Harliss C. Jackson, Revenue Officer
Group #1, Dallas, Texas

SUBJECT: Jack Ruby - Sensitive Case Report

Pursuant to RC-DAL Memorandum No. 12-19, CR 51-10, Rev. 4-7-60, the attached Sensitive Case Report is being submitted.

Harliss C. Jackson
Harliss C. Jackson
Revenue Officer

HCJ:ns
attachment

Approved:
SM Orenbaun (GS)

COMMISSION EXHIBIT NO. 1728

SENSITIVE CASE REPORT

November 27, 1963

Initial Report

1. Identification
Jack Ruby
3929 Rawlins Street
Dallas, Texas
Night Club Operator

2. Principal Issue, Kind of Tax, and Period Involved
Income Tax - $3,626.97; Excise Tax - $35,440.87
Income Tax due for 1959 and 1960
Excise Tax due for 1st ¼ 56 through 2nd ¼ 59 Addl. and
9-1-59 through 6-30-62

The issue involved regarding the Income Tax, Mr. Ruby had not filed a 1040 ES and paid quarterly and did not pay the amount due when filing the Income Tax Returns for the years involved. With respect to the Excise Tax, Mr. Ruby and his lawyer contended that they were of the belief that he was not liable for the Cabaret Tax based on a case then in the Federal Courts which was later decided in favor of the Federal Government.

The taxpayer has had a long history of tax delinquencies dating back to 1958. This office has been in continuous contact with the taxpayer in an effort to get taxpayer on a current basis, and the recently submitted Offer in Compromise was a final effort to get taxpayer on a current basis and prevent further tax delinquencies.

During the period from 1958 to the present date, liabilities were incurred on quarterly withholding returns and on personal income tax returns. Efforts to get the taxpayer on a current basis by use of depositary receipts on the quarterly returns, and by 1040 ES on the income tax liabilities have not been successful in that the taxpayer was using current income to pay on past delinquencies and was never able to get current.

The excise tax liability arose from misinterpretation of tax laws. It was the opinion of the taxpayer and his tax advisors that the business was primarily a dance-hall and that sales were not taxable as a cabaret. Taxpayer further contends that the reason he did not file returns for later periods following the initial assessment was due to pending litigation of this particular issue. Litigation was later decided in favor of the Government, and the additional excise tax against the taxpayer resulted.

An Offer in Compromise is pending wherein taxpayer offers $3,000.00 with which to compromise the entire assessment, which funds are to be borrowed from a friend.

2

COMMISSION EXHIBIT No. 1728—Continued

Sensitive Case Report - 2 - November 27, 1963

3. Reasons for Sensitivity
Jack Ruby is alleged to have shot and killed one Lee Harvey Oswald on Sunday, November 24, 1963. Lee Harvey Oswald is alleged to have shot and killed United States President John F. Kennedy.

4. Action Planned or Taken
Recent revelations of money found on the taxpayer's person and in his apartment as a result of his arrest, necessitates an investigation to determine the source and ownership of the monies.

The Revenue Officer has been alerted to reactivate his investigation on the case and to make a determination as to the source of the monies confiscated and to determine the taxpayer's claim to such monies.

If a determination is made that the money is the property of the taxpayer, we will request rejection of the Offer in Compromise and take immediate levy action to protect the interests of the Government.

Completion date is undeterminable inasmuch as Mr. Ruby is in custody of law enforcement authorities.

Other Divisions involved are Audit and Intelligence.

COMMISSION EXHIBIT No. 1728—Continued

SENSITIVE CASE REPORT

December 6, 1963

First Periodic Monthly Report

1. Identification
Jack Ruby
3929 Rawlins Street (now in Dallas County Jail, Dallas, Texas)
Dallas, Texas

2. Action Taken
None, other than outlined in initial report, dated 11/26/63.

3. Contemplated Actions
None, other than outlined in initial report, dated 11/26/63.

COMMISSION EXHIBIT No. 1728—Continued

Commission Exhibit No. 1729

FORM 668-A
(REV. JANUARY 1962)

U. S. TREASURY DEPARTMENT — INTERNAL REVENUE SERVICE

NOTICE OF LEVY

TO: Sheriff's Dept.,
Dallas County, Texas
Attn; Sheriff Decker

DATE 11-26-63

You are hereby notified that there is now due, owing, and unpaid from (Name and Address of Taxpayer)

Jack Ruby, 3929 Rawlins St., Dallas, Texas

to the United States of America the sum of

Forty-four thousand four hundred thirteen and 86/100 Dollars $ 44,413.86

CLASS OF TAX AND PERIOD	DATE OF ASSESSMENT	REFERENCE NO.	UNPAID BALANCE	STATUTORY ADDITIONS	TOTAL
Income 1959	5-27-60	60 BP 300661	$ 1,501.80	$ 344.77	$ 1,846.57
Income 1960	6-23-61	61 OP 401231	2,125.17	436.97	2,562.14
Excise; 1st ½ '56 thru 2nd ½ '59 Additional.	11-20-59	(EXC 59 A 11 545077	16,879.05	3,725.24	20,604.29
Excise; 9-1-59 thru 6-30-62	1-18-63	(EXC 63 A 1 547000	18,561.82	839.04	19,400.86
				TOTAL AMOUNT DUE	$ 44,413.86

You are further notified that demand has been made upon the taxpayer for the amount set forth herein, and that such amount is still due, owing, and unpaid from this taxpayer, and that the lien provided for by Section 6321, Internal Revenue Code of 1954, now exists upon all property or rights to property belonging to the aforesaid taxpayer. Accordingly, you are further notified that all property, rights to property, moneys, credits, and bank deposits now in your possession and belonging to this taxpayer (or with respect to which you are obligated) and all sums of money or other obligations owing from you to this taxpayer are hereby levied upon and seized for satisfaction of the aforesaid tax, together with all additions provided by law, and demand is hereby made upon you for the amount necessary to satisfy the liability set forth herein, or for such lesser sum as you may be indebted to him, to be applied as a payment on his tax liability.

DISTRICT DIRECTOR OF INTERNAL REVENUE	BY (Signature)	TITLE
Ellis Campbell, Jr.	Harlin C. Jackson	Revenue Officer

CERTIFICATE OF SERVICE

I hereby certify that this levy was served by delivering a copy of this notice of levy to the person named at the right hereof.	NAME	TITLE
	DATE AND TIME	SIGNATURE OF REVENUE OFFICER

U. S. GOVERNMENT PRINTING OFFICE: 1962—626262 Part 1 - To be returned to Internal Revenue Service FORM 668-A (REV. 1-62)

Commission Exhibit No. 1730

FORM 668-A
(REV. JANUARY 1962)

U. S. TREASURY DEPARTMENT — INTERNAL REVENUE SERVICE

NOTICE OF LEVY

TO: City of Dallas
Dallas, Texas
Attn; Chief Curry

DATE 11-26-63

You are hereby notified that there is now due, owing, and unpaid from (Name and Address of Taxpayer)

Jack Ruby, 3929 Rawlins St., Dallas, Texas

to the United States of America the sum of

Forty-four thousand four hundred thirteen and 86/100 Dollars $ 44,413.86

CLASS OF TAX AND PERIOD	DATE OF ASSESSMENT	REFERENCE NO.	UNPAID BALANCE	STATUTORY ADDITIONS	TOTAL
Income 1959	5/27/60	60 BP 300661	$ 1,501.80	$ 344.77	$ 1,846.57
Income 1960	6/23/61	61 OP 401231	2,125.17	436.97	2,562.14
Excise; 1st ½ '56 thru 2nd ½ '59 Add'l	11/20/59	(EXC 59 A 11 545077	16,879.05	3,725.24	20,604.29
Excise; 9-1-59 thru 6-30-62	1-18-63	63 A 1 547000	18,561.82	839.04	19,400.86
				TOTAL AMOUNT DUE	$ 44,413.86

You are further notified that demand has been made upon the taxpayer for the amount set forth herein, and that such amount is still due, owing, and unpaid from this taxpayer, and that the lien provided for by Section 6321, Internal Revenue Code of 1954, now exists upon all property or rights to property belonging to the aforesaid taxpayer. Accordingly, you are further notified that all property, rights to property, moneys, credits, and bank deposits now in your possession and belonging to this taxpayer (or with respect to which you are obligated) and all sums of money or other obligations owing from you to this taxpayer are hereby levied upon and seized for satisfaction of the aforesaid tax, together with all additions provided by law, and demand is hereby made upon you for the amount necessary to satisfy the liability set forth herein, or for such lesser sum as you may be indebted to him, to be applied as a payment on his tax liability.

DISTRICT DIRECTOR OF INTERNAL REVENUE	BY (Signature)	TITLE
Ellis Campbell, Jr.	Harlin C. Jackson	Revenue Officer

CERTIFICATE OF SERVICE

I hereby certify that this levy was served by delivering a copy of this notice of levy to the person named at the right hereof.	NAME	TITLE
	DATE AND TIME	SIGNATURE OF REVENUE OFFICER

U. S. GOVERNMENT PRINTING OFFICE: 1962—626262 Part 1 - To be returned to Internal Revenue Service FORM 668-A (REV. 1-62)

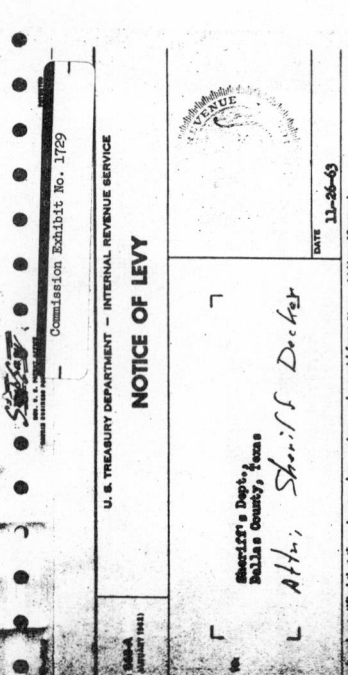

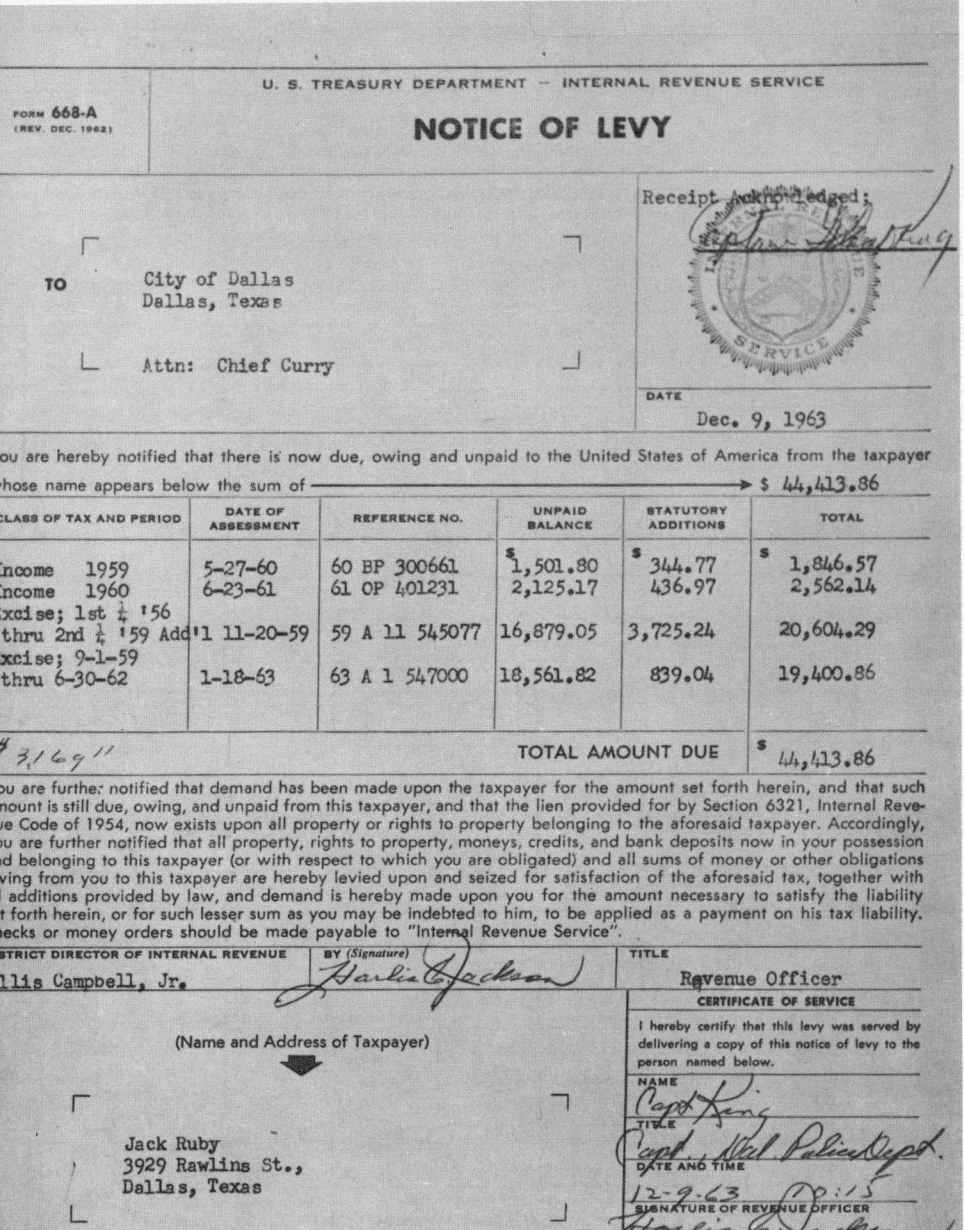

FORM 668-A (REV. DEC. 1962)

U. S. TREASURY DEPARTMENT — INTERNAL REVENUE SERVICE

NOTICE OF LEVY

TO City of Dallas
Dallas, Texas

Attn: Chief Curry

Receipt Acknowledged;
Captain Will Fritz King

DATE Dec. 9, 1963

You are hereby notified that there is now due, owing and unpaid to the United States of America from the taxpayer whose name appears below the sum of → $ 44,413.86

CLASS OF TAX AND PERIOD	DATE OF ASSESSMENT	REFERENCE NO.	UNPAID BALANCE	STATUTORY ADDITIONS	TOTAL
Income 1959	5-27-60	60 BP 300661	$ 1,501.80	$ 344.77	$ 1,846.57
Income 1960	6-23-61	61 OP 401231	2,125.17	436.97	2,562.14
Excise; 1st ¼ '56 thru 2nd ¼ '59 Add'l	11-20-59	59 A 11 545077	16,879.05	3,725.24	20,604.29
Excise; 9-1-59 thru 6-30-62	1-18-63	63 A 1 547000	18,561.82	839.04	19,400.86
#3169"				TOTAL AMOUNT DUE	$ 44,413.86

You are further notified that demand has been made upon the taxpayer for the amount set forth herein, and that such amount is still due, owing, and unpaid from this taxpayer, and that the lien provided for by Section 6321, Internal Revenue Code of 1954, now exists upon all property or rights to property belonging to the aforesaid taxpayer. Accordingly, you are further notified that all property, rights to property, moneys, credits, and bank deposits now in your possession and belonging to this taxpayer (or with respect to which you are obligated) and all sums of money or other obligations owing from you to this taxpayer are hereby levied upon and seized for satisfaction of the aforesaid tax, together with all additions provided by law, and demand is hereby made upon you for the amount necessary to satisfy the liability set forth herein, or for such lesser sum as you may be indebted to him, to be applied as a payment on his tax liability. Checks or money orders should be made payable to "Internal Revenue Service".

DISTRICT DIRECTOR OF INTERNAL REVENUE	BY (Signature)	TITLE
Ellis Campbell, Jr.	Harlie C. Jackson	Revenue Officer

(Name and Address of Taxpayer)

Jack Ruby
3929 Rawlins St.,
Dallas, Texas

CERTIFICATE OF SERVICE

I hereby certify that this levy was served by delivering a copy of this notice of levy to the person named below.

NAME Capt King

TITLE Capt., Dal. Police Dept.

DATE AND TIME 12-9-63 10:15

SIGNATURE OF REVENUE OFFICER Harlie C. Jackson

FORM 668-A (REV. 12-62)

PART 1 — TO BE RETURNED TO INTERNAL REVENUE SERVICE

COMMISSION EXHIBIT No. 1731

Form 668 (REV. MAY 1958)

U. S. TREASURY DEPARTMENT - INTERNAL REVENUE SERVICE

NOTICE OF FEDERAL TAX LIEN UNDER INTERNAL REVENUE LAWS

DISTRICT: Dallas, Texas

NO.: B-3665

Pursuant to the provisions of Sections 6321, 6322, and 6323 of the Internal Revenue Code of 1954, notice is hereby given that there have been assessed under the Internal Revenue laws of the United States against the following-named taxpayer, taxes (including interest and penalties) which after demand for payment thereof remain unpaid, and that by virtue of the above-mentioned statutes the amount of said taxes, together with penalties, interest, and costs that may accrue in addition thereto, is a lien in favor of the United States upon all property and rights to property belonging to said taxpayer, to wit:

NAME OF TAXPAYER: Jack Ruby

RESIDENCE OR PLACE OF BUSINESS: Club Vegas, 3508 Oak Lawn, Dallas, Texas

NATURE OF TAX	ACCOUNT NO.	YEAR OR TAXABLE PERIOD	ASSESSMENT DATE	AMOUNT OF ASSESSMENT
Excise	59 A 11 545077	1st 1/4 56 thru 2nd 1/4 59	11/20/59	$ 16,879.05
			TOTAL	$ 16,879.05

WITNESS my hand at Dallas, Texas, on this, the 11th day of Jan., 1960

R. C. Davis

DISTRICT DIRECTOR OF INTERNAL REVENUE	BY (Signature)	TITLE
Ellis Campbell, Jr.		Group Supervisor, #2

(NOTE: Certificate of officer authorized by law to take acknowledgments is not essential to the validity of Notice of Federal Tax Lien. G.C.M. 26419, C.B. 1950-1, 125.) Dallas Co., Dallas, Texas

COLLECTION OFFICER

COMMISSION EXHIBIT No. 1732

No. ....

UNITED STATES

vs.

NOTICE OF TAX LIEN

Filed this ______________ *day of*

______________, *19*____, *at* ____ *m.*

____
Clerk (or Registrar).

FORM 668 (REV. 5-58)

INTERNAL REVENUE CODE OF 1954

SEC. 6321. LIEN FOR TAXES.

If any person liable to pay any tax neglects or refuses to pay the same after demand, the amount (including any interest, additional amount, addition to tax, or assessable penalty, together with any costs that may accrue in addition thereto) shall be a lien in favor of the United States upon all property and rights to property, whether real or personal, belonging to such person.

SEC. 6322. PERIOD OF LIEN.

Unless another date is specifically fixed by law, the lien imposed by section 6321 shall arise at the time the assessment is made and shall continue until the liability for the amount so assessed is satisfied or becomes unenforceable by reason of lapse of time.

SEC. 6323. VALIDITY AGAINST MORTGAGEES, PLEDGEES, PURCHASERS, AND JUDGMENT CREDITORS.

(a) INVALIDITY OF LIEN WITHOUT NOTICE.—Except as otherwise provided in subsection (c), the lien imposed by section 6321 shall not be valid as against any mortgagee, pledgee, purchaser, or judgment creditor until notice thereof has been filed by the Secretary or his delegate—

(1) Under State or Territorial Laws.—In the office designated by the law of the State or Territory in which the property subject to the lien is situated, whenever the State or Territory has by law designated an office within the State or Territory for the filing of such notice; or

(2) With Clerk of District Court.—In the office of the clerk of the United States district court for the judicial district in which the property subject to the lien is situated, whenever the State or Territory has not by law designated an office within the State or Territory for the filing of such notice; or

(3) With Clerk of District Court for District of Columbia.—In the office of the clerk of the United States District Court for the District of Columbia, if the property subject to the lien is situated in the District of Columbia.

(b) FORM OF NOTICE.—If the notice filed pursuant to subsection (a)(1) is in such form as would be valid if filed with the clerk of the United States district court pursuant to subsection (a)(2), such notice shall be valid notwithstanding any law of the State or Territory regarding the form or content of a notice of lien.

(c) EXCEPTION IN CASE OF SECURITIES.—

(1) Exception.—Even though notice of a lien provided in section 6321 has been filed in the manner prescribed in subsection (a) of this section, the lien shall not be valid with respect to a security, as defined in paragraph (2) of this subsection, as against any mortgagee, pledgee, or purchaser of such security, for an adequate and full consideration in money or money's worth, if at the time of such mortgage, pledge, or purchase such mortgagee, pledgee, or purchaser is without notice or knowledge of the existence of such lien.

(2) Definition of Security.—As used in this subsection, the term "security" means any bond, debenture, note, or certificate or other evidence of indebtedness, issued by any corporation (including one issued by a government or political subdivision thereof), with interest coupons or in registered form, share of stock, voting trust certificate, or any certificate of interest or participation in, certificate of deposit or receipt for, temporary or interim certificate for, or warrant or right to subscribe to or purchase, any of the foregoing; negotiable instrument; or money.

(d) DISCLOSURE OF AMOUNT OF OUTSTANDING LIEN.—If a notice of lien has been filed under subsection (a), the Secretary or his delegate is authorized to provide by rules or regulations the extent to which, and the conditions under which, information as to the amount of the outstanding obligation secured by the lien may be disclosed.

SEC. 6325. RELEASE OF LIEN OR PARTIAL DISCHARGE OF PROPERTY.

(a) RELEASE OF LIEN.—Subject to such rules or regulations as the Secretary or his delegate may prescribe, the Secretary or his delegate may issue a certificate of release of any lien imposed with respect to any internal revenue tax if—

(1) Liability Satisfied or Unenforceable.—The Secretary or his delegate finds that the liability for the amount assessed, together with all interest in respect thereof, has been fully satisfied, has become legally unenforceable, or, in the case of the estate tax imposed by chapter 11 or the gift tax imposed by chapter 12, has been fully satisfied or provided for; or

(2) Bond Accepted.—There is furnished to the Secretary or his delegate and accepted by him a bond that is conditioned upon the payment of the amount assessed, together with all interest in respect thereof, within the time prescribed by law (including any extension of such time), and that is in accordance with such requirements relating to terms, conditions, and form of the bond and sureties thereon, as may be specified by such rules or regulations.

GPO : 1958 O - 108053

COMMISSION EXHIBIT No. 1732—Continued

Form 668
(REV. MAY 1958)

U. S. TREASURY DEPARTMENT · INTERNAL REVENUE SERVICE

NOTICE OF FEDERAL TAX LIEN UNDER INTERNAL REVENUE LAWS

DISTRICT
Dallas, Texas

NO.
H-9762

Pursuant to the provisions of Sections 6321, 6322, and 6323 of the Internal Revenue Code of 1954, notice is hereby given that there have been assessed under the Internal Revenue laws of the United States against the following-named taxpayer, taxes (including interest and penalties) which after demand for payment thereof remain unpaid, and that by virtue of the above-mentioned statutes the amount of said taxes, together with penalties, interest, and costs that may accrue in addition thereto, is a lien in favor of the United States upon all property and rights to property belonging to said taxpayer, to wit:

NAME OF TAXPAYER
Jack Ruby

RESIDENCE OR PLACE OF BUSINESS
3727 Homer, Dallas, Texas

NATURE OF TAX	ACCOUNT NO.	YEAR OR TAXABLE PERIOD	ASSESSMENT DATE	AMOUNT OF ASSESSMENT
Income	60 BP 300661	1959	5/27/60	$ 3,321.36
			TOTAL	$ 3,321.36

WITNESS my hand at Dallas, Texas, on this,

the 28th day of July, 1960

DISTRICT DIRECTOR OF INTERNAL REVENUE	BY (Signature)	TITLE
Ellis Campbell, Jr.	Oscar E. Horton	R. C. Davis Acting Group Supervisor,

(NOTE: Certificate of officer authorized by law to take acknowledgments is not essential to the validity of Notice of Federal Tax Lien. G.C.M. 26419, C.B. 1950-1, 125.) Dallas Co., Dallas, Texas

COLLECTION OFFICER'S COPY

COMMISSION EXHIBIT No. 1733

No. ____________

UNITED STATES

vs.

NOTICE OF TAX LIEN

Filed this ______________ day of

____________, 19____, at ____ m.

____

Clerk (or Registrar).

FORM 668 (REV. 5-58)

INTERNAL REVENUE CODE OF 1954

SEC. 6321. LIEN FOR TAXES.

If any person liable to pay any tax neglects or refuses to pay the same after demand, the amount (including any interest, additional amount, addition to tax, or assessable penalty, together with any costs that may accrue in addition thereto) shall be a lien in favor of the United States upon all property and rights to property, whether real or personal, belonging to such person.

SEC. 6322. PERIOD OF LIEN.

Unless another date is specifically fixed by law, the lien imposed by section 6321 shall arise at the time the assessment is made and shall continue until the liability for the amount so assessed is satisfied or becomes unenforceable by reason of lapse of time.

SEC. 6323. VALIDITY AGAINST MORTGAGEES, PLEDGEES, PURCHASERS, AND JUDGMENT CREDITORS.

(a) INVALIDITY OF LIEN WITHOUT NOTICE.—Except as otherwise provided in subsection (c), the lien imposed by section 6321 shall not be valid as against any mortgagee, pledgee, purchaser, or judgment creditor until notice thereof has been filed by the Secretary or his delegate—

(1) Under State or Territorial Laws.—In the office designated by the law of the State or Territory in which the property subject to the lien is situated, whenever the State or Territory has by law designated an office within the State or Territory for the filing of such notice; or

(2) With Clerk of District Court.—In the office of the clerk of the United States district court for the judicial district in which the property subject to the lien is situated, whenever the State or Territory has not by law designated an office within the State or Territory for the filing of such notice; or

(3) With Clerk of District Court for District of Columbia.—In the office of the clerk of the United States District Court for the District of Columbia, if the property subject to the lien is situated in the District of Columbia.

(b) FORM OF NOTICE.—If the notice filed pursuant to subsection (a)(1) is in such form as would be valid if filed with the clerk of the United States district court pursuant to subsection (a)(2), such notice shall be valid notwithstanding any law of the State or Territory regarding the form or content of a notice of lien.

(c) EXCEPTION IN CASE OF SECURITIES.—

(1) Exception.—Even though notice of a lien provided in section 6321 has been filed in the manner prescribed in subsection (a) of this section, the lien shall not be valid with respect to a security, as defined in paragraph (2) of this subsection, as against any mortgagee, pledgee, or purchaser of such security, for an adequate and full consideration in money or money's worth, if at the time of such mortgage, pledge, or purchase such mortgagee, pledgee, or purchaser is without notice or knowledge of the existence of such lien.

(2) Definition of Security.—As used in this subsection, the term "security" means any bond, debenture, note, or certificate or other evidence of indebtedness, issued by any corporation (including one issued by a government or political subdivision thereof), with interest coupons or in registered form, share of stock, voting trust certificate, or any certificate of interest or participation in, certificate of deposit or receipt for, temporary or interim certificate for, or warrant or right to subscribe to or purchase, any of the foregoing; negotiable instrument; or money.

(d) DISCLOSURE OF AMOUNT OF OUTSTANDING LIEN.—If a notice of lien has been filed under subsection (a), the Secretary or his delegate is authorized to provide by rules or regulations the extent to which, and the conditions under which, information as to the amount of the outstanding obligation secured by the lien may be disclosed.

SEC. 6325. RELEASE OF LIEN OR PARTIAL DISCHARGE OF PROPERTY.

(a) RELEASE OF LIEN.—Subject to such rules or regulations as the Secretary or his delegate may prescribe, the Secretary or his delegate may issue a certificate of release of any lien imposed with respect to any internal revenue tax if—

(1) Liability Satisfied or Unenforceable.—The Secretary or his delegate finds that the liability for the amount assessed, together with all interest in respect thereof, has been fully satisfied, has become legally unenforceable, or, in the case of the estate tax imposed by chapter 11 or the gift tax imposed by chapter 12, has been fully satisfied or provided for; or

(2) Bond Accepted.—There is furnished to the Secretary or his delegate and accepted by him a bond that is conditioned upon the payment of the amount assessed, together with all interest in respect thereof, within the time prescribed by law (including any extension of such time), and that is in accordance with such requirements relating to terms, conditions, and form of the bond and sureties thereon, as may be specified by such rules or regulations.

GPO : 1958 O - 106051

COMMISSION EXHIBIT No. 1733—Continued

OPTIONAL FORM NO. 10
5010-104
UNITED STATES GOVERNMENT
Memorandum

Commission Exhibit No. 1734

TO :Mr. Harlis Jackson, Revenue Officer DATE:December 9, 1963

FROM :Robert W. Klein, Special Agent

SUBJECT:Jack Ruby
Dallas, Texas

This memorandum will serve as a receipt to you for the $3,169.11 belonging to Jack Ruby which you and I received from the Dallas Police Department.

I will retain this money in the Intelligence Division office for the purpose of examining serial numbers.

Robert W. Klein
Robert W. Klein

COMMISSION EXHIBIT NO. 1734

POSTING VOUCHER

Nº 8158225

ACCOUNT NUMBER	T. D. A. F. P.	T. D. A. P. P.	NOTICE	OTHER	BALANCE AFTER THIS PAYMENT
60BP300661	✓				—0—

CLASS OF TAX	CASH	CHECK	MONEY ORDER	DEPOSITARY RECEIPT
Income	✓			

PERIOD COVERED	DISTRICT	DATE
1959	Dallas, Texas	12-9-63

RECEIVED OF: (Name and address)—Print
Dallas Police Dept.,
Property of; Jack Ruby
3929 Rawlins St.,
Dallas, Texas

TAX	$1,501.80
PENALTY (dr.)	$
INTEREST (dr.)	$ 343.77
Lien (dr.)	$ 1.00
AMOUNT RECEIVED (cr.)	$1,846.57

SIGNATURE OF OFFICER
Harlin C. Jackson

U. S. TREASURY DEPARTMENT—INTERNAL REVENUE SERVICE U. S. GOVERNMENT PRINTING OFFICE 16—29653ᵃ-8 Form 809—Part 1 (Rev. 1-57)

MEMO COPY

(NOT A POSTING VOUCHER)

Nº 8158225

ACCOUNT NUMBER	T. D. A. F. P.	T. D. A. P. P.	NOTICE	OTHER	BALANCE AFTER THIS PAYMENT
60BP300661	✓				—0—

CLASS OF TAX	CASH	CHECK	MONEY ORDER	DEPOSITARY RECEIPT
Income	✓			

PERIOD COVERED	DISTRICT	DATE
1959	Dallas, Texas	12-9-63

IF CASH CONVERTED, IDENTIFY MONEY ORDER OR BANK DRAFT
Dallas Police Dept.,
Property of; Jack Ruby
3929 Rawlins St.,
Dallas, Texas

TAX	$1,501.80
PENALTY	$
INTEREST	$ 343.77
Lien	1.00
AMOUNT RECEIVED	$1,846.57

SIGNATURE OF OFFICER
Harlin C. Jackson

U. S. TREASURY DEPARTMENT—INTERNAL REVENUE SERVICE U. S. GOVERNMENT PRINTING OFFICE 16—29653ᶜ-8 Form 809—Part 3 (Rev. 1-57)

COMMISSION EXHIBIT No. 1734—Continued

POSTING VOUCHER

№ 815822

ACCOUNT NUMBER	T. D. A. F. P.	T. D. A. P. P.	NOTICE	OTHER	BALANCE AFTER THIS PAYMENT
61 OP 401231		✓			802.63

CLASS OF TAX	CASH	CHECK	MONEY ORDER	DEPOSITARY RECEIPT
Income	✓	✓		

PERIOD COVERED	DISTRICT	DATE
1960	Dallas, Texas	12-9-63

RECEIVED OF: (Name and address)—Print

Dallas Police Dept.,
Property of; Jack Ruby
3929 Rawlins St.,
Dallas, Texas

TAX	$1,322.54
PENALTY (dr.)	$
INTEREST (dr.)	$
(dr.)	$
AMOUNT RECEIVED (cr.)	$1,322.54

SIGNATURE OF OFFICER: Harlen C. Jackson

U. S. TREASURY DEPARTMENT—INTERNAL REVENUE SERVICE — U. S. GOVERNMENT PRINTING OFFICE 16—29653-4 — Form 809—Part I (Rev. 1

MEMO COPY

(NOT A POSTING VOUCHER)

№ 815822

ACCOUNT NUMBER	T. D. A. F. P.	T. D. A. P. P.	NOTICE	OTHER	BALANCE AFTER THIS PAYMENT
61 OP 401231		✓			802.63

CLASS OF TAX	CASH	CHECK	MONEY ORDER	DEPOSITARY RECEIPT
Income	✓	✓		

PERIOD COVERED	DISTRICT	DATE
1960	Dallas, Texas	12-9-63

IF CASH CONVERTED, IDENTIFY MONEY ORDER OR BANK DRAFT

Dallas Police Dept.,
Property of; Jack Ruby
3929 Rawlins St.,
Dallas, Texas

TAX	$1,322.54
PENALTY	$
INTEREST	$
AMOUNT RECEIVED	$1,322.54

SIGNATURE OF OFFICER: Harlen C. Jackson

U. S. TREASURY DEPARTMENT—INTERNAL REVENUE SERVICE — U. S. GOVERNMENT PRINTING OFFICE 16—29653-4 — Form 809—Part 3 (Rev. 1

COMMISSION EXHIBIT No. 1734—Continued

FEDERAL BUREAU OF INVESTIGATION

1

Date November 26, 1963

ALFRED DAVIDSON, JR., was personally contacted by the writer at his temporary residence, Hollywood Parkway Motel, 11034 Ventura Boulevard, North Hollywood, California, Room 7 (telephone 763-8803) at which time he furnished substantially the following information:

During late September-early October, he was in Dallas, Texas, on business promoting a radio show, "The World of Fashion." He represented OLEG CASSINI, Women's Fashions, New York City. He was first introduced by phone to JACK RUBY by the Credit Manager of the Neiman-Marcus Department Store in Dallas. He thereafter went over to see RUBY at his Carousel Night Club, and for approximately the next six weeks (until November 15 or thereabouts) was befriended by RUBY. He saw him many times both during the day and at night at his night club.

Although he never met RUBY before, RUBY extended every hospitality to DAVIDSON, and RUBY refused to allow him to pick up any checks. DAVIDSON was toured about the city in RUBY's car from time to time. DAVIDSON stated that RUBY was apparently known by everyone in Dallas, was a friend of anyone who needed any help, knew everyone on the police force, treated them to free drinks, had a press pass on his car, had a police pass, and carried a revolver in the glove compartment of his car at all times although he did not have a permit. He claimed that he needed this revolver for protection inasmuch as he carried large sums of money with him from time to time, paying off his employees in cash, and not believing in the use of checking accounts. RUBY also indicated that he had friends and financial interests in Las Vegas, no details, and also had friends in Los Angeles, no details. As to the club itself, DAVIDSON always observed it as well run and proper. He considers RUBY as well fixed financially.

DAVIDSON characterizes RUBY as a glad-hander and a crusader for anyone who was wronged. As to the killing of OSWALD, he, DAVIDSON, was not surprised when RUBY was identified as the killer, and in fact had stated to a motel acquaintance when he had only been indicated on television as a night club owner, "I'll bet that was JACK RUBY."

It is DAVIDSON's opinion that RUBY, being of the nature that he is, and an admirer of President KENNEDY, took it upon

On 11/25/63 at North Hollywood, California File # Los Angeles 44-895

by SA JOHN P. ANDREWS:ps Date dictated 11/26/63

381

COMMISSION EXHIBIT No. 1735

2
LA 44-895

himself to avenge what he considered to be a personal wrong. DAVIDSON stated that RUBY does not have the intelligence, education, or foresight to look ahead to the consequences of his act. DAVIDSON is certain, however, that RUBY cannot be considered insane.

Contrary to published reports, during his acquaintance with RUBY, he never saw any acts of violence or violent temper or any other abusive conduct on the part of RUBY.

DAVIDSON is not aware whether RUBY was acquainted with OSWALD.

RUBY telephonically contacted DAVIDSON at his current residence about four days ago merely for a social call.

DAVIDSON will soon move into his own business to be known as Alfred Davidson and Associates, Suite 107, in a building next to the KLAC Building, 5800 block, Wilshire Boulevard, Los Angeles, California. In about two weeks, he will also move to another residence address on Rodeo Drive, Beverly Hills, specific address not at hand immediately. He can always be reached through the law firm of his ex-father-in-law, J. ARTHUR WARNER, New York Financier, which in Los Angeles is Bautzer, Irwin, Schutzbank, and Schwab, 190 North Cannon Drive, Beverly Hills, California, telephone number CR 5-1212.

382

COMMISSION EXHIBIT No. 1735—Continued

FD-302 (Rev. 3-3-59)

FEDERAL BUREAU

Commission Exhibit No. 1736

1

Date 12/16/63

JOSEPH CODY, Detective, Dallas Police Department, advised that he has known JACK RUBY for twelve or thirteen years. CODY stated that he went to work for the Dallas Police Department in 1950 and was assigned to the Patrol Division, which covered South Ervay Street, where JACK RUBY was operating the Silver Spur. CODY stated he saw RUBY around his place of business on several occasions.

CODY stated he was in the Korean War and was assigned in the Counter Intelligence Corps. He stated that while on that assignment he had been assigned in Dallas part of the time and, during that time, had gone into the Silver Spur, The Carousel, and the Vegas Clubs, on several occasions. He stated that RUBY liked any kind of officer and always wanted to be in a position of helping them. CODY advised he recalled one incident in particular when three individuals had jumped on two officers in Ruby's place, at which time RUBY got into the fight and gave a good account of himself. He stated RUBY is an unusually good "rough-and-tumble fighter" and he believed RUBY could have whipped all three of these characters, inasmuch as he is very strong and also fast with it.

CODY stated that after World War II was over and he returned to the Police Department in Dallas he saw RUBY occasionally on official business. He mentioned that about three years ago RUBY had a sign stolen from the front of the Carousel Club, which was valued at approximately $100.00. CODY stated at that time he was in the Theft Bureau and had gone over there in his official capacity. CODY also stated that, approximately one month before RUBY shot OSWALD, RUBY had called and asked him to come by the Carousel. CODY stated he did not know the nature of the call until he arrived there, but found out RUBY wanted his advice on where he could locate a new safe which he was planning on purchasing to put in the Carousel. CODY stated RUBY had said he wanted to put it where it wouldn't be noticeable and yet it could easily be heard in the event burglars tried to get into it. CODY stated he told RUBY, "You might as well put it out in the middle of the dance floor," and

on 12/12/63 at Dallas, Texas File # DL 44-1639

by Special Agent LEO L. ROBERTSON/eah Date dictated 12/14/63

68

This document contains neither recommendations nor conclusions of the FBI. It is the property of the FBI and is loaned to your agency; it and its contents are not to be distributed outside your agency.

COMMISSION EXHIBIT No. 1736

DL 44-1639

2

added that there wasn't anyplace where RUBY could have located it to get the results he desired.

CODY also stated that he, CODY, had been a hockey player and he goes out to Fair Park and skates occasionally. He stated that RUBY prides himself on his fighting prowess and tries to stay in pretty good shape and that RUBY also goes out and skates. CODY stated he had never gone out with RUBY socially and had never made previous arrangements to go skating with RUBY, but he estimated there had been at least a half dozen times in the last two or three years that RUBY had arrived at Fair Park while he, CODY, had been skating. CODY stated that on these occasions they had skated together; that RUBY was not in the pro class, but he was a much better skater than average. CODY stated he was sure RUBY did consider him a friend and added RUBY liked to be in a position of having police officers for friends, although RUBY never asked or expected anything from policemen to CODY's knowledge. CODY further advised he had heard RUBY carried a gun and imagined it was true, although he had never personally seen a gun on RUBY. He was sure that RUBY carries large amounts of money with him, especially late at night when he closed down his "joints" and stated, in view of this, he had no doubt about RUBY carrying a gun at times.

CODY also advised he had not been in Dallas the day that RUBY shot OSWALD. CODY advised he had a pilot's license and while flying had some trouble with the plane and, while flying low, had hit a high wire with the wing of the plane and had been forced down on Lake Bistineau near Shreveport, Louisiana. CODY stated he did not know that RUBY had killed OSWALD until he had heard it on the radio Sunday night, November 24, 1963. CODY stated he had really been surprised when he heard RUBY had shot OSWALD, as he never figured RUBY was the type who would do anything of that nature, although he apparently liked to fight. CODY stated he was high-tempered and would get worked up to a fighting pitch over nothing.

CODY did not know anything about the plans for security at the time OSWALD was supposed to be moved from the City to the County Jail. He never worked for RUBY and does not know any other person who did.

69

This document contains neither recommendations nor conclusions of the FBI. It is the property of the FBI and is loaned to your agency; it and its contents are not to be distributed outside your agency.

COMMISSION EXHIBIT No. 1736—Continued

Date December 4, 1963

1

Mrs. MARILYN PATRICIA JOYCE, nee DE LONG, 1132 Webber Drive, Lansing, Michigan, advised that she was employed as a hostess by Braniff Airlines with headquarters at Dallas, Texas in 1960 and 1961. During this period she resided in an apartment located at 4812 Alcot, Dallas, Texas.

Shortly after moving into this apartment, she met JACK L. RUBY, who also had an apartment in the building. Shortly after meeting RUBY she and her roommates and their dates, the identities of whom she could not recall, at RUBY's invitation attended the Sovereign Club, located on Commerce Street. She stated that RUBY owned this club, and that she has heard that RUBY also owned the Carousel and Vegas, both being nightclubs in the city of Dallas.

Mrs. JOYCE stated that she never talked to RUBY alone, always in the company of others, and that most of the times that she saw RUBY were at the swimming pool located at 4812 Alcot, Dallas.

Mrs. JOYCE described RUBY as a "glad hander" and one who tried to impress people of the fact that he knew everyone. She stated that she had never heard of RUBY being ill or having any mental problems. She stated she has no knowledge of his political beliefs.

Mrs. JOYCE advised that she does not know any members of the Dallas Police Department and has no knowledge that RUBY was friendly with any members of the Police Department. She also stated that she is not acquainted with nor does she know of any known criminals in Dallas, nor does she have any knowledge of RUBY's acquaintance with any known criminals.

Mrs. JOYCE advised that she had never heard of LEE HARVEY OSWALD prior to the assassination of President KENNEDY.

Mrs. JOYCE stated that her former roommates in Dallas were NANCY RITTS, now Mrs. WILLIAM McMILLAN, and

On 12/4/63 at East Lansing, Michigan File # Detroit 44-563
Dallas 44-1639

by SA ROBERT F. BOYLE and
SA DENNIS M. GIBBS :vwm Date dictated 12/4/63

393

DE 44-563
DL 44-1639
2

FRANCES WARLICK, now Mrs. JAMES LEAK, both residing Dallas, Texas. She stated that JAMES LEAK is a "wealthy attorney and gambler who possibly knows RUBY very well".

394

FD-302 (Rev. 1-25-60)

FEDERAL BUREAU OF INVESTIGATION

[redacted] Commission Exhibit No. 1738

1

Date 12/19/63

Mr. SAMUEL SCHWARTZ, 133 North Yarmouth Avenue, advised he is the Vice President and Sales Manager of the Embassy Manufacturing Company, 1919 West Oxford Street, Philadelphia, Pennsylvania. He advised his company makes metal stampings for the lighting fixture industry and in his capacity he travels all over the United States. He stated he contacts the General Lighting Company, Kirschner Company and the Columbia Lighting Company in Dallas, Texas.

Mr. SCHWARTZ related that on one of his trips to Dallas, about ten or twelve years ago, he was staying at the Baker Hotel and was watching a television boxing match at the hotel and at that time JACK RUBY was also at the hotel watching the fight. During the fight they began talking together and later that night they went out to dinner together.

Mr. SCHWARTZ advised that RUBY seemed to be a high-caliber type of individual so he called RUBY the next time he was in Dallas and spent some time with him. SCHWARTZ stated from that time on, he would call RUBY whenever he was in Dallas and they would visit together or go out to supper together. SCHWARTZ stated he has not seen RUBY for over a year since he has not been in Dallas for over a year. He advised he was in Dallas about every six months.

He related that RUBY had mentioned he was from Chicago and had talked about going to Chicago for a visit and at one time, he, SCHWARTZ, had given RUBY his home address in Philadelphia so RUBY could contact him in the event RUBY came to Philadelphia. Mr. SCHWARTZ stated he could not recall when this incident had taken place but did know that it had been several years ago. He added that RUBY had never visited at the SCHWARTZ home and had never contacted him in Philadelphia, Pennsylvania.

SCHWARTZ related as a rule he would arrive in Dallas, Texas, on a Friday night, spend the weekend in Dallas and call on his business contacts on Monday or Tuesday. During this period of time, he stated he might see RUBY once or twice, and they would meet at the hotel and go out for dinner. He stated he had been to RUBY's apartment only once and could not recall where the apartment was located.

On 12/17/63 at Longport, New Jersey File # Newark 44-443

by SAs LLOYD A. NELSON and ROBERT L. TAGG/mab Date dictated 12/17/63

79

2

NK 44-443

SCHWARTZ also sated that he had been at RUBY's clubs, the Vegas and the Carousel, to visit RUBY but added that these clubs were not to his liking and therefore did not frequent these clubs other than to call on RUBY.

SCHWARTZ related it was his opinion that RUBY did not like the night club business, and he, SCHWARTZ, always felt that RUBY wanted to be a business man and was looking for status in the community. SCHWARTZ stated it was his impression that RUBY thought he could learn something about the business field from SCHWARTZ and that was one reason he, RUBY, liked to associate with him. He added that RUBY very seldom discussed business with him; however, at one time he did mention that he was contemplating going into the hot dog machine business. He stated apparently this business did not come into being.

Mr. SCHWARTZ advised that he makes it a practice not to enter into discussions revolving around politics or religion; however, he stated it has been his experience that anyone who had strong feelings in these matters will make his feelings known and will discuss these fields voluntarily.

Mr. SCHWARTZ added that he could not recall RUBY ever entering into any discussion concerning politics.

He stated RUBY had never discussed President KENNEDY or any political systems, and it was his, SCHWARTZ's, opinion that RUBY had no strong political views.

SCHWARTZ related that RUBY seemed to be well known in Dallas and the acquaintances of RUBY whom he met all seemed to be very highly respected people. He recalled one night RUBY invited him to dinner at the 3225 Club in Dallas, which he described as a very elite club, and while there, RUBY introduced him to GREER GARSON and her husband. SCHWARTZ advised that during his association with RUBY, he did not know him to associate with anyone who did not have a good reputation.

Mr. SCHWARTZ also advised that RUBY appeared to be the type of person he would call a "handshaker" and knew many people, but he did not know of any close friends which RUBY might have.

Concerning LEE HARVEY OSWALD, Mr. SCHWARTZ stated he had seen his photograph many times during the past few days and could

80

not recall ever seeing this person in RUBY's clubs or in Dallas and never heard RUBY mention this person. Judging from what he had read about OSWALD, Mr. SCHWARTZ stated it was his opinion that RUBY would not associate with or be affiliated in any way with such a person. He stated he based this on the fact that all the persons he had met when in the company of RUBY had been persons of stature.

SCHWARTZ stated that RUBY seemed to be well acquainted with several police officers in Dallas, but he did not know the names of any of these men. He pointed out that he did not believe this was anything out of the ordinary, since Dallas seems to be the type of town where everyone knows everyone else. He added that the way RUBY spoke to the police officers, there seemed to be a familiarity between them.

SCHWARTZ described RUBY as a soft-spoken and gentle type of person who would never try to antagonize anyone. He added he was a clean-living person who did not drink or smoke and was interested in physical culture and wanted to see how long he could live and be healthy. He was pleased with himself and his success and liked Dallas and people in general. He was not a bitter person and was easy to get along with and a person would feel comfortable in his presence. He never had any show of obvious emotions and never made any derogatory statement or threatening statement about anyone.

SCHWARTZ added that RUBY was the type of person who could take care of himself and could be tough if necessary. He related that RUBY had told him that he had to keep his customers in line and on more than one occasion had to remove them from his place of business. RUBY related to SCHWARTZ that on one occasion, he became involved in an altercation with one person and the person bit off part of one of his fingers.

SCHWARTZ also stated on one occasion, several years ago, he met RUBY at one of his clubs at closing time to go out to dinner. At that time RUBY had a paper sack which contained the day's receipts and in the sack was a revolver. They got into the car and RUBY put the gun in the glove compartment. At that time, he, SCHWARTZ, asked RUBY whyyhe had the gun, and RUBY stated he had the gun because of the money he was carrying and added he needed that protection in Dallas. SCHWARTZ stated he did not question RUBY any further in this matter, but he gained the impression that RUBY carried a gun when he carried large amounts of money. He stated he did

81

not see RUBY with a gun after that. SCHWARTZ advised he could not recall any more details concerning this event.

SCHWARTZ advised he was shocked when he learned that RUBY had shot OSWALD and stated that it was inconceivable to him that RUBY would be capable of doing such a thing. He stated as far as he was concerned, this would have to have been a spontaneous act on the part of RUBY, and he was certain that RUBY did not have any dictation from anyone to do such an act.

He added that RUBY was strong willed and egotistical and would not allow himself to be talked into anything. He also added RUBY was not the type who would align himself with any radical group and did not believe he had the education to become involved in any such group.

SCHWARTZ again stated it was his opinion that the action taken by RUBY was due to a spontaneous action on his part and not due to any political involvements.

8V

FD-302 (Rev. 1-25-60) FEDERAL BUREAU OF — Commission Exhibit No. 1739

1

Date November 29, 1963

JOE HOWARD LINTHICUM, Texas Department of Correctios Number 171455, was interviewed in the Warden's Office, Texas State Prison, Texas Department of Corrections.

He advised that he has been a resident of Dallas, Texas, for many years. In about 1950, he frequented the "Silver Spur Club" in Dallas and became acquainted with the owner, JACK RUBY. In 1952, LINTHICUM received a prison sentence at the Federal Correctional Institute, Seagoville, Texas, and was not released until April, 1954. After returning to Dallas and while again frequenting the "Silver Spur Club", he witnessed JACK RUBY engage in a fight with three customers, and LINTHICUM went to RUBY's assistance. Afterwards, RUBY offered him a job at the club and he worked for RUBY for about eight months and then another month at RUBY's "Vegas Club". He then terminated his employment but continued his association with RUBY until 1962.

LINTHICUM stated RUBY was "hot headed" and would brawl at the slightest provocation. He never discussed politics and evidenced no indication that he was a "patriot". His primary concern was in "making the dollar". RUBY dated some of his "strippers" and occasional female customers of his clubs. He was friendly with members of the Dallas Police Department and would permit them to have "drinks on the house".

On 11/27/63 at Huntsville, Texas File # HO 44-939

by SA ROBERT E. WIATT : mem Date dictated 11/27/63

138

FD-302 (Rev. 3-3-59) FEDERAL BUREAU OF INVESTIGATION Commission Exhibit No. 1740

1

Date December 3, 1963

ROBERT MC EWAN was interviewed at the Galaxie Club, 613 Monmouth Street, Newport, Kentucky. He advised as follows:

Mr. MC EWAN is an entertainer working as a Master of Ceremonies, commedian and song and dance man. He works under the stage name of BOBBY O'DAY. His current address is the Metropole Hotel, Cincinnati, Ohio; however, around the first of December he expects to leave the Cinciannati, Ohio area and go to Nashville, Tennessee, where he will appear in the Rainbow Room.

He has no fixed permanent address, but can be located at any time through his booking agent, MIKE RIEFF, 818 Olive Street, St. Louis, Missouri, telephone number Central 1-4552. He can also be located through his cousin, JAMES MAWATT, 16219 East Seven Mile Road, Detroit, Michigan. He considers this as his permanent address.

During the period of one week before Christmas, 1962, until two weeks in January, 1963, Mr. MC EWAN appeared as an entertainer at the Carousel Club, in Dallas, Texas. He there became acquainted with JACK RUBY, who managed this club. While there, he saw RUBY on a daily basis, but he did not become particularly friendly with RUBY. He pointed out that it was his general policy when working at an establishment to in fact, avoid as much contact as was feasible with the manager of the establishment, inasmuch as he always considered such an individual was very busy and did not have time to take up with the various entertainers unless he had some actual business with them.

He recalled that RUBY lived in a single room behind the Club and also kept in this room two dogs. He said that the room had a very untidy appearance.

MC EWAN's act at the Carousel Club went well for approximately one and one-half weeks. After he had been appearing there approximately one and one-half weeks, one night, he, MC EWAN, told two or three jokes, relative to Jewish people. He said that these jokes in his opinion, were completely "inoffensive". Immediately upon MC EWAN finishing his act, RUBY confronted him. RUBY at this time was excited; had taken offense at the jokes relative to Jewish people; and stated "My people have suffered enough". MC EWAN had previously

on 11/30/63 at Newport, Kentucky 325 File # DL 44-1639 LS 44-542

by Special Agents JOHN M. BARRY and CHARLES V. SHIPLEY CVS/mjr/jn Date dictated 11/30/63

been telling jokes relative to various nationalities and racial groups to which jokes RUBY had taken no exception. He said that RUBY was easily excited and seemed to be "erratic" and nervous. He could cite no specific statements or instances, however, except the above one which he based this opinion or conclusion.

On New Year's Eve, 1962-1963, Mr. MC EWAN was staying at a motel in Dallas, the name of which he cannot now recall. There were some other entertainers whose names he does not recall also staying at this motel. There was a New Year's party held by the entertainers and RUBY attended this party. He said he recalled RUBY throwing firecrackers and "cherry bombs" fireworks in the swimming pool, but this activity was not out of keeping with the activities of the others at the party. This was not done through any spirit of anger on the part of RUBY, but was done in the spirit of having fun.

Mr. MC EWAN had never heard of LEE HARVEY OSWALD prior to the assassination of President KENNEDY. He knows of no association between RUBY and OSWALD, and knows of no connection of RUBY with any organization or group of society.

He said further, he did not know of the connection, if any, of Mr. RUBY with the Dallas Police, or any of the police, other than that it did appear that Mr. RUBY knew some of the police, which Mr. MC EWAN said was common in any town for a night club operator.

Mr. MC EWAN stated that he would have no idea whatsoever why JACK RUBY would kill LEE HARVEY OSWALD, if in fact he had done this as was reported by the press.

376

COMMISSION EXHIBIT No. 1740—Continued

Date 12-10-63

1

BRYCE G. BRADY, II, 4931 Eastside Avenue, Dallas, Texas, telephone TA 4-7488, who is employed as a fitter for Austin Brothers Steel Company, Dallas, advised he was interviewed by Special Agents of the FBI on December 4, 1963, concerning his association with JACK LEON RUBY. Additionally, BRADY advised as follows:

BRADY met RUBY in the latter part of 1951 when he went to work for RUBY part-time as a "bouncer", bartender, and handy man at RUBY's Silver Spur Club in Dallas. BRADY said he left this employment about seven months later which was approximately in the Spring of 1952.

In December, 1951, ED (LNU), a bartender at the Silver Spur at that time, suggested to BRADY that the two of them buy RUBY a .38 revolver for a Christmas present. Until that time, according to BRADY, RUBY carried a small caliber pistol at times for protection, since RUBY did handle the club's receipts. He stated he gave ED (LNU) $30.00 for his half, and ED (LNU) purchased a .38 Colt snub-nose he believes from Titche - Goettinger Department Store in Dallas, and they gave it to RUBY for Christmas. BRADY said the gun was wrapped and he saw it only at a glance when RUBY opened it at Christmas.

BRADY said since he left RUBY's employ in 1952, he has seen him around Dallas streets, but has had no actual contact with him. The last time he saw RUBY was about three years ago, when he visited the Vegas Club and as he entered the club RUBY was leaving. He said they greeted each other, but had no conversation.

BRADY stated he has not seen or heard of ED (LNU) mentioned above since he, BRADY, left the Silver Spur and BRADY does not know where ED (LNU) is presently residing or employed.

He related that while employed by RUBY in 1951-1952, he

on 12-10-63 at Dallas, Texas File # DL 44-1639

by Special Agent JAMES E. GARRIS - md Date dictated 12-10-63

286

COMMISSION EXHIBIT No. 1741

2

DL 44-1639

observed that RUBY was a nervous, emotional person, who lost his temper frequently and occasionally RUBY would physically remove a "trouble maker" from his club. BRADY said that to the best of his knowledge RUBY was a law abiding citizen and business man, who operated a "clean" club and had nothing to do with prostitution, gambling or narcotics. BRADY added that he heard from an unrecalled source in recent months, that one could go to RUBY's Vegas Club in Dallas and get any kind of narcotics he wanted.

BRADY advised that although he never heard RUBY discuss politics, he appeared to be a devoted American citizen and nothing ever came to his attention that would cause him to question his loyalty to the United States.

BRADY advised that while he was employed by RUBY, a Dallas police officer, name unknown, was also employed there part-time on weekends as a "bouncer." BRADY said that during the time he was employed at the Silver Spur, Dallas Police Officers, names unknown, frequently came to the club to check on the performances. He added that he saw some of the officers patronize the Silver Spur while they were off duty and they never paid cover charges, but did pay for beer and food served to them. He related that during the Christmas holidays of 1951, he saw RUBY pass out fifths of whiskey to Dallas Police Officers, names unknown, as well as to others, names unknown, as Christmas gifts.

BRADY related that when he was employed by RUBY he had occasions to call RUBY at his apartment regarding business matters and each time a woman, believed by him to be the same woman, would answer the telephone. This woman was un-

387

3

DL 44-1639

known to BRADY. He suspected that RUBY was living in common-law relationship with this woman. BRADY added that RUBY never mentioned being married to anyone.

BRADY advised that father, BRYCE BRADY, who resides at 6606 Avondale Drive, Nichols Hills, Oklahoma City, Oklahoma, suffered a light heart attack early in November, 1963, and as a result, he left Dallas on November 8, 1963, to be with his father. BRADY returned to Dallas the weekend of November 16 - 17, 1963, to pick up his pay check and exchange his clothing. He then drove back to Oklahoma City to be with his father. BRADY returned to Dallas on the afternoon of November 22, 1963, and to his job on November 23, 1963.

BRADY stated he never heard of LEE HARVEY OSWALD and knew of no association between OSWALD and RUBY.

388

FD-302 (Rev. 1-25-60) FEDERAL BUREAU OF Commission Exhibit No. 1742

1.

Date 12/8/63

NORMAN SMITH, Gardiner's Neck Road, Swansea, Massachusetts, age 33, an insurance salesman, advised as follows:

He is a native of Swansea, Massachusetts. After completing service in the U.S. Air Force in 1953, he continued his education at Southern Methodist University (SMU), graduating in 1955. Thereafter he went into the theater acting business, specializing in jazz poetry and opened up the Dallas Little Theater on Oaklawn Avenue in Dallas, Texas. This closed on June 15, 1957. In the fall of 1958, he opened a coffee house called "The Poet" on Mc Kinney Avenue in Dallas. In the spring of 1959 he closed this and opened another coffee house called "The Eighth Day", and this was followed in the fall of 1959 with still another coffee house venture called "The Fat Man", all in the same general location in Dallas. In the spring of 1960, realizing that this was not his business, he left Dallas and returned to Swansea, Massachusetts where he has resided since.

During the approximate period 1957 - 1960, he knew JACK RUBY as the owner of "The Vegas", a stripper club in Dallas. He met RUBY in the "Artist's Club" in Dallas, which was an after hours club catering to musicians, actors and club owners. On occasions he played $1 limit poker with RUBY and others, although he did not consider RUBY a gambling addict. He also met RUBY in "The Vegas" on occasions when RUBY booked a band from SMU called the "Cell Block Seven", which was a favorite of SMITH.

On one occasion, while in the "Artist's Club", RUBY became involved in a drunken brawl with someone and was kicking his adversary while the latter was on the floor. SMITH interceded and took a punch at RUBY to stop the melee.

In all, he had been in RUBY's company about 20 times during this period of time, but he would not consider himself anything more than a casual, social acquaintance of RUBY, based on their allied types of business. He had never been to RUBY's apartment, or had RUBY ever been to his home. He had never met any of RUBY's relatives, and RUBY had never met any of SMITH's family.

On 12/7/63 at Swansea, Mass. File # Dallas 44-1639 BS 44-337

by SA JOHN E. KEARY/mab Date dictated 12/8/63

245

COMMISSION EXHIBIT No. 1742

2.

BS 44-337

He had only one business dealing with RUBY, and that involved the purchase of 20 or 30 chairs from RUBY to outfit one of SMITH's coffee houses.

He knows little of RUBY's background, other than the fact that RUBY came from Chicago. He had heard that RUBY attempted unsuccessfully to get a union started of waitors and club personnel in the mid 1950's. RUBY was also supposed to be interested in some pizza making machine around 1960 when SMITH left Dallas. Prior to running "The Vegas", RUBY was rumored to have had a hillbilly joint in the south end of Dallas where an irate customer was supposed to have bitten off the end of RUBY's finger.

RUBY, like other club owners, carried a gun in his money bag containing the club's money. However, he never knew RUBY to have carried a gun on his person or to have threatened anyone with it.

SMITH knew nothing inparticular concerning RUBY's relationship with Dallas Police.

RUBY was a very friendly type, an extrovert and generally well liked. He was a brawler and a bully in the sense that he only picked a fight with those he could physically beat up. He was a publicity hound always looking for publicity for his business, and he was reputed to be a successful club operator by competitors. He did not suspect RUBY of being a homosexual.

He is confident that RUBY had no connection with any secret organization either subversive or criminal, and he believes this due to the fact that RUBY was an intellectual moron, was irresponsible, had an unpredictable temper and consequently would be an untrustworthy member of any such organization.

RUBY was not overly patriotic, but seemed to have an inordinate respect for people in high places.

SMITH has no personal knowledge of OSWALD. SMITH was shocked of hearing that RUBY shot OSWALD and he has no explanation as to why RUBY would do such a thing.

246

COMMISSION EXHIBIT No. 1742—Continued

Commission Exhibit No. 1743

FD-302 (Rev. 3-3-59)

FEDERAL BUREAU OF INVESTIGATION

1

Date 11/30/63

FRANK H. FISHER, 2377 Dalworth Street, Grand Prairie, Texas, voluntarily furnished the following information:

FISHER advised he worked for JACK RUBY at the Carousel Club from May 1, 1961, until August 13, 1963, as a musician and band leader. He stated he knew RUBY only in a business way, but once attended a party for all employees at the club on July 4, 1962, at RUBY's home.

FISHER further advised he knew RUBY to be a real fine fellow at times, and on other occasions he showed a very nasty temper. He stated RUBY was a conflicting personality with both friends and employees at times.

FISHER stated he never heard RUBY discuss politics or make any statements about the President of the United States or the Governor of Texas. He stated he had no information that might connect RUBY to any of the recent happenings or to LEE OSWALD. He advised that RUBY seemed to be known by many of the police officers in Dallas, and that they seemed to have a good relationship existing.

FISHER advised he could furnish no further information of value.

on 11/27/63 at Dallas, Texas File # DL 44-1639

by Special Agent DONALD E. BRINKLEY /cv Date dictated 11/28/63

155

This document contains neither recommendations nor conclusions of the FBI. It is the property of the FBI and is loaned to your agency; it and its contents are not to be distributed outside your agency.

Commission Exhibit No. 1744

FD-302 (Rev. 1-25-60)

ERAL BUREAU OF INVEST

Date December 20, 1963

JOEY GERARD, Room 432, Baltimore Hotel, stated he is in show business as a master of ceremonies, singer, and comedian and can always be located through contact with his agent, MIKE RIAFF, St. Louis, Missouri.

GERARD stated he has known JACK RUBY since May, 1961, and in terms of actual contact has been with him about five months. He said he worked as master of ceremonies at the Carousel Club, Dallas, Texas, for JACK RUBY on three separate occasions. Another occasion in December, 1961, he worked for RUBY as a bartender at the Carousel Club.

GERARD said the last time he worked for JACK RUBY was in January, 1962, when he appeared at the Carousel Club for two weeks. Since this time he saw RUBY about three times when he would drop in at the Carousel Club to see the show, at which time he would also talk with RUBY. The last time he saw JACK RUBY at the Carousel Club on such an occasion was in the latter part of April, 1962.

GERARD said on the previous evening he studied a photograph of OSWALD which appeared in a current magazine and is positive he never saw OSWALD in the Carousel Club. He said to determine whether or not OSWALD was acquainted with RUBY contact should be made with RUBY's close associates named BUDDY KING and JIMMY RHODES.

BUDDY KING is a former entertainer and in 1961 was employed by JACK RUBY as Manager at the Carousel Club. GERARD was unable to furnish KING's current whereabouts, but said he heard in 1962 that he was "fronting" a night club in Dallas, Texas. He explained "fronting" is a show business term for a person who runs a night club for a person who actually has the license. He also explained that by "fronting" he means a person who operates a night club and tries to give the appearance of owning it when actually he does not.

GERARD said JIMMY RHODES was a photographer for JACK RUBY and helped him set up the lighting and staging at the Carousel Club. RHODES currently resides at 1022 Mulberry, Sulphur Springs, Texas, telephone TU 5-4323.

On 12/18/63 at St. Louis, Missouri File # SL 44-496

by SA EDWARD M. MORELAND:jc Date dictated 12/19/63

This document contains neither recommendations nor conclusions of the FBI. It is the property of the FBI and is loaned to your agency; it and its contents are not to be distributed outside your agency.

-171-

GERARD described BUDDY KING and JIMMY RHODES as individuals who "busted out" of the entertainment racket. He said JACK RUBY liked to surround himself with these type of persons.

GERARD said JACK RUBY was a very "erratic" type of individual and was "given to having fits of temper". GERARD said three or four times nightly he recalled RUBY would become very angry and would shout, using very profane and verbally abusive language. These outbursts usually occurred as a result of arguments with waitresses and bartenders who RUBY would accuse of stealing or not performing their duties satisfactorily.

GERARD said in the five months contact with JACK RUBY he only saw him actually "lay his hands" on one person. This situation occurred when the band leader and trumpet player named FRANK FISHER came into the Carousel Club in an intoxicated condition. RUBY refused to allow FISHER to go on stage and when FISHER insisted RUBY grabbed him and pushed him toward the door. GERARD said FISHER currently resides at 2377 Dalworth, Apartment 103, Grand Prairie, Texas.

GERARD related that JACK RUBY especially disliked his sister, EVA, and every time she came to the Carousel Club a loud argument between the two would usually ensue. EVA operated another club either owned by RUBY or partly owned by him.

Concerning RUBY's acquaintance and association with police officers, GERARD said that uniformed officers were always in the Carousel Club at the end of the bar RUBY always had a pot of coffee at the bar and the officers would congregate there. GERARD said he remembered a Lieutenant JOHN TONY, a plain-clothes detective of the Dallas Police Department, was frequently in the club. He estimated that Lieutenant TONY would be in the Carousel Club two or three times weekly either off duty or on duty. On a number of occasions he observed Lieutenant TONY come into the Carousel Club with a group of persons and have a small party and see the show.

-172-

JACK RUBY always had a special price for police officers and other close friends of his and would sell beer and setups to these individuals at approximately his cost.

GERARD said he vaguely remembered seeing the late officer TIPPETT at the club but was unable to furnish details or be positive about this.

GERARD said he was aware that RUBY had a revolver in his desk at the Carousel Club inasmuch as on one occasion he saw it. He never remembered ever seeing RUBY carrying a gun.

GERARD remembered that frequently JACK RUBY went to the Dallas Police Station for the purpose of getting FRANK FISHER out of jail. GERARD explained FISHER would usually be in jail on a drunk charge. He remembered this jail was near the Post Office in downtown Dallas.

GERARD also stated that he remembered JACK RUBY was very strict concerning any acts or jokes pertaining to either religion or politics. GERARD said RUBY especially resented any jokes pertaining to the Jewish religion.

GERARD said he remembered that he was the master of ceremonies when SYRA, an exotic dancer, whose stage name is "The Dutch Doll" first played at the Carousel Club.

GERARD was unable to furnish any information concerning any association with JACK RUBY and subversive elements or membership in any type of "extremist" organizations.

-173-

FD-302 (Rev. 1-25-60)

Commission Exhibit No. 1745

FEDERAL BUREAU OF INVESTIGATION

1

Date November 27, 1963

AUGUST DE ANGELO, 2038 Sombero, Captain of the Show Room, Flamingo Hotel, advised he knows JACK RUBY but not socially. He stated during 1956 and 1957, he was Maitre'D, Hilton Hotel, Dallas, and recalls RUBY coming into the hotel on numerous occasions. He informed that to his knowledge, RUBY had never been to Las Vegas and was not considered by those who knew him in Dallas to be interested in gambling. DE ANGELO claimed RUBY was more interested in show business and was always energetic in his promotion of the Vegas Club, which RUBY owned in Dallas. He described RUBY as a person who liked talent and the entertainment field, in general, and whenever he frequented the Hilton Hotel, he would make it a point to inform DE ANGELO of persons appearing at the Vegas Club. DE ANGELO stated he liked RUBY personally, even though he had a very boring personality and was extremely hard to get rid of. RUBY was known to DE ANGELO to be very arrogant at times and considered him very tempermental. He claimed he avoided RUBY since you could never determine what type of reaction you might get from the simplest of statements to him.

DE ANGELO stated that although he had played cards with RUBY on a couple of occasions at the Artist Club, Dallas, he did not know him well enough to even guess at the motivation behind OSWALD's murder. He recalled that RUBY used to employ Dallas Police Officers at the Vegas Club as "door watchers" but knew of no other association between RUBY and the Police Department with the exception that he seemed to know all policemen.

On 11/26/63 at Las Vegas, Nevada File # LV 44-48

by SA JAMES E. DOYLE JED:alf Date dictated 11/26/63

79

FD-302 (Rev. 1-25-60)

Commission Exhibit No. 1746

FEDERAL BUREAU OF INVESTIGATION

Date November 29, 1963

1

WALTER C. CLEWIS, Manager, Municipal Auditorium, Mobile, Alabama, advised that he had met JACK RUBY in Dallas and had known him over a period of several years. CLEWIS stated that RUBY had a partner, name not recalled, who was in partnership with RUBY in The Carousel and booked rock and roll shows throughout Texas. CLEWIS stated that in his business as Manager of the Municipal Coliseum Auditorium, San Angelo, Texas, he knew the partner of RUBY first, and was subsequently introduced to RUDY at The Carousel. CLEWIS stated it was his opinion on the basis of information he had obtained from unrecalled sources, that RUBY booked striptease shows for smokers through the State of Texas.

CLEWIS stated that although he had tried, he had been unable to recall the name of the individual who contacted him and identified himself as RUBY's partner, but he is sure that the name appears in the files of the Municipal Coliseum Auditorium at San Angelo, Texas as they had much correspondence with this individual since the individual wrote them a check which bounced.

CLEWIS stated that he did not personally like RUBY as RUBY always attempted to be the big shot and boasted not only to him but to other people in his presence that he could do anything he wanted in Dallas as he had enough information on the Police Department and judges that he could not be convicted.

CLEWIS stated that while in San Angelo, he had a secretary named JEAN PIERCE, nee OLSON, who resided with her parents, the C. H. OLSONS, 121 Howard Street. He stated this secretary did not have a particularly good reputation as she was alleged to have dated Negroes in addition to numerous individuals. CLEWIS stated that in October, 1961, he fired his secretary and then permitted her to resign. She then, through the above mentioned unrecalled partner of RUBY, obtained a position working for RUBY at one of his clubs in Dallas. He stated he subsequently met JEAN PIERCE and she advised that she did not stay long in her position as there was something "funny" about the place and that she was dissatisfied with the costume

On 11/27/63 at Mobile, Alabama File # MO 44-1070 Dallas 44-1639

by SA JAMES A. DAY:pei Date dictated 11/27/63

67

MO 44-1070

2

she wore. CLEWIS stated he did not pursue the subject with PIERCE at the time and had no further information as to why she left RUBY's employ.

68

COMMISSION EXHIBIT No. 1746—Continued

Date 12/31/63

LEO UKIE SHERIN, 525 North Crescent Heights, Los Angeles, telephone 651-1426, was interviewed at the Mauna Loa Motel, 80-880 Highway 111, Indio, California.

SHERIN said he met JACK RUBY during August, 1958 when RUBY came into the "University Club", Dallas, Texas, where SHERIN was playing piano. RUBY introduced himself to SHERIN and mentioned they had mutual friends, names not recalled by SHERIN. SHERIN saw RUBY occasionally thereafter at the "University Club" and also at RUBY's nightclub, "The Carousel." RUBY on occasions attempted to hire SHERIN to work for RUBY at "The Carousel", but SHERIN refused this employment because he did not want to play in a burlesque house.

SHERIN did not know RUBY's background and did not believe RUBY had any hoodlum connections. RUBY never discussed Communism, or ever mentioned "The Fair Play for Cuba Committee." He never expressed any radical or extremist views to SHERIN. SHERIN described RUBY as a lonely, overly dramatic person, who wanted to be liked by everyone. RUBY was constantly paying for dinner checks and giving people presents in order to have people like him. He was always inviting members of the Dallas Police Department to see the show at "The Carousel" and gave them coffee and sandwiches. On occasion a Dallas police officer would buy a drink and send it to one of the female performers at the burlesque house. RUBY would advise the officer not to waste his money on that girl as she had a boy friend and would then point to, or name, another girl and advise the officer "She will play." SHERIN could not recall the names of any police officers who frequented RUBY's club and did not know whether any officer ever "followed through" with girls suggested by RUBY.

RUBY never exhibited any great interest in politics, but had made statements to SHERIN that former President KENNEDY was a great man. SHERIN felt RUBY was over-sensitive, explaining that if one of the entertainers of the club was a couple of minutes late, he would go into a tirade.

On 12/27/63 at Indio, California File # Los Angeles 44-895

by SAA J. CLAYTON TAYLOR:dsh Date dictated 12/28/63

53

COMMISSION EXHIBIT No. 1747

LA 44-895
2

SHERIN met RUBY's sister, EVA GRANT, who ran the "Las Vegas Club" in Dallas for RUBY, but SHERIN did not know her well, or become acquainted with her friends or associates. SHERIN said he feels that if RUBY determines where SHERIN resides he will try to call SHERIN as a character witness. SHERIN feels RUBY is a nice person and he would consider being a character witness for RUBY if he could first talk to RUBY. He feels RUBY would tell him why he killed OSWALD.

RUBY did not know LEE HARVEY OSWALD, or have any association with OSWALD, to the best of SHERIN's knowledge. The only close associate of RUBY known to SHERIN was RUBY's roommate, GEORGE SENATOR. SHERIN departed Dallas about one week prior to the assassination of President KENNEDY. He recalled that about one week prior to his departure he observed the owner of the "Largo Club", a Los Angeles, California club, in Dallas visiting with RUBY. SHERIN did not recall the name of the owner of the "Largo Club."

54

COMMISSION EXHIBIT No. 1747—Continued

Commission Exhibit No. 1748

FD-302 (Rev. 3-3-59)

FEDERAL BUREAU OF INVESTIGATION

Date 11/25/63

1

JOE CAMPISI, 4445 Ashford Drive, Dallas, partner in the ownership of the Egyptian Lounge, 5610 Mockingbird Lane, furnished the following information concerning his knowledge of JACK RUBY, owner and operator of the Carousel Club in Dallas:

CAMPISI stated he has known JACK RUBY since about 1949 when RUBY was operating the Spur Club in Dallas, also known as the Silver Spur. CAMPISI described RUBY as a "very high-strung, very excitable person" who would "belt someone at the drop of a hat." CAMPISI stated that if RUBY disagreed with somebody or had trouble with them concerning anything, RUBY would immediately take the offensive and assault the person with his fists.

CAMPISI stated RUBY is probably well known to every businessman and restaurant owner in Dallas, through RUBY's operation of night clubs since his arrival in Dallas in about 1949. CAMPISI cited that RUBY goes to every football game in the Cotton Bowl simply for the purpose of meeting people, "glad-handing" and promoting his night club, by inviting these people to come to them. CAMPISI stated that RUBY does not know the first thing about football. RUBY would also, according to CAMPISI, attend the fights and the musicals for the same purpose. CAMPISI described RUBY as "one hell of a hustler who would do anything to earn a buck."

CAMPISI advised that RUBY had a great love for dogs and would have as many as three dogs living with him at his apartment or house. Also CAMPISI described RUBY as quite a "ladies man" but that for a few years in about 1955 to about 1958 RUBY spent most of his social time with one particular girl whose name CAMPISI could not recall. CAMPISI was of the opinion that this girl's name would be known to CAMPISI's partner RALPH PAUL.

CAMPISI stated that during the 14 years he has known RUBY, RUBY has never mentioned politics and has never expressed any great dislikes or likes concerning any particular political party. He further stated that RUBY "operated out of his hip pocket" meaning that RUBY would carry money received at the club in his pocket and pay his bills with this money in cash.

on 11/24/63 at Dallas, Texas 5/14 File # DL 44-1639

by Special Agent S IVAN D. LEE & ROBERT M. BARRETT/gtd Date dictated 11/25/63

COMMISSION EXHIBIT No. 1748

2

DL 44-1639

This was CAMPISI's explanation of why RUBY had over $2,000 in his pocket at the time of his arrest on November 24, 1963. CAMPISI stated that when it was announced that RUBY had shot LEE HARVEY OSWALD, this announcement did not surprise CAMPISI based on his knowledge of RUBY and RUBY's temperament.

CAMPISI stated that RUBY made a practice of becoming acquainted with all police officers and he, RUBY, would cooperate with the police in the operation of his night club. CAMPISI stated RUBY did this for his own protection as police officers would, at RUBY's request and cooperation, keep undesirable characters and prostitutes out of RUBY's club. Police officers would also advise RUBY whenever he would hire a girl to work as a stripper who also had a record for prostitution. CAMPISI was of the opinion RUBY gained entrance to the City Hall basement on November 24, 1963, through this friendship with and knowledge of numerous Dallas police officers.

CAMPISI stated that he has been in RUBY's clubs, both the Carousel on Commerce Street and the Vegas on Oak Lawn Avenue, numerous times and he had never observed LEE HARVEY OSWALD at either place. He had never heard RUBY ever mention anyone by the name of LEE or LEE HARVEY OSWALD or O. D. LEE or ALEK HIDELL.

CAMPISI was asked to identify persons that he knew were acquainted with RUBY. He again stated that RUBY would be known to every night club operator and beer hall operator in Dallas and probably numerous Dallas businessmen. When asked if RUBY was ever known to partake in gambling CAMPISI stated he had never heard of RUBY ever gambling or engaging in bookmaking either as a bookie or a person placing bets. CAMPISI did state that RUBY was acquainted with Dallas gamblers JOHNNIE ROSS PATRONO, BOBBY CHAPMAN, RUSSELL DOUGLAS MATTHEWS and JIMMY VOURIS. He also stated that he was of the opinion RUBY was acquainted with known Dallas police character MARVIN RALPH PRESTRIDGE. He also stated that he had never observed RUBY at any time "flash" the money he was carrying. CAMPISI estimated that the receipts from RUBY's club would easily total over $2,000 in any one week.

CAMPISI advised he would attempt to ascertain the name of RUBY's former girl friend and immediately furnish same to the FBI.

575

COMMISSION EXHIBIT No. 1748—Continued

Commission Exhibit No. 1749

FD-302 (Rev. 3-3-59)

FEDERAL BUREAU OF INVESTIGATION

1

Date 12/4/63

Patrolman JOHN WAYNE BARNETT, Dallas Police Department, Northwest Sub-Station, 2828 Shore Crest Drive, Dallas, furnished the following information:

He stated he has known of JACK RUBY for an unrecalled period of time and that he operated the Carousel Club. Continuing, he stated prior to his assignment to the Northwest Sub-Station, he worked District 114 out of the downtown station, and while on duty one evening, approximately one and one-half years ago, specific date unrecalled, he met JACK RUBY for the first time with two unknown individuals, attempting to enter the Top Hat Club, a "private Negro Club," located on Hall and Thomas Streets. BARNETT related that he stopped RUBY and his companions and "asked them to leave, as they had no business in that club." BARNETT advised that "RUBY stated he would, and returned to a parked car with the two unknown individuals." BARNETT stated that he then left the area of the Top Hat Club and returned approximately ten minutes later to find the car that RUBY and his companions had gotten into parked in front of the Top Hat Club, and thus assumed that "they had returned and gone into the club." BARNETT stated he did not enter the club to contact RUBY the second time inasmuch as the Top Hat is a private club and he could not enter.

BARNETT related that he also worked District 104, which covers the downtown area, a short time before being assigned to the Northwest Sub-Station. He continued that while on duty, he occasionally entered the Carousel Club to make a "check." He advised that whenever he entered the Carousel Club, RUBY would offer him coffee or cokes. He further advised that RUBY on some occasions would appear to be "overly friendly" and on other occasions would say nothing to him. He stated that RUBY, in his opinion, was the type that liked to be "in the spotlight." He said he never saw RUBY lose his temper, and that RUBY never asked favors of him. BARNETT advised he had heard that RUBY did not permit his "girls" to go out with any of the police officers, but could not elaborate further.

BARNETT related that in his contact with RUBY, he never conversed with him at great length. He further related that to his knowledge, he has never heard of RUBY being interested in political affairs or being a member of a political or any other type of organization.

on 12/4/63 at Dallas, Texas File # DL 44-1639

by Special Agents GARY S. WILSON and JAMES W. SWINFORD :lp Date dictated 12/4/63

209

COMMISSION EXHIBIT No. 1749

BARNETT advised that he was not assigned to the "detail" regarding the transfer of LEE HARVEY OSWALD and that he did not see the shooting. He further advised that h has never worked for RUBY, stating that Dallas police regulations prohibit officers to work anywhere liquor is sold.

BARNETT related he last saw JACK RUBY approximatel nine months ago and has never seen LEE HARVEY OSWALD. BARNE continued that he does not know RUBY well enough to comment RUBY's character or stability.

ABADIE advised that he had no knowledge as to RUBY's association with OSWALD. ABADIE was never in RUBY's Carousel Club or in any of his other clubs, pointing out that his social status and income did not incline him to be in places such as this. He stated that the only thing he knew about any background was hearsay to the effect that RUBY had come to Dallas from Detroit, Michigan, in 1934 or 1935; that he was related to the RUBINSTEINs, who were mixed up in the "poker crowd" and a part of the old "Purple Gang" in Detroit. ABADIE stated that he had heard this type information while a bellhop at the Wolverine in Detroit, Michigan, at about this time. ABADIE advised that he did not know who RUBY's parents were, did not know their names, or whether or not JOSEPH and FANNIE RUBINSTEIN were in fact part of the family described just previously by him.

He also stated that he knew of no associates of RUBY amongst the gamblers in Dallas or amongst the other racketeers. He stated that working in his warehouse, however, it was obvious that to operate gambling in the manner that he did, that he must have racketeering connections with other individuals in the City of Dallas, as well as Fort Worth, Texas. He also said that this opinion applied also to police connection with the two cities and that this had to be obvious in order to operate. While he was making book for RUBY's establishment, he did observe police officers in and out of the gambling establishment on occasion. He knew none of these officers and could not identify any.

During his employment with the two enterprises owned by JACK RUBY he observed nothing to indicate that RUBY had any subversive connections, any interest in the Fair Play for Cuba Committee, or any radical or extremist views, either communistic or views of the far right.

Because of his lack of closeness to RUBY, himself, he knew none of RUBY's close relatives, associates, or girl friends. He stated that RUBY's reputation in the working establishment was that he had no close friends, stayed completely to himself, and was interested solely and entirely in his businesses and in gambling.

279

COMMISSION EXHIBIT No. 1750

His particular impressions of RUBY were that he was a quiet, intense racketeer, gambler and hustler. He advised that he never saw him angry or appearing upset during the period of time that he was an employee. He appeared calm, not one to express his emotions; had the reputation amongst the workers of neither drinking nor being addicted to narcotics. His one outstanding characteristic, which was mentioned, was his own personal intense interest in gambling of any kind.

ABADIE advised that he had no gun in his possession; that to the best of his memory, which he said is extremely clouded because of his constant drinking, the last time that he had his 1941 Colt blue, single-action revolver was in February, 1960, when he hocked it in a Birmingham, Alabama, pawn shop, along with his watch. He could not recall the name of the pawn shop but stated that there are only three or four in the city; that they are all in one block and it was one of these. He stated that he had no gun at the time that he was employed by RUBY; that he had not sold him any gun, loaned him any gun, or, along with the previous information mentioned, had not even had any contacts with him of any kind.

As to his wife, Mrs. RUBY ABADIE, whose whereabouts is not known to him, ever having met RUBY in his, ABADIE's company, he maintained that this was absolutely not true. He said his wife was never around either of RUBY's establishments where he was employed and he at no time ever met RUBY out any place socially when his wife was present, or any other time. He further advised that Mrs. SHIRLEY GATLIN was a friend of both him and his wife, but that she had not been in Dallas during the time that he was employed by RUBY, which was the only time that he ever knew who RUBY was or had ever observed him any place. He advised, therefore, that it would have been impossible for the three of them to have ever run into RUBY in Dallas.

280

COMMISSION EXHIBIT No. 1750—Continued

He advised that he had other guns as follows:

One was a .38 caliber snub-nose Smith & Wesson revolver, traded to an aircraft surplus dealer in San Antonio, Texas, in 1959. This individual has a wife who runs a motel and can be identified by the Piper Airplane dealers in Houston, CUMMINGS and GROVES, as there was a law suit between the two. In 1957 he had a .38 automatic, which was stolen while he lived at 106 Newhouse Street, Houston, Texas. Earlier than that his previous wife, BARBARA JEAN ABADIE, stole a .32 caliber Police Colt Special and gave it to some girl friend somewhere in the State of California.

ABADIE concluded by saying that he wanted to make it plain that he had never had any close association with RUBY, although RUBY had known his father, ULYSSES G. ABADIE, many years prior to the time of employment. Even this was never mentioned to him by RUBY. He advised that while he was employed by RUBY he received no impressions of extremism any place he worked on RUBY's part or on the part of anyone else, except that everyone in the shop and everyone he worked with were anti-integrationists in their views. He said they did not like Negroes; that he, himself, did not; that they would not allow Negroes to place bets and did not want to associate with them. ABADIE heard no views expressed indicating that anyone he worked with wanted to take any extremist action in support of their views.

The following descriptive data was obtained by personal observation and interview:

Name	WILLIAM B. ABADIE
Sex	Male
Race	White
Date of Birth	September 3, 1908
Place of Birth	Houston, Texas
Hair	Black with grey temples
Eyes	Brown
Height	5' 10½"
Weight	138 pounds

281

Immediate Relatives	Wife: RUBY ABADIE, address unknown.
Education	High school, plus night school, Detroit University.
Profession	Instrument mechanic
Employment	October 14, 1963, to present: Scott Instrument Company, 3734 West Slauson, Los Angeles, California
Arrest Records	1930: Illegal possession of liquor; fined $100. at Wichita, Kansas.
	1932: Disturbing the peace; fined $10. at Wichita, Kansas.
	1960: Fraud; $25.00, Houston, Texas.
Peculiarities	Both hands crippled by arthritis.

In addition, at the time of the interview ABADIE described himself as an alcoholic and "bum," advising that he had been a constant alcoholic for the past ten years.

He advised that prior to going to work for Scott Instrument Company he was employed by the Salvation Army, San Bernardino, California, for five weeks, and in the hospital for three weeks, both San Bernardino.

282

FD-302 (Rev. 3-3-59) FEDERAL BUREAU OF Commission Exhibit No. 1751

1

Date Dec. 7, 1963

WILLIAM J. HARRIS, President, Dallas Federation of Muscians, Local 147, Room 505-B, 1416 Commerce Street Building, telephone RI 2-3077, furnished the following information:

He first met JACK RUBY in 1947 or 1948 when RUBY and his sister opened the Silver Spur Club in Dallas. The club remained opened for only 6 or 8 weeks when the club closed . RUBY did not pay the band then playing at the club. HARRIS called on RUBY in an effort to obtain the money for the band. RUBY advised he would pay the band when he sold his beer stock at the club. Shortly thereafter, RUBY did pay the band.

HARRIS only spoke with RUBY about a half dozen times in the course of the past 15 years and has never had any social relations with RUBY. He has never played poker with RUBY, although HARRIS used to play cards in the early evening at the Artists of Dallas Club, 418½ North St. Paul, which is now the American Legion Club. HARRIS understands RUBY used to drop in late at the club to play poker.

NORMAN SMITH, a former member of the Local 147, also played cards at the Artists of Dallas Club. SMITH graduated from Southern Methodist University (SMU) 7 or 8 years ago and during his last year at SMU, produced a large musical variety show. HARRIS was cosignor on a $500.00 note for SMITH several years ago and when SMITH "skipped" town, HARRIS had to repay the note. HARRIS has heard SMITH, after leaving Dallas, went to Hollywood, California, where he worked in the T.V. show "The Deputy" with ALLEN CHASE, who was a classmate of SMITH's at SMU. SMITH was originally from Massachusetts and HARRIS has heard recently SMITH ran for a constable office somewhere in the East, possibly in New Jersey. To HARRIS's knowledge, SMITH has not been in Dallas for over four years.

HARRIS recalls RUSTY BROWN, 2300 Avalon, Fort Worth, Texas, telephone numbers JE 4-5381 and ED 6-2801,

on 12/6/63 at Dallas, Texas File # DL 44-1639

by Special Agent R. NEIL QUIGLEY/csh Date dictated 12/7/63

166

COMMISSION EXHIBIT No. 1751

2

DL 44-1639

who travels around the country with a dixie land band, worked for a long time at RUBY's clubs.

RUBY always impressed HARRIS as wanting to do something big. At one time RUBY had an act built around a small Negro boy who RUBY thought would "make it big." However, nothing ever came of the act.

RUBY was always fair and honest in his dealings with Local 147.

167

COMMISSION EXHIBIT No. 1751—Continued

FD-302 (Rev. 1-25-60) FEDERAL BUREAU OF INVESTIGATION

Commission Exhibit No. 1752

1

Date December 3, 1963

ROBERT DONALD LAWRENCE, was interviewed at his residence, 237 Lana Street, Apartment 1A, Las Vegas, telephone number 736-4785.

LAWRENCE was questioned concerning his knowledge of, and/or association with, JACK RUBY. LAWRENCE advised that he has not seen RUBY since he departed Dallas, Texas, approximately six or seven years ago. He advised that he was acquainted with RUBY in Dallas, when the latter owned and operated the "Vegas Club" in that city. He recalled RUBY as at one time the operator of the "Professional Club" in Dallas.

LAWRENCE related that he knew RUBY well, describing him as a "hot head" with a "short fuse."

He stated that he has no information that RUBY has been in the Las Vegas area recently and added that he has never seen RUBY in Las Vegas, Nevada.

LAWRENCE recalled that RUBY at one time operated a beer and wine establishment in Dallas, Texas. He further recalled that RUBY was always friendly with the police in Dallas. He mentioned that RUBY was a very excitable person and used to become heated in the midst of poker games when things did not go his way. He also advised that RUBY spoke like a high pressure salesman when in conversation with others. LAWRENCE related that he knew the following persons were friends and associates of RUBY in the Dallas, Texas area:

JOHNNY ROSS, liquor store owner;
"Chicken Louie," well known hood, deceased;
R. D. MATTHEWS, strong arm man;
CHARLEY TISH, employed Prime Rib Restaurant, Las Vegas;
ABE WEINSTEIN and BARNEY WEINSTEIN, brothers who operated the Colony Club and Theatre Lounge respectively.

LAWRENCE advised that he had never heard of LEE HARVEY OSWALD until his name appeared in the newspapers.

On 11/26/63 at Las Vegas, Nevada File # Las Vegas 44-48

by SAS FRANCIS J. SCHMIDT and JOSEPH A. MURRAY: JAM/nph Date dictated 11/26/63

198

Commission Exhibit No. 1753

Form No. 1588 (Revised) Memorandum Report (7-1-60)

UNITED STATES SECRET SERVICE
TREASURY DEPARTMENT

d 1t

ORIGIN Field OFFICE Los Angeles, California FILE NO. 4-3-601.0

TYPE OF CASE	STATUS	TITLE OR CAPTION
Protective Research	Closed	Jack Ruby - PRS Subject C 14 b
INVESTIGATION MADE AT: Los Angeles, California	PERIOD COVERED: 11/29/63 - 11/30/63	
INVESTIGATION MADE BY: SAIC Guy H. Spaman & SA Darwin D. Horn		

DETAILS

DETAILS OF INVESTIGATION

On the afternoon of November 29, 1963, SAIC Spaman received a phone call from a man who said he was Irving Cassidy. Mr. Cassidy said that he had just visited Harry Hall in Terminal Island Federal Reformatory, Los Angeles, and Mr. Hall asked that Mr. Cassidy call SAIC Spaman to tell him that Harry Hall had information concerning Jack Ruby from Dallas, Texas, and would like to talk with the Secret Service.

Harry Hall was an informant for the Los Angeles Office several years ago, giving information which resulted in the seizure of a counterfeiting plant. He has since given information to the Intelligence Division of the Treasury and the Federal Bureau of Investigation.

Harry Hall is serving a sentence of 30 months in Terminal Island for defrauding boxing promoter Truman Gibson of a large sum of money. His confidence scheme involved forging United States Attorney Francis Whelan's signature and other fraudulent Federal papers resulting in his conviction in Federal Court after an investigation by the FBI.

On the same date SA Horn interviewed Harry Hall at Terminal Island Reformatory in the presence of a prison official. Hall stated that he had had business dealings with Jack Ruby and was well acquainted with him, but advised SA Horn that he did not want to talk in the reformatory in the presence of witnesses, but would talk to SAIC Spaman if he could be taken out of Terminal Island to the Secret Service Office.

On November 30, 1963, SAIC Spaman discussed this matter with Inspector Kelley at Dallas, Texas, advising Inspector Kelley that Harry Hall had been of assistance to other agencies in addition to the Secret Service, and that his information in many cases had been reliable.

DISTRIBUTION	COPIES	REPORT MADE BY	DATE
Chief	Orig.	Guy H. Spaman (signed), Special Agent in Charge	12/4/63
Los Angeles	cc	APPROVED	DATE
Dallas	2 cc	SPECIAL AGENT IN CHARGE	454
	GHS:sr		

(CONTINUE ON PLAIN PAPER)

U. S. GOVERNMENT PRINTING OFFICE

SAIC Spaman discussed with Inspector Kelley the advisability of interviewing Hall with an FBI agent, inasmuch as the FBI had been in close contact with Hall recently, and Hall was in the custody of the Department of Justice. Inspector Kelley agreed to this procedure. SAIC Spaman then made arrangements with SAC William Simon, FBI, Los Angeles, for SA William Knowland, FBI, to meet with Spaman at Terminal Island.

On November 30, 1963, SAIC Spaman and SA Knowland, FBI, interviewed Harry Hall at Terminal Island without prison officials being present. Hall stated that around 1950 to 1952 his Uncle, Marty Fields, introduced him to Jack Ruby in Dallas, Texas. At that time Ruby ran a small cheap bar and night club in Dallas. Harry Hall had checked into a Dallas Hotel using the alias of Harry Sinclair, Jr. and was looking for high stake gambling games to get into or to place bets on football games or horse races.

His method of operation at that time was to use the name of a well known person and ingratiate himself with persons with money. He would then make bets or gamble putting over fictitious checks if he lost and leaving town. Ruby on occasion provided Hall with a bankroll and introduced him to likely victims, with Ruby taking 40% of any deal while Hall collected 60%. Ruby's cut was because he was supposed to have influence with the police, so that he would have no worry about any gambling arrest.

Hall said that during this period through influential people, he was able to meet in Dallas, he was able to place bets with a bookie in Montreal by telephone, winning about $5,000. Ruby and Hall then went to Chicago enroute to Montreal to collect their winnings, but Ruby remained in Chicago while Hall went to Montreal and collected the money, returning to join Ruby in Chicago.

At that time Ruby was staying at the Devonshire Hotel on the near north side in Chicago, while Hall stayed at the Palmer House. During their stay in Chicago Ruby visited and seemed quite friendly with a man who had a store which sold what Hall called "schlox" meaning off-brand merchandise similar to expensive appliances, etc. This man's store was located on the west side of State street in the middle of the block south of Grand. This man was supposed to be able to get for a person any type of merchandise that a person wanted. Hall did not know what Ruby's dealings were with this man. They returned to Dallas by way of Tulsa, Oklahoma, where Ruby seemed to have good connections in gambling circles, and Shreveport, Louisiana, where Ruby had similar good connections.

Hall stated that there was a Texas millionaire named Bill Byers, who came from Tyre, Texas, who was friendly with two other Texas millionaires named Murchison and Andraddy. Bill Byers circulated between Texas and Los Angeles. Ruby knew that Byers carried large sums of money with him and wanted Hall, who also knew Byers, to find out when Byers would be alone. Ruby said he had a couple of men who would hold Byers up without injuring him, and that Ruby and Hall could divide whatever

money Byers had. Hall said he did not go through with this deal, but he heard later that Byers was robbed while at the Del Charro Hotel, La Jolla, California. This hotel is owned by Mr. Murchison.

Hall further stated that some time during this period, while he was going under the name of Harry Sinclair, Jr. or Ed Pauley, Jr. he met H. L. Hunt, another Texas millionaire; that he and Ruby bet Hunt on the Cotton Bowl and Rose Bowl games, winning a large sum of money from Hunt, which they split.

Hall stated that also during this time he and Ruby came to Los Angeles and Ruby continued to San Francisco, where he said he was going to see one "Stony" and "Solly" or "Hecky" Schuman on some deal. These men were supposed to be known racketeers or gamblers in San Francisco. Hall stated that one time when he was associating with Ruby, he recalls that Ruby said that he was going to Florida to buy a load of "contraband" to send to Israel. Hall said that Ruby was the type who was interested in any way to make money and seemed to have good contacts with the police. He said that he could not conceive of Ruby doing anything out of patriotism.

Hall further stated that he was acquainted with one Eugenia Elson, who is a manicurist at the Beverly Wilshire Hotel, Los Angeles. He said she has a son, Eugene, who is 8 or 9 years old. She was born in Russia and formerly lived in Dallas, being married to a wealthy Dallas man whom she has since divorced. Hall stated that this woman, he believed, had some Russian friends in Dallas. He said he knew of no connection between her and Ruby.

Hall stated that he was sentenced to State Reformatory, Chino, California, in 1955 for checks, being released in 1956. He said all of the above information related to events before that time; that he had no dealings or no contact with Ruby since 1955. However, he stated that he was close enough to Ruby so that if he were permitted to talk to Ruby he believed he could persuade him to tell the whole story.

SA Knowland stated that the information he secured at this joint questioning of Hall would be teletyped to their Dallas Office.

DISPOSITION

Closed Los Angeles.

Commission Exhibit No. 1754

UNITED STATES DEPARTMENT OF JUSTICE

FEDERAL BUREAU OF INVESTIGATION

In Reply, Please Refer to
File No.

WASHINGTON 25, D. C.

June 10, 1964

Individuals and Organizations
Involved or Interviewed

JACK L. RUBY
LEE HARVEY OSWALD - VICTIM

ISADORE MAX MILLER, Also
Known As Isadore "Izzy" Miller

INFORMATION CONCERNING

An investigation of Isadore Max Miller was instituted to ascertain if his gambling activities were in violation of Federal antigambling statutes.

It was determined that for the past several years Miller has operated as a bookmaker in the Dallas, Texas, area. In his gambling activities he is closely associated with known Dallas, Texas, bookmakers John Eli Stone, Henry Clinton Winfrey and James Woodrow Stone, brother of Eli Stone. These individuals use various apartments in Dallas as bookmaking headquarters and frequently change their base of operations. In most instances the apartments are rented and telephone service acquired under assumed names.

No violation of Federal statutes was developed and no prosecution resulted in connection with this investigation of Miller.

Jack Ruby's name does not appear in this file and he was not connected in any way in this investigation.

COMMISSION EXHIBIT No. 1754

Commission Exhibit No. 1755

DL 44-1639
PLS:gj
1

The following investigation was conducted by SA PAUL L. SCOTT:

On January 22, 1964, ISADORE MILLER, also known as IZZY MILLER, 11144 Valleydale Drive, Dallas, Texas, owner of Enquire Shine and Press Shop, 1322 Commerce Street, whose name appeared in the personal effects of RUBY, advised he has known RUBY since 1949 or 1950. At that time RUBY was operating the Silver Spur Club on South Ervay Street. MILLER has been in the Silver Spur Club on a few occasions and also the Vegas and Carousel Clubs subsequently operated by RUBY. RUBY has been a customer at the Enquire Shine and Press Shop since he began operation of the Carousel Club and most of MILLER's contacts with him have been business contacts. RUBY was well known in the downtown section of Dallas. He was a friendly individual and was always doing things for people. On occasion when MILLER would be at one of RUBY's clubs, he would observe RUBY "flare up" when some customer in his club misbehaved. MILLER has no knowledge of any close associates of RUBY other than a girl friend, name unknown, whom RUBY dated a number of years. MILLER has only been to the Carousel Club one time during the past two years. He has no knowledge of RUBY's activities other than the operation of the club in Dallas.

MILLER did not know LEE HARVEY OSWALD and has no knowledge of any connection between RUBY and OSWALD.

On January 22, 1964, SAM HICKS, shoe shine boy, Enquire Shine and Press Shop, residence 1201 - 7th Street, Dallas, an acquaintance of RUBY, advised he has known RUBY for the past three or four years as a customer at this shop. He has occasionally delivered cleaning to RUBY at the Carousel Club. RUBY was a generous individual and was always giving things to the shoe shine boys and other employees at the shop. HICKS has no knowledge of any associates of RUBY other than ANDREW ARMSTRONG who helped RUBY operate the Carousel Club.

HICKS did not know LEE HARVEY OSWALD and has no knowledge of any connection between RUBY and OSWALD.

51

COMMISSION EXHIBIT No. 1755

FD-302 (Rev. 3-3-59) FEDERAL BUREAU OF INVESTIGATION

1 [redacted]

Commission Exhibit No. 1756

Date Dec. 20, 1963

JAMES C. BARRAGAN, owner, The Town Pump of Dallas, 5021 West Lovers Lane, associate of JACK RUBY, furnished the following information:

He opened The Town Pump of Dallas in about 1956, which is the same year he first met JACK RUBY, as RUBY made it a practice to visit all of the night spots in Dallas at least once a year. At this time RUBY was operating the Vegas Club, which he understood was owned by RUBY's mother, and as far as he knows, RUBY did not have any funds of his own to operate such an establishment. He described RUBY as a man who would have a pocketful of money one day and was broke the next day. On one occasion five years ago RUBY attempted to sell him a diamond ring, saying he was broke and needed the money. He last saw RUBY in the Carousel Club about two years ago, at which time there were approximately six uniformed officers of the Dallas Police Department present. He recalls thinking at the time that RUBY must have friends in the police department as drinks were still being served after midnight even though the police were present.

He had no personal contact with RUBY outside of an occasional visit from RUBY at The Town Pump, and he was only in one of RUBY's clubs, the Carousel Club, on one occasion, as noted above. He does not know of any connection between LEE HARVEY OSWALD or of any direct connection RUBY had with the Dallas Police Department.

on 12/17/63 at Dallas, Texas File # DL 44-1639

by Special Agent EDWARD J. MABEY/csh Date dictated 12/19/63

23

COMMISSION EXHIBIT NO. 1756

FD-302 (Rev. 1-25-60) FEDERAL BUREAU OF INVESTIGATION

Date 12/3/63

1

GLADWIN HILL, who resides at 7874 Fairholm Drive, Hollywood, California, telephone OL 2-2846, voluntarily appeared at the Los Angeles FBI Office and advised as follows:

He is a reporter for the <u>New York Times</u> stationed in the Los Angeles area.

Shortly after noon on November 22, 1963, he departed Los Angeles for Dallas. He arrived Dallas at approximately 4:45 p.m. on November 22, 1963. He arrived at the Dallas Police Department (PD) at approximately 6:30 p.m. November 22, 1963, and remained there until approximately 1:00 a.m., November 23, 1963. HILL advised that OSWALD was being detained by the Dallas PD on the fourth floor and that each time he was interrogated by the police it was necessary to bring him from the fourth floor to the third floor of the Dallas PD through a public corridor. The public corridor was crowded in each instance and at no time was HILL required to show identification, nor did he observe any of the other reporters show identification.

On Saturday, November 23, 1963, he returned to the PD at approximately 9:00 a.m. and remained until 9:30 p.m. that evening. OSWALD was transferred between the third and fourth floor on numerous occasions and again through a crowded public corridor. He was not challenged on November 23, nor did he see anyone question other reporters regarding their identity. HILL stated at this time it occurred to him that it would have been possible and quite easy for anyone who desired to enter the building and kill OSWALD.

Just before he departed the PD at approximately 9:30 p.m. on November 23, Chief of Police CURRY volunteered to a number of the press who were standing around, that OSWALD would be transferred from the PD to County authorities on Sunday morning. The Chief indicated that if the press were at the building about 10 o'clock Sunday morning they would be on time. HILL also stated he recalled the Chief indicate that the case against OSWALD had developed to such an extent it was no longer necessary to have him available to confront him with new evidence.

On 12/3/63 at Los Angeles, California File # Los Angeles 44-895

by SAs CHESTER E. ST. VINCENT and JOSEPH C. ALSTON/ AY Date dictated 12/3/63

COMMISSION EXHIBIT NO. 1757

HILL returned to the PD at approximately 9:45 Sunday morning November 24, 1963 and immediately upon arrival talked to Chief CURRY. The Chief stated that if he had not told the press Saturday evening that he was going to transport OSWALD at 10 o'clock he would have transferred him earlier to the County Jail. He said the Chief did not indicate in any way that he had been pressured by the press regarding this transfer but that he was merely trying to keep his word. At about 11:00 a.m. HILL together with several other reporters accompanied the Chief and a number of officers from the third floor to the basement by elevator. As he approached the area where OSWALD was to pass through on his way to a van which would take him to the County Jail, HILL was challenged by a police officer and the police officer examined his credentials. HILL stated this is the first time he was compelled to display his credentials. At approximately 11:20 OSWALD appeared through a door leading out to a ramp where the van was located waiting to take him to the County Jail. As OSWALD proceeded through the door, police officers filled in behind him and HILL was unable to observe his movements. HILL heard a shot and immediately realizing what had happened he ran out of the police building through another exit to take up a position by the van. At no time did he see RUBY nor did he see who fired the shot at OSWALD.

HILL stated the security at the police building was "terrible and haphazard". He added it would have been possible for anyone to get in, proceed to the third floor and shoot OSWALD as he was being moved to and from the fourth floor.

HILL stated, Sunday night he returned to the basement area where OSWALD had been shot, where he ran into Attorney TOM HOWARD. He stated HOWARD indicated he was at the PD on behalf of RUBY and he introduced HILL to Attorney FRED BRUNER, a former assistant District Attorney who told HILL that he had represented RUBY in the past in some legal matters.

HILL stated the transfer of RUBY from the police department building to the County Jail was handled in a much different manner and the press was not aware of this transfer until after it had actually taken place. HILL stated he heard

from unrecalled sources after OSWALD's death that RUBY owned the Carousel Club and managed the Vegas Club, which was owned by his sister. He also heard talk that RUBY was a homosexual and that RUBY hung around both at the Police Department and City Hall. He also heard from unrecalled sources that RUBY was acquainted with MICKEY COHEN, and that COHEN had met his girl friend, CANDY BAR through RUBY.

HILL stated the following individuals were in Dallas covering the assassination and the related events from the Los Angeles area:

GENE BONDS, ABC

TOM PETTIT and TED MANN, NBC

ED HADDAD, KPOL

GENE BLAKE, Los Angeles Times

HILL stated that he knew of no unauthorized persons in police basement; he knows of no one who was permitted in the basement without properly identifying themselves; that he has received no information indicating that anyone conspired with RUBY to kill OSWALD and that he received no information indicating that any police officer or any other official conspired with RUBY or willingly permitted OSWALD's killing. He further stated that he could not recall ever observing RUBY in the police department at any time and that he had no knowledge of any relationship between RUBY and OSWALD.

FD-302 (Rev. 3-3-59) FEDERAL BUREAU OF — Commission Exhibit No. 1758 —

Date 11/26/63

DEAN M. JENNINGS was telephonically interviewed at his employment, Gallo Wine Company, 225 Shaw Road, South San Francisco, California, telephone JU 9-6802. He advised that he lives on a houseboat in Sausalito, California, and uses Box Office Box 591, Sausalito, as his home address.

He was questioned about his acquaintance with JACK RUBY, the man who was alleged to have shot LEE HARVEY OSWALD in the Dallas Police Department. JENNINGS stated he had met RUBY while he, JENNINGS, was employed as a branch manager of the American Guild Variety Artists (AGVA) in Dallas, Texas during 1956 and 1957. JENNINGS stated he may have contacted RUBY in his official capacity, but he was mainly acquainted with RUBY socially. Both he and RUBY belonged to the Musicians Union Club, located in the Musicians Union Building, Dallas, Texas. RUBY, together with JENNINGS, BILL HARRIS and a NORMAN SMITH used to play poker regularly there. JENNINGS stated that he had an honorary membership card but that RUBY appeared to be a regular member although he was not a musician. BILL HARRIS is the President of the Musicians Union and would be very well acquainted with any other persons who might know RUBY. NORMAN SMITH had something to do with Little Theater groups in the Dallas area.

JENNINGS' impression of RUBY was that he was "a night club character." By this, he meant that he was a small time operator who was always on the fringe of going broke but liked to leave the impression that he was a big shot. RUBY had the reputation of being somewhat of a tough guy and had a very bad temper. He appeared to always be playing the part of a junior version of MICKEY COHEN. JENNINGS stated that he had heard that RUBY used to own a night club in Chicago before he moved to Dallas. If this were true, the AGVA in Chicago would be able to tell more about it.

When questioned about OSWALD or any radical inclinations or acquaintances which RUBY may have had, JENNINGS stated that as far as he knows, RUBY was not smart enough to have any radical ideas. He, JENNINGS, did not know OSWALD.

When questioned about the family of RUBY, JENNINGS stated he had never met any family and assumed that RUBY was single inasmuch

on 11/25/63 at San Francisco, California File # SF 44-494

by Special Agent SA EWING H. RAUCH/jl Date dictated 11/26/63

This document contains neither recommendations nor conclusions of the FBI. It is the property of the FBI and is loaned to your agency; it and its contents are not to be distributed outside your agency.

198

COMMISSION EXHIBIT NO. 1758

2
SF 44-494
EHR:jl

as he was always "chasing the strippers around." In connection with this, JENNINGS stated that CANDY BAR was stripping in Dallas at that time and that he believed RUBY had dated her several times. JENNINGS stated that he had heard that CANDY BAR had been paroled and is now leading a legitimate life but he does not know her address.

199

COMMISSION EXHIBIT NO. 1758—Continued

Commission Exhibit No. 1759

BANK OF DALLAS 3708 LEMMON AVENUE AT WELBORN • P. O. BOX 6667 • DALLAS 19, TEXAS

JAMES A. DONNELL
VICE PRESIDENT AND CASHIER

August 18, 1964

Mr. J. Lee Rankin
General Counsel
President's Commission on the
Assassination of President Kennedy
200 Maryland Ave., N. E.
Washington, D. C. 20002

Dear Mr. Rankin:

The savings account maintained by Eva L. Grant and/or Jack L. Ruby was opened on July 6, 1962, using a cash deposit of $100.00. The account had very little activity and was closed on February 19, 1964, when Mrs. Grant took cash for the balance of the account in the amount of $116.15. The signature card reflected the signature of Eva L. Grant and Jack L. Ruby. The home address given was 3929 Rawlins, telephone number Lakeside 6-6258 and the occupation given was manager of the Club Vages, telephone number Lakeside 8-4775.

This is all the information we have regarding this joint account and should you need additional information, we will be happy to comply with your request.

Yours very truly,

James A. Donnell
Vice President

JAD:ji

Your *Bank in Dallas*

Commission Exhibit No. 1760

Item 1

In connection with a survey of crime conditions in the Dallas Division of the FBI in March, 1962, it was established that there were three burlesque houses located in downtown Dallas; however, there was no information any of these were frequented by any known criminal element. They were night clubs catering to tourists, mostly, and featured "strip-tease" dancers and exorbitant prices for food, beer, wine and setups. They were as follows:

Theater Lounge, 1326 Jackson, operated by Barney Weinstein;

Abe's Colony Club, 1322½ Commerce, operated by Abe Weinstein;

The Carousel, 1312½ Commerce, operated by Jack Ruby.

COMMISSION EXHIBIT NO. 1760

Item 3

In connection with certain information concerning James Breen which was forwarded to our Dallas Office from our Los Angeles Office by communication dated March 20, 1956, the following interview with Bunny Breen, whose true name is Eileen Curry, is set forth.

On March 18, 1956, Bunny Breen, presently known as Carol Connor, requested the Los Angeles Office to have Special Agent Ambrose K. Law call her collect at Davis 74784, Dallas, Texas. She had been interviewed twice for information she might furnish in the case entitled "Unknown Subject, Abraham Davidian - Victim. Obstruction of Justice." She was acting as was James Breen as informants for the Federal Narcotics Bureau and the Los Angeles Police Department Vice Squad. She indicated she had formerly been with Stanley Adams, a subject in this case. Bunny, at that time, was operating a house of prostitution in Los Angeles on a call girl basis. She furnished no information of particular significance. James Breen was interviewed two or three times as a possible prospective confidential source, but both were constantly in trouble with local authorities and contact could not be maintained with them. Bunny, on March 18, 1956, advised she and James had jumped a local bond on narcotics charges about the first of the year and gone to Dallas. James was driving a cab for the City Transportation Company, and she was apparently operating in some branch of the prostitution racket. Bunny was told by James he had made connection with large narcotics setup operating between Mexico, Texas and the East. James made several trips and returned. He left about three weeks ago and has not returned. He purposely did not give details so she could not get into trouble. He took his clothes about three weeks ago and said he was going on another trip. She heard later that he had left her but heard also from a bondsman named Schott this was not true and that James had contacted him and asked him to look out for her if she got into any trouble. She believes James made connections with the narcotics ring through a former associate from Seagoville Prison where James served time. In some fashion James got the okay to operate through Jack Ruby of Dallas. Several days ago, one Jack (last name unknown) of Houston came to see Bunny with one Gordon Winter

COMMISSION EXHIBIT No. 1761

of Houston, a friend of hers and James. Jack told her that James was trying to hijack a 300 to 400 thousand load of narcotics from Mexico and was going to try to go with another distribution setup. Jack questioned her as to whether she had information regarding James' whereabouts and threatened her if she was withholding information about James. Also, he stated his life would not be worth anything if he was trying to double-cross the group. Bunny fears James has been killed or kidnapped and wanted to talk to someone she could trust.

- 2 -

COMMISSION EXHIBIT No. 1761—Continued

FD-302 (Rev. 1-25-60)

FEDERAL BUREAU — Commission Exhibit No. 1762

Date 6/11/64

EILEEN CURRY, residing at the Regency Hotel, 19 East Ohio Street, Chicago, Illinois, under the name of CAROL SCOTT, furnished the following information:

In December, 1955, CURRY advised, she was living with JAMES ECKFORD BREEN and that about that time arrived with BREEN in Dallas, Texas.

CURRY planned to have two girls employed as prostitutes at the Statler Hilton Hotel, which was then nearing completion. On arriving in Dallas BREEN and CURRY rented a two-bedroom apartment in a modern apartment building located on Gaston Boulevard near Fitzhugh Street in Dallas. This apartment building was a two-story structure located on a corner and had a covered parking area in the rear. There were approximately 24 to 30 one and two-bedroom apartments in the building, which was U-shaped. CURRY and BREEN rented a first floor apartment and resided in this apartment for approximately two months.

After arriving in Dallas, Texas, BREEN secured employment as a cab driver. Approximately four weeks after their arrival in Dallas, BREEN brought JACK RUBY to the apartment house, where he introduced RUBY to CURRY as a friend of his. A few days after this first meeting JACK RUBY, accompanied by a white male, who was short and dark, drove to the CURRY apartment in a late model, blue-green automobile, make unrecalled. They waited outside of the apartment until joined by BREEN, at which time they departed. Later that day BREEN told CURRY that he had accompanied RUBY to an unnamed location, where he had been shown moving pictures of various border guards, both Mexican and American. In addition, included among the movies were films of persons described by BREEN as various "narcotic agents," as well as persons who were "contacts" on the "Mexican side." BREEN was enthused over what he considered an extremely efficient operation in connection with narcotics traffic.

CURRY advised that she had a large argument with BREEN at about this time, indicating to him that she did not want him to engage in the narcotics business, particularly

On 6/9/64 at Chicago, Illinois File # CG 44-645

by SAs CHARLES E. BRUNNER DENNIS W. SHANAHAN/kmg Date dictated 6/10/64

10

"heavy" narcotics such as heroin and cocaine.

A day or two later BREEN left Dallas for a purported trip to Chihuahua, Mexico. BREEN was gone from the apartment for four or five days and on his return indicated that he had made $2400. CURRY was of the opinion that BREEN could not have made this large a sum on marijuana and accused him of transporting "heavy" narcotics. BREEN denied this to CURRY, but nevertheless CURRY told BREEN that if he left again on a similar trip she would leave him.

During BREEN's absence CURRY was visited on one or two occasions by JACK RUBY, who evidenced an interest in her. On one of these occasions RUBY took her to his night club, which was then closed as it was after the closing time. She recalled RUBY's club as having an angled entrance and a long bar on the left side as one entered. She recalled a row of small windows located high on the front wall of the club. She further recalled a hanging vertical sign outside of the club. She could not recall the name of this club nor did she recall its location other than to state that it was in the city of Dallas. She advised that there was a large gas station located on the corner of the same street to the right of RUBY's club as one faced the club entrance.

CURRY advised that she did not become intimate with RUBY despite his statement that he could send her influential clients if she were "friendly." CURRY advised that RUBY was aware that she was employing two prostitutes during that period of time and, in fact, sent two or three customers through CURRY to these girls at about this time.

CURRY recalled that RUBY attempted to interest her in selling pornographic photographs to her customers, indicating that he had a large quantity of such material available to him. CURRY stated that she declined to sell such material since, if arrested, she did not want to be found with this type of material, which she felt would make any charges against her more serious.

On the occasion of CURRY's trip to RUBY's night club RUBY was driving the same blue-green car in which he

11

had been a passenger at the time that BREEN had accompanied RUBY and the heavy set man to view the movies of the border guards.

At about this time the Statler Hilton Hotel was officially opened and the two girls employed by CURRY then took up residence in the hotel with the knowledge of certain hotel employees, whose identity CURRY refused to divulge. Within a few days after the opening of the Statler Hilton Hotel, BREEN left town to go to Mexico. Believing that BREEN was once more engaged in narcotics traffic, CURRY decided to leave him and move out of her apartment. She moved to the Casa Linda, located on Gaston Boulevard in a suburb of Dallas. She stated that the Casa Linda was an extremely large apartment development, consisting of approximately 150 apartments and included, for tenant use, a swimming pool and bar. Approximately two weeks after CURRY moved to the Casa Linda Apartments, three white males forced their way into her apartment. One of these men was JACK SULLIVAN, who originally came from Houston, Texas. The second and third men were unknown to CURRY. She stated that these three men wanted to know the whereabouts of BREEN, indicating that BREEN had either run out with the money advanced him to purchase narcotics or had purchased the narcotics and then failed to deliver them to his superiors. During the course of their conversation with CURRY, these men indicated that $180,000 was involved in BREEN's disappearance. At the time that these three individuals entered CURRY's apartment she had with her a young prostitute, whom she knew as DEBBIE. She stated that she did not know DEBBIE's true name, nor did she know any other name utilized by this girl at any time. She advised that SULLIVAN beat her in an attempt to learn from CURRY the whereabouts of BREEN. In addition, he severely beat DEBBIE and on leaving the apartment took DEBBIE with him. She said it was her understanding that DEBBIE had been forced by SULLIVAN, acting as her pimp, to work in a house of prostitution located somewhere in Texas City, Texas. She said that she had learned at a later occasion that DEBBIE had gotten a message out by means of one of her customers to the effect that she was being held prisoner at this particular house of prostitution in Texas City. CURRY advised that she had never

learned the exact whereabouts of DEBBIE, nor has she seen or heard from this girl since 1956.

CURRY advised that SULLIVAN, accompanied by the same two men, returned to her apartment the next day following the abduction of DEBBIE. The second visit occurred in the morning, at which time she again told SULLIVAN and his companions that she did not know the whereabouts of BREEN. The same men returned again during the late afternoon of the same day. During this third visit SULLIVAN, in an attempt to frighten CURRY, fired a shot, which apparently pierced a closet door and must have entered an adjacent apartment. Immediately thereafter SULLIVAN and his companions left the apartment.

CURRY advised that SULLIVAN and his companions did not mention JACK RUBY but indicated that they were employed by the people interested in BREEN's narcotic business, and from this she concluded that these three men were connected in some way with BREEN.

CURRY advised that she has had no contact with BREEN since the above described incidents and has no knowledge as to his present whereabouts. She stated that she has not seen nor heard from JACK RUBY since 1956 but recognized him from the various newspaper photographs taken of RUBY in connection with the murder of OSWALD in November, 1963. She advised that the two girls working for her in Dallas at the time of RUBY's visit to her apartment were one "SKY" (Last Name Unknown) and one CONNIE (Last Name Unknown). She said that "SKY" was about 21 years old, slender, extremely pretty with silver blond hair and, she believed, was from Dallas, Texas. CONNIE was believed to be from Longview, Texas. She stated that she did not know whether either girl had ever been arrested but both had been employed as prostitutes at various locations in Texas for two or three years prior to 1956.

CURRY advised that one RALPH HEDRICK had been a close friend of BREEN's when both were incarcerated at the Federal Correctional Institution at Seagoville, Texas.

5
CG 44-645

She stated that HEDRICK, in 1956, was in his 30's and had already completed 15 years of various penal servitude. She said that HEDRICK was, at that time, employed in a print shop in Dallas, Texas, and was active in some type of lecture tour wherein he spoke about his criminal background before youth groups. CURRY advised that she had no knowledge as to whether BREEN would have confided in HEDRICK or whether HEDRICK would have known RUBY but felt that HEDRICK was BREEN's closest friend in the Dallas area.

CURRY advised that she had heard rumors in Dallas, Texas, the source not now recalled, to the effect that BREEN's contact and protection in Muskogee, Oklahoma, was allegedly the Chief of Police of Muskogee.

14

FD-302 (Rev. 1-25-60) FEDERAL BUREAU OF INVESTIGATIC

1

[redacted]

Commission Exhibit No. 1763

Date December 26, 1963

JACK HARDEE, JR. was interviewed at the Mobile County Jail, Mobile, Alabama, where he is incarcerated in federal custody. He was advised that he did not have to speak with interviewing agents; that anything he said could be used against him in a court of law; and that he could have the advice of an attorney prior to the interview. No threats, promises, or duress were used to induce him to make this statement.

HARDEE stated that he was born near Memphis, Tennessee, and he was 38 years old. He stated that he has travelled extensively throughout the southern part of the United States.

HARDEE stated that he has spent some time in Dallas, Texas, and he had met JACK RUBY during the course of his contacts in Dallas. He stated that approximately one year ago, while in Dallas, Texas, he attempted to set up a numbers game, and he was advised by an individual, whom he did not identify, that in order to operate in Dallas it was necessary to have the clearance of JACK RUBY. He stated that this individual, whom he did not identify, told him that RUBY had the "fix" with the county authorities, and that any other fix being placed would have to be done through RUBY.

HARDEE stated that he did not like RUBY upon their first contact, and this, coupled with a change in his plans, which was unrelated to this, caused him to change his mind about operating the numbers game, and the plan fell through.

HARDEE stated that he had also met JACK RUBY because a girlfriend of his, whom he refused to identify, went to the Bent Elbow Club in Dallas in an effort to obtain a job as a stripper. He stated that she was referred to the Cow Girl Club, and, from there, to JACK RUBY, where she went to work. He stated that he was out of town at the time, and, upon his return, he learned from an undisclosed source that RUBY was "messing around" with his girlfriend. He stated that he felt fondly towards this girl, because she is the

On 12/24/63 at Mobile, Alabama File # MO 44-1070

by SA JAMES A. DAY and SA STANLEY J. ORENSTEIN :jes Date dictated 12/24/63

- 65 -

mother of an illegitimate daughter by him. He stated in the course of the interview that the girlfriend was a Canadian Citizen and the adopted daughter of an American woman. He indicated that she had had some trouble with Immigration Authorities in Dallas recently and was granted her citizenship approximately three years ago.

HARDEE stated that when he heard that RUBY was attempting to have sexual relations with his girlfriend, he, with two friends of his, went to RUBY's business place, and he personally warned RUBY to keep his hands off the girl. He stated that at that time RUBY exhibited to him a nickel-plated .357 Magnum Revolver, which he was wearing on his left hip stuffed inside his trousers. Because HARDEE had two friends with him, and RUBY had only two of his friends present, the encounter was a "Mexican Stand-Off", and RUBY accepted HARDEE's warning.

HARDEE stated that upon his insistence his girlfriend quit working for RUBY as of that time.

During the period that HARDEE was in Dallas approximately one year ago, he was in RUBY's presence on several occasions. He stated that RUBY impressed him as being the type of individual who would kill without much provocation.

HARDEE also stated that the police officer whom HARVEY LEE OSWALD allegedly killed after he allegedly assassinated the president was a frequent visitor to RUBY's night club, along with another officer who was a motorcycle patrol in the Oaklawn Section of Dallas. HARDEE stated from his observation there appeared to be a very close relationship between these three individuals.

HARDEE also stated that he had seen RUBY in the Dallas Police Department wearing a gun, and officers there, whom he did not know, were aware that RUBY was wearing a gun at the time.

HARDEE stated that he knew TOM LASSISTER, the "Second Floor Shoe Buyer" for Volks Brothers Shoe Company,

and his wife, whose name he could not recall, a former barmaid for RUBY, were well-acquainted with RUBY and could furnish information about him.

HARDEE stated that he knows of his own personal knowledge that RUBY hustled the strippers and other girls who worked in his club. RUBY made dates for them, accepting the money for the dates in advance, and kept half, giving the other half to the girls. These dates were filled in the new hotel in downtown Dallas and the Holiday Motel in Irvington, where RUBY had an associate, whom HARDEE could only identify as a Negro who drove a big Cadillac.

HARDEE also stated that an individual he knows only as SOL, who operates and owns SOL's Bar And Restaurant on either Main Street or Elm Street in Dallas, Texas, was well-acquainted with RUBY.

[redacted]

Commission Exhibit No. 1764

Item 8

On August 11, 1953, Special Agent Ralph J. Miles chanced to be in the office of Vincent Lee, Branch Manager, American Guild of Variety Artists, 1818 Live Oak Street, Dallas, Texas, on official business. An individual later identified by Mr. Lee as Jack Ruby, operator of the Silver Spur, 1717 South Ervay Street, Dallas, Texas, came blustering into Lee's office. Ruby demanded of Lee that Lee supply Ruby with some "girls" to put on entertainment at his Silver Spur. Lee told Ruby that Ruby would have to put up a cash bond to guarantee the girls' salary whereupon Ruby began to curse Lee, claiming that he was short on money and that Lee did not make his, Ruby's, competitors put up such a cash bond. Lee maintained that he still could not furnish girl entertainers to Ruby unless Ruby put up some cash at which time Ruby arose and in a threatening tone of voice asked Lee: "Do you want to know whether or not I'm packing a gun?", and "What are you trying to do, be a tough guy in Dallas? Well, I'm just as tough as they come" or words to that effect.

After Ruby stormed out of Lee's office, cursing all the while, Lee confidentially advised Special Agent Miles that Ruby considered himself a very tough Dallas character and was an associate of Joe Bonds, operator of the Sky Club, who was also a "tough" character who bore a grudge against Lee because Lee one time attempted to collect a $700.00 bad check Bonds had given a girl entertainer at which time either Bonds or one of his henchmen had struck Lee across the forehead with a pistol. Lee continued that both Ruby and Bonds always carried concealed pistols and were in constant association with James Robert Todd, better known as Jack Todd, FBI number 1805383, Dallas Police Department number 22255, a well-known Dallas safe-cracker. Lee informed that Ruby, Bonds and Todd, together with other hoodlums and safe-crackers, whose identities were unknown to Lee, usually hung around Sue's Used Car Lot, 3400 Live Oak, Dallas, Texas.

COMMISSION EXHIBIT No. 1764

FD-302 (Rev. 1-25-60)

FEDERAL BUREAU OF INVESTIGA.

[redacted]

Commission Exhibit No. 1765

Date 12/5/63

JOSEPH GLASER, President, Associated Booking Corporation, 50 West 57th Street, New York City, advised that approximately five or six weeks ago he was informed by the corporation's Dallas representative, namely ANTHONY POPPA, that POPPA had been contacted by JACK RUBY, a night club operator in Dallas, Texas, relative to employing an entertainer named JEWEL BROWN.

GLASER explained that about a year or so ago through the assistance of his corporation, JEWEL BROWN, who had been formerly employed with JACK RUBY, was employed by the LOUIS ARMSTRONG band which was then on and overseas tour for the United States Department of State. When ARMSTRONG returned to the United States for vacation RUBY attempted to rehire JEWEL BROWN, who in turn referred RUBY to ANTHONY POPPA. RUBY thereafter contacted POPPA for the above purpose during which time he claimed to be a personal friend of JOE GLASER having known him when both resided in Chicago, Illinois. POPPA instructed RUBY to contact GLASER concerning his interest in JEWEL BROWN. According to GLASER, RUBY made several telephone calls to him, however, GLASER refused to speak to him.

On August 5, 1963, RUBY personally contacted him at his New York Office along with one Dr. DANTE, a hypnotist performer, and suggested that GLASER sign DANTE to an exclusive contract. GLASER denied this request and later on reprimanded RUBY for telling people in the entertainment field that they were long time personal friends, whereas this was the first time they ever met. As the interview developed RUBY asked two favors, one, to have GLASER contact the American Guild of Variety Artists for the purpose of settling a dispute RUBY was having with night club competitors in Dallas, Texas, and, two, asked permission to rehire JEWEL BROWN. GLASER refused RUBY on both these requests and immediately thereafter terminated the interview. GLASER said he considers RUBY a "mental case" and described him as being a "phony" as well as a "namedropper". He also said RUBY could be

On 12/3/63 at 50 West 57th Street New York City File # NY 44-974

by SA EDWARD S. LENEHAN :vmc 310 Date dictated 12/5/63

COMMISSION EXHIBIT No. 1765

NY 44-974

classified as a typical "DAMON RUNYON character of the past".

GLASER extended his complete cooperation in this matter and stated that should he develop any additional information concerning RUBY he will make it available to the Federal Bureau of Investigation.

311

COMMISSION EXHIBIT No. 1765—Continued

Commission Exhibit No. 1766

Date April 16, 1964

1

JACK MARCUS, Attorney, 134 North La Salle Street, Chicago, Illinois, advised he visited Havana, Cuba, for four days and three nights early in September, 1959, during the Labor Day weekend. He stated he was accompanied on this visit by SHERWIN BRAUN and JAY BISHOV, also of Chicago, Illinois.

MARCUS informed that they traveled to Miami, Florida, in BRAUN's privately owned automobile and stayed at the Nautilus Hotel located on Collins Avenue in Miami Beach, Florida. MARCUS stated they checked out of the Nautilus Hotel the day prior to leaving for Havana, Cuba, from Key West, Florida. He explained that he and his friends knew they would be out most of the night and planned to drive to Key West, Florida, early in the morning, so they checked out of the hotel the day before leaving for Key West. After driving to Key West, Florida, they left their automobile in an adjacent parking lot and purchased tickets on the "Q" Airlines, which MARCUS described as a Cuban-owned airline. He stated further that they obtained their visas or travel permits to Cuba at the same place where they purchased their travel tickets. MARCUS stated there was little or no problem in obtaining these permits or visas, and that little background data was requested for same. He recalled that they flew to Havana in the afternoon, and that the airplane was definitely Cuban as the personnel on the plane were Cuban.

MARCUS stated he believes that it was on the third night or last night that they were in Havana, Cuba, that he saw JACK RUBY at the Tropicana Night Club. He added that he could not elaborate any further concerning this meeting other than that information furnished on November 25, 1963.

MARCUS reiterated that he is certain this visit to Havana took place over the Labor Day weekend of 1959;

On 4/14/64 at Chicago, Illinois File # CG 44-645

by SAs RAYMOND E. STOELTING and LESTER K. ESAREY/rms Date dictated 4/16/64

COMMISSION EXHIBIT No. 1766

2

CG 44-645

however, he did not recall the exact days and nights he was there. He stated that they returned to Key West, Florida, via the same airlines they had used in going over to Havana, Cuba.

3

FD-302 (Rev. 1-25-60)

FEDERAL BUREAU OF INVESTIGATION

Commission Exhibit No. 1767

Date April 16, 1964

1

JAY (No Middle Name) BISHOV, Attorney, business address 5152 North Clark Street, Chicago, Illinois, advised he visited Havana, Cuba, for a period of four days and three nights over the Labor Day weekend of 1959. He advised he was accompanied on this visit by his friends, JACK MARCUS and SHERWIN BRAUN.

BISHOV stated that they traveled to Miami, Florida, in SHERWIN BRAUN's privately owned automobile and stayed in the Nautilus Hotel in Miami Beach while there. He stated further that they checked out of this hotel the day before leaving for Havana, Cuba, from Key West, Florida. He continued by saying that they drove from Miami Beach to Key West, Florida, where they left the automobile in a parking lot at or near the airport. He stated further that they purchased tickets from the Airways "Q" for their flight to Havana, Cuba, and also obtained their visas or travel permits at the same counter where they purchased their tickets. BISHOV advised he could not recall exactly what these visas or travel permits consisted of; however, he noted they had to furnish little background information in order to obtain them. He informed that the Airways "Q" was a Cuban airline and the personnel on the airplane were Cuban.

BISHOV stated he could not elaborate any further concerning the previous information he furnished on November 25, 1963, regarding seeing JACK RUBY at the Tropicana Night Club in Havana, Cuba.

- O -

4

On 4/15/64 at Chicago, Illinois File # CG 44-645

by SAs RAYMOND E. STOELTING and LESTER K. ESAREY/rms Date dictated 4/16/64

FD-302 (Rev. 1-25-60) FEDERAL BUREAU OF INVESTIGAT

Commission Exhibit No. 1768

Date April 16, 1964

1

SHERWIN BRAUN, Architect, business address 140 East Ontario, Chicago, Illinois, advised that on the Labor Day weekend of 1959, he, accompanied by JAY BISHOV and JACK MARCUS, visited Havana, Cuba, for a period of three nights and four days. He stated they were on a Florida vacation prior to returning to their respective schools in Chicago, Illinois.

BRAUN stated he drove his privately owned automobile on this trip to Miami, Florida, and that they stayed at the Nautilus Hotel located on Collins Avenue in Miami Beach, Florida. BRAUN informed that the day after checking out of the Nautilus Hotel, they drove to Key West, Florida, and left the automobile in a lot nearby the airport at Key West, Florida. He stated further that they flew to Havana, Cuba, via the Airways "Q", a Cuban airlines, and that the personnel on the airplane were Cuban. BRAUN also stated that they obtained their visas or entry permits to Cuba at the same counter where they purchased their travel tickets. He advised he could not recall exactly what this visa or entry permit consisted of; however, he described it as a small piece of paper or document with little background information on it.

BRAUN stated he could not recall exactly what days they were in Havana, Cuba; however, he is certain it was over the Labor Day weekend of 1959. He advised that it was on the third or last night in Havana that the meeting with JACK RUBY took place at approximately 4 a.m. in the casino section of the Tropicana Night Club. He added he could not elaborate any more concerning this meeting other than the information he had furnished on November 25, 1963.

BRAUN advised he and his friends returned to Key West, Florida, via the Airways "Q", and reiterated that he is certain this was a Cuban airline.

5

On 4/15/64 at Chicago, Illinois File # CG 44-645

by SAs RAYMOND E. STOELTING and LESTER K. ESAREY/rms Date dictated 4/16/64

COMMISSION EXHIBIT No. 1768

Commission Exhibit No. 1769

1
CG 44-645
DWS:jmn

On April 14, 1964, at the request of IC* RICHARD D. ALLEN, Mrs. JENNIE BEATO, Chief, Mail and File Unit, Immigration and Naturalization Service, Chicago, checked that agency's records for any information concerning JACK MARCUS, JAY BISHOV, and SHERWIN BRAUN. No record of any kind was found for these three individuals.

*Investigative Clerk

6

COMMISSION EXHIBIT No. 1769

FD-302 (Rev. 1-25-60)

ERAL BUREAU OF I [redacted]

Commission Exhibit No. 1770

Date 4/16/64

Mrs. MANUEL QUEVEDO, Secretary, Aero Cender Airlines, McAllister Hotel, advised that she and her husband formerly owned and operated an airlines known as Aerovisa Q. She said this was commonly known as the "Q" Airlines and as part of its service maintained a regular schedule between Key West, Florida, and Havana, Cuba. She related that on January 1, 1959, FIDEL CASTRO seized this airlines and she and her husband were removed from any control of the airlines. She said they never had any further management of the airlines and she has no idea what became of any records after January 1, 1959. She noted the airlines no longer is in operation.

7

On 4/16/64 at Miami, Florida File # Miami 44-1412

by SA ROBERT K. LEWIS:jkj Date dictated 4/16/64

This document contains neither recommendations nor conclusions of the FBI. It is the property of the FBI and is loaned to your agency; it and its contents are not to be distributed outside your agency.

COMMISSION EXHIBIT No. 1770

FD-302 (Rev. 1-25-60)

ERAL BUREAU OF INVESTIGATIO [redacted]

Commission Exhibit No. 1771

Date 4/16/64

LOUIS POLLACK, Assistant Manager, Nautilus Hotel, 1825 Collins Avenue, advised that this hotel was closed from 1960 to 1962. He stated that when the hotel reopened, many of the old records were destroyed. He searched his old files kept in a storage room and was able to locate a box of registration cards for the years 1958 and 1959. He made a complete search of these cards, but could locate no registration under the names JACK MARCUS, JAY BISHOV or SHERWIN BRAUN. POLLACK said he had no way of determining whether or not this box of cards was complete for the years 1958 and 1959. He further advised that a check of all his records since the hotel reopened was negative for any registration in the above names.

8

On 4/16/64 at Miami Beach, Florida File # Miami 44-1412

by SA ROBERT K. LEWIS:jkj Date dictated 4/16/64

This document contains neither recommendations nor conclusions of the FBI. It is the property of the FBI and is loaned to your agency; it and its contents are not to be distributed outside your agency.

COMMISSION EXHIBIT No. 1771

Commission Exhibit No. 1772

Date 12/2/63

1

JACK (NMI) MARCUS, age 27, advised he is an attorney, business address, 134 North LaSalle Street, Suite 1508, Chicago, Illinois, phone number CE 6-3938, and resides at 812 Brown, Evanston, Illinois.

Mr. MARCUS stated he visited Havana, Cuba, for four days during the Labor Day week end, 1959, with two companions, JAY BISHOV and SHERWIN BRAUN. During this vacation trip, the three were approached by a man in the Tropicana Night Club Havana, Cuba, who gave his name as JACK RUBY. RUBY stated he heard the three men were from the United States and indicated he was familiar with Chicago, Illinois, had some acquaintances in Chicago and may possibly have been originally from Chicago. RUBY stated he owned a night club in Texas which MARCUS believes was in Dallas and possibly called the "Carousel". He indicated he had "everything" at the night club including gambling. RUBY told MARCUS if he ever passed through Dallas, he should stop in at RUBY's night club.

MARCUS stated RUBY was alone and appeared to have been on vacation but may have been friendly with the employees in the gambling section of the Tropicana.

MARCUS further stated the meeting lasted only about ten minutes and no other questions were asked or other information obtained. No radical or political type statements were made by RUBY nor were there any indications he belonged to any particular organizations.

MARCUS described JACK RUBY as follows:

Race	White
Sex	Male
Nationality	American
Age	Mid-forties
Height	5'11"
Weight	175 pounds
Build	Medium to large
Hair	Brownish, balding slightly
Accent	Midwestern rather than Texan
Complexion	Fair

On 11/24/63 at Evanston, Illinois File # DL 44-1639 CG 44-645

by SAs LANSING P. LOGAN and DANIEL P. BLAKE/mav Date dictated 11/29/63

434

COMMISSION EXHIBIT No. 1772

DL 44-1639
CG 44-645

2

Characteristics	Appeared to have been of Jewish extraction. Also described as a gregarious type and an extrovert.

Mr. MARCUS advised when the shooting incident in Dallas, Texas, took place concerning LEE HARVEY OSWALD by a JACK RUBY, November 24, 1963, the name struck MARCUS as being familiar and when he saw the newspaper picture of JACK RUBENSTEIN, it bore a sharp resemblance to the JACK RUBY he met in Havana, Cuba, in 1959.

435

COMMISSION EXHIBIT No. 1772—Continued

1

PHYLLIS F. (Mrs. SAMUEL DAVID) RUBY, 11616 Jamestown Road, Dallas, Texas, was interviewed telephonically as a result of an anonymous telephone call received at the Dallas Office of the Federal Bureau of Investigation, on November 29, 1963, wherein a female, who refused to identify herself by name, address, or telephone number, furnished the following information:

She had talked with Mrs. SAM RUBY, 11616 Jamestown Road, Dallas, Texas, sister-in-law of JACK RUBY, and Mrs. SAM RUBY had advised that her brother-in-law, JACK RUBY, accompanied by a gambler and racketeer of Fort Worth, Texas, name and further identity unknown, had flown to Havana, Cuba, shortly after CASTRO had taken command, for the purpose of meeting GEORGE RAFT, the movie star and reputed gambler.

Mrs. RUBY advised that she has never made any such statement to anyone and, in fact, has never been aware that JACK RUBY has ever taken a trip to Cuba at any time for any reason. She advised, after being made aware of the contents of the anonymous telephone call, that she suspects the source of this call may have been EVA L. GRANT, her sister-in-law. She advised she and EVA L. GRANT have never liked each other and EVA GRANT, from time to time in the past, has tried to cause rifts between her and her husband, SAM.

She said specifically that within the past day or two EVA L. GRANT has been in touch with SAM RUBY for the purpose of attempting to gain his assistance in the operation of the Carousel Club in Dallas, inasmuch as JACK RUBY, who normally operates that club, is in jail and someone is needed to look after things at the club. She said she feels that EVA probably believes that she cannot get SAM RUBY to work at the Carousel Club without first getting him away from the influence of her, Mrs. RUBY.

Mrs. RUBY said this is only supposition on her part and mentions it only because she cannot figure out who the anonymous caller would have been unless it was EVA L. GRANT. She repeated that she has

on 12/5/63 at Dallas, Texas File # DL 44-1639

by Special Agent ALBERT SAYERS/eah Date dictated 12/5/63

436

DL 44-1639

2

no knowledge and has never had any knowledge of JACK RUBY ever having made a trip to Cuba. She, therefore, could not have made any statement to anyone about such a trip.

Mrs. RUBY said that the only trip by JACK RUBY that she knows about, other than various trips he has made to Chicago from time to time, is a trip he made with several other businessmen, one of whom was the attorney, STANLEY KAUFMAN, from Dallas to Hot Springs, Arkansas, to attend the races. She said this was about seven years ago and they took a train, which was specially assembled in Dallas for that trip.

437

Commission Exhibit No. 1773

FD-302 (Rev. 3-3-59)

FEDERAL BUREAU OF INVESTIGATION

1

Date 11/25/63

SHERWIN JACK BRAUN, Architect, 6238 North Hoyne, business address 140 East Ontario, Chicago, Illinois, advised on the Labor Day weekend of 1959, he, JACK MARCUS and JAY BISHOV visited Havana, Cuba for three or four days while on a Florida vacation prior to returning to school in Chicago, Illinois.

On the first or second night in Havana, the three men had visited the Tropicana night club in Havana, Cuba and were standing by the roulette wheel or crap table when a man walked up and introduced himself. BRAUN adised he thought the man gave his name as JACK RUBY but was not sure. BRAUN stated he did not know the man who said he had originally been from Chicago, Illinois, but now owned some sort of night club or gambling establishment in Texas, possibly Dallas. The man invited the three men to visit his night club whenever they got to Texas.

BRAUN stated he believed RUBY was alone but appeared to know his way around and was familiar with the employees of the Tropicana. BRAUN stated RUBY did not give him a business card nor did he know how long RUBY stayed in Cuba nor where he stayed.

BRAUN described the man known as JACK RUBY as a white male American, large or heavy build, with round or oval face, had a "Jewish appearance", and did not have a Texas or southern accent. BRAUN stated no radical or political type statements were made, nor were any comments made other than the above casual remarks made by RUBY.

on 11/25/63 at Chicago, Illinois File # CG 44-645 DL 44-1639

by Special Agent DANIEL P. BLAKE/tjd 651 Date dictated 11/26/63

This document contains neither recommendations nor conclusions of the FBI. It is the property of the FBI and is loaned to your agency; it and its contents are not to be distributed outside your agency.

COMMISSION EXHIBIT No. 1773

FD-302 (Rev. 3-3-59)

FEDERAL BUREAU OF INVESTIGATION

1

Commission Exhibit No. 1774

Date 11/25/63

JAY (NMI) BISHOV, Attorney, 6060 North Ridge, business address 5152 North Clark, Chicago, Illinois, advised he visited Havana, Cuba for three or four days about the first of September, as it was the Labor Day weekend in 195?, BISHOV stated he was with two other companions, a JACK MARCUS and SHERWIN BRAUN, both of Chicago, Illinois.

BISHOV stated that the second or third night in Havana, Cuba, he, BRAUN and MARCUS were standing near a crap table or roulette wheel at the Tropicana night club when a man approached and introduced himself by a name which BISHOV believed was JACK RUBY. RUBY asked where the three men were from and when BISHOV stated he was from the West Side of Chicago, Illinois, RUBY stated that he was also from that sectin of Chicago, Illinois, but had moved to Dallas, Texas some years before. BISHOV stated RUBY did not specify any particular street names or individuals with whom he had been acquainted in Chicago, Illinois.

BISHOV stated JACK RUBY extended an invitation to the three men to visit him at one of his night clubs in Dallas, Texas. BISHOV stated he was under the impression RUBY owned more than one night club in Dallas, Texas and indicated that these clubs were somewhat plush.

BISHOV stated RUBY appeared to know his way around the Tropicana night club, Havana, Cuba and may have been familiar with some of the employees. BISHOV stated the conversation lasted only about ten minutes and nothing other than the above casual comments were made. BISHOV stated no radical political type statements were made nor was there any indication RUBY belonged to any particular organizations. BISHOV stated he did not know how long RUBY had been in Havana, Cuba, where he was staying nor when he was supposed to return to the United States.

BISHOV stated he was not sure of the name nor of the picture appearing in the daily newspaper, that it was identical to the JACK RUBY he met in Cuba but described this individual as a white male American, of average build, 5'7" - 6', 165 - 200 pounds, dark hair, with a "Jewish appearance", and was in his mid or late forties. BISHOV stated RUBY was an extrovert and loud talker but appeared to be friendly.

on 11/25/63 at Chicago, Illinois File # DL 44-1639 CG 44-645

by Special Agent DANIEL P. BLAKE/tjd 652 Date dictated 11/26/63

This document contains neither recommendations nor conclusions of the FBI. It is the property of the FBI and is loaned to your agency; it and its contents are not to be distributed outside your agency.

COMMISSION EXHIBIT No. 1774

DL 89-43
WFO 44-520
DL 44-1639
KJH:mpc:eah

1

Miss VIRGINIA CARROLL, Passport Office, State Department, advised SA KENNETH J. HASER, November 25, 1963, Passport files contain no record of JACK LEON RUBY, aka JACK LEON RUBENSTEIN. Records of Validation and Denial of Validation for travel to Cuba checked re subject with negative results. Check was made of records of Swiss Protection Passports issued to American citizens who were in Cuba and desired to return to the United States, but no record of subject could be located.

Mr. DONALD J. SIMON, Records Management Research, State Department, advised SA HASER the post files sent to Washington, D. C., from American Embassy at Havana, Cuba, contain no indices but he and his staff had checked all logical boxes of these records re subject with negative results.

Miss CARROLL also advised that there was no record of LEE HARVEY OSWALD in the records for Validation and Denial of Validation for travel to Cuba and no record of him in the files concerning Swiss Protection Passports, issued to American citizens desiring to return to United States since January, 1961.

653

FORM FS-511 (7-15-56)

UNIT ES OF AMERICA

IMMIGRANT VISA AND ALIEN REGISTRATION

I- 1229544

OF: (Family name) OSWALD, (First name) Marina (Middle name) Nikolaevna

PORT OF

I certify that the immigrant named herein arrived in the United States at this port on the MAASDAM (Name of vessel or flight No. of aircraft) IMM. & NATZ. SERVICE NEW YORK N. Y. ADMITTED JUN 13 1962 CLASS

on (Day) (Month) (Year) O

and was inspected by me and {admitted / detained} for further inquiry by special inquiry officer under

Symbol M-1

Section .... of the Immigration and Nationality Act.

Immigrant Inspector.

AMERICAN Embassy

AT Moscow, U.S.S.R.

Jack F. Matlock

Consul of the United States of America.

Service No. 1152096
Tariff Item No. 21
Fee Paid $20
Local Cy equiv. 18.00 rubles

ACTION OF SPECIAL INQUIRY OFFICER

The immigrant herein was (admitted) (excluded) and {no appeal taken / appeal taken} under

Symbol

Section .... of the Immigration and Nationality Act.

Special Inquiry Officer.

ACTION ON APPEAL

ADMITTED

EXCLUDED

DATE

This visa is issued under Section 221 of the Immigration and Nationality Act, and upon the basis of the facts stated in the application.

IMMIGRANT CLASSIFICATION

NONQUOTA (Symbol) M-1 QUOTA (Symbol)

VISA PETITION NO. IF ANY: Petition approved on February 28, 1962.

IMMIGRANT VISA NO. 52 QUOTA

ISSUED ON (Day) 24 (Month) May (Year) 1962

THE VALIDITY OF THIS VISA EXPIRES MIDNIGHT AT THE END OF (Day) 23 (Month) September (Year) 1962

NATIONALITY (If stateless, so state, and give previous nationality) Soviet

PASSPORT

NO. KU-37790

OR OTHER TRAVEL DOCUMENTS (Describe) Soviet Vid na Zhitelstvo

ISSUED TO Marina Nikolaevna OSWALD

BY Ministry of Foreign Affairs of Moscow, U.S.S.R.

ON 11 January 1962

EXPIRES 11 January 1964

Commission Exhibit No. 1776

15

Oswald, Marina - 4

May 9, 1962 CO 243.1-P

Mr. Michel Cieplinski
Acting Administrator
Bureau of Security and Consular Affairs
Department of State
Washington, D. C.

Dear Mr. Cieplinski:

The Service file relating to the case of Mrs. Marina N. P. Oswald, subject of your letter of March 27, 1962, has been carefully reviewed in this office.

On February 28, 1962, the District Director at San Antonio wrote the Assistant Director of the Visa Office that he declined to waive in Mrs. Oswald's case the sanctions against the issuance of immigrant visas in the Soviet Union imposed pursuant to Section 342(g) of the Immigration and Nationality Act. Your letter states that preventing Mrs. Oswald from accompanying her husband and child to the United States would weaken the attempts of the Embassy in Moscow to encourage positive action by the Soviet authorities in other cases involving Soviet relatives of United States citizens. Your letter also states that waiving of sanctions in behalf of Mrs. Oswald would be in the best interests of the United States.

In view of the strong representations made in your letter of March 27, 1962, you are hereby advised that sanctions imposed pursuant to Section 243(g) of the Immigration and Nationality Act are hereby waived in behalf of Mrs. Oswald.

Sincerely yours,

/s/ Robert H. Robinson

Robert H. Robinson
Deputy Associate Commissioner
Travel Control

CC: REGIONAL COMMISSIONER, SAN PEDRO, CALIFORNIA
For your information.
DISTRICT DIRECTOR, SAN ANTONIO, TEXAS
For your information.

CC: OFFICER IN CHARGE, DALLAS, TEXAS
For your information and inclusion in file A12 530 645 herewith attached.

COMMISSION EXHIBIT No. 1777

FD-302 (Rev. 3-3-59)

FEDERAL BUREAU OF INVESTIGATION

1

Date 11/23/63

MARINA OSWALD, 2515 West Fifth Street, Irving, Texas, phone BLackburn 3-1628, was interviewed at the Dallas Police Department through interpreters Mrs. RUTH PAINE, 2515 West Fifth Street, Irving, phone BLackburn 3-1628, and ILYA A. MANANTOV, 6911 East Mockingbird Lane, Dallas, TAylor 1-2817, inasmuch as MARINA OSWALD speaks only the Russian language.

OSWALD advised that she is the wife of LEE HARVEY OSWALD. She will have been married to OSWALD three years April, 1963, having married him in Minsk, U.S.S.R.

She arrived with her husband June 13, 1962, in the United States of America at New York City. They immediately came to Fort Worth, Texas, and resided with ROBERT OSWALD; who is the brother of her husband. ROBERT OSWALD now resides in Denton, Texas. After staying one month with ROBERT OSWALD, they rented an apartment in Fort Worth, Texas. About October, 1962, they moved to Dallas, Texas, and rented an apartment on Elsbeth Street and thereafter moved to an apartment on Neely Street. About May, 1963, they moved to New Orleans, Louisiana. MARINA OSWALD moved back to Dallas about September 24, 1963, and LEE HARVEY OSWALD moved to Dallas about two weeks later. About October 15, 1963, LEE HARVEY was employed by the Texas School Book Depository. He has been renting a room (at 1026 North Beckley, Dallas) and visits her on the weekends at 2515 West Fifth Street, Irving.

On the night of November 21, 1963, LEE HARVEY OSWALD spent the night with her at 2515 West Fifth. He left early on the morning of November 22, 1963, before she or Mrs. RUTH PAINE awakened.

MARINA OSWALD advised that LEE HARVEY OSWALD owned a rifle which he used in Russia about two years ago. She observed what she presumed to be the same rifle in a blanket in the garage at 2515 West Fifth, Irving. On November 22, 1963, she observed the same blanket in the garage but the rifle was missing. MARINA OSWALD stated that on November 22, 1963, she had been shown a rifle in the Dallas Police Department, reportedly found at the Texas School Book

Commission Exhibit No. 1778

on 11/22/63 at Dallas, Texas File # DL 89-43

by Special Agent JAMES W. BOOKHOUT/cah Date dictated 11/23/63

104

COMMISSION EXHIBIT No. 1778

2

DL 89-43

Depository, and was unable to positively identify it as the same one she had observed in the above mentioned garage. She stated that it was a dark color like the one she had seen, but she did not recall the sight. She stated she had never closely observed the rifle seen in the garage and that she would not be able to identify it if seen again, as all guns looked alike to her.

MARINA OSWALD added that LEE HARVEY OSWALD had not been back to 2515 West Fifth Street, Irving, anytime during the day of November 22, 1963, after he left early that morning.

105

FD-302 (Rev. 3-1-59)

FEDERAL BUREAU OF INVESTIGATION

Date 11/23/63

1

On this date, MARINA OSWALD, residence 2515 W. 5th Street, Irving, Texas, was interviewed at the Adolphus Hotel with the assistance of Dr. MARIA ADELMAN, 3144 D. Hudnall, Dallas, Texas, who interpreted the English questions of SA ODUM into Russian and interpreted MARINA OSWALD's Russian replies into English.

SA ODUM advised MARINA OSWALD that he was a Special Agent of the Federal Bureau of Investigation and MARINA OSWALD observed his credentials. She was advised she did not have to make any statement but that any statement she did make might be used against her in a court of law and that she was entitled to an attorney. She was also advised that it was desired that she be interviewed for any information that would assist in the solution of the assassination of President JOHN KENNEDY.

She stated she had no additional information to furnish and expressed dislike for the FBI since the FBI had investigated her and her husband previously and knew everything they had done since they arrived in the United States. She also stated she desired to help her husband, LEE OSWALD, and that she did not desire to be interviewed by representatives of the FBI.

Commission Exhibit 1779

on 11/23/63 at Dallas, Texas File # DL 89-43

by Special Agents BARDWELL D. ODUM and ROBERT J. ANDERSON:vm Date dictated 11/23/63

106

FD-302 (Rev. 3-3-59)

FEDERAL BUREAU OF INVESTIGATION

Date 11/28/63

Mrs. MARINA NIKOLAEVNA OSWALD was interviewed in the Russian language by SA LEON I. GOPADZE of the U. S. Secret Service, with SA MAX D. PHILLIPS of the U. S. Secret Service also present. SA GOPADZE introduced himself as Mr. LEE, an agent of the Government, and introduced the two interviewing FBI agents as agents of the Federal Bureau of Investigation.

At the outset of the interview, before SA GOPADZE could advise MARINA OSWALD of her constitutional rights, she stated, "Do I have a right not to answer questions if I do not want to." MARINA OSWALD was advised she did not have to talk if she did not want to, that she had a right to an attorney, and anything she did say could be used against her.

She was asked if she would mind answering questions that were to be asked. She replied that she did not wish to be asked anything, as anything she had to say she had said before and she had no further information.

MARINA OSWALD was advised that there were many unanswered questions and would she care to be asked these questions. She replied that she was tired and worried about one of her children, who was slightly ill, and for this reason she did not care to be interviewed. She was told that her cooperation in this investigation was needed and she was asked whether she would consider an interview at a later date or on some other occasion. She indicated that she did not wish to be interviewed.

MARINA OSWALD stated the Government knows all the facts and she has no further facts except what is known to the Government. MARINA OSWALD stated she did not have a friendly attitude toward the FBI because she felt the FBI had caused her husband to lose his job following his arrest in New Orleans for distributing pro-Castro literature and disturbing the peace.

When asked if she intended to stay in the United States, MARINA OSWALD stated she would like to stay in the United States because of her children and to be near where her husband is buried. She then asked for assurance that she would be allowed to stay in the United States and she was advised that this was a matter coming under the jurisdiction of the Immigration and Naturalization

— Commission Exhibit 1780 —

on 11/27/63 at Arlington, Texas File # DL 89-43

by Special Agents CHARLES T. BROWN, JR., and JAMES P. HOSTY, JR. / mac Date dictated 11/28/63

107

COMMISSION EXHIBIT No. 1780

2

DL 89-43

Service. She was advised that the Government needs her cooperation and this might help. MARINA OSWALD then stated if she was not allowed to stay in the United States, then that was all right also. When asked how she intended to live and support her children, she stated she would find some type of work. She was then advised that if she cooperated with the Government this could be of some assistance to her.

MARINA OSWALD then stated she was tired of answering questions. When told that the Government only wanted the facts, she stated she had the same facts as everyone else and no other. MARINA OSWALD was then asked if she ever had any conversations with her husband about former President JOHN F. KENNEDY. MARINA OSWALD stated "No." She was then asked if her husband, LEE OSWALD, ever indicated in any way that he intended to kill former President KENNEDY. She stated "No, I feel he did not do it because he never spoke against President KENNEDY at any time." When asked if he had ever said anything against Texas Governor JOHN CONNALLY, she stated she could not recall any statements that LEE OSWALD made against Texas Governor JOHN CONNALLY. When asked if LEE OSWALD could have had a grudge against Texas Governor CONNALLY, she stated she did not know. MARINA OSWALD then stated "I swear before God that LEE OSWALD did not intend to kill President KENNEDY." When asked if she believed in God, MARINA OSWALD stated she has believed in God since the death of her mother. When asked if she was a Christian, she said "Yes." MARINA OSWALD was then asked if she knew any of her husband's associates, and she stated "No," that LEE OSWALD was a "loner" and was always by himself. MARINA OSWALD also stated her husband never expressed political views or opinions to her since he felt that women did not belong in politics. When asked if LEE OSWALD had any friends in Russia, she stated "No," as he was a "loner" in Russia also and he was always reading Marxist books, such as "Das Kapital." MARINA OSWALD stated that one time she became so exasperated with LEE OSWALD she asked him "What are you trying to do, start another revolution?" She stated that LEE OSWALD was strong-willed and stubborn; he was hot-headed and had his own ideas about everything. MARINA OSWALD was asked if she had ever seen LEE OSWALD with a gun and she stated "No." When asked if she had ever seen him go hunting, MARINA OSWALD stated there was no place around Dallas or Fort Worth where he could hunt and he had no transportation to go hunting and could not drive an automobile.

108

COMMISSION EXHIBIT No. 1780—Continued

3

DL 89-43

When asked if she would like to have another visit from the FBI , she stated that there is no reason for another visit. MARINA OSWALD stated that she was treated satisfactorily, however, she hoped she would not be bothered again, that the Government has all the facts and in her mind, due to what has been told her, she is satisfied that LEE OSWALD had killed President JOHN F. KENNEDY.

MARINA OSWALD was then asked if she would help furnish additional facts so that it might be possible to clear her husband, LEE OSWALD, if he had not killed the President. MARINA OSWALD stated if she knew any additional facts she would furnish them to clear up the case. She stated that "the Government knows more than I do".

The conversation was momentarily interrupted, at which time MARINA OSWALD snapped "Let's come to the business of this conversation". MARINA OSWALD then requested termination of the interview and it was discontinued immediately at this point.

109

Commission Exhibit No. 1781

FD-302 (Rev. 3-3-59)

FEDERAL BUREAU OF INVESTIGATION

Date November 29, 1963

Mrs. MARINA NIKOLAEVNA OSWALD, nee PRUSAKOVA, was interviewed at the Inn of the Six Flags, Dallas - Fort Worth Turnpike, in the Russian language. SA BOGUSLAV did the actual conversing with Mrs. OSWALD.

Mrs. OSWALD appeared rather tired, her face was drawn, and there was a look of fatigue in her eyes. She expressed great concern for her babies, and at the outset of the interview said that if it would be all right she would like to leave the interview for whatever time it might take to take care of her babies if they needed her. It was agreed that she would be allowed to leave for this purpose at any time.

She said that due to the events of the past few days, she had become extremely tired and on the day before, particularly November 27, 1963, she had been very irritable, but now on reflection felt that she would like to talk to the FBI and be of any assistance that she could be in this regard.

From the outset of the interview, Mrs. OSWALD appeared to be friendly and cooperative and she answered each of the questions asked her freely. If she did not understand the question, she was not hesitant in asking for a clarification. She expressed concern at one point that the interviewing agents did not like her. She was assured, however, that there was no personal animosity toward her by the interviewing agents or the FBI, and she seemed satisfied with this explanation.

She was interviewed from approximately 9:20 p.m. until 11:30 p.m.

She advised she had married LEE HARVEY OSWALD in Russia, and they had returned from Russia to the United States on June 13, 1962, and had thereafter arrived in Fort Worth, Texas, on June 14, 1962. She said that following their return to Fort Worth, they had resided in Fort Worth, where OSWALD had been employed for awhile and then they had resided at Dallas, Texas. They lived in Dallas, Texas, until sometime in May, 1963. In early May, 1963, OSWALD left Dallas and went to New Orleans, Louisiana, to find work. He said he

on 11/28/63 at Dallas, Texas File # DL 89-43

by Special Agents WALLACE R. HEITMAN and SA ANATOLE A. BOGUSLAV/gm Date dictated 11/29/63

546

would send for his wife and child upon finding work. After he had been in New Orleans for a few days, Mrs. OSWALD and her child were taken to New Orleans by Mrs. OSWALD's friend, Mrs. RUTH PAINE, in PAINE's station wagon. She does not recall the exact date they arrived in New Orleans but believes it was during the latter part of May, 1963. She said OSWALD had a job upon their arrival with the Louisiana Coffee Company on Magazine Street. She said OSWALD had rented an apartment at 4907 Magazine Street and that is the address where they lived during this period of time in New Orleans. They lived at no other address.

At this point, Mrs. OSWALD said that she did not like New Orleans and did not want to return there. She said that it was a good place for tourists to go as there were a lot of bars where nude women danced, but that she did not like the town and would rather have the baby born in Texas.

She said Mrs. PAINE had written a Quaker friend who lived in New Orleans, and this friend, whose name Mrs. OSWALD does not remember, dropped by their apartment shortly after Mrs. OSWALD arrived to pay her respects, but she did not return.

Mrs. OSWALD said she did not speak English and understood very little English and for that reason she did not make any friends herself in New Orleans. She said her husband was very retiring, quiet, and secretive and did not make friends, and for that reason they had no friends at New Orleans, and she does not recall anyone dropping by their apartment. She said that she had told OSWALD on occasion that she would appreciate it if he would become acquainted with any Russians in New Orleans in order that she could have friends and someone with whom to converse. She said that OSWALD had not done this, however.

Mrs. OSWALD said OSWALD had worked at the coffee company until about the middle or latter part of August, 1963, at which time he had lost his job. He had been earning about $1.35 or $1.50 per hour at the job. After he lost this job, he made application for unemployment compensation with the unemployment office in New Orleans and had thereafter begun to receive regular weekly unemployment checks in the amount of $33.00 each until she left New Orleans.

She said that her husband had always handled the family finances and that she was not allowed to handle money.

She said they had talked of saving money for the coming baby which was due in October, 1963, but she does not know how much money OSWALD had saved. She said OSWALD had a wallet which he kept in the apartment in New Orleans with this money that he was saving. She said the money that was saved came from his pay check from the coffee company and from the unemployment check. When asked how much this money amounted to, she replied that it might be $100.00 or $200.00, or maybe less, but that it was not very much. She said they had no bank account or safe-deposit box in New Orleans or any other place that they had lived. She said that she does not know of any other moneys OSWALD ever had besides that which he had earned from his jobs or unemployment compensation and that he had no other sources of income. She said that OSWALD felt it was a shameful thing for him because he could not support his wife and family. She said she realized that OSWALD felt shame about this, and as a consequence she very seldom spoke to him about finances or money or finding a job.

After he lost his job at the coffee company in August, 1963, they talked about what they should do because Mrs. OSWALD was due to give birth to a baby in October. It was decided that they would see if Mrs. PAINE would keep Mrs. OSWALD during the time the baby was due. Mrs. PAINE agreed to do this and wrote them a letter that she would be in New Orleans to pick up Mrs. OSWALD and the older child and take them back to Dallas.

Mrs. PAINE arrived in New Orleans on about September 20, 1963, although Mrs. OSWALD does not remember the exact date. She said Mrs. PAINE keeps a meticulous diary, and she undoubtedly would know the date she had arrived in New Orleans. Mrs. OSWALD recalls that on the date Mrs. PAINE arrived, she and OSWALD had waited at the house for Mrs. PAINE because they knew this was the day Mrs. PAINE was to arrive. She said that on the previous night she and OSWALD had gone to the grocery store to pick up some groceries, and having realized on the day of Mrs. PAINE's arrival she had forgotten something, she went back to the grocery store and upon her return to the apartment, Mrs. PAINE had arrived. Mrs. PAINE's arrival time on that date, believed to be September 20, 1963, was about 2:30 or 3:00 in the afternoon.

Mrs. PAINE stayed in New Orleans at the OSWALDS' house for about four or five days, and then she left with

DL 89-43

Mrs. PAINE and her older child on about September 24 or 25, 1963, in the PAINES' station wagon.

Mrs. OSWALD said that on the day immediately prior to Mrs. PAINE's arrival that she had stayed in the house all day with her child and that she does not exactly recall what OSWALD did but knows that he was in the house at least part of the time and certainly spent the night at the house. It was on that evening (the day before Mrs. PAINE's arrival) that they went to the grocery store together. She said that OSWALD generally would go to town during the day, and when he did, he was gone about two hours as it took one-half hour to ride on the bus each way.

She said that two days before Mrs. PAINE's arrival, OSWALD was also at the house and it was the usual day. She said she could not recall exactly what he had done but knows he was there at least part of the day and spent the night at the apartment.

She said OSWALD had been at the apartment each day during Mrs. PAINE's stay with them at this time and had spent each night at the apartment.

Mrs. OSWALD advised that upon her departure from New Orleans with Mrs. PAINE, it was agreed by her and her husband that OSWALD would remain in New Orleans to find work and if he could not find work, he would return to Dallas. OSWALD also made a statement that he had a friend in another city and that he might contact this friend to see if he could find work. Mrs. OSWALD said she did not think that this was true — she did not believe OSWALD had a friend anywhere. She said that it is possible that Mrs. PAINE would know who this friend was and what the name of the city was. She said she could not remember.

When asked what the arrangements were at the time she left New Orleans, Mrs. OSWALD said that her husband was to remain there in New Orleans or return to Dallas, but no arrangements were made for him to go to Mexico City. Inasmuch as Mexico City had not been mentioned, she was asked why she had said no arrangements had been made for OSWALD to go to Mexico City. She replied she had been looking

549

5
DL 89-43

at television the past few days and had seen or heard that OSWALD had been in Mexico City. She said she was only trying to be helpful and that is the reason she had mentioned Mexico City as she did.

Mrs. OSWALD said that she did not know anything about any trip that OSWALD may have made to Mexico City. She said that upon OSWALD's return to Dallas, which was in early October, 1963, that she had not asked him where he had been or what he had done since she had left him in New Orleans because she knew that he had not found work and that it would only embarrass him to ask. She said that OSWALD had not volunteered any information about where he had been or what he had done.

Mrs. OSWALD was asked what OSWALD did during the time he was unemployed. She said he sat around the house all day reading. She said he read so much she often wondered why he did not get sores from sitting down so much. She said OSWALD visited the library regularly at New Orleans, where he checked out mostly books on history, but he also read books by HEMINGWAY, JACK LONDON, and REMARQUE. She said that she cannot accurately recall, but she believes that OSWALD went to the library and checked out books the day before Mrs. PAINE arrived. She said OSWALD went every Tuesday to pick up his unemployment check.

She said they did not make plans very far ahead at the time she left New Orleans to have the baby in Texas because it was not known whether or not OSWALD would find a job, and if he did where it would be.

She advised OSWALD had come to Dallas early in October, 1963. She could not remember the exact date and again said that Mrs. PAINE would probably know the exact date because she kept a meticulous diary. She advised OSWALD had called her at Mrs. PAINE's residence and told her that he had arrived in Dallas the day before and had rented a room. He left a telephone number where he could be contacted. Mrs. OSWALD said she did not have this number but felt sure Mrs. PAINE had it in her diary.

Mrs. OSWALD was asked if OSWALD had used any other names, and she replied that he had not to her knowledge. She was then asked if he had not used a different name in

550

Dallas when he had rented a room upon his return to Dallas on October 3, 1963, and she said that she now recalled OSWALD had used another name. She said that on one occasion Mrs. PAINE had telephoned the place where OSWALD was staying and had asked to speak to Mr. OSWALD, and the man who answered the phone said there was no one by the name of OSWALD at the place. Mrs. OSWALD said she herself called this number and talked to OSWALD, at which time he said he had been there the day before when someone had called and asked for Mr. OSWALD, but that he was using another name at the house and had not answered to the name OSWALD. He told Mrs. OSWALD he was using another name because he did not want any questions asked about himself.

Mrs. OSWALD was asked if OSWALD could drive a car, and she replied that he did not have a driver's license. She said Mrs. PAINE had taught him something about driving a car after he returned to Dallas in October, 1963. She said also that OSWALD's cousin who lived on French Street in New Orleans had taught him something about driving. She said she believes OSWALD could have passed a driver's test.

551

COMMISSION EXHIBIT No. 1781—Continued

1 Date 11/29/63

Mrs. MARINA NIKOLAEVNA OSWALD was interviewed at the Inn of Six Flags. She advised that OSWALD had arrived in Dallas, Texas, in early October, 1963. She cannot remember the exact date but knows it was prior to October 8, 1963, which was the date that she was expecting her second baby to arrive. She also pinpoints the date by the fact that OSWALD found work in Dallas on October 15, 1963, and she knows he had arrived in Dallas over a week before that. She said her husband called her on the phone at the PAINE residence sometime during the day after he had arrived and mentioned that he had arrived the evening before. She asked him why he had not called when he arrived, and he said he did not want to disturb her.

Mrs. OSWALD was asked where OSWALD had stayed the night of his arrival, and she replied that she did not know, but she presumed that he had stayed at the YMCA or some room. On this first telephone call to her, OSWALD said he was already in Irving, Texas, and asked that Mrs. PAINE come to pick him up at the bus stop. This bus stop is about a twenty minute walk from the house. Mrs. PAINE left immediately and picked OSWALD up at the bus stop and brought him back to her house.

OSWALD stayed at the PAINE residence that afternoon and night and then the next morning Mrs. PAINE and Mrs. OSWALD took him to downtown Dallas where he was let out of Mrs. PAINE's station wagon with his valise as he was to look for a place to stay and to start looking for work.

OSWALD had a medium-size valise when he arrived at the PAINE house containing both clean and dirty clothing. He gave Mrs. OSWALD his washing and extracted from his valise his shaving equipment. Mrs. OSWALD said that she did not notice anything in the valise that was out of the ordinary. She did not notice any weapons nor any money.

She said that OSWALD had some money in a wallet, and that he left this wallet at the PAINE house on the day that Mrs. PAINE took him to Dallas after extracting some

on 11/29/63 at Dallas, Texas File # DL 89-43

by Special Agents WALLACE R. HEITMAN & ANATOLE A. BOGUSLAV /cv Date dictated 11/29/63

568

COMMISSION EXHIBIT No. 1782

DL 89-43
WRH:AAB:cv
2

money for his own use. She said she does not know how much money was in the wallet or how much money OSWALD took but knows that it was not very much.

She stated that on the day he came to the PAINE residence, OSWALD fooled around with a typewriter with a Russian keyboard belonging to Mrs. PAINE because one of the keys was broken.

Mrs. OSWALD was asked what she and OSWALD had talked about on this afternoon and night that OSWALD had spent with her at the PAINE house. She replied that OSWALD was the type that could sit in front of a television set all day and not say a word. She said they had talked about family matters such as how she was feeling and how the child was feeling, but they did not talk too much because she, Mrs. OSWALD, was not feeling well. They also talked about a wedding in the MURRETT family that was supposed to take place on or about October 5, 1963. Mrs. MURRETT is OSWALD's aunt.

On the following day when Mrs. PAINE accompanied by Mrs. OSWALD dropped OSWALD off in downtown Dallas, OSWALD stated he was going to find a place to live, and he would then call Mrs. OSWALD. She said he called about 5 p.m. that day and said he had found a place to live in the Oak Cliff section near a lake. He furnished the telephone number where he could be reached, and Mrs. PAINE made a note of this telephone number in her diary or on some paper. Mrs. OSWALD does not remember th s number. She said that thereafter OSWALD did call her about twice a day to ask her about her condition and how their child was. It was agreed that Mrs. PAINE would contact OSWALD on the telephone because the place OSWALD was staying had other people using this telephone, and Mrs. OSWALD would not be able to make herself understood.

569

COMMISSION EXHIBIT No. 1782—Continued

CO-2-34030

~~Oswald, Marina~~ -2
Inv 3-2 U. S. Secret Service

Chief | Nov. 25, 1963

SA Patterson - Dallas

Information obtained at the Dallas Office

During the interview of the subject's wife she advised that the FBI had contacted her about the location of her husband about 10 days prior to the assassination and she had told them that her husband worked in the building from which the President was killed. She also stated that she had been interviewed in October and gave the same basic information to the FBI.

While I was at the police station, I engaged an FBI agent in a conversation and found out that he was on the subversive desk. He stated that Oswald had contacted two known subversive agents about 15 days before the shooting but the entire information was top secret and he could not tell us any more but he felt sure that the file would be turned over to our Chief.

The wife also advised that she had seen the rifle that was used in the shooting at her home about three weeks before the shooting.

She advised that she was a Castro supporter and from the interview it was felt that she is still a hard core communist.

She stated that he had never mentioned killing the President but would not mention anything about shooting Connally.

She stated that she did not know the man that killed her husband.

It was felt by the interviewer that she was not telling the truth and still believed in communism.

William H. Patterson
Special Agent

[redacted]

Commission Exhibit 1783

COMMISSION EXHIBIT No. 1783

Date December 5, 1963

1

MARINA OSWALD was interviewed at 11611 Farrar Street.

The English translation of a letter originally written in Russian was read to her. The letter was re-translated into the Russian language as it was read by SA BOGUSLAV. This English translation had been furnished to the FBI Office at Dallas by the U. S. Secret Service. Upon the reading of the letter, MARINA stated immediately it was a letter written in the original by LEE OSWALD in the Russian language. She stated she had found the original letter in a room at the former OSWALD address on Neeley Street in Dallas. She related the incident concerning this letter as follows:

One night during the spring while she and OSWALD were in residence at the Neeley Street address, she became worried about OSWALD because he had not returned to their home very late in the evening. She said OSWALD had informed her that he was going to a typewriting class at the Dallas Evening School that evening. When he had not returned by 10:00 o'clock, she went into a room in which he kept his personal things and in this room she noticed a letter hand-written in the Russian language. This is the letter which is referred to above. She stated the letter gave her certain instructions concerning a Post Office box and other family matters and appeared to be a farewell letter.

She advised that about midnight that night, OSWALD came rushing into the house in a very agitated and excited state and his face was very pale. As soon as he entered the house, he turned on the radio. Later, he laid down on the bed and MARINA again noticed how very pale he was. She asked him what was wrong and he confessed to her that he had tried to kill General WALKER by shooting at him with a rifle but didn't know whether he had hit him or not. He said he wanted to find out on the radio whether or not he had hit him. MARINA said she became angry with OSWALD for shooting at General WALKER and he replied to her that General WALKER was the leader of the fascist organization here and it was

Commission Exhibit 1784

on 12-3-63 at Dallas, Texas File # DL 89-43

by Special Agents ANATOLE A. BOGUSLAV
WALLACE R. HEITMAN
mvs Date dictated 12-3-63

This document contains neither recommendations nor conclusions of the FBI. It is the property of the FBI and is loaned to your agency; it and its contents are not to be distributed outside your agency.

282

COMMISSION EXHIBIT No. 1784

2
DL 89-43

best to remove him. MARINA said she was quite relieved when she found out that OSWALD had missed General WALKER with the rifle bullet. She said she and OSWALD were listening to the radio reports about the rifle shot at General WALKER and OSWALD was translating the reports for her.

She stated OSWALD did not have the rifle with him when he returned to the house. She also advised that OSWALD to her knowledge did not take the rifle with him when he left the house that evening. She stated she thought OSWALD had used the same rifle he had at the house on Neeley Street and at the PAINE house.

She said that the following evening she talked to OSWALD about the attempted assassination of General WALKER again. OSWALD told her that he had hidden the rifle which he used to shoot at General WALKER in some bushes or in the ground, she did not remember which.

MARINA advised that she told OSWALD she was going to keep the letter written in Russian by OSWALD, which was evidently a farewell letter, in order that she could use it against him if he ever had another "crazy" scheme. She said that if OSWALD started to do anything like this, that she would go to the police with the letter. She also made OSWALD promise that he would never do anything like this again.

She advised that for a period of about a month before this attempt on WALKER's life, OSWALD had been very agitated and had closed himself in his room for long periods of time while he wrote and read. She said that it was evident that he had been thinking about the assassination attempt for some period of time. She said OSWALD did not mention General WALKER in her presence before the night of the attempted assassination. She said they did not speak of the incident again after the second night following the assassination attempt.

She said that she had insisted that they move from Dallas to another city because she felt that if they moved OSWALD would be less likely to repeat such a deed.

MARINA asked OSWALD how he had arrived at the WALKER house on the night of the attempted assassination.

283

COMMISSION EXHIBIT No. 1784—Continued

3
DL 89-43

He said he had gone there on foot. He said that after he fired the rifle, he ran away and that he could run very fast. He said the police thought the would-be assassin had an automobile. He came home on the bus.

284

Form No. 1580 (Revised)
Memorandum Report
(7-1-60)

UNITED STATES SECRET SERVICE [redacted]
TREASURY DEPARTMENT

Commission Exhibit No. 1785

ORIGIN Field (Dallas) OFFICE Dallas, Texas FILE NO. CO-2-34030

TYPE OF CASE	STATUS	TITLE OR CAPTION
Protective Research	Continued	Assassination of President Kennedy Mrs. Marina Oswald
INVESTIGATION MADE AT Dallas, Texas	PERIOD COVERED 12/2/63 to 12/5/63	
INVESTIGATION MADE BY ATSAIC Leon I. Gopadze		

DETAILS

SYNOPSIS

The note written in Russian and recovered from the Russian book entitled "Book of Helpful Instructions" was translated and traced to Lee Harvey Oswald. Marina Oswald was questioned about the note and statement obtained. She was also questioned concerning other matters pertaining to the case.

DETAILS OF INVESTIGATION

Reference is made to M/R of ATSAIC Gopadze dated 12-3-63. Further reference is made to office memorandum of 12-3-63.

On 12-2-63 the reporting agent, with SA Kunkel, proceeded to the Martin residence where Marina Oswald was questioned by the reporting agent as to whether she knew anything about telegrams allegedly sent and received by Lee Oswald prior to his death. She stated that she has no knowledge of any telegrams sent or received by her husband. She was also questioned about Lee Oswald's rooming house where he registered under the assumed name and about placing a phone call to this place as related by Mrs. Ruth Paine. Marina Oswald stated that when Lee Oswald did not show up over the weekend (believed to be November 16 and 17, 1963) she asked Ruth Paine to telephone the rooming house and upon contacting the house, Ruth Paine was told that they had no one by the name of Lee Oswald. According to Marina Oswald, when her husband telephoned her the following day from his place of employment, she (Marina) asked him why he gave her a telephone number where he was not known and he stated that it was none of her business. Marina Oswald also stated that they had a quarrel over the telephone and when Lee showed up on Thursday evening (November 21, 1963) he more or less indicated that his arrival was to patch up the quarrel. Marina Oswald was also asked the reason she moved, for about a week, when they lived at 602 Elsbeth Street and she stated that it happened before Thanksgiving Day of 1962 when her husband beat her up and that she moved, first to stay with a friend by the name of Anna Meller, and then with Anna Ray, whose addresses she did

DISTRIBUTION	COPIES	REPORT MADE BY	DATE
Chief Dallas	Orig.&2cc 2 cc	ATSAIC Leon I. Gopadze	536 12-5-63
		APPROVED SPECIAL AGENT IN CHARGE	DATE 12-5-63

(CONTINUE ON PLAIN PAPER)

not know. Both women are Russians and she has met them through Mr. Peter P. Gregory. Further questioning of Marina Oswald was discontinued due to the arrival of FBI Agents Wallace Heistman and Anatole Bogoslov. Agent Bogoslov spoke Russian and acted as translator between Agent Heistman and Marina Oswald.

Upon return of the reporting agent to the office, he was given two Russian books to examine, which were entitled "Our Child" and "Book of Helpful Instructions" and other items written in Russian which were received the same day from the Irving Police Department, Irving, Texas. There were two letters written in Russian by Ruth Paine concerning various offers received by her for Marina Oswald to live and work, post cards, and one unsigned page taken from a writing pad, written in pencil, giving various instructions concerning a post office box, disposition of the writer's personal belongings, about the paid bills, his possible apprehension and where he could be located in the event of his arrest. In view of the contents of the note and indication that the note was written by Lee Oswald prior to his assassination of the President, Marina Oswald was interviewed over the telephone by the reporting agent at her place of residence but she disclaimed any knowledge of such note. The note was constructed in very poor Russian and many words were misspelled which were hard to understand. Translation of this note was furnished to Chief with office memorandum of the reporting agent dated 12-3-63, together with the statement later obtained from Marina Oswald in her own handwriting. In the evening of the same day, Ruth Paine was interviewed by the reporting agent and SA Brady regarding the above-mentioned note as set forth in the M/R of SA Brady dated 12-3-63.

On December 3, 1963 the reporting agent, with SA Brady, proceeded to the Martins' residence where Marina Oswald was questioned about the note between 11:30 A.M. and 12:30 P.M. Marina Oswald immediately stated that she did not want to talk about the note over the telephone the previous evening but that the note has nothing to do with the assassination of the President. She went on to say that the note was written by her husband, Lee Oswald, prior to his attempted assassination of former General Walker, the head of the Fascist organization in the United States who lived in Dallas, Texas, when they lived on Neeley Street in Dallas; that the note, together with a post office key, was left on a dresser of their bedroom and after reading the note she was afraid that her husband was planning to do something dreadful due to his hatred toward the Fascist organizations and their beliefs. She also stated that when her husband returned home late that night he was very nervous and finally told her that he shot Walker with his rifle and that it was best for everybody that he got rid of him. She further stated that when the following day they learned from radios and newspapers that the rifle shot fired by an unknown person missed Walker, she decided to keep the note as a threat against her husband so that he would not repeat the same thing again, which he promised not to do. She also stated that she did not report this matter to the police as she loved her husband and, particularly, on account of their child. However, she stated

536

if the shot had taken it's mark, she would have reported the matter to the police. She also stated that prior to the shooting, her husband was seen drawing all kinds of maps, etc. which he did not do prior to shooting the President. Statement concerning the Walker incident was obtained from Marina Oswald in her own handwriting. She requested that the matter not be reported to the police but that, if asked by the FBI, she would tell them everything.

On December 4, 1963, the reporting agent interviewed Marina Oswald as to whether she knew of any place or of a rifle range where her husband could do some practicing with a rifle, and whether she ever saw her husband taking the rifle out of the house. She said that she never saw Lee going out or coming in to the house with the rifle and that he never mentioned to her doing any practice with a rifle. She also said that every time he came home over the weekend he either would call, requesting Mrs. Paine to pick him up at the bus point, or he would request Mrs. Paine to take him to the bus point to return to Dallas. Marina Oswald was asked again about a school where her husband took his typing lessons and she again stated that she did not know the name of the school, its location and suggested that Mr. George A. Bouhe be contacted as she believed that Mr. Bouhe attended the same school many years ago. At the time of interview with Marina Oswald, Jim Martin arrived at the house with a man who was introduced as Attorney John M. Thorne, with offices at 302 West College Street, Grand Prairie, Texas, telephone number AN 2-2608. Prior to this date, Mr. Martin indicated that, in view of legal matters involving money received by Marina Oswald, establishing funds and various offers, he was contemplating the hiring of a lawyer and that Mr. Thorne agreed to act in such capacity.

The reporting agent acted only in the capacity of interpreter between Marina Oswald, Mr. Martin and Mr. Thorne who were making arrangements to establish a bank account, to find a business manager who would represent Marina as an agent, to deal with various offers received, and will be received, by her in the future. Apparently Marina Oswald is satisfied with her life with the Martins and trusts Mr. Martin implicitly. Therefore, she agreed that Mr. Martin will represent her in the business capacity, as her manager.

At the conclusion of the above-mentioned interview, the reporting agent and SA Brady returned to the office before the arrival of FBI agents Heistman and Bogoslov.

By checking the telephone directory, it was ascertained that George A. Bouhe resides at 4740 Homer, Dallas, Texas, phone number TAylor 7-2288. Mr Bouhe was interviewed over the telephone by the reporting agent about the night school that Lee Oswald may have attended and he stated that in all possibility Lee attended the Crozier Technical School, located on Bryan Street in Dallas, as he recommended the same school to Marina Oswald to learn the English language.

536

CO-2-34030
12-5-63

Upon return of the reporting agent to his hotel, a message was received to telephone Mr. Martin at his residence. An effort was made to talk to Mr. Martin but SA James Johnson advised that Mr. Martin was not in, that he was conferring with his lawyer and that he wanted totalk to the reporting agent about newspaper reporters who are requesting a personal interview with Marina Oswald. At the time of placing the call to the Martin residence, Inspector Tom Kelley was in the room and the above information was related to him. Inspector Kelley requested to advise Mr. Martin in the event of his call to the reporting agent to tell him not to agree on any conferences between Marina Oswald and the newspapermen, or any other people, until such conference will be approved by either this Service or by the FBI. Later, when Mr. Martin telephoned the reporting agent at his room concerning the matter, he was advised of Inspector Kelley's request and he said that he would try to convince the newspaperman to postpone the interview until he would allow it.

On December 5, 1963, SA Seale made inquiry at the Crozier Technical School, 2218 Bryan Street, Dallas, Texas. This was done in an effort to determine if Lee H. Oswald had ever attended this school. Mr. Troy C. Bond, Principal, produced a registration form which reflected that Lee H. Oswald registered here on January 28, 1963.

The application form further reflected that Oswald took a typing course; that he attended classes each week from 6:15 P.M. to 7:15 P.M. Mr. Bond stated that Oswald attended classes on Monday, Tuesday and Thursday of each week. The application form indicated that Oswald dropped out of school on April 8, 1963; however, Mr. Bond stated that it is possible that Oswald had stopped attending classes prior to this date.

Mr. Bond stated that this registration card is the only existing record of Oswald's attendance at this school. He said that, since Oswald did not desire high school credit for the typing course, all the other records of his attendance were destroyed.

Neither Mr. Bond, Mrs. Gladys Yoakum, Oswald's typing teacher, nor Mrs. Juanita Richey, who registered Oswald, were able to recall him personally.

A copy of Oswald's registration card is attached to the original of this report.

UNDEVELOPED LEADS

Further information will be reported as developed.

LIG:mla

536

COMMISSION EXHIBIT No. 1785—Continued

CO-2-34,030

U. S. Secret Service

Chief

December 3, 1963

ATSAIC Leon I. Gopadze, Dallas

Assassination of President Kennedy, Dallas, Texas

The attached is literal translation from Russian to English of the statement obtained from Marina Oswald and her interpretation of the letter written in Russian by her deceased husband Lee Harvey Oswald prior to his attempted assassination of former General Walker at Dallas, Texas, on April 10, 1963.

The statement was obtained from Marina Oswald on December 3, 1963, by Assistant to the Special Agent in Charge Leon I. Gopadze between 11:30 A.M. and 12:30 P.M., at the residence of Mr. and Mrs. James Martin, 11611 Farrar Street, Dallas, Texas, regarding a note written in Russian which was found in a book entitled Book of Helpful Instructions belonging to Mrs. Marina Oswald.

Leon I. Gopadze
Leon I. Gopadze
Assistant to the
Special Agent in Charge

LIG:amr

Encl.

322

COMMISSION EXHIBIT No. 1786

December 3, 1963
Dallas, Texas

I, Marina Oswald, verify that letter which was shown to me by Agent L van Lynch Goparinef who is working for the Secret Service of the Government of the United States of America, is the letter which was written by my deceased husband Lee Oswald. This letter was written on Neely Street, Dallas, Texas, prior to his departure to New Orleans. For the proper understanding the contents of this letter I will try to write in proper Russian language.

"(1) This key for the Post Office Box in the Main Post Office which is located in the city on Ervay Street on the same street where the drug store where we always have met, 4 blocks from the drug store on the same street is located the Post Office. There you will find our box. I paid for the box last month so don't worry.

(2) Send the information to the consulate what happened to me and also get clippings from the newspapers (if the newspapers will write anything about me). I think that the consulate will help you faster if they will learn everything.

(3) I paid for the house on the 2nd, so don't worry about it.

(4) I have recently paid for the water and gas.

(5) Perhaps that my wages from the work also will be forthcoming. They will send it (the money) to our Post Office Box. Go to the bank where you will change the check for cash.

(6) My clothes, etc. you can throw away or give away. Do not keep it. My personal papers (military, working papers, etc.) I prefer that you keep.

(7) Several of my documents located in the small blue suitcase.

(8) My address book is located on my table in my room if you want it.

(9) Here we have friends and Red Cross who will also help you.

(10) I left you money as much as I could, $60 on second and you and June could exist on $10 a week for two months more.

(11) If I am still alive and will be taken to the city prison, the prison is located at the end of the bridge through which we always travel to the city (in the beginning of the city immediately after the bridge)."

This letter was found by me in the evening of the same day when attempted assassination was made on the person by the name of Walker. Late that night when he (Lee) came home he confessed to me that he shot this person, he was very nervous and refused to answer any questions asked by me but said only that this person is head of the fascist organization and

322

COMMISSION EXHIBIT NO. 1786—Continued

had better be gotten rid of. This letter I did not destroy for the purpose of having evidence in case my husband in the event he will repeat the same thing. He promised me that he would not repeat the same thing. That was the main reason why I insisted for him to go to some other town, for instance in New Orleans. I did not report about this matter to the police on the account of personal feeling toward my husband and also wanted to save my family.

Everything that I have wrote is the truth.

/s/ Marina Oswald

December 3, 1963

Dallas

322

COMMISSION EXHIBIT NO. 1786—Continued

3го дек. 1963г.
Даллас, Тех.

-1-

Я, Марина Освальд, подтверждаю, что письмо, которое было показано мне агентом Ливаном Ильичом Гопарзо, который служит в секретном отделе правительства США, является письмом написанным моим покойным мужем Ли Освальдом. Это письмо написано на Neely street, Даллас, Техас до его отъезда в Нов. Орлеан. Для правильного понятия содержания этого письма постараюсь написать его правильно по-русски.

1) „Этот ключ от почтового ящика на главном почтамте, который находится в городе на улице „Ervay", на той же улице где аптека, у которой мы всегда встречались. Четыре блока от аптеки на этой улице находится почтамт. Там найдешь наш ящик. Я заплатил за наш в прошлом м-це, так ты не переживай об этом.

М. Освальд

323

-2-

2) Посылай в посольство информацию, что со мной случилось и тоже вырезки из газеты (если в газетах что-нибудь обо мне напишут). Я думаю, что посольство быстрей тебе поможет, когда всё узнает.

3) Я заплатил за дом на 2е число, так не переживай об этом.

4) За воду и газ тоже платил недавно.

5) Возможно, что деньги с работы будут. Они пошлют на наш ящик на почтамт. Пойдешь в банк и поменяешь чек на деньги.

6) Мою одежду и т.п. ты можешь выбросить или отдать, не сохраняй их. Но мои личные бумаги (военные, заводские и т.д.) я предпочитаю, чтобы ты держала.

322

М. Освальд

7) Некоторые мои документы находятся в синем маленьком чемодане.

8) Адресная книга на моем столе в моей комнатке, если тебе надо.

9) Тут есть у нас друзья и „красный крест" - тоже тебе помогут. (Red cross - по английски)

10) Я оставил тебе деньги так много, как я мог, 60 долларов на 2ое число и ты и Джун можете жить на 10 долларов в неделю еще 2 м-ца.

11) Если я жив и взят в городскую тюрьму, ~~которая наход~~ то городская тюрьма находится на конце того моста, через который ты всегда ехала в город. (Самое начало города сразу через мост.)

Марина Освальд. 322
WC

Это письмо было найдено много вечером того дня когда было совершено покушение на человека по имени Вокер. Поздно вечером, когда он пришел домой, то сознался мне, что он стрелял в этого человека, был очень взволнован и не отвечал на вопросы, предложенные мною. Только сказал, что этот человек возглавляет фашистскую организацию и лучше от него избавиться. Это письмо я не уничтожила, чтобы иметь улику против моего мужа, если он он захотел повторить подобное. Он обещал мне, что такое более не повторится. И это было основной причиной, почему я настаивала уехать в другой город, например в Нов Орлеан. Я не сообщила об этом полиции из-за моих естественных чувств к мужу, я хотела сохранить семью. Всё что я написала здесь - правда.

WC

Марина Освальд. 322
3 дек. 1963 года Даллас

COMMISSION EXHIBIT No. 1786—Continued

COMMISSION EXHIBIT No. 1786—Continued

Form No. 1589 (Revised)
Memorandum Report
(7-1-60)

UNITED STATES SECRET SERVICE
TREASURY DEPARTMENT [redacted]

Commission Exhibit 1787

ORIGIN: Field	OFFICE: Dallas	FILE NO. CO-2-34,030
TYPE OF CASE: Protective Research	STATUS: Continued	TITLE OR CAPTION: ASSASSINATION OF PRESIDENT KENNEDY, DALLAS, TEXAS
INVESTIGATION MADE AT: Dallas, Texas	PERIOD COVERED: November 29 - December 1, 1963	
INVESTIGATION MADE BY: ATSAIC Leon I. Gopadze		

DETAILS

SYNOPSIS

Additional information received from Marina Oswald concerning her life with Lee Harvey Oswald and other pertinent information regarding the case.

DETAILS OF INVESTIGATION

Reference is made to memorandum report of ATSAIC Gopadze dated November 29, 1963, relative to the investigation conducted in this case.

On the afternoon of November 29, 1963, the reporting agent, accompanied by SA Art Blake, proceeded to the Six Flags Inn in the anticipation of Marina Oswald and her children to be moved to the residence of the Martin's residence the same evening. Mr. James Martin is the assistant manager of the Inn and had invited Marina Oswald and her children to stay at his house.

Upon arrival of agents at the cottage, Robert Oswald was also there, and he asked for assistance of the reporting agent to translate important information concerning his brother Lee Oswald. He stated that apparently the cemetary officials through the Miller's Funeral Home, Fort Worth, are concerned about retaining Lee Oswald's body at the cemetary due to the pressure of families who have relatives buried there as the cemetary officials received all kinds of threats, even to the extent that the body would be exhumed. According to Robert Oswald, the funeral home officials suggested to him either the body be removed from the cemetary or be cremated. He also stated that he had been told that it would take three signatures of Marina Oswald, his mother's and his to accomplish the necessary action. The information furnished by Robert Oswald was translated to Marina Oswald who at first refused to consider such request but after various reasons for such action were explained to her she agreed for cremation of her husband's body inpreference that the body be removed to another cemetary.

DISTRIBUTION	COPIES	REPORT MADE BY	DATE
Chief Dallas	Orig. & 2 2	[signature] SPECIAL AGENT	12-3-63
		APPROVED: Forrest V. Sorrels SPECIAL AGENT IN CHARGE	12-3-63

(CONTINUE ON PLAIN PAPER)   U. S. GOVERNMENT PRINTING OFFICE

41E

CO-2-34,030
Page 2

During the ensuing general conversation with Marina Oswald she indicated that she was very tired from the previous evening due to the interrogation by the FBI agents and that she was worried whether the Martin family liked her during the time she spent with them on Thanksgiving Day. She was also worried as to the length of time she could stay with the Martins and what sort of work they are expecting from her. Upon arrival of James Martin at the cottage occupied by Marina Oswald, the above mentioned problems were related to him and he stated that Marina could stay with them as long as she wanted and that all they wanted her to do was to be happy and for her to feel as a member of their family. Marina Oswald also indicated that she would rather move from the cottage the following day than the same evening which was agreeable to Mr. Martin. During that evening the reporting agent felt that Marina Oswald expressed additional confidence in the reporting agent and in fact she was very disappointed when the agent departed.

On November 30, 1963, the reporting agent accompanied by SA Blake proceeded to the Six Flags Inn for the purpose of additional questioning of Marina Oswald about some matters which were of interest to the Service. Marina Oswald was questioned concerning the origin of the black wallet containing $180.00 in cash and the identity of Byron Phillips of the Wilbarger County, Texas, who executed an affidavit of financial responsibility for her entree into the United States. She stated that the money in the amount of $170.00 represented their savings from her husband's wages and that $10.00 was given to her by the newspaper man; that Lee Oswald was very stingy with his money, tried to exist and eat on little as possible and never bought anything for himself. She was asked whether he was lazy and did not like to work and she replied in the negative as he needed to work and was very concerned about his financial responsibility.

Regarding Byron Phillips, she stated that neither she or Lee ever saw Byron Phillips, that she has heard that her mother-in-law Mrs. Marguerite Oswald worked for him as a practical nurse during the time she (Mrs. Oswald) was residing in Vernon, Texas, and that Mrs. Oswald asked Mr. Phillips to execute the necessary affidavit. Marina Oswald further stated that the wallet in question was given to her husband by his mother upon their arrival in Fort Worth, Texas, from Russia, and that she kept it always in the places where they lived. She was also questioned concerning whether or not she ever saw in Lee's possession pamphlets showing pictures of the late President Kennedy requesting that he be indicted for treason and she replied in the negative. In connection with curtain rods mentioned by Lee Oswald to Wesley Frazier as the latter drove Lee to work Friday morning, she stated that she never saw any rods in the Paine's house or in the garage as Mrs. Ruth Paine only had venetian blinds.

Marina Oswald also stated that when she was shown, by the reporting agent, pictures of Lee Oswald holding a rifle she did not advise at that time that she had the same pictures but in smaller sizes pasted in her family album but that upon suggestion of Mrs. Marguerite Oswald she destroyed them upon learning that

41E

her husband was a prime suspect in the shooting of the President. She also related that the Thursday evening (November 21, 1963) when Lee Oswald appeared at the Paine's house unexpectedly, he told her to buy anything the children needed from their savings, that he appeared to be nervous, that he tried to make up to her due to their previous domestic quarrel and that he went to bed at about 8:00 P.M. the same evening. According to Marina Oswald, when she went to bed around 10:00 P.M., she felt that he was not asleep as shortly after he touched her to see if she were asleep. Marina Oswald further stated that the following day (Friday) when she got up from her bed, after the departure of her husband, she noticed his wedding ring laying on the top of their bedroom dresser. She stated that he never, to her knowledge, took off his ring before, and that at that time she thought it was a strange thing for him to do.

During the ride transporting Marina Oswald and her two children to the Martin's residence located at 11611 Farrar Street, Dallas, Texas, Marina Oswald was constantly talking concerning her husband trying to analyze his emotions and possible reason for killing the President. She said that on numerous occasions he would drop on his knees in front of her crying, saying that he was lost, did not know what to do and was confused in his way of life. Marina Oswald also stated that her husband always tried to improve himself, but that he mostly was concentrating in reading books about the great men of the world, their achievements and their contribution to the world. Marina Oswald is of the opinion that her husband was an ego-maniac who wanted to be a "big man" but that in failing to be so he decided to show the whole world who he was by killing the President so that the whole world would know his name. Marina Oswald also stated tlat while they were living in the Soviet Union, Lee Oswald indicated the lack of freedom of speech in Russia, the travel restrictions and in some way he was disappointed in the way he was treated there.

The trip from the Six Flags Inn to the Martin's residence was without any incidents and no further pertinent information was received from Marina Oswald in this case.

On December 1, 1963, the reporting agent accompanied by SA Gintz proceeded to the Martin's residence for the purpose of taking Marina Oswald and her family to the cemetary which visit she previously requested. Upon arrival of the Robert Oswald family from Denton, Texas, with Special Agents James Lackey and Talmage Bailey, the Oswalds decided that only Marina and Robert Oswald would go to the cemetary. Both Oswalds, including Marina's daughter Junie, were taken to the Rose Hill cemetary located in Fort Worth, Texas, in the government car preceded by plain police car occupied by two plain clothes police officers. On the way to the cemetary Marina Oswald bought azalea plant and one dozen white carnations from a florist shop. Upon arrival at the cemetary Marina Oswald placed the flowers at the Lee Oswald grave with two separate notes written in Russian that the azalea plant was from his wife and for him to rest in peace. The carnations were from his children. Marina Oswald was very pleased to see that the grave contained a white flowered cross with many other flowers. There were not many onlookers and the grave was guarded by the Fort Worth police car with a uniform policeman.

416

COMMISSION EXHIBIT No. 1787—Continued

Marina Oswald remained at the grave for about twenty minutes, and the party returned to the Martin's residence. At the residence Mrs. Martin suggested that Marina Oswald change her appearance for the security reasons while residing at their house and Marina Oswald did not object to that request. Mrs. Robert Oswald, who is a professional beauty operator, cut Marina Oswald's hair, making it short. No other conversation was conducted by the reporting agent with Marina Oswald that day.

UNDEVELOPED LEADS

Further contacts will be maintained with Marina Oswald for any possible information she may have in this case.

LIG:amr

416

COMMISSION EXHIBIT No. 1787—Continued

MP
INV-3-2
O MARINA-2 ✓

[redacted]

1
RPG:vm
DL 100-10461

Commission Exhibit 1788

The following information is set forth concerning the circumstances surrounding the recent publication of a photograph of LEE HARVEY OSWALD holding a rifle and a pamphlet with a revolver on his hip which appeared in LIFE Magazine and other publications:

The original photograph in question is one of 47 photographs found during the search of property of LEE HARVEY OSWALD in the garage of Mrs. RUTH PAINE's residence, 2515 W. 5th Street, Irving, Texas, on November 23, 1963, by homicide and robbery detectives G. F. ROSE, H. M. MOORE, R. S. STOVALL, and J. D. ADAMCIK, Dallas Police Department.

These 47 photographs were turned over to the FBI on December 2, 1963, by Captain J. W. FRITZ, Homicide and Robbery Bureau, Dallas Police Department.

On February 27, 1964, MARINA OSWALD advised SAs WALLACE R. HEITMAN and ANATOLE A. BOGUSLAV that she had originally taken the photograph of LEE HARVEY OSWALD with a rifle and pistol which had recently appeared on the front page of LIFE Magazine. She stated she took this picture with the American-made Imperial Reflex camera owned by OSWALD and that the picture was taken in the yard at their Neeley Street address in Dallas, Texas. She stated she could only recall that she snapped the camera one time but she stated she must have snapped it twice because there were two different poses of OSWALD with the rifle. She stated she believes OSWALD developed the film and printed one copy each of the poses as far as she knows. These prints he gave her and inscribed each on the back to his daughter JUNE. He told MARINA for her to show them to JUNE after he had gone away. He did not explain to MARINA what he meant by going away.

MARINA stated she had placed the pictures in the baby photograph album which she had. On November 22, 1963, following her questioning by the Dallas Police she and MARGUERITE OSWALD, mother of LEE HARVEY OSWALD, were at the residence of Mrs. RUTH PAINE, 2515 W. 5th Street, Irving, Texas, and she (MARINA) showed MARGUERITE OSWALD the photographs of LEE HARVEY OSWALD with the rifle. MARGUERITE told MARINA to hide the photographs and MARINA did hide them in a shoe at the PAINE residence. On the next day,

2
DL 100-10461

MARINA was again questioned by the Dallas Police following which questioning MARGUERITE OSWALD asked MARINA what she had done with the pictures of LEE HARVEY OSWALD with the rifle. She replied she had hid them and MARGUERITE told her to burn them. MARINA advised she burned these two photographs on November 23, 1963, at the PAINE residence. She does not recall that there were other prints in existence. She stated however that there must have been other prints in existence because of subsequent happenings. She stated while she was residing at the home of JAMES HERBERT MARTIN, her former business advisor, and prior to the release of the LIFE Magazine which contained the photograph of OSWALD on the cover, she was told by MARTIN that he had sold the photograph of OSWALD with the rifle to LIFE Magazine for $5,000.

MARINA OSWALD advised that her former attorney, JOHN M. THORNE, on about February 11, 1964, told her at the home of Mr. and Mrs. DECLAN P. FORD, 14057 Brookcrest, Dallas, Texas, that it was he who had sold the photograph of OSWALD with the rifle to LIFE Magazine for $5,000.

MARINA OSWALD stated as far as she knows, LIFE Magazine has not paid $5,000. She has not received any money for the photograph. She stated further that neither MARTIN nor THORNE asked her permission to sell the photograph and she had not given authority to either of them to sell the photograph.

The following investigation was conducted by SA JAMES W. BOOKHOUT:

On February 27, 1964, Captain J. W. FRITZ, Homicide and Robbery Bureau, Dallas Police Department, advised he did not know how many copies of the photograph of OSWALD with a rifle which had appeared in several publications had been made. Captain FRITZ recalled that on November 23, 1963, he had requested the Identification Division of the Dallas Police Department to make up a few enlarged copies of said photograph for aid in the investigation and one copy of the enlarged photograph was furnished to the FBI at Dallas, Texas, and one to U. S. Secret Service, Dallas, Texas, on November 23, 1963. The enlarged copy received by the FBI at Dallas was furnished to FBI Headquarters on November 24, 1963.

Captain FRITZ stated to his knowledge copies of said photograph and others have been furnished to the Texas Attorney General's Office and to Assistant District Attorney for Dallas County, BILL ALEXANDER. Captain FRITZ stated no copies of said photograph, to his knowledge, were furnished to any news media and that Assistant Chief of Police GEORGE LUMPKIN reportedly has a record of the dissemination made of the photographs in this case.

Captain FRITZ advised it would have been possible for some member of the OSWALD family to have had another copy of the photograph in question, however; he felt that the photograph with the cards of OSWALD's which appeared in LIFE Magazine, had to have come from those originally in the possession of the Dallas Police Department.

On February 27, 1964, Captain GEORGE M. DOUGHTY, Identification Division, Dallas Police Department, advised his department has no record of the number of copies made of the photograph in question or of the dissemination made of same. DOUGHTY recalled that a number of photographs in instant case had been made up by Assistant Chief of Police GEORGE LUMPKIN.

Captain DOUGHTY stated to his knowledge no photographs in instant case were ever disseminated to any news media of any type.

On March 2, 1964, Assistant Chief of Police GEORGE LUMPKIN, Dallas Police Department, advised he did not know how many copies had been made of the photograph in question. He stated the only copies of said photograph known to have been disseminated were to the FBI, U. S. Secret Service, Attorney General's Office, and to the Dallas County District Attorney's Office. Assistant Chief LUMPKIN stated no copies were ever authorized for dissemination to any news media of any type.

On March 2, 1964, Lt. CARL DAY, Identification Division, Dallas Police Department, advised that on November 23 and 24, 1963, a large number of copies were made of the photograph in question and were laid out for use of investigating officers. Lt. DAY stated his instructions had been to give the FBI and the U. S. Secret Service anything they wanted. Lt. DAY advised when he returned to work on November 25, 1963, he found all of the photographs gone and it was necessary to make up some more. He stated he has no record of the dissemination of these photographs. He recalls when the photographs were laid out, numerous officers examined them and it is possible some were taken by these

COMMISSION EXHIBIT No. 1788—Continued

unrecalled officers without his knowledge. Lt. DAY estimated he had made at least 24 copies of said photograph and possibly more. Lt. DAY stated that about four days to a week after November 22, 1963, an order was put into effect that photographs in instant case were to be disseminated only on authority of the Chief's Office. Prior to this time, there is no way to tell how many photographs were given out or to whom given.

Lt. DAY stated that since said order, six sets of photographs (50 to 60 photographs which would include the photograph of OSWALD holding the rifle) were made for Assistant Chief of Police GEORGE LUMPKIN on December 7, 1963, and later five additional sets were sent to Assistant Chief LUMPKIN reportedly for the Attorney General's Office. Lt. DAY stated also that on December 4, 1963, Patrolman GLASSCOCK, Department of Public Safety, was given two sets of eleven photographs for Governor CONNALLY, however, he is not sure that the photograph of OSWALD holding the rifle was included in this group.

Lt. DAY stated he has no knowledge of said photograph being given to any news media of any type.

On March 2, 1964, Captain J. W. FRITZ, Homicide and Robbery Bureau, Dallas Police Department, advised that NEWSWEEK Magazine of March 2, 1964, has an article on Page 80 concerning the photograph of OSWALD holding a rifle wherein it is stated that said photograph was purchased from JAMES MARTIN, business advisor of MARINA OSWALD, by LIFE Magazine. This article further stated that "unfortunately for LIFE, at least two other packets of OSWALD's photographs were subsequently being circulated (but not by MARTIN). GENE ROBERTS, an enterprising 31-year-old reporter for the Detroit Free Press, decided to go after them and managed to buy some twenty photographs (including the two LIFE had bought)."

COMMISSION EXHIBIT No. 1788—Continued

748-379 O—64—vol. XXIII——28

Form No. 1588 (Revised)
MEMORANDUM REPORT
(7-1-50)

UNITED STATES SECRET SERVICE
TREASURY DEPARTMENT

ORIGIN Field	OFFICE Dallas	FILE NO. CO-2-34,030
TYPE OF CASE: Protective Research	STATUS: Continued	TITLE OR CAPTION: Assassination of President Kennedy, Dallas, Texas
INVESTIGATION MADE AT: Dallas, Texas	PERIOD COVERED: December 10, 1963	
INVESTIGATION MADE BY: ATSAIC Leon I. Gopadze		

[redacted]

— Commission Exhibit No. 1789 —

DETAILS

SYNOPSIS

Additional information received from Marina Oswald regarding attempted assassination of former General Walker. Also concerning whereabouts of Lee Oswald during the month of October 1962.

DETAILS OF INVESTIGATION

Reference is made to memorandum report of ATSAIC Gopadze dated December 10, 1963.

On December 10, 1963, the reporting agent accompanied by SA Kunkel proceeded to the Martin's residence where Marina Oswald was questioned for additional information she may have relative to the attempted assassination of former General Walker by her husband Lee Harvey Oswald. She stated that Lee Oswald also told her that once before prior to taking shot at General Walker on April 10, 1963, he went to the Walker residence for the same purpose but that he changed his mind as the place did not look just right for him, that three days prior to April 10 he took his rifle out of the house and buried it in a field near the Walker's house. According to Marina Oswald, upon her husband's return to the house after he tried to kill General Walker and telling her about it, three days later she saw him taking his military green rain coat for the purpose of wrapping the rifle and bringing it home. However, stated that when he returned home she did not see the rifle but several days later she saw the rifle on a shelf in the apartment where he always kept it. Marina Oswald also stated that the evening her husband shot at Walker, he told her that the church which is located near the Walker's house had some gathering, that there was plenty of noise and that after shooting at Walker he buried the rifle in the same place. Lee Oswald also told her, after reading in newspapers

DISTRIBUTION	COPIES	REPORT MADE BY	DATE
Chief	Orig. & 2	[signature] SPECIAL AGENT	12-11-63
Dallas	2	APPROVED SPECIAL AGENT IN CHARGE	12-11-63

U. S. SECRET SERVICE

(CONTINUE ON PLAIN PAPER)

U. S. GOVERNMENT PRINTING OFFICE 16—61500-1

632

CO-2-34,030
Page 2

that some young man saw an automobile containing three men pulling away from the scene of shooting, that the Americans always think they should have a car to get away from the scene of the crime and that he would rather use his feet to do so than to have a car. He also told her that he took buses to go to the Walker residence and that he took a different bus to return homeafter the shooting.

In connection with Lee Oswald's places of residence after he moved from the YMCA on October 19, 1962, she stated that at that time she was staying with Elena Hall, that Lee had some apartment in Dallas but that she did not know where and that when she was moved from the Hall's home to 602 Elsbeth Street in the early part of November, Lee and his friend Gary Taylor moved her there. Regarding Gary Taylor, she stated that Gary was the son-in-law of George De Mohrenschildt and his wife, being married to the daughter of George's wife from the previous marriage by the name of Alexie; that Gary was a taxi driver and that after his divorce from Alexie he moved to live with his parents in Dallas but she did not know where. Marina Oswald was asked if she ever saw her husband doing any dry practice with the rifle either in their apartments or any place else, and she replied in the negative. She also was asked how she was able to explain to her mother-in-law, Marguerite Oswald, concerning the attempted assassination of General Walker by her husband, and she replied that she did to the best of her knowledge of English language and that no one else knew about the shooting except her and her mother-in-law.

Concerning Lee Oswald's being in Mexico City and his visits to the Cuban and Russian Embassies, Marina Oswald stated that she had no prior knowledge of him going to Mexico City, but that due to their family difficulties she on several occasions expressed her desire to return to Russia on which he agreed and that he also expressed a desire to return to Russia to save their marriage and on account of their children. She also stated that in order to return to Russia she wrote to the Russian Embassy in Washington, D. C.

Marina Oswald was asked why her husband used the name of "Aleck" and she stated that the name of "Aleck" was given to him by his co-workers in Russia because they did not like the name of Lee as it usually is connected with Chinese persons. She was also asked if to her knowledge her husband used the name of Aleck Hidell, and she replied in the negative. During the interview with Marina Oswald, she advised the reporting agent that she signed contracts the previous evening with Attorney John M. Thorne to handle her business on 10% commission basis for a period of ten years; that she also signed a contract with Jim Martin to receive 15% as her business manager; and that Robert Oswald also would receive 10% as her adviser. Marina Oswald stated that Robert Oswald examined and approved the contents of the contracts.

UNDEVELOPED LEADS

Possible additional interview with Marina Oswald.

LIG:amr

632

Form No. 1588 (Revised)
Memorandum Report
(7-1-60)

UNITED STATES SECRET SERVICE
TREASURY DEPARTMENT

ORIGIN Field (Dallas)	OFFICE Dallas, Texas		FILE NO. CO-2-34030
TYPE OF CASE Protective Research	STATUS Continued	TITLE OR CAPTION Assassination of President Kennedy	
INVESTIGATION MADE AT Dallas, Texas	PERIOD COVERED 12/6/63	Marina Oswald [redacted]	
INVESTIGATION MADE BY ATSAIC Leon I. Gopadze			

— Commission Exhibit No. 1790 —

DETAILS

SYNOPSIS

Marina Oswald states that her husband had no other means of transportation but by a bus or walking. She also states that Mrs. Marguerite Oswald had information concerning the attempted assassination of former General Walker.

DETAILS OF INVESTIGATION

Reference is made to M/R of ATSAIC Gopadze dated 12-5-63.

In order to ascertain the mode of transportation used by Lee Oswald during his stay in Dallas and its vicinity, and because of reports that he had been seen practicing a rifle at the Sports Dome Gun Range, Grand Prairie, Texas (M/R of SA Kunkel dated December 3 and 4, 1963), Marina Oswald was interviewed by the reporting agent on 12-6-63 at the Martin residence. She stated that she is positive that her husband had no car nor ever borrowed one from anybody. They were too poor to buy one and he was too independent to be obligated to anyone by borrowing anything from them. According to Marina Oswald, whenever they needed transportation to move from place to place they were helped by either Ruth Paine or Elena Hall and that when they moved from the apartment on Elsbeth Street to the apartment on Neeley Street they moved their own belongings as the apartments were only a few blocks apart.

As set forth in the M/R of SA Kunkel, Lee Oswald has been identified as being at a rifle range on October 28 and 30, 1963 and on November 2 and 16, 1963. By furnishing Marina Oswald with a calendar and also by calling her attention to a notation found in Lee Oswald's address book, the name of FBI Agent James P. Hosty, his phone number, his address and the date of November 1, 1963, she stated that this notation was made by her husband the same day (November 1, 1963) when she and Ruth Paine advised him that two FBI agents were at their house asking for him. Her husband arrived at the house about an hour after the agents

DISTRIBUTION	COPIES	REPORT MADE BY	DATE
Chief	Orig.&2cc	(signature) ATSAIC Leon I. Gopadze, Special Agent	554 12-9-63
Dallas	2 cc	APPROVED (signature) Special Agent in Charge	DATE 12-9-63

(CONTINUE ON PLAIN PAPER) U.S. GOVERNMENT PRINTING OFFICE 16—61808-1

COMMISSION EXHIBIT NO. 1790

CO-2-34030
12-9-63
Page 2

departure. She said she would like to correct her previous statement concerning the visit of two agents either on November 3 or 4, 1963, as previously reported, as she is sure now the visit was on November 1, 1963.

Marina Oswald went on to say that her husband was with them over the weekend of November 2 and 3, 1963, that he did not go any place, that the following weekend, November 9 and 10, he also spent with them, and that it was the weekend of November 16 and 17 when he did not show up at their house. Marina Oswald further said that she did not think herhusband had the rifle any place but Mrs. Paine's garage as she or Mrs. Paine would have seen him with the rifle during the weekends. According to Marina Oswald, she saw the rifle in the garage about three weeks prior to November 22nd and she thinks that the rifle was taken out of the garage by her husband in the morning of the assassination of the President.

Marina Oswald was further questioned concerning the attempted assassination of former General Walker by her husband on April 10, 1963, and whether any one else knew beside herself about this act. She stated that the day of her husband's arrest and after she and her mother-in-law returned to the Paine's from visiting Lee Oswald at the City Jail, she told her mother-in-law that she thought Lee was responsible for shooting the President as he previously unsuccessfully tried to kill General Walker with his rifle. That was the same day when Mrs. Oswald, Sr., told her to destroy Lee's pictures in her album showing him standing with the rifle. Marina Oswald further stated that her husband twice saw the TV showing of a moving picture depicting a plot to kill a Cuban dictator with a bomb where the plotters had to dig a tunnel and that Lee did not like the picture as he said that was the way they did in the old days. She also thought Lee saw a TV showing of a movie where an attempt was made to kill a President at the railroad station with a rifle, from a house, but she was not sure about it. The way Marina Oswald was describing the later picture, it leaves very little doubt that this picture is entitled "Suddenly" starring Frank Sinatra.

Marina Oswald also was asked for assistance in transcribing various names, words and addresses written in Russian by her husband in his small notebook, reproduced pages of which were furnished this Service by the FBI. Nothing was found there of interest to this Service except various names of their friends while they were living in Russia, their addresses, and telephone numbers, various names of Government offices, Russian calendar, proper pronunciation of Russian words, items to be obtained for Marina's departure from Russia and a hand-drawn map of the Kremlin and its vicinity.

English meaning of notations found in Lee Oswald's book and written in Russian are set forth by pages in the attached separate page.

UNDEVELOPED LEADS

Further contacts will be maintained with Marina Oswald for possible additional information she may have.

LIG:mla

554

COMMISSION EXHIBIT NO. 1790—Continued

English translation of Russian words found in Lee Oswald's book:

Page 1 - Russian word for "to-day"

Page 4 - Hand-drawing of Kremlin, its vicinity and names of streets

Page 5 - Items to be obtained for departure from Russia

Page 6 - Addresses of various establishments in Russia

Page 9 - Russian word for a wedding ring. Bank

Page 12 - Russian word for "thanks"

Page 13 - Name of a street

Page 14 - Hand-drawing of Russian calendar

Page 15 - Proper pronunciation of Russian words

Page 16 - Name of Colonel Aksanov in Foreign Section - Minsk

Page 17 - Bank of Commerce and address in Moscow - Name of Mr. Koslov and phone number

Page 19 - Names and addresses of friends in Minsk

Page 20 - Name, address and phone number of their child doctor

Page 21 - South Germany Consulate. Address of a friend in Minsk.

Page 22 - Names of Russian Government Departments

Page 23 - Russian names in Russia and Minsk. Name "Rose Kooznetzova" - employed by Intourist Hotel in Minsk

Page 24 - Communist Party in USA and its address.

Page 25 - Name of "Lucy", her address and phone number - a girl Lee knew in Minsk who attended a medical school

Page 26 - The name and address of Yura Moreshanski who introduced Marina to Lee

Page 27 - Office of the Government Attorney

Page 28 - "Ostankino" - name of a hotel in Moscow

Page 29 - Marina's address while she was on vacation

554

COMMISSION EXHIBIT No. 1790—Continued

Form No. 1588 (Revised)
MEMORANDUM REPORT
(7-1-50)

UNITED STATES SECRET SERVICE
TREASURY DEPARTME[redacted]

Commission Exhibit 1791

ORIGIN	OFFICE	FILE NO.
Field (Dallas)	Dallas, Texas	CO-2-34030

TYPE OF CASE	STATUS	TITLE OR CAPTION
Protective Research	Continued	Assassination of President Kennedy Mrs. Marina Oswald
INVESTIGATION MADE AT: Arlington, Texas	PERIOD COVERED: 11/27 - 12/10/63	
INVESTIGATION MADE BY: ATSAIC Leon I. Gopadze		

DETAILS

SYNOPSIS

Details of interview of Marina Oswald by FBI Agents Hosty and Brown at the Six Flags Inn on 11-27-63 which was translated by ATSAIC Gopadze.

DETAILS OF INVESTIGATION

Reference is made to M/R of ATSAIC Gopadze dated 11-29-63, page 2, setting forth general information as to what transpired during the interview between the FBI agents and Marina Oswald, at the Six Flags Inn, on 11-27-63. However, it was deemed advisable that additional information concerning the meeting be furnished.

After the reporting agent introduced himself to Marina Oswald under the name of "Lee" and as being a Government agent, the following statements were made by Marina Oswald in reply to questions asked by the FBI agents:

At the outset of the interview before reporting agent could advise Marina Oswald of her rights, she asked, "Do I have a right not to answer questions if I do not want to?" She was advised by the FBI agents she did not have to talk; that anything she said could be held against her. She was asked if she would mind answering questions to be asked; she replied that she did not wish to be asked, as anything she had to say she had said before and she had no further information. Marina Oswald was advised that there were many unanswered questions. She stated that she would not care to be asked. She stated she was tired and worried about one of her babies who was ill and she did not care to be interviewed. Marina Oswald was told that her cooperation was needed in this investigation and she was asked whether she would consider an interview later on some other occasion. She stated she desired no further interview. Marina Oswald stated the Government knows the facts and that she has no other facts except what is known. Asked why she did not want to be interviewed, she

DISTRIBUTION	COPIES	REPORT MADE BY	DATE
Chief Dallas	Orig.&2cc 2 cc	ATSAIC Leon I. Gopadze, SPECIAL AGENT	12-10-63
		APPROVED: [signature] SPECIAL AGENT IN CHARGE	12-10-63

562

(CONTINUE ON PLAIN PAPER)

U. S. GOVERNMENT PRINTING OFFICE 16—61306-4

COMMISSION EXHIBIT No. 1791

CO-2-34030
12-10-63
Page 2

replied that she did not have a friendly feeling toward the FBI. When asked if she intended to stay in the United States, Marina Oswald stated she would like to remain in the United States because of her children and also to be near where her husband is buried. She then asked for assurance that she would be allowed to remain in the United States and she was advised that this was a matter coming within the jurisdiction of the Immigration and Naturalization Service. Marina Oswald was told that the Government needs her cooperation and this might help her. She stated if she were not allowed to remain in the United States then that was all right, too. Marina Oswald was asked how she intended to make a living for herself and her children; she said she would find some type of work. She was then told that her cooperation with the Government could also be of assistance. Marina then stated she was tired of answering questions and she was told the Government just wanted the facts; she stated that she had the same facts as everyone else. When asked if Lee Oswald had ever had any conversations about President Kennedy, Marina Oswald said "no"; asked if he ever stated he intended to kill President Kennedy, she stated "no, but I feel he did not because he never spoke of President Kennedy." When asked if he had ever spoken against Governor John Connally, Marina stated that Lee Oswald had no grudge against Connally; she then stated "I swear before God Lee did not intend to kill the President." Asked if she believed in God, Marina Oswald stated that she has believed in God since the death of her mother. Asked if she were a Christian, she stated "yes".

Marina Oswald was then asked about associates of Lee Oswald and she stated she knew of no associate as he was a "loner". He was always by himself and he never expressed political views to her and he was of the opinion that women did not belong in politics. When asked if he had any friends in Russia, she said "no"; he was always studying and reading Marxist books like "Das Kapital". Marina stated that one time she said to Lee Oswald, "What are you trying to do, start another revolution?" Marina described Lee Oswald as strong-willed and stubborn; he was hot-headed and had his own ideas about everything. She was asked if she had ever seen Lee Oswald with a gun, had she seen him go hunting? She stated that there was no place to hunt where they lived and he had no transportation to go hunting and he did not know how to drive an automobile. When asked if she would resent another visit by the FBI, she stated that there was no reason for such a visit. Marina Oswald stated that she had been treated well; that she hoped she would not be bothered again. Marina Oswald stated that the Government has all the facts and, in her mind, due to what she has been told, she is satisfied that Lee Oswald had killed the President. Marina Oswald was advised that they desired to get all the facts and that if she had any additional facts that he had not killed the President it might possibly clear Lee Oswald. She stated that if she knew any additional facts to clear Lee Oswald she would furnish them. Marina Oswald stated the Government knows more than she does. At one point during the conversation, when momentarily interrupted, she snapped "Let's come to the business". Marina Oswald then requested termination of the interview.

LIG:mla

562

Commission Exhibit No. 1791—Continued

Form No. 1588 (Revised)
Memorandum Report
(7-1-60)

UNITED STATES SECRET SERVICE
TREASURY DEPARTMENT

ORIGIN (Dallas) Field OFFICE Dallas, Texas FILE NO. CO-2-34030

TYPE OF CASE	STATUS	TITLE OR CAPTION
Assassination of the President	Continued	Lee Harvey Oswald
INVESTIGATION MADE AT: Washington, D. C. and Dallas, Texas	PERIOD COVERED: 11/26/63 - 11/28/63	
INVESTIGATION MADE BY: ATSAIC Leon L. Gopadze		

DETAILS

SYNOPSIS

This report relates to listening of the tape recording interview of Marina Oswald by SAs Charles Kunkel and James F. Howard, which was translated by Russian interpreter Peter P. Gregory. The report also relates to the personal interview with Marina Oswald witnessed by Mr. Gregory.

DETAILS OF INVESTIGATION

Per Chief's orders the reporting agent reported to Washington in connection with interview of Marina Oswald, by Special Agents of the Dallas office.

Upon arrival of the reporting agent to Washington, D. C., on November 26, 1963, arrangements were made to transcribe the tape recording of the questions and answers during the questioning of Marina Oswald by SAs Kunkel and Howard which was translated by Russian Interpreter Mr. Gregory. The translation was faultless without deviation and at no time was there any indication that Mr. Gregory was translating otherwise. It also appeared that Mr. Gregory had a complete confidence of Marina Oswald and she was answering to the best of her ability.

On November 26, 1963, as instructed by Chief, the reporting agent and SA Max Phillips of the PRS proceeded to Dallas, Texas, for the purpose of personal interview with Marina Oswald and to be of any assistance to the Dallas office. Upon arrival to the Dallas office, the agents were advised by Inspector Tom Kelley that the FBI agents would like to use the reporting agent as interpreter for their proposed interview with Marina Oswald the same day. Inspector Kelley was advised that the reporting agent was not a finished interpreter to be used by the FBI for any official interrogation as used by the State Department or for the Court purposes, however, the reporting agent was willing to assist the FBI to the best of his ability. Upon arrival of FBI agents Charles

DISTRIBUTION	COPIES	REPORT MADE BY / APPROVED	DATE
Chief	Orig & 2 cc	Leon L. Gopadze, SPECIAL AGENT 319	11-29-63
Dallas	2 cc	APPROVED: Forrest V. Sorrels, SPECIAL AGENT IN CHARGE rås	11-29-63

(CONTINUE ON PLAIN PAPER)

U. S. GOVERNMENT PRINTING OFFICE 16—61500-1

Commission Exhibit No. 1792

T. Brown and James P. Hosty, Jr. of their Dallas office, the reporting agent explained to them the problems of a finished translator or interpreter for their particular need but they requested for assistance as their interview with Marina Oswald would be very limited. At this time it was agreed that the reporting agent would represent himself as a Government Agent without disclosing his true name or his official capacity.

11-27-63

Upon arrival of FBI Agents Hosty and Brown, SA Phillips and reporting agent went to the Six Flags Inn where Marina Oswald was staying, and entered her cottage. Marina Oswald was sitting on a davenport in the living room holding her infant child. The reporting agent introduced himself to Marina Oswald as being a Government agent by the name of Mr. Lee. He also introduced FBI Agents Hosty and Brown in their true capacity. Marina Oswald was told the purpose of the visit and she immediately asked whether she has a right not to answer any questions if she did not wish to do so. This was translated to the FBI agents and Marina Oswald was assured that she had rights not to answer any questions if she did not want to. The agents asked Marina Oswald whether she would object to be questioned in the future by their agents as there are many questions to be asked which were not previously answered by her or propounded to her. Marina Oswald replied that she had no other information that had not been given by her before and that she would decline any other interview by the FBI agents, by explaining that she and her husband, Lee, felt that the FBI was responsible for Lee in losing his jobs. Many attempts were made by interviewing agents to change her mind by convincing that they were not responsible for Lee's loss his jobs or to obtain one but she repeatedly refused to be interrogated. The agents also tried to explain to her that if she felt that Lee was not responsible in killing the President, it was their duty to find the guilty person. Marina Oswald was constantly indicating that she was tired to be questioned by various agencies and persons and that she would like to terminate the interview. Prior to the departure of the interviewing agents and the reporting agent, Marina Oswald was asked if she would decline to see the reporting agent the following day and she had no objection for such visit. Upon return of the agents to the Dallas office of the Secret Service, FBI Agent Hosty made notations as to answers made by Marina Oswald during the interview in narrative form and a copy of it was promised by FBI Agent Hosty to be furnished to this Service. During the conference with the FBI agents, the reporting agent mentioned to FBI Agent Hosty that Marina Oswald has recognized him as the FBI agent who had interviewed her on or about October 27, 1963, concerning the whereabouts of Lee Oswald. Agent Hosty admitted that he had talked to Mrs. Oswald and that Mrs. Paine had acted as his translator. This admission was made by FBI Agent Hosty in presence of Inspector Thomas Kelley, SAIC Sorrels and SA Max Phillips.

The following day, November 28, 1963, the reporting agent felt that in order to interview Marina Oswald, the assistance of Mr. Peter P. Gregory who acted as the interpreter between Marina Oswald and SAs Kunkel and Howard, would be beneficial to the cause as it was felt that Marina Oswald during the prior interview had an idea that the reporting agent was also an FBI agent. A contact by the agents of

319

the Dallas office was made with Mr. Gregory who agreed to be present and assist the reporting agent in obtaining any possible information needed by this office and particularly to convince Marina Oswald that the reporting agent is not the FBI agent due to her indicated feeling toward the FBI.

About 11 A.M. on November 28, 1963, the reporting agent, accompanied by SA Max Phillips and ~~SA Robert A. Steuart,~~ proceeded to the Six Flags Inn, where they met Mr. Gregory who arrived about the same time. After being introduced to Mr. Gregory, the two of us proceeded to a separate room, reserved by our agents. After explaining to Mr. Gregory, the problem and particularly to explain to Marina Oswald that the reporting agent was not an FBI agent and for her to cooperate in the matter with me. Mr. Gregory, after exchanging the mutual personal background, was more than willing to do anything he could. As to Mr. Gregory's relationship with the Oswalds, he stated that he is an Oil-Consultant, was born in Russia, and that he came to the United States in 1923; that he arrived in the U. S. on the West Coast and that he studied at the University of California at Berkley, California, and that when he moved to Dallas, Texas, being employed in his particular profession, he also was engaged on his own to teach Russian to any Americans who expressed a desire for the language.

He said that sometime in latter part of June 1962, he received a phone call at his office in Dallas from a man who said his name was Oswald. He said he learned Mr. Gregory was teaching Russian and that he would like to see him as soon as possible concerning this matter. In a few days, Lee Oswald came to his business office where he indicated that he would like to be an interpreter in Russian language. According to Gregory, Lee spoke fairly well in Russian, but with somewhat Polish accent. That in order to satisfy himself whether Lee could be an interpreter, he asked Lee to read some Russian books and to translate them. Lee did this and then Lee asked if he could give him a letter to anyone concerned certifying re his ability to be a translator. Such letter was given to Lee by Mr. Gregory. At this time, Mr. Gregory said he has grown-up children who are gainfully employed and his youngest son, Paul, was still a student at Oklahoma University, Norman, Oklahoma. However, Mr. Gregory stated that about 4 years ago only Paul indicated to him that he would like to learn Russian which was contrary to wishes of the older children, and which they never did.

At the time he talked to Lee Oswald, he also learned that Lee was in Russia, that he returned with a Russian wife and that he was living with his brother, Robert Oswald. When he was helping his son Paul to learn Russian, he thought of the idea that Paul would learn more polished Russian from Marina Oswald and also about life in Russia. Upon this idea, he contacted Lee Oswald by phone and asked him if his wife, Marina, would mind teaching his son the language. At that time, the Oswalds were living on Mercedes Street in Fort Worth and ~~that~~ Paul used to go to their residence once or twice a week to study the language. After Paul Gregory departed for Oklahoma City, to further study at the University in the latter part of September 1962, Mr. Gregory invited several Russian people to his home for dinner. He invited the Oswalds as well as other Russian friends, among whom was invited was George A. Bouhe, who was born in Leningrad, Russia. Mr. Gregory thought that inasmuch as Marina lived in Leningrad and studied there, Mr. Bouhe would enjoy meeting her. As result of this

319

evening Mr. Bouhe found a job for Lee Oswald and he started working in some photostat or photographing shop in Dallas. However, up to then Lee was working in Ft. Worth as a sheet metal worker.

The Oswalds moved to Dallas either the latter part of September 1962 or early October of the same year. When they moved to Dallas he lost all contact with them and never saw them again. However, he has heard through other Russian friends that they were very disappointed in the Oswalds and one of his friends told him that Lee Oswald was a turncoat and that his name was mentioned in the Ft. Worth papers as being such. This happened in February 1963 when he invited for a dinner George Bouhe, Mr. and Mrs. Clark and Meller, who also told him that the Oswalds did not deserve any help because of their attitude. Mr. Gregory also advised that everybody was sympathetic and liked Marina but everyone disliked Lee. He also heard that Oswald beat ~~upon~~ Marina on several occasions. Ann Meller also told him that on one occasion Marina moved to her (Ann's) house due to such bad treatment.

According to Mr. Gregory the next time he heard of Lee Oswald was Friday when he shot our President, and that Lee Oswald was considered a prime suspect in the shooting. Mr. Gregory said he himself disliked Lee Oswald as Lee was arrogant, stubborn and would not discuss anything but his particular type of politics, which was definitely radical.

Mr. Gregory appeared to be a very sincere man, highly educated, and there was no question that he stands for good Americanism and is very patriotic, and loyal to this country.

Marina Oswald was then interviewed only in presence of Mr. Gregory. Mr. Gregory assured her that the reporting agent was not an FBI Agent and told her to cooperate to the fullest extent. She stated she was born on July 17, 1941, in the city of Molotovsk in Archangel District. She said during the war between Germany and Russia she lost her father, and that when the war was over she and her mother moved to Moldavia District located in the southern part of Russia. She said up to the fourth grade in elementary school, they lived in the Moldvin District and then moved to Leningrad where she entered the fifth grade at the 374 Women's School, located on Kiev Street. She went there up to the seventh grade when she decided to enter a Pharmaceutical school, even though she did not graduate from the elementary school which had 10 grades.

While attending the Pharmaceutical school she also worked which helped her make her living and stay in school. According to her, Marina's mother died in Leningrad on April 8, 1956. After finishing the Pharmaceutical school in 1959 she decided to go to the city of Minsk to live with her uncle (her mother's brother) who then was employed by the Government as a military engineer.

In March of 1961, she met Lee Oswald. The circumstances of this meeting are set forth in a tape recording transcription prepared and previously furnished Chief, with the exception that after meeting and marrying Lee, he decided to return to the U. S. and after correspOnding with the American consulate in Moscow, they finally were able to obtain a visa for their trip to the United States. According to Marina

319

COMMISSION EXHIBIT No. 1792—Continued

Oswald, in order to obtain the visa, and after receiving the permission, she and Lee went to Moscow where the transportation was supplied by the American consulate. She said they arrived in New York by air on 2-13-62; they stayed in some hotel in New York City for one day and then went by train to Texas. She said when they got to Texas, they were met by Robert Oswald in the town where he lived with his family; that they stayed with Robert Oswald for about 1½ months and then moved to live with Lee's mother in Ft. Worth, Texas. She said after staying with her mother-in-law for about 3 weeks, she and Lee moved to an apartment on Mercedes Street, that was some time the latter part of July, 1962. She said they lived there until October 1962 when Lee lost his job in the sheet metal factory as it was seasonal work. In October 1962 Lee left for Dallas to look for work and she, with her daughter June, moved to live with Mrs. Elena Hall, whose address she could not recall but whose husband was a dental technician.

She stated that Elena Hall was born in Russia but was married to an American. Marina went on to say that while in Dallas, Lee lived at the YMCA but after Lee was able to obtain employment in either a photostat or photography shop, she moved to Dallas where Lee already had an apartment on Elsbeth Street. They lived there until January 1963, when they moved to an apartment on Neely Street. She could not remember the exact addresses on both streets. However, upon request of interviewing agent she described the type of buildings. She said that on Elsbeth St. it was a one story, red brick building, but that on Neely St. it was a two story frame building and that they lived upstairs. Subsequently Marina Oswald pointed out to SA Charles E. Kunkel the exact apartment houses where they lived on Elsbeth and Neely Streets. She said they lived there until May 1963, when she and her daughter moved to live with the Paines in Irving, Texas. According to Marina Oswald, the same day she moved to Irving, Lee bought a bus ticket to go to New Orleans; that this move was upon the insistance of Marina as she suggested he would have a better chance of getting work there where he was born and had relatives. The following day she received a phone call at Mrs. Paine's home from Lee in New Orleans saying he was staying with his aunt whose name she did not know. Marina said that about a week later Lee phoned her again from New Orleans and said he had found a job at the Louisiana Coffee Company. He wanted her to join him there. About a week later she and her daughter were taken to New Orleans by Mrs. Paine and she joined Lee in an apartment which he rented before she arrived. This apartment was on Magazine Street.

Lee continued working for the Louisiana Coffee Company but he lost his job in August 1963. Marina Oswald remained with Lee until the last of September 1963, depending on unemployment compensation checks, for about 7 weeks. As Lee could not find a job, and due to somewhat marital difficulties, Marina wrote to Mrs. Paine concerning these troubles and asked her if she could come down and take her back to Irving, Texas. Mrs. Paine agreed to do so and while Mrs. Paine was on her vacation traveling in unknown places she arrived in New Orleans and took Marina back to Irving, Texas. As far as Marina can remember, this occurred in the latter part of September 1963. Lee remained in New Orleans looking for work. During the time Lee remained in New Orleans for about a week, he did not call her or communicate with her in any way. However, in early October 1963 she received a phone call from Lee at Mrs. Paine's house, telling her he was in Dallas, Texas; that he had taken a room, but he did not tell her the address, he gave her only a telephone number. She did not remember that phone number as that number, as that number was given to Mrs. Paine to put in Mrs. Paine's phone book. She remembers that Lee said it was a rooming

319

COMMISSION EXHIBIT No. 1792—Continued

house with many rooms with no private toilet facilities. Later he phoned again and said he moved to another rooming house without disclosing the address but leaving a phone number where he could be reached. This number was also given to Mrs. Paine and she put it down in her phone book. According to Marina Oswald, Lee has been phoning her from Dallas almost every day due to his worries about their children, and that when she left New Orleans, she took all their belongings except leaving his personal things with him there.

After obtaining the foregoing information the reporting agent felt she was very sincere in her statements and that she was furnishing the information voluntarily without trying to hold anything back. In connection with Lee's and her finances, she said they lived very frugally; that Lee was very stingy; and that at no time was Lee giving her funds — but that while he was working, they tried to save up as much as they could, and that Lee never told her the amount of his salary while working.

At this time Marina was asked if she knew of any clubs that Lee belonged to in Russia. She replied the only club he belonged to was a Hunters Club in Minsk. In asking her whether he had freedom of travel in Russia, she replied negatively and said he had only limited permission to travel while living in Russia. She was asked if to her knowledge Lee was in Leningrad and whether she knew of a club named "Inter-Club". She said she knows Lee was not in Leningrad as his visa which he obtained directed him to report directly to Moscow from Helsinky, Finland. However, she said she knows the INTER CLUB in Leningrad as this place is mostly patronized by foreign sailors for their entertainment, such as dancing, seeing films, and the club could be entered by any person by paying the entrance fee.

She was asked whether she had any knowledge of Lee's trips to Mexico or Washington, D. C. She replied in the negative. She was asked whether she or Lee had any cameras and she replied that Lee bought one camera in Russia and a second one in the United States. She said one was a small camera and the other was a box camera. She added that she was not proficient with operating any cameras as she never had an opportunity to do so.

She was asked whether Lee had any guns and she said yes; that he had a rifle while they were living in New Orleans but did not know what kind of a gun it was as she was not familiar with firearms of any kind. She added that when she moved from New Orleans she cannot tell whether she brought the gun to Irving, Texas, but that she found a rifle wrapped in one of their blankets and that it was in Mrs. Paine's garage. She said she did not examine this gun but only saw the barrell.

Concerning visits by FBI agents, Marina stated that while living on Mercedes Street in Fort Worth, Texas, they were visited by two agents who talked to Lee at length outside the house in their automobile; that while living in Irving, Texas, to her knowledge only on two occasions did agents visit there; however, she had been advised by her neighbors that some agents made inquiries concerning Lee while they were gone from the house. By furnishing Marina a calendar she established that the first visit of a FBI agent in Irving, Texas, was either on October 22 or 23, 1963, which she learned from neighbors; that the second visit was on October 25, 1963, by one FBI agent who talked with her, but Lee was not there. It was a very short conversation and was translated by Mrs. Paine and the agent then left.

The next visit was about a week later, either on November 5 or 6, 1963, when two agents called together, but she did not see the agents then but was told by Mrs. Paine that they had been there asking for Lee. According to her, she could not understand the conversation between Mrs. Paine and the agents, but Mrs. Paine explained they were asking about Lee. In connection with FBI agents' visit in Fort Worth, Marina Oswald said that after the agents left, Lee was very nervous. Lee never told her what this was all about but was very nervous concerning the interview.

On the last occasion when Mrs. Paine's home was visited by FBI agents, Lee was already working for the Texas Schoolbook Depository.

Apparently Marina was very much concerned that Mr. Gregory and I had any doubts as to her sincerity and truthfulness in her answers to our questions. She repeatedly would remark "I hope you believe me, as I swear by God, this is the truth." Her religious convictions concerning belief in God she expressed the previous evening when she was asked by the reporting agent if she believed in God, she replied that she did not believe in God until her mother died but that after her death she started to believe in God, and particularly since she came to the United States. During the conversation she also indicated that Lee was a loner, stubborn, hot headed, and some times violent just like his mother Mrs. Oswald, Sr., who on numerous occasions exhibited her temper by shrieking at her, stamping her feet, and insisting that she have her own way in any aspect of Marina's life.

Before showing Marina Oswald photographs of Lee Oswald holding the rifle, she was forewarned to tell me the truth about the photographs. She replied she would. At this time two photographs of Lee holding the rifle, a newspaper, and a revolver strapped to his side were shown to her and by seeing them it seemed somewhat of a shock to her. She started crying but after composing herself, she said that the pictures were taken while they were living in the duplex on Neely Street at Dallas, Texas, as she recognized the background of the picture. She was then asked who took the pictures. Marina hesitatingly said she didn't think she knew but immediately stated that there was no use to tell a lie, and added that it was taken by her upon Lee's request, even though she did not know how to operate the camera. The operation of the camera was explained to her by Lee who also measured the distance where she should stand when taking the photographs. After Marina Oswald examined the pictures it was pointed out to her Lee was holding a rifle containing the scope and she said honestly that she does not remember noticing the scope but that it was Lee's rifle and the same one which she had previously seen in their apartment in New Orleans. The fact that Lee had a revolver in a holster on his right side was pointed out to her but she said she did not notice the revolver while taking the picture as Lee was dressed in black and it would have been hard to see. She said the reason Lee asked her to take the photographs was for the purpose of sending photographs to the Militant magazine to show that he was ready for anything. Marina Oswald said this was also probably for the purpose of showing that he was here and that he was ready to do anything even if it involves possible use of arms. She was very much concerned that her first version to the police concerning the gun was false, as she had tried to protect Lee whom she loved and still loves but feels that the truth should be known. She asked that information given concerning the gun be withheld from the Police as she does not want to be branded as a liar.

Marina Oswald further stated that there was no question but that that was Lee's rifle, that she was now satisfied that he was responsible for killing the President, but that she had never had any inkling that he would be so violent to anybody. She was asked whether Lee, to her knowledge, was an expert rifle-shot, and she said Lee was boastful that he was a good shot and that he learned this while in the military service. Marina also expressed her deep sorrow and concern over the killer of her husband and said she has no malice toward him, and hoped he would not be killed for his crime.

Marina Oswald said that at no time had she seen Lee carrying guns away from the house for any purpose or had seen him practice shooting any guns. She said he would go to work either by a bus or be taken by a neighbor who also worked where he did.

Marina Oswald inquired of the reporting agent and Mr. Gregory if she should give the same information to the FBI or any other agency of the Government, and she was told for her own sake and her children's sake to tell the truth during all of this investigation which would help her in the long run, and particularly with her desire to remain in the United States. She was also told this Service was willing to help her all they could.

At the conclusion of the interview, as it was felt that she was very tired, Marina on her own accord stated that on Thursday night about 6:30 P.M., on November 21, 1963, Lee appeared at the Paine's house; that this surprised her because Lee had never visited her on week days while working for the Texas Schoolbook Depository but only on weekends; that he told her he had something very important to do. The following morning Lee left the Paine's house, but she did not see Lee's actual departure from the area. Prior to Lee's departure he told Marina not to expect him home over the weekend, a statement Lee had never made before, as he had spent every weekend with his family.

Marina further stated that after the assassination of the President, Mrs. Paine told her that during the Thursday evening of November 21, 1963, Lee was doing something in the Paine's garage, but Mrs. Paine did not know what Lee was doing in the garage.

After the reporting agent's return to the U. S. Secret Service Office, Dallas, Texas, Marina Oswald had one of the Secret Service agents phone the office and asked for the reporting agent. She apologized for not giving the following information: She stated that while pointing out to our agents the apartment on Neely Street as well as Ellsbeth Street, it came to her mind that on her departure from New Orleans with Mrs. Paine, Lee told her and Mrs. Paine that he might go to some other cities to look for work, and particularly to a city where one of his friends was living; that the name of both cities were furnished by Lee to Mrs. Paine who no doubt will remember the names and may remember the name of his friend he mentioned. She also said tha while living on Neely Street in Dallas, Lee was attending some night school where they teach all kinds of languages, typing, etc. She said he attended this school twice a week and usually would go to the school direct from his work and would get

home about 8:30 P.M. She knows he was studying typing as he was bringing home some of his home work; that he attended this school for about a month.

UNDEVELOPED LEADS

Further interrogation of Marina Oswald if an opportunity presents itself.

Form No. 1588 (Revised)
MEMORANDUM REPORT
(7-1-60)

UNITED STATES SECRET SERVICE
TREASURY DEPARTMENT

Oswald, Marina 2

ORIGIN Field	OFFICE Dallas	FILE NO. CO-2-34,030
TYPE OF CASE: Protective Research	STATUS: Pending	TITLE OR CAPTION: ASSASSINATION OF PRESIDENT KENNEDY, DALLAS, TEXAS
INVESTIGATION MADE AT: Dallas, Texas	PERIOD COVERED: November 22 - 29, 1963	
INVESTIGATION MADE BY: ATSAIC Leon L. Gopadze & SA Max D. Phillips		

DETAILS

— Commission Exhibit 1793 —

SYNOPSIS

Mrs. Marina Oswald interviewed by Federal Bureau of Investigation while ATSAIC Leon L. Gopadze of Los Angeles acted as Russian translator. FBI SA Hosty, Jr. admitted interviewing Mrs. Marina Oswald on or about October 27, 1963, twenty-seven days before the assassination.

DETAILS OF INVESTIGATION

Per Chief Rowley, the reporting Special Agent returned to Dallas, Texas, with ATSAIC Leon Gopadze of Los Angeles for the purpose of assisting ATSAIC Gopadze during his interview with Mrs. Marina Oswald and of assisting Inspector Thomas J. Kelley with subject investigation.

It should be noted, however, that the reporting Special Agent was first ordered by Chief Rowley on November 22, 1963, to deplane at Dallas, Texas, while enroute from Austin, Texas, to Washington, D. C. Chief Rowley's orders were to act as a coordinator and to relay investigative information from Dallas to the Chief's Office. From approximately 4:00 P.M., November 22, 1963, through 10:30 PM, November 23, 1963, the reporting Special Agent performed coordinating duties, upon which time Chief Rowley gave orders to return to Washington and resume duties in Protective Research Section.

Other Investigations

On November 27, 1963, the reporting agent, ATSAIC Gopadze, SAIC Sorrels, and Inspector Kelley conducted a pre-interview briefing with two FBI Special Agents. These FBI Special Agents were Charles T. Brown, Jr. and James P. Hosty, Jr. of the Dallas Office. It was discussed at this pre-interview briefing that ATSAIC Gopadze would act as a Russian interpreter for the Federal Bureau of Investigation.

DISTRIBUTION	COPIES	REPORT MADE BY	DATE
Chief	Orig. & 1	Max D Phillips — SPECIAL AGENT Max D. Phillips	11-30-63
Dallas	2	APPROVED — SPECIAL AGENT IN CHARGE	DATE 204 11-30-63

(CONTINUE ON PLAIN PAPER)

COMMISSION EXHIBIT NO. 1793

CO-2-34,030
Page 2

During this pre-interview briefing, SA James P. Hosty, Jr. casually mentioned that he had talked to Mrs. Marina Oswald at the Irving Street address about two months ago.

SA Hosty was asked by the reporting Special Agent, "How did you talk to her - doesn't she only speak Russian?" SA Hosty replied that Ruth Paine, acted as a translater. SA Hosty was further asked by the reporting Special Agent, "Did you interview her (Mrs. Marina Oswald) before or after the new baby was born?" SA Hosty replied that it was about ten days after the baby was born. (Mrs. Marina Oswald's baby was born on October 17, 1963.)

Upon terminating the pre-interview conference above, the reporting Special Agent and ATSAIC Gopadze were transported in the FBI vehicle to Six Flags Inn, Arlington, Texas. FBI Special Agents Brown and Hosty were the accompanying agents. While at the Six Flags Inn, FBI Special Agents Brown and Hosty questioned Mrs. Marina Oswald using ATSAIC Gopadze as a translater. (See ATSAIC Gopadze's memorandum report regarding his interview with Mrs. Marina Oswald on this occasion.)

Upon terminating the interview above, the reporting Special Agent, ATSAIC Gopadze and FBI Special Agents Brown and Hosty then returned to the U. S. Secret Service Dallas Office wherein the foregoing interview with Mrs. Marina Oswald was reduced to narrative form for the benefit of FBI Special Agents Brown and Hosty. Inspector Kelley and SAIC Sorrels were also present during this period. FBI SA Hosty stated that this Service would be provided with a copy of his report concerning this interview.

At 9:27 P.M., the reporting Special Agent heard ATSAIC Gopadze remark to FBI SA Hosty that Mrs. Marina Oswald had recognized him as the FBI agent who had interviewed Mrs. Marina Oswald on or about October 27, 1963, concerning the whereabouts of Mr. Lee Harvey Oswald. At this time, FBI SA Hosty admitted that he had talked to Mrs. Marina Oswald on or about October 27, 1963, and that Mrs. Paine had acted as his translater at that meeting.

UNDEVELOPED LEADS

Investigation continued

MDP:amr

204

COMMISSION EXHIBIT NO. 1793—Continued

Date December 1, 1963

(1)

MARINA OSWALD was interviewed at the home of JAMES HERBERT MARTIN, 11611 Farrar Street, Dallas, Texas, telephone DAvis 7-6569.

She advised that after OSWALD returned to Dallas in early October, 1963, and found a room in Oak Cliff, he had called her an average of twice a day to inquire about her condition as her second child was due on about October 8, 1963. She said OSWALD found a job at the Texas School Book Depository on October 15, 1963. She said Mrs. PAINE had talked to one of her neighbors about OSWALD needing a job and a woman neighbor said there was a vacancy where her brother was employed, and suggested that OSWALD contact this place. Mrs. OSWALD does not recall the name of the neighbor, except that she is called LENNIE. Mrs. PAINE found that the place of employment of this neighbor's brother was the Texas School Book Depository and she called that place several times asking for the person it had been recommended that she call, but she could not locate this person. She finally was able to locate this person by telephone, and upon inquiring about possible employment for OSWALD was told that OSWALD should call about the job. MARINA said that the date of contact by Mrs. PAINE of this person at the Texas School Book Depository must have been on Monday, October 14, 1963, as she knows OSWALD went to the Texas School Book Depository on the following day, which was October 15, 1963, and got a job.

The second weekend following his return to Dallas, which was the weekend of October 11-13, 1963, OSWALD had no job. He spent that weekend at the PAINE residence and MARINA believes it was during that weekend sometime that Mrs. PAINE talked to her neighbor, LENNIE, about the job for OSWALD.

She recalls he came to the PAINEs for the weekend on October 18, 1963, as this is OSWALD's birthday. He spent the night of October 18th at the PAINE house, spent all day Saturday

[redacted]

Commission Exhibit No. 1794

on 11/30/63 at Dallas, Texas File # DL 89-43
DL 100-10461

by Special Agent S ANATOLE A. BOGUSLAV and WALLACE R. HEITMAN:bnm/jj Date dictated 12/1/63

64

COMMISSION EXHIBIT NO. 1794

and Saturday night, and then on October 20, a Sunday, Mrs. PAINE took MARINA to the Parkland Hospital as her baby was due. OSWALD stayed with the children at the PAINE house. She was released from the hospital on Tuesday morning, October 22, and PAINE brought her back to her house. When she returned to the PAINE home, OSWALD was at work.

While she was in the hospital, OSWALD visited her on Monday night, October 21, with Mrs. PAINE and the children, but only OSWALD was allowed to see her and the newborn baby. She believes that he came about 7 or so in the evening and stayed for about 1½ hours. She said that after his visit OSWALD returned with Mrs. PAINE and the children to the PAINE residence where he stayed overnight.

Following her return from the hospital to the PAINE home, OSWALD visited her each weekend, with two exceptions, and would usually call her at least once a day. He usually came on Friday, after work, with the neighbor who worked at the School Book Depository and would return to work on Monday morning with this same neighbor. On the two exceptions noted, one occurred when OSWALD called her from work on a Friday, exact date not remembered, to inform her that he had an appointment to see about another job the next day, Saturday, and therefore would not be at the PAINE residence that night, Friday. He said that he did not like the work at the Texas School Book Depository and wanted to try to find another job, but did not want Mrs. PAINE to know it as she had helped him get the job at the School Book Depository. He said he had seen an ad in the newspaper and was going to answer that ad. MARINA advised that the ad was by some photographic concern. She said OSWALD had appeared at the PAINE residence on that Saturday, and said that he had applied for the job but had been unsuccessful. He arrived at the PAINE residence on that day before lunch.

Concerning his job at the School Book Depository, OSWALD told MARINA that his job was to fill out orders and pack them in boxes. He said he did not like his work and it was for that reason that he was looking for other work.

65

COMMISSION EXHIBIT NO. 1794—Continued

DL 89-43
(3)

MARINA asked OSWALD about the people at the School Book Depository and each time she would try to engage him in conversation about his fellow employees, he would turn her questions aside and say that he was not interested in any of them. She asked him about his boss and he said the boss was a nice man. She said she told OSWALD that he should make friends at the School Book Depository but she knew that he was not interested in making friends. OSWALD mentioned to her that they had coffee breaks at the Depository and that the atmosphere down there was very congenial. He did not tell MARINA on which floor he worked.

The other weekend on which OSWALD did not visit the PAINE residence occurred on November 15-17, 1963. On this Friday, November 15, 1963, OSWALD called MARINA and she told him not to come that weekend because one of the PAINE children was having a birthday and Mr. PAINE would be over and it was not convenient for OSWALD to spend the weekend. He did not come to the PAINE house that weekend. MARINA advised she became lonesome that weekend and on Sunday, November 17, 1963, had Mrs. PAINE call the telephone number where OSWALD was staying as she wanted to talk to him. Mrs. PAINE called the number and asked the person who answered the telephone for LEE OSWALD, but could not locate OSWALD at that number. She advised the next day, Monday, November 18, 1963, OSWALD called her about 3 o'clock in the afternoon. She told him that she had tried to locate him the day before and had Mrs. PAINE call the number he had left. OSWALD then became angry and told MARINA that Mrs. PAINE should not have called for him under his right name, LEE OSWALD, because he was staying there under another name. MARINA asked him why he was staying there under another name and he replied that he did not want people asking questions. MARINA became mad at OSWALD because he was staying at this house under another name. OSWALD also was mad. He told MARINA to tear his telephone number out of Mrs. PAINE's book and MARINA refused to do this. She then hung up the telephone on OSWALD.

On Thursday, November 21, 1963, OSWALD appeared unannounced at the PAINE residence, at about 5:45 p.m., with

DL 89-43
(4)

the neighbor boy who worked at the School Book Depository and with whom he usually caught a ride. She asked him why he had come and he replied that he had gotten lonesome. He wanted to make up with MARINA. She said that she was still mad at him because he was staying at his rooming house under a false name. Even though OSWALD wanted to make up, she did not make up, and as a consequence did not talk to him much during that evening of November 21. She said that OSWALD had played with the children outside for a while and then had gone to bed about 8:30 in the evening. She said that she retired about midnight. She advised that she did not know if OSWALD went to the PAINE garage that night, but advised he could have easily done so because he was outside with the children a good deal. She said that generally OSWALD would go to the garage on the weekends because many of their things were stored there and she would ask him to get something for her from these things. She said she did not pay any particular attention to when he went or what he did if he went to the garage.

On the morning of November 22, 1963, the alarm rang at 6:40 a.m. and she awoke and OSWALD remained asleep. She began feeding the baby and at about 7 o'clock she awoke OSWALD and told him he had better get up or he would be late for work. He got up and as he finished dressing, said he would take care of his own breakfast. He then went into the kitchen, but she does not believe he fixed anything because the coffee pot was not warm when she went in later, about 7:20, and she saw no signs of breakfast preparations. She said the last time she saw OSWALD was when he left her bedroom to go to the kitchen.

On November 21, 1963, the previous evening, OSWALD told her that he would not be able to come to the PAINE residence on the coming weekend, November 22-24, 1963. She asked him why and he said it was not convenient to disturb people so often. She also remembers that on Thursday, November 21, she came running from the kitchen to see OSWALD in another part of the house, and asked him how it would be to see a real live President. She was referring to the visit of President KENNEDY, scheduled for the next day. OSWALD was extremely short in his answer, said something like "I don't know," and abruptly terminated the conversation. Mrs. OSWALD said she liked President KENNEDY and JACKIE KENNEDY because both of them appeared, in their photographs, to be very sympathetic people. She said that she would often have OSWALD read the captions under photographs of President KENNEDY and JACKIE. She said she admired them both. She stated she has asked OSWALD on one occasion what kind of a President Mr. KENNEDY was and he had replied that KENNEDY was a good President. She said OSWALD never gave any indication whatsoever that he intended any harm to the President.

She said she feels intuitively that if OSWALD was trying to kill the President, that one shot would have been enough, and that she feels, therefore, that he might have been aiming at the other person (Governor CONNALLY). She said OSWALD never mentioned any possible plans that he might have about assassinating the President. She said she cannot understand this thing.

She recalled on one occasion, quite a while ago, she made the remark to OSWALD that she couldn't imagine one person killing another. She asked him if he could kill another person and he replied "HITLER needed killing," and implied that by killing HITLER, others could be saved.

The rifle that was owned by OSWALD she had seen many times. She recalled specifically seeing it when they lived on Neeley Street, and she knows that OSWALD had the rifle in the garage at the PAINE residence. She advised she did not know that the rifle had a scope on it. She recalls that she had asked OSWALD why he had the rifle and he told her that it was for hunting purposes. She replied that he could not expect to go hunting if he did not have a car. He assured her that one day they would have a car.

MARINA advised that the only sources of income that OSWALD had, to her knowledge, were his pay for his employment and previously his unemployment compensation. She said that he was paid each 2 weeks when he worked at the School Book Depository and she believes he received about $100 each pay day. She also said OSWALD got one $33 unemployment check after he began work at the School Book Depository.

She said that when she was at the police station in Dallas, following the assassination of the President, she talked to Mrs. PAINE and asked her to bring some things to her at the police chief's residence where she spent the night. She told Mrs. PAINE that OSWALD had been saving money in a wallet which was in one of the drawers of a chest in the PAINE house and asked Mrs. PAINE to bring that to her also. She said the wallet and the other things were brought to her at the police station and she extracted the money from the wallet, counted it, and found it to be $170. A <u>Life</u> reporter who was standing nearby threw in $10 and that made $180. She said this is the money that OSWALD had saved, beginning in New Orleans.

Mrs. OSWALD advised she had been thinking about how OSWALD had come to the PAINE residence on the first occasion following his return to Dallas in early October, 1963. She said upon reflection she believed that OSWALD had called from the bus station, stating that he was already in Irving and asked Mrs. PAINE to pick him up. She said Mrs. PAINE was busy at the time and could not go. OSWALD later appeared at the house and said that he had hitchhiked a ride with a Negro on a truck.

FD-302 (Rev. 3-3-59)

FEDERAL BUREAU OF INV[redacted] Commission Exhibit No. 1795

1

Date 2/20/64

MAURICE CARLSON, President, Reliance Life and Accident Insurance Company, and a close friend of RICHARD NIXON, advised that NIXON was invited to Dallas in April 1963 to the South and East Dallas Chamber of Commerce to receive the Good American award. At the last minute NIXON was unable to attend and cancelled his trip. Mr. CARLSON does not know if any press coverage of NIXON's contemplated visit in April, 1963 was given in the Dallas newspapers.

Mr. CARLSON advised that he is certain RICHARD NIXON was in Dallas, Texas, on November 21, 1963, having arrived by private plane with the President of the Pepsi Cola Company.

on 2/19/64 at Dallas, Texas File # DL 100-10461

by Special Agent VINCENT E. DRAIN/ds 279 Date dictated 2/19/64

This document contains neither recommendations nor conclusions of the FBI. It is the property of the FBI and is loaned to your agency; it and its contents are not to be distributed outside your agency.

COMMISSION EXHIBIT No. 1795

FD-302 (Rev. 3-3-59)

FEDERAL BUREAU OF INVESTIGATION

1

Date 2/26/64

Mrs. EMMA R. REID, Executive Secretary and Manager of South and East Dallas Chamber of Commerce, 1106 Graham Street, telephone TAylor 6-4159, advised she handles all correspondence emanating from that office and through her are issued all invitations to persons who are invited to speak before this organization.

Mrs. REID made a positive statement that no invitation to appear as a speaker had been issued by South and East Dallas Chamber of Commerce to former Vice President of the United States RICHARD M. NIXON. She stated the speaker at the annual membership banquet held April 2, 1963, was former Governor of Texas, ALLAN SHIVERS.

on 2/25/64 at Dallas, Texas File # DL 100-10461

by Special Agent ROBERT C. LISH:vm 280 Date dictated 2/25/64

This document contains neither recommendations nor conclusions of the FBI. It is the property of the FBI and is loaned to your agency; it and its contents are not to be distributed outside your agency.

COMMISSION EXHIBIT No. 1795—Continued

Date 2/25/64

1

At the Dallas Public Library there were reviewed issues of "The Dallas Morning News," a daily newspaper published at Dallas, Texas. This review of microfilm copies of all editions was examined for the period March 16 to May 15, 1963.

There was not found in any of the above-mentioned issues of this daily newspaper any mention concerning a proposed visit or an invitation which might have been issued to former Vice President of the United States RICHARD M. NIXON.

on 2/25/64 at Dallas, Texas File # DL 100-10461

by Special Agent ROBERT C. LISH:vm 281 Date dictated 2/26/64

Date 2/27/64

1

At the Dallas Times Herald Newspaper Library, there were reviewed issues of the "Dallas Times Herald," a daily newspaper published at Dallas, Texas. This review of microfilm copies of all editions was conducted for the period March 16 to May 15, 1963.

There was not found in any of the above-mentioned issues of this daily newspaper any mention concerning a proposed visit or an invitation which might have been extended to the former Vice President of the United States, RICHARD M. NIXON.

on 2/25/64 at Dallas, Texas File # DL 100-10461

by Special Agent RAYMOND P. YELCHAK:vm 282 Date dictated 2/26/64

FD-302 (Rev. 3-3-59)

FEDERAL BUREAU OF INVESTIGATI

Date 2/25/64

1

Mr. MAURICE CARLSON, President of Reliance Life and Accident Insurance Company, Reliance Building, Dallas, Texas, advised he was previously confused as to the South and East Dallas Chamber of Commerce inviting RICHARD NIXON to speak in April, 1963, to their annual banquet.

He stated efforts were made to get BARRY GOLDWATER, U. S. Senator from Arizona, but they did not work out. He stated Mr. ROBERT R. PARKS was Chairman of the Speakers Committee during that time and he could furnish the details on this. CARLSON stated to his knowledge NIXON was not in Dallas in 1962 and was here only once in 1963 that being November 21, 1963.

CARLSON stated he had previously advised this office that he thought that NIXON was invited to speak before the South and East Dallas Chamber of Commerce in November, 1963, but since refreshing his memory, he remembered it was Senator BARRY GOLDWATER of Arizona and not NIXON.

on 2/25/64 at Dallas, Texas File # DL 100-10461

by Special Agent VINCENT E. DRAIN:vm 283 Date dictated 2/25/64

FD-302 (Rev. 3-3-59)

FEDERAL BUREAU OF INVESTIGATI

Date 2/25/64

1

Mr. ROBERT R. PARKS, President of Robert R. Parks Machinery Company, 3909 Main Street, Dallas, Texas, advised he was the Committee Chairman of obtaining a speaker for the annual banquet for the South and East Dallas Chamber of Commerce in April, 1963. He stated efforts were made to get Senator BARRY GOLDWATER to speak but this never did work out. Instead, former Governor ALLAN SHIVERS of Texas was invited and was the speaker. He said to his knowledge at no time was NIXON ever invited to speak before the South and East Dallas Chamber of Commerce and particularly was not invited to do so in April, 1963.

on 2/25/64 at Dallas, Texas 284 File # DL 100-10461

by Special Agent VINCENT E. DRAIN:vm Date dictated 2/25/64

COMMISSION EXHIBIT NO. 1796

COMMISSION EXHIBIT NO. 1797

Form No. 1668 (Revised)
Memorandum Report
(7-1-50)

Oswald, Marina 2

UNITED STATES SECRET SERVICE
TREASURY DEPARTMENT

Oswald, Marguerite

ORIGIN Field	OFFICE Dallas	FILE NO. CO-2-34,030
TYPE OF CASE: Protective Research	STATUS: Pending	TITLE OR CAPTION: ASSASSINATION OF PRESIDENT KENNEDY, DALLAS, TEXAS
INVESTIGATION MADE AT: Dallas, Texas	PERIOD COVERED: November 27, 1963 - December 1, 1963	
INVESTIGATION MADE BY: SA Max D. Phillips		

DETAILS

SYNOPSIS

Wallet which contained $180.00 and was in the possession of Mrs. Marina Oswald was investigated. Wallet was given to Lee Harvey Oswald about a year ago by his mother and the $180.00 was believed to be Lee Harvey Oswald's savings.

DETAILS OF INVESTIGATION

— Commission Exhibit 1798

Reference previous reports concerning this case.

Other Investigations

Incidental to accompanying ATSAIC Gopadze to the Six Flags Inn, Arlington, Texas, on November 27, 1963, the reporting Special Agent learned that Mrs. Marina Oswald had in her possession $180.00. Permission was obtained from Mr. Robert Oswald to view the money for possible investigative leads.

Upon viewing the $180.00 the following salient facts were observed: There were eight (8) $20's and two (2) $10's. The condition of the notes was relatively good. The ten notes came from the following Federal Reserve Banks: New York; San Francisco; Dallas; Atlanta. The serial numbers on these notes did not follow any sequence.

The $180.00 was contained in a new wallet, the type that is given out by banks as an advertising medium. The description of the wallet is black plastic with an advertisement that reads: "WAGGONER NATIONAL BANK VERNON, TEXAS."

ATSAIC Gopadze asked Marina Oswald about the money. Marina Oswald stated that the money was the money that Lee Harvey Oswald was saving, but

DISTRIBUTION	COPIES	REPORT MADE BY	DATE
Chief Dallas	Orig. & 2 2	Max D. Phillips (signature) Max D. Phillips SPECIAL AGENT	12-2-63 339
		APPROVED: (signature) SPECIAL AGENT IN CHARGE	DATE 12-2-63

COMMISSION EXHIBIT No. 1798

Page 2

she did not know where the money actually came from. Marina Oswald further stated that the wallet was the one that Lee Harvey Oswald's mother had given him.

On December 1, 1963, the reporting Special Agent interviewed Mrs. Marguerite Oswald, mother of Lee Harvey Oswald, at her home, 2220 Thomas Place, Fort Worth, Texas, regarding the $180.00 and the wallet. Mrs. Marguerite Oswald stated that she did not know anything specifically about how Lee Harvey Oswald got the $180.00, but she did say that he was accustomed to saving his money. As to the wallet, Mrs. Marguerite Oswald said that she gave the wallet to Lee Harvey Oswald when he returned from Russia, which was over a year; that she was working in Vernon, Texas, at the time and obtained the wallet from the Waggoner National Bank, Vernon, Texas.

UNDEVELOPED LEADS

Continued investigation.

MDP:amr

339

COMMISSION EXHIBIT No. 1798—Continued

ASSISTANCE RENDERED BY THE POSTAL INSPECTION SERVICE
IN INVESTIGATION OF PRESIDENT KENNEDY'S ASSASSINATION

Immediately upon learning of the assassination of President Kennedy, the cooperation of the Postal Inspection Service was offered to agencies investigating the murder. By 2:00 p.m., November 22, our Fort Worth Division had established liaison with the Secret Service, the FBI, the Dallas Police Department, the Fort Worth Police, and Sheriff's offices.

At the outset it was not known who had primary responsibility for the investigation. Accordingly, cooperation was offered to all. As soon as President Johnson made clear that the FBI was in charge of the investigation, we assured them, both here in Washington and at Dallas, of our complete cooperation.

The following summarizes the more significant Inspection Service participation:

At Dallas, Texas

A postal employee of the Terminal Annex, Dallas post office, after hearing early broadcasts of Oswald's apprehension on November 22, recalled that he had rented a box to a person by that name. He checked his rental applications and determined that Box 6225 had been rented to Lee H. Oswald on November 2, 1963, and promptly furnished this information to a postal inspector. The business on the application was shown as "Fair Play for Cuba Committee, Chairman." This information was passed on to the Secret Service.

At the request of the Secret Service, Box 6225 was kept under constant personal surveillance by postal inspectors from about 5:00 p.m., November 22 until midnight November 24, as it was anticipated that an accomplice might call for mail in the box. The only mail in the box consisted of a Russian magazine addressed to Oswald. A modified surveillance was maintained thereafter. No one called for mail out of this box. The only outstanding key was recovered from Oswald immediately after he was taken into custody.

On November 23, in accordance with a request of the Secret Service, Mr. and Mrs. M. F. Tobias, manager of the apartments at 602 Elsbeth, Dallas, were interviewed. They stated that the Oswalds had lived at that apartment from November 3, 1962 to about March 1, 1963. Mrs. Tobias stated that the Oswalds had had considerable domestic trouble, and their fights disturbed other tenants so that they finally were requested to move. Mrs. Tobias mentioned that the

COMMISSION EXHIBIT No. 1799

- 2 -

Oswalds frequently used her telephone to make and receive telephone calls and that all such conversations were in a foreign language. Three visitors of the Oswalds were described. Oswald was described as queer acting, and his wife as being quite lonely but very friendly. The foregoing information was furnished to the Secret Service.

Mrs. Tobias also stated that an information form completed by the Oswalds incident to renting the apartment was in the possession of Mrs. Marian Jurek, 9211 Hathaway, Dallas. The FBI was informed of the possibility that Mrs. Jurek might have handwriting specimens of Lee Oswald.

Advice was received on the morning of November 23 from the FBI that a rifle similar to that found in the sniper's nest had been purchased from Kleins Sporting Goods Company, Chicago, Illinois, for $21.95, with a postal money order issued March 20, 1963. Search at the main post office, Dallas, by a postal inspector failed to disclose such an order; however, the inspector upon checking undeliverable sporting goods magazines in the post office found an add of Kleins showing the price of an identical rifle for $21.45. The Postal Inspector in Charge at Chicago was so informed immediately and determined through examination of bank deposit slips that Kleins had deposited a money order for $21.45 about March 14, 1963. Further search by an inspector at the Dallas post office disclosed record of the issuance of money order No. 2,202,130,462, for $21.45, on March 12, 1963. This paid order was located at the Records Center in Alexandria, Virginia on the early evening of November 23. The order showed the remitter as A. Hidell, P. O. Box 2915, Dallas, Texas. This box was rented in the name of J. H. Oswald at that time and a forwarding order was later entered to have mail sent to New Orleans. Hidell is the same name as was used by Lee Oswald on a draft registration card which he had in his pocket, and his name was also shown on his box application card in New Orleans as being entitled to receive mail in the box.

The paid money order was immediately turned over to a Secret Service agent at Washington, D. C., who flew it to Dallas.

Postal inspectors furnished to the FBI at their request the originals of applications for Post Office Boxes 6225 (Terminal Annex) and 2915 (General post office). The original forwarding request was turned over to the Secret Service at their request.

On the morning of November 24, in accordance with a request of the FBI, postal inspectors obtained and furnished the address of Miss Ruth Willis, a Terminal Annex box patron, who worked on the fourth floor of the Texas School Book Depository on November 22 and heard footsteps overhead just after shots were fired.

COMMISSION EXHIBIT No. 1799—Continued

- 3 -

A postal inspector took part in the interrogation session of Oswald for about two hours just prior to the shooting of Oswald on November 24. A memorandum covering the interview was furnished by him to the FBI at their request. Two copies of the memorandum are attached.

On December 2, the Secret Service advised that they had a letter from Oswald to his wife, written in Russian prior to the assassination, indicating there might be a sudden, permanent separation between him and his wife. Because the Secret Service surmised that Mrs. Oswald would receive further word through a post office on Ervay Street, postal inspectors gave the matter attention but could not locate the letter.

At New Orleans, Louisiana

On the evening of November 22, postal inspectors determined from records of the Lafayette Square Station, New Orleans, that post office box 30061 was rented to L. H. Oswald on June 3, 1963. Others authorized to receive mail were A. J. Hidell and Marina Oswald. The home address was shown at that time as 657 French Street, but there is no such number. On September 24, 1963, the New Orleans post office received a request to forward mail from Box 30061 to 2515 West Fifth Street, Irving, Texas. The box was closed September 26, 1963. Two copies of a newspaper "The Militant" were on hand. The FBI was furnished the originals of the application and forwarding order on Box 30061 on November 23.

Inquiry by postal inspectors on the evening of November 22 of Mr. Jesse Gardner, manager of apartments at 4905 and 4907 Magazine Street, New Orleans, elicited the information that Oswald had rented a furnished apartment at 4905 Magazine, but had used the 4907 address probably through error. Mr. Gardner stated that Mrs. Oswald became pregnant while living there, and was picked up by another woman, name unknown, in a station wagon, who said she was taking her to Texas to have her baby, and that Oswald left shortly thereafter. The letter carrier from Station B, serving the Magazine Street address, recalled that most of the mail for Oswald was second-class matter including some foreign newspapers. One Russian magazine was on hand at Station B.

On the evening of November 22, postal inspectors determined from New Orleans police records that Lee H. Oswald was arrested on August 9, 1963 in the 700 block of Canal Street, charged with disturbing the peace, and fined $10 or 10 days. The arrest occurred after he became involved in an argument with three students who were anti-Castro, as he was distributing pro-Castro circulars. He had no other record of arrest to our knowledge.

- 4 -

At Irving, Texas

Inquiry on November 22 by postal inspectors at Irving, at the request of the Secret Service, disclosed a forwarding order, dated May 15, 1963, directing that mail for Lee Oswald be sent from 2515 West Fifth Street to 4907 Magazine Street, New Orleans, Louisiana. As far as could be determined the address at 2515 West Fifth Street was the only one ever used by Oswald at Irving.

Carriers who served 2515 West Fifth Street from the latter part of July 1963 until November 22, had continued to deliver mail to the Oswalds to the 2515 West Fifth Street address. One of the carriers recalled that only circulars and newspapers of foreign origin had been delivered.

Postal inspectors interviewed Mr. and Mrs. C. P. Schneider, 2707 West Fifth Street, on the early evening of November 22. They stated that they first saw Mrs. Oswald at the 2515 West Fifth Street address in August 1963, and that Mrs. Ruth Paine, who resided in the residence at the latter address, said that she (Mrs. Paine) had taken Mrs. Oswald to New Orleans at least once since August 1963, and had last returned from there with Mrs. Oswald on about October 22, so that the latter could have an expected baby. Both stated that Mrs. Oswald apparently could speak only Russian, and that Mrs. Paine had taught Russian in a Catholic church school.

Mr. Schneider said he had seen Oswald in front of the 2515 West Fifth Street residence at approximately 6:00 p.m., November 21. He stated that a neighbor, Mrs. Ed Roberts of 2519 West Fifth Street, had told him that Willie Randle, 2439 West Fifth Street, had driven Oswald to work on the morning of November 22, and that Oswald was carrying a package large enough to have contained a rifle.

On November 25, it was determined that a postage due parcel had been on hand in the Irving post office for Mrs. or Mr. Oswald earlier in the week of the assassination and was delivered about November 20 or 21.

At Fort Worth, Texas

At the request of the Secret Service on November 22, for information on Robert L. Oswald, brother of the assassin, and listed in the Fort Worth city directory as living at 7313 Davenport Street, Fort Worth, inspectors maintained surveillance at that residence, and checked license plates of vehicles parked at that address. Their inquiries disclosed that he had moved on March 5, 1962 to Route 5, Box 32-C, Malvern, Arkansas, and from there on September 10, 1963, to

- 5 -

1009 Sienna Drive, Denton, Texas. They also determined that there was no criminal record for him in the Tarrant County Sheriff's office or the Fort Worth Police Department. Secret Service was so advised.

On November 22, inspectors checked records of the Fort Worth Motel for possible registration by Oswald on November 20 to 21. This was based on a report that on the morning of November 21 at breakfast in the motel an unidentified man remarked that "Benedict Arnold is coming to town." The identity of the person making this remark was not established.

At midnight on November 22, postal inspectors, at the request of the Secret Service, accompanied two agents to the residence of Peter Gregory, 3513 Dorothy Lane, South, where the agents went inside to interview Mr. Gregory. Their information was that Gregory had taught Russian to Oswald and that his son was friendly with Oswald.

COMMISSION EXHIBIT No. 1799—Continued

Lee Harvey Oswald on bridge in Minsk.

COMMISSION EXHIBIT No. 1800

FD-302 (Rev. 3-3-59)

FEDERAL BUREAU OF INVESTIGATION

Date January 7, 1964

1

Mrs. MARGUERITE OSWALD, 2220 Thomas Place, mother of LEE HARVEY OSWALD, was contacted to ascertain some addresses of LEE HARVEY OSWALD during 1944-46. Mrs. OSWALD furnished the following information:

She stated that in 1944, she and her family resided on Bartholomew Street, in New Orleans, Louisiana. She said she does not recall the exact address, but that the home was located near the Nola Theater on this street. She said that in the latter part of 1944, or the early part of 1945, exact dates not recalled, she sold the house on Bartholomew Street and moved to 4801 Victor Street, in Dallas, Texas. She said that her son, LEE HARVEY, moved with her to Dallas, from New Orleans, but that the other two boys stayed at a Lutheran home in New Orleans. Mrs. OSWALD said she lived on Victor Street, in Dallas, during 1945; and in 1946, exact date not recalled, she moved to Fort Worth, Texas.

Commission Exhibit No. 1801

on 1/6/64 at Fort Worth, Texas File # DL 100-10461

by Special Agents EARLE HALEY and ROBLEY D. MADLAND:mja Date dictated 1/7/64

COMMISSION EXHIBIT No. 1801

DL 44-1639
AS:gj
1

The name "THOMAS" and the number FL 7-8574 was found among the property in JACK L. RUBY's automobile at the time of his arrest on November 24, 1963, at Dallas, Texas.

The number FL 7-8574 was listed in the Dallas Criss-Cross Directory to RUTH WAFFORD, 908 Mount Aubrin, whose current telephone number is TA 4-8761. It was determined that RUTH WAFFORD has a son named THOMAS currently residing at 43 Constitution, Charleston Heights, South Carolina.

The following information was received from the Savannah Division pursuant to the above information:

On December 23, 1963, THOMAS DUDLEY WAFFORD, 43 Constitution, Charleston Heights, South Carolina, advised SA HARRY C. BELK that he does not know JACK L. RUBY or LEE HARVEY OSWALD. He said he does not know how the slip of paper with his mother's telephone number and his first name got into RUBY's automobile.

287

COMMISSION EXHIBIT No. 1802

OFFICE OF THE DIRECTOR

UNITED STATES DEPARTMENT OF JUSTICE

FEDERAL BUREAU OF INVESTIGATION

WASHINGTON, D.C. 20535

September 4, 1964

BY COURIER SERVICE

Honorable J. Lee Rankin
General Counsel
The President's Commission
200 Maryland Avenue, N. E.
Washington, D. C.

Dear Mr. Rankin:

An article captioned "California Crowd Hears Harangue by Bircher" written by Julius Duscha, staff reporter, under the date line of Santa Ana, California, August 29, appeared in the "Washington Post" on August 30, 1964. This article stated that Professor Revilo P. Oliver of the University of Illinois spoke for more than one hour before 1,300 men and women in the auditorium of the Santa Ana Valley High School. A copy of this article is enclosed.

In response to you equest of Inspector James R. Malley of this Bureau on Sep. ber 2, 1964, that we locate and interview Mr. Oliver for the purpose of determining the basis for the remarks attributed to him in the aforementioned article, we determined Mr. Oliver is staying at the Argonaut Hotel, Denver, Colorado, until September 5, 1964. Accordingly, we contacted Mr. Oliver in Denver at which time he advised that his speech for the most part contained the same material that was published in his articles which appeared in the "American Opinion" magazine in February and March, 1964. Mr. Oliver identified this magazine as an organ published by the John Birch Society. Mr. Oliver further stated that all of his material used in his articles was obtained by him from public sources and he added that he has no confidential sources.

Mr. Oliver advised that the source of his statement that communists, with the help of the Central Intelligence Agency (CIA), were responsible for the assassination, was a book entitled "Oswald: Assassin or Fall Guy?" written by Joachim Joesten which was published by Marzani and Munsell Publishers, Inc., New York City.

— Commission Exhibit No. 1803 —

COMMISSION EXHIBIT No. 1803

Honorable J. Lee Rankin

Mr. Oliver advised that in connection with his statement that he did not know whether Oswald was paid by CIA or by the Soviet secret police and that it might be just a matter of bookkeeping anyway, he believed his source for this statement was either the aforementioned book by Joesten or an article by John Henshaw which appeared in the "National Enquirer." Mr. Oliver also stated that his source for the statement that under orders from Secretary of Defense Robert McNamara the Army "began to rehearse for the funeral more than a week before the funeral," was a news article which appeared in the "Clarion Ledger" on February 21, 1964. He identified the "Clarion Ledger" as a newspaper published in Jackson, Mississippi. According to Mr. Oliver, this article pertained to statements made by Army Captain Richard Cloy who reportedly was in charge of protocol for state funerals.

In conclusion, Mr. Oliver stated that he always furnishes the sources of his material during his speeches but that unfortunately, the newspaper accounts usually do not identify these sources.

In connection with Mr. Oliver's statements that material in his speech was for the most part contained in his articles which appeared in the "American Opinion" magazine, there is enclosed for the information of the Commission a copy of a pamphlet entitled "Dallas Marxmanship by Revilo P. Oliver, Parts I and II," which was furnished this Bureau by Mr. Roy J. Evans, President of the Evans Distributing Company, Shreveport, Louisiana. Mr. Evans stated he received this pamphlet through the mail and upon reading its contents, he did not agree with it and consequently desired to furnish it to this Bureau for information.

You will note that Part I of the enclosed pamphlet appeared in "American Opinion" magazine for February, 1964, and Part II of the pamphlet appeared in the March, 1964, issue of "American Opinion" magazine.

In connection with Mr. Oliver's statements that certain material in his speech was based on the book "Oswald: Assassin or Fall Guy?" your attention is directed to chapter 16 of Mr. Joesten's book entitled "Oil Thicker Than Blood," which contains a number of statements alleging a conspiracy in

- 2 -

COMMISSION EXHIBIT No. 1803—Continued

connection with the assassination of President John F. Kennedy. Your attention is also directed to the report of Special Agent Robert P. Gemberling dated May 15, 1964, at Dallas, Texas, captioned "Assassination of John Fitzgerald Kennedy, 11-22-63, Dallas, Texas; Miscellaneous - Information Concerning." This report, which is in the possession of the Commission, sets forth information on pages 561 through 595 concerning Joachim Joesten.

In connection with Mr. Oliver's statement that some of the material in his speech may have been based upon an article by John Henshaw which appeared in the "National Enquirer," your attention is directed to the Commission's letter of May 5, 1964, requesting this Bureau to make certain inquiries in connection with Mr. Henshaw's article. Your attention is also directed to our letter of May 8, 1964, which furnished the Commission with results of our inquiries in such matter.

In connection with Mr. Oliver's statement that data in his speech alleging that under orders from Secretary of Defense Robert McNamara the Army "began to rehearse for the funeral more than a week before the funeral" was based upon an article in the "Clarion Ledger" for February 21, 1964, please be advised that we have determined that the Friday, February 21, 1964, issue of the "Clarion Ledger," Jackson, Mississippi daily newspaper, contained an article entitled "A Lot to Remember." This article reported an interview with Captain Richard C. Cloy and identified Captain Cloy as being in charge of the caisson section which carried the President's coffin, the saluting battery which fired the 21-gun final salute and the fife and drum corps which marched with the cortege. Captain Cloy is quoted as saying "We were preparing the actual funeral arrangements less than an hour after the President was shot." Captain Cloy is also quoted as saying "We were in a state of readiness and had just finished a funeral rehearsal because there was grave concern for President Hoover's health, but we never expected that our practice was preparing us for President Kennedy."

The article also reported that Captain Cloy had been visiting in Mississippi but was en route to his new assignment with the General Staff of the Third Infantry Division in Germany.

For your information, we are obtaining a copy of the news article which appeared in the "Clarion Ledger" for February 21, 1964, and such article will be immediately forwarded to the Commission upon receipt.

For your added information, Mr. Albert E. Jenner, Jr., of your staff, has requested that he be immediately apprised of data in this letter upon receipt by the Commission.

Sincerely yours,

J. Edgar Hoover

Enclosures (2)

'The Warren Gang'

California Crowd Hears Harangue by Bircher

By Julius Duscha
Staff Reporter

SANTA ANA, Calif., Aug. 29—Outside the night air was cool and refreshing. Inside it was stuffy and frightening.

Thirteen hundred men and women filled the auditorium of the Santa Ana Valley High School to hear Prof. Revilo P. Oliver of the University of Illinois speak for more than an hour. Outside there were a few pickets.

Duscha

His speech included such phrases as "the Warren gang," "Bobby Socks Kennedy," "a hole called Harvard University," and "the supreme directorate of conspiracy, whoever they may be."

But the speech by Oliver (whose first name is his last name spelled backward) occasioned few comments in California's Orange County.

Solid-Looking Audience

Almost every night of the week in the Los Angeles area, of which Orange County is the southernmost part, right-wing extremists are haranguing well dressed audiences made up of middle-class businessmen and their stylishly dressed wives.

These are not little old ladies in tennis shoes from Pasadena. They are not food faddists, religious fanatics or some other kind of cultists. They are solid middle-class Americans.

Oliver, a member of the council of the John Birch Society, got his greatest response during his address on Friday night when he praised the energy and intelligence of the American people.

Then, in mocking tones, he spoke of "the bipeds who are too lazy, too stupid, too savage to work for themselves." His listeners laughed and cheered.

Foreign Aid Ripped

Oliver solemnly warned his audience against becoming entangled in such programs as foreign aid, assistance for underdeveloped countries, world peace and civil rights.

The clear implication of

News Analysis

Oliver's words was that white Americans are a super-race and that other peoples are inferior.

At one point he spoke of the "profound biological differences between human races."

He also was openly anti-Semitic. He read, for example, in a mocking Yiddish accent, a letter of criticism that he had received.

There was no question, though, that his audience responded best to his suggestions that they were successful only because they had worked hard and that anyone who was not successful was simply lazy and inferior and, in Mr. Doolitle's words in "My Fair Lady," among "the undeserving poor."

Kennedy's Assassination

Most of Oliver's speech was devoted to a rehashing of charges he made last winter in the Birch Society magazine, American Opinion, that President Kennedy's assassination was part of a Communist plot and engineered with the help of the Central Intelligency Agency.

"I don't know," Oliver said, "whether Oswald was paid by the CIA or by the Soviet secret police—and it's just a matter of bookkeeping anyway."

Oliver also said that under orders from Secretary of Defense Robert S. McNamara the Army "began to rehearse for the funeral more than a week before the funeral," and there were gasps from his audience.

Teacher of Classics

Oliver, a professor of classics at Illinois, is a large man who speaks with a flat Midwestern accent.

He has become one of the star attractions on the right-wing speaking circuit, and a profitable circuit it is.

It cost $1.50 to hear him. In addition to the speech, delivered in a dark auditorium from a bright lighted stage on which a huge American flag had been pinned as a backdrop, each listener got a ticket stub telling him how he could obtain more information about the John Birch Society.

DALLAS

MARXMANSHIP

by

REVILO P. OLIVER

PARTS I & II

Compliments of:

DUO OIL & GAS CO.
P. O. Box 5296
Shreveport, La.

Reprinted by permission

Part 1..... American Opinion Magazine, Feb., 1964
Part 2..... American Opinion Magazine, Mar., 1964

COMMISSION EXHIBIT No. 1803—Continued

MARXMANSHIP

In Dallas

Revilo P. Oliver is Professor of Classics in the University of Illinois. During World War II, he was Director of Research in a secret agency of the War Department. He has traveled widely. Dr. Oliver is an academician of international reputation who has published scholarly articles in four languages within the pages of twelve learned periodicals in the United States and Europe.

■ We all know what happened in Dallas on the twenty-second of November. It is imperative that we understand it.

Lee Harvey Oswald was a young punk who defected to the Soviet, taking with him the operational codes of the Marine Corps and such other secrets as a fledgling traitor had been able to steal while in military service. He not only forfeited his American citizenship by his acts, but also officially repudiated it under oath in the American Embassy in Moscow. He was then trained in sabotage, terrorism, and guerrilla warfare (including accurate shooting from ambush) in the well-known school for international criminals near Minsk, and while there he married the daughter of a colonel in the Soviet military espionage system (and possibly also in the Secret Police).* In 1962, after he had been trained for three years in Russia, the Communist agent and his Communist wife were brought to the United States, in open violation of American law, by our Communist-dominated State Department.

On his arrival in this country, Oswald took up his duties as an agent of the Conspiracy, spying on anti-Communist Cuban refugees, serving as an agitator for "Fair Play for Cuba,"and participating in some of the many other forms of subversion that flourish openly in defiance of law through the connivance of the Attorney General, Robert F. Kennedy. In April of 1963, he was sent to Dallas, where he tried to murder General Edwin Walker. The failure does not reflect on the assassin's professional training: General Walker happened to turn his head at the instant the shot was fired. According to a story that has been neither confirmed nor denied officially at the time that I write, Oswald was arrested as a suspect, but was released through the personal intervention of Robert F. Kennedy, and all inquiry into the attempted assassination of a great American was halted.†

In November, Oswald was sent back to Dallas, where a job in a suitably located building had been arranged for him. He shot the President of the United States from ambush, left the building undetected, and would have escaped to Mexico but for some mischance. He was stopped for questioning by a vigilant policeman, whom he killed in a moment of panic. Arrested and identified, he, despite his training, was so vain as to pose for photographs while triumphantly giving the Communists' clenched-fist salute; he asked for a noted Communist attorney, who had been a member of the little Communist cell that included the noted traitor, Alger Hiss; and he began to tell contradictory stories. He was accordingly liquidated before he could make a complete confession.

There are many other significant data, but I have stated the essentials. They are known to you.

The fact that they are known to you should give you—if you are an American—hope and courage. You will need both.

Obviously, something went wrong in Dallas—in our favor, this time. The best laid schemes o' mice and men gang aft a-gley—and so do schemes of Communists, sometimes. The identification of the murderer was a near-miracle. If not the result of divine intervention, it was the result of a series of coincidences of the same order as might enable a bum with a dollar in his pocket to enter a casino in Reno and emerge with a thousand.

It is highly significant that, after Oswald was arrested, you learned the facts. That proves that the Communist Conspiracy's control of the United States is not yet complete.

I firmly believe that in our nation as a whole the overwhelming majority of local policemen, whom we shamefully neglect and take for granted, are brave and honorable Americans. But I know nothing of the police in Dallas. It is quite possible that, as is usual in our large cities, they are subject to great pressures from a corrupt municipal government. I shall not be greatly astonished if, in the course of the Conspiracy's frantic efforts to confuse us with irrelevancies, it should be disclosed that pay-offs had been made by Jakob Leon Rubenstein, alias Ruby, and other members of the underworld that pander to human vice and folly. It is by no means impossible that crypto-Communists have been planted in that police force. But paint the picture as dark as you will, it remains indisputably true that, at the very least, there were enough honest and patriotic men on that police force to bring about the arrest of Oswald, to identify him, and to prevent both his escape and his assassination "while trying to escape." It required a gunman from outside to do the job.

It is quite true that the Communist Conspiracy, through the management of great broadcasting systems and news agencies, through the many criminals lodged in the Press, and through many indirect pressures (such as allocation of advertising and harassment by bureaus of the federal government), has a control over our channels of communication that seems to us, in our moments of discouragement, virtually total. As was to be expected, a few moments after the shot was fired in Dallas, the vermin, probably in obedience to general or specific orders issued in advance of the event, began to screech out their diseased hatred of the American people, and, long after the facts were known to everyone, went on mechanically repeating, like defective phonograph records, the same vicious lies about the "radical right" until fresh orders reached them from headquarters. But the significant fact is that there were enough honest American newsmen, in the United States and abroad, to make it impossible to conceal the Conspiracy's connection with the bungled assassination. That is very encouraging.

The Show And The Sorrow

All that could be done at the moment to obscure the Communists' mischance was to stage an elaborate spectacle with

* If you missed the detail about Mrs. Oswald's father, see the *Congressional Record* for December 4, page 22215.

† Reprinted in *The Councilor* (228 Oil & Gas Bldg., Shreveport, La.), December 20, 1963.

all the technical virtuosity seen in a performance of *Aida* in the Baths of Caracalla or the amphitheatre at Verona, supplemented with the cruder devices of Hollywood's expert vulgarians. Every effort was made to incite an orgy of bathos and irrationality. For the most part, the good sense of the American people frustrated the efforts of the showmen. But we need to consider the facts clearly and objectively.

There are two basic reasons why the American people were shocked and grieved by the assassination. Neither has anything to do with either the personal character of the victim or the identity of the assassin.

(1) The victim was the President of the United States; he was therefore symbolically representative of the nation, and his assassination was a form of armed attack on our country. The alarm, indignation, and sorrow excited by such an attack made on American soil should have no relation to either the private or public character of the person who was President. To put the matter as clearly as possible, the crime would have been every bit as horrible and shocking, had it (*per impossibile*) been absolutely certain that on the very next day the President would be impeached, tried, convicted, removed from office, and executed for his own crimes. That would be tomorrow, and would not affect today, when he is still legally invested with the dignity of his high office.

All decent men feel instinctively that the order, the stability, the preservation of civilized society requires that the officers whom that society has appointed in conformity with its own constitution be inviolate so long as they are clothed with the dignity of office, however mistaken and unfortunate their appointment may have been. So long as the officer has not outlawed himself by violent usurpation, any misuse of the powers legally bestowed upon him indicates either a defect in the constitution (which may grant excessive powers or provide inadequate checks) or the fatuity of citizens who tolerate abuses for which constitutional remedies are available. In either case, the abuse is primarily evidence of a weakness that the society must learn to correct legally. And if the society cannot learn from experience, there is no hope for it anyway.

(2) Regardless of office, political violence is always shocking and a warning of impending collapse. The Roman Republic was doomed as soon as it became clear that the wealthy and high-born renegade, Clodius, could send his gangsters into the streets with impunity; when the decent people of Rome tried to protect themselves by hiring gangsters of their own under Milo, that was not an answer: It was a confession of defeat. The assassination of Kennedy, quite apart from consideration of the office that he held, was an act of violence both deplorable and

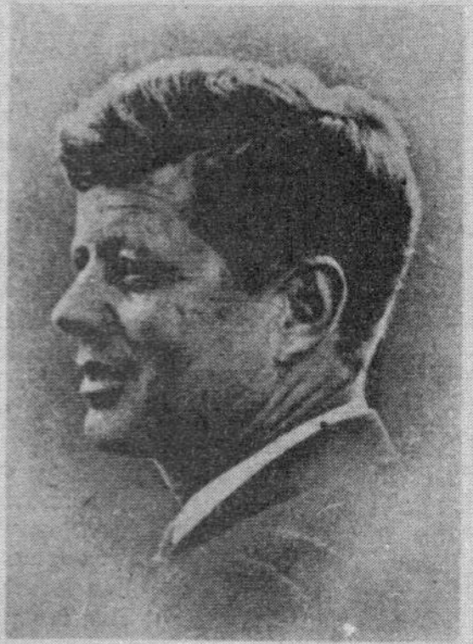

de mortuis nil nisi . . . ?

ominous—as ominous as the violence excited by the infamous Martin Luther King and other criminals engaged in inciting race war with the approval and even, it is said, the active co-operation of the White House. It was as deplorable and ominous as the violence of the uniformed goons (protected by reluctant and ashamed soldiers) whom Kennedy, in open violation of the American Constitution, sent into Oxford, Mississippi, to kick into submission American citizens, whom the late Mr. Kennedy had come to regard as his subjects.

Such lawlessness, regardless of the identity of the perpetrators or their professed motives, is as alarming as the outbreak of a fire in a house; and if not speedily extinguished, will destroy the whole social order. That is a fact that all conservatives know, for it is they who read the lessons of human history and understand how hard it is to build and how easy it is to destroy — how perishable and precious are the moral restraints and the habitual observance of them by which civilization shelters itself from the feral barbarism that is latent in all peoples. That is the very fact that "Liberal intellectuals" try to conceal with the contorted sophistries that they are perpetually devising to justify as "social good" or "progress" the murders and massacres that secretly fascinate and excite them. That is why conservatives try to conserve what "Liberals" seek to destroy.

The foregoing are two good and sufficient reasons why Americans were shocked and grieved by the assassination in Dallas. Let them suffice us. It is imperative that we do not permit ourselves to be confused at this critical time by a twisted proverb and residual superstition.

Taboo

The maxim, *de mortuis nil nisi bonum*, has long been a favorite dictum of Anglo-Saxons (for some reason, it is seldom cited on the continent of Europe). Reference books usually attribute it to one of the Seven Sages, Chilo, who lived in the early part of the Sixth Century B.C.; but that is a mistake. In his precepts for prudent conduct, roughly similar to Benjamin Franklin's, Chilo urges us not to *malign* the dead (*ton technekota me kakologein*). He was interested in our own integrity, not the comfort or reputation of the deceased, and the precept is on a par with his advice that we should not utter idle threats in a quarrel because that is womanish.

Whatever the source of the phrase so glibly and frequently quoted these days, the notion that one should speak only good of the departed is compounded of various sentiments. It undoubtedly had its origin in man's deep-seated and primitive fear of the dead—a fear lest the Manes may somehow hear what we say and, if angered, use their mysterious powers to work harm upon us. That residual awe is supplemented by our infinite pity for the dead, and our hope that after life's fitful fever they sleep well. Pity is reinforced by the strong impulse toward generosity and kindness that, although biologically inexplicable, is found in all decent men. And that kindness is directed in part toward the living, for even the most odious and despicable beings may be survived by someone who grieves for them. Even Nero had one concubine who loved him. Acte wept for him and saw to it that his body was decently buried. And we honor her for it.

The dictum has become a fixed convention. We all know the story of the old men in a rural community who attend the funeral of one of their contemporaries. Having known the old reprobate all his life, they stand silently in a circle, tongue-tied, uneasily shuffling their feet, eyeing one another and searching their memories, until one is at last able to say, "Well, when Jake

COMMISSION EXHIBIT No. 1803—Continued

COMMISSION EXHIBIT No. 1803—Continued

was a boy, he was mighty nigh the best speller in the sixth grade."

As an expression of courtesy and personal kindness, the dictum is unexceptionable. In politics and history it is utter nonsense — and everyone knows that it is. Were the dictum taken seriously, history would be impossible, for no page of it can be written without recording the follies and the crimes of the dead. Not even the sentimental innocents who now, under expert stimulation, weep over the "martyred President" believe in the dictum *de mortuis* — at least, I have yet to hear one of them utter a lament for Adolf Hitler, although Adolf is certainly as defunct as Jack and therefore presumably as much entitled to post-mortem consideration.

Taboos are for barbarians, who indulge in tribal howling and gashing of cheeks and breast whenever a big chief dies or an eclipse portends the end of the world. We are a civilized race.

In memoriam aeternam

Rational men will understand that, far from sobbing over the deceased or lying to placate his vengeful ghost, it behooves us to speak of him with complete candor and historical objectivity. Jack was not sanctified by a bullet.

The departed Kennedy is the John F. Kennedy who procured his election by peddling boob-bait to the suckers, including a cynical pledge to destroy the Communist base in Cuba. He is the John F. Kennedy with whose blessing and support the Central Intelligence Agency staged a fake "invasion" of Cuba designed to strengthen our mortal enemies there and to disgrace us — disgrace us not merely by ignominious failure, but by the inhuman crime of having lured brave men into a trap and sent them to suffering and death. He is the John F. Kennedy who, in close collaboration with Khrushchev, staged the phoney "embargo" that was

Communist Oswald trained in Minsk.

improvised both to befuddle the suckers on election day in 1962 and to provide for several months a cover for the steady and rapid transfer of Soviet troops and Soviet weapons to Cuba for eventual use against us. He is the John F. Kennedy who installed and maintained in power the unspeakable Yarmolinsky-McNamara gang in the Pentagon to demoralize and subvert our armed forces and to sabotage our military installations and equipment. He is the John F. Kennedy who, by shameless intimidation, bribery, and blackmail, induced weaklings in Congress to approve treasonable acts designed to disarm us and to make us the helpless prey of the affiliated criminals and savages of the "United Nations."

I have mentioned but a few of the hundred reasons why we shall never forget John F. Kennedy. So long as there are Americans, his memory will be cherished with distaste. If the United States is saved by the desperate exertions of patriots, we may have a future of true greatness and glory—but

we shall never forget how near we were to total destruction in the year 1963. And if the international vermin succeed in completing their occupation of our country, Americans will remember Kennedy while they live, and will curse him as they face the firing squads or toil in a brutish degradation that leaves no hope for anything but a speedy death.

Three Explanations

Why was Kennedy murdered by the young Bolshevik? With a little imagination, it is easy to excogitate numerous explanations that are not absolutely impossible. For example: (a) Oswald was a "madman" who acted all alone just to get his name in the papers; (b) Oswald was a poor shot who was really trying to kill Governor Connally or Mrs. Kennedy and hit the President by mistake; (c) the person killed was not Kennedy but a double, and the real Kennedy is now a guest aboard a "flying saucer" on which he is heroically negotiating with Martians or Saturnians to Save the World. With a little time and a fairly wide reading in romantic fiction, anyone can think of sixty or seventy fantasies as good or better than those that I have mentioned.

On the evidence, however, and with consideration of human probabilities, there are only three explanations that are not preposterous, viz.:

(1) That Kennedy was executed by the Communist Conspiracy because he was planning to turn American. For this comforting hypothesis there is no evidence now known. Ever since January, 1961, some hopeful Americans have maintained that Jack was a conservative at heart, that he deliberately packed his administration with Schlesingers, Rostows, and Yarmolinskys so that these would bring our nation so near to disaster that even the stupidest "Liberal," not in the employ of the Conspiracy, could not overlook the obvious, and that when an unmistakable crisis at last made it politically feasible, Kennedy would carry out a sudden and dramatic *volte-face*, sweep the scum out of Washington, and rally the forces of the great majority of loyal and patriotic Americans.

I wish I could believe that. It is true that the late Senator McCarthy praised young Kennedy, but although the Senator was a great American whose memory we must all revere, he was not preternaturally gifted: He could have been either deceived by a smooth-talking hypocrite (as have been greater men than he in the past) or mistaken in his estimate of a person who, although then sincere in his allegiance to what then seemed to be the winning side, later thought it expedient to change sides. It is also true that Kennedy said some fine things in speeches delivered just before his death, but those statements did not significantly differ from the pro-American flourishes normally used as seasoning in the boob-bait manufactured by Salinger's technicians during the past three years.

If Kennedy did entertain laudable designs, he cannot have kept them entirely *in petto;* he must have disclosed them to a few persons, perhaps including his father, in whom he had confidence. And if he did, the time for those persons to give evidence is now, while there is still a chance to clear the reputation of the deceased.

(2) That the assassination was the result of one of the rifts that not infrequently occur within the management of the Communist Conspiracy, whose satraps sometimes liquidate one another without defecting from the Conspiracy, just as Persian satraps, such as Tissaphernes and Pharnabazus, made war on one another without revolting or intending to revolt against the King of Kings.

Now it was generally suspected for some time before the assassination that

COMMISSION EXHIBIT No. 1803—Continued

Khrushchev and Kennedy were planning to stage another show to bamboozle the American suckers just before the election next November. According to this plan, a fake "revolt" against Castro would be enacted by the Communist second team, which has long been kept in reserve for such an eventuality. (Cf. *American Opinion*, March, 1962, p. 33.) The "democratic revolution" was to be headed by a Communist agent who differed from Fidel only in being less hairy and less well known to Americans, so that the *New York Times*, the State Department, the Central Intelligence Agency, and our other domestic enemies could swear once again that the vicious criminal was an "agrarian reformer," an "anti-Communist," and the "George Washington of Cuba." (It is confidently believed in conspiratorial circles that the dumb brutes in the United States will never learn—until it is much too late.)

What is not certain is the script for the third act of the comedy. Most (but not all) informed observers believe that this performance in Cuba was to accomplish two things: (a) the re-election of Kennedy and most of his stooges in Congress, which would, of course, be impossible without some seasonably contrived and major "crisis"; and (b) the endlessly repeated and trite device of making the tax-paying serfs in the United States, who have financed every important Communist conquest since 1917, work to provision and fortify another conquest under the pretext that by so doing they in some mysterious way "fight Communism."

Now, if those observers are correct in their projections, the scenario called for the "success" of the "democratic revolution." And that would involve, if the play was to be convincing, the liquidation of Fidel and a few of his more notorious accomplices. And that, as is well known to everyone who has made even the slightest study of Communism, would be merely commonplace and normal.

The rabid rats of Bolshevism devour one another—and no one knows that better than the rats themselves. Almost all of the Conspiracy's most famous murderers—Trotsky, Zinoviev (Apfelbaum), Kirov (Kostrikov), Kamenev (Rosenfeld), Yezhov, Beria, and a hundred others, possibly including Stalin—were murdered by their insatiably blood-thirsty confederates. Indeed, it is a general rule that only accident or disease can save a Communist "leader" from assassination or execution by other Communists as soon as his usefulness to the Conspiracy is ended or his liquidation will provide an opportunity for useful propaganda.

Cornered rats will fight for their lives. Castro, of course, knew of the planned "revolution," and if the dénouement was correctly foreseen by American observers, he also knew that, whatever solemn pledges may have been given him by his superiors, he would not survive. It is possible, therefore, that Fidel arranged the assassination of Jack in the hope of averting, or at least postponing, his own. Now that Oswald is silenced and superiors who gave him his orders are unidentified, it may never be possible completely to disprove that hypothesis, although there are a number of considerations that weigh against it.

We should note, also, that a few American observers believed that the Communist scenario had a different third act. According to their forecast, the Communist second team was to stage an indecisive "revolt" against the first team. Jack, pretending to carry out after four years the pledge that he made to get himself elected, would commit the United States to support the second team. At the scheduled moment on the eve of elections Nick would "intervene" and yell about a

"nuclear holocaust," thus producing a "crisis" which would call for a "bi-partisan" cancellation of the election. The gang in the Pentagon, hypocritically wringing its greasy hands, would claim that we were even weaker than its concerted sabotage of our defenses had in fact made us by that time. That would suffice to set craven "intellectuals" and neurotic females to running through our streets howling for "peace" and the "United Nations." After much tension, a great "statesmanlike solution" would be found: surrender of our sovereignty and weapons to an "international" body, with the Russians agreeing to do likewise. Then the savages in the "international police force" would move in, and the glorious and long-awaited butchery of the American boobs would get under way.

Those who make this prognosis support it by pointing out that the Conspiracy has already fallen far behind its schedule for the United States, and that the slow but ever increasing awakening of the American people from their hypnotic lethargy makes it necessary for the Conspiracy to adopt drastic and precipitate measures now, if it is not to fail utterly. If those observers are right, then interference by Castro is excluded, for the plan itself would guarantee his safety until the United States had been abolished.

(3) That the Conspiracy ordered the assassination as part of systematic preparation for a domestic take-over. If so, the plan, of course, was to place the blame on the "right-wing extremists" (if I may use the Bolsheviks' code-word for informed and loyal Americans), and we may be sure that a whole train of "clues" had been carefully planted to lead or point in that direction as soon as Oswald was safe in Mexico. These preparations were rendered useless when Oswald was, through some mischance, arrested—probably in consequence of some slip-up of which we as yet know nothing. He may, for example, have missed connections with some agent of the Conspiracy who was to transport him to the airport, and it may be significant that, when observed on the street, he was walking directly toward the apartment of the Jakob Rubenstein (alias Jack Ruby) who later silenced him.

Two objections to this explanation are commonly raised, but neither is cogent.

The first is the assumption that, if the International Conspiracy had planned the assassination, there would have been no slip-up. That is absurd. The degenerates are not Supermen. Their agents make blunders all the time—blunders that could destroy whole segments of the apparatus, if the Conspiracy did not have so many criminals planted in communications and politics to cover up the blunders and to paralyze the normal reactions of a healthy society. It would take pages even to list the mistakes that the Conspiracy's agents, including their branch manager, Castro, have made in the course of the Cuban operation. For that matter, a potentially serious and quite unnecessary mistake was made when the Communist Party's *official* publication, *The Worker*, yelled for the appointment of Earl Warren to "investigate" the assassination *before* the appointment was made—or at least, before the appointment was disclosed to the public. Nothing was gained by that mistake in timing, which serves only to give away the whole show.

The second argument is that the Conspiracy could not have wanted to eliminate Kennedy, who was doing so much for it. But that is a miscalculation. For one thing, the job was not being done on schedule. A few measures had been forced through Congress, but not, for example, what is called "Civil Rights," a very vital part of the vermin's preparations for the final take-over. Virtually nothing was done to speed up national

Commission Exhibit No. 1803—Continued

bankruptcy and the total economic collapse that is doubtless scheduled to accompany the subjugation of the American people. The Congress was, on the whole, the most American Congress that we have had for many years, and it blocked the measures most cunningly designed to destroy the nation. It was not the fault of any one man, to be sure, but the record for 1963 was, for all practical purposes, a stalemate. Our "Liberals," always impatient for open dictatorship and terrorism, were beginning to feel frustrated; some of them were screeching in our more prominent daily, weekly, and monthly liepapers about the "standpatism" of Congress and hinting that that nasty relic of the Constitution must be abolished in the interests of "effective democracy." Others were beginning to lose confidence.

That is what the Conspiracy cannot afford. It is already sadly behind schedule. Of course, its secret plans, like the identity of its master strategists, are undisclosed, but at the end of 1958 some competent observers, after the most careful and painstaking study of all available indications, concluded that 1963 was the year scheduled for the effective capture of the United States. And those analysts—without exception, so far as I know—still believe that they were right; they believe that the Communist schedule was retarded and partly disrupted by the awakening of the American people and their growing awareness of the Communist Conspiracy and its designs. It is known from past operations that the Conspiracy's plans always call for constantly *accelerated* subversion in the final phase of a conquest, and so even a stalemate is, from the standpoint of our enemies, an alarming tactical failure. They cannot afford many more without suffering total defeat.

The Conspiracy, we must remember, does not have the resilience of a nation at war, which, unless thoroughly rotted, can rely on the powerful cohesive force of patriotism. To be sure, a frenzied hatred of mankind and human civilization is an even more powerful cohesive force among the born Bolsheviks who direct and manage the Conspiracy, and it has been able to excite race hatred among certain "minorities" and so acquire some fanatical shock-troops; but for a very large part of the work of subversion it must rely on low-grade criminals, opportunistic collaborators,

Is this Communist Rubenstein?

and stupid employees. And its power of discipline over those groups largely depends on their complete confidence that the Conspiracy's triumph is inevitable.

Careful observers were aware of the feeling of crisis in conspiritorial circles before the assassination. In June of 1963, an experienced American military man made a careful analysis of the situation at that time, and in his highly confidential report concluded, on the basis of indications in Communist and crypto-Communist sources, that the

Conspiracy's schedule called for a major incident to create national shock ***before Thanksgiving***. Taylor Caldwell, who combines feminine sensitivity with artistic perception, sensed in the tone of Communist and "Liberal" publications a direction that made the assassination of Kennedy "very probable"—and she said so in an explicit warning published on October thirty-first and written about a week earlier. Other observers, who saw that Communist plans called for some sensational act of violence in the United States naturally considered the assassination of Kennedy (possibly in a crash of his airplane so arranged as to show unmistakable sabotage) as one of the expedients that the Conspiracy might adopt, although they did not, so far as I know, regard it as the *most* likely at the present juncture.

But, aside from the Conspiracy's obvious need for some drastic means of checking the growth of American patriotism, there is the consideration that Kennedy was rapidly becoming a political liability. Despite the best efforts of the lie-machines, it was clear that his popularity was diminishing so rapidly that some observers doubted whether even the most cunningly contrived and timed "crisis" could procure his re-election. His conduct was exciting ever increasing disgust even among the credulous; and what was worse, the vast cesspool in Washington was beginning to leak badly.

The bandits of the New Frontier, of whom Billie Sol Estes was but a puny specimen, had operated a little too openly. It had not been possible entirely to conceal the theft of wheat worth $32 million in a single raid or the probable "disappearance" of another $109 million in the same way. It had not been possible completely to suppress the TFX scandal, which would incense the entire nation if it were really exposed; it had not been possible to prevent the public from finding out *something* about little Bobby Baker; and a hundred other boils of corruption (including, it is rumored, some murders thus far successfully disguised as "accidental deaths") are ready to burst at the slightest pressure. Only the most desperate exertions, involving the *personal* intervention of two of the most prominent members of the Administration, have kept the lid — precariously and temporarily—on the modernized badger game that is operated (at the taxpayers' expense and partly on government property) to entrap and subject to blackmail members of Congress not responsive to bribery and other routine pressures from the Administration. There are rumors that an even more filthy scandal, involving both sadistic sexual perversions and the use of governmental powers for the importation and distribution of hallucinatory narcotics, is simmering dangerously near to the surface. I am told that documentary evidence of secret shipments of secret munitions of war to the Soviet by the Administration in treasonable defiance of law is available in a place in which it is secure from both burglary and bribery. Even so minor a matter as the recent exposure of "scientists" in the employ of the Department of Health, Education and Welfare as having forged spectrographic data for use in a smear-job on an American physician disquieted some theretofore complacent and somnolent citizens. For aught I know to the contrary, the assassination of Kennedy may have been necessary as the *only* means of avoiding, or even long deferring, national scandals so flagrant as to shock the whole of our brainwashed and hypnotized populace back to sanity.

In summary, then, there is not a single indication that the Conspiracy did not plan and carry out the assassination of Kennedy. On the other hand, there is evidence which very strongly suggests that it did.

COMMISSION EXHIBIT No. 1803—Continued

COMMISSION EXHIBIT No. 1803—Continued

First of all, there is the suspicious celerity with which the broadcasting agency sardonically called Voice of America, Tass in Moscow, Earl Warren, and many publicists and politicians noted for their services to the Conspiracy in the past, began to screech that the murder was the work of "right-wing extremists" almost as soon as the shot was fired. One is justified in asking whether the leaders of this chorus went into action as soon as they received news *that they were expecting*. Or, if they did not know the precise moment, were they not prepared in advance for news of that kind? Is it conceivable that the same story would have occurred independently to so many different persons, however intense their hatred of the American people, or that they would have dared to announce *as fact* a malicious conjecture, if they had no assurance that their statements would be confirmed by "evidence" to be discovered subsequently? Not even the most addle-pated emulator of Sherlock Holmes would pretend to identify a murderer without a single clue. But the screechers went much farther than that: What they said was the precise *opposite* of what was suggested by the first indications available (the arrest of a Negro, reported on the radio while the Presidential automobile was starting for the hospital) — an indication which, although it later proved to be wrong, no prudent person could have disregarded at the time, unless he had assurance, from some source that he trusted, that contrary indications would soon be produced.

Persons whose business it is to tamper with the news are naturally accustomed to lying, but even they do not lightly take the risk of being caught promptly in a particularly improbable and offensive lie. The case of Earl Warren is even more puzzling. No one would suspect him of concern for truth, but surely the Chief Justice of the Supreme Court must be shrewd enough not to make allegations without some reason to believe that he will be able to produce some shreds of "evidence" to support them.

It seems that preparations had been made for rioting and murder throughout the country. Americans known to be opponents of the Conspiracy, including General Walker, prominent members of the John Birch Society, and leaders of other conservative organizations, began to receive threats of death by telephone from creatures who somehow knew that Kennedy was dead *before* he reached the hospital. In many communities, mobs composed of the dregs of humanity and openly proposing to burn the homes and murder the families of known conservatives, began to form in the evening, as though in obedience to orders that had not been countermanded to all sectors. I do not suggest that the local vermin were entrusted with a fore-knowledge of precisely what was to happen in Dallas,

Officer J. D. Tippit

but it seems very likely that they had been prepared to respond to a signal and told what to do when the signal came.

It is easy to see what could have happened, had everything gone smoothly in Dallas. There could have been a complete break-down of law and order everywhere. The numerous vermin that have been living for years in ill-concealed anticipation of the glorious day when they will be able to hack Americans to pieces and drag bodies through the streets, could have "spontaneously" started looting, burning, and murdering. In many places they could have mustered strength beyond the control of the police, and even if checked and arrested, they could have claimed, like Rubenstein, that they had been "crazed" by "sorrow" for martyred Jack, and, of course, unlimited funds would have been available for legal defense. What is more, the great nest of traitors in Washington could have begun a pseudo-legal reign of terror, for which the infamous "Sedition Trial" in Washington in 1944 was obviously a small-scale and premature pilot-study. In an atmosphere of hysteria, maintained by the anti-American television, radio, and Press, all the leading American patriots could have been dragged in chains to Washington. The "Federal Marshals," fresh from Alcatraz and the like, whom the juvenile Czar had used for his invasion of Mississippi, could have been counted on to beat some of them to death or murder them while "trying to escape." The sadists whom we have imported as "mental health experts" could have tortured others into fake "confessions" or have destroyed their minds with drugs. There could have been a national Saturnalia of *legalized* violence under cover of which the International Conspiracy could have gained a control of the whole nation that could not subsequently have been broken.

You, who read these lines, may owe your life or at least your liberty to the vigilance and sagacity of Officer J. D. Tippit, the policeman who stopped Oswald on the street and was murdered by the Conspiracy's well-trained but not infallible agent.

There is other evidence, including definite indications that certain persons, whom observers have long regarded as members or at least auxiliaries of the Conspiracy, knew days in advance that *something* was going to happen to Kennedy in Dallas. But when one considers the enormous gains that the Conspiracy could have reaped from the assassination, had it been carried out without mishap, and when one remembers that the Conspiracy had an urgent and even desperate need of precisely such an event, one cannot avoid the conclusion that the weight of probability lies overwhelmingly on the side of the view that the murder was arranged by the Conspiracy as a strategic operation.

Be Ye Not Comforted

Many Americans, while giving thanks for their deliverance, strangely assume that the Communists' mishap in Dallas will give us a respite from danger of at least several months. On the contrary, the danger is greater than ever, for the partial failure merely augments the criminals' need for some signal victory over Americans to preserve enthusiasm in their own ranks. As I write, shortly before Christmas, it does not seem that that victory can be attained before the New Year, but we may be sure that every effort will be made to attain it as soon as possible thereafter.

The first expedient was primarily defensive. In a hasty and thus far successful attempt to thwart an investigation by legally constituted authorities, i.e. the Senate Subcommittee on Internal Security and the Attorney General of the State of Texas, both of whom had already announced their de-

inquiry, an illegal and un-Constitutional "special commission" was improvised with the obvious hope that it could be turned into a Soviet-style kangaroo court. The best-known members of this packed "commission" are:

(1) Earl Warren, so notorious as the chief of the quasi-judicial gang engaged in subverting the Constitution of the United States that many thousands of the finest and most prominent American citizens have for two years been demanding with increasing insistence his impeachment and trial. A favorite subject of speculation and debate among some informed observers is whether Warren, if brought to trial, would try to dodge behind the Fifth Amendment or would take it on the lam and disappear behind the Iron Curtain. Warren, who spends his vacations with Little Comrade Tito in Yugoslavia or with Big Comrade Khrushchev in the Crimea, began to traduce and defame loyal and informed Americans minutes after the murder in Dallas; and it is easy to see why the Communist Party, through some indiscretion or mis-timing, officially nominated him as head of the "special commission" two days before his appointment was announced in Washington.

(2) T. Hale Boggs, the loud-mouthed agitator who disgraces the State of Louisiana in Congress. *The Councilor* has reproduced a press photograph which shows young Boggs in the act of giving the Communist clenched-fist salute while he was head of the Communist-front "American Student Union" in Tulane University, ridiculing our Army, and urging young men not to fight for their country. The same publication reports that it has indisputable evidence that Boggs "served three years before entering Congress" as chairman of a Communist-front "Peace Drive," and reports that he is a member of the "Interparliamentary Union," a sinister abroad to plot the liquidation of the United States. As promptly as Warren, Boggs began to yell that the "right-wing" (as he and his kind call Americans who don't want to be liquidated) was guilty of having shot Mister Jack.

(3) Allen W. Dulles, one of the founders of the malodorous Council On Foreign Relations and currently its Director. Dulles was the head of an American spy ring in Switzerland during the Second World War and is said to have done a fairly good job, although it was believed at the time that his organization was infested with double agents who were really in the employ of the Soviet—and even more serious implications can be drawn from the testimony given in Karlsruhe last July by Heinz Felfe, a Soviet agent who had been Mr. Dulles' German counterpart and supposed competitor in Switzerland.

Our Central Intelligence Agency, although it was infected from the very beginning by the incorporation of scum from the notorious O.S.S., was still an American agency while it was under the command of Admiral Hillenkoetter. Under Mr. Dulles it was transformed into the bizarre gang of seventeen thousand or more secret and faceless agents, some of them expert assassins so recently imported into the United States that they cannot speak English. Mr. Dulles' C.I.A. is also the gang that helped Castro attain power in Cuba, staged the fake "invasion" to destroy anti-Communist organizations in Cuba, recently carried out (in close cooperation with the Soviet Secret Police) the murders in South Vietnam as a prelude to complete and open Communist occupation, and is known to have served the Soviet in many other ways, while, so far as is known, it has never done anything at all for the United States, whose taxpayers provide the gang with unlimited funds. Some perhaps frenetic

COMMISSION EXHIBIT No. 1803—Continued

The Worker proposed Warren.

observers believe—based upon this and other "coincidences"—that the C.I.A. is now the major branch of the Soviet Secret Police in the United States.

It was to Mr. Dulles personally that the late Bang-Jensen trustingly confided evidence that very important members of the C.I.A. were officers in the Soviet Secret Police, and Mr. Dulles did nothing at all about it—unless, indeed, it was the C.I.A. that murdered Bang-Jensen to prevent him from ever giving testimony.

One writer has recently suggested that it was the C.I.A. that arranged the assassination of Kennedy; I know of no evidence to support that opinion, but obviously Mr. Dulles' creation is open to suspicion. Perhaps that is why he is a member of the "special commission."

(4) John J. McCloy, of the Council On Foreign Relations, the Ford Foundation, the World Brotherhood, and other mysteriously powerful organizations whose un-American or anti-American activities should have been McCloy is reputed to be the principal author of the present plan to disarm the United States and prepare it for occupation by Soviet troops and associated savages of the "United Nations," which he, as an assistant of Alger Hiss, helped to design and foist on the American people.

Well, those four form a majority of the "fact-finding commission" and their records offer a guarantee of the kind of "facts" they will find or devise. Two of the other members are self-styled "Liberals" of little political experience, and it is obviously idle to speculate concerning what Senator Russell may be able to do alone in such company.

It should be noted that the very creation of this Soviet-style "commission" in violation of our Constitution and for the express purpose of superseding legal and Constitutional procedures represents in itself a victory for which the Communist Conspiracy would have been willing to pay almost any price, since it accelerates the disintegration of legality and accustoms Americans to dictatorial acts that subvert the authority of Congress.

The functions of a "commission" so constituted are obvious. It will:

(1) Cover up for the Communist Conspiracy as much as possible by claiming that Comrade Oswald was a poor, lone critter who done it all alone. Probably "psychiatrists" will be produced to prove he done it 'cause, at the age of six months, he had to wait an extra five minutes for his bottle. That will establish the need for more Welfare and Civil Rights.

(2) Suppress permanently the report of the F.B.I., which it has already acted to conceal from the American people, an. if permanent suppression proves impossible, to have the report watered down or at least kept secret until a "crisis" can be arranged that will make its publication pass almost unnoticed.

COMMISSION EXHIBIT No. 1803—Continued

(3) Smother and suppress the evidence of close contacts between Oswald and Rubenstein in both Waco and Dallas during the period immediately preceding the assassination of Kennedy, and other evidence connecting both of them with mysteriously prosperous persons of unknown antecedents in the vicinity of New York City. Every effort will be made to conceal Rubenstein's connections with Communist Cuba, including such items as a clandestine visit to Havana about a year ago, when he stayed with a long-time and close associate of Castro's named Praskin, who operates, as a cover for his other activities, a "novelty store" on the Prado opposite the Seville Hotel.* It may even be possible to prevent the public from learning definitely whether or not the "Jack" Rubenstein who executed Oswald is the person of the same name who has a published record of Communist associations and activities in this country going back for many years.

(3) Harass the Dallas police as much as possible. This will convey to police forces everywhere an understanding of the inadvisability of interfering with Communists engaged in the discharge of their duties. I doubt that the "commission" will go farther than this, although I confess that I am disturbed by the persistence with which the "Liberal" columnists around the world, from France to Australia, insist that poor Oswald, an innocent little Communist, was "framed" by the "Fascist" police of Dallas.

(4) Try to smear and intimidate loyal Americans in every way possible. Much can be accomplished in this direction if the Congress can be pressured into voting un-Constitutional powers of subpoena to an un-Constitutional "commission" dominated by persons who

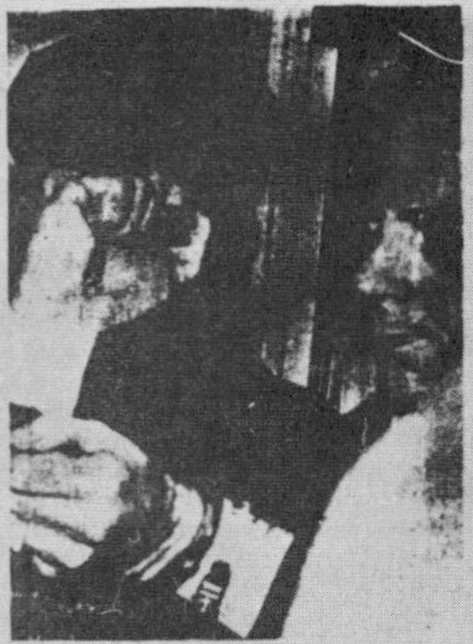

The Communist clenched-fist salute.

should themselves be on trial for their efforts to subvert and destroy the Constitution. Since no American cow is wealthy after having been milked by the Income-Tax collectors, and since the majority of conspicuously loyal Americans are persons of very modest means, just one item, the cost of employing attorneys, could give the gang the power to inhibit and even paralyze most of the opposition to treason in the crucial year of 1964. It is possible, of course, that the "commission" may simply assume such powers. If so, Congress will probably object; but, if it should be necessary, the august Chief Justice could dash over to the Supreme Court Building, put on his black robe, and rule that Congress, like God, is un-Constitutional. It's just a ten-minute trip by cab.

(5) To go as much further as may be feasible. It is reported in the Press that the "commission" has requested the power to "extort" testimony from "unwilling witnesses." At the time at which I write, it seems unlikely that any such un-Constitutional power will be un-Constitutionally granted. Of course, the original plan, to have been carried out *eventually*, if everything went according to schedule in Dallas, called for nice, rubber-lined torture chambers (such as you may glimpse in that excellent film, *My Latvia*) in which the hated Americans could be scientifically tortured into "confession," and the remains of those who proved "uncooperative" could be efficiently washed down the drains.

(6) To create propaganda for other Communist projects to facilitate the final conquest of the United States. A number are likely, but the most obvious is the one that was contemplated when Comrade Oswald was careful to provide evidence that the rifle used in the assassination had been purchased by mail. It is eminently desirable that firearms now in the possession of Americans be confiscated, partly to convince the Conspiracy's serfs how helpless they are, and especially to reduce the occupational hazards to the Balubas, Outer Mongolians, or other beasts who may form the "international police force" that is to occupy the United States and butcher its white inhabitants.

(7) To co-operate when the Conspiracy arranges for further violence. We may be sure that such will occur at the earliest feasible moment, and that every precaution will be taken to avoid a slip-up such as occurred in Dallas. It is impossible to predict at this moment when such an incident will occur or what form it will take—except, of course, that the blame will fall on "right-wing extremists." The assassination of other high government officials is an obvious possibility—perhaps too obvious, despite the sudden yapping of "Liberals" that something must be done quick to prevent the succession of John McCormack, as now provided by law. (*Newsweek*, THE WEEKLY LIEPAPER published by the *Washington Post*, had the effrontery to state the cause for alarm: McCormack is suspected of "anti-Communism"!) The Conspiracy, however, might go so far as to arrange the assassination of some Justice: That could, perhaps, be made to seem plausible after the Warren Court has maltreated a number of Americans in its latest usurpation of un-Constitutional powers, and it is, furthermore, the only *sure* way of preventing an impeachment and trial by Congress.

But another assassination would seem a bit monotonous, unless preceded by several other incidents of a different pattern. A hundred varieties of incidents are possible, such as first-class race riots, an "accidental" nuclear explosion to pep up agitation for "*disarmament*," or a well planned series of *almost* convincing "suicides" of American "rightists." A properly timed "crisis" in Latin America, preferably near to our borders, would be a suitable intermezzo during the performance. We cannot now predict precisely what arrangements the unknown Directorate of the Conspiracy will deem most expedient, for it is likely that their choice of both time and events will be made after they have seen how much advantage they will have been able to extract from the Kennedy assassination.

One thing is certain, however: The bungle in Dallas, far from justifying the slightest relaxation, should summon us to the utmost vigilance. It should warn us that we have come to the year of decision, and that only our most devoted and united efforts can prevail against a gang of international murderers rendered desperate by the awareness that their time is running out. ■ ■

(*End of Part One.*)

*I understand that full report on this and other known activities of Rubenstein will probably appear in a future issue of *The Herald of Freedom* (Box 333, Staten Island 1, N.Y.).

MARXMANSHIP

In Dallas [Part II]

Revilo P. Oliver is Professor of Classics in the University of Illinois. During World War II, he was Director of Research in a secret agency of the War Department. He has traveled widely. Dr. Oliver is an academician of international reputation who has published scholarly articles in four languages within the pages of twelve learned periodicals in the United States and Europe.

■ HENCEFORTH, no American has an excuse for illusion. He has had an ocular demonstration of who and what his enemies are. And that lesson is repeated every day as his enemies, recklessly exposing themselves, try to carry out their original plan in spite of Comrade Oswald's bungling.

The assassination and its aftermath must have given to many Americans the shock that each of us must somehow feel in his own being before he can understand what Communists really are and why they are seeking to kill or enslave him. That understanding does not automatically come from mere information. We all carry in our minds a great accumulation of items of information, such as that a continent lies under the ice of Antarctica or that the natives of the Andaman Islands are pygmies, which have no effect on our thinking because such facts seem irrelevant to our own lives. By this time, every literate American has in his own mind a good deal of information about Communists, although often as detached and unrelated items that seem remote from his quotidian concerns. Even copious and systematic information may remain, so to speak, inert in the mind until illumined by a perception that carries conviction.

The Moment Of Truth

The perception usually comes from some personal experience or observation. It may be some minor shock, such as the falling apple is said to have given Newton; but at that shock a thousand bits of scattered knowledge latent in the mind arrange themselves into a coherent whole and exhibit a basic truth.

When I was a youngster, I knew a man of substance who told me that he had almost been enlisted in a Communist-front operation to release from prison a creature named Mooney, who had murdered nine persons in California to show how much he loved Humanity. Although moved by the plausible and pathetic story told him by the Editor of a "literary" periodical, the gentleman was canny enough to check a few facts and then visit the headquarters of the organization soliciting his support. His unannounced visit gave him his moment of perception. He returned with the conviction that he had seen specimens of a criminal gang that was burrowing its way beneath the foundations of society, bent on undermining the whole nation. I thought his alarm preposterous, and, I am afraid, smiled at it.

In college, I could not overlook the

great acumen to see that their idealistic squeakings about "social justice" and the "downtrodden" were mere pretense to cover the malice and phrenetic rancors seething within them. But I did not really understand them until I met, during the great Crusade to Save the Soviet, a young lawyer who had been provided with a direct commission and a "vital" job in Washington to preserve him from the kind of military service that may be bad for the skin. He explained to me the wickedness of making a profit, and he told me how "social justice" would come to businessmen. "We'll shoot them in the belly," he said rapturously; "they die longer that way." And the greasy-faced creature licked its dry lips.

A professional man tells me that his moment came at the time that Irreproachable Ike, violating the Constitution he had sworn to uphold, used the Army to help the Warren Crew get the race war under way. He was talking to a clergyman of the "social gospel" variety whose emotional perturbation he did not understand until some indiscreet exclamations let him see that the holy man was inwardly trembling with eagerness for news that Americans had been bayonetted or machine-gunned on the streets of Little Rock.

The moment came to another man when he was one of a party of four in the bar of a private club. One of the four, an evidently urbane and cultivated gentleman — who had come to the United States as a refugee and had been given a salary and security that he could never have attained in the land whence he came — took a Scotch or two too many and began to make it painfully clear that he regarded Americans as detestable swine who need to be taught, with the toe of a boot, their place in One World.

A university professor tells me that his moment came two years ago when a years pontificated about the market-place of ideas," and, serene as a seated Buddha, had beamed benignly when Gus Hall and Gordon Hall spoke on the campus, "because we need to hear all sides," began to yell like a Comanche at a scalp-dance. What had shattered academic serenity was the discovery that there was a horrible "hate-sheet" read by "Fascist war-mongers" who must be "stamped out" or, at least, have their teeth kicked in. As for contributors to the hate-sheet, said the Sakya Muni of Academic Freedom, whom I quote verbatim, "they must be exterminated. Shooting is *too good* for them." The hate-sheet in question was that mild and self-consciously "moderate" fortnightly, *National Review*, and my informant believes that the Double Dome would have run amok with a kris, had he even suspected the existence of AMERICAN OPINION. As it was, however, the yells sufficed to make my informant suddenly realize what makes "Liberals" tick — and he compared them to certain well wrapped and disguised packages that are occasionally discovered by a postal inspector or the baggage master of an airline because they also tick.

A New Yorker says that his moment came early in December when he read a column by Walter Lippmann, whom he had long supposed to be suffering from nothing more serious than a cerebrum bloated with ideals. In that column the punctate pundit, wrapping his feet about his neck in one of his customary verbal twists, claimed that "in a free [*sic*] country" criticism of "Civil Rights and Russia" is "inherently subversive." Not content with having thus exposed himself, Big-Brained Walt went on tactlessly to yowl that because Oswald scored a bull's-eye, "the *only* solace for the nation's [*sic*] shame and grief can come from a Purge"—a purge, of course, of the awful Americans who think they still have a country. Thus, said my correspondent, was long covert hatred of Americans and dissembled blood-lust made manifest for all to see. It is possible, to be sure, that the quoted phrase was just lipography, and that Lippmann meant something else, such as forced feeding of castor oil to Americans; but the phrase served to give at least one of his readers an impulse to put together and comprehend many data that his mind was holding in suspension.

Ex uno disce omnes

Oswald was a young Communist punk, but, aside from his fortuitous notoriety, there was nothing unusual about him. You have seen thousands like him, and you are paying taxes to breed or nourish swarms of them.

You saw a representative selection of them in that excellent film, *Operation Abolition,* which is now more timely than ever. You saw the veteran criminals, who should have been deported or imprisoned long ago, riot and yell at the House Committee, an official delegation of the highest governmental authority in our nation. You will not have failed to recognize in them rabid beasts grown insolent with long impunity. You saw also the rioting swarms of young creatures that had crawled out from the woodwork of the University of California and other tax-supported institutions of "higher learning." You had an opportunity to study their hate-contorted faces.

You can see fledgling Oswalds in the flesh whenever, as occasionally happens, a loyal American is permitted to speak on or near a college campus. The young "progressives" will be there to jeer and quibble. It will be instructive to observe how many are deformed in body or feature as well as mind, and, if you approach near enough, you can see the hatred glistening in beady eyes. (For a close approach, a handkerchief sprinkled with ammonia will minimize the discomfort.) And you should reflect that you are financing, directly through taxes or contributions or indirectly through the institution's tax-exemption, the hatching and "education" of young murderers.

You can see the species wherever you look. And with just a little patience and dexterity, you can make all but the most hardened and experienced disclose their inner emotions — perhaps in a spate of verbiage, but at least for a moment in an unguarded word or glare in the eyes; and you will feel like a swimmer who has glimpsed, six fathoms down, the flat, greenish flicker of a turning shark.

You can see them on television, on the floor of Congress, and in their pulpits; you can read them in the Press. And you need have no doubts. Whether they are trying crudely or subtly to use the Communists' assassination of Kennedy to incite hatred against "right-wing extremists," you can no longer fancy that they are just ignorant "intellectuals" with mixed-up ganglia. They are lying. They are lying with conscious calculation. They are lying with murderous intent.

You cannot mistake them when, in your very presence and with breath-taking effrontery, they discharge the diseased hatreds and homicidal lusts that fester in their gangrenous little minds.

From direct observation, you, as an American, can now recognize your enemy and know what he is. And if ever you are tempted to doubt the evidence of your own eyes and ears, remember that such monsters are no novelty — that in the brief span of man's sad and dolorous history one can find almost innumerable recorded instances of recrudescent savagery and of the frenzied and exacerbated rage of anthropoid beasts that cannot bear to be dragged toward civilization and humanity. The best illustration in a book that I have

seen is Louis Zoul's *Thugs and Communists* (Public Opinion, Long Island City 4; cf. American Opinion, January, 1962, pp. 29-36).

The vital thing is that you, as an American, realize that you are being hunted by a feral and stealthy pack. And that this is no nightmare, from which you will automatically awaken in a moment, nor yet is it a vision excited by the writers who strove to be more *outré* than Poe. That is a reality which you must face, if you are to survive at all:

The Time Is Now

With the nature of our enemies thus made manifest, and with such unmistakable indications of their numbers and power, an American who does not wilfully close his eyes and drug his mind can scarcely escape a perception of the magnitude and immediacy of our peril. This is the year of decision. We cannot hope for a complete victory this year, but we must end thirty years of unvaried retreat and, for a change, advance a little to recover some of the ground we have lost and to turn the tide of battle. A mere stalemate is scarcely possible, and another defeat will be our last. With another defeat, you and I may not be alive in 1965—or, if we are, we may regret it.

Now that Providence has given us a last chance, we must use it wisely and well. We must act with courage and determination, and, above all, with a rational and realistic understanding of our situation. We are fighting against enormous, though not insuperable odds, and we shall need the utmost effort of every American who will work with us. Our greatest handicap is that we, unlike our enemies, do not have a unified and secret command which plans the total strategy without need to disclose or explain it to anyone, and which carries out that strategy by issuing orders that are obeyed without question. Against a conspiracy that makes its decisions in secret and coordinates with the efficiency of a single organism the movements of its numerous and often hidden tentacles, we can oppose only the voluntary efforts of individuals who are loosely organized into a large number of voluntary organizations, which must, in turn, voluntarily cooperate with one another. In these circumstances a secret strategy is impossible, and we must rely on the rationality and self-control of responsible individuals to supply that minimum of unity and coordination without which we could do nothing against a conspiracy that has almost absolute control over its agents through its appeal to their criminal instincts, their complicity in past crimes, and, if need be, fear.

Our enemies plan in secret, but they have a standard technique for dealing with Americans that has long been obvious to every observer. While the vast majority of Americans are kept, so far as possible, in a state of ignorant complacency and confusion by the lie-machine, conservative and patriotic organizations are destroyed by inciting them to fight one another and by paralyzing each one with internal dissension. That technique has been used for more than forty years, and, without exception until the past few years, accomplished its purpose speedily and infallibly. Its success depended partly upon our enemies' vast financial resources and long experience in covert and subtle manipulation of individuals, but even more on the fact that loyal Americans are divided in their personal interests and beliefs.

That we Americans are so divided is our basic weakness in the present struggle, but it is not one of which we need be ashamed. It is the weakness of all societies of free men, and hence it is, in large part, precisely what we are trying to preserve. But our conflicts of interest and belief must be candidly ad-not to succumb to the manipulations of our enemies.

The Unity Of Dissension

As Americans, our one bond of effective unity is the American tradition, which is, in its essentials, a severely *practical* one. It is our first and most urgent duty to take a lesson from our forefathers, the citizens of the thirteen colonies, who, confronted by overwhelming odds, achieved independence because they had the intelligence and self-control never to lose sight of their real objective; although the colonies were deeply divided by opposed economic interests, vehement religious dissensions, and cultural differences that were, within the ambit of Western civilization, comparatively great. The governing bodies of each colony well knew that they could make an extremely advantageous settlement by deserting the other twelve. And the larger colonies must have been often tempted to seek opportunities, during the long struggle, of extending their influence and power at the expense of others in the hope of dominating whatever confederation might come out of independence.

A desperate undertaking, which most political analysts would have pronounced impossible *a priori* for peoples so sundered by divergent interests and creeds, succeeded because — and only because — our forefathers were able to transcend those differences and maintain an effective unity for the specific and strictly limited purpose of attaining political freedom.

Our task as Americans today is to attain and maintain an effective unity for the specific and strictly limited purpose of (a) preserving our national independence by recovering our federal government from the international vermin who have stealthily captured it, and (b) restoring as rapidly as may be than a decade—our Constitutional government that those vermin have all but totally subverted. As a *practical* imperative, all other purposes, however passionately important they may be to us personally, must be recognized as secondary and even irrelevant, so far as the cause in which we must unite is concerned.

Our problem, I grant, is far more complex and delicate than that which confronted our forefathers. Their opponents were men who frankly and honorably declared themselves and disdained disguise. Our enemies are secret criminals whose principal weapon has always been deceit, dissimulation, and stealthy subversion. But our problem, surely, is not beyond the power of reason. And we should derive a stimulus to use it from the consideration that we have much more at stake than did our forefathers.

Who Is The Enemy?

Every one of us who tries to calculate our chances of victory must be continually astonished, and not infrequently dismayed, by the fantastic fact that what should be our greatest strength is also our greatest weakness. We have so indulged our human propensities to sentimentality and emotionalism, and we have been so subtly conditioned to fear shibboleths and bugaboos, that we squander in acrimonious debate over conjectures the energies which, if rationally directed, could save us from annihilation.

Our enemy is the International Communist Conspiracy. Of that, there can be no possible doubt. Every time the fetid nest of vermin in Washington spends our money and (usually) the lives of American soldiers to enslave and barbarize another country, that country is invariably handed over to Communists — never to Fabian Socialists, Illuminati, or similar groups. East

China, Cuba, and the many others are all obviously and notoriously *Communist* provinces. And it is perfectly obvious that what the nest is preparing for the United States, through "civil rights," disarmament, and the like, is a *Communist* regime.

Although the Conspiracy is secret, we have learned a great deal about it by (a) studying its operations, and (b) utilizing the testimony of defectors from the Conspiracy and of our own counter-espionage agents who were able to penetrate some distance into the organization. The information thus obtained is necessarily incomplete, and, for obvious reasons, it becomes the more scanty, the nearer we approach the Conspiracy's inner core; and fails us completely before we reach that core.

The information that we have is sufficient to give us a good working knowledge of the general structure of the Conspiracy, although, of course, there are a great many details and possibly some very important elements about which we urgently need to know more.

Only the most naive persons today are puzzled by the operations of what is the lowest level in the Conspiracy (although it includes persons of great social or political prominence). The Conspiracy, engaged in total subversion, naturally finds and exploits all the weaknesses that are inherent in our society as in all human societies. It finds, and uses as its unconscious instruments, fat-heads and dunces who can be stirred to glutinous sentimentality or a rancorous resentment of their betters. But it uses above all the criminal tendencies that always have been present in all large populations and always will be present to the utmost verge of the foreseeable future. Every large aggregation of human beings produces, by biological necessity, its sneak-thieves, robbers, shysters, "intellectuals," As is known to everyone who has thought about it at all, the continued existence of a civilization, like that of a large city, depends on the efficiency of the sewage system that disposes of its organic waste: On this level, all that the Conspiracy has to do is stop up the sewers (which civilized societies seem naturally disposed to neglect anyway, since no one likes to think about such unpleasant necessities). By this time, we have all learned not to waste time arguing whether a given person, who is knowingly serving the Conspiracy's ends, is a member, an accomplice, a hireling, or just a petty criminal who has been given opportunity and encouragement.

The structure of the main Communist apparatus in this country is reasonably clear. There is a large number of them and, so far as is known, they operate independently of one another. The official Communist Party, the more concealed "Trotskyite" apparatus, the military and naval espionage rings directed from the various Soviet embassies, the industrial and technological espionage directed from the various consulates, and the Secret Police are all controlled directly from Moscow, and are believed to have no contact with one another in this country, except that the Secret Police watch all the others and probably supervise the transfer of talented criminals, recruited by the Party, to the more secret units. The vast crypto-Communist apparatus no longer has large cells, such as the one of which the infamous Hiss was a member; and is now so organized that no cell has more than three members and most of the criminals know the identity only of the superior from whom they receive orders. Most observers believe that this operation is handled by the Secret Police. There are other apparatus and transmission belts, some possibly of strategic importance, which *may* operate in this country independently of the ones I have mentioned. But given the criminals' success in preventing or halting all official inquiry into their more clandestine activities in the United States, we can only speculate about the chain of command in operations that we cannot even *prove* to be Communist. Most observers would agree in identifying some of these by cogent inference from copious circumstantial evidence; about others, so little is known that competent observers differ widely in the surmises that they base on admittedly fragmentary indications; and it is quite possible that there are some whose true nature has not even been suspected.

So far as we know, however, the various Bolshevik apparatus are controlled from Moscow. Whenever we can trace their organization at all, we can follow the wires until they disappear in the massive walls of the Kremlin. (In recent years, some circuits have been rewired so that the lines from this country go to Peking; cf. AMERICAN OPINION, January, 1964, p. 71. That merely shows that a new exchange has been installed for operational convenience.) All observers, I believe, would agree that, so far as is known, the criminals in our country get their orders, directly or indirectly, from Moscow.

Now there are very good reasons for believing that the foul brute that is titular Boss in the Kremlin is merely a subordinate, an executive of limited powers. So long as the unspeakable thing called Stalin was alive, most (but not all) observers thought that he was the real head of the Conspiracy. Events subsequent to the death (or, perhaps, liquidation) of that monster have made it increasingly apparent to judicious observers that the organization of the Conspiracy is more complex than was once generally supposed — that the bloody beast named Khrushchev is like a "star" in a show on Broadway in that his personal appetites and eccentricities will, within rather narrow limits, be tolerated, since he represents a considerable investment in publicity; but who can always be fired by the producers of the show, and *will be* eliminated the minute that he gets out of hand so far as to endanger the success of production. So, who are the producers?

The question may be too precipitately asked. Let us state it first in more simple terms: Who controls Khrushchev and the organizations on which his power is evidently based?

An experienced and highly qualified anti-Communist organization, which has probably penetrated as far into the Kremlin and its secrets as any human beings, summarized its findings in a report that the Honorable Timothy P. Sheehan read to the House of Representatives on August 5, 1957. (You probably never heard of it. The unanimity with which daily liepapers ignored sensational, and therefore potentially profitable, news, and the extraordinary exertions made by prominent subhumans to avert the re-election of Congressman Sheehan, serve only, so far as prudent and rational Americans are concerned, to validate and confirm the report he communicated to Congress.)

The kernel of this long and circumstantial report is that, superior to Krushchev and similar administrators, and superior even to the Secret Police, is another and more select organization of truly international scope, the Communist Security System (CSS), which has penetrated and controls even the Secret Police. The existence of such an inner organization was first suspected by cautious observers in 1939, when the purulent blob of anti-human protoplasm called Nicolai Yezhov was blotted out and replaced by the equally loathesome thing called Lavrenti Beria. That suspicion, however, remained hypothetical, in the eyes of most observers,

until 1953, when the ease with which the Beria-thing was in turn liquidated made it apparent to thoughtful analysts that the Secret Police, of which Beria had been the absolute and unchallenged master, must be in turn subordinate to some inner and even more secret apparatus. The CSS, as described in the report, precisely corresponds to that more secret apparatus, as its characteristics were deduced by many observers before the report was made public by a courageous and patriotic Congressman at the cost of his own political career.

Not all qualified observers find the report on the Communist Security System as convincing and cogent as I do, although I know of none who would categorically reject it. Since no member of the CSS has ever defected and confessed, the intelligence report concerning it can be corroborated only by deduction and inference from numerous, scattered, often ambiguous, and sometimes conflicting data. The most that any observer can say, therefore, is that he accepts the report's description of the CSS as highly probable, since it fits the known pattern of conspiratorial organization and provides the most comprehensive and consistent explanation thus far proposed of the facts which indicate that the Conspiracy is controlled by some inner circle.

But if the CSS is the controlling organism, we have merely pushed the ultimate question one step farther back. Who controls the CSS?

That, of course, must be the darkest and most jealously guarded secret of all. As was to be expected, the report can only state that "the guiding [i.e. controlling] members of the Communist Security System" are "fellow travellers, rich financiers, and secret Communists" whose identity is known only to themselves and the few trusted agents through whom they, as an invisible government, transmit their orders. That description suggests — even implies — that most or all of the real directors of the Conspiracy live outside of Soviet territory. There is nothing implausible in that. Indeed, there never was any real evidence to support the gratuitous assumption that the Conspiracy's headquarters were moved to Russia after the conquest of that country in 1917.

Our Secret Enemy

Whatever hypothesis we may form concerning the inmost structure of the Communist Conspiracy, we can scarcely do other than postulate that the supreme direction must come from some supreme council which, in all probability, has not less than ten nor more than five hundred members. Whatever we may suspect, we do not know who they are; we do not know where they meet or how they communicate with one another; we do not even know what rational end (if any) they propose to themselves other than a Satanic dominion over the whole world. We only know that they must be phenomenally intelligent and unutterably evil.

Now, at the risk of laboring the obvious, we cannot too often remind ourselves that our ultimate enemies are the members of that council, *whoever* they are, *however* they work, and *whatever* their secret designs. And the International Communist Conspiracy by definition consists of the unknown members of that council and *all* of the instrumentalities and subordinate organizations that they direct. That is the conspiracy that we must defeat, at least in our own country, if we are not to perish most miserably at its hands. And I do not see how any American who has observed what has been done to his nation in recent years, and thought about it, could disagree with either the definition or a statement that only the most dedicated and united efforts of American patriots can save us from an imminent and unspeakable horror.

No reader of AMERICAN OPINION, I

am sure, will be confused, even for an instant, by the semantic quibble made possible by the fact that the Communist Conspiracy is not directed by Communists, if by that term we mean persons who believe in "Marxism." The barbarous jargon and confusing twaddle of "dialectical materialism" has always been what Marx designed it to be, an elaborate deception triply useful for enlisting recruits, stultifying ignorant "intellectuals," and concealing serious purposes. On the lower levels of the Conspiracy, many members of the Communist Party believe, or pretend to believe, that drivel as an article of faith; while the more sincere and intelligent rack their brains trying to solve a set of quadratic equations that were designed to be insoluble (and eventually they either defect or get the point and move upward to the next level). We may be quite sure, I think, that anyone who attains the rank of assistant to an immediate subordinate of a branch manager, such as Castro, has left belief in "Marxism" as far behind him as belief in Santa Claus. So, unless we find an adolescent's pleasure in the paradox that Khrushchev and his kind are not Communists, we must understand that by "Communist" we mean a conscious participant in the International Conspiracy, without reference to his real or feigned reasons for participation.

Some Theories

It has long been apparent that the Communist Conspiracy was something quite different from the picture that its members tried to hold before the general public. It was clear to judicious observers a century ago that the degenerates who publicly headed or secretly financed the International were not in the least interested in the "workers" or the "proletariat" about whose "oppression" they pretended to snivel. When the Conspiracy effected its first territorial conquest in 1917, only the simple-minded could describe as "Russian" a revolution whose leaders and executives had, almost without exception, swarmed into Russia a few months before the take-over, and had been financed from both Germany and the United States, although those two nations were technically at war with one another. And after the conquest of Russia, it was clear that the total resources of that hapless and more than decimated land were utterly inadequate to finance an international conspiracy. And although Trotsky, Lenin, Stalin, and the rest were, without doubt, viciously cunning monsters, it was extremely improbable that they had either the brains or the time to direct such a conspiracy while discharging their duties as executives in Russia and, incidentally, clawing at one another's throats.

Long ago, therefore, observers very reasonably began to look for a conspiracy behind the Soviet. The existence of such an inner or directing conspiracy was strongly suggested, as I have said, by the known facts in the history of Communism from the time of Marx to the present. It was also indicated by analogy to the structure of criminal conspiracies known to history. For example, Weishaupt's Illuminati* were organized in a set of concentric circles; all members, even those in the outer circle, were given the impression that they were "on the inside," but the members of each inner circle regarded the members of outer circles as neophytes to be prepared for more advanced work or as suckers who were useful because they could be made to believe anything. The Assassins, founded by Hasan-i-Sabbah, were similarly organized: The members of the lowest grade (*Lasiqs*) were fanatical believers in the *Koran* and Islam, while guru members of the grade next to the top (*Da'i i-Kabir*) found it difficult to

---

* See American Opinion, June, 1962, pp. 33-37.

keep a straight face while talking to boobs they considered so stupid as to believe in Allah or any god.

Since it was clear that there was a conspiracy inside the outer (Marxist) shell, it was only natural that attempts should be made to identify it. Various sincere and thoughtful writers have positively identified the inner conspiracy as composed of one of the following: "Force X," Illuminati, Satanists, "Bilderbergers," Zionists, Pharisees, Khazars, Fabian Socialists, International Bankers, Rockefellers, Rothschilds, or a gang of otherwise unidentified "messianic materialists." Good and authentic evidence drawn from the present or the recent past can be assembled to support each of these identifications, and it is easy to argue convincingly that each is right, provided that we can assume an extraordinary degree of stupidity or short-sighted venality in some or all of the others. And although some of the groups I have listed overlap others, or may do so, it is clear that *all* of them cannot be the *one* central conspiracy. Furthermore, we cannot assume that there are a number of *major* conspiracies independent of one another but all blithely working together today with no thought of the morrow.

Let me take as my example the "Force X," recently brought into prominence by Kenneth de Courcy in his excellent and generally reliable *Intelligence Digest*. And let me hasten to add that, although I feel confident that I recognize the entity to which Mr. de Courcy refers, I do not pretend to have at my disposal the mass of information and documentation that has presumably been assembled by Mr. de Courcy's private intelligence organization, which largely consists of former members of British Military Intelligence now stationed throughout the world as representatives of British industries or in similar capacities.

Mr. de Courcy has *not* said that "Force X" was the inner core of the Communist Conspiracy, but many of his readers have drawn that inference from the indications that he has provided. Mr. de Courcy has described "Force X" as "basically a criminal group," which "directs the entire drug traffic of the world," high-class prostitution and homosexual rings, and many other forms of profitable crime. But he says that it "has made use of Communism," that "its power far exceeds that of Communism," that "in Russia, Trotsky, Zhdanov, Beria, and Litvinov" were its agents (as were, in Germany, "both Ludendorff and Himmler"), and that its executive head, a homosexual and necrophilic degenerate, gave advice to Stalin and now advises both Khrushchev and Mao Tse-tung. Mr. de Courcy concludes that "the alliance between this person and Communism is very close, although there are fundamental clashes of aim. Neither seems to mind this at present."

It is at that point that I have my doubts. As Communist agents and fuddled fops are forever telling us, there is only one world—and, what is worse, it is less than 25,000 miles in circumference at the equator. It is much, much too small for *two* conspiracies of "One Worlders," and if, perchance, there are two, the heads of both must have realized long ago that the more successful they were, the sooner one would have to liquidate the other to escape liquidation itself. I could believe that "Force X" is subordinate to the International Communist Conspiracy, and I could believe that "Force X" is the inner core of that Conspiracy and so controls Khrushchev and similar vermin, but I cannot believe that two wolves are peacefully munching one rabbit.

Less Blood-Pressure, Please

If not two, then not three or five or ten. What we have said about "Force X" will apply, ***mutatis mutandis,*** to any other conspiratorial group that we may consider in connection with the Communists. Let us, therefore, draw some conclusions.

On the basis of the information supplied by Mr. de Courcy, and on the basis of our own deductions concerning the probable structure of the Conspiracy, we recognize that "Force X" may be:

(1) An inner circle, comparable to, if not identical with, the Communist Security System.

(2) A formal arm of the Conspiracy, comparable to the official Communist Party in the United States or the Secret Police, and like them controlled from above.

(3) A large and highly organized gang of racketeers, who, like all ordinary criminals, "take the cash and let the credit go," intent only on loot today and loot tomorrow, but with no long-range plans or cosmocratic ambitions. Such a gang would naturally be encouraged and protected by the Communists, and would naturally perform services for cash fees or in exchange for protection and opportunities. (Note that China is now the principal source of the narcotics commonly used by drug-addicts, so that one of the most profitable branches of the gang's business depends on supplies from Communist territory.) This, however, would make the gang, for all practical purposes, a Communist subsidiary or instrumentality, and it could not be "more powerful" than its employers.

Those are, I think, the three most probable explanations, but others are possible, viz.:

(4) That our inferences about the Conspiracy are incorrect, and that "Force X" and the Communists really are independent in the sense that neither controls the other.

(5) That the data supplied by Mr. de Courcy are wrong, in part or in their entirety, either because his informants were mistaken or because they were supplied with false information (a common trick in all intelligence work) or because they or Mr. de Courcy have some interest in deceiving us. Thus "Force X," as described to us, may not exist at all.

Now we may differ widely in the percentage of probability that we assign to each of those five explanations, and it will certainly do no harm to argue about them for the purpose of clarifying our own thinking and of eliciting from one another such incidental information as each of us may have that is relevant to the subject. But obviously, no one of the five hypotheses is *certainly* right or *certainly* wrong. And I trust that no one will place an extraordinary strain on his neuro-vascular system to shout at the rest of us.

Serious argument is futile when what we obviously need is more evidence. That evidence is available. A great deal must now be in the possession of various police forces throughout the United States and either has not been assembled or has been suppressed by political pressures. A vast amount of evidence was concealed when the gang around Mr. Macmillan succeeded in covering up most of the Profumo scandals, but the greater part of it is still there. In the opinion of the best informed observers, a *thorough* investigation of the activities of Bobbie Baker, and his high-ranking accomplices in the Administration, would uncover a vast cesspool of corruption necessarily connected with the one in England, because some specialists in vice and crime shuttle back and forth from one country to the other. Probably any one of the hundreds of known nests of drug-addicts, perverts, and degenerates in Washington (or others found in any other large city) would expose a trail that could be followed back to the lair of some criminal syndicate or subsidiary thereof.

What "Force X" is or is not can be ascertained only by systematic and relentless inquiry conducted with governmental powers; and while it might take a long time for such an investigation to attain certainty, every bit of additional evidence would enable us to calculate probabilities more accurately. In the meantime, you can't prove anything by waving your arms.

Horrid Hypotheses

So far as I can see, all hypotheses regarding conspiracies that may be associated with the Communist Conspiracy are in the same status as views about "Force X." The evidence comes, of course, from other sources, is of varying degrees of probability, can be reconciled with more or less difficulty with what we know or think we can deduce with some assurance concerning the Communists, and is susceptible to different ranges of alternative interpretations. In some cases religious belief will strongly affect our estimates: A formidable and powerful conspiracy of Satanists will seem likely only to those who believe in a Devil having the power to intervene, directly or indirectly, in the affairs of this world. In others, a recognition of adverse interests or inveterate antipathies is very likely to color our opinions. But we are certainly dealing with hypotheses based on inadequate data. The most probable cannot be reasonably stated as a certainty; the least probable cannot reasonably be pronounced an impossibility. To prove or disprove anything, we shall need many more facts than we now have at our disposal.

I confess that I cannot understand the extraordinary amount of passion that can be generated by violent asseverations and hysterical denunciations of theses that can be established or refuted only by ascertaining facts. Quarrels on this subject remind me of two men whom I once saw engage in a violent brawl to determine which of two teams would win a ball game on the following day. I could not but wonder whether they imagined that their exertions would, through some sympathetic or methectic magic, affect the result.

Less Heat, More Light

No display of temper will change historical facts. The hair-pulling matches in which some Americans engage to vindicate their favorite hypotheses would be comic, if they were not tragic in their consequences: personal antagonisms, disruption of conservative organizations, and, quite possibly, defeat and death for all of us. I should suppose that even the most perfervid champions of antithetical hypotheses would realize, if they paused to think about it for a moment, that the only way to settle their argument — to say nothing of accomplishing something for their country — is to unite in demanding of their state and federal governments the kind of searching and unremitting inquiry into the Communist Conspiracy that we have urgently needed for fifty years and have never had.

Few Americans realize that all of our uncertainties and the futile quarrels that they occasion are directly caused by the International Communist Conspiracy's success in stifling, frustrating, or preventing official investigation. A raid, carried out jointly by the State of Michigan and Federal officers in 1922 on the headquarters of a nest of homicidal vermin disclosed evidence that should have scared every sober American as much as though a bullet had whizzed past his ear. But the net result was that a gang of subversives, headed by the malodorous Felix Frankfurter, stopped in 1925 all Federal investigation of the enemies in our midst. Nothing more was done by our Federal government, despite its obligation under the Constitution to protect us from foreign enemies, until a great American, Martin

Activities (see his new book, MARTIN DIES' STORY; The Bookmailer, New York; $5.00). Mr. Dies' committee accomplished a great deal, despite open opposition and clandestine harassment from the great War Criminal in the White House and the scabrous louts with which that being surrounded himself.

In the Senate, a valiant beginning was made by Senator McCarthy, but we all know what happened to him; and we know that all inquiry into treason in Washington was effectively stopped when Eisenhower issued his un-Constitutional order to protect the vicious vermin lodged in our government from interrogation.

Both the House and the Senate Committees have done the best that they could, I believe, in the face of enormous pressures from the criminals who had captured the Treasury of the United States and could use our money to prevent us from learning about our blood-thirsty enemies. But such inquiries were necessarily limited to the peripheral and superficial.

Some years ago, Judge Robert Morris, one of the most experienced and staunch of all Congressional investigators, in a radio broadcast, stated that *no* Congressional committee had *ever* been able to investigate subversion and treason effectively, because the investigation, whenever it began to approach the higher echelons of the Conspiracy, was stopped by *"irresistible pressures."*

Obviously, what we Americans must do, if we wish to go on living, is to generate pressures which make those that once seemed "irresistible" seem as puny as the waving of a cockroach's antennae.

The information is there and available in vast quantities. It is constantly and almost automatically coming to light; the trouble is that, if you read the

Rangers, on the authority of the Attorney General of Texas, raided a criminal hang-out and discovered documents that astonished even seasoned observers. The membership of the Communist Party in Texas had been officially estimated at about five hundred. That was obviously too low, but few were prepared for the discovery of a list containing the names of *ten thousand* international criminals, members or conscious accomplices of the Conspiracy, residing in Texas. As I write, it is rumored that Earl Warren, if not soon impeached and brought to trial, will make heroic efforts to suppress that list, acting either in his capacity as Boss of the Warren Crew in the Supreme Court Building or in his capacity as chairman of Johnson's special Committee to Conceal. Whether those efforts succeed will depend on you, my fellow Americans.

Armageddon

I venture to suggest—even to urge—that we Americans suspend our vexatious *disputaillerie* about conjectures and concentrate our united efforts on obtaining the basic information that we need, not merely to settle our arguments, but to survive.

I do not see how there can be a reasonable objection to that policy, with which even the most incensed should concur. We are prudent men and we therefore know that every prudent man knows that—if it happens that he is unjustly accused of a crime of which he is innocent—he cannot destroy public documents and sandbag witnesses on their way to the Grand Jury without arousing some grave suspicions that he may be less innocent than a new-born lamb on the hills of Arcadia.

We must obtain all possible information quickly, and we must be willing, as reasonable and practical men, to pay

demoralization of American life falls on you and me, who were too timid, too busy, or too lazy to do anything about it during the past fifty years. That means, specifically, that we must be prepared to condone and forget venial sins in public life—anything, that is, which is short of treason. We could all argue for a year, vehemently and inconclusively, about what should be a general standard of sexual morality. I hope that we would agree, however, that that standard, however much we prize it, is less important than our lives and those of our children. That question is vital, if, as informed sources in Washington assert, fifty-five Senators — a majority, mind you — are now kept in line by blackmail made possible by highly-trained and expert "call girls" operating, at the expense of American taxpayers, in collaboration with secret agents who installed concealed microphones and hidden cameras, including infra-red equipment. That, it is said, explains votes for "disarmament" and also explains the massive resistance that would be opposed to any proposal for an open and searching investigation. In the present crisis, I think it not too much to ask of even Mrs. Grundy that she look the other way for a while.

In the meantime, we certainly know enough about our enemies to attack effectively the Conspiracy on fronts that can absorb all our energies. Enough of

into their motives or antecedents a waste of time. And time is what we cannot afford to waste: We have so little of it left.

It is entirely possible that we may never be able to identify the head of the octopus, but that will matter little, if we can lop off enough of its tentacles.

I know that apocalyptic visions of cosmic disaster are usually born of disordered imaginations. I know that men tend always to exaggerate the importance of their own countries and hence of the crises of the moment. But look as I will, I cannot see a future for Western civilization anywhere in the world, if the United States is lost. What another race may do in five hundred or a thousand or ten thousand years is beyond our prevision; but the fate of human civilization as we know it depends, I fear, on what we do this year.

This is not Valley Forge: Had our forefathers lost, they would have reverted to the status of British colonies and still have enjoyed a good fortune greater than that of most of the rest of civilized mankind. This is Châlons or Tours, and the issue, quite simply, is whether the world's most hated minority, the Christian West, shall be forever obliterated by the infinite barbarism of irrational hordes. Or, to put it in less general terms, the issue is whether your children will regret having been born. ■ ■

SAINTED RELICS

■ A vase for flowers, purchased for $27, brought the highest price among 250 items sold at an auction conducted at Valkill, for many years the home of the late Mrs. Franklin D. Roosevelt.

A "nice crowd" gathered at the cottage off Route 9G in Hyde Park where many items, once used by Mrs. Roosevelt and her husband, the late President Roosevelt, had been stored, said auctioneer Wilson Proper. Two old trunks, carved with the initials "F.D.R." brought $2.50 each and a third was sold for $3.

Mr. Proper said a rosewood chair used by the President "didn't bring $10," and went unsold. He also said he kept a tray that Mrs. Roosevelt had used in bed. "I couldn't get an offer of $2 for it," he observed.

The sale brought less than $300. "I just don't understand what happened," Proper said. "I had as many as 300 people standing out there on the lawn of the cottage at one time or another but they practically laughed in my face when I started asking reasonable prices."—FROM THE POUGHKEEPSIE JOURNAL

Form No. 1588 (Revised)
Memorandum Report
(7-1-60)

(7)

Oswald, Lee H. Pre-Russian Period
K.P.

UNITED STATES SECRET SERVICE
TREASURY DEPARTMENT

ORIGIN Field (Dallas)	OFFICE Dallas, Texas	FILE NO. CO-2-34030
TYPE OF CASE Protective Research	STATUS Continued	TITLE OR CAPTION Assassination of President Kennedy Lee Harvey Oswald
INVESTIGATION MADE AT Dallas, Texas	PERIOD COVERED 12/10/63	
INVESTIGATION MADE BY Special Agent Gary R. Seale		

— Commission Exhibit No. 1804 —

DETAILS

SYNOPSIS

New York office requested to make inquiry at the schools which Lee Harvey Oswald attended while residing in New York City.

DETAILS OF INVESTIGATION

Reference is made to previous reports in this case, particularly the M/R of Special Agent George J. Sershen, New York, dated 12-5-63.

The purpose of this phase of the investigation is to develop all possible background information on Lee Harvey Oswald up until the time of his return from Russia.

Other Investigations (K.P.)

On December 10, 1963, Marguerite Oswald was interviewed at her home, 2220 Thomas Place, Fort Worth, Texas. She stated that she and Lee Harvey Oswald moved to New York City in September 1952, and that, for a short while, they resided with her oldest son, John E. Pic. She is unable to remember Pic's address. She said they left New York in January 1954. (K.P.)

Mrs. Oswald stated that, while she and Lee Oswald were living in Manhattan, he attended a Lutheran school. She stated that he attended a public school located off the concourse in the Bronx; that this school is the one from which he became truant. Mrs. Oswald stated that they then moved to E. 178th Street near the Bronx Zoo, and that Lee Oswald attended a public school near there.

DISTRIBUTION	COPIES	REPORT MADE BY	DATE
Chief	Orig.&2cc	Gary R. Seale (signature), SPECIAL AGENT	12-12-63
New York	2 cc	APPROVED (signature) 615, SPECIAL AGENT IN CHARGE	DATE 12-12-63
Dallas	2 cc		

(CONTINUE ON PLAIN PAPER)

CO-2-34030
12-12-63
Page 2.

Mrs. Oswald was unable to provide any addresses where they lived in New York, and she was unable to furnish the names of any of the schools which Oswald attended in New York.

UNDEVELOPED LEADS

The New York Office is requested to make inquiry at the schools which Lee Harvey Oswald attended while living in New York, and to obtain copies of all available records.

New York's M/R should be directed to the Protective Research Section, marked for the attention of Inspector Kelley.

GRS:mla

615

FD-302 (Rev. 3-3-59)

FEDERAL BUREAU OF INVESTIGATION

1

Date ~~11/22/63~~ NOV 30 1963

At 5:26 PM, Mrs. MARGUERITE CLAVERIE OSWALD, 2220 Thomas Place, Fort Worth, Texas, was interviewed, at which time she was advised that she did not have to make any statement, any statement she did make could be used in a court of law, and further that she had the right to consult an attorney before making a statement. Mrs. OSWALD stated she desired to make a statement to a representative of the Government from Washington. SAs CHARLES T. BROWN, JR. and W. HARLAN BROWN had previously identified themselves to Mrs. OSWALD as being Special Agents of the Federal Bureau of Investigation and as representing this Bureau with headquarters in Washington, D. C. During the interview, Mrs. OSWALD said she did not desire to make a written statement in this matter.

Mrs. OSWALD advised she is a practical nurse. She stated LEE HARVEY OSWALD is her son and he was born October 19, 1939, at New Orleans, Louisiana. She has another son, ROBERT OSWALD, a Certified Public Accountant, who resides in Denton, Texas, and another son in the U. S. Air Force during the past 15 years, whereabouts of whom is unknown.

When LEE HARVEY OSWALD was approximately 5 years of age, she moved with her family from New Orleans, Louisiana, to Fort Worth, Texas. LEE HARVEY OSWALD attained 11th grade at Arlington Heights High School in Fort Worth after having attended grammar schools in the same city.

At the age of 17, LEE HARVEY OSWALD entered the Marine Corps, serving in that organization for approximately two years until he received a "dire need" discharge. At the time of his discharge Mrs. OSWALD was ill and after the Red Cross had investigated her illness, LEE HARVEY OSWALD was discharged from the service. When he returned home to Fort Worth, it was her recollection that he remained at home for about three days and left her home for the purpose of going to work. She stated she received a letter postmarked New Orleans, Louisiana, which stated that he was going to Europe aboard a ship. She said that the next time she heard of her son, LEE HARVEY OSWALD, was when she read in the newspapers that he was in the U.S.S.R. The newspaper accounts showed that he had defected to the Soviets; however, Mrs. OSWALD said she could not believe this because he had never expressed an affinity for Communism, nor had he been known to belong to any hate groups or use words which would indicate hatred for anyone. It was her

— Commission Exhibit No. 1805 —

on 11/22/63 at Dallas, Texas File # DL 89-43

by Special Agent W. HARLAN BROWN and CHARLES T. BROWN, JR. /rmb Date dictated 11/22/63

113

This document contains neither recommendations nor conclusions of the FBI. It is the property of the FBI and is loaned to your agency; it and its contents are not to be distributed outside your agency.

COMMISSION EXHIBIT NO. 1805

2
DL 89-43

recollection that he went to Russia about 1958 and remained there about 2½ years.

About February, 1960, Mrs. OSWALD stated she made a trip to Washington, D. C., and while there had a conference with State Department officials there whom she described as top officials in the State Department. She stated they were GENE BOSTER, officer in charge of Soviet affairs, DENMAN STANFIELD, Office of Special Consular Service, and ED HICKEY, Deputy Director of the Passport Department. She also said she had the telephone number of Secretary of State DEAN RUSK, but never contacted him. She did talk to Mr. RUSK's secretary who, in turn, made her appointment with BOSTER, STANFIELD and HICKEY.

After her return to her home in Fort Worth, Texas, the State Department wrote her giving the address of her son about three weeks later. She stated she felt this was strange in that the State Department had professed no knowledge of his whereabouts when she was in Washington. The State Department first informed her that he had gone to Finland and later told her that he was living in Minsk, U.S.S.R. She said that her son, LEE HARVEY OSWALD, did not have any knowledge of her having gone to Washington and does not have such knowledge at the present time. She said the State Department arranged for him to return to the United States with his wife MARINA, a Soviet citizen who is still a Soviet alien. She stated had her son remained in Russia, she would have written the newspaper concerning her son's life before he went to the U.S.S.R. She did not know why he had defected as he had never indicated any sympathy for Russia and "loved" the Marines. At one time LEE HARVEY OSWALD stated in a letter to her that she should have no fear because he would never become a Russian citizen. She stated that he held no animosity toward anyone as far as she knew, but never had any close friends.

Mrs. OSWALD stated that LEE HARVEY's wife MARINA was a registered pharmacist in the Soviet Union and spoke French fluently, in addition to Russian. When she last heard from MARINA, she was trying to learn English.

It was Mrs. OSWALD'S recollection LEE HARVEY OSWALD returned to the United States about the last of September, 1962, and stayed with a brother for about a week or two before they moved to her home, where LEE HARVEY and his wife stayed about one month.

Mrs. OSWALD stated that about a year ago, or a little more, LEE HARVEY OSWALD kissed her good-bye and she stated she had

114

COMMISSION EXHIBIT NO. 1805—Continued

3
DL 89-43

not heard from him since that time, but inspfar as she knew he had moved to Dallas. She did know that they had one child and that he had had difficulty in finding employment in Fort Worth because no one wanted a defected Communist in his employ.

Mrs. OSWALD stated that she had never seen a rifle or any other firearms in LEE HARVEY's possession at any time and did not know anything about his activities during the past year. She could not give any information regarding the friends or associates of LEE HARVEY OSWALD, nor did she know anything concerning any organizations to which he belonged.

Mrs. OSWALD did not believe that her son had actually defected to Russia, stating he could have been shanghaied and made to remain there, although she said this was her opinion only.

During her son's Marine service, she recalled he was in the "Formosa crisis" in the summer of 1957 or 1958, having entered the Marine Corps about 1956 and being released in September, October, or November, 1958.

Mrs. OSWALD stated that her son was a brilliant boy and wanted to attend college. He did receive a high-school diploma while a member of the U. S. Marines. She stated that she raised LEE HARVEY OSWALD as an orphan because his father died before he was born.

While in high school he played football, belonged to the Y.M.C.A. and seemed to get along with others, but had no friends. He was aloof, spending spare time reading, listening to the radio and television and playing monopoly. Mrs. OSWALD stated she worked as a practical nurse and on many occasions did not have the money to pay for her children's lunches. While her sons were in school, they came home before she did almost every afternoon. LEE HARVEY OSWALD, she stated, had never caused her any trouble and she did not know of any instances in which he had been arrested. Her son, ROBERT OSWALD, attended Texas Christian University and MARINA attended that school for a short time.

She read in the papers that LEE HARVEY spoke Russian fluently and it was her belief if this were true he studied Russian in the service. He had never had any mental trouble and had never been examined by a psychiatrist at any time, Mrs. OSWALD stated. He at no time indicated any animosity toward the Government of the United States or the President.

'15

Form No. 1588 (Revised)
MEMORANDUM REPORT
(7-1-60)

UNITED STATES SECRET SERVICE
TREASURY DEPARTMENT

Oswald, Marguerite

ORIGIN Field	OFFICE Dallas, Texas	FILE NO. CO-2-34,030
TYPE OF CASE Protective Research	STATUS Continued	TITLE OR CAPTION Assassination of President Kennedy
INVESTIGATION MADE AT Dallas, Ft.Worth, Texas	PERIOD COVERED 4-30-64	Tape Recording held by Mrs. Marguerite Oswald
INVESTIGATION MADE BY SA's John Joe Howlett & Robert A. Stouart		

DETAILS

Commission Exhibit No. 1806

SYNOPSIS

Mrs. Marguerite Oswald would not allow the Secret Service to have a copy of a tape recording she has in her possession.

DETAILS OF INVESTIGATION

Inspector Kelley requested that an attempt be made to obtain a copy of a tape recording that Mrs. Oswald told the President's Commission that she had.

Other Investigations

On 4-30-64 at about 10:07 am, I telephoned Mrs. Marguerite Oswald in Ft. Worth, Texas, telephone PE-7-7677. I talked with Mrs. Oswald and SA Robert A. Steuart monitored the phone call.

I informed Mrs. Oswald that the President's Commission had requested that I obtain a copy of the tape recording that she had discussed with them. Mrs. Oswald said that she had received a letter from the President's Commission informing her that either the FBI or the Secret Service would contact her to obtain a copy of the tape. She said that she phoned the President's Commission and told them that this would not be acceptable to her and that she would handle it her own way. Mrs. Oswald said that the recording had been copied and that it was in the hands of authorities, however, she would not identify who she was talking about when she said authorities. When I asked Mrs. Oswald if I could obtain a copy of the recording she said that she had discussed the matter with the President's Commission and suggested that I contact them. Mrs. Oswald was informed that the President's Commission had requested that I obtain a copy of the tape recording. She said that she would not specifically refuse to give me a copy of the tape, but simply suggested that I contact the President's Commission again. Mrs. Oswald would give no reason for not letting

DISTRIBUTION	COPIES	REPORT MADE BY	DATE
Chief ✓	Orig. & 1 cc	SPECIAL AGENT	4-30-64
Dallas	2 cc's	APPROVED Forrest V. Sorrels — SPECIAL AGENT IN CHARGE	4-30-64

1468

(CONTINUE ON PLAIN PAPER)

U. S. GOVERNMENT PRINTING OFFICE 16—61600-4

me have a copy of the tape and would not tell me what she told the President's Commission. She said that she suggested that I contact the President's Commission and they could tell me what she told them, if they wanted to, however, she wouldn't.

During the conversation Mrs. Oswald said that she was going back to Washington to appear before the President's Commission and I asked her if she planned to present the Commission with a copy of this tape at that time and she would make no comment.

Mrs. Oswald was very cautious and evasive during the conversation and would not allow herself to be pinned down to a particular answer. She was also very careful not to reveal any information or her plans

In summary, Mrs. Oswald would not refuse to give us a copy of the tape but at the same time would not talk about arrangements for us to obtain a copy. She said it was not acceptable for her for the FBI or Secret Service to obtain a copy of this tape; that a copy was already in the hands of "authorities" and she would handle the matter in her own way.

DISPOSITION

Case remains open. This phase of the investigation is considered closed.

JJH:VS

SECRET SERVICE
RECEIVED

COMMISSION EXHIBIT NO. 1806—Continued

FD-302 (Rev. 1-25-60)

FEDERAL BUREAU OF INVESTIGATION

OSWALD, ROBERT
PIC, JOHN
Oswald, Marguerite

1 Involved or Interviewed

Date April 6, 1964

EDWIN GREWE, Resident Director, Bethlehem Children's Home (formerly Evangelical Lutheran Bethlehem Orphan Asylum), 9100 Grant Street, was recontacted. He advised that the records he previously furnished were all the records in his files which pertain to LEE HARVEY OSWALD, ROBERT OSWALD and JOHN PIC, who in early 1940 were at the home when it was called the Evangelical Lutheran Bethlehem Orphan Asylum.

GREWE advised there was no one at the children's home at present who was there when the OSWALDS and PIC attended. GREWE furnished the following information concerning persons who were at the children's home in early 1940 or who were associated with the children's home during the period the OSWALD boys were at the home:

1) Pastor HENRY L. HONOLD, Christ Lutheran Church; residence - 627 Caffin Avenue, New Orleans, Louisiana; was pastor for the children at the Evangelical Lutheran Bethlehem Orphan Asylum.

2) Reverend M. R. LE CRON - deceased; Reverend LE CRON baptized LEE HARVEY OSWALD.

3) Mr. MARTIN GUND, deceased.

4) Mr. M. GERSTNER, deceased.

5) Pastor JOHN NAU - presently professor of religion and philosophy at the University of Southern Mississippi, Hattiesburg, Mississippi; NAU succeeded Pastor LE CRON at Redeemer Lutheran Church, New Orleans, and the application of OSWALD for admittance to the home went through NAU.

6) Mr. FRED GROTH - presently a teacher in a Lutheran school at Manawa, Wisconsin, and his address is 762 Depot Street, Manawa, Wisconsin. GROTH was superintendent at the children's home during the time the OSWALDS and PIC were at the home and Mrs. GROTH was the matron at the home.

7) Mr. ED KOSCHMANN was a teacher who lived at the children's home during the time the OSWALDS and PIC [redacted]

— Commission Exhibit No. 1807 —

On 3/30/64 at New Orleans, Louisiana File # NO 100-16601

by SA DONALD C. STEINMEYER /lyc Date dictated 4/1/64

20

COMMISSION EXHIBIT NO. 1807

NO 100-16601
2

were at the home. KOSCHMANN presently resides at 5511 Morningside Drive, Cleveland 29, Ohio. KOSCHMANN is principal of St. Mark's Lutheran School, Cleveland, Ohio.

21

COMMISSION EXHIBIT No. 1807—Continued

NO 89-69

Set forth are copies of the records of the Bethlehem Childrens Home previously furnished by Mr. Grewe.

22

COMMISSION EXHIBIT No. 1807—Continued

Evangelical Lutheran Bethlehem Orphan Asylum

(APPLICATION FOR RELEASE OF CHILDREN.)

New Orleans, La., Jan. 19 1944

TO THE BOARD OF DIRECTORS,

GENTLEMEN:

I, the undersigned, respectfully apply for the release of

Lee Oswald

from your ~~asylum~~ Home to me

I promise to take him under my personal supervision and give him a Christian training according to the teachings and Tenets of the Ev. Lutheran Church.

I also agree and promise to pay all arrears for board, amounting to $——

Applicant Mrs. Marguerite C. Oswald

Relation of Applicant Mother

The Committee on Applications hereby approves and recommends the above application.

H. L. Harold, Chairman

Granted by the Board of Directors at a meeting held Jan. 11, 1944

M. Grund President

M. Gerstner Secretary

23

COMMISSION EXHIBIT No. 1807—Continued

APPLICATION BLANK.

New Orleans, La., Dec. 26 1942

To the President and Board of Directors of the
Evangelical Lutheran Bethlehem Orphan Asylum Association.

I, We, the undersigned, hereby make application for the admission to your Home of

Name in full	Age	Born: Date	Born: Place	Christened: When (Date)	Christened: Where Place and Church	Christened: By Whom (Pastor)
Oswald, Lee	3	10/18/39	New Orleans		Redeemer	Rev. M. R. Le Crone

Father Robert Lee Oswald ~~living~~ dead Address

Mother Mrs L. Oswald living ~~dead~~ Address 111 Sherwood Forest Blvd

Date and place of marriage

Tutor Address

Occupation of party making application Telephone Operator

Business Address Residence

Can you contribute? Yes If so, how much per month $10.00

Will you supply shoes and clothing? Yes

If application is accepted, I hereby agree to sign and abide by the Association's contract, and leave the boys in the Asylum until at least one year after confirmation, and girl's until they have reached the age of 18 years.

x Mrs Marguerite Oswald

The Committee on Applications hereby approves and recommends the above application.

H. L. Harold Chairman

Pastor

Redeemer Church

Approved 192 Rec. Secty.

Date entered Asylum 12/26/42 192 A. C. Schorr Supt.

Date Confirmed 192 Age

Pastor , Church

Date of release 192 Age

24

COMMISSION EXHIBIT No. 1807—Continued

Name

ate entered Asylum 192 Board per month $

Year 192	Board per month	Amount Paid	Date Paid	Year 192	Board per month	Amount Paid	Date Paid	Year 192	Board per month	Amount Paid	Date Paid
alance due											
nuary											
ebruary											
arch											
pril											
ay											
ne											
ly											
ugust											
ptember											
ctober											
ovember											
ecember											
tal											
alance due											
nuary											
bruary											
arch											
pril											
ay											
ne											
ly											
ugust											
ptember											
ctober											
ovember											
ecember											
tal											
alance due											
nuary											
bruary											
arch											
ril											
ay											
ne											
ly											
ugust											
ptember											
tober											
vember											
cember											

Whooping Cough
Measles
Mumps
Chicken Pox

Diph.
Toxoid
Given.

25

APPLICATION BLANK.

New Orleans, La., 12-23 1941

To the President and Board of Directors of the
Evangelical Lutheran Bethlehem Orphan Asylum Association.

I, We, the undersigned, hereby make application for the admission to your Home of

Name in full	Age	Born: Date	Born: Place	Christened: When (Date)	Christened: Where Place and Church	Christened: By Whom (Pastor)
PIC, JOHN EDWARD	9	1-17-32	New Orleans, La.		Trinity Ev. Church	Rev. [illegible]
OSWALD, ROBERT	7	4-7-34	" "		Redeemer Church	Rev. H.R. [illegible]

Father Edward John Pic living/dead Address New Orleans, La.

Mother Marguerite [illegible] Oswald living/dead Address 1010 Bartholomew St.

Date and place of marriage Gulfport / New Orleans, La. Aug. 29, 1929.

Tutor — Address

Occupation of party making application Housewife

Business Address 1010 Bartholomew Street Residence —

Can you contribute? Yes. If so, how much per month $ 20.00 [illegible]

Will you supply shoes and clothing? Yes,

If application is accepted, I hereby agree to sign and abide by the Association's contract, and leave the boys in the Asylum until at least one year after confirmation, and girl's until they have reached the age of 18 years.

The Committee on Applications hereby approves and recommends the above application.

H. L. [illegible] Chairman Pastor J. H. [illegible]

Redeemer Church, Church

Approved 192 Rec. Secty.

Date entered Asylum 192 [illegible] Supt.

Date Confirmed 192 Age

Pastor Church

26

Date of release 192 Age

Name

Date entered Asylum 192 \ Board per month $

Year 192	Board per month	Amount Paid	Date Paid	Year 192	Board per month	Amount Paid	Date Paid	Year 192	Board per month	Amount Paid	Date Paid
Balance due											
January											
February											
March											
April											
May	House - Rent - 45.00 per mo.										
June	[illegible] home 2100.00 - 2000.00 [illegible]										
July	5000.00 insurance - [illegible] 2 yrs on insurance										
August	22.00 [illegible] - - - - -										
September	25.00 Income - [illegible] - 20.00 [illegible] 500, -										
October											
November											
December					[illegible] Washington, [illegible]						
Total Balance due	By John Oswald [illegible]										
January											
February											
March											
April											
May											
June											
July											
August											
September											
October											
November											
December											
Total Balance due											
January											
February											
March											
April											
May											
June											
July											
August											
September											
October											
November											

27

COMMISSION EXHIBIT No. 1807—Continued

New Orleans, La., Jan 2 1942

To the President and Board of Directors of the
Evangelical Lutheran Bethlehem Orphan Asylum Association.

I, We, the undersigned, hereby make application for the admission to your Home of

Name in full	Age	Born: Date	Born: Place	Christened: When (Date)	Christened: Where Place and Church	Christened: By Whom (Pastor)
Oswald, Robert Edward Jr.	7	4/7/34	New Orleans	4/29/34	N. O. LA. Evangelical	Rev. A. J. Schroer

Father Robert Ed. Oswald ~~living~~ dead Address 831 Pauline St. - Aug 28

Mother Marg. Clavenie Oswald living ~~dead~~ Address (1010 [illegible])

Date and place of marriage July 19, 1933 - New Orleans, La

Tutor ______ Address ______

Occupation of party making application ______

Business Address ______ Residence ______

Can you contribute? 10.00 If so, how much per month $ 10.00

Will you supply shoes and clothing? Yes

If application is accepted, I hereby agree to sign and abide by the Association's contract, and leave the boys in the Asylum until at least one year after confirmation, and girl's until they have reached the age of 18 years.

The Committee on Applications hereby approves and recommends the above application.

x Mrs. Lee Oswald
Mother

______ Chairman

Pastor ______

______ Church

Approved 12/9/41 192

______ Rec. Secty

Date entered Asylum 1/3/42 192

A. C. Goetsch Supt.

Date Confirmed ______ 192 Age ______

Pastor ______ Church

Date of release ______ 192 Age ______

28

To whom released ______

______ Supt.

COMMISSION EXHIBIT No. 1807—Continued

Name Oswald, Mrs. L. + Mother

Date entered Asylum Jan. 3, 1942 192 Board per month $20.00

Year 1942	Board per month	Amount Paid	Date Paid	Year 192	Board per month	Amount Paid	Date Paid	Year 192	Board per month	Amount Paid	Date Paid
Balance due											
January		20.00	[illegible]								
February		10.00	2/1								
March		20.00	3/15								
April		20.00	4/21								
May		20.00	5/23								
June		10.00	6/11								
July											
August		20.00	8/27								
September		20.00	9/18								
October		[illegible]	10/20								
November											
December											
Total Balance due											
January											
February											
March											
April											
May											
June											
July											
August											
September											
October											
November											
December											
Total Balance due											
January											
February											
March											
April											
May											
June											
July											
August											
September											
October											
November											

29

Rejected

Feb. 1, 1945
4801 Victor
Dallas, Texas

My Dear Rev. Honald,

I have just received your letter and it is apparent to me that there is a misunderstanding somewhere. My reasons for wishing to have the children return are due to the fact that when I marry I shall have to travel with my husband to such places as he may have to work. We are not able to establish a home now for the children because Mr. Ekdahl's work takes him from city to city. He was only in Dallas a few months when he was transferred to New York then to Austin & now Fort Worth. He expects shortly to be transferred to New York but then expects to be sent out again to some other locality for a few months. Under the circumstances it is impossible for us to take the children, traveling, living at hotels and attempting to arrange for their schooling. For these reasons I think you will understand better why I wish to have the boys return to the home. They are more than willing to go since it was their home for the past few years I would rather they stay there than in some strange boarding school. I must ask you if you will please present these

30

circumstances to the Board of Directors again and prevail upon them to reconsider their decision so that the boys may have a permanent place of abode in preference to moving them from school to school

Yours Truly
Mrs Marguerite Oswald

31

COMMISSION EXHIBIT No. 1807—Continued

EVANGELICAL LUTHERAN BETHLEHEM ORPHAN ASYLUM
5413 N. PETERS STREET
PHONE FRANKLIN 5031
NEW ORLEANS, LA.

Dec. 9, 1941

Page No. 3.

APPLICATION COMMITTEE: No written report received, however, Pastor Honold reported verbally on several cases as follows:-

A member of the Board of Directors of the Home for Incurables advised that they would return $150.00 of the money paid them for the care of Miss. Hilda Poeck.

A case was submitted by Pastor Nau from Redeemer Church involving a boy 10 years of age, 1 boy 8 years and another 2 years. The mother was married to a Mr.Pic ~~who died~~, later married to a Mr. Oswald who has also died. While she has some money left from insurance policies finds it necessary to seek employment and would like to have the children placed in the home. Pastor Nau was informed we could do nothing about the boy 2 years old, but something might be done about the other two children. Matter placed in the hands of the Committee with full power to act.

HAUPT CASE: Mr. & Mrs.Geo.Haupt requested permission to take their niece 8 years old with them for the Christmas Holidays. The mother has given permission. They would like to take the child permanently and Pastor Honold suggested they take lexgal adoption proceedings. The mother is not willing to agree to such proceedings. Another plan was suggested. The fos ter home arrangements whereby we would release the child to Mr.& Mrs.Haupt and still retain guardianship over her. The mother is willing to agree to such an arrangement, which would have to be worked through the Juvenile Court. On motion made seconded and passed the matter left in the hands of the committee with full power to act.

The report was then adopted as a whole.

SUPERINTENDENT'S REPORT: Superintendent reported no change in the enrollment since last report. Fifty children on roll, forty nine in the home and Leonard King at Austin. Superintendet also advised that all children has been placed in different homes Thanksgiving Day. The Film of the home had been shown in Passcagoula and while the attendance was not very good the collection amounted to $20.50. Pastor Honold suggested we try and get the parents and relatives of the children to take them from the home during the Christmas Holidays after the Christmas Eve. celebration. The matter was left to the discretion of the Superintendent.

SCHOOL BOARD: No report. Mr. Heintzen suggested that we include in the Pension Plan our teachers Mr. Koschmann and Miss.Anna Wegner. On motion made, seconded and passed this was approved.

32

COMMISSION EXHIBIT No. 1807—Continued

EVANGELI[illegible] [illegible]UTHERAN [illegible]LEHEM [illegible]RPHAN ASYLUM
[illegible]13 N. PETERS STREET
PHONE FRANKLIN 5031
NEW ORLEANS, LA.

Sept. 12, 1942.

Page No. 2.

Victor was living in a very nice appartment and the income was $34.00 per week between Mrs. Victor and Betty. Motion made and seconded and passed that if the proper signatures for the release could be obtained that Clara be Released to her mother.

Pic-Oswald Case. The young boy having reached the proper age the committee was authorized to accept the boy into the home. Board to be paid $10.00 per month.

Helmers Case: It was moved seconded and passed that the two other Hellmers children be released.

It was decided that Mr Supt. Groth furnish the board the names and amounts being paid by different families for board.

Superintendent's report: Report shows 2 admitted, releaseded 3 on roll 46, in the home 35. Dorothy Tuesch will remain with Mr. & Mrs. Mell Ott until February at least. She is now attending Nicholls High School.

Festival Committee: No report.

Communications:

Ladies Auxiliary proceedings for August 1942, received, read and filed as part of these records.

Letter received from Rayl & Lob enclosing release from Mercy Soniat Hospital for services rendered to Mr. Wm. Heinrichs.

Letter received from Rayl & Lob requesting payment of $23.72 amount expended in the Heinrichs Estate over and above the amount tendered them in signed checks. It was moved seconded and passed that this amount be paid.

Unfinished Business.

Heinrichs nam[illegible]sed on vault in Hope Mausoleum. This matter is being attended to.

General Assembly. It was approved that the General Assembly be held Monday Nov. 30,1942. at St.Paul's School House.

Tires for Truck. If it is found necessary that tires are needed application will have to be made to the rationing board.

New Business.

Mr. Webert suggested that we circulate the film prepared showing activities of the home in Texas before Christmas which might bring in larger contributions. The matter left in the hands of Supt.

A Ledger Book at the Bethlehem Children's Home, 9100 Grant Street, contained the following entries concerning LEE OSWALD, ROBERT OSWALD and JOHN PIC:

Name	Born	Baptized	Parents	Monthly Payment	Admitted to Home	Released
OSWALD, ROBERT	4/7/34 New Orleans, La.	4/29/34 by Rev. SCHERER, Evangelical.	Mrs. LEE OSWALD, New Orleans, La.	$10.00	1/3/42, age 7	To mother Mrs. LEE OSWALD, June 1944
OSWALD, LEE	10/18/39 New Orleans, La.	(no date) by Rev. H. R. LeCRON, Redeemer.	Mrs. LEE OSWALD, New Orleans, La.	$10.00	12/26/43 age 3	To mother Mrs. LEE OSWALD, 1/20/44
PIC, JOHN	1/17/32 New Orleans, La.	1/31/32 by Rev. A. SCHERER, Evangelical.	Mrs. LEE OSWALD	$10.00	1/3/42, age 9	To mother Mrs. LEE OSWALD, June 1944

34

COMMISSION EXHIBIT No. 1807—Continued

TRANSLATION FROM FRENCH

"MY SON DID NOT ASSASSINATE KENNEDY"

Exclusive Story by the Mother of Oswald.

(From "Le Nouveau Candide" No. 153, week of April 2 to April 9, 1964.)

This woman bears an accursed name. To the whole world her son is the presumed assassin of President Kennedy. But Marguerite Oswald refuses to believe what the world says.

In her eyes, a mischievous youngster who played hooky in order to go to look at animals at the zoo, a good young man who sent small gifts to her, could not have committed this frightful crime. The Dallas tragedy uprooted Marguerite Oswald. At 55 years of age, this old nurse without resources, this simple woman who has neither experience nor connections, threw herself into an unbelievable enterprise: she wants to proclaim her son's innocence.

To tear down the structure of presumptions raised against Lee Harvey Oswald, she probed her memory, sifted police reports and conceived a strange theory: her son appears to have been an agent of the American Intelligence Service.

We present, without pronouncing any judgment, her arguments, which express perhaps more maternal love than shrewdness.

Even if this was only a desperate appeal of a mother refusing to believe that she gave birth to a monster, this document would deserve to be included in the record. But it contains likewise some disturbing revelations.

COMMISSION EXHIBIT No. 1808

The Warren Commission - charged with the investigation of the assassination of Kennedy - has apparently already decided on a verdict of guilty for Oswald. The argument of the mother of Lee Harvey raises questions to which the report of this Commission should give answers, if it is to dissipate once and for all the doubts which still hang heavy over the Dallas affair.

* * *

The Mother of Oswald Says: "MY SON IS INNOCENT." They Doctored a Photo to Ruin Him.

"Lee Harvey Oswald, my son, was a victim of a trap. He was betrayed, killed, and then shamefully calumniated. I am convinced of it today.

"But the American press poisoned the public mind by printing indiscriminately false information furnished by the police and echoing fantastic rumors. The same attitude abroad was demonstrated by a French magazine, which put on its cover a photo of my son holding a rifle in his hand, having this caption: 'With this photo, there is no more mystery in Dallas.'

They Pasted On the Face

"How absurd! Tens of thousands of Texans and millions of Americans own rifles or revolvers. Millions of Americans have their pictures taken with their weapons in hand. This does not mean that they are potential criminals. On the other hand, there is no proof that this rifle was used to kill President Kennedy, or even that it was of the same type as the assassin's weapon.

- 2 -

COMMISSION EXHIBIT No. 1808—Continued

"Furthermore, if my son intended to commit a political crime or if he already fired at a general, as they claim (1), he was intelligent enough not to leave such a photograph lying about.

Note (1): Lee Oswald is suspected of being the man who last year in Dallas attempted to kill General Walker, one of the heads of the John Birch Society, a rightist-extremist organization.

"Moreover, I doubt the authenticity of this document. My son was very thin since his return from Russia. But he appeared fairly heavy in this photo. I asked some experts. They told me that it seemed to be a composite picture. Apparently, the face of my son was pasted upon someone else's body.

"My daughter-in-law never talked to me about this photo during the weeks we lived together after Lee's arrest. Yet, we discussed the affair interminably, recalling the smallest details. She never made an allusion to this photo.

Absurd Stories

"And then, three months later, she appears to have sold this document which could be used against her husband.

"The police minutely searched my daughter-in-law's belongings as well as mine, seizing all our photographs. Why was that one not published immediately? Why would one wait for three months before revealing it? It is curious that this document was put in circulation at the moment when serious doubts were expressed in the Warren Commission and when new testimony tended to establish my son's innocence.

"Newspapers spread the most absurd stories about our family. We were good and loyal Americans. We never had a brush with justice. Lee never was in trouble. My children were and still are patriots. My three boys joined the Army as volunteers. One of my sons has been a career army man for fourteen years.

"I was born fifty-five years ago at New Orleans. My father was of French origin. His name was Jean Claverie;he spoke French all the time. He was one of the first streetcar conductors in the city; those famous streetcars which we see in films. He was a model employee. My mother was of German origin; her name was Dora Stucke. As soon as I completed my high school studies, I started to work as a secretary for a lawyer.

"In 1929, at the age of twenty-one, I married Edward J. Eic (sic). He was a railway porter. He left me after I had my first-born, John Edward, now a sergeant in the Air Force. We were divorced in 1932. The following year I married Robert Edward Lee Oswald, a young man of Irish origin, who was in the insurance business.

General's Given Name

"My first born Robert (sic) works today at a brick and cement factory. My husband and I were very happy.

"Alas, he died in August 1939, of a heart attack, a few days before Poland was invaded by Hitler. I expected a child at the time, the one whom I named Lee Harvey. He was born a few months later, on October 18, 1939. The name "Lee" is traditional with the Oswald family, in honor of General Lee, Commander in Chief of the Southern forces during the War of Secession (sic), a hero for all patriots. Harvey was the name of my husband's mother.

"It was not easy to raise three small children by myself during the war, but my youngsters did not lack anything. Lee was an extremely intelligent child for his age, to the point that parents in the neighborhood were jealous.

He Cut Classes

"In 1945, I married for the third time. He was an engineer from Boston, Edwin A. Ekdahl. The two eldest boys were sent to a military college. Lee stayed with me. After my divorce in 1948, I went to join my son Edward, who was stationed in New York.

"We lived modestly. I had to work hard, but Lee was not unhappy. What he, who had grown up in Texas, missed was the great open spaces and the fresh air. He was suffocating in the midst of skyscrapers and under the elevated railroad. He was bored in class, where his comrades were less advanced than he. Fascinated by the zoological gardens he "cut" classes to see the animals in their cages. It was his passion. When it rained, he read in the public libraries.

"New York authorities are very strict with school children who skip classes. In Texas, teachers close their eyes to it. In New York Lee was brought back to school by a policeman and reprimanded. But he stayed away from school again. This time he was taken, as the law demands, and brought before the judge who sent him to a "rehabilitation" school.

"Subsequently they returned him to me and advised me to go back to Texas, for New York was a very hard place in which to live, for a child who needed the open air. Thus, we returned to New Orleans. Not once did Lee cut school and easily earned his high-school diploma.

Recruited by the C. I. A.

"No one has ever told me that he was examined by psychiatrists and that it was discovered that he could be dangerous. What a ridiculous invention! If it were so, why did they return him to me? Why didn't they treat him?

"If Lee was an unbalanced boy, a delinquent, would they have accepted him at sixteen in the ranks of the Aviation Cadet Corps, i. e., in the student pilot corps of the U. S. Air Force? They require from the members of the Cadet Corps moral and physical qualities of future officers. If my son had a tainted medical record, he would not have been admitted among the cadets.

"I am making public, at the same time as this statement, a photo of my son Lee in a cadet uniform stressing the fact that police, who so generously distributed other documents, had this one carefully hidden. No doubt, it did not fit in with the image of Lee they wanted to create.

"Lee was sixteen years old when he wanted to enlist in the Marines. The circumstances in which he chose this elite branch of service,

- 5 -

COMMISSION EXHIBIT No. 1808—Continued

in my opinion, are in glaring contradiction to reports, according to which, Lee frequented with communists at that time, and was, himself, a 'red' and an admirer of Karl Marx.

"For my part, and taking into consideration what I know about the life of my son, I think that, on the contrary, he was recruited by the C. I. A. (2), that he was sent by this organization to Russia, then to Dallas to infiltrate subversive organizations and - who knows - to expose a conspiracy against Kennedy.

Note (2): C. I. A.: Central Intelligence Agency, American federal intelligence and counterespionage organization.

"This is a theory, but it seems to me that it conforms to my son's conduct from the day in 1954, when he came home accompanied by an officer in uniform.

"This officer told me that the country needed boys like Lee - alert, educated and loyal - and that I should let him enlist in the Marines, despite his youth. I hesitated a little, then gave my consent.

"But military authorities thought later that Lee was a little too young and delayed his enlistment by six months. Lee brought to the house a big volume, 'The Marine Training Manual,' and learned it by heart to such a point, that I teased him calling him 'general.' In my heart I was proud of him.

"At the same time that he studied the Marines' manual, Lee read 'Das Kapital' by Karl Marx. I have never asked him questions on this subject. I was sure that military authorities - who supervised the training of my son - required him to study this work. The Marines are an expeditionary force and I suppose that officers expected to make a type of intelligence agent out of Lee and that they asked him to gather documentary evidence on communism. This is a current practice for candidates for the C. I. A.

- 6 -

COMMISSION EXHIBIT No. 1808—Continued

A Happy "Marine"

"Sure enough, Lee never told me that he worked for an espionage agency and I never asked him about it. But since when does a secret agent reveal his true profession to his mother? Did the parents of pilot Powers, brought down in Russia while he was at the controls of his U 2 reconnaissance plane, know that their son worked for the C. I. A.?

"No one came forward to say that Lee was an intelligence agent. But is it not a rule in the secret services never to divulge the name of those who work for them? It is possible that even now, in order to track down the real criminals, Lee's superiors keep silent.

"The fact remains that, when he became seventeen years old, Oswald enlisted in the Marines and was sent to camp where he specialized in electronics and aviation. The Chief of Staff of the Marines sent me a diploma, told me that I should be proud to be the mother of Lee Harvey Oswald and suggested that I frame the diploma and hang it on the wall.

"Lee was always very happy to be in the Marines. All his letters showed his enthusiasm. When he was on leave he wore his uniform all the time. He repeated on every occasion how proud he was to be a Marine. He sent me money from time to time and presents from foreign countries such as the Philippines and Japan. If he had difficulties in the service, I never knew anything about them. His 'bad conduct' seems to me an invention. The fact was that he was promoted to the rank of corporal.

"I wish to straighten out another error here. The press stated that my son appeared to have been decorated as a champion carbine marksman. What a fib! It was not my son but his battalion which was decorated. It was a collective decoration for the whole team. There is nothing to prove that Lee was the best shot of the battalion or even that he was an excellent marksman.

A Bed in the Kitchen

"After returning to California from Japan, Lee often telephoned me. Thus he learned that I had an accident. I wanted to hide it from him, so as not to worry him. I was then a department manager in a store at Fort Worth, Texas. A big glass demijohn fell on me from above and I was seriously injured. I had to go to a hospital, for an X-ray examination, and all this cost so much. I was not insured. I had to sell my furniture. I lost my job.

- 7 -

"Lee sent me a telegram saying that he had been in contact with the Red Cross concerning me. Later on, in September 1959, he came home. He had an emergency discharge because of my illness. This procedure is called 'dire (need) discharge' (discharge because of necessity).

"I put a bed in the kitchen and Lee slept there.

While Reading a Newspaper

"Next morning he said to me: 'Mother, I madea decision. I am going to work on a cargo boat. I wish to engage in export and import. I would not be able to earn enough money here.'

"On the third day he said good-bye to me.

"I was stunned by this sudden departure. And now I think that it was impossible for him to decide like this, in one night, to go to Russia. He must have received an order.

"Lee left me one hundred dollars. One week later he wrote to me from New Orleans that he was shipping out on a boat going to Europe.

"It was only in November 1959, when reading a newspaper, that I learned that my son was in Moscow and that he wanted to renounce his American citizenship.

"Borrowing some money I got together the sum necessary to take me to Washington in order to obtain my son's address. They gave it to me: it was Hotel Metropole. [illegible]ote to him and he replied: 'Mamma, please send me some money.' With the return mail I sent him a check for twenty dollars. He wrote to me for the second time in June, 1961, to tell me that he had just gotten married.

"Afterwards he wrote to me more often, telling me about his life, his wife, a new-born child, and small daily problems. He wanted books, shaving soap, razor blades; but he also sent me some presents: a shawl, some figurines, and many photos. He never talked about politics and never about his plans.

- 8 -

"Later he wrote asking me to help him return to Texas. I took some steps without success. Where did Lee find money for a trip? At the U. S. Embassy in Moscow which gave it to him and returned him his passport, which seemed logical if Lee was an intelligence agent.

"It appears that the Soviets conveyed to the American Government my son's file. But they denied me the right to consult this file. I am going to the Soviet Embassy myself shortly in order to ask the Russians for this file. It proves, I am sure, that the communists discovered that Lee was an American agent.

A Colonel's Niece

"My son, his wife and little daughter lived with me for over a month after their return. Marina Nikolaevna was pretty and charming. I always had good relations with her. It is not true to insinuate that there was coldness between us or that Lee went to live elsewhere because of that. Lee was always independent as are we all in our family.

"Marina has never repudiated the Soviets. She has never renounced communism. She was born at Arkhangelsk but grew up in Leningrad where she went to school. Her father and mother are dead but she has an uncle, a retired Red Army colonel. She went to the university. She is a doctor of pharmaceutics (sic).

"I have to destroy here two legends. The first one alleges that Lee learned Russian because he was a Marxist. Lee learned Russian during his service in the Marines. His teachers were military men and the course was a part of military training.

"According to the second, Lee did not want Marina to learn English. It would be ridiculous for a husband to forbid his wife to learn the language of a country where she lives.

"The fact is that Marina spoke English badly, but she did speak it, and so we could chat together all day.

- 9 -

COMMISSION EXHIBIT No. 1808—Continued

"She told me that she loved Lee deeply, was attached to him forever, and devoted to his child. However, there were moments, it is true, when she talked of returning to Russia. One time I saw her come in with a black eye. 'It was Lee who did this to me,' she confessed to me.

"Lee told me that he adored his wife. He did not earn much; however, he bought her a gold ring with a ruby, ruby being Marina's birth stone. Lee often occupied himself with the baby; pampered her; told her stories. He was a very good father.

"Later they left me. I did not see Lee and Marina again for almost a year. He had finally found a job in a factory. Marina cried with joy. 'Thank your God; Lee is working,' she said to me.

"On November 22, 1963, at three thirty, I was returning to my home in Fort Worth, having finished my work. I was then employed as a nurse. I was driving in my car. I turned on the radio. They announced the death of Kennedy. I was upset because I admired the President. And then there was this frightening shock: the arrest of my son."

* * *

Next Week: "THE DAY BEFORE MY SON'S MURDER,

A POLICEMAN SHOWED ME A PICTURE

OF RUBY AND ASKED ME:

'DO YOU KNOW THIS MAN?'"

- 10 -

COMMISSION EXHIBIT No. 1808—Continued

Captions of pictures appearing in the text:

Page 1 (from left to right):

1. "For Marguerite Oswald, her son Lee is innocent. He was betrayed and calumniated."

2. "At fourteen, Lee Oswald preferred walks in the neighboring zoo to school."

3. "In the eyes of his mother, Lee Oswald at the age of 16 was a well-behaved young man, affectionate and industrious. There was nothing unbalanced about him, she said."

Page 5:

1. "Lee Harvey Oswald at 16, in his uniform of the U. S. Air Force cadet. This photo was entrusted to us by Oswald's mother. According to her, police had good reasons to keep it secret."

A statement in large type under this picture: "THIS PORTRAIT PROVES THAT HE WAS AN AMERICAN PATRIOT."

2. "Mother Oswald was a nurse. She was dismissed after her son's arrest."

A statement on the left of the picture: "HE WAS NOT UNBALANCED AS THEY SAID."

3. "At 17, Oswald enlisted in the elite Marine Corps."

Statement on the left of the picture: "A CHAMPION MARKSMAN OF THE MARINES? THIS IS FALSE."

Statement on the right of the picture: "HE READ MARX AT 16, BUT ON ORDERS."

4. "His diploma was sent to his mother 'so that she could frame it.' "

Page 6:

"At 11, Lee Oswald (on the bottom, smiling) attended a school at Fort Worth, Texas. His teacher judged him very intelligent."

COMMISSION EXHIBIT No. 1808—Continued

DL 100-10461
JPH:BL
1

The following investigation was conducted by SA JAMES P. HOSTY, JR.:

On October 18, 1963, Dallas Confidential Informant T-1 advised that in March, 1963 ROBERT L. OSWALD of 7313 Davenport Avenue, Fort Worth, Texas, moved from Fort Worth to Box 32-C, Malvern, Arkansas.

On October 18, 1963, Mrs. EDITH SHANNON, 2701 Mercedes Street, Fort Worth, Texas, advised that she could not recall LEE OSWALD or his wife when they lived at 2703 Mercedes Street, Fort Worth, Texas.

On October 18, 1963, Mrs. M. M. BOYD, 2705 Mercedes Street, Fort Worth, Texas, advised that she could not recall LEE OSWALD when he resided at 2703 Mercedes Street, Fort Worth, Texas.

On October 29, 1963, a pretext interview by a Special Agent of the FBI at 2919 West Fifth Street, Irving, Texas, reflected that Mrs. RUTH PAINE resided at 2515 West Fifth Street. Mrs. PAINE was separated from her husband, MICHAEL R. PAINE. It was determined that Mrs. PAINE was employed at St. Mark's School, Dallas, Texas, on a part-time basis as a teacher of the Russian language and she had a Russian born woman living with her. This Russian born woman gave birth to a girl about a week ago and Mrs. PAINE was taking care of this woman. It was determined that the husband of the Russian born woman visited his wife at this address periodically but did not reside there.

On October 31, 1963, Mrs. DOROTHY SMITH, Irving, Texas, Credit Bureau, advised that they had a credit record for MICHAEL R. PAINE and his wife RUTH PAINE, who resided at 2515 West Fifth Street, Irving, Texas. Mrs. SMITH advised their credit was satisfactory and that Mr. PAINE was employed by Bell Helicopter Company in Fort Worth as a Design Engineer. Mrs. PAINE was employed as a housewife.

On October 31, 1963, Mr. EDWARD T. OVIATT, Assistant Head Master, St. Mark's School of Texas, Dallas, Texas, advised that Mrs. PAINE was a satisfactory employee and was loyal to this country and he considered her to be a stable individual. Mr. OVIATT stated that Mrs. PAINE was employed on a part-time basis as a teacher of Russian language. He also advised that he had recently learned from

— Commission Exhibit No. 1809 — 137

COMMISSION EXHIBIT No. 1809

DL 100-10461
2

a conversation with Mrs. PAINE that she had a Russian born woman living with her and she was assisting this woman in view of the fact that she had recently had a new baby and she, Mrs. PAINE, was improving her Russian speaking ability by having this Russian speaking person in her house.

On October 31, 1963, J. H. KITCHING, Dallas County Sheriff's Office, and LEON POWERS, Irving, Texas, Police Department, advised that they had no record for RUTH PAINE.

On October 31, 1963, Mr. TED SCHURMAN, Security Officer, Bell Helicopter, Fort Worth, Texas, advised that MICHAEL R. PAINE was presently employed by that company as an engineer and he holds a security clearance.

On November 1, 1963, Mrs. RUTH PAINE, 2515 West Fifth Street, Irving, Texas, was interviewed at which time she advised that MARINA OSWALD, wife of LEE HARVEY OSWALD, was staying with her following the recent birth of her baby. Mrs. PAINE furnished OSWALD's place of employment as the Texas School Book Depository, 411 Elm Street, Dallas, Texas, where he was employed as a laborer. Mrs. PAINE stated that she did not know where OSWALD was residing in Dallas at this time but that it was his plan as soon as he had enough money, to get an apartment for his family and take his wife and children to live with him. Mrs. PAINE volunteered that she would be glad to furnish this address to the FBI as soon as she determined where the OSWALDs were residing.

On November 5, 1963, Mrs. RUTH PAINE advised SAs JAMES P. HOSTY, JR. and GARY S. WILSON that she had not been able to obtain the address of LEE OSWALD in Dallas, Texas, but that she would furnish it to the FBI as soon as she was able to obtain it. Mrs. PAINE advised that LEE OSWALD had visited his wife, MARINA OSWALD on November 2 and 3, 1963, at Irving, Texas.

Mrs. PAINE then expressed the opinion that she considered LEE OSWALD to be a very illogical person and recalled that he admitted to her being a "Trotskyite Communist."

138

COMMISSION EXHIBIT No. 1809—Continued

Form No. 1888 (Revised)
MEMORANDUM REPORT
(7-1-60)

UNITED STATES SECRET SERVICE
TREASURY DEPARTMENT

ORIGIN Field | OFFICE Dallas | FILE NO. CO-2-34,030

TYPE OF CASE	STATUS	TITLE OR CAPTION
Protective Research	Continued	Assassination of President Kennedy, Dallas, Texas
INVESTIGATION MADE AT: Dallas, Texas	PERIOD COVERED: December 3, 1963	George Senator
INVESTIGATION MADE BY: SA Elmer W. Moore		

—Commission Exhibit No. 1810—

DETAILS

SYNOPSIS

Results of interview with George Senator, Ruby's roommate.

DETAILS OF INVESTIGATION

Reference is made to previous reports.

George (NMN) Senator (white; male; 5-7½; 192; brown eyes; brown-grey hair; dark complexion, mole left cheek; appendectomy scar, cut scar tip of ring finger of left hand) was interviewed at the Dallas Office December 3, 1963, for the purpose of ascertaining his background and association with Jack Ruby, who shot and killed Lee Harvey Oswald.

George Senator stated that he was born of Jewish parents at Gloversville, New York on September 4, 1913. He has one brother living in Gloversville, another brother at Rochester, and three married sisters living in New York City. He completed his formal education upon graduation from grammar school at Gloversville in June 1929. He went to New York City and worked in a hat factory, for Western Union, in the wholesale silk industry, and was unemployed at times. About 1932 he developed lung trouble and returned to Goversville for about one year, part of which he worked for a brother who operated a small restaurant. He returned to New York City and again worked in the silk industry. About 1934 he again returned to Gloversville and left there with neighbors, the Sebring family, to go to Florida. He worked at Miami in various resorts as a kitchen worker. Between 1934 and 1941 he lived and worked in both New York City and Miami.

On August 21, 1941, he entered the Army Air Force and was assigned serial number 12,006,042. He served mainly as an aerial armourer with the 5th Bomber Command, 33rd Group in Australia and Pacific Theater during World War II.

DISTRIBUTION	COPIES	REPORT MADE BY	DATE
Chief Dallas	Orig. & 2 2	Elmer W. Moore SPECIAL AGENT	12-7-63
		APPROVED Forrest V. Sorrels 590 SPECIAL AGENT IN CHARGE	12-7-63

(CONTINUE ON PLAIN PAPER)

U. S. GOVERNMENT PRINTING OFFICE 16—61800-1

COMMISSION EXHIBIT No. 1810

He was discharged as a Staff Sergeant on September 9, 1945.

He then operated a lunch counter in New York City for about one year. In January 1946, he married Shirley Baron of the Bronx. A son, Robert, was born of this marriage on October 6, 1947. He was divorced in 1956 in Dallas and his former wife later married a man named Wexler.

Senator went to Miami in 1947 and worked as a lunch counterman for about two years. He then became a dress salesman for the Reha Manufacturing Company of Milwaukee for about nine months. The next ten years he sold dresses for Smoler Bros. of Chicago and moved to Dallas for that company about May 1954. He traveled considerably as a clothing salesman out of Dallas until about 1959 - 1960. He then worked at odd jobs and in selling various lines, including novelities for the Volume Sales Co. of Dallas. He worked for Jack Ruby at the Carousel Club from March to August 1962, and at various other short periods since. He is presently a salesman of colored post cards for Dexter Press, West Nyack, New York.

About one and one-half years ago, Senator moved into an apartment with Jack Ruby, however, he stayed only about five months. He explained that Ruby "isn't very neat about the house." Senator then moved into the Grandbury Apartments on Maple Avenue with Stanton Corbat, a dress buyer. In November, Corbat and Senator moved to Apartment 206, 223 S. Ewing Street, next to Ruby who by then occupied Apartment 207. Corbat married on August 10, 1963, and on November 1, 1963, Senator moved into Apartment 207 with Ruby. The apartment had a living-dining room, kitchen, bath and two bedrooms and rented for $125.00 a month.

Senator stated that Ruby is a big-hearted man who has helped many people who were down on their luck. He said that Ruby was very emotional and, although he did not appear to be very religious, took his faith very seriously, observing all the Orthodox Jewish Holidays and particularly the memorial services for the dead. Ruby, he said, was a clean living man; did not smoke; rarely drank; liked to exercise by bar bells with occasional golf and swimming; and was concerned about the fact that Senator drank too much in his opinion. Senator said he had heard rumors since "the trouble" that Ruby is a homosexual and felt that such ideas cast a reflection him as he had lived with Ruby. He said he could assure anyone that Ruby is not a homosexual and has a normal man's interest in women. Ruby has no firm political convictions but regarded himself as a Democrat. Senator said Ruby was a man who liked people and had a strong desire to be liked. He sometimes talked rough but actually was a gentle person. Senator discounted reports that Ruby is a "street brawler" but said that he can "handle himself" if necessary as he often had to act as bouncer at his club. Senator stated that he did not know Oswald and that he was certain that Ruby did not.

Senator was questioned regarding his movements from November 22 to the 24th. He stated that he left the apartment at 223 S. Ewing Street at approximately 8:30 A.M., and that Ruby was still asleep when he departed. He made business calls and stopped for lunch at a place called Jacques, believed to

be at Carol Street and the Expressway. It was there that he learned of the shooting of President Kennedy. He said that he did probably what everybody else did that day, listen to the news and grieved over the President's death. He returned to the apartment and went to bed at approximately 10:30 P.M. He does not recall seeing Ruby again that day.

At about 3:00 A.M., Saturday, November 23, 1963, Jack came to Senator's room and woke him. Jack told him he had been at his sister Eva's place, said that he had bought food for her, and that both had cried over the death of the President. Ruby then phoned a man known to Senator as Larry at the Carousel Club and told him to get out the polaroid camera and meet them on the street in front of the club. In the meantime, Ruby had asked Senator to get up and go some place with him. Ruby and Senator drove to the Carousel Club where they picked up Larry with the camera and drove to Hall Street and Expressway where Ruby took three pictures of a poster bearing the words, "Impeach Earl Warren." Senator said that Ruby was quite incensed about this poster and that he could not understand how anyone would have the nerve to put up such a sign and that whoever they were they would have to be commies or birchers. At the same time Ruby was carrying an ad which he had cut from a newspaper in which a number of questions were put to President Kennedy by a Bernard Wiessman. Senator said that Ruby was also very "hot" about this article and commented that Wiessman did not spell his name as a Jew, but if he were a Jew he should be ashamed of himself. They went to the Southland Hotel Coffee Shop and had coffee, Ruby drinking grapefruit juice. While there, Ruby reread the ad and made comments about it. They left the Coffee Shop and went to the Main Dallas Post Office on Ervay Street where Ruby rang the night bell. A postal clerk responded and Ruby asked him who Bernard Wiessman was and who had rented the Post Office Box, the number of which appeared in the article. The postal clerk told Ruby that he did not know anything about the matter and the only person who could answer Ruby's questions would be the Postmaster. After this Ruby took Larry back to the Carousel Club and both Senator and Ruby went to their apartment at approximately 6:00 A.M.

Senator said that he awoke about 10.30 A.M. and shortly after woke Ruby. They fixed breakfast and watched television. Senator said that Ruby was very emotional and kept asking what would happen to the President's family, his wife and his children. He also expressed sorrowfor the policeman who had been killed by Oswald. Ruby said that both the killings were in cold blood, but Senator could not recall that at any time he expressed any hatred for Oswald. Ruby repeated over and over "Why did this have to happen?" and expressed pity for the entire Kennedy family. time and time again.

Senator left the apartment along about noon on Saturday and spent the afternoon shopping for food and drinking beer at various places where he talked with different people regarding the shooting. At about 7:30 P.M. he went home and prepared dinner, however, Ruby did not come in for dinner. Senator left about 8:30 P.M. and visited with friends named Bill Downey and Mike Barkley.

Senator returned to the apartment about 10:30 P.M. and found that Jack was there and had eaten some of the food the Senator had cooked earlier. Ruby, he said, had been crying and was brooding without saying very much. Ruby went out and Senator went to bed. Senator awoke on Sunday morning at approximately 9:00 A.M. and spent some time doing laundry while Ruby was asleep. At about 9:30 A.M. Ruby awoke. They had breakfast and Senator said that Jack was "worse in his grief" and described him as being very upset with a strange look on his face, almost as if he were in shock. During the morning a stripper, Little Lynn, telephoned to Ruby from Fort Worth as she needed money. Jack said he would send her some by Western Union. After that Ruby took his dachshund Sheba and said he was going to drive to the club. Senator did not see Ruby again until after his arrest for shooting Oswald.

Senator said that it was his opinion that there was no premeditation on the part of Ruby in shooting Oswald and that he must have done so on the spur of the moment. Senator said he had heard later that Ruby had spent some time at the Carousel Club just sitting around and crying on Saturday. He added that Ruby was the first club owner to announce that he would close for three days. Senator said there were several things that may not have come to the attention of the authorities which would indicate to him that Ruby had not planned to shoot Oswald. He said the fact that Ruby had the dog Sheba, to which he was very attached, in the car when he went to the police station alone would indicate that he intended to return soon. Also the fact that he had the cash receipts from the club in the car. Senator said he was convinced that Ruby had emotionally worked himself up to such a pitch that when he saw Oswald in the basement of the police station he went out of his head.

Senator said that he did not think that Ruby carried a gun at all times as he had seen Ruby's revolver stored in a blue canvass bag at both the club and at the apartment. He said Ruby always carried the gun when he carried money from the club to the apartment or to the bank. Senator stated that it was ridiculous to think that Ruby had any connection with subversive organizations or with Oswald.

EWM:amr

590

COMMISSION EXHIBIT No. 1810—Continued

FD-302 (Rev. 1-25-60)

FEDERAL BUREAU OF INVESTIGATION

Date December 6, 1963

(1)

WILLIAM MILTON BURLEY, III, was interviewed at the Denver Office of the Federal Bureau of Investigation, at which time he was advised that he need not make any statement; that any statement made by him could be used against him in a court of law, and that he could consult a lawyer prior to making any statement.

Mr. BURLEY advised that he formerly resided at 7039 Conley Street, Baltimore, Maryland, and that he is presently employed by the Encyclopaedia Britannica Company, 126 West 12th Avenue, Denver, Colorado. He said he is now residing at 3353 West 33rd Avenue in Denver.

BURLEY stated that he graduated from Patterson Park High School, Baltimore, Maryland, in 1954, and thereafter attended Baltimore Junior College from February, 1955, to June, 1955, and also the University of Maryland at Munich, Germany, from January, 1963, to April, 1963.

He said that in August, 1961, he was drafted into the United States Army and assigned to Fort Jackson, South Carolina, for basic training. He said that he later took military police training at Fort Gordon, Georgia, and after completing this training, was stationed with the United States Army at Munich, Germany, from January, 1962, to July, 1963.

BURLEY stated that while assigned at Munich, Germany, he became acquainted with BERNARD WEISSMAN and LARRY SCHMIDT and during many discussions of political activities, determined that they all shared the same views regarding their approach to American politics. He explained that by this he meant that all favored a conservative type of government and were opposed to the liberals in the United States Government.

He said that thereafter he attended many discussions of political activities with WEISSMAN and SCHMIDT and also other service men who were assigned at Munich. During one of these discussions, toward the end of their time at Munich, someone proposed [redacted]

—Commission Exhibit No. 1811—

On 12/4/63 at Denver, Colorado File # DN 89-41

by Special Agents RAYMOND J. FOX and BRENDAN P. WALSH:jkr Date dictated 12/5/63

- 4 -

COMMISSION EXHIBIT No. 1811

DN 89-41
RJF:jkr
(2)

that they all meet in the United States, after their discharge from the Army and continue active support of the conservative groups in the United States. BURLEY stated that while they all agreed to this, actually no such meeting was later held in the United States, and, to his knowledge, only he, WEISSMAN and SCHMIDT actually met for this purpose.

BURLEY advised that LARRY SCHMIDT was the first one to receive his discharge from the service, and that he returned to the United States, where he lived for a short period of time with his wife in the State of Louisiana.

SCHMIDT continued to communicate by letter with WEISSMAN and BURLEY and later informed them that he had moved to Dallas, Texas. In his letters SCHMIDT told WEISSMAN and BURLEY that there was a large group of influencial businessmen in the Dallas area who shared the same political views as he and WEISSMAN and BURLEY, and that he, SCHMIDT, felt that WEISSMAN and BURLEY should come to Dallas, and become active in political affairs.

BURLEY stated that he returned to the United States from Munich, Germany, in July, 1963, and was discharged honorably from the United States Army at Fort Hamilton, Brooklyn, New York, in August, 1963.

He said that he immediately went to Baltimore, Maryland, to reside with his wife, WINIFRED BURLEY, at 7039 Conley Street, in Baltimore.

He said he obtained employment with the Beltone Schwartz Company at Baltimore, Maryland, selling hearing aids and was so employed from September, 1963, until October, 1963.

He said that during this time, although he had only been home one month, he learned that his wife was four months' pregnant, and that he separated from his wife for this reason.

5

DN 89-41
RJF:jkr
(3)

Mr. BURLEY stated that while in Munich, Germany, he had become acquainted with Miss ELSA SILBERNAGEL, a naturalized German citizen, and had previously discussed with her the possibility of her coming to the United States. He said that he learned, while at Baltimore, that she planned to enter the United States for the purpose of immigrating on October 25, 1963. He advised that since his marital relations had become strained and he planned to separate from his wife, he left Baltimore, Maryland, on October 23, 1963, and went to Mount Vernon, New York, for the purpose of meeting Miss SILBERNAGEL when she landed at New York City, on October 25, 1963.

Upon arriving at Mount Vernon, New York, he contacted BERNARD WEISSMAN at the home of WEISSMAN's father, HARRY WEISSMAN, 439 South Columbus Avenue, Mount Vernon, New York, and resided with the WEISSMANs during his New York stay.

He said that he met ELSA SILBERNAGEL at New York City, upon her arrival and assisted her in getting settled in New York. He stated that ELSA SILBERNAGEL was invited by the WEISSMANs to stay at their home, and that she accepted this offer.

BURLEY advised that while at Mount Vernon, New York, WEISSMAN told him that LARRY SCHMIDT had been in touch with him, WEISSMAN, and continued to urge WEISSMAN to come to Dallas, Texas. He said that according to SCHMIDT an opportunity existed for WEISSMAN and BURLEY to obtain business opportunities in Dallas by joining the conservative group in that city and becoming active in their affairs.

He stated that WEISSMAN was in favor of going to Dallas, and BURLEY subsequently agreed to accompany him on this trip.

He said he left Mount Vernon, on October 31, 1963; returned to Baltimore, Maryland, to pack his clothes, and remained at Baltimore until November 2, 1963.

6

BURLEY advised on November 2, 1963, BERNARD WEISSMAN, accompanied by ELSA SILBERNAGEL, came to Baltimore, in WEISSMAN's 1957 Ford automobile, at which time BURLEY joined them.

He said that all three left Baltimore on November 2, 1963, and drove to Greensboro, North Carolina, where they visited with BURLEY's father for about five hours.

He said they then drove to Charlotte, North Carolina, where they spent the remainder of the night of November 2-3, 1963, with BURLEY's mother.

On the afternoon of November 3, 1963, all three left Charlotte, North Carolina, and drove straight through to Dallas, Texas, arriving at Dallas, at approximately 3:00 P.M., on November 4, 1963.

Upon arriving at Dallas, BURLEY made arrangements through the Preston Travel Agency, which is located in a bank building on Preston Road in North Dallas, for ELSA SILBERNAGEL to obtain plane transportation that same day from Dallas, to Denver, Colorado. He said that they then drove ELSA to Love Field, where she was due to leave for Denver, in approximately two hours, at about 8:00 P.M. that evening.

BURLEY advised that he and WEISSMAN then called LARRY SCHMIDT who resides at 5735 Gaston, in Dallas, and spent the night with him.

On the following day, November 5, 1963, he and WEISSMAN obtained an apartment at 4618 Reiger Street, Dallas, Texas, and on the following day, November 6, 1963, they obtained employment at Carpet Engineers Company in the 2,000 Block of South Beckley Street in Dallas, as salesmen.

BURLEY advised that from November 6, 1963, through November 21, 1963, he and WEISSMAN were frequently in the company of LARRY SCHMIDT and all had numerous discussions at their apartment concerning the conservative political group in Dallas, Texas.

He said that after they had been in Dallas, approximately ten days, SCHMIDT, who he knew to be a member of the Young Americans for Freedom at Dallas, and also a member of the John Birch Society (JBS), approached WEISSMAN and himself to become members of the JBS. He said SCHMIDT made available application forms for them and that he and WEISSMAN completed these forms and returned them to SCHMIDT. He said they were also given the "Blue Book" of the JBS to read and that both he and WEISSMAN did read this book.

BURLEY stated that he never attended an actual meeting of the JBS or any other organization at Dallas, and that he did not pay the $2.00-per-month fee which all members are required to pay in the JBS. He added, however, that he considered that his application form for membership actually did make him a member of the JBS.

Mr. BURLEY stated that through LARRY SCHMIDT he met JOE GRINNAN, a Dallas, Texas, oil man, who has an office on Southern Street in Dallas, approximately four times, and he found that JOE GRINNAN is a volunteer co-ordinator in the JBS at Dallas.

He said he also met JOE's brother, ROBERT GRINNAN, who is a real estate investor in Dallas, and he understood that ROBERT GRINNAN is also a member of the JBS.

BURLEY stated that during the time he was in Dallas, he met several groups of businessmen, usually in a cafeteria, and was introduced to these businessmen by SCHMIDT. He could not recall the names of these people since he met them on one occasion only; however, he understood from conversation later with SCHMIDT,

DN 89-41
RJF:jkr
(6)

that all were members of the JBS.

BURLEY advised that about November 12, 1963, while he and WEISSMAN were at their apartment that evening, WEISSMAN told him that LARRY SCHMIDT had approached him with the proposition that they place an ad in a Dallas Newspaper timed to coincide with the visit of President KENNEDY to Dallas, in which they would list questions concerning the Administration of the President. WEISSMAN told BURLEY at this time that the contents of the ad would be taken from JBS literature and that SCHMIDT wanted WEISSMAN to sponsor the ad and have it contain his name.

He stated that he and WEISSMAN discussed this proposition at length that evening; that he told WEISSMAN that he did not believe it would be wise to use his name, but that WEISSMAN was in favor of it since he felt that the Dallas businessmen who were members of the JBS would be favorably inclined toward them because of this action.

Mr. BURLEY said that WEISSMAN told him that it had been decided to place the ad in the "Dallas Morning News" since this was a conservative newspaper.

He advised that in another meeting at the apartment on November 14, 1963, LARRY SCHMIDT and WEISSMAN examined a brochure of the JBS containing approximately fifty questions attacking the KENNEDY Administration, and that from these fifty questions, twelve questions were eventually chosen to be placed in the ad.

He said that the main twelve questions which were subsequently used, were reduced to writing that evening by WEISSMAN and SCHMIDT, and that on the following day, November 15, 1963, WEISSMAN and SCHMIDT took this final proof to JOE GRINNAN's office for approval. He said that he understood from later conversation that GRINNAN approved of the advertisement and it was generally under

DN 89-41
RJF:jkr
(7)

stood during that visit with GRINNAN, that he would raise enough money from business associates to pay for the ad.

BURLEY stated that on Monday, November 18, 1963, he, LARRY SCHMIDT and WEISSMAN were in JOE GRINNAN's office at Dallas, at which time there was a great deal of discussion as to whether the newspaper would accept the ad. He said that WEISSMAN was instructed by GRINNAN and SCHMIDT to take a typed copy of the ad to the newspaper and ask them if they would run it.

BURLEY said that WEISSMAN took the copy to the newspaper on that date, at which time he was informed by the newspaper people that they saw no reason why the ad couldn't be run, but would like to take the matter up with the legal advisors of the newspaper first.

He said that on Tuesday, November 19, 1963, WEISSMAN again contacted the newspaper people at the "Dallas Morning News" and was informed that they had agreed to run the ad.

He said that on the following day, November 20, 1963, JOE GRINNAN gave $1,000.00 to BERNARD WEISSMAN as part payment for the ad, which was to be placed in the newspaper on the morning of November 22, 1963. He said that GRINNAN told WEISSMAN to give the $1,000.00 to the newspaper people and agreed to pay the balance on the following day.

He stated that on November 21, 1963, the balance of $463.00 was given to WEISSMAN by GRINNAN and WEISSMAN then turned this money over to the newspaper people. BURLEY pointed out that he was not present when this money was given to WEISSMAN to pay for the ad, but learned of it later from WEISSMAN.

He said he understood from WEISSMAN that JOE GRINNAN raised the money for the ad from other Dallas businessmen and possibly from other members of the JBS. He said that neither he

DN 89-41
RJF:jkr
(8)

nor WEISSMAN contributed money toward the cost of the ad since neither of them had any money, and he does not believe that LARRY SCHMIDT contributed money either. BURLEY stated that he does not know the names of any businessmen or JBS members who may have contributed any amount of money toward the cost of the ad.

He said that during discussion of the proposed ad, it had been pointed out to WEISSMAN and himself by LARRY SCHMIDT that SCHMIDT and JOE GRINNAN had discussed the possible name of the person who would sponsor the ad and had agreed that since BERNARD WEISSMAN was Jewish, it would be desirable to have his name appear in the ad in order to show members of the JBS that there were Jewish people in the conservative movement. SCHMIDT emphasized that GRINNAN felt that there were too many conservatives who were anti-Jewish and that this would tend to lessen the anti-Jewish sentiment among members of the conservative group.

SCHMIDT also stated to WEISSMAN and BURLEY that GRINNAN had brought to his attention that STANLEY MARCUS, a prominent Dallas businessman, had boasted that he held the Jewish vote in Dallas, and that WEISSMAN's name appearing on this ad would indicate to MARCUS that he did not control all of the Jewish vote.

BURLEY stated that there is no such group as the American Fact Finding Committee; that this was an ad hoc committee name which originated with JOE GRINNAN and LARRY SCHMIDT. He said that GRINNAN and SCHMIDT explained that there didn't need to be any such group and that any fictitious name would suffice for the ad.

BURLEY stated that he and WEISSMAN were aware that GRINNAN and SCHMIDT were using them by having WEISSMAN sponsor this ad; however, they consented to this procedure because their main purpose in going to Dallas, was to find some business, such as a bar or tavern, and felt that by their active support of the conservative group they

11

COMMISSION EXHIBIT No. 1811—Continued

DN 89-41
RJF:jkr
(9)

would gain favor with the Dallas businessmen who were members of this group.

BURLEY advised that during the time he was in Dallas, he never heard any of the people with whom he came into contact in the JBS or other conservatives, mention the name LEE HARVEY OSWALD or the name JACK RUBY. He said that he never heard WEISSMAN, SCHMIDT or JOE or ROBERT GRINNAN ever refer to either RUBY or OSWALD. BURLEY advised that neither did he hear any of these people mention any violence toward President KENNEDY and it was his opinion that the people he met in this group were sound, sensible businessmen who disagreed with the policies of President KENNEDY and his Administration, and he cannot seriously believe that they ever entertained thoughts of assassinating the President of the United States.

BURLEY stated that he is positive, based upon his knowledge of the JBS members and other conservatives in Dallas, that none of these persons were associated with LEE HARVEY OSWALD or had any connection with the assassination of President KENNEDY.

He advised that when he learned of the assassination of the President, he was shocked and immediately made arrangements to leave his employment in Dallas.

He said that after the assassination, many vitriolic letters were mailed to the box number which appeared in the advertisement in the "Dallas Morning News" and it became apparent to him that because of the reaction of the people, he and WEISSMAN were not going to be successful in any business venture in Dallas.

He said that he and WEISSMAN remained at their apartment until November 27, 1963, when he left Dallas, by bus to come to Denver, Colorado, and WEISSMAN left in his personal auto to drive to Mount Vernon, New York.

12

COMMISSION EXHIBIT No. 1811—Continued

DN 89-41
RJF:jkr
(10)

BURLEY stated that prior to leaving Dallas, he had one more meeting with LARRY SCHMIDT and WEISSMAN at JOE GRINNAN's home, at which time all expressed sympathy for the KENNEDY family and he was convinced that GRINNAN and SCHMIDT were shocked at the violent assassination of President KENNEDY.

BURLEY stated that it is his intention to remain at Denver, Colorado, and continue employment with the Encyclopaedia Britannica Company.

He said that he anticipates that he will reside at his current Denver address for at least six months and thereafter will continue residence at another address in Denver.

BURLEY furnished the following background and descriptive data concerning himself:

Name:	WILLIAM MILTON BURLEY, III
Born:	July 17, 1935 Ohiopyle, Pennsylvania
Race:	White
Sex:	Male
Height:	5'11"
Weight:	170 pounds
Hair:	Dark brown
Eyes:	Blue (wears dark horn-rimmed glasses)
Scars:	Burn scar right forearm; appendectomy scar
Military service:	United States Army, August, 1961, to August, 1963, honorable discharge August 7, 1963
Military Service Number:	US 53 331 300
Relatives:	
Mother:	MARY BURLEY,

DN 88-41
RJF:jkr
(11)

	724 East Moorhead Street Charlotte, North Carolina
Father:	WILLIAM M. BURLEY Greensboro, North Carolina, salesman for Mobile Homes Company, Market Street, Greensboro.
Brothers:	RICHARD BURLEY, 4758th DSES, Box 762, Biggs Air Force Base, El Paso, Texas;
	SAMUEL BURLEY, 724 East Moorhead Street, Charlotte, North Carolina;
	GERALD BURLEY, 724 East Moorhead Street, Charlotte, North Carolina.
Sisters:	ARMINDA OLIVE, husband, CALVIN OLIVE, Orlando, Florida;
	MILLICENT HORNE, husband, PAUL HORNE, 1533 Belvedere Avenue, Charlotte, North Carolina.
Wife:	WINIFRED BURLEY, 7039 Conley, Baltimore, Maryland.
Former employments:	June, 1953, to June, 1956 - Night shift at Chevrolet Division,

DN 89-41
RJF:jkr
(12)

Baltimore, Maryland, assembly line;

June, 1956, to August, 1956,
Remington Rand Company,
Baltimore, Maryland, salesman;

September, 1956, to March, 1958,
Trojan Boat Company,
Lancaster, Pennsylvania, salesman;

March, 1958, to January, 1959,
in business for self as trucking
contractor, Toledo, Ohio
(Unable to make go of business.);

January, 1959, to June, 1959,
West Toledo Marine Company,
Toledo, Ohio, salesman;

July, 1959, to August, 1961,
Albright Boat and Marine Company,
Pineville, North Carolina, salesman.

15

COMMISSION EXHIBIT No. 1811—Continued

D 302 (Rev. 1-25-60)

FEDERAL BUREAU OF INVESTIGATION

1

Date July 4, 1964

RICHARD LEE HOUSTON, United States Marine Corps 2081759, assigned to Platoon 138, B Company, First Battalion, Marine Corps Recruit Depot, Parris Island, South Carolina, advised that he enlisted in the United States Marine Corps on May 8, 1964, at Dallas, Texas. He advised he was employed by the "Dallas Morning News" in the Retail Advertising Department for approximately one and one-half years and frequently during the political seasons he engaged in accepting political advertisements for the newspaper. He advised that due to the number of the political advertisements, anyone in the department was eligible to handle them.

On one date, which he was unable to recall, an individual who informed HOUSTON that he was BERNARD WEISSMAN entered the office while he, HOUSTON, was on duty and informed HOUSTON that he wanted to place an advertisement in the newspaper. HOUSTON explained that WEISSMAN identified himself verbally and did not exhibit any papers to verify his identification.

HOUSTON described WEISSMAN as being between 25 and 28 years of age, six feet tall, thin, slight build, dark wavy hair, dark complexion as that of an individual of the Jewish descent, and spoke with a slight New York accent. HOUSTON said that possibly WEISSMAN wore glasses, but he was unable to make a definite statement to that effect.

Upon entering the office, WEISSMAN gave HOUSTON a copy of the advertisement he wanted to place in the newspaper. After HOUSTON looked at it, there was some question in his mind as to whether it could be placed due to the contents of the advertisement, and he then took the copy to JOHN RECTOR, whom HOUSTON identified as the Advertising Manager.

HOUSTON recalled that RECTOR then took the advertisement to CY WAGNER, the Advertising Director.

HOUSTON stated that at that point he returned to his location, and he was unable to state what happened with the advertisement from there on. [redacted]

—Commission Exhibit No. 1812

On 7/3/64 at Parris Island, South Carolina File # Savannah 44-1200

by SA WILLIAM P. FRIDAY/bah 93 Date dictated 7/4/64

COMMISSION EXHIBIT No. 1812

SV 44-1200
2

Upon returning to his location, HOUSTON informed WEISSMAN that they would need some money and would have an attorney look at the advertisement to be sure it would be all right to place in the newspaper. HOUSTON recalled that the cost of the advertisement was $1,400.00 and WEISSMAN made a deposit of $500.00 cash to the cashier. Since HOUSTON did not handle the deposit transaction, he did not know how this deposit was made except that it was in cash. WEISSMAN informed HOUSTON that he would bring in the remainder of the cost when he came to check the proof.

To the best of HOUSTON's recollection, WEISSMAN came in approximately two days later to check the proof and after looking at the proof, WEISSMAN made some changes to the questions contained in the advertisement. HOUSTON said he then took the advertisement back to the Advertising Manager and to his knowledge the advertisement was approved.

HOUSTON stated that at this time WEISSMAN also paid the remainder of the charges for the ad.

HOUSTON stated he recalled that the advertisement carried the name of BERNARD WEISSMAN as Chairman of the American Fact-Finding Committee.

HOUSTON said this was the last time he saw WEISSMAN. He was unable to recall the exact date that WEISSMAN appeared for the second time but is of the opinion that it must have been the 15th or 16th of November, 1963.

HOUSTON recalled that WEISSMAN stated that other members of the Committee had to approve the advertisement and took some proofs of the ad with him. WEISSMAN furnished HOUSTON an address which, according to HOUSTON, he gave to the Advertising Manager.

HOUSTON stated that he was acquainted with JACK RUBY since RUBY had come into the office almost on a weekly basis to place ads in the newspaper concerning the night clubs. HOUSTON stated he knew RUBY only by sight and was not acquainted with him. He advised that RUBY at no time made any mention to him about the ad placed by WEISSMAN in

SV 44-1200
3

the newspaper. HOUSTON also stated that RUBY was not mentioned by WEISSMAN in the two visits to the office with HOUSTON.

HOUSTON voluntarily furnished an opinion that the advertisement was placed in the morning paper since it would be on the streets in time for the impact to hit the public prior to the visit of President KENNEDY.

FEDERAL BUREAU OF INVESTIGATION

1

Date 12/4/63

Mr. NORMAN SIEGEL, Manager, Carpet Engineers of Dallas, 2006 South Beckley, telephone WHitehall 3-7371, home telephone ADams 5-0607, advised that BERNARD D. WEISSMAN had answered an advertisement in the newspapers and had been employed by Carpet Engineers about November 6, 1963. SIEGEL stated that WEISSMAN had applied for a position as salesman for the firm and with him was WILLIAM M. BURLEY, who was likewise employed by the firm as a salesman. He understood that WEISSMAN and BURLEY had served in the United States Army together and had recently come from New York City. WEISSMAN and BURLEY worked for the Carpet Engineers up to, and including November 22, 1963, but did not report for work thereafter. SIEGEL said that as salesmen, they went out together on appointments but did not make any sales while working for the company. When WEISSMAN made application for a job, he requested that his phone number not be given out to anyone and SIEGEL said that he heard from someone, whose name he does not recall, that WEISSMAN was engaged in politics. WEISSMAN received telephone calls every day from a man who gave his name as LARRIE SCHMIDT. SIEGEL stated that to the best of his recollection, WEISSMAN was attending a sales meeting at 2006 South Beckley on November 22, 1963, from sometime in the morning until about 12:00 Noon. At noon on Friday, the men came out of the sales meeting and someone asked WEISSMAN if he had paid for the full page ad which had appeared in "The Dallas Morning News". WEISSMAN acknowledged that he had inserted and paid for the ad. SIEGEL did not know of any other income that WEISSMAN or BURLEY had but remembered that on that morning, WEISSMAN received a telephone call and when the operator told the caller that WEISSMAN was tied up in a conference, the individual left a message to the effect that LARRY JONES had called and wanted to meet him (WEISSMAN) where his brother hangs out for lunch. It was believed by SIEGEL that this was just a few minutes before President KENNEDY was assassinated and when the message was called to the attention of WEISSMAN, WEISSMAN said something like "Somebody is crazy, I don't know anyone named LARRY JONES".

It was SIEGEL's recollection that WEISSMAN attended all of the sales meeting on that date but he said that WILLIAM M. BURNEY did not come into the Carpet Engineers office on Beckley until about 2:00 PM on November 22, 1963. BURNEY did not attend

[redacted]

—Commission Exhibit No. 1813—

on 12/3/63 at Dallas, Texas File # DL 89-43

by Special Agents W. HARLAN BROWN & EDWIN D. KUYKENDALL/cah 683 Date dictated 12/4/63

This document contains neither recommendations nor conclusions of the FBI. It is the property of the FBI and is loaned to your agency; it and its contents are not to be distributed outside your agency.

COMMISSION EXHIBIT No. 1813

2

DL 89-43

the sales meeting that morning.

SIEGEL said that FRANK DiMARIA, the Sales Manager for Carpet Engineers of Dallas, had gone out to WEISSMAN's and BURNEY's apartment and picked up a kit which had been issued to them by the company. It was his recollection that DiMARIA had told him that WEISSMAN and BURNEY had 2 or 3 other people in the apartment when he came out and picked up the kit.

SIEGEL recalled that WEISSMAN listed employment with Great Books, 300 Madison Avenue, New York City, and requested the company not to check on this employment because he said he was still working for them and they owed him money. He said he was afraid he would not get his money if they knew he was employed elsewhere.

SIEGEL stated that he had no knowledge that either WEISSMAN or BURNEY were acquaintances of JACK RUBY or LEE HARVEY OSWALD.

SIEGEL made available verifax copies of WEISSMAN's application for employment which is dated November 6, 1963, and signed by WEISSMAN. WEISSMAN's Social Security Number is listed as 113-28-1879 and his residence shown as 4618 Reiger, Dallas, Texas. He was born November 1, 1937, and stated he was a United States citizen. His employer was listed as Carpet Engineers, Inc., 2006 Beckley, Dallas, Texas, and his position was salesman. He listed his marital status as married and stated that he held no interest in real estate. His personal property consisted of a 1957 Ford convertible automobile, valued at $675.00. There were no debts or liabilities listed and he said he did not have any private income. He said he had been in the costume jewelry business working on the party plan but had been drafted in the United States Army. WEISSMAN had never been bankrupt or insolvent according to his application, and had never been in arrears or default in a previous employment. The application showed that he had never been discharged from any position but had been bonded while employed by the Underwood-Olivetti Corporation, and the Great Books of the Western World. He did not know the names of the surety companies. He listed his wife as JANE WEISSMAN, Rural Free Delivery 4, Jefferson Valley, New York, and stated from June, 1956 to December, 1957, he was employed by the Nuclear Development Corporation, White Plains, New York, as a model and tool maker by Dr. A. E. SUROSKY.

693

COMMISSION EXHIBIT No. 1813—Continued

He was terminated because of a layoff. In January 1957 to July, 1961, he was employed by the Jayne-Williams Company, Inc. and American Sellers of Music, Inc. as President and Sales Manager, at 1108 Clinton Avenue, Irvington, New Jersey, and 160 Renner Avenue, Newark, New Jersey. He left this employment because he was drafted. He listed employment from June, 1960 to July, 1961 with the Underwood-Olivetti Corporation, Broad Street, Newark, New Jersey, as a sales supervisor, under FRANK SELLERS, Sales Manager, but was drafted. He served in the United States Army from August, 1961 to August, 1963, being discharged. From September, 1963, to October, 1963, he was employed by Great Books, 300 Madison Avenue, New York City, as district manager under ART GARDINER. He left this employment to re-locate in Dallas. He listed his military service discharge as being honorable, attaining the rank of Corporal, E-4, MPC (Military Police), Serial Number US 51474607. His references were LARRY SCHMIDT, insurance salesman, 5735 Gaston Avenue, Dallas, Texas, and SOL WEIL, President-Owner, Swiss Knitting Mills, 5 Stanwix Street, Brooklyn, New York.

He made an application again on November 6, 1963, listing the person to be notified in case of accident as HARRY WEISSMAN, 439 South Columbus Avenue, Mount Vernon, New York, telephone MO 4-6994. WEISSMAN signed an agreement on November 21, 1963, to pay Carpet Engineers, Inc., 345 North Cannon Drive, Beverly Hills, California, the sum of $300 for one complete kit and samples. He also signed a sales executive agreement which is in blank and not signed by the company. His Employee's Withholding Exemption Certificate reflected that WEISSMAN had one dependent.

WILLIAM M. BURLEY likewise signed application for employment on November 6, 1963, with Carpet Engineers, Inc., listing his Social Security Number as 218-30-6968. He was married and had four persons to support. He gave references as LARRY SCHMIDT, 5735 Gaston, Dallas, and BERNARD MAIER, 6018 Eastern Avenue, Baltimore, phone ME 3-8095. In case of ~~accident~~, MARY BURLEY, 724 East Morehead, Charlotte, North Carolina, phone ED 2-8410, was to be notified. His wife was listed as WINIFRED BURLEY, 7039 Conley Street, Baltimore, Maryland, phone 282-0454 and his

children were listed as BILL, DAVE and MELANIE. WILLIAM M BURNEY served in the United States Army as a policeman at $122.50 per month from August, 1961, to August, 1963, and was discharged. From June, 1959, to August, 1961, he was employed by the Albright Boat Company, Pineville, North Carolina as sales manager at $200 per month. He left this employment because he was drafted. From September, 1958, to June, 1959, he received $150 per week while sales manager of the West Toledo Marine, Toledo, Ohio, leaving for a better position. From September, 1956, to September, 1958, he received $150 per week as district manager for the Trojan Boat Company, Lancaster, Pennsylvania, leaving there because of a pay cut. He worked for the Fuller Brush Company, Baltimore, Maryland, as a salesman at $125 per week from August, 1953, to August, 1958, leaving because he wanted to travel. In another application for a surety bond, to the Fidelity Insurance Company at 111 West Jackson Boulevard, Chicago, Illinois, he stated his residence was 4618 Apartment 7, Reiger, Dallas, Texas. He was born July 17, 1935, and is a United States citizen. He listed his father's name as WILLIAM M. BURLEY, 729 East Morehead Street, Charlotte, North Carolina, and his mother, MARY M. BURLEY, of the same address. WINIFRED BURLEY, his wife, was listed as residing at 7039 Conley Street, Baltimore, Maryland. He likewise had filed an Employee's Withholding Exemption Certificate and a sales application agreement which was in blank.

The verifax copies of the applications for employment, employees withholding exemption certificates, and sales executive agreements of BURLEY and WEISSMAN have been retained in this file.

1
DL 89-43
EDK:BJD

RICHARD K. MARKS, Assistant Cashier, Republic National Bank, Dallas, Texas, on December 3, 1963, advised SAs W. HARLAN BROWN and EDWIN D. KUYKENDALL that he met BERNARD WEISSMAN and WILLIAM M. BURLEY on about November 12, 1963, when BURLEY was at the Republic National Bank considering opening a bank account. He understood WEISSMAN was only there with BURLEY and was not engaged in any business transaction himself although WEISSMAN was heard to remark that he might want to open an account later at that bank. BURLEY told Mr. MARKS on about November 26, 1963, that he thought the check he has used in opening his account at the bank might possibly be returned because of insufficient funds; that his father might not have enough funds in his account in North Carolina to cover same.

Mr. MARKS understood that BURLEY and WEISSMAN were in the armed forces together and were good friends. He believes they are both friends of one LARRIE H. SCHMIDT, an employee of Mutual of New York, Dallas, Texas. He believes SCHMIDT would know a great deal about BERNARD WEISSMAN's background and activities. He said SCHMIDT is a "right winger" and has been very outspoken in his thinking as a "right winger". He said SCHMIDT is a friend of WARREN CARROLL, 4326 Mc Kinney Avenue, Dallas, a writer employed by "Lifeline", an enterprize believed controlled by H. L. HUNT, a wealthy Dallas oil man.

Mr. MARKS said LARRIE SCHMIDT on December 3, 1963, told him that he thought BURLEY had gone to South Texas "for the holidays" and presumed WEISSMAN may have gone with him.

Mr. MARKS stated he has no information indicating WEISSMAN and BURLEY are affiliated with any specific organizations. Mr. MARKS does not know LEE HARVEY OSWALD or JACK RUBY and has no information that would indicate any association between WEISSMAN and BURLEY with either OSWALD or RUBY.

—Commission Exhibit No. 1814 —

701

COMMISSION EXHIBIT No. 1814

FD-302 (Rev. 3-3-59) FEDERAL BUREAU — Commission Exhibit No. 1815

1

Date 12/5/63

LARRIE HENRY SCHMIDT, 5735 Gaston Avenue, Apartment E, Dallas, Texas, advised that he is employed as an insurance salesman by Mutual of New York, 2505 Turtle Creek Boulevard, Dallas. He advised that BERNARD WEISSMAN and WILLIAM M. BURLEY are two friends of his who served in the U. S. Army with him at Munich, Germany, during 1962. All three then were attached to the Headquarters, Southern Area Command, U. S. Army, at Munich. They spoke then about Dallas and how well he, SCHMIDT, liked Dallas. BURLEY and WEISSMAN said then they would like to come to Dallas and at least visit SCHMIDT there after they got out of service. SCHMIDT originally resided at Lincoln, Nebraska. SCHMIDT entered the Army in 1954 and was discharged in 1957 as an enlisted man. He then worked for a while in 1959 as editor of the Culver City Citizen, Culver City, California. After that he again served in the U. S. Army from 1959 to October, 1962. SCHMIDT has resided in Dallas since October, 1962. He has on occasions corresponded with his friend, BERNARD WEISSMAN who after being released from the Army in about August, 1963, resided at Mt. Vernon, New York. Recently WEISSMAN and his wife separated and WEISSMAN decided to come to Dallas more or less toward seeking a new location because of his domestic difficulties and pending divorce proceedings. WEISSMAN, accompanied by WILLIAM BURLEY, arrived in Dallas around the first of November, 1963. WEISSMAN had been employed as a salesman at or near Mt. Vernon, New York. His permanent home address was 439 South Columbus Avenue, Mt. Vernon, New York, c/o his father, name unknown.

He said that he (SCHMIDT) at about the time BERNARD WEISSMAN and BURLEY arrived in Dallas, conceived the idea of placing an advertisement in a newspaper pertaining to President KENNEDY's visit to Dallas on November 22, 1963. He exhibited a newspaper clipping entitled "'Riot' Tag Denied by Demonstrator" which article had appeared in the "Dallas Times Herald", Dallas, Texas, October 27, 1963.

He said that article pertained to a demonstration put on by college students when ADLAI STEVENSON, United Nations Ambassador, visited in Dallas shortly before that date. The article identified himself as the leader of the collegiate demonstrators. SCHMIDT said he had told the "Dallas Times Herald" that the 14 students participating in that demonstration

on 12/3/63 at Dallas, Texas File # 89-43

by Special Agents W. HARLAN BROWN and EDWIN D. KUYKENDALL/BJD Date dictated 12/5/63

EDK 710

COMMISSION EXHIBIT No. 1815

2

were from the University of Dallas, Irving, Texas. He said these students did some picketing at the time of ADLAI STEVENSON's appearance in Dallas but these students were not the ones who struck or "spat" upon STEVENSON at that time. SCHMIDT said the students were only picketing in an orderly manner. SCHMIDT said he himself is not a student.

SCHMIDT described himself as a "conservative" and felt that no demonstration such as picketing should be given at an appearance of a President of the United States but he felt that some type of activity should be engaged in which would indicate disapproval of President KENNEDY's policies. He therefore conceived the idea of inserting an ad in the newspaper instead of engaging in any other type of a demonstration. He first considered placing his own name in the ad. BERNARD WEISSMAN appeared in Dallas at about the time he was thinking about this ad. He said BERNARD WEISSMAN is a "good conservative" and is of the Jewish Faith. SCHMIDT said on numerous occasions "anti-Semitism charges" had been made against "conservatives" and he thought the use of BERNARD WEISSMAN's name in the ad would to some extent counteract the anti-Semitism charges that had been leveled against "conservatives". He believed the appearance of the name of a person of the Jewish faith in such an ad might attract persons of that faith to reply to the ad. Also SCHMIDT said he was interested in finding out if replies would prove "left wing" persons are just as anti-Semitic as persons in the "right wing". It was decided, therefore, that BERNARD WEISSMAN's name with his permission would be placed in the ad. He said the ad was written as if an organization known as The American Fact Finding Committee had inserted it with BERNARD WEISSMAN being shown as its chairman. SCHMIDT said that there is no such organization as The American Fact Finding Committee; that it is simply a name thought of by him for this advertisement. He said no organization participated in the preparation or placing of this ad in the "Dallas Morning News" which appeared on November 22, 1963. He said it was written by himself at his apartment at 5735 Gaston and was assisted some in its preparation by JOSEPH P. GRINNAN, 4640 Southern, Dallas, an independent oil man who has an office in the Wilson Building, Dallas. He said he began writing this advertisement by himself about a week before it was taken

711

3

to the "Dallas Morning News"; that he and GRINNAN took it to the "Dallas Morning News" four or five days before the ad appeared. The ad cost $1463. The funds to pay for same were solicited by Mr. GRINNAN from prominent Dallas businessmen. That amount of money was said to have been contributed by five or six prominent Dallas businessmen whose names he does not know. He denied that any organization backed this ad and said it was handled by himself and GRINNAN only as individuals.

SCHMIDT stated Post Office Box 1792, Dallas 21, Texas, was rented by BERNARD WEISSMAN one or two days before the ad was placed. SCHMIDT said it was felt there was a "great basis for the ad" but said the ad would never have been placed had they known what they know now. He said "conservatives" are not pro-KENNEDY but certainly they did not wish him any personal harm. He said he and GRINNAN wanted to place tough questions in the ad in order to put President KENNEDY on the spot regarding such questions, but certainly there was no desire to cause him any physical harm.

SCHMIDT said WEISSMAN and BURLEY did not come to Dallas specifically in connection with the placing of this ad and in fact had nothing to do with the ad until after they had arrived in Dallas. SCHMIDT said he and JOSEPH P. GRINNAN are both members of the John Birch Society but their activities in connection with this ad were solely as individuals. SCHMIDT does not know if GRINNAN is affiliated with any other organizations but knows of none. SCHMIDT said he (SCHMIDT) also is a member of Young Americans for Freedom, which has headquarters at Washington, D.C., Post Office Box 1731. He identified it as a national "conservative" organization, the primary function of which is to inform and interest young persons of high school and college age concerning "conservative" politics. He said by "conservative" he means conservation of the United States Constitution and Bill of Rights; preservation of our freedoms and our traditional way of life; and preservation of individual responsibilities rather than collective responsibilities.

712

COMMISSION EXHIBIT No. 1815—Continued

He said President KENNEDY has put it beautifully as "not what your country can do for you but what you can do for it", and further defining the word "conservative" he said responsibility should start with the individual and be retained on a family or local level as opposed to the "big brother" aspect of "welfare state at the Federal Government level". SCHMIDT identified the John Birch Society as a patriotic organization, the basic function of which is to fight Communism by informing people of the threat of Communism at the grass roots level.

SCHMIDT stated WEISSMAN and BURLEY left Dallas on November 27, 1963, and as of the time of this interview were supposed to be in El Paso, Texas, visiting BURLEY's brother, full name unknown. He said BURLEY has in the past resided at Baltimore, Maryland. They left Dallas because the reaction to the advertisement bearing WEISSMAN's name was far greater with the assassination of President KENNEDY than it would have been otherwise. He said WEISSMAN was employed by Carpet Engineers of Dallas but lost his job there. The Jewish Welfare Committee in Dallas was trying desperately to find WEISSMAN and numerous other persons were trying to get in touch with him. He said BERNARD obtained the mail from Post Office Box 1792, Dallas, the first time after the ad appeared and found 25 correspondents who favored the ad and 27 who opposed the ad. SCHMIDT said those favoring the ad were written prior to the time of President KENNEDY's assassination and those opposing were written subsequent to the assassination. The second time WEISSMAN obtained the mail from that Post Office box a large man wearing a "ten gallon hat" appeared to be waiting for him and tried to follow him from the Post Office. He said WEISSMAN did not know the man's identity. He said BERNARD told him "if there are the kind of "nuts" on the other side who don't hesitate to attack and kill the President of the United States, there are some who wouldn't hesitate to do the same to me". SCHMIDT said WEISSMAN being afraid of possible physical harm to himself left Dallas. SCHMIDT recalled WEISSMAN also had been interviewed by a representative of the "Dallas Morning News" on November 23 following which an article appeared in that newspaper on November 24, concerning that interview with WEISSMAN.

SCHMIDT stated he does not know LEE HARVEY OSWALD or JACK RUBY. He further stated that BERNARD WEISSMAN, WILLIAM BURLEY and JOSEPH P. GRINNAN do not know either OSWALD or RUBY so far as he knows.

713

COMMISSION EXHIBIT No. 1815—Continued

Identifying data pertaining to LARRIE HENRY SCHMIDT as obtained by interview and observation is as follows:

Race	White
Sex	Male
Birth	December 29, 1936 Oakland, California
Height	About 5'8"
Weight	165 lbs.
Hair	Brown
Eyes	Brown
Complexion	Medium
Marital status	Married
Relatives	Father, REUBEN SCHMIDT, died 1958; Mother, LUCILLE SCHMIDT, nee STALL, died 1937; (Parents prior to death resided at 345 F Street, Lincoln, Nebraska) Wife, BARBARA KAY ORR SCHMIDT, 5735 Gaston, Apartment E, Dallas.

714

COMMISSION EXHIBIT No. 1815—Continued

FD-302 (Rev. 3-3-59)

FEDERAL BUREAU OF INVESTIGATION

—Commission Exhibit No. 1816 — Date 11/26/63

1

STANLEY F. KAUFMAN, 1520 Mercantile Securities Building, advised that he has known JACK RUBY since 1954 and has represented him in several civil matters pertaining to his night night club business in Dallas.

KAUFMAN stated he knows nothing about RUBY's activities while in Chicago prior to coming to Dallas, but knows that for the past nine or ten years he has attended the same synagogue as he attends and he considers RUBY one of the most active Jewish bachelors in the synagogue.

KAUFMAN stated he knows of no trips that RUBY has made, with the exception of a vacation trip to Cuba some years back prior to the time CASTRO took over, at which time he went down to visit some acquaintance, name not now recalled, who worked in a casino there, as well as a trip to Chicago some years back in connection with the death of his father. He stated he does not know LEE HARVEY OSWALD and never heard OSWALD mentioned by RUBY. KAUFMAN stated he heard over TV that RUBY had asked for three attorneys and that his name was mentioned, but he has received no contact from RUBY since his arrest and, since he does not handle criminal cases, he would not represent RUBY in connection with this pending charge against RUBY. He stated RUBY has never had a bank account to his knowledge and has always paid for his services in cash. He stated he knows of only two persons who might be able to furnish pertinent information concerning RUBY, one RALPH PAUL, of Dallas, who has or had some business connection with RUBY, and ALICE NICHOLS, a girl friend or former girl friend of RUBY, who resides at 8707 Redondo.

KAUFMAN stated that on the morning of November 23, 1963, RUBY called him, appeared to be very upset, and asked him if he had read the article placed in the Dallas News by a BERNARD WEISSMAN. KAUFMAN stated that he told RUBY he had seen it and RUBY asked, "Did you notice that this ad was bordered in black, which makes it look like a death tip?" KAUFMAN stated that RUBY wanted to know who WEISSMAN was and how he could get in touch with him and if Mr. FREEDMAN, of the Anti-Defamation League, could furnish him any information as to the whereabouts of BERNARD WEISSMAN. He stated RUBY also told him that he had tried to locate this WEISSMAN through the Post Office Department, but was

on 11/26/63 at Dallas, Texas File # DL 44-1639

by Special Agents ALFRED D. NEELEY & J. CALVIN RICE Date dictated 11/26/63

eah

DL 44-1639

2

unable to do so. KAUFMAN stated that RUBY told him that he had been to the Dallas News Advertising Department and had raised "hell" with the Ad Department for accepting such an ad.

KAUFMAN stated that from his contacts with RUBY and the civil matters he has handled for him he is aware that RUBY is quick tempered, and that it is his opinion RUBY had no assistance or guidance in connection with his shooting of OSWALD.

654

FD-302 (Rev. 3-3-59) FEDERAL BUREAU OF INVESTIGATION

Date December 18, 1963

1

MARINA OSWALD was interviewed at 11611 Farrar Street.

She advised that in the late fall of 1962 when she and OSWALD were living at the Elsbeth Street address in Dallas, they had a quarrel. MARINA decided to move away from OSWALD. She contacted GEORGE DE MOHRENSCHILDT, who came out to the Elsbeth Street address in his convertible and took MARINA, her daughter JUNE, and a few baby things to the ANNA MELLER house at 5930½ La Vista. OSWALD was supposed to come to the MELLER house where they could talk over their domestic problems, but he did not. Later the same day, GEORGE DE MOHRENSCHILDT took MARINA back to the Elsbeth Street address, where she packed up some belongings. GEORGE DE MOHRENSCHILDT then took her back to the MELLER house. She stayed there about six days with ANNA MELLER, and then stayed for a while with KATHY FORD, the wife of DECLAN FORD, who lives at 14057 Brookcrest.

— Commission Exhibit No. 1817 —

on 12/17/63 at Dallas, Texas File # DL 44-1639

by Special Agents ANATOLE A. BOGUSLAV and WALLACE R. HEITMAN:mja Date dictated 12/18/63

365

COMMISSION EXHIBIT No. 1817

Date December 20, 1963

MARINA OSWALD was interviewed at 11611 Farrar Street.

A faded blue cloth jacket with padding bearing label "Sir Jac" with zipper front was exhibited to MARINA. She immediately identified this jacket as being the property of her husband, LEE HARVEY OSWALD. She said she recognized the jacket because she has handled it and washed it for OSWALD.

MARINA was further questioned concerning JOE R. FRANKLIN, who is presently confined at the Texas Department of Corrections at Huntsville, Texas. She reiterated she does not know this person and that she does not believe OSWALD ever knew him. She said in October, 1962, she was residing either at Mercedes Street in Fort Worth or in the homes of friends in Dallas. She did not reside in the Oak Cliff section during the period of October, 1962. She recalls living in a white frame house with a front porch, but this was located on Mercedes Street in Fort Worth. It was a duplex. The people who lived on the other side were a young couple. The woman was pregnant. MARINA does not recall she and OSWALD having any neighbor identified as an older woman who might have caused trouble between MARINA and OSWALD. She does not recall OSWALD ever bringing a man to her house either on Mercedes Street or where she was living with friends in Dallas. She said she does not recall any occasion when she walked from her house to a car with OSWALD and thereafter OSWALD got in the car and drove off with a man.

MARINA advised that to her knowledge she has never heard of the Texas Import-Export Company of Fort Worth, Texas. She said she has had no employment in the United States, nor has she been connected with any mercantile or commercial enterprise. She does not recall OSWALD being connected with any concern by this name.

— Commission Exhibit No. 1818 —

on 12/19/63 at Dallas, Texas File # DL 100-10,461

by Special Agents ANATOLE A. BOGUSLAV and WALLACE R. HEITMAN/gm Date dictated 12/20/63

353

COMMISSION EXHIBIT No. 1818

2
DL 100-10,461

MARINA said she knows of no Russian officials or intelligence officers that OSWALD contacted in Russia with the exception of those individuals he may have contacted for the purpose of obtaining the necessary documentation relating to his stay in Russia or his subsequent departure with her.

She advised of further information concerning Col. NICOLAI AKSIONOV. She had a girl friend whose boy friend was a distant relative of AKSIONOV. This girl friend and her boy friend did on occasions visit the OSWALDs at their apartment. She recalls this boy mentioning the AKSIONOVs. She recalls he mentioned on one occasion that AKSIONOV's wife had had an affair with another man. She said that this boy had several conversations with OSWALD out of her hearing, and it is entirely possible he may have furnished other facts concerning the background and family of AKSIONOV without her knowledge.

MARINA said she was not interested in conversing on political matters with OSWALD. Whenever he began a conversation along these lines, she would simply tell him that she was not interested. She recalls telling him in New Orleans at the time he was passing out the "Hands Off Cuba" circulars that no one would join his movement as most people had families and had to take care of them. She recalls telling OSWALD that the United States is a rich country and that almost everyone owns a home and OSWALD could not promise land or other things and thereby gain followers.

354

FD-302 (Rev. 3-3-59)

FEDERAL BUREAU OF INVESTIGATION

Date December 20, 1963

MARINA OSWALD was interviewed at 11611 Farrar Street.

MARINA identified certain of her friends and relatives in Russia as follows:

1. INESSA YAKHLIEL is a graduate engineer. She presently resides on Leningradskaya Street in Minsk. Her present employment is not known.

2. OLGA PETROVNA DMOVSKAYA is a girl friend of MARINA's who was employed as a pre-school age teacher in Minsk. She is not presently employed as she has a small child.

3. LIUBOV AKSIONOV is the aunt of MARINA. She is MARINA's mother's sister and resides in Minsk. She is believed to be divorced but is still using her husband's name. She has been living with VASILI (LNU) for the past eight years although her legal marital status is not known to MARINA. She is a bookkeeper by profession. Her place of work is unknown. As far as MARINA is concerned, neither this aunt nor her former husband is known kin to Col. NICOLAI AKSIONOV.

4. LIALIA PETRUSEVICH was a neighbor of MARINA's in Minsk. She was a graduate of the lumber building institute at Minsk and at the present time holds some administrative position in the lumber building industry.

5. LUDMILLA LARIONOVA-SEMIONOVA resides in Leningrad at the address Zaozernaya Street #6, Apt. #4. She is in charge of a government import store in Leningrad.

6. ELLY SOBOLEVA is a pharmacist. She was MARINA's schoolmate in the Leningrad pharmacy school. Because of the low pay of a pharmacist, she is now studying microbiology in Leningrad University.

Commission Exhibit No. 1819

on 12/19/63 at Dallas, Texas File # DL 100-10,461

by Special Agents ANATOLE A. BOGUSLAV and WALLACE R. HEITMAN/gm Date dictated 12/20/63

190

7. (FNU) TARUSINA lives in Leningrad. She is the mother of OLEG TARUSIN, who is a former boy friend of MARINA's. Mrs. TARUSINA is the mother who encouraged her boy to marry MARINA.

8. LEONIDA (LNU) is a practical nurse at the Third Clinical Hospital in Minsk. She is a spinster.

9. ALFRED (LNU) is a young man from Cuba who is apparently an admirer of ANITA ZIEGER, who is a member of the ZIEGER family from Argentina who were friends of the OSWALDs in Minsk. ALFRED (LNU) and ANITA ZIEGER both spoke Spanish.

10. ALEXANDER ROMANOVICH ZIEGER is the father of ANITA ZIEGER.

11. ERIC TITOVETS, Leningradskaya 1-11 in Minsk. MARINA does not know whether he is attending a school or not. If he has completed the school, he may have changed his address.

181

COMMISSION EXHIBIT No. 1819—Continued

FD-302 (Rev. 3-3-59)

FEDERAL BUREAU OF INVESTIGATION

Date January 16, 1964

1

MARINA OSWALD was interviewed at 11611 Farrar Street, in the Russian language, SA BOGUSLAV translating.

She was exhibited a silver-colored bracelet with the name MARINA on it, which is contained in a gold-colored box. This bracelet is among the personal effects of MARINA and LEE HARVEY OSWALD acquired by the Dallas Police Department through a search of the RUTH PAINE residence, 2515 Fifth Street, Irving, Texas, on November 22, 1963, and subsequently made available to the FBI Office at Dallas.

MARINA identified this bracelet as a gift to her from LEE HARVEY OSWALD. She said it had been given to her immediately after OSWALD had returned from New Orleans, in early October, 1963. She said that now everybody knows OSWALD had been to Mexico immediately prior to his return to Dallas, in October, 1963, although she had not known this at the time, thinking he had returned to Dallas directly from New Orleans. She said the bracelet was too small for her and she had not particularly liked it, and as a consequence had not worn it. She said OSWALD had purchased a similar bracelet for himself with his name on it prior to the time they moved from Dallas to New Orleans, in the spring of 1963. She said OSWALD had wanted her to have a bracelet like his.

MARINA said OSWALD did not state where he had bought the bracelet, which he gave her as a gift, and that she definitely did not know that he had been to Mexico prior to his return to Dallas.

MARINA stated she had not discovered OSWALD'S wedding ring on the dresser in her room at the RUTH PAINE home the morning of November 22, 1963, upon getting up that morning. She said she had not seen it until the police came to her house to search it, following the arrest of

[redacted]

— Commission Exhibit No. 1820 —

on 1/15/64 at Dallas, Texas File # DL 100-10461

by Special Agents ANATOLE A. BOGUSLAV and WALLACE R. HEITMAN :mja Date dictated 1/16/64

COMMISSION EXHIBIT No. 1820

2
DL 100-10461

OSWALD on November 22, 1963. She had not noticed the ring on the dresser before the police came. She advised she recalled calling RUTH PAINE later in that day, November 22, 1963, or the following day, to tell her about the ring.

MARINA was questioned concerning her prior statement that she could not understand how OSWALD could commit a killing, in view of his prior admission to her that he had attempted to assassinate General WALKER, at Dallas. She stated that upon reflection, and in view of the WALKER incident, that she now felt that LEE HARVEY OSWALD had been capable of murder. She stated he had evidently been a man of some strong will to have carried out the attempted assassination of WALKER, even though he became highly nervous later when he returned to their home, following that assassination attempt. She said that if it is true that OSWALD committed the assassination of President KENNEDY, that he very possibly would not have been caught if he had not lost control of himself when accosted by Policeman TIPPIT, resulting in the killing of Officer TIPPIT.

MARINA was asked if, while she resided in New Orleans, she had attended any meetings alone, or in the company of OSWALD, or any other person. She answered she had not attended any such meetings on any occasion in New Orleans, or in Dallas. She stated while she was in New Orleans with OSWALD, she had been visited on occasion by OSWALD'S uncle and aunt and their family, and had been visited on two occasions by a Quaker friend of RUTH PAINE. RUTH PAINE had written this friend that MARINA OSWALD was in New Orleans and requested that the friend contact MARINA.

3
DL 100-10461

MARINA said she had previously stated this friend had visited her on one occasion. She now remembers that this Quaker friend of RUTH PAINE, whose name MARINA does not recall, visited her on two occasions--the first time she came alone to their house on Magazine Street and the second time she came accompanied by her two daughters. MARINA said this woman's husband is a Professor in a medical school in New Orleans, she believes. She said LEE HARVEY OSWALD had been at the house on the occasion of both visits of this Quaker woman. MARINA recalled that one of the daughters of the Quaker woman had toured the Soviet Union and the other daughter was a student of the Russian language.

MARINA was questioned concerning her religious belief. She advised she has always had a religious feeling, which dates back to a very young age. She said her grandmother, who had taken care of her when she was very young, had been very religious, in fact almost fanatically so. The grandmother taught her prayers, which she said for a number of years, but no longer recites. MARINA said she crosses herself before going to sleep each night, but she did not let LEE HARVEY OSWALD know this because he did not believe in a God and would have resented her doing this.

She said she has more religious belief now because of her recent experiences.

She volunteered the opinion that most every Russian, whether he shows it or not, down deep in his heart has a religious belief of sorts.

MARINA was further questioned concerning the events of the night of November 21, 1963. She said OSWALD had told her when he arrived unexpectedly at the PAINE residence on the evening of November 21, 1963, that he was lonesome for her and for the children. MARINA said at the time, she thought that OSWALD had arrived primarily to patch up the quarrel between them. She was asked if OSWALD had made the statement that he had something important to do, and she replied that she did not recall that he made such a statement.

She said she recalls OSWALD had retired to his bed approximately two hours before she had, but she does not believe he was asleep when she retired. She said, in fact, she believes he did not go to sleep until the early morning hours and for that reason, he did not awaken when the alarm clock went off. She said upon reflection, that she would now say that OSWALD had been nervous because he had not gone to sleep as he usually did. She did not think at the time of his being nervous.

On the morning of November 22, 1963, after OSWALD had arisen and was leaving the bedroom, and while MARINA was in bed feeding the baby, she mentioned to him that she had not had time previously to purchase the shoes which they had agreed she needed. OSWALD then told her to buy the shoes and to buy anything that was necessary for the children out of the money which they had saved, and which was in the wallet in the dresser drawer. MARINA states that in reflection, now she believes this to be strange, because OSWALD had always been most frugal and did not allow her to spend hardly any money.

MARINA said OSWALD told her he would not be back to the PAINE house that weekend because he did not want to disturb the PAINE family any more than necessary.

MARINA was questioned regarding her personal relationships with LEE HARVEY OSWALD. She stated that she can recall that after a series of arguments, which had culminated in her writing a letter to the Soviet Embassy in the United States, requesting permission to return with her daughter, JUNE, to the Soviet Union, OSWALD had begged her not to leave him alone; and she had thereafter agreed that the whole family could return to Russia together. She said OSWALD had on occasion asked her not to laugh at him, or his ideas. She advised she had the impression that OSWALD had become lost in his relationship with the people of the world and was trying to find himself and to make something out of himself. She said she had been sorry for him.

FD-302 (Rev. 3-3-59)

FEDERAL BUREAU OF INVESTIGATION

Date January 17, 1964

1

MARINA OSWALD was interviewed at her place of residence, 11611 Farrar Street. She was again questioned about her recollection of the activities of OSWALD on Saturday, November 9, 1963. She stated OSWALD had called her on the previous day, November 8, 1963, which was a Friday, and told her he would not come to the PAINE residence on that day because he had an appointment to see about a job the following day, November 9, 1963. She stated OSWALD appeared at the PAINE residence about 9:00 A.M. to the best of her recollection on November 9, 1963. About mid-morning that date, Mrs. PAINE took OSWALD, MARINA and JUNE to Oak Cliff in Dallas to the Drivers License Office, but the office was closed because it was an election day. Mrs. PAINE then took the OSWALDs back to her house. MARINA states OSWALD stayed in the house the rest of the day, and, in fact, stayed at the house until the following Monday morning when he went to work. She stated she does not know of any occasion when OSWALD talked to anybody about the purchase of an automobile. She said she is positive that he did not leave the PAINE residence on November 9, 1963 for such a purpose. She said that if OSWALD had talked to anybody about purchasing an automobile, that she did not know about it.

MARINA was again questioned concerning the trip taken by LEE HARVEY OSWALD to Mexico in September-October of 1963. She said OSWALD had not told her anything whatsoever about any intentions on his part to go to Mexico. She said he had not told her upon his return to Dallas in early October, 1963 that he had been to Mexico. She said she received no intimation whatsoever that he had intentions of going to Mexico or that he had been to Mexico. She said her first knowledge of OSWALD's travel to Mexico had been that which she gained from television programs at Dallas immediately following the assassination of President KENNEDY.

In this connection, MARINA OSWALD said that although she had in the spring of 1963 petitioned the Soviet representative in the United States to return to Russia, that by the fall of 1963 she had no desire to return to Russia. She

on 1-16-64 at Dallas, Texas File # DL 100-10461

by Special Agent s ANATOLE A. BOGUSLAV / WALLACE R. HEITMAN mvs 23 Date dictated 1-17-64

2
DL 100-10461

said she had originally petitioned the Soviet government for a return to Russia mainly because OSWALD had found it difficult and almost impossible to support his family in the United States. She wanted to help OSWALD and she felt that she could do this by returning to Russia with their baby daughter.

Portions of the diary of OSWALD in Russian were discussed with MARINA. She said she knew RIMMA SHERIKOVA who was the guide of OSWALD during his first trip to Moscow. She met this guide when the latter came to Minsk with a tourist group.

She advised she is aware that OSWALD had girl friends in Minsk before he met her, and she has met some of these friends. She recalls a girl named ENNA from Riga Estonia worked in the same factory as did OSWALD and had been a friend of his. She also recalled that a girl named TAMARA had been a friend of OSWALD before their marriage. She remembers a friend of OSWALD's had been a Jewish girl named ELLA GERMAN. She does not know these friends of OSWALD well because they were friends of his rather than hers, and OSWALD did not maintain a social relationship after their marriage.

MARINA reiterated that OSWALD had never attempted suicide to her knowledge since she had known him. She stated she had observed the scars on his left wrist and had asked him on several occasions about the scars but he was embarrassed and refused to talk to her about the scars.

MARINA said upon reflecting on the entries of OSWALD in his diary pertaining to his suicide attempt, that it was her belief he had done this in order to obtain from the Russian government permission to stay in that country, and that he had not truly wanted to take his life.

MARINA advised OSWALD had told her on an occasion that he had walked into the American Embassy in Moscow and

231

thrown his passport on the table and told the officials that he considered himself no longer an American.

MARINA said OSWALD was the type of person who thought that there were green pastures in other countries. She said he had been disappointed in the Soviet Union. MARINA advised that he would like to have combined the job opportunities in the Soviet Union with the freedom of press and other freedoms enjoyed in the United States.

MARINA said in Russia OSWALD had enjoyed meeting people, but frequently he would grow tired of people after he knew them for a while. PAVEL GOLOVACHEV, however, was his best friend. OSWALD and PAVEL enjoyed talking to each other. PAVEL was very clever; he was a good story teller. PAVEL was an expert in electronics and read many periodicals and books on the subject. Although neither OSWALD nor MARINA were interested in electronics, they would listen to PAVEL talk about electronics. OSWALD and PAVEL also discussed politics. PAVEL was very frank and direct in his approach to things and in his conversation. He was candid in his views. MARINA thinks he was honest in his opinions. PAVEL and OSWALD played chess a good bit.

ERIC TITOVIETS, a medical student in Minsk, presented a better appearance than did PAVEL and was more handsome than PAVEL. MARINA stated she was more attracted to ERIC at first than to PAVEL, but when she became better acquainted with each of them, she found that PAVEL being more direct and more honest in his opinions was the more attractive of the two. She found ERIC to be afraid to openly discuss political questions.

In his letter of September 9, 1963 to the OSWALDs, ERIC mentioned the "Z's". MARINA said this was a reference to the ZIEGER family who lived in Minsk and were friends of the OSWALDs. When he first went to work in the TV factory, OSWALD could not speak adequate Russian. Mr. ZIEGER, whose full name is ALEXANDER ROMANOVICH ZIEGER, can speak

COMMISSION EXHIBIT No. 1821—Continued

Russian, English, Spanish and Polish, and he acted as OSWALD's interpreter. ZIEGER was one of the chief engineers in the plant. OSWALD did not work in the same section as did ZIEGER. OSWALD and ZIEGER became good friends and associated socially before and after OSWALD's marriage. Concerning ZIEGER, MARINA stated he was of Jewish blood, she believed. He had been raised in a land which was a part of Poland. He had spent 25 years in Argentina and had then returned to his homeland. Meanwhile, his homeland had become part of Russia and is now known as Belorussia.

MARINA stated ERIC TITOVIETS had become acquainted with the ZIEGERs. ERIC knew the ZIEGERs when she met OSWALD. ERIC, like the OSWALDs, was a friend of the ZIEGERs. She said it was therefore natural for ERIC to comment regarding the ZIEGERs in his letter to the OSWALDs. Concerning her friend LIALIA, MARINA stated this girl's full name is LARISSA PETROVANA PETRUSEVICH, and her nickname is LIALIA. She lived in the same apartment house as did the OSWALDs in Minsk. Although she had been raised in Belorussia, she had relatives living in Moscow. MARINA stated LIALIA on occasion had visited her relatives in Moscow. MARINA does not recall the occasions but knows that LIALIA had been in Moscow.

MARINA stated LIALIA was a few months older than she, and would, therefore, be 22 or almost 23 years of age at the present time. She estimated the height of LIALIA to be about 5' 4". LIALIA has brown eyes and dark hair. She had a pretty figure which was somewhat girlish. She had well-shaped legs, and although she was not pretty, was very attractive. She had a lively personality. MARINA described LIALIA as a child who was not at all sophisticated. She said

COMMISSION EXHIBIT No. 1821—Continued

5
DL 100-10461

LIALIA was very definitely of Russian descent although she might have some Polish blood as her mother had possibly come from Poland. MARINA stated that to her knowledge, LIALIA had never lived in Moscow but had only visited there for short occasions to see her relatives.

234

COMMISSION EXHIBIT No. 1821—Continued

FD-302 (Rev. 3-3-59)

FEDERAL BUREAU OF INVESTIGATION

Date January 18, 1964

1

MARINA OSWALD was interviewed at her place of residence, 11611 Farrar Street.

She was questioned concerning a notation on a sheet of autobiographical notes of OSWALD. This notation showed his wife as MARINA NIKILIEVNA OSWALD, and written underneath that was the name "DAVID LEE OSWALD, son, American". MARINA OSWALD said that this had been a note made by OSWALD before the birth of her first daughter, JUNE. OSWALD thought the first child would be a son and had already selected the name as DAVID LEE. It was in anticipation of this that he made this note on this autobiographical sketch.

MARINA was asked if she recalled that OSWALD had in his possession a phonograph record when he returned to Dallas, on October 3, 1963. She said she did not know if he had a phonograph record and that if he had brought a phonograph record back to Dallas on that occasion, she did not know about it.

She also said OSWALD had never spoken to her about Jai-lai games.

MARINA said she had never been in, nor seen, the residence at 1026 North Beckley, where OSWALD last lived.

MARINA was asked the direct question if OSWALD had ever said anything, or did anything, to indicate to her he was thinking of, or intended to, kill or attempt to assassinate or harm the late President KENNEDY, or Governor JOHN CONNALLY. She answered that OSWALD had not said anything, or done anything, to indicate any intentions to harm either late President KENNEDY, or Governor CONNALLY. She said that the accusation of OSWALD as the assassin of President KENNEDY had

on 1/17/64 at Dallas, Texas File # DL 100-10461

by Special Agents ANATOLE A. BOGUSLAV and WALLACE R. HEITMAN:mja Date dictated 1/18/64

COMMISSION EXHIBIT No. 1822

2
DL 100-10461

come as a "thunder clap" to her.

She said that she cannot recall that OSWALD ever said anything, or wrote anything, against Governor JOHN CONNALLY. She said OSWALD had told her he had written to the United States Navy, protesting his undesirable discharge, and that he had received a form letter from the Navy, stating that his request would be considered. He made the remark to her that the bureaucracy in the United States was just as bad as it was in Russia.

MARINA identified two additional acquaintances of hers in Russia. These persons are TAMARA ALEXANDROVNA SANKOVSKAYA, who is approximately age 34, and was an employee of the Third Clinical Hospital at the same time as was MARINA. This woman is married and has a child and is a pharmacist by profession. Another friend of MARINA'S was SOFIA VASILEVSKAYA, now about age 25, who also was employed at the Third Clinical Hospital at the same time as was MARINA. She was also a pharmacist by profession.

MARINA said if JACK RUBY is found guilty of the slaying of LEE HARVEY OSWALD, she would hope RUBY would not forfeit his life, as she believes enough blood has been shed in this matter.

236

COMMISSION EXHIBIT No. 1822—Continued

FD-302 (Rev. 3-3-59)

FEDERAL BUREAU OF INVESTIGATION

Date January 22, 1964

1

MARINA OSWALD was interviewed at her residence, 11611 Farrar Street. She was questioned concerning the trip of LEE HARVEY OSWALD to Mexico in September-October, 1963. She recalls seeing the English-Spanish dictionary and the other dictionary along with some picture postal cards of Mexico scenes in the RUTH PAINE residence, and she knows that these were the property of LEE OSWALD, but she did not think anything about the origination of the articles nor did she know that they had come from Mexico.

She said the bracelet given her by OSWALD had been given to her immediately after OSWALD returned to Dallas in early October, 1963. She did not ask OSWALD where he had acquired the bracelet and she did not know where he acquired it. It did not occur to her that this bracelet might have been purchased in Mexico as she did not know that OSWALD had been to Mexico.

Shortly after the assassination of President KENNEDY, she showed a coin to Mrs. PAINE which coin had a hole in it. She said this coin had been given her by OSWALD after his return to Dallas in early October, 1963, but not immediately after his return. She cannot recall the exact date that he gave her the coin. She read the inscriptions on the coin and knew that it was a Mexican coin, but she did not think about it being acquired by OSWALD in Mexico.

She stated she does not recall OSWALD ever mentioning to her that he saw a jai alai game or intended seeing one or was interested in jai alai. She does not recall that OSWALD brought a phonograph record with him to Dallas in early October, 1963.

MARINA was exhibited the rough draft handwritten letter of OSWALD in which information was set out that he had been to Mexico City. She said this handwriting appeared to be OSWALD's. She could not remember ever seeing the letter before. She said she cannot read English and had not read the letter.

on 1-21-64 at Dallas, Texas 284 File # DL 100-10461

by Special Agents WALLACE R. HEITMAN
ANATOLE A. BOGUSLAV
mvs
Date dictated 1-22-64

COMMISSION EXHIBIT No. 1823

2

MARINA expressed surprise that Mrs. PAINE knew the contents of the letter. She said Mrs. PAINE had never discussed with her this letter nor its contents. She said Mrs. PAINE had not discussed with her a trip made by OSWALD to Mexico.

Concerning this trip by OSWALD to Mexico, MARINA said that she did not know that he intended going to Mexico nor did she know that he had taken a trip to Mexico. She said OSWALD was most secretive and close-mouthed about many things. She said there was much that OSWALD did or thought about that she knew nothing about. She said she had in times past asked OSWALD questions to which he had replied words to the effect, "none of your business". For this reason, she always hesitated to ask him questions about anything even though she might want to ask him.

287

COMMISSION EXHIBIT No. 1823—Continued

FD-302 (Rev. 3-3-59)

FEDERAL BUREAU OF INVESTIGATION

1

Date ____________

MARINA OSWALD was interview in the English language on January 31, 1964. She was questioned concerning a letter which had been received by her from "ANITA", which letter had been addressed to "Dear MARINA, ALEC and JUNE MARIE". This letter was written in Russian. In the letter "ANITA" mentioned "ALFRED" from Cuba and another person named "FREDERICK".

MARINA advised the writer of this letter was ANITA ZIEGER, one of the daughters of Mr. and Mrs. ALEXANDER ROMANOVICH ZIEGER, who were friends of the OSWALDs in Minsk. She said that "ANITA" in this letter was indulging in a bit of "girl talk" about her boy friends.

MARINA stated "ALFRED", whose last name she did not know, is a Cuban citizen and a resident of Cuba who for some time has been studying in Russia. He studied at the University of Minsk for about six months and later studied at the University of Moscow, where he is believed to presently be studying.

MARINA said "ALFRED's" parents have visited him in Russia both in Minsk and Moscow. She said although she did not personally know "ALFRED", LEE HARVEY OSWALD had known him as he had met "ALFRED" at Minsk through ANITA ZIEGER on one occasion when they visited at the University of Minsk to attend some social or scholastic affair. MARINA also related "ALFRED" had wanted to marry ANITA but the latter had not wanted to marry him.

Concerning "FREDERICK", MARINA said this young man had worked in the same television and radio factory as had LEE OSWALD and he and LEE OSWALD were acquaintances. "FREDERICK" is a Hungarian and at the present time he lives with his parents in a part of Russia other than Belorussia, believed to be the Ukraine. She believes "FREDERICK" is the person depicted in the photograph, which is photograph No. 2 in inventory item No. 37. This photograph depicted three individuals, "FREDERICK" believed to be the person on the left, ANITA ZIEGER the person in the middle, and LEE OSWALD the person on the right. MARINA said she had met "FREDERICK" but does not recall under what circumstances she first became acquainted with him. She also advised "FREDERICK" at one time had been interested in marrying ANITA, but she had not been interested in marrying him.

on 1/31/64 at Dallas, Texas 291 File # DL 100-10461

by Special Agent WALLACE R. HEITMAN /rmb Date dictated 2/1/64

COMMISSION EXHIBIT No. 1824

FD-302 (Rev. 3-3-59) FEDERAL BUREAU OF INVESTIGATION

O-RUSS
O-POST
O-MARINA
INV I-1

(3)

Date 2/1/64

1

MARINA OSWALD was interviewed at her place of residence, 11611 Farrar Street, Dallas, Texas. During this interview, a number of photographs were exhibited to her, which photographs are identified by item number and photograph number, i.e., "Item 1 P 1." Photographs depicted on Item Nos. 1 through 65, 70, 276, 287, 367 through 370, as well as 107, were shown to MARINA OSWALD.

MARINA OSWALD identified these photographs, where known, as follows:

ITEM 1:

P 1: Subject matter unknown. Probably taken by LEE HARVEY OSWALD while in U. S. Marine Corps as photograph shows date of December 1958.

P 2: Believed to be JOHN PIC, half-brother of OSWALD.

P 3: Office building in Minsk.

P 4: Unknown.

P 5: Unknown. It is possible that the building on the extreme left is General WALKER's house at Dallas because LEE HARVEY OSWALD told her that he had taken photographs of WALKER's house and she is not familiar with the scene herein depicted. To her knowledge, she has not seen the WALKER house.

P 6: Unknown.

on 1/31/64 at Dallas, Texas 292 File # DL 100-10461

by Special Agents RICHARD L. WIEHL and WALLACE R. HEITMAN - LAC Date dictated 1/31/64

COMMISSION EXHIBIT No. 1824-A

LEE HARVEY OSWALD

ITEM 2:

P 1: Unknown.

P 2: Unknown.

P 3: A scene in Japan taken by OSWALD.

P 4: ROBERT OSWALD's baby, CATHY.

P 5: Nevsky Prospect in Leningrad, Russia, showing the subway building.

ITEM 3:

P 1: Believed to be scene in Japan taken by OSWALD.

P 2: Marine Corps friend of OSWALD's in Japan.

P 3: Marine Corps friend of OSWALD's in Japan.

P 4: Scene in Japan.

P 5: Scene in Japan.

P 6: Scene in Japan.

ITEM 4:

P 1: Friend of OSWALD in Marine Corps in Japan.

P 2: Japanese scene taken by OSWALD.

P 3: Marine Corps friends of OSWALD in Japan.

P 4: Japanese street scene.

P 5: Japanese street scene.

293

COMMISSION EXHIBIT No. 1824-A—Continued

LEE HARVEY OSWALD

ITEM 5:

P 1: Believed to be rural scene in Japan.

P 2: Japanese monument.

P 3: Japanese scene.

P 4: Japanese scene.

P 5: Japanese scene.

ITEM 6:

P 1: Believed to be photograph taken in Japan.

P 2: Believed to be photograph taken in Japan.

P 3: OSWALD in Japan in Marine Corps.

P 4: Believed to be Japanese scene.

P 5: Unknown. MARINA recalls that OSWALD mentioned to her there was a railroad track near the WALKER home in Dallas as he told her he had taken a photograph of the WALKER home; and as this scene depicts a railroad track, she believes it possible this may be the railroad track near the WALKER home.

ITEM 7:

P 1: Japanese scene.

P 2: Unknown.

P 3: Believed to be a Japanese scene or monument in New Orleans, Louisiana.

P 4: Photograph of Czar's palace in Leningrad.

394

COMMISSION EXHIBIT No. 1824-A—Continued

LEE HARVEY OSWALD

ITEM 8:

P 1: Post card sent to OSWALDS in Russia by Mrs. MARGUERITE OSWALD, mother of LEE OSWALD. Picture is believed to be of the Alamo.

P 2: Post card showing a government office in Leningrad.

P 3: View of Minsk from OSWALD apartment.

P 4: Scene in Leningrad.

ITEM 9:

P 1: Photograph taken in Japan.

P 2: Unknown.

P 3: Carnival time in New Orleans.

P 4: Unknown.

P 5: Unknown.

P 6: The Black Sea in Russia in moonlight.

P 7: Carnival time in New Orleans.

ITEM 10:

P 1: Photograph depicting bridge on Nevsky Prospect in Leningrad.

P 2: Photograph depicting another scene on Nevsky Prospect in Leningrad.

P 3: Unknown.

P 4: A building in Leningrad.

395

COMMISSION EXHIBIT No. 1824-A—Continued

ITEM 11:

P 1: A photograph believed to be of LEE OSWALD as small boy in zoo in New York.

P 2: MARINA OSWALD on street in Minsk.

P 3: Carnival time in New Orleans.

P 4: Photograph taken inside of OSWALD quarters on Elsbeth Street, Dallas, Texas.

P 5: Believed to be carnival scene in New Orleans.

P 6: Appears to be the same as P 6 on Item 1, also unknown.

ITEM 12:

A line of people waiting to see LENIN's tomb in Moscow.

ITEM 13:

Unknown building in unknown place.

ITEM 14:

P 1: Unknown building; is possibly the WALKER home in Dallas, Texas, as MARINA does not know the identity of the building.

P 2: Unknown.

P 3: MARINA on New Year's Day near the "Dacha"--recreation cabin--of MIKHAIL SMOLSKI near Minsk. SMOLSKI is an engineer, and his father is a professor. This photograph taken before MARINA's marriage.

(ITEM 14 CONT.):

P 4: The other half of photograph P 3. Also taken near the "Dacha." This photograph depicts LARISSA PETROVANA PETRUSEVICH.

P 5: PAVEL GOLOVACHEV, a friend of LEE OSWALD and MARINA in Minsk.

P 6: Unknown.

ITEM 15:

P 1: LEE HARVEY OSWALD in Moscow.

P 2: A photograph of LEE HARVEY OSWALD taken at the Hotel Berlin, Moscow.

ITEM 16:

P 1: OLGA PETROVNA DMOVSKAYA, a girl friend of MARINA's who is employed as a pre-school age teacher in Minsk.

P 2: The burial crypt of GREBOEDOV (phonetic) at some town in Georgia, Russia, which is the home town of PUSHKIN.

P 3: Another view of this crypt.

P 4: A scene at Sochi, Russia, a Black Sea resort.

P 5: Unknown.

ITEM 17:

Photograph of GALINA KHONTULEVA, a friend of MARINA's, and inscription by GALINA on back, partly translated by MARINA as, "MARINA, this is for you from me--now I have changed my looks--your friend regardless of the change."

LEE HARVEY OSWALD

ITEM 18:

P 1: OSWALD photograph taken at radio factory in Minsk.

P 2: Monument to womanhood in Republic of Georgia in Russia.

P 3: Cousin of MARINA, VALENTIN MIKHAILOV, whose mother is POLINA VASILIEVNA MIKHAILOVA. Cousin lives in Kharkov, Russia, and is now believed to be in the Russian Army in Germany.

P 4: Photograph of MARINA in Leningrad.

P 5: Statue to womanhood in Republic of Georgia, Russia.

ITEM 19:

Photograph of MARINA's sixth grade class at Leningrad. MARINA is in first row, first on left.

ITEM 20:

P 1: Photograph of a group of young Russian people taking a rest period while harvesting potato crop near Minsk. The young girl in the foreground is ELLY SOBLEVA, a pharmacist by profession who is a friend of MARINA. She is now studying Microbiology in Leningrad University. It is required of all young people that they aid in bringing in Russian crops where necessary.

P 2: A photograph depicting flowers on a grave, taken in Republic of Georgia, Russia, sent to OSWALDS by PAVEL GOLOVACHEV.

P 3: Photograph depicting three persons identified from left as (a) LUDMILLA LARIONOVA SEMIONOVA, a friend of MARINA's who resides at Zaozernaya Street # 6, Apartment 4, Leningrad. She is in charge of a government import store in Leningrad;

298

LEE HARVEY OSWALD

(ITEM 20 CONT.)

(b) Unknown; (c) Unknown.

P 4: A photograph depicting LEE OSWALD on left and the Russian tourist guide known to OSWALD in Minsk, first name ROSA, last name not recalled by MARINA.

P 5: Photograph depicting Nevsky Prospect in Leningrad.

ITEM 21:

P 1: Statue in Leningrad.

P 2: Statue of STALIN in Minsk, which was later torn down.

P 3: Nevsky Prospect in Leningrad.

P 4: Unknown.

ITEM 22:

P 1: LEE OSWALD.

P 2: Unknown.

P 3: Theater in Leningrad.

P 4: LEE OSWALD.

P 5: Unknown.

P 6: CATHY OSWALD, ROBERT OSWALD's baby.

P 7: Mrs. ZIEGER, a friend of the OSWALDS in Minsk. Her husband is ALEXANDER ROMANOVICH ZIEGER, who was employed by the same television factory as OSWALD in Minsk.

ITEM 23:

Nevsky Prospect, Minsk.

299

LEE HARVEY OSWALD

ITEM 24:

Photograph of students in one of LEE OSWALD's school classes. LEE OSWALD is third from left on first row.

ITEM 25:

P 1: MARINA OSWALD in Russia.

P 2: Photograph of MARINA OSWALD and LEE OSWALD with daughter JUNE, taken in photograph booth in bus station at Dallas, Texas.

P 3: Photograph of MARINA OSWALD and LEE OSWALD with daughter JUNE, taken in photograph booth in bus station at Dallas, Texas.

P 4: LEE OSWALD in Minsk.

ITEM 26:

P 1: LEE and MARINA OSWALD on train leaving Russia.

P 2: Mrs. MARGUERITE OSWALD, mother of LEE HARVEY OSWALD.

P 3: Scene at Moscow Zoo.

P 4: LEE OSWALD on steps of an apartment house in Minsk.

ITEM 27:

P 1: Unknown.

P 2: Unknown.

P 3: Unknown.

P 4: MARINA and LEE OSWALD on train leaving Russia.

P 5: Photograph of flowers taken by PAVEL GOLOVACHEV and sent to the OSWALDS.

300

COMMISSION EXHIBIT No. 1824-A—Continued

LEE HARVEY OSWALD

ITEM 28:

P 1: Photograph of shrubbery taken by PAVEL GOLOVACHEV and sent to OSWALDS.

P 2: JUNE OSWALD at Minsk.

P 3: LEE OSWALD in apartment at Minsk.

P 4: LEE OSWALD in apartment at Minsk a day or so before leaving Russia, ironing diapers on suitcase placed on floor.

ITEM 29:

P 1: Unknown.

P 2: LARISSA PETROVANA PETRUSEVICH, mentioned above, and cousin, name unknown, at Minsk.

P 3: MARINA on train leaving Russia.

P 4: Photograph of flowers taken by PAVEL GOLOVACHEV.

ITEM 30:

P 1: Moscow Zoo.

P 2: Scene at marriage of ROBERT OSWALD, brother of LEE HARVEY OSWALD, and his wife, VADA.

P 3: Not recognizable.

P 4: Photograph of persons, from left:
(a) VASILY (Last Name Unknown);
(b) his wife, LUBOVA AKSIONOVA (LNU);
(c) MARINA, standing;
taken in Minsk.

301

COMMISSION EXHIBIT No. 1824-A—Continued

LEE HARVEY OSWALD

ITEM 31:

P 1: PAVEL GOLOVACHEV near one of NAPOLEON's cannon at Brest, Poland.

P 2: Unknown.

P 3: PAVEL GOLOVACHEV by a cannon, place unknown.

P 4: LEE OSWALD on train leaving Russia.

ITEM 32:

P 1: Photograph of building in Minsk, Russia.

P 2: Building in Leningrad.

P 3: River scene in Minsk.

P 4: Scene in Leningrad.

P 5: Scene in Leningrad.

P 6: Scene in Leningrad.

ITEM 33:

P 1: Scene in Leningrad.

P 2: Scene in Brest, Poland.

P 3: Scene in Brest, Poland.

P 4: A square in Minsk.

P 5: Photograph of individuals, from left:
(a) INNA (LNU), from Medical Institute, Minsk;
(b) Mrs. ZIEGER, friend of OSWALD's, and
(c) LEE OSWALD, photograph taken near Minsk.

P 6: Picture of JUNE OSWALD taken on Elsbeth Street, Dallas, Texas.

302

COMMISSION EXHIBIT No. 1824-A—Continued

LEE HARVEY OSWALD

ITEM 34:

P 1: LEE and MARINA OSWALD on train leaving Russia.

P 2: Scene at Moscow Zoo.

P 3: MARINA on train leaving Russia.

P 4: Scene at Sochi, Black Sea Resort.

ITEM 35:

P 1: OSWALD at Minsk at time of marriage.

P 2: Another photograph of OSWALD ironing diapers on back of suitcase in apartment at Minsk.

P 3: Photograph of persons, from left:
(a) LEE OSWALD;
(b) ANATOLE (LNU), friend of OSWALD, not known by MARINA, and
(c) Mr. ZIEGER, above mentioned.

P 4: Photograph of grave of flowers taken by PAVEL GOLOVACHEV.

ITEM 36:

P 1: OSWALD on steps near an apartment house in Minsk.

P 2: OSWALD on train leaving Russia.

P 3: OSWALD on train leaving Russia.

P 4: Photograph of individuals, from left:
(a) with flowered blouse, a neighbor in apartment house at Minsk, name unknown;
(b) and (c) two female acquaintances of MARINA who visited at Minsk, names not recalled.

303

COMMISSION EXHIBIT No. 1824-A—Continued

LEE HARVEY OSWALD

ITEM 37:

P 1: Photograph of Mrs. MARGUERITE OSWALD.

P 2: Photograph of persons, from left:
(a) unknown friend of ELEANOR ZIEGER;
(b) ELEANOR ZIEGER; ELEANOR ZIEGER is daughter of Mr. and Mrs. ZIEGER, mentioned above.
(c) LEE OSWALD.

P 3: Scene in Brest, Poland.

P 4: ROBERT OSWALD and his daughter, CATHY, in Fort Worth, Texas.

ITEM 38:

P 1: OSWALD on train leaving Russia.

P 2: A photograph of AUDREY HEPBURN.

P 3: MARINA on train leaving Russia.

ITEM 39:

P 1: Photograph of MARINA OSWALD on left and Mrs. ZIEGER on right. MARINA is holding JUNE.

P 2: PAVEL GOLOVACHEV's photographs of Russian nature scenes.

P 3: PAVEL GOLOVACHEV's photographs of Russian nature scenes.

P 4: PAVEL GOLOVACHEV's photographs of Russian nature scenes.

ITEM 40:

P 1: VADA OSWALD, wife of ROBERT OSWALD, standing, and CATHY OSWALD in car.

304

COMMISSION EXHIBIT No. 1824-A—Continued

LEE HARVEY OSWALD

(ITEM 40 CONT.)

P 2: CATHY OSWALD at Fort Worth, Texas.

P 3: PAVEL GOLOVACHEV in Brest, Poland.

P 4: Unknown.

P 5: LARISSA PETROVANA PETRUSEVICH and her friend, IGOR (LNU).

ITEM 41:

Photograph taken at Minsk. From left: MARINA OSWALD; IGOR, friend of LARISSA, mentioned above.

ITEM 42:

P 1: Monument in Leningrad.

P 2: Electrical building in Leningrad.

P 3: Minsk park scene.

P 4: Museum--Leningrad.

P 5: Children's Square in Minsk.

P 6: ROBERT LEE OSWALD, son of ROBERT OSWALD, brother of LEE HARVEY OSWALD.

ITEM 43:

P 1: A boat at Amsterdam, Holland.

P 2: A boat at Amsterdam, Holland.

305

COMMISSION EXHIBIT No. 1824-A—Continued

LEE HARVEY OSWALD

ITEM 44:

P 1: A Neva River scene, Leningrad.

P 2: Moskovsky Prospect in Leningrad showing entrance to subway building.

P 3: Czar's palace at Leningrad.

P 4: Public Library, Leningrad.

ITEM 45:

P 1: A Leningrad monument.

P 2: Inside subway building at Leningrad.

P 3: Czar's palace, Leningrad.

ITEM 46:

P 1: Leningrad street scene.

P 2: Unknown building in unknown city.

P 3: Czar's palace, Leningrad.

ITEM 47:

P 1: Russian post card for 8th of March (Woman's Day).

P 2: Russian post card for October Revolution Day.

P 3: Russian post card for Russian May Day.

ITEM 48:

P 1: Russian cartoon post card.

P 2: Scene at Leningrad.

P 3: Leningrad scene, with PUSHKIN monument in foreground and Museum of Russian Art in background.

306

COMMISSION EXHIBIT No. 1824-A—Continued

LEE HARVEY OSWALD

ITEM 49:

P 1: Leningrad street scene, with Neva River to left.

P 2: Building in Leningrad.

P 3: Neva River at Leningrad.

ITEM 50:

Nevsky Prospect in Leningrad.

ITEM 51:

P 1: Post card showing nature scene in Bellorussia, sent to OSWALDS at Dallas, Texas on Elsbeth Street.

P 2: Post card depicting masonry map of Texas on highway, sent to OSWALDS at Minsk, Russia, by Mrs. MARGUERITE OSWALD.

P 3: Russian post card glorifying October Revolution.

ITEM 52:

P 1: Theater in Leningrad.

P 2: Moskovsky Prospect in Leningrad.

P 3: Carnival scene, New Orleans, Louisiana.

ITEM 53:

P 1: Scene in New Orleans.

P 2: Boat on Mississippi River at New Orleans.

P 3: Mississippi River Bridge at New Orleans.

307

COMMISSION EXHIBIT No. 1824-A—Continued

LEE HARVEY OSWALD

ITEM 54:

P 1: Street scene in New Orleans, Louisiana.

P 2: Street scene in New Orleans.

P 3: Downtown Fort Worth, Texas.

P 4: Picture post card of rural scene in Bellorussia.

ITEM 55:

P 1: Museum, Leningrad.

P 2: Scene in New Orleans.

P 3: Scene in New Orleans.

P 4: Scene in New Orleans.

ITEM 56:

P 1: Russian art post card.

P 2: Russian art post card.

P 3: A building in Moscow.

P 4: A post card showing rural scene in Bellorussia.

ITEM 57:

P 1: Minsk Stadium.

P 2: Bellorussia Theater in Minsk.

P 3: Russian art post card.

P 4: Russian art post card.

308

COMMISSION EXHIBIT No. 1824-A—Continued

LEE HARVEY OSWALD

ITEM 58:

P 1: Russian art post card.

P 2: Russian art post card.

P 3: Russian art post card.

P 4: Russian art post card.

ITEM 59:

P 1: Scene on Neva River, Leningrad.

P 2: Kremlin in Moscow.

P 3: Russian post card with picture of PUSHKIN.

P 4: Russian art post card.

ITEM 60:

P 1: Russian art post card.

P 2: Russian art post card.

P 3: River scene in Holland or England.

P 4: Russian art scene.

ITEM 61:

P 1: Russian art post card.

P 2: Russian art post card.

P 3: Russian art post card.

P 4: Russian art post card.

ITEM 62:

P 1: Russian art post card.

P 2: Russian art post card.

309

COMMISSION EXHIBIT No. 1824-A—Continued

LEE HARVEY OSWALD

ITEM 63:

P 1: Post card to OSWALDS in Russia from Mrs. OSWALD (front and back).

P 2: Post card from LEE OSWALD in New Orleans to RUTH PAINE in Irving, Texas, for MARINA (front and back).

ITEM 64:

P 1: Russian post card celebrating May Day.

P 2: Address side of post card from LEE OSWALD to RUTH PAINE for MARINA.

ITEM 65:

P 1: Appears to be negative of photograph of Leningrad street scene.

P 2: Unrecognizable.

P 3: Unrecognizable.

P 4: Unrecognizable.

P 5: Unrecognizable.

P 6: Unrecognizable.

ITEM 70:

P 1: Picture of railroad track, place unknown to MARINA.

P 2: JUNE OSWALD at one month in Minsk.

P 3: OSCAR SEMIONOVA, son of LUDMILLIA LARIONOVA SEMIONOVA, friend of MARINA's in Minsk, with inscription on back, "For my darling MARINA and her family, from OSCAR ALEXANDER, 2 years old 30/Aug/62."

P 4: Unknown.

ITEM 276:

P 1: Arch in Leningrad.

P 2: Arch in Leningrad.

COMMISSION EXHIBIT No. 1824-A—Continued

LEE HARVEY OSWALD

ITEM 287:

Roll of film, photos not shown.

ITEM 367:

P 1: River scene in Minsk from OSWALD apartment.

P 2: Scene at Minsk.

P 3: OSWALD apartment house in Minsk, with balcony to OSWALD apartment marked.

P 4: Airport building at Minsk.

P 5: Picture post card of scene at Botanic Garden in Minsk.

P 6: OSWALD and MARINA OSWALD on balcony of apartment in Minsk.

ITEM 368:

P 1: Japanese scene, probably taken by OSWALD in Japan.

P 2: Same as P 1.

P 3: Same as P 1.

P 4: Photograph of person, taken by OSWALD in Japan.

P 5: Same as P 4.

P 6: Same as P 1.

P 7: Same as P 1.

P 8: Same as P 1.

P 9: Mrs. JOHN HALL, with an unknown child. Mrs. HALL is a friend of MARINA's at Dallas, Texas.

P 10: Unknown.

COMMISSION EXHIBIT No. 1824-A—Continued

LEE HARVEY OSWALD

ITEM 369:

Unknown building, believed possibly by MARINA to be a photograph of General WALKER house in Dallas although she has not seen this house. The building depicted is unfamiliar to her. OSWALD told her he had taken a photograph of WALKER house.

ITEM 370:

Photographs 1 through 13 believed to have been taken by OSWALD in Japan. Persons in Photograph 12 unknown to MARINA.

ITEM 107:

This is a photograph of a sign which says, "No Admittance." MARINA advised she has never seen this sign, to her knowledge, and she does not know to whom it belongs. She has no information whatsoever concerning it.

312

COMMISSION EXHIBIT No. 1824-A—Continued

FD-302 (Rev. 3-3-59)

FEDERAL BUREAU OF INVESTIGATION

O-MARINA 2
INV 1-1
KP

1

Date 2/3/64

MARINA OSWALD was interviewed in the English language, at her residence 11611 Farrar Street.

She was exhibited four photographs which appeared to be of street scenes in Russian cities. These four photographs are appropriately identified as DL - 7, DL - 8, DL - 9, and DL - 10. She identified these photographs as depicting the following scenes or buildings:

DL - 7: The white building in the background of this photograph is identified as the Palace of Culture for Professional Unions in Minsk, where she first met LEE HARVEY OSWALD.

DL - 8: This photograph depicts the Minsk Circus in the right background and a monument to a Russian hero in the left foreground. This photograph was taken by LEE HARVEY OSWALD in Minsk.

DL - 9: This is a close-up of the Palace of Culture for Professional Unions at Minsk. PAVEL GOLOVACHEV took this picture.

DL - 10: This is a photograph of the Admiralty Office in Leningrad.

MARINA OSWALD made available a four-page handwritten letter in the Russian language dated December 27, 1963, 2515 West 5th Street, Irving, Texas, to MARINA OSWALD from RUTH PAINE. This letter is being forwarded to the FBI Laboratory for appropriate translation and will thereafter be recorded in its English translation.

315

on 2/2/64 at Dallas, Texas File # DL 100-10461

by Special Agent WALLACE R. HEITMAN - gj Date dictated 2/3/64

COMMISSION EXHIBIT No. 1825

UNITED STATES DEPARTMENT OF JUSTICE

FEDERAL BUREAU OF INVESTIGATION

In Reply, Please Refer to File No.

Cincinnati, Ohio
March 26, 1964

RE: TELEPHONE INTERVIEW WITH MRS. MARGUERITE OSWALD, RADIO STATION WHIO, DAYTON, OHIO, MARCH 19, 1964

On March 19, 1964, a telephone interview was conducted by Mr. Phil Donahue, Radio Station WHIO, Dayton, Ohio, on the program called "Conversation Piece." The interview was with Mrs. Marguerite Oswald, mother of Lee Harvey Oswald, and was by long-distance telephone with Mrs. Oswald at Little Rock, Arkansas. Also in the interview were listeners to WHIO who telephoned their questions to be answered by Mrs. Oswald.

The interviewer introduced his guest as Mrs. Marguerite Oswald, mother of the accused presidential assassin, and stated she was participating in the program by way of long-distance telephone from Little Rock, Arkansas. He stated that she would answer questions put to her by the listeners of "Conversation Piece" at telephone number 253-8866.

She was asked by the interviewer for some of the reasons she was offering to support her assertion that her son did not kill President Kennedy.

Mrs. Oswald stated she knew Lee Harvey Oswald is innocent of this terrible tragedy. She stated she believes he was an agent of his government and that he was framed for the assassination of the President. She said he was supposed to be a Marxist and known defector. He was in Dallas at that particular time and was offered a job at the Book Depository three days prior to the motorcade. The route of the motorcade was changed to pass by the Book Depository. Lee did not get the job himself; he was offered the job. He was out of work at that time. She indicated everything points to the fact that this boy's past record of his defection to Russia and his views on Marxism would be a perfect setup for an assassin

COMMISSION EXHIBIT NO. 1826

of the President. She stated she believes that this is what happened and believes that her son was meant to be killed at the Book Depository, but this failed for some reason or other and he was able to get away. She thinks that officer Tippet was not killed by Lee Harvey Oswald. She thinks the assassins are still at large. She advanced the supposition that if Lee was framed and he was supposed to be killed in the building, then someone else would have to be killed in order for Lee to be arrested and then be killed himself. She believes that Jack Ruby only came into the case as a paid killer in order to shut Lee up.

When questioned by a listener as to why Lee did not have psychiatric care, she stated she did not know and was never informed that Lee should have psychiatric treatment. She explained his truancy in New York and that he was placed in a children's home by a judge. He was there about six to seven weeks. She denied having fled from New York because she did not want Lee to have psychiatric treatment, stating that she remained in New York for 11 months after this. She stated that she did not know Lee had psychiatric treatment, but would assume he had psychiatric treatment at the children's home as it was possible that the children there were given tests of some sort.

In answer to a question, she stated she believes it was normal for her son to defect to Russia because she believes he was an agent of the United States Government, and that he was sent to Russia as a defector and went there as a United States Government Agent.

With regard to a quotation by her in "U. S. News and World Report" in February, that President Johnson was in the White House through the actions of her son, she claimed that this was a misquotation.

She indicated she had received no information that her son was an agent of the United States from the United States Government.

She stated she believes President Kennedy was shot from the overpass directly in front of the motorcade, and not

COMMISSION EXHIBIT NO. 1826—Continued

from the Book Depository.

She described her family as an average American family and a very patriotic family, in answer to a question indicating she had not discharged her duty as a good mother. She described her son as a brilliant boy, and stated the press is becoming a little more sympathetic toward her.

She stated that someone could have put Lee's rifle in the window of the Book Depository, and that a photograph taken at the time of the shooting shows the car had passed the window of the Book Depository, making it impossible for anyone to shoot at this car from that window.

She indicated that she believed her son was a Government agent because he was not under surveillance and that he was framed because of his Marxist views and because of his defection. She indicated that perhaps the person who framed him did not know he was a Government agent and he was found to be one only after being framed.

With regard to the shot at General Walker, she explained that if her son was an agent, he might become involved in a threat on General Walker's life, and, in his note to his wife, was telling his wife he might be arrested. If this did happen, she, as a Russian citizen, should get in touch with the Russian Embassy.

She stated she believes that more than one person was involved in the assassination. She admitted that her son could have been the one who had killed the President, but that she does not think so. She stated the car had bullet shatters on the left hand side which was not facing the Book Depository, and this car was immediately sent to be renovated. She questioned why this evidence was taken away.

She refused to speak for the opinions of any other members of her family, stating that Lee's brothers did not have the information concerning him that she has..

- 3 -

COMMISSION EXHIBIT No. 1826—Continued

She stated she doubted if she would believe the Warren Commission if they find Lee was the assassin. She indicated she thinks someone in the Government that wanted President Kennedy out of the way used her boy.

- 4 -

COMMISSION EXHIBIT No. 1826—Continued

— Commission Exhibit No. 1827 —

KRLD-TV reel 55
Monday, November 25, 1963 a.m.

PRESS INTERVIEW WITH POLICE CHIEF CURRY

CURRY. -- but I don't see that my resigning could help the situation any. Officials have expressed their confidence in me and as long as I have their confidence and backing I will continue to try to make a good police chief.

Q. Chief Curry, when did you first start out in the law enforcement field?

CURRY. 1936.

Q. And how long have you been with the Dallas Police Department?

CURRY. Since that time.

Q. And how long have you been Chief?

CURRY. Since January 21, 1960. I was assistant chief seven years prior to that.

Q. Chief Curry, there has been much said about the extreme gallantry displayed by Officer J. D. Tippit whose funeral will be this afternoon. Would you make one final comment on that before I switch this.

CURRY. Certainly. My heart goes out to Mrs. Tippit and the family. (Choked up) That's all I want to say.

NO 89-69
JDVE/ush

The following were contacted by SA J. DAWSON VAN EPS on December 2, 1963, and advised that their records include no information concerning Dr. A. J. HIDEEL:

Miss GERTRUDE BARBIER
Doctors Exchange
2337 Bruxells
New Orleans, Louisiana

Miss HILMA McAULIFFE, Secretary,
Orleans Parish Medical Society
1430 Tulane Avenue
New Orleans, Louisiana

Mrs. ROBERT WILSON, Clerk
Louisiana State Board of Medical Examiners
521 Hibernia Bank Building
New Orleans, Louisiana

Mrs. WILSON said that all private practitioners in the State of Louisiana are listed with the Louisiana State Board of Medical Examiners and have been since 1894.

She also advised that the 22nd edition of the American Medical Directory, published in 1963 does not include a listing for a Dr. A. J. HIDEEL.

CBS-TV
Thursday, November 28, 1963

INTERVIEW WITH DIAL RYDER, IRVING GUNSMITH SHOP, DALLAS, TEXAS

Q. It has been pretty well established that Oswald, the accused assassin of the President, used a 6.5 Carcano rifle, which is an Italian make, I think, with a Mauser action. Do you remember working on any gun like that?

RYDER. No. sir, I don't. I sure don't.

Q. You have attached a lot of scopes, telescopic sights recently. How would you mount a scope on a gun like that?

RYDER. Well, actually there is really one way to mount it on there. It would be with a side mount, and I don't recall putting a side mount on any bolt action that I've worked on.

Q. What do you mean by a side mount? Can you show me on this rifle here? Let's look at the gun.

RYDER. A side mount is mounted on the side of the gun, on, most likely, on the lefthand side of the gun. Now on this particular rifle here, which is an Argentine Mauser, it would be best on the top rather than on the side, over here.

Q. What do you do when you mount it?

COMMISSION EXHIBIT No. 1829

RYDER. Well, you have to drill holes and attach the threads, which are supposed to pass from the scope to the mount through that.

Q. On this gun it would be on top, but on the gun that has been established as the one that was used or found, let's say, in the School Book Building, it was, it would have to have been a side mount?

RYDER. Yes, sir. It sure would. And the pictures that the agent has shown me, it was a side mount.

Q. You were shown pictures by the FBI of the gun they found?

RYDER. Yes, sir.

Q. And that was a side-mounted telescopic sight?

RYDER. It sure was.

Q. And you don't remember mounting any side mounts?

RYDER. No, sir, I sure don't. Not on special or a bolt-action gun, I don't.

COMMISSION EXHIBIT No. 1829—Continued

FD-204 (Rev. 3-3-59)

UNITED STATES DEPARTMENT OF JUSTICE
FEDERAL BUREAU OF INVESTIGATION

Copy to:

Report of: SA DARREL B. CURRIE
Office: Boston, Massachusetts
Date: 12/23/63

Field Office File #: 105-10942
Bureau File #: 105-126128, 105-126129

Title:

RUTH HYDE PAINE;
MICHAEL RALPH PAINE

Character:

INTERNAL SECURITY - R

Synopsis:

Mrs. ARTHUR M. YOUNG and family, 35 E. 75th St., New York City, N.Y., resided at Kimball House, a seasonal hotel, Northeast Harbor, Maine, summer of 1950. No record of MICHAEL RALPH PAINE at this hotel. Hotel records show Mrs. STANLEY GOODWIN of New York and her daughter, JANE L. GOODWIN, also summer guests in 1950. Credit and arrest checks at Northeast Harbor, Maine, were negative. Prof. VLADIMIR SAJKOVIC, Mt. Holyoke College, South Hadley, Mass., vaguely recalls name RUTH HYDE as possibly a student in his Russian language course at University of Pennsylvania, summer of 1957, but has no pertinent information. MICHAEL RALPH PAINE attended Harvard College from 1947-49 as a member of the Class of 1951. Harvard College record contained no adverse information concerning his character or loyalty. On 6/30/49 the Administrative Board of Harvard College voted that PAINE's connection with Harvard be severed for failure to meet minimum requirements. Harvard College Registrar stated MICHAEL PAINE's father, GEORGE LYMAN PAINE, JR., known to him by reputation as "an enthusiastic Marxist and Trotskyite." Background data concerning GEORGE LYMAN PAINE, JR. set out. Harvard College Registrar did not know how closely MICHAEL R. PAINE had been associated with his father.

- RUC -

BS 105-10942

DETAILS:

At Northeast Harbor, Maine:

The following investigation was conducted by SA RAYMOND G. ROSS on December 12 and 13, 1963:

ARTHUR M. YOUNG and Mrs. ARTHUR M. YOUNG, nee FORBES, are not residents of Northeast Harbor, Maine, or regular summer visitors and are unknown to the following:

RICHARD A. SMITH, Postmaster, Northeast Harbor, Maine

Mrs. ESTHER S. BROWN, Part Owner, F. T. Brown Company, Main Street, Northeast Harbor, Maine

CARLO NINFI, Tax Collector and Treasurer, Northeast Harbor, Maine

The 1950 Directory and Handbook of Northeast Harbor, Maine, which contains the names of summer visitors discloses Mrs. ARTHUR M. YOUNG and family, 35 East 75th Street, New York City, N. Y., resided at the Kimball House, a seasonal hotel, Northeast Harbor, during the summer of 1950, exact period of residence not stated.

Mr. LOREN KIMBALL, Proprietor of the Kimball House, advised his 1950 hotel register disclosed Mr. and Mrs. ARTHUR YOUNG occupied Hillside #2, a large cottage owned by the hotel, as of June 29, 1950. Date of departure from this cottage was not listed. His hotel register also reflects CAMERON F. PAINE, no address listed, resided at this same cottage as of June 29, 1950. His date of departure was not listed. There is no record of MICHAEL RALPH PAINE.

The hotel register further disclosed that Mrs. STANLEY GOODWIN of New York and her daughter, JANE L. GOODWIN, occupied Hillside Cottage #2 as of July 13, 1950. Date of departure from the cottage was not listed but the register did contain a mailing address of Mrs. STANLEY GOODWIN as 830 Park Avenue, New York 21, N. Y.

Mrs. MARION KIMBALL, wife of the priprietor of the Kimball House, Northeast Harbor, Maine, could not recall the foregoing.

- 2 -

On December 12, 1963, Reverend MALCOLM S. SAWTELLE, Pastor, St. Mary's Episcopal Church, Northeast Harbor, Maine, advised that the Directory of the Protestant Episcopal Church of America reflects that Reverend ANTHONY PAUL TREASURE, former Pastor of St. Mary's Episcopal Church, Northeast Harbor, is presently located at the All Saints Church, Heaton Norris, Stockport, England.

There is no credit bureau located at Northeast Harbor, Maine.

On December 13, 1963, CARLO NINFI, Tax Collector and Treasurer, Northeast Harbor, Maine, advised that the arrest records located at the Northeast Harbor, Maine, Town Office contain no arrest record for these persons.

At South Hadley, Massachusetts:

On December 23, 1963, Professor VLADIMIR SAJKOVIC, Professor of Russian Language, Mt. Holyoke College, advised SA WALTER F. BRADY that he taught an elementary Russian language course at the University of Pennsylvania at the 1957 summer session.

Professor SAJKOVIC stated he only vaguely remembers the name RUTH HYDE as possibly a student in this Russian language course. He stated he could not be helpful as he recalled nothing about her and knew nothing of her background.

At Cambridge, Massachusetts:

The following investigation was conducted by SA JAMES T. SULLIVAN on December 23, 1963:

The 1960 edition of the Harvard Alumni Directory identifies MICHAEL RALPH PAINE as a member of the Harvard College Class of 1951. The directory shows PAINE was in attendance at Harvard College from 1947 to 1949. As of 1960 his residence address was listed as Rural Delivery #1, Malvern, Pennsylvania.

On December 23, 1963, Mrs. ADELINE DAILEY, Registrar's Office, Harvard College, stated records of that office identify MICHAEL RALPH PAINE as a member of the Class of 1951. He was born June 25, 1928, at New York, N.Y., to GEORGE LYMAN PAINE, JR. and RUTH FORBES PAINE. The file showed that PAINE's reports were to be forwarded to his mother, Mrs. GILES W. THOMAS. This latter name was scratched out and listed under

it was PAINE's mother's name, Mrs. ARTHUR YOUNG.

MICHAEL RALPH PAINE was admitted to Harvard College in May, 1947, from the Horace Mann Lincoln School, New York, N. Y. He was in attendance at Harvard College during the Fall Term 1947-1948, the Spring Term 1947-1948, and the academic year 1948-1949. His field of concentration was shown as Physics.

The file showed that the Administrative Board, Harvard College, on December 2, 1947, voted that no action be taken on the unsatisfactory mid-term record compiled by PAINE.

The file showed further that the Administrative Board, on June 30, 1949, voted that PAINE's connection with the college be severed on account of failure to meet minimum requirements, and further voted that PAINE be discouraged regarding re-admission.

Transcripts of his scholastic record were sent to PAINE on September 14 and 15, 1950.

On December 23, 1963, SARGENT KENNEDY, Registrar, Harvard College, stated that although he was well aware that MICHAEL PAINE's mother is a member of the well-known FORBES family of Milton, Massachusetts, he had not known MICHAEL PAINE, her son.

He stated he had reviewed MICHAEL PAINE's folder and noted that it contained nothing reflecting adversely upon his character and loyalty. He said he felt PAINE's academic trouble stemmed solely from the fact "he never came to grips with studying." He pointed out he had heard nothing derogatory concerning MICHAEL PAINE.

KENNEDY stated that MICHAEL PAINE's father, GEORGE LYMAN PAINE, JR., was known to him by reputation as "an enthusiastic Marxist and Trotskyite," who, in the 25th and 35th annual reports of the Harvard College Class of 1922, had set out much of his basic philosophy. KENNEDY stated he did not know how closely MICHAEL R. PAINE has been associated with his father.

In the 25th Anniversary Report, Harvard College Class of 1922, GEORGE LYMAN PAINE, JR., born November 16, 1901, at New York, N. Y., to GEORGE LYMAN PAINE, Harvard College Class of 1896, and to CLARA MAY, identified himself in 1947 as a resident of 629 Hudson Street, New York, N.Y., and as an architect.

He stated he had married RUTH FORBES at Milton, Massachusetts, on March 20, 1926, and had been divorced in 1934. He had married FRANCES DRAKE at New York, N.Y., in 1939.

PAINE wrote in part as follows:

". . . My office closed. I got a job through the Civil Works Administration with the New York City Housing Authority. Up to my neck in housing research and community planning, I shared the hard work and the dreams of liberals whose baby it was. I joined the Federation of Architects, Engineers, Chemists, and Technicians, a union of professional men. There, through those most active in it, the members of the various radical political parties, I came into contact with Marxism. The writings of Marx, Engels, Lenin and Trotsky opened new doors upon an old world. The theory of historical materialism began to make clear much that had eluded me these many years; the relations between the movement of society and the movement of ideas, between the world of the mass (action) and the world of the intellectual, between the individual and society.

"This theory and its derivative, the theory of class struggle, provided the only comprehensible explanation of the new phenomena on the American scene, the radio squad cars called out to disperse the too-great throngs of workers crowding to hear Shakespeare and Beethoven in the park (WPA) and to break up the hunger marches, the historic movement to the left of intellectuals flocking to Marxism and workers to the sit-down strikes and the CIO. It gave substance and coherence to the great events of the past ten years of which I, like most Harvard men, had been but dimly conscious though deeply, vaguely disturbed; from Sacco and Vanzetti, through the defeats of the European revolutions, to the rise of Hitler.

"I could no longer escape the reality of the class struggle nor the responsibility for action. I became a follower of Leon Trotsky and a partisan of the world working class.

"In the twelve years which have followed, life, both for me and for my wife, has been an interweaving harmony of reading and hard work, activity in the labor movement and Marxist politics, of theory and practice. Architecture, three years as a shipfitter during the

"war, organizing, speaking, labor defense, teaching, and writing have been among the facets of a unified, creative life. To my way of thinking this joy is no result of accident or personal whim. Creation and frustration are but the reciprocal expressions of the relation of the individual to his society. Today the world-wide contradictions, decay and incapacity of capitalism are a paralyzing reality for all society, therefore also for the individual. The upward path from the old to the new has been a path of struggle, a concrete struggle, a class struggle. I am free and I am content because I have chosen my side in that struggle and chosen to act."

In the Thirty-fifth Anniversary Report of the Harvard College Class of 1922, GEORGE LYMAN PAINE, JR. identified himself as an architect and as a resident of 2331 Holgate Square, Los Angeles 31, California.

He wrote in part as follows:

". . . I am still married to the same remarkable woman, still earning a living as an architect, still consumed by the urge to contribute as I am able to the solution of those ills of society which today frustrate most marriages and most architects along with other human beings.

"I continue to express such creative energies as I may have in a stubborn, active and uncompromising hostility to all forces, all aspects of society which deny to man both order and human dignity and which, furthermore, oppose a positive barrier to his every effort to achieve such a goal.

"By 1950 it finally became clear that the solution to the problems of humanity, and therefore of individual creativity, lay not in the education of people nor in the character of leaders. The problem lay in the concept itself of leadership over people. The solution lay in the liberation of people to achieve their own destiny, apart from and in opposition to domination by any elite or group whatsoever.

"Because the Trotskyites shared in this concept of the role of an elite, of a mission to lead, I broke with them, along with a number of colleagues, in 1951.

BS 105-10942

"Since then I have become part owner and part editor of a small paper, CORRESPONDENCE. For the past five years it has been an arduous and exciting experiment toward the creation of an instrument, a form, through which the ordinary worker can freely express his real concerns and can communicate with others, and through which the intellectual can re-establish contact with the driving force of society and contribute thereto as a colleague whose function is not to dominate but to give of his historical knowledge and, particularly experience. . . . ."

- 7* -

COMMISSION EXHIBIT No. 1830—Continued

UNITED STATES DEPARTMENT OF JUSTICE
FEDERAL BUREAU OF INVESTIGATION

Copy to:

Report of: SA JAMES P. HOSTY, JR. Office: DALLAS
Date: DECEMBER 11, 1963

Field Office File No.: DL 105-1716 Bureau File No.:

Title: RUTH HYDE PAINE

Character: INTERNAL SECURITY - RUSSIA

Synopsis: RUTH HYDE PAINE, the daughter of WILLIAM A. HYDE and Mrs. CAROL HYDE, is married to MICHAEL RALPH PAINE. Mrs. PAINE advised she became acquainted with MARINA OSWALD and LEE HARVEY OSWALD in early 1963, and in May of 1963, she assisted MARINA OSWALD and her child in moving to New Orleans, La. Mrs. PAINE stated she assisted MARINA OSWALD and child in moving from New Orleans to Irving, Texas, in September of 1963. Mrs. PAINE stated that MARINA OSWALD then resided with her since MARINA's husband was unemployed and she was expecting another child. On 11/1/63 RUTH PAINE advised a Special Agent of the FBI that LEE HARVEY OSWALD was employed at the Texas School Book Depository (TSBD) but was unable to furnish his residence. Mrs. PAINE advised on 11/23/63 LEE HARVEY OSWALD came to her residence on 11/21/63 allegedly to visit his wife and children. Mrs. PAINE advised she later learned from MARINA OSWALD that among the OSWALDs' personal property stored in her garage was a rifle belonging to LEE HARVEY OSWALD.

- P -

Details:

I. BACKGROUND

A. Residence

On November 1, 1963, Mrs. RUTH PAINE adised she resided at 2515 West 5th Street, Irving, Texas.

COMMISSION EXHIBIT No. 1831

DL 105-1716
JPH:mam

B. Employment

On October 31, 1963, Mr. EDWARD T. OVIATT, Assistant Headmaster, St. Marks School of Texas, Dallas, Texas, advised that Mrs. PAINE had been employed on a part-time basis as a teacher of the Russian language. At this time, however, she was not teaching on a full-time basis but tutoring students at their homes.

C. Education

On November 25, 1963, Mrs. RUTH PAINE advised that she formerly attended Antioch College in Ohio and studied the Russian language at a summer school session at the University of Pennsylvania two years ago.

D. Marital Status

On November 1, 1963, Mrs. RUTH PAINE advised that she is married to MICHAEL RALPH PAINE.

E. Identification Record

On October 31, 1963, J. H. KITCHING, Dallas County Sheriff's Office, and LEON POWERS, Irving, Texas, Police Department, advised that they had no record for RUTH PAINE.

COMMISSION EXHIBIT No. 1831—Continued

DL 105-1716
JPH:gmf

II. FAMILY BACKGROUND OF RUTH HYDE PAINE

On December 2, 1963, SAs JOHN W. LILL, JR., and BERNARD D. MALONEY contacted CARL D. HYDE, M.D., 1405 President Street, Yellow Springs, at his office located at 1425 Xenia Avenue, Yellow Springs, Ohio, who furnished the following information:

He is a brother of RUTH HYDE PAINE, 2515 West Fifth Street, Irving, Texas, with whom the wife of LEE HARVEY OSWALD is presently residing. He said that OSWALD was not known personally to him and that he had not heard of him prior to the assassination of President JOHN F. KENNEDY in Dallas, Texas, November 22, 1963.

He related that his sister, RUTH, had visited him at Yellow Springs in September, 1963, and mentioned she was leaving for New Orleans, Louisiana, at that time to contact a woman of Russian birth and invite her to stay with her in her home at Irving, Texas. He could not recall whether his sister had mentioned the woman's last name but recalled she had told him that the woman's husband was a communist and although the woman was a Russian, she did not share her husband's views. It was mentioned that the husband had not allowed this woman to learn English, that the woman was pregnant at the time, and that she was experiencing marital difficulties. The circumstances of his sister's acquaintance with this woman were not mentioned.

Dr. HYDE said that his sister, RUTH, was also experiencing marital difficulties at this time and it was his opinion that RUTH's actions to assist this woman were to lend moral support to this woman and herself in view of their mutual difficulties.

He said that following the assassination of President KENNEDY he learned of the identity of the woman previously mentioned by his sister, RUTH, as being the wife of LEE HARVEY OSWALD. He said that his father, WILLIAM A. HYDE, Park Street, Columbus, Ohio, had told him that he had received mail from RUTH, in which she mentioned that LEE HARVEY OSWALD had been to his sister's home prior to the assassination for the purpose of visiting his wife. It was not indicated to him that OSWALD himself was actually residing at his sister's home.

COMMISSION EXHIBIT No. 1831—Continued

Dr. HYDE said that all of the family, including himself, were "tolerant of others point of view" and explained by this he meant that should a person make it known that he is a communist and not engaged in subversion, they would not feel duty-bound to advise respective authorities of this person's views. He claimed to have no further knowledge of the OSWALDs and appeared cooperative during the interview.

The following investigation was conducted by SAs ROBERT F. MAHLER and FRANCIS X. SHORTT at Columbus, Ohio:

Efforts to locate Mrs. CAROL HYDE, mother of Mrs. RUTH PAINE, nee HYDE, were made December 2, 1963, at 4400 Glenmawr Avenue. It was observed this residence was empty.

Mrs. JOAN BARKER, neighbor, 4390 Glenmawr Avenue, advised on December 2, 1963, she was more closely associated with Mrs. CAROL HYDE than any other neighbor. CAROL HYDE, she said, has not lived next door since 1961. She presently attends Oberlin Theological Seminary, Oberlin, Ohio, and lives there. During the summer of 1963, she said, CAROL HYDE was ordained a minister in the First Unitarian Chruch, 93 West Wiseheimer Road, Columbus, Ohio.

Mrs. BARKER said the residence of 4400 Glenmawr Avenue had been rented to a JEAN JOLLIFF, who has recently moved away to 758 Racine Avenue, Columbus, Ohio. The residence is now empty.

Mrs. BARKER said CAROL HYDE was divorced from her husband, WILLIAM HYDE, at Franklin County in 1961. During an unknown period, 1960, her ex-husband had Mrs. HYDE committed to the Harding Sanitarium, Worthington, Ohio, as a mental patient.

CAROL HYDE is not expected to return to Columbus in the near future. Her last visit to Columbus was during September, 1963, at which time her daughter, RUTH PAINE, stayed overnight in Columbus, then went to visit her brother, CARL HYDE, in Yellow Springs, Ohio.

Mrs. BARKER said she had never heard Mrs. HYDE mention the name OSWALD until the two spoke via a long-distance telephone call November 29, 1963, concerning the property next door, at which time Mrs. HYDE mentioned that a Mrs. OSWALD had been living with her daughter, RUTH PAINE, at Irving, Texas. During this conversation, CAROL HYDE also told Mrs. BARKER after she graduates from the theological seminary her ambition is to become a chaplain in a mental institution.

WILLIAM AVERY HYDE, Apartment 105, 580 Park Street, Columbus, Ohio, born June 4, 1902, Palo Alto, California, employed as a actuary, Nationwide Insurance Company, 246 North High Street, was interviewed December 2, 1963. He said he is the father of RUTH PAINE, nee HYDE, who is married to MICHAEL PAINE, Irving, Texas. He is also the father of Mrs. SYLVIA HOKE, 5421 Waneta Road, Bethesda, Maryland, and the father of Dr. CARL D. HYDE, 1405 President Street, Yellow Springs, Ohio. He said he is divorced from CAROL ELIZABETH HYDE, nee HYDE. He explained he and his ex-wife are sixth cousins with the same surname. He advised their divorce took place at Franklin County, Ohio, in 1961. He said CAROL HYDE is a divinity student at Oberlin Theological Seminary, Oberlin, Ohio.

He related he last visited with his daughter, RUTH PAINE, at the residence of RUTH's husband's mother, Mrs. RUTH YOUNG, Paoli, Pennsylvania, during Labor Day weekend, 1963. He stayed at this place two days. His daughter, RUTH, and her two children were there but her husband, MICHAEL PAINE, remained at Dallas, Texas.

During this visit his daughter related that she had met Mrs. MARINA OSWALD, through circumstances not recalled by WILLIAM HYDE, and that MARINA, who had separated from her husband, LEE HARVEY OSWALD, had been living with RUTH PAINE, who was also temporarily separated from her husband, at RUTH's home, Irving, Texas, during the summer of 1963. During their visit over Labor Day weekend WILLIAM HYDE understood that MARINA OSWALD and her daughter had joined LEE HARVEY OSWALD at New Orleans, Louisiana, where the latter went to seek employment.

During this visit, RUTH PAINE expressed concern about

MARINA OSWALD, who was pregnant. She wanted MARINA to join her at Irving, Texas, so MARINA could have her child there. RUTH PAINE returned to Texas via New Orleans, where she picked up MARINA and her daughter. WILLIAM HYDE believed LEE HARVEY OSWALD remained in New Orleans since he did not return to Texas with RUTH and MARINA.

WILLIAM HYDE could not explain why his daughter and MARINA OSWALD were so closely attached, except that his daughter was interested in studying the Russian language and through her membership in the Society of Friends she felt learning the Russian language would assist in lessening the tensions between the United States and Russia. He added MARINA OSWALD was apparently very interesting to his daughter and could offer her substantial comfort or his daughter would not have had anything to do with her. He said he knew of no subversive connections MARINA OSWALD may have had.

WILLIAM HYDE continued and said RUTH and MARINA and MARINA's daughter lived together, away from their respective husbands, from September, 1963, until just recently when MARINA OSWALD was placed in protective custody by the U. S. Secret Service. A daughter, RACHAEL OSWALD, was born to MARINA October 20, 1963.

WILLIAM HYDE said he received a letter from RUTH PAINE, written October 19, 1963, in which she mentioned that MARINA and her daughter were a comfort to her. She also mentioned that LEE HARVEY OSWALD was a weekend visitor, that he had taken a room in Dallas, separate from his wife, and had obtained employment at Dallas, Texas. The time of OSWALD's arrival at Dallas was not mentioned, nor was the type of employment described. In a sentence, RUTH PAINE said LEE HARVEY OSWALD had proven himself to be a "fine family man after all." WILLIAM HYDE did not know the significance of this sentence.

He received another letter from RUTH, dated November 6, 1963, which announced the birth of MARINA's child.

WILLIAM HYDE said during his visit with his daughter, during the Labor Day weekend, the information concerning MARINA

OSWALD was not significant to him. He explained he had never met either MARINA nor LEE HARVEY OSWALD, and knew nothing more concerning what he had related.

He explained that late in the day of November 22, 1963, as he was watching television concerning news developments of the assassination, the name of LEE HARVEY OSWALD was mentioned. It was further mentioned that he had a Russian wife. This sounded familiar to WILLIAM HYDE so he searched through correspondence from his daughter and learned that this was the OSWALD his daughter had referred to in her letter to him of October 19, 1963.

Being concerned over his daughter's safety, WILLIAM HYDE attempted to telephone her at Irving, Texas, but received a reply from a juvenile babysitter to the effect that Mrs. PAINE "had left with a lot of people." He decided to travel to Texas and boarded a plane which took him to Chicago, Illinois. At Chicago, he again telephoned his daughter at Irving, Texas, talked with her, and learned his daughter had accompanied MARINA OSWALD to the Police Station and that both women were safe. His daughter convinced him it would be useless to fly to Texas, so he returned to Columbus.

He has since communicated with his daughter by telephone calls to and from her.

WILLIAM HYDE said he had never heard the name JACK RUBY or RUBENSTEIN mentioned by anyone until this name became public news.

WILLIAM HYDE said he had been interviewed on November 29, 1963, by a reporter from the "Columbus Citizen Journal," furnished background information concerning his daughter, RUTH PAINE, and a photograph of her with her two children, which he had taken earlier.

HYDE mentioned to the interviewing Agents that he was proud to have sent his three children to Antioch College, Yellow Springs, Ohio, and pointed out two of his children married Antioch graduates, and the third married a Swarthmore College graduate.

The February 14, 1948, issue of the "Ohio State News," a newspaper published by students at the Ohio State University, contained an article which was captioned, "Ohio College Students Initiate Educational Democracy Drive." The article stated that more than 100 students from colleges and universities throughout Ohio have initiated a drive for democracy in education. The article indicated the Ohio Council for Educational Democracy was formed in Columbus over the past weekend to obtain this goal. This organization would work to do away with racial and religious discrimination in Ohio colleges. CARL HYDE of Antioch College was elected as vice chairman of the organization.

Confidential Informant T-1, another U. S. Government Agency which conducts intelligence investigations, advised on December 17, 1952, that Mrs. WILLIAM A. HYDE, 1986 Summit Street, Columbus, Ohio, had admitted to many neighbors during the past years that she was a "Communist." Mrs. HYDE's daughter was a student at Antioch College, Yellow Springs, Ohio.

This same informant advised that RUTH AVERY HYDE, 1986 Summit Street, Columbus, Ohio, was listed in the 1951-1952 Antioch Student Directory of Antioch College, Yellow Springs, Ohio.

Confidential Informant T-2 advised on December 27, 1954, that the Women's International League for Peace and Freedom met on December 20, 1954, at 70 E. Como Street, Columbus, Ohio. Mrs. CAROL HYDE was the speaker of the evening and she showed a film entitled, "The Toymaker." The theme of the film was that although men are different, they are all made by one Creator and only this realization makes them conscious of the fact that when they destroy others they are also destroying themselves.

A characterization of the Women's International League for Peace and Freedom is contained in the appendix of this report.

Mr. LOREN G. WINDOM, Assistant United States Attorney, Southern District of Ohio, Columbus, Ohio, sent a letter to the

Cincinnati Office of the FBI, dated June 4, 1953, requesting an investigation of CARL DUDLEY HYDE to determine the validity of his claim of "Conscientious Objector" in connection with his classification under the Selective Service System. This investigation revealed that his parents were WILLIAM AVERY HYDE and CAROL ELIZABETH HYDE, and he resided at 1986 Summit Street, Columbus, Ohio, from 1945 to 1948. He joined the Religious Society of Friends, Cleveland, Ohio, in 1949 and based his objections to military service on religious convictions and beliefs. He travelled to England in 1953 to study the possibility of living in a religious community, the Society of Brothers.

The February 12, 1947, issue of the "Dayton Daily News," a daily newspaper published in Dayton, Ohio, contained an article which indicated that CARL DUDLEY HYDE was one of fifteen residents of Yellow Springs, Ohio, who sent their draft registration cards to Representative Joseph Martin, Speaker of the House, accompanied with a letter which stated in part, "We see any military program involving peacetime conscription as a drastic violation of civil rights and a threat to the peace-making efforts of the United Nations." Most of the senders were students of Antioch College.

DL 105-1716
JPH:mam

III. CONNECTIONS WITH LEE HARVEY OSWALD AND MARINA NIKOLAEVNA OSWALD

On October 29, 1963, a pretext interview by a Special Agent of the FBI at 2519 West 5th Street, Irving, Texas, reflected that Mrs. RUTH PAINE resided at 2515 West 5th Street. Mrs. PAINE was separated from her husband, MICHAEL RALPH PAINE, and it was determined that Mrs. PAINE was employed at St. Marks School of Texas, Dallas, Texas, on a part-time basis as a teacher of the Russian language, and she had a Russian-born woman living with her. This Russian-born woman gave birth to a baby girl about a week ago, and Mrs. PAINE was taking care of this woman. It was determined that the husband of the Russian-born woman visited his wife at this address periodically but did not reside there.

On October 31, 1963, Mrs. DOROTHY SMITH, Irving, Texas, Credit Bureau, advised that they had a credit record for MICHAEL R. PAINE and his wife, RUTH PAINE, who resided at 2515 West 5th Street, Irving, Texas. Mrs. SMITH advised their credit was satisfactory, and that Mr. PAINE was employed by Bell Helicopter Company in Fort Worth, Texas, as an engineer. Mrs. PAINE's employment was shown as a housewife.

On October 31, 1963, Mr. EDWARD T. OVIATT, Assistant Headmaster, St. Marks School of Texas, Dallas, Texas, advised that Mrs. PAINE was a satisfactory employee and was loyal to this country. He considered her to be a stable individual. Mr. OVIATT advised that Mrs. PAINE was employed on a part-time basis as a teacher of the Russian language. He also learned in a conversation with Mrs. PAINE that she had a Russian-born woman living with her, and she was assisting this woman in view of the fact that she had recently had a new baby and she, Mrs. PAINE, was improving her Russian speaking ability by having this Russian-speaking person in her house.

DL 105-1716
JPH:mam

On October 31, 1963, Mr. TED SCHURMAN, Security Officer, Bell Helicopter Company, Fort Worth, Texas, advised that MICHAEL R. PAINE was presently employed by that company was an engineer, and he holds a security clearance.

On November 1, 1963, Mrs. RUTH PAINE was interviewed, at which time she advised that MARINA OSWALD, wife of LEE HARVEY OSWALD, was staying with her following the recent birth of her baby. Mrs. PAINE furnished OSWALD's place of employment as the Texas School Book Depository (TSBD), 411 Elm Street, Dallas, Texas, where he was employed as a laborer. Mrs. PAINE stated she did not know where OSWALD was residing in Dallas at this time, but it was his plan as soon as he had enough money to get an apartment for his family and then take his wife and children to live with him. Mrs. PAINE volunteered that she would be glad to furnish this address to the FBI as soon as she determined where the OSWALDs were residing.

On November 5, 1963, Mrs. RUTH PAINE advised that she had been unable to obtain the address of LEE OSWALD in Dallas, but she would furnish it to the FBI as soon as she was able to obtain it. Mrs. PAINE advised that LEE OSWALD had visited his wife, MARINA OSWALD, on November 2 and 3, 1963, at Irving, Texas. Mrs. PAINE then expressed the opinion that she considered LEE OSWALD to be an illogical person and recalled that he admitted to her being a "Trotskyite Communist".

On November 22, 1963, Mrs. RUTH PAINE advised Special Agent JAMES W. BOOKHOUT upon interview at the Dallas Police Department that she first met LEE HARVEY OSWALD and his wife, MARINA OSWALD, during the early part of 1963 at a party. Inasmuch as she was interested in the Russian language and was a teacher of the Russian language, she became friendly with MARINA OSWALD.

About May, 1963, Mrs. PAINE brought MARINA OSWALD to New Orleans, Louisiana, and later brought her from New Orleans to Irving, Texas, to reside with her, Mrs. PAINE, due to the fact that she was about to have a baby and her husband was unemployed.

On November 23, 1963, Mrs. RUTH PAINE advised Special Agents JAMES P. HOSTY, JR., and JOE B. ABERNATHY that she first met LEE HARVEY OSWALD and his wife, MARINA OSWALD, during the winter of 1963, possibly February 22, 1963. They met at a social gathering, at which time Mrs. PAINE, who speaks the Russian language, became acquainted with Mrs. MARINA OSWALD, who speaks only Russian and has a very limited knowledge of the English language. Mrs. PAINE stated that in approximately April of 1963, LEE OSWALD and his wife, MARINA, visited them at their home where they had dinner together. Mrs. PAINE stated that during this period, OSWALD was employed at Jaggars - Chiles - Stovall, a blueprinting company in Dallas, Texas. OSWALD lost his job in either late April or early May and went to New Orleans, Louisiana, to find a job in early May, 1963. Mrs. PAINE stated that on May 10, 1963, she drove MARINA OSWALD and her child to New Orleans to join LEE OSWALD. Mrs. PAINE stated that following OSWALD's arrest for "Disturbing the Peace" and "Distributing Pro-Castro Literature" in New Orleans, he lost his job and Mrs. MARINA OSWALD was in the late stages of pregnancy with their second child. Mrs. PAINE stated she is very fond of MARINA OSWALD and felt sorry for her, so she drove to New Orleans on September 23, 1963, and took Mrs. MARINA OSWALD and her child, JUNE OSWALD, back to Irving, Texas, with her. They arrived in Irving, Texas, on September 24, 1963. When they left Louisiana, LEE OSWALD was still residing in that city; however, Mrs. PAINE stated that she later determined that LEE OSWALD apparently went to Mexico City after September 24, 1963.

Mrs. PAINE stated on October 4, 1963, LEE OSWALD contacted his wife at the PAINE residence and advised her that he was now in Dallas. He indicated he had arrived in Dallas

on October 3, 1963, and had a room somewhere in Dallas, which address he did not give. Mrs. PAINE stated she did learn that OSWALD had moved to another room a few days later, and it was in this place that OSWALD was residing at the time of his arrest on November 22, 1963.

Mrs. PAINE stated that on November 18, 1963, MARINA OSWALD telephonically contacted LEE OSWALD at a telephone number which Mrs. PAINE stated she cannot recall. She had Mrs. PAINE ask for LEE OSWALD by his true name. OSWALD apparently became quite incensed with his wife for giving out his true name, since he was apparently living at this address under another name. Mrs. PAINE stated that after October 5, 1963, OSWALD started receiving mail at her address, which mail included newspapers and periodicals from the Soviet Union.

Mrs. PAINE further stated that on October 15, 1963, OSWALD obtained a job as a laborer at the TSBD, 411 Elm Street, Dallas, Texas. Mrs. PAINE stated that after OSWALD returned to Dallas on October 3, 1963, he usually visited his wife and children at Mrs. PAINE's residence on weekends and sometimes spent the night at her house. Mrs. PAINE stated that the OSWALDs had many of their personal effects stored in her garage, and on the night of November 21, 1963, a Thursday, LEE OSWALD appeared at the PAINE residence allegedly to visit his famil and asked to stay overnight. That evening, OSWALD went out to the garage, allegedly to rearrange some of his personal effects. Mrs. PAINE stated she later determined that LEE HARVEY OSWALD had a rifle wrapped up inside of a blanket among some of his personal effects in her garage. Mrs. PAINE stated she did not realize this until Mrs. OSWALD admitted it to Dallas Police detectives on the afternoon of November 22, 1963. Mrs. PAINE stated that she did not think LEE HARVEY OSWALD was a very logical individual, but at no time did he ever give any indications to her that he would do a violent thing, such as killing an individual. Mrs. PAINE insisted that her friendship with the OSWALDs was with MARINA, and not with LEE HARVEY OSWALD.

DL 105-1716
JPH:mam

On November 27, 1963, Mrs. RUTH KLOEPFER, 306 Pine Street, New Orleans, Louisiana, advised Special Agents TROY H. GIST and EUGENE E. BJORN that she received a long distance telephone call from Mrs. RUTH PAINE in Irving, Texas, asking her to visit a Mrs. LEE OSWALD at 4907 Magazine Street, New Orleans. Mrs. PAINE stated that she had learned of Mrs. KLOEPFER through a fellow Quaker. Mrs. PAINE asked Mrs. KLOEPFER to look after Mrs. OSWALD who was about to have a baby and needed help. Mrs. KLOEPFER promised Mrs. PAINE she would visit Mrs. OSWALD to see if she could help her.

105-1716

APPENDIX

WOMEN'S INTERNATIONAL LEAGUE FOR PEACE AND FREEDOM

CINCINNATI, OHIO, CHAPTER

A confidential informant who conducted investigations of subversive organizations for a national veterans organization advised on May 8, 1940, that a Cincinnati Chapter of the Women's International League for Peace and Freedom (WILPF) was then in existence and was suspected of being a Communist front organization.

Another confidential informant advised on October 31, 1955, that the Cincinnati Chapter of the WILPF is an affiliate of the international organization, and that its aims and objectives are to promote world peace and disarmament.

A third confidential informant advised on May 16, 1957, that while the Communist Party (CP) in Cincinnati had in the past expressed an interest in the Cincinnati Chapter of the WILPF, that interest does not exist at the present time and the CP at Cincinnati is making no attempts to infiltrate or control the WILPF.

The Communist Party has been designated by the Attorney General of the United States pursuant to Executive Order 10450.

FD-302 (Rev. 3-3-59)

FEDERAL BUREAU OF INVESTIGATION

1

Oswald, Marina

Date 2/25/64

MARINA OSWALD was interviewed at the home of Mr. and Mrs. DECLAN P. FORD, 14057 Brookcrest, Dallas, Texas. Mr. HENRY BAER, law partner of Mr. WILLIAM A. McKENZIE, Attorney for MARINA, was present during this interview.

MARINA was asked if she or her husband, LEE HARVEY OSWALD, had known an individual by the name of ALBERT OSBORNE or JOHN HOWARD BOWEN. She advised she did not know any persons by these names. She said she had never heard him mention the names. She was asked if OSWALD had mentioned making an acquaintance on his trip to Mexico in September-October, 1963. MARINA said she cannot recall that OSWALD said he made any such acquaintances. She said OSWALD took the trip to Mexico alone and returned alone.

MARINA was exhibited a photograph of one JOHN HOWARD BOWEN which depicts him standing on a grassy lawn before a castle-like edifice. She said she could not identify this person. She was exhibited a mug type photograph of one ALBERT OSBORNE taken October, 1963, and she advised she had never seen this person to her knowledge.

on 2/24/64 at Dallas, Texas File # DL 100-10461

by Special Agent WALLACE R. HEITMAN and ANATOLE A. BOGUSLAV:vm Date dictated 2/25/64

-79-

COMMISSION EXHIBIT No. 1832

UNITED STATES DEPARTMENT OF JUSTICE
FEDERAL BUREAU OF INVESTIGATION

In Reply, Please Refer to
File No.

WASHINGTON 25, D.C.

February 25, 1964

LEE HARVEY OSWALD

Marina Oswald was interviewed on February 24, 1964. She stated that approximately two weeks after the General Walker incident and while they resided on Neeley Street in Dallas, Oswald, some time between 11 a.m. and 1 p.m., dressed himself in a suit and tie and put a pistol underneath his jacket. (The General Walker incident occurred on April 10, 1963.) She said Oswald was unemployed at this time. She said she inquired where he was going, to which Oswald replied approximately, "Nixon is coming and I'm going to take a look."

Mrs. Oswald said that at the time she realized she had to act fast, whereupon she walked into the bathroom and told Oswald to come into the bathroom with her, which he did. She said she then quickly jumped outside the door, closing it as she left the bathroom. She said she forcibly held the bathroom door shut holding on to the knob and bracing her feet against the wall. She said Oswald attempted to get out of the bathroom and was yelling, "Open the door." She said she forcibly held the door shut for about three minutes. In this respect she said that she cannot at this time accurately recall the length of time she forcibly held the bathroom door closed. She said she told Oswald it was difficult for her to hold the door and commented to him that something might happen to the baby. She said that she was pregnant at this time.

She said she told Oswald he was not going to shoot at anyone else and that if he wanted to come out of the bathroom, he would have to walk across her body. She said she reminded Oswald of his promise to her after the Walker incident that he would not try to do anything else like that. She recalled she said something like, "How can you deceive me after you gave me your word?" She said she told Oswald she would open the door if he would give his word to remain in the bathroom and not go anywhere and if he would undress and give her his clothing and pistol. Mrs. Oswald said that her husband agreed to this and she opened the bathroom door after holding it, as stated, for approximately three minutes.

COMMISSION EXHIBIT No. 1833

Oswald then took off his outer garments, including his shoes, and gave them and his pistol to her. She said that she put the pistol under the mattress and that she does not know whether or not the pistol was loaded. Later that day Oswald took the pistol from under the mattress and put it on the shelf where he usually kept it.

Mrs. Oswald said that the bathroom door at their Neeley Street residence opened toward the inside and there was no lock on the outside of the door, although she believes there was a lock on the inside. She said that she feels that she kept Oswald in the house on the occasion in question by persuasion and that this was one of the times he did something that she wanted him to do.

Mrs. Oswald commented that Oswald remained in the bathroom approximately three hours. She said he asked her for a book and that he spent the time in the bathroom reading with the door shut. She recalled that at about 4 p.m. she told Oswald he could come out of the bathroom if he desired, and he did so. He thereafter sat in the living room in his shorts reading. She said that he did not leave the house that day.

Mrs. Oswald said that at the time she did not know who Richard M. Nixon was and she did not recall Oswald ever mentioning Mr. Nixon's name prior to the occasion in question. She said she knows at this time that Mr. Nixon once ran for the presidency, but she said she still knows very little about him. She maintained that she and Oswald did not talk about this incident or about Mr. Nixon after the incident and, in fact, did not discuss the matter during the time Oswald was sitting in the bathroom or after he came out of the bathroom.

Mrs. Oswald said that she told Mr. and Mrs. James H. Martin about the Nixon incident approximately three to four weeks after she moved into the Martin residence and, thereafter, she repeated it to Robert Oswald. She stated she cannot recall whether she told Robert Oswald about the Nixon incident in the presence of the Martins or whether she spoke to him about it alone.

Mrs. Oswald was again asked if she could remember anything which might have indicated to her that Oswald was to do anything unusual on November 22, 1963. She said that she could not remember anything which would indicate this and that the news of her husband's arrest had come as a "thunderclap" to her.

Mrs. Oswald stated that while she and her husband resided in New Orleans on Magazine Street toward the end of August or early in September, 1963, for a period of about two weeks, Oswald was making plans to hijack an airplane and force the pilot to take him to Cuba. She said he subsequently revised his plans to the extent that he included her as part of his planning. She said he told her that he was to sit at the front of the airplane with a pistol and that she was to sit at the back of the plane with a pistol. They were to be accompanied by their daughter June and were to attempt to force the crew to fly the plane to Cuba. Mrs. Oswald stated that she refused to have anything to do with the plan and told Oswald, "Only a crazy man would think this up." She said Oswald told her he would buy a lightweight pistol for her and that he wanted her to at least learn how to hold it. She said she refused to do this. She said her husband told her that he had seen some lightweight pistols, but that she told him not to purchase one as she would not participate in the scheme.

She said she recalled that Oswald, during the period of time when he was planning to hijack the airplane, studied a world map and figured out distances to various places. She said he told her it would be necessary to hijack a plane with sufficient gas to get them to Cuba. She recalled that Oswald wrote out timetables of airlines on a piece of paper. She does not know what happened to the map or to the paper on which he wrote the timetables. During this period she stated that Oswald began to take physical exercise to increase his physical strength.

She said that when she refused to take part in the scheme to hijack an airplane, she counseled Oswald to attempt to enter Cuba legally. Thereafter, her husband began planning to go to Mexico alone for the purpose of obtaining permission to enter Cuba.

Concerning James H. Martin, Mrs. Oswald stated that Martin told her while she was in residence at his home that he had undergone an operation and could not father children.

1 — Commission Exhibit No. 1834 — Date 7/3/64

L. S. BROTHERTON, 10537 Fern Drive, Dallas, was interviewed at his place of business, Service, Inc., 4936 Columbia, Dallas. He said he had never owned the DuCharme Club in Dallas, did not know the owner, and had never visited the place.

He said that in about the late spring or early summer of 1963 he had been approached by three individuals at the Beachcomber Club on Lovers Lane in Dallas, which he then owned. He remembered that one of them was named LARRIE SCHMIDT, but he could not remember the names of SCHMIDT's two friends. These men represented themselves as having a great deal of money at their disposal and being interested in buying a night club in Dallas. BROTHERTON said that at the time he was losing money on the Beachcomber Club and would have been glad to have sold it, but from the first approach made to him by this trio he had them tabbed as "phonies," who probably had no money.

BROTHERTON said thereafter one or the other of the three would drop into the Lavender Room in Dallas, which BROTHERTON was then operating and which he still owns, to discuss the possible purchase of the Beachcomber Club. This went on for a matter of four or five weeks. No serious negotiations were ever entered into and BROTHERTON felt that the three men had no money and were not in a financial position to buy any business. Accordingly, he never took their talk very seriously. After a few weeks, BROTHERTON said he got tired of talking to the three, and told them he had had a firm offer for the Beachcomber Club and was not interested in talking further with them. He did not thereafter see them again.

BROTHERTON said the three of them never mentioned JACK RUBY, nor did they discuss with BROTHERTON any club other than the Beachcomber which they might be considering buying. He said he had no reason to believe that any of the three had ever met or talked with RUBY.

BROTHERTON said he had known JACK RUBY as a fellow night

on 7/2/64 at Dallas, Texas File # DL 44-1639

by Special Agent W. JAMES WOOD/eah Date dictated 7/2/64

COMMISSION EXHIBIT No. 1834

2
DL 44-1639

club owner for many years, that he first got acquainted with RUBY about eight years ago when the latter tried to get BROTHERTON to put some money into a night club venture which he recalled may have been the Vegas Club. BROTHERTON said that at the time he did not have any money and was not able to go into this business with RUBY. He said he had seen RUBY a number of times at a place RUBY owned on South Ervay Street in Dallas. However, BROTHERTON explained, he is crippled, has trouble climbing stairs, and seldom saw RUBY at the Carousel Club, where he had to climb stairs to get to the club.

BROTHERTON said he now owns the Lavender Room, the Purple Room, the Copa Club, the Streamliner Club, and the Roadrunner Club in the Dallas area, but has the latter three clubs leased out. He said that he made it a practice to go two or three times a week to night clubs owned by other individuals to keep up with what was going on at the clubs, and from time to time visited RUBY's clubs in this way. He said he was never a social friend of RUBY's, however, and never visited in RUBY's home or had RUBY to his home.

He said he last saw RUBY about a month before RUBY shot OSWALD in Dallas. He said he had never known OSWALD, nor did he have any reason to believe RUBY had ever been acquainted with OSWALD.

BROTHERTON said HENRY LEM BROTHERTON is his cousin. He said he had no knowledge about a liquor violation charged to JACK RUBY which had been dismissed at the instigation of HENRY LEM BROTHERTON. He also said he had no reason to believe that any one of the three men who purported to be interested in purchasing the Beachcomber Club had ever contacted HENRY LEM BROTHERTON in any connection whatsoever.

COMMISSION EXHIBIT No. 1834—Continued

Form No. 1588 (Revised)
Memorandum Report
(7-1-60)

UNITED STATES SECRET SERVICE
TREASURY DEPARTMENT

ORIGIN / TYPE OF CASE	OFFICE / STATUS	FILE NO. / TITLE OR CAPTION
Field Protective Research	Dallas, Texas Continued	CO-2-34,030 Assassination of President Kennedy Robert A. Surrey
INVESTIGATION MADE AT: Dallas, Texas	PERIOD COVERED: 5-14/15-64	
INVESTIGATION MADE BY: SA John Joe Howlett and SA Gene Wofford		

DETAILS

SYNOPSIS

Unable to identify customer of Robert A. Surrey.

— Commission Exhibit No. 1835 —

DETAILS OF INVESTIGATION

Reference is made to my M/R dated 4-14-64.

Other Investigations

At 5:50 P.M. on May 14, 1964, SA Wofford and I attempted to interview Mr. Robert A. Surrey at his home, 3506 Lindenwood, Dallas. Mrs. Surrey answered the door and I asked if Mr. Surrey was in. She replied that he was and left us standing outside while she went to get him. Mr. Surrey came to the front door and I identified myself and SA Wofford and told Mr. Surrey that we would like to talk with him for a few minutes. He asked what we wanted to talk to him about and I told him it was about some leaflets. He asked what leaflets I was referring to and I told him the "Wanted for Treason" leaflets. He replied that he knew what I wanted to talk with him about and I asked him if we could come in and talk with him a few minutes. Mr. Surrey replied that he was "not in the information giving business." I asked him if we could talk with him a few minutes about his customer and the leaflets and he said no. I asked him if he was refusing to talk with us and he replied that he guessed I could put it that way. I then asked him if it was not a fact that he was refusing to talk with us and he replied yes. This completed our conversation with Mr. Robert A. Surrey.

On 5-15-64 SA Wofford and I interviewed Mr. Emil L. Borak, President, Johnston Printing Company, 2700 North Haskell, Dallas, Texas, Telephone TAylor 3-6191. Mr. Borak was shown a copy of the "Wanted for Treason" leaflet and asked if it was a job that had been printed by his company. Mr. Borak said that the leaflet had not been printed by his company as he reviews everything that goes through

DISTRIBUTION	COPIES	REPORT MADE BY	DATE
Chief ✓	Orig & 2 cc	[signature] SPECIAL AGENT	5-15-64
Dallas	2 cc	APPROVED [signature] SPECIAL AGENT IN CHARGE	5-15-64

(CONTINUE ON PLAIN PAPER)

U. S. GOVERNMENT PRINTING OFFICE 16—61800-1

2.
CO-2-34,030

his print shop. He was advised that one of his salesmen had taken the job to another print shop to be run. Mr. Surrey was identified to Mr. Borak as being the salesman. Mr. Borak did not appear to be upset or disturbed when informed that the job was done at the request of his salesman, Mr. Surrey.

Mr. Borak took SA Wofford and I back in his print shop where he had one of his printers identify the type and set the first line of the left hand column of the leaflet. This line of type appears to be identical in every respect to the type used in printing the "Wanted for Treason" leaflet. Mr. Borak stated that this was a fairly common type and he felt sure several other printing shops in the city of Dallas would have the same type.

Mr. Borak was asked if Mr. Surrey was experienced at setting type. Mr. Borak said that it takes a relatively skilled man to operate the hot lead type machine. Mr. Borak admitted that it was possible that a printer might have typeset for Mr. Surrey.

Mr. Borak explained that his printers are required to account for all of their time during the day. Any time a printer works on a job, he records on the job jacket the minute that he starts the job and the minute that he completes the job. The printer is also required to have a work order before doing any job on the equipment. Mr. Borak said that should a printer not properly record his time or work on a job without a job order, that the employee was risking a reprimand and possible firing.

Mr. Borak was notified two or three different times that his salesman, Mr. Surrey, took this job to another printer and that Mr. Surrey also provided the copy from which the leaflet was printed. However, this did not appear to disturb Mr. Borak and he gave no indication that he would reprimand or discharge Mr. Surrey for his actions.

Mr. Borak, during the conversation, asked me if Klause printed the job and I said yes. Mr. Borak went on to say that Klause formerly worked for him for about a year or maybe two, and that Klause knew just about all of the employees at Johnston Printing Company.

UNDEVELOPED LEADS

The investigation continues.

ATTACHMENTS - Chief

Three copies of "Wanted for Treason" leaflets
(NOTE: The type line obtained from Johnston Printing Company is shown in purple above the first line of the text.)

JJH:wd

UNITED STATES SECRET SERVICE
TREASURY DEPARTMENT

ORIGIN	OFFICE	FILE NO.
Field	Dallas, Texas	CO-2-34,030

TYPE OF CASE	STATUS	TITLE OR CAPTION
Protective Research	Continued	Assassination of President Kennedy
INVESTIGATION MADE AT: Dallas, Texas	PERIOD COVERED: May 13, 1964	(Robert A. Surrey)
INVESTIGATION MADE BY: SAIC Sorrels, SA William Patterson, SA Roger Warner, SA John Joe Howlett and SA Cone F. Wofford		

DETAILS

SYNOPSIS

Robert A. Surrey, 3506 Lindenwood, Dallas, identified as person for whom Robert Klause printed the "Wanted for Treason" leaflets.

DETAILS OF INVESTIGATION

Reference my M/R dated 5-12-64.

Other Investigations

On 5-13-64, SA Wofford and SA Howlett interviewed Mrs. Ruth Klause at her place of employment, Union Bankers Insurance Co., 2551 Elm St., Dallas. Mrs. Klause agreed to accompany us to the Secret Service Office, Dallas, so that we might talk in private. This arrangement was also acceptable to her employer.

SAIC Sorrels and SA Howlett interviewed Mrs. Ruth Klause at the Dallas Secret Service Office. Mrs. Klause readily admitted that she and her husband, Robert Klause, printed the "Wanted for Treason" leaflets at Lettercraft Printing Co., 2615 Oak Lawn, Dallas, late one evening. Mrs. Klause said that she was unable to recall the date that the leaflets were printed and that she has been trying to remember the date for the last few days since we had been talking with her husband and she knew that we would more than likely be talking with her. Mrs. Klause said that she did not see the copy that the text of the leaflet was taken from and that she only saw the negatives of President Kennedy's picture. Mrs. Klause said that she did not know for sure where the negatives were made but assumed that her husband had the negatives made at Monk Bros. as that was where they had most of the work done. Mrs. Klause said that to the best of her memory they printed 10,000 copies of the leaflet. When they completed printing the leaflet she said they packed them into two boxes and left them in a storeroom at Lettercraft. She and her husband then went home and she said she never saw the

DISTRIBUTION	COPIES	REPORT MADE BY	DATE
Chief ✓	Orig.& 1 cc	SPECIAL AGENT	5-14-64
Dallas	2 cc's	APPROVED / SPECIAL AGENT IN CHARGE	DATE 5-14-64

(CONTINUE ON PLAIN PAPER) U. S. GOVERNMENT PRINTING OFFICE 16—61500-1

COMMISSION EXHIBIT No. 1836

2.
CO-2-34,030

leaflets again. However, she said she kept one sample copy which she later destroyed after the assassination. She said her husband talks very little and that he never told her for whom he printed the leaflets. She said that she asked him when she first saw the leaflet who it was for and her husband told her that it was none of her business.

Mrs. Klause said that she did not know the price of the job but estimated it to be about $60. She said a few days after they printed the leaflets that her husband gave her $20. She said her reason for helping print the leaflets was because she needed the money and that she thought the "Wanted for Treason" leaflet was a joke until the President was assassinated.

While Mrs. Klause was being interviewed at the Secret Service Office, Dallas, her husband, Robert Klause, came into the office and said that he wanted to tell the story about the "Wanted for Treason" leaflet. Mrs. Klause said that she did not want her husband to know that she had talked with us and she was escorted out of the office through a back door.

SAIC Sorrels, SA Patterson and SA Warner interviewed Robert Klause in the Dallas Secret Service Office. Robert Klause identified his customer as Mr. Robert A. Surrey, 3506 Lindenwood, Dallas, Texas, telephone LA 6-7741. He said Surrey was a salesman for the Johnston Printing Co., 2700 North Haskell, Dallas, Texas, telephone TA 3-6191. Klause said that Surrey came to him and said that he had a printing job that he wanted him to do for him. Klause agreed to do the job for $40 and Surrey provided two pictures from a magazine and the text copy on what printers call a "railroad board". Klause was unable to make a negative of the magazine pictures and took them to Monk Bros. to be photographed. Klause himself shot a photograph of the text copy on the camera at Lettercraft Printing Company. Klause then made the plate from the negatives that Monk Bros. had made and the negatives that he had made. Klause said that he printed the leaflets by himself late one evening, and Mr. Surrey picked the leaflets up the next evening.

Klause said that Surrey told him that he, Surrey, had a customer who wanted these printed up and that he, Surrey, could not handle the job. Surrey never did name the individual for whom he was placing the order.

Robert Klause said that the leaflets were printed about a week or maybe two weeks before the assassination and his wife, Ruth Klause, said that it was about three weeks prior to the assassination. Efforts were made to more accurately determine the date, but Mr. and Mrs. Klause were unable to do so.

Mr. Klause said that to the best of his memory he printed 5,000 copies of the leaflet. Mrs. Klause said that to the best of her memory they printed 10,000 copies of the leaflet.

The interviews with Mr. and Mrs. Klause were recorded on a portable dictaphone and the belts are being held in the files at Dallas.

Mr. Robert A. Surrey is known to be associated with General Edwin Walker. Information at the Criminal Intelligence Section, Dallas Police Department, indicates that Mr. Surrey is an aide to General Walker.

COMMISSION EXHIBIT No. 1836—Continued

3.
CO-2-34,030

It is also reported that the picket signs used when the Dallas Theatre Center was picketed in 1962 were made at the home of Robert Surrey.

Karen Surrey, daughter of Robert Surrey, presented a bouquet of flowers to Madam Ngo Dinh Nhu when she visited Dallas. This was supposed to be during an "American Day" celebration. The "American Day" celebration was to counteract United Nations Day.

The American Eagle Publishing Company published a book containing the news stories from the Dallas Times Herald and the Dallas Morning News. The back cover of this book contained a letter on the letterhead of "American Eagle Publishing Company" and was signed by Robert A. Surrey, President American Eagle Publishing Company. This book which sells for $6.00 was distributed by the American Book Store Company, 6930 Snyder Plaza, Dallas 5, Texas.

The American Eagle Publishing Company is believed to be controlled by General Edwin Walker. Lt. Jack Revill, Criminal Intelligence Section, Dallas Police Department, reports that he has received numerous complaints that the American Eagle Publishing Company is anti-Jewish, anti-negro, etc. Lt. Revill reports that some organizations from the opposite end of the spectrum try to keep tab on what the American Eagle Publishing Co. is doing. For this reason, it is possible that Mr. Surrey did not want to print the "Wanted for Treason" leaflets at the American Eagle Publishing Company.

On Sept. 30, 1962, Ashland Frederic Burchwell (CO-2-36,862) was arrested in Dallas, Texas, with several guns and a large quantity of ammunition in his car. Burchwell stated at that time that he was enroute to Mississippi to assist General Walker. Burchwell had in his personal effects the unlisted telephone number of Mr. Robert A. Surrey. Burchwell also admitted working for General Walker.

UNDEVELOPED LEADS

Investigation continued.

JJH:VS

COMMISSION EXHIBIT No. 1836—Continued

Form No. 1588 (Revised)
MEMORANDUM REPORT
(7-1-60)

UNITED STATES SECRET SERVICE
TREASURY DEPARTMENT

ORIGIN Field — OFFICE Dallas, Texas — FILE NO. CO-2-34,030

TYPE OF CASE	STATUS	TITLE OR CAPTION
Protective Research	Continued	Assassination of President Kennedy
INVESTIGATION MADE AT: Dallas, Texas	PERIOD COVERED: May 26, 1964	Robert A. Surrey
INVESTIGATION MADE BY: SAIC Forrest V. Sorrels		

— Commission Exhibit No. 1837 —

DETAILS

SYNOPSIS

Robert Klause claims he did not talk to Robert A. Surrey regarding "Wanted for Treason" leaflets until the day he, Klause, came to the Secret Service Office in Dallas.

DETAILS OF INVESTIGATION

Reference is made to memorandum reports submitted by Special Agent John Joe Howlett, Dallas, dated May 14 and 15, 1964.

Other Investigations

On May 26, 1964, Robert Klause was contacted by telephone and questioned as to whether or not Robert A. Surrey had contacted him or discussed with him the "Wanted for Treason" leaflets after Surrey had picked up the leaflets a week or two before November 22, 1963. He was specifically asked if Surrey had contacted him after the assassination of President Kennedy. Klause stated that Surrey had not mentioned the leaflets to him at any time after the leaflets had been delivered to Surrey. Klause stated that on May 13, 1964, before coming to the Secret Service Office in Dallas, he had contacted Surrey and informed him that he was coming to the Secret Service Office at our request and that Surrey had remarked, "Well, that's the way the ball bounces."

Mr. Klause stated that if Surrey had talked to him about this matter or if he knew anything else that he would gladly tell us, as he feels much better after having visited our Dallas office and telling what he knew about the leaflets.

It might be stated here that Robert A. Surrey was requested to appear for an interview at Dallas, Texas, with a representative of the President's Commission on the Assassination of President Kennedy, and he declined to do so, with the

DISTRIBUTION	COPIES	REPORT MADE BY	DATE
Chief ✓	Orig & 2 cc	SPECIAL AGENT	
Dallas	2 cc	APPROVED [signature] SPECIAL AGENT IN CHARGE	6-3-64

(CONTINUE ON PLAIN PAPER)

U. S. GOVERNMENT PRINTING OFFICE 16—61806-1

COMMISSION EXHIBIT No. 1837

remark that he did not think much of the Warren Commission, and later on when he was contacted with the view of finding out who his attorney is, he stated he did not have an attorney and again emphasized the fact that he does not think much of the Warren Commission.

UNDEVELOPED LEADS

Investigation continues.

FVS:wd

COMMISSION EXHIBIT No. 1837—Continued

FD-302 (Rev. 3-3-59)

FEDERAL BUREAU OF INVESTIGATION

Date 3/3/64

MARINA OSWALD accompanied interviewing Special Agents in a Bureau automobile to the vicinity of the former residences of LEE HARVEY and MARINA OSWALD in the Oak Cliff Section of Dallas. MARINA stated she had never been to the residence of LEE HARVEY OSWALD at 1026 North Beckley. Upon viewing this residence, MARINA stated she had often seen this house because it was situated near a bus stop which she and her husband had used.

She stated she had never realized the exact location of the last residence of OSWALD until seen by her on this date.

Interviewing Agents and MARINA traced the route of herself and OSWALD on the night in March, 1963, when OSWALD took from the Neely Street Address his rifle wrapped in a raincoat. This route, as traced by MARINA, is herewith described:

> Leave the Neely Street Address and proceed east to Elsbeth Street a distance of ½ block, then turn left or north and proceed one block to Canty Street, then turn right or east again and proceed one block to Zangs Boulevard. At this point, MARINA is not sure as to whether they proceeded north on Zangs or traversed Zangs and continued to Beckley which parallels Zangs and proceeded north on Beckley. She stated she believed OSWALD caught the bus at the corner where Beckley and Zangs meet which is a distance of three blocks north of Canty Street. It will be noted that at a point two blocks north of Canty, Zangs makes an abrupt northeast oblique and crosses Beckley a block later. MARINA pointed out the fish store and the ice cream store to which she was headed that night. These stores are located a block northeast on Zangs from the point where Zangs and Beckley intersect.

MARINA was questioned again concerning the possibility that LEE HARVEY OSWALD had attempted suicide. She reiterated that she did not have any information to indicate that OSWALD had attempted suicide. She repeated she had seen a scar on his inner left wrist and when she questioned OSWALD about the scar, he would not discuss it.

— Commission Exhibit No. 1838 —

473

on 3/2/64 at DALLAS, TEXAS File # DL 100-10461

by Special Agents WALLACE R. HEITMAN & ANATOLE A. BOGUSLAV/les Date dictated 3/3/64

COMMISION EXHIBIT No. 1838

DL 100-10461
2

MARINA stated she had no further information in this regard to furnish.

MARINA's attorney, WILLIAM A. MC KENZIE, was picked up in front of his office in downtown Dallas and accompanied the interviewing agents and MARINA to Oak Cliff.

Following the tour of Oak Cliff, MC KENZIE was dropped off at his office and the interviewing agents returned MARINA to her home in Richardson.

474

COMMISSION EXHIBIT No. 1838—Continued

FD-302 (Rev. 3-3-59)

FEDERAL BUREAU OF INVESTIGATION Oswald, Marina

1

Date 3/13/64

MARINA OSWALD was interviewed at 14057 Brookcrest, the home of Mr. and Mrs. DECLAN P. FORD.

MARINA was questioned concerning two thick books which she believes to be history books on the subject of the United States which she recalled were read and studied by LEE HARVEY OSWALD. She said she can recall that OSWALD had two such books which she believed were concerning the history of the United States. These books were written in English and had dark blue covers and the pages had red edges. It was a two volume work she believes. She can recall last seeing these books at the Magazine Street address in New Orleans. She cannot recall seeing them since they left New Orleans. It is her belief the books were owned by OSWALD prior to his trip to Russia and they were among other effects OSWALD left with his brother ROBERT. She can recall the books were in good condition. She cannot recall that OSWALD made notes in the books.

MARINA was questioned as to the names under which she, Mr. JAMES HERBERT MARTIN, and Mr. JOHN M. THORNE had traveled en route from Washington, D. C., to Dallas, Texas, following her testimony before the President's Commission. She said she cannot now remember what name she traveled under or the names which MARTIN and THORNE used. She was asked if she could recall the name "HOBBS" as being the name which was used by her. She said the name sounds familiar but she cannot exactly recall if that is the name used by her.

MARINA was asked if to her knowledge OSWALD had any American acquaintances in Russia other than persons he had met in the U. S. Embassy or connected therewith. She replied the only such acquaintance she can now recall is the American woman news correspondent who interviewed LEE HARVEY OSWALD in Moscow prior to the time he went to Minsk. MARINA said the name MARY LOU PATTERSON is not familiar to her. She said she cannot recall OSWALD ever mentioning this name. She does not believe OSWALD knew other Americans in Moscow or Minsk.

MARINA stated that in the past two weeks she has written

— Commission Exhibit No. 1839 —

485

on 3/12/64 at Dallas, Texas File # DL 100-10461

by Special Agent WALLACE R. HEITMAN and ANATOLE A. BOGUSLAV:vm Date dictated 3/13/64

COMMISSION EXHIBIT No. 1839

2
DL 100-10461

her friend, GALINA KHONTULEVA, who resides in Leningrad, Russia. She did not expect this letter to be delivered nor did she expect a reply from GALINA. She did however receive an answer from KHONTULEVA a few days ago. She wrote that there is criticism in Russia of the Dallas police for not finding more than one suspect in the assassination of the President. GALINA said that none of MARINA's friends thought that LEE HARVEY OSWALD had assassinated the President.

486

COMMISSION EXHIBIT No. 1839—Continued

FD-302 (Rev. 3-3-59)

FEDERAL BUREAU OF INVESTIGATION

Date 3/13/64

1

At approximately 11:30 p.m., MARINA OSWALD was telephonically contacted at the home of Mr. and Mrs. DECLAN P. FORD, 14057 Brookcrest in Dallas, following a telephonic request from MARINA to the FBI Office in Dallas that Agent BOGUSLAV call her.

MARINA stated that during the testimony she had given the President's Commission in Washington she had been shown a book written in Russian entitled "The Eyes Which Inquire". This book was written by a Bulgarian author. She was asked by the Commission to explain why some letters had been cut out of this book and at the time she could not explain this. She said she could now remember that LEE HARVEY OSWALD had cut certain letters from a book to form her name, MARINA NIKOLAEVNA OSWALD. He told her he intended to place the assembled name over the bell at the Elsbeth Street address. She asked him why he would do this because her name was spelled out in Russian letters. She said this was one of LEE HARVEY OSWALD's pranks. Thereafter, OSWALD assembled her name in English letters; photographed it at his place of employment, and put it over the bell at the Elsbeth Street address.

The Russian book entitled "The Eyes Which Inquire" (English translation) is Item No. 324 in the list of personal effects of MARINA and LEE HARVEY OSWALD.

on 3/12/64 at Dallas, Texas 487 File # DL 100-10461

by Special Agent ANATOLE A. BOGUSLAV:vm Date dictated 3/13/64

COMMISSION EXHIBIT No. 1840

FD-302 (Rev. 3-3-59)

Oswald, Marina

FEDERAL BUREAU OF INVESTIGATION

Date 3/14/64

1

Mrs. MARINA OSWALD was located at the residence of DECLAN P. FORD, 14057 Brookcrest, at which time she furnished the following information:

Upon being exhibited Volume I and Volume II of "The Outline of History" by H. G. WELLS, published by Garden City Books, Garden City, New York, she identified them as books which belonged to LEE HARVEY OSWALD and as being the "two thick books on the history of the United States" which were carefully read by LEE HARVEY OSWALD while they were residing on Elsbeth Street in Dallas, Texas.

488

on 3/13/64 at Dallas, Texas File # DL 100-10461

by Special Agent ANATOLE A. BOGUSLAV and R. NEIL QUIGLEY:vm Date dictated 3/14/64

This document contains neither recommendations nor conclusions of the FBI. It is the property of the FBI and is loaned to your agency; it and its contents are not to be distributed outside your agency.

COMMISSION EXHIBIT No. 1841

FD-302 (Rev. 3-3-59)

Oswald, Marina

FEDERAL BUREAU OF INVESTIGATION

Date 3/31/64

1

MARINA OSWALD was interviewed at her residence, 629 Belt Line Road.

She stated ISAAC DON LEVINE has contacted her on several occasions in the past when she resided at the MARTIN residence and at the FORD residence with respect to writing a book. She does not have a contract with LEVINE and does not expect to sign a contract with him or to authorize him to write anything concerning her. She advised she has not given LEVINE any material whatsoever, such as letters, photographs, or other documents. She has conversed with LEVINE on a number of occasions concerning her background and her life with LEE HARVEY OSWALD.

MARINA was also questioned concerning a statement made by PAVEL GOLOVACHEV in a letter to her on September 15, 1962. GOLOVACHEV wrote this letter from Minsk, Russia, and commented on Pogodin's Play, "A Man With The Rifle." In a prior letter to GOLOVACHEV, MARINA had inquired as to the basic idea of the play on behalf of PAUL GREGORY, an acquaintance of hers, to whom she was teaching Russian.

MARINA explained one of the key thoughts in the play is that "now we do not have to fear a man with a rifle." This thought came about in the following manner: World War I followed by the revolution in Russia made a man with a rifle in Russia a feared person. In the play, an old woman is explaining to her audience how at a time, which was after World War I and after the Russian revolution, she had been in the forest picking mushrooms and had suddenly noticed a man with the rifle. She became afraid. However, the man with the rifle did not harm her but, instead, helped her pick the mushrooms. So she told her audience that "now we do not have to fear a man with the rifle." MARINA explained this was one of the central themes of the play. She said PAUL GREGORY had questioned her about this theme and it was for that reason she had questioned GOLOVACHEV.

501

on 3/31/64 at Dallas, Texas File # 100-10461

by Special Agents WALLACE R. HEITMAN & W. JAMES WOOD/eah Date dictated 3/31/64

This document contains neither recommendations nor conclusions of the FBI. It is the property of the FBI and is loaned to your agency; it and its contents are not to be distributed outside your agency.

COMMISSION EXHIBIT No. 1842

FD-302 (Rev. 3-3-59) FEDERAL BUREAU OF INVESTIGATION Oswald, Marina

INV. 3-7

K, P

Date 4/3/64

1

MARINA OSWALD, who resides at 629 Belt Line Road, Richardson, Texas, was interviewed.

She advised that the person whose nickname is "Tolia" is one ANATOLI, last name unknown, who is a friend of her girl friend, LARISSA PETROVNA PETRUSEVICH, who resided in the same apartment house as did the OSWALDs in Minsk, Russia.

MARINA identified a personal note addressed to herself signed "Tolia" (Inventory Item No. 144) as being from ANATOLI.

MARINA advised she had identified a photograph of this ANATOLI which photograph was among other snapshots in her personal possessions which were acquired by the Dallas Police Department in the search of the RUTH PAINE residence on November 22-23, 1963.

MARINA was questioned further concerning clothing jackets which had been owned by LEE HARVEY OSWALD. She said to the best of her recollection LEE HARVEY OSWALD had only two jackets, one a heavy jacket, blue in color, and another light jacket, grey in color. She said she believes OSWALD possessed both of these jackets in Russia and had purchased them in the United States prior to his departure for Russia. She said she cannot recall that OSWALD ever sent either of these jackets to any laundry or cleaners anywhere. She said she can recall washing them herself. She advised to her knowledge OSWALD possessed both of these jackets at Dallas on November 22, 1963.

on 4/1/64 at Richardson, Texas 502 File # DL 100-10461

by Special Agent WALLACE R. HEITMAN:vm Date dictated 4/2/64

COMMISSION EXHIBIT No. 1843

FD-302 (Rev. 3-3-59) FEDERAL BUREAU OF INVESTIGATION Oswald, Marina 2

Date 4/6/64

1

MARINA OSWALD was interviewed at her place of residence, 629 Belt Line Road, Richardson, Texas.

She was questioned further concerning the silver-colored bracelet, which LEE HARVEY OSWALD had given her following his return to Dallas, Texas, after his trip to Mexico. She said this bracelet was very similar to a bracelet which LEE HARVEY OSWALD wore. His bracelet had the name "LEE" engraved upon it. She stated she believed OSWALD purchased his bracelet about the time they were residing on Elsbeth Street, or perhaps during the time they rented a place on Neely Street.

She recalled OSWALD's watch had been in disrepair and, instead of having the watch fixed, he bought the bracelet and wore it in place of the watch. On a previous occasion, when OSWALD's watch was in disrepair, he had had it fixed at Leonard's Department Store in Fort Worth, Texas. This was at a time when they resided in Fort Worth.

She believes OSWALD was working at Jaggars-Chiles-Stovall at the time he purchased the bracelet.

MARINA said she does not know where OSWALD purchased the bracelet which he presented her. OSWALD did not say he had purchased it in Mexico. He presented it to her within the first hour after they were reunited following his trip to Mexico. She recalls seeing a bracelet very much like the bracelet which he gave her in the Woolworth Store at New Orleans.

She did not like the bracelet and never wore it.

on 4/3/64 at Richardson, Texas 503 File # 100-10461

by Special Agent WALLACE R. HEITMAN/eah Date dictated 4/6/64

COMMISSION EXHIBIT No. 1844

FD-302 (Rev. 3-3-59)

FEDERAL BUREAU OF INVESTIGATION

Date 4/29/64

1

MARINA OSWALD was interviewed at her residence, 629 Belt Line Road.

She was questioned concerning information received from PHILIPPE VAN DER VORM regarding the difficulty a young American had at Kilometer 26 while riding on the Del Norte bus from Mexico City en route to the United States Border, which was the same bus on which OSWALD traveled from Mexico to the Border. MARINA stated OSWALD had not told her about any difficulty he had with any Mexican officials or other persons while he was on his visit to Mexico in September - October, 1963. She said she does not believe OSWALD had any such difficulty or that he was removed from a bus in Mexico. She said he did not speak of being fined or otherwise approached for payments of any money on leaving Mexico.

MARINA was also shown photographs of MARY LOUISE CAMACHO, nee Patterson, as information has been received that this person possibly knew OSWALD while he was in Russia. Upon viewing these photographs, MARINA said she did not recognize the person therein depicted and did not know this person by name. She said she did not believe OSWALD knew this person, as she had never heard him speak of such a person.

MARINA was questioned concerning the possibility that LEE HARVEY OSWALD was photographed with a Mrs. MARIE LORETTA HYDE, of Port Angeles, Washington; Miss RITA NAMAN, and Mrs. MONIKA KRAMER, all residents of the United States, while they were on a visit in Minsk, Russia, in August, 1961. MARINA said she did not know of any such photograph which had been taken, although it was entirely possible OSWALD had become acquainted with such persons and had had his picture made. She was not aware, however, that such had occurred.

591

on 4/27/64 at Richardson, Texas File # DL 100-10461

by Special Agents WALLACE R. HEITMAN & RICHARD L. WIEHL/eah Date dictated 4/29/64

Re: LEE HARVEY OSWALD

Photographs of the fragmentary stickers and tag on Commission Exhibit C-254 were shown to Mrs. PAINE, at which time she stated she does not recall seeing these before and does not know when they were put on Commission Exhibit C-254.

On April 24, 1963, RUTH PAINE recalls taking LEE HARVEY OSWALD to the Continental Trailways Bus depot in Dallas, Texas, at which time he took his luggage into the bus station, apparently checked it, and returned to her car. She recalled he had two green duffel bags, a tan, portable, Russian-made radio, and some suitcases, but cannot specifically recall whether these suitcases resembled the photographs of Commission Exhibits A-1 and C-254.

Mrs. PAINE advised, after examining replicas of the fragmentary tag and stickers found on Commission Exhibit C-254, that she cannot recall seeing any such items, or fragments of such, at any time on Commission Exhibit C-254 or any bag resembling this exhibit.

Mrs. PAINE advised that she is unable to explain the significance of the number "7" appearing in the photograph of a fragmentary sticker found on Commission Exhibit C-254, and advised that if this is a part of an address, she has no idea as to what address it is.

On May 4, 1964, MARINA OSWALD was interviewed at her residence, 629 Belt Line Road, Richardson, Texas.

MARINA was questioned concerning the traveling bags used by OSWALD on his trip to New Orleans, Louisiana, in April 1963 and on his trip to Mexico in September-October 1963. She said she cannot recall exactly, but believes OSWALD took two bags on his trip from Dallas to New Orleans in April 1963 when he preceded the family on that move. She emphasized that her memory on this point was not very good. She said she believed OSWALD took the blue canvas zipper bag which he owned and which is depicted in the photograph labeled Commission Exhibit A-1, and the larger folding green canvas bag, which is labeled Commission Exhibit C-254. She was exhibited both of these photographs and identified each as being the property of OSWALD.

- 10 -

She said again she cannot remember well, but believes OSWALD took only the blue zipper canvas bag (Commission Exhibit A-1) on his trip from New Orleans to Mexico. She emphasized that she had not been in New Orleans at the time OSWALD left, and, therefore, could not be sure what he had taken with him. She seems to recall that the larger green canvas bag (Commission Exhibit C-254) was at the PAINE garage at the time OSWALD was in Mexico, but again she cannot be sure of this. She said she cannot recall what bags or bag OSWALD had in his possession at the time he first came to the PAINE house after his Mexico trip, but she believes that he did have the blue zipper bag with him (Commission Exhibit A-1).

MARINA was also exhibited photographs depicting torn baggage stickers and check, each labeled C-254, and she said she cannot recall specifically that she had seen these torn stickers or check on any bags owned by her husband, LEE HARVEY OSWALD.

She was also exhibited the new and unused stickers and baggage check obtained at the Continental Trailways in Dallas, but she could not identify them as being similar to any stickers or tags she had previously seen on any bags owned by LEE HARVEY OSWALD.

MARINA was again questioned concerning the method of transportation of LEE HARVEY OSWALD to the PAINE house on his first visit after his Mexico trip. She said she recalled she previously had advised in an interview with the FBI that Mrs. PAINE had picked OSWALD up at the bus stop in Irving, Texas, after he telephoned the PAINE house and brought him to the PAINE house. She said she cannot be definite in this, however, because she does recall that on one occasion OSWALD caught a ride with a Negro person somewhere in Irving and was brought to the PAINE house. She said it was possible that Mrs. PAINE had not driven OSWALD from the bus stop in Irving to the PAINE house on the occasion of his first visit to the PAINE house after the Mexico trip. She said she recalled on one occasion when OSWALD visited the PAINE house that Mrs. PAINE's automobile was being repaired. She said it was possible this was the same occasion that OSWALD had caught the ride with the Negro person. She said, however, that she is not completely sure of this as she has no way of connecting the two incidents.

COMMISSION EXHIBIT No. 1846—Continued

MARINA OSWALD was questioned as to which bus line OSWALD had used when he traveled from Dallas to New Orleans in April 1963. MARINA said she cannot remember the names of the bus lines but can recall that she and Mrs. PAINE accompanied OSWALD to the bus station on the day before he left when he checked a bag or two bags at the bus station. She said this bus station was located near the bridge separating Oak Cliff from downtown Dallas and the buses in the terminal were large, light-colored buses with a picture of a running dog thereon. She also recalls the bus station was quite near the Texas School Book Depository Building where OSWALD held his last job.

In this connection, it is noted the Greyhound Bus Station is located within a few blocks of the bridge separating Oak Cliff and downtown Dallas, and within a few blocks of the Texas School Book Depository Building, whereas the other bus station in Dallas, the Continental Trailways, is located a few blocks east of the Greyhound Bus Station and further away from the described bridge and the Texas School Book Depository Building.

MARINA was asked if the numbers "9/26" which appear on one side of the valise depicted in Commission Exhibit C-254 bore any significance or if she recalled seeing these numbers. She said that these numbers had no significance to her and she could not specifically recall them appearing on the bag.

MARINA also advised that the partial number which appears on the address sticker of Commission Exhibit C-254 does not have any significance to her because she cannot recall seeing this sticker on the bag.

MARINA was questioned as to what valise OSWALD took with him when he left the PAINE residence for Dallas immediately following his visit to the PAINE residence after his Mexico trip. She said she believed OSWALD took his blue zipper case to Dallas, and perhaps also the other green valise, but she cannot now recall which he took or if he took both.

COMMISSION EXHIBIT No. 1846—Continued

Re: LEE HARVEY OSWALD

On May 5, 1964, ROBERT OSWALD was interviewed at the office of WILLIAM A. MC KENZIE, attorney, Fidelity Union Life Building, Dallas, Texas, at which time he furnished the following information:

He examined colored photographs of items designated as Commission Exhibits A-1 and C-254.

OSWALD advised that he is sure that these are photographs of two bags belonging to his brother, LEE HARVEY OSWALD, deceased, and that he first saw them about June 1962, at which time LEE HARVEY OSWALD and his wife, MARINA, moved into the ROBERT OSWALD home at 7313 Davenport Street, Fort Worth, Texas. This was after LEE and MARINA had returned from Russia. They stayed at ROBERT OSWALD's house for three or four weeks, leaving about July 1962 and taking the two bags, depicted in the photographs, with them when they moved.

ROBERT OSWALD examined the photographs of fragmentary stickers and a tag found on C-254 and stated that he does not recall ever seeing these items on Commission Exhibit C-254. He further stated he does not know when they were affixed to Commission Exhibit C-254. He examined what appears to be a "7" in the photograph of one of the fragmentary stickers and stated that while he had never noticed this sticker before, he believes that the "7" is a part of the address 7313 Davenport Street, Fort Worth, Texas, which is ROBERT OSWALD's previous address where he lived from May 1, 1957, to March 4, 1963. He stated that from time to time, his brother, LEE HARVEY OSWALD, used this as a home address since ROBERT OSWALD was the only one in the family whose residence was fixed during this period. On March 4, 1963, ROBERT OSWALD moved to Route 5, Box 140, Malvern, Arkansas.

ROBERT OSWALD examined the marking "9/26", above which appears an initial in the photograph of Commission Exhibit C-254, and stated that he does not recall seeing this marking previously and does not know the significance of this marking and does not know when it was placed on the bag.

ROBERT OSWALD examined replicas of the fragmentary tag and stickers found on Commission Exhibit C-254 and stated that he

Re: LEE HARVEY OSWALD

cannot recall seeing any such items or fragments thereof at any time on Commission Exhibit C-254.

ROBERT OSWALD stated that he has no idea whether LEE HARVEY OSWALD had the bags, identified as Commission Exhibits A-1 and C-254, with him in New Orleans, Louisiana, or in Mexico City, or whether he had them in his possession when he arrived in Dallas in October 1963, since he did not see LEE HARVEY OSWALD from Thanksgiving 1962 until November 22, 1963, when he saw him in the Dallas City Jail.

ROBERT OSWALD advised that he has no knowledge of what, if any, busses were utilized by LEE HARVEY OSWALD between Dallas and New Orleans, New Orleans and Mexico City, or Mexico City and Dallas; and, in fact, knows first-hand of no bus trips made by LEE HARVEY OSWALD using Continental Trailways buses.

On May 6, 1964, Mrs. RUTH PAINE, 2515 West 5th Street, Irving, Texas, personally accompanied a Special Agent of the Dallas Office of the Federal Bureau of Investigation to the Greyhound Bus Depot at Jackson and Lamar Streets, Dallas, Texas, and to the Continental Trailways Bus Depot, 1500 Jackson Street, Dallas, Texas, in order that she could positively identify to which of these two bus depots she took LEE HARVEY OSWALD on April 24, 1963.

After viewing both of the above-mentioned bus depots at Dallas, Texas, Mrs. PAINE stated that she is positive she took OSWALD to the Continental Trailways Bus Depot.

Date 5/5/64

MARINA OSWALD was interviewed at her residence, 629 Belt Line Road, Richardson, Texas.

She was exhibited a colored photograph which is labeled D-209 and which depicts three women, two men and a small boy standing near a small white automobile, with a large building in the background, and a statue of JOSEF STALIN on the left. She stated that the person standing to the extreme right in this photograph with his right hand (the only one visible) in his pocket is LEE HARVEY OSWALD. She said she can recognize his features, his stance and his shirt.

She was also shown a photograph in black and white which depicts two of the women shown in the previous photograph, number D-209, the small boy, the two men and an additional man standing to the extreme right. This photograph also had what appears to be the same large building in the background and had the same automobile in the foreground. She identified the man standing with both hands in his pocket, second from the right, as being LEE HARVEY OSWALD. She said she can recognize his features, his stance and his shirt.

She was also shown a colored photograph which appears to be the same scene as that depicted in the black and white photograph described above. She again identified positively the person standing second from the right as being identical with LEE HARVEY OSWALD.

MARINA OSWALD said she can recall that sometime during the summer of 1961, which was the year of her marriage, LEE HARVEY OSWALD had mentioned he had met some American people in Minsk. She said she recalls OSWALD had gone to the store for some groceries and, upon returning, mentioned that he had seen these people. She said she remembers OSWALD remarked the American people had told him, OSWALD, he could speak very good English. OSWALD did not tell the American people that he was an American himself.

— Commission Exhibit No. 1847 —

592

on 5/4/64 at Richardson, Texas File # DL 100-10461

by Special Agent RICHARD L. WIEHL and WALLACE R. HEITMAN/ds Date dictated 5/5/64

COMMISSION EXHIBIT No. 1847

2

DL 100-10461

MARINA OSWALD said she cannot recognize any of the other people in the above-described photographs. She does not know whether or not the occasion when OSWALD met the American people in Minsk is the same as depicted in these photographs.

MARINA was questioned concerning the traveling bags used by OSWALD on his trip to New Orleans, Louisiana, in April 1963 and on his trip to Mexico in September-October 1963. She said she cannot recall exactly, but believes OSWALD took two bags on his trip from Dallas to New Orleans in April 1963 when he preceded the family on that move. She emphasized that her memory on this point was not very good. She said she believed OSWALD took the blue canvas zipper bag which he owned and which is depicted in the photograph labeled Commission Exhibit A-1, and the larger folding green canvas bag, which is labeled Commission Exhibit C-254. She was exhibited both of these photographs and identified each as being the property of OSWALD.

She said again she cannot remember well, but believes OSWALD took only the blue zipper canvas bag (Commission Exhibit A-1) on his trip from New Orleans to Mexico. She emphasized that she had not been in New Orleans at the time OSWALD left, and, therefore, could not be sure what he had taken with him. She seems to recall that the larger green canvas bag (Commission Exhibit C-254) was at the PAINE garage at the time OSWALD was in Mexico, but again she cannot be sure of this. She said she cannot recall what bags or bag OSWALD had in his possession at the time he first came to the PAINE house after his Mexico trip, but she believes that he did have the blue zipper bag with him (Commission Exhibit A-1).

MARINA was also exhibited photographs depicting torn baggage stickers and check, each labeled C-254, and she said she cannot recall specifically that she had seen these torn stickers or check on any bags owned by her husband, LEE HARVEY OSWALD.

She was also exhibited the new and unused stickers and baggage check obtained at the Continental Trailways in Dallas, but

593

COMMISSION EXHIBIT No. 1847—Continued

DL 100-10461

she could not identify them as being similar to any stickers or tags she had previously seen on any bags owned by LEE HARVEY OSWALD.

MARINA was again questioned concerning the method of transportation of LEE HARVEY OSWALD to the PAINE house on his first visit after his Mexico trip. She said she recalled she previously had advised in an interview with the FBI that Mrs. PAINE had picked OSWALD up at the bus stop in Irving, Texas, after he telephoned the PAINE house and brought him to the PAINE house. She said she cannot be definite in this, however, because she does recall that on one occasion OSWALD caught a ride with a Negro person somewhere in Irving and was brought to the PAINE house. She said it was possible that Mrs. PAINE had not driven OSWALD from the bus stop in Irving to the PAINE house on the occasion of his first visit to the PAINE house after the Mexico trip. She said she recalled on one occasion when OSWALD visited the PAINE house that Mrs. PAINE's automobile was being repaired. She said it was possible this was the same occasion that OSWALD had caught the ride with the Negro person. She said, however, that she is not completely sure of this as she has no way of connecting the two incidents.

MARINA OSWALD was questioned as to which bus line OSWALD had used when he traveled from Dallas to New Orleans in April 1963. MARINA said she cannot remember the names of the bus lines but can recall that she and Mrs. PAINE accompanied OSWALD to the bus station on the day before he left when he checked a bag or two bags at the bus station. She said this bus station was located near the bridge separating Oak Cliff from downtown Dallas and the buses in the terminal were large, light-colored buses with a picture of a running dog thereon. She also recalls the bus station was quite near the Texas School Book Depository Building where OSWALD held his last job.

In this connection, it is noted the Greyhound Bus Station is located within a few blocks of the bridge separating Oak Cliff and downtown Dallas, and within a few blocks of the

DL 100-10461

Texas School Book Depository Building, whereas the other bus station in Dallas, the Continental Trailways, is located a few blocks east of the Greyhound Bus Station and further away from the described bridge and the Texas School Book Depository Building.

MARINA was asked if the numbers "9/26" which appear on one side of the valise depicted in Commission Exhibit C-254 bore any significance or if she recalled seeing these numbers. She said that these numbers had no significance to her and she could not specifically recall them appearing on the bag.

MARINA also advised that the partial number which appears on the address sticker of Commission Exhibit C-254 does not have any significance to her because she cannot recall seeing this sticker on the bag.

MARINA was questioned as to what valise OSWALD took with him when he left the PAINE residence for Dallas immediately following his visit to the PAINE residence after his Mexico trip. She said she believed OSWALD took his blue zipper case to Dallas, and perhaps also the other green valise but she cannot now recall which he took or if he took both.

FD-302 (Rev. 3-3-59) FEDERAL BUREAU OF INVESTIGATION

— Commission Exhibit No. 1848 — Date 5/14/64

1

MARINA OSWALD was interviewed at her residence, 629 Belt Line Road.

She was questioned concerning her aunt, POLINA VASILIEVNA PRUSAKOVA MIKHAILOVA, who is her mother's sister. She stated her aunt's husband is YURI MIKHAILOV. They have three sons, VALENTINE YURIEVICH MIKHAILOV, ALEXANDER YURIEVICH MIKHAILOV, and VLADIMIR YURIEVICH MIKHAILOV. Her uncle, YURI, is a building engineer. She said her aunt, POLINA, had sent money to her and her sister when they were young. She said she had never sent any money to her aunt.

MARINA said her aunt and uncle live in Kharkov, Russia, at the address Trinkler Drive. She said she believed the address on that street was House 5, Apartment 7. Her aunt and uncle lived at this address when she visited them on a vacation trip in 1961 after she was married to LEE HARVEY OSWALD.

MARINA said she personally does not know anyone by the name of IRINA ALEKSEYEVNA MIKHAYLOVICH, VAVA, OLECHKA, MARUSYA, or OLYA, and she has never heard her aunt or uncle in Kharkov mention these names.

MARINA cannot recall any other address where her aunt and uncle have lived in Kharkov.

MARINA said the name "MIKHAILOVICH," if a Russian name, would be used as a middle name rather than as a last name. If this name "MIKHAILOVICH" or "MIKHAYLOVICH" was a Belorussian name, it would very probably be used as a last name rather than a middle name.

MARINA was also questioned concerning her knowledge of LYDIA DYMITRUK.

She advised she first met LYDIA DYMITRUK at Mrs. DECLAN FORD's house in Dallas, Texas, about the time she had temporarily resided with Mrs. FORD. She said this was about a year and a half or more ago. She again came in contact with LYDIA DYMITRUK when

596

on 5/13/64 at Richardson, Texas File # DL 100-10461

by Special Agent WALLACE R. HEITMAN and RICHARD L. WIEHL:vm Date dictated 5/14/64

COMMISSION EXHIBIT NO. 1848

the latter used her automobile to take MARINA, her baby JUNE, and LEE HARVEY OSWALD to Parkland Hospital in Dallas for the purpose of having JUNE examined by a doctor there. At this time, the OSWALDs lived on Elsbeth Street in Dallas. MARINA cannot recall exactly how it came about that LYDIA DYMITRUK took them to the hospital but she believes she requested DYMITRUK for this favor. She recalls DYMITRUK came into their home on this occasion. When they arrived at Parkland Hospital it was found the doctor who was to examine the baby was not there. DYMITRUK returned MARINA and JUNE (LEE HARVEY OSWALD was not present on this trip) to the Elsbeth address and in the early evening DYMITRUK again took MARINA and JUNE to Parkland Hospital. LEE HARVEY OSWALD accompanied them on this trip.

MARINA cannot recall the exact details of what transpired at the hospital on this occasion. She cannot recall whether any questions were asked LEE HARVEY OSWALD as to his employment or whether any request was made that he pay for the treatment of his daughter, JUNE.

She can recall again seeing LYDIA DYMITRUK at a store in Irving, Texas, when she was living with Mrs. RUTH PAINE. Mrs. PAINE and MARINA went into this store. MARINA saw LYDIA DYMITRUK and the latter came over to greet MARINA. MARINA introduced her to Mrs. PAINE. The three of them thereafter had a cup of coffee. MARINA was pregnant at this time and LYDIA DYMITRUK commented on this fact. MARINA said she had gone to New Orleans to join her husband in May of 1963 and as her second daughter, RACHEL, was born in October of 1963, this meeting with LYDIA DYMITRUK must have taken place about April or May of 1963 but no later.

MARINA has again seen LYDIA DYMITRUK recently at the Russian Orthodox Church in Dallas. This last time that MARINA saw LYDIA DYMITRUK was on May 4, 1964, when the Russian Easter services were celebrated at the Russian Orthodox Church in Dallas.

597

COMMISSION EXHIBIT NO. 1848—Continued

3

DL 100-10461

MARINA said she does not particularly like LYDIA DYMITRUK and has never been friendly with her. She said LYDIA has spoken very little about her past life. She advised she does know LYDIA lived in Belgium prior to coming to the United States. She knows LYDIA is divorced and the husband lives in the Dallas area. She has heard LYDIA state that the latter has a sister in Belgium at the present time. MARINA does not know PAUL DYMITRUK, the former husband of LYDIA. She said LYDIA DYMITRUK speaks good Russian and she understands that she also speaks Flemish.

598

COMMISSION EXHIBIT NO. 1848—Continued

UNITED STATES DEPARTMENT OF JUSTICE

FEDERAL BUREAU OF INVESTIGATION

In Reply, Please Refer to File No.

Dallas, Texas
June 9, 1964

Oswald, Marina

LEE HARVEY OSWALD

On June 5, 1964, Marina Oswald, 629 Belt Line Road, Richardson, Texas, was interviewed to determine if she was possibly confused when she stated on February 24, 1964, that approximately two weeks after the attempted assassination of Major General Edwin A. Walker at Dallas, Texas, on April 10, 1963, Lee Harvey Oswald had indicated that he was going out because "Nixon is coming and I'm going to take a look," it being noted that previous investigation had established that the then Vice President Lyndon B. Johnson was in Dallas, Texas, on April 23, 1963.

Marina Oswald was asked if it was possible that she had become confused as to the name used by Oswald on the above referred to occasion. Specifically, she was asked if she recalled if Oswald had said, "Nixon is coming and I'm going to take a look," as previously reported by her. She stated these were the words of Oswald as best she could remember. She stated she is positive Oswald said "Nixon" was coming. She stated she was familiar with the name "Nixon" because of the publicity received by him in connection with his nomination as the Republican candidate for President.

Marina Oswald was asked if there was a possibility she had confused the name "Nixon" with the name "Johnson." She reiterated she is positive Oswald used the name "Nixon." She stated she was not familiar with the name "Johnson" at that time.

On June 8, 1964, Marina Oswald advised that to the best of her recollection the words used by Oswald on this occasion were "Nixon is coming and I'm going to take a look." She is positive Oswald said "Nixon." She said she was very familiar with the word "Nixon" and was not familiar at all with the word "Johnson." She pointed out Richard Nixon was well known in Russia and had been even prior to 1960. She said she can recall being familiar with the name Richard Nixon as far back as the famous "kitchen debate" between Nixon and Khrushchev. She said also she

COMMISSION EXHIBIT No. 1849

LEE HARVEY OSWALD

can recall seeing news pictures of Nixon with President Eisenhower. She can recall seeing Nixon's picture in newsreels in movie theaters in Leningrad and Minsk, Russia. She was well aware of the importance of Richard Nixon prior to the time she met Lee Harvey Oswald.

She pointed out she had not gained any familiarity with the name of President Johnson until after the assassination of President Kennedy.

COMMISSION EXHIBIT No. 1849—Continued

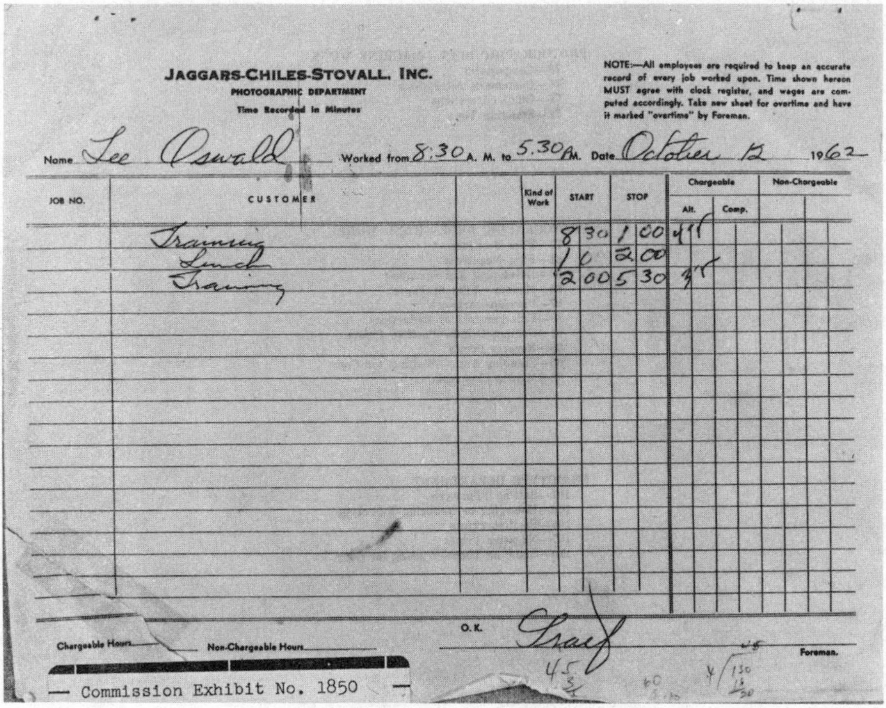

JAGGARS-CHILES-STOVALL, INC.
PHOTOGRAPHIC DEPARTMENT
Time Recorded in Minutes

NOTE:—All employees are required to keep an accurate record of every job worked upon. Time shown hereon MUST agree with clock register, and wages are computed accordingly. Take new sheet for overtime and have it marked "overtime" by Foreman.

Name Lee Oswald Worked from 8:30 A. M. to 5.30 P.M. Date October 12 1962

JOB NO.	CUSTOMER		Kind of Work	START	STOP	Chargeable Alt.	Chargeable Comp.	Non-Chargeable
	Training			8 30	1 00	4½		
	Lunch			1 0	2 00			
	Training			2 00	5 30	3½		

Chargeable Hours Non-Chargeable Hours O.K. Graef Foreman.

— Commission Exhibit No. 1850 —

COMMISSION EXHIBIT No. 1850

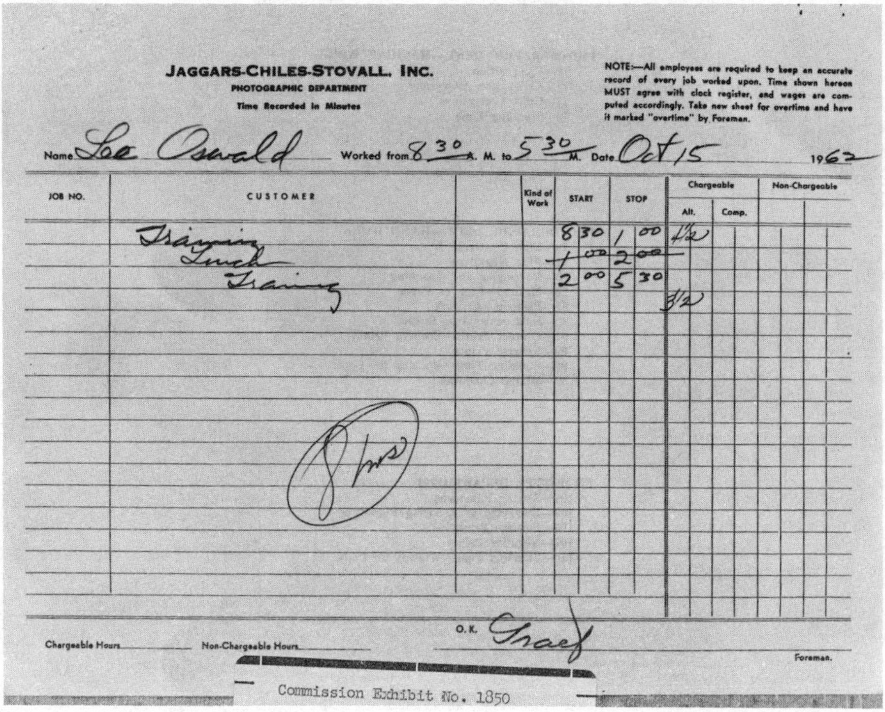

JAGGARS-CHILES-STOVALL, INC.
PHOTOGRAPHIC DEPARTMENT
Time Recorded in Minutes

NOTE:—All employees are required to keep an accurate record of every job worked upon. Time shown hereon MUST agree with clock register, and wages are computed accordingly. Take new sheet for overtime and have it marked "overtime" by Foreman.

Name Lee Oswald Worked from 8 30 A. M. to 5 30 M. Date Oct 15 1962

JOB NO.	CUSTOMER		Kind of Work	START	STOP	Chargeable Alt.	Chargeable Comp.	Non-Chargeable
	Training			8 30	1 00	4½		
	Lunch			1 00	2 00			
	Training			2 00	5 30	3½		

8 hrs

Chargeable Hours Non-Chargeable Hours O.K. Graef Foreman.

Commission Exhibit No. 1850

COMMISSION EXHIBIT No. 1850—Continued

JAGGARS-CHILES-STOVALL, INC.
PHOTOGRAPHIC DEPARTMENT
Time Recorded in Minutes

NOTE:—All employees are required to keep an accurate record of every job worked upon. Time shown hereon MUST agree with clock register, and wages are computed accordingly. Take new sheet for overtime and have it marked "overtime" by Foreman.

Name lee Oswald Worked from 8.30 A. M. to ____ M. Date October 16th, 1962

JOB NO.	CUSTOMER		Kind of Work	START		STOP		Chargeable Alt.	Chargeable Comp.	Non-Chargeable
23001	titches			8	30	8	45			
22683	Dallas Chamber of commerce			8	45	9	00			
21046	Glenn			9	00	9	20			
22938	Calonic corp.			9	20	9	45			
22846	army map service			9	45	10	10			
22983	Sears			10	10	10	40			
20005	Dallas magazine			10	40	11	30			
22983	Sears and Roebuck enlargment			11	30	12	30	4–		
	Lunch			12	30	1	30			
23046	Tracy Locke			1	30	1	45			
22197	Rogers + smith			1	45	2	30			
22788	Continental			2	30	3	00			
23040	Cumming carpets			3	00	3	30			
22262	ttl Industries			3	30	4	00			
23117	Paul mcfain			4	00	5	00			
22815	Tracy Locke			5	00	5	20			
22967	Ikonographics			520	530	5	40	4.9–		

Chargeable Hours ____ Non-Chargeable Hours ____ 8 10 O.K. ____ Foreman.

Commission Exhibit No. 1850

COMMISSION EXHIBIT NO. 1850—Continued

JAGGARS-CHILES-STOVALL, INC.
PHOTOGRAPHIC DEPARTMENT
Time Recorded in Minutes

NOTE:—All employees are required to keep an accurate record of every job worked upon. Time shown hereon MUST agree with clock register, and wages are computed accordingly. Take new sheet for overtime and have it marked "overtime" by Foreman.

Name Lee Oswald Worked from 8.30 A. M. to 5.00 M. Date October 17, 1962

JOB NO.	CUSTOMER		Kind of Work	START		STOP		Chargeable Alt.	Chargeable Comp.	Non-Chargeable
23258	Trinity Labs			8	30	9	00			
23222	american printing			9	00	9	15			
23092	Phillips Browns			9	15	10	00			
23261	cliff Hopper			10	00	10	15			
23168	florida press			10	15	10	30			
22192	Rogers + Smith			10	30	10	45			
23198	Tracy - Locke			10	45	11	15			
23189	Sam Bloom			11	15	11	45			
23331	Robert Wilma			11	45	12	15			
21659	Robert Buttes			12	15	12	30	4–		
	LUNCH			12	30	1	00			
23153	Louisiana Gas			1	00	1	30			
20954	Rogers + Smith			1	30	2	00			
22197	Rives, Dyke			2	00	2	30			
2325	McCauly Tape			2	30	3	15			
23222	Floyd Hotman			3	15	4	15			
23223	BBD + O			4	15	5	00	4–		

8 1 O.K.

Chargeable Hours ____ Non-Chargeable Hours ____ ____ Foreman.

Commission Exhibit No. 1850

COMMISSION EXHIBIT NO. 1850—Continued

JAGGARS-CHILES-STOVALL, INC.
PHOTOGRAPHIC DEPARTMENT
Time Recorded in Minutes

NOTE:—All employees are required to keep an accurate record of every job worked upon. Time shown hereon MUST agree with clock register, and wages are computed accordingly. Take new sheet for overtime and have it marked "overtime" by Foreman.

Name Lee Oswald Worked from 8:30 A. M. to ____ M. Date Oct. 18, 1962

JOB NO.	CUSTOMER	Kind of Work	START	STOP	Chargeable Alt.	Chargeable Comp.	Non-Chargeable
23430	Paul Cretain		8:30	8:45			
23408	August compton + assc.		8:45	9:00			
23408	ayres		9:00	9:25			
23299	WFAA T.V.		9:25	9:55			
23383	Tom Lennies		9:55	10:10			
20963	ark Louisiana Gas Co.		10:10	10:30			
23409	Glenn adv.		10:30	11:00			
23203	Vic Thomas Bros.		11:00	11:30			
23409	Glenn advert. (enlarg)		11:30	12:40	4 10		
	Lunch		12:40	1:10			
23455	Pollack Paper CO		1:10	1:30			
23408	ayres		1:30	1:55			
22883	foot care + building		1:55	2:50			
23517	McKay Travis		2:50	3:45			
23456	Electro Type Service		3:45	4:30			
23581	Evans Young Wyatt		4:30	5:00	3 50		

Chargeable Hours ______ Non-Chargeable Hours ______ O.K. ______ Foreman.

Commission Exhibit No. 1850

COMMISSION EXHIBIT No. 1850—Continued

JAGGARS-CHILES-STOVALL, INC.
PHOTOGRAPHIC DEPARTMENT
Time Recorded in Minutes

NOTE:—All employees are required to keep an accurate record of every job worked upon. Time shown hereon MUST agree with clock register, and wages are computed accordingly. Take new sheet for overtime and have it marked "overtime" by Foreman.

Name Lee Oswald Worked from 8:30 A. M. to 5:00 M. Date Oct. 19th 1962

JOB NO.	CUSTOMER	Kind of Work	START	STOP	Chargeable Alt.	Chargeable Comp.	Non-Chargeable
23163	P&L Company		8:30	8:45			
23008	Sam Bloom		8:45	9:00			
23059	Cunningham & Walsh		9:00	9:10			
23569	Lucy Locke		9:10	9:25			
23575	Southwestern Inc.		9:25	9:55			
23547	Warren H. Breedlove adv.		9:55	10:10			
23502	Galloway-Wallace		10:10	10:20			
23287	Electrotype Service		10:20	10:30			
23282	Mercantile Ins CO.		10:30	10:50			
23465	Electrotype service		10:50	11:30			
23282	Electrotype		11:30	12:40	4 10		
	Lunch		~~12:40~~	~~1:10~~			
23219	Rogers & Smith		1:10	2:05			
23133	Smith Ayles Bros Inc.		2:05	3:00			
	Dallas Times Herald		3:00	3:45			
23689	ano		3:45	5:00	3 50		

Chargeable Hours ______ Non-Chargeable Hours ______ O.K. ______ Foreman.

Commission Exhibit No. 1850

COMMISSION EXHIBIT No. 1850—Continued

JAGGARS-CHILES-STOVALL, INC.
PHOTOGRAPHIC DEPARTMENT
Time Recorded in Minutes

NOTE:—All employees are required to keep an accurate record of every job worked upon. Time shown hereon MUST agree with clock register, and wages are computed accordingly. Take new sheet for overtime and have it marked "overtime" by Foreman.

Name Lee H Oswald Worked from 8:30 A. M. to 5:05 M. Date Oct 22 1962

JOB NO.	CUSTOMER	Kind of Work	START	STOP	Chargeable Alt.	Chargeable Comp.	Non-Chargeable
22831	Cunningham Wabash		8 30	9 10			
23819	C & W		9 10	9 35			
22798	Alfred Lawrence		9 35	10 15			
23381	Don Baxter		10 15	10 45			
23942	J C S		10 45	11 15			
23859	Harold Binder		11 15	11 50			
23884	Rogers & Smith		11 50	12 45	4½		
	Lunch		12 45	1 15			
23869	Sanger advert.		1 15	2 00			
23587	Bob Charbeneau		2 00	2 15			
23357	Cunningham Corp		2 15	2 50			
23959	Tel Industries		2 50	3 10			
23853	Binder		3 10	3 45			
23631	Wilson Rozelle adv		3 45	4 30			
			4 30	5 05	3 50		

8 05'

Chargeable Hours______ Non-Chargeable Hours______ O.K. ______ Foreman.

Commission Exhibit No. 1850

COMMISSION EXHIBIT No. 1850—Continued

JAGGARS-CHILES-STOVALL, INC.
PHOTOGRAPHIC DEPARTMENT
Time Recorded in Minutes

NOTE:—All employees are required to keep an accurate record of every job worked upon. Time shown hereon MUST agree with clock register, and wages are computed accordingly. Take new sheet for overtime and have it marked "overtime" by Foreman.

Name L H Oswald Worked from 8:30 A. M. to 5:00 M. Date Oct 23 1962

JOB NO.	CUSTOMER	Kind of Work	START	STOP	Chargeable Alt.	Chargeable Comp.	Non-Chargeable
24032	Sam Bloom		8 30	8 45			
24036	Tom Ennis		8 45	8 55			
24044	nick adrens		8 55	9 15			
24035	Bales adv.		9 15	10 00			
23964	William Volker Co.		10 00	10 15			
27349	R. N. B.		10 15	10 30			
24038	Sam Bloom		10 30	10 45			
23858	Jack E. Holmes		10 45	10 55			
24406	Glen Mason		10 55	12 15	3 45		
	Lunch		12 15	~~12 45~~			
24085	Poms adv.		12 45	12 55			
24149	magnuson adv.		12 55	1 35			
24081	Sam Bloom		1 35	2 15			
24053	fidelity adv		2 15	3 05			
22798	alfred lawrence		3 05	4 00			
24093	Rogers & Smith		4 00	4 15			
23747	Sam Bloom		4 15	5 00	4 15		

8'

Chargeable Hours______ Non-Chargeable Hours______ O.K. ______ Foreman.

Commission Exhibit No. 1850

COMMISSION EXHIBIT No. 1850—Continued

JAGGARS-CHILES-STOVALL, INC.
PHOTOGRAPHIC DEPARTMENT
Time Recorded in Minutes

NOTE:—All employees are required to keep an accurate record of every job worked upon. Time shown hereon MUST agree with clock register, and wages are computed accordingly. Take new sheet for overtime and have it marked "overtime" by Foreman.

Name L H Oswald Worked from 8:30 A. M. to 5:00 M. Date Oct. 24 1962

JOB NO.	CUSTOMER		Kind of Work	START		STOP		Chargeable Alt.	Chargeable Comp.	Non-Chargeable
24093	Rogers & Smith			8	30	9	00			
24257	Sam Bloom			9	00	9	25			
23506	Sam Bloom			9	25	9	55			
24106	Glenn-Moon			9	55	10	30			
23381	Don L Baxter			10	30	10	45			
24198	Zale's adv.			10	45	10	55			
24204	Ed. Beard			10	55	11	25			
24093	Rogers & Smith			11	25	12	10			
24190	Ayres-Compton			12	10	12	50	4 20		
	Lunch			12	50	1	20			
24207	Rogers & Smith			1:	20	1	40			
24334	Autograph Mascot			1	40	2	10			
24211	Blanff ads.			2	10	2	30			
24285	Samenthanis			2	30	2	50			
24283	Campbell-Dickey			2	50	3	30			
24100	Hesse Envelope			3	30	4	25			
24250	Sears Roebuck			4	25	5	00	3 40		

Chargeable Hours______ Non-Chargeable Hours______ O.K. Foreman.

Commission Exhibit No. 1850

COMMISSION EXHIBIT NO. 1850—Continued

JAGGARS-CHILES-STOVALL, INC.
PHOTOGRAPHIC DEPARTMENT
Time Recorded in Minutes

NOTE:—All employees are required to keep an accurate record of every job worked upon. Time shown hereon MUST agree with clock register, and wages are computed accordingly. Take new sheet for overtime and have it marked "overtime" by Foreman.

Name Lee H. Oswald Worked from 8:30 A. M. to 5:00 M. Date Thur. Oct. 25th 1962

JOB NO.	CUSTOMER		Kind of Work	START		STOP		Chargeable Alt.	Chargeable Comp.	Non-Chargeable
24453	BBD&O			8	30	8	55			
23631	Wilson-Rozelle ads.			8	55	9	30			
24401	Robinson Printers			9	30	10	:00			
24128	Gulf States			10	00	10	15			
24479	L Jak Wyatt			10	15	10	45			
23372	Tracey Locke			10:	45	11	40			
24398	Delfolds			11	40	1	10	4 40		
	Lunch			1	10	1	40			
24128	Gulf			1:	40	2	30			
24397	Lelands			2	30	3:	20			
24489	Tom Gates			3	20	4:	15			
24353	Stafford Person			4	15	5:	00	3 20		

Chargeable Hours______ Non-Chargeable Hours______ O.K. Foreman.

Commission Exhibit No. 1850

COMMISSION EXHIBIT NO. 1850—Continued

JAGGARS-CHILES-STOVALL, INC.
PHOTOGRAPHIC DEPARTMENT
Time Recorded in Minutes

NOTE:—All employees are required to keep an accurate record of every job worked upon. Time shown hereon MUST agree with clock register, and wages are computed accordingly. Take new sheet for overtime and have it marked "overtime" by Foreman.

Name Lee H Oswald Worked from 8:30 A. M. to 5:00 M. Date Friday Oct 26th 196–

JOB NO.	CUSTOMER		Kind of Work	START		STOP		Chargeable Alt.	Chargeable Comp.	Non-Chargeable
24614	R + S			8	30	9	40			
24665	Goodloe Stark			9	10	9	45			
24669	W. W. Sewell Co			9	45	10	20			
24567	Sam Bloom			10	20	10	45			
24528	Fry Hammond Barr			10	45	11	10			
24501	Industrial printing			11	10	11	20			
24444	Rogers + Smith			11	20	11	40			
24659	Don Boyles			11	40	12	15			
24741	Creative Design			12	15	12	35			
24606	Mojikon Corp			12	35	12	45	4 15 –		
	Lunch			12	45	1	15			
24042	anonmous			1	15	1	35			
24464	West Texas Utilities			1	35	2	05			
24467	Goodman paper co.			2	05	2	55			
24537	McLendon			2	55	3	35			
24188	Riverside Press			3	35	4	20			
24641	Tracy Locke			4	20	5	00	3 45 –		

J

Chargeable Hours _____ Non-Chargeable Hours _____ O.K. _____ Foreman.

Commission Exhibit No. 1850

COMMISSION EXHIBIT No. 1850—Continued

JAGGARS-CHILES-STOVALL, INC.
PHOTOGRAPHIC DEPARTMENT
Time Recorded in Minutes

NOTE:—All employees are required to keep an accurate record of every job worked upon. Time shown hereon MUST agree with clock register, and wages are computed accordingly. Take new sheet for overtime and have it marked "overtime" by Foreman.

Name Lee H. Oswald Worked from 8:30 A. M. to 5:00 M. Date Monday Oct. 29 1962

JOB NO.	CUSTOMER		Kind of Work	START		STOP		Chargeable Alt.	Chargeable Comp.	Non-Chargeable
24895	advertising artists assoc.			8	30	8	55			
22192	Rogers + Smith			8	55	9	20			
24718	Tracy Locke			9	20	9	40			
24878	Electronics Service			9	40	10	05			
24644	Cunningham Walsh			10	05	10	35			
24959	Paul E. Edwards Studios			10	35	11	25			
24578	Sam Bloom			11	25	12	30	4 –		
	Lunch			12	30	1	00			
24875	adv. artists			1	00	1	35			
24904	Bratcher			1	35	2	30			
24861	Walter H. Allen Co.			2	30	2	55			
24939	David Reeves			2	55	3	30			
24925	Chamber of Commerce			3	30	4	20			
24932	Jay Hays			4	20	4	40			
2468	Addeta company			4	40	5	00	4 –		

J

Chargeable Hours _____ Non-Chargeable Hours _____ O.K. _____ Foreman.

Commission Exhibit No. 1850

COMMISSION EXHIBIT No. 1850—Continued

JAGGARS-CHILES-STOVALL, INC.
PHOTOGRAPHIC DEPARTMENT
Time Recorded in Minutes

NOTE:—All employees are required to keep an accurate record of every job worked upon. Time shown hereon MUST agree with clock register, and wages are computed accordingly. Take new sheet for overtime and have it marked "overtime" by Foreman.

Name Lee H. Oswald Worked from 8:30 A. M. to 5:00 P M. Date Oct. 30th Tues. 1962

JOB NO.	CUSTOMER		Kind of Work	START	STOP	Chargeable Alt.	Chargeable Comp.	Non-Chargeable
25071	Dallas Civic Opera			8 30	9 30			
25002	Aylin adve.			9 30	10 20			
24874	Payk-survey			10 20	10 45			
24538	Graphic Illus.			10 45	11 15			
24957	Mississippi Power			11 15	12 05			
22192	Rogers & Smith			12 05	12 30	4		
	Lunch			12 30	1 00			
24957	Miss. Power			1 00	1 35			
24635	Gulf Insulator			1 35	2 20			
24644	C&W			2 20	3 05			
25151	Jack Holmes			3 05	3 40			
25104	Zales adv.			3 40	4 10			
24876	adver. artist			4 10	4 30	4		
25195	Rod Lambert	8		4 30	5 00			

Chargeable Hours ________ Non-Chargeable Hours ________ O.K. ________ Foreman.

Commission Exhibit No. 1850

COMMISSION EXHIBIT NO. 1850—Continued

JAGGARS-CHILES-STOVALL, INC.
PHOTOGRAPHIC DEPARTMENT
Time Recorded in Minutes

NOTE:—All employees are required to keep an accurate record of every job worked upon. Time shown hereon MUST agree with clock register, and wages are computed accordingly. Take new sheet for overtime and have it marked "overtime" by Foreman.

Name Lee H. Oswald Worked from 8:30 A. M. to 5:00 M. Date Oct. 31st Wed. 1962

JOB NO.	CUSTOMER		Kind of Work	START	STOP	Chargeable Alt.	Chargeable Comp.	Non-Chargeable
25234	Republic National Life			8 30	8 45			
25117	Bob Baird			8 45	9 20			
25126	Contain - Corp of America			9 20	9 40			
25261	Tracy Locke			9 40	10 15			
25247	D'Arcy			10 15	11 05			
25119	Max K Bredlow			11 05	11 35			
25232	Rominger adve.			11 35	12 30	4		
	Lunch			12 30	1 00			
24875	advertis. artist assoc			1 00	1 25			
24729	Ray Hanword, Box & Rd. Co			1 25	2 10			
25127	Container Corp of America			2 10	2 55			
25344	Bryan & Bryan			2 55	3 40			
20058	Southwestern Life			3 40	4 30			
25218	Lambert Williamson			4 30	5 00	4		

Chargeable Hours ________ Non-Chargeable Hours ________ O.K. ________ Foreman.

Commission Exhibit No. 1850

COMMISSION EXHIBIT NO. 1850—Continued

JAGGARS-CHILES-STOVALL, INC.
PHOTOGRAPHIC DEPARTMENT
Time Recorded in Minutes

NOTE:—All employees are required to keep an accurate record of every job worked upon. Time shown hereon MUST agree with clock register, and wages are computed accordingly. Take new sheet for overtime and have it marked "overtime" by Foreman.

Name Lee H Oswald Worked from 8:30 A. M. to 5:15 M. Date Nov. 1st THUR 1962

JOB NO.	CUSTOMER	Kind of Work	START	STOP	Chargeable Alt.	Chargeable Comp.	Non-Chargeable
25282	Crum Thomas		8 30	9 10			
25443	J. Morgan		9 10	9 55			
25445	Braniff adv.		9 55	10 25			
25404	Sam Bloom		10 25	11 05			
25377	Cunningham Cooper & Co.		11 05	11 45			
?	Pollock Paper Co.		11 45	12 10			
25456	Rogers & Smith		12 10	12 30	4		
	Lunch		12 30	1 00			
25487	Mulley of Potty adv.		1 00	1 40			
25543	Bemod printing CO		1 40	2 25			
25365	White auto		2 25	3 05			
25550	Wilson Engin.		3 05	3 45			
25569	Indust. Printing CO.		3 45	4 20			
25127	Container Corp		4 20	5 15	4 15		

8 15

Chargeable Hours ______ Non-Chargeable Hours ______ O.K. ______ Foreman.

— Commission Exhibit No. 1851 —

COMMISSION EXHIBIT No. 1851

JAGGARS-CHILES-STOVALL, INC.
PHOTOGRAPHIC DEPARTMENT
Time Recorded in Minutes

NOTE:—All employees are required to keep an accurate record of every job worked upon. Time shown hereon MUST agree with clock register, and wages are computed accordingly. Take new sheet for overtime and have it marked "overtime" by Foreman.

Name Lee H. Oswald Worked from 8:30 A. M. to 5:00 M. Date Nov. 2 FRIDAY 1962

JOB NO.	CUSTOMER	Kind of Work	START	STOP	Chargeable Alt.	Chargeable Comp.	Non-Chargeable
25628	Braniff adv.		8 30	9 20			
25620	Brandenburg adv.		9 20	10 15			
25631	Evan Young - negs		10 15	11 25			
25608	Sam Bloom		11 25	12 10			
25192	Bullock		12 10	12 30	4		
	Lunch		12 30	1 00			
25468	GREEN-BUSH ADVER		1 00	1 25			
25380	Cunningham Cooper & CO		1 25	2 15			
25440	Sam Bloom		2 15	2 55			
25750	Fleming & Sons		2 55	3 30			
25628	Braniff adv.		3 30	3 40			
12224	Lone Star Gas		3 40	3 55			
25660	Rogers & Smith		3 55	4 20			
25813	Paymaster		4 20	5 00	4		

8

Chargeable Hours ______ Non-Chargeable Hours ______ O.K. ______ Foreman.

— Commission Exhibit No. 1851 —

COMMISSION EXHIBIT No. 1851—Continued

JAGGARS-CHILES-STOVALL, INC.
PHOTOGRAPHIC DEPARTMENT
Time Recorded in Minutes

NOTE:—All employees are required to keep an accurate record of every job worked upon. Time shown hereon MUST agree with clock register, and wages are computed accordingly. Take new sheet for overtime and have it marked "overtime" by Foreman.

Name Lee H Oswald Worked from 8:15 A. M. to 4:00 M. Date Sat. Nov. 3 19—

JOB NO.	CUSTOMER		Kind of Work	START		STOP		Chargeable Alt.	Chargeable Comp.	Non-Chargeable
25479	C & W			8	15	8	30			
25735	White auto			8	30	8	55			
25734	White auto			8	55	9	25			
25714	Glenn adv.			9	25	9	45			
25817	Container corp			9	45	10	15			
25518	Stefan Kromas			10	15	10	50			
25723	Crook adv.			10	50	11	15			
25841	Kers			11	15	11	30			
25086	Medallion Stove			11	30	12	00			
25852	Chas Beall			12	00	12	45	4 1/2		
	Lunch			~~12~~	~~45~~	~~1~~	~~15~~			
25881	BBD & O			1	15	2	10			
25702	Rogers & Smith			2	10	3	05			
25887	Bob Pierce			3	05	4	00			

7 1/4 O.K.

Chargeable Hours ______ Non-Chargeable Hours ______ Foreman.

Commission Exhibit No. 1851

COMMISSION EXHIBIT NO. 1851—Continued

JAGGARS-CHILES-STOVALL, INC.
PHOTOGRAPHIC DEPARTMENT
Time Recorded in Minutes

NOTE:—All employees are required to keep an accurate record of every job worked upon. Time shown hereon MUST agree with clock register, and wages are computed accordingly. Take new sheet for overtime and have it marked "overtime" by Foreman.

Name Lee H Oswald Worked from 8:30 A. M. to 5:00 M. Date Mon Nov. 5 1962

JOB NO.	CUSTOMER		Kind of Work	START		STOP		Chargeable Alt.	Chargeable Comp.	Non-Chargeable
25853	Paul McCain Typog.			8	30	9	35			
25862	White auto			9	35	10	10			
25951	McCarty			10	10	10	30			
25303	Jack Wyatt			10	30	10	55			
25086	Medallion			10	55	11	15			
24837	Container			11	15	11	35			
25576	Tracy Locke			11	35	11	55			
25804	Sam Bloom			11	55	12	10			
25887	Bob Pierce			12	10	12	20			
25903	Bagelwolf			12	20	12	30	4		
—	Lunch			12	30	1	00			
25967	Earl Webb			1	00	1	45			
25881	BBD & O			1	45	2	35			
25984	BBD & O			2	35	3	40			
25667	Ducker adv.			3	40	4	15			
26006	Southwestern Life Ins.			4	15	5	00	4		

O.K.

Chargeable Hours ______ Non-Chargeable Hours ______ Foreman.

Commission Exhibit No. 1851

COMMISSION EXHIBIT NO. 1851—Continued

JAGGARS-CHILES-STOVALL, INC.
PHOTOGRAPHIC DEPARTMENT
Time Recorded in Minutes

NOTE:—All employees are required to keep an accurate record of every job worked upon. Time shown hereon MUST agree with clock register, and wages are computed accordingly. Take new sheet for overtime and have it marked "overtime" by Foreman.

Name Lee H Oswald Worked from 8:30 A. M. to 5:00 P.M. Date Nov 6 1962

JOB NO.	CUSTOMER	Kind of Work	START	STOP	Chargeable All.	Chargeable Comp.	Non-Chargeable
25936	Tom Grimes		8 30	9 10			
26027	Stanley Campbell		9 10	9 25			
26003	Southland Life Insure.		9 25	10 05			
26058	Medallion		10 05	10 30			
25632	Tracy Locke		10 30	11 00			
25935	Sears Roebuck & Co.		11 00	11 35			
25971	Stefan Kramer		11 35	12 20			
26093	Foote-Cone & Belding		12 20	1 00	4 1/2		
	Lunch		1 00	1 30			
26062	Sam Bloom		1 30	2 20			
25660	Rogers & Smith		2 20	3 05			
26165	Jack Wyatt		3 05	3 20			
26204	Pollock		3 20	3 40			
26095	Dallas Civic Opera		3 40	4 10			
26057	Sam Bloom		4 10	4 20			
26102	Bif? Rolnick		4 20	5 00	3 1/2		

Chargeable Hours ____ Non-Chargeable Hours ____ 8 O.K. ____ Foreman.

Commission Exhibit No. 1851—Continued

JAGGARS-CHILES-STOVALL, INC.
PHOTOGRAPHIC DEPARTMENT
Time Recorded in Minutes

NOTE:—All employees are required to keep an accurate record of every job worked upon. Time shown hereon MUST agree with clock register, and wages are computed accordingly. Take new sheet for overtime and have it marked "overtime" by Foreman.

Name Lee H Oswald Worked from 8:30 A. M. to 5:30 P.M. Date Nov 7 1962

JOB NO.	CUSTOMER	Kind of Work	START	STOP	Chargeable All.	Chargeable Comp.	Non-Chargeable
26266	Nancy Jones		8 30	8 55			
26089	Braniff adv.		8 55	9 20			
26135	Harold Peacock		9 20	10 05			
25616	Glenn adver.		10 05	10 45			
26257	Linz Jewelers		10 45	11 30			
22801	Rogers & Smith		11 30	12 15			
26348	L. M. Brooks		12 15	12 30			
26213	Stanley Campbell		12 30	12 45	4 1/4		
	Lunch		12 45	1 15			
26266	Nancy Jones		1 15	2 05			
25949	Titche's (22)		2 05	3 00			
25517	International Public Relations		3 00	3 55			
25660	Rogers & Smith		3 55	4 30			
26293	Jack Wyatt		4 30	5 30	4 1/4		

8 3/4

Chargeable Hours ____ Non-Chargeable Hours ____ O.K. ____ Foreman.

Commission Exhibit No. 1851

Commission Exhibit No. 1851—Continued

JAGGARS-CHILES-STOVALL, INC.
PHOTOGRAPHIC DEPARTMENT
Time Recorded in Minutes

NOTE:—All employees are required to keep an accurate record of every job worked upon. Time shown hereon MUST agree with clock register, and wages are computed accordingly. Take new sheet for overtime and have it marked "overtime" by Foreman.

Name Lee H. Oswald Worked from 8:30 A. M. to 5:15 M. Date Thurs. Nov 8 1962

JOB NO.	CUSTOMER		Kind of Work	START		STOP		Chargeable Alt.	Chargeable Comp.	Non-Chargeable
26425	Rogers & Smith			8	30	9	05			
26273	Jack Wyatt			9	05	9	35			
26423	Great Southwest In.			9	35	9	55			
26402	Hooker Ptg. Co.			9	55	10	20			
26418	J. Frank Parker & Son			10	20	11	00			
26310	Sam Bloom			11	00	11	25			
26419	Prewitt Printing			11	25	11	55			
26465	Campbell-Dickey adv.			11	55	12	15			
26159	Lloyd Mades			12	15	12	35			
26289	Southwest Invest.			12	35	12	55	4 25		
	Lunch			12	55	1	25			
25517	Inter. Public Relation			1	25	2	10			
25671	Glenn adv.			2	10	2	45			
26400	Sam Bloom			2	45	3	20			
26525	Bryan & Bryan			3	20	3	55			
26533	AMS			3	55	4	30	50		
26561	Crandell corp.			4	30	5	15	3		

Chargeable Hours______ Non-Chargeable Hours______ 8 1/50 O.K. ______ Foreman.

Commission Exhibit No. 1851

COMMISSION EXHIBIT No. 1851—Continued

JAGGARS-CHILES-STOVALL, INC.
PHOTOGRAPHIC DEPARTMENT
Time Recorded in Minutes

NOTE:—All employees are required to keep an accurate record of every job worked upon. Time shown hereon MUST agree with clock register, and wages are computed accordingly. Take new sheet for overtime and have it marked "overtime" by Foreman.

Name Lee H Oswald Worked from 8:30 A. M. to 5:30 M. Date Friday nov. 9 1962

JOB NO.	CUSTOMER		Kind of Work	START		STOP		Chargeable Alt.	Chargeable Comp.	Non-Chargeable
26606	Wilson engraving			8	30	9	10			
26531	AMS			9	10	9	50			
26442	Sam Bloom			9	50	10	20			
24709	Sam Bloom			10	20	11	05			
26518	Crandell corp			11	05	11	35			
26615	Jack T Holmes			11	35	12	20			
26705	Taylor Norsbury			12	20	12	40	4 50		
	Lunch			12	40	1	10			
26630	Cunningham corp			1	10	2	00			
26603	Ayling			2	00	2	45			
26638	Glenn adv			2	45	3	10			
26712	Glen adv.			3	10	3	50			
26493	BBD & O.			3	50	4	20			
26730	Ditchie			4	20	4	55			
26659	Ayres Compton			4	55	5	30	4 20		

8 3/4

O.K.

Chargeable Hours______ Non-Chargeable Hours______ ______ Foreman.

Commission Exhibit No. 1851

COMMISSION EXHIBIT No. 1851—Continued

JAGGARS-CHILES-STOVALL, INC.
PHOTOGRAPHIC DEPARTMENT
Time Recorded in Minutes

NOTE:—All employees are required to keep an accurate record of every job worked upon. Time shown hereon MUST agree with clock register, and wages are computed accordingly. Take new sheet for overtime and have it marked "overtime" by Foreman.

Name Lee H Oswald Worked from 8:15 A. M. to 5:30 M. Date sat nov 10 1962

JOB NO.	CUSTOMER		Kind of Work	START		STOP		Chargeable Alt.	Chargeable Comp.	Non-Chargeable
26630	Cunningham-Cooper			8	15	9	00			
26805	Sanger Harris			9	00	9	45			
26658	ayers Compton			9	45	10	55			
26531	AMS			10	55	11	50			
26818	W. W. Sherrill			11	50	12	30	4 15		
	Lunch			12	30	1	00			
26737	Rogers + Smith			1	00	2	10			
26697	Bryan - Bryan			2	10	3	00			
—	~~Wm~~. Brook			3	00	3	55			
26847	Bob Knight			3	55	4	45	4 30		
26055	Medallion Stori			4	45	5	30			

8 45

Chargeable Hours______ Non-Chargeable Hours______ O.K.______ Foreman.

Commission Exhibit No. 1851

COMMISSION EXHIBIT NO. 1851—Continued

JAGGARS-CHILES-STOVALL, INC.
PHOTOGRAPHIC DEPARTMENT
Time Recorded in Minutes

NOTE:—All employees are required to keep an accurate record of every job worked upon. Time shown hereon MUST agree with clock register, and wages are computed accordingly. Take new sheet for overtime and have it marked "overtime" by Foreman.

Name Lee H Oswald Worked from 8:15 A. M. to 6:00 M. Date mon. nov 12 1962

JOB NO.	CUSTOMER		Kind of Work	START		STOP		Chargeable Alt.	Chargeable Comp.	Non-Chargeable
26813	Evans Young & Wyatt			8	15	8	50			
26952	McCarty Co of Texas			8	50	9	40			
26835	Gulf States			9	40	10	20			
26868	Lone Star Gas			10	20	10	55			
26332	Jack Adams			10	55	11	55	7 4		
26849	W. A. Green			11	55	1	00	4		
	Lunch			1:	00	1	30			
26696	R W Lemberton			1	30	2	10			
26882	Chester County Plan. Comm.			2	10	2	45			
26913	Cepart associates			2	45	3	30			
26579	~~Glen~~ adves			3	30	4	00			
26962	Bearden			4	00	4	20			
26699	Jersey Production Res.			4	20	4	40			
26884	White's auto			4	40	5	10			
26813	Evans Young - Wyatt			5	10	5	20	4 30		
26988	KRLD			5	20	6	00			

9 4

Chargeable Hours______ Non-Chargeable Hours______ O.K.______ Foreman.

Commission Exhibit No. 1851

COMMISSION EXHIBIT NO. 1851—Continued

JAGGARS-CHILES-STOVALL, INC.
PHOTOGRAPHIC DEPARTMENT
Time Recorded in Minutes

NOTE:—All employees are required to keep an accurate record of every job worked upon. Time shown hereon MUST agree with clock register, and wages are computed accordingly. Take new sheet for overtime and have it marked "overtime" by Foreman.

Name Lee H. Oswald Worked from 8:30 A. M. to 5:30 M. Date Tues Nov 13 1962

JOB NO.	CUSTOMER		Kind of Work	START	STOP	Chargeable Alt.	Chargeable Comp.	Non-Chargeable
26952	McCarty of Texas			8 30	9 10			
27055	Containers Corp			9 10	9 40			
26952	McCarty Co.			9 40	10 30			
26873	Evans Young & Wyatt			10 30	11 00			
26949	[illegible]			11 00	11 20			
18554	T. C. J			11 20	11 50			
27036	Grace Crockett			11 50	12 30	4—		
	Lunch			12 30	1 00			
27033	Tracy-Locke			1 00	1 30			
26900	Walraven Book Cover Co			1 30	2 10			
27104	Sears Roebuck Co.			2 10	2 45			
27079	Titches			2 45	3 25			
27127	Todd Co.			3 25	4 15			
26662	Ennis Business Form			4 15	5 00			
27184	Robert Curran			5 00	5 30	4 30 —		

Chargeable Hours______ Non-Chargeable Hours______ 4 30 O.K. ______ Foreman.

Commission Exhibit No. 1851

COMMISSION EXHIBIT NO. 1851—Continued

JAGGARS-CHILES-STOVALL, INC.
PHOTOGRAPHIC DEPARTMENT
Time Recorded in Minutes

NOTE:—All employees are required to keep an accurate record of every job worked upon. Time shown hereon MUST agree with clock register, and wages are computed accordingly. Take new sheet for overtime and have it marked "overtime" by Foreman.

Name Lee H Oswald Worked from 8 30 A. M. to 5 00 M. Date Wed. Nov 14 1962

JOB NO.	CUSTOMER		Kind of Work	START	STOP	Chargeable Alt.	Chargeable Comp.	Non-Chargeable
27113	White Auto			8 30	9 10			
27119	Phillips Brown			9 10	9 45			
26464	Bob Knight			9 45	10 20			
27232	Wal Lingle			10 20	11 05			
27093	Taylor-Norsworthy			11 05	11 25			
27229	Dallas Chamber of Commerce			11 25	11 45			
27110	Cunningham & Walsh			11 45	12 10			
27097	RPLD			12 10	12 30	4—		
	Lunch			12 30	1 00			
27260	Fleming & Sons			1 00	1 30			
27336	Tracy Locke			1 30	2 10			
27309	Darcy			2 10	2 45			
27055	Containers			2 45	3 30			
27323	Braniff Adv.			3 30	4 05			
27230	Tracy Locke			4 05	4 40			
27211	Sam Bloom			4 40	5 00	4—		

Chargeable Hours______ Non-Chargeable Hours______ 8 O.K. ______ Foreman.

Commission Exhibit No. 1851

COMMISSION EXHIBIT NO. 1851—Continued

JAGGARS-CHILES-STOVALL, INC.
PHOTOGRAPHIC DEPARTMENT
Time Recorded in Minutes

NOTE:—All employees are required to keep an accurate record of every job worked upon. Time shown hereon MUST agree with clock register, and wages are computed accordingly. Take new sheet for overtime and have it marked "overtime" by Foreman.

Name Lee H Oswald Worked from 8:30 A. M. to 6:00 M. Date Thurs. Nov 15 1962

JOB NO.	CUSTOMER		Kind of Work	START		STOP		Chargeable Alt.	Chargeable Comp.	Non-Chargeable
27408	Zales adv.			8	30	9	10			
26792	Jack T. Holmes			9	10	9	40			
27412	Don Baits			9	40	10	10			
27288	Malco Products			10	10	10	20			
27354	McCormick			10	20	10	45			
27403	Gulf Pub.			10	45	11	05			
27309	D-arcy adv.			11	05	11	25			
26464	Bob Knight			11	25	11	55			
27365	Lone Star			11	55	12	20			
27356	Container Corp			12	20	12	50	4 30		
	— Lunch —			12	50	1	20			
27247	White auto			1	20	1	50			
27300	Hal Lindgren			1	50	2	30			
27042	Burton & Gray			2	30	3	30			
27463	Skorgenics			3	30	4	15			
27506	Jack T. Holmes			4	15	5	10			
27396	Don Manning Studio			5	10	6	00	4 30		

Chargeable Hours ________ Non-Chargeable Hours ________ 9 O.K. ________ Foreman.

Commission Exhibit No. 1851

COMMISSION EXHIBIT NO. 1851—Continued

JAGGARS-CHILES-STOVALL, INC.
PHOTOGRAPHIC DEPARTMENT
Time Recorded in Minutes

NOTE:—All employees are required to keep an accurate record of every job worked upon. Time shown hereon MUST agree with clock register, and wages are computed accordingly. Take new sheet for overtime and have it marked "overtime" by Foreman.

Name Lee H Oswald Worked from 8:30 A. M. to 5:30 M. Date Friday Nov 16 1962

JOB NO.	CUSTOMER		Kind of Work	START		STOP		Chargeable Alt.	Chargeable Comp.	Non-Chargeable
27506	Jack T Holmes			8	30	9	10			
27618	Bud Biggs			9	10	9	45			
27477	Palmer Printing Co			9	45	10	15			
27570	Epling Laundry			10	15	10	50			
27626	Electrodyne Service			10	50	11	20			
27566	J. F. Parker & Son			11	20	11	45			
27603	McCallen			11	45	12	05			
27249	Southwestern Elec.			12	05	12	20			
7547	Nancy Jones			12	20	12	40			
27249	Southwestern Elec. Power			12	40	1	00	4 30		
	Lunch			1	00	1	30			
27204	Tracy Locke			1	30	2	15			
27737	Zond Grimm			2	15	3	05			
27634	D'arcy			3	05	4	00			
25894	J C B			4	00	4	30			
27509	Butler			4	30	5	30	4 —		

8 1/2

Chargeable Hours ________ Non-Chargeable Hours ________ O.K. ________ Foreman.

Commission Exhibit No. 1851

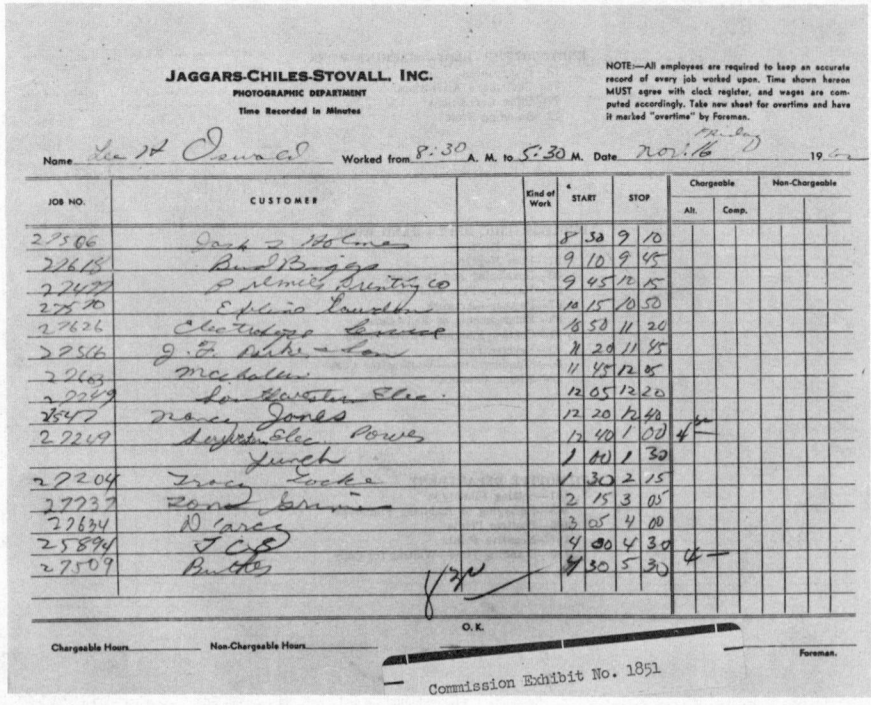

COMMISSION EXHIBIT NO. 1851—Continued

JAGGARS-CHILES-STOVALL, INC.
PHOTOGRAPHIC DEPARTMENT
Time Recorded in Minutes

NOTE:—All employees are required to keep an accurate record of every job worked upon. Time shown hereon MUST agree with clock register, and wages are computed accordingly. Take new sheet for overtime and have it marked "overtime" by Foreman.

Name Lee H. Oswald Worked from 8:30 A. M. to 5:00 M. Date Nov 17 (Sat.) 1962

JOB NO.	CUSTOMER	Kind of Work	START		STOP		Chargeable Alt.	Chargeable Comp.	Non-Chargeable
27758	Sears		8	30	9	20			
27805	J.W. Doug Co.		9	20	10	05			
27788	Sam Bloom		10	05	10	45			
27700	Cunningham + Walsh		10	45	11	10			
27807	Scott		11	10	11	35	3½		
27704	Adcraft adv. Agency		11	35	12	00			
	— Lunch —		12	00	12	30			
27826	Brandenberg adv		12	30	1	20			
27677	B B D & O		1	20	2	10			
?	J C S		2	10	3	00			
27848	Braniff		3	00	3	30			
26910	Standford agency		3	30	4	10			
27819	Fry Hammond Fed.		4	10	4	30			
27758	Sears		4	30	5	00			
	8								

Chargeable Hours______ Non-Chargeable Hours______ O.K.______ Foreman.

Commission Exhibit No. 1851

COMMISSION EXHIBIT NO. 1851—Continued

JAGGARS-CHILES-STOVALL, INC.
PHOTOGRAPHIC DEPARTMENT
Time Recorded in Minutes

NOTE:—All employees are required to keep an accurate record of every job worked upon. Time shown hereon MUST agree with clock register, and wages are computed accordingly. Take new sheet for overtime and have it marked "overtime" by Foreman.

Name Lee H. Oswald Worked from 8:15 A. M. to 5:45 M. Date (monday) Nov 19 1962

JOB NO.	CUSTOMER	Kind of Work	START		STOP		Chargeable Alt.	Chargeable Comp.	Non-Chargeable
27230	Tracy Locke		8	15	8	45			
27858	Chapman McClain		8	45	9	20			
27778	Prewitt Printing Co.		9	20	9	55			
26670	Ling-Temco Vought		9	55	10	30			
27150	[illegible]		10	30	11	00			
27929	Big Town		11	00	11	20			
27858	Charles McLain		11	20	12	00			
27929	Big Town		12	00	12	30	4½		
	Lunch —		12	30	1	00			
27856	Stanley Martin		1	30	2	30			
27851	Neals + Hickok		2	30	3	10			
18554	J C S		3	10	3	50			
27970	[illegible]		3	50	4	00			
27881	Sears Roebuck + Co		4	00	4	20			
27897	Cunningham + Coggins		4	20	5	10			
22950	J C S		5	10	5	45			

8¾

Chargeable Hours______ Non-Chargeable Hours______ O.K. ______ Foreman.

Commission Exhibit No. 185

COMMISSION EXHIBIT NO. 1851—Continued

JAGGARS-CHILES-STOVALL, INC.
PHOTOGRAPHIC DEPARTMENT
Time Recorded in Minutes

NOTE:—All employees are required to keep an accurate record of every job worked upon. Time shown hereon MUST agree with clock register, and wages are computed accordingly. Take new sheet for overtime and have it marked "overtime" by Foreman.

Name Lee H Oswald Worked from 8:15 A. M. to 5:45 M. Date Tues Nov 20 1962

JOB NO.	CUSTOMER		Kind of Work	START		STOP		Chargeable Alt.	Chargeable Comp.	Non-Chargeable
27632	Ken Reid			8	15	9	10			
27787	Sam Bloom			9	10	10	00			
27971	Sam Bloom			10	00	10	50			
28084	Charles Beale			10	50	11	40			
28644	Don L Baxter			11	40	12	20	4[05]		
	— Lunch —			12	20	12	50			
28106	Internat. Publication			12	50	1	20			
28087	Jack Wyatt			1	20	1	45			
28149	Industrial printing tech.			1	45	2	30			
28101	Lone Star Boat			2	30	3	15			
28123	Graphic arts Center			3	15	4	00			
28077	Jack Wyatt			4	00	4	20			
27339	Sam Bloom			4	20	4	40			
27897	Cunningham & Cooper			4	40	5	10			
22566	J Frank Parker & Son			5	10	5	45	4[55]		

O.K.

Chargeable Hours______ Non-Chargeable Hours______ Foreman.

Commission Exhibit No. 1851

COMMISSION EXHIBIT NO. 1851—Continued

JAGGARS-CHILES-STOVALL, INC.
PHOTOGRAPHIC DEPARTMENT
Time Recorded in Minutes

NOTE:—All employees are required to keep an accurate record of every job worked upon. Time shown hereon MUST agree with clock register, and wages are computed accordingly. Take new sheet for overtime and have it marked "overtime" by Foreman.

Name Lee H Oswald Worked from 8:30 A. M. to 6:00 M. Date Wed. Nov 21 1962

JOB NO.	CUSTOMER		Kind of Work	START		STOP		Chargeable Alt.	Chargeable Comp.	Non-Chargeable
22832	Dallas Chamber of Comm.			8	30	9	20			
27898	J. C. S.			9	20	9	45			
28106	International Publication			9	45	10	15			
28148	BBD & O			10	15	10	50			
28240	Dallas—Fed World Art Dir.			10	50	11	15			
28258	Bob Knight			11	15	11	30			
27924	Big Town			11	30	12	00			
22854	Bob Knight			12	00	12	20			
22568	Zitaker Edises.			12	20	12	30	4		
	Lunch			12	30	1	00			
?	Hepworth Adv. Co			1	00	1	45			
28176	Don Baxter			1	45	2	15			
28366	Lining Jenkins			2	15	2	50			
28319	Jack O. Anglin			2	50	3	20			
27609	Taylor Norsworthy Inc.			3	20	4	05			
27936	Delhi Taylor			4	05	5	00			
28348	Robert Williams			5	00	6	00	5		
28280	Medallion									

O.K.

Chargeable Hours______ Non-Chargeable Hours______

9

Commission Exhibit No. 1851

COMMISSION EXHIBIT NO. 1851—Continued

JAGGARS-CHILES-STOVALL, INC.
PHOTOGRAPHIC DEPARTMENT
Time Recorded in Minutes

(Page I)

NOTE:—All employees are required to keep an accurate record of every job worked upon. Time shown hereon MUST agree with clock register, and wages are computed accordingly. Take new sheet for overtime and have it marked "overtime" by Foreman.

Name Lee H Oswald Worked from 8:30 A. M. to 6:00 M. Date Friday nov 23 1962

JOB NO.	CUSTOMER	Kind of Work	START	STOP	Chargeable Alt.	Chargeable Comp.	Non-Chargeable
27805	Southwestern Drug co		8 30	9 10			
28412	Sam Bloom		9 10	9 40			
28360	Prewitt Printing co.		9 40	10 05			
28443	Marvin Krieger		10 05	10 25			
28056	Container Corp		10 25	10 40			
28416	Cotton Bowl Rodeo		10 40	11 00			
28071	Wyatt adver.		11 00	11 20			
28201	Rogers + Smith		11 20	11 40			
27849	Monte Rosenwald + assoc.		11 40	12 00			
28056	Container Corp.		12 00	12 20			
28427	Dravy Locke		12 20	12 35			
28486	Container Corp		12 35	12 50			
27787	Sam Bloom		12 50	1 05	4 25		
	— Lunch —		1 05	1 35			
27433	Sam Bloom		1 35	2 10			
28501	AMS		2 10	2 45			
28334	advertis. service agency		2 45	3 20			

O.K.

Chargeable Hours ______ Non-Chargeable Hours ______ ______ Foreman.

COMMISSION EXHIBIT NO. 1851—Continued

JAGGARS-CHILES-STOVALL, INC.
PHOTOGRAPHIC DEPARTMENT
Time Recorded in Minutes

(Page II)

NOTE:—All employees are required to keep an accurate record of every job worked upon. Time shown hereon MUST agree with clock register, and wages are computed accordingly. Take new sheet for overtime and have it marked "overtime" by Foreman.

Name Oswald Worked from 8:30 A. M. to 6:00 M. Date ______ 19__

JOB NO.	CUSTOMER	Kind of Work	START	STOP	Chargeable Alt.	Chargeable Comp.	Non-Chargeable
28106	International Publicity		3 20	4 15			
27833	Dallas Chamber of Commerce		4 15	4 50			
28461	Wyatt		4 50	5 15			
28509	Teleaideo		5 15	5 35			
28510	Teleaideo		5 35	6 00	4 25		

9 —

O.K.

Chargeable Hours ______ Non-Chargeable Hours ______ ______ Foreman.

Commission Exhibit No. 1851

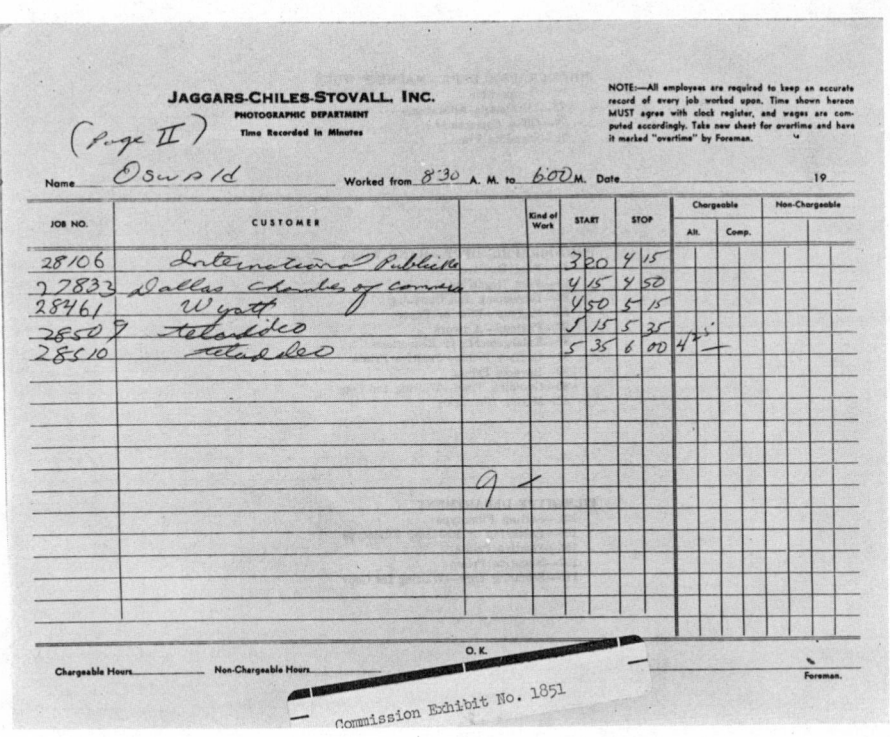

COMMISSION EXHIBIT NO. 1851—Continued

JAGGARS-CHILES-STOVALL, INC.
PHOTOGRAPHIC DEPARTMENT
Time Recorded in Minutes

NOTE:—All employees are required to keep an accurate record of every job worked upon. Time shown hereon MUST agree with clock register, and wages are computed accordingly. Take new sheet for overtime and have it marked "overtime" by Foreman.

Name Lee H Oswald Worked from 8:15 A. M. to 4:00 M. Date (Sat.) nov 24 1962

JOB NO.	CUSTOMER		Kind of Work	START		STOP		Chargeable Alt.	Comp.	Non-Chargeable
28614	Tom Bloom			8	15	9	20			
25894	JCS			9	10	9	50			
28553	Bob Pierce			9	50	10	30			
28635	Robert K Butlake Fav			10	30	11	20			
28457	John I Thompson			11	20	12	00			
28544	Marith Royd			12	00	12	20			
28314	Whites auto			12	20	12	40			
28658	Glen			12	40	1	00	4 40		
	Lunch			1	00	1	30			
28649	Illaddro			1	30	2	10			
28621	Tracy Locke			2	10	3	15			
	-maintance-			3	15	4:	00	2 30		

Chargeable Hours ____ Non-Chargeable Hours ____ O.K. ____ Foreman.

Commission Exhibit No. 1851—Continued

JAGGARS-CHILES-STOVALL, INC.
PHOTOGRAPHIC DEPARTMENT
Time Recorded in Minutes

NOTE:—All employees are required to keep an accurate record of every job worked upon. Time shown hereon MUST agree with clock register, and wages are computed accordingly. Take new sheet for overtime and have it marked "overtime" by Foreman.

Name Lee H Oswald Worked from 830 A. M. to 5:30 M. Date mon Nov 26 1962

JOB NO.	CUSTOMER		Kind of Work	START		STOP		Chargeable Alt.	Comp.	Non-Chargeable
28201	Rogers + Smith			8	30	9	20			
28678	Gordon mask.			9	20	10	15			
28230	Gordon masks			10	15	11	00			
28621	Tracy Locke			11	00	11	45			
28726	Klaf mailer			11	45	12	30	4 —		
	Lunch			12	30	1	00			
28656	Glenn adver.			12	30	1	20			
28693	Abe Berger ads			1	20	2	10			
28689	Powell Ptg.			2	10	3	00			
28713	Glenn Adv			3	00	4	10			
28799	Ikonogenics			4	10	5	30	5 —		

Chargeable Hours ____ Non-Chargeable Hours ____ O.K. ____ Foreman.

Commission Exhibit No. 1851

Commission Exhibit No. 1851—Continued

JAGGARS-CHILES-STOVALL, INC.
PHOTOGRAPHIC DEPARTMENT
Time Recorded in Minutes

NOTE:—All employees are required to keep an accurate record of every job worked upon. Time shown hereon MUST agree with clock register, and wages are computed accordingly. Take new sheet for overtime and have it marked "overtime" by Foreman.

Name Lee H Oswald Worked from 830 A. M. to 5:45 M. Date tues. nov 27 1962

JOB NO.	CUSTOMER		Kind of Work	START	STOP	Chargeable Alt.	Chargeable Comp.	Non-Chargeable
28842	Baptist Public Rel.			8 30	9 10			
28829	Swang			9 10	9 40			
28834	Republic Nat. Life			9 40	10 15			
28657	Glenn advg			10 15	10 35			
28849	Gulf States Oil			10 35	10 50			
28848	Crandall Corp.			10 50	11 05			
28484	Taylor Norsworthy			11 05	11 25			
28922	Don Baptist			11 25	11 40			
28918	Wright Plan & Rep			11 45	12 20			
25899	J C S			12 20	12 40			
28978	Park and Survey			12 40	1 00	4 30		
	Lunch			1 00	1 40			
28427	Sam Bloom			1 40	2 20			
28679	National Survey			2 20	3 00			
28555	Longhorns			3 00	3 35			
28852	C C of A			3 35	4 20			
28920	Rogers & Smith			4 20	4 55			
28701	Charles Beale			4 55	5 45	1 05		

Chargeable Hours 8 35 O.K. Foreman.

Commission Exhibit No. 1851

COMMISSION EXHIBIT No. 1851—Continued

JAGGARS-CHILES-STOVALL, INC.
PHOTOGRAPHIC DEPARTMENT
Time Recorded in Minutes

NOTE:—All employees are required to keep an accurate record of every job worked upon. Time shown hereon MUST agree with clock register, and wages are computed accordingly. Take new sheet for overtime and have it marked "overtime" by Foreman.

Name Lee H Oswald Worked from 8:15 A. M. to 6:00 M. Date wed nov 28 1962

JOB NO.	CUSTOMER		Kind of Work	START	STOP	Chargeable Alt.	Chargeable Comp.	Non-Chargeable
28977	Judy Bonnes			8 15	9 10			
28831	Messina Kreiger			9 10	9 45			
29412	Tracy Locke			9 45	10 10			
25894	JCS (1)			10 10	10 35			
25894	JCS (2)			10 35	11 05			
28948	Robert K Butts			11 05	11 30			
29082	Jack Wyatt			11 30	11 50			
29010	Robert Curran			11 50	12 10			
28999	Crook Advg agcy			12 10	12 45	4 30		
	Lunch			12 45	1 15			
29066	Robinson Service			1 15	2 10			
29132	Goodman Paper Pro			2 10	2 40			
25894	JCS			2 40	3 20			
29081	Keitz & Herndon			3 20	4 10			
29058	Glenn advg			4 10	4 45			
29131	Crowe Guild Cement CO			4 45	5 15			
29211	Ikonogenics			5 15	6 00	4 45		

Chargeable Hours 9 45 Non-Chargeable Hours O.K. Foreman.

Commission Exhibit No. 1851

COMMISSION EXHIBIT No. 1851—Continued

JAGGARS-CHILES-STOVALL, INC.
PHOTOGRAPHIC DEPARTMENT
Time Recorded in Minutes

NOTE:—All employees are required to keep an accurate record of every job worked upon. Time shown hereon MUST agree with clock register, and wages are computed accordingly. Take new sheet for overtime and have it marked "overtime" by Foreman.

Name Lee H Oswald Worked from 8:15 A. M. to 6:00 M. Date Thurs nov 29 1962

JOB NO.	CUSTOMER		Kind of Work	START		STOP		Chargeable Alt.	Chargeable Comp.	Non-Chargeable	
29249	Beddoe Printing			8	15	8	45				
29235	Lone Star Gas			8	45	9	20				
29253	Rogers + Smith			9	20	10	00				
29070	Arkansas Western Gas			10	00	10	20				
29338	Goodwin			10	20	10	40				
29330	Will printing co			10	40	11	05				
29282	Peerless Mfg			11	05	11	25				
29348	Wilson Eng.			11	25	12	05				
29353	H – H			12	05	12	25				
29061	Taylor Norsbury			12	25	1	00	4			
	Lunch			1	00	1	30				
29277	W. M. Leap.			1	30	1	50				
29058	Glenn			1	50	2	30				
29337	Tracy - Locke (1)			2	30	3	10				
29339	Tracy Lock (2)			3	10	3	55				
29319	White auto			3	55	4	40				
28503	Lloyd modes			4	40	5	25				
29379	Harmon Bass			5	25	6	00	4			

Chargeable Hours ____ Non-Chargeable Hours ____ O.K. R15 ____ Foreman.

Commission Exhibit No. 1851

COMMISSION EXHIBIT NO. 1851—Continued

Page I

JAGGARS-CHILES-STOVALL, INC.
PHOTOGRAPHIC DEPARTMENT
Time Recorded in Minutes

NOTE:—All employees are required to keep an accurate record of every job worked upon. Time shown hereon MUST agree with clock register, and wages are computed accordingly. Take new sheet for overtime and have it marked "overtime" by Foreman.

Name Lee H Oswald Worked from 8:15 A. M. to 5:30 M. Date Monday nov 30 19 62

JOB NO.	CUSTOMER		Kind of Work	START		STOP		Chargeable Alt.	Chargeable Comp.	Non-Chargeable	
29453	Ennis Business Forms			8	15	9	05				
27630	Evans Young + Wyatt			9	05	9	50				
29228	W M Zemp + asso.			9	50	10	20				
29197	continental cdies			10	20	10	45				
29196	Leo adams			10	45	11	15				
29488	walter D allen			11	15	11	45				
26560	Johnston Printing Co			11	45	12	10				
29499	Tracy - Locke			12	10	12	30				
29542	addressograph mult.			12	30	1	0	4 45			
	lunch			1	00	1	20				
29462	container corp			1	20	1	35				
29495	Wright allen			1	35	2	10				
29545	John a Scott + CO			2	10	2	30				
28477	west			2	30	2	50				
29229	cunningham coope			2	50	3	10				
28728	Park Aerial Servic			3	10	3	35				
	Robert K Buttles			3	35	4	10				

O. K.

Chargeable Hours ________ Non-Chargeable Hours ________ ________ Foreman.

Commission Exhibit No. 1851

COMMISSION EXHIBIT No. 1851—Continued

Page II

JAGGARS-CHILES-STOVALL, INC.
PHOTOGRAPHIC DEPARTMENT
Time Recorded in Minutes

NOTE:—All employees are required to keep an accurate record of every job worked upon. Time shown hereon MUST agree with clock register, and wages are computed accordingly. Take new sheet for overtime and have it marked "overtime" by Foreman.

Name Lee H Oswald Worked from ______ A. M. to ______ M. Date ______ 19__

JOB NO.	CUSTOMER		Kind of Work	START		STOP		Chargeable Alt.	Chargeable Comp.	Non-Chargeable	
29581	ad artist			4	10	4	30				
29513	Sears + Roebuck			4	30	5	30	4 1			

8 5

O. K.

Chargeable Hours ________ Non-Chargeable Hours ________ ________ Foreman.

Commission Exhibit No. 1851

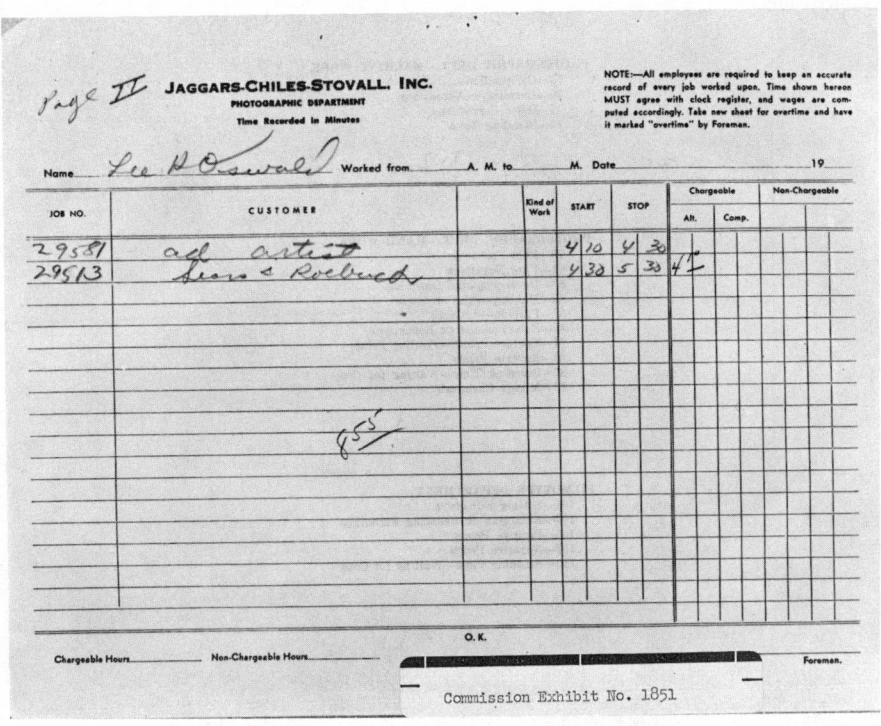

COMMISSION EXHIBIT No. 1851—Continued

JAGGARS-CHILES-STOVALL, INC.
PHOTOGRAPHIC DEPARTMENT
Time Recorded in Minutes

NOTE:—All employees are required to keep an accurate record of every job worked upon. Time shown hereon MUST agree with clock register, and wages are computed accordingly. Take new sheet for overtime and have it marked "overtime" by Foreman.

Name Lee H. Oswald Worked from 8:00 A. M. to 5:30 M. Date Dec 1st (Sat.) 1962

JOB NO.	CUSTOMER		Kind of Work	START		STOP		Chargeable Alt.	Chargeable Comp.	Non-Chargeable
29618	Eldred J Robinson			8	00	8	35			
28106	International Public Relat.			8	35	9	10			
29641	Cozy ... adv.			9	10	9	45			
29608	Budd Biggs			9	45	11	15			
29372	Walraven Book Cover			11	15	11	35			
29527	AMS			11	35	12	05			
29656	Goodloe Studio			12	05	12	30	4 3/4		
	Lunch			12	30	1	00			
29425	Park aerial Survey			1	00	1	55			
29591	Bud Biggs			1	55	2	20			
29614	Mary Hammond, Cars			2	20	2	50			
29668	John A Scott			2	50	3	20			
?	Robert Curran			3	20	3	50			
29691	Crandell Corp.			3	50	4	15			
29637	Medallion Stores			4	15	4	50			
29655	Goodloe Studio			4	50	5	10			
29591	Cain			5	10	5	30	4 1/4		

Chargeable Hours________ Non-Chargeable Hours________ 9 1/2 O.K.

Foreman.

— Commission Exhibit No. 1852 —

Commission Exhibit No. 1852

JAGGARS-CHILES-STOVALL, INC.
PHOTOGRAPHIC DEPARTMENT
Time Recorded in Minutes

NOTE:—All employees are required to keep an accurate record of every job worked upon. Time shown hereon MUST agree with clock register, and wages are computed accordingly. Take new sheet for overtime and have it marked "overtime" by Foreman.

Name Lee H Oswald Worked from 8:15 A. M. to 5:30 M. Date Dec 3 Mon. 1962

JOB NO.	CUSTOMER		Kind of Work	START		STOP		Chargeable Alt.	Chargeable Comp.	Non-Chargeable
29633	Rogers + Smith			8	15	9	20			
29700	Sam Bloom			9	20	9	50			
29607	Bud Biggs			9	50	10	15			
29654	McCain			10	15	10	45			
29749	Sears Roebuck & Co			10	45	11	10			
29651	Wyatt adv			11	10	11	50			
29691	Crandell Corp.			11	50	12	10			
29778	American Fashion			12	10	12	45	4 1/2		
	Lunch			12	:45	1	:15			
29645	Margorie Phillips			1	15	1	35			
29574	Irwin Thomas			1	35	2	10			
29742	TP&L			2	10	2	40			
29535	ICS			2	40	3	00			
29767	Glenn			3	00	3	20			
29659	Goodloe Stuck adv.			3	20	3	45			
29709	White auto			3	45	4	20			
29656	Goodloe Studio			4	20	5	05			
29253	Rogers + Smith			5	05	5	30	4 1/2		

Chargeable Hours________ Non-Chargeable Hours________ 8 45 O.K.

Foreman.

Commission Exhibit No. 1852—Continued

Page I

JAGGARS-CHILES-STOVALL, INC.
PHOTOGRAPHIC DEPARTMENT
Time Recorded in Minutes

NOTE:—All employees are required to keep an accurate record of every job worked upon. Time shown hereon MUST agree with clock register, and wages are computed accordingly. Take new sheet for overtime and have it marked "overtime" by Foreman.

Name Lee H Oswald Worked from 8:15 A. M. to 5:45 M. Date Dec 4 1962

JOB NO.	CUSTOMER		Kind of Work	START		STOP		Chargeable Alt.	Chargeable Comp.	Non-Chargeable
29832	Zules			8	15	8	40			
29838	Rayles - Nosworthy			8	40	8	55			
29884	Gray - Locke			8	55	9	15			
29826	Lone Star Gas			9	15	9	40			
29863	Bob Knight			9	40	10	05			
29851	Robinson Bowl			10	05	10	35			
29787	Jack Wyatt			10	35	11	05			
29058	Glenn			11	05	11	30			
28848	Crandell Co.			11	3[illegible]	11	55			
12224	Lone Star Gas			11	55	12	10			
29859	Romingers adv			12	10	12	45	4½		
	Lunch			12	45	1	:15			
29955	Elaine Collins			1	15	1	50			
29484	Walter A Allen			1	50	2	30			
29910	Braniff adv			2	30	2	55			
29970	American Gas Journal			2	55	3	40			
27081	J C S			3	40	4	05			
29995	Sears Roebuck			4	05	4	45			

O.K.

Chargeable Hours ______ Non-Chargeable Hours ______ ______ Foreman.

Commission Exhibit No. 1852

COMMISSION EXHIBIT NO. 1852—Continued

Page II

JAGGARS-CHILES-STOVALL, INC.
PHOTOGRAPHIC DEPARTMENT
Time Recorded in Minutes

NOTE:—All employees are required to keep an accurate record of every job worked upon. Time shown hereon MUST agree with clock register, and wages are computed accordingly. Take new sheet for overtime and have it marked "overtime" by Foreman.

Name Oswald Worked from ______ A. M. to ______ M. Date ______ 19__

JOB NO.	CUSTOMER		Kind of Work	START		STOP		Chargeable Alt.	Chargeable Comp.	Non-Chargeable
29955	Elaine Collins			4	45	5	15			
29988	Dallas Theatre Center			5	15	5	45	4½		

9 —

O.K.

Chargeable Hours ______ Non-Chargeable Hours ______ ______ Foreman.

Commission Exhibit No. 1852

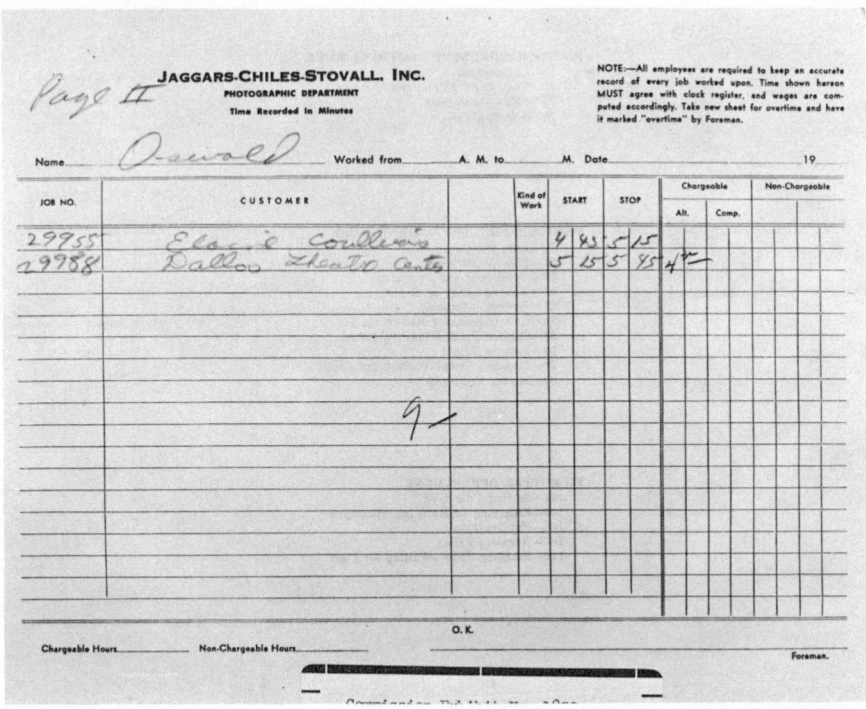

COMMISSION EXHIBIT NO. 1852—Continued

JAGGARS-CHILES-STOVALL, INC.
PHOTOGRAPHIC DEPARTMENT
Time Recorded in Minutes

NOTE:—All employees are required to keep an accurate record of every job worked upon. Time shown hereon MUST agree with clock register, and wages are computed accordingly. Take new sheet for overtime and have it marked "overtime" by Foreman.

Name Lee H Oswald Worked from 8:15 A. M. to 5:45 M. Date Wed Nov 5 19 62

JOB NO.	CUSTOMER	Kind of Work	START		STOP		Chargeable Alt.	Chargeable Comp.	Non-Chargeable
30088	Glenn (1)		8	15	8	45			
29724	Hesse Envelopes		8	45	9	20			
30008	Crook Advertising		9	20	9	40			
1240	M Beckley agency		9	40	9	55			
29920	abe Burges		9	55	10	40			
30084	Glenn		10	40	11	05			
30126	containers		11	05	11	55			
29818	concrete corporation		11	55	12	30			
29815	TP 4		12	30	1	05	4 50		
	Lunch		1	05	1	35			
30026	Cunningham corp		1	35	2	10			
29929	Glenn Mason		2	10	2	50			
30135	Horace Peacock		2	50	3	30			
30088	Glenn (2)		3	30	4	05			
30197	Lin		4	05	4	55			
29814	J C S (1-2)		4	55	5	45	4 10		

Chargeable Hours ______ Non-Chargeable Hours 9 — O.K. ______ Foreman.

Commission Exhibit No. 1852

COMMISSION EXHIBIT No. 1852—Continued

page I

JAGGARS-CHILES-STOVALL, INC.
PHOTOGRAPHIC DEPARTMENT
Time Recorded in Minutes

NOTE:—All employees are required to keep an accurate record of every job worked upon. Time shown hereon MUST agree with clock register, and wages are computed accordingly. Take new sheet for overtime and have it marked "overtime" by Foreman.

Name Lee H Oswald Worked from 8:15 A. M. to 5:15 M. Date Thurs Dec 6 19 62

JOB NO.	CUSTOMER	Kind of Work	START		STOP		Chargeable Alt.	Chargeable Comp.	Non-Chargeable
30257	Marbo Production		8	15	8	45			
30171	AMS		8	45	9	20			
30215	Tom Greene		9	20	9	40			
30132	Southwestern Life		9	40	10	00			
30244	Ozzie Sons		10	00	10	20			
30299	Pitaluk		10	20	10	45			
29656	Goolot Steck adv		10	45	11	05			
30252	Collins commercial art		11	05	11	25			
30199	The Epling Lowdon		11	25	11	55			
30250	Marbo Productions		11	55	12	15			
30304	Mell douglas		12	15	12	45	4 1/2		
	Lunch		12	45	1	15			
30166	Sears Roebuck & Co		1	15	1	40			
30135	Horace Peacock		1	40	2	10			
30368	Hicks Printing Co		2	10	2	45			
30352	Braniff		2	45	3	25			
30310	Lone Star Gas		3	05	3	25			

Chargeable Hours ______ Non-Chargeable Hours ______ O.K. ______ Foreman.

Commission Exhibit No. 1852

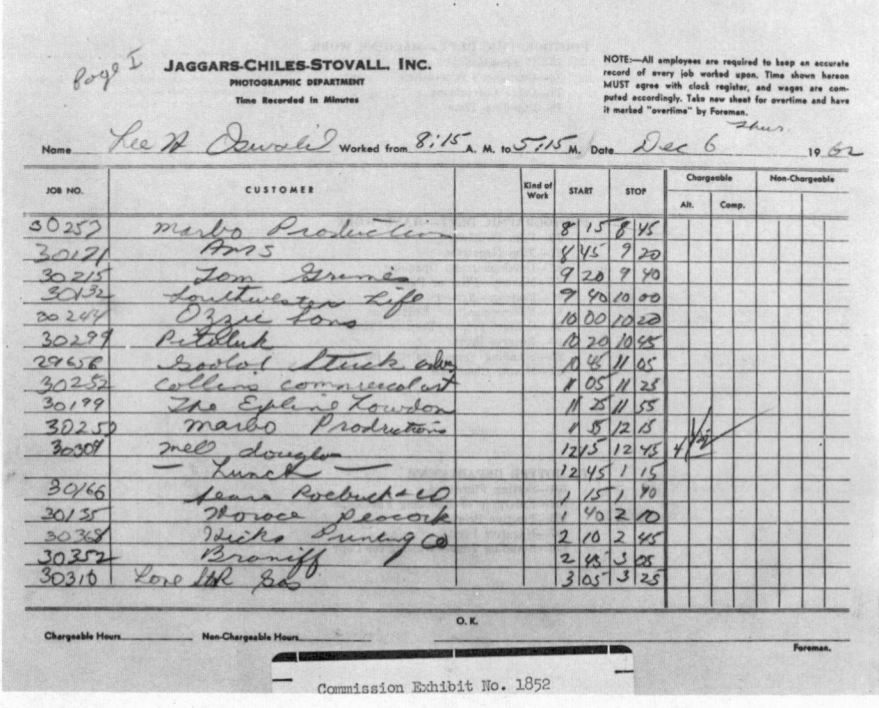

COMMISSION EXHIBIT No. 1852—Continued

Page II

JAGGARS-CHILES-STOVALL, INC.
PHOTOGRAPHIC DEPARTMENT
Time Recorded in Minutes

NOTE:—All employees are required to keep an accurate record of every job worked upon. Time shown hereon MUST agree with clock register, and wages are computed accordingly. Take new sheet for overtime and have it marked "overtime" by Foreman.

Name Lee Oswald Worked from ______ A. M. to ______ M. Date ______ 19__

JOB NO.	CUSTOMER	Kind of Work	START	STOP	Chargeable Alt.	Chargeable Comp.	Non-Chargeable
30322	Don L. Baytes		3 25	4 05			
30102	Lile advertising		4 05	4 25			
30231	Sprigkas sop		4 25	4 40			
30348	al Baines		4 40	5 15	4		

8 15

8 1/2

O.K. ______

Chargeable Hours ______ Non-Chargeable Hours ______ ______ Foreman.

Commission Exhibit No. 1852

COMMISSION EXHIBIT NO. 1852—Continued

JAGGARS-CHILES-STOVALL, INC.
PHOTOGRAPHIC DEPARTMENT
Time Recorded in Minutes

NOTE:—All employees are required to keep an accurate record of every job worked upon. Time shown hereon MUST agree with clock register, and wages are computed accordingly. Take new sheet for overtime and have it marked "overtime" by Foreman.

Name Lee H Oswald Worked from 8:15 A. M. to 5:30 M. Date Friday Dec 7 19 62

JOB NO.	CUSTOMER	Kind of Work	START	STOP	Chargeable Alt.	Chargeable Comp.	Non-Chargeable
29814	J. C. S.		8 15	8 35			
29851	Robbins - Cover - Paper		8 35	8 55			
26560	Johnson Printing Co		8 55	9 40			
30374	Rogers + Smith		9 40	10 30			
30578	Tracy Locke		10 30	11 15			
25083	Bolt Pierce		11 15	11 50			
30500	Wyatt adv		11 50	12 15	4		
	lunch		12 15	12 45			
20455	R + S		12 45	1 20			
30523	Linz Jewelers		1 20	1 50			
27977	Sam Bloom		1 50	2 30			
30525	Keitz Herndon		2 30	3 20			
27081	J C S		3 20	4 10			
29696	Litches adv		4 10	4 45			
30494	Container corp		4 45	5 10		45	
30580	Les adarts		5 10	5 30	4		

8 45

O.K. ______

Chargeable Hours ______ Non-Chargeable Hours ______ ______ Foreman.

Commission Exhibit No. 1852

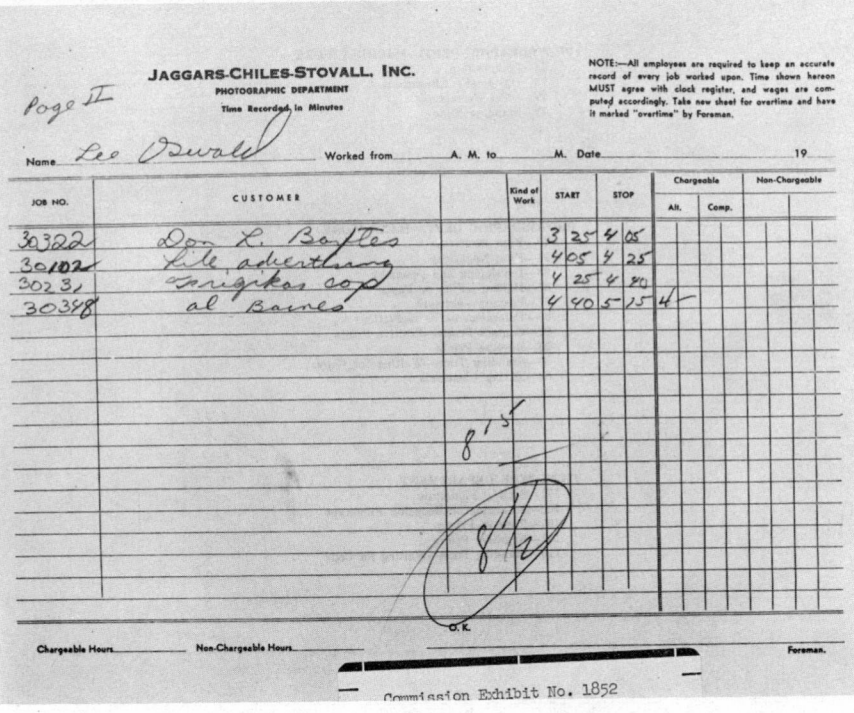

COMMISSION EXHIBIT NO. 1852—Continued

JAGGARS-CHILES-STOVALL, INC.
PHOTOGRAPHIC DEPARTMENT
Time Recorded in Minutes

NOTE:—All employees are required to keep an accurate record of every job worked upon. Time shown hereon MUST agree with clock register, and wages are computed accordingly. Take new sheet for overtime and have it marked "overtime" by Foreman.

Name Lee H. Oswald Worked from 8:00 A. M. to 3:30 M. Date (Sat.) Dec 8 1962

JOB NO.	CUSTOMER	Kind of Work	START	STOP	Chargeable Alt.	Chargeable Comp.	Non-Chargeable
30662	Container corp.		8 00	9 10			
30661	Ivory-Lock		9 10	9 55			
30572	Electrotype service		9 55	10 40			
30565	Robbins cover page		10 40	11 10			
30621	Ivory Locke		11 10	11 25			
30637	Shattuck adver		11 25	11 45			
30505	A. Accurate		11 45	12 00	4 —		
	— lunch —		12 00	12 30			
30694	S W adver.		12 30	1 10			
30714	(1) James H Stall		1 10	1 50			
30714	(2) Ja. H. Stall		2 30	2 55			
30580	Les adams & asso		2 55	3 10			
30583	Park aerial survey		3 10	3 30	3 —		

Chargeable Hours ______ Non-Chargeable Hours ______ O.K. ______ Foreman.

Commission Exhibit No. 1852

COMMISSION EXHIBIT NO. 1852—Continued

JAGGARS-CHILES-STOVALL, INC.
PHOTOGRAPHIC DEPARTMENT
Time Recorded in Minutes

Page I

NOTE:—All employees are required to keep an accurate record of every job worked upon. Time shown hereon MUST agree with clock register, and wages are computed accordingly. Take new sheet for overtime and have it marked "overtime" by Foreman.

Name Lee H. Oswald Worked from 8:15 A. M. to 5:30 M. Date monday Dec 10 1962

JOB NO.	CUSTOMER	Kind of Work	START	STOP	Chargeable Alt.	Chargeable Comp.	Non-Chargeable
30696	Tuller-Smith-Ross		8 15	8 40			
30711	Kinney CO		8 40	8 55			
30732	Pollock Paper CO		8 55	9 20			
30527	S.W. States Telephone		9 20	9 45			
30083	Fitches adv		9 45	10 05			
30703	Webb Printing CO		10 05	10 25			
30575	Industrial Printing		10 25	10 45			
29818	J C S		10 45	11 05			
30677	Braniff		11 05	11 30			
22950	J.C.S		11 30	11 45			
20455	12 & S		11 45	12 10			
28446	containers		12 10	1 00	4 45		
	lunch		1 00	1 30			
30685	International Public Relat		1 30	2 05			
30784	(1) J C S		2 05	2 55			
30598	Glen		2 55	3 45			
30711	Kinney CO		3 45	4 15			

Chargeable Hours ______ Non-Chargeable Hours ______ O.K. ______ Foreman.

Exhibit No. 1852

COMMISSION EXHIBIT NO. 1852—Continued

JAGGARS-CHILES-STOVALL, INC.
PHOTOGRAPHIC DEPARTMENT
Time Recorded in Minutes

NOTE:—All employees are required to keep an accurate record of every job worked upon. Time shown hereon MUST agree with clock register, and wages are computed accordingly. Take new sheet for overtime and have it marked "overtime" by Foreman.

Page II

Name Lee Oswald Worked from ______ A. M. to ______ M. Date ______ 19__

JOB NO.	CUSTOMER		Kind of Work	START		STOP		Chargeable Alt.	Chargeable Comp.	Non-Chargeable
30915	Stanley Kromes			4	15	4	55			
30784	(2) J C S			4	55	5	30	4		

8 45

O.K.

Chargeable Hours ______ Non-Chargeable Hours ______ ______ Foreman.

Commission Exhibit No. 1852

Commission Exhibit No. 1852—Continued

JAGGARS-CHILES-STOVALL, INC.
PHOTOGRAPHIC DEPARTMENT
Time Recorded in Minutes

NOTE:—All employees are required to keep an accurate record of every job worked upon. Time shown hereon MUST agree with clock register, and wages are computed accordingly. Take new sheet for overtime and have it marked "overtime" by Foreman.

Name Lee H Oswald Worked from 8:15 A. M. to 5:15 M. Date Dec 11 (Tuesday) 19 62

JOB NO.	CUSTOMER		Kind of Work	START		STOP		Chargeable Alt.	Chargeable Comp.	Non-Chargeable
22950	J C S			8	15	8	45			
30881	Hormogenics			8	45	9	20			
30752	Interstate Map			9	20	9	50			
30749	Electro Plastics			9	50	10	30			
30782	Tracy Locke			10	30	11	05			
30859	Bonoff			11	05	11	35			
30942	Bob Pierce			11	35	12	05			
30832	Glenn Alves			12	05	12	30	4 15		
	Lunch			12	30	1	00			
30799	Evans Young - Wyatt			1	00	1	20			
30752	(2) Interstate Maps			1	20	1	45			
30968	John A Scott			1	45	2	15			
31010	Linz Jewelers			2	15	2	40			
30877	Rogers - Smith			2	40	3	30			
30918	Tom Asmnes			3	30	3	55			
30728	A. A. Allen Reynolds			3	55	4	30			
30749	Electro Plastics			4	30	5	15	4 15		

O.K. JG

Chargeable Hours ______ Non-Chargeable Hours ______ ______ Foreman.

Commission Exhibit No. 1852—Continued

Page I

JAGGARS-CHILES-STOVALL, INC.
PHOTOGRAPHIC DEPARTMENT
Time Recorded in Minutes

NOTE:—All employees are required to keep an accurate record of every job worked upon. Time shown hereon MUST agree with clock register, and wages are computed accordingly. Take new sheet for overtime and have it marked "overtime" by Foreman.

Name Lee H Oswald Worked from 8:15 A. M. to 5:15 M. Date wed Dec 12 19 [illegible]

JOB NO.	CUSTOMER	Kind of Work	START	STOP	Chargeable Alt.	Chargeable Comp.	Non-Chargeable
31108	Crook advs.		8 15	8 35			
31124	Don Baxter		8 35	8 55			
17610	Don Baxter		8 55	9 20			
31098	Glenn advs		9 20	9 50			
31030	Electrotype service		9 50	10 25			
30582	Park aerial maps		10 25	10 45			
22950	JCS		10 45	11 00			
30975	Sam Bloom		11 00	11 15			
30987	Crandell corp		11 15	11 30			
31125	Ed Bearden		11 30	11 45			
31128	Hormes		11 45	12 05			
30833	Southwestern Drug		12 05	12 15			
2.	Jack Wyatt		12 15	12 30	4½		
	lunch		12 30	1 00			
31129	Rives Dyke		1 00	1 20			
30084	Glenn		1 20	1 50			
31131	Rives Dyke + Co.		1 50	2 15			

Chargeable Hours ______ Non-Chargeable Hours ______ O.K. ______ Foreman.

Commission Exhibit No. 1852

COMMISSION EXHIBIT No. 1852—Continued

Page II

JAGGARS-CHILES-STOVALL, INC.
PHOTOGRAPHIC DEPARTMENT
Time Recorded in Minutes

NOTE:—All employees are required to keep an accurate record of every job worked upon. Time shown hereon MUST agree with clock register, and wages are computed accordingly. Take new sheet for overtime and have it marked "overtime" by Foreman.

Name Lee H Oswald Worked from ______ A. M. to ______ M. Date ______ 19__

JOB NO.	CUSTOMER	Kind of Work	START	STOP	Chargeable Alt.	Chargeable Comp.	Non-Chargeable
22950	JCS		2 15	2 45			
31156	Lone Star Gas		2 45	3 10			
31187	Wilson Eng.		3 10	3 25			
31132	Rives Dyke		3 25	3 50			
31206	D + O		3 50	4 15			
31220	Zimi Jewelers		4 15	4 35			
31176	Rogers & Smith		4 35	5 15	4½		

Chargeable Hours ______ Non-Chargeable Hours ______ O.K. ______ Foreman.

Commission Exhibit No. 1852

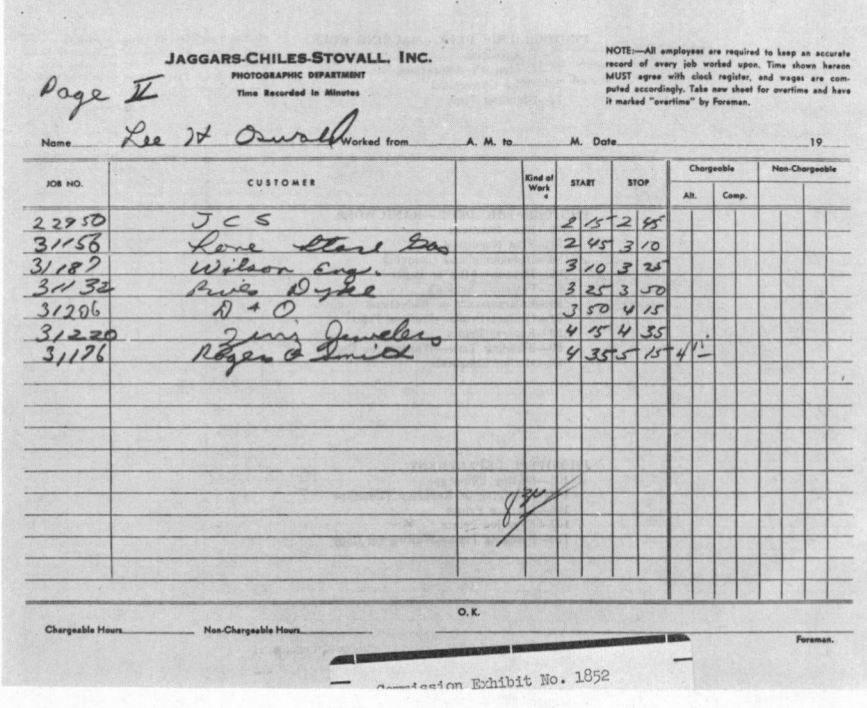

COMMISSION EXHIBIT No. 1852—Continued

JAGGARS-CHILES-STOVALL, INC.
PHOTOGRAPHIC DEPARTMENT
Time Recorded in Minutes

NOTE:—All employees are required to keep an accurate record of every job worked upon. Time shown hereon MUST agree with clock register, and wages are computed accordingly. Take new sheet for overtime and have it marked "overtime" by Foreman.

Name Lee H Oswald Worked from 8:30 A. M. to 5:30 M. Date Dec 14 Friday 1962

JOB NO.	CUSTOMER		Kind of Work	START	STOP	Chargeable Alt.	Chargeable Comp.	Non-Chargeable
31450	Bud Biggs			8 30	8 45			
22950	ICS			8 45	9 10			
30157	Graduate Reserve center			9 10	9 40			
31083	Ken Ronaly			9 40	10 05			
31505	Wyatt adver			10 05	10 50			
31341	(1) White auto			10 50	11 30			
31021	(1) White auto Stores			11 30	11 55			
31331	Bud Biggs			11 55	12 15			
30919	Tracy Locke			12 15	1 00	4½ ✓		
	Lunch			~~1 00~~	~~1 30~~			
31511	Bud Biggs			1 30	2 20			
31466	adver art studios	8½ ✓		2 20	3 10			
31535	Bob chaveran			3 10	3 50			
31548	Acco menu co			3 50	4 45			
31021	(2) White auto			4 45	5 30	4		

Chargeable Hours ____ Non-Chargeable Hours ____ O.K. ____ Foreman.

Commission Exhibit No. 1852

COMMISSION EXHIBIT NO. 1852—Continued

JAGGARS-CHILES-STOVALL, INC.
PHOTOGRAPHIC DEPARTMENT
Time Recorded in Minutes

NOTE:—All employees are required to keep an accurate record of every job worked upon. Time shown hereon MUST agree with clock register, and wages are computed accordingly. Take new sheet for overtime and have it marked "overtime" by Foreman.

Name Lee H Oswald Worked from 8:10 A. M. to 5:45 M. Date Dec 17 Monday 1962

JOB NO.	CUSTOMER		Kind of Work	START	STOP	Chargeable Alt.	Chargeable Comp.	Non-Chargeable
31702	Hepworth adv			8 10	9 25			
31431	Goodman Paper			9 25	9 55			
31692	Evans Party Pastes			9 55	10 40			
31708	Doug Pritchett			10 40	11 35			
31407	Korjeguies			11 35	1 00	4⁵⁰		
	Lunch			1 00	1:30			
31718	Ed Bearden			1 30	1 55			
31698	Standford			1 55	2 25			
31557	Bill Elliott			2 25	3 05			
31109	Jack Wyatt			3 05	3 35			
31743	Sitzurk adver			3 35	4 05			
31678	Electr Type Sprocco			4 05	4 25			
31698	Standford			4 25	4 40			
31748	Ed Bearden			4 40	5 05			
31845	Tel-Industries			5 05	5 45	4¹⁵		

9⁰⁵

Chargeable Hours ____ Non-Chargeable Hours ____ O.K. ____ Foreman.

Commission Exhibit No. 1852

COMMISSION EXHIBIT NO. 1852—Continued

Page I

JAGGARS-CHILES-STOVALL, INC.
PHOTOGRAPHIC DEPARTMENT
Time Recorded in Minutes

NOTE:—All employees are required to keep an accurate record of every job worked upon. Time shown hereon MUST agree with clock register, and wages are computed accordingly. Take new sheet for overtime and have it marked "overtime" by Foreman.

Name Lee H Oswald Worked from 8:15 A. M. to 5:45 M. Date Tues. Dec 18 1962

JOB NO.	CUSTOMER	Kind of Work	START	STOP	Chargeable Alt.	Chargeable Comp.	Non-Chargeable
31396	Braniff adv. Dept		8 15	9 05			
31817	Electrotypal Service Co		9 05	9 25			
31392	Bud Biggs		9 25	9 48			
31774	Pollock Paper Co		9 45	10 15			
31830	Wyatt ado.		10 15	10 35			
31811	Lone Star Gas		10 35	11 05			
31742	Pitluk adver		11 05	11 25			
31718	McCullen		11 25	11 55			
31888	Skorogness		11 55	12 30	45		
	Lunch		12 30	1 00			
—	Doug Pritchett		1 00	1 20			
31943	Container Corp of Amer		1 20	1 45			
31941	Industrial Printing		1 45	2 05			
31869	Ratcliff		2 05	2 35			
31918	Lom Graves		2 35	2 50			
31097	Cunningham		2 50	3 20			
31096	Cunningham and Cooper		3 20	3 40			

Chargeable Hours_____ Non-Chargeable Hours_____ O.K. _____ Foreman.

Commission Exhibit No. 1852

COMMISSION EXHIBIT NO. 1852—Continued

Page II

JAGGARS-CHILES-STOVALL, INC.
PHOTOGRAPHIC DEPARTMENT
Time Recorded in Minutes

NOTE:—All employees are required to keep an accurate record of every job worked upon. Time shown hereon MUST agree with clock register, and wages are computed accordingly. Take new sheet for overtime and have it marked "overtime" by Foreman.

Name Lee Oswald Worked from_____ A. M. to_____ M. Date_____ 19__

JOB NO.	CUSTOMER	Kind of Work	START	STOP	Chargeable Alt.	Chargeable Comp.	Non-Chargeable
22950	T.C.S.		3 40	3 55			
31934	Hepworth		3 55	4 10			
31900	Peacock		4 10	4 25			
31800	Marvin Krieger		4 25	4 40			
31942	T. N.		4 40	4 55			
31671	White auto		4 55	5 10			
32003	McCormick		5 10	5 25			
32006	Robert Williams		5 25	5 35			
31708	Doug Pritchett		5 35	5 45	45		

9—

Chargeable Hours_____ Non-Chargeable Hours_____ O.K. _____ Foreman.

Commission Exhibit No. 1852

COMMISSION EXHIBIT NO. 1852—Continued

Page I

JAGGARS-CHILES-STOVALL, INC.
PHOTOGRAPHIC DEPARTMENT
Time Recorded in Minutes

NOTE:—All employees are required to keep an accurate record of every job worked upon. Time shown hereon MUST agree with clock register, and wages are computed accordingly. Take new sheet for overtime and have it marked "overtime" by Foreman.

Name Lee H Oswald Worked from 8:15 A. M. to 5:45 M. Date Dec. 19 (noted) 19

JOB NO.	CUSTOMER		Kind of Work	START		STOP		Chargeable Alt.	Chargeable Comp.	Non-Chargeable
32074	Medallion Stores			8	15	8	40			
32044	Braniff			8	40	9	00			
31969	Cunningham Cooper			9	00	9	15			
31939	Hepworth			9	15	9	35			
32102	L. G. Balfour			9	35	9	50			
31902	Taylor-Norsworthy			9	50	10	10			
32081	Fred Locke			10	10	10	30			
31811	Lone Star Gas			10	30	10	45			
32140	Industrial Printing			10	45	11	10			
32053	Hepworth advtg			11	10	11	30			
31954	Cunningham & Cooper			11	30	11	50			
32069	R. J. Burke advtg.			11	50	12	30	4		
	Lunch			12	30	1	00			
32112	Effler - Rowdon			1	00	1	20			
31028	Sam Bloom			1	20	1	40			
31131	Stepp J. Kraus			1	40	2	05			
32077	Robbins Cares-Page			2	05	2	35			

Chargeable Hours ______ Non-Chargeable Hours ______ O.K. ______ Foreman.

Commission Exhibit No. 1852

COMMISSION EXHIBIT NO. 1852—Continued

Page II

JAGGARS-CHILES-STOVALL, INC.
PHOTOGRAPHIC DEPARTMENT
Time Recorded in Minutes

NOTE:—All employees are required to keep an accurate record of every job worked upon. Time shown hereon MUST agree with clock register, and wages are computed accordingly. Take new sheet for overtime and have it marked "overtime" by Foreman.

Name Lee H Oswald Worked from ______ A. M. to ______ M. Date ______ 19

JOB NO.	CUSTOMER		Kind of Work	START		STOP		Chargeable Alt.	Chargeable Comp.	Non-Chargeable
32045	Braniff Adv. Dept			2	35	3	30			
31028	Sam Bloom			3	30	4	25			
32202	Lins			4	25	5	05			
32018	Ratcliff adv			5	05	5	25			
31622	L. O. Bellflower			5	25	5	45	4 45		

Chargeable Hours ______ Non-Chargeable Hours ______ O.K. ______ Foreman.

Commission Exhibit No. 1852

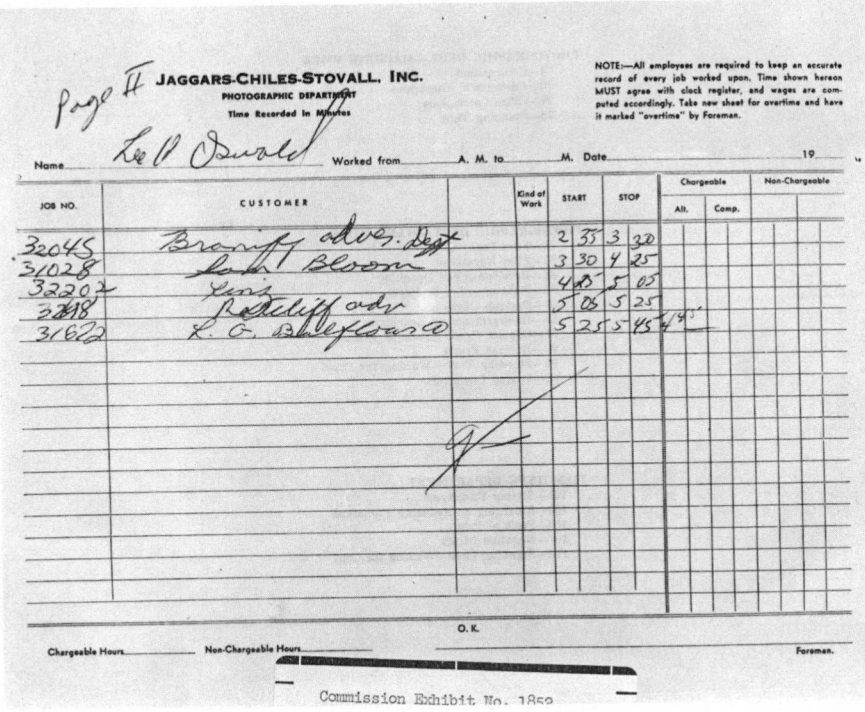

COMMISSION EXHIBIT NO. 1852—Continued

JAGGARS-CHILES-STOVALL, INC.
PHOTOGRAPHIC DEPARTMENT
Time Recorded in Minutes

NOTE:—All employees are required to keep an accurate record of every job worked upon. Time shown hereon MUST agree with clock register, and wages are computed accordingly. Take new sheet for overtime and have it marked "overtime" by Foreman.

Name Lee H Oswald Worked from 8:15 A. M. to 5:45 M. Date Thurs Dec 20 19__

JOB NO.	CUSTOMER		Kind of Work	START		STOP		Chargeable Alt.	Chargeable Comp.	Non-Chargeable
32146	Industrial Ptg			8	15	9	10			
32281	Braniff			9	10	10	00			
32257	Bob Knight			10	00	10	40			
32199	Tom Evans			10	40	11	20			
32115	Bozell & Jacobs			11	20	11	50			
32081	Tracy Locke			11	50	12	20			
32080	(1) Tracy-Locke			12	20	12	40	4 25		
	Lunch			12	40	1	10			
32153	Lone Star Sa			1	10	1	30			
32277	Robbie's Cook Bag			1	30	1	55			
31740	Pitluk			1	55	2	35			
31742	Pitluk			2	35	2	50			
32080	(2) Tracy Lock			2	50	3	25			
32123	Tracy Lock			3	25	4	10			
32346	A H Allen			4	10	5	00			
32297	Hepworth adv			5	00	5	45	4 35		

Chargeable Hours____ Non-Chargeable Hours____ O.K. ____ Foreman.

Commission Exhibit No. 1852

Commission Exhibit No. 1852—Continued

JAGGARS-CHILES-STOVALL, INC.
PHOTOGRAPHIC DEPARTMENT
Time Recorded in Minutes

NOTE:—All employees are required to keep an accurate record of every job worked upon. Time shown hereon MUST agree with clock register, and wages are computed accordingly. Take new sheet for overtime and have it marked "overtime" by Foreman.

Name Lee H Oswald Worked from 8:15 A. M. to 5:45 M. Date Dec 21 1962

JOB NO.	CUSTOMER		Kind of Work	START		STOP		Chargeable Alt.	Chargeable Comp.	Non-Chargeable
32390	General adv			8	15	8	40			
32307	Glenn adv			8	40	9	05			
32157	Scott			9	05	9	35			
32436	David Reeves			9	35	9	55			
32420	Dallas Times Herald			9	55	10	20			
32446	R K Butch			10	20	10	45			
32423	Pitluk adv			10	45	11	00			
32358	Republic National			11	00	11	50			
32466	Doug Pritchett			11	50	12	30	4 1		
	Lunch			12	30	1	00			
32483	T.P. & L			1	00	1	35			
32511	Howard Peacock			1	35	1	55			
32341	Gulf States			1	55	2	30			
32335	Gulf States			2	30	3	10			
	J C S			3	10	3	50			
32510	Nardis			3	50	4	50			
32528	Sears			4	50	5	45	4 15		

Chargeable Hours____ Non-Chargeable Hours____ O.K. ____ Foreman.

Commission Exhibit No. 1852

Commission Exhibit No. 1852—Continued

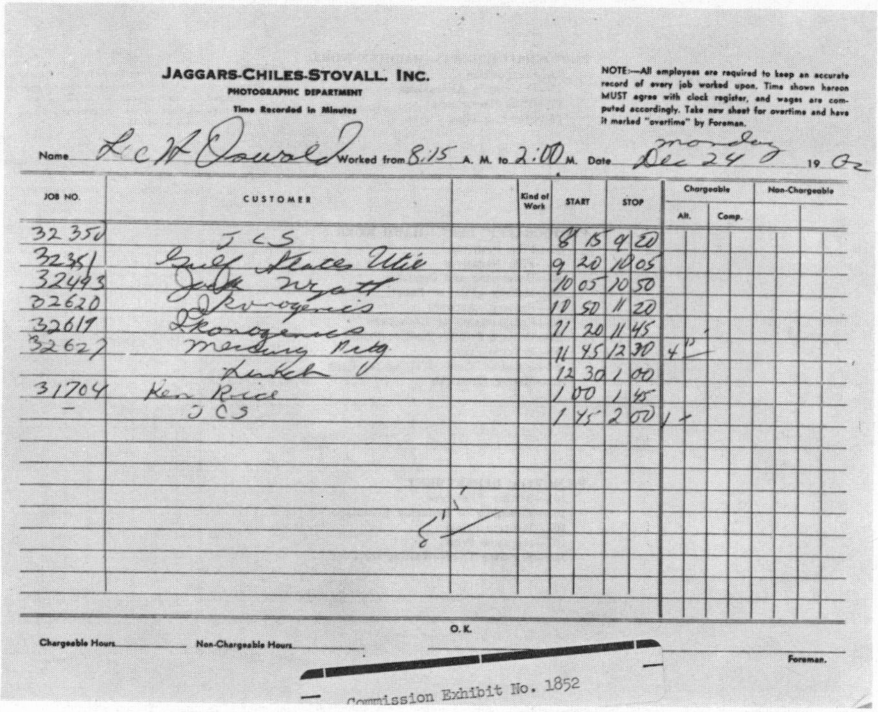

JAGGARS-CHILES-STOVALL, INC.
PHOTOGRAPHIC DEPARTMENT
Time Recorded in Minutes

NOTE:—All employees are required to keep an accurate record of every job worked upon. Time shown hereon MUST agree with clock register, and wages are computed accordingly. Take new sheet for overtime and have it marked "overtime" by Foreman.

Name Lee H Oswald Worked from 8:15 A. M. to 2:00 M. Date monday Dec 24 19 62

JOB NO.	CUSTOMER		Kind of Work	START		STOP		Chargeable Alt.	Chargeable Comp.	Non-Chargeable
32350	JCS			8	15	9	20			
32351	Gulf States Util			9	20	10	05			
32493	Jack Wyatt			10	05	10	50			
32620	Ikonogenics			10	50	11	20			
32619	Ikonogenics			11	20	11	45			
32627	Mercury Mktg			11	45	12	30	4½		
	Lunch			12	30	1	00			
31704	Ken Rice			1	00	1	45			
—	JCS			1	45	2	00	1		

Chargeable Hours ____ Non-Chargeable Hours ____ O.K. ____ Foreman.

Commission Exhibit No. 1852

COMMISSION EXHIBIT No. 1852—Continued

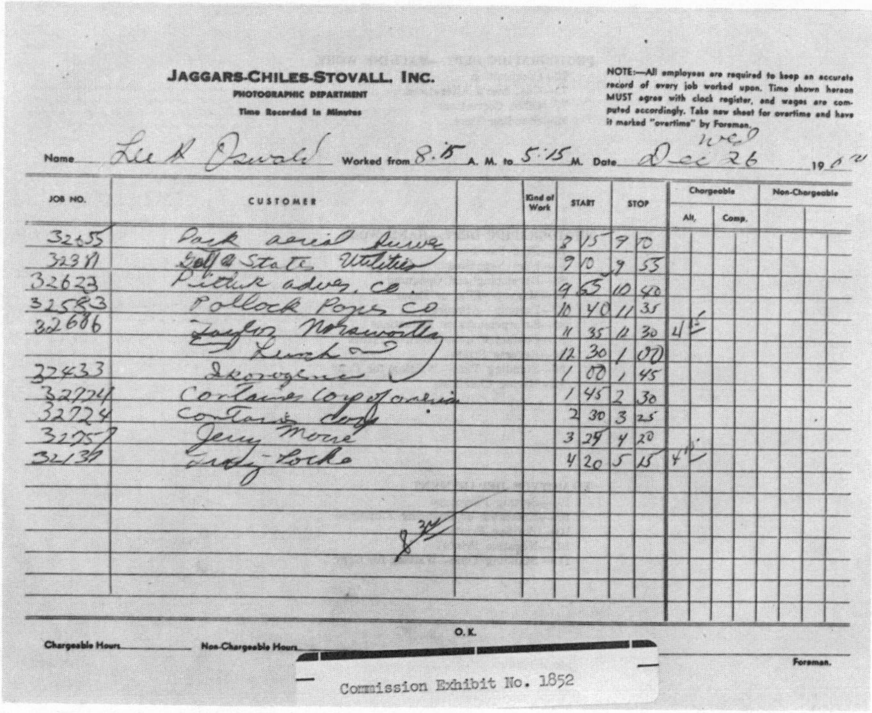

JAGGARS-CHILES-STOVALL, INC.
PHOTOGRAPHIC DEPARTMENT
Time Recorded in Minutes

NOTE:—All employees are required to keep an accurate record of every job worked upon. Time shown hereon MUST agree with clock register, and wages are computed accordingly. Take new sheet for overtime and have it marked "overtime" by Foreman.

Name Lee H Oswald Worked from 8:15 A. M. to 5:15 M. Date wed Dec 26 19 62

JOB NO.	CUSTOMER		Kind of Work	START		STOP		Chargeable Alt.	Chargeable Comp.	Non-Chargeable
32655	Jack aerial Survey			8	15	9	10			
32381	Gulf States Utilities			9	10	9	55			
32623	Pitluk adver. Co.			9	55	10	40			
32583	Pollock Paper Co			10	40	11	35			
32686	Taylor Norsworthy			11	35	12	30	4½		
	Lunch			12	30	1	00			
32433	Ikonogenics			1	00	1	45			
32724	Container Corp of America			1	45	2	30			
32724	Container Corp			2	30	3	25			
32757	Jerry Moore			3	25	4	20			
32139	Trady-Locke			4	20	5	15	4½		

Chargeable Hours ____ Non-Chargeable Hours ____ O.K. ____ Foreman.

Commission Exhibit No. 1852

COMMISSION EXHIBIT No. 1852—Continued

JAGGARS-CHILES-STOVALL, INC.
PHOTOGRAPHIC DEPARTMENT
Time Recorded in Minutes

NOTE:—All employees are required to keep an accurate record of every job worked upon. Time shown hereon MUST agree with clock register, and wages are computed accordingly. Take new sheet for overtime and have it marked "overtime" by Foreman.

Name Lee H Oswald Worked from 8:15 A. M. to 5:30 M. Date Thur. Dec 27 1962

JOB NO.	CUSTOMER	Kind of Work	START	STOP	Chargeable Alt.	Chargeable Comp.	Non-Chargeable
31866	Ratcliff adv.		8 15	9 10			
32724	Cornett Co.		9 10	9 40			
32307	Glenn adv.		9 40	9 55			
32083	McCrary		9 55	10 15			
32381	Gulf State		10 15	10 35			
—	B B D & O		10 35	11 10			
32867	The Todd Co		11 10	11 45			
32857	Herald		11 45	12 30	4 45		
	Lunch		12 30	1 00			
32895	Sears Roebuck		1 00	1 20			
32380	Gulf State		1 20	1 45			
32887	Goldmer Paper Co.		1 45	2 20			
32894	John A Scott		2 20	3 05			
32884	Al Barnes		3 05	3 40			
32244	Marvin R Bredlow		3 40	3 55			
3208	Clavelle I Sherman		3 55	4 30			
32932	S C Z		4 30	4 50			
32380	Gulf State util		4 50	5 30	4 30		

Chargeable Hours _____ Non-Chargeable Hours _____ 8 45 O.K. _____ Foreman.

Commission Exhibit No. 1852

COMMISSION EXHIBIT NO. 1852—Continued

JAGGARS-CHILES-STOVALL, INC.
PHOTOGRAPHIC DEPARTMENT
Time Recorded in Minutes

NOTE:—All employees are required to keep an accurate record of every job worked upon. Time shown hereon MUST agree with clock register, and wages are computed accordingly. Take new sheet for overtime and have it marked "overtime" by Foreman.

Name Lee H Oswald Worked from 8:30 A. M. to 5:15 M. Date Dec 28 1962

JOB NO.	CUSTOMER	Kind of Work	START	STOP	Chargeable Alt.	Chargeable Comp.	Non-Chargeable
32378	Gulf States		8 30	9 15			
32493	Jack Wyatt Co.		9 15	10 00			
33018	Bob Knight		10 00	10 45			
32535	Riverside		10 45	11 10			
32942	John T Thompson		11 10	11 40			
33021	Baptist Publications		11 40	12 30	4		
	Lunch		12 30	1 00			
32964	Fitzgerald art		1 00	1 45			
32350	T C S		1 45	2 20			
33100	Ikonogenics		2 20	2 50			
33101	Ikonogenics		2 50	3 30			
33074	Boswell Jacobs		3 30	4 20			
33069	Klein Co		4 20	5 15	4 15		

8 15

Chargeable Hours _____ Non-Chargeable Hours _____ O.K. _____ Foreman.

Commission Exhibit No. 1852

COMMISSION EXHIBIT NO. 1852—Continued

Page I

JAGGARS-CHILES-STOVALL, INC.
PHOTOGRAPHIC DEPARTMENT
Time Recorded in Minutes

NOTE:—All employees are required to keep an accurate record of every job worked upon. Time shown hereon MUST agree with clock register, and wages are computed accordingly. Take new sheet for overtime and have it marked "overtime" by Foreman.

Name Lee H. Oswald Worked from 8:15 A. M. to 5:45 M. Date Sat. Dec 29 1962

JOB NO.	CUSTOMER		Kind of Work	START	STOP	Chargeable Alt.	Chargeable Comp.	Non-Chargeable
33167	Hepworth adves			8 15	9 10			
33070	Rogers & Smith			9 10	9 25			
33188	L D Brandenberg			9 25	9 50			
32276	Taylor Norsworthy			9 50	10 15			
33005	Rogers & Smith			10 15	10 35			
33168	Tracy - Locke			10 35	10 55			
32984	Bob Baird			10 55	11 20			
32637	C & W			11 20	11 45			
33165	Charleen McClain			11 45	12 20	40 5		
	Lunch			12 20	12 50			
33172	B B D & O			12 50	1 10			
33182	AB AR			1 10	2 05			
33066	Robert Curran			2 05	2 25			
—	AMS			2 25	3 05			
32858	Bozell & Jacobs			3 05	3 30			
32858	Bragg adves			3 30	3 55			
32881	Dixie maps			3 55	4 10			
32812	SW Life Ins. CO			4 10	4 35			

O.K.

Chargeable Hours______ Non-Chargeable Hours______ Foreman.

Commission Exhibit No. 1852

COMMISSION EXHIBIT No. 1852—Continued

Page II

JAGGARS-CHILES-STOVALL, INC.
PHOTOGRAPHIC DEPARTMENT
Time Recorded in Minutes

NOTE:—All employees are required to keep an accurate record of every job worked upon. Time shown hereon MUST agree with clock register, and wages are computed accordingly. Take new sheet for overtime and have it marked "overtime" by Foreman.

Name Lee Oswald Worked from______ A. M. to______ M. Date______ 19__

JOB NO.	CUSTOMER		Kind of Work	START	STOP	Chargeable Alt.	Chargeable Comp.	Non-Chargeable
32378	Gulf States			4 35	5 10			
32379	"			5 10	5 25			
32381	"			5 25	5 45	4 5		

9 –

O.K.

Chargeable Hours______ Non-Chargeable Hours______ Foreman.

Commission Exhibit No. 1852

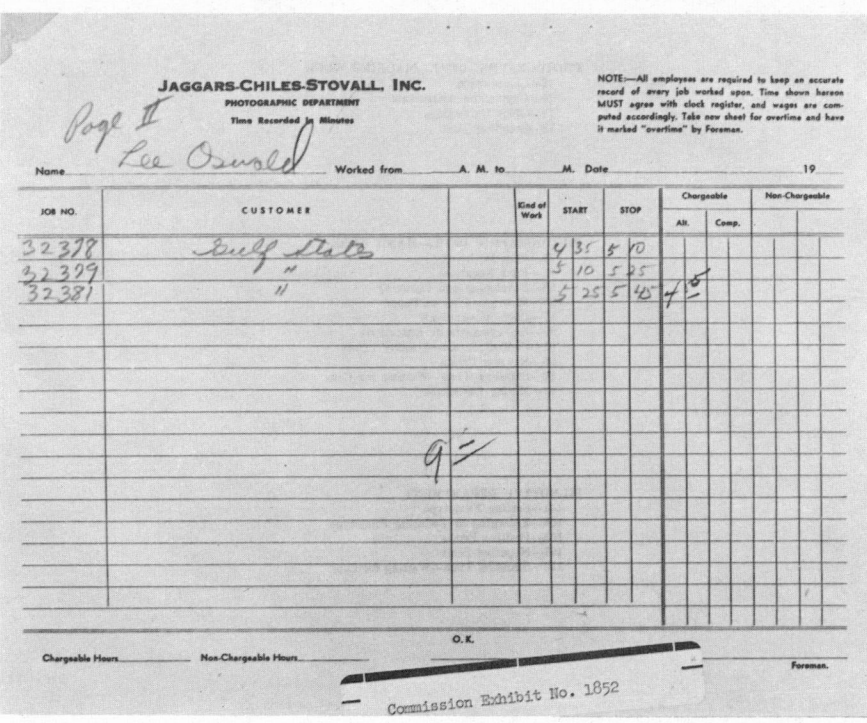

COMMISSION EXHIBIT No. 1852—Continued

JAGGARS-CHILES-STOVALL, INC.
PHOTOGRAPHIC DEPARTMENT
Time Recorded in Minutes

NOTE:—All employees are required to keep an accurate record of every job worked upon. Time shown hereon MUST agree with clock register, and wages are computed accordingly. Take new sheet for overtime and have it marked "overtime" by Foreman.

Mon.

Name Lee H Oswald Worked from 8:00 A. M. to 5:15 M. Date Dec 31st 1962

JOB NO.	CUSTOMER		Kind of Work	START	STOP	Chargeable Alt.	Chargeable Comp.	Non-Chargeable
33199	Clay Stephen			8 00	8 55			
33204	Clay Stephen			8 55	9 30			
33218	Dale Boyce			9 30	10 15			
32704	Photo-Stat corp			10 15	10 50			
32660	Wyatt adv.			10 50	11 30			
33187	Grulle, Smith & Ross			11 30	12 00	4		
	— Lunch —			12 00	12 30			
—	Lile adv			12 30	1 25			
33231	Campbell Ducky			1 25	2 10			
32856	Frage adv.			2 10	3 00			
33290	Tracy-Locke			3 00	3 45			
33257	Cobco Industries			3 45	4 25			
33303	Harper Standard Eng			4 25	5 15	4 45		
	8 45							

Chargeable Hours____ Non-Chargeable Hours____ O. K.____ Foreman.

Commission Exhibit No. 1852

COMMISSION EXHIBIT No. 1852—Continued

JAGGARS-CHILES-STOVALL, INC.
PHOTOGRAPHIC DEPARTMENT
Time Recorded in Minutes

NOTE:—All employees are required to keep an accurate record of every job worked upon. Time shown hereon MUST agree with clock register, and wages are computed accordingly. Take new sheet for overtime and have it marked "overtime" by Foreman.

Name Lee H Oswald Worked from 8:15 A. M. to 5:15 M. Date Jan 2nd Wed 19 62

JOB NO.	CUSTOMER		Kind of Work	START		STOP		Chargeable Alt.	Chargeable Comp.	Non-Chargeable
33046	Wyatt adv.			8	15	8	50			
33186	Fuller Smith & Ross			8	50	9	20			
33300	CCA			9	20	9	40			
33328	Guild adv			9	40	10	15			
33349	Sam Bloom			10	05	10	35			
30322	Don L Baxter			10	35	11	05			
33299	Pollock			11	05	11	25			
33205	Fidelity adv.			11	25	11	55			
33309	Sam Bloom			11	55	12	45	4 3/4		
	Lunch			12	45	1	15			
32812	S.W. Life Insurance			1	15	1	45			
33403	Goodman Paper Co			1	45	2	30			
33413	Tom Thumb			2	30	3	15			
33399	Zeigler Norsworth			3	15	4	05			
33424	King			4	05	4	50			
33231	Campbell Dicky			4	50	5	15	4–		

8 3/4 O.K.

Chargeable Hours ______ Non-Chargeable Hours ______ Foreman.

Commission Exhibit No. 1853

COMMISSION EXHIBIT NO. 1853

JAGGARS-CHILES-STOVALL, INC.
PHOTOGRAPHIC DEPARTMENT
Time Recorded in Minutes

NOTE:—All employees are required to keep an accurate record of every job worked upon. Time shown hereon MUST agree with clock register, and wages are computed accordingly. Take new sheet for overtime and have it marked "overtime" by Foreman.

Name Lee H Oswald Worked from 8:15 A. M. to 5:15 M. Date Jan 3 Thur. 19 62

JOB NO.	CUSTOMER		Kind of Work	START		STOP		Chargeable Alt.	Chargeable Comp.	Non-Chargeable
33023	Rogers & Smith			8	15	9	10			
33488	Republic Nat. Life			9	10	9	40			
33430	Taylor-Norsworthy			9	40	9	55			
33459	Allen adv			9	55	10	15			
33360	CC of A			10	15	10	35			
33413	Tom Thumb			10	35	10	50			
33574	Gordon Marks & Co.			10	50	11	40			
33172	BBD&O			11	40	12	15	4		
	Lunch			12	15	12	45			
33022	BBD&O			12	45	1	25			
33594	Jamieson Film			1	25	2	05			
33238	Sealy Southwest			2	05	2	45			
33540	Conference Cops			2	45	3	10			
33497	Cunningham & Walsh			3	10	3	55			
33523	Bryant & Bryan			3	55	4	35			
33618	General Adv			4	35	5	15	4 3/4		

8 3/4 O.K.

Chargeable Hours ______ Non-Chargeable Hours ______ Foreman.

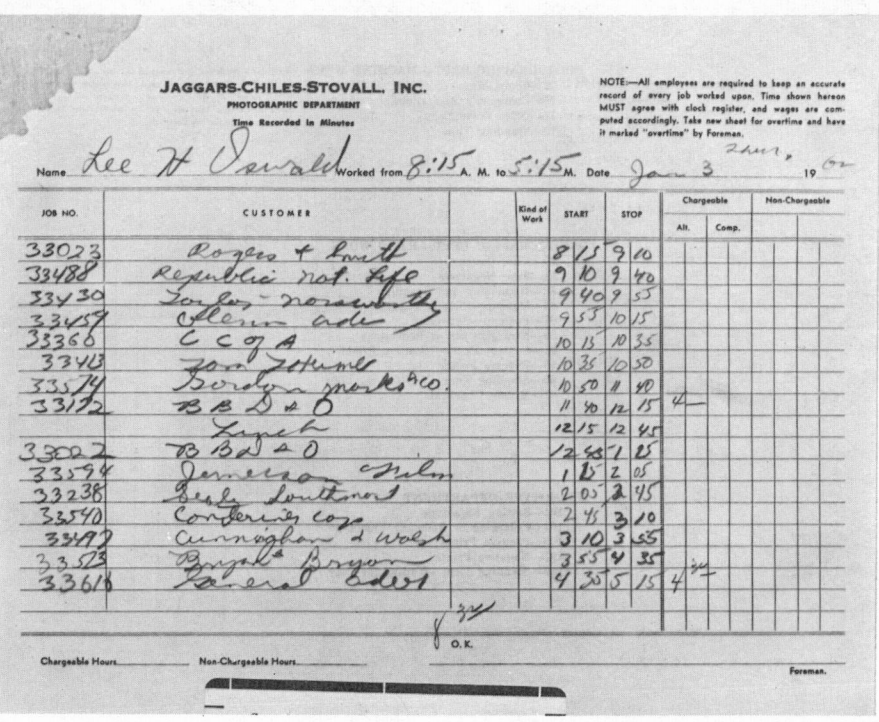

COMMISSION EXHIBIT NO. 1853—Continued

JAGGARS-CHILES-STOVALL, INC.
PHOTOGRAPHIC DEPARTMENT
Time Recorded in Minutes

NOTE:—All employees are required to keep an accurate record of every job worked upon. Time shown hereon MUST agree with clock register, and wages are computed accordingly. Take new sheet for overtime and have it marked "overtime" by Foreman.

Name Lee H. Oswald Worked from 8:15 A. M. to 5:15 M. Date Jan 4 Fri 19 63

JOB NO.	CUSTOMER	Kind of Work	START	STOP	Chargeable Alt.	Chargeable Comp.	Non-Chargeable
33360	Container Corp of Ams		8 15	9 10			
33553	Engineering Supply		9 40	10 05			
33714	Bud Biggs		10 05	10 30			
33734	Baptist Public Rel.		10 30	11 05			
33743	The McCarty Co. of Tex.		11 05	11 25			
33769	Goodman Paper Co		11 25	11 40			
33768	Goodman Paper		11 40	11 55			
33740	Tracy-Locke		11 55	12 15	4—		
	Lunch		12 15	12 45			
33801	Bud Biggs		12 45	1 10			
33773	S W Engraving Co		1 10	1 30			
33522	J C S		1 30	2 00			
33289	Tom Bruns		2 05	2 40			
33771	Goodman Paper Co		2 40	3 20			
33753	Robert K Butcher		3 20	4 05			
33758	Boyell & Jacobs		4 05	4 40			
33819	Ditch		4 40	5 00			
33749	Harris Goode		5 00	5 15	4 3[illegible]—		

Chargeable Hours ________ Non-Chargeable Hours ________ 8 30 O.K. ________ Foreman.

Commission Exhibit No. 1853—Continued

JAGGARS-CHILES-STOVALL, INC.
PHOTOGRAPHIC DEPARTMENT
Time Recorded in Minutes

NOTE:—All employees are required to keep an accurate record of every job worked upon. Time shown hereon MUST agree with clock register, and wages are computed accordingly. Take new sheet for overtime and have it marked "overtime" by Foreman.

Name Lee H Oswald Worked from 8:15 A. M. to 6:00 M. Date Jan 7 mon 19 63

JOB NO.	CUSTOMER	Kind of Work	START	STOP	Chargeable Alt.	Chargeable Comp.	Non-Chargeable
33787	(1) Sam Bloom		8 15	8 40			
34009	Wyatt adv.		8 40	9 10			
33785	Sam Bloom		9 10	9 45			
33918	Evans Young & Wyatt		9 45	10 20			
33898	Collins Printing		10 20	10 45			
32316	S W Telephone Co		10 45	11 05			
33787	(2) Sam Bloom		11 05	11 40			
33833	Rogers & Smith		11 40	12 15	4—		
	Lunch		12 15	12 45			
34054	Sears Roebuck & Co		12 45	1 20			
33853	Lone Star Gas		1 20	2 05			
34060	Continental Engs.		2 05	2 40			
3460	Robert Williams		2 40	3 20			
33949	Don L Boyle		3 20	4 00			
34086	Industrial Printing		4 00	4 50			
34093	D'art Studios		4 50	5 20			
32316	Southwestern Telephone Co		5 20	6 00	5 15—		

Chargeable Hours ________ Non-Chargeable Hours ________ 9 15 O.K. ________ Foreman.

Commission Exhibit No. 1853

Commission Exhibit No. 1853—Continued

JAGGARS-CHILES-STOVALL, INC.
PHOTOGRAPHIC DEPARTMENT
Time Recorded in Minutes

NOTE:—All employees are required to keep an accurate record of every job worked upon. Time shown hereon MUST agree with clock register, and wages are computed accordingly. Take new sheet for overtime and have it marked "overtime" by Foreman.

Name Lee H Oswald Worked from 8:15 A. M. to 6:00 M. Date Tues Jan 8 1963

JOB NO.	CUSTOMER	Kind of Work	START	STOP	Chargeable Alt.	Chargeable Comp.	Non-Chargeable
33787	Sam Bloom		8 15	9 10			
34182	Braniff		9 10	9 25			
34150	Braniff Sales Dept.		9 25	9 40			
34126	Wright / Allen / Rye		9 40	10 05			
34034	Paymaster Feed mill		10 05	10 25			
34230	Goodman Paper		10 25	10 45			
34194	Alfred Lawrence + Ass.		10 45	11 05			
34235	Pat. Eng		11 05	11 20			
34249	Pat. Eng		11 20	11 50			
34244	Tract, Inc.		11 50	12 30	4 15		
	Lunch		12 30	1 00			
34265	Industrial Pntg + ads.		1 00	1 50			
33787	Sam Bloom		1 50	2 50			
34034	Paymaster		2 50	3 30			
34209	Riverside Press		3 30	4 10			
34147	Texas Instruments		4 10	4 50			
34199	Irving Locke		4 50	5 20			
34127	Warren K Bredlow		5 20	6 00	5		

Chargeable Hours ______ Non-Chargeable Hours ______ O.K. ______ Foreman.

915

COMMISSION EXHIBIT NO. 1853—Continued

Page I

JAGGARS-CHILES-STOVALL, INC.
PHOTOGRAPHIC DEPARTMENT
Time Recorded in Minutes

NOTE:—All employees are required to keep an accurate record of every job worked upon. Time shown hereon MUST agree with clock register, and wages are computed accordingly. Take new sheet for overtime and have it marked "overtime" by Foreman.

Name Lee H Oswald Worked from 8:30 A. M. to 5:00 M. Date Jan 9 1963

JOB NO.	CUSTOMER	Kind of Work	START	STOP	Chargeable Alt.	Chargeable Comp.	Non-Chargeable
34361	Ratcliff		8 30	9 10			
34401	Irving Locke		9 10	9 25			
33874	Hill Printing		9 25	10 05			
34330	Taylor Restaurants		10 05	10 20			
33735	Gulf States		10 20	10 40			
34406	Ken Rice		10 40	11 00			
34415	McCarty of Texas		11 00	11 15			
34296	State Fed. Com		11 15	11 30			
34395	Irving Locke		11 30	11 45			
34309	Bill Elliott		11 45	12 00			
33735	(1) Gulf States		12 00	12 10			
34244	Offset Inc.		12 10	12 20			
34381	Coachmen ads		12 20	12 30	4		
	Lunch		12 30	1 00			
33735	(2) Gulf States		1 00	1 20			
34446	Container Corp		1 20	1 45			
34366	Glenn adver		1 45	2 10			

Chargeable Hours ______ Non-Chargeable Hours ______ O.K. ______ Foreman.

Commission Exhibit No. 1853

COMMISSION EXHIBIT NO. 1853—Continued

Page II

JAGGARS-CHILES-STOVALL, INC.
PHOTOGRAPHIC DEPARTMENT
Time Recorded In Minutes

NOTE:—All employees are required to keep an accurate record of every job worked upon. Time shown hereon MUST agree with clock register, and wages are computed accordingly. Take new sheet for overtime and have it marked "overtime" by Foreman.

Name Lee H Oswald Worked from ______ A. M. to ______ M. Date ______ 19__

JOB NO.	CUSTOMER		Kind of Work	START	STOP	Chargeable Alt.	Chargeable Comp.	Non-Chargeable
34299	Tracy - Locke			2 10	2 25			
34450	Humphrey Williamson			2 25	2 45			
34419	ads			2 45	3 00			
34085	Sam Bloom			3 00	3 20			
34504	Stanford			3 20	4 05			
2.	Sulf State Mtl.			4 05	4 25			
34423	Electric Coaches			4 25	5 00	4		

O.K.

Chargeable Hours______ Non-Chargeable Hours______ Foreman.

Exhibit No. 1853

COMMISSION EXHIBIT NO. 1853—Continued

JAGGARS-CHILES-STOVALL, INC.
PHOTOGRAPHIC DEPARTMENT
Time Recorded In Minutes

NOTE:—All employees are required to keep an accurate record of every job worked upon. Time shown hereon MUST agree with clock register, and wages are computed accordingly. Take new sheet for overtime and have it marked "overtime" by Foreman.

Name Lee H Oswald Worked from 8:15 A. M. to 5:45 M. Date Jan 10 1963

JOB NO.	CUSTOMER		Kind of Work	START	STOP	Chargeable Alt.	Chargeable Comp.	Non-Chargeable
34509	Park aerial			8 15	8 40			
34469	Tracy - Locke			8 40	9 10			
34466	Tracy - Lock			9 10	9 25			
34591	Evans - Young - Wyatt			9 25	9 45			
34484	Electrographic service			9 45	10 10			
34426	Toastmaster			10 10	10 30			
32464	Industrial Realty			10 30	11 05			
34488	Linz Jewelers			11 05	11 25			
34573	Rogers & Smith			11 25	11 50			
34454	Tracy - Locke			11 50	12 30	4 15		
	Lunch			12 30	1 00			
33934	Braniff			1 00	1 20			
34579	couchman adv			1 20	1 40			
34657	American Beauty			1 40	2 20			
34652	American Beauty			2 20	2 50			
34634	wyatt adv.			2 50	3 40			
34579	couchman adv			3 40	4 35			
34426	Stefor Kramer			4 35	5 05	4	+	

O.K.

Chargeable Hours______ Non-Chargeable Hours______ Foreman.

COMMISSION EXHIBIT NO. 1853—Continued

JAGGARS-CHILES-STOVALL, INC.
PHOTOGRAPHIC DEPARTMENT
Time Recorded in Minutes

Page II

NOTE:—All employees are required to keep an accurate record of every job worked upon. Time shown hereon MUST agree with clock register, and wages are computed accordingly. Take new sheet for overtime and have it marked "overtime" by Foreman.

Name Lee H Oswald Worked from ______ A. M. to ______ M. Date ______ 19__

JOB NO.	CUSTOMER		Kind of Work	START		STOP		Chargeable Alt.	Chargeable Comp.	Non-Chargeable
34721	R B moreland			5	35	5	45	4 15		

O.K.

Chargeable Hours ______ Non-Chargeable Hours ______ Foreman.

Commission Exhibit No. 1853

COMMISSION EXHIBIT No. 1853—Continued

→ To: New Address 602 Elsbeth St Dallas

JAGGARS-CHILES-STOVALL, INC.
PHOTOGRAPHIC DEPARTMENT
Time Recorded in Minutes

Page I

NOTE:—All employees are required to keep an accurate record of every job worked upon. Time shown hereon MUST agree with clock register, and wages are computed accordingly. Take new sheet for overtime and have it marked "overtime" by Foreman.

Name Lee H Oswald Worked from 8:30 A. M. to 5:15 M. Date Jan 11 Friday 19__

JOB NO.	CUSTOMER		Kind of Work	START		STOP		Chargeable Alt.	Chargeable Comp.	Non-Chargeable
34607	Braniff adv.			8	30	9	10			
34374	C & W			9	10	9	25			
34463	Dupree Way			9	25	9	50			
34734	Rogers + Smith			9	50	10	10			
34634	Wyatt adv			10	10	10	30			
34800	Bob Knight			10	30	10	45			
34782	Sam Bloom			10	45	11	05			
34829	Goodman Papers			11	05	11	20			
34823	Goodman Papers			11	20	11	50			
34822	Goodman Papers			11	50	12	45	4 15		
	Lunch			12	45	1	15			
34721	R.B. moreland			1	15	1	35			
34639	Alabama Eng. Co			1	35	2	10			
34769	Bob Ritzel			2	10	2	30			
34753	Jordan			2	30	2	45			
34394	Ikonogenics			2	45	3	10			
34837	Brattle Engraving			3	10	3	20			

O.K.

Chargeable Hours ______ Non-Chargeable Hours ______ Foreman.

Commission Exhibit No. 1853

COMMISSION EXHIBIT No. 1853—Continued

JAGGARS-CHILES-STOVALL, INC.
PHOTOGRAPHIC DEPARTMENT
Time Recorded in Minutes

Page II

NOTE:—All employees are required to keep an accurate record of every job worked upon. Time shown hereon MUST agree with clock register, and wages are computed accordingly. Take new sheet for overtime and have it marked "overtime" by Foreman.

Name ______ Worked from ______ A. M. to ______ M. Date ______ 19__

JOB NO.	CUSTOMER		Kind of Work	START		STOP		Chargeable Alt.	Chargeable Comp.	Non-Chargeable
34734	Rogers & Smith			3	40	3	45			
34895	Johnston Ptg			3	45	4	20			
34909	Wease Envelope			4	20	4	45			
34625	Lendon			4	45	5	00			
34175	Rickog creative Bto			5	00	5	15	4		
		8 15								

Chargeable Hours ______ Non-Chargeable Hours ______ O.K. ______ Foreman.

Commission Exhibit No. 1853

COMMISSION EXHIBIT NO. 1853—Continued

JAGGARS-CHILES-STOVALL, INC.
PHOTOGRAPHIC DEPARTMENT
Time Recorded in Minutes

NOTE:—All employees are required to keep an accurate record of every job worked upon. Time shown hereon MUST agree with clock register, and wages are computed accordingly. Take new sheet for overtime and have it marked "overtime" by Foreman.

Name Lee H Oswald Worked from 8:00 A. M. to 5:45 P. M. Date Sat. Jan 12 1963

JOB NO.	CUSTOMER		Kind of Work	START		STOP		Chargeable Alt.	Chargeable Comp.	Non-Chargeable
32660	J C S			8	00	8	40			
30999	C & W			8	40	9	30			
34878	Rogers & Smith			9	30	10	05			
34804	Rogers & Smith			10	05	10	45			
34622	John T. Holmes			10	45	11	15			
34883	Adver Service Co			11	15	12	05			
34985	Mullen Smith & Ross			12	05	12	15	15		
	Lunch			12	15	12	45			
33630	Tom Miles Display			12	45	1	35			
34943	Forth W ado			1	35	2	20			
34869	Electrotype Service			2	20	3	10			
35007	J.C.S.			3	10	4	00			
34872	Safeway			4	00	4	55			
33881	Ratcliff			4	55	5	45	5		
		9 14								

Chargeable Hours ______ Non-Chargeable Hours ______ O.K. ______ Foreman.

Commission Exhibit No. 1853

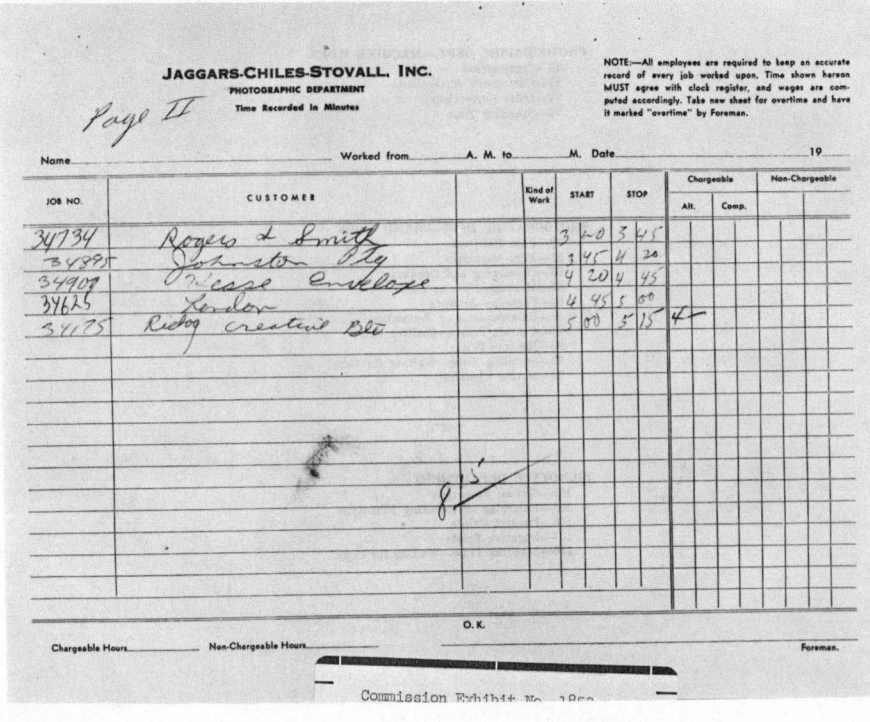

COMMISSION EXHIBIT NO. 1853—Continued

Page I

JAGGARS-CHILES-STOVALL, INC.
PHOTOGRAPHIC DEPARTMENT
Time Recorded in Minutes

NOTE:—All employees are required to keep an accurate record of every job worked upon. Time shown hereon MUST agree with clock register, and wages are computed accordingly. Take new sheet for overtime and have it marked "overtime" by Foreman.

Name Lee H. Oswald Worked from 8:10 A. M. to 5:15 M. Date Jan. 14. monday 1963

JOB NO.	CUSTOMER		Kind of Work	START		STOP		Chargeable Alt.	Chargeable Comp.	Non-Chargeable
34983	Glen Mason & Assoc			8	10	8	25			
35011	Florida Press			8	25	8	40			
34244	Fact, Inc.			8	40	9	10			
34968	Victor Bruner			9	10	9	35			
35028	Robert Williams			9	35	10	10			
34795	Gulf States			10	10	10	40			
35021	Ross Cunningham			10	40	11	05			
35025	auld advs.			11	05	11	50			
34992	T.C.S.			11	50	12	30	4 20		
	~~Lunch~~			~~12~~	~~30~~	~~1~~	~~00~~			
35057	Container Corp			1	00	1	20			
34965	White auto			1	20	1	45			
32682	International Public Rel			1	45	2	15			
34981	Jack T. Holmes			2	15	2	35			
35090	Ivey-Locke			2	35	3	10			
35073	Cliff [illegible] advs.			3	10	3	25			
35130	Wyatt advs			3	25	4	10			

O.K.

Chargeable Hours____ Non-Chargeable Hours____ Foreman.

Commission Exhibit No. 1853

COMMISSION EXHIBIT No. 1853—Continued

Page II

JAGGARS-CHILES-STOVALL, INC.
PHOTOGRAPHIC DEPARTMENT
Time Recorded in Minutes

NOTE:—All employees are required to keep an accurate record of every job worked upon. Time shown hereon MUST agree with clock register, and wages are computed accordingly. Take new sheet for overtime and have it marked "overtime" by Foreman.

Name Lee H. Oswald Worked from ____ A. M. to ____ M. Date ____ 19__

JOB NO.	CUSTOMER		Kind of Work	START		STOP		Chargeable Alt.	Chargeable Comp.	Non-Chargeable
34246	Cunningham Cooper			4	10	4	45			
34085	Sam Bloom			4	45	5	15	4 15		

8 35 (circled)

O.K.

Chargeable Hours____ Non-Chargeable Hours____ Foreman.

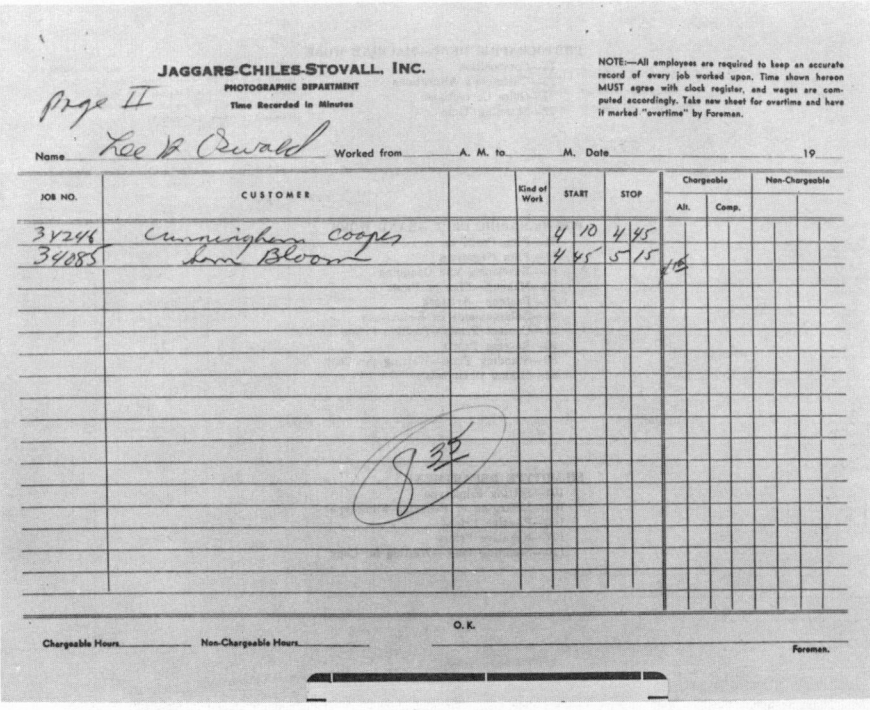

COMMISSION EXHIBIT No. 1853—Continued

JAGGARS-CHILES-STOVALL, INC.
PHOTOGRAPHIC DEPARTMENT
Time Recorded in Minutes

NOTE:—All employees are required to keep an accurate record of every job worked upon. Time shown hereon MUST agree with clock register, and wages are computed accordingly. Take new sheet for overtime and have it marked "overtime" by Foreman.

Name Lee H. Oswald Worked from 8.05 A. M. to 5:15 M. Date Jan 15 1963

JOB NO.	CUSTOMER		Kind of Work	START		STOP		Chargeable Alt.	Chargeable Comp.	Non-Chargeable
35147	Purnell & Co.			8	05	8	20			
35150	Wellmon Land Engs.			8	20	8	40			
34085	Sam Bloom			8	40	9	05			
35118	Crook adver			9	05	9	40			
35153	Container Corp			9	40	10	10			
35236	Fidelity adver			10	10	10	25			
34782	Bloom			10	25	10	45			
35042	andy anderson			10	45	11	25			
35202	Cleveland Alderman			11	25	11	35	4 / 0		
32885	Inter. Public Relations			11	35	12	45	4		
	~~Lunch~~			~~12~~	~~45~~	~~1~~	~~15~~			
35115	General Drafting			1	15	2	10			
35208	Clay Stephenson			2	10	3	05			
35233	L. O. Balfour Co			3	05	4	10			
32885	Inter. Public Relations			4	10	5	15	✓		

Chargeable Hours ______ Non-Chargeable Hours ______ (8 45) O.K. ______ Foreman.

Commission Exhibit No. 1853—Continued

page I

JAGGARS-CHILES-STOVALL, INC.
PHOTOGRAPHIC DEPARTMENT
Time Recorded in Minutes

NOTE:—All employees are required to keep an accurate record of every job worked upon. Time shown hereon MUST agree with clock register, and wages are computed accordingly. Take new sheet for overtime and have it marked "overtime" by Foreman.

Name Lee H. Oswald Worked from 8:00 A. M. to 5:45 M. Date Jan 16 (Wed) 1963

JOB NO.	CUSTOMER		Kind of Work	START		STOP		Chargeable Alt.	Chargeable Comp.	Non-Chargeable
35414	allied artist			8	00	8	20		20	4
35381	Glen			8	20	8	40		20	
35291	King			8	40	9	10		30	
35283	R B moreland			9	10	9	40		30	
35423	marvin krieger			9	40	10	05		25	
35426	Don L. Bayles			10	05	10	10		5	
~	T C S			10	10	10	25		15	
35127	Container Corp			10	25	10	45		20	
35153	Bud Biggs			10	45	11	00		15	
35401	S. W. Bell			11	00	12	15		75	
35276	Fichler			12	15	12	30	4½	15	
—	~~Lunch~~			~~12~~	~~30~~	~~1~~	~~00~~			
35458	Sargo adv			1	00	1	30		30	
35321	Sargo adv			1	30	1	45		15	
35323	McCormick			1	45	2	10		25	
34964	[illegible]			2	10	2	20		10	
35127	Service			2	20	2	40		20	

Chargeable Hours ______ Non-Chargeable Hours ______ O.K. ______ Foreman.

Commission Exhibit No. 18..

Commission Exhibit No. 1853—Continued

Page II

JAGGARS-CHILES-STOVALL, INC.
PHOTOGRAPHIC DEPARTMENT
Time Recorded in Minutes

NOTE:—All employees are required to keep an accurate record of every job worked upon. Time shown hereon MUST agree with clock register, and wages are computed accordingly. Take new sheet for overtime and have it marked "overtime" by Foreman.

Name Lee H Oswald Worked from ____ A. M. to ____ M. Date ____ 19__

JOB NO.	CUSTOMER		Kind of Work	START	STOP	Chargeable Alt.	Chargeable Comp.	Non-Chargeable
35573	Hepworth			2 40	2 55		15	
34290	Tom Browne			2 55	3 25		30	
34804	Rogers & Smith			3 25	3 50		25	
35502	Electrotype Service			3 50	4 20		30	
34512	Safeway			4 20	4 45		25	
35514	Trocc - Locke			4 45	5 00		15	
35585	Titches adv.			5 00	5 15	15	15	
34825	Hoernes Boyles			5 15				
		8 45					525	

Chargeable Hours ____ Non-Chargeable Hours ____ O.K. ____ Foreman.

COMMISSION EXHIBIT No. 1853—Continued

Page I

JAGGARS-CHILES-STOVALL, INC.
PHOTOGRAPHIC DEPARTMENT
Time Recorded in Minutes

NOTE:—All employees are required to keep an accurate record of every job worked upon. Time shown hereon MUST agree with clock register, and wages are computed accordingly. Take new sheet for overtime and have it marked "overtime" by Foreman.

Name Lee H. Oswald Worked from 8:15 A. M. to 5:30 M. Date Thurs Jan 17 1963

JOB NO.	CUSTOMER		Kind of Work	START	STOP	Chargeable Alt.	Chargeable Comp.	Non-Chargeable
35149	Anderson Clayton			8 15	9 10		55	
12224	Lone Star Gas			9 10	9 45		35	
35215	Braniff			9 45	10 15		30	
35516	W. W. Sherrill			10 15	10 40		25	
35689	McCann Erickson			10 40	11 00		20	
35533	adv. Service			11 00	11 20		20	
35274	Rogers & Smith			11 20	11 50		30	
35592	Rogers & Smith			11 50	12 10		20	
	~~Lunch~~			~~12 10~~	~~12 40~~			
—	J.C.S. —			12 40	12 55		15	
35655	Pollock Paper Co			12 55	1 10		15	
32885	Internat'l P. R.			1 10	1 25		15	
35604	McCann Erickson			1 25	2 05		40	
34238	Gulf States			2 05	2 25		20	
35651	Wyatt			2 25	2 50		25	
3070	Ayres			2 50	3 10		20	
35752	Continental Corp			3 10	3 35		25	
35754	Boardman Paper Co			3 35	3 50		15	

Chargeable Hours ____ Non-Chargeable Hours ____ O.K. ____ Foreman.

Commission Exhibit No. 1853

COMMISSION EXHIBIT No. 1853—Continued

JAGGARS-CHILES-STOVALL, INC.
PHOTOGRAPHIC DEPARTMENT
Time Recorded in Minutes

NOTE:—All employees are required to keep an accurate record of every job worked upon. Time shown hereon MUST agree with clock register, and wages are computed accordingly. Take new sheet for overtime and have it marked "overtime" by Foreman.

Page II

Name Lee H. Oswald Worked from ____ A. M. to ____ M. Date Jan 17th 19__

JOB NO.	CUSTOMER		Kind of Work	START	STOP	Chargeable Alt.	Chargeable Comp.	Non-Chargeable	
35756	Goodman Paper Co.			3 50	4 30		40		
35667	Ivey-Locke [?]			4 30	5 10		40		
34290	Sam Sumner [?]	8 55		5 10	5 30	450	20		
		8 3/4					525		

O. K.

Chargeable Hours ________ Non-Chargeable Hours ________ ________ Foreman.

COMMISSION EXHIBIT No. 1853—Continued

JAGGARS-CHILES-STOVALL, INC.
PHOTOGRAPHIC DEPARTMENT
Time Recorded in Minutes

NOTE:—All employees are required to keep an accurate record of every job worked upon. Time shown hereon MUST agree with clock register, and wages are computed accordingly. Take new sheet for overtime and have it marked "overtime" by Foreman.

Name Lee H Oswald Worked from 8:05 A. M. to 5:30 M. Date Jan 18 Friday 1963

JOB NO.	CUSTOMER		Kind of Work	START	STOP	Chargeable Alt.	Chargeable Comp.	Non-Chargeable	
35751	Goodman Paper			8 :05	9 00				
35656	Hepworth adver.			9 00	9 40				
35831	Howard Reecroft [?]			9 40	10 10				
35820	The Jordan Co.			10 10	10 45				
35587	Cunningham & Walsh			10 45	11 05				
35524	Adver. Service Co.			11 05	11 40	45			
35867	assoc. adver agency			11 40	12 30	4			
	Lunch			12 30	1 00				
35850	Goodman Paper Co			1 00	1 40				
35821	Rogers & Smith			1 40	2 15				
35853	Dixie Wax Paper Co			2 15	3 45	30			
35890	[illegible]			3 45	4 30	4			
35440	Raymonds [?]			4 30	5 30				
		8 1/2 [?]							

O. K.

Chargeable Hours ________ Non-Chargeable Hours ________ ________ Foreman.

Commission Exhibit No. 1853

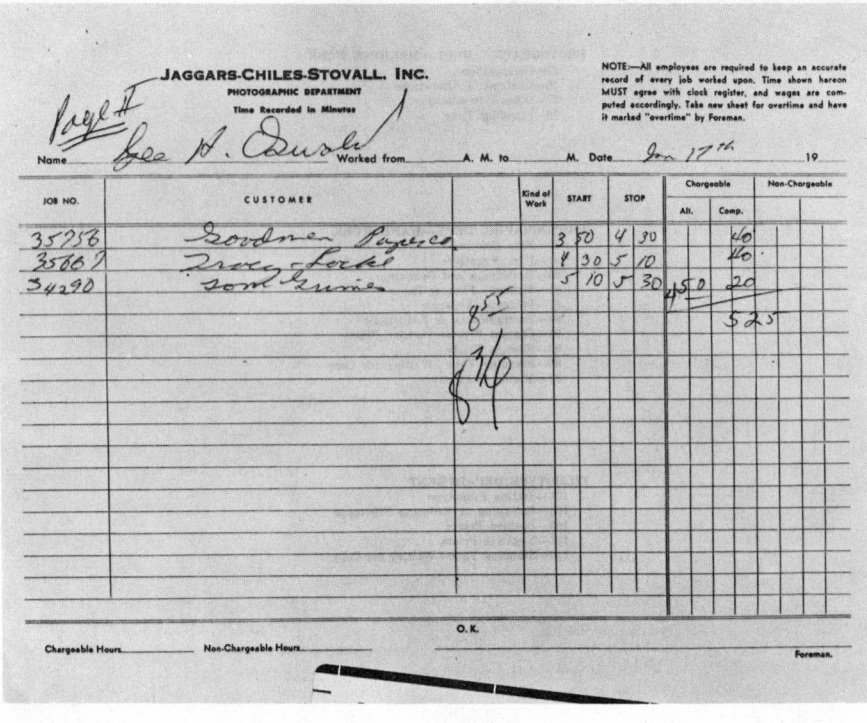

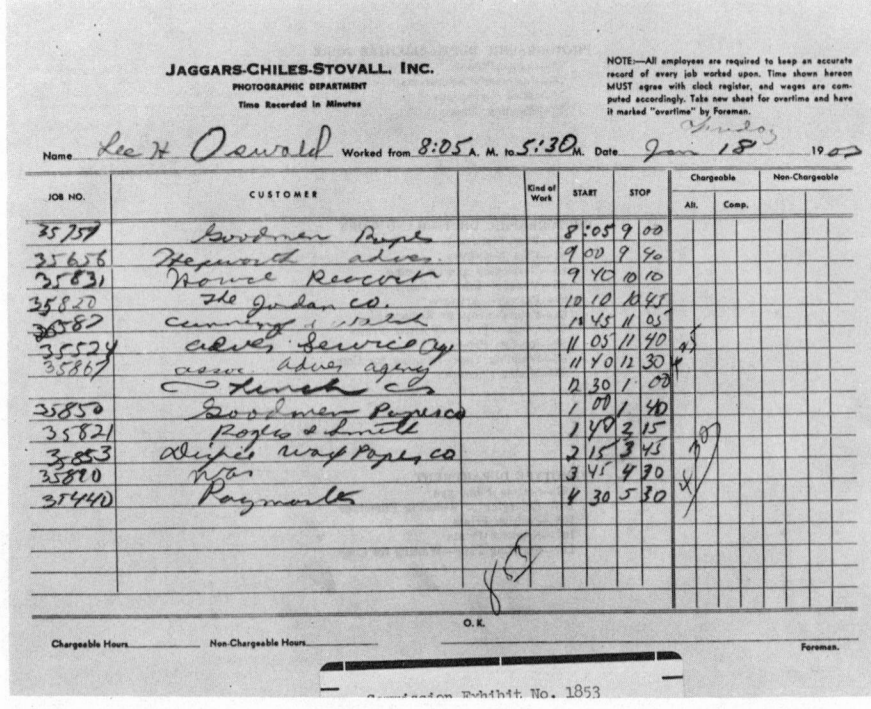

COMMISSION EXHIBIT No. 1853—Continued

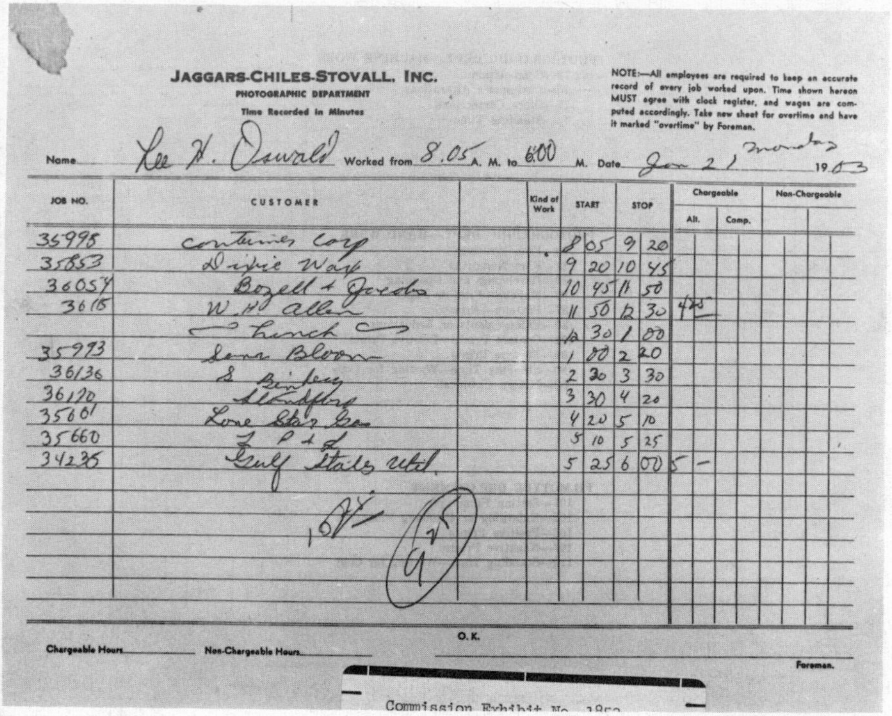

JAGGARS-CHILES-STOVALL, INC.
PHOTOGRAPHIC DEPARTMENT
Time Recorded in Minutes

NOTE:—All employees are required to keep an accurate record of every job worked upon. Time shown hereon MUST agree with clock register, and wages are computed accordingly. Take new sheet for overtime and have it marked "overtime" by Foreman.

Name Lee H. Oswald Worked from 8.05 A. M. to 6.00 M. Date Jan 21 Monday 1963

JOB NO.	CUSTOMER	Kind of Work	START	STOP	Chargeable Alt.	Chargeable Comp.	Non-Chargeable
35998	container corp		8 05	9 20			
35853	Dixie Wax		9 20	10 45			
36057	Bozell & Jacobs		10 45	11 50			
3615	W. H. Allen		11 50	12 30	4 25		
	Lunch		12 30	1 00			
35993	Sam Bloom		1 00	2 20			
36136	S. Binkley		2 30	3 30			
36120	Standford		3 30	4 20			
35601	Lone Star Gas		4 20	5 10			
35660	T P & L		5 10	5 25			
34235	Gulf States util.		5 25	6 00	5 –		

Chargeable Hours ______ Non-Chargeable Hours ______ O.K. ______ Foreman.

Commission Exhibit No. 1853

Commission Exhibit No. 1853—Continued

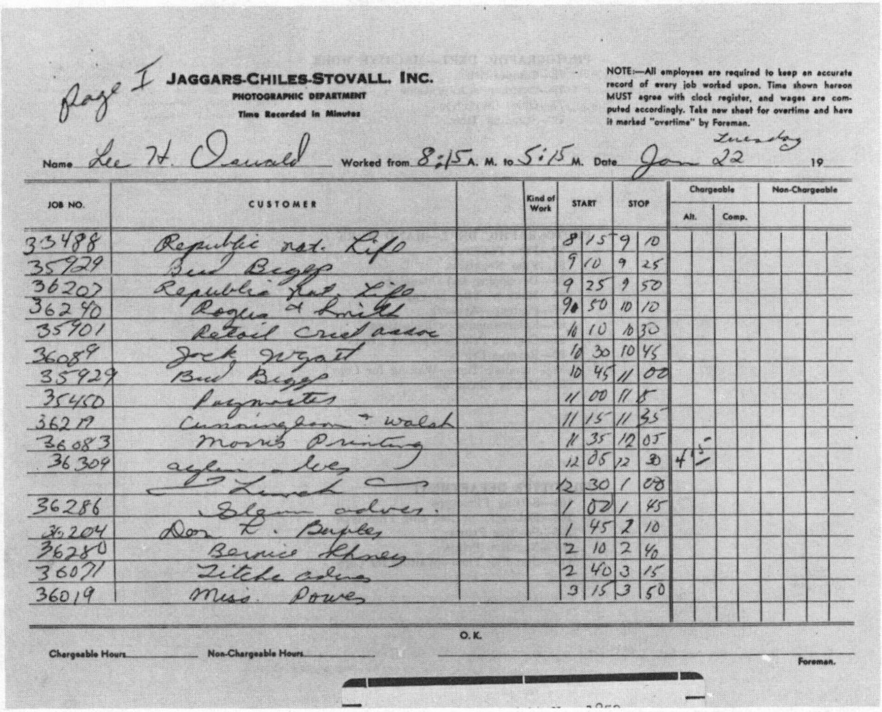

Page I

JAGGARS-CHILES-STOVALL, INC.
PHOTOGRAPHIC DEPARTMENT
Time Recorded in Minutes

NOTE:—All employees are required to keep an accurate record of every job worked upon. Time shown hereon MUST agree with clock register, and wages are computed accordingly. Take new sheet for overtime and have it marked "overtime" by Foreman.

Name Lee H. Oswald Worked from 8:15 A. M. to 5:15 M. Date Jan 22 Tuesday 19

JOB NO.	CUSTOMER	Kind of Work	START	STOP	Chargeable Alt.	Chargeable Comp.	Non-Chargeable
33488	Republic nat. Life		8 15	9 10			
35929	Bud Biggs		9 10	9 25			
36207	Republic nat. Life		9 25	9 50			
36240	Rogers & Smith		9 50	10 10			
35901	Retail Credit assoc		10 10	10 30			
36089	Jack Wyatt		10 30	10 45			
35929	Bud Biggs		10 45	11 00			
35450	Paymaster		11 00	11 15			
36219	Cunningham & Walsh		11 15	11 35			
36083	Morris Printing		11 35	12 05			
36309	aglen advs		12 05	12 30	4 15		
	Lunch		12 30	1 00			
36286	Glenn advs.		1 00	1 45			
36204	Don L. Bugles		1 45	2 10			
36280	Bernice Shney		2 10	2 40			
36071	Fitche adv		2 40	3 15			
36019	Miss Powers		3 15	3 50			

Chargeable Hours ______ Non-Chargeable Hours ______ O.K. ______ Foreman.

Commission Exhibit No. 1853—Continued

JAGGARS-CHILES-STOVALL, INC.
PHOTOGRAPHIC DEPARTMENT
Time Recorded in Minutes

Pog II

NOTE:—All employees are required to keep an accurate record of every job worked upon. Time shown hereon MUST agree with clock register, and wages are computed accordingly. Take new sheet for overtime and have it marked "overtime" by Foreman.

Name Lee H Oswald Worked from ______ A. M. to ______ M. Date ______ 19__

JOB NO.	CUSTOMER		Kind of Work	START		STOP		Chargeable Alt.	Chargeable Comp.	Non-Chargeable
36208	T.P.&L			3	50	4	25			
36308	Cliff Harper			4	25	4	45			
34290	Tom Grime			4	45	5	15	4 15		
									510	
		8 30								

O.K.

Chargeable Hours ______ Non-Chargeable Hours ______ ______ Foreman.

Commission Exhibit No. 1853

COMMISSION EXHIBIT NO. 1853—Continued

JAGGARS-CHILES-STOVALL, INC.
PHOTOGRAPHIC DEPARTMENT
Time Recorded in Minutes

Pog I

NOTE:—All employees are required to keep an accurate record of every job worked upon. Time shown hereon MUST agree with clock register, and wages are computed accordingly. Take new sheet for overtime and have it marked "overtime" by Foreman.

Name Lee H Oswald Worked from 8:15 A. M. to 5:30 M. Date wed Jan 23 19[illegible]

JOB NO.	CUSTOMER		Kind of Work	START		STOP		Chargeable Alt.	Chargeable Comp.	Non-Chargeable
36236	Cunningham & Walsh			8	15	9	10			
36289	Linz Jewelers			9	10	9	25			
36343	American Beauty			9	25	9	45			
36449	Fritzwold Art			9	45	10	10			
36286	Glenn adv.			10	10	10	30			
36465	Linz			10	30	10	45			
36508	Wyatt ad Service			10	45	11	10			
35007	T.C.S.			11	10	11	40			
34290	Tom Grime			11	40	12	15	4		
	lunch			12	15	12	45			
36454	Marvin Kruegg			12	45	1	10			
36442	Jack Wyatt			1	10	1	35			
36491	Norsworthy - Mercer			1	35	2	05			
36484	Sears Roebuck & Co.			2	05	2	25			
36126	Gulf State			2	25	2	50			
36010	Paymaster Feed			2	50	3	10			
36531	Glenn			3	10	3	25			

O.K.

Chargeable Hours ______ Non-Chargeable Hours ______ ______ Foreman.

Commission Exhibit No. 1853

COMMISSION EXHIBIT NO. 1853—Continued

Page II

JAGGARS-CHILES-STOVALL, INC.
PHOTOGRAPHIC DEPARTMENT
Time Recorded in Minutes

NOTE:—All employees are required to keep an accurate record of every job worked upon. Time shown hereon MUST agree with clock register, and wages are computed accordingly. Take new sheet for overtime and have it marked "overtime" by Foreman.

Name Lee H Oswald Worked from ______ A. M. to ______ M. Date ______ 19__

JOB NO.	CUSTOMER	Kind of Work	START	STOP	Chargeable Alt.	Chargeable Comp.	Non-Chargeable
36465	Lizzy		3 25	3 50			
36494	Norsworthy - Mercer Co		3 50	4 10			
36506	White Auto		4 10	4 25			
36491	Baron Store		4 25	4 50			
36514	R. B. Moreland		4 50	5 30	[illegible]	5 25	

8 3/4

Chargeable Hours ______ Non-Chargeable Hours ______ O. K. ______ Foreman.

Commission Exhibit No. 1853

COMMISSION EXHIBIT No. 1853—Continued

Page I

JAGGARS-CHILES-STOVALL, INC.
PHOTOGRAPHIC DEPARTMENT
Time Recorded in Minutes

NOTE:—All employees are required to keep an accurate record of every job worked upon. Time shown hereon MUST agree with clock register, and wages are computed accordingly. Take new sheet for overtime and have it marked "overtime" by Foreman.

Name Lee H. Oswald Worked from 8:15 A. M. to 5:15 M. Date Thurs. Jan 24 1963

JOB NO.	CUSTOMER	Kind of Work	START	STOP	Chargeable Alt.	Chargeable Comp.	Non-Chargeable
36621	Rogers & Smith		8 15	8 40			
33408	Republic Nat'l Bank		8 40	9 10			
36591	Jack Taylor		9 10	9 25			
36587	Sam Bloom		9 25	9 50			
34290	Tom Grimes		9 50	10 10			
36567	Tom Grimes		10 10	10 30			
36001	Ikonogenics		10 30	10 50			
36019	Mississippi Power		10 50	11 10			
36530	Glenn Adv		11 10	11 35			
36633	Virgil Naylor		11 35	11 55			
36630	Glen Adv		11 55	12 30	4 15		
	Lunch		12 30	1 00			
36680	Fidelity		1 00	1 25			
36472	Rogers & Smith		1 25	1 50			
36624	Bayles		1 50	2 20			
36644	Bryan & Bryan		2 20	2 45			
34389	Don L. Bayles		2 45	3 10			

Chargeable Hours ______ Non-Chargeable Hours ______ O. K. ______ Foreman.

Commission Exhibit No. 1853

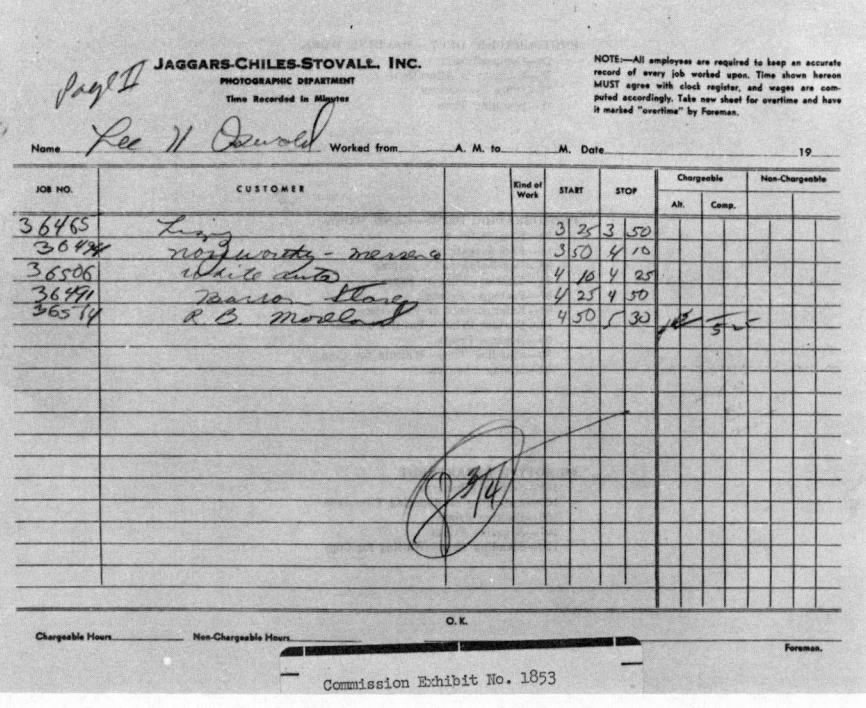

COMMISSION EXHIBIT No. 1853—Continued

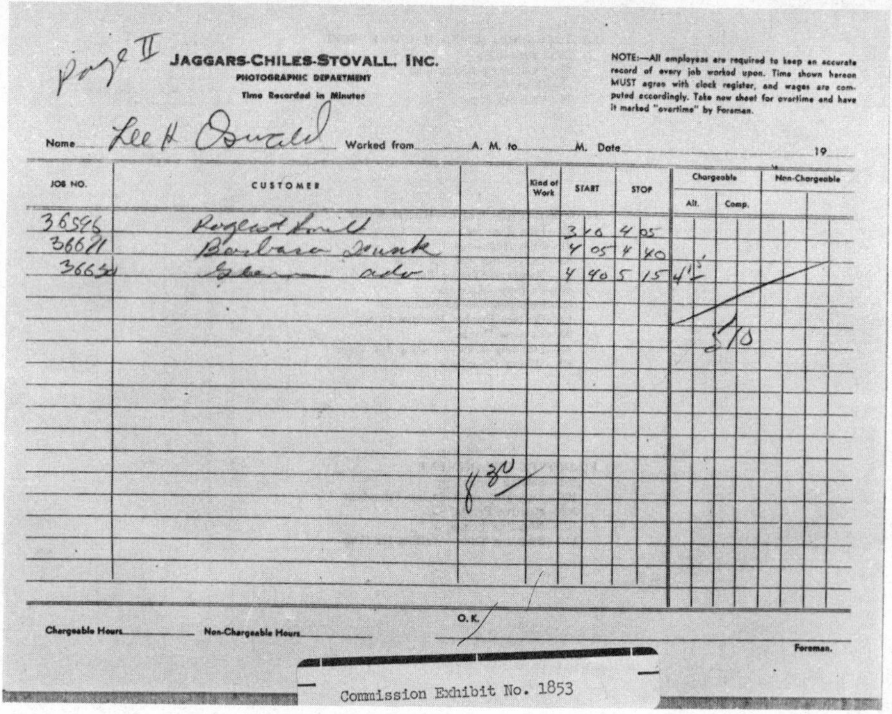

Page II

JAGGARS-CHILES-STOVALL, INC.
PHOTOGRAPHIC DEPARTMENT
Time Recorded in Minutes

NOTE:—All employees are required to keep an accurate record of every job worked upon. Time shown hereon MUST agree with clock register, and wages are computed accordingly. Take new sheet for overtime and have it marked "overtime" by Foreman.

Name Lee H Oswald Worked from ______ A. M. to ______ M. Date ______ 19__

JOB NO.	CUSTOMER		Kind of Work	START		STOP		Chargeable Alt.	Chargeable Comp.	Non-Chargeable
36596	Rogers Advt [?]			3	40	4	05			
36671 [?]	Barbara Munk [?]			4	05	4	40			
36650 [?]	Glenn Advt			4	40	5	15	4 15		

8 30

510

Chargeable Hours ______ Non-Chargeable Hours ______ O.K. ______ Foreman.

Commission Exhibit No. 1853

COMMISSION EXHIBIT No. 1853—Continued

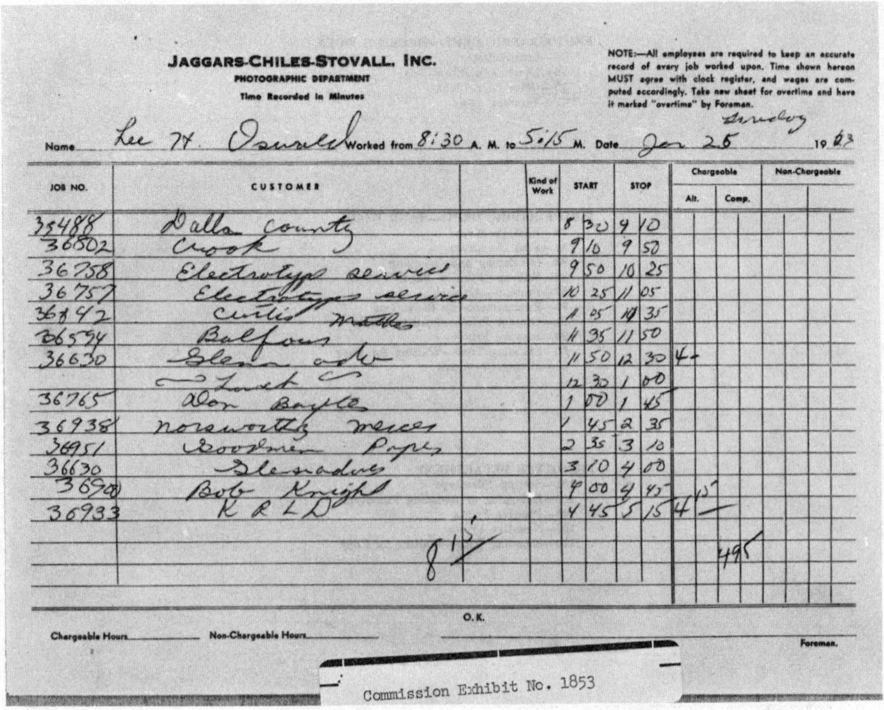

JAGGARS-CHILES-STOVALL, INC.
PHOTOGRAPHIC DEPARTMENT
Time Recorded in Minutes

NOTE:—All employees are required to keep an accurate record of every job worked upon. Time shown hereon MUST agree with clock register, and wages are computed accordingly. Take new sheet for overtime and have it marked "overtime" by Foreman.

Name Lee H. Oswald Worked from 8:30 A. M. to 5:15 M. Date Jan 25 Friday 1963

JOB NO.	CUSTOMER		Kind of Work	START		STOP		Chargeable Alt.	Chargeable Comp.	Non-Chargeable
35488	Dallas County			8	30	9	10			
36502	Crook			9	10	9	50			
36758	Electrotype service			9	50	10	25			
36757	Electrotype service			10	25	11	05			
36842 [?]	Curtis Mathes			11	05	11	35			
36594	Balfour			11	35	11	50			
36630	Glenn Advt			11	50	12	30	4		
	Lunch			12	30	1	00			
36765	Don Boyles			1	00	1	45			
36938	Norsworthy Mercer			1	45	2	35			
36951	Goodman Papers			2	35	3	10			
36630	Glenn Advt			3	10	4	00			
3690[?]	Bob Knight			4	00	4	45			
36933	KRLD			4	45	5	15	4 15		

8 15

495

Chargeable Hours ______ Non-Chargeable Hours ______ O.K. ______ Foreman.

Commission Exhibit No. 1853

COMMISSION EXHIBIT No. 1853—Continued

JAGGARS-CHILES-STOVALL, INC.
PHOTOGRAPHIC DEPARTMENT
Time Recorded in Minutes

NOTE:—All employees are required to keep an accurate record of every job worked upon. Time shown hereon MUST agree with clock register, and wages are computed accordingly. Take new sheet for overtime and have it marked "overtime" by Foreman.

Name Lee H Oswald Worked from 8:00 A. M. to 5:30 M. Date Sat. Jan 26 1963

JOB NO.	CUSTOMER	Kind of Work	START	STOP	Chargeable Alt.	Chargeable Comp.	Non-Chargeable
36678	(1) Park aerial survey		8 00	8 20			
36678	(2) Park aerial		8 20	9 10			
35488	Dallas county		9 10	9 45			
37016	Tom Irvine		9 45	10 10			
36620	Bob Bond		10 10	10 45			
36744	Electrotype		10 45	11 10			
36933	KRLD		11 10	11 40			
	Ayly		11 40	12 30	4 30		
	lunch		12 30	1 00			
37070	[illegible]		1 00	1 45			
37073	[illegible]		1 45	2 40			
34753	Jordon Co.		2 40	2 55			
37039	[illegible] Co.		2 55	3 35			
37030	Jesse Caesar		3 35	4 10			
37082	Gordon Marks		4 10	4 35			
37085	Bob Knight		4 35	5 05	3 30		
35642	Robert K Butler		5 05	5 30	4		

Chargeable Hours ______ Non-Chargeable Hours ______ O.K. 9 ______ Foreman.

Commission Exhibit No. 1853

COMMISSION EXHIBIT NO. 1853—Continued

JAGGARS-CHILES-STOVALL, INC.
PHOTOGRAPHIC DEPARTMENT
Time Recorded in Minutes

NOTE:—All employees are required to keep an accurate record of every job worked upon. Time shown hereon MUST agree with clock register, and wages are computed accordingly. Take new sheet for overtime and have it marked "overtime" by Foreman.

Payl

Name Lee H Oswald Worked from 8:00 A. M. to 6:00 M. Date Monday Jan 28 1963

JOB NO.	CUSTOMER	Kind of Work	START	STOP	Chargeable Alt.	Chargeable Comp.	Non-Chargeable
35264	White auto		8 00	8 20			
37074	Bloom		8 20	9 05			
36875	Jack Wyatt		9 05	9 45			
36757	Electrotype service		9 45	10 10			
36746	West Texas util		10 10	10 35			
36895	Crook adv		10 35	10 50			
37116	Ed Bearden		10 50	11 10			
37111	Campbell		11 10	11 45			
36903	Miss Honey		11 45	12 30	4 30	2 70	
	lunch		12 30	1 00			
37085	Bob Knight		1 00	1 25			
36765	Ron L. Boyles		1 25	2 10			
36676	Park aerial		2 10	3 05			
37088	advertising service		3 05	3 55			
37176	Tom Irvine		3 55	4 40			
37024	Sparrow		4 40	5 00			
37049	[illegible] party		5 00	5 20			
37153	Norworthy [illegible]		5 20	6 00	5	3 00	

Chargeable Hours ______ Non-Chargeable Hours ______ 9 50 O.K. 5 70 ______ Foreman.

COMMISSION EXHIBIT NO. 1853—Continued

Page I

JAGGARS-CHILES-STOVALL, INC.
PHOTOGRAPHIC DEPARTMENT
Time Recorded in Minutes

NOTE:—All employees are required to keep an accurate record of every job worked upon. Time shown hereon MUST agree with clock register, and wages are computed accordingly. Take new sheet for overtime and have it marked "overtime" by Foreman.

Name Lee H Oswald Worked from 8:00 A. M. to 5:45 M. Date Tues. Jan 29 1963

JOB NO.	CUSTOMER		Kind of Work	START		STOP		Chargeable Alt.	Chargeable Comp.	Non-Chargeable
37154	McCormick			8	00	8	20			
36934	Bob Knight			8	20	8	40			
37144	Glenn			8	40	9	10			
37145	Zitche			9	10	9	40			
37124	Art Johnson			9	40	10	10			
37129	Ed Bearden			10	10	10	25			
37135	Tom Ramsey			10	25	10	40			
34290	Tom Irvine			10	40	11	10			
37170	Braniff			11	10	11	25			
37326	Rives Dyke & Co.			11	25	11	45			
37325	R K Buthe			11	45	12	05			
37282	Ebeco			12	05	12	30	4 30		
	— lunch —			12	30	1	00			
36676	Park aerial			1	00	1	25			
37281	Ike Stack Comp.			1	25	1	50			
37225	T - L			1	50	2	30			
37087	Chester County Planning			2	30	2	55			

Chargeable Hours ________ Non-Chargeable Hours ________ O.K. ________ Foreman.

Commission Exhibit No. 1853

COMMISSION EXHIBIT No. 1853—Continued

Page II

JAGGARS-CHILES-STOVALL, INC.
PHOTOGRAPHIC DEPARTMENT
Time Recorded in Minutes

NOTE:—All employees are required to keep an accurate record of every job worked upon. Time shown hereon MUST agree with clock register, and wages are computed accordingly. Take new sheet for overtime and have it marked "overtime" by Foreman.

Name Lee H Oswald Worked from ________ A. M. to ________ M. Date ________ 19__

JOB NO.	CUSTOMER		Kind of Work	START		STOP		Chargeable Alt.	Chargeable Comp.	Non-Chargeable
36947	Electrotype Service			2	55	3	20			
37132	Roberts Cover & Page			3	20	3	50			
37290	Pollock			3	50	4	35			
36657	Schwagley			4	35	5	10			
37297	McCormick adv			5	10	5	45	4 45		
								55		
		9 15								

Chargeable Hours ________ Non-Chargeable Hours ________ O.K. ________ Foreman.

Commission Exhibit No. 1853

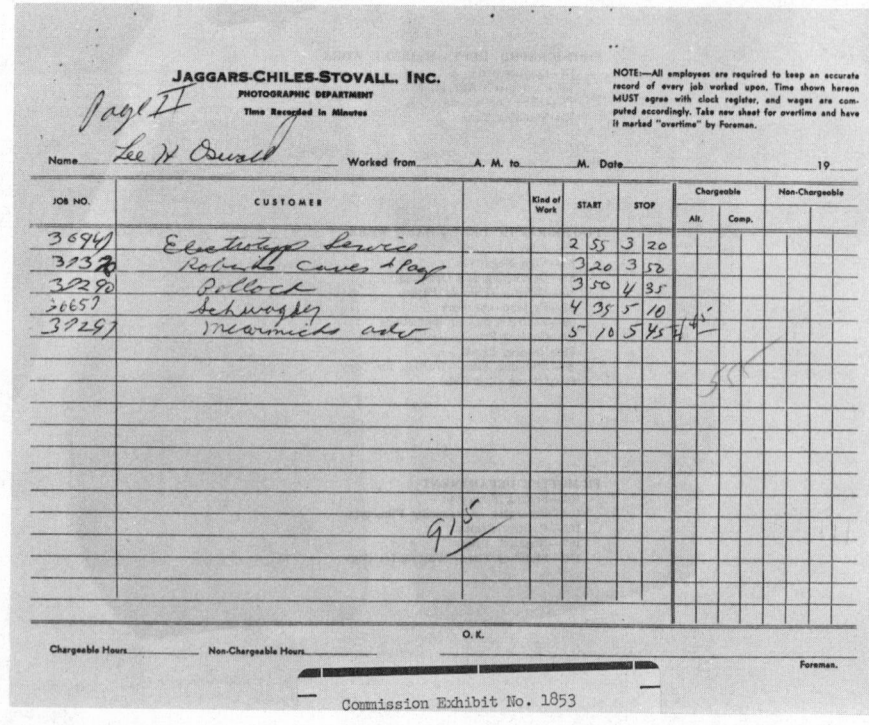

COMMISSION EXHIBIT No. 1853—Continued

JAGGARS-CHILES-STOVALL, INC.
PHOTOGRAPHIC DEPARTMENT
Time Recorded in Minutes

NOTE:—All employees are required to keep an accurate record of every job worked upon. Time shown hereon MUST agree with clock register, and wages are computed accordingly. Take new sheet for overtime and have it marked "overtime" by Foreman.

Name Lee H. Oswald Worked from 8:00 A. M. to 6:30 M. Date Jan 30 wed. 19

JOB NO.	CUSTOMER	Kind of Work	START		STOP		Chargeable Alt.	Chargeable Comp.	Non-Chargeable
37261	White auto		8	00	8	25			
37337	(1) Jack T Holme		8	25	9	10			
37337	(2) Jack T Holme		9	10	9	45			
37438	Tracy-Locke		9	45	10	10			
37365	R H S		10	10	10	35			
37325	Robert Buttles		10	35	11	10			
37311	Graphic Industries		11	10	12	15	4 45		
	Lunch		12	15	12	45			
37035	Mel Douglas		12	45	1	10			
37381	Lodd Co		1	10	1	55			
37325	Robert K Buttles		1	55	2	50			
36778	Cunningham & Walsh		2	50	3	30			
37256	Tracy-Locke		3	30	4	05			
35261	White auto		4	05	4	55			
36976	Elliott McCain		4	55	5	35			
37552	Seminary South		5	35	6:	30	5 45		
							6 00		

O.K.

Chargeable Hours______ Non-Chargeable Hours______ ______ Foreman.

Commission Exhibit No. 1853

COMMISSION EXHIBIT NO. 1853—Continued

JAGGARS-CHILES-STOVALL, INC.
PHOTOGRAPHIC DEPARTMENT
Time Recorded in Minutes

NOTE:—All employees are required to keep an accurate record of every job worked upon. Time shown hereon MUST agree with clock register, and wages are computed accordingly. Take new sheet for overtime and have it marked "overtime" by Foreman.

Name Lee H Oswald Worked from 8:00 A. M. to 6:00 M. Date Jan 01 Thurs. 1963

JOB NO.	CUSTOMER	Kind of Work	START		STOP		Chargeable Alt.	Chargeable Comp.	Non-Chargeable
37239	Glen Adams		8	00	8	45			
37538	Sherrill		8	45	9	25			
37630	Tom Greene		9	25	10	10			
37629	Rogers & Smith		10	10	10	40			
36592	L B Balfour		10	40	11	10			
37555	Caudle Engraving		11	10	11	25			
37728	Sparrow ad. agency		11	25	11	40			
37871	Standford		11	40	11	55			
36744	West Texas Util		11	55	12	10			
37729	Doug Printer		12	10	12	35			
37743	Tracy-Locke		12	35	12	50	4 50		
	Lunch		12	50	1	20			
35261	White auto		1	20	2	05			
37242	Bob Knight		2	05	2	55			
37720	Campbell Stirley		2	55	3	45			
32358	Republic Nat'l Bank		3	45	4	45			
37559	Standford		4	45	5	20			
37728	Kirby		5	20	6.	00	4 40		

O.K.

Chargeable Hours______ Non-Chargeable Hours______ ______ Foreman.

Commission Exhibit No. 1853

COMMISSION EXHIBIT NO. 1853—Continued

page I

JAGGARS-CHILES-STOVALL, INC.
PHOTOGRAPHIC DEPARTMENT
Time Recorded in Minutes

NOTE:—All employees are required to keep an accurate record of every job worked upon. Time shown hereon MUST agree with clock register, and wages are computed accordingly. Take new sheet for overtime and have it marked "overtime" by Foreman.

Name Lee H Oswald Worked from 8:15 A. M. to 5:15 M. Date Feb Monday 1st 19

JOB NO.	CUSTOMER		Kind of Work	START		STOP		Chargeable Alt.	Chargeable Comp.	Non-Chargeable
37699	R & S			8	15	9	10			
35488	Dallas county			9	10	9	45			
37664	Blume			9	45	10	10			
36155	Creative Design			10	10	10	30			
37757	Graphics corp			10	30	10	50			
37762	Dibil NSD			10	50	11	10			
37765	R G Balfour			11	10	11	30			
37847	Sam Bloom			11	30	11	45			
37584	Hirsch			11	45	12	05			
36575	Jack Wyatt			12	05	12	30	4 15		
	Lunch			12	30	1	00			
37877	Zitokes			1	00	1	30			
37921	Doug Pruett			1	30	2	00			
37647	Contours			2	00	2	20			
37636	Braniff ords dept			2	20	2	55			
37194	Rogle & Smith			2	55	3	20			
37554	Stanford agency			3	20	3	50			

Chargeable Hours ______ Non-Chargeable Hours ______ O. K. ______ Foreman.

Commission Exhibit No. 1854

COMMISSION EXHIBIT NO. 1854

page II

JAGGARS-CHILES-STOVALL, INC.
PHOTOGRAPHIC DEPARTMENT
Time Recorded in Minutes

NOTE:—All employees are required to keep an accurate record of every job worked upon. Time shown hereon MUST agree with clock register, and wages are computed accordingly. Take new sheet for overtime and have it marked "overtime" by Foreman.

Name Lee H Oswald Worked from ______ A. M. to ______ M. Date ______ 19

JOB NO.	CUSTOMER		Kind of Work	START		STOP		Chargeable Alt.	Chargeable Comp.	Non-Chargeable
37928	Collins comm. art			3	50	4	15			
37765	Lon Runkle			4	15	4	50			
37925	Braniff			4	50	5	15	4 15		

5/10

8 3/4

Chargeable Hours ______ Non-Chargeable Hours ______ O. K. ______ Foreman.

Commission Exhibit No. 1854

COMMISSION EXHIBIT NO. 1854—Continued

JAGGARS-CHILES-STOVALL. INC.
PHOTOGRAPHIC DEPARTMENT
Time Recorded in Minutes

NOTE:—All employees are required to keep an accurate record of every job worked upon. Time shown hereon MUST agree with clock register, and wages are computed accordingly. Take new sheet for overtime and have it marked "overtime" by Foreman.

Name Lee H Oswald Worked from 8:00 A. M. to 5:30 M. Date Jan 4 monday 1963

JOB NO.	CUSTOMER		Kind of Work	START	STOP	Chargeable Alt.	Chargeable Comp.	Non-Chargeable
38100	Lone Star Gas			8 00	9 10			
39805	Riverside Press			9 10	9 55			
37916	Lone Star Gas			9 55	10 40			
38110	Keity-Herndone			10 40	11 35			
38166	Glenn			11 35	12 30	4 30		
	~ lunch ~			12 30	1 00			
37099	Rhinehart Oil news			1 00	1 30			
38120	Standford			1 30	2 00			
33451	Cliff Harper			2 00	2 50			
38122	Crook			2 50	3 20			
38178	Cowan			3 20	3 35			
38060	Container Corp			3 35	3 55			
38143	King			3 55	4 10			
38156	Mervin Kruger			4 10	4 30			
38069	Wyatt Stores			4 30	4 45			
38207	Jack T. Holmes			4 45	5 05			
37959	R & S	9		5 05	5 30	4 30		

O.K.

Chargeable Hours _____ Non-Chargeable Hours _____ 540 _____ Foreman.

Commission Exhibit No. 1854—Continued

JAGGARS-CHILES-STOVALL. INC.
PHOTOGRAPHIC DEPARTMENT
Time Recorded in Minutes

NOTE:—All employees are required to keep an accurate record of every job worked upon. Time shown hereon MUST agree with clock register, and wages are computed accordingly. Take new sheet for overtime and have it marked "overtime" by Foreman.

Name Lee H Oswald Worked from 8:15 A. M. to 5:30 M. Date Feb 5 1963

JOB NO.	CUSTOMER		Kind of Work	START	STOP	Chargeable Alt.	Chargeable Comp.	Non-Chargeable
38271	Don L. Bapter			8 15	9 10			
38299	(1) Chas Beall			9 10	9 45			
38242	Sam Bloom			9 45	10 10			
38299	Charles Beale			10 10	10 35			
38269	Pollock Paper Co			10 35	11 05			
39805	Riverside Press			11 05	11 35			
36268	Riverside Press			11 35	12 30	4 15		
	Lunch			12 30	1 00			
38323	Womack Nelson			1 00	1 20			
38257	Tracy Locke			1 20	1 40			
37906	Sam Bloom			1 40	2 05			
38366	Wyatt Adv			2 05	2 25			
38023	McCormick			2 25	3 05			
36747	West Tex Util			3 05	3 50			
38070	Ragland Smith			3 50	4 30			
38296	Lone Star Gas			4 30	5 10			
38299	(2) Charles Beal			5 10	5 30	4 30		

Chargeable Hours _____ Non-Chargeable Hours _____ 8 45 S.K. 1 525 _____ Foreman.

Commission Exhibit No. 1854—Continued

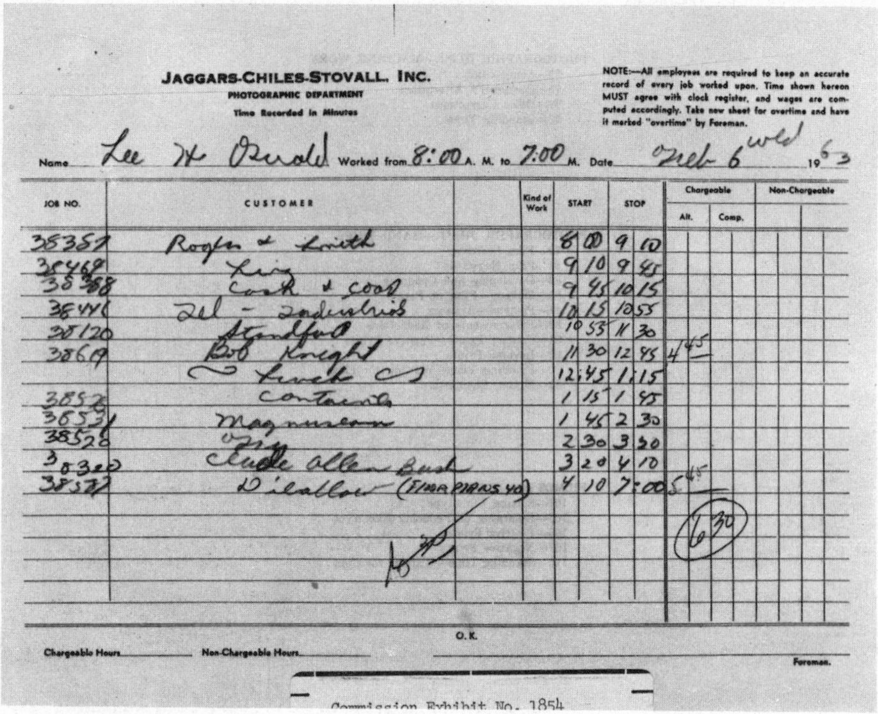

JAGGARS-CHILES-STOVALL, INC.
PHOTOGRAPHIC DEPARTMENT
Time Recorded in Minutes

NOTE:—All employees are required to keep an accurate record of every job worked upon. Time shown hereon MUST agree with clock register, and wages are computed accordingly. Take new sheet for overtime and have it marked "overtime" by Foreman.

Name Lee H Oswald Worked from 8:00 A. M. to 7:00 M. Date Feb 6 wed 1963

JOB NO.	CUSTOMER	Kind of Work	START	STOP	Chargeable Alt.	Chargeable Comp.	Non-Chargeable
38357	Rogers & Smith		8 00	9 10			
38469	King		9 10	9 45			
38388	Cook & Cook		9 45	10 15			
38441	Tel - Industries		10 15	10 55			
38120	Standford		10 55	11 30			
38619	Bob Knight		11 30	12 45	4 45		
	Lunch CS		12 45	1 15			
3852	Containers		1 15	1 45			
38531	Magnuson		1 45	2 30			
38528	Ozig		2 30	3 20			
38300	Clyde Allen Bush		3 20	4 10			
38537	Dilallow (Time plans 40)		4 10	7:00	5 45		
					6 30		

Chargeable Hours ______ Non-Chargeable Hours ______ O.K. ______ Foreman.

Commission Exhibit No. 1854

COMMISSION EXHIBIT No. 1854—Continued

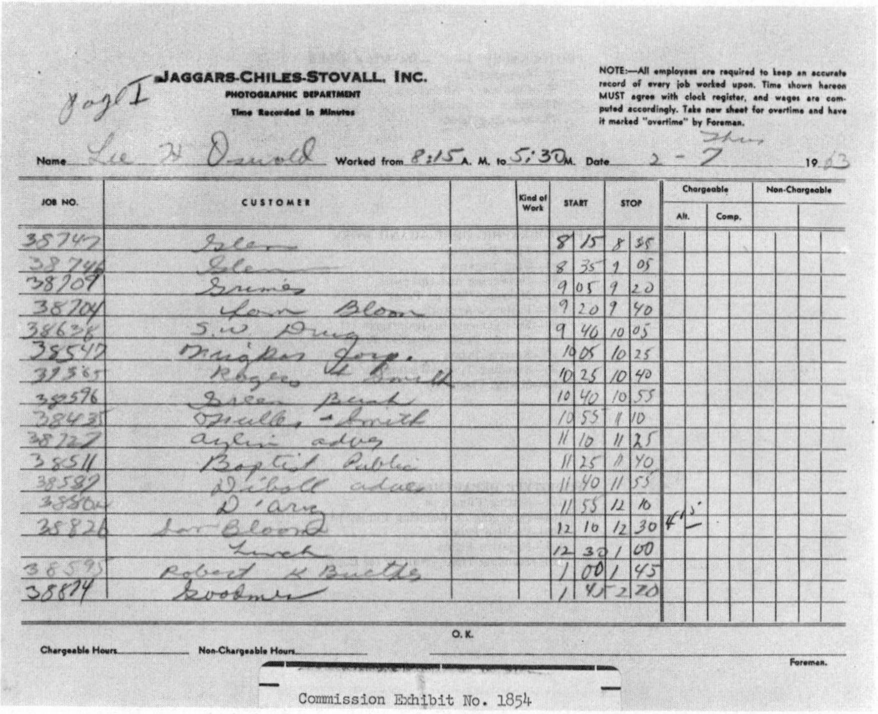

JAGGARS-CHILES-STOVALL, INC.
PHOTOGRAPHIC DEPARTMENT
Time Recorded in Minutes

NOTE:—All employees are required to keep an accurate record of every job worked upon. Time shown hereon MUST agree with clock register, and wages are computed accordingly. Take new sheet for overtime and have it marked "overtime" by Foreman.

Name Lee H Oswald Worked from 8:15 A. M. to 5:30 M. Date 2-7 Thurs 1963

JOB NO.	CUSTOMER	Kind of Work	START	STOP	Chargeable Alt.	Chargeable Comp.	Non-Chargeable
38747	Glenn		8 15	8 35			
38746	Glenn		8 35	9 05			
38709	Grimes		9 05	9 20			
38704	Sam Bloom		9 20	9 40			
38638	S.W. Drug		9 40	10 05			
38547	Mighas Corp.		10 05	10 25			
38365	Rogers & Smith		10 25	10 40			
38596	Green Bush		10 40	10 55			
38435	Mueller & Smith		10 55	11 10			
38727	Aylin adv.		11 10	11 25			
38511	Baptist Public		11 25	11 40			
38589	Dibrell adv.		11 40	11 55			
38806	D'Arcy		11 55	12 10			
38826	Sam Bloom		12 10	12 30	4 45		
	Lunch		12 30	1 00			
38595	Robert K Buethe		1 00	1 45			
38874	Goodman		1 45	2 20			

Chargeable Hours ______ Non-Chargeable Hours ______ O.K. ______ Foreman.

Commission Exhibit No. 1854

COMMISSION EXHIBIT No. 1854—Continued

Page II

JAGGARS-CHILES-STOVALL, INC.
PHOTOGRAPHIC DEPARTMENT
Time Recorded in Minutes

NOTE:—All employees are required to keep an accurate record of every job worked upon. Time shown hereon MUST agree with clock register, and wages are computed accordingly. Take new sheet for overtime and have it marked "overtime" by Foreman.

Name Lee H Oswald Worked from ____ A. M. to ____ M. Date ____ 19__

JOB NO.	CUSTOMER		Kind of Work	START		STOP		Chargeable Alt.	Chargeable Comp.	Non-Chargeable
38873	Goodman			2	20	2	55			
38390	6th Church of Crist			2	55	3	35			
38779	Sam Bloom			3	35	4	15			
38836	KRLD art Dept			4	15	4	50			
38782	Draffins & Sons			4	50	5	10			
38853	Stanford			5	10	5	30	1½		

8 45'

5 25

Chargeable Hours ____ Non-Chargeable Hours ____ O.K. ____ Foreman.

Commission Exhibit No. 1854

COMMISSION EXHIBIT No. 1854—Continued

JAGGARS-CHILES-STOVALL, INC.
PHOTOGRAPHIC DEPARTMENT
Time Recorded in Minutes

NOTE:—All employees are required to keep an accurate record of every job worked upon. Time shown hereon MUST agree with clock register, and wages are computed accordingly. Take new sheet for overtime and have it marked "overtime" by Foreman.

Name Lee H Oswald Worked from 8:30 A. M. to 5:30 M. Date Feb 8 Fri 19__

JOB NO.	CUSTOMER		Kind of Work	START		STOP		Chargeable Alt.	Chargeable Comp.	Non-Chargeable
38850	Pollard			8	30	9	10			
38959	a.P.R.L			9	10	10	05			
38871	Jack T Holmes			10	05	10	35			
38691	continental adv			10	35	10	50			
38860	Balfour			10	50	11	10			
38820	Gulf Pub. Co.			11	10	11	45			
38848	Braniff advertising			11	45	12	30	4		
	Lunch			12	30	1	00			
38880 (1)	Gulf States			1	00	1	30			
38991	Malone			1	30	2	05			
38877	Lone Star Gas			2	05	2	40			
38929	Hepworth adv. co.			2	40	2	55			
38789	Aylin adv			2	55	3	20			
38723	Frigikas corp			3	20	3	45			
38898	Edward J. Robinson			3	45	4	15			
38880 (2)	Gulf State			4	15	4	50			
39024	Pollock			4	50	5	10			
38970	White Auto			5	10	5	30	4¾		

Chargeable Hours ____ 8¾ Non-Chargeable Hours ____ 510 Foreman.

Commission Exhibit No. 1854

COMMISSION EXHIBIT No. 1854—Continued

JAGGARS-CHILES-STOVALL, INC.
PHOTOGRAPHIC DEPARTMENT
Time Recorded in Minutes

NOTE:—All employees are required to keep an accurate record of every job worked upon. Time shown hereon MUST agree with clock register, and wages are computed accordingly. Take new sheet for overtime and have it marked "overtime" by Foreman.

Name Lee H Oswald Worked from 8:15 A. M. to 5:45 M. Date 2-11 mans. 19

JOB NO.	CUSTOMER		Kind of Work	START	STOP	Chargeable Alt.	Chargeable Comp.	Non-Chargeable
39222	Beldens assoc			8 15	9 10			
38575	Beddoe Printing			9 10	9 50			
38201	Don L. Baptist			9 50	10 45			
38860	Balfour			10 45	11 35			
39015	Lowe-Runkle			11 35	12 30	4 15		
	~ lunch ~			12 30	1 00			
34054	The Turner Co.			1 02	1 40			
36887	Don L. Baptist			1 40	2 15			
39289	W.Z. Temp			2 15	2 50			
37153	Norsworthy-Mercer Inc.			2 50	3 25			
38387	R & B			3 25	3 55			
39339	Goodman Paper Prod.			3 55	4 10			
39340	"			4 10	4 25			
39341	"			4 25	4 40			
39292	Sam Bloom			4 40	4 55			
39290	"			4 55	5 30			
39291	Sam Bloom 9	✓		5 30	5 45	4 45		

Chargeable Hours ____ Non-Chargeable Hours ____ O.K. ____ (540) Foreman.

COMMISSION EXHIBIT NO. 1854—Continued

Page I

JAGGARS-CHILES-STOVALL, INC.
PHOTOGRAPHIC DEPARTMENT
Time Recorded in Minutes

NOTE:—All employees are required to keep an accurate record of every job worked upon. Time shown hereon MUST agree with clock register, and wages are computed accordingly. Take new sheet for overtime and have it marked "overtime" by Foreman.

Name Lee H Oswald Worked from 8:30 A. M. to 5:45 P. M. Date Tues. 12-2 19

JOB NO.	CUSTOMER		Kind of Work	START	STOP	Chargeable Alt.	Chargeable Comp.	Non-Chargeable
39377	Sam Bloom			8 30	9 10			
37319	Eptine Cowdon			9 10	9 25			
39176	Star Engraving			9 25	9 40			
39381	Sam Bloom			9 40	9 55			
38455	S. M. U.			9 55	10 10			
39286	Electrotype Service			10 10	10 25			
39466	Peacock			10 25	10 50			
38410	R & S			10 50	11 05			
39249	Collins County			11 05	11 20			
38201	Don L. Baxter			11 20	11 40			
35261	White Auto			11 40	12 00			
39405	Peacock			12 00	12 15			
39418	Eger			12 15	12 30	4 —		
	← Lunch →			12 30	1 00			
37330	Marvin A. Kruger			1 00	1 30			
39324	Sam Bloom			1 30	2 10			
38566	AMS			2 10	2 40			

Chargeable Hours____ Non-Chargeable Hours____ O.K.____ Foreman.

Commission Exhibit No. 1854

COMMISSION EXHIBIT NO. 1854—Continued

Page II

JAGGARS-CHILES-STOVALL, INC.
PHOTOGRAPHIC DEPARTMENT
Time Recorded in Minutes

NOTE:—All employees are required to keep an accurate record of every job worked upon. Time shown hereon MUST agree with clock register, and wages are computed accordingly. Take new sheet for overtime and have it marked "overtime" by Foreman.

Name Lee H. Oswald Worked from____ A. M. to____ M. Date____ 19

JOB NO.	CUSTOMER		Kind of Work	START	STOP	Chargeable Alt.	Chargeable Comp.	Non-Chargeable
38363	International Public			2 40	3 05			
39504	Sam Bloom			3 05	3 25			
39355	Homart Devel.			3 25	3 40			
36747	West Texas Utilities			3 40	4 10			
38387	R & S			4 10	4 55			
37466	Horace Peacock			4 55	5 45	4 15'		

5 25

8 45'

Chargeable Hours____ Non-Chargeable Hours____ O.K.____ Foreman.

Commission Exhibit No. 1854

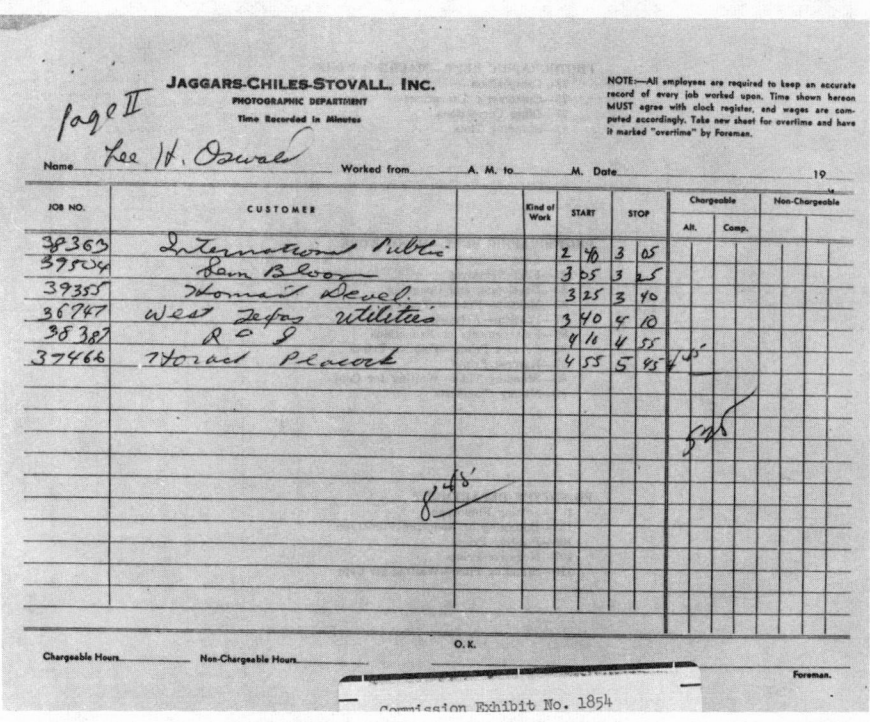

COMMISSION EXHIBIT NO. 1854—Continued

Page I

JAGGARS-CHILES-STOVALL, INC.
PHOTOGRAPHIC DEPARTMENT
Time Recorded in Minutes

NOTE:—All employees are required to keep an accurate record of every job worked upon. Time shown hereon MUST agree with clock register, and wages are computed accordingly. Take new sheet for overtime and have it marked "overtime" by Foreman.

Name Lee H. Oswald Worked from 8:00 A. M. to 5:30 M. Date Feb 13 1962

JOB NO.	CUSTOMER		Kind of Work	START		STOP		Chargeable Alt.	Chargeable Comp.	Non-Chargeable
39602	Electrolyte Service			8	00	8	15			
39424	Bud Biggs			8	15	8	40			
39401	Collin's Commercial art			8	40	9	05			
39591	Pollock Paper Co.			9	05	9	20			
39431	Jack Wyatt			9	20	9	45			
39305	World Gift			9	45	10	05			
34246	Cunningham - Coxes			10	05	10	20			
39516	Cunningham Coxes			10	20	10	40			
39488	Green Bush ale			10	40	11	00			
39609	Tracy - Locke			11	00	11	15			
39992	Riverside Press			11	15	11	35			
39645	Glenn			11	35	11	55			
39058	KRLD			11	55	12	15	4 15		
	Lunch			12	15	12	45			
39398	BBD + O			12	45	1	15			
39533	Tracy - Locke			1	15	1	50			
39214	E Farrel Morrow			1	50	2	25			

O.K.

Chargeable Hours____ Non-Chargeable Hours____ ____ Foreman.

Commission Exhibit No. 1854

COMMISSION EXHIBIT NO. 1854—Continued

Page II

JAGGARS-CHILES-STOVALL, INC.
PHOTOGRAPHIC DEPARTMENT
Time Recorded in Minutes

NOTE:—All employees are required to keep an accurate record of every job worked upon. Time shown hereon MUST agree with clock register, and wages are computed accordingly. Take new sheet for overtime and have it marked "overtime" by Foreman.

Name Lee H Oswald Worked from____ A. M. to____ M. Date____ 19__

JOB NO.	CUSTOMER		Kind of Work	START		STOP		Chargeable Alt.	Chargeable Comp.	Non-Chargeable
39708	Bel art			2	25	3	10			
39157	Creation Design			3	10	3	55			
39662	Industrial Printing			3	55	4	25			
39330	Marvin A. Krieger			4	25	4	50			
39709	W. W. Sherill			4	50	5	20	4 5		

510

8 30

O.K.

Chargeable Hours____ Non-Chargeable Hours____ ____ Foreman.

Commission Exhibit No. 1854

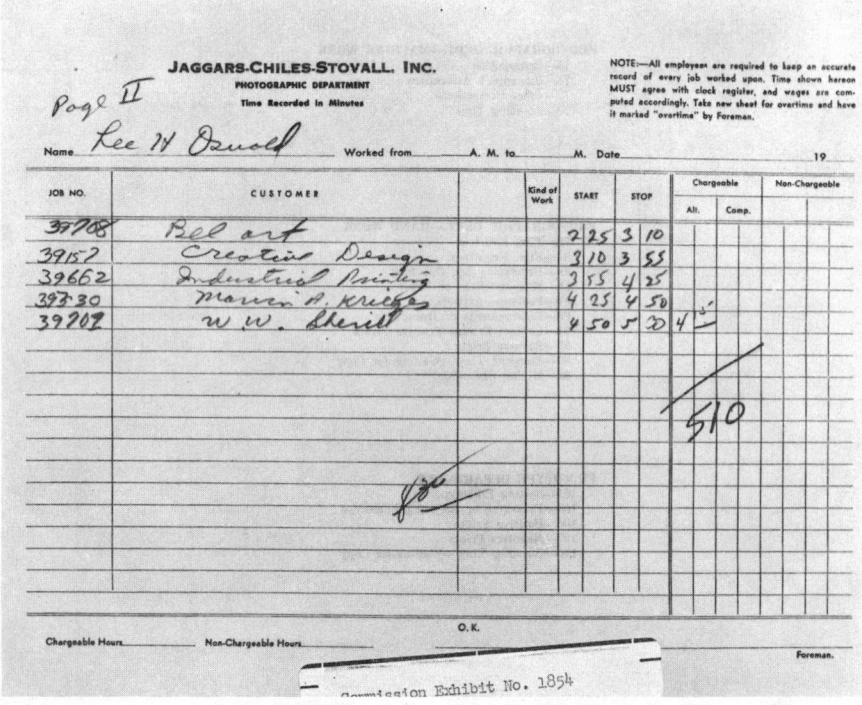

COMMISSION EXHIBIT NO. 1854—Continued

Page I

JAGGARS-CHILES-STOVALL, INC.
PHOTOGRAPHIC DEPARTMENT
Time Recorded in Minutes

NOTE:—All employees are required to keep an accurate record of every job worked upon. Time shown hereon MUST agree with clock register, and wages are computed accordingly. Take new sheet for overtime and have it marked "overtime" by Foreman.

Name Lee H Oswald Worked from 8:00 A. M. to 5:30 M. Date Dec. Feb 14 1963

JOB NO.	CUSTOMER		Kind of Work	START		STOP		Chargeable Alt.	Chargeable Comp.	Non-Chargeable
39455	Republic Natl Bank			8	00	8	15			
39429	Baller + Grey			8	15	8	35			
39795	Sam Bloom			8	35	9	10			
39657	American Beauty			9	10	9	45			
38704	Sam Bloom			9	45	10	10			
39741	Sam Bloom			10	10	10	25			
39033	Seleaddo			10	25	10	50			
39676	Platemakers Inc			10	50	11	10			
39808	K & J			11	10	11	30			
38410	Rogers + Smith			11	30	11	45			
39992	Pinnacle Press			11	45	12	00			
38592	Safeway			12	00	12	15			
38396	C & W			12	15	12	30	4¾		
	Lunch			12	30	1	00			
39836	Graphic Ill			1	00	1	20			
39871	R.K. Bittles			1	20	1	40			
39495	Steplon Kromes			1	40	2	15			

Chargeable Hours________ Non-Chargeable Hours________ O.K.________ Foreman.

COMMISSION EXHIBIT No. 1854—Continued

Page II

JAGGARS-CHILES-STOVALL, INC.
PHOTOGRAPHIC DEPARTMENT
Time Recorded in Minutes

NOTE:—All employees are required to keep an accurate record of every job worked upon. Time shown hereon MUST agree with clock register, and wages are computed accordingly. Take new sheet for overtime and have it marked "overtime" by Foreman.

Name Lee H Oswald Worked from ______ A. M. to ______ M. Date ______ 19__

JOB NO.	CUSTOMER		Kind of Work	START		STOP		Chargeable Alt.	Chargeable Comp.	Non-Chargeable
39639	Pollock			2	15	2	40			
39016	Union Life Insurance			2	40	3	05			
39828	S M Brooks			3	05	3	20			
39483	Stefan Kramer			3	20	3	40			
39884	AMS			3	40	3	55			
39474	Paymaster			3	55	4	10			
39263	Collins Commissary			4	10	4	30			
39999	Goodman			4	30	4	50			
39985	Gooden Paper Co.			4	50	5	30	4¾		

9—

540

Chargeable Hours________ Non-Chargeable Hours________ O.K.________ Foreman.

Commission Exhibit No. 1854

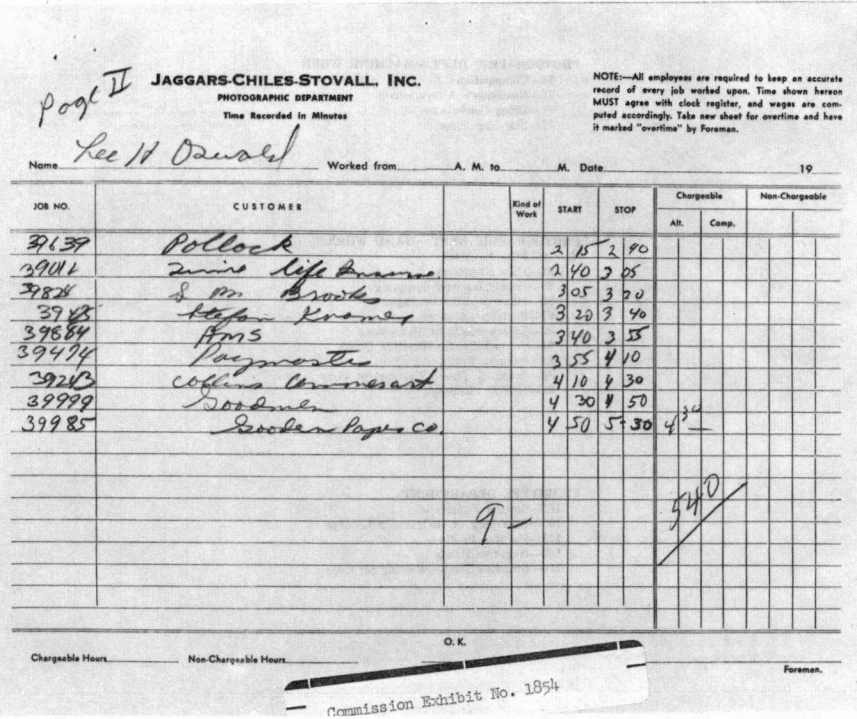

COMMISSION EXHIBIT No. 1854—Continued

JAGGARS-CHILES-STOVALL, INC.
PHOTOGRAPHIC DEPARTMENT
Time Recorded in Minutes

Page I

NOTE:—All employees are required to keep an accurate record of every job worked upon. Time shown hereon MUST agree with clock register, and wages are computed accordingly. Take new sheet for overtime and have it marked "overtime" by Foreman.

Name Lee H. Oswald Worked from 8:00 A. M. to 5:15 M. Date Friday Feb 15 1963

JOB NO.	CUSTOMER		Kind of Work	START	STOP	Chargeable Alt.	Chargeable Comp.	Non-Chargeable
40029	Petroleum Engineers			8 00	8 40			
40011	Norsworthy - Mercer			8 40	9 10			
40026	Snack - Lock			9 10	9 30			
39746	Sam Bloom			9 30	9 50			
40039	Mary E. Kerr			9 50	10 05			
40011	King			10 05	10 20			
39955	Jordon			10 20	10 40			
37153	Norsworthy - Mercer Ins			10 40	10 55			
39808	R & S			10 55	11 10			
39331	Continental Adv			11 10	11 35			
39947	Sam Bloom			11 35	12 05			
39822	Stofan Krones			12 05	12 30	4½		
				12:30	1:00			
38410	Robert Smith			1 00	1 15			
39882	R. K. Bulske			1 15	1 45			
39925	Norsworthy - Mercer			1 45	2 00			
39744	Sam Bloom			2 00	2 25			

Chargeable Hours ____ Non-Chargeable Hours ____ O.K. ____ Foreman.

COMMISSION EXHIBIT NO. 1854—Continued

JAGGARS-CHILES-STOVALL, INC.
PHOTOGRAPHIC DEPARTMENT
Time Recorded in Minutes

Page II

NOTE:—All employees are required to keep an accurate record of every job worked upon. Time shown hereon MUST agree with clock register, and wages are computed accordingly. Take new sheet for overtime and have it marked "overtime" by Foreman.

Name Lee H. Oswald Worked from ____ A. M. to ____ M. Date ____ 19__

JOB NO.	CUSTOMER		Kind of Work	START	STOP	Chargeable Alt.	Chargeable Comp.	Non-Chargeable
39883	Bill Collins Advertising			2 25	2 55			
38410	R & S			2 55	3 30			
39892	Walter H. Allen			3 30	3 55			
40130	Floyd Patterson			3 55	4 15			
40113	Industrial Prints			4 15	4 30			
40091	Dallas Chamber of Commerce			4 30	4 45			
39984	Goodman Paper Co.			4 45	5 15	4½		
						5¾		

8¾

Chargeable Hours ____ Non-Chargeable Hours ____ O.K. ____ Foreman.

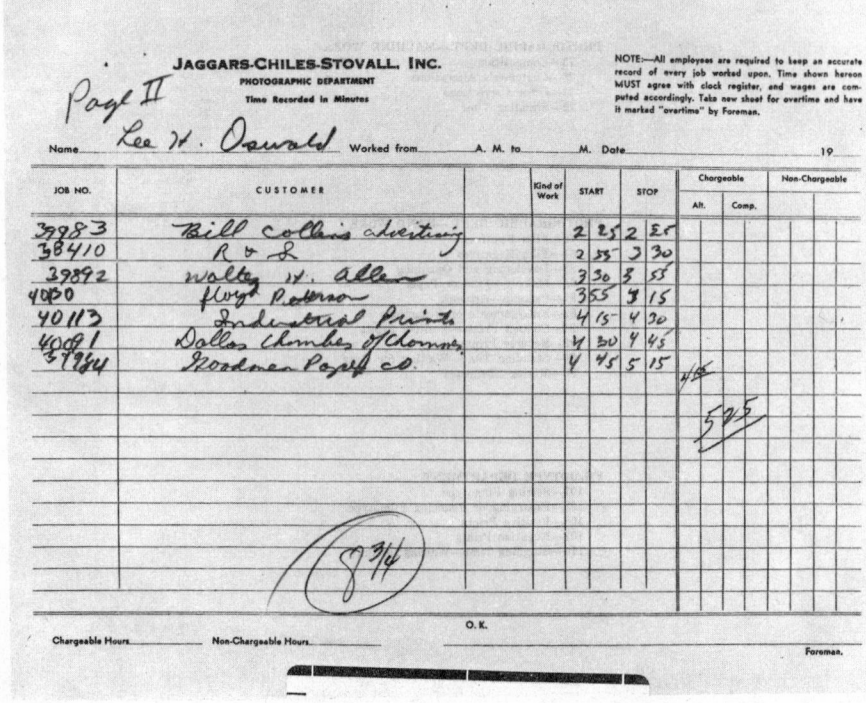

COMMISSION EXHIBIT NO. 1854—Continued

Page I

JAGGARS-CHILES-STOVALL, INC.
PHOTOGRAPHIC DEPARTMENT
Time Recorded in Minutes

NOTE:—All employees are required to keep an accurate record of every job worked upon. Time shown hereon MUST agree with clock register, and wages are computed accordingly. Take new sheet for overtime and have it marked "overtime" by Foreman.

Name Lee H. Oswald Worked from 9:00 A. M. to 5:30 M. Date Oct 16 Sat. 1963

JOB NO.	CUSTOMER		Kind of Work	START		STOP		Chargeable Alt.	Chargeable Comp.	Non-Chargeable
40179	Tracy - Locke			9	00	9	20			
40188	Lone Star Gas			9	20	9	45			
40134	R & S			9	45	10	05			
28970	Rogers & Smith			10	05	10	25			
39277	Hal Lindgren			10	25	10	50			
40154	Texas Envelope Co			10	50	11	20			
39882	Robert K Butcher			11	20	11	45			
39763	Sam Bloom			11	45	12	30	3¾		
	Lunch			12	30	1	00			
40218	Gulf States			1	00	1	30			
37858	Don L. Baxter			1	30	1	55			
39763	Sam Bloom			1	55	2	25			
40259	Industrial Rammy			2	25	3	05			
37237	Glenrado			3	05	3	45			
40238	Ernest L. Mentz			3	45	4	20			
40074	Campbell mfg.			4	20	4	40			
40242	Mithoff			4	40	4	55			

(cont.)

O. K.

Chargeable Hours______ Non-Chargeable Hours______ Foreman.

Commission Exhibit No. 1854

COMMISSION EXHIBIT No. 1854—Continued

Page II

JAGGARS-CHILES-STOVALL, INC.
PHOTOGRAPHIC DEPARTMENT
Time Recorded in Minutes

NOTE:—All employees are required to keep an accurate record of every job worked upon. Time shown hereon MUST agree with clock register, and wages are computed accordingly. Take new sheet for overtime and have it marked "overtime" by Foreman.

Name Lee H. Oswald Worked from 9:00 A. M. to 5:30 M. Date 19

JOB NO.	CUSTOMER		Kind of Work	START		STOP		Chargeable Alt.	Chargeable Comp.	Non-Chargeable
40036	Alabama Engraving			4	55	5	10			
38363	International Public			5	10	5	30	4½		

480

8

O. K.

Chargeable Hours______ Non-Chargeable Hours______ Foreman.

Commission Exhibit No. 1854

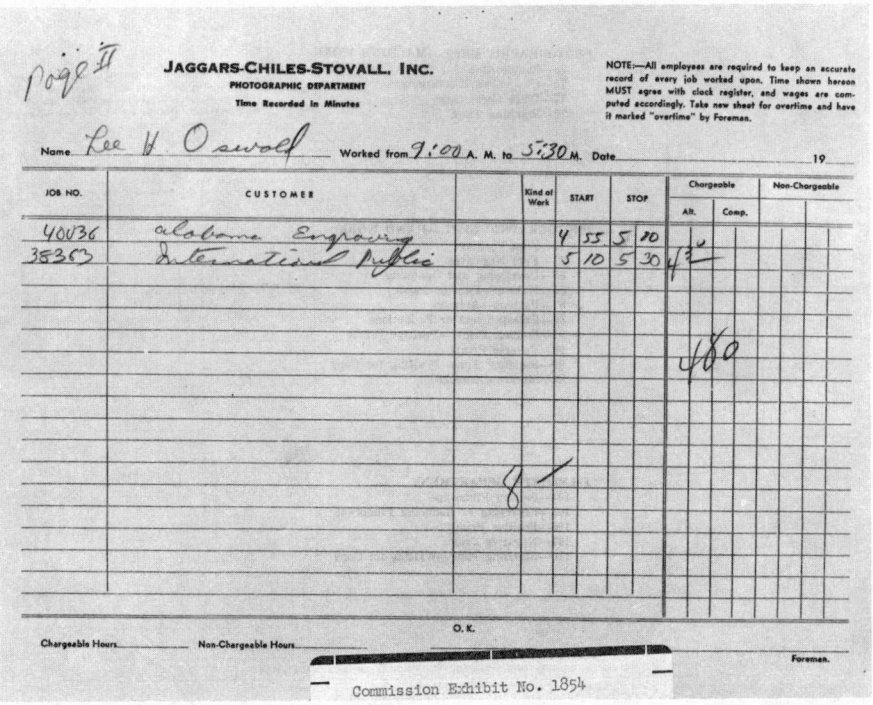

COMMISSION EXHIBIT No. 1854—Continued

JAGGARS-CHILES-STOVALL, INC.
PHOTOGRAPHIC DEPARTMENT
Time Recorded in Minutes

NOTE:—All employees are required to keep an accurate record of every job worked upon. Time shown hereon MUST agree with clock register, and wages are computed accordingly. Take new sheet for overtime and have it marked "overtime" by Foreman.

Name Lee H. Oswald Worked from 8:00 A. M. to 5:30 M. Date Feb 18 mon 1963

JOB NO.	CUSTOMER		Kind of Work	START		STOP		Chargeable Alt.	Chargeable Comp.	Non-Chargeable
40197	Glenn adver.			8	00	8	20			
40269	Industrial Printing			8	20	8	35			
40248	Auld adver.			8	35	9	10			
40205	Troy Locke			9	10	9	50			
40217	(1) Gulf State util			9	50	10	10			
40245	Bobkent aud.			10	10	10	30			
40206	Mission Power co			10	30	10	55			
31887	Don L. Baxter			10	55	11	15			
38363	Inter. Public Relat			11	15	11	45			
40288	(1) R.K. Butcher + assoc.			11	45	12	30	4 30		
	Lunch			12	30	1	00			
40217	(2) Gulf State			1	00	1	30			
38410	R + S			1	30	2	30			
40244	Godwin adver			2	30	3	25			
40288	(2) K.K. Butcher			3	25	4	20			
39292	Sam Bloom			4	20	5	10	4 30.		
40362	Troy Lock			5	10	5	30			

Chargeable Hours ______ Non-Chargeable Hours ______ 9 O.K. ______ Foremen.

Commission Exhibit No. 18...

COMMISSION EXHIBIT NO. 1854—Continued

pay 1

JAGGARS-CHILES-STOVALL, INC.
PHOTOGRAPHIC DEPARTMENT
Time Recorded in Minutes

NOTE:—All employees are required to keep an accurate record of every job worked upon. Time shown hereon MUST agree with clock register, and wages are computed accordingly. Take new sheet for overtime and have it marked "overtime" by Foreman.

Name Lee H Oswald Worked from 8:00 A. M. to 5:30 M. Date Feb 19 Tues 1963

JOB NO.	CUSTOMER		Kind of Work	START		STOP		Chargeable Alt.	Chargeable Comp.	Non-Chargeable
40216	R.K. Butcher			8	00	8	20			
40086	Glenn			8	20	8	45			
40126	(1) Gulf State utilities			8	45	9	30			
39763	Sam Bloom			9	30	10	20			
39759	Tom Greives			10	20	11	05			
40417	T P + L			11	05	11	30			
40349	King Jewelers			11	30	11	50			
40475	Glenn adv			11	50	12	15	4 15'		
	and lunch co			12	15	12	45			
40126	(2) Gulf State			12	45	1	15			
40274	Continental Corp			1	15	1	35			
40018	Sam Bloom			1	35	1	50			
40361	Purnell & Case			1	50	2	10			
34242	Sam Bloom			2	10	2	35			
40487	Arkie W. Gas Co.			2	35	2	55			
37984	Pittluck ads.			2	55	3	10			
40529	BBD + O			3	10	3	35			

Chargeable Hours ______ Non-Chargeable Hours ______ O.K. ______ Foremen.

Commission Exhibit No. 1854

COMMISSION EXHIBIT NO. 1854—Continued

Page II

JAGGARS-CHILES-STOVALL, INC.
PHOTOGRAPHIC DEPARTMENT
Time Recorded in Minutes

NOTE:—All employees are required to keep an accurate record of every job worked upon. Time shown hereon MUST agree with clock register, and wages are computed accordingly. Take new sheet for overtime and have it marked "overtime" by Foreman.

Name Lee H Oswald Worked from ______ A. M. to ______ M. Date ______ 19__

JOB NO.	CUSTOMER		Kind of Work	START		STOP		Chargeable Alt.	Chargeable Comp.	Non-Chargeable
40545	W. K. Bredlow			3	35	3	50			
40288	Robert R. Butches			3	50	4	15			
36621	R & S			4	15	4	40			
40526	BBD&O			4	40	5	30	4 45		

5 40

9

Chargeable Hours ______ Non-Chargeable Hours ______ O.K. ______ Foreman.

Commission Exhibit No. 1854

COMMISSION EXHIBIT No. 1854—Continued

Page I

JAGGARS-CHILES-STOVALL, INC.
PHOTOGRAPHIC DEPARTMENT
Time Recorded in Minutes

NOTE:—All employees are required to keep an accurate record of every job worked upon. Time shown hereon MUST agree with clock register, and wages are computed accordingly. Take new sheet for overtime and have it marked "overtime" by Foreman.

Name Lee H Oswald Worked from 8:15 A. M. to 6:30 M. Date Wed April 20 1963

JOB NO.	CUSTOMER		Kind of Work	START		STOP		Chargeable Alt.	Chargeable Comp.	Non-Chargeable
40541	Oak Cliff Typesetting			8	15	9	10			
40545	Bredlow Adv			9	10	9	58			
40497	Pollock			9	50	10	10			
37984	Pitluk adv			10	10	10	35			
39892	W.H. Allen			10	35	11	05			
40276	Pugnacle Mills			11	05	11	30			
40728	Container Corp.			11	30	12	05			
40376	Sam Bloom			12	05	12	30	4 15		
	Lunch			12	30	1	00			
40673	Glenn advs			1	00	1	30			
40676	BBD&O			1	30	2	00			
40728	Container			2	00	2	40			
39291	Sam Bloom			2	40	3	05			
40585	J.C.S.			3	05	3	25			
40576	Stanford ads			3	25	4	15			
40656	Hal Mayes ads			4	15	4	35			
40638	Auld			4	35	5	10			
				(con.)						

Chargeable Hours ______ Non-Chargeable Hours ______ O.K. ______ Foreman.

Commission Exhibit No. 1854

COMMISSION EXHIBIT No. 1854—Continued

Page II

JAGGARS-CHILES-STOVALL, INC.
PHOTOGRAPHIC DEPARTMENT
Time Recorded in Minutes

NOTE:—All employees are required to keep an accurate record of every job worked upon. Time shown hereon MUST agree with clock register, and wages are computed accordingly. Take new sheet for overtime and have it marked "overtime" by Foreman.

Name Lee H. Oswald Worked from ______ A. M. to ______ M. Date ______ 19__

JOB NO.	CUSTOMER		Kind of Work	START		STOP		Chargeable Alt.	Chargeable Comp.	Non-Chargeable
40536	Pollock Razor			5	10	5	35			
40768	Container Corp			5	25	5	40			
40766	Sam Bloom			5	40	6	05			
40641	ad P.R.			6	05	6	30	5 3/4		

585

945

Chargeable Hours ______ Non-Chargeable Hours ______ O.K. ______ Foreman.

Commission Exhibit No. 1854

COMMISSION EXHIBIT NO. 1854—Continued

Page I

JAGGARS-CHILES-STOVALL, INC.
PHOTOGRAPHIC DEPARTMENT
Time Recorded in Minutes

NOTE:—All employees are required to keep an accurate record of every job worked upon. Time shown hereon MUST agree with clock register, and wages are computed accordingly. Take new sheet for overtime and have it marked "overtime" by Foreman.

Name Lee H Oswald Worked from 8:00 A. M. to 5:45 M. Date Feb 21 Thur. 1963

JOB NO.	CUSTOMER		Kind of Work	START		STOP		Chargeable Alt.	Chargeable Comp.	Non-Chargeable
40216	Robert K Butcher			8	00	8	15			
40199	Bob Knight			8	15	8	30			
40735	Arms			8	30	8	55			
40603	Continental ads			8	55	9	10			
40858	Cleveland Herman			9	10	9	45			
41614	D P & L			9	45	10	05			
40638	auld ad			10	05	10	20			
40851	Norsworthy-Mercer			10	20	10	40			
40838	Lone Star Gas			10	40	11	00			
38410	R & S			11	00	11	30			
40790	Braniff ads			11	30	11	45			
40849	Zoby-Rock			11	45	12	00			
40207	Ratcliff shoes			12	00	12	15	4 15		
	~~Robert~~			12	15	12	45			
40199	Signal magazine			12	45	1	05			
40903	Republic National			1	5	1	30			
40484	Arkla Gas			1	30	1	50			

Chargeable Hours ______ Non-Chargeable Hours ______ O.K. ______ Foreman.

Commission Exhibit No. 1854

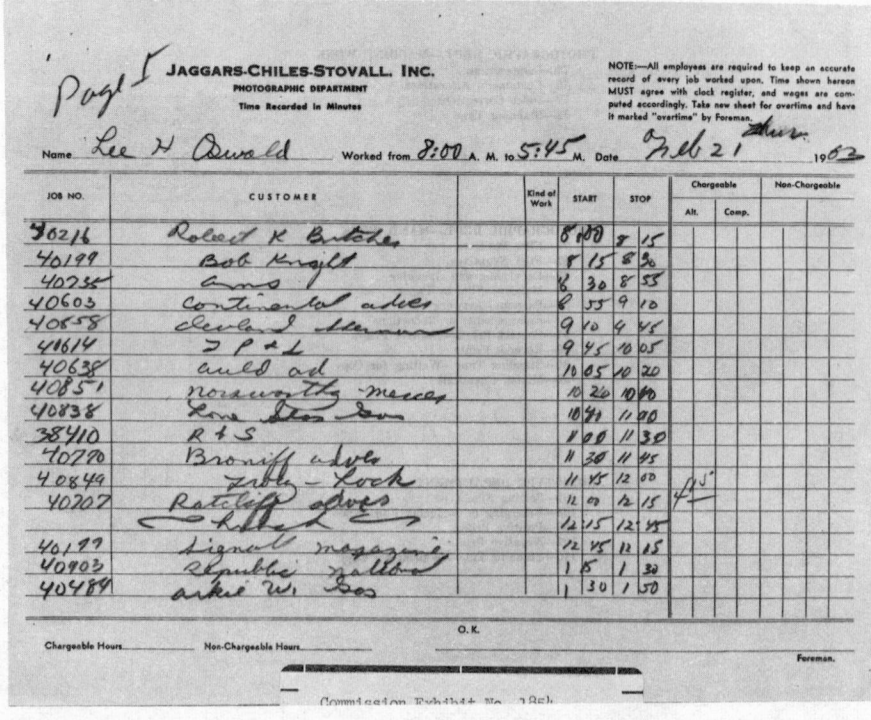

COMMISSION EXHIBIT NO. 1854—Continued

Page II

JAGGARS-CHILES-STOVALL, INC.
PHOTOGRAPHIC DEPARTMENT
Time Recorded in Minutes

NOTE:—All employees are required to keep an accurate record of every job worked upon. Time shown hereon MUST agree with clock register, and wages are computed accordingly. Take new sheet for overtime and have it marked "overtime" by Foreman.

Name Lee H. Oswald Worked from ______ A. M. to ______ M. Date ______ 19__

JOB NO.	CUSTOMER	Kind of Work	START	STOP	Chargeable Alt.	Chargeable Comp.	Non-Chargeable
40870	DMG		1 50	2 10			
40293	Curtis		2 10	2 25			
40829	d'Arcy		2 25	2 40			
40940	Glenn		2 40	2 55			
40925	Tom Grume		2 55	3 10			
40429	D'Arcy		3 10	3 35			
40889	White auto		3 35	3 55			
40585	ad P.R.		3 55	4 10			
40900	White auto		4 10	4 35			
40653	Johnson Printing		4 35	4 55			
40840	Wilkins		4 55	5 20			
40668	Union Bankers Life		5 20	5 45	5—		

915'

555

Chargeable Hours ______ Non-Chargeable Hours ______ O. K. ______ Foreman.

Commission Exhibit No. 1854

COMMISSION EXHIBIT No. 1854—Continued

Page I

JAGGARS-CHILES-STOVALL, INC.
PHOTOGRAPHIC DEPARTMENT
Time Recorded in Minutes

NOTE:—All employees are required to keep an accurate record of every job worked upon. Time shown hereon MUST agree with clock register, and wages are computed accordingly. Take new sheet for overtime and have it marked "overtime" by Foreman.

Name Lee H. Oswald Worked from 8:15 A. M. to 5:30 P.M. Date Feb 22 19[illegible]

JOB NO.	CUSTOMER	Kind of Work	START	STOP	Chargeable Alt.	Chargeable Comp.	Non-Chargeable
40970	Oak Cliff Type.		8 15	9 10			
41007	Ayres Compton		9 10	9 50			
41045	Al Barnes		9 50	10 40			
40976	Lone Star Gas		10 40	11 00			
41064	Glenn adv		11 00	11 20			
40474	North Jewels		11 20	11 50			
40344	Braniff		11 50	12 10			
41159	Goodman Paper Co.		12 10	12 30			
40948	Glenn adv		12 30	12 45	4 3/4		
	Lunch		12 45	1 15			
40728	containers		1 15	1 40			
40561	Tom Grimes		1 40	2 05			
40845	Tracy-Locke		2 05	2 35			
41168	R. B. Moreland		2 35	2 55			
41104	Godwin		2 55	3 20			
41054	Ad Recorder		3 20	3 45			
40993	Molesworthy-Mercer		3 45	4 10			

Chargeable Hours ______ Non-Chargeable Hours ______ O. K. ______ Foreman.

Commission Exhibit No. 1854

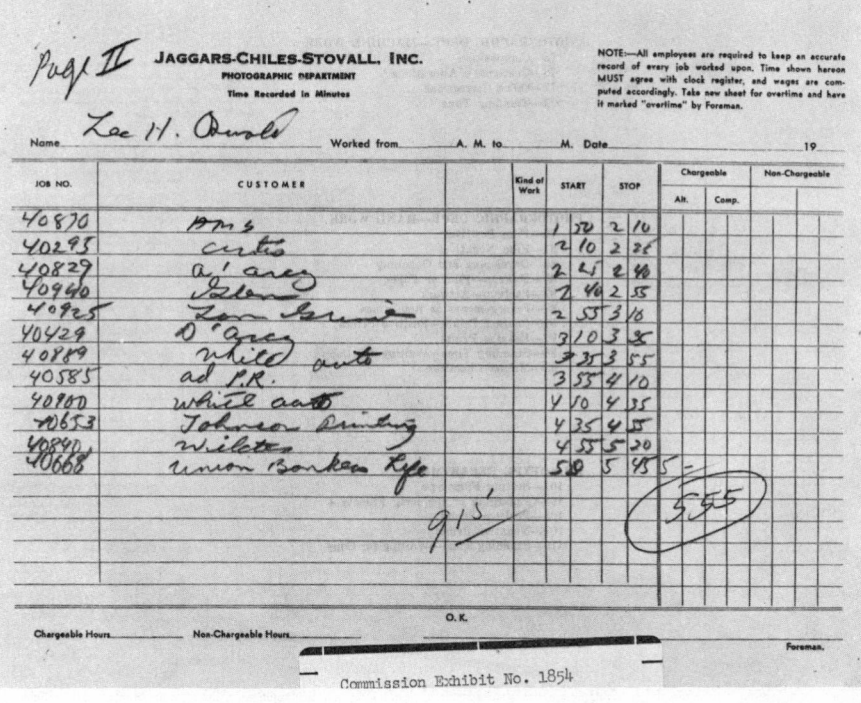

COMMISSION EXHIBIT No. 1854—Continued

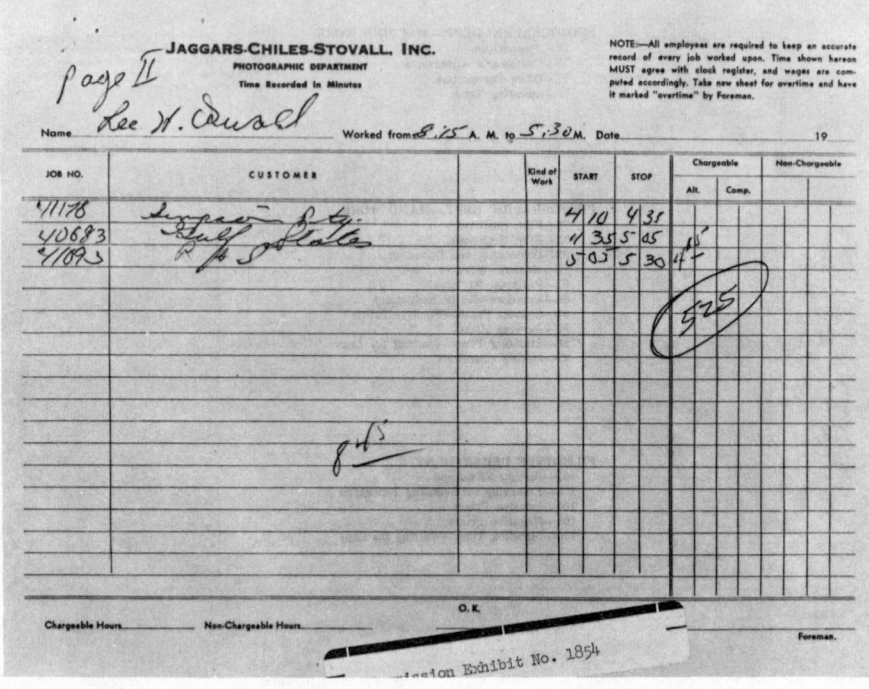

JAGGARS-CHILES-STOVALL, INC.
PHOTOGRAPHIC DEPARTMENT
Time Recorded in Minutes

NOTE:—All employees are required to keep an accurate record of every job worked upon. Time shown hereon MUST agree with clock register, and wages are computed accordingly. Take new sheet for overtime and have it marked "overtime" by Foreman.

page II

Name Lee H. Oswald Worked from 8:15 A. M. to 5:30 M. Date ______ 19__

JOB NO.	CUSTOMER	Kind of Work	START	STOP	Chargeable Alt.	Chargeable Comp.	Non-Chargeable
41178	Simpson Pty.		4 10	4 35			
40683	Gulf States		4 35	5 05	4 15		
41893	R & S		5 05	5 30			

525

8 45

Chargeable Hours______ Non-Chargeable Hours______ O. K. ______ Foreman.

Commission Exhibit No. 1854

COMMISSION EXHIBIT NO. 1854—Continued

JAGGARS-CHILES-STOVALL, INC.
PHOTOGRAPHIC DEPARTMENT
Time Recorded in Minutes

NOTE:—All employees are required to keep an accurate record of every job worked upon. Time shown hereon MUST agree with clock register, and wages are computed accordingly. Take new sheet for overtime and have it marked "overtime" by Foreman.

Name Lee H. Oswald Worked from 8:00 A. M. to 6:00 M. Date Feb 25 1963

JOB NO.	CUSTOMER	Kind of Work	START	STOP	Chargeable Alt.	Chargeable Comp.	Non-Chargeable
41247	Dixon Rock		8 00	8 45			
41306	Excel Sign Co.		8 45	9 20			
41073	Crook adv.		9 20	10 05			
41147	(1) Walter H. Allen		10 05	10 40			
40683	Gulf State		10 40	11 10			
41330	W. R. Hayes		11 10	11 35			
40770	Braniff		11 35	12 15	4 15		
	~ Little "		12 15	12 45			
40561	Tom Jennie		12 45	1 15			
41331	Fuller Smith & Ross		1 15	2 55			
41421	Farmer Flachman		2 55	3 50			
41381	C.F. Riley		3 50	4 10			
41333	arcade Lithography		4 10	5 00			
4147	(2) Walter H. Allen		5 00	6 00	5 15		

9 30

570

Chargeable Hours______ Non-Chargeable Hours______ O. K. ______ Foreman.

Commission Exhibit No. 1854

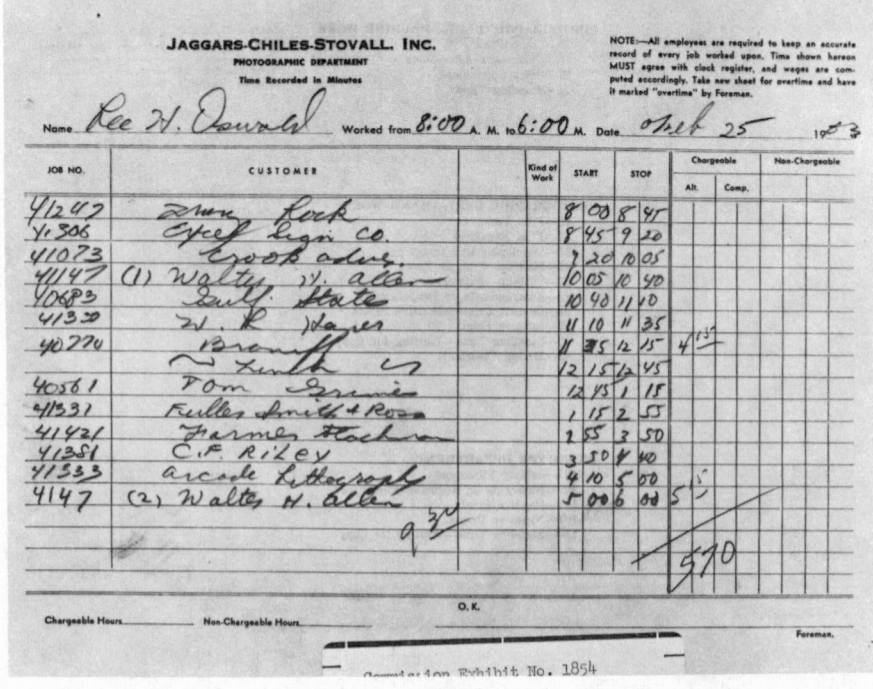

COMMISSION EXHIBIT NO. 1854—Continued

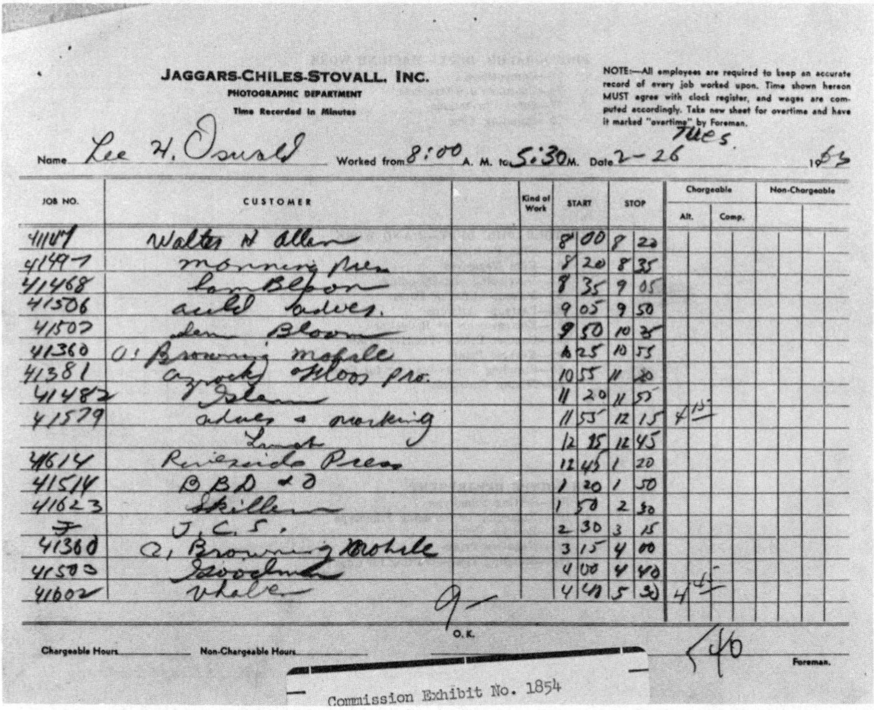

JAGGARS-CHILES-STOVALL, INC.
PHOTOGRAPHIC DEPARTMENT
Time Recorded in Minutes

NOTE:—All employees are required to keep an accurate record of every job worked upon. Time shown hereon MUST agree with clock register, and wages are computed accordingly. Take new sheet for overtime and have it marked "overtime" by Foreman.

Name Lee H. Oswald Worked from 8:00 A. M. to 5:30 M. Date Tues. 2-26 1963

JOB NO.	CUSTOMER		Kind of Work	START		STOP		Chargeable Alt.	Chargeable Comp.	Non-Chargeable
41147	Walter H Allen			8	00	8	20			
41497	morning news			8	20	8	35			
41468	Sam Bloom			8	35	9	05			
41506	auld adves.			9	05	9	50			
41507	Sam Bloom			9	50	10	25			
41360	A. Browning Mobile			10	25	10	55			
41381	Azrock Floor Pro.			10	55	11	20			
41482	Islam			11	20	11	55			
41579	adves & marking			11	55	12	15	4 15		
	Lunch			12	15	12	45			
41614	Riverside Press			12	45	1	20			
41514	BBD&O			1	20	1	50			
41623	Skillern			1	50	2	30			
J	J. C. S.			2	30	3	15			
41380	A. Browning Mobile			3	15	4	00			
41503	Goodman			4	00	4	40			
41602	Whalen			4	40	5	30	4 15		

Chargeable Hours ______ Non-Chargeable Hours ______ 9 O.K. 5 40 Foreman.

Commission Exhibit No. 1854

COMMISSION EXHIBIT No. 1854—Continued

JAGGARS-CHILES-STOVALL, INC.
PHOTOGRAPHIC DEPARTMENT
Time Recorded in Minutes

NOTE:—All employees are required to keep an accurate record of every job worked upon. Time shown hereon MUST agree with clock register, and wages are computed accordingly. Take new sheet for overtime and have it marked "overtime" by Foreman.

Name Lee H Oswald Worked from 8:10 A. M. to 5:40 M. Date Wed. Feb 27 1963

JOB NO.	CUSTOMER		Kind of Work	START		STOP		Chargeable Alt.	Chargeable Comp.	Non-Chargeable
41700	Hal Lindgren			8	10	9	25			
41648	Goodman Apes			9	15	9	50			
41618	OAK Cliff Typography			9	50	10	25			
41619	Oak Cliff Typography			10	25	10	45			
41783	Bloom			10	45	11	20			
41767	Zemco			11	20	11	50			
41702	Containers Corp.			11	50	12	30	4 30		
	Lunch			12	30	1	00			
41729	Bridgman ext			1	00	1	30			
41652	T P & L			1	30	2	00			
41700	Hal Lindgren			2	00	2	45			
41177	T L			2	45	3	15			
41561	Henry Shields			3	15	4	00			
41625	BBD&O			4	00	4	25			
41826	Hepworth			4	25	4	55			
41725	Electrotype Service			4	55	5	15			
41297	Jamison Film			5	15	5	40	4 15		

Chargeable Hours ______ Non-Chargeable Hours ______ 9 O.K. 5 40 Foreman.

COMMISSION EXHIBIT No. 1854—Continued

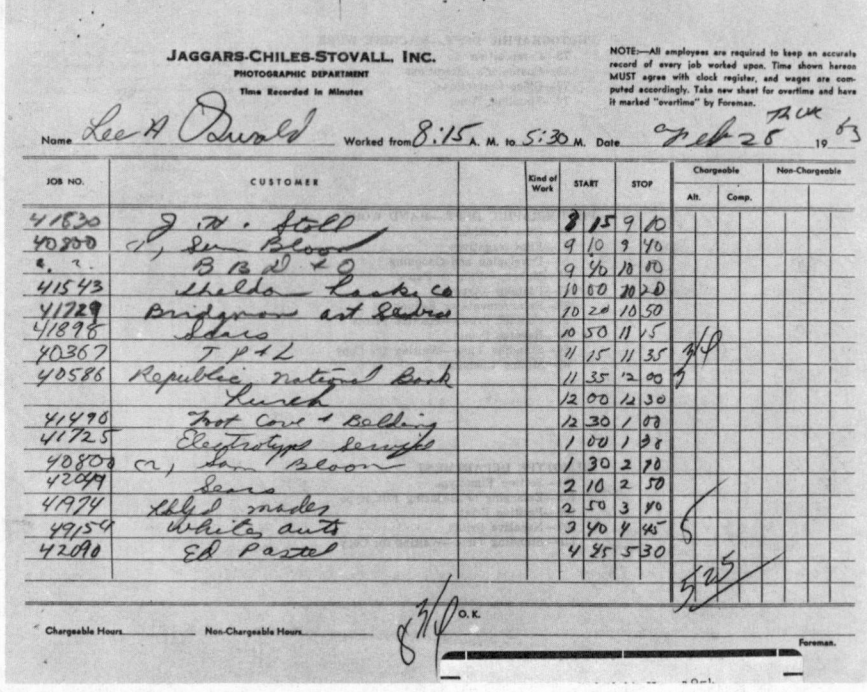

JAGGARS-CHILES-STOVALL, INC.
PHOTOGRAPHIC DEPARTMENT
Time Recorded in Minutes

NOTE:—All employees are required to keep an accurate record of every job worked upon. Time shown hereon MUST agree with clock register, and wages are computed accordingly. Take new sheet for overtime and have it marked "overtime" by Foreman.

Name Lee H Oswald Worked from 8:15 A. M. to 5:30 M. Date Feb 28 Thur 19 63

JOB NO.	CUSTOMER		Kind of Work	START		STOP		Chargeable Alt.	Chargeable Comp.	Non-Chargeable
41830	J. H. Stoll			8	15	9	10			
40800	(1) Sam Bloom			9	10	9	40			
c. 2.	B B D + O			9	40	10	00			
41543	Sheldon Leaks Co			10	00	10	20			
41729	Bridgman art Studio			10	20	10	50			
41898	Sears			10	50	11	15			
40367	T P + L			11	15	11	35	3/4		
40586	Republic National Bank			11	35	12	00			
	Lunch			12	00	12	30			
41490	Foot Cone + Belding			12	30	1	00			
41725	Electrotype Service			1	00	1	30			
40800	(2) Sam Bloom			1	30	2	10			
42049	Sears			2	10	2	50			
41974	Lloyd Mader			2	50	3	40			
49154	Whites auto			3	40	4	45	5		
42090	Ed Pastel			4	45	5	30			
								5 1/4		

Chargeable Hours ______ Non-Chargeable Hours ______ 8 3/4 O.K.

Foreman.

COMMISSION EXHIBIT No. 1854—Continued

Page I

JAGGARS-CHILES-STOVALL, INC.
PHOTOGRAPHIC DEPARTMENT
Time Recorded in Minutes

NOTE:—All employees are required to keep an accurate record of every job worked upon. Time shown hereon MUST agree with clock register, and wages are computed accordingly. Take new sheet for overtime and have it marked "overtime" by Foreman.

Name Lee H. Oswald Worked from 8:00 A. M. to 5:30 M. Date March 1 1963

JOB NO.	CUSTOMER	Kind of Work	START	STOP	Chargeable Alt.	Chargeable Comp.	Non-Chargeable
42033	Al Barnes		8 00	8 20			
42028	Continental Eng		8 20	8 40			
41939	General		8 40	9 05			
41991	Affiliated Food		9 05	9 30			
41677	Story Locke		9 30	10 15			
42100	ad PR		10 15	11 05			
42103	Bud Briggs		11 05	11 40			
42179	Middaugh		11 40	12 15	4 15		
	Lunch		12 15	12 45			
41965	B B D & O		12 45	1 15			
40490	T.C.S.		1 15	2 00			
42214	Rogers & Smith		2 00	2 25			
41842	Shelby Smith & Ross		2 25	3 10			
12224	Rose Stos Bros		3 00	3 40			
41908	Norsworthy-Mercer		3 40	4 00			
?	Hal Ringrat		4 00	4 20			
42030	Cameron & Newman		4 20	4 40			
			(con.)				

Chargeable Hours ________ Non-Chargeable Hours ________ O.K. ________ Foreman.

Commission Exhibit No. 1855

COMMISSION EXHIBIT NO. 1855

Page II

JAGGARS-CHILES-STOVALL, INC.
PHOTOGRAPHIC DEPARTMENT
Time Recorded in Minutes

NOTE:—All employees are required to keep an accurate record of every job worked upon. Time shown hereon MUST agree with clock register, and wages are computed accordingly. Take new sheet for overtime and have it marked "overtime" by Foreman.

Name Lee H. Oswald Worked from ________ A. M. to ________ M. Date ________ 19__

JOB NO.	CUSTOMER	Kind of Work	START	STOP	Chargeable Alt.	Chargeable Comp.	Non-Chargeable
40416	T C S		4 40	5 30	4 40		

5 40

9—

Chargeable Hours ________ Non-Chargeable Hours ________ O.K. ________ Foreman.

Commission Exhibit No. 1855

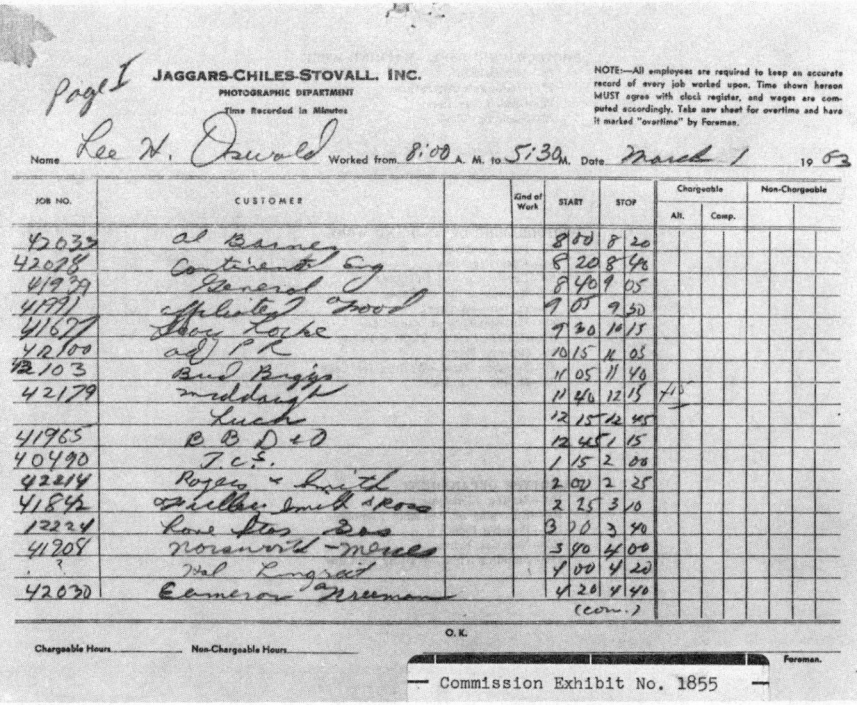

COMMISSION EXHIBIT NO. 1855—Continued

JAGGARS-CHILES-STOVALL, INC.
PHOTOGRAPHIC DEPARTMENT
Time Recorded in Minutes

NOTE:—All employees are required to keep an accurate record of every job worked upon. Time shown hereon MUST agree with clock register, and wages are computed accordingly. Take new sheet for overtime and have it marked "overtime" by Foreman.

Name Lee H. Oswald Worked from 8:00 A. M. to 5:30 M. Date Monday March 4 1963

JOB NO.	CUSTOMER	Kind of Work	START	STOP	Chargeable Alt.	Chargeable Comp.	Non-Chargeable
42161	Gulf States util		8 00	8 15			
41939	General Electric		8 15	9 00			
40800	Sam Bloom		9 00	9 50			
42296	Branifforder		9 50	10 45			
42407	the County of Dallas		10 45	11 30			
4220	R & S		11 30	11 55			
42324	Wilson Engraving		11 55	12 30	4		
	Lunch		12 30	1 00			
42138	Glenn		1 00	1 30			
42245	R & S		1 30	2 15			
42437	Sears & Roebuck		2 15	3 05			
41493	W. Texas util.		3 05	3 35			
42368	Ready to Print		3 35	3 50			
42308	Tietche		3 50	4 20			
42200	Tom Jones		4 20	4 50			
42480	Mc allister Berke		4 50	5 30	4		

9 540

Chargeable Hours ______ Non-Chargeable Hours ______ O.K. ______ Foreman.

Commission Exhibit No. 1855

COMMISSION EXHIBIT No. 1855—Continued

JAGGARS-CHILES-STOVALL, INC.
PHOTOGRAPHIC DEPARTMENT
Time Recorded in Minutes

NOTE:—All employees are required to keep an accurate record of every job worked upon. Time shown hereon MUST agree with clock register, and wages are computed accordingly. Take new sheet for overtime and have it marked "overtime" by Foreman.

Name Lee H. Oswald Worked from 8:00 A. M. to 5:30 M. Date March 5 1963

JOB NO.	CUSTOMER	Kind of Work	START	STOP	Chargeable Alt.	Chargeable Comp.	Non-Chargeable
42540	multi-Paper Products		8:00	9 00			
42200	Tom Frazer		9 00	9 40			
42488	Glenn		9 40	10 20			
42418	Norsworthy-Mercer		10 20	10 55			
41587	Jack L Holmes		10 55	11 35			
42218	(1) adver. Service		11 35	12 05			
42522	Tom Grimis		12 05	12 30	4		
	Lunch		12 30	1 00			
42597	Production art Select		1 00	1 30			
42609	Cunningham & Walsh		1 30	2 10			
41954	White auto		2 10	3 00			
42593	Wyatt adver.		3 00	3 35			
4228	(1) ad. Service		3 35	4 05			
42600	R & S		4 05	4 30			
42654	Reitz & Herndon		4 30	4 50			
29803	Riverside Press		4 50	5 30	4		

9 540

Chargeable Hours ______ Non-Chargeable Hours ______ O.K. ______ Foreman.

Commission Exhibit No. 1855

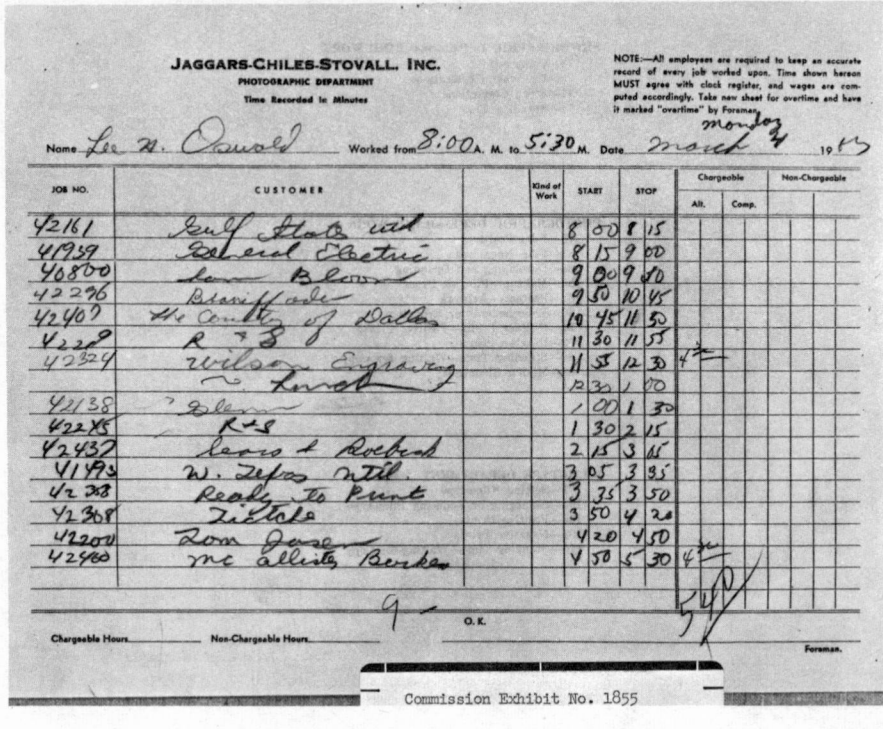

COMMISSION EXHIBIT No. 1855—Continued

Page I

JAGGARS-CHILES-STOVALL, INC.
PHOTOGRAPHIC DEPARTMENT
Time Recorded in Minutes

NOTE:—All employees are required to keep an accurate record of every job worked upon. Time shown hereon MUST agree with clock register, and wages are computed accordingly. Take new sheet for overtime and have it marked "overtime" by Foreman.

Name Lee H. Oswald Worked from 8:00 A. M. to 5:30 M. Date March 8 196

JOB NO.	CUSTOMER		Kind of Work	START		STOP		Chargeable Alt.	Chargeable Comp.	Non-Chargeable
42758	Crook			8	00	8	30			
42686	Lew Ramsey			8	30	9	10			
40800	Sam Bloom			9	10	9	40			
42662	KRLD art Dept.			9	40	10	00			
42733	Cunningham & Cooper			10	00	10	15			
42630	Sam Bloom			10	15	10	35			
42722	ad PR			10	35	10	50			
42645	Fuller & Smith & Ross			10	50	11	05			
42645	Collins Comm. art.			11	05	11	25			
42732	W. A. Green			11	25	11	40	#		
42776	Beals			11	40	12	00			
	Lunch			12	00	12	30			
41493	West Texas Util			12	30	1	00			
42576	State of Maryland			1	00	1	50			
42570	R.B. Moreland			1	50	2	30			
42833	S.W. Life			2	30	3	10			
42554	Seminary South			3	10	3	55			

Chargeable Hours ________ Non-Chargeable Hours ________ O.K. ________ Foreman.

Commission Exhibit No. 1855

COMMISSION EXHIBIT No. 1855—Continued

Page II

JAGGARS-CHILES-STOVALL, INC.
PHOTOGRAPHIC DEPARTMENT
Time Recorded in Minutes

NOTE:—All employees are required to keep an accurate record of every job worked upon. Time shown hereon MUST agree with clock register, and wages are computed accordingly. Take new sheet for overtime and have it marked "overtime" by Foreman.

Name Lee H. Oswald Worked from ________ A. M. to ________ M. Date ________ 19

JOB NO.	CUSTOMER		Kind of Work	START		STOP		Chargeable Alt.	Chargeable Comp.	Non-Chargeable
42882	Reitz-Her.			3	55	4:	35			
42563	Riverside Press			4:	35	5:	30	5		

540

Chargeable Hours ________ Non-Chargeable Hours ________ O.K. ________ Foreman.

Commission Exhibit No. 1855

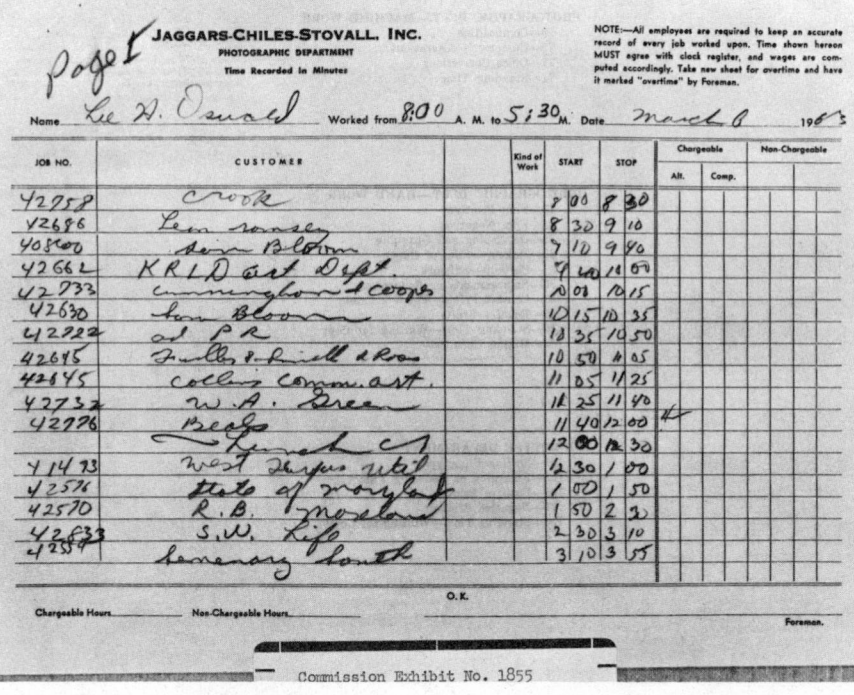

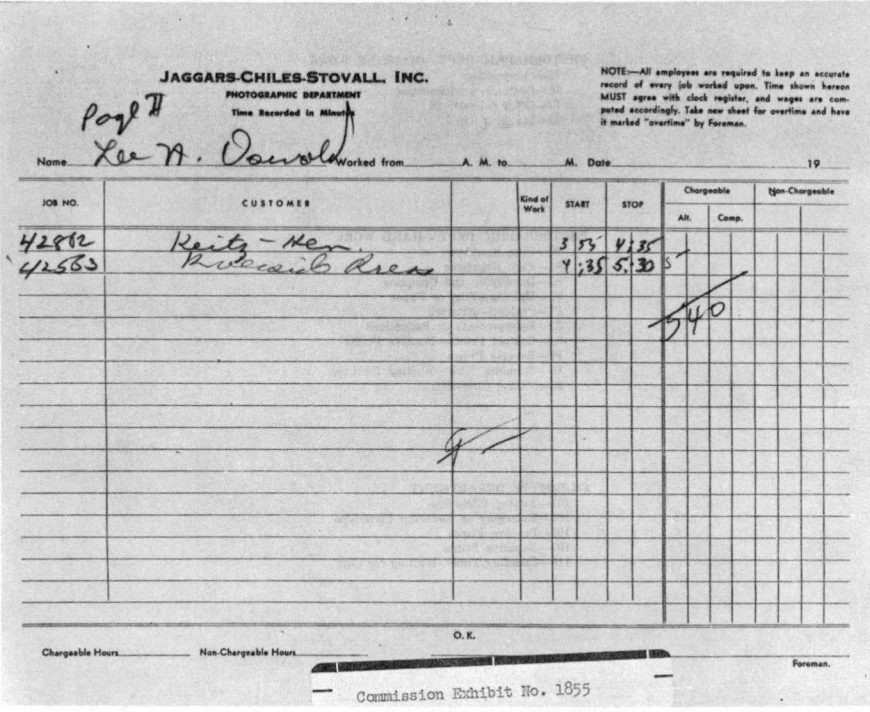

COMMISSION EXHIBIT No. 1855—Continued

Page I

JAGGARS-CHILES-STOVALL, INC.
PHOTOGRAPHIC DEPARTMENT
Time Recorded in Minutes

NOTE:—All employees are required to keep an accurate record of every job worked upon. Time shown hereon MUST agree with clock register, and wages are computed accordingly. Take new sheet for overtime and have it marked "overtime" by Foreman. Thurs.

Name Lee H. Oswald Worked from 8:00 A. M. to 5:30 M. Date March 7 1963

JOB NO.	CUSTOMER		Kind of Work	START		STOP		Chargeable Alt.	Chargeable Comp.	Non-Chargeable
42583	Riverside Press			8	00	8	15			
42504	Bud Biggs			8	15	8	45			
42971	Tom Graves			8	45	9	10			
42924	Nonnworthy - Mecca			9	10	9	45			
42833	S.W. Life Insurance			9	45	10	25			
42033	Al Barnes			10	25	10	55			
42929	S.W. Life			10	55	11	35			
43003	Glen Adv			11	35	12	15	4[15]		
	Lunch		1	12	15	12	45			
42033	Al Barnes			12	45	1	15			
—	Standard Book Cover			1	15	2	00			
29805	Riverside Press			2	00	2	25			
42950	Continental			2	25	2	50			
42928	Jack Wyatt			2	50	3	25			
42625	Collins Commercial			3	25	3	55			
42981	Butler & Hayes			3	55	4	10			
43003	Glen			4	10	4	35			

Chargeable Hours______ Non-Chargeable Hours______ O.K. ______ Foreman.

Commission Exhibit No. 1855

COMMISSION EXHIBIT No. 1855—Continued

Page II

JAGGARS-CHILES-STOVALL, INC.
PHOTOGRAPHIC DEPARTMENT
Time Recorded in Minutes

NOTE:—All employees are required to keep an accurate record of every job worked upon. Time shown hereon MUST agree with clock register, and wages are computed accordingly. Take new sheet for overtime and have it marked "overtime" by Foreman.

Name Lee H. Oswald Worked from______ A. M. to______ M. Date______ 19__

JOB NO.	CUSTOMER		Kind of Work	START		STOP		Chargeable Alt.	Chargeable Comp.	Non-Chargeable
43070	Glen			4	35	5	05			
42297	Braniff order			5	05	5	30	4[41]		
								5[49]		

9/

Chargeable Hours______ Non-Chargeable Hours______ O.K. ______ Foreman.

Commission Exhibit No. 1855

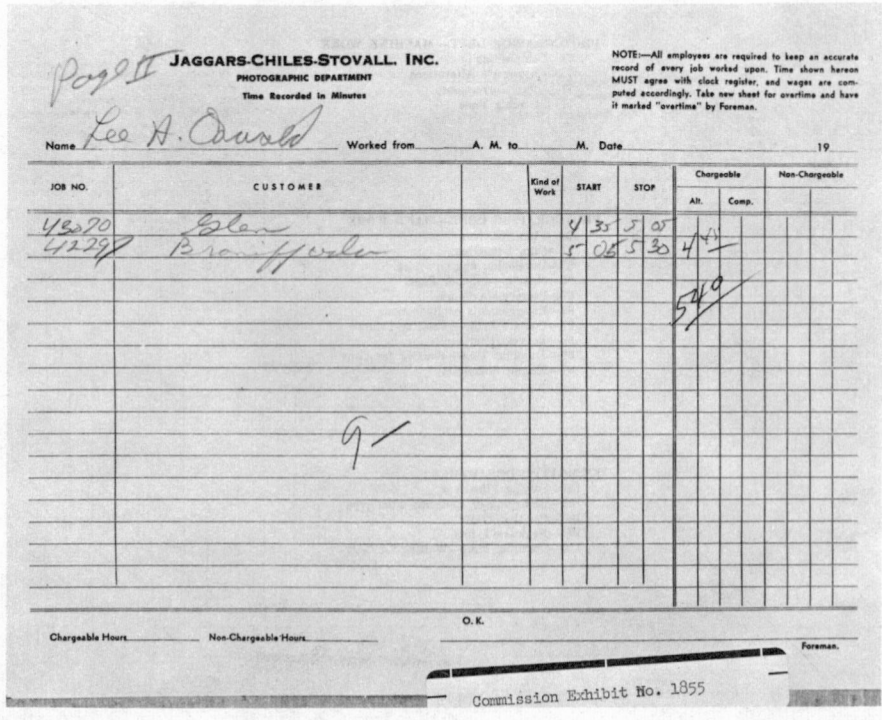

COMMISSION EXHIBIT No. 1855—Continued

JAGGARS-CHILES-STOVALL, INC.
PHOTOGRAPHIC DEPARTMENT
Time Recorded in Minutes

NOTE:—All employees are required to keep an accurate record of every job worked upon. Time shown hereon MUST agree with clock register, and wages are computed accordingly. Take new sheet for overtime and have it marked "overtime" by Foreman.

Name Lee H. Oswald Worked from 8:00 A. M. to 5:15 M. Date Friday Mar 8 1963

JOB NO.	CUSTOMER		Kind of Work	START	STOP	Chargeable Alt.	Chargeable Comp.	Non-Chargeable
43136	Hesse Envelope			8 00	8 25			
43164	Baxter			8 25	9 05			
43120	Bloom			9 05	9 40			
42904	Space Corp			9 40	10 10			
43131	Rominger			10 10	10 45			
42937	Bill Bond			10 45	11 10			
43158	Sam Bloom			11 10	11 35			
42584	Chyka Productions			11 35	12 30	4		
	lunch			12 30	1 00	—		
43163	Rogers & Smith			1 00	1 30			
43255	Arrade Lithographing			1 30	2 10			
43088	TP & L			2 10	2 40			
43040	Braniff			2 40	3 05			
43190	Goodman Paper Co.			3 05	3 55			
43253	Bryan & Bryan			3 55	4 40			
43254	Mrs Rowe			4 40	5 15	4 1/4		
						5 25		

(8 3/4) O.K.

Chargeable Hours ______ Non-Chargeable Hours ______ Foreman.

Commission Exhibit No. 1855

COMMISSION EXHIBIT NO. 1855—Continued

JAGGARS-CHILES-STOVALL, INC.
PHOTOGRAPHIC DEPARTMENT
Time Recorded in Minutes

NOTE:—All employees are required to keep an accurate record of every job worked upon. Time shown hereon MUST agree with clock register, and wages are computed accordingly. Take new sheet for overtime and have it marked "overtime" by Foreman.

Name Lee H. Oswald Worked from 8:00 A. M. to 4:00 M. Date Sat. March 9 1963

JOB NO.	CUSTOMER		Kind of Work	START	STOP	Chargeable Alt.	Chargeable Comp.	Non-Chargeable
43315	Sam Bloom			8 00	8 25			
43338	Sam Grimes			8 25	9 05			
29805	Riverside Press			9 05	9 40			
42548	George Chelka			9 40	10 10			
42645	Collins Comm Art			10 10	10 35			
43023	Continental adv.			10 35	10 55			
43211	ad. Service agency			10 55	11 10			
43429	Mithoff			11 10	11 30			
43376	Sam Bloom			11 30	12 00	4		
	lunch			12 00	12 30			
43395	Baxter & Kay			12 30	2 30			
43430	Wilson	7 1/2		2 30	4:00	3 1/2		
						4 50		

(7 1/2)

O.K.

Chargeable Hours ______ Non-Chargeable Hours ______ Foreman.

Commission Exhibit No. 1855

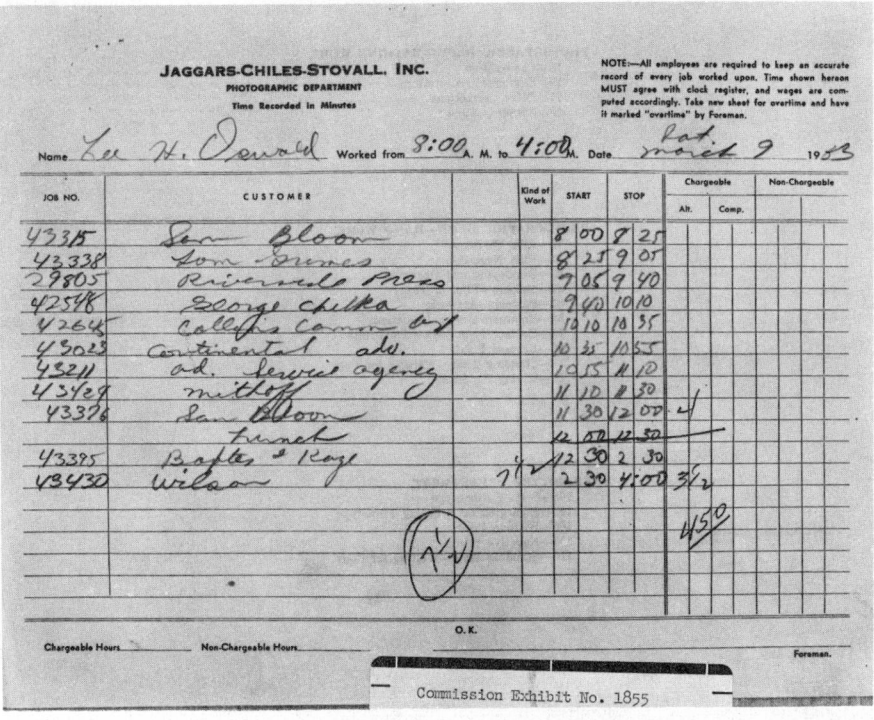

COMMISSION EXHIBIT NO. 1855—Continued

Page I

JAGGARS-CHILES-STOVALL, INC.
PHOTOGRAPHIC DEPARTMENT
Time Recorded in Minutes

NOTE:—All employees are required to keep an accurate record of every job worked upon. Time shown hereon MUST agree with clock register, and wages are computed accordingly. Take new sheet for overtime and have it marked "overtime" by Foreman.

Name Lee H. Oswald Worked from 8:00 A. M. to 5:00 M. Date Monday March 11 1963

JOB NO.	CUSTOMER		Kind of Work	START	STOP	Chargeable Alt.	Chargeable Comp.	Non-Chargeable
38195	J.C.S.			8 00	8 30			
43511	Morris Kreuges			8 30	9 10			
43356	Egan Co			9 10	9 40			
43211	ad service			9 40	10 00			
43152	art Johnson			10 00	10 20			
42980	Betty Welzigdes			10 20	10 50			
43086	S.W. O'Neil Labat.			10 50	11 15			
43437	Frey Hammond + Sears			11 15	11 45			
43352	Goodman Paper			11 45	12 15	4 1/4		
	lunch		✓	12 15	12 45			
43664	Craig-Thomas			12 45	1 15			
43372	Sam Bloom			1 15	1 40			
43315	Sam Bloom			1 40	2 05			
41723	Curtis Prty			2 05	2 40			
43237	Texas Electric			2 40	3 05			
43424	Mithoff Adv			3 05	3 50			
43572	Stallford			3 50	4 10			

Chargeable Hours____ Non-Chargeable Hours____ O.K.____ Foreman.

COMMISSION EXHIBIT No. 1855—Continued

Page II

JAGGARS-CHILES-STOVALL, INC.
PHOTOGRAPHIC DEPARTMENT
Time Recorded in Minutes

NOTE:—All employees are required to keep an accurate record of every job worked upon. Time shown hereon MUST agree with clock register, and wages are computed accordingly. Take new sheet for overtime and have it marked "overtime" by Foreman.

Name Lee H. Oswald Worked from____ A. M. to____ M. Date____ 19__

JOB NO.	CUSTOMER		Kind of Work	START	STOP	Chargeable Alt.	Chargeable Comp.	Non-Chargeable
43559	C C of A			4 10	4 25			
43510	[illegible] Mickelson			4 25	4 45	1/4		
43500	E.A. Lester + assoc			4 45	5 00	4 1/4		
						5 1/2		

8 1/2

Chargeable Hours____ Non-Chargeable Hours____ O.K.____ Foreman.

Commission Exhibit No. 1855

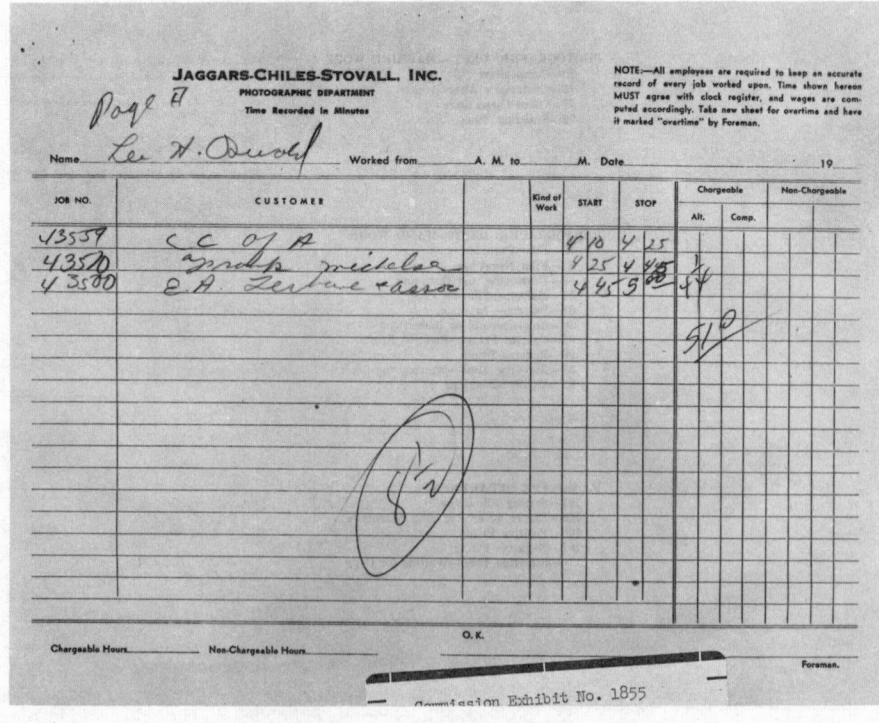

COMMISSION EXHIBIT No. 1855—Continued

JAGGARS-CHILES-STOVALL, INC.
PHOTOGRAPHIC DEPARTMENT
Time Recorded in Minutes

NOTE:—All employees are required to keep an accurate record of every job worked upon. Time shown hereon MUST agree with clock register, and wages are computed accordingly. Take new sheet for overtime and have it marked "overtime" by Foreman.

Name Lee H. Oswald Worked from 8:00 A. M. to 5:15 M. Date Thurs. Nov 12 1963

JOB NO.	CUSTOMER		Kind of Work	START		STOP		Chargeable Alt.	Chargeable Comp.	Non-Chargeable
43539	Electrotype Service			8	00	8	25			
42584	George Chyka Productions			8	25	9	05			
43577	Sam Bloom			9	05	9	50			
42671	Action Ad. Service			9	50	10	10			
43405	Stefan Kramer			10	10	10	35			
43600	Frank Oliver			10	35	10	55			
43633	Lone Star Gas			10	55	11	10			
43494	Bud Biggs			11	10	11	45			
43506	Mote Rapelwald			11	45	12	15	4 15		
	~ Lunch ~			12	15	12	45			
37858	Don L Bayles			12	45	1	15			
42584	George Chyka			1	15	1	35			
43094	Continental Adv.			1	35	1	50			
43637	R.K. Butler			1	50	2	10			
43621	Graphic Ill.			2	10	2	30			
43149	Cunningham & Walsh			2	30	2	55			
43029	Universal Colors			2	55	3	10			

Chargeable Hours __________ Non-Chargeable Hours __________ O.K. __________ Foreman.

Commission Exhibit No. 1855

COMMISSION EXHIBIT No. 1855—Continued

JAGGARS-CHILES-STOVALL, INC.
PHOTOGRAPHIC DEPARTMENT
Time Recorded in Minutes

NOTE:—All employees are required to keep an accurate record of every job worked upon. Time shown hereon MUST agree with clock register, and wages are computed accordingly. Take new sheet for overtime and have it marked "overtime" by Foreman.

Name Lee H. Oswald Worked from ______ A. M. to ______ M. Date ______ 19__

JOB NO.	CUSTOMER		Kind of Work	START		STOP		Chargeable Alt.	Chargeable Comp.	Non-Chargeable
43350	I P + A			3	10	3	30			
43600	Frank Oliver			3	30	3	55			
43686	Electrotype Service			3	55	4	10			
43208	Gatty Evans			4	10	4	25			
43559	Container Corp			4	25	4	40			
43492	Rominger ad.			4	40	4	50			
43652	Wilson Eng.			4	50	5	05			
43739	Jack Wiggatt			5	05	5	15	4 30		
								5 45		

8 45

Chargeable Hours __________ Non-Chargeable Hours __________ O.K. __________ Foreman.

COMMISSION EXHIBIT No. 1855—Continued

JAGGARS-CHILES-STOVALL, INC.
PHOTOGRAPHIC DEPARTMENT
Time Recorded in Minutes

NOTE:—All employees are required to keep an accurate record of every job worked upon. Time shown hereon MUST agree with clock register, and wages are computed accordingly. Take new sheet for overtime and have it marked "overtime" by Foreman.

Name Lee H. Oswald Worked from 8:00 A. M. to 5:30 M. Date Wed. March 13 1963

JOB NO.	CUSTOMER		Kind of Work	START	STOP	Chargeable Alt.	Chargeable Comp.	Non-Chargeable
43800	Republic National Life			8 00	9 40			
43814	Trade-Locke			8 40	9 10			
43690	Wyatt adv			9 10	9 50			
43942	Gardner Paper Co.			9 50	10 20			
43723	Trade-Locke			10 20	10 55			
43819	Continental adv			10 55	11 20			
43881	Stanford			11 20	11 45			
43884	White Auto			11 45	12 15	4 15		
	lunch			12 15	12 45			
43916	Addressograph-Mult			12 45	1 15			
43425	Universal Schools			1 15	1 45			
43855	McCarty of Texas			1 45	2 10			
43847	S.W. Electric			2 10	2 40			
43864	W.W. Sherrill			2 40	3 05			
43355	Aylin adv			3 05	3 50			
43354	Aylin adv			3 50	4 15			
43351	adver			4 15	4 50			
43931	Trade Lock 9			4 30	5 30	4 15		

Chargeable Hours______ Non-Chargeable Hours______ O.K.______ 540 Foreman.

Commission Exhibit No. 1855

COMMISSION EXHIBIT NO. 1855—Continued

JAGGARS-CHILES-STOVALL, INC.
PHOTOGRAPHIC DEPARTMENT
Time Recorded in Minutes

NOTE:—All employees are required to keep an accurate record of every job worked upon. Time shown hereon MUST agree with clock register, and wages are computed accordingly. Take new sheet for overtime and have it marked "overtime" by Foreman.

Name Lee H. Oswald Worked from 8:00 A. M. to 5:30 M. Date Thur March 14 1963

JOB NO.	CUSTOMER		Kind of Work	START	STOP	Chargeable Alt.	Chargeable Comp.	Non-Chargeable
41224	(1) Tom Miller			8:00	9 10			
43120	(1) Sam Bloom			9 10	9 50			
41224	(2) Tom Miller			9 50	10 35			
43884	White Auto			10 35	11 05			
43238	International PR			11 05	11 25			
44120	Aylin ad			11 25	11 45			
44053	Glenn Mason & as			11 45	12 15	4 15		
	lunch			12:15	12:45			
44166	Standford			12 45	1 15			
43120	(2) Sam Bloom			1 15	1 40			
44162	C & W			1 40	2 20			
44190	Rogers & Smith			2 20	3 05			
44192	Rogers & Smith			3 05	3 30			
43931	Trade Locke			3 30	3 50			
44097	Scott			3 50	4 20			
44184	Lekne Kut			4 20	4 45			
43653	Titches			4 45	5 05			
42516	Sam Bloom			5 05	5:30	4 15		

Chargeable Hours______ Non-Chargeable Hours______ O.K. 9 540 Foreman.

Commission Exhibit No. 1855

COMMISSION EXHIBIT NO. 1855—Continued

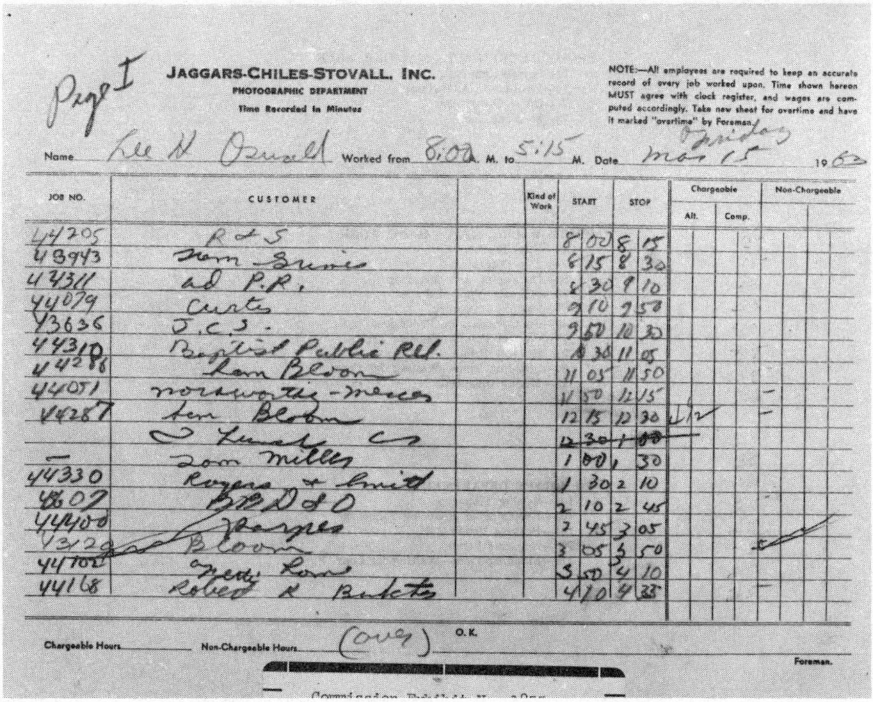

Page I

JAGGARS-CHILES-STOVALL, INC.
PHOTOGRAPHIC DEPARTMENT
Time Recorded in Minutes

NOTE:—All employees are required to keep an accurate record of every job worked upon. Time shown hereon MUST agree with clock register, and wages are computed accordingly. Take new sheet for overtime and have it marked "overtime" by Foreman.

Name Lee H Oswald Worked from 8:00 A. M. to 5:15 M. Date Friday Mar 15 1963

JOB NO.	CUSTOMER		Kind of Work	START		STOP		Chargeable Alt.	Chargeable Comp.	Non-Chargeable
44205	R & S			8	00	8	15			
43943	Sam Swies			8	15	8	30			
44311	ad P.R.			8	30	9	10			
44079	Curtis			9	10	9	50			
43636	J.C.S.			9	50	10	30			
44310	Baptist Public Rel.			10	30	11	05			
44288	Sam Bloom			11	05	11	50			
44051	Norsworthy-Mercer			11	50	12	15			—
44287	Sam Bloom			12	15	12	30	4 1/2		—
	Lunch			~~12~~	~~30~~	~~1~~	~~00~~			
—	Tom Miller			1	00	1	30			
44330	Rogers & Smith			1	30	2	10			
4607	BBD&O			2	10	2	45			
44400	Harpes			2	45	3	05			
43129	Bloom			3	05	3	50			
44102	Neiman Lowe			3	50	4	10			
44168	Robert R Bullocks			4	10	4	35			

Chargeable Hours______ Non-Chargeable Hours______ (over) O.K. ______ Foreman.

COMMISSION EXHIBIT No. 1855—Continued

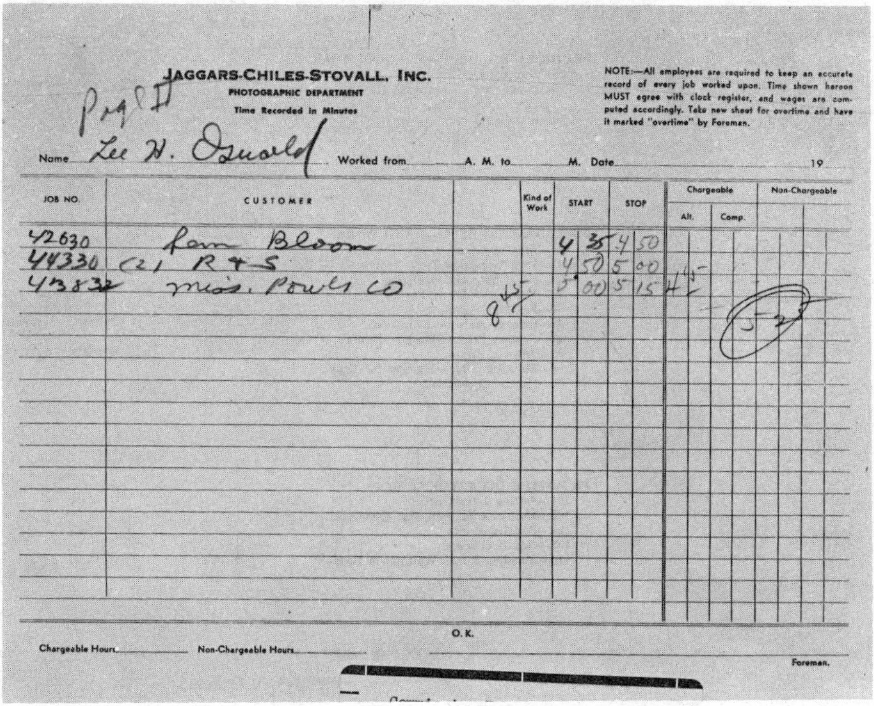

Page II

JAGGARS-CHILES-STOVALL, INC.
PHOTOGRAPHIC DEPARTMENT
Time Recorded in Minutes

NOTE:—All employees are required to keep an accurate record of every job worked upon. Time shown hereon MUST agree with clock register, and wages are computed accordingly. Take new sheet for overtime and have it marked "overtime" by Foreman.

Name Lee H. Oswald Worked from______ A. M. to______ M. Date______ 19__

JOB NO.	CUSTOMER		Kind of Work	START		STOP		Chargeable Alt.	Chargeable Comp.	Non-Chargeable
42630	Sam Bloom			4	35	4	50			
44330	(2) R & S			4	50	5	00			
43832	Miss. Power Co	8 45		5	00	5	15	4 45		

Chargeable Hours______ Non-Chargeable Hours______ O.K. ______ Foreman.

COMMISSION EXHIBIT No. 1855—Continued

Page I

JAGGARS-CHILES-STOVALL, INC.
PHOTOGRAPHIC DEPARTMENT
Time Recorded in Minutes

NOTE:—All employees are required to keep an accurate record of every job worked upon. Time shown hereon MUST agree with clock register, and wages are computed accordingly. Take new sheet for overtime and have it marked "overtime" by Foreman.

Name Lee H. Oswald Worked from 7:45 A. M. to 5:45 M. Date (Sat.) March 16 19

JOB NO.	CUSTOMER		Kind of Work	START		STOP		Chargeable Alt.	Chargeable Comp.	Non-Chargeable
44493	Goodman			7	45	8	10			
44346	Oden ad			8	10	8	45			
44330	Rogers & Arnett			8	45	9	15			
44506	Hal Mayes			9	15	9	40			
44467	Monte Rosenberg			9	40	10	00			
42471	I. C. S.			10	00	10	20			
44351	Monte Rosenwald			10	20	10	45			
44040	I.C.S.			10	45	11	10			
44287	Sam Bloom			11	10	11	35			
44443	ad PR			11	35	12	00	4:15		
	Lunch			12	00	12	30			
44479	Sears & Roebuck			12	30	1	00			
43952	Ad P.R.			1	00	1	30			
44566	Glenn adver.			1	30	2	05			
44539	B B D & O			2	05	2	30			
44543	Baptist Public Rel.			2	30	3	20			
44502	Sam Bloom			3	20	4	10			

Chargeable Hours ______ Non-Chargeable Hours ______ O.K. ______ Foreman.

Commission Exhibit No. 1855

COMMISSION EXHIBIT No. 1855—Continued

Page II

JAGGARS-CHILES-STOVALL, INC.
PHOTOGRAPHIC DEPARTMENT
Time Recorded in Minutes

NOTE:—All employees are required to keep an accurate record of every job worked upon. Time shown hereon MUST agree with clock register, and wages are computed accordingly. Take new sheet for overtime and have it marked "overtime" by Foreman.

Name Lee H. Oswald Worked from 7:45 A. M. to ______ M. Date 3-16 Sat 1963

JOB NO.	CUSTOMER		Kind of Work	START		STOP		Chargeable Alt.	Chargeable Comp.	Non-Chargeable
44528	Whites auto			4	10	4	35			
44541	Al Barnes			4	35	5	10			
44320	Beals ado			5	10	5	45	8 15		

570

930

Chargeable Hours ______ Non-Chargeable Hours ______ O.K. ______ Foreman.

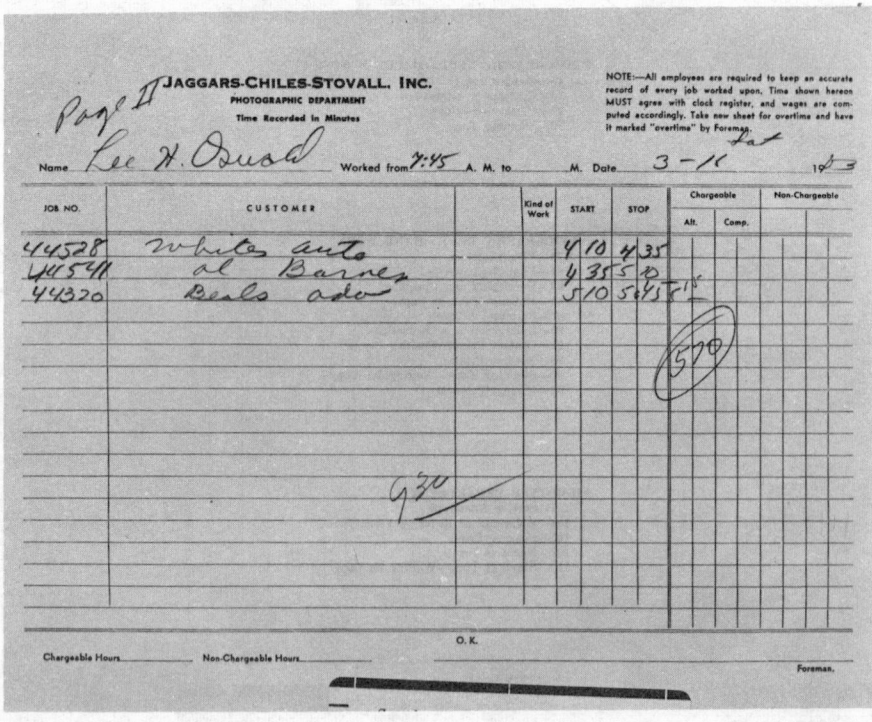

COMMISSION EXHIBIT No. 1855—Continued

JAGGARS-CHILES-STOVALL, INC.
PHOTOGRAPHIC DEPARTMENT
Time Recorded in Minutes

page 5

NOTE:—All employees are required to keep an accurate record of every job worked upon. Time shown hereon MUST agree with clock register, and wages are computed accordingly. Take new sheet for overtime and have it marked "overtime" by Foreman.

Name Lee H. Oswald Worked from 8:00 A. M. to 5:00 M. Date Mar. 18 19

JOB NO.	CUSTOMER		Kind of Work	START	STOP	Chargeable Alt.	Chargeable Comp.	Non-Chargeable
44503	BBD&O			8 00	8 15			
44481	R B Moreland			8 15	8 30			
44355	Sam Bloom			8 30	9 10			
44424	Sam Bloom			9 10	9 30			
41093	Rogers & Smith			9 30	10 00			
44583	Wilson			10 00	10 20			
44096	Electrotype Service			10 20	10 45			
43998	Universal Schols			10 45	11 05			
44562	Pan Moshie			11 05	11 35			
44498	Fla Jordan Co.			11 35	11 55			
44804	Hardy & Hawks			11 55	12 15	4 15		
	Lunch			12 15	12 45			
44537	Sam Bloom			12 45	1 15			
44328	Jack Taylor			1 15	1 48			
43607	BBD&O			1 48	2 20			
44216	Alabama Engr.			2 20	3 00			
43722	Container Corp.			3 00	3 20			

Chargeable Hours ______ Non-Chargeable Hours ______ O.K. ______ Foreman.

Commission Exhibit No. 1855

COMMISSION EXHIBIT No. 1855—Continued

JAGGARS-CHILES-STOVALL, INC.
PHOTOGRAPHIC DEPARTMENT
Time Recorded in Minutes

Page 11

NOTE:—All employees are required to keep an accurate record of every job worked upon. Time shown hereon MUST agree with clock register, and wages are computed accordingly. Take new sheet for overtime and have it marked "overtime" by Foreman.

Name Lee H. Oswald Worked from ____ A. M. to ____ M. Date ____ 19

JOB NO.	CUSTOMER		Kind of Work	START	STOP	Chargeable Alt.	Chargeable Comp.	Non-Chargeable
44514	White Auto			3 20	3 45			
44014	Braniff			3 45	4 10			
44576	Collins Commercial Art			4 10	4 30			
44804	Robert R. Butler			4 30	5 00	4 15		
						5 10		

8 3/4

Chargeable Hours ______ Non-Chargeable Hours ______ O.K. ______ Foreman.

Commission Exhibit No. 1855

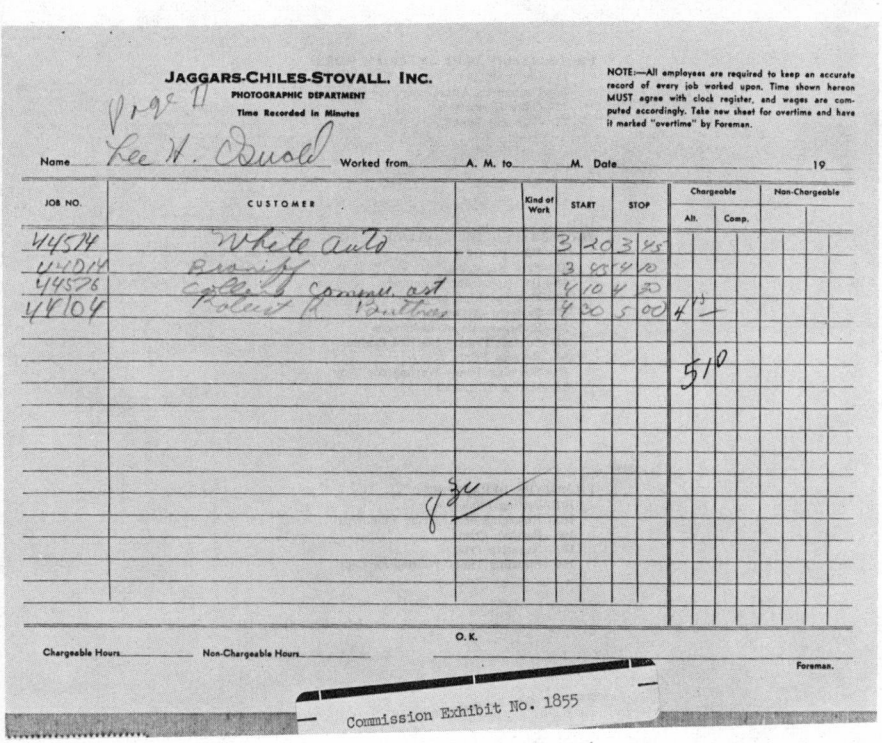

COMMISSION EXHIBIT No. 1855—Continued

Page I

JAGGARS-CHILES-STOVALL, INC.
PHOTOGRAPHIC DEPARTMENT
Time Recorded in Minutes

NOTE:—All employees are required to keep an accurate record of every job worked upon. Time shown hereon MUST agree with clock register, and wages are computed accordingly. Take new sheet for overtime and have it marked "overtime" by Foreman.

Name Lee H. Oswald Worked from 8:00 A. M. to 5:30 M. Date Tues. May 19 1963

JOB NO.	CUSTOMER		Kind of Work	START		STOP		Chargeable Alt.	Chargeable Comp.	Non-Chargeable
44711	Graphic Oil.			8	00	8	15			
44774	Titches			8	30	9	10			
44694	Davis & Boaz			9	10	9	40			
44752	Jack Wyatt			9	40	10	10			
44627	Crook Ads			10	10	10	30			
44604	Harde & Heiks			10	30	10	50			
44688	Rogers & Smith			10	50	11	10			
44407	Sun Bloom			11	10	11	35			
44758	Goodman Poges			11	35	12	05			
44719	Simpson Prtg.			12	05	12	30	4 30		
	Lunch			12	30	1	00			
44397	Hal Copeland			1	00	1	30			
44527	White Autos			1	30	2	10			
44856	Dowe-Rinke			2	10	2	45			
44577	Jim Lofelly			2	45	3	10			
44325	Bill Bond			3	10	3	45			
44708	Glenn Ads			3	45	4	15			

Chargeable Hours_____ Non-Chargeable Hours_____ O.K. _____ Foreman.

Commission Exhibit No. 1855

COMMISSION EXHIBIT No. 1855—Continued

Page II

JAGGARS-CHILES-STOVALL, INC.
PHOTOGRAPHIC DEPARTMENT
Time Recorded in Minutes

NOTE:—All employees are required to keep an accurate record of every job worked upon. Time shown hereon MUST agree with clock register, and wages are computed accordingly. Take new sheet for overtime and have it marked "overtime" by Foreman.

Name Lee H. Oswald Worked from_____ A. M. to_____ M. Date_____ 19__

JOB NO.	CUSTOMER		Kind of Work	START		STOP		Chargeable Alt.	Chargeable Comp.	Non-Chargeable
44831	American Home Real.			4	15	4	30			
44574	Gulf State			4	30	4	45			
44356	Empire Distrib.			4	45	5	10			
44983	Don Bap Co.			5	10	5	30	4 30		

540

Chargeable Hours_____ Non-Chargeable Hours_____ O.K. _____ Foreman.

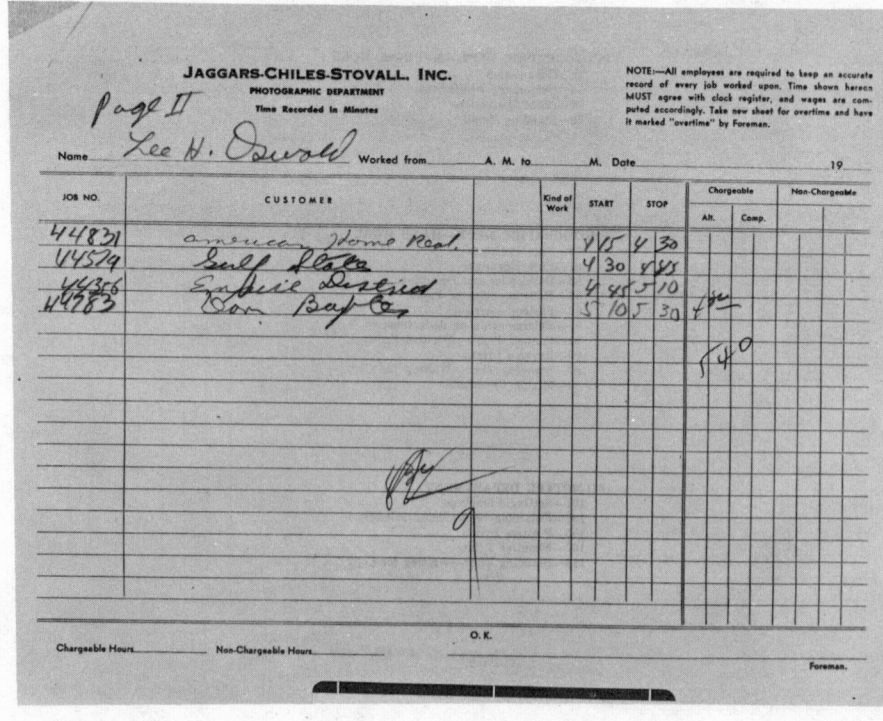

COMMISSION EXHIBIT No. 1855—Continued

JAGGARS-CHILES-STOVALL, INC.
PHOTOGRAPHIC DEPARTMENT
Time Recorded in Minutes

NOTE:—All employees are required to keep an accurate record of every job worked upon. Time shown hereon MUST agree with clock register, and wages are computed accordingly. Take new sheet for overtime and have it marked "overtime" by Foreman.

Name Lee H. Oswald Worked from 8:00 A. M. to 5:15 P. M. Date Mar 20 (wed) 1963

JOB NO.	CUSTOMER	Kind of Work	START		STOP		Chargeable Alt.	Comp.	Non-Chargeable
42149	Don L Baxter		8	00	8	30			
41224	Tom Miller		8	30	9	10			
45055	Duncan Coffee		9	10	9	45			
44984	Blanks Engraving		9	45	10	10			
44754	Texas Nameplate		10	10	10	35			
44924	Bill Stout		10	35	10	55			
45028	Padgett		10	55	11	30			
44780	ad P.R.		11	30	12	15	4 15		
	Lunch		12	15	12	45			
44555	Sam Bloom		12	45	1	15			
45070	Wyatt		1	15	2	00			
44356	Empire Elec.		2	00	2	20			
44833	Al Barnes		2	20	2	45			
44989	Rominger		2	45	3	10			
44579	E. S. U.		3	10	3	55			
45005	Glen Mason		3	55	4	35			
45118	Standford		4	35	5	15	4 30		

Chargeable Hours 8 45 Non-Chargeable Hours O.K. 5 45 Foreman.

Commission Exhibit No. 1855—Continued

page I

JAGGARS-CHILES-STOVALL, INC.
PHOTOGRAPHIC DEPARTMENT
Time Recorded in Minutes

NOTE:—All employees are required to keep an accurate record of every job worked upon. Time shown hereon MUST agree with clock register, and wages are computed accordingly. Take new sheet for overtime and have it marked "overtime" by Foreman.

Name Lee H. Oswald Worked from 8:00 A. M. to 5:00 P. M. Date Mar 21 (THUR) 1963

JOB NO.	CUSTOMER	Kind of Work	START		STOP		Chargeable Alt.	Comp.	Non-Chargeable
45084	Rogers & Smith		8:	00	8	20			
44981	American Beauty		8	20	8	45			
45049	B B D & O		8	45	9	10			
45106	R & S		9	10	9	25			
45040	Randell		9	25	9	45			
45173	Sam Bloom		9	45	10	00			
44578	E S U		10	00	10	15			
44074	Curtis		10	15	10	35			
41325	Bill Bond		10	35	10	50			
45134	Braniff		10	50	11	30			
45160	B B D & O		11	30	12	30	4 30		
	Thought U		12	30	1	00			
45241	Ben Ramsey		1	00	1	15			
45278	Dec. of Dallas		1	15	1	35			
45260	Mary Hammond		1	35	1	55			
45183	Rogers & Smith		1	55	2	30			
45285	Newton adv		2	30	3	05			

(cont.)

Chargeable Hours Non-Chargeable Hours O.K. Foreman.

Commission Exhibit No. 1855

Commission Exhibit No. 1855—Continued

Page II

JAGGARS-CHILES-STOVALL, INC.
PHOTOGRAPHIC DEPARTMENT
Time Recorded in Minutes

NOTE:—All employees are required to keep an accurate record of every job worked upon. Time shown hereon MUST agree with clock register, and wages are computed accordingly. Take new sheet for overtime and have it marked "overtime" by Foreman.

Name Lee H. Oswald Worked from ______ A. M. to ______ M. Date ______ 19__

JOB NO.	CUSTOMER	Kind of Work	START		STOP		Chargeable Alt.	Chargeable Comp.	Non-Chargeable
45315	S. Bloom	.	3	05	3	35			
45026	T P & L		3	35	3	55			
45166	B B D & O		3	55	4	20			
45299	Bloom		4	20	4	45			
45356	Monte Ressin		4	45	5	00	4—		

5 10

8 3/4

Chargeable Hours ______ Non-Chargeable Hours ______ O.K. ______ Foreman.

Commission Exhibit No. 1855

COMMISSION EXHIBIT No. 1855—Continued

Page I

JAGGARS-CHILES-STOVALL, INC.
PHOTOGRAPHIC DEPARTMENT
Time Recorded in Minutes

NOTE:—All employees are required to keep an accurate record of every job worked upon. Time shown hereon MUST agree with clock register, and wages are computed accordingly. Take new sheet for overtime and have it marked "overtime" by Foreman.

Name Lee H. Oswald Worked from 7:45 A. M. to 5:15 M. Date Mar 22 Friday 1963

JOB NO.	CUSTOMER	Kind of Work	START		STOP		Chargeable Alt.	Chargeable Comp.	Non-Chargeable
45261	Dallas Times Her.		7	45	8	05			
44694	Davis – Box Mgf		8	05	8	25			
45144	Industrial Prtg		8	25	9	10			
45414	McClenns Dress		9	10	9	40			
45096	Sam Bloom		9	40	10	10			
45153	Highland Park		10	10	10	35			
45202	Sandmen Papers		10	35	10	55			
45398	Borton & Serey		10	55	11	10			
45335	Rogers Smith		11	10	11	35			
45424	Zales		11	35	11	55			
45153	Hi Parks		11	55	12	30	4 45		
	Lunch		~~12~~	~~30~~	~~1~~	~~00~~			
45107	R & S		1	00	1	30			
45356	Tom Cruning		1	30	2	00			
45215	The Stuck Co		2	00	2	15			
45477	Cortinies		2	15	3	05			
44288	Sam Bloom		3	05	3	35			

(Con.)

Chargeable Hours ______ Non-Chargeable Hours ______ O.K. ______ Foreman.

Commission Exhibit No. 1855

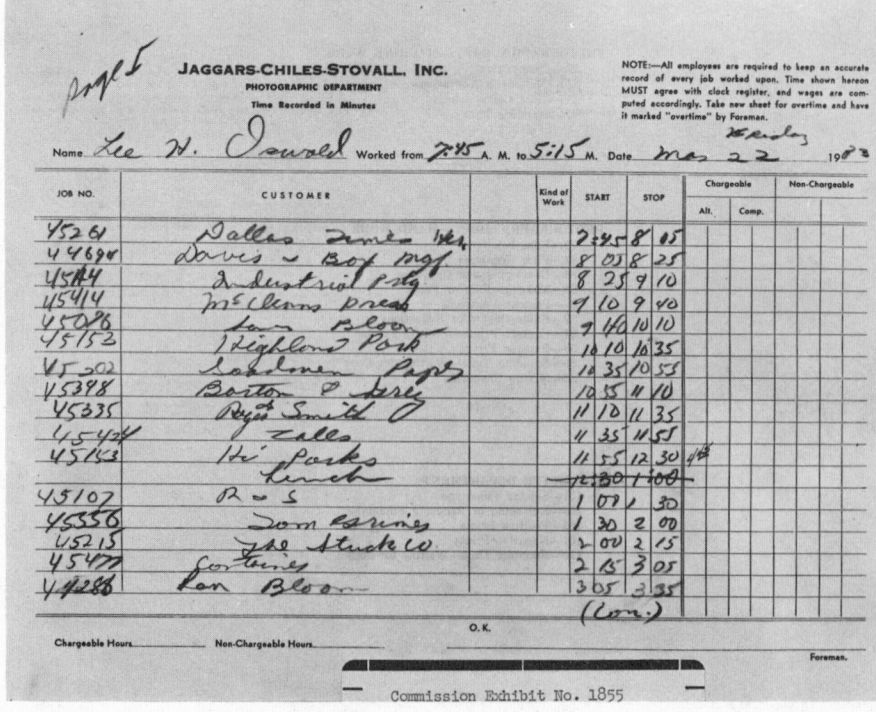

COMMISSION EXHIBIT No. 1855—Continued

Page II

JAGGARS-CHILES-STOVALL, INC.
PHOTOGRAPHIC DEPARTMENT
Time Recorded in Minutes

NOTE:—All employees are required to keep an accurate record of every job worked upon. Time shown hereon MUST agree with clock register, and wages are computed accordingly. Take new sheet for overtime and have it marked "overtime" by Foreman.

Name Lee H. Oswald Worked from ____ A. M. to ____ M. Date ____ 19__

JOB NO.	CUSTOMER		Kind of Work	START	STOP	Chargeable Alt.	Chargeable Comp.	Non-Chargeable
44201	Fry & Hammond			3 35	3 55			
43859	Tom Greene			3 55	4 15			
45204	Wilson Eng			4 15	4 35			
45118	Standford			4 35	4 50			
45335	R-S			4 50	5 05			
45490	McCarty Co. of Texas			5 05	5 15	1/6		

5 40

9 hrs

Chargeable Hours ____ Non-Chargeable Hours ____ O.K. ____ Foreman.

Commission Exhibit No. 1855—Continued

Page I

JAGGARS-CHILES-STOVALL, INC.
PHOTOGRAPHIC DEPARTMENT
Time Recorded in Minutes

NOTE:—All employees are required to keep an accurate record of every job worked upon. Time shown hereon MUST agree with clock register, and wages are computed accordingly. Take new sheet for overtime and have it marked "overtime" by Foreman.

Name Lee H. Oswald Worked from 7:30 A. M. to 6:00 M. Date Mar 23 Sat. 1963

JOB NO.	CUSTOMER		Kind of Work	START	STOP	Chargeable Alt.	Chargeable Comp.	Non-Chargeable
45504	R K Butler			7:30	8 10			
45518	Ed Preas			8 10	8 40			
4560	Grant			8 40	9 10			
45220	White auto			9 10	9 35			
45592	continental			9 35	10 05			
45335	R & S.			10 05	10 50			
45604	Hal Myers Co			10 50	11 15			
44617	Gordon Co.			11 15	11 35			
45351	Goodwin ad.			11 35	12 00			
	Lunch			12:00	12:30	5-		
45700	al Barnes			12 30	1 00			
45622	Ewald Sendefur			1 00	1 55			
4565	R & S			1 55	2 30			
45671	Wilson			2 30	3 20			
45689	Campbell-Dickey			3 20	4 05			
37850	Boyles			4 05	4 40			
45526	S.W. Electric			4 40	5 15			
				(Con.)				

Chargeable Hours ____ Non-Chargeable Hours ____ O.K. ____ Foreman.

Commission Exhibit No. 1855

Commission Exhibit No. 1855—Continued

page II

JAGGARS-CHILES-STOVALL, INC.
PHOTOGRAPHIC DEPARTMENT
Time Recorded in Minutes

NOTE:—All employees are required to keep an accurate record of every job worked upon. Time shown hereon MUST agree with clock register, and wages are computed accordingly. Take new sheet for overtime and have it marked "overtime" by Foreman.

Sat

Name Lee H. Oswald Worked from 7:30 A. M. to ____ M. Date Mar 23 1963

JOB NO.	CUSTOMER		Kind of Work	START		STOP		Chargeable Alt.	Chargeable Comp.	Non-Chargeable
45620	Grant ad.			5	15	6:00		45		

100

10

Chargeable Hours ____ Non-Chargeable Hours ____ O.K. ____ Foreman.

Commission Exhibit No. 1855

COMMISSION EXHIBIT No. 1855—Continued

page I

JAGGARS-CHILES-STOVALL, INC.
PHOTOGRAPHIC DEPARTMENT
Time Recorded in Minutes

NOTE:—All employees are required to keep an accurate record of every job worked upon. Time shown hereon MUST agree with clock register, and wages are computed accordingly. Take new sheet for overtime and have it marked "overtime" by Foreman.

mon.

Name Lee H. Oswald Worked from 8:10 A. M. to 5:10 M. Date Mar 25 1963

JOB NO.	CUSTOMER		Kind of Work	START		STOP		Chargeable Alt.	Chargeable Comp.	Non-Chargeable
45671	Wilson Eng			8	10	8	45			
45782	Tom Sims			8	45	9	10			
45501	TP&L			9	10	9	50			
45649	AMS			9	50	10	15			
45477	Container Corp.			10	15	10	40			
45782	Ed Bearden			10	40	11	05			
45511	Belfour			11	05	11	35			
45735	Goodman Paper.			11	35	12	00	350		
	Lunch			12:00		12:30				
44617	Jackson Co.			12	30	1	00			
45834	Ed Bearden			1	00	1	15			
45490	McCarty Co			1	15	1	35			
44205	R&S			1	35	2	05			
45615	R & S			2	05	2	30			
45703	Padgett			2	30	2	45			
45325	Bennett Pety			2	45	3	05			
45620	Grant ad.			3	05	3	40			

(con.)

Chargeable Hours ____ Non-Chargeable Hours ____ O.K. ____ Foreman.

COMMISSION EXHIBIT No. 1855—Continued

Page II

JAGGARS-CHILES-STOVALL, INC.
PHOTOGRAPHIC DEPARTMENT
Time Recorded in Minutes

NOTE:—All employees are required to keep an accurate record of every job worked upon. Time shown hereon MUST agree with clock register, and wages are computed accordingly. Take new sheet for overtime and have it marked "overtime" by Foreman.

Name Lee H Oswald Worked from ______ A. M. to ______ M. Date ______ 19__

JOB NO.	CUSTOMER		Kind of Work	START		STOP		Chargeable Alt.	Chargeable Comp.	Non-Chargeable
45667	Balfours			3	40	3	55			
45770	Len Ramsey			3	55	4	10			
45689	BBD&O			4	10	4	30			
45551	Continental ads			4	30	4	45			
45728	Tom Ferris			4	45	5	10	4 40		

Chargeable Hours ______ Non-Chargeable Hours ______ O.K. ______ Foreman.

Commission Exhibit No. 1855

COMMISSION EXHIBIT NO. 1855—Continued

Page I

JAGGARS-CHILES-STOVALL, INC.
PHOTOGRAPHIC DEPARTMENT
Time Recorded in Minutes

NOTE:—All employees are required to keep an accurate record of every job worked upon. Time shown hereon MUST agree with clock register, and wages are computed accordingly. Take new sheet for overtime and have it marked "overtime" by Foreman.

Name Lee H. Oswald Worked from 8:00 A. M. to 5:45 M. Date Tues. Nov 25 1962

JOB NO.	CUSTOMER		Kind of Work	START		STOP		Chargeable Alt.	Chargeable Comp.	Non-Chargeable
45718	Dallas C of C			8	00	8	25			
45676	Hall ad			8	25	9	05			
45364	Hardwood Book			9	05	9	40			
45793	Frigidaires			9	40	10	10			
45981	Sears Roebuck			10	10	10	35			
45677	Hall Prtg			10	35	11	00			
46060	Curtis Prtg			11	00	11	20			
46005	(1) BBD&O			11	20	11	40			
45956	Continental			11	40	12	00			
46088	Star Richards			12	00	12	30	4 40		
	Lunch			12:	00	12:	30			
45672	Clarke & Courts			12	30	1	00			
45825	I.P.A.			1	00	1	20			
45436	A.O. P.R.			1	20	1	45			
46005	(2) BBD&O			1	45	2	05			
45437	A.O. P.R.			2	05	2	25			
46060	Lowe-Runkle			2	25	2	45			

Con.

Chargeable Hours ______ Non-Chargeable Hours ______ O.K. ______ Foreman.

Commission Exhibit No. 1855

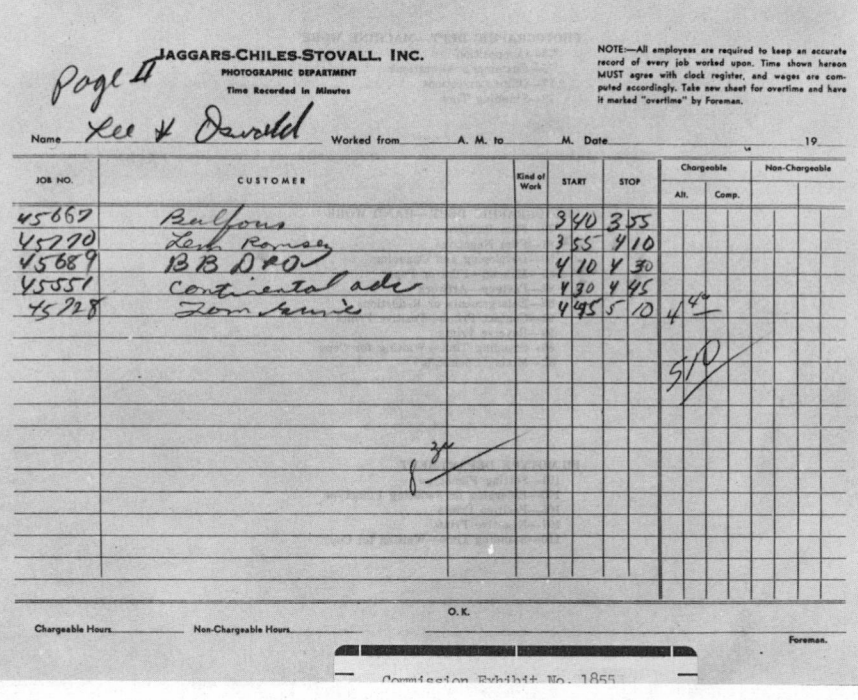

COMMISSION EXHIBIT NO. 1855—Continued

page II

JAGGARS-CHILES-STOVALL, INC.
PHOTOGRAPHIC DEPARTMENT
Time Recorded in Minutes

NOTE:—All employees are required to keep an accurate record of every job worked upon. Time shown hereon MUST agree with clock register, and wages are computed accordingly. Take new sheet for overtime and have it marked "overtime" by Foreman.

Name Lee H. Oswald Worked from ____ A. M. to ____ M. Date ____ 19__

JOB NO.	CUSTOMER		Kind of Work	START	STOP	Chargeable Alt.	Chargeable Comp.	Non-Chargeable
45708	BBD+O			2 45	3 05			
42149	Dor Boyles			3 25	3 30			
46103	BBDO			3 30	3 45			
46034	Zing Jewelers			3 45	4 00			
45949	Coachman ad.			4 00	4 15			
46139	Containers Corp.			4 15	4 35			
43822	Sam Bloom			4 35	4 55			
45388	R+S			4 55	5 20	5 15		
44406	Sam Bloom			5 20	5 45			

O.K.

Chargeable Hours ____ Non-Chargeable Hours ____ Foreman.

Commission Exhibit No. 1855—Continued

page I

JAGGARS-CHILES-STOVALL, INC.
PHOTOGRAPHIC DEPARTMENT
Time Recorded in Minutes

NOTE:—All employees are required to keep an accurate record of every job worked upon. Time shown hereon MUST agree with clock register, and wages are computed accordingly. Take new sheet for overtime and have it marked "overtime" by Foreman.

Name Lee H. Oswald Worked from 7:40 A. M. to 6:40 M. Date wed Mar 27 19 63

JOB NO.	CUSTOMER		Kind of Work	START	STOP	Chargeable Alt.	Chargeable Comp.	Non-Chargeable
45946	Containers Corp.			7 40	8 00			
45842	Braniff ad.			8 00	8 15			
45845	Braniff ad. Dept			8 15	8 35			
45696	West Texas Util			8 35	8 55			
46028	Etheridge Printing			8 55	9 15			
46171	Sam Bloom			9 15	9 40			
45767	Sam Bloom			9 40	10 00			
46188	Sam Bloom			10 00	10 20			
46131	Sam Bloom			10 20	10 40			
44985	Glenn ad			10 40	11 00			
46154	McCann			11 00	11 20			
—	S. Gas assoc.			11 20	11 50			
45918	Braniff Intr. ad.			11 15	12 15	4 35		
	[illegible]			12 15	12 45			
46230	Print-Pak			12 45	1 15			
44424	Sam Bloom			1 15	1 40			
46290	W-S Hayes			1 40	2 05			

con,

O.K.

Chargeable Hours ____ Non-Chargeable Hours ____ Foreman.

Commission Exhibit No. 1855

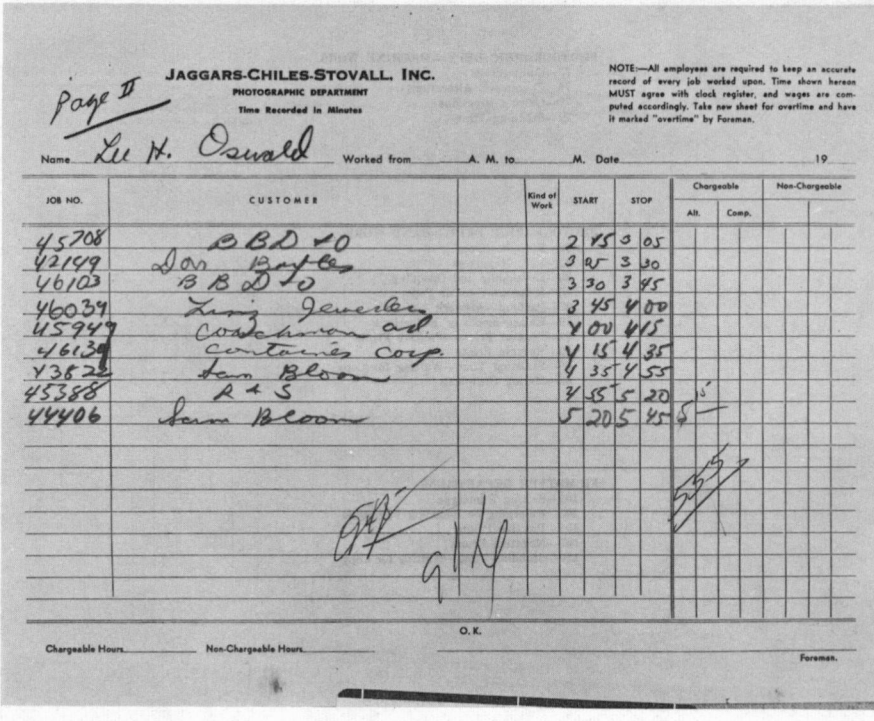

Commission Exhibit No. 1855—Continued

Page II

JAGGARS-CHILES-STOVALL, INC.
PHOTOGRAPHIC DEPARTMENT
Time Recorded in Minutes

NOTE:—All employees are required to keep an accurate record of every job worked upon. Time shown hereon MUST agree with clock register, and wages are computed accordingly. Take new sheet for overtime and have it marked "overtime" by Foreman.

Name Lee H. Oswald Worked from ______ A. M. to ______ M. Date ______ 19__

JOB NO.	CUSTOMER		Kind of Work	START		STOP		Chargeable Alt.	Chargeable Comp.	Non-Chargeable
46288	City Prtg Co.			2	05	2	35			
40215	Dunllaps Smith ad			2	35	3	00			
46137	Rogers & Smith			3	00	3	20			
44528	White auto			3	20	3	45			
44999	Isle[illegible] ad			3	48	4	00			
46312	Romanjes			4	00	4	15			
45671	Willson Eng.			4	15	4	45			
45811	Hal Ringgsen			4	45	5	15			
46377	S. W. Life			5	15	5	40			
46362	(1) Rogers & Smith			5	40	6	30	5		
46362	(2) R & S			6	30	6	40	5		

6 30

7 10

Chargeable Hours______ Non-Chargeable Hours______ O.K. ______ Foreman.

Commission Exhibit No. 1855

COMMISSION EXHIBIT No. 1855—Continued

Page I

JAGGARS-CHILES-STOVALL, INC.
PHOTOGRAPHIC DEPARTMENT
Time Recorded in Minutes

NOTE:—All employees are required to keep an accurate record of every job worked upon. Time shown hereon MUST agree with clock register, and wages are computed accordingly. Take new sheet for overtime and have it marked "overtime" by Foreman.

Name Lee H. Oswald Worked from 7:30 A. M. to 5:30 M. Date Thur May 28 1963

JOB NO.	CUSTOMER		Kind of Work	START		STOP		Chargeable Alt.	Chargeable Comp.	Non-Chargeable
46250	Braniff			7	30	7	55			
37858	Don W. J. Bapla			7	55	8	20			
46325	Gail Klaf			8	20	9	00			
45956	(1) Containers			9	00	9	15			
45778	B. Dallas C of C			9	15	9	35			
45709	(1) B BD & O			9	35	10	00			
46368	Crook			10	00	10	20			
46335	Music & Sound			10	20	10	45			
46138	Tracy Locke			10	45	11	05			
45071	Willson Eng			11	05	11	35			
45888	Braniff			11	35	12	15	4 40		
	~ Lunch ~			12	15	12	45			
46078	Etheridge Prtg			12	45	1	15			
46526	Rogers & Smith			1	15	1	35			
46425	Beals adv			1	35	2	00			
46254	Mercury Prt.			2	00	2	20			
46326	Export Service			2	20	2	45			

Con.

Chargeable Hours______ Non-Chargeable Hours______ O.K. ______ Foreman.

Commission Exhibit No. 1855

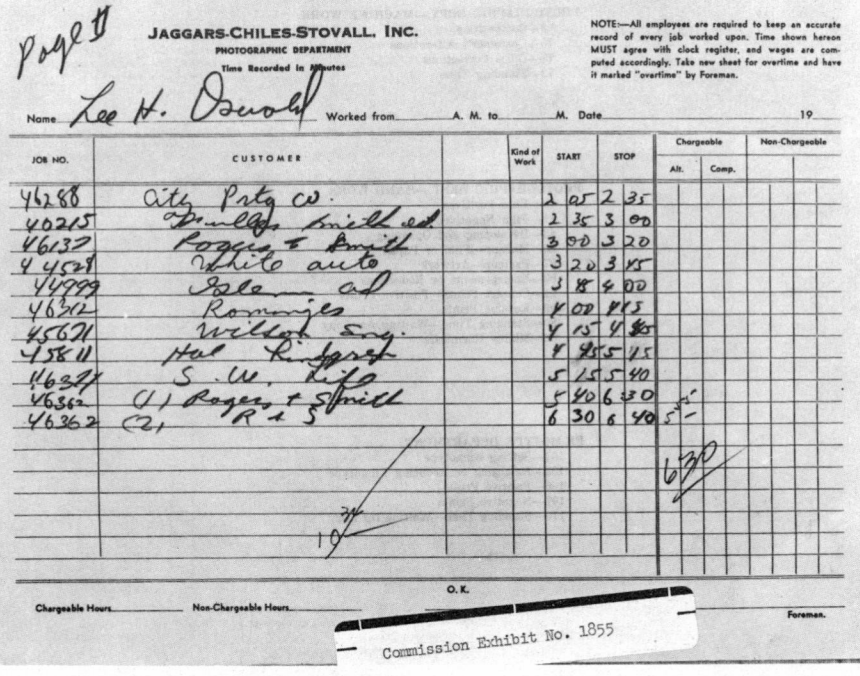

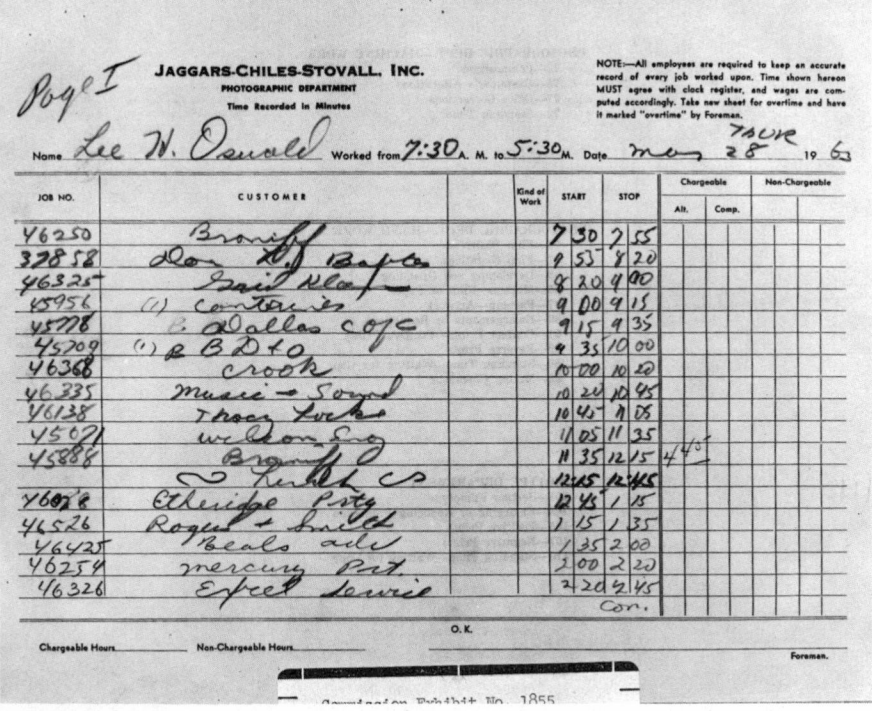

COMMISSION EXHIBIT No. 1855—Continued

Page II

JAGGARS-CHILES-STOVALL, INC.
PHOTOGRAPHIC DEPARTMENT
Time Recorded in Minutes

NOTE:—All employees are required to keep an accurate record of every job worked upon. Time shown hereon MUST agree with clock register, and wages are computed accordingly. Take new sheet for overtime and have it marked "overtime" by Foreman.

Name Lee H Oswald Worked from ______ A. M. to ______ M. Date ______ 19__

JOB NO.	CUSTOMER	Kind of Work	START	STOP	Chargeable Alt.	Chargeable Comp.	Non-Chargeable
46401	Electrotype service		2 45	3 10			
45956	(2) containers corp		3 10	3 35			
46418	Glenn		3 35	4 10			
46546	Les adams		4 10	4 35			
45709	(2) B B D &O		4 35	4 50			
37858	Bayfle		4 50	5 10			
46171	Sam Bloom		5 10	5 30	4 45		
					5 70		
	9 34						

O. K.

Chargeable Hours ______ Non-Chargeable Hours ______ ______ Foreman.

Commission Exhibit No. 1855

COMMISSION EXHIBIT No. 1855—Continued

Page I

JAGGARS-CHILES-STOVALL, INC.
PHOTOGRAPHIC DEPARTMENT
Time Recorded in Minutes

NOTE:—All employees are required to keep an accurate record of every job worked upon. Time shown hereon MUST agree with clock register, and wages are computed accordingly. Take new sheet for overtime and have it marked "overtime" by Foreman.

Name Lee H. Oswald Worked from 8:00 A. M. to 5:45 M. Date Friday mar 29 1963

JOB NO.	CUSTOMER	Kind of Work	START	STOP	Chargeable Alt.	Chargeable Comp.	Non-Chargeable
46594	Titches		8 00	8 20			
46569	Rogers & Smith		8 20	8 45			
46354	(1) Norsworthy mercer		8 45	9 10			
46171	Sam Bloom		9 10	9 35			
43933	Sam Bloom		9 35	10 00			
46515	Goodner Paper		10 00	10 20			
46490	Aldas Leathercraft		10 20	10 50			
46456	Jack T. Holmes		10 50	11 25			
46461	Electrotype service		11 25	12 00	4		
	2 Lunch [illegible]		12 00	12 30			
46716	Curtis		12 30	1 00			
44985	Glenn		1 00	1 20			
46648	Print Pak		1 20	1 50			
46607	Dallas Times Her.		1 50	2 25			
—	Pollock		2 25	2 55			
46036	Creative Designs		2 55	3 25			
46614	Ad. Artist		3 25	3 55			
			(Con)				

O. K.

Chargeable Hours ______ Non-Chargeable Hours ______ ______ Foreman.

Commission Exhibit No. 1855

COMMISSION EXHIBIT No. 1855—Continued

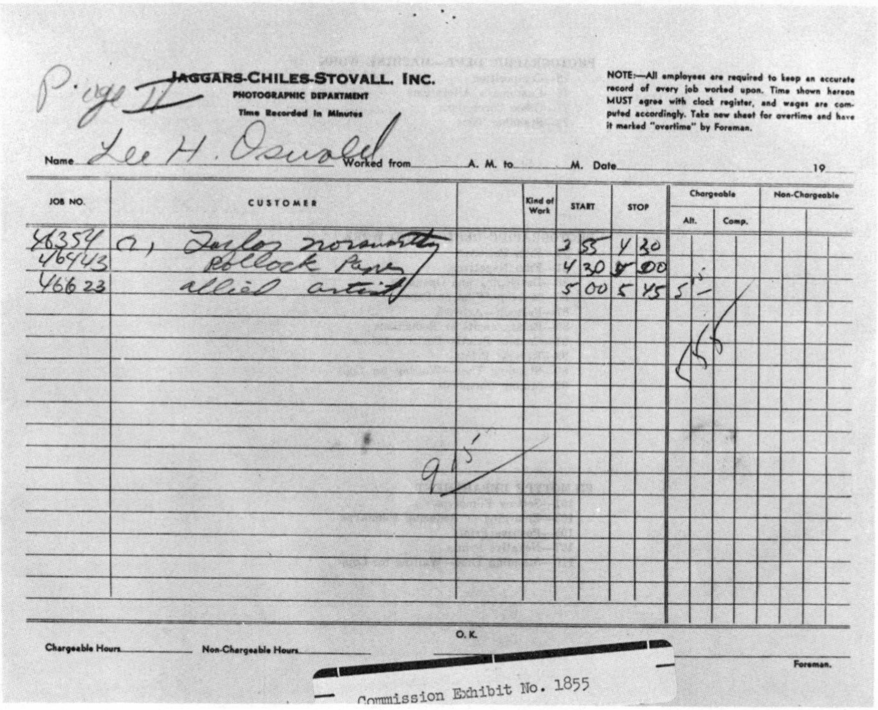

Page II

JAGGARS-CHILES-STOVALL, INC.
PHOTOGRAPHIC DEPARTMENT
Time Recorded in Minutes

NOTE:—All employees are required to keep an accurate record of every job worked upon. Time shown hereon MUST agree with clock register, and wages are computed accordingly. Take new sheet for overtime and have it marked "overtime" by Foreman.

Name Lee H. Oswald Worked from ______ A. M. to ______ M. Date ______ 19__

JOB NO.	CUSTOMER	Kind of Work	START	STOP	Chargeable Alt.	Chargeable Comp.	Non-Chargeable
46354	a, Taylor Norsworthy		3 55	4 20			
46443	Pollock Paper		4 30	5 00			
46623	allied artist		5 00	5 45	5'-		

155

915

Chargeable Hours ______ Non-Chargeable Hours ______ O.K. ______ Foreman.

Commission Exhibit No. 1855

COMMISSION EXHIBIT No. 1855—Continued

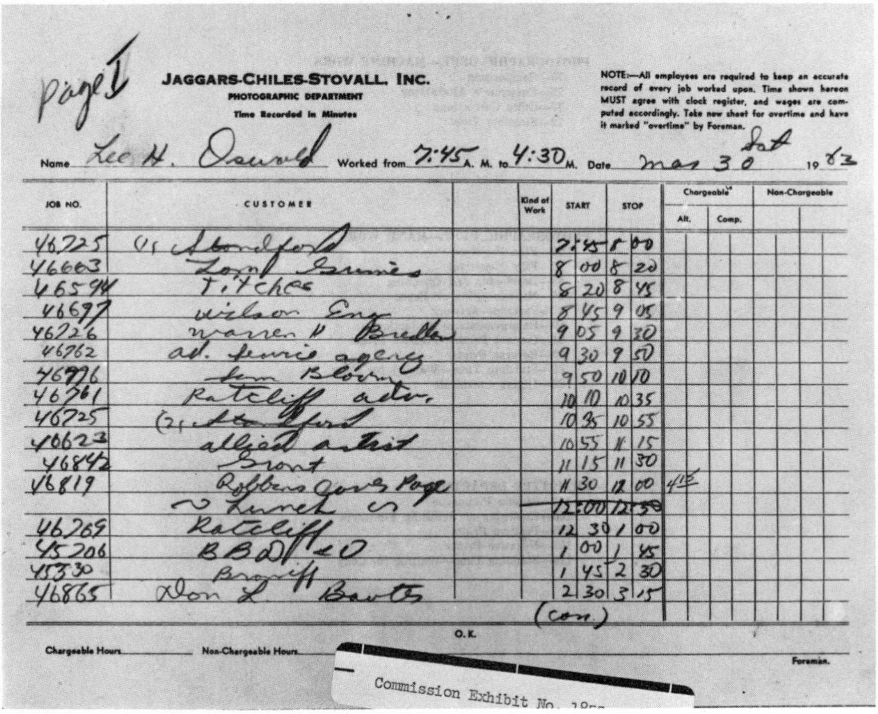

Page I

JAGGARS-CHILES-STOVALL, INC.
PHOTOGRAPHIC DEPARTMENT
Time Recorded in Minutes

NOTE:—All employees are required to keep an accurate record of every job worked upon. Time shown hereon MUST agree with clock register, and wages are computed accordingly. Take new sheet for overtime and have it marked "overtime" by Foreman.

Name Lee H. Oswald Worked from 7:45 A. M. to 4:30 M. Date Mar 30 Sat 1963

JOB NO.	CUSTOMER	Kind of Work	START	STOP	Chargeable Alt.	Chargeable Comp.	Non-Chargeable
46725	a, Stanford		7:45	8 00			
46663	Tom Grimes		8 00	8 20			
46594	Titches		8 20	8 45			
46697	Wilson Eng		8 45	9 05			
46726	Warren H Bradley		9 05	9 30			
46762	ad. service agency		9 30	9 50			
46776	Sam Bloom		9 50	10 10			
46761	Ratcliff adv.		10 10	10 35			
46725	(2) Stanford		10 35	10 55			
46623	allied artist		10 55	11 15			
46842	Grant		11 15	11 30			
46819	Robbins Jones Page		11 30	12 00	415		
	~ Lunch ~		~~12:00~~	~~12 30~~			
46769	Ratcliff		12 30	1 00			
45206	BBD&O		1 00	1 45			
45330	Braniff		1 45	2 30			
46865	Don L. Bartos		2 30	3 15			

(con)

Chargeable Hours ______ Non-Chargeable Hours ______ O.K. ______ Foreman.

Commission Exhibit No. 1855

COMMISSION EXHIBIT No. 1855—Continued

Page II

JAGGARS-CHILES-STOVALL, INC.
PHOTOGRAPHIC DEPARTMENT
Time Recorded in Minutes

NOTE:—All employees are required to keep an accurate record of every job worked upon. Time shown hereon MUST agree with clock register, and wages are computed accordingly. Take new sheet for overtime and have it marked "overtime" by Foreman.

Name Lee H Oswald Worked from ______ A. M. to ______ M. Date ______ 19__

JOB NO.	CUSTOMER		Kind of Work	START		STOP		Chargeable Alt.	Chargeable Comp.	Non-Chargeable	
46705	Robert K. Bethel			3	15	3	55				
46722	James H. Lugong			3	35	4	00				
46841	Muller Smith Ross			4	00	4	15				
46880	S. Gas			4	15	4	30	4			

4 9/5

8 1/4

Chargeable Hours______ Non-Chargeable Hours______ O. K. ______ Foreman.

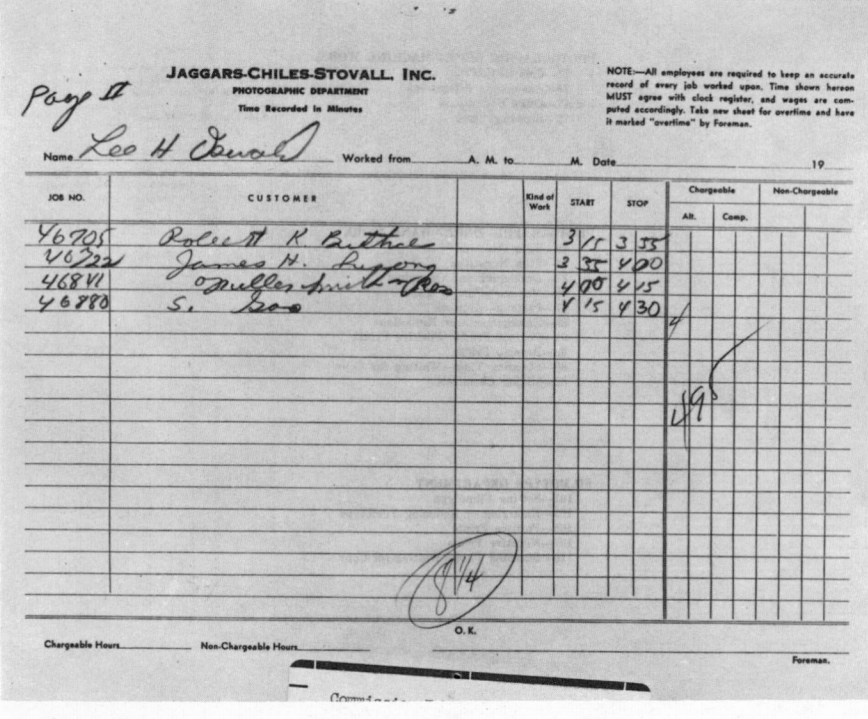

COMMISSION EXHIBIT No. 1855—Continued

Page I

Please note new mailing add.
P.O. Box 2915

JAGGARS-CHILES-STOVALL, INC.
PHOTOGRAPHIC DEPARTMENT
Time Recorded in Minutes

NOTE:—All employees are required to keep an accurate record of every job worked upon. Time shown hereon MUST agree with clock register, and wages are computed accordingly. Take new sheet for overtime and have it marked "overtime" by Foreman.

Name Lee H Oswald Worked from 8:00 A. M. to 6:30 M. Date April 2nd mon. 1963

JOB NO.	CUSTOMER		Kind of Work	START		STOP		Chargeable Alt.	Chargeable Comp.	Non-Chargeable
46885	BBD+O			8	00	8	15			
46352	C+W			8	15	8	35			
46171	Sam Bloom			8	35	9	05			
46880	S. Gas assn			9	05	9	25			
45765	Gilgray circus			9	25	9	45			
46879	S. Gas assn			9	45	10	00			
46922	Jones Duggin			10	00	10	15			
46768	Bill Bond J.			10	15	10	30			
46852	Campbell Dickey			10	30	10	45			
44558	Sam Bloom			10	45	11	00			
46171	Sam Bloom			11	00	11	25			
46841	Wylie Smith			11	25	11	55			
46971	Print Pak			11	50	12	15	4 45		
	~ lunch			12	15	12	45			
46965	Continental Eng			12	45	1	15			
46958	Green Stallion			1	15	1	35			
46981	Sam Bloom			1	35	2	05			
						con.				

O.K.

Chargeable Hours______ Non-Chargeable Hours______ Foreman.

— Commission Exhibit No. 1856 —

COMMISSION EXHIBIT NO. 1856

Page II

JAGGARS-CHILES-STOVALL, INC.
PHOTOGRAPHIC DEPARTMENT
Time Recorded in Minutes

NOTE:—All employees are required to keep an accurate record of every job worked upon. Time shown hereon MUST agree with clock register, and wages are computed accordingly. Take new sheet for overtime and have it marked "overtime" by Foreman.

Name Lee H. Oswald Worked from ______ A. M. to ______ M. Date ______ 19__

JOB NO.	CUSTOMER		Kind of Work	START		STOP		Chargeable Alt.	Chargeable Comp.	Non-Chargeable
46262	adv Lewis			2	05	2	35			
46853	Texas Leather			2	35	2	55			
46882	Hepworth			2	55	3	20			
46843	Miss. Power Co.			3	20	3	45			
46839	S.W. ad.			3	45	4	35			
46914	Tom Grimes			4	35	5	20			
46437	Universal School			5	20	5	55			
46824	Les odoms			5	55	6	30	5 45		
								600		
	10 —									

O.K.

Chargeable Hours______ Non-Chargeable Hours______ Foreman.

— Commission Exhibit No. 1856 —

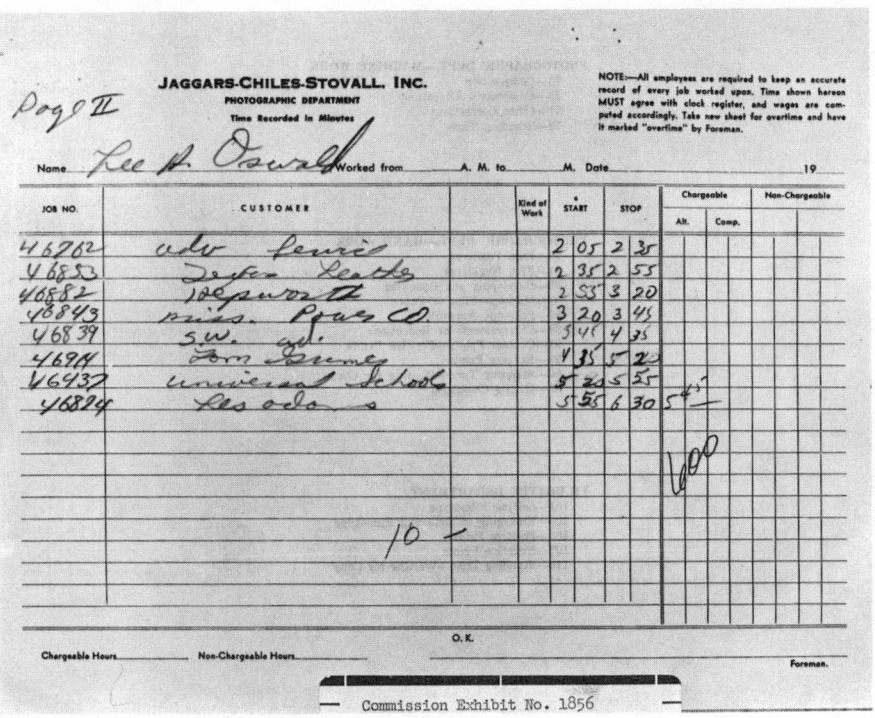

COMMISSION EXHIBIT NO. 1856—Continued

Pg I **JAGGARS-CHILES-STOVALL, INC.**
PHOTOGRAPHIC DEPARTMENT
Time Recorded in Minutes

NOTE:—All employees are required to keep an accurate record of every job worked upon. Time shown hereon MUST agree with clock register, and wages are computed accordingly. Take new sheet for overtime and have it marked "overtime" by Foreman.

Name Lee H. Oswald Worked from 7:30 A. M. to 5:00 M. Date Apr. 2 TUES 19 6

JOB NO.	CUSTOMER		Kind of Work	START		STOP		Chargeable Alt.	Chargeable Comp.	Non-Chargeable
47031	Electrotype Service			7	30	7	55			
47014	Spurs prints			7	55	8	15			
47033	ayres compton			8	15	8	35			
47061	Lone Star Gas			8	35	9	05			
47079	Bill Bond			9	05	9	35			
45677	W Texas util.			9	36	10	05			
47012	(1) Ed Bearden			10	05	10	30			
45868	Braniff			10	30	10	55			
47060	Taylor Pub.			10	55	11	10			
47155	and Denny			11	10	11	45	10		
47176	Containers			11	45	12	20	5		
	Lunch			12	20	12	50			
46712	Draughon			12	50	1	10			
47107	Loftin Shepard			1	10	1	55			
46954	S. W. Telephone			1	35	2	05			
47092	R&S			2	05	2	45			
47012	(2) Ed Bearden			2	45	3	20			

Chargeable Hours____ Non-Chargeable Hours____ O.K.____ Foreman.

Commission Exhibit No. 1856

COMMISSION EXHIBIT No. 1856—Continued

Pg II **JAGGARS-CHILES-STOVALL, INC.**
PHOTOGRAPHIC DEPARTMENT
Time Recorded in Minutes

NOTE:—All employees are required to keep an accurate record of every job worked upon. Time shown hereon MUST agree with clock register, and wages are computed accordingly. Take new sheet for overtime and have it marked "overtime" by Foreman.

Name Lee H. Oswald Worked from ____ A. M. to ____ M. Date ____ 19__

JOB NO.	CUSTOMER		Kind of Work	START		STOP		Chargeable Alt.	Chargeable Comp.	Non-Chargeable
45886	Braniff			3	20	4	00			
46762	Ad. Texas Service			4	00	4	30			
—	JCS			4	30	5	00	4		

600

10

Chargeable Hours____ Non-Chargeable Hours____ O.K.____ Foreman.

Commission Exhibit No. 1856

COMMISSION EXHIBIT No. 1856—Continued

JAGGARS-CHILES-STOVALL, INC.
PHOTOGRAPHIC DEPARTMENT
Time Recorded in Minutes

NOTE:—All employees are required to keep an accurate record of every job worked upon. Time shown hereon MUST agree with clock register, and wages are computed accordingly. Take new sheet for overtime and have it marked "overtime" by Foreman.

Name Lee H. Oswald Worked from 7:45 A. M. to 5:00 M. Date Wed apr. 3 1963

JOB NO.	CUSTOMER		Kind of Work	START		STOP		Chargeable Alt.	Chargeable Comp.	Non-Chargeable
47066	Tracy Locke			7	45	8	20			
46606	Crook adv			8	20	9	00			
46881	Campbell			9	00	9	45			
47340	Cleveland Sherman			9	45	10	15			
47257	The Zodd Co			10	15	11	00			
47341	Wilson D'arcy			11	00	11	40			
46322	Sam Bloom			11	40	12	15	4 30		
	Lunch			12	15	12	45			
42639	J.C.S.			12	45	1	25			
47381	Tracy-Locke			1	25	2	05			
47284	R & S			2	05	2	40			
46758	James H. Lusary			2	40	3	10			
47067	Lone Sta Gas			3	10	3	30			
47475	Bennett Prtg			3	30	4	05			
47450	Couchman adv.			4	05	4	25			
47340	Cleveland Sherman			4	25	4	45			
46789	Braniff			4	45	5	00	4 15		

Chargeable Hours (4 4) Non-Chargeable Hours O.K. 525 Foreman.

Commission Exhibit No. 1856

COMMISSION EXHIBIT NO. 1856—Continued

page I

JAGGARS-CHILES-STOVALL, INC.
PHOTOGRAPHIC DEPARTMENT
Time Recorded in Minutes

NOTE:—All employees are required to keep an accurate record of every job worked upon. Time shown hereon MUST agree with clock register, and wages are computed accordingly. Take new sheet for overtime and have it marked "overtime" by Foreman.

Name Lee H. Oswald Worked from 8:00 A. M. to 5:30 M. Date Thurs apr. 4 1963

JOB NO.	CUSTOMER		Kind of Work	START		STOP		Chargeable Alt.	Chargeable Comp.	Non-Chargeable
47411	Jack Wyatt			8	00	8	20			
47550	Ken Bell			8	20	8	45			
47075	Stevenson			8	45	9	05			
47122	Johnston Prtg			9	05	9	25			
47388	Gardner Papers			9	25	9	50			
46606	Crook adv			9	50	10	10			
47526	Cunningham & Walsh			10	10	10	35			
47170	T P - L			10	35	11	05			
47459	Cunningham Compact			11	05	11	20			
47531	Wright Allen & Ryan			11	20	11	40			
47536	Sam Bloom			11	40	11	55			
47094	R & S			11	55	12	10	4 10		
	Lunch			~~12~~	~~10~~	~~12~~	~~40~~			
47384	Miss. Power Co			12	40	1	10			
45498	Hal Mayes			1	10	1	30			
47381	Tracy Locke			1	30	2	05			
47488	Ams			2	05	2	40			

Chargeable Hours Non-Chargeable Hours O.K. Foreman.

Commission Exhibit No. 1856

COMMISSION EXHIBIT NO. 1856—Continued

Page II

JAGGARS-CHILES-STOVALL, INC.
PHOTOGRAPHIC DEPARTMENT
Time Recorded in Minutes

NOTE:—All employees are required to keep an accurate record of every job worked upon. Time shown hereon MUST agree with clock register, and wages are computed accordingly. Take new sheet for overtime and have it marked "overtime" by Foreman.

Name Lee H. Oswald Worked from ______ A. M. to ______ M. Date ______ 19__

JOB NO.	CUSTOMER		Kind of Work	START	STOP	Chargeable Alt.	Chargeable Comp.	Non-Chargeable
47560	Lone Star Gas			2 40	3 05			
47478	The Zold Co			3 05	3 30			
47593	Wilson Engrav.			3 30	3 50			
47556	S.W. Drug			3 50	4 05			
47530	Ackerman associat.			4 05	4 20			
47658	Tom [illegible]			4 20	4 40			
4744[illegible]	Morbo Productions			4 40	5 00			
47652	BBD&O			5 00	5 30	4 50		
		9				5 40		

Chargeable Hours ______ Non-Chargeable Hours ______ O.K. ______ Foreman.

Commission Exhibit No. 1856

COMMISSION EXHIBIT NO. 1856—Continued

Page I

JAGGARS-CHILES-STOVALL, INC.
PHOTOGRAPHIC DEPARTMENT
Time Recorded in Minutes

NOTE:—All employees are required to keep an accurate record of every job worked upon. Time shown hereon MUST agree with clock register, and wages are computed accordingly. Take new sheet for overtime and have it marked "overtime" by Foreman.

Name Lee H. Oswald Worked from 8:05 A. M. to 5:05 M. Date FRIDAY Apr. 5 1963

JOB NO.	CUSTOMER		Kind of Work	START	STOP	Chargeable Alt.	Chargeable Comp.	Non-Chargeable
47743	Story-Locke			8 05	8 25			
47710	(1) Hal Mayes			8 25	8 50			
46171	Sam Bloom			8 50	9 10			
47710	(2) Hal Mayes			9 10	9 35			
47288	Glenn adver.			9 35	10 05			
47597	BBD&O			10 05	10 40			
47741	Wilson Engr.			10 40	10 55			
44555	Sam Bloom			10 55	11 10			
47757	Sam Bloom			11 10	11 35			
47624	Ussery Prtg CO			11 35	12 15	4 10		
	~ Lunch ~			12 15	12 45			
47715	Wilson Eng.			12 45	1 15			
47868	(1) Dunc[illegible] Coffee			1 15	1 35			
4744[illegible]	Sears Roebuck			1 35	1 55			
4669[illegible]	Titches ad			1 55	2 30			
47659	Curtis Mathes			2 30	3 15			
47783	Gordon Marks			3 15	3 50			
				con.				

Chargeable Hours ______ Non-Chargeable Hours ______ O.K. ______ Foreman.

Commission Exhibit No. 1856

COMMISSION EXHIBIT NO. 1856—Continued

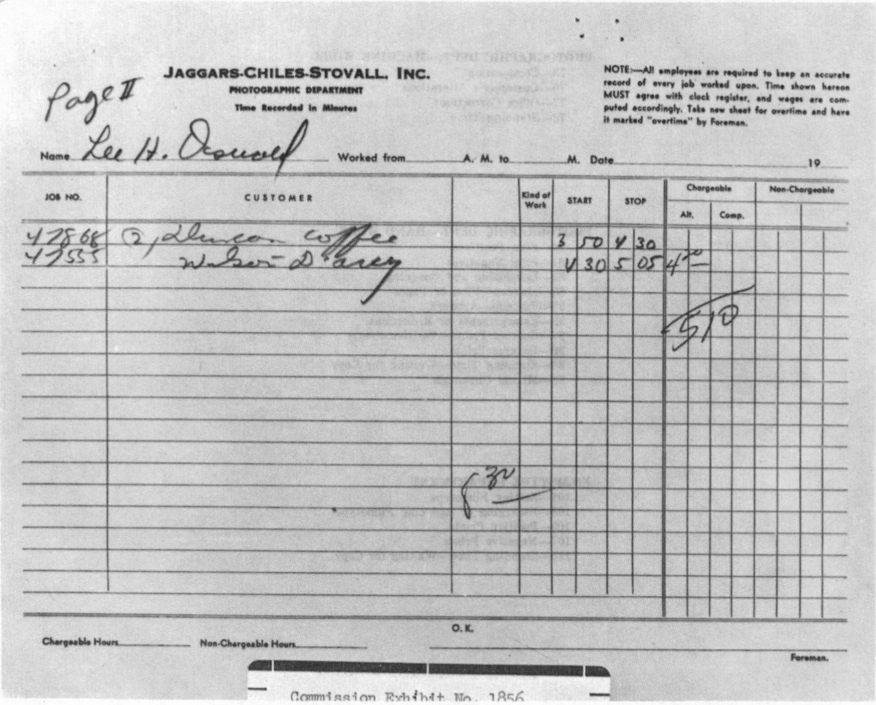

Page II

JAGGARS-CHILES-STOVALL, INC.
PHOTOGRAPHIC DEPARTMENT
Time Recorded in Minutes

NOTE:—All employees are required to keep an accurate record of every job worked upon. Time shown hereon MUST agree with clock register, and wages are computed accordingly. Take new sheet for overtime and have it marked "overtime" by Foreman.

Name Lee H. Oswald Worked from ______ A. M. to ______ M. Date ______ 19__

JOB NO.	CUSTOMER		Kind of Work	START	STOP	Chargeable Alt.	Chargeable Comp.	Non-Chargeable
47868	(2) Duncan Coffee			3 50	4 30			
47555	Wilson D'Arcy			4 30	5 05	4 20		
		8 30				5 10		

Chargeable Hours______ Non-Chargeable Hours______ O.K. ______ Foreman.

Commission Exhibit No. 1856

COMMISSION EXHIBIT NO. 1856—Continued

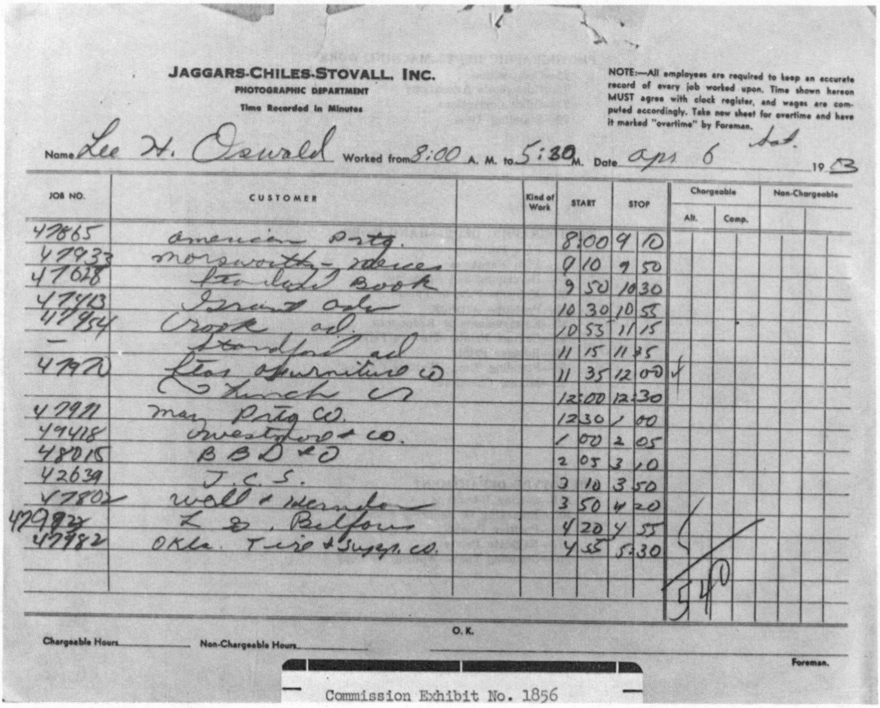

JAGGARS-CHILES-STOVALL, INC.
PHOTOGRAPHIC DEPARTMENT
Time Recorded in Minutes

NOTE:—All employees are required to keep an accurate record of every job worked upon. Time shown hereon MUST agree with clock register, and wages are computed accordingly. Take new sheet for overtime and have it marked "overtime" by Foreman.

Name Lee H. Oswald Worked from 8:00 A. M. to 5:30 M. Date Apr 6 Sat. 1963

JOB NO.	CUSTOMER		Kind of Work	START	STOP	Chargeable Alt.	Chargeable Comp.	Non-Chargeable
47865	American Prtg.			8:00	9 10			
47933	Morsworthy-Reeves			9 10	9 50			
47628	Standard Book			9 50	10 30			
47413	Grant Ad			10 30	10 55			
47954	Crook ad.			10 53	11 15			
—	Standford ad			11 15	11 35			
47920	Leos Furniture Co			11 35	12 00			
	Lunch			12:00	12:30			
47921	May Prtg Co.			12 30	1 00			
49418	Westford & Co.			1 00	2 05			
48015	B B D & O			2 05	3 10			
42639	J. C. S.			3 10	3 50			
47802	Wall & Herndon			3 50	4 20			
47982	L. D. Belfour			4 20	4 55			
47982	Okla. Tire & Supply Co.			4 55	5:30			
						5 40		

Chargeable Hours______ Non-Chargeable Hours______ O.K. ______ Foreman.

Commission Exhibit No. 1856

COMMISSION EXHIBIT NO. 1856—Continued

FD-302 (Rev. 3-3-59)

FEDERAL BUREAU OF INVESTIGATION

Date January 16, 1964

1

Mrs. MAX E. CLARK (nee GALI), 4312 Selkirk Drive West, furnished the following information:

Mrs. CLARK was reared in France but her mother and father were from Russia and left Russia after the 1917 Revolution. She speaks Russian and is acquainted with most of the Russian-speaking people around Dallas and Fort Worth. Mrs. CLARK stated around June of 1962 she received a telephone call from a man identifying himself as OSWALD, and she believed that his first name might have been LEE. OSWALD told her that he had obtained her name from the Texas Employment Commission in Fort Worth and was contacting her as he understood that she spoke Russian, and possibly some of her family had originally come to this country from Russia. OSWALD stated he would like to get acquainted with Mrs. CLARK and her husband, and would like to visit with them sometime. She stated that she would have her husband contact him at some future date and maybe they could visit.

In September or October of 1962, her husband, MAX CLARK, contacted LEE OSWALD who was at that time living in Fort Worth. OSWALD could not come to their house and asked the CLARKs to come out to see them, but MAX CLARK could not go and told OSWALD if he wanted to visit with them, he and his wife would have to come to their home. In about October, 1962, Mrs. CLARK went to the home of the OSWALDs on Mercedes Street with GEORGE BOUHE from Dallas. BOUHE was taking some clothes to Mrs. OSWALD for herself and her baby. She visited with Mrs. OSWALD only a few minutes and LEE HARVEY OSWALD was not at home. During the latter part of October, 1962, MARINA OSWALD was staying at the home of ELENA HALL on Trail Lake Drive in Fort Worth. At that time LEE OSWALD was in Dallas. Mrs. HALL was injured in an automobile accident and was in the hospital for about seven days. During this time, she visited MARINA OSWALD nearly every day to help her with her shopping and to buy some groceries. She talked to her in Russian, generally about personal matters in Fort Worth and in this country. She did not see LEE OSWALD during this period of time. On one occasion during the latter part of October, 1962, she and her husband went to the HALL's residence

[redacted]

— Commission Exhibit No. 1857 —

on 1-13-64 at Fort Worth, Texas File # DL 100-10461

by Special Agent [illegible]LE HALEY [illegible]LEY D. MADLAND MVS Date dictated 1-15-64

COMMISSION EXHIBIT NO. 1857

2
DL 100-10461

for a visit and some other Russians from Dallas were there. At that time she met LEE HARVEY OSWALD for the first time. She talked very little to him but had most of her conversation with MARINA OSWALD. She stated that MAX CLARK, her husband, talked to LEE OSWALD a large part of the evening as he was interested in obtaining information about Russia.

During the conversations with MARINA OSWALD, MARINA told her that her parents died when she was a small girl. She later moved into the home of an uncle and aunt in Russia and she made the remark that this uncle was a member of the Communist Party in Russia. She stated that this uncle was not very happy when she married LEE HARVEY OSWALD. Mrs. CLARK stated that she had never discussed politics or government with MARINA OSWALD, but she indicated she was very happy to be in the United States. She was unable to furnish any information concerning LEE HARVEY OSWALD other than the one conversation that she had with him.

COMMISSION EXHIBIT NO. 1857—Continued

FD-302 (Rev. 1-25-60) FEDERAL BUREAU OF INVESTIGAT

1

Date 12/18/63

Mrs. TATIANA BIGGERS, 2805 West Lane Drive, Houston, Texas, was interviewed at her place of employment, 810 Medical Towers Building, Houston. Mrs. BIGGERS advised that she was born in Russia and speaks Russian and French fluently. She advised that she left Russia in 1920, the year of her birth, and resided from 1920 to the late 1940's in France. She advised that she entered the United States as a GI Bride.

BIGGERS advised that over the Christmas Holidays, 1962, she was a house guest of ANNA MELLER, 5903½ La Vista Drive, Dallas, Texas. She advised that while in Dallas, she attended a party at the home of the DECLAN FORDS in Dallas, on December 28, 1962. She stated also at the party was subject OSWALD and his wife, MARINA. BIGGERS advised she recalls being introduced to OSWALD at the party but did not talk with him. She stated that she talked considerably to MARINA OSWALD because she felt sorry for MARINA in that MARINA was unable to speak English and was more or less left by herself at the party.

She stated MARINA was very hard to talk to and volunteered no information other than answering direct questions put to her. She stated MARINA made no attempt to carry on a conversation. She described MARINA as being a shy and withdrawn person.

BIGGERS advised ANNA MELLERS told her that on one occasion MARINA had come to the MELLER's home in Dallas with her child after a quarrel at home. MELLER said MARINA at that time had a black eye. BIGGERS stated from this she got the impression that OSWALD was cruel to MARINA.

She advised when she first heard OSWALD's name after the assassination it meant nothing to her and she did not recognize him until information concerning his background appeared in the newspapers. She stated she immediately recognized the photograph of MARINA OSWALD which appeared in the newspapers as being of the woman she had met at the FORD's party.

— Commission Exhibit No. 1858 —

On 12/18/63 at Houston, Texas File # HO 105-1291

by SA WILLIAM J. SCHMIDT:pak Date dictated 12/18/63

COMMISSION EXHIBIT No. 1858

2

HO 105-1291

BIGGERS advised also attending at the FORD party was GEORGE BOUHE, former secretary of the Russian Orthodox Church, presently at Bacliff, Texas, and VICTOR and IRENA VYSLEP, Dallas, Texas.

COMMISSION EXHIBIT No. 1858—Continued

FD-302 (Rev. 3-3-59) FEDERAL BUREAU OF INVESTIGATION

1 Date 12/24/63

Mrs. THOMAS RAY (NATALIE) was interviewed at her home approximately six miles northeast of Blossom, Texas, but prior to the interview she was advised of the identity of SA DEL D. DRAKE, JR.

Mrs. RAY stated that she had been born in Russia and had married her husband in 1946 in Germany, where she was a displaced person. He was a former GI who had taken a job as a civilian radio operator. She subsequently moved to her present home in Blossom, had become a naturalized American Citizen, and had received her papers in Federal Court, Paris, Texas.

Mrs. RAY stated that in 1962, through mutual friends, Mr. and Mrs. CHARLES E. HARRIS, Georgetown, Texas, (Mrs. HARRIS is Russian born, but now an American Citizen) the RAYS were invited to attend a New Year's celebration in Dallas, Texas, at the home of Mr. and Mrs. DECLAN FORD, 14057 Brookcrest Drive, on December 28, 29, 1962. She said that they met the FORDS in Dallas; went to this party at the FORDS; and to the best of her recollection the following persons attended the party and she wished to explain that she had never met any of these people prior to the party with the exception of the HARRIS':

1. FNU JACKSON, apparently very prominent people in Dallas, who apparently were close friends of GEORGE BOUHE, and to whose home some of the people went after the party at the FORDS. (The JACKSON home was a very lavish home in a big residential district of Dallas).

2. Mr. and Mrs. FRANK RAY, no relation to Mr. and Mrs. THOMAS RAY. (Mrs. FRANK RAY was Russian born) Mrs. THOMAS RAY stated that this couple was apparently having marital difficulties and was supposed to have obtained a divorce.

3. GEORGE BOUHE, a bachelor, 4740 Homer Street, Apartment O, telephone TA 7-2288, who Mrs. RAY described as a person who was very much interested in all of the Russian people keeping track of one another and giving a helping hand to one another. She said BOUHE was considered

Commission Exhibit No. 1859

on 12/19/63 at Blossom, Texas File # DL 100-10461

by Special Agent DEL D. DRAKE, JR./sah Date dictated 12/20/63

COMMISSION EXHIBIT No. 1859

2

DL 100-10461

the leader of the Social group.

4. JOHN and ELAIN HALL - No known address and nothing more known of them.

5. TATIANA BIGGERS, apparently a divorcee, who was from somewhere around Houston, Texas.

6. TEOFIL and ANNA MELLER, 5930½ LaVista Drive, Dallas, Texas, telephone TA 3-2219. Both of these persons were apparently Russian born.

7. LYDIA DYMITRUK - apparently a single person who resided somewhere in Dallas, Texas.

8. A Russian man and a Chinese woman, whose names are unrecalled were at the party and nothing more is known or recalled about them. These persons came together.

9. Mr. and Mrs. DANIEL F. SULLIVAN, Lafayette, Louisiana - a divisional geologist for Continental Oil Company, telephone number 232-6998.

Mrs. RAY estimated that there were from 15 to 25 couples at the party during the evening and the morning hours of December 29, 1962 prior to the time that some of the persons at the party went to the JACKSON residence for a drink. She stated that among the group at the FORD residence were LEE HARVEY OSWALD and his Russian wife, MARINA, who could not speak English. She said that the OSWALDS had been brought to the party by an unknown couple from Fort Worth, Texas, or at least a couple who resided somewhere close to the area where the OSWALDS were residing. She pointed out that most of the persons who were Russian born enjoyed talking to Mrs. OSWALD and that the people who did not understand Russian very well, did not pay too much attention to any of the conversation that took place. She said her husband was one of these persons. However, LEE HARVEY OSWALD was questioned at considerable length by

COMMISSION EXHIBIT No. 1859—Continued

different persons at the party including herself, and many questions were asked of him about his stay in Russia, his work, and whether he would like to return to Russia sometime in the future. Mrs. RAY explained that OSWALD was very proud of the fact that he spoke Russian so well and that she was amazed that he had such good command of the language. OSWALD stated that he might someday return to Russia, and again Mrs. RAY said that she was amazed that OSWALD had such an understanding of the Russian Government and of the workings of the Russian Government. He did not exactly say anything that she could recall that sounded like he was advocating the Russian way of life and she was positive he never did say anything about the Kennedy Administration, of American politics, nor did OSWALD mention Cuba or CASTRO. Furthermore the name of JACK RUBY was never mentioned.

Mrs. RAY said that many of the persons tried to talk a little English to Mrs. OSWALD, and OSWALD did not seem to care that his wife attempted to talk English. On many occasions when Mrs. OSWALD was asked a question OSWALD would interpret and answer the question for her, and this made some of the other Russian speaking guests quite angry because they felt that since Mrs. OSWALD was the latest arrival from Russia, she was more or less the "main attraction" at the party. OSWALD drank quite a bit and after some of the guests talked to him briefly, they would apparently get tired of him and would turn their attention to his wife. However, Mrs. RAY said that she did understand Mrs. OSWALD to say that she and her husband had had no trouble getting married in Russia, and furthermore, they had no trouble getting permission to leave the country to come to the United States. This was a point that caused several of native Russians to wonder, since they knew that this does not happen in Russia. Mrs. OSWALD also pointed out to Mrs. RAY that in Russia the Russian people were more or less afraid to talk to her husband, because they did not trust him and that since they did not welcome her husband, this was one of his reasons for wanting to come back to the United States.

However, as Mrs. RAY pointed out, OSWALD said several times that he liked Russia and that he "might go back". She said that both the OSWALDS talked about Minsk, Russia, and that from what OSWALD said, he liked this location and the way things were run in Minsk.

Mrs. RAY recalled that when OSWALD was leaving the party he said that he did not actually want to leave, but that it was necessary since he did not have a car and that he was riding with another couple. (This was apparently the couple who lived somewhere near OSWALDS.) She also recalled that OSWALD was not employed at the time of the party.

She also recalled that OSWALD was introduced to her under a Russian name but she has not been able to recall just what that name was but in the event she recalls it she will advise the FBI later.

After the departure of the OSWALDS, Mrs. RAY related that GEORGE BOUHE said he had tried to help the OSWALDS and had tried to help him take care of his family, but that OSWALD had done nothing to help himself. BOUHE said that when OSWALD would go somewhere to seek employment and was asked where he was last employed, he would reply, "Minsk, Russia", and then never give an explanation, and therefore he would not hear from his application. She said that BOUHE offered an explanation about OSWALD that seemed to be the consensus of opinion of several of the persons who knew him, and that was that OSWALD was a "mental case". However, on Sunday, December 30, 1962, while several of the persons from the party, and some others, all of whom Mrs. RAY cannot identify, were at the MELLER residence, OSWALD was discussed at considerable length by the Russians at the party. Mrs. RAY said that there was considerable speculation offered about the possibility that OSWALD was possibly a Russian Agent as that would explain why it had been no trouble for the OSWALDS to get married and to leave Russia for the United States.

5
DL 100-10461

But this theory was thrown out because OSWALD was "broke" and had "no connections in the United States, and Russia did not allow their Agents to be in this predicament in the United States. This was not like the Russian Government according to Mrs. RAY.

Mrs. RAY also said that the thought had arisen in her mind that since the Russian people had not aparently accepted OSWALD that he had been given an assignment in the United States by the Russian Government so that when he returned he would be accepted and that would probably explain his reason for wanting to return to Russia. However, Mrs. RAY said that after giving more consideration to OSWALD, she finally decided that he was a mental case, but she cannot get out of her mind that you cannot trust the Russian Government and that they are capable of doing anything.

Mrs. RAY said that she felt sorry for Mrs. OSWALD at the party and since this was the only time she had ever seen her she knew that some of the others felt the same way because several had said that OSWALD really mistreated MARINA and they were trying to help her. Mrs. RAY said that GEORGE BOUHE seemed to have some very definite opinions on the OSWALD family and that she felt that he would be very glad to discuss them with the FBI.

Mrs. RAY finally closed her remarks by saying again that she could not understand how OSWALD and his wife had so little trouble, if any, in leaving Russia, and she knew that several of the other guests felt the same way about it. She also said that she was sorry that she could not recall any more, but explained that this was the only time she had seen these people and that much of the details had been forgotten until she saw OSWALD's picture on television at the time of his arrest in Dallas, Texas and many of the remarks made about him had come back to her. She said the FBI could talk to her at any time it was necessary.

COMMISSION EXHIBIT No. 1859—Continued

FD-302 (Rev. 1-25-60)

FEDERAL BUREAU OF INVESTIGATION

Commission Exhibit No. 1860

Date December 7, 1963

CHARLES EDWARD HARRIS, JR., 904 E. 12th, Georgetown, Texas, partner, Troy Laundry and Dry Cleaners, 303 W. 6th, Georgetown, Texas, furnished the following information:

Between Christmas and New Years Day, about December 28, 1962, he and his wife attended a party at the residence of Mr. and Mrs. DECLAN FORD at Dallas, Texas. The party was attended by about fifty people, some of whom had an interest or background in Russia - either Russian born or married to a Russian born person. Others present at the party were friends of the FORDS, without any apparent Russian connection or interest. He stated that his wife, Mrs. HARRIS, and Mrs. DECLAN FORD were both Russian born and it was that mutual interest that initiated their acquaintance.

HARRIS recalled that the first night they were in Dallas they attended the party at the FORD residence. During the party he met and conversed with LEE HARVEY OSWALD, whose photograph he observed and recognized. He could not recall the specific topic of their casual conversation and did not recall any comments made by OSWALD concerning political ideology, foreign travel or activity. HARRIS recalled that he judged OSWALD as a "nut" but could not specify the exact basis for this judgment other than that he may have pre-judged OSWALD since he had been informed by Mrs. FORD prior to the party that OSWALD had recently returned from Russia and had married a Russian girl. He stated that he had not met OSWALD before the party and did not see him again afterwards.

HARRIS stated that the day following the party, he and his wife attended an open house or afternoon party in Dallas at the residence of ANNA MELLER, another Russian born acquaintance of Mrs. HARRIS. She stated that to the best of his recollection, neither OSWALD or OSWALD's wife were at the MELLER residence.

HARRIS added that in the evening, the day following the party, he and his wife attended another smaller gathering

On 12/5/63 at Georgetown, Texas File # SA 105=2909

by SA HAROLD LEO FABRIZ/cbl Date dictated 12/6/63

This document contains neither recommendations nor conclusions of the FBI. It is the property of the FBI and is loaned to your agency; it and its contents are not to be distributed outside your agency.

29

SA 105-2909

at the home of the FORDS; however, the OSWALDS were not present. On the third day in Dallas, HARRIS and his wife attended another open house at the residence of GEORGE BEUHE, who is interested in the welfare of newcomers to the Dallas area who have Russian backgrounds. HARRIS stated that OSWALD was not at the BEUHE residence; however, BEUHE was acquainted with OSWALD and was also a friend of Mrs. HARRIS and Mrs. FORD.

HARRIS added that Mr. and Mrs. THOMAS RAY, who were from Blossom, Texas, which is near Paris, Texas, were at the party at the FORD residence the night that OSWALD was there. Mrs. RAY is Russian born, according to HARRIS.

HARRIS stated that another couple, present at the party at the FORD residence was Mr. and Mrs. FRANK RAY of Dallas, no relation to the THOMAS RAYS, above. HARRIS advised that after he returned to Georgetown, Texas, his wife stayed an additional day at the residence of Mr. and Mrs. FRANK RAY at Dallas.

HARRIS also recalled that a man named ALLEN JACKSON of Dallas was at the party at the FORD residence which was also attended by OSWALD; however, he did not believe that JACKSON had any Russian background but was merely a friend of the FORDS.

HARRIS stated that he married his wife, who was a Russian refugee, in Iran in September, 1946, after he had been discharged from the U.S. Army and while he was employed by TWA. He added that his wife became a naturalized United States citizen in the summer of 1963 and that they have two daughters, aged 8 and 12.

COMMISSION EXHIBIT No. 1860—Continued

FD-302 (Rev. 1-25-60)

FEDERAL BUREAU OF INVESTIGATION

Commission Exhibit No. 1861

Date December 9, 1963

Mrs. CHARLES EDWARD HARRIS, 904 E. 12th, Georgetown, Texas, furnished the following information:

On December 28, 1962, she and her husband attended a party at the residence of Mr. and Mrs. DECLAN FORD at Dallas, Texas. The party was attended by about forty or fifty people, some of whom were Russian born as Mrs. FORD (first name KATSHA - phonetic) and Mrs. HARRIS, and others who had no apparent Russian background.

Mrs. HARRIS stated that at the party she met and conversed in Russian with LEE HARVEY OSWALD, whose photograph she observed and recognized. She advised that OSWALD asked her why she left Russia and what was wrong with Russia. Her reply was something to the effect that she left because everything was wrong and she countered OSWALD by asking him why he left Russia if everything was so good over there. Upon her query, OSWALD was annoyed with her and was obviously upset by her remark, whereupon she ignored him and joined in the singing of Russian songs with a group of other guests.

She recalled that about an hour after her brief encounter with OSWALD, she was sitting on a sofa with ALLEN JACKSON with whom she was conversing when LEE HARVEY OSWALD's wife walked by and JACKSON made some remark to Mrs. OSWALD which Mrs. OSWALD apparently ignored. When JACKSON asked what was the matter with Mrs. OSWALD, Mrs. HARRIS advised him that Mrs. OSWALD did not speak English. Mrs. HARRIS then proceeded to act as an interpreter for Mrs. OSWALD and JACKSON as they conversed for several minutes. Mrs. HARRIS added that she tried to teach Mrs. OSWALD some English words and was telling her about American customs when LEE HARVEY OSWALD came over to where they were talking and chided Mrs. HARRIS, in strong Russian language, for telling his wife anything of the English language or of local customs. He asserted that his wife had no need of learning anything of either subject and escorted Mrs. OSWALD from the presence of Mrs. HARRIS.

On 12/5/63 at Georgetown, Texas File # SA 105-2909

by SA HAROLD LEO FABRIZ/cbl Date dictated 12/6/63

COMMISSION EXHIBIT No. 1861

SA 105-2909

Mrs. HARRIS stated that she had never met either LEE HARVEY OSWALD or his wife at any time prior to the party at the FORD residence and did not see them subsequent to that evening.

She recalled that during her two short conversations with OSWALD she did not hear him express any political ideas, his travel or employment in Russia of his activities in the United States. She added that she did not believe OSWALD attended any of the other functions she and her husband attended at Dallas during the last week of December 1962.

Mrs. HARRIS stated that in addition to the party at the FORD residence, she and her husband attended an open house or afternoon party at the residence of ANNA N. MELLER, 5903 1/2 La Vista Drive, Dallas, Texas, on December 29, 1962. She did not believe that OSWALD was present at that gathering, however. Also at the MELLER residence was another Russian born woman, named LYDIA DYMITRUK, 4635 McKinny Avenue, Apartment 51-A, Dallas, Texas; however, Mrs. HARRIS did not know whether or not LYDIA was acquainted with OSWALD.

Mrs. HARRIS also stated that on December 30, 1962, she and her husband attended an open house or afternoon party at the residence of GEORGE BEUHE, 4740 Homer Street, Dallas, Texas. She stated that BEUHE was acquainted with OSWALD and Mrs. OSWALD since he takes an interest in recently arrived individuals of Russian background and is interested in their welfare.

She added that at the party at the BEUHE residence she met a man named JOHN HALL, whose wife, ELAINA (phonetic) was from Iran and was of Russian extraction. She recalled that the HALLS resided in Fort Worth but did not know whether or not they were acquainted with OSWALD.

Mrs. HARRIS also stated that Mr. and Mrs. THOMAS RAY, Blossom, Bexas (near Paris, Texas) were in attendance at the party at the FORD residence on December 28, 1962. She stated that Mrs. THOMAS RAY is Russian born.

Mrs, HARRIS also stated that at the residence of ANNA MELLER in Sallas she met TATIANA BIGGERS, 2805 West Lane Drive, Houston, Texas, phone MO 50350. She did not know if

3.

SA 105-2909

TATIANA was acquainted with OSWALD.

Mrs. HARRIS added that ALLEN and MARGARET JACKSON, 3735 West Bay Circle, Dallas, Texas, phone TA 4-0216 or TA 7-7165, were at the party at the FORD residence on December 28, 1962; however, she believed that the JACKSONS were merely friends of the FORDS and did not believe that either of the JACKSONS had any Russian background. It was Mr. JACKSON who conversed with Mrs. OSWALD through the translation of Mrs. HARRIS.

Mrs. HARRIS stated that Mrs. OSWALD had come to the United States about six or seven months prior to the time of the party, or in the Spring or summer of 1962, to the best of her understanding. She stated that she understood that Mrs. OSWALD had been living for several weeks with Mrs. DECLAN FORD (KATSHA FORD - phonetic) because OSWALD had beatened her. She added that she understood that Mrs. OSWALD worked for Mrs. FORD just to earn her keep there. Mrs. HARRIS also advised that she understood that Mrs. OSWALD had lived with ANNA RAY (Mrs. FRANK RAY) at Dallas, Texas, for a shorter period of time.

Mrs. HARRIS added that it was a private joke between her and Mrs. FORD concerning the inability of OSWALD to obtain a job and they saw the humor in it when they considered the reaction of prospective employers where OSWALD would tell them that he was last employed in Minsk, Russia. They observed that naturally, no one was going to hire someone who had last worked in Russia. Mrs. HARRIS reported that she received the impression from OSWALD that he wanted to impress people that he had been in Russia and that he had worked there. She added that he made it sound important that he had been in Russia and he appeared to feel that others should have been impressed by his adventure there.

Mrs. HARRIS added that she was unfavorably impressed by OSWALD and considered him an eccentric from the outset of their meeting. She stated that prior to the time she met OSWALD at the party, she had been informed by Mrs. FORD of OSWALD's recent stay in Russia and marriage to a Russian woman.

UNITED STATES DEPARTMENT OF JUSTICE

FEDERAL BUREAU OF INVESTIGATION

In Reply, Please Refer to File No.

Dallas, Texas

May 6, 1964

LEE HARVEY OSWALD

By letter dated April 30, 1964, the President's Commission requested that Miss YAEKO OKUI be interviewed, as witnesses had testified to her presence at a year-end combination Christmas - New Year's Party, December 28 - 30, 1962, at the residence of Mr. and Mrs. DECLAN P. FORD, at 14057 Brookcrest Drive, Dallas, Texas, at which party MARINA and LEE HARVEY OSWALD were also in attendance.

On May 5, 1964, Miss YAEKO OKUI, 5646 Loring Drive, Apartment 149, Dallas, Texas, was contacted at her residence for interview.

Miss OKUI advised she was born January 19, 1933, Tokyo, Japan, and resided at the residence of her parents, 843 Yamashita-Cho, Sumoto City, Hyogo Prefecture, Japan, until her travel to the United States in 1959.

As a matter of background, Miss OKUI advised her father was a practicing attorney in Sumoto City, Japan, until the time of his death approximately four years ago, and that her mother, Mrs. TOYO OKUI, is presently a Certified Public Accountant operating accounting firms in Sumoto City and Wakayamac City. Miss OKUI advised she attended Wasada University in Tokyo for three and one-half years, majoring in Business Administration and Economics. She advised she did not receive a degree from this university, but lacks only the submission of a thesis, which she plans to submit upon her return. In addition, Miss OKUI completed seven years of study at the Sogetsu School of Professional Flower Arrangement at Tokyo, for which she received a Teacher's Certificate, allowing her to practice professional flower arrangement teaching throughout the world. Miss OKUI advised she is further proficient in Kato music, which Miss OKUI described as a large, thirteen-string instrument, which is quite popular in Japanese symphony orchestras. Miss

COMMISSION EXHIBIT No. 1862

Re: LEE HARVEY OSWALD

OKUI stated she, likewise, holds a Teacher's Certificate in this instrument and she, accordingly, has conducted several classes in Kato music during her residence in Dallas.

Miss OKUI advised that in the Spring of 1959, upon completing her studies at the Sogetsu School in Tokyo, she came in contact with a Mr. OZAWA, President of Ozawa & Company, Osaka, Japan, which company is the Japanese agent for Schwabach Perutz & Company, a Dallas corporation dealing in cotton exchange. Miss OKUI expressed a desire to Mr. OZAWA to visit the United States for cultural purposes and, accordingly, Mr. OZAWA arranged for her employment with Mr. GERARDO WEINSTEIN, President of Schwabach Perutz & Company, in his offices in the Cotton Exchange Building, Dallas. Mr. WEINSTEIN agreed to act as Miss OKUI's sponsor for a two-year period during her employment by him in the United States and, accordingly, she arrived in the United States and Dallas, Texas, in the Summer of 1959.

Miss OKUI explained that, due to the diversity between her home land and that of the United States, she requested Mr. WEINSTEIN employ her as a governess in his home in the beginning to allow her to acquaint herself with western world customs, such as buying her groceries and other domestic differences.

Miss OKUI stated she continued her employment with Mr. WEINSTEIN until approximately June or July, 1961, when she obtained a position with Nippon Service, Inc., 13 West 46th Street, New York City, whereupon she took up residence in New York at 22 East 95th Street. Miss OKUI explained that Nippon Service is operated as an American representative for the Takashamaya (phonetic) Department Stores, Japan's largest department store chain. Miss OKUI advised she was employed by Nippon Service under the direct supervision of Mr. MICHIO KUSHI, President of that company, until her return to Dallas, in August, 1962. She advised she returned to Dallas at the request of Mr. KUSHI to act as the southwestern representative for Nippon Service, Inc. She explained her duties were primarily in the public relations field, in that she was required to make numerous contacts with southwestern firms having Japanese connections in the name of her company.

-2-

COMMISSION EXHIBIT No. 1862—Continued

Re: LEE HARVEY OSWALD

Miss OKUI stated that, upon her return to Dallas in August, 1962, she took up residence with the family of Mr. & Mrs. WARREN LESLIE, 11415 Hillcrest, Dallas, Texas. Mr. LESLIE, at that time, was Vice President of the Neiman-Marcus Department Store in Dallas. She advised she resided with the LESLIE family until the Spring of 1963, when Mr. & Mrs. LESLIE became separated and she then occupied a guest house to the rear of the residence of Mr. & Mrs. LEE STARR, 5710 Chatham Hill, Dallas, President of Titche-Goettinger Department Stores, at their invitation. Miss OKUI stated she has lived at her present address for about six months.

Miss OKUI stated further she is no longer employed by Nippon Service, Inc., as she has terminated her position with that firm in preparation for return to her home in Japan. Miss OKUI is scheduled to depart the United States on June 10, 1964, via NYK Lines from San Francisco, California; however, she intends to remain in Dallas until the end of May, 1964.

Miss OKUI related that, in addition to her services with Nippon Service, Inc., in the southwestern area of the United States, she lectures on an average of two to three times a week before ladies' clubs and other similar groups on the art of Ikebana, the Japanese art of flower arrangement, and in Origami, the Japanese art of paper folding. Miss OKUI engages in these teaching lectures as a free-lance speaker, for which she receives a fee.

Miss OKUI stated that, while attending a chamber music concert in Dallas approximately four years ago, she became acquainted with a Mr. LEV ARONSON, who is a widely acclaimed cellist and music teacher in the Dallas area. Miss OKUI characterized Mr. ARONSON as a Latvian by birth, who speaks Russian fluently, and is conversant in several other languages, and it was through Mr. ARONSON she had occasion to become acquainted with Mr. & Mrs. DECLAN FORD. She advised she has attended several functions in the company of Mr. ARONSON as a guest of the FORD family, and she recalls attending a party at the FORD residence, in the company of Mr. ARONSON, in the latter part of December, 1962. Miss OKUI

-3-

COMMISSION EXHIBIT No. 1862—Continued

Re: LEE HARVEY OSWALD

advised this party was held at the North Dallas residence of Mr. & Mrs. FORD, 14057 Brookcrest Drive, and that this party was occasioned by the celebration of the Russian holiday season which, she explained, is held a few days following the Christmas season in this country.

Miss OKUI recalled that, upon arrival at this party, she was introduced to a large number of people in attendance, none of whom she can recall now, but she does recall being introduced to an individual, who she now knows was LEE HARVEY OSWALD, and his wife, MARINA, who were also in attendance at the party. Miss OKUI stated she recalls further having a conversation with MARINA OSWALD, through Mr. ARONSON as interpreter, and she received a good deal of attention from the guests at the party, inasmuch as she was the only Oriental in attendance. Miss OKUI recalled she discussed with MARINA OSWALD the fact that she, MARINA, had recently arrived in the United States and had had little or no opportunity to see the country and get acquainted with the people.

Miss OKUI further stated she does recall having a discussion with MARINA's husband, whom she now knows to be LEE HARVEY OSWALD, concerning Ikebana, or flower arrangement, and OSWALD, to the best of her recollection, queried her about how she liked the United States in relation to Japan, insofar as the customs of the people were concerned. She stated OSWALD did not, at any time, broach the subject of politics and, if he had, she would have been inadequate in that regard, as she takes little interest in that subject.

Miss OKUI stated that, if there was some consternation by any of the guests at her discussion with OSWALD, she was not aware of it and, in fact, feels certain Mr. ARONSON was at her side at all times that evening. Miss OKUI stated further that that was the first and last time she had ever met or talked to either LEE HARVEY OSWALD or his wife, MARINA OSWALD, and, in fact, did not, at any time, know his name until OSWALD received notoriety

-4-

COMMISSION EXHIBIT No. 1862—Continued

Re: LEE HARVEY OSWALD

as a result of the assassination of President KENNEDY. Miss OKUI also stated that, to the best of her recollection, Mr. ARONSON did not, at least not to her, express any displeasure over her discussion with LEE HARVEY OSWALD, and she stated she feels certain he would have mentioned it had that been true.

-5-

COMMISSION EXHIBIT No. 1862—Continued

UNITED STATES DEPARTMENT OF JUSTICE

FEDERAL BUREAU OF INVESTIGATION

In Reply, Please Refer to
File No.

New York, New York
May 14, 1964

Lee Harvey Oswald
Internal Security - R - Cuba

Michio Kushi, 67-77 136th Street, Queens, New York, was contacted by a Special Agent of the Federal Bureau of Investigation on May 12, 1964 at the offices of the Nippon Service, Inc., 13 West 46th Street, New York City. Mr. Kushi is the President of this company.

He said he is acquainted with Miss Yaeko Okui and that she is a young, attractive lady who resides in Dallas, Texas. She is a native of Japan and is a charming person possessing above-average intelligence. He described her as a person who has many friends and acquaintances and one who has an engaging personality.

To the best of his knowledge, Miss Okui arrived in the United States from Japan in the spring or summer of 1959. She moved to Dallas, Texas and was employed by an unknown firm in Dallas for approximately two years.

Kushi advised that he was formerly a Vice-President of the Takashimaya Department Store, 562 5th Avenue, New York City, which is Japan's largest department store chain. The Nippon Service, Inc. represents several Japanese firms in the United States and his representatives contact numerous firms throughout the United States. He wanted to explain the above since it was in this connection he met Miss Okui. In the summer of 1961 he travelled to Dallas on business and he met Miss Okui while contacting firms. He offered employment to her and in the summer of 1961 she came to New York City . She was employed by the Nippon Service, Inc. but assigned to the Takashimaya Department Store for sales training. She worked until the summer of 1962 when she returned to Dallas to serve in the public relations field for his firm. She was required to contact firms in the Southwest with whom his company had business relations. Miss Okui contacted him about two weeks ago and telephonically advised she was returning to Japan around the last part of May, 1964.

He advised he is not aware that Miss Okui attended a party in December 1962 which was also attended by Lee Harvey Oswald and his wife, Marina. He said he is not closely associated with

COMMISSION EXHIBIT No. 1863

Lee Harvey Oswald

Miss Okui but he feels sure she would not have had an opportunity to meet Oswald in her business contacts. This party evidently was a social affair and not in relation to her business contacts. He felt sure she is not in a position to discuss politics in the United States, and based upon his association with her, she would not enter into any discussion of politics.

He pointed out Miss Okui is a professional flower arrangement teacher and is quite proficient in Kato music. She engages in teaching and has held lectures in regard to the above in the Southwest, but he would doubt she ever met Oswald through these lectures.

He has no basis for his statement but stated Miss Okui probably met Oswald once and only once and probably did not even recall him.

He has no record of Okui's employment to the best of his knowledge, but while in New York City she resided with Mrs. Kazuko Ogura, an accomplished flower arranger in New York City.

COMMISSION EXHIBIT No. 1863—Continued

UNITED STATES DEPARTMENT OF JUSTICE

FEDERAL BUREAU OF INVESTIGATION

In Reply, Please Refer to
File No.

Dallas, Texas
May 21, 1964

LEE HARVEY OSWALD

The following investigation supplements that contained in a memorandum of this agency dated May 6, 1964, relating to Miss YAEKO OKUI, who was in attendance at a year-end combination Christmas - New Year's Party, December 28 - 30, 1962, at the residence of Mr. and Mrs. DECLAN P. FORD at 14057 Brookcrest Drive, Dallas, Texas, at which party MARINA and LEE HARVEY OSWALD were also in attendance.

On May 18, 1964, GERARDO WEINSTEIN, President, Schwabach Perutz and Company, Room 1610, Cotton Exchange Building, 608 North St. Paul, Dallas, Texas, was interviewed at his offices regarding the employment of Miss YAEKO OKUI in the spring of 1959.

WEINSTEIN advised that his firm deals in the purchase, sale, and exchange of cotton throughout the world, principally in the Orient, and that his company is represented in Japan by Ozawa and Company, a brokerage firm located in Osaka, Japan. He advised that in the spring of 1959 he desired to employ a Japanese girl as governess for his children and discussed this matter at length with Mr. GEORGE PERUTZ, a member of the board of Schwabach Perutz and Company, and that Mr. PERUTZ advised him at that time that his wife, Mrs. PERUTZ, was acquainted with a well-educated, English-speaking Japanese girl residing at that time on Awaji Island located about ten miles off the coast of Kobi, Japan. WEINSTEIN stated Mrs. PERUTZ accordingly contacted this Japanese girl, whom he now knows to be Miss YAEKO OKUI, and inquired of her availability for a position in the United States as governess for Mr. WEINSTEIN's children. WEINSTEIN stated Miss OKUI answered Mrs. PERUTZ's inquiry by

COMMISSION EXHIBIT No. 1864

return mail to the effect she would be very much interested in employment in the United States for a period of two years and that upon being advised of this by Mrs. PERUTZ, WEINSTEIN communicated with Mr. OZAWA of the Ozawa Company in Osaka, Japan, and requested his assistance in arranging a two-year temporary visa for Miss OKUI. WEINSTEIN stated he, through his attorneys, submitted the appropriate forms to the Immigration Service reflecting his intentions to act as sponsor for Miss OKUI in the event her visa were granted, and promising round trip transportation from Japan to the United States and return.

WEINSTEIN advised arrangements were made by Mr. OZAWA through the U. S. Consul in Tokyo for a two-year temporary visa for Miss OKUI and that Miss OKUI arrived by ocean liner to San Francisco and subsequently Dallas in the middle of the summer of 1959. He advised Miss OKUI immediately took up her duties as governess at his residence and remained in that position through the entire two-year period, ending in approximately July 1961. He advised Miss OKUI then arranged through subsequent friends she had made in Dallas for an extension on her visa, and, upon the expiration of her employment period with him, she subsequently obtained a position with the Nippon Service Company, Incorporated, in New York City, which Mr. WEINSTEIN stated he understands acts as United States representative for the Takashimaya (phonetic) Department Store chain of Japan. WEINSTEIN stated to the best of his recollection she remained in New York approximately one year, at which time she returned to Dallas as a Southwestern States representative for that firm. WEINSTEIN advised he and his family have lost contact with Miss OKUI subsequent to her employment in New York City, and have seen her on only three or four occasions since her return to Dallas.

WEINSTEIN stated that during the tenure of her employment at his home, he and his family thought very highly of Miss OKUI and found her to be a highly intelligent, well-educated, and talented girl. He stated she accepted her responsibilities fully and was always quietly polite and unassuming while a resident in his household.

WEINSTEIN advised he was not aware that Miss OKUI had attended a dinner party at which LEE HARVEY and MARINA OSWALD were also in attendance; however, he knew that she had become friendly with many of the Russian-speaking people in the Dallas-Fort Worth area, inasmuch as she had become a close friend and companion to Mr. LEV ARONSON, whom he believed to have been of Russian origin, and who was fluent in the Russian language. WEINSTEIN attributed this association to their mutual enjoyment of parlor music in which both were quite gifted rather than to any amorous relationship.

WEINSTEIN advised that around the first of May, 1964, he received a letter from Miss OKUI expressing her intentions to return to Japan; and, as he, WEINSTEIN, remained obligated to pay for her passage home, he accordingly arranged passage aboard the Africa Maru scheduled to depart San Francisco June 8, 1964. He advised, further, he has arranged for her belongings to be shipped to San Francisco in care of William Diamond and Company, Pier 23, for subsequent shipment to Japan.

On May 18, 1964, GEORGE PERUTZ, Director, Schwabach Perutz and Company, Room 1610, Cotton Exchange Building, 608 North St. Paul, Dallas, Texas, advised he first became acquainted with Miss YAEKO OKUI through his wife, SIDNEY PERUTZ, who he recalls met Miss OKUI at a flower arrangement show in a Tokyo park sometime during 1956 or 1957. PERUTZ explained that he and his wife make frequent trips to the Orient and most notably Japan as a result of his business interests in that area of the world, and that these trips are usually made in the spring of each year for the purpose of selling cotton futures to Japanese textile mills and other purchasers. He advised that Miss OKUI and his wife became close friends and, in fact, his wife has visited the OKUI home on several occasions and he recalls his wife spending a full week with the OKUI family on one occasion. PERUTZ stated that following their return to the United States, Miss OKUI and his wife corresponded frequently regarding floral arrangements and other Japanese cultural arts in which Miss OKUI was quite proficient.

Mr. PERUTZ recalled that Mr. GERARDO WEINSTEIN, President of Schwabach Perutz and Company mentioned to him early in 1959 the need of a governess for his children and that he, Mr. PERUTZ, suggested to WEINSTEIN that he discuss his needs with Mrs. PERUTZ as she was acquainted with a number of talented Japanese girls who would be desirous of employment in the United States. He advised Mrs. PERUTZ recommended Miss OKUI to Mr. WEINSTEIN, and WEINSTEIN subsequently made arrangements with Mr. OZAWA of Ozawa and Company, the Schwabach Perutz and Company representatives, for a two-year temporary visa for Miss OKUI to the United States. He stated Mr. WEINSTEIN was required to furnish proof of his intentions to act as sponsor for Miss OKUI during her stay in the United States, and he recalls Miss OKUI arrived in the United States and in Dallas in the early summer of 1959. PERUTZ stated Miss OKUI and Mrs. PERUTZ continued on friendly terms while Miss OKUI was employed for Mr. WEINSTEIN in Dallas, but that following her employment in New York Miss OKUI and Mrs. PERUTZ drifted apart as Miss OKUI found many new friends in Dallas, and neither he nor Mrs. PERUTZ has seen Miss OKUI more than five or six times in the last three years.

Mr. PERUTZ advised he could furnish little information regarding Miss OKUI's background or family other than that she was a well-bred, highly intelligent young lady of obviously good heritage; however, he felt his wife, Mrs. PERUTZ, could furnish more information of value in this vein.

On May 19, 1964, Mrs. SIDNEY PERUTZ, 11405 St. Michaels, Dallas, Texas, advised she first met Miss YAEKO OKUI at a flower arrangement show being held in a Tokyo, Japan, park early in the summer of 1957 and that due to their mutual interest in flower arrangements, and, as Miss OKUI had a fluent mastery of the English language, she and Miss OKUI became well acquainted. She stated Miss OKUI expressed an avid interest for life in the United States and its customs, and that she and Miss OKUI exchanged ideas on this subject. She advised she, too, was interested in the customs of Japan, and, accordingly, visited the residence of Miss OKUI and family at

Miss OKUI's request on several occasions. She advised that Miss OKUI at that time was residing with her mother and two younger sisters on Awaji Island off the coast of Kobi, Japan, and that on one occasion Mrs. PERUTZ spent a week on Awaji Island with the OKUI family.

Mrs. PERUTZ advised she recalls that Mr. OKUI, YAEKO's father, had been a prominent attorney in Japan at one time, but that in 1957 he was already a bedridden invalid and that she knows he has subsequently passed away. She stated Mrs. TOYO OKUI, mother of YAEKO, is a Certified Public Accountant and operates one or more accounting businesses in Japan, from which she has sent her youngest daughters, including YAEKO, to college. Mrs. PERUTZ advised from her recollection the family consists of an older sister whom Mrs. PERUTZ has not met, but whom she knows to be married to an English naval officer who is now retired from the service and living in California, name unrecalled. She stated YAEKO is the next oldest sister and that she has two other younger sisters who are both, to her knowledge, still living in Japan after having completed their college education, names unrecalled. She advised she has heard indirectly through Miss OKUI that she also has a half brother living in Tokyo who is married to a member of the prominent MITSUBISHI family. Mrs. PERUTZ believed she also has another brother who has been hospitalized for some years in a mental institution somewhere in Japan. Mrs. PERUTZ was unable to furnish any other information regarding the family or background of YAEKO OKUI.

In regard to the attendance of Miss YAEKO OKUI at a party at which LEE HARVEY and MARINA OSWALD were also in attendance, Mrs. PERUTZ stated she did not find this unusual as Miss OKUI frequently attended Russian gatherings in the company of Mr. LEV ARONSON, a noted Dallas cellist and music teacher whom she believes to be of Russian origin and who has many Russian-speaking friends in this area. Mrs. PERUTZ advised she is of the opinion Miss OKUI would have had no social relationship with either LEE HARVEY or MARINA OSWALD other than through mutual attendance at one of these Russian gatherings, and knows that Miss OKUI has never mentioned the OSWALDS to her at any time, either before or after the assassination of President KENNEDY. Mrs. PERUTZ stated, further, that she feels positive there could be no social relationship between Miss YAEKO OKUI and LEE HARVEY OSWALD, inasmuch as their obvious cultural and educational levels are so diverse.

COMMISSION EXHIBIT No. 1864—Continued

February 17, 1964

Captain W. P. Gannaway
Special Service Bureau
Dallas Police Department

Thru:
Lieutenant Jack Revill
Criminal Intelligence Section
Special Service Bureau
Dallas Police Department

SUBJECT: CRIMINAL INTELLIGENCE (6)
LEV ARONSON

Sir:

Pursuant to the instructions of Captain W. P. GANNAWAY, SUBJECT was interviewed by the undersigned officers and the following report submitted.

SUBJECT, who is Russian born, resides at 8418 Swananoah. He gives music lessons and is a cello player for the DALLAS SYMPHONY ORCHESTRA. His telephone number is FL7-5150.

SUBJECT stated that he met LEE HARVEY and MARINA OSWALD on December 28, 1962, at a party at the residence of DECLAN FORD. However, he talked to OSWALD very little and so could not furnish much information about him. That was the only time he saw the OSWALDS. SUBJECT said that GEORGE de MOHRENSCHILDT probably knew LEE HARVEY OSWALD best. He also stated that he had never heard of JACK RUBY until OSWALD was slain.

Respectfully submitted,

F. A. Hellinghausen

F. A. Hellinghausen, Detective
Criminal Intelligence Section

P. M. Parks

P. M. Parks, Detective
Criminal Intelligence Section

COMMISSION EXHIBIT No. 1865

FD-302 (Rev. 3-3-59) FEDERAL BUREAU OF INVESTIGATION

1

Date 5/5/64

Miss YAEKO OKUI, 564_ Loring Drive, Apartment 149, Dallas, Texas, was contacted at her residence for interview.

Miss OKUI advised she was born January 19, 1933, Tokyo, Japan, and resided at the residence of her parents, 843 Yamashita-Cho, Sumoto City, Hyogo Prefecture, Japan, until her travel to the United States in 1959.

As a matter of background, Miss OKUI advised her father was a practicing attorney in Sumoto City, Japan, until the time of his death approximately four years ago, and that her mother, Mrs. TOYO OKUI, is presently a Certified Public Accountant operating accounting firms in Sumoto City and Wakayamac City. Miss OKUI advised she attended Wasada University in Tokyo for three and one-half years, majoring in Business Administration and Economics. She advised she did not receive a degree from this university, but lacks only the submission of a thesis, which she plans to submit upon her return. In addition, Miss OKUI completed seven years of study at the Sogetsu School of Professional Flower Arrangement at Tokyo, for which she received a Teacher's Certificate, allowing her to practice professional flower arrangement teaching throughout the world. Miss OKUI advised she is further proficient in Kato music, which Miss OKUI described as a large, thirteen-string instrument, which is quite popular in Japanese symphony orchestras. Miss OKUI stated she, likewise, holds a Teacher's Certificate in this instrument and she, accordingly, has conducted several classes in Kato music during her residence in Dallas.

Miss OKUI advised that in the Spring of 1959, upon completing her studies at the Sogetsu School in Tokyo, she came in contact with a Mr. OZAWA, President of Ozawa & Company, Osaka, Japan, which company is the Japanese agent for Schwabach Perutz & Company, a Dallas corporation dealing in cotton exchange. Miss OKUI expressed a desire to Mr. OZAWA to visit the United States for cultural purposes and, accordingly, Mr. OZAWA arranged for her employment with Mr. GERARDO WEINSTEIN, President of Schwabach

— Commission Exhibit No. 1866 —

570

on 5/5/64 at Dallas, Texas File # DL 100-10461

by Special Agents EUGENE F. PETRAKIS & A. RAYMOND SWITZER/eah Date dictated 5/5/64

COMMISSION EXHIBIT NO. 1866

2
DL 100-10461
EFP:eah

Perutz & Company, in his offices in the Cotton Exchange Building, Dallas. Mr. WEINSTEIN agreed to act as Miss OKUI's sponsor for a two-year period during her employment by him in the United States and, accordingly, she arrived in the United States and Dallas, Texas, in the Summer of 1959.

Miss OKUI explained that, due to the diversity between her home land and that of the United States, she requested Mr. WEINSTEIN employ her as a governess in his home in the beginning to allow her to acquaint herself with western world customs, such as buying her groceries and other domestic differences.

Miss OKUI stated she continued her employment with Mr. WEINSTEIN until approximately June or July, 1961, when she obtained a position with Nippon Service, Inc., 13 West 46th Street, New York City, whereupon she took up residence in New York at 22 East 95th Street. Miss OKUI explained that Nippon Service is operated as an American representative for the Takashamaya (phonetic) Department Stores, Japan's largest department store chain. Miss OKUI advised she was employed for Nippon Service under the direct supervision of Mr. MICHIO KUSHI, President of that company, until her return to Dallas, in August, 1962. She advised she returned to Dallas at the request of Mr. KUSHI to act as the southwestern representative for Nippon Service, Inc. She explained her duties were primarily in the public relations field, in that she was required to make numerous contacts with southwestern firms having Japanese connections in the name of her company.

Miss OKUI stated that, upon her return to Dallas in August, 1962, she took up residence with the family of Mr. & Mrs. WARREN LESLIE, 11415 Hillcrest, Dallas, Texas. Mr. LESLIE, at that time, was Vice President of the Neiman-Marcus Department Store in Dallas. She advised she resided with the LESLIE family until the Spring of 1963, when Mr. & Mrs. LESLIE became separated and she then occupied a guest house to the rear of the residence of Mr. & Mrs. LEE STARR, 5710 Chatham Hill, Dallas, President of Titche-Goettinger Department Stores, at their invitation. Miss

571

OKUI stated she has lived at her present address for about six months.

Miss OKUI stated further she is no longer employed by Nippon Service, Inc., as she has terminated her position with that firm in preparation for return to her home in Japan. Miss OKUI is scheduled to depart the United States on June 10, 1964, via NYK Lines from San Francisco, California; however, she intends to remain in Dallas until the end of May, 1964.

Miss OKUI related that, in addition to her services with Nippon Service, Inc., in the southwestern area of the United States, she lectures on an average of two to three times a week before ladies' clubs and other similar groups in the art of Ikebana, the Japanese art of flower arrangement, and in Origami, the Japanese art of paper folding. Miss OKUI engages in these teaching lectures as a free-lance speaker, for which she receives a fee.

Miss OKUI stated that, while attending a chamber music concert in Dallas approximately four years ago, she became acquainted with a Mr. LEV ARONSON, who is a widely acclaimed cellist and music teacher in the Dallas area. Miss OKUI characterized Mr. ARONSON as a Latvian by birth, who speaks Russian fluently, and is conversant in several other languages, and it was through Mr. ARONSON she had occasion to become acquainted with Mr. & Mrs. DECLAN FORD. She advised she has attended several functions in the company of Mr. ARONSON as a guest of the FORD family, and she recalls attending a party at the FORD residence, in the company of Mr. ARONSON, in the latter part of December, 1962. Miss OKUI advised this party was held at the North Dallas residence of Mr. & Mrs. FORD, 14057 Brookcrest Drive, and that this party was occasioned by the celebration of the Russian holiday season which, she explained, is held a few days following the Christmas season in this country.

Miss OKUI recalled that, upon arrival at this party, she was introduced to a large number of people in attendance, none of whom she can recall now, but she does recall being introduced to an individual, who she now knows was LEE HARVEY OSWALD, and his wife, MARINA, who were also in attendance at the party. Miss OKUI stated she recalls further having a conversation with MARINA OSWALD, through Mr. ARONSON as interpreter, and she received a good deal of attention from the guests at the party, inasmuch as she was the only Oriental in attendance. Miss OKUI recalled she discussed with MARINA OSWALD the fact that she, MARINA, had recently arrived in the United States and had had little or no opportunity to see the country and get acquainted with the people.

Miss OKUI further stated she does recall having a discussion with MARINA's husband, whom she now knows to be LEE HARVEY OSWALD, concerning Ikebana, or flower arrangement, and OSWALD, to the best of her recollection, queried her about how she liked the United States in relation to Japan, insofar as the customs of the people were concerned. She stated OSWALD did not, at any time, broach the subject of politics and, if he had, she would have been inadequate in that regard, as she takes little interest in that subject.

Miss OKUI stated that, if there was some consternation by any of the guests at her discussion with OSWALD, she was not aware of it and, in fact, feels certain Mr. ARONSON was at her side at all times that evening. Miss OKUI stated further that that was the first and last time she had ever met or talked to either LEE HARVEY OSWALD or his wife, MARINA OSWALD, and, in fact, did not, at any time, know his name until OSWALD received notoriety as a result of the assassination of President KENNEDY. Miss OKUI also stated that, to the best of her recollection, Mr. ARONSON did not, at least not to her, express any displeasure over her discussion with LEE HARVEY OSWALD, and she stated she feels certain he would have mentioned it had that been true.

FD-302 (Rev. 3-3-59) FEDERAL BUREAU OF INVESTIGATION

Date 5/19/64

1

GERARDO WEINSTEIN, President, Schwabach Perutz and Company, Room 1610, Cotton Exchange Building, 608 N. St. Paul, Dallas, Texas, was interviewed at his offices regarding the employment of Miss YAEKO OKUI in the spring of 1959.

WEINSTEIN advised that his firm deals in the purchase, sale, and exchange of cotton throughout the world, principally in the Orient, and that his company is represented in Japan by Ozawa and Company, a brokerage firm located in Osaka, Japan. He advised that in the spring of 1959 he desired to employ a Japanese girl as governess for his children and discussed this matter at length with Mr. GEORGE PERUTZ, a member of the board of Schwabach Perutz and Company, and that Mr. PERUTZ advised him at that time that his wife, Mrs. PERUTZ, was acquainted with a well-educated, English-speaking Japanese girl residing at that time on Awaji Island located about ten miles off the coast of Kobi, Japan. WEINSTEIN stated Mrs. PERUTZ accordingly contacted this Japanese girl, who he now knows to be Miss YAEKO OKUI, and inquired of her availability for a position in the United States as governess for Mr. WEINSTEIN's children. WEINSTEIN stated Miss OKUI answered Mrs. PERUTZ' inquiry by return mail to the effect she would be very much interested in employment in the United States for a period of two years and that upon being advised of this by Mrs. PERUTZ, WEINSTEIN communicated with Mr. OZAWA of the Ozawa Company in Osaka, Japan, and requested his assistance in arranging a two year temporary visa for Miss OKUI. WEINSTEIN stated he, through his attorneys, submitted the appropriate forms to the Immigration Service reflecting his intentions to act as sponsor for Miss OKUI in the event her visa were granted and promising round trip transportation from Japan to the United States and return.

WEINSTEIN advised arrangements were made by Mr. OZAWA through the U. S. Consul in Tokyo for a two year temporary visa for Miss OKUI and that Miss OKUI arrived by ocean liner to San Francisco and subsequently Dallas in the middle of the summer of 1959. He advised Miss OKUI immediately took up her duties as governess at his residence and remained in that position through the entire two year period ending in approximately July, 1961. He advised Miss OKUI then arranged through

— Commission Exhibit No. 1867 —

574

on 5/18/64 at Dallas, Texas File # DL 100-10461

by Special Agent EUGENE F. PETRAKIS and A. RAYMOND SWITZER:vm Date dictated 5/19/64

This document contains neither recommendations nor conclusions of the FBI. It is the property of the FBI and is loaned to your agency; it and its contents are not to be distributed outside your agency.

2
DL 100-10461

subsequent friends she had made in Dallas for an extension on her visa and upon the expiration of her employment period with him she subsequently obtained a position with the Nippon Service Company, Incorporated, in New York City which Mr. WEINSTEIN stated he understands acts as United States representative for the Takashamaya (phonetic) Department Store chain of Japan. WEINSTEIN stated to the best of his recollection she remained in New York approximately one year at which time she returned to Dallas as a southwestern states representative for that firm. WEINSTEIN advised he and his family have lost contact with Miss OKUI subsequent to her employment in New York City and have seen her on only three or four occasions since her return to Dallas.

WEINSTEIN stated that during the tenure of her employment at his home he and his family thought very highly of Miss OKUI and found her to be a highly intelligent, well-educated, and talented girl. He stated she accepted her responsibilities fully and was always quietly polite and unassuming while a resident in his household.

WEINSTEIN advised he was not aware that Miss OKUI had attended a dinner party at which LEE HARVEY and MARINA OSWALD were also in attendance; however, he knew that she had become friendly with many of the Russian-speaking people in the Dallas-Fort Worth area inasmuch as she had become a close friend and companion to Mr. LEV ARONSON, who he believed to have been of Russian origin, and who was fluent in the Russian language. WEINSTEIN attributed this association to their mutual enjoyment of parlor music in which both were quite gifted rather than to any amorous relationship.

WEINSTEIN advised that around the first of May, 1964, he received a letter from Miss OKUI expressing her intentions to return to Japan and as he, WEINSTEIN, remained obligated to pay for her passage home he accordingly arranged passage aboard the Africa Maru scheduled to depart San Francisco June 8, 1964. He advised further he has arranged for her belongings to be shipped to San Francisco in care of the William Diamond and Company, Pier 23, for subsequent shipment to Japan.

575

FD-302 (Rev. 3-3-59) FEDERAL BUREAU OF INVESTIGATION

Date 5/19/64

1

GEORGE PERUTZ, Director, Schwabach Perutz and Company, Room 1610, Cotton Exchange Building, 608 N. St. Paul, Dallas, Texas, advised he first became acquainted with Miss YAEKO OKUI through his wife, SIDNEY PERUTZ, who he recalls met Miss OKUI at a flower arrangement show in a Tokyo park sometime during 1956 or 1957. PERUTZ explained that he and his wife make frequent trips to the Orient and most notably Japan as a result of his business interests in that area of the world and that these trips are usually made in the spring of each year for the purpose of selling cotton futures to Japanese textile mills and other purchasers. He advised that Miss OKUI and his wife became close friends and, in fact, his wife has visited the OKUI home on several occasions and he recalls his wife spending a full week with the OKUI family on one occasion. PERUTZ stated that following their return to the United States Miss OKUI and his wife corresponded frequently regarding floral arrangements and other Japanese cultural arts in which Miss OKUI was quite proficient.

Mr. PERUTZ recalled that Mr. GERARDO WEINSTEIN, President of Schwabach Perutz and Company mentioned to him early in 1959 the need of a governess for his children and that he, Mr. PERUTZ, suggested to WEINSTEIN that he discuss his needs with Mrs. PERUTZ as she was acquainted with a number of talented Japanese girls who would be desirous of employment in the United States. He advised Mrs. PERUTZ recommended Miss OKUI to Mr. WEINSTEIN and WEINSTEIN subsequently made arrangements with Mr. OZAWA of Ozawa and Company, the Schwabach Perutz and Company representatives, for a two year temporary visa for Miss OKUI to the United States. He stated Mr. WEINSTEIN was required to furnish proof of his intentions to act as sponsor for Miss OKUI during her stay in the United States and he recalls Miss OKUI arrived in the United States and in Dallas in the early summer of 1959. PERUTZ stated Miss OKUI and Mrs. PERUTZ continued on friendly terms while Miss OKUI was employed for Mr. WEINSTEIN in Dallas but that following her employment in New York Miss OKUI and Mrs. PERUTZ drifted apart as Miss OKUI found many new friends in Dallas and neither he nor Mrs. PERUTZ have seen Miss OKUI more than five or six times in the last three years.

— Commission Exhibit No. 1868 —

576

on 5/18/64 at Dallas, Texas File # DL 100-10461

by Special Agent EUGENE F. PETRAKIS and A. RAYMOND SWITZER:vm Date dictated 5/19/64

COMMISSION EXHIBIT NO. 1868

2
DL 100-10461

Mr. PERUTZ advised he could furnish little information regarding Miss OKUI's background or family other than that she was a well-bred, highly intelligent young lady of obviously good heritage; however, he felt his wife, Mrs. PERUTZ, could furnish more information of value in this vein.

577

COMMISSION EXHIBIT NO. 1868—Continued

FD-302 (Rev. 3-3-59)

FEDERAL BUREAU OF INVESTIGATION

Date 5/19/64

1

Mrs. SIDNEY PERUTZ, 11405 St. Michaels, Dallas, Texas, advised she first met Miss YAEKO OKUI at a flower arrangement show being held in a Tokyo, Japan park early in the summer of 1957 and that due to their mutual interest in flower arrangements and as Miss OKUI had a fluent mastery of the English language, she and Miss OKUI became well acquainted. She stated Miss OKUI expressed an avid interest for life in the United States and its customs and that she and Miss OKUI exchanged ideas on this subject. She advised she too was interested in the customs of Japan and accordingly visited the residence of Miss OKUI and family at Miss OKUI's request on several occasions. She advised that Miss OKUI at that time was residing with her mother and two younger sisters on Awaji Island off the coast of Kobi, Japan, and that on one occasion Mrs. PERUTZ spent a week on Awaji Island with the OKUI family.

Mrs. PERUTZ advised she recalls that Mr. OKUI, YAEKO's father, had been a prominent attorney in Japan at one time but that in 1957 he was already a bedridden invalid and that she knows he has subsequently passed away. She stated Mrs. TOYO OKUI, mother of YAEKO, is a Certified Public Accountant and operates one or more accounting businesses in Japan from which she has sent her youngest daughters, including YAEKO, to college. Mrs. PERUTZ advised from her recollection the family consists of an older sister whom Mrs. PERUTZ has not met but who she knows to be married to an English naval officer who is now retired from the service and living in California, name unrecalled. She stated YAEKO is the next oldest sister and that she has two other younger sisters who are both to her knowledge still living in Japan after having completed their college education, names unrecalled. She advised she has heard indirectly through Miss OKUI that she also has a half brother living in Tokyo who is married to a member of the prominent MITSUBISHI family. Mrs. PERUTZ believed she also has another brother who has been hospitalized for some years in a mental institution somewhere in Japan. Mrs. PERUTZ was unable to furnish any other information regarding the family or background of YAEKO OKUI.

In regard to the attendance of Miss YAEKO OKUI at a party

— Commission Exhibit No. 1869 —

578

on 5/19/64 at Dallas, Texas File # DL 100-10461

by Special Agent EUGENE F.PETRAKIS and A. RAYMOND SWITZER:vm Date dictated 5/19/64

This document contains neither recommendations nor conclusions of the FBI. It is the property of the FBI and is loaned to your agency; it and its contents are not to be distributed outside your agency.

COMMISSION EXHIBIT NO. 1869

2
DL 100-10461

at which LEE HARVEY and MARINA OSWALD were also in attendance, Mrs. PERUTZ stated she did not find this unusual as Miss OKUI frequently attended Russian gatherings in the company of Mr. LEV ARONSON, a noted Dallas cellist and music teacher who she believes to be of Russian origin and who has many Russian-speaking friends in this area. Mrs. PERUTZ advised she is of the opinion Miss OKUI would have had no social relationship with either LEE HARVEY or MARINA OSWALD other than through mutual attendance at one of these Russian gatherings and knows that Miss OKUI has never mentioned the OSWALDs to her at any time either before or after the assassination of President KENNEDY. Mrs. PERUTZ stated further that she feels positive there could be no social relationship between Miss YAEKO OKUI and LEE HARVEY OSWALD inasmuch as their obvious cultural and educational levels are so diverse.

579

COMMISSION EXHIBIT NO. 1869—Continued

1.

Date 5/20/64

MICHIO KUSHI, 67-77 136th Street, Queens, New York, was interviewed at the offices of the Nippon Service, Incorporated, 13 West 46th Street, New York, New York. Mr. KUSHI is the President of the Nippon Service, Incorporated.

He said he is acquainted with Miss YAEKO OKUI and that she is a young attractive lady who resides in Dallas, Texas. She is a native of Japan and is a charming person, possessing above average intelligence. He described her as a person who has many friends and acquaintances and one who has an engaging personality.

To the best of his knowledge, Miss OKUI arrived in the United States from Japan in the spring or summer of 1959. She moved to Dallas, Texas, and was employed by an unknown firm in Dallas for approximately two years.

KUSHI advised that he was formerly a Vice-President of the Takashimaya Department Store, 562 5th Avenue, New York City, which is Japan's largest department store chain. The Nippon Service, Incorporated represents several Japanese firms in the United States and his representatives contact numerous firms throughout the United States. He wanted to explain the above since it was in this connection he met Miss OKUI. In the summer of 1961, he travelled to Dallas on business and he met Miss OKUI while contacting firms. He offered employment to her and in the summer of 1961, she came to New York City. She was employed by the Nippon Service Incorporated, but assigned to the Takashimaya Department Store for sales training. She worked until the summer of 1962, when she returned to Dallas to serve in the public relations field for his firm. She was required to contact firms in the Southwest with whom his company had business relations. Miss OKUI contacted him about two weeks ago and telephonically advised she was returning to Japan around the last part of May, 1964.

— Commission Exhibit No. 1870 —

380

On 5/12/64 at New York, New York File # NY 105-38431

by SA JAMES O. INGRAM/tmm Date dictated 5/14/64

COMMISSION EXHIBIT No. 1870

2.

NY 105-38431

He advised he is not aware that Miss OKUI attended a party in December, 1962 which was also attended by LEE HARVEY OSWALD and his wife, MARINA. He said he is not closely associated with Miss OKUI but he feels sure she would not have had an opportunity to meet OSWALD in her business contacts. This party evidently was a social affair and not in relation to her business contacts. He felt sure she is not in a position to discuss politics in the United States, and based upon his association with her she would not enter into any discussion of politics.

He pointed out Miss OKUI is a professional flower arrangement teacher and is quite proficient in Kato music. She engages in teaching and has held lectures in regard to the above in the Southwest but he would doubt she ever met OSWALD through these lectures.

He has no basis for his statement but stated Miss OKUI probably met OSWALD once and only once and probably did not even recall him.

He has no record of OKUI's employment to the best of his knowledge but, while in New York City she resided with Mrs. KAZUKO OGURA, an accomplished flower arranger in New York City.

381

COMMISSION EXHIBIT No. 1870—Continued

Form No. 1588 (Revised)
MEMORANDUM REPORT
(7-1-60)

UNITED STATES SECRET SERVICE
TREASURY DEPARTMENT

ORIGIN Field	OFFICE Dallas, Texas		FILE NO. CO-2-34,030
TYPE OF CASE: Assassination of President Kennedy	STATUS: Continued		TITLE OR CAPTION: Lee Harvey Oswald
INVESTIGATION MADE AT: Dallas, Texas	PERIOD COVERED: 7-22-64		[redacted]
INVESTIGATION MADE BY: SA John Joe Howlett			— Commission Exhibit No. 1871 —

DETAILS

SYNOPSIS

Locations of two other job opportunities of Lee Harvey Oswald.

DETAILS OF INVESTIGATION

Investigation was requested by Mr. Jenner on 7-22-64 via telephone. Information phoned back to him at his request on 7-22-64.

Other Investigations

Padgett Printing Company, 1313 Industrial Boulevard, between Cole and Leslie Streets, Dallas. It is about .4 mile from planned motorcade route on Stemmons Freeway. Buildings across the street completely block any view of the freeway from Padgett Printing Company, at the street level.

A map marked with the location of Padgett Printing Company, the Texas Schoolbook Depository, and the Trade Mart is attached with original of this report. The route from the Texas Schoolbook Depository to the Trade Mart is also marked.

On 7-22-64, I interviewed Mr. Richard Uher, Assistant Station Manager, Trans-Texas Airways in his office at Love Field. Mr. Uher said that men employed as Cargo Handlers worked around the Terminal Building and the Air Freight Building. They would unload baggage, cargo, and express from Trans-Texas airplanes and take it to the air freight building, baggage area, or to another airline. They would also pick up baggage, cargo, and express from Trans-Texas passenger area, or the air freight building and load it onto Trans-Texas airplanes.

A map is attached which has the general areas marked in blue where they would pick up and/or deliver baggage, cargo, etc. The location of the President's airplane is marked in red.

DISTRIBUTION	COPIES	REPORT MADE BY	DATE
✓ Chief	Orig & 2 cc	John Joe Howlett, SPECIAL AGENT	7-22-64
Dallas	2 cc	APPROVED: Forrest V. Sorrels, SPECIAL AGENT IN CHARGE	7-22-64

(CONTINUE ON PLAIN PAPER)   U. S. GOVERNMENT PRINTING OFFICE 16—61806-1

2.
CO-2-34,030

DISPOSITION

This phase of the investigation is considered closed.

ATTACHMENT

Two maps

JJH:wd

COMMISSION EXHIBIT No. 1871—Continued

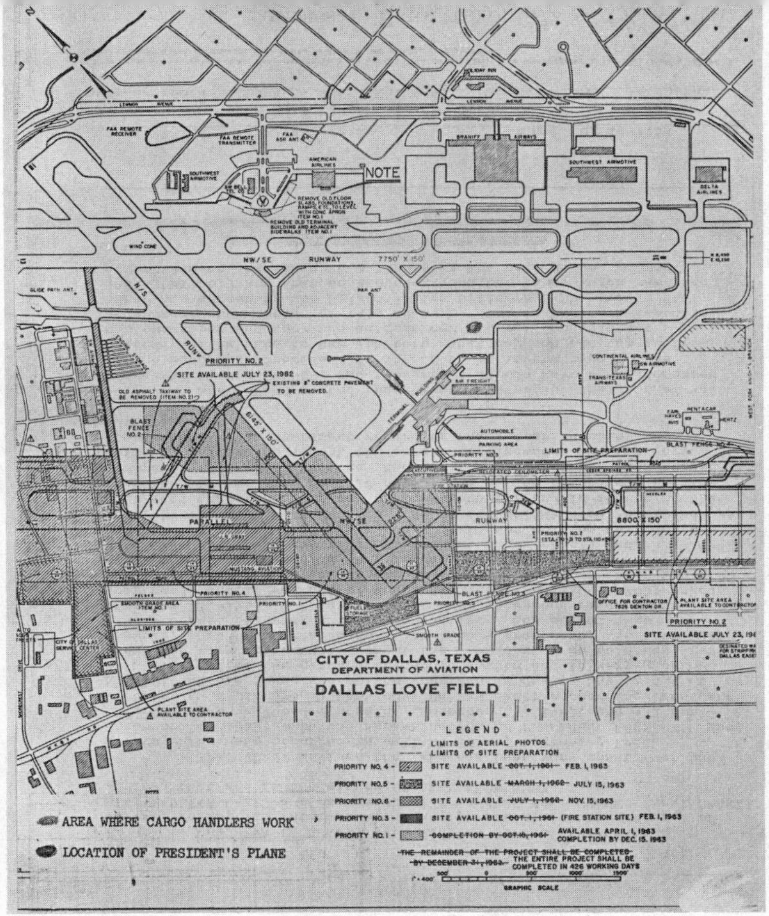

Commission Exhibit No. 1871—Continued

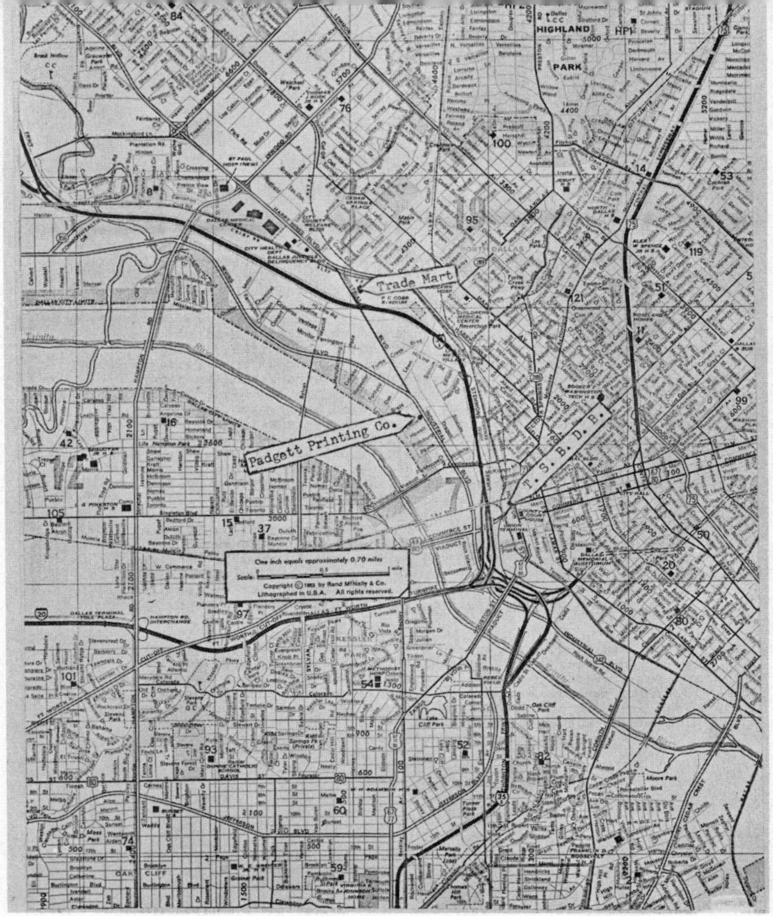

Commission Exhibit No. 1871—Continued

FD-302 (Rev. 3-3-59)

FEDERAL BUREAU OF INVESTIGATION

1

Date 11/25/63

Mrs. EVA L. GRANT, 3929 Rawlins Street (Apartment I), Dallas, Texas, was interviewed at her apartment in the presence of Mrs. PAULINE HALL, a close personal friend of Mrs. GRANT. Mrs. GRANT advised that she is the sister of JACK LEON RUBY.

Mrs. GRANT advised that she has been very upset over the events which have occurred in Dallas, Texas, beginning Friday, November 22, 1963, with the assassination of President KENNEDY. She informed that on Tuesday morning, November 19, 1963, she and her brother saw a picture in the local Dallas paper concerning President KENNEDY and his young son at the President's desk. She said that JACK RUBY called the picture to her attention and in very glowing terms was very enthusiastic about the President. He told her, for example, that "That man doesn't act like a President. He acts just like a normal everyday man with a family." She stated that on November 22, 1963, a Friday morning, her telephone rang at her apartment, and it was her brother, JACK RUBY, calling. RUBY asked her if she saw the advertisement in the morning paper which was a full-page ad addressed to "Mr. Kennedy" by BERNARD WEISMANN. She said that JACK RUBY was very upset about this article and, undoubtedly it bothered him a great deal, not only on that day but for the next two or three days. He called WEISMANN an "SOB" and also said that the newspaper was completely wrong in accepting the ad. She advised that he told her he had called the "Times Herald" newspaper in Dallas, and they had advised him that they had turned down and refused to accept the same advertisement. He was very commending in his statement regarding that paper refusing the advertisement.

Mrs. GRANT stated that he was most upset that the ad was addressed to Mr. KENNEDY and thought it should have been addressed to the Honorable President if it had to be in the paper. She stated that he came to her apartment that day and had the ad from his own paper and took the ad from her paper. She said she understood both copies of this ad were found in RUBY's automobile after his arrest by the Dallas Police Officers. She stated that JACK RUBY told her that he had contacted the paper which ran the advertisement and asked them "Where in the hell do you get off

— Commission Exhibit No. 1872 —

on 11/25/63 at Dallas, Texas File # DL 44-1639

by Special Agent S JACK B. PEDEN & GASTON C. THOMPSON: mam Date dictated 11/25/63

164

COMMISSION EXHIBIT No. 1872

DL 44-1639
JBP,GCT:mam
2

"taking an ad like that? Are you money hungry?" She said that RUBY felt it was a rotten thing for any person to question the way the President was running this country. She said that RUBY made a statement regarding the advertisement and regarding WEISMANN, whose name appeared at the bottom of the ad, that "If that guy is a Jew they ought to whack the hell out of him." By that, she advised since RUBY is a Jew he felt that this reflected against the Jewish race.

She advised that RUBY told her that he went to the Post Office in downtown Dallas and looked at the box, which box number appears in the advertisement. He told her that the box was full of mail. According to Mrs. GRANT, after he told her this, he made the statement, "I bet Weismann is a Communist", or words to that effect.

Mrs. GRANT advised that she personally "had a crush on President Kennedy". She stated that she and her brother both had a great admiration for President KENNEDY and felt he was a wonderful President. She said that JACK RUBY is not greatly interested in political affairs as a rule, but he would fuss at her if she did not pay her poll tax, since he felt it was a patriotic thing to do. She informed that early Thursday morning, November 21, 1963, JACK RUBY, as was his custom, placed advertisements in both Dallas papers concerning the entertainment to be offered at the Carousel and Vegas Night Clubs, Dallas, Texas, which clubs he has an interest in. She advised that after President KENNEDY was assassinated on November 22, 1963, he called the newspapers to change the advertisements to show that the clubs would be closed Friday, Saturday, and Sunday, November 22, 23, and 24, 1963. She said that DON SAFFERN (PH), a newspaper reporter for the Dallas "Times Herald", called him and wanted to know if he was sure

165

COMMISSION EXHIBIT No. 1872—Continued

he was not going to operate those clubs on any of those three days. He pointed out that some of the other clubs apparently were not going to be closed for even one night. When RUBY heard that the other clubs were not going to be closed, he became quite upset and asked DON how anyone with any kind of conscience could dance and have a good time after the President had been killed. He ended up by telling DON that he did not care what anyone else did, that he was going to close for those three days.

Mrs. GRANT displayed a page from the Dallas "Morning News", dated Saturday, November 23, 1963, in Section 1, Page 19, containing a one-column ad, approximately four inches in length, stating the Carousel Club on Main Street, Dallas, would be closed "Friday, Saturday, and Sunday".

Mrs. GRANT recalled that on the day of the President's assassination, November 22, 1963, JACK RUBY telephoned her at least eight times and made three personal visits to her apartment. She said that he was most upset over the assassination of the President and described OSWALD as a "creep" and said, "He has no class." She said that the phrase "He has no class" was a phrase which RUBY used to indicate his complete dislike for a person.

Mrs. GRANT informed that her father passed away several years ago. She said that on Friday when JACK RUBY was in her apartment they had discussed both the death of her father and the assassination of President KENNEDY. She advised both she and her brother, JACK, stated that they were more upset over the assassination of President KENNEDY than they were over the death of their own father. She pointed

166

out that when their father died, JACK RUBY seemed well composed and displayed very little outward emotion. She said, however, that on Friday afternoon, November 22, 1963, following the President's assassination, he was terribly upset. She also pointed out that on Saturday morning, when JACK RUBY was at her apartment, he cried very noticeably about the President's assassination. She stated that he discussed sending flowers to the place near the spot where the President was assassinated, and she feels sure that he did have flowers delivered to that spot.

Mrs. GRANT informed that JACK RUBY was in her apartment on November 22, 1963, from approximately 5:30 PM until approximately 7:15 PM, and then he dressed and went to the synagogue for prayer.

She stated that on Saturday morning he told her that he "bummed around with" a person whose first name is LARRY, an employee of the Carousel Club, all night Friday night. On Saturday morning he and LARRY drove out to a point on the North Central Expressway in Dallas, Texas, where there is a large billboard sign to the effect "Impeach Earl Warren" or some similar phraseology. He advised that he had shown LARRY how to take the picture, and LARRY had taken the picture of this sign. In connection with this sign, she stated that it has been situated there for some period of time, and that it has constantly bothered and annoyed RUBY. She stated that he did not like the sign and on numerous occasions had mentioned the sign to her.

Mrs. GRANT informed that on Saturday, November 23, 1963, RUBY called STANLEY KAUFMAN, a Dallas attorney, and

167

DL 44-1639
JBP,GCT:mam
5

discussed with KAUFMAN the sign and the advertisement in the newspaper, as well as the assassination of President KENNEDY by OSWALD. In the conversation with KAUFMAN, he told KAUFMAN that "I don't know why I want to connect that sign and the mail box with Oswald, but I do." Also in the course of conversation, he explained to KAUFMAN that he had taken a picture of the sign and had gone and physically observed the mail box which was listed in the advertisement mentioned above.

Mrs. GRANT related that after RUBY made the telephone call to Attorney STANLEY KAUFMAN, he left her apartment and did not return thereto until approximately 4:00 PM, Saturday, November 23, 1963. She advised he remained at her apartment from about 4:00 PM to around 8:00 PM, November 23, 1963, when he again left in his automobile. She advised she did not hear from RUBY again until approximately 10:20 PM, at which time she received a telephone call from RUBY, stating that among other things he was going to Radio Station KLIF in Dallas, Texas. She stated that from remarks made by RUBY during the 10:20 PM telephone conversation that she gained the impression RUBY had been at his residence, 223 S. Ewing (Apartment 207), Dallas, Texas, since a short time after leaving her place around 8:00 PM the same date.

At 11:30 PM, that same night, he called and told her he had been at Radio Station KLIF where he had talked with HENRY WADE, District Attorney, Dallas County, Texas, and RUSS KNIGHT, of Radio Station KLIF, Dallas, Texas.

Mrs. GRANT stated that she next heard from her brother, JACK RUBY, about 12:40 AM, Sunday, November 24, 1963,

168

DL 44-1639
JBP,GCT:mam
6

at which time he called her by telephone. She said she gained the impression that he was at his residence. She volunteered this was the last time that she heard from her brother, JACK RUBY, prior to contacting him at the City Jail, Dallas, Sunday afternoon, November 24, 1963, following the shooting of OSWALD. On this last call, RUBY was worried about her, GRANT's, health and told her "to go to bed".

Mrs. GRANT stated that although her brother has used her address, 3929 Rawlins Street, Dallas, for mailing purposes, he has never lived there.

Mrs. GRANT said, to the best of her knowledge, JACK RUBY has never been a "joiner" of organizations and does not belong to any group or organization of any kind and has no particular political philosophy. She described him as an "American" and a great admirer of President KENNEDY. She further advised she has never seen or heard anything which might indicate her brother, JACK RUBY, is connected or affiliated in any way with any Communist or Cuban organization. She was very emphatic in stating that she and JACK RUBY are very strongly opposed to any Communist organization or any group which they felt might be backed by Communists.

Mrs. GRANT further stated that she has heard through a television or news media that an individual made a remark to the effect that OSWALD had been seen in the night club operated by JACK RUBY. She stated in most emphatic terms that she is absolutely positive that RUBY has never had any connection with OSWALD in any way. She admitted that she did not know every individual her brother knew, but she is still certain he did not know OSWALD.

Mrs. GRANT said she was permitted to visit her brother, JACK RUBY, at the City Jail, Dallas, Texas, on the

169

COMMISSION EXHIBIT No. 1872—Continued

DL 44-1639
JGP,GCT:mam
7

afternoon of Sunday, November 24, 1963; however, she did not engage him in any conversation as to why he shot OSWALD, nor did RUBY volunteer any information to her in this regard.

170

CITY OF DALLAS
TEXAS
POLICE DEPARTMENT

February 6, 1964

The Honorable Waggoner Carr
Attorney General of Texas
Austin, Texas

Dear Sir:

I am attaching additional information pertaining to Lee Harvey Oswald which has been submitted to me by Detective Hart.

This is all the information that could be obtained.

Sincerely yours,

J. E. Curry
Chief of Police

es
Att.

COMMISSION EXHIBIT No. 1873

28 January 1964

Captain W.P. Gannaway
Special Service Bureau
Dallas Police Department

Thru:
Lieutenant Jack Revill
Criminal Intelligence Section
Special Service Bureau
Dallas Police Department

Subject: Criminal Intelligence (1)
LEE HARVEY OSWALD
DPD# 54018

Sir:

Pursuant to the instructions of CHIEF J.E. CURRY the following is submitted.

The cumulative record from the FORT WORTH PUBLIC SCHOOLS is included as enclosure # 1. The schools attended by SUBJECT are shown by numbers rather than names. These schools are identified as follows:
18- GEORGE C. CLARKE ELEMENTARY SCHOOL-3300 S. HENDERSON
19- LILY B. CLAYTON ELEMENTARY SCHOOL-2000 PARK PLACE AVE.
28- ARLINGTON HEIGHTS ELEMENTARY SCHOOL-5100 EL CAMPO AVE.
48- RIDGLEA WEST ELEMENTARY SCHOOL-7325 KERMIT AVE.
#266- ARLINGTON HEIGHTS HIGH SCHOOL-4501 W. ROSEDALE AVE.

Cumulative records do not show SUBJECT'S attendance at ARLINGTON HEIGHTS HIGH SCHOOL because SUBJECT only attended three weeks and received no grades or credits. Photostatic copy of enrollment card is unavilable however this card indicates that SUBJECT enrolled in that school 8-30-56 and attended classes in the tenth (10th) grade until 9-28-56 at which time he quit school to enlist in the U.S. MARINE CORPS. SUBJECT had transferred from BEAUREGARD SCHOOL in NEW ORLEANS,LA. which he had attended in 1954 and 1955. The principal at BEAUREGARD SCHOOL was MR. H.T. GARLAND. At the time of his enrollment at ARLINGTON HEIGHTS HIGH SCHOOL, SUBJECT gave his home address as 4936 COLLINWOOD AVE., FORT WORTH, TEXAS. SUBJECT had moved back to FORT WORTH 1 July 1956 from NEW ORLEANS,LA. .

COMMISSION EXHIBIT No. 1873—Continued

Page 2- LEE HARVEY OSWALD- 28 January 1964-

A copy of SUBJECT'S enrollment card from DALLAS INDEPENDENT SCHOOL DISTRICT, PUBLIC EVENING SCHOOL is included as enclosure # 2. SUBJECT enrolled for a typing course and paid $ 9.00. This card does not show an attendance record. No attendance record is kept since SUBJECT would not receive school credit for this course. The attached record is the only record kept by the school. Grade records are not kept on non-credit courses .

Respectfully submitted,
H M Hart
H.M. Hart, Detective
Criminal Intelligence Section

COMMISSION EXHIBIT No. 1873—Continued

FORT WORTH PUBLIC SCHOOLS
CUMULATIVE RECORD

NAME Oswald, Lee (SURNAME / CHRISTIAN NAME)
BIRTH YEAR 39 MONTH Oct. DAY 18
PARENT or Guardian Edwin Ekdall (Deceased) Mrs. Marguerite Oswald
ADDRESS 1505 8th Ave. PHONE none
ADDRESS 7408 Ewing PHONE PE-7995
ADDRESS PHONE
VACCINATION EXPIRES 1951 - 419
M.A.
C.A.
IQ 103
DATE [illegible]-50

Date of Entry	School	Grade	Room	Days Present	Days Absent	Tardy	Dis. Early	Reading	Spelling	H'Writing	English	Spanish	S. Studies	El. Science	Arithmetic	Art	Music		Phys. Ed.	Health		Citizenship		Date of Withdrawal	Destination	Teacher
1-27-47	19	1	33	87	1			B		B	B		B	B	B	B	B		a	a		B		5-30-47	2	[illegible]
3-18-48 Destination #18																										
9-5-48	28	3	34	155	23	2		C	[illegible]	C	C		a	a	B	a	B		B	B		B		6-3-49	Gr. 4	R. Hailey
9-7-49	49	4	108	163	10	1	1	B	C	B	B	C	B	B	B	B	B		B	B		B		6-2-50	Gr. 5	Livingston
9-6-50	[illegible]	6	105	[illegible]	[illegible]	3	-	C	D	B	C		B	B	D	B	B		B	B		B		6-1-51	Gr. 6	Darnor
9-5-51	[illegible]	6	[illegible]	[illegible]	[illegible]			B	[illegible]	C	D	C	C	C	D	B	B		a	a		B		5-29-52	Gr. 7	Bratton

		Date	Norm	Gr. Eq.	High Score		Low Score	
Met. Ach.	Form	2-8-50	4.5	4.0	Read.	4.7	Spell	3.3
Stanford.	Ach.	2-13-51	5.5	7.0	[illegible]	4.9	Elem. Sci.	3.0
"	"	2-11-52	6.5	7.4	Word M.	8.6	Spell	4.4

School Lily B. Clayton Millicent Keeble Principal
FORM 9

COMMISSION EXHIBIT No. 1873—Continued

NAME Oswald, Lee (First, Middle) BIRTH: YEAR 1939 MONTH Oct. DAY 18 SEX: MALE / FEMALE
ADDRESS 1505 8th Ave.
FATHER'S NAME Edwin Ekdall GUARDIAN'S NAME
MOTHER'S NAME ORIGINAL RECORD SENT TO DATE

DATE OF ENTRY	School	Grade	Days Present	Days Absent	Tardy	Dismissed Early	Citizenship	Reading	Spelling	Handwriting	English	Spanish	Soc. Sci. St. Soc. Studies	Arithmetic	Art	Music	Instrumental Music	Health Sci.-Health	Speech	Industrial Arts	Homemaking	Band Orchestra		Phys. Ed.		Reading Level	Date of Withdrawal	Destination	Home Room Teacher
9-9-47	19	2	120	5	2																						3-13-48	#18	[illegible]
3-19-48	18	2	40	6			B	C	D	B	B		A	A	B	A								A			6-2-48	3	[illegible]

(Residual Copy—Cumulative Record—Grades K-6—Fort Worth Public Schools)

COMMISSION EXHIBIT No. 1873—Continued

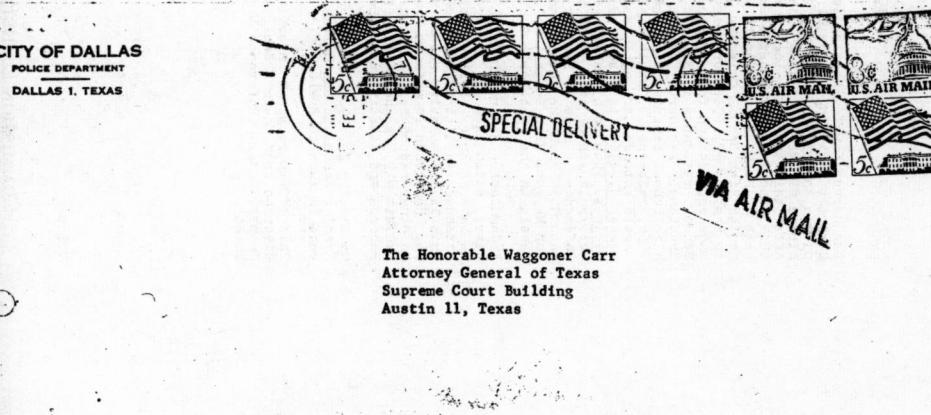

CITY OF DALLAS
POLICE DEPARTMENT
DALLAS 1, TEXAS

SPECIAL DELIVERY

VIA AIR MAIL

U.S. AIR MAIL 8¢

The Honorable Waggoner Carr
Attorney General of Texas
Supreme Court Building
Austin 11, Texas

COMMISSION EXHIBIT No. 1873—Continued

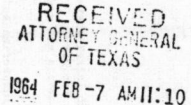

RECEIVED
ATTORNEY GENERAL
OF TEXAS
1964 FEB -7 AM 11:10

COMMISSION EXHIBIT No. 1873—Continued

CITY OF FORT WORTH

TEXAS

February 4, 1964

Honorable Waggoner Carr
Attorney General of Texas
Supreme Court Building
Austin 11, Texas

Dear Mr. Carr:

In answer to your recent letter wherein you requested information relating to Lee Harvey Oswald, I herewith submit the enclosed documents and summary pertaining thereto.

Officer V. T. Sommers, Inspection and Intelligence Division, was responsible for securing these documents which include scholastic records primarily.

I trust the information enclosed will be beneficial to the Commission on the assassination of President Kennedy.

If this department can be of further assistance, please let me know.

Very sincerely,

Cato S. Hightower
Cato S. Hightower
CHIEF OF POLICE

CSH:dt

Encls.

COMMISSION EXHIBIT NO. 1873-A

SUMMARY

Lee Harvey Oswald attended school in the Fort Worth Public School District beginning in the First Grade, January 27, 1947, and completed the Sixth Grade, May 29, 1952. Reference is made to Exhibits #1, #2, #3, #4, #5, and #6, (copies of School Records). After this time, nothing can be found in the files or records of this School District until September, 1956. A Transfer Certificate of High School Credits was received by the Arlington Heights Senior High School from New Orleans Public High Schools, reference to Exhibit #7, (Copy of Transfer), at which time Lee Harvey Oswald made application for registration at the Arlington Heights High School, reference to Exhibit #8, (Copy of Application for Registration). Lee Harvey Oswald was classified by the Fort Worth High School Department in Class 10 at this time, dated August 30, 1956, reference to Exhibit #9, (Copy of Classification Card). Lee Oswald attended Arlington Heights High School, Date Entered: September 5, 1956, to Date Withdrawn: September 28, 1956, Reason: Marines. (Due to his short attendance of only a few days -- approximately 18 school days -- at this time he did not receive any credits.) Reference is made to Exhibit #10, (Copy of Permanent High School Record.) From the date withdrawn, September 28, 1956, from Arlington Heights High School, no other record is available of Lee Harvey Oswald in the Fort Worth Public School District.

A Cumulative Record of Lee Oswald was obtained and this records yearly attendance and average grades. First shown on the Record is Date of Entry, followed by school number, indicating school attended. (A list of these schools by number is also furnished.) This is a cumulative record of Exhibits #1, #2, #3, #4, #5, and #6. Reference is made to Exhibit #11, (Copy of Cumulative Record). No other record can be found of Lee Harvey Oswald, reference to Exhibit #12, (a check of Fort Worth Police Department Files -- Records and Identification Bureaus).

On January 28, 1963, Lee Harvey Oswald registered in a Public Evening School in the Dallas Independent School District. Reference is made to Exhibit #13, (Copy of Registration Card).

This office received information that Mrs. Marguerite Oswald was divorced from Edwin Ekdahl in 1948, 17th District Court of Tarrant County, Texas. Reference is made to Exhibit #14, (Information Sheet).

Respectfully submitted,

V. T. Sommers
V. T. Sommers, Investigator,
Inspection & Intelligence Unit,
Fort Worth Police Department.

VTS:bcr

COMMISSION EXHIBIT NO. 1873-A—Continued

MATERIAL LIST

EXHIBIT #1	Copy of School Record -- First Grade.
EXHIBIT #2	Copy of School Record -- Second Grade.
EXHIBIT #3	Copy of School Record -- Third Grade.
EXHIBIT #4	Copy of School Record -- Fourth Grade.
EXHIBIT #5	Copy of School Record -- Fifth Grade.
EXHIBIT #6	Copy of School Record -- Sixth Grade.
EXHIBIT #7	Copy of Transfer: New Orleans, Louisiana, Public High Schools to Fort Worth Public High School.
EXHIBIT #8	Copy of Application for Registration.
EXHIBIT #9	Copy of Classification Card.
EXHIBIT #10	Copy of Permanent High School Record.
EXHIBIT #11	Copy of Cumulative Record and List of Schools Attended In Fort Worth, Texas.
EXHIBIT #12	Information Sheet, Re: A Check of the Fort Worth Police Department Files.
EXHIBIT #13	Copy of Registration Card: Dallas Independent School District.
EXHIBIT #14	Information Sheet, Re: Divorce of Mrs. Marguerite Oswald from Edwin Ekdahl.

COMMISSION EXHIBIT No. 1873-A—Continued

FIRST GRADE

January 29, 1947

to

May 30, 1947

Lee Oswald attended School #19,

Lily B. Clayton Elementary School,

2000 Park Place,

Fort Worth, Texas.

Home Room Teacher: Lois Lowimore, (The Fort Worth Public School District Personnel Office received a letter of resignation from this teacher dated October 8, 1947, resignation to be effective December 19, 1947. Reason: To be married. After resignation, therefore, the Personnel Office does not have her married name.)

No other records available except copy of Cumulative Record, attached.

Note: Policy of the School District has been to keep the Teacher's Daily Register for only five years. Therefore, this register has been disposed of, due to the fact that it has been approximately sixteen years. Received information that this policy has been changed, now that it has been proved there could be a need for these registers.

This also applies to the following exhibit -- Exhibit #2.

COMMISSION EXHIBIT No. 1873-B

NAME Oswald (Last) Lee (First) (Middle) BIRTH: YEAR 1939 MONTH Oct. DAY 18 SEX: MALE ~~FEMALE~~

ADDRESS 1505 8th Ave.

FATHER'S NAME Edwin Ekdahl GUARDIAN'S NAME

MOTHER'S NAME ORIGINAL RECORD SENT TO #28 DATE 5-9-49

DATE OF ENTRY	School	Grade	Days Present	Days Absent	Tardy	Dismissed Early	Citizenship	Reading	Spelling	Handwriting	English	El. Science / Spanish	Soc. Sci. St. Soc. Studies	Arithmetic	Art	Music	Instrumental Music	Health Saf.-Health	Speech	Industrial Arts	Homemaking	Band Orchestra		Phys. Ed.		Reading Level	Date of Withdrawal	Destination	Home Room Teacher
6-27-47	19	1	103	87	1			B		B	B	B	B	B	B	B		A						A			5-30-47	2	Lowrimore
						3-18-48 Destination #18																							

(Residual Copy—Cumulative Record—Grades K-8—Fort Worth Public Schools)

COMMISSION EXHIBIT No. 1873-B—Continued

SECOND GRADE

September 9, 1947

to

March 18, 1948

Lee Oswald attended School #19,

Lily B. Clayton Elementary School,

2000 Park Place,

Fort Worth, Texas.

Home Room Teacher: Florine Murphy,
(Mrs.) Robert Dale Murphy,
8032 Pinewood Drive,
Fort Worth, Texas
Telephone: CI4-0366.
(Still teaching at same School.)

March 19, 1948

to

June 2, 1948
(Same school year)

Lee Oswald transferred from School #19,

above date of withdrawal March 18, 1948,

transferred to School #18,

George C. Clark Elementary School,

3300 S. Henderson.

Date of Entry: March 19, 1948

Home Room Teacher: Glenada Press,
(Mrs.) E. R. Press,
1708 Oak Hill Road,
Fort Worth, Texas
Telephone: GL1-5400.
(Still teaching at same School.)

— Commission Exhibit No. 1873-C —

No other records available except copy of Cumulative Record, attached.

COMMISSION EXHIBIT No. 1873-C

NAME Oswald, Lee (Last, First, Middle) BIRTH: YEAR 1939 MONTH Oct. DAY 18 SEX: MALE / FEMALE

ADDRESS 1505 8th Ave.

FATHER'S NAME Edwin Ekdall GUARDIAN'S NAME

MOTHER'S NAME ORIGINAL RECORD SENT TO DATE

DATE OF ENTRY	School	Grade	Days Present	Days Absent	Tardy	Dismissed Early	Citizenship	Reading	Spelling	Handwriting	English	Spanish	Soc. Sci. St. Soc. Studies	Arithmetic	Art	Music	Instrumental Music	Health Sci.-Health	Speech	Industrial Arts	Homemaking	Band Orchestra	Phys. Ed.	Reading Level	Date of Withdrawal	Destination	Home Room Teacher
9-9-47	19	2	120	5	2																				3-18-48	#18	Murphy
3-19-48	18	2	40	-			B	C	D	B	B		A	A	B	A							A		6-2-48	3	Prels

FORM (Residual Copy—Cumulative Record—Grades K-9—Fort Worth Public Schools)

COMMISSION EXHIBIT No. 1873-C—Continued

THIRD GRADE

September 8, 1948

to

June 3, 1949

Lee Oswald attended School #28,

Arlington Heights Elementary School,

5100 El Campo,

Fort Worth, Texas.

Home Room Teacher: Rosina Hailey,
Now (Mrs.) Lee E. Sattawhite, Jr.,
5817 Malvey Avenue,
Fort Worth, Texas
Telephone: PE8-8534.
(Married and is not teaching anywhere at this time.)

No other records available except copy of Cumulative Record, attached.

Note: This school sustained a burglary in which there was reported an excessive amount of vandalism, destroying School Records. This being after Lee Oswald attended the school, his records were among those destroyed.

COMMISSION EXHIBIT No. 1873-D

FORT WORTH PUBLIC SCHOOLS
CUMULATIVE RECORD

NAME Oswald, Lee (SURNAME, CHRISTIAN NAME) ADDRESS 1505 8th Ave. PHONE none

BIRTH YEAR 39 MONTH Oct. DAY 18 ADDRESS 7408 Ewing PHONE PE-7995 M.A.

PARENT Edwin Ekdall (Deceased) ADDRESS PHONE C.A.

or Guardian Mrs. Marguerite Oswald VACCINATION EXPIRES 1951 - #19 I.Q. 103

DATE [illegible] 50

Date of Entry	School	Grade	Room	Days Present	Days Absent	Tardy	Dis. Early	Language Arts: Reading	Spelling	H'Writing	English	Spanish	S. Studies	El. Science	Arithmetic	Fine Arts: Art	Music	Phys. Ed.	Health	Citizenship	Date of Withdrawal	Destination	Teacher
1-27-47	19	1	103	87	1			B		B	B		B	B	B	B	B	a	a	B	5-30-47	2	[illegible]
3-18-48 Destination #48																							
1-8-48	28	3	34	154	23	2		C	B	C	C		a	a	B	a	a	B	B	a	6-3-49	Gr. 4	R. Hailey
9-7-49	48	4	108	163	10	1	1	B	C	B	B	C	B	B	B	B	B	B	B	B	6-2-50	Gr. 5	Livingston
9-6-50	48	5	105	157½	17½	3	-	C	L	B	C		B	B	D	B	B	B	B	B	6-1-51	Gr. 6	Darsey
9-5-51	48	6	115	[illegible]	[illegible]			B	L	C	D	C	C	C	D	B	B	a	a	B	5-29-52	Gr. 7	Bratton

		Date	Norm	Gr. Eq.	High Score		Low Score	
Met. Ach.	Form	2-8-50	4.5	4.0	Read.	4.7	Spell.	3.3
Stanford.	Ach.	2-13-51	5.5	4.0	Read.	4.9	Elem. Sci.	3.0
"	"	2-11-52	6.5	[illegible]	Word M.	8.6	Spell	4.4

School Lily B. Clayton — Millicent Keeble Principal

FORM D

COMMISSION EXHIBIT No. 1873-D—Continued

FOURTH GRADE

September 7, 1949
to
June 2, 1950

Lee Oswald attended School #48,

Ridglea West Elementary School,

7325 Kermit,

Fort Worth, Texas.

Home Room Teacher: Emma Dee Livingston,
(Mrs.) Clyde I. Livingston,
7304 Pensacola Avenue,
Fort Worth, Texas.
Telephone: PE8-1485.
(Now married, not teaching.)

Reference is made to copy of Teacher's Daily Register, attached. (Two copies of this same register are furnished. The first copy is untouched. The second copy is retouched for legibility.)

COMMISSION EXHIBIT No. 1873-E

FORM M-191

TEXAS TEACHER'S

Daily Register

FOR PUBLIC SCHOOLS

1949-50

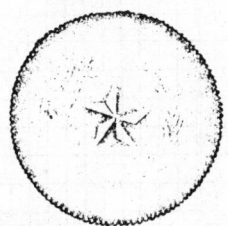

Ridglea West #48 — Fort Worth

Name of School and No. — Post Office

Tarrant — Mrs. E. D. Livingston

County — Name of Teacher

FOR GRADE IV Room 108

Note.—This register is the property of the State of Texas. Each classroom teacher must keep the register neatly and accurately according to instructions, completely fill in all data, and return the register at the close of the school term to the office of the principal, county superintendent, or local superintendent to be filed before the teacher's salary for the last month can be drawn. It becomes an important official record for the school. PLEASE READ AND FOLLOW DIRECTIONS.

Authorized by

STATE DEPARTMENT OF EDUCATION

STATE OF TEXAS

K853-749-50m

COMMISSION EXHIBIT No. 1873-E—Continued

SCHOOL TERM

Beginning ________ 19____
Ending ________ 19____

Boys

Put (√) before names of all pupils transported.

RECORD OF ATTENDANCE

Write E in square to show date pupil was admitted; W to denote date pupil withdrew or dropped; and R to show date pupil was re-admitted. A for Absence; T for Tardy; blank space for Present and On Time.

ATTENDANCE ANALYSIS

Pupil Classification
R—Resident; N—Non-Resident
T—Transfer; B—Eligible Bus

RECORD OF WORK (LIST SUBJECTS TAUGHT)

O'Connor, Albert B.
(Last Name) (First Names)
Born: Month 4 Day 3 Year 41
Age Sept. 1, 1949. Years 9
Entered 4TH grade
Promoted to 5TH grade
Retained in ________ grade
O'Connor, Albert B.
(Name of Parent or Guardian)
Address: 7404 Culver
Occupation: apprentice Ed. ordinator
*Source of Pupil (Check one): B1, B2, C1, C2, C3, C4, C5, C6, C7, C8
No. of yrs. in this grade ________ (Include this year)
No. yrs. in school previous to this yr.: ________
†Loss or withdrawal due to (check one): D1, D2, D3, D4.

Month	1st Week	2nd Week	3rd Week	4th Week	Days Absent	Days Present	Times Tardy
1		A		a E	[illegible]	20	0
2					1	[illegible]	[illegible]
3					[illegible]	27	
4	a				[illegible]	[illegible]	
5		a a	a	H H	[illegible]	[illegible]	0
6			a		1	27	0
7			a				
8	a a				3	27	
9		a a a a		H H	5	[illegible]	0
10							
Tot.						[illegible]	0

Month	Reading	Spelling	Writing	English	Language	Social	Science	Arith.	Art	Music	Phys. Ed.	Health	Citizenship
1	a	a	B	B	a	a	B	C	B	a	a	a	a
2	a	B	B	B	B	B	a	B	a	a	a	a	a
3	a	a	B	a	a	B	a	B	a	a	a	a	a
4	a	a	B	B	a	B	a	a	a	a	a	a	a
5	B	B	B	B	a	B	a	a	a	a	a	a	a
6	B	a	B	a	a	B	B	a	a	a	a	a	a
7	a	a	B	a	a	a	a	a	a	a	a	a	a
8	B	a	B	a	a	B	B	a	a	a	a	a	a
9	a	a	B	B	a	B	a	a	a	a	a	a	a
10													
Tot.													

Oswald, Lee
(Last Name) (First Names)
Born: Month 10 Day 18 Year 39
Age Sept. 1, 1949. Years 9
Entered 4TH grade
Promoted to 5TH grade
Retained in ________ grade
Oswald, Mrs. M.
(Name of Parent or Guardian)
Address: 7408 Ewing
Occupation: [illegible]
*Source of Pupil (Check one): B1, B2, C1, C2, C3, C4, C5, C6, C7, C8
No. of yrs. in this grade ________ (Include this year)
No. yrs. in school previous to this yr.: ________
†Loss or withdrawal due to (check one): D1, D2, D3, D4.

Month	1st Week	2nd Week	3rd Week	4th Week	Days Absent	Days Present	Times Tardy
1	E	a a a a					
2					3	[illegible]	1
3			H H	a a	2	25	
4			H H a	a	[illegible]	[illegible]	
5	a	H		H H	[illegible]	[illegible]	1
6					1	27	0
7	a						
8				T	1	29	0
9				H H	[illegible]	[illegible]	0
10					[illegible]	[illegible]	0
Tot.					10	[illegible]	1

Month	Reading	Spelling	Writing	English	Language	Social	Science	Arith.	Art	Music	Phys. Ed.	Health	Citizenship
1	B	B	C	B	a	B	C	C	C	B	B	B	B
2	B	B	B	B	B	B	B	C	B	B	B	B	B
3	B	B	B	C	C	C	C	C	B	C	B	B	C
4	B	B	B	B	B	B	C	C	B	B	B	B	B
5	C	C	B	C	C	B	C	B	B	C	C	B	C
6	B	C	B	B	C	B	C	B	B	B	C	B	C
7	B	C	B	B	C	B	B	C	B	B	B	B	B
8	B	C	B	B	C	B	B	B	B	a	B	a	B
9	B	C	B	B	C	B	B	B	B	B	B	B	B
10													
Tot.													

Parker, Wyman H.
(Last Name) (First Names)
Born: Month 9 Day 4 Year 40
Age Sept. 1, 1949. Years 8
Entered 4TH grade
Promoted to 5TH grade
Retained in ________ grade
Parker, S. H.
(Name of Parent or Guardian)
Address: 7317 Brazos
Occupation: aircraft mechanic
*Source of Pupil (Check one): B1, B2, C1, C2, C3, C4, C5, C6, C7, C8
No. of yrs. in this grade ________ (Include this year)
No. yrs. in school previous to this yr.: ________
†Loss or withdrawal due to (check one): D1, D2, D3, D4.

Month	1st Week	2nd Week	3rd Week	4th Week	Days Absent	Days Present	Times Tardy
1	E						
2	T	T			0	[illegible]	2
3				H		27	
4			H H			27	
5		H		H H	[illegible]	[illegible]	2
6	T					28	1
7							
8					0	30	2
9	T			H H	[illegible]	[illegible]	1
10							2
Tot.						[illegible]	4

Month	Reading	Spelling	Writing	English	Language	Social	Science	Arith.	Art	Music	Phys. Ed.	Health	Citizenship
1	a	a	B	B	a	B	a	C	B	a	a	a	B
2	B	a	B	a	a	a	a	a	B	a	B	a	B
3	a	a	B	a	a	a	a	a	B	a	B	a	B
4	a	a	B	B	a	a	a	a	B	a	B	a	B
5	B	a	B	C	a	B	B	B	a	a	a	a	a
6	a	a	B	a	a	a	a	a	a	a	a	a	B
7	a	a	B	a	a	a	a	B	a	a	a	a	a
8	a	a	B	a	a	a	a	B	a	a	a	a	a
9	a	a	B	B	a	a	a	B	B	a	a	a	B
10													
Tot.													

*Code each pupil as soon as he is placed on your roll. See explanation of Terms.
†Code each pupil upon withdrawal. A pupil is absent until the teacher knows of **his permanent withdrawal.**
Disregard heavy black lines unless your school reports on the six-weeks basis.

SCHOOL TERM	RECORD OF ATTENDANCE	ATTENDANCE ANALYSIS	RECORD OF WORK IN SUBJECTS TAUGHT
Beginning ____ 19__ Ending ____ 19__	Write E in square to show date pupil was admitted; W to denote date pupil withdrew or dropped; and R to show date pupil was re-admitted. A for Absence; T for Tardy; blank space for Present and On Time.	Pupil Classification: R—Resident; N—Non-Resident; T—Transfer; B—Eligible Bus	Reading, Spelling, Writing, English, Spanish, Social St., Science, Arith., Art, Music, Phys. Ed., Health, Citizenship

Boys

Put (√) before names of all pupils transported.

Columns: MONTH | 1st Week M T W T F | 2nd Week M T W T F | 3rd Week M T W T F | 4th Week M T W T F | Days Absent | Days Present | Times Tardy — MONTH | I R Ab. Pr. | II N Ab. Pr. | III T Ab. Pr. | IV B Ab. Pr.

O'Connor, Albert B.
(Last Name) (First Names)

Born: Month 4 Day 3 Year 41

Age Sept. 1, 1949. Years 9

Entered 4TH grade

Promoted to 5TH grade

Retained in ____ grade

O'Connor, Albert B.
(Name of Parent or Guardian)

Address: 7404 Culver

Occupation: apprentice Coordinator

*Source of Pupil (Check one): B1, B2, C1, C2, C3, C4, C5, C6, C7, C8

No. of yrs. in this grade ____ (Include this year)
No. yrs. in school previous to this yr.: ____
†Loss or withdrawal due to (check one): D1, D2, D3, D4.

Month	Reading	Spelling	Writing	English	Spanish	Social St.	Science	Arith.	Art	Music	Phys. Ed.	Health	Citizenship
1	a	a	B	B	a	a	B	C	B	a	a	a	a
2	a	B	B	B	B	B	a	B	a	a	a	a	a
3	a	a	B	a	a	B	a	B	a	a	a	a	a
4	a	a	B	B	a	a	B	a	B	a	a	a	a
5	B	B	B	B	a	a	B	B	a	a	a	a	a
6	B	a	B	a	a	B	B	a	a	a	a	a	a
7	a	a	B	a	a	a	a	a	a	a	a	a	a
8	B	a	B	a	a	B	B	a	a	a	a	a	a
9	a	a	B	B	a	B	a	a	a	a	a	a	a
10													
Tot.													

Oswald, Lee
(Last Name) (First Names)

Born: Month 10 Day 18 Year 39

Age Sept. 1, 1949. Years 9

Entered 4TH grade

Promoted to 5TH grade

Retained in ____ grade

Oswald, Mrs. M.
(Name of Parent or Guardian)

Address: 7408 Ewing

Occupation: Father deceased

*Source of Pupil (Check one): B1, B2, C1, C2, C3, C4, C5, C6, C7, C8

No. of yrs. in this grade ____ (Include this year)
No. yrs. in school previous to this yr.: ____
†Loss or withdrawal due to (check one): D1, D2, D3, D4.

Days Absent	Days Present	Times Tardy
3	30	1 1
2	25	
3	24	
8	79	1-1
1	27	0-0
1	29	0-0
0	28	0-0
2	84	0-0
10-	163	1-1

Month	Reading	Spelling	Writing	English	Spanish	Social St.	Science	Arith.	Art	Music	Phys. Ed.	Health	Citizenship
1	B	a	C	B	a	B	C	C	C	B	B	B	B
2	B	a	B	B	B	B	B	C	B	B	B	B	B
3	B	a	B	C	C	C	C	C	B	C	B	B	C
4	B	a	B	B	B	B	C	C	B	B	B	B	B
5	C	C	B	C	C	B	C	B	B	C	C	B	C
6	B	C	B	B	B	B	B	C	B	B	B	B	B
7	B	C	B	B	C	B	B	B	B	a	B	a	B
8	B	C	B	B	C	B	B	B	B	B	B	B	B
9	B	C	B	B	C	B	B	B	B	B	B	B	B
10													
Tot.													

Parker, Wyman H.
(Last Name) (First Names)

Born: Month 9 Day 4 Year 40

Age Sept. 1, 1949. Years 8

Entered 4TH grade

Promoted to 5TH grade

Retained in ____ grade

Parker, S. H.
(Name of Parent or Guardian)

Address: 7317 Brazos

Occupation: aircraft mechanic

*Source of Pupil (Check one): B1, B2, C1, C2, C3, C4, C5, C6, C7, C8

No. of yrs. in this grade ____ (Include this year)
No. yrs. in school previous to this yr.: ____
†Loss or withdrawal due to (check one): D1, D2, D3, D4.

Month	Reading	Spelling	Writing	English	Spanish	Social St.	Science	Arith.	Art	Music	Phys. Ed.	Health	Citizenship
1	a	a	B	B	a	B	a	C	B	a	a	a	B
2	B	a	B	a	a	a	a	a	B	a	a	B	B
3	a	a	B	a	a	a	a	C	B	a	B	a	B
4	a	a	B	a	a	a	a	C	B	a	B	a	B
5	B	a	B	C	B	B	B	B	a	a	a	a	a
6	a	a	B	a	a	a	a	a	a	a	a	a	B
7	a	a	B	a	a	a	a	B	a	a	a	a	a
8	a	a	B	a	a	a	a	B	a	a	a	a	a
9	a	a	B	B	a	a	a	B	B	a	a	a	B
10													
Tot.													

*Code each pupil as soon as he is placed on your roll. See explanation of Terms.
†Code each pupil upon withdrawal. A pupil is absent until the teacher knows of his permanent withdrawal.
Disregard heavy black lines unless your school reports on the six-weeks basis.

COMMISSION EXHIBIT No. 1873-E—Continued

FIFTH GRADE

September 6, 1950
to
June 1, 1951

Lee Oswald attended School #18,

Ridglea West Elementary School,

7325 Kermit,

Fort Worth, Texas.

Home Room Teacher: Mattie Lee Darsey,
Now (Mrs.) John Warren Smith,
4009 Anita Street,
Fort Worth, Texas.
Telephone: WA6-4952.
(Married, not teaching.)

Reference is made to copy of Teacher's Daily Register, attached. (Two copies of the same register are attached. First copy is untouched. Second copy is retouched for legibility.)

COMMISSION EXHIBIT No. 1873-F

FORM M-191

Teacher's Daily Register

19 50 - 19 51

Ridglea West #48 Fort Worth
Name of School and No. Post Office

Tarrant M. L. Darsey
County Name of Teacher

FOR GRADE Five

Note.—This register is the property of the State of Texas. Each classroom teacher must keep the register neatly and accurately according to instructions, completely fill in all data, and return the register at the close of the school term to the office of the principal, county superintendent, or local superintendent to be filed before the teacher's salary for the last month can be drawn. It becomes an important official record for the school. PLEASE READ AND FOLLOW DIRECTIONS.

Authorized by
TEXAS EDUCATION AGENCY
STATE OF TEXAS

B2163-550-60m

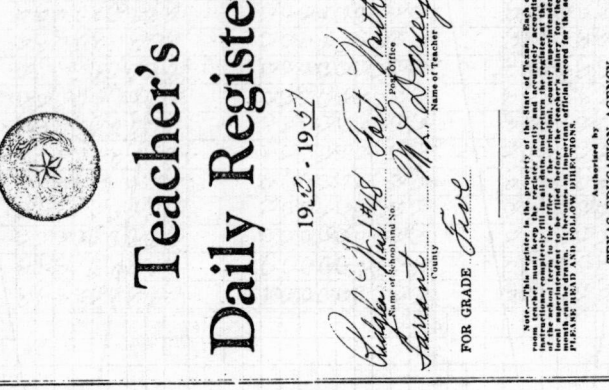

COMMISSION EXHIBIT No. 1873-F—Continued

Beginning 9-6 1950
Ending 6-1 1951

Write E in square to show date pupil was admitted; W to denote date pupil withdrew or dropped; and R to show date pupil was re-admitted. A for Absence; T for Tardy; blank space for Present and On Time.

Pupil Classification
R—Resident; I—Ineligible
T—Transfer; B—Eligible Bus

Boys

Put (√) before names of all pupils transported.

Oswald, Lee Harvey
(Last Name) (First Names)
Born: Month Oct Day 18 Year 1939
Age Sept. 1, 1950 Years 10
Entered fifth grade
Promoted to ______ grade
Retained in ______ grade
Marguerite Oswald
(Name of Parent or Guardian)
Address: 7408 Ewing
Occupation: Insurance
*Source of Pupil (Check one): (B1) B2, C1, C2, C3, C4, C5, C6, C7, C8
No. of yrs. in this grade 1 (Include this year)
No. yrs. in school previous to this yr.:
†Loss or withdrawal due to (check one): D1, D2, D3, D4.
PE - 9995

Month	Reading	Spelling	Writing	Language	Social Studies	Elem. Science	Arith.	Art	Music	Physical Ed.	Health	Citizenship
1	B	C	B	B	B	B	C	B	C	B	A	B
3	B	D	B	B	B	B	D	B	C	B	A	B
5	C	C	B	C	B	B	D	B	C	B	A	C
7	B	D	C	B	B	C	D	B	B	B	A	B
9	C	D	C	C	B	B	D	B	B	B	A	B
Tot.	C	D	B	C	B	B	D	B	B	B	B	B

Owen, Michael Richard
(Last Name) (First Names)
Born: Month Jan Day 14 Year 1940
Age Sept. 1, 1950 Years 10
Entered fifth grade
Promoted to sixth grade
Retained in ______ grade
J. E. Owen
(Name of Parent or Guardian)
Address: 4405 Fairfax
Occupation: Consolidated
*Source of Pupil (Check one): B1, B2, C1, C2, C3, C4, C5, C6, C7, C8
No. of yrs. in this grade 1 (Include this year)
No. yrs. in school previous to this yr.:
†Loss or withdrawal due to (check one): D1, D2, D3, D4.
PE - 7434
84

Month	Reading	Spelling	Writing	Language	Social Studies	Elem. Science	Arith.	Art	Music	Physical Ed.	Health	Citizenship
1	B	A	B	A	A	A	B	B	B	A	A	A
3	A	A	B	B	B	B	B	B	A	A	A	A
5	B	A	B	C	C	B	B	C	B	B	A	B
7	B	A	B	B	B	B	B	A	B	A	A	B
9	B	B	B	B	B	B	C	B	B	A	A	B

Parker, Wyman Wayne
(Last Name) (First Names)
Born: Month Sept Day 4 Year 1940
Age Sept. 1, 1950 Years 10
Entered fifth grade
Promoted to sixth grade
Retained in ______ grade
Samuel Parker
(Name of Parent or Guardian)
Address: 7317 Brazos
Occupation: Convair
*Source of Pupil (Check one): (B1) B2, C1, C2, C3, C4, C5, C6, C7, C8
No. of yrs. in this grade 1 (Include this year)
No. yrs. in school previous to this yr.:
†Loss or withdrawal due to (check one): D1, D2, D3, D4.
PE - 2647

Month	Reading	Spelling	Writing	Language	Social Studies	Elem. Science	Arith.	Art	Music	Physical Ed.	Health	Citizenship
1	A	A	B	B	A	A	B	B	B	A	A	B
3	A	B	B	B	B	B	B	B	A	A	A	B
5	A	B	B	B	B	B	B	B	B	B	A	C
7	A	B	B	A	B	A	C	B	B	A	A	B
9	A	A	B	A	A	A	C	B	A	A	A	B
Tot.	A	A	B	A	A	A	C	B	B	A	A	B

*Code each pupil as soon as he is placed on your roll. See explanation of Terms.
†Code each pupil upon withdrawal. A pupil is absent until the teacher knows of his permanent withdrawal.
Disregard heavy black lines unless your school reports on the six-weeks basis.

COMMISSION EXHIBIT No. 1873-F—Continued

SCHOOL TERM

Beginning 9-6 19 50
Ending 6-1 19 51

Boys

Put (V) before names of all pupils transported.

RECORD OF ATTENDANCE

Write E in square to show date pupil was admitted; W to designate date pupil withdrew or dropped; and R to show date pupil was re-admitted. A for Absence; T for Tardy; blank space for Present and On Time.

Columns: Month | 1st Week (M T W T F) | 2nd Week (M T W T F) | 3rd Week (M T W T F) | 4th Week (M T W T F) | Days Absent | Days Present | Times Tardy

ATTENDANCE ANALYSIS

Pupil Classification
R—Resident; I—Ineligible
T—Transfer; B—Eligible Bus

Columns: Month | I R (Ab. Pr.) | II I (Ab. Pr.) | III T (Ab. Pr.) | IV B (Ab. Pr.)

RECORD OF WORK (LIST SUBJECTS TAUGHT)

Oswald, Lee Harvey
(Last Name) (First Names)
Born: Month Oct Day 18 Year 39
Age Sept. 1, 1950 Years 10
Entered fifth grade
Promoted to ________ grade
Retained in ________ grade
Marguerite Oswald
(Name of Parent or Guardian)
Address: 7408 Erving
Occupation: Insurance [illegible]
*Source of Pupil (Check one): B1, B2, C1, C2, C3, C4, C5, C6, C7, C8
No. of yrs. in this grade 1 (Include this year)
No. yrs. in school previous to this yr.: ________
†Loss or withdrawal due to (check one): D1, D2, D3, D4.

Month	Days Absent	Days Present	Times Tardy
1	2	26	2
3	2	25	1
5	3	30	0
7	3	20	0
8	4	25	0
10	[illegible]	31	0
	3½	31½	0

PE-7995

Month	Reading	Spelling	Writing	Language	Social Studies	Elem. Science	Arith.	Art	Music	Physical Ed.	Health	Citizenship
1	B	C	B	B	B	B	C	B	C	B	A	B
3	B	D	B	B	B	B	D	B	C	B	A	B
5	C	C	B	C	B	B	D	B	C	B	A	C
7	B	D	C	B	B	C	D	B	B	B	A	B
9	C	D	C	C	B	B	D	B	B	B	A	B
Tot.	C	D	B	C	B	B	D	B	B	B	B	B

Owen, Michael Richard
(Last Name) (First Names)
Born: Month Jan. Day 14 Year 1940
Age Sept. 1, 1950 Years 10
Entered fifth grade
Promoted to sixth grade
Retained in ________ grade
O. F. Owen
(Name of Parent or Guardian)
Address: 4405 Fairfax
Occupation: Consolidated
*Source of Pupil (Check one): B1, B2, C1, C2, C3, C4, C5, C6, C7, C8
No. of yrs. in this grade 1 (Include this year)
No. yrs. in school previous to this yr.: ________
†Loss or withdrawal due to (check one): D1, D2, D3, D4.

Month	Days Absent	Days Present	Times Tardy
1			1
8	[illegible]	[illegible]	1
10	[illegible]	[illegible]	0

PE-7404
84

Month	Reading	Spelling	Writing	Language	Social Studies	Elem. Science	Arith.	Art	Music	Physical Ed.	Health	Citizenship
1	B	A	B	A	A	A	B	B	B	A	A	A
3	A	A	B	B	B	B	B	B	A	A	A	A
5	B	A	B	B	B	B	B	B	B	B	A	B
7	B	A	B	B	B	B	B	A	B	A	A	B
9	B	B	B	B	B	B	C	B	B	A	A	B

(Entry crossed through on the form.)

Parker, Wyman Wayne
(Last Name) (First Names)
Born: Month Sept Day 4 Year 1940
Age Sept. 1, 1950 Years 10
Entered fifth grade
Promoted to sixth grade
Retained in ________ grade
Samuel Parker
(Name of Parent or Guardian)
Address: 7317 Brazos
Occupation: Carswell
*Source of Pupil (Check one): B1, B2, C1, C2, C3, C4, C5, C6, C7, C8
No. of yrs. in this grade 1 (Include this year)
No. yrs. in school previous to this yr.: ________
†Loss or withdrawal due to (check one): D1, D2, D3, D4.

Month	Days Absent	Days Present	Times Tardy
1		[illegible]	1
5	1	[illegible]	4
7		23	
8	0	29	0
10	1½	33½	

PE-2647
85

Month	Reading	Spelling	Writing	Language	Social Studies	Elem. Science	Arith.	Art	Music	Physical Ed.	Health	Citizenship
1	A	A	B	B	A	A	B	B	B	A	A	B
3	A	B	B	B	B	B	B	B	A	A	A	B
5	A	B	B	B	B	B	B	B	B	B	A	C
7	A	B	B	A	B	A	C	B	B	A	A	B
9	A	A	B	A	A	A	C	B	B	A	A	B
Tot.	A	A	B	A	A	A	C	B	B	A	A	B

(Entry crossed through on the form.)

---

*Code each pupil as soon as he is placed on your roll. See explanation of Terms.
†Code each pupil upon withdrawal. A pupil is absent until the teacher knows of his permanent withdrawal.
Disregard heavy black lines unless your school reports on the six-weeks basis.

SIXTH GRADE

September 5, 1951

to

May 29, 1952

Lee Oswald attended School #18,

Ridglea West Elementary School,

7325 Kermit,

Fort Worth, Texas.

Home Room Teacher: Betty Bratton,
Now (Mrs.) Howard L. Green,
7316 Oakland Lane,
Fort Worth, Texas.
Telephone: BU1-3216.
(Married -- not teaching.)

Reference is made to copy of Teacher's Daily Register, attached. (Two copies of same register are furnished. First copy is untouched. Second copy is retouched for legibility.)

COMMISSION EXHIBIT No. 1873-G

FORM M-191

THE STATE OF TEXAS

Teacher's Daily Register

195__ - 195__

Ridglea West #18 ________
Name of School and No. Post Office

Tarrant ____ Betty Bratton
County Name of Teacher

FOR GRADE 6

Note.—This register is the property of the State of Texas. Each classroom teacher must keep the register neatly and accurately according to instructions, completely fill in all data, and return the register at the close of the school term to the office of the principal, county superintendent, or local superintendent to be filed before the teacher's salary for the last month can be drawn. It becomes an important official record for the school. PLEASE READ AND FOLLOW DIRECTIONS.

Authorized by

TEXAS EDUCATION AGENCY

STATE OF TEXAS

81406-451-75m

COMMISSION EXHIBIT No. 1873-G—Continued

SCHOOL TERM

Beginning Sept. 5 1951
Ending May 29 1952

Boys

Put (V) before names of all pupils transported.

RECORD OF ATTENDANCE

Write E in square to show date pupil was admitted; W to denote date pupil withdrew or dropped; and R to show date pupil was re-admitted. A for Absence; T for Tardy; blank space for Present and On Time.

ATTENDANCE ANALYSIS

Pupil Classification
R—Resident; I—Ineligible
T—Transfer

RECORD OF WORK (LIST SUBJECTS TAUGHT)

Pupil 1

9-5-51
Keeling, Michael
(Last Name) (First Name)
Born: Month Jan Day 14 Year 1940
Age Sept. 1, 1951 Years 11
Entered 6th grade
Promoted to 7 grade
Retained in ____ grade
C. B. Raven
(Name of Parent or Guardian)
Address: 4405 Fairfax
Occupation: foreman
*Source of Pupil (Check one): B1, B2, C1, C2, C3, C4, C5, C6, C7, C8

Month	Days Absent	Days Present	Times Tardy
1	3	25	0
2	0	22	0
3	3½	35½	0
4			
5	2	30	0
6	6	27	0
7	1½	27	0
8			
9			
10			
Tot.			

No. of yrs. in this grade 1 (Include this year)
No. yrs. in school previous to this yr.: 2
†Withdrawal due to (check one): D1, D2, D3, D4.
Eligible Bus Pupil (check one): Yes____ No____
Bus Route____ Run No.____
‡Was this pupil enrolled on 1st Monday in Feb. of this year? Yes____ No____

Month	Reading Lit.	Spelling	Handwriting	Lang. English	Lang. Grammar	Social St.	Elem. Science	Arithmetic	Art	Music	Phy. Ed.	Health	Citizenship
1	[illegible]	[illegible]	[illegible]	B	a	[illegible]	[illegible]	C	[illegible]	a	a	[illegible]	[illegible]
2	B	a	[illegible]	C	B	B	B	a	[illegible]	B	[illegible]	C	a
3	[illegible]	a	B	C	a	[illegible]	[illegible]	a	[illegible]	[illegible]	a	[illegible]	a
4	[illegible]	[illegible]	[illegible]	[illegible]	a	B	B	B	[illegible]	[illegible]	a	[illegible]	a
5	a	a	B	a	a	B	B	a	[illegible]	a	a	a	a
6	a	a	B	B	B	a	a	a	B	a	a	a	a
7	a	a	B	B	a	a	a	a	B	a	a	a	a
8	a	a	C	B	a	a	a	a	B	a	a	a	a
9	a	a	B	B	a	B	B	B	B	a	a	a	a
10													
Tot.													

Pupil 2

9-5-51
O'Connor, Patrick
(Last Name) (First Names)
Born: Month Apr. Day 3 Year 1940
Age Sept. 1, 1951 Years 11
Entered 6th grade
Promoted to 7 grade
Retained in ____ grade
C. B. O'Connor
(Name of Parent or Guardian)
Address: 4404 Culver
Occupation: teacher
*Source of Pupil (Check one): C1, C2, C3, C4, C5, C6, C7, C8

Month	Days Absent	Days Present	Times Tardy
1	0	38	0
2	3	35	0
3	2	26	0
4			
5	0	32	0
6	1	26	0
7	1	29	0
8			
9			
10			
Tot.			

No. of yrs. in this grade 1 (Include this year)
No. yrs. in school previous to this yr.: 2
†Withdrawal due to (check one): D1, D2, D3, D4.
Eligible Bus Pupil (check one): Yes____ No____
Bus Route____ Run No.____
‡Was this pupil enrolled on 1st Monday in Feb. of this year? Yes____ No____

Month	Reading Lit.	Spelling	Handwriting	Lang. English	Lang. Grammar	Social St.	Elem. Science	Arithmetic	Art	Music	Phy. Ed.	Health	Citizenship
1	[illegible]	[illegible]	[illegible]	[illegible]	[illegible]	[illegible]	[illegible]	C	C	a	a	[illegible]	[illegible]
2	[illegible]	a	[illegible]	[illegible]	a	B	[illegible]	[illegible]	a	[illegible]	a	a	a
3	a	a	[illegible]	B	a	B	[illegible]	a	a	B	[illegible]	a	B
4	a	[illegible]	[illegible]	B	a	[illegible]	[illegible]	[illegible]	B	B	[illegible]	a	a
5	a	a	B	a	a	a	a	a	B	B	a	a	a
6	a	a	B	B	B	a	a	C	C	a	a	a	B
7	B	a	B	B	a	B	a	B	B	B	a	a	B
8	a	a	B	B	a	a	a	B	B	B	a	a	B
9	a	B	B	B	a	B	B	B	B	B	a	a	B
10													
Tot.													

Pupil 3

1-2-51
[illegible], [illegible]
(Last Name) (First Names)
Born: Month Oct. Day 18 Year 1940
Age Sept. 1, 1951 Years 11
Entered 4th grade
Promoted to 7 grade
Retained in ____ grade
Marguerite [illegible]
(Name of Parent or Guardian)
Address: 1400 Ewing
Occupation: [illegible]
*Source of Pupil (Check one): B1, B2, C1, C2, C3, C4, C5, C6, C7, C8

Month	Days Absent	Days Present	Times Tardy
1	2	26	0
2	1	31	1
3	0	35	0
4			
5	2	30	0
6	1	26	0
7	0	29	0
8			
9			
10			
Tot.			

No. of yrs. in this grade 1 (Include this year)
No. yrs. in school previous to this yr.: 2
†Withdrawal due to (check one): D1, D2, D3, D4.
Eligible Bus Pupil (check one): Yes____ No____
Bus Route____ Run No.____
‡Was this pupil enrolled on 1st Monday in Feb. of this year? Yes____ No____

Month	Reading Lit.	Spelling	Handwriting	Lang. English	Lang. Grammar	Social St.	Elem. Science	Arithmetic	Art	Music	Phy. Ed.	Health	Citizenship
1	[illegible]	[illegible]	[illegible]	[illegible]	[illegible]	C	[illegible]	[illegible]	[illegible]	[illegible]	[illegible]	[illegible]	[illegible]
2	[illegible]	B	C	C	a	C	C	B	a	[illegible]	[illegible]	C	B
3	[illegible]	[illegible]	[illegible]	[illegible]	C	B	[illegible]	[illegible]	[illegible]	[illegible]	[illegible]	a	[illegible]
4	[illegible]	[illegible]	[illegible]	[illegible]	[illegible]	[illegible]	[illegible]	[illegible]	[illegible]	[illegible]	[illegible]	[illegible]	[illegible]
5	a	B	C	B	B	C	C	C	B	B	a	a	a
6	B	a	B	B	C	a	a	B	C	C	a	a	B
7	a	B	B	C	B	B	B	C	B	B	a	a	B
8	a	C	B	B	B	B	B	C	B	B	a	a	B
9	B	B	C	D	C	C	C	D	B	B	a	a	B
10													
Tot.													

*Code each pupil as soon as he is placed on your roll. See explanation of Terms.
†Code each pupil upon withdrawal. A pupil is absent until the teacher knows of his permanent withdrawal.
¹ Disregard heavy black lines unless your school reports on the six-weeks basis.
‡"This year" means this school year. You cannot answer this question until next February.

Beginning Sept. 5, 1951
Ending May 29, 1952

Write E in square to show date pupil was admitted; W to denote date pupil withdrew or dropped; and R to show date pupil was re-admitted. A for Absence; T for Tardy; blank space for Present and On Time.

R—Resident; I—Ineligible
T—Transfer

Boys

Put (√) before names of all pupils transported.

9-5-51
Kenney, Michael
(Last Name) (First Names)
Born: Month Jan. Day 14 Year 1940
Age Sept. 1, 1951 Years 11
Entered 6th grade
Promoted to 7 grade
Retained in ______ grade
[illegible]
(Name of Parent or Guardian)
Address: 4405 Fairfax
Occupation: [illegible]
Source of Pupil (Check one): B1, B2, C1, C2, C3, C4, C5, C6, C7, C8

No. of yrs. in this grade 1 (Include this year)
No. yrs. in school previous to this yr.: 2
†Withdrawal due to (check one): D1, D2, D3, D4.
Eligible Bus Pupil (check one): Yes____ No____

Bus Route____ Run No.____
‡Was this pupil enrolled on 1st Monday in Feb. of this year? Yes____ No____

MONTH	Days Absent	Days Present	Times Tardy
1	3	[illegible]	0
2	0	[illegible]	0
3	2½	25½	0
4			
5	2	30	0
6	0	27	0
7	1½	[illegible]	
8			
9			
10			

Mo.	Reading	Spelling	Handwriting	Lang.-Eng. (oral)	Lang.-Eng. (written)	Social Studies	Elem. Science	Arith.	Art	Music	Phy. Ed.	Health	Citizenship
1	[illegible]	[illegible]	B	B	a	B	B	C	B	a	a	a	[illegible]
2	B	a	B	C	B	B	B	a	[illegible]	B	a	a	a
3	B	a	B	C	a	[illegible]	[illegible]	a	B	B	a	a	a
4	B	[illegible]	[illegible]	[illegible]	[illegible]	B	B	B	B	[illegible]	a	a	a
5	a	a	B	a	a	B	B	a	[illegible]	a	a	a	a
6	a	a	B	B	B	a	a	a	B	a	a	a	a
7	a	a	B	B	a	a	a	a	B	a	a	a	a
8	a	a	B	B	a	a	a	a	B	a	a	a	a
9	a	a	B	B	a	B	B	B	B	a	a	a	a
10													
Tot.													

9-5-51
O'Connor, Patrick
(Last Name) (First Names)
Born: Month [illegible] Day 3 Year 1940
Age Sept. 1, 1951 Years 11
Entered 6th grade
Promoted to 7 grade
Retained in ______ grade
[illegible] O'Connor
(Name of Parent or Guardian)
Address: 7404 [illegible]
Occupation: teacher
Source of Pupil (Check one): B1, B2, C1, C2, C3, C4, C5, C6, C7, C8

No. of yrs. in this grade 1 (Include this year)
No. yrs. in school previous to this yr.: 2
†Withdrawal due to (check one): D1, D2, D3, D4.
Eligible Bus Pupil (check one): Yes____ No____

Bus Route____ Run No.____
‡Was this pupil enrolled on 1st Monday in Feb. of this year? Yes____ No____

MONTH	Days Absent	Days Present	Times Tardy
1	0	23	0
2	[illegible]	[illegible]	[illegible]
3	2	26	0
4			
5	0	32	0
6	1	[illegible]	0
7	1	[illegible]	0
8			
9			
10			

Mo.	Reading	Spelling	Handwriting	Lang.-Eng. (oral)	Lang.-Eng. (written)	Social Studies	Elem. Science	Arith.	Art	Music	Phy. Ed.	Health	Citizenship
1	a	B	[illegible]	B	a	B	B	C	C	a	B	[illegible]	[illegible]
2	B	a	B	B	a	B	[illegible]	[illegible]	[illegible]	B	a	a	C
3	a	a	B	[illegible]	[illegible]	[illegible]	[illegible]	a	B	B	[illegible]	[illegible]	B
4	a	B	[illegible]	B	a	[illegible]	[illegible]	B	[illegible]	B	[illegible]	[illegible]	a
5	a	a	B	a	a	a	a	a	B	B	a	a	a
6	a	a	B	B	B	a	a	C	C	a	a	a	B
7	B	a	B	B	a	B	B	B	B	B	a	a	B
8	a	a	B	B	a	a	a	B	B	B	a	a	B
9	a	B	B	B	a	B	B	B	B	B	a	a	B
10													
Tot.													

1-5-52
Oswald, Lee
(Last Name) (First Names)
Born: Month Oct. Day 18 Year 1939
Age Sept. 1, 1951 Years 11
Entered 6th grade
Promoted to 7 grade
Retained in ______ grade
Marguerite Oswald
(Name of Parent or Guardian)
Address: 7408 Ewing
Occupation: insurance
Source of Pupil (Check one): (B1) B2, C1, C2, C3, C4, C5, C6, C7, C8

No. of yrs. in this grade 1 (Include this year)
No. yrs. in school previous to this yr.: 2
†Withdrawal due to (check one): D1, D2, D3, D4.
Eligible Bus Pupil (check one): Yes____ No____

Bus Route____ Run No.____
‡Was this pupil enrolled on 1st Monday in Feb. of this year? Yes____ No____

MONTH	Days Absent	Days Present	Times Tardy
1	2	26	0
2	1	31	1
3	0	28	0
4			
5	2	30	0
6	1	26	0
7	0	29	0
8			
9			
10			

Mo.	Reading	Spelling	Handwriting	Lang.-Eng. (oral)	Lang.-Eng. (written)	Social Studies	Elem. Science	Arith.	Art	Music	Phy. Ed.	Health	Citizenship
1	B	D	C	D	D	C	C	D	B	B	B	a	C
2	D	D	C	D	a	C	C	D	a	C	a	a	B
3	B	D	C	C	C	B	B	D	B	C	a	a	a
4	C	D	C	D	C	C	C	D	B	C	a	a	B
5	a	D	C	D	B	C	C	C	B	B	a	a	a
6	B	a	B	D	C	a	a	D	C	C	a	a	B
7	a	D	B	C	B	B	B	C	B	B	a	a	B
8	a	C	B	D	B	B	B	C	B	B	a	a	B
9	B	D	C	D	C	C	C	D	B	B	a	a	B
10													
Tot.													

*Code each pupil as soon as he is placed on your roll. See explanation of Terms.
†Code each pupil upon withdrawal. A pupil is absent until the teacher knows of his permanent withdrawal.
Disregard heavy black lines unless your school reports on the six-weeks basis.
‡"This year" means this school year. You cannot answer this question until next February.

COMMISSION EXHIBIT No. 1873-G—Continued

TRANSFER:

Certificate of High School Credits

From: Warren Easton High School of New Orleans, Louisiana, September 18, 1956.

Principle H. T. Garland.

September, 1954 to June 1955 - - - - Beauregard.

September 8, 1955 to October 10, (1956), corrected to 1955.

To: Arlington Heights Senior High School, 4501 W. Rosedale, Fort Worth, Texas.

Note: The above date of October 10, 1956 on the transfer from New Orleans must be incorrect as Lee Oswald transferred to, and attended school in Fort Worth, Texas -- Arlington Heights High School -- in September, 1956, and left the same month to go into service of the U. S. Marine Corps. Therefore, he could not have attended school in New Orleans in October 1956. This would be after he had already transferred to Fort Worth. To further substantiate this correction, note that the dates on the transfer are September 8, 1955 to October 10, 1956. This would be thirteen months and two days when a school year is only nine months. Therefore, it is believed that the correct date on the transfer should be October 10, 1955, instead of 1956.

COMMISSION EXHIBIT No. 1873-H

Transfer Certificate of High School Credits

For Lee Harvey Oswald who attended the Warren Easton High School of New Orleans, Louisiana
from Sept. 8, 1955 [Sept. 1954] to Oct. 10, 1956 [June 1955 – Beauregard]
Date 9-18-56 Principal H. T. Garland

	SUBJECTS	Year Taken (1, 2, 3, 4)	No. of Course	No. of Weeks	Periods Per Week	Minutes Per Week	GRADE	Unit Credit	Names of Schools for Outside Credits
ENGLISH	English	1	I	38	5	300	70 D	1.0	Beauregard
		2	II	2			Inc		
	Speech								
	Journalism								
SOCIAL STUDIES	General History	2	I	2			Inc.		
	Geography								
	U. S. History								
	English History								
	Civics	1	I	38	5	300	83 C	1.0	"
	Economics								
	Sociology								
MATHEMATICS	General Mathematics	1	I	38	5	300	75 D	1.0	"
	Secondary Arithmetic								
	Algebra								
	Plane Geometry								
	Solid Geometry								
	Trigonometry								
SCIENCE	General Science	1	I	"	"	"	76 D	1.0	"
	Biology	1	I	2			Inc.		
	Physics								
	Chemistry								
FOREIGN LANGUAGES	Latin								
	French								
	Spanish								
	German								
	Italian								
HOME ECONOMICS BUSINESS EDUCATION INDUSTRIAL ARTS	Homemaking								
	Industrial Arts								
	Woodworking								
	Electricity								
	Motor Mechanics								
	Metals								
	Graphic Arts								
	Mechanical Drawing								
	Typewriting								
	Bookkeeping								
	Shorthand								
	Commercial Law								
	Distributive Education								
MUSIC, ART, PHYSICAL EDUCATION	General Music								
	Instrumental Music								
	Music Appreciation								
	Music Theory								
	Art	1	I	"	"	"	80.8	1.0	"
	Physical Education	1	I	"	"	"	78	.25	"
		2	II				Inc.		

There are Three (3) years of 39 weeks each in the senior high school course. Length of recitation periods 60 minutes.
Passing grade is 70.

Form 239-4M-7-53

COMMISSION EXHIBIT No. 1873-H—Continued

APPLICATION FOR REGISTRATION,

(Copy)

FORT WORTH PUBLIC SCHOOLS.

COMMISSION EXHIBIT NO. 1873-I

R	K	U	T	N

APPLICATION FOR REGISTRATI
FORT WORTH PUBLIC SCHOOLS

SCHOOL NUMBER 26th DATE Sept. 6 1956

NAME OF PUPIL Oswald (LAST) LEE (FIRST) HARVEY (MIDDLE) TELEPHONE PE-87259

DATE OF BIRTH Oct. (MONTH) 18 (DAY) 1939 (YEAR) AGE 16 SEX M PRESENT GRADE 10

AUTHORITY GIVEN IN ESTABLISHING BIRTH DATE ______ (TO BE FILLED IN FOR FIRST GRADE OR KINDERGARTEN CHILD ONLY)

RESIDENCE OF PUPIL 4936 (NUMBER) Collinwood (STREET) BIRTHPLACE NEW ORLEANS (CITY) (COUNTY), LA. (STATE)

NAME OF PERSON WITH WHOM CHILD LIVES, IF NOT WITH PARENTS ______

SCHOOL ATTENDED LAST YEAR WARREN EASTERN (NAME) NEW ORLEANS (CITY) (COUNTY), LA. (STATE)

CHILD'S ADDRESS WHEN ENUMERATED IN SCHOLASTIC CENSUS LAST JANUARY —

FATHER'S NAME Dead (LAST) (FIRST) ADDRESS ______ (NUMBER) (STREET) (CITY) (STATE)

MOTHER'S NAME Oswald, (LAST) MARGRET (FIRST) ADDRESS 4936 (NUMBER) Collinwood, (STREET) Ft.Wo. (CITY) T (STATE)

FATHER'S OCCUPATION —— MOTHER'S OCCUPATION ______

DATE PUPIL MOVED TO FORT WORTH July (MONTH) 1st (DAY) 1956 (YEAR)

IS THIS PUPIL A MEMBER OF ANY HIGH SCHOOL FRATERNITY OR SORORITY?* YES ______ NO ✓

*Members of high school fraternities and sororities are banned from attendance in public schools by act of the Texas Legislature, October, 1949.

FORM 8

WHEN SUCCESSFULLY VACCINATED? 1952 (YEAR) PHYSICIAN —— CITY Fort Worth

(A pupil whose vaccination was expired or who was not regularly enrolled in the Fort Worth Public Schools last year must present a certificate of successful vaccination signed by a licensed physician.)

HAS CHILD BEEN IMMUNIZED AGAINST DIPHTHERIA? (YES) 1940 (YEAR) WHOOPING COUGH? (YES) 1940 (YEAR)

IS CHILD HARD OF HEARING, NEAR-SIGHTED, OR HAS HE ANY OTHER PHYSICAL DEFECT OR WEAKNESS? NO

(This information is necessary in order for the teacher to understand the pupil's needs)

IN CASE OF SUDDEN ILLNESS OR ACCIDENT, IF FAMILY CANNOT BE CONTACTED, CALL DR. ——

TELEPHONE ______

PLEASE LIST BELOW THE NAMES OF ALL OTHER CHILDREN IN THE FAMILY UNDER EIGHTEEN (18) YEARS OF AGE.

	LAST NAME	FIRST NAME	BIRTHDAY			AGE		SCHOOL ATTENDING
			MONTH	DAY	YEAR	MALE	FEMALE	
1								
2								
3								
4								
5								

I HEREBY CERTIFY THAT THE CHILDREN WHOSE NAMES ARE GIVEN HEREON ARE IN MY CHARGE AND CUSTODY AND THE DATES OF THEIR BIRTHS ARE TRUE AND CORRECT.

NOTE: This application must be signed by the father, mother, legal guardian, or person certifying to be in full legal control of pupil.

SIGNED Marguerite C. Oswald

ADDRESS 4936 Collinwood

CLASSIFICATION CARD

(Copy)

FORT WORTH PUBLIC SCHOOLS,

HIGH SCHOOL DEPARTMENT.

COMMISSION EXHIBIT No. 1873–J

P 14

CLASSIFICATION CARD, FORT WORTH SCHOOLS
HIGH SCHOOL DEPARTMENT

NAME Oswald, Lee Harvey DATE 8.30.56

LAST SCHOOL ATTENDED Warren Easton HS New Orleans La. DATE LEFT Oct 10, 1956

ASSIGNMENT ROOM N 10 CLASS 12 COURSE

	MATH	ENGLISH	HISTORY	SCIENCE	LATIN	MOD. LGS.	VOC. SUB.	Art	P.E.	TO CR.
SUBDIVISIONS	Gen 1,2	1,2	Civ 1,2	Gen 1,2				1,2	1,2	
CREDITS ALLOWED V	1	1	1	1				1	½	5½
EXAMINED FOR										
GRADE										
PRESENT STANDING										
COURSES ASSIGNED		3	W1	Bio 1			W Shop 1		P.E. 3	

V ARE CONDITIONED ON GOOD WORK IN THIS SCHOOL

J.B. Sharp assistant – PRINCIPAL

H.S. 56

COMMISSION EXHIBIT No. 1873–J—Continued

PERMANENT HIGH SCHOOL RECORD,
(Copy)
FORT WORTH PUBLIC HIGH SCHOOLS,

ARLINGTON HEIGHTS HIGH SCHOOL,

NUMBER 266,

4501 W. ROSEDALE,

FORT WORTH, TEXAS.

COMMISSION EXHIBIT No. 1873-K

SCHOOL HISTORY (Give Activity and Year)
1.
2.
3.
4.
5.
6.
7.

Arlington Heights **HIGH SCHOOL** NO. 266 Recorded in School No.

Date of Graduation
No. in Class Rank
Transcripts Sent Date
1. Secret Service (Mr. Sorels) 12-11-63
2. Presidents Investigation (Mr. Summers) [illegible]
3. N. Worth Police Dept. 1-30-64

Name Oswald, Lee Harvey
Address 4936 Collinwood Parent Marguerite C. Oswald
Date of Birth October 18, 1939 Place of Birth New Orleans, La.
Date Entered Sept. 5 1956 School Last Attended
Date Withdrawn 9-28-56 Reason Marines Destination
I. Q. Test Given Date of Test

DAYS ATTENDED / CITIZENSHIP: Beauregard, New Orleans La. (1954, 1955); Warren Easton H.S., New Orleans La. (1955, 1956)

		1954 S Div.	Gr.	Cr.	1955 S Div.	Gr.	Cr.	1955 S Div.	Gr.	Cr.	1956 S Div.	Gr.	Cr.	1956 S Div.	Gr.	Cr.	S 19 Div.	Gr.	Cr.	S 19 Div.	Gr.	Cr.	S 19 Div.	Gr.	Cr.	S Total	
LANGUAGE ARTS—	English	1	D	1/2	2	D	1/2	Attended from 9-8-55 to 10-10-55 No Credits						No credits													English
	Journalism																										Journalism
	Speech																										Speech
MATHEMATICS—	Gen. Mathematics	1	D	1/2	2	D	1/2																				Gen. Mathematics
	Algebra																										Algebra
	Plane Geometry																										Plane Geometry
	Solid Geometry																										Solid Geometry
	Plane Trigonometry																										Plane Trigonometry
	Adv. Arithmetic																										Adv. Arithmetic
SOCIAL STUDIES—	Jr. Social Studies																										Jr. Social Studies
	Anc.-World History																										Anc.-World History
	Modern History																					CONSTITUTION					Modern History
	American History																										American History
	Texas History																										Texas History
	Civics	1	C	1/2	2	C	1/2																				Civics
	Economics																										Economics
SCIENCE—	General Science	1	D	1/2	2	D	1/2																				General Science
	Biology-Botany																										Biology-Botany
	Health Education																										Health Education
	Chemistry																										Chemistry
	Physics																										Physics
LANGUAGES—	Latin																										Latin
	French																										French
	Spanish																										Spanish
VOCATIONAL—	Mech. Drawing																										Mech. Drawing
	Shop																										Shop
	Foods																										Foods
	Clothing																										Clothing
	Home Management																										Home Management
COMMERCIAL—	Com. Arithmetic																										Com. Arithmetic
	Com. Law																										Com. Law
	Shorthand																										Shorthand
	Typewriting																										Typewriting
	Bookkeeping																										Bookkeeping
	Salesmanship																										Salesmanship
MISCELLANEOUS—	Art	1	D	1/2	2	D	1/2																				Art
	Bible																										Bible
	Distrib. Education																										Distrib. Education
	Driver Education																										Driver Education
MUSIC—	Music Orientation																										Music Orientation
	Music History																										Music History
	Band																										Band
	Orchestra																										Orchestra
	Chorus																										Chorus
PHYSICAL EDUCATION—	R.O.T.C.																										R.O.T.C.
	Physical Education	1	D	1/8	2	D	1/8																				Physical Education
	TOTAL						5 1/4																				TOTAL

COMMISSION EXHIBIT No. 1873-K—Continued

CUMULATIVE RECORD,
(Copy)
FORT WORTH PUBLIC SCHOOLS.

Also,

LIST OF SCHOOLS, BY NUMBER,

LEE OSWALD ATTENDED IN THE

FORT WORTH PUBLIC SCHOOL DISTRICT.

COMMISSION EXHIBIT No. 1873-L

FORT WORTH PUBLIC SCHOOLS
CUMULATIVE RECORD

NAME Oswald, Lee (SURNAME / CHRISTIAN NAME) — ADDRESS 1505 8th Ave. PHONE none

BIRTH YEAR 39 MONTH Oct. DAY 18 — ADDRESS 7408 Ewing PHONE PE-7995 — M. A.

PARENT Edwin Ekdall (Deceased) — ADDRESS PHONE — C. A.

or Guardian Mrs. Marguerite Oswald — VACCINATION EXPIRES 1951 - #19 — I.Q. 103

DATE 1-16-50

Date of Entry	School	Grade	Room	Days Present	Days Absent	Tardy	Dis. Early	LANGUAGE ARTS: Reading	Spelling	H'Writing	English	Spanish	S. Studies	El. Science	Arithmetic	FINE ARTS: Art	Music		Phys. Ed.	Health		Citizenship		Date of Withdrawal	Destination	Teacher
1-27-47	19	1	103	87	1			B		B	B		B	B	B	B	B		a	a		B		5-30-47	2	Lowrimore
3-18-48 Destination #18																										
9-8-48	28	3	34	154	23	2		C	D	C	C		a	a	B	a	a		B	B		a		6-3-49	Gr. 4	R. Hailey
9-7-49	19	4	108	163	10	1	1	B	C	B	B	C	B	B	B	B	B		B	B		B		6-2-50	Gr. 5	Livingston
9-6-50	48	5	105	157½	17½	3	-	C	D	B	C		B	B	D	B	B		B	B		B		6-1-51	Gr. 6	Darsey
9-5-51	48	6	113	170½	5½			B	D	C	D	C	C	C	D	B	B		a	a		B		5-29-52	Gr. 7	Bratton

		Date	Norm	Gr. Eq.	High Score		Low Score	
Met. Ach.	Form	2-8-50	4.5	4.0	Read.	4.7	Spell.	3.3
Stanford.	Ach.	2-13-51	5.5	5.0	Read.	4.9	Elem. Sci.	3.0
"	"	2-11-52	6.5	7.4	Word M.	8.6	Spell	4.4

School Lily B. Clayton — Millicent Keeble Principal

COMMISSION EXHIBIT No. 1873-L—Continued

NAME Oswald, Lee (Last / First / Middle) — BIRTH: YEAR 1939 MONTH Oct. DAY 18 — SEX: MALE / FEMALE

ADDRESS 1505 8th Ave.

FATHER'S NAME Edwin Ekdall — GUARDIAN'S NAME

MOTHER'S NAME — ORIGINAL RECORD SENT TO — DATE

DATE OF ENTRY	School	Grade	Days Present	Days Absent	Tardy	Dismissed Early	Citizenship	Reading	Spelling	Handwriting	English	Spanish	Soc. Sci. St. Soc. Studies	Arithmetic	Art	Music	Instrumental Music	Health Sci.-Health	Speech	Industrial Arts	Homemaking	Band Orchestra		Phys. Ed.		Reading Level	Date of With-drawal	Destination	Home Room Teacher
9-9-47	19	2	120	5	2																						3-18-48	#18	Murphy
3-19-48	18	2	40	6			B	C	D	B	B		A	A	B	A								A			6-2-48	3	Peels

(Residual Copy—Cumulative Record—Grades K-9—Fort Worth Public Schools)

COMMISSION EXHIBIT No. 1873-L—Continued

LIST OF ELEMENTARY SCHOOLS IN FORT WORTH

ATTENDED BY LEE HARVEY OSWALD.

Ft. Worth Public School Number:	Name of School:	Address of School:
# 18	George C. Clarke	3300 So. Henderson St.
# 19	Lily B. Clayton	2000 Park Place Ave.
# 28	Arlington Heights	5100 El Campo
# 48	Ridglea West	7325 Kermit

SENIOR HIGH SCHOOL IN FORT WORTH

ATTENDED BY LEE HARVEY OSWALD.

# 266	Arlington Heights High	4501 W. Rosedale

COMMISSION EXHIBIT No. 1873-L—Continued

CITY OF FORT WORTH

TEXAS

January 24, 1964

INFORMATION SHEET

Nothing in our files, Records Bureau, and I. D. Bureaus on this subject, Lee Harvey Oswald. However, I did receive information that Lee Harvey Oswald brought his Russian born wife and child by the I. D. Bureau after their return to the United States, at which time she was fingerprinted by this Bureau for the Immigration Authorities.

No records were maintained in the I. D. Bureau, or the prints, as they were forwarded to the Immigration Office.

V. T. Sommers

V. T. Sommers, Investigator,
Inspection & Intelligence Unit,
Fort Worth Police Department.

VTS:bcr

COMMISSION EXHIBIT No. 1873-M

REGISTRATION CARD,

(Copy)

DALLAS INDEPENDENT SCHOOL DISTRICT,

PUBLIC EVENING SCHOOL.

(Received from Dallas Police Intelligence Office.)

COMMISSION EXHIBIT No. 1873–N

COPY

(NON-CREDIT)

Mr. Mrs. Miss OSWALD LEE H.
LAST NAME FIRST MIDDLE

602 ELSBETH
RESIDENCE ADDRESS

COMM. PHOTO.
OCCUPATION

JAGGERS PRNT. CO.
EMPLOYER

532 Browder.
BUSINESS ADDRESS

Original Fees Due —
Add'n'l (Mid-Term)

PAYMENTS

Date	Receipt No.	Amt.
1/28/63	24817	9.00

Res. Phone ______ Business Phone ______ 23 Yrs. of Age

Fall 19__ H.S. Spring 19__

SUBJECT	INSTRUCTOR	RM.	TIME	RM.	SUBJECT	INSTRUCTOR
			4:15 to 5:15			
			5:15 to 6:15			
Typing	Yoakum	118	6:15 to 7:15			
			7:15 to 8:15			
			8:15 to 9:15			

DALLAS INDEPENDENT SCHOOL DISTRICT
PUBLIC EVENING SCHOOL
REGISTRATION CARD
E-6—10M—810—60

Schedule arranged by R
Date enrolled 1-14-63
FALL SPRING

COMMISSION EXHIBIT No. 1873–N—Continued

CITY COUNCIL
WILLARD BARR
R. E. HARDING, JR.
T. Z. HAMM
HARRIS P. HOOVER

BAYARD H. FRIEDMAN, MAYOR

CITY OF FORT WORTH
TEXAS

CITY COUNCIL
SCRANTON JONES
MARVIN B. SHANNON
R. M. STOVALL
DOYLE WILLIS

CATO S. HIGHTOWER
CHIEF OF POLICE

February 3, 1964

INFORMATION SHEET

Mrs. Marguerite Oswald, mother of Lee Harvey Oswald, was divorced from Edwin Ekdahl in 1948 in the 17th District Court of Tarrant County, Texas. Mr. Ekdahl won the divorce suit charging harsh and cruel treatment.

Respectfully submitted,

H. F. Hopkins

Lt. H. F. Hopkins, Investigator,
Inspection & Intelligence Unit,
Fort Worth Police Department.

HFH:bcr

COMMISSION EXHIBIT No. 1873-O

UNITED STATES DEPARTMENT OF JUSTICE

FEDERAL BUREAU OF INVESTIGATION

In Reply, Please Refer to
File No.

Dallas, Texas

April 3, 1964

LEE HARVEY OSWALD

By letter dated March 20, 1964, the President's Commission requested that investigation be conducted concerning LEE HARVEY OSWALD's possible attendance at a day nursery in Dallas, Texas, during the School Year 1944 - 1945, in an effort to obtain school records and information from individuals who recalled LEE HARVEY OSWALD's personality, interests and abilities.

The President's Commission also advised that ROBERT OSWALD had testified before the President's Commission that LEE HARVEY OSWALD had attended elementary school in Benbrook, Texas, during 1946 and 1947. It was requested that in obtaining information concerning LEE HARVEY OSWALD that efforts be made to obtain information concerning his brother, ROBERT LEE OSWALD, JR., and his half brother, JOHN EDWARD PIC.

Mr. ROYDON SCHULTZ, 4726 Victor Street, Dallas, Texas, on March 30, 1964, advised he has resided at this address for approximately forty-five years, and recalls that in 1945 LEE HARVEY OSWALD resided with his mother, brother, and half brother at 4801 Victor Street for a period of one or two years. He stated LEE HARVEY OSWALD, to his recollection, was a young boy of five or six years of age, with whom he became quite familiar, as LEE HARVEY made it a practice to visit his residence on almost a daily basis to play in a sandbox in his back yard. He advised LEE HARVEY generally would come to his house between 6:00 or 7:00 AM in the morning and, on many occasions, would remain in his back yard all day playing in the sandbox and, on occasion, engage in play with other children in the neighborhood.

He advised he is quite certain LEE HARVEY OSWALD attended no school of any type while residing at 4801 Victor Street, as he saw him too frequently about the neighborhood.

COMMISSION EXHIBIT No. 1874

RE: LEE HARVEY OSWALD

On March 30, 1964, Mr. JACK SCHULTZ, 4726 Victor Street, Dallas, Texas, advised he has resided at this address his entire life and recalls that when he was nine or ten years old LEE HARVEY OSWALD resided near his residence at 4801 Victor Street. He stated that, although he was three or four years older than LEE HARVEY, he recalls him quite well visiting his residence on almost a daily basis to play in his back yard.

He stated to the best of his recollection LEE HARVEY was prone to "run wild" in the neighborhood for a young boy of his age and that, to his knowledge, he attended no school of any type while residing in this neighborhood.

On March 30, 1964, Mrs. JOE FISCHER, Fischer's Day Nursery, 4951 Victor, Dallas, Texas, advised she was formerly employed by Miss Pat's Pre-School in Dallas, having become associated with this institution in 1945 under its owner, Mrs. PAT REED. She stated at the time the school opened in 1945 it was located at the Munger Baptist Church located at 3919 Munger, Dallas, Texas.

Mrs. FISCHER stated she remained at this school until 1948, during which time the school was moved to its present location at 4525 Junius Street, Dallas. She stated that in 1945 there were only two other nursery schools in the neighborhood in addition to Miss PAT's, those being the Minnie and Mickey Mouse Nursery School and the Mother Goose Kindergarten. She stated she is quite certain LEE HARVEY OSWALD did not attend Miss PAT's, as she has a facility for remembering children she has supervised in the past, and his name is in no way familiar to her.

On March 31, 1964, Mrs. LEITHA BRANDON, Owner, Miss Pat's Pre-School, 4525 Junius Street, Dallas, Texas, advised she purchased this school in December, 1949, from Mrs. PAT PLACKARD and has operated it at 4525 Junius Street since that time.

Mrs. BRANDON advised there are no records available prior to 1949 of children attending this pre-school, and she has no information that LEE HARVEY OSWALD ever attended this institution.

-2-

COMMISSION EXHIBIT No. 1874—Continued

RE: LEE HARVEY OSWALD

On March 31, 1964, Mrs. PAT PLACKARD, Exchange Bank Building, Dallas, Texas, advised she operated a nursery school in Dallas, Texas, from 1945 until December, 1949, under the name of Miss Pat's Pre-School. She advised at the time she opened the school its location was at the Munger Baptist Church, 3919 Munger, Dallas, Texas, and shortly thereafter she moved the school to 4525 Junius, where it currently operates under the name of Miss Pat's Pre-School, although she no longer has any connection with it.

Mrs. PLACKARD advised she has no records available of children attending her pre-school in the past, but that she was very familiar with all of the children and their families who attended her pre-school, and she has no recollection whatsoever of LEE HARVEY OSWALD having attended her pre-school.

Mrs. PLACKARD advised, to her knowledge, the only other schools of this type of operation in this neighborhood in 1945 were the Minnie and Mickey Mouse School, operated by a Miss LOTTIE VANDERPOOL, and the Mother Goose Kindergarten, operated by a Mrs. R. H. CHOWNING.

On March 31, 1964, Mrs. PAULINE CRISWELL, 3926 Worth Street, Dallas, Texas, advised she is the owner of Minnie and Mickey Mouse Nursery School located at this address, having purchased it on January 1, 1964, from Miss LOTTIE VANDERPOOL.

Mrs. CRISWELL advised there are no records available of children formerly attending this school at the time it was operated by Mrs. VANDERPOOL, and she has no information in her possession that LEE HARVEY OSWALD ever attended this nursery school.

On March 31, 1964, Miss LOTTIE VANDERPOOL, 634 North Hill Drive, Dallas, Texas, advised she started the Minnie and Mickey Mouse Nursery School at 3926 Worth Street, Dallas, Texas, in 1942, and operated it herself until she sold it on January 1, 1964. She stated at the time she sold the school she had a number

-3-

COMMISSION EXHIBIT No. 1874—Continued

of incomplete records in her possession of former children who attended this school, but that at the time she sold the school she destroyed all records except those for the past three years.

She stated she can usually remember the names of all children down through the years who attended her nursery school, and is certain LEE HARVEY OSWALD never attended this nursery school.

On March 31, 1964, Mrs. R. H. CHOWNING, 5327 Junius Street, Dallas, Texas, advised she operated the Mother Goose Kindergarten in Dallas from 1945 to 1958, but that all records kept by her during this period have been destroyed. She stated she operated her school as a morning kindergarten, wherein children would attend for only three hours, and did not conduct her institution as a nursery school.

She stated she is quite certain LEE HARVEY OSWALD never attended this school, as his name is completely unfamiliar to her as a past student.

On March 31, 1964, Mr. ROBERT OSWALD, 1009 Sierra, Denton, Texas, brother of LEE HARVEY OSWALD, advised that he recently testified before the President's Commission on the assassination of President KENNEDY, and he does not recall giving any testimony to the effect that LEE HARVEY OSWALD attended a nursery school while their family resided in Dallas, Texas.

OSWALD pointed out, to the best of his recollection, that LEE HARVEY OSWALD did not attend any type of school until the family moved to Fort Worth, Texas, when LEE HARVEY commenced his education in the first grade at Benbrook, Texas, in early 1946.

On March 31, 1964, Mr. A. R. CARTWRIGHT, SR., Box 21006, Superintendent of Water Department at Benbrook, Texas, furnished the following information:

He recalled that the OSWALD family lived in the house next door to where the Water Department is now located. CARTWRIGHT was not personally acquainted with this family, but recalled that Mrs. OSWALD lived there and had three sons. The youngest son was LEE HARVEY OSWALD and he believed LEE did attend the first grade at Benbrook School.

On March 31, 1964, Mr. R. W. WOOD, Superintendent of Benbrook Elementary School, Benbrook, Texas, 800 Mercedes Street, furnished the following information:

In 1945, 1946 and 1947, the Benbrook Elementary School was under the jurisdiction of Tarrant County. Mr. WOOD advised he did not have any records dating back to 1945-1947. WOOD was not with the school at that time and was not acquainted with LEE HARVEY OSWALD or the OSWALD family.

Mr. WOOD made inquiry among the teachers at the Benbrook Elementary School at this time and none of them was teaching in the school during 1945-1947. Mr. WOOD believed that the school records for that period of time would be in the possession of the County Superintendent of Schools in Fort Worth.

On March 31, 1964, Mr. O. H. STOWE, County Superintendent of Schools, Fort Worth, Texas, furnished the following information from his records:

They have a card reflecting that LEE OSWALD, Route 5, Box 567, Benbrook, Texas, entered the Benbrook Common School at Benbrook, Texas, on October 31, 1945. His age was shown as 6, birth shown as July 9, 1939. (It is noted that this is a different birth date for LEE HARVEY OSWALD.) Mr. STOWE advised that the family probably gave a different birth date, as September 1 of each year is the cut-off date for children to enter school. He had to be six years of age on September 1, 1945, and they probably showed his birth date as July 9, 1939, to qualify for this entrance.

RE: LEE HARVEY OSWALD

OSWALD entered in the low first grade; he took five subjects and made all "A's" and "B's" and received an "A" in citizenship. He was present 82 school days and was absent 15 school days. There is nothing on the card reflecting any derogatory information. Parent or guardian was listed as E. A. EKDAHL.

Mr. STOWE checked his records further and determined that Mrs. ELLA RUSSELL was a teacher of the first grade at the Benbrook School at that time. He stated Mrs. RUSSELL is now deceased.

On March 31, 1964, Mr. OTIS R. CARLTON, 104 Mildred Drive, Benbrook, Texas, furnished the following information:

In 1945, 1946 and 1947, he was living on San Saba Street in Benbrook, Texas. At that time, this street was part of Route 5 in Benbrook. He recalled that Mrs. OSWALD and her three sons lived in the house which is now 100 San Saba Street in Benbrook. He believed they lived there for a period of six to eight months. Mrs. OSWALD was the owner of this property.

On one occasion while they were living there, Mrs. OSWALD contacted Mr. CARLTON and asked him to come up and inspect her house and give her an estimate as to what she might be able to sell this property for, as she was planning on leaving Benbrook. Mr. CARLTON told her he was a schoolteacher, not a real estate man, but she insisted on him helping her, and he agreed to go up and look at the property.

He did inspect the property one night and told her that he believed she could sell the house and lot for $2,750.00. The next night Mrs. OSWALD came to the home of Mr. CARLTON and told him that she was going to accept his offer. Mr. CARLTON asked her what offer she was talking about. She said the offer to buy her house for $2,750.00. CARLTON told her he had never

made any such offer and that he merely told her that she might obtain this price when she was ready to sell it. She insisted that he had made her this offer and that she was going to hold him to it and that she wanted him to buy this house. CARLTON, at that time, was buying some rent property and he finally agreed to buy the house for $2,750.00.

During the next few weeks, he was in and out of the OSWALD home on several occasions. One night he was in the living room of the OSWALD home talking to Mrs. OSWALD about the real estate transaction. LEE OSWALD, the youngest boy, came running through the kitchen door and was chasing JOHN PIC, his older brother. LEE OSWALD had a long butcher knife in his hand and he threw the knife at JOHN PIC but missed him, and it hit the wall. Mrs. OSWALD only made the remark that "they have these little scuffles all the time and don't worry about it."

CARLTON stated that the OSWALD family left Benbrook sometime in 1946 or possibly in 1947. He has not seen or had any dealings with them since then. He did recall that LEE OSWALD attended the first grade at Benbrook School because his daughter was teaching in the school at that time, but was teaching the fifth and sixth grades. His daughter never had any dealings with LEE OSWALD.

CARLTON stated that ROBERT OSWALD and JOHN PIC appeared to be boys of a little more even disposition than LEE OSWALD.

FD-302 (Rev. 3-3-59) FEDERAL BUREAU OF INVESTIGATION

1

Date 5/1/64

Mrs. RUTH PAINE, 2515 West 5th Street, furnished the following information, after examining colored photographs of items designated as Commission Exhibits A-1 and C254. A-1 is a blue cloth zipper bag, approximately 21" x 11" x 9½". C254 is a green cloth bag known as a "Bee 4", approximately 24" x 18" x 11":

On October 4, 1963, when Mrs. PAINE arrived at her residence in Irving, Texas, LEE HARVEY OSWALD had already arrived at her home and she did not see what luggage, if any, he brought with him at that time.

On October 7, 1963, when OSWALD left Mrs. PAINE's home for Dallas, Texas, he had with him a bag similar to that depicted in the photograph of Commission Exhibit C254, and she believes this is a photograph of the bag which he had with him at that time.

Mrs. PAINE advised she does not recall seeing the figures "9/26" at any time on the bag carried by OSWALD on October 7, 1963, or on a similar bag at any time.

At the time RUTH PAINE and MARINA OSWALD moved some of the OSWALD effects from New Orleans, Louisiana, to Irving, Texas, in Mrs. PAINE's Chevrolet Station Wagon, she does not specifically recall any bags resembling Commission Exhibits A-1 and C254.

Photographs of the fragmentary stickers and tag on Commission Exhibit C254 were shown to Mrs. PAINE, at which time she stated she does not recall seeing these before and does not know when they were put on Commission Exhibit C254.

On April 24, 1963, RUTH PAINE recalls taking LEE HARVEY OSWALD to the Continental Trailways Bus Depot in Dallas, Texas, at which time he took his luggage into the bus station, apparently checked it, and returned to her car. She recalled he had two green duffel bags, a tan, portable, Russian-made radio, and some suitcases, but cannot specifically recall whether these suitcases resembled the photographs of Commission Exhibits A-1 and C254.

— Commission Exhibit No. 1875 —

185

on 5/1/64 at Irving, Texas File # DL 100-10461

by Special Agent BARDWELL D. ODUM and J. DOYLE WILLIAMS/eah;ds Date dictated 5/1/64

COMMISSION EXHIBIT No. 1875

2

DL 100-10461

Mrs. PAINE advised, after examining replicas of the fragmentary tag and stickers found on Commission Exhibit C254, that she cannot recall seeing any such items, or fragments of such, at any time on Commission Exhibit C254 or any bag resembling this exhibit.

Mrs. PAINE advised that she is unable to explain the significance of the number "7" appearing in the photograph of a fragmentary sticker found on Commission Exhibit C-254, and advised that if this is a part of an address, she has no idea as to what address it is.

186

COMMISSION EXHIBIT No. 1875—Continued

FD-302 (Rev. 3-3-59)

FEDERAL BUREAU OF INVESTIGATION

— Commission Exhibit No. 1876 — Date 5/19/64

1

Physical observation of the rear of the residence of Major GENERAL EDWIN A. WALKER, 4011 Turtle Creek Boulevard, Dallas, was made by SAs ROBERT M. BARRETT and IVAN D. LEE on May 18, 1964. It was determined from this observation that the photograph depicting the residence of Major General EDWIN A. WALKER, marked as Commission exhibit No. 5 and as FBI inventory No. 369, is identical with the rear of WALKER's residence.

Physical observation on May 18, 1964, of the alley behind the residence of Major General EDWIN A. WALKER and comparing the photograph taken by SA IVAN D. LEE on February 1, 1964, determined that the photograph listed as photograph No. 2, Item No. 7, was taken in the alley at the northeast edge of the property line of Major General EDWIN A. WALKER's residence looking to the southwest.

On May 18, 1964, physical observation of the Missouri, Kansas, and Texas railroad tracks which are located in the vicinity of the residence of Major General EDWIN A. WALKER was made by SAs ROBERT M. BARRETT and IVAN D. LEE. It was determined that photograph No. 5, Item No. 6, was taken with the individual taking the photograph facing south by southeast approximately 67 yards from where the curb line of Newman Street if extended would cross the railroad tracks. It is noted that Newman Street runs in a south-easterly to a northwesterly direction and it would intersect the railroad at a point almost due east of the Dallas Theater Center.

In the photograph marked as photograph No. 5, Item No. 6, the bridge railing observed in the middle of the picture is identical with the one which crosses over Lemmon Avenue East. The building in the left center of the photograph is identical with the Stoneleigh Hotel. What appears to be a building or structure to the left of the Stoneleigh Hotel and just to the right of the metal utility pole (which is on the left-hand side of photograph) is a large air conditioning water cooler. To the left of the metal utility pole is a dark object which appears to be a building. This is identical to the apartment house roof line of the Turtle Creek Apartments. In the middle of the photograph and just to the right of the railroad

258

on 5/18/64 at Dallas, Texas File # DL 100-10461

by Special Agent IVAN D. LEE and ROBERT M. BARRETT:vm Date dictated 5/19/64

2
DL 100-10461

bridge railing an electric utility pole with a transformer can be observed extending above the trees. Also observed on the right-hand edge of the photograph are telephone poles with a heavy telephone cable running between the poles. In the physical observation of the area all of the above items were noted by SAs BARRETT and LEE.

By automobile mileage from the parking lot at the Dallas Theater Center which is located approximately 200 feet from where the photograph was taken it is 0.7 mile from Major General EDWIN A. WALKER's residence.

259

FD-302 (Rev. 3-3-59)

FEDERAL BUREAU OF INVESTIGATION

— Commission Exhibit No. 1877 — Date 5/20/64

1

Mr. BEN B. PASSMORE, 314 Cottonwood, Richardson, Texas (AD 5-2838), stated he is a Construction Inspector with the Dallas Insuring Office, Federal Housing Administration, 1621 Main Street, Dallas, Texas.

Mr. PASSMORE said he has been assigned since sometime in 1962 as the inspector on a high-rise apartment now being completed at 3883 Turtle Creek Boulevard, Dallas, Texas, same being known as 21 Turtle Creek Square. Mr. PASSMORE said he maintained daily construction progress logs on the construction of 21 Turtle Creek Square.

Mr. PASSMORE viewed Photograph No. 2, Item No. 7, and identified the high-rise building under construction depicted in that photograph as 21 Turtle Creek Square. Mr. PASSMORE, with Special Agents ROBERT M. BARRETT, IVAN D. LEE, and EMORY E. HORTON visited the area where Photograph No. 2, Item No. 7, was taken, at which time Mr. PASSMORE viewed the building known as 21 Turtle Creek Square as it now appears from that position and compared its present appearance to the view depicted in Photograph No. 2, Item No. 7.

Mr. PASSMORE produced a 35 mm slide, taken by himself, that depicts 21 Turtle Creek Square, and said this slide was made at the time the building was completed to its full height, but before the penthouses were constructed. After studying the slide and Photograph No. 2, Item No. 7, Mr. PASSMORE stated Photograph No. 2, Item No. 7, appears to show one more bay on the construction elevator tower than does his slide. From this, Mr. PASSMORE opined that Photograph No. 2, Item No. 7, was taken after the twenty-second floor of the building was completed and the form for the shear wall was being raised on the northeast corner of the building so the concrete could be run thereby forming the supports for the roof.

Mr. PASSMORE then referred to his daily construction logs and determined that the building was at the stage of

261

on 5/20/64 at Dallas, Texas File # DL 100-10461

by Special Agent EMORY E. HORTON/eah Date dictated 5/20/64

COMMISSION EXHIBIT No. 1877

2
DL 100-10461

construction referred to above on March 8 - 12, 1963. He pointed out there do not appear to be any workmen depicted in Photograph No. 2, Item No. 7, which suggests that the photograph may have been made on a weekend, as they did not work on Saturday and Sunday. Mr. PASSMORE referred to his calendar and determined that March 9 and 10, 1963, were a Saturday and Sunday.

262

COMMISSION EXHIBIT No. 1877—Continued

FD-302 (Rev. 3-3-59)

FEDERAL BUREAU OF INVESTIGATION

Commission Exhibit No. 1878

Date 4/22/64

1

Mr. JOSEPH P. GRINNAN, 811 Wilson Building, who resides at 4640 Southern, and is employed as an independent oil operator, advised he had solicited funds which had been used to pay for the advertisement which appeared in the "Dallas Morning News," on November 22, 1963. This full-page ad was signed by the American Fact-Finding Committee, BERNARD WEISSMAN, Chairman. GRINNAN said he could think of four individuals who contributed somewhere around $1,500 "give or take a hundred," which was used to pay for the ad in the "Dallas Morning News."

He said that he had become acquainted with LARRIE SCHMIDT, a friend of BERNARD WEISSMAN, at a meeting of an organization called the "Young Americans for Freedom." He said LARRIE SCHMIDT and BERNARD WEISSMAN were soldier friends, having served in the Army together, and through LARRIE SCHMIDT he became acquainted with BERNARD WEISSMAN. LARRIE SCHMIDT wanted to protest the visit of President KENNEDY to Dallas on November 22, 1963, in a dignified way; therefore, they got together and LARRIE SCHMIDT wrote the ad with some suggestions by GRINNAN. GRINNAN stated he did not write out anything when the advertisement was being written. He said the four contributors for the advertisement read the advertisement before publication.

GRINNAN stated that the American Fact-Finding Committee was a paper name only and that no organization sponsored this advertisement, other than the American Fact-Finding Committee, which name they made up. He said that if anyone composed the American Fact-Finding Committee it was himself, LARRIE SCHMIDT, and a fellow named BILL from Baltimore, Maryland, who was a friend of LARRIE SCHMIDT and BERNARD WEISSMAN. He said he was pretty sure that BERNARD WEISSMAN took the advertisement to the "Dallas Morning News" and made arrangements for its publication. He said they intended no personal harm to come to the President.

Regarding the source of the funds to pay for the advertisement, he said he was reluctant to give the names of the contributors, because he did not want to hurt anyone. He said

298

on 4/20/64 at Dallas, Texas File # DL 100-10461

by Special Agents W. HARLAN BROWN & EDWIN D. KUYKENDALL /mh Date dictated 4/22/64

DL 100-10461

2

he desired to contact these contributors, who in turn may have solicited funds from other sources, prior to making these names available.

He was told that the President's Commission on the Assassination of President KENNEDY had specifically requested he be interviewed to determine the source of the funds used to pay for the "Dallas Morning News" advertisement. He stated he would contact the contributors to determine if they had any objection to the release of their names, and would call the interviewing Agents on April 21, 1964.

299

FD-302 (Rev. 3-3-59)

FEDERAL BUREAU OF INVESTIGATION

1

Date 4/22/64

JOSEPH P. GRINNAN, 811 Wilson Building, an independent oil operator, advised by telephone that he had not contacted all the contributors to the "Dallas Morning News" advertisement on November 22, 1963, consisting of a full page signed by American Fact-Finding Committee, BERNARD WEISSMAN, Chairman, but would do so and would advise of the outcome of his contacts on April 23, 1964.

— Commission Exhibit No. 1879 —

300

on 4/22/64 at Dallas, Texas File # DL 100-10461

by Special Agent W. HARLAN BROWN/eah Date dictated 4/22/64

This document contains neither recommendations nor conclusions of the FBI. It is the property of the FBI and is loaned to your agency; it and its contents are not to be distributed outside your agency.

COMMISSION EXHIBIT No. 1879

FD-302 (Rev. 3-3-59)

FEDERAL BUREAU OF INVESTIGATION

1

Date 4/23/64

At 3:15 PM, Mr. JOSEPH P. GRINNAN, 811 Wilson Building, an independent oil operator, advised by telephone that he did not desire to be interviewed on April 23, 1964, because he wanted to consult with his lawyer, Doctor ROBERT MORRIS, who is currently in the race for the Republican nomination for the United States Senate. He said Doctor MORRIS was believed to be in Amarillo, Texas, and would be in Dallas on April 24, 1964. He said that after consulting with Doctor MORRIS he would contact the Dallas FBI Office.

— Commission Exhibit No. 1880 —

301

on 4/23/64 at Dallas, Texas File # DL 100-10461

by Special Agent W. HARLAN BROWN/eah Date dictated 4/23/64

This document contains neither recommendations nor conclusions of the FBI. It is the property of the FBI and is loaned to your agency; it and its contents are not to be distributed outside your agency.

COMMISSION EXHIBIT No. 1880

FD-302 (Rev. 3-3-59)

FEDERAL BUREAU OF INVESTIGATION

1

Date 4/24/64

At 1:11 PM, Mr. JOSEPH P. GRINNAN, 811 Wilson Building, independent oil operator, was contacted by telephone and advised that he was still waiting to hear from Doctor ROBERT MORRIS regarding information concerning the source of funds for the "Dallas Morning News" advertisement on which he had previously been contacted. He was told that the President's Commission on the Assassination of President KENNEDY had contacted our Bureau Headquarters in Washington, D. C., and had requested to be advised on April 24, 1964, whether he would make this information available.

Mr. GRINNAN advised he would call the Dallas FBI Office on April 24, 1964, after he had made contact with his attorney, Doctor MORRIS.

Commission Exhibit No. 1881

on 4/24/64 at Dallas, Texas 302 File # DL 100-10461

by Special Agent W. HARLAN BROWN/eah Date dictated 4/24/64

Commission Exhibit No. 1882

UNITED STATES DEPARTMENT OF JUSTICE

FEDERAL BUREAU OF INVESTIGATION

In Reply, Please Refer to File No.

Dallas, Texas
April 24, 1964

LEE HARVEY OSWALD

The President's Commission, by letter dated April 7, 1964, requested investigation be conducted to determine the source of the funds used to pay for an advertisement appearing in "The Dallas Morning News" on November 22, 1963. Certain information concerning this advertisement appears on pages 684 to 721 of the report of Special Agent ROBERT P. GEMBERLING dated December 10, 1963, at Dallas, Texas.

On April 20, 1964, Mr. JOSEPH P. GRINNAN, 811 Wilson Building, who resides at 4640 Southern, Dallas, Texas, and is employed as an independent oil operator, advised he had solicited funds which had been used to pay for the advertisement which appeared in "The Dallas Morning News", on November 22, 1963. This full-page advertisement was signed by the American Fact-Finding Committee, BERNARD WEISSMAN, Chairman. GRINNAN said he could think of four individuals who contributed somewhere around $1,500.00, "give or take a hundred", which was used to pay for the advertisement in "The Dallas Morning News".

He said that he had become acquainted with LARRIE SCHMIDT, a friend of BERNARD WEISSMAN, at a meeting of an organization called the "Young Americans for Freedom". He said LARRIE SCHMIDT and BERNARD WEISSMAN were soldier friends, having served in the Army together, and through LARRIE SCHMIDT he became acquainted with BERNARD WEISSMAN. LARRIE SCHMIDT wanted to protest the visit of President KENNEDY to Dallas on November 22, 1963, in a dignified way; therefore, they got together and LARRIE SCHMIDT wrote the advertisement with some suggestions by GRINNAN. GRINNAN stated he did not write out anything when the advertisement was being written. He said the four contributors for the advertisement read the advertisement before publication.

GRINNAN stated that the American Fact-Finding Committee was a paper name only and that no organization

COMMISSION EXHIBIT No. 1882

sponsored this advertisement, other than the American Fact-Finding Committee, which name they made up. He said that if anyone composed the American Fact-Finding Committee it was himself, LARRIE SCHMIDT, and a fellow named BILL from Baltimore, Maryland, who was a friend of LARRIE SCHMIDT and BERNARD WEISSMAN. He said he was pretty sure that BERNARD WEISSMAN took the advertisement to "The Dallas Morning News" and made arrangements for its publication. He said they intended no personal harm to come to the President.

Regarding the source of the funds to pay for the advertisement, he said he was reluctant to give the names of the contributors, because he did not want to hurt anyone. He said he desired to contact these contributors, who in turn may have solicited funds from other sources, prior to making these names available.

He was told that the President's Commission on the Assassination of President KENNEDY had specifically requested he be interviewed to determine the source of the funds used to pay for "The Dallas Morning News" advertisement. He stated he would contact the contributors to determine if they had any objection to the release of their names, and would call the interviewing Agents on April 21, 1964.

On April 22, 1964, JOSEPH P. GRINNAN advised by telephone that he had not contacted all the contributors to "The Dallas Morning News" advertisement on November 22, 1963, consisting of a full page signed by American Fact-Finding Committee, BERNARD WEISSMAN, Chairman, but would do so and would advise of the outcome of his contacts on April 23, 1964.

On April 23, 1964, at 3:15 P.M., Mr. JOSEPH P. GRINNAN advised by telephone that he did not desire to be interviewed on April 23, 1964, because he wanted to consult with his lawyer, Doctor ROBERT MORRIS, who is currently in the race for the Republican nomination for the United States Senate. He said Doctor MORRIS was believed to be in Amarillo, Texas, and would be in Dallas on April 24, 1964. He said that after consulting with Doctor MORRIS he would contact the Dallas Office of the Federal Bureau of Investigation.

COMMISSION EXHIBIT No. 1882—Continued

On April 24, 1964, at 1:11 P.M., Mr. JOSEPH P. GRINNAN was contacted by telephone and advised that he was still waiting to hear from Doctor ROBERT MORRIS regarding information concerning the source of funds for "The Dallas Morning News" advertisement on which he had previously been contacted. Mr. GRINNAN advised he would call the Dallas Office of the Federal Bureau of Investigation on April 24, 1964, after he had made contact with his attorney, Doctor MORRIS.

On April 24, 1964, at 3:35 P.M., Mr. JOSEPH P. GRINNAN telephoned the Dallas Office of the Federal Bureau of Investigation and stated he wanted to give the information concerning the funds for "The Dallas Morning News" advertisement which had previously been requested of him. Mr. GRINNAN stated he preferred to give the information on the telephone at that time.

Mr. GRINNAN stated that the reason the full-page advertisement was placed in "The Dallas Morning News" on November 22, 1963, signed by the American Fact-Finding Committee, BERNARD WEISSMAN, Chairman, was because he and the other individuals responsible for this advertisement considered it a dignified way of protesting the policies of President JOHN FITZGERALD KENNEDY, with due respect to the office of the President. Mr. GRINNAN stated the contributors to the fund which was used in payment of "The Dallas Morning News" advertisement were as follows:

H. R. BRIGHT, an independent oil operator with offices in the Mercantile Commerce Building, Dallas, Texas

EDGAR CRISSEY, an insurance man with offices in the Fidelity Union Life Building, Dallas, Texas, who resides at 3320 Villanova Street, Dallas, Texas

NELSON BUNKER HUNT, an independent oil man with offices in the Mercantile Securities Building, Dallas, Texas, who is the son of H. L. HUNT, a well-known Dallas oil man.

COMMISSION EXHIBIT No. 1882—Continued

Re: LEE HARVEY OSWALD

All of the aforementioned persons reside in Dallas, Texas, and Mr. GRINNAN advised that Doctor ROBERT MORRIS, his attorney, was at that time present while Mr. GRINNAN was furnishing the above information.

Mr. GRINNAN stated he did not know the amounts each of the contributors gave to the fund, but felt that they had solicited funds from others for the purpose of paying for the advertisement. He stated that at first, he thought he (GRINNAN) had been a contributor to the fund, but had determined, upon checking, that he had not contributed anything toward the fund used for the payment of the advertisement in the newspaper.

- 4 -

COMMISSION EXHIBIT No. 1882—Continued

FD-302 (Rev. 3-3-59) FEDERAL BUREAU OF INVESTIGATION

— Commission Exhibit No. 1883 — Date 5/15/64

1

Mr. HARVEY ROBERT BRIGHT, who is also known as "Bum" Bright, an independent oil operator of the firm of Bright and Schiff, Mercantile Continental Building, was interviewed commencing at 10:48 a.m. and was advised that he did not have to make any statement and that any statement he did make could be used against him in a court of law. He was advised he had a right to consult with a lawyer before making any statement.

BRIGHT stated he desired to be interviewed in the presence of his attorney, ROBERT PAYNE, who sat in on the interview.

Mr. BRIGHT stated he did not know JACK RUBY or LEE HARVEY OSWALD and had had no contact or dealings with them at any time.

BRIGHT stated that sometime prior to the time the full page advertisement which was signed by the American Fact Finding Committee appeared in the "Dallas Morning News" on November 22, 1963, he had been solicited to contribute to such an advertisement. BRIGHT declined to give the names of the persons who had contacted him, terming them "A" and "B." He said that "A" first called him and asked him if he would make a contribution to such an advertisement and BRIGHT agreed. He said that later "A" and "B" came to his office in the Mercantile Continental Building in Dallas which was two or three days or perhaps a week prior to the time the "Dallas Morning News" ran this advertisement. "B," according to BRIGHT, stated he did not have the money to put up for the advertisement and Mr. BRIGHT stated he put up "B's" money for him and considered it in the nature of a loan. He said he currently carries it on his books and it is believed that "B" owes him $300 or $400 now but did not remember whether all of this was for the advertisement. BRIGHT stated he wrote out a check for "B's" contribution for the advertisement as well as for his contribution and that "B" signed notes for the amount owed BRIGHT. BRIGHT stated he had not collected any money from "B" and that the money contributed for the advertisement was his own and was not supplied by any other persons. He advised he did not solicit any funds from others in connection with this matter. He remarked that he might have "bankrolled" "B" for this contribution as he did not know whether "B" was going to pay him back or not. On the other hand, he said "B" might

305

on 5/15/64 at Dallas, Texas File # DL 100-10461

by Special Agent W. HARLAN BROWN and EDWIN D. KUYKENDALL:vm Date dictated 5/15/64

COMMISSION EXHIBIT No. 1883

2
DL 100-10461

make the full contribution and then he, BRIGHT, would not be a contributor. He said he would have to contact "B" to determine if "B" would pay the entire amount of the contribution. BRIGHT declined to give the names of the people who had contacted him as well as the amount of his contribution as well as the amount of the contribution of "B." BRIGHT stated that the advertisement which appeared in the "Dallas Morning News" on November 22,1963, had been read to him over the telephone but declined to give the name of the individual who read it to him.

The interview was terminated at 11:05 a.m.

306

COMMISSION EXHIBIT No. 1883—Continued

FD-302 (Rev. 3-3-59)

FEDERAL BUREAU OF INVESTIGATION

1 — Commission Exhibit No. 1884 —

Date 5/15/64

Mr. EDGAR R. CRISSEY, an insurance man associated with E. F. White & Associates, 1115 Fidelity Union Building, who resides at 3320 Villanova Street, Dallas, Texas, was advised that he did not have to make any statement and that any statement he did make could be used against him in a court of law. He was advised that he could consult with a lawyer prior to making any statement.

CRISSEY stated he was not acquainted with LEE HARVEY OSWALD or JACK RUBY and never had had any contact with either of them. CRISSEY collected contributions, he related, for the insertion of an advertisement in the "Dallas Morning News," on November 22, 1963, which advertisement was edged in black, and signed by the American Fact-Finding Committee, BERNARD WEISSMAN, Chairman. CRISSEY stated he had never known WEISSMAN, but solicited contributions at the request of a friend, JOE GRINNAN. CRISSEY stated he contributed $15.00 in cash for this advertisement in the "Dallas Morning News" and had collected, in all, approximately $135.00 from two or three other people. He declined to give the names of these individuals, stating the money was collected as a matter of confidence and he promised them at the time that their names would not be divulged. He stated that these people who had contributed to him, he was sure, did not know OSWALD or RUBY. The approximately $135.00 collected by him was turned over to JOE GRINNAN for expense concerning the insertion of the advertisement.

JOE GRINNAN contacted CRISSEY about one week prior to November 22, 1963, stating he desired to place the advertisement in the "Dallas Morning News," and requested him to solicit funds for an advertisement to be placed in the "Dallas Morning News." CRISSEY understood that the Legal Department, of the "Dallas Morning News," had reviewed the advertisement prior to its being run in the November 22, 1963, issues of the "Dallas Morning News." CRISSEY stated that they had very little time in which to obtain contributions and he understood that BUNKER HUNT had contributed and a person known as "BUM" BRIGHT, with offices in the Mercantile Continental Building, was also a contributor.

307

on 5/15/64 at Dallas, Texas File # DL 100-10461

by Special Agent W. HARLAN BROWN and EDWIN D. KUYKENDALL/eah:ds Date dictated 5/15/64

COMMISSION EXHIBIT No. 1884

2

DL 100-10461

CRISSEY stated the last thing they wanted was for something to happen to President KENNEDY, terming the insertion of the advertisement as being ill-timed. He said that no organization sponsored the advertisement that he knew of, although it was signed by BERNARD WEISSMAN, whom he did not know.

CRISSEY stated the article was written by a man whose name he did know at the time, but whose name he had forgotten. CRISSEY stated he saw a proof copy of the advertisement prior to its being run in the newspaper. He believed the newspaper advertisement cost approximately $1,500.00, and stated he did not wish to reveal the names of persons who contributed.

308

COMMISSION EXHIBIT No 1884—Continued

FD-302 (Rev. 3-3-59) FEDERAL BUREAU OF INVESTIGATION

— Commission Exhibit No. 1885 — Date 5/15/64

1

Mr. NELSON BUNKER HUNT, 4508 Lakeside Drive, with offices on the 7th Floor, Mercantile Securities Building, an independent oil operator, at the outset of interview requested that his secretary call his attorney prior to being interviewed. He was, therefore, interviewed in the presence of his attorney, IVAN IRWIN.

HUNT readily admitted having contributed cash to JOE GRINNAN for the purpose of placing an advertisement in the "Dallas Morning News." This advertisement appeared on November 22, 1963, and was signed by the American Fact-Finding Committee. HUNT termed it an article which asked some embarrassing questions of President KENNEDY. He said he could not recall the amount he contributed, but believed it to be between $200.00 and $300.00. He gave the contribution to JOE GRINNAN in cash, merely reaching in his pocket and pulling forth the contribution. He exhibited this by reaching in his pocket and exposing a roll of bills while being interviewed. He said JOE GRINNAN contacted him several days before the "Dallas Morning News" ran the advertisement and told him by telephone that the "Dallas Morning News" would publish this advertisement. He later came by the Hunt office and received the money, Mr. HUNT related.

HUNT was unable to state whether he had read the article prior to publication, but stated that GRINNAN might have read some of it over the telephone or might have told him about it. He stated the article was a criticism of President KENNEDY in a dignified way. He stated the money contributed by him was his own money and he did not solicit or obtain contributions from any other person.

HUNT stated he did not know LEE HARVEY OSWALD or JACK RUBY and stated he had never had any contact with them. He did not know the names of others who had contributed toward the cost of the advertisement and did not know BERNARD WEISSMAN, whose name appeared on the advertisement. He understood that WEISSMAN came from New York from reading the papers, he said.

309

on 5/15/64 at Dallas, Texas File # DL 100-10461

by Special Agents W. HARLAN BROWN & EDWIN D. KUYKENDALL/eah Date dictated 5/15/64

COMMISSION EXHIBIT No. 1885

2
DL 100-10461

HUNT did not know of any organization who had sponsored the advertisement and did not know anything concerning the American Fact-Finding Committee. He did not know who prepared this advertisement for publication and remarked that the timing of the advertisement was not too good.

310

COMMISSION EXHIBIT No. 1885—Continued

FD-302 (Rev. 1-25-60) FEDERAL BUREAU OF INVESTIGATION

1

Date 3/24/64

Mr. S. L. MALONE, Secretary-Treasurer, Jaggars-Chiles-Stovall, Incorporated, 522 Browder, stated all company records pertaining to the employment of LEE H. OSWALD were turned over to Mr. JAMES M. DePRATO, Special Agent, Internal Revenue Service, 2101 Pacific Avenue, Dallas, Texas, on November 23, 1963. He said these records consist of the following:

(1) Employee Identification Questionnaire (employment application) prepared by LEE HARVEY OSWALD.

(2) Twenty-six (26) checks paid to OSWALD by Jaggars-Chiles-Stovall, Incorporated, as salary during his employment.

(3) Correspondence with Texas Employment Commission to Jaggars-Chiles-Stovall, Incorporated. He said OSWALD was referred to that company by Texas Employment Commission.

Mr. MALONE stated the only other records he has that pertain to OSWALD's employment by Jaggars-Chiles-Stovall, Incorporated, are his Employee's Withholding Exemption Certificate, dated October 12, 1963, signed LEE H. OSWALD, prepared in the name of LEE H. OSWALD, 3519 Fairmount, Dallas, Texas, Social Security Number 433-56-3739, and the Time Records maintained by OSWALD. He said OSWALD prepared a Time Record on each day worked during his employment of October 12, 1962, through April 6, 1963. He exhibited the Time Records and it was noted each contains OSWALD's name, hours worked, and date at the top and below that is a listing of the jobs worked on that are listed by job number and customer's name. The Time Records are for the following days:

10/12/62
10/15-19/62
10/22-27/62
10/30-11/3/62
11/5-10/62
11/12-17/62

— Commission Exhibit No. 1886 —

459

On 3/18/64 at Dallas, Texas File # DL 100-10461

by SA EMORY E. HORTON:vm Date dictated 3/21/64

COMMISSION EXHIBIT No. 1886

2
DL 100-10461

11/19-21/62
11/23-24/62
11/26-12/1/62
12/3-8/62
12/10-14/62
12/17-21/62
12/24/62
12/26-29/62
12/31/62
1/2-4/63
1/7-12/63
1/14-18/63
1/21-26/63
1/28-2/1/63
1/4-2/8/63
2/11-16/63
2/18-22/63
2/25-3/1/63
3/4-9/63
3/11-16/63
3/18-23/63
3/25/63 (two reports, one for "Mon" and one for "Tues.")
3/27-30/63
4/1-6/63.

Mr. MALONE stated that all handwriting and handprinting appearing on each of the above-described documents was prepared by LEE HARVEY OSWALD except the foreman's signature appearing at the bottom of each of the employee time records.

Mr. MALONE stated the above-described records constitute the only records still in possession of Jaggars-Chiles Stovall, Incorporated, that pertained in any way to the employment of LEE HARVEY OSWALD. Mr. MALONE furnished the above-described Employee's Withholding Exemption Certificate and Time Records.

460

COMMISSION EXHIBIT No. 1886—Continued

FD-302 (Rev. 1-25-60)

FEDERAL BUREAU OF INVESTIGATION

Date 3/24/64

1

Mr. O. V. CAMPBELL, Vice President, Texas School Book Depository (TSBD), 411 Elm (RI 7-3521), stated that all records pertaining to LEE HARVEY OSWALD's employment at TSBD have previously been furnished to Agents of the FBI. He stated the only employee records maintained by TSBD that would contain OSWALD's handwriting and/or signature are OSWALD's application for employment and Employee's Withholding Exemption Certificate which have previously been furnished.

Mr. CAMPBELL stated the only records maintained by Texas School Book Depository that would show the hours worked by OSWALD are the payroll records reflecting the employment of OSWALD from October 16 through November 22, 1963. Mr. CAMPBELL pointed out that these records are prepared in their entirety by Mr. H. S. AIKEN, employee of TSBD, and OSWALD did not participate in any manner in preparation of same. He stated TSBD does not utilize a time clock or other device to record an individual's times of arrival and departure as such information is maintained by Mr. AIKEN and employees in the warehouse are paid in cash; are not required to sign any type of receipt for their pay; therefore, there is no additional record pertaining to OSWALD's employment at TSBD. Regarding the payroll records maintained by TSBD, Mr. CAMPBELL pointed out that copies of same had previously been furnished to an Agent of the FBI.

— Commission Exhibit No. 1887 —

461

On 3/18/64 at Dallas, Texas File # DL 100-10461

by SA EMORY E. HORTON:vm Date dictated 3/21/64

COMMISSION EXHIBIT No. 1887

Date 5/14/64

1

Mr. PETER PAUL GREGORY, Geologist, Continental National Bank Building, was recontacted and furnished the following information:

GREGORY recalled that when LEE HARVEY OSWALD first contacted him he told him that he had obtained GREGORY's name from someone at the Fort Worth Public Library. GREGORY has conducted classes in Russian at the Fort Worth Public Library for about four years. He stated he had made inquiry at the Fort Worth Public Library but had been unable to locate anyone who had talked to OSWALD and might have given his name to OSWALD.

— Commission Exhibit No. 1888 —

on 5/13/64 at Fort Worth, Texas 547 File # DL 100-10461

by Special Agent EARLE HALEY and ROBLEY D. MADLAND:vm Date dictated 5/14/64

COMMISSION EXHIBIT No. 1888

Date 5/14/64

1

Mr. MAX CLARK, Attorney, Ridglea State Bank Building, furnished the following information:

CLARK recalled that during the first interview he was not sure as to the source of OSWALD in obtaining the name of Mrs. CLARK but first thought it might have been the Fort Worth Public Library. He later talked to his wife, Mrs. GALI CLARK, and she said that when OSWALD called her the first time he told her he had obtained her name from some person at the Texas Employment Commission. CLARK further advised that his wife vaguely recalled that OSWALD might have told her the name of this person was SMITH but she was not certain as to this information. CLARK advised that his sister works at the Texas Employment Commission and one of his aunts was employed there for many years until her death three years ago. He related that many persons at the Texas Employment Commission are acquainted with him and also know that his wife is from France and is of Russian descent. CLARK stated he and his wife had made some inquiry out of curiosity to try to learn the name of the person who gave Mrs. CLARK's name to OSWALD but they had not been successful.

— Commission Exhibit No. 1889 —

548

on 5/13/64 at Fort Worth, Texas File # DL 100-10461

by Special Agent EARLE HALEY and ROBLEY D. MADLAND:vm Date dictated 5/14/64

COMMISSION EXHIBIT No. 1889

FD-302 (Rev. 3-3-59)

FEDERAL BUREAU OF INVESTIGATION

Date 5/14/64

1

Mr. ARLISS NIXON, Manager, Fort Worth Public Library, furnished the following information:

He and his assistants had checked all library records in the past but had failed to develop the names of any individuals at this library who might have given the name of PETER GREGORY to LEE HARVEY OSWALD. NIXON was unable to furnish any information concerning any person who might have given this name to OSWALD.

— Commission Exhibit No. 1890 —

549

on 5/13/64 at Fort Worth, Texas File # DL 100-10461

by Special Agent EARLE HALEY and ROBLEY D. MADLAND:vm Date dictated 5/14/64

COMMISSION EXHIBIT NO. 1890

FD-302 (Rev. 3-3-59)

FEDERAL BUREAU OF INVESTIGATION

Date 5/14/64

1

Mrs. VIRGINIA HALE, 6475 Fortune Road, employed in the Job Placement Division of Texas Employment Commission, furnished the following information:

She recalled LEE HARVEY OSWALD quite well and she sent him out on the job to the Leslie Welding Company. Mrs. HALE stated she did not give the names of MAX CLARK or PETER GREGORY to OSWALD but she believed that Mrs. ANNIE LAURIE SMITH of Texas Employment Commission might have furnished the name of CLARK to OSWALD.

— Commission Exhibit No. 1891 —

550

on 5/13/64 at Fort Worth, Texas File # DL 100-10461

by Special Agent EARLE HALEY and ROBLEY D. MADLAND:vm Date dictated 5/14/64

COMMISSION EXHIBIT NO. 1891

FD-302 (Rev. 3-3-59) FEDERAL BUREAU OF INVESTIGA N

Date 5/14/64

1

Mrs. ANNIE LAURIE SMITH, 301 S. Bowen Road, Arlington, Texas, employed as a Counselor at the Texas Employment Commission, furnished the following information:

She has been so employed for the past nine years. She interviewed LEE HARVEY OSWALD in June of 1962 when he came to this office seeking a job. OSWALD had not been to the employment office before and was not sure as to his qualifications for any particular type of job. In applicants of this type, the Counselors interview these persons to obtain their background, their job experience, and try to advise them the type of job they might best be qualified for. Mrs. SMITH talked to LEE HARVEY OSWALD on two different occasions. She recalled that at times he was quite cooperative then other times he acted rather moody and did not want to furnish some of the information.

Near the close of the last interview, LEE HARVEY OSWALD mentioned to Mrs. SMITH that his wife was from Russia; that she could only speak the Russian language, and he would like to get acquainted with any persons in Fort Worth who might speak the Russian language and in this way his wife could talk to them and maybe they could make more friends in Fort Worth. Mrs. SMITH advised she is personally acquainted with Mr. and Mrs. PETER PAUL GREGORY and she wrote the name of Mr. GREGORY on a piece of paper showing the office number and phone number of Mr. GREGORY and she gave this to LEE HARVEY OSWALD. During part of this conversation, a Mrs. HALL, sitting at the next desk to Mrs. SMITH, overheard the conversation and mentioned to Mrs. SMITH that Mrs. MAX CLARK who lives in Fort Worth is of Russian descent and speaks Russian and also French. Mrs. SMITH recalls Mrs. HALL wrote the name and phone number of Mrs. CLARK on a slip of paper, handed it to Mrs. SMITH, and she in turn passed it on to LEE HARVEY OSWALD.

Mrs. SMITH advised she was not personally acquainted with Mr. or Mrs. MAX CLARK but had heard of them. She stated that Mrs. HALL never talked to OSWALD and she only furnished the name of Mrs. CLARK to Mrs. SMITH and she in turn gave it to OSWALD.

— Commission Exhibit No. 1892 — 551

on 5/13/64 at Fort Worth, Texas File # DL 100-10461

by Special Agent EARLE HALEY and ROBLEY D. MADLAND:vm Date dictated 5/14/64

COMMISSION EXHIBIT NO. 1892

2
DL 100-10461

Mrs. SMITH stated that LEE HARVEY OSWALD did not discuss any politics or anything about the governments of the United States or Russia and that she only talked to him about his past employment and the type of work he had done prior to going to Russia, also the work he had done in Russia, and if he had done any work since he had returned from Russia. She stated he wanted the names of these individuals so that he and his wife might visit them and OSWALD's wife would then be able to talk to these people in Russian since she could not speak any English.

552

COMMISSION EXHIBIT NO. 1892—Continued

FD-302 (Rev. 1-25-60)

FEDERAL BUREAU OF INVESTIGATION

Date 11/27/63

1

Mr. LYNN COBENA, Manager, Commercial Employment Agency, 1001 National Bank of Commerce Building, was interviewed and made available an application with his agency made by LEE HARVEY OSWALD on May 7, 1963. The application reflected he had been employed from 1962 to 1963 at Jaggers-Chiles-Stoval on 522 Browder Street, D llas, Texas as a photographer and was laid off because of a cut in the night shift. He was applying for a position as a photographer and gave the following description of his duties with his former employer:

> Development of films on standard commercial modification camera, use of lens, enlargers, etc.; setting up and shooting of "live" and "perspective" photo shots as well as modification shots.

In checking his incoming log sheet for May 7, 1963, COBENA advised that OSWALD had been in his office twice that day. The reason for the second visit was not indicated. COBENA stated the interviewer who talked to OSWALD was Mr. DON PECOT, who is no longer employed by the agency. He furnished PECOT's last known address as 1200 Lowerline Avenue, New Orleans, Louisiana. The application also indicates OSWALD was referred to Darrell DeMoss Company in New Orleans; however, there is no indication on the application as to the results of OSWALD's interview at that company.

COBENA made available both the application and the agency agreement which were signed by OSWALD on May 7, 1963.

— Commission Exhibit No. 1893 —

On 11/26/63 at New Orleans, Louisiana File # NO 89-69

by SA THEODORE R. VIATER /bda,lyc Date dictated 11/26/63

37

This document contains neither recommendations nor conclusions of the FBI. It is the property of the FBI and is loaned to your agency; it and its contents are not to be distributed outside your agency.

COMMISSION EXHIBIT NO. 1893

FD-302 (Rev. 1-25-60)

FEDERAL BUREAU OF INVESTIGATION

1 — Commission Exhibit No. 1894 — Date 11/23/63

Mr. WILLIAM I, MONAGHAN, Vice President - Finance, William B. Reily and Co., Inc., 640 Magazine Street, advised that records of his company reflect that LEE HARVEY OSWALD was employed by that company from May 10, 1963, until July 19, 1963, as an oiler - machinist assistant in the coffee plant at 640 Magazine Street. He explained that OSWALD's duties were routine, that he tended to and greased fittings in the machines. He advised that OSWALD's superior, EMMETT BARBE, reported that OSWALD wandered off the job and would not be available when needed. For this reason, OSWALD's employment was terminated on July 19, 1963, for inefficiency.

Mr. MONAGHAN furnished the original of an Application for Employment which he states was apparently filled out by OSWALD on May 9, 1963. He pointed out that this lists OSWALD's residence address as 757 French Street and his residence telephone as HUnter 8-4326.

This application reflects OSWALD was born on October 18, 1939. The birth place is not reflected. The application reflects that OSWALD attended Beauregard Junior High School and Warren Eastern Senior High School, graduating in 1959. The application further reflects he was in the United States Marine Corps from 1959 - 1963 and was honorably discharged. He listed as personal character references the following:

> JOHN MURRETT, Pharmacist, 757 French Street, telephone HUnter 8-4326
>
> Sgt. ROBERT HIDELL, Active Duty, U.S.M.C.
>
> W. S. OSWALD, Retired, 136 Elmeer Street, VErnon 5-7869. (This name, occupation and address has a line drawn through it.)
>
> Lieut. (illegible, possibly T or J) EVANS, Active Duty, U.S.M.C.

Mr. MONAGHAN also furnished a Xerox copy of a Character - Financial Report, dated May 16, 1963, on LEE HARVEY OSWALD, 757 French Street, New Orleans, Louisiana.

On 11/23/63 at New Orleans, Louisiana File # NO 89-69

by SA LESTER G. DAVIS: mam Date dictated 11/23/63

30

This document contains neither recommendations nor conclusions of the FBI. It is the property of the FBI and is loaned to your agency; it and its contents are not to be distributed outside your agency.

COMMISSION EXHIBIT NO. 1894

This report reflects the following:

"1. Lee Harvey Oswald is employed as a Maintenance Man for the Standard Coffee Company, and has been so engaged in this occupation for the past one week, and enjoys a favorable business reputation. Previous to this, he was in the U. S. Marines for some three years. He enjoys a favorable business reputation, and his prospects for the future appear to be favorable.

"FINANCES: His present and past financial standing is good, and he is regarded as an individual who lives within his means. Learned of no illiness or physical impairments that might affect his earning capacity.

"CHARACTER-HOME SURROUNDINGS: His character, habits, and Morals are good, and he is known to keep good associates, and well regarded. He resides with his wife, and child. They live in a middle class residential section with frame homes that are well kept, and living conditions are adequate. Stability and class of residencts in this section is good."

OSWALD is employed as a maintenance man for the Standard Coffee Company.

In connection with the above, Mr. MONAGHAN pointed out that the Standard Coffee Company is the "house-to-house sales branch" of the William B. Reily and Co., Inc.

Mr. MONAGHAN also furnished Xerox copies of employment reports filled out by LEE HARVEY OSWALD in connection with his regular duties. He explained that these are made out in long hand and printing by OSWALD and were filed with OSWALD's supervisor, Mr. EMMETT C. BARBE, JR. These are employment reports for OSWALD's

31

activities of the following dates: Thursday, July 11; Friday, July 12; Monday, July 15; Tuesday, July 16; Wednesday, July 17; Thursday, July 18; and Friday, July 19.

Mr. MONAGHAN explained that the originals of these reports had been turned over to Mr. A. G. VIAL of the United States Secret Service on November 23, 1963, in connection with investigation being conducted by that agency.

Mr. MONAGHAN further furnished a Xerox copy of Employee's Withholding Exemption Certificate, Form W4, which was allegedly filled out by LEE H. OSWALD and reflects his Social Security Number to be 433-54-3937. It reflects OSWALD claimed withholding exemption as a married man with one additional dependent. This is dated May 16, 1963, and signed LEE H. OSWALD.

Mr. MONAGHAN advised that the original of this certificate was turned over to Mr. A. G. VIAL, United States Secret Service, New Orleans, Louisiana, on November 23, 1963, in connection with investigation being conducted by that agency.

Mr. MONAGHAN advised that OSWALD's immediate superior was EMMETT C. BARBE, JR., maintenance foreman. He stated that other employees who worked with OSWALD at the William B. Reily Co. were CHARLES JOSEPH LE BLANC, a maintenance man, and ATURO RODRIGUEZ, maintenance man.

Mr. MONAGHAN stated that he did not know OSWALD personally.

32

OFFICE OF THE DIRECTOR

UNITED STATES DEPARTMENT

FEDERAL BUREAU OF INVE

WASHINGTON, D.C. 20535

June 18, 1964

BY COURIER SERVICE

Honorable J. Lee Rankin
General Counsel
The President's Commission
200 Maryland Avenue, N. E.
Washington, D. C.

Dear Mr. Rankin:

Reference is made to your letter of June 2, 1964, requesting that this Bureau obtain for the Commission copies of all of the records concerning Lee Harvey Oswald that are maintained by the Texas Employment Commission, Fort Worth, Texas.

On June 5, 1964, Mr. William H. Hefner, Supervisor, Texas Employment Commission, Fort Worth, Texas, made available to this Bureau a work order concerning Lee Harvey Oswald. According to Mr. Hefner, this work order reflects that Oswald was sent to the Louv-R-Pak, Division of Leslie Welding Company, Fort Worth, Texas, to make an application for a job with that company. Two photographic copies of the work order made available by Mr. Hefner are enclosed for the Commission.

Mr. Hefner further advised that the aforementioned work order is the only record available at the Texas Employment Commission, Fort Worth, Texas, regarding Lee Harvey Oswald. He stated that in November, 1963, he and Mrs. Virginia Hale, a fellow employee, checked through all records of the Texas Employment Commission, Fort Worth, Texas, in an effort to find the original application filed by Oswald when he first came to the Texas Employment Commission office. He added that they were not able to find such original application, but pointed out that a number of old applications had been destroyed and it is possible the application of Lee Harvey Oswald was destroyed.

— Commission Exhibit No. 1895

COMMISSION EXHIBIT NO. 1895

Honorable J. Lee Rankin

Mr. Hefner rechecked his records during our interview with him on June 5, 1964, but was unable to locate any other information regarding Lee Harvey Oswald.

This concludes our inquiries in this particular matter.

Sincerely yours,

J. Edgar Hoover

Enclosures (2)

- 2 -

COMMISSION EXHIBIT NO. 1895—Continued

FIRM NAME: Louv-R-Pak

ADDRESS: Div. of Leslie Welding Co. 200 E. No. Vacek

TELEPHONE: ED 2-8187

BUSINESS:

PERSON TO SEE: Tommy Bargas — TITLE: Foreman

HOW TO REACH:

NO. OPENINGS: 1

DURATION: P T

AGE RANGE: up to 40

SEX: M F

MAR. STAT.

OCCUPATIONAL TITLE: Sheet Metal Worker

OCC. CODE: 4-80.010

EMPLOYER JOB TITLE: Trainee

PART IV CODE: 4-X6

PAY RATE: $ 1.25 HR. DAY WK. MO.

HOURS: FROM Days AM TO 4 PM

NO. DAYS:

IND. CODE: 34

MASTER ORDER

WHEN TO APPLY: DATE ______ TIME __ AM __ PM BY APPOINTMENT No

EDUCATION AND TRAINING REQUIREMENTS:

EMPLOYER REQUIREMENTS (DUTIES – EXPERIENCE, ETC.): JUL 1 1962

Some exp with sheet metal. – familiarity with spot welding, a beader, fly shear & groover. Will train in making louvers.

EXPERIENCE REQUIREMENTS:	TEST SELECTED APPLICANTS:	KIND OF TESTS
IN OCC: YES ✓ NO __	YES __ NO __	TYPE ____
IN IND: YES ✓ NO __	TESTS BY EMPLOYERS:	S/H ____
TRAINEE: YES __ NO ✓	YES __ NO __	S ____

PERSONAL CHARACTERISTICS:

MACHINES OR EQUIPMENT TO OPERATE (TYPE AND MAKE):

PHYSICAL REQUIREMENTS: COMPANY EXAM: YES __ NO __

COMMENTS: Order brought in by Will.

EMPLOYEE BENEFITS:

DATE: 7-12-62 TIME: 2:00 TAKEN BY: VH ASSIGNED TO: VH

FORM G-81A (281) GENERAL PURPOSE ORDER

REFERRAL AND PLACEMENT RECORD

NO.	CALL IN DATE	CALL IN MET.	DATE REF.	APPLICANT'S NAME	OCC. CODE	SEX	VET	HD CP	CLM STAT.	AGE	TEST SEL.		RE-SULT	REMARKS
1	7-12	T	7-13 DR	Oswald, Lee H	4-X6	M	–	–	–	39			H	LM
2														
3														
4														
5														
6														
7														
8														
9														
10														

DATE | EMPLOYER CONTACT INFORMATION:

DATE ORDER WAS FILLED ~~CANCELLED~~ 7-13-62

REASONS FOR CANCELLATION:

SUPERVISOR'S INSTRUCTIONS:

COMMISSION EXHIBIT No. 1895—Continued

FD-302 (Rev. 1-25-60)

FEDERAL BUREAU OF INVESTIGATION

Date 11/25/63

1

Mr. WILLIAM I. MONAGHAN, Vice President, William B. Reily and Company, Inc., 640 Magazine Street, furnished the original of the payroll checks payable to LEE H. OSWALD who was employed by that company from May 10, 1963, to July 19, 1963. These checks are all drawn on the National Bank of Commerce in New Orleans, New Orleans, Louisiana, and all are payable to LEE H. OSWALD with the exception of one, which is payable to LEE OSWALD, the latter is the payroll check # 1941, dated June 21, 1963.

The following is the data contained on each of these payroll checks of William B. Reily and Company, Inc., New Orleans, Louisiana:

DATE	CHECK #	AMOUNT	FIRST ENDORSEMENT	SECOND ENDORSEMENT
5/17/63	882	$53.72	LEE H. OSWALD	ROLAND MARTIN
5/24/63	1079	53.72	LEE H. OSWALD	Martin's Rest.
5/31/63	1274	53.72	LEE H. OSWALD	Martin's Rest.
6/7/63	1486	55.59	LEE H. OSWALD	Martin's Rest.
6/14/63	1684	52.97	LEE H. OSWALD	Foltz Tea & Coffee Co.
6/21/63	1941	53.72	LEE H. OSWALD	Martin's Rest.
6/28/63	1995	53.72	LEE H. OSWALD	ROLAND MARTIN
7/5/63	2185	53.72	LEE H. OSWALD	Martin's Rest.
7/12/63	2368	52.97	LEE H. OSWALD	Martin's Rest.
7/19/63	2549	53.72	LEE H. OSWALD	Martin's Rest.
7/22/63	2621	10.84	LEE H. OSWALD 4907 Magazine HU 8-4226	Endorsement stamp illegible.

— Commission Exhibit No. 1896 —

On 11/25/63 at New Orleans, Louisiana File # NO 89-69

by SA's LESTER G. DAVIS and JOHN WILLIAM MILLER /jm Date dictated 11/25/63

34

COMMISSION EXHIBIT No. 1896

NO 89-69
2

In addition, Mr. MONAGHAN made available a group insurance enrollment and record card which bears the signature of OSWALD.

Data on this card reflects that LEE H. OSWALD resided at 757 French Street, New Orleans, Louisiana; that he was born October 18, 1939, and employed May 10, 1963. Death benefits were designated to be paid to MARINA N. OSWALD, his wife, who resided at 757 French Street, New Orleans, Louisiana. This card is dated May 10, 1963.

MONAGHAN further advised he could not determine if OSWALD completed the information on this card other than the signature of employee.

Mr. MONAGHAN also furnished data taken from time punch cards of employee, LEE H. OSWALD. The following is a compulation reflecting the time OSWALD arrived at his place of employment and the time he left each day while employed by the William B. Reily and Company, Inc., as reflected on these time cards:

DAY	TIME IN	TIME OUT
Friday, 5/10/63	7:59 AM	4:30 PM
Monday, 5/13/63	8:24 AM	5:00 PM
Tuesday, 5/14/63	8:18 AM	5:00 PM
Wednesday, 5/15/63	8:23 AM	5:00 PM
Thursday, 5/16/63	8:29 AM	5:00 PM
Friday, 5/17/63	8:25 & 9:57 AM (stamped twice)	5:00 PM
Monday, 5/20/63	8:25 AM	5:00 PM
Tuesday, 5/21/63	8:22 AM	5:00 PM
Wednesday, 5/22/63	8:20 AM	5:00 PM
Thursday, 5/23/63	8:24 AM	5:01 PM
Friday, 5/24/63	9:58 AM	6:30 PM
Monday, 5/27/63	9:53 AM	6:35 PM
Tuesday, 5/28/63	8:50 AM	5:31 PM
Wednesday, 5/29/63	9:45 AM	6:30 PM
Thursday, 5/30/63	9:00 AM	5:30 PM
Friday, 5/31/63	9:53 AM	7:32 PM

35

COMMISSION EXHIBIT No. 1896—Continued

NO 89-69
3

DAY	TIME IN	TIME OUT
Monday, 6/3/63	9:47 AM	6:30 PM
Tuesday, 6/4/63	9:50 AM	6:30 PM
Wednesday, 6/5/63	9:58 AM	6:30 PM
Thursday, 6/6/63	10:05 AM	6:30 PM
Friday, 6/7/63	8:57 AM	5:30 PM
Monday, 6/10/63	8:52 AM	5:30 PM
Tuesday, 6/11/63	8:44 AM	5:30 PM
Wednesday, 6/12/63	8:56 AM	5:31 PM
Thursday, 6/13/63	8:50 AM	5:30 PM
Friday, 6/14/63	8:29 AM	5:30 PM
Monday, 6/17/63	8:53 AM	5:31 PM
Tuesday, 6/18/63	8:53 AM	5:30 PM
Wednesday, 6/19/63	8:53 AM	5:30 PM
Thursday, 6/20/63	8:52 AM	5:30 PM
Friday, 6/21/63	8:53 AM	5:30 PM
Monday, 6/24/63	8:57 AM	5:30 PM
Tuesday, 6/25/63	8:58 AM	5:30 PM
Wednesday, 6/26/63	8:54 AM	5:30 PM
Thursday, 6/27/63	8:53 AM	5:30 PM
Friday, 6/28/63	9:01 AM	5:30 PM
Monday, 7/1/63	8:59 AM	5:30 PM
Tuesday, 7/2/63	8:49 AM	5:30 PM
Wednesday, 7/3/63	8:53 AM	5:30 PM
Thursday, 7/4/63	-------	-------
Friday, 7/5/63	8:53 AM	5:30 PM
Monday, 7/8/63	8:47 AM	5:30 PM
Tuesday, 7/9/63	8:49 AM	5:30 PM
Wednesday, 7/10/63	8:54 AM	5:30 PM
Thursday, 7/11/63	8:58 AM	5:30 PM
Friday, 7/12/63	8:27 AM	5:01 PM
Monday, 7/15/63	8:19 AM	5:00 PM
Tuesday, 7/16/63	8:26 AM	5:00 PM
Wednesday, 7/17/63	9:37 AM	6:00 PM
Thursday, 7/18/63	8:26 AM	5:00 PM
Friday, 7/19/63	8:22 AM	4:30 PM (terminated)

COMMISSION EXHIBIT No. 1896—Continued

FD-302 (Rev. 1-25-60)

FEDERAL BUREAU OF INVESTIGATION

Date 11/23/63

Mr. CHARLES JOSEPH LE BLANC, 2824 South Romain Street, New Orleans, Louisiana, advised that he is employed as maintenance man for William B. Reily and Company, Inc., 640 Magazine Street, New Orleans, Louisiana. He stated that he knew LEE H. OSWALD only while OSWALD was employed as an oiler-machinist assistant for William B. Reily Company, Inc. He recalled that he "broke OSWALD in on the job". He stated that OSWALD was a man of very few words and usually seemed to avoid conversation. He recalled that on one occasion the exact date of which he could not recall OSWALD asked him, "Do you like it here?" Mr. LE BLANC stated he replied, "I ought to like it. I have been with them ten years". He continued that OSWALD explained that he did not mean whether LE BLANC liked working for the company whereupon LE BLANC stated he asked, "Well, what do you mean?" He stated OSWALD said,"Here", and he asked, "New Orleans?" whereupon OSWALD said, "No, the country". He stated he replied, "Why, certainly" whereupon OSWALD discontinued the conversation and walked away. He advised that he never discussed this matter further with OSWALD and in fact he and OSWALD had very little to say to each other except conversation concerning the oiling of some of the machines.

Mr. LE BLANC advised that OSWALD was not attentive to his job and wandered about the building considerably and was usually gone when he was needed. He continued that he would have to "run OSWALD down" in the building and would ask him where he had been and why he was not on the job whereupon OSWALD would merely shrug his shoulders and state that he had "just been around".

He advised that he recalled that OSWALD had a habit of pointing his finger at someone when he would approach them and make a sound as if he were shooting the person like children do in playing "cops and robbers".

Mr. LE BLANC advised that he has never heard OSWALD make any statements that he would shoot someone nor has he discussed in any manner the shooting of another. He merely attributed the above to an idiosyncrasy.

[redacted]

— Commission Exhibit No. 1897

On 11/23/63 at New Orleans, Louisiana File # NO 89-69

by SA LESTER G. DAVIS /cv 41 Date dictated 11/23/63

COMMISSION EXHIBIT No. 1897

NO 89-69/cv
2

Mr. LE BLANC stated he knew of no associate, friend or relative of LEE H. OSWALD and could furnish no information as to whether OSWALD owned a firearm. He did recall, however, that he had observed OSWALD looking at gun magazines maintained in the waiting room of the Crescent City Garage located next door to William B. Reily Company, Inc. He explained that employees of the Reily Company would go to the waiting room of the Crescent City Garage for soft drinks on their breaks and that someone in the garage apparently collected guns and maintained gun magazines on a coffee table which were available to employees. He stated he, however, had never discussed guns with OSWALD.

Mr. LE BLANC advised that the only other employee with whom OSWALD would have been in contact was ARTURO RODRIGUEZ, maintenance man.

42

COMMISSION EXHIBIT No. 1897—Continued

FD-302 (Rev. 1-25-60)

FEDERAL BUREAU OF INVESTIGATION

Date 11/25/63

1

Mr. ARTURO MENDEZ RODRIGUEZ, 323 Marais Street, Apartment U, New Orleans, Louisiana, voluntarily furnished the following information:

He stated that he recalled LEE OSWALD as a fellow employee at the William B. Reily Company, 640 Magazine Street. He stated that as best as he can recall, OSWALD worked there about three months and he recalled that OSWALD was working there when he, RODRIGUEZ, took his vacation in June, 1963.

He emphasized that he was never closely associated with OSWALD and that his only contact with him was when OSWALD started working for the Reily Company, in that he instructed him how to oil and clean the machines. He also stated that as far as he could tell, OSWALD was not friendly with any of the employees and he described OSWALD as a person who did not talk much, was very quiet and did not associate with any employees.

He stated that when the workers took a break, OSWALD always stayed by himself, sometimes he went to the driveway and smoked a cigarette, and sometimes he just sat in a chair and appeared to stare into space.

OSWALD never discussed his past and RODRIGUEZ knew nothing about his background. Shortly after he began working he did state that he had just gotten out of the military service and came to work for Reily Company. RODRIGUEZ stated that he did not know that OSWALD was married and did not know where he lived. RODRIGUEZ said that to the best of his knowledge, he did not believe that OSWALD had an automobile as he sometimes saw him come to work on a bus.

RODRIGUEZ advised that he has never received any mail from OSWALD and did not know where he went when he quit working for the Reily Company. He stated that he believed OSWALD did not quit his job voluntarily, but was asked to leave by the company. He informed he did not know anyone by the name of HIDELL.

The following description of ARTURO MENDEZ RODRIGUEZ was obtained by personal observation and questioning:

[redacted]

— Commission Exhibit No. 1898 —

On 11/23/63 at New Orleans, Louisiana File # NO 89-69

by SA's JOSEPH L. FLEMING & G. MYRYWIN ALDERSON/lrs Date dictated 11/23/63

43

COMMISSION EXHIBIT No. 1898

NO 89-69
2

Name	ARTURO MENDEZ RODRIGUEZ
Sex	Male
Race	White
Date of Birth	September 18, 1929
Place of Birth	Merida, Yucatan, Mexico
Height	5'10"
Weight	135
Hair	Black
Eyes	Black
Build	Medium
Nationality	Mexican
Alien Registration	A-11889286
Occupation	Oiler - mechanic
Marital Status	Married
Relatives	Wife - ANNA MARIA RODRIGUEZ; 3 minor children
Residence	323 Marais Street, Apartment U, New Orleans, Louisiana

44

COMMISSION EXHIBIT No. 1898—Continued

FD-302 (Rev. 1-25-60)

FEDERAL BUREAU OF INVESTIGATION

— Commission Exhibit No. 1899 —

1

Date November 25, 1963

Mr. JOHN C. CLARK, Assistant Vice President in Charge of Production, William B. Reily and Company, Inc., 640 Magazine Street, advised that he knew LEE H. OSWALD only while OSWALD was employed by that company and only because he was so employed. He continued that his only contact with OSWALD was to reprimand him a couple of times. He explained that OSWALD was not an aggressive worker and had to be reprimanded concerning this.

Mr. CLARK stated that he had no conversation with OSWALD concerning outside activities and that he did not know any of OSWALD's friends or associates nor any member of OSWALD's family.

Mr. CLARK stated that an inquiry of all employees of the plant revealed that only the following individuals employed by William B. Reily and Company, Inc., had had any conversation whatsoever with OSWALD.

EMMETT CHARLES BARBE, JR., maintenance foreman, OSWALD's immediate superior.

CHARLES JOSEPH LE BLANC, a maintenance man who worked with OSWALD."

ARTURO RODRIGUEZ, a maintenance man who worked with OSWALD.

Miss ROSE SCHAMBRA, a floor lady in the plant.

Mr. CLARK advised that OSWALD was actually employed by ALFRED A. CLAUDE, who was plant manager at the time. He continued that CLAUDE is no longer employed by this company, but he understands CLAUDE is presently employed by the Chrysler Aerospace Division in New Orleans.

He explained that Mr. CLAUDE had not necessarily had conversation with OSWALD.

He advised that the only other person who perhaps would have necessarily had contact and conversation with OSWALD would be JOHN D. BRANYON, 7937 Oak Street, New Orleans.

On 11/25/63 at New Orleans, Louisiana File # NO 89-69

by SA LESTER G. DAVIS
SA JOHN WILLIAM MILLER /cjo Date dictated 11/25/63

45

COMMISSION EXHIBIT No. 1899

NO 89-69 /cjo
2

Louisiana, who is believed to be presently employed by Boeing Aircraft Corporation. He explained that BRANYON would have worked with OSWALD while OSWALD was employed at the Reily Company.

46

COMMISSION EXHIBIT No. 1899—Continued

FD-302 (Rev. 1-25-60)

FEDERAL BUREAU OF INVESTIGATION

1 — Commission Exhibit No. 1900 — Date November 25, 1963

Miss ROSE SCHAMBRA, 5528 Catina Street, advised she is a "floor lady" at William B. Reily and Company, Inc., 640 Magazine Street, and as such supervises the packaging of coffee.

She stated she has supervision over three coffee packaging machines which machines have to be greased regularly by maintenance men employed by the company. She continued that during the Summer of 1963, LEE OSWALD was employed as a maintenance man and as such would grease the machines under her supervision. She stated she found OSWALD to be a quiet and shy person who never seemed to converse with anyone. She recalled that when he did make his rounds to grease a machine, she would sometimes tell him which machine needed oiling and he would make no reply to anything she said. She recalled that on occasions she would tell him not to put too much oil in the fittings and he merely shrugged his shoulders without comment. Because of this shyness and quiet attitude, she felt sorry for him and one day approached him asking him his name. He merely replied "LEE", and kept walking.

Miss SCHAMBRA said that this more or less seemed to be typical of his attitude while he was employed at that company. She added that his mind seemed to be on something else instead of his work and never about conversation with employees. She stated she did not know any people with whom he might have been in contact and certainly none of his friends, associates, or members of his family. She added that she had had no contact with OSWALD away from the plant where they worked.

Miss SCHAMBRA advised that she knew no one by the name of HIDELL or name similar to that and certainly had never heard OSWALD speak of anyone by this name.

On 11/25/63 at New Orleans, Louisiana File # NO 89-69

by SA LESTER G. DAVIS
SA JOHN WILLIAM MILLER /cjo Date dictated 11/25/63

47

COMMISSION EXHIBIT No. 1900

1 — Commission Exhibit No. 1901 — Date 11/25/63

Mr. CHARLES JOSEPH LEBLANC, Maintenance Man, William B. Reily and Company, Inc., 640 Magazine Street, was questioned further concerning his inability to find LEE H. OSWALD on occasion while OSWALD was employed by that company.

Mr. LEBLANC explained that plant employees have two breaks during the day, one at 9:00 AM and the other at 1:30 PM. He continued that on several occasions he had noted that OSWALD would overstay the 15 minute break and would be missing for 20 to 30 minutes at a time. He further recalled that OSWALD was also gone from his employment on other than extended breaks for 20 to 30 minutes and on a few occasions as long as 45 minutes. He added that the extended periods of 45 minutes were not often.

When questioned as to how frequently OSWALD would be gone from his employment during the day, he stated that while it happened several times it was not as often as once a day during his period of employment there but came close to being on the average of once a day.

Mr. LEBLANC could not say where OSWALD had been during periods that he was missing from his place of employment and although he asked OSWALD on several occasions where he had been he had not received an answer to this. He stated that he had never observed OSWALD to come into the plant from the outside except on break periods and had never observed OSWALD leave the plant except to go next door to the Crescent City Garage where employees frequently obtained soft drinks from dispensing machines. He commented that it was at this place where he had observed OSWALD reading gun magazines and thought perhaps OSWALD may have overstayed his break periods to read such magazines.

Mr. LEBLANC advised that OSWALD was a "loner" even at lunch period. He continued that OSWALD usually ate his lunch out and he recalls having seen OSWALD eat lunch at Martin's Restaurant located at the corner of Tchoupitoulas and Girod Streets near the plant.

Mr. LEBLANC advised that he knew no one by the name of HIDELL or names similar to that and that he had never heard LEE OSWALD speak of anyone by this name.

On 11/25/63 at New Orleans, Louisiana File # NO 89-69

by SA'S LESTER G. DAVIS & JOHN WILLIAM MILLER /bal Date dictated 11/25/63

48

COMMISSION EXHIBIT No. 1901

Date November 30, 1963

ROY RICHARDSON, residing 7730 Sycamore Street, New Orleans, Louisiana, phone number, 866-4777, employed at Brick and Stone Center, Inc., 401 North Jefferson Davis Parkway, New Orleans, was contacted and advised that OSWALD was there and applied for a job during July, 1963, date unknown. RICHARDSON stated that the owner S. KENAN MANSON, residing 401 Park Road, Metairie, phone number VE 3-6770, of both Brick and Stone Center, Inc., and Mason, Marble, and Granite, 501 North Jefferson Davis Parkway, advised him that he had furnished OSWALD's application for employment to the New Orleans FBI Office several days ago.

RICHARDSON further stated that he had never met OSWALD and had no information concerning him.

— Commission Exhibit No. 1902 —

On 11/29/63 at New Orleans, Louisiana File # NO 89-69 DALLAS 89-43

by SA MICHAEL F. CAMPBELL :dc Date dictated 11/29/63

52

COMMISSION EXHIBIT No. 1902

FD-302 (Rev. 1-25-60)

FEDERAL BUREAU OF INVESTIGATION

1

Date 11/25/63

Mr. ROBERT HEDRICK, Manager, Factory Outlet Shoes, 729 Canal Street, New Orleans, Louisiana, advised that this business has been in operation since August 1, 1963, however, from July 1, 1963 he had possession of the building and was preparing for his original opening August 1, 1963. He advised that LEE HARVEY OSWALD was not employed at any time by his company. Mr. HEDRICK further advised that this location was previously under the name of Rhealee Millinery Company, whose home office is in Dallas, Texas. He advised that he has no knowledge of the employment record of this company or whether or not OSWALD was in fact employed by Rhealee Millinery Company.

Mr. HEDRICK advised that sometime during the month of August, 1963 he recalled seeing LEE OSWALD at the corner of Canal and Carondelet in the bus stop area distributing leaflets, however, he himself had no contact with OSWALD. He further advised that on one occasion he recalled seeing OSWALD in conversation with another individual whom he described as heavy set with swarthy, Latin complexion. He was not able to identify this individual carrying on conversation with OSWALD except to say he is of opinion that perhaps they were arguing in view of the motions of their hands and arms.

Mr. HEDRICK stated that when he saw OSWALD it was usually in the late evening around 5:00 PM when he would make his trip to the bank to make a deposit in the National Bank of Commerce night deposit box.

Mr. HEDRICK advised that he is unable to furnish further information regarding the Dolly Shoe Company but suggested a contact be made with Southern Shoe Company, 214 Decatur Street, since this company is the wholesale outlet for shoes in this area.

Commission Exhibit No. 1903

On 11/25/63 at New Orleans, Louisiana File # NO 89-69

by SA JAMES E. SCHMIDT, JR. and SA THEODORE R. VIATER/jab Date dictated 11/25/63

53

This document contains neither recommendations nor conclusions of the FBI. It is the property of the FBI and is loaned to your agency; it and its contents are not to be distributed outside your agency.

COMMISSION EXHIBIT No. 1903

FD-302 (Rev. 1-25-60)

FEDERAL BUREAU OF INVESTIGATION

Date November 30, 1963

TEDDY GUICHARD, residing at 1226 St. Phillips Street, New Orleans, phone number 523-1337, employed Brick and Stone Center, Inc., 401 North Jefferson Davis Parkway, New Orleans, was contacted and advised that he works as laborer in stone yard and approximately the end of July he saw OSWALD when he came to apply for work. OSWALD was introduced to GUICHARD but that was the extent of the conversation. GUICHARD advised that to the best of his knowledge OSWALD was alone at this time. GUICHARD had never seen OSWALD before this time and did not see him again until newspaper accounts of the weekend of November 22 through 25. GUICHARD advised that he has no further information regarding OSWALD.

Commission Exhibit No. 1904

On 11/29/63 at New Orleans, Louisiana File # NO 89-69 DALLAS 89-43

by SA MICHAEL F. CAMPBELL :dc Date dictated 11/29/63

54

This document contains neither recommendations nor conclusions of the FBI. It is the property of the FBI and is loaned to your agency; it and its contents are not to be distributed outside your agency.

COMMISSION EXHIBIT No. 1904

FD-302 (Rev. 1-25-60)

FEDERAL BUREAU OF INVESTIGATION

Date November 26, 1963

Mr. S. K. MANSON, President of the Manson Marble and Granite Company, 501 North Jefferson Davis Parkway, New Orleans, Louisiana, telephone number 488-0165, advised that he recalled that LEE H. OSWALD had filed an application for employment with his company in July, 1963.

Mr. MANSON stated that his company ran an advertisement in the local newspaper for a yard man for a building materials yard and that OSWALD applied as the result of reading this advertisement in the newspaper.

MANSON advised that OSWALD was not hired in view of the fact that he made several errors on his application such as listing his age as 25 when he appeared much younger, and listing a telephone number Hunter 8-4326 which was supposed to be his residence phone. MANSON stated that when he called this number he was advised that while OSWALD was known at that number he did not reside there. MANSON stated that he left word with the person answering this telephone number to advise OSWALD that the job had been filled.

Mr. MANSON furnished the application blank filled out by LEE H. OSWALD which is set out as follows:

"APPLICATION

"Name: LEE H. OSWALD

Address: 757 French St.

Phone: HU - 84326

Age: 25

Education: H.S. (Warren Easton)

Previous Employment: (State length of time employed)
Wm. B. Riely Co. 3 months May - July
640 Magazine St. as maintance michianic

[redacted]

Commission Exhibit No. 1905

On 11/26/63 at New Orleans, Louisiana File # NO 89-69

by SA G. MYRYWIN ALDERSON :sms Date dictated 11/26/63

This document contains neither recommendations nor conclusions of the FBI. It is the property of the FBI and is loaned to your agency; it and its contents are not to be distributed outside your agency.

55

COMMISSION EXHIBIT No. 1905

NO 89-69/sms
2

Reason for leaving: Reduction by company of maintance crew

Military status: 3 yrs. U.S.M.C. Honourable Discharge May 1960 - May 1963

Marital status: married, 1 child

References: (Give three)
JOHN MURRETT 801 Florida Av.
CHARLES HARRISON Tulane Un.
WM. OSWALD"

56

COMMISSION EXHIBIT No. 1905—Continued

FD-302 (Rev. 1-25-60)

FEDERAL BUREAU OF INVESTIGATION

1

Date 11/25/63

On this date, a review of New Orleans Street Directory reflected that there is no 640 Rampart Street in New Orleans. Likewise, there is no 640 North Rampart in New Orleans. At 640 South Rampart Street in New Orleans there are the Louisiana Weekly Publishing Company, Inc. (Negro newspaper); HENRY B. DEJOIE, Printer for the Louisiana Weekly Publishing Company; H. L. WILCOX, Real Estate; and Mrs. THELMA BOUTEE, Physician.

Commission Exhibit No. 1906

On 11/25/63 at New Orleans, Louisiana File # NO 89-69

by SA RAYMOND E. BECK and SA FRANK A. SASS, JR. :sab Date dictated 11/25/63

51

This document contains neither recommendations nor conclusions of the FBI. It is the property of the FBI and is loaned to your agency; it and its contents are not to be distributed outside your agency.

COMMISSION EXHIBIT NO. 1906

FD-302 (Rev. 1-25-60)

FEDERAL BUREAU OF INVESTIGATION

1

Date November 27, 1963

Mrs. G. M. WATSON, Bookkeeper, The Louisiana Weekly, 640 South Rampart Street, observed a photograph of LEE HARVEY OSWALD, New Orleans Police Department no. 112723 and advised that OSWALD was never employed by the Louisiana Weekly. Mrs. WATSON pointed out that she keeps all the employee records and prepares all of the salary checks for her company and would certainly know OSWALD if he had worked there in September, 1963.

Commission Exhibit No. 1907

On 11/26/63 at New Orleans, Louisiana File # NO 89-69

by SA MILTON R. KAACK SA ERNEST C. WALL, JR. /sw Date dictated 11/26/63

58

This document contains neither recommendations nor conclusions of the FBI. It is the property of the FBI and is loaned to your agency; it and its contents are not to be distributed outside your agency.

1 Date 11/27/63

Mr. GEORGE REPPEL, 5508 Wilton Drive, dba Reppel Studio, 5220 Elysian Fields Avenue, advised that he has not employed any help during the year 1963. He stated that his is a small business run primarily by he and his wife.

REPPEL further stated that he does not take applications from anyone nor does he take names and addresses of persons to be considered for employment in the future, as he seldom needs help. He further stated that he has received calls from persons (names or addresses not recalled) within the past year seeking employment with him, but his business during the year has not required having extra help.

— Commission Exhibit No. 1908 —

On 11/27/63 at New Orleans, La. File # NO 89-69

by SA JOHN WILLIAM MILLER :dmm Date dictated 11/27/63

59

This document contains neither recommendations nor conclusions of the FBI. It is the property of the FBI and is loaned to your agency; it and its contents are not to be distributed outside your agency.

COMMISSION EXHIBIT No. 1908

NO 89-69/sms

On November 27, 1963, Special Agent PETER VIAL, United States Secret Service, advised that he heard from a source that he could not recall that LEE HARVEY OSWALD made application for work at Michoud and that he went to work at Michoud.

The following investigation was conducted by SA G. MYRYWIN ALDERSON:

On November 29, 1963, Mrs. LILLIAN GLEASON, Personnel Officer, National Aeronautics and Space Administration (NASA), Michoud, Louisiana, reviewed her records and advised that LEE HARVEY OSWALD had never filed an application for employment with NASA.

On November 29, 1963, Mr. JOHN H. CANERDAY, Personnel Officer, Mason-Rust Contractors, Michoud Operations, Michoud, Louisiana, advised that LEE HARVEY OSWALD had never made application for employment with Mason-Rust Contractors at NASA.

On November 29, 1963, Mr. W. H. JOHNSON, Personnel Officer, Chrysler Corporation Space Division, Michoud, Louisiana, advised that a review of the records of his office failed to reflect that LEE HARVEY OSWALD had applied for employment with Chrysler Corporation Space Division at NASA.

On November 30, 1963, Mr. JOHN A. ALLAN, Chief of Security, The Boeing Company, Claiborne Towers, New Orleans, Louisiana, advised that a review of the files of the personnel office failed to reflect that LEE HARVEY OSWALD had filed an application for employment at NASA.

— Commission Exhibit No. 1909 —

60

COMMISSION EXHIBIT No. 1909

NO 89-69:jas

At New Orleans, Louisiana

The following investigation was conducted by SA THEODORE R. VIATER:

On November 29, 1963, the following establishments were contacted and disclosed no record of LEE HARVEY OSWALD's ever having been employed or registered:

Falstaff Brewing Corporation,
2601 Gravier Street;
Miss EARLINE BENSON,
Personnel Clerk.

Regal Brewing Company,
233 St. Maurice Street;
Mr. PAUL R. SPELLMAN,
Assistant Comptroller.

Nationwide Employment Bureau, Inc.,
1414 National Bank of Commerce Building;
Mr. PAUL MILES, Manager.

Nunes Employment Service, Inc.,
231 Carondelet Street,
Mrs. SARA BAS NUNES, Owner.

The following investigation was conducted by SA EMIL HENRY BECKER:

On November 29, 1963, the followimg employment agencies were contacted with regard to LEE HARVEY OSWALD with negative results:

Dot Romer Employment Service,
234 Loyola Avenue;
Mrs. DOROTHY ROMER, Owner.

Accredited Personnel Service, Inc.;
no longer in business.

Accurate Placement Service;
no longer in business.

61

— Commission Exhibit No. 1910 —

COMMISSION EXHIBIT No. 1910

2 NO 89-69:jas

Domestic Employment Service;
no longer in business.

The following investigation was conducted by SA EUGENE E. BJORN:

On November 29, 1963, the following employment agencies were contacted regarding LEE HARVEY OSWALD, with negative results:

Manpower, Inc., 305 Baronne Street;
Miss RUTH T. SCHRODER, Manager.

Employers Overload Company,
1409 National Bank of Commerce Building;
MILDRED SICARD, Manager.

62

COMMISSION EXHIBIT No. 1910—Continued

On November 29, 1963, the following individuals were interviewed at their places of employment, and all advised that LEE H. OSWALD was never employed by them, never applied for employment with their concern, and was unknown to them until they began reading about him in the newspapers:

Mrs. C. FRANCK HOFFMAN, Partner and Manager, Franck's Studio, 926 Poydras Street, New Orleans, Louisiana;

RICHARD RELF, Manager, Relf Studios, 113 Royal Street, New Orleans, Louisiana;

ELIZABETH POLIT, Proprietor, Red Seafood, 1341 Elysian Fields Avenue, New Orleans, Louisiana, who advised that her building was once occupied by South Central Studio.

PEDRO CASANAVE, Proprietor, Pedro Art Studio, 5112 Freret Street, New Orleans, Louisiana;

Mrs. E. L. TILLON, Lee Tillon Studio, 1504 South Carrollton Avenue, New Orleans, Louisiana;

Mrs. GISELE SCHULTZ, Proprietor, Schultz Bookkeeping, 4228 South Roman Street, New Orleans, Louisiana;

Mrs. THOMAS BARBERITO who advised that her concern is not a photographic studio, but that her husband, THOMAS BARBERITO, is an independent accountant who works out of his home, 1007 Dwn. Street, Metairie, Louisiana.
Mrs. LAURA SCACCIA, Guccione Studio, 26 Beverly Gardens Drive, Metairie, Louisiana;

Mr. WILLIAM CORAN, Proprietor, Bill Coran Studio, 206 Pasadena, Metairie, Louisiana.

EARL FORSTALL, Manager, The Ad Shop, 1201 South Rampart Street, New Orleans, Louisiana.

63

— Commission Exhibit No. 1911 —

COMMISSION EXHIBIT No. 1911

GEORGE BLESTEL, Photographer, The Ad Shop, 1201 South Rampart Street;

Mrs. GLORIA STYRND, Clerk-Receptionist, E. S. Upton Printing Company, 746 Carondelet Street;

LAWRENCE SMITH, Production Manager, E. S. Upton Printing Company, 746 Carondelet Street;

ALONZO EMERSON, Office Manager, American Metals, Inc., successor to American Sheet Metal Works, 4401 Bienville Avenue;

L. L. MC INTYRE, Manager, Electrolux Corporation, 1935 Tulane Avenue;

BEN SMITH, Manager, Electrolux Corporation, 3407 Metairie Road, formerly located at 616 North Rampart Street;

Mrs. FRANK RENTON, Bookkeeper, Printing Press, Inc., 518 Conti Street;

BENNY LA BRUYERE, Manager, Printers Supply Mart, 610 Magazine Street;

JUDSON CRANE, JR., Manager, Crane Shoes, 1726 Tulane Avenue;

HENRY C. HARTMANN, Owner, Hartmann Studio, 1123½ Royal Street;

MARGARET MICHEL, Personnel Manager, Times-Picayune and States-Item, 615 North Street;

64

COMMISSION EXHIBIT No. 1911—Continued

LEO SCHEUERMAN, Manager,
Camera Center, Katz & Besthoff,
841 Canal Street;

JACK MORROW, Personnel Section,
Humble Oil & Refining Company (Esso),
1410 Canal Street;

HARRY SKILES, Assistant Superintendent,
Sales Terminal, Humble Oil & Refining
Company, Chalmette;

LEON TRICE, Owner, Leon Trice Photographers, 727 Poydras Street;

JAMES KENNEDY, Sackett Studios,
1102 Canal Street;

ROBERT SACKETT, Sackett Studios,
1102 Canal Street;

CAROL AMBERG, Couble Chek,
2107 Banks Street;

CLARENCE J. LEFTWICH, Apex Sales
Company, 2727 South Broad Street;

MILTON HELLMERS, Rathborne Land &
Lumber Company, 4th Street, Harvey, La.;

SIDNEY MOLAISON, Rathborne Land &
Lumber Company, 4th Street, Harvey, La.;

RALPH PLAIDEAU, Owner, Primary Color Lab,
619 Poydras Street;

LAWRENCE STOULIG, Manager,
Dumas-Milner Leasing Corporation,
740 Baronne Street;

RICHARD J. SANUCHEAU, Rental Agent,
Dumas-Milner Leasing Corporation,
1000 Common Street;

65

DONALD ENTRINGER, Manager,
McKenzie Pastry Shops,
3908 Downman Road;

RAY DECOTEAU, Plant Superintendent,
McKenzie Pastry Shops, 3908 Downman Road;

JACK BEECH, Owner, Industrial
Photographers, 709 Royal Street;

JULIUS E. WEISS, Owner,
Bernadas-Weiss Photography,
621 Chartres Street;

Mrs. MARGARET NELSON, Secretary,
Marine & Industrial Equipment,
4659 Evangeline Street;

F. N. MAITRE, Personnel Director,
Louisiana Coca Cola Bottling Company,
1050 South Jefferson Davis Parkway;

Mrs. R. LATIMER, President,
Nifty Printing Company, Inc.,
3923 Tulane Avenue;

EUGENE L. COLLEY, Owner,
Winston's Printing Shop,
5019 Tchoupitoulas Street;

Miss HANNA LEE KATZ, Personnel Manager,
Godchaux's, 828 Canal Street (contacted
November 30, 1963.)

Mrs. ETHEL ABRAMSON, Personnel Department,
Godchaux's, 828 Canal Street (contacted
November 30, 1963.)

Mrs. BETTY VON, Owner, Krause-Von
Studios, 613 Canal Street, (contacted
November 30, 1963.)

66

PAUL ROSSETTER, Manager, Doubleday Book Shop, 633 Canal Street, (contacted November 30, 1963,);

JUANITA ACCARDO, Owner, Apex Southern Sales Company, 8725 Oak Street, (contacted November 30, 1963)

Through inquiries at the New Orleans Retailers Credit Bureau and other appropriate sources and by review of the city and telephone directories, no address was found for the following individuals or companies:

Rachael Photo Studio,
Doubl-Ad Shop,
Art Studios,
Print Rollers, Inc.

Ables Commercial Photography

Rex Photography,
Lincola Photo Studios,
Jasimer Company,
Ansco Photo Supplies,
Ajax, Inc, Photographers,
W. B. Simson, Shipping,
B. O or B. D. Company,
532 Magazine Street.

The above investigation at New Orleans was conducted by Special Agents MICHAEL F. CAMPBELL, DONALD L. HUGHES, JOHN M. MC CARTHY, WILLIAM L. NEWBROUGH, JAMES R. RIORDAN, and CLAUDE L. SCHLAGER.

67

COMMISSION EXHIBIT No. 1911—Continued

FD-302 (Rev. 1-25-60) FEDERAL BUREAU OF INVESTIGATION

Date 11/29/63

1

Mr. PHILIP A. BLAPPERT, Manager, Rosen Photography, 859 Front Street, New Orleans, Louisiana, after being advised of the identity of the interviewing Agent, furnished the following information:

Mr. BLAPPERT advised that LEE H. OSWALD applied for a position of Clerk-Typist at his concern some time in the middle of August, but he could not recall the exact date. BLAPPERT advised that he destroyed OSWALD's application after he decided not to employ him but could remember that OSWALD listed his address as 4809 Magazine Street, New Orleans, and listed the fact that he was married. BLAPPERT stated that OSWALD was neatly dressed, well spoken, and looked too good to be applying for a $50.00 a week job as Clerk-Typist. BLAPPERT stated further that based on the latter, he became suspicious of OSWALD.

BLAPPERT could furnish no further information.

Commission Exhibit No. 1912

On 11/29/63 at New Orleans, Louisiana File # NO 89-69

by SA JAMES R. RIORDAN :jas Date dictated 11/29/63

74

COMMISSION EXHIBIT No. 1912

FD-302 (Rev. 1-25-60)

FEDERAL BUREAU OF INVE

Commission Exhibit No. 1913

Date 11/30/63

1

FRED MADDEN, Personnel Manager, American Metals, Inc., 4401 Bienville Avenue, advised as follows:

Upon seeing various photographs of LEE HARVEY OSWALD beginning on November 22, 1963, he had a vague recollection that this individual had, in possibly the past six months, been in his place of business inquiring for employment. Upon returning to his office the following work day, he had checked all available applications and records and found that no proof of such an inquiry by OSWALD could be located.

On 11/29/63 at New Orleans, Louisiana File # NO 89-69

by SA DONALD L. HUGHES/lrs Date dictated 11/29/63

75

COMMISSION EXHIBIT No. 1913

FD-302 (Rev. 1-25-60)

FEDERAL BUREAU OF INVI

Commission Exhibit No. 1914

Date 11/30/63

1

FRED OLSEN, Personnel Director, Katz-Besthoff, Inc., 900 Camp Street, furnished the following voluntary information:

He stated that he recalled LEE HARVEY OSWALD applying for employment with Katz-Besthoff and as best he can recall, this was in the latter part of July or early part of August, 1963. He stated that he could not locate the application executed by OSWALD and inasmuch as it is company policy to destroy applications after two months, it was quite possible that OSWALD's application was destroyed.

OLSEN stated that the reason he is able to recall OSWALD applying for employment, was that it was only a short time prior to OSWALD applying for employment that he had been involved in passing out handbills on Canal Street in regards to Fair Play for Cuba or something in that regards. OLSEN stated that in the event that the application would be located, he would notify the FBI of same.

On 11/30/63 at New Orleans, Louisiana File # 89-69

by SA WILLIAM L. NEWBROUGH:lav Date dictated 11/30/63

76

COMMISSION EXHIBIT No. 1914

FD-302 (Rev. 1-25-60) FEDERAL BUREAU OF INVESTIGATION

[redacted]

1 Commission Exhibit No. 1915 — Date 11/27/63

Mr. ERIC ROGERS, 407 Magazine Street, front apartment, advised that he and his wife moved into this apartment on about July 16, 1963 and that OSWALD and his wife were already living in the adjoining apartment at 4905 Magazine. ROGERS said that he was out of work and that it was not until October 1, 1963 that he, ROGERS obtained a part-time job at the Meal-A-Minute, 1000 Canal Street, as a waiter. He said that up until he went to work he believes that he saw OSWALD at least once every day, up until the time OSWALD left.

He recalls that OSWALD had packed household effects and clothes in a station wagon one afternoon and that OSWALD's wife and child departed with the woman who drove the station wagon on the following morning. He said on the following day he saw OSWALD running to catch a bus on the corner, carrying two suitcases. That was the last time he saw him.

Shortly after ROGERS moved into the neighborhood he observed an individual whom ROGERS thought to be of Spanish descent called to visit OSWALD. The exact time of this visit not recalled by ROGERS, but he is certain that it was before the time OSWALD was arrested by the New Orleans Police Department.

ROGERS never saw any guns or firearms in the OSWALD apartment and never saw OSWALD with anything resembling a firearm. He recalls that although OSWALD spent the majority of his time reading either on the porch or in the front room of his apartment, in the afternoons he would walk to the corner and catch a bus going toward the business section or would walk in that direction. He said occasionally OSWALD would walk up to the confectionary on the corner of Magazine and Dufosset to buy ice cream, since he would see him returning to the apartment with it. He said that OSWALD always spoke Russian to his wife, in fact, Mrs. OSWALD could not speak any English.

He said that it was rumored in the neighborhood that Mrs. OSWALD was pregnant at the time she moved and he believed that on one occasion OSWALD took her to a physician. The date and time of this visit was not recalled by ROGERS, nor was the identity of the physician known to him.

On 11/27/63 at New Orleans, Louisiana File # NO 89-69

by SA'S JOHN B. LEE & MILTON R. KAACK /bal Date dictated 11/27/63

This document contains neither recommendations nor conclusions of the FBI. It is the property of the FBI and is loaned to your agency; it and its contents are not to be distributed outside your agency.

COMMISSION EXHIBIT No. 1915

FD-302 (Rev. 1-25-60)

FEDERAL BUREAU OF INVESTIGATION

Date 11/24/63

1

Mr. NORMAN OSWALD, 706 Division Street, Metairie, Louisiana, advised he has had no association whatsoever with LEE HARVEY OSWALD. He advised his only recollection of this person is when his father died in New Orleans about the time of his birth, that his mother, MARGUERITE, thereafter raised LEE in Texas and no one in his family has had any occasion to meet him or in any manner associate with him. He advised he knows of no instance when LEE has returned to New Orleans, that they have never exchanged holiday greetings or in other ways associated with each other and he knows nothing whatsoever about his background. He stated he had never heard of anyone by the name of HIDELL and knew knowledge whether or not LEE had ever used this name.

— Commission Exhibit No. 1916 —

On 11/23/63 at Metairie, Louisiana File # NO 89-69

by SA's REED W. JENSEN & RAY E. ROCKHOLD/lrs Date dictated 11/23/63

146

This document contains neither recommendations nor conclusions of the FBI. It is the property of the FBI and is loaned to your agency; it and its contents are not to be distributed outside your agency.

COMMISSION EXHIBIT No. 1916

FD-302 (Rev. 1-25-60)

FEDERAL BUREAU OF INVESTIGATION

Date 11/25/63

1

WILLIAM STOUT OSWALD, JR., 136 Elmeer Street, Metairie, Louisiana, advised he is the son of WILLIAM STOUT OSWALD, SR., and HAZEL OSWALD and a first cousin of LEE HARVEY OSWALD. Mr. OSWALD stated the last he had seen or heard of LEE OSWALD was when LEE was in New Orleans with his mother, MARGUERITE, when LEE was about age 14. He did not know how long LEE had stayed in New Orleans and he could provide no further personal information concerning LEE's activities since that time.

OSWALD said the name HIDELL did not mean anything to him.

— Commission Exhibit No. 1917 —

On 11/23/63 at Metairie, Louisiana File # NO 89-69

by SA's REED W. JENSEN & RAY E. ROCKHOLD/lrs Date dictated 11/23/63

147

This document contains neither recommendations nor conclusions of the FBI. It is the property of the FBI and is loaned to your agency; it and its contents are not to be distributed outside your agency.

COMMISSION EXHIBIT No. 1917

FD-302 (Rev. 1-25-60) FEDERAL BUREAU OF INVESTIGATION

Date 11/25/63

1

LOWELL OSWALD, 132 Elmeer Street, Metairie, Louisiana, advised he is the son of HAZEL OSWALD, who resides at 136 Elmeer Street. He stated he is a first cousin of LEE OSWALD. He recalled LEE OSWALD spent some time in his childhood in the New Orleans area. He said he would not know him if he were to meet him and could provide no information whatsoever concerning LEE's activities since childhood.

OSWALD said the name HIDELL did not mean anything to him.

Commission Exhibit No. 1918

On 11/23/63 at Metairie, Louisiana File # NO 89-69

by SA's REED W. JENSEN & RAY E. ROCKHOLD/lrs Date dictated 11/23/63

This document contains neither recommendations nor conclusions of the FBI. It is the property of the FBI and is loaned to your agency; it and its contents are not to be distributed outside your agency.

COMMISSION EXHIBIT No. 1918

FD-302 (Rev. 1-25-60) FEDERAL BUREAU OF INVESTIGATION

Commission Exhibit No. 1919

Date 11/24/63

Mrs. HAZEL OSWALD, 136 Elmeer Street, Metairie, Louisiana, advised she is the widow of WILLIAM STOUT OSWALD, SR. She stated her husband's brother, LEE OSWALD, SR., and wife, MARGUERITE, nee Claverie, had been residing in New Orleans, in the 1930's. LEE SR. died in 1939 and approximately two months after his death, a son, LEE HARVEY OSWALD, was born. When LEE was approximately 2½ years of age, MARGUERITE left New Orleans, going to the Fort Worth, Texas, area where she continued to raise LEE and an older brother, ROBERT E. OSWALD and another son by a previous marriage whose name was not known to Mrs. OSWALD. Mrs. OSWALD stated she lost all track of MARGUERITE and LEE until one day she received a telephone call from MARGUERITE. During the conversation, MARGUERITE indicated LEE was then 14 years of age, that she was living in the City of New Orleans with him and employed at the Burt Shoe Store on Canal Street.

According to Mrs. OSWALD, sometime after this call she went by this store and talked with MARGUERITE for a short time. After that she lost all contact with MARGUERITE and apparently MARGUERITE and LEE left New Orleans, date unknown. She said she did not know how long MARGUERITE had actually resided in New Orleans.

Mrs. OSWALD stated the next time she heard from either MARGUERITE or LEE was one day in about April, 1963, when LEE telephoned her saying he was in New Orleans and wanted to visit and obtain some information about his father's relatives, specifically a HARVEY OSWALD, the grandfather, then deceased. LEE came to her residence and arrived alone by bus. They talked about his father's folks and she gave him a photograph of his father. During her conversation with LEE he said he left his wife and child in Texas until he could find some employment in New Orleans and that he wanted to find employment as a photographer. He did not specifically say where he was living but she received the impression that one of his mother's sisters was in New Orleans, address unknown, and that LEE was living with her. Mrs. OSWALD stated sometime prior to LEE's visit she had read in the newspapers that LEE had been in Russia and had indicated a desire to become a Russian citizen. During the conversation they were talking about LEE's wife and LEE exhibited her photograph. Mrs. OSWALD asked him if his wife

On 11/23/63 at Metairie, Louisiana File # NO 89-69

by SA's REED W. JENSEN & RAY E. ROCKHOLD/lrs Date dictated 11/23/63

This document contains neither recommendations nor conclusions of the FBI. It is the property of the FBI and is loaned to your agency; it and its contents are not to be distributed outside your agency.

COMMISSION EXHIBIT No. 1919

NO 89-69
2

were Russian and LEE replied "Why do you ask that?". She said that other than this one exchange, all of her conversation was about relatives.

She stated she did not hear from nor see LEE thereafter and to her knowledge he was not in personal contact with any of the other relatives in the OSWALD family. With respect to any contacts or associates in New Orleans, she stated she had no knowledge whatsoever as to what his activities may have been. As to other members of the OSWALD family, she said she had a son, NORMAN A. OSWALD, at 706 Division Street, Metairie. He has a son, WILLIAM STOUT OSWALD, III, who is a school teacher in Metairie, and has some responsible position in one of the military reserve units. WILLIAM OSWALD, III, had talked to Mrs. OSWALD on the morning of November 23, 1963, indicating someone had questioned him about LEE OSWALD and he indicated that he knew nothing whatsoever about him. She said she does not know what school or organizations LEE might have been associated with while he resided in New Orleans and that the name HIDELL meant nothing to her and she was positive it was not an OSWALD family name. She had never heard LEE use this name.

In conclusion, Mrs. OSWALD advised that after the death of LEE's father, the mother had severed relations with the OSWALD family and after moving to Texas, did not maintain any association with any member of the family and she could not furnish any further details concerning his background.

150

COMMISSION EXHIBIT No. 1919—Continued

FD-302 (Rev. 1-25-60)

FEDERAL BUREAU OF INVESTIGATION

—Commission Exhibit No. 1920 — Date November 25, 1963

1

Mr. and Mrs. CHARLES MURRET advised that LEE HARVEY OSWALD is Mrs. MURRET's nephew, Mrs. MURRET's sister being OSWALD's mother. Sometime after Easter, 1963, exact date not recalled, OSWALD called Mrs. MURRET on the telephone and advised that he had just arrived in New Orleans by bus. He asked if he could spend a few nights at her residence while he was seeking employment in New Orleans. They said that he spent from three to five nights at their residence, and that he spent the daytime seeking employment. He would never eat breakfast but would leave early in the morning and return to their residence shortly before dinner and would eat the evening meal with them. OSWALD had but few clothes consisting of a change of pants and shirt although he claimed to have several duffel bags at the bus station. He also had a few cardboard boxes in which he stated were clothes belonging to his wife and baby which he kept in the MURRET garage. OSWALD did not possess any firearms while residing at the MURRET residence to their knowledge. He had no visitors while staying there and only received one letter which he claimed was from his wife. He did receive several telephone calls after he left regarding jobs. OSWALD obtained a job, according to his statement to them, as a mechanic at the Reily Coffee Company which they believe he obtained by answering a newspaper advertisement. He told them he found an apartment on the same day on which he got the job and that he moved to this apartment either the next day or the day following it. OSWALD's wife and baby arrived several days later from Texas in a station wagon which was driven by a woman who spoke the Russian language. Mr. and Mrs. MURRET did not know this woman's name but they did recall the station wagon bore Texas license plates.

Mrs. MURRET advised that she and her sister, OSWALD's mother, did not get along very well and that when OSWALD was about two years of age, her sister and her children moved to Texas. She said she has had no contact with LEE OSWALD over the years until he telephonically contacted her requesting permission to stay at her home while seeking employment.

Mr. and Mrs. MURRET knew of no friends or acquaintances of OSWALD in the New Orleans area. Mr. and Mrs. MURRET had no knowledge of when OSWALD left New Orleans or by what means he may have traveled.

On 11/23/63 at New Orleans, Louisiana File # NO 89-69

by SAs MILTON R. KAACK and ERNEST C. WALL, JR. /lyc Date dictated 11/25/63

COMMISSION EXHIBIT No. 1920

FD-302 (Rev. 1-25-60)

FEDERAL BUREAU OF INVESTIGATION

1

Date November 27, 1963

Mrs. ARTHUR A.P. BARRE, nee ALICE OSWALD, 2311 St. Charles Avenue, furnished the following information:

She is an aunt of LEE HARVEY OSWALD. The only time she may have seen LEE's mother was at the funeral of his father, ROBERT EDWARD LEE OSWALD, in 1939. She has never met LEE OSWALD and knows nothing concerning him.

Commission Exhibit No. 1921

On 11/26/63 at New Orleans, Louisiana File # NO 89-69

by SA JOSEPH G. ENGELHARDT /sms Date dictated 11/26/63

152

This document contains neither recommendations nor conclusions of the FBI. It is the property of the FBI and is loaned to your agency; it and its contents are not to be distributed outside your agency.

COMMISSION EXHIBIT No. 1921

FD-302 (Rev. 1-25-60)

FEDERAL BUREAU OF INVESTIGATION

1

Date 11/27/63

Miss ADELE OSWALD, 2018 General Pershing Street, furnished the following information:

She is the daughter of THOMAS and ADELE OSWALD and the cousin of LEE HARVEY OSWALD. She has not seen or heard from LEE HARVEY OSWALD or his mother since the death of LEE's father in 1939. She knows nothing concerning him.

Commission Exhibit No. 1922

On 11/26/63 at New Orleans, Louisiana File # NO 89-69

by SA JOSEPH G. ENGELHARDT /bda Date dictated 11/26/63

153

This document contains neither recommendations nor conclusions of the FBI. It is the property of the FBI and is loaned to your agency; it and its contents are not to be distributed outside your agency.

COMMISSION EXHIBIT No. 1922

FD-302 (Rev. 1-25-60)

FEDERAL BUREAU OF INVESTIGATION

1

Date 11/27/63

MRS. TONY BEVINETTO, nee SHIRLEY OSWALD, 1914 South Carrollton Avenue, furnished the following information:

She is the daughter of HARVEY N. OSWALD, uncle of LEE HARVEY OSWALD. Both her mother and father are deceased. She left New Orleans in 1939 and returned in 1942. She has never seen LEE OSWALD or his mother and knows nothing concerning them.

Commission Exhibit No. 1923

On 11/26/63 at New Orleans, Louisiana File # NO 89-69

by SA JOSEPH G. ENGELHARDT /mrk Date dictated 11/26/63

154

COMMISSION EXHIBIT No. 1923

FD-302 (Rev. 1-25-60)

FEDERAL BUREAU OF INVESTIGATION

1

Date 11/27/63

Mrs. WILLIAM BROWN, nee FLOY OSWALD, 3944 Virgil Boulevard, furnished the following information:

She is a daughter of HARVEY OSWALD, uncle of LEE HARVEY OSWALD. Bother her father and mother are dead. She is of the opinion she may have seen LEE's mother twice before LEE's father died in 1939. She has not seen her since and has never seen LEE OSWALD and knows nothing concerning him.

Commission Exhibit No. 1924

On 11/26/63 at New Orleans, Louisiana File # NO 89-69

by SA JOSEPH G. ENGELHARDT /bda Date dictated 11/26/63

155

COMMISSION EXHIBIT No. 1924

FD-302 (Rev. 1-25-60)

FEDERAL BUREAU OF INVESTIGATION

1

Date 11/27/63

Mrs. ADELE F. OSWALD, 2018 General Pershing Street, furnished the following information:

She is the widow of THOMAS OSWALD, uncle of LEE HARVEY OSWALD. She has not seen the mother of LEE HARVEY OSWALD since the death of LEE's father in 1939 and has never seen LEE HARVEY OSWALD and knows nothing concerning him.

[redacted]

Commission Exhibit No. 1925

On 11/26/63 at New Orleans, Louisiana File # NO 89-69

by SA JOSEPH G. ENGELHARDT /bda Date dictated 11/26/63

This document contains neither recommendations nor conclusions of the FBI. It is the property of the FBI and is loaned to your agency; it and its contents are not to be distributed outside your agency.

COMMISSION EXHIBIT NO. 1925

FD-302 (Rev. 1-25-60)

FEDERAL BUREAU OF INVESTIG

1

Date November 27, 1963

Mrs. EDMOND C. CARTER, nee ETHEL OSWALD, apartment 1005, Pontchartrain Hotel, 2031 St. Charles Avenue, furnished the following information:

She is the sister of ROBERT EDWARD LEE OSWALD, father of LEE HARVEY OSWALD. She has never seen LEE OSWALD, knows nothing concerning him, and has had no communication of any type with LEE's mother subsequent to the death of his father in 1939.

On 11/26/63 at New Orleans, Louisiana File # NO 89-69

by SA JOSEPH G. ENGELHARDT /sms Date dictated 11/26/63

This document contains neither recommendations nor conclusions of the FBI. It is the property of the FBI and is loaned to your agency; it and its contents are not to be distributed outside your agency.

COMMISSION EXHIBIT NO. 1926

FD-302 (Rev. 1-25-60) FEDERAL BUREAU OF INVESTIGATION

Date November 27, 1963

Mrs. JAMES COKER, nee HATTIE OSWALD, Apartment 2G, Andrew Jackson Apartments, Second Street and St. Charles Avenue, furnished the following information:

She is a ister of ROBERT EDWARD LEE OSWALD, father of LEE HARVEY OSWALD. Her mother had the following children: THOMAS, WILLIAM, ALICE, HARVEY, ETHEL, HATTIE, and ROBERT. THOMAS, WILLIAM, HARVEY, and ROBERT are deceased. THOMAS' widow, Mrs. ADELE F. OSWALD, and her daughter, ADELE, live at 2018 General Pershing Street. WILLIAM's widow, HAZEL, lives at 136 Elmeer Street, Metairie. ALICE is married to ARTHUR A. P. BARRE and lives at 2311 St. Charles Avenue. HARVEY's wife is also deceased. They were the parents of Mrs. WILLIAM BROWN, 3944 Virgil Boulevard and Mrs. TONY BEVINETTO, 1914 South Carrollton Avenue. ETHEL is Mrs. EDMOND C. CARTER, Apartment 1005, Pontchartrain Hotel, 2031 St. Charles Avenue.

Mrs. COKER advised she never saw LEE HARVEY OSWALD or his mother. LEE's father was divorced from his first wife and this met with disapproval from his family. She knew nothing concerning the woman he then married and who became the mother of LEE HARVEY OSWALD.

Mrs. COKER advised she and her husband left New Orleans in 1924 and lived in New York City. They moved to Washington, D.C. in 1942 and returned to New Orleans in 1958. She could furnish no information whatsoever concerning LEE HARVEY OSWALD.

[redacted]

Commission Exhibit No. 1927

On 11/26/63 at New Orleans, Louisiana File # NO 89-69

by SA JOSEPH G. ENGELHARDT /sms Date dictated 11/26/63

COMMISSION EXHIBIT No. 1927

FD-302 (Rev. 1-25-60) FEDERAL BUREAU OF INVESTIGATION

1

Date November 27, 1963

ROBERT LAWRENCE HELLER, 4703 Freret Street, advised he resides in the upstairs apartment at this address and has a telephone number 899-8631. He advised that at this time he is employed part time with television station WYES and also Motion Picture Advertising, 1032 Carondelet Street. HELLER stated that he is not personally acquainted with LEE HARVEY OSWALD as he has never met this individual, however, some time during the month of August, 1963, he was at the location on Canal and Carondelet Streets when he observed OSWALD handing out leaflets for Fair Play for Cuba. At this time he observed that OSWALD was being "pushed around" by several male individuals he identified as Cubans and that these individuals were actually taking the leaflets from OSWALD and destroying same and causing a considerable disturbance. As a result of this disturbance, OSWALD was arrested by the New Orleans Police Department and he believes was taken to jail. HELLER advised that he is unable to give the specific date of OSWALD's arrest at this time but believes this can be checked with the New Orleans Police Department. He is of the opinion that this was some time during the month of August, 1963.

As a result of this arrest he contacted attorney JACK NELSON and advised him of OSWALD's predicament because he felt OSWALD would probably be needing an attorney in this instance. He advised that he is not aware of what action, if any, NELSON may have taken in connection with OSWALD. HELLER advised that this was the only occasion he has ever seen OSWALD and has no further information as far as OSWALD is concerned.

HELLER advised that he is not acquainted with any of the following individuals:

JACK RUBY
O. H. LEE
A. J. HIDELL

[redacted]

Commission Exhibit No. 1928

On 11/27/63 at New Orleans, Louisiana File # NO 44-2064
NO 89-69

by SAs JAMES E. SCHMIDT, JR. and DEAN S. LYTLE :sms Date dictated 11/27/63

COMMISSION EXHIBIT No. 1928

FD-302 (Rev. 1-25-60) FEDERAL BUREAU OF INVESTIGATION

[redacted]

Commission Exhibit No. 1929 Date November 27, 1963

Mrs. RUTH KLOEPFER, 306 Pine Street, furnished the following information:

At some time in July, 1963 she received a long distance call from a Mrs. RUTH PAINE in Irving, Texas. Mrs. PAINE said she had gotten Mrs. KLOEPFER's name from a Mrs. ELEANOR HAMMOND, 1202 Bandera Lane, Garland, Texas. Mrs. KLOEPFER knew Mrs. HAMMOND to be a Quaker and active in the Friends Meeting Group. Mrs. PAINE wanted to ask a favor of Mrs. KLOEPFER, going on to say she would like Mrs. KLOEPFER to visit a Mrs. LEE OSWALD at 4907 Magazine Street. Mrs. PAINE identified Mrs. OSWALD as a friend of Mrs. PAINE who was having domestic trouble and feared her husband might send her back to Russia. Mrs. PAINE wanted Mrs. KLOEPFER to find someone who could speak Russian in case Mrs. OSWALD, who was about to have a baby, needed help. Mrs. KLOEPFER agreed to do this but did not do so as soon as she had anticipated.

About two or three days later she received a second long distance call from Mrs. PAINE. She told Mrs. PAINE she had not been to see Mrs. OSWALD as yet. Mrs. PAINE stated that was fine because in the meantime she had received a letter from Mrs. OSWALD who informed that Mr. OSWALD had returned, that they were not separating, and that Mr. OSWALD was not sending her back to Russia. She promised Mrs. PAINE she would visit Mrs. OSWALD anyway to see if she could help.

She then received a letter from Mrs. PAINE which was dated July 18, 1963 and with which was included a copy of a letter Mrs. PAINE had written to Mrs. PAUL BLANCHARD. Mrs. KLOEPFER furnished these two letters and they read as follows:

"July 18

"Dear Ruth Kloepfer -

"The enclosed speaks for itself. I don't know, of course, whether Mrs. Blanchard is on vacation, or will get this letter promptly. I have only her home address, which might go to her directly on Saturday, but on Monday she would be at the Unitarian Church (I

On 11/27/63 at New Orleans, Louisiana File # NO 89-69

by SA'S TROY H. GIST & EUGENE E. BJORN :dc Date dictated 11/27/63

This document contains neither recommendations nor conclusions of the FBI. It is the property of the FBI and is loaned to your agency; it and its contents are not to be distributed outside your agency.

189

COMMISSION EXHIBIT No. 1929

2

NO 89-69/dc

"judge) and not see her home mail until evening.

"As you see, I feel finding a Russian speaker is very important not only to get the present news, but to act as a contact for Marina should she need emergency help. I doubt one year of college Russian would be sufficient, although your daughter would probably find contact with Marina rewarding. What they could say to each other, however, would be severely limited.

"I very much appreciate your taking interest in this matter.

"Sincerely
/S/: Ruth Paine".

"2515 W. 5th Street
Irving, Texas
July 18, 1963

"Mrs. Paul Blanchard
4721 Perrier
New Orleans 15, La.

"Dear Mrs. Blanchard,

"Mrs. Philip Harper, the secretary at the Dallas Unitarian Church suggested I write to you when I told her of the following problem.

"I have a girl friend in New Orleans whom I have not heard from for over a month. She is from the Soviet Union and came to this country over a year ago with her husband, an american whom she met and married there.

"Marina's contact with speakers of English has been small and she still speaks and understands very little in English. (She and I speak and correspond in Russian.) Her last letter stated that she thought

190

COMMISSION EXHIBIT No. 1929—Continued

"she might have to go back to the Soviet Union, something she would prefer not to do. But she and her husband have not been getting along, and he has said that he would like her to go back. They have a baby girl 1½ years old, and are expecting a second child in October. Marina's last letter also stated that she has not been able to make contact with any Russian speaking people in N.O.

"Frankly, I'm worried. I have no way of calling them and getting current information directly. I would like to ask you to seek a Russian speaking person there who would be able to go and visit with Marina, thereby making contact for her with someone of the N.O. Russian community. With such a contact she could seek help if she needs it.

"Yesterday evening, in my concern, I telephoned Mrs. Ruth A. Kloepfer (Mrs. Warner) 306 Pine Street, New Orleans 18, UN 6-0389. She is clerk of the N.O. Friends Meeting. (Quakers) I asked her also to look for someone who could speak Russian and go to visit Marina. She could not think of anyone she knew who could speak the language, but said she would go. It is a great kindness on her part to do this. She does not know me any more than you do.

"Marina's full name and address is: Mrs. Lee Oswald, 4907 Magazine, N.O. It is my impression that this address is not far from your church.

"If you would be so kind, please call Mrs. Kloepfer and see if she has any news. I am asking for your help in addition to hers because of her mention that she knew no one in the Russian community. Perhaps between you you can find some Russian speakers. There must be quite a few in N. O. The language barrier is very real; I don't believe Marina would be able to convey much to a person speaking only English. (Russian is her only language.)

"On July 27th I plan to leave here for vacation in the East. If there is any point to my doing so I will plan to drive (to Mass.) via New Orleans. If Marina has already left for the Soviet Union, of course, there would be no point in my coming.

"My address July 31 to 12 will be c/o Young, Naushon Island, Woods Hole, Mass. After that time until Sept. 17 it will be c/o Arthur Young, Paoli, Penna. I am hoping, of course, to know something by the 27th, but add these addresses in case they should prove useful.

"Any help you can give on this whole matter will be greatly appreciated.

"Sincerely,

/S/: Ruth Paine

"Ruth Paine
(Mrs. Michael R. Paine)

"carbon to:
"Ruth A. Kloepfer
306 Pine Street
New Orleans, 18, La. "

One evening, probably during latter July or early August, 1963 she went to visit Mrs. OSWALD at 4907 Magazine Street. LEE OSWALD met her at the door and was not receptive to her visit until she stated Mrs. PAINE had requested she drop by to see Mrs. OSWALD. During this brief visit, LEE OSWALD translated her conversation with Mrs. OSWALD. She asked OSWALD if he was working. He said he was not but was looking for work. She asked him what kind of work he did and he replied that he was a mechanic and had also done dark room and photographic work. She asked OSWALD if he or Mrs. OSWALD had relatives in the New Orleans area who could assist Mrs. OSWALD in the event he was away. He identified an aunt of his as Mrs. (FNU) MURRETT, telephone HU 84326.

Mrs. KLOEPFER stated she made no attempt to locate any Russian speaking person to visit with Mrs. OSWALD and she had no further contact with Mrs. PAINE or OSWALD until in September, 1963. On Friday, September 20, 1963 she received a call from Mrs. PAINE who stated she was in New Orleans and visiting in the OSWALD residence. Mrs. KLOEPFER told Mrs. PAINE she would visit with them the following Sunday September 22, 1963. On Sunday afternoon about 2:00 P.M., she and her two daughters, KAROL and RUTH ANN, both of whom speak Russian, called upon LEE and Mrs. OSWALD and Mrs. PAINE at 4907 Magazine Street. They visited the above for approximately one hour. Upon entering this residence they noticed the PAINE station wagon was packed and asked OSWALD about this. He stated Mrs. OSWALD was going to Texas with Mrs. PAINE and they were about ready to leave. OSWALD indicated he was staying in New Orleans for a couple of days after which he was going north or to Philadelphia, or to "somewhere in the East". They asked him why he was making this trip and he was very evasive and indefinite about where he was going or why but said something to the effect that his trip pertained to business.

She recalled that in conversation during the above visit, OSWALD expressed a fondness for Russia. They asked him why he left Russia and returned to the United States if he was fond of it there. OSWALD stated living conditions in Russia were not very good and he did not want to raise his children there. They asked him how he was able to stay in Russia for an extended visit. OSWALD said everyone who stays in Russia has to be a citizen, after which he related he had been a tourist in Russia for about a month and then became a citizen. He also made mention on the fact that he had a rather difficult time in getting back into the United States, adding that it usually takes six months to get into Russia and about six months to get out.

193

Mrs. KLOEPFER stated she had never known Mrs. PAINE and had never heard of LEE or Mrs. OSWALD prior to the above two contacts. She stated she had not seen Mrs. PAINE or the OSWALDS subsequent to the September 22, 1963 visit. Mrs. KLOEPFER furnished the above two letters in order that copies could be made of them.

194

FD-302 (Rev. 1-25-60)

FEDERAL BUREAU OF INVESTIGATION

Date 11/29/63

1 Reverend ALBERT D'ORLANDO, Unitarian Church, 1800 Jefferson Avenue, who resides at 7700 Nelson Street, advised that in or about the last week in July, 1963, he received a letter from Mrs. PAUL BLANCHARD in Connecticut. She enclosed a letter she had received from a Mrs. RUTH PAINE, Irving, Texas, which asked for assistance to Mrs. LEE OSWALD. The letter also mentioned that Mrs. PAINE had called Mrs. RUTH KLOEPFER about Mrs. OSWALD, so he talked to Mrs. KLOEPFER about the matter. Mrs. KLOEPFER said she had already talked with the OSWALD family once and would do so again, taking along her two daughters who could speak Russian. He pursued the matter no further and never met the OSWALD family. He said he knew of no one in his Church, other than Mrs. KLOEPFER, who knew the OSWALD family or ever talked to them.

—Commission Exhibit No. 1930

On 11/29/63 at New Orleans, Louisiana File # NO 89-69

by SA TROY H. GIST /jas Date dictated 11/29/63

229

This document contains neither recommendations nor conclusions of the FBI. It is the property of the FBI and is loaned to your agency; it and its contents are not to be distributed outside your agency.

COMMISSION EXHIBIT NO. 1930

FD-302 (Rev. 1-25-60)

FEDERAL BUREAU OF INVESTIGATION

Date November 29, 1963

1 DEAN ANDREWS, Attorney, Room 202, Hotel Dieu Hospital, advised that his physicians will permit him to return home November 29, 1963 and within a few days he hopes to be strong enough to go to his office, where he will attempt to identify this individual whom he believed to be named CLAY BERTRAND. ANDREWS advised he had been unable to identify the individual who called him and asked him to defend LEE HARVEY OSWALD in Dallas, Texas. He stated this individual had called him on Saturday, November 23, 1963.

—Commission Exhibit No. 1931

On 11/29/63 at New Orleans, Louisiana File # NO 89-69

by SA REGIS L. KENNEDY /lyc Date dictated 11/29/63

230

This document contains neither recommendations nor conclusions of the FBI. It is the property of the FBI and is loaned to your agency; it and its contents are not to be distributed outside your agency.

COMMISSION EXHIBIT NO. 1931

FD-302 (Rev. 1-25-60) **FEDERAL BUREAU OF INVESTIGATION**

Date 11/29/63

1 Mrs. PAUL BLANCHARD, 4721 Perrier Street, advised that sometime in July, she was in Connecticut visiting relatives when she received a letter from a Mrs. RUTH PAINE, Irving, Texas, who said she had obtained her name from some person in Texas. Mrs. PAINE was concerned about the welfare of Mrs. LEE OSWALD. She was on an extended visit and knew that she could not visit Mrs. OSWALD, so she forwarded the letter to Reverend ALBERT D'ORLANDO, Unitarian Church, 1800 Jefferson Avenue. She never inquired about the matter further and never met LEE or Mrs. OSWALD.

Commission Exhibit No. 1932

On 11/29/63 at New Orleans, Louisiana File # NO 89-69

by SA TROY H. GIST /jas 231 Date dictated 11/29/63

This document contains neither recommendations nor conclusions of the FBI. It is the property of the FBI and is loaned to your agency; it and its contents are not to be distributed outside your agency.

COMMISSION EXHIBIT No. 1932

FD-302 (Rev. 1-25-60) **FEDERAL BUREAU OF INVESTIGATION**

Commission Exhibit No. 1933 — Date 11/23/63

Mr. ADRIAN T. ALBA, residence 624 Focis Street, Metairie, Louisiana, advised that he owns and operates the Crescent City Garage, 618 Magazine Street, New Orleans, Louisiana.

Mr. ALBA advised that he knew LEE OSWALD while OSWALD was employed at the William B. Reily and Company, Inc. next door to his garage. He stated that employees of the latter company would occasionally get cold drinks from the dispensing machine at his place of business and would sit in the waiting room of his office, drink their soft drinks and look at magazines which he maintained there. He explained that he, ALBA, was a gun collector and recalled that OSWALD showed an intense interest in guns and talked freely about guns. He stated OSWALD seemed to have quite a good knowledge of firearms. He recalled that on one occasion, the exact date of which he could not set, he had ordered a carbine from the National Rifle Association at a cost of $30.00. In discussing this, OSWALD wanted to know if ALBA could get one for him also. Mr. ALBA stated he advised OSWALD that he could get this gun at this price as a member of the National Rifle Association and each member was allowed to purchase only one. He continued that OSWALD told him to go ahead and get the carbine and that he, OSWALD, would make an offer on the gun that Mr. ALBA could not afford to turn down.

Mr. ALBA stated he did not sell this or any other gun to OSWALD nor has he ordered a gun of any type for OSWALD.

He further recalled that OSWALD showed an intense interest in a Japanese rifle that Mr. ALBA had had customized as a part of his gun collection. He recalled that OSWALD was interested in the number of inches that had been cut from the barrel of this gun and was interested in the twist of the rifling. Mr. ALBA pointed out that he usually cleaned his guns at his office to avoid any accident to his children at home, and this is why OSWALD knew of his guns and saw some of them. He recalled that OSWALD would "bury himself" in the gun magazines kept on the coffee table in the waiting room of the garage and otherwise seemed very quiet and smug.

On 11/23/63 at New Orleans, Louisiana File # NO 89-69

by SA LESTER G. DAVIS /cv 264 Date dictated 11/23/63

This document contains neither recommendations nor conclusions of the FBI. It is the property of the FBI and is loaned to

COMMISSION EXHIBIT No. 1933

NO 89-69/cv
2

Mr. ALBA recalled that on one occasion, the exact date of which he could not set, OSWALD asked to borrow one of his gun magazines and took it with him. He could not identify the magazine which OSWALD borrowed recalling that OSWALD was reading it and had it open at the time he asked to borrow it. He therefore did not see the magazine cover and did not ask OSWALD which magazine he was referring to. He further recalled that a few days later OSWALD mentioned to him that he had returned the magazine indicating he had replaced it on the coffee table. Mr. ALBA stated he did not see OSWALD return the magazine or check concerning it. He advised he in fact maintained no check on the magazines which he gets by subscription and by purchase from magazine counters and keeps no track of persons who read them.

In order to determine if he was talking about the right man, Mr. ALBA checked the photograph of LEE HARVEY OSWALD in the November 23, 1963, issue of the Times-Picayune, New Orleans newspaper. Upon looking at the photograph of OSWALD who was described as being in custody at Dallas, Texas, in connection with the assassination of President JOHN FITZGERALD KENNEDY, Mr. ALBA stated that this was a photograph of the LEE OSWALD he was referring to and the person who borrowed his gun magazine.

Mr. ~~OSWALD~~ Alba made available his supply of gun magazines which were maintained in the waiting room of the Crescent City Garage referred to above. These consist of the following:

June, 1963 issue of "The American Rifleman"

July, 1963 issue of "The American Rifleman"

September, 1963 issue of "The American Rifleman"

October, 1963 issue of "The American Rifleman"

November, 1963 issue of "The American Rifleman"

265

COMMISSION EXHIBIT No. 1933—Continued

NO 89-69/cv
3

January, 1964 issue of "Guns and Hunting"

December, 1958 issue of "Field and Stream"

266

COMMISSION EXHIBIT No. 1933—Continued

FD-302 (Rev. 1-25-60)

FEDERAL BUREAU OF INVESTIGATION

1

Date 11/25/63

Mr. ADRIAN ALBA, 624 Focis Street, Metairie, Louisiana, who operates the Crescent City Garage, 618 Magazine Street, New Orleans, advised that he now recalls an additional conversation he had with LEE H. OSWALD who was formerly employed at William B. Reily and Company, Inc. Coffee Plant next door to his garage. He explained that being a gun collector, he, ALBA, had one of his rifles at the garage office, cleaning it, and OSWALD saw it. He was interested in the gun and during conversation concerning it spoke about and discussed the merits of small caliber and larger caliber bullets. He recalled that OSWALD mentioned that a smaller caliber bullet was more deadly than a larger one, to which point ALBA agreed.

Mr. ALBA stated that in the several conversations he had with OSWALD concerning firearms, OSWALD was only interested in rifles. He explained that OSWALD never spoke of pistols or other guns but on one occasion commented that the carbine was indeed the finest of all rifles. He believed that OSWALD preferred the carbine over any gun made, although he did show interest in other type rifles such as a Japanese rifle ALBA had at his office on one occasion cleaning it.

Mr. ALBA expressed the opinion that OSWALD would necessarily have had a great deal of practice in firing a rifle with a scope sight to have been able to "get off as many shots" as he did during the assassination of President KENNEDY at Dallas, Texas. He further explained that having had experience in shooting rifles with scope sights he knows that it takes a period of time for one to adjust his eyesight to the image at which he is firing after each shot. He added that this is not as easy as an open sight and that a bolt action rifle would add to the time necessarily consumed in firing such a rifle. He therefore believed that OSWALD had much practice in firing a gun of this type.

Mr. ALBA advised, however that he knew of no rifle practice which OSWALD had engaged in while in New Orleans, adding that from his conversation with OSWALD he did not believe that OSWALD belonged to any of the local gun clubs. He added that it would have been almost impossible for OSWALD to practice with a rifle around New Orleans unless he belonged to a gun club.

—Commission Exhibit No. 1934

On 11/25/63 at New Orleans, Louisiana File # NO 89-69

by SA'S LESTER G. DAVIS & JOHN WILLIAM MILLER /bal Date dictated 11/25/63

324

COMMISSION EXHIBIT NO. 1934

FD-302 (Rev. 1-25-60)

FEDERAL BUREAU OF INVESTIGATION

1

Date November 25, 1963

Mr. FORD O'NEAL, (NA), Identification Bureau, Mississippi Highway Safety Patrol, Wiggins, Mississippi, a lifelong resident of Wiggins, advised telephonically that he was not acquainted with anyone in the Wiggins or Stone County area identifiable with YVES LEANDEZ. Mr. O'NEAL advised he would make inquiry in an effort to develop background information, if any, concerning this individual.

Mr. O'NEAL subsequently telephonically advised that he had contacted the following officials, all lifelong residents of the Wiggins area, none of whom were personally aware of anyone in the area identifiable with YVES LEANDEZ and none of whom had any reference to this person in their respective records.

H. W. PRESTON, Sheriff of Stone County;

Mrs. ESTELLE BOWDEN, Clerk, Local Draft Board;

Mrs. MYRTLE BAKER, Postmistress;

Mrs. JAMES ALFORD, Credit Bureau of Wiggins.

Mr. O'NEAL advised he felt certain if LEANDEZ had lived for any period of time in the Wiggins area, under this name that one or more of the persons named would have heard of him.

—Commission Exhibit No. 1935

On 11/25/63 at Gulfport, Mississippi File # NO 89-69

by SA WILLIAM F. DUKES /sw Date dictated 11/25/63

325

COMMISSION EXHIBIT NO. 1935

FD-302 (Rev. 1-25-60)

FEDERAL BUREAU OF INVESTIGATION

1 — Commission Exhibit No. 1936 — Date November 26, 1963

JULIAN EVANS, 1910 Prytania Street, New Orleans, Louisiana, was interviewed at his place of residence, and supplied the following information:

The first time that EVANS met the OSWALD family was one day, exact date and time unknown, while EVANS was in the Covington area. He said that at that time LEE HARVEY OSWALD was approximately seven years old. EVANS and his wife, MYRTLE EVANS, maintained a friendship with the OSWALDs, who, at that time he believed resided in a house on Alvar Street, New Orleans, which was owned by Mrs. OSWALD. Subsequently, Mrs. OSWALD sold her house at Alvar Street he believed, and then moved in with her sister, address unknown. He advised that in approximately May of 1954, Mrs. OSWALD and her son, LEE HARVEY OSWALD, moved into 1454 St. Mary Street, apartment six, where they resided until approximately November, 1954. He stated that at that time, namely May, 1954, Mrs. OSWALD decided to move from the upstairs apartment because the rent was too high. He advised that she took an apartment next door at 1452 St. Mary Street and resided in that apartment until approximately May, 1955. He advised that at the time OSWALD lived at the above residences, which are owned by him, LEE HARVEY OSWALD appeared to be a head strong, boisterous individual. He stated that on occasions he would holler in a loud tone of voice to his mother. He advised that he could not recall, nor could he make out the exact language he did use when he had arguments with his mother.

He advised generally OSWALD appeared to be a quiet fellow who did not associate much with the neighbors. He said he could not remember any close associates which OSWALD had during the period of time he resided at 1454 and 1452 St. Mary Street. He advised that recently he mentioned to some of the neighbors in that area, as well as the grocery store owners, that OSWALD had resided at the above addresses, but none of these people could recall him. He advised that he never noticed any of the literature which OSWALD did read, nor did he ever hear him make any comments regarding either the Communist or Marxist philosophy. He advised he never knew of any incident where OSWALD was involved in any fights in the neighborhood, although he recalls one time when OSWALD came home from school apparently suffering from an injury which he assumed OSWALD suffered as a result of a fight.

On 11/26/63 at New Orleans, Louisiana File # NO 89-69

by SA JOHN M. MC CARTHY /cjo Date dictated 11/26/63

327

NO 89-69 /cjo
2

EVANS advised that he had no indication from any of OSWALD's actions while he was a young boy, that he was in any way disloyal to the United States.

EVANS recalled that his wife had told him that MARGURITE OSWALD was married twice. He recalled that his wife informed him that at the time LEE HARVEY OSWALD's father, who was MARGURITE's second husband, died, MARGURITE OSWALD was about seven months pregnant with LEE HARVEY OSWALD. He advised that his wife also had told him that when MARGURITE OSWALD want out for an evening, she would leave LEE with a babysitter (name and address unknown), and when Mrs. OSWALD would return, she would notice that LEE had welts on his body which he apparently received as a result of a beating.

EVANS advised that in approximately May of 1955, the OSWALD family moved from the apartment they occupied at 1452 St. Mary Street, and moved to an apartment on Exchange Place in New Orleans, exact address unknown. He advised he hadn't seen LEE HARVEY OSWALD from the time that he left 1452 St. Mary, until about the Spring of 1963, exact date unknown, when OSWALD returned to New Orleans.

In the spring of 1963, exact date unknown, LEE HARVEY OSWALD came to his home looking for an apartment. He stated that his wife, MYRTLE EVANS, answered the door and asked him if he recalled LEE HARVEY OSWALD. He advised that he did remember the boy and was surprised to see him again. EVANS advised that his wife told OSWALD that she had no apartment currently available, at which time they conversed for about an hour in the house. EVANS advised that during that brief period of time OSWALD mentioned nothing concerning his association or activity with the Fair Play for Cuba Committee or any attachment with any other official organization. He advised that OSWALD had told him that he had married while he was in Russia and when MYRTLE EVANS queried him as to whether OSWALD had given up his United States Citizenship,

328

NO 89-69 /cjo
3

OSWALD replied in the negative. EVANS stated that he did not notice at that time whether or not OSWALD had any baggage with him. He advised that to the best of his recollection, OSWALD arrived at his home by public transportation. He advised that in March of 1963, OSWALD was working for the Reily Coffee House in New Orleans, but cannot definitely be sure.

EVANS stated that after this brief conversation, MYRTLE EVANS accompanied OSWALD in his search for an apartment. He advised that it took them approximately one-half day to find the apartment on Magazine Street, exact address unknown. He stated that his wife informed him that OSWALD seemed pleased with the apartment at that time, but said that he did not believe his wife would like it because while OSWALD and his wife were in Russia, they lived in a new apartment. OSWALD advised EVANS, had also mentioned that he was going to establish an apartment in New Orleans and then send for his wife, who he believed at that time was in Russia.

EVANS advised that during the time he has known LEE HARVEY OSWALD, he cannot recall any mention on the part of OSWALD to assassinate President KENNEDY. He stated that from his association with OSWALD, he did not think that OSWALD would be the type to assassinate President KENNEDY. He based this conclusion on the fact that he felt that OSWALD was an introvert and a a recluse individual, who did not have time to associate generally in social circles. He advised that he could be wrong in his opinion.

JULIAN EVANS advised that he recalls that sometime, exact date unknown, MARGURITE OSWALD worked in a stocking place on Canal Street near the Audubon Building as a manager and buyer.

He stated that he cannot recall the exact name or location of this particular establishment. He further advised that he does not have any records available concerning the occupant of 1454 St. Mary Street and 1452 St. Mary Street, New Orleans, during the period May, 1954, and 1955. He stated that the present occupants of these residences are fairly current and would not have any knowledge concerning OSWALD. He advised that his memory fails him as to the name of the people who occupied the building during the above period.

329

COMMISSION EXHIBIT No. 1936—Continued

NO 89-69 /cjo
4

JULIAN EVANS stated that his recollection of the OSWALD family and their activities is not too clear and complete. He stated that his wife, MYRTLE EVANS, would be in a better position to know more about the OSWALDs since she had been in closer contact with them than he.

330

COMMISSION EXHIBIT No. 1936—Continued

KRLD reel 23"B" Item 1 November 23, 1963

Q. Dan, is there any further information on that name we had earlier about a Mr. Abt in New York?

RATHER. That came about in this manner. Oswald was being taken past a group of reporters. There is a very large contingent of reporters from all over the world in the corridors of the Dallas Police Headquarters. On numerous occasions when Oswald is transported from one office to another or from one floor of the building to another, he is brought right past the newsmen. This morning, Oswald was brought past that contingent. He spotted a microphone and as police whisked him past the microphone Oswald reached in the direction of the microphone and said, "I would like to contact Mr. Abt, A-B-T, Mr. Abt in New York to defend me." Now that is the only quote that we have had out of Mr. Oswald as to who he would like to have defend him.

Q. We had a report up here a while ago that Oswald had refused to take the lie detector test.

RATHER. That is our understanding -- that he has refused to take a lie detector test. There wasn't much talk about a lie detector test until about 4 or 5 hours ago and at that time police began to speak in terms of possibly submitting him to a lie detector test but we understand from the police detectives who have been interrogating him that he was asked on several occasions to take a lie detector test and that he declined.

COMMISSION EXHIBIT NO. 1937

KRLD reel 25"A" November 23, 1963

DAN RATHER IN DALLAS REPORTING

Jose Rodriguez Molina was brought in for questioning this morning. He was not held for any long period of time nor has he been charged. But Molina has been identified by, I believe, the Justice Department, and you might correct me on this Allen, I believe he has been identified by the Justice Department as a possible subversive but at any rate Molina has a long record of being connected with suspicious organizations and a lot of people are talking in terms of, well, you know, maybe there is more to this than just the case of one man and one act. But it is going to take a long time before we ever know for sure, if we ever do.

COMMISSION EXHIBIT NO. 1937—Continued

FD-302 (Rev. 1-25-60) FEDERAL BUREAU OF INVESTIGATION

Date 11/27/63

1

Dr. CUTHBERT J. BROWN, 1110 Maison Blanche Building, New Orleans, Louisiana, advised that he had no personal recollection of LEE HARVEY OSWALD or his relatives. Dr. BROWN stated that his records showed that he treated a Mrs. L. OSWALD, 1010 Bartholomew Street, New Orleans, Louisiana, on October 14, 1941. She was 31 years of age at that time. He treated her again on September 10, 1942, at which time she advised him that she resided at 227 Atlantic Avenue, Algiers, Louisiana.

Dr. BROWN stated that the above Mrs. OSWALD brought her 3 year old son, LEE OSWALD, in for treatment of impetigo, a disease of the skin, on August 17, 1942. The records further showed that Dr. BROWN removed a wart from a finger of LEE OSWALD on July 12, 1943. OSWALD's address at the latter date was shown as 2136 Broadway, New Orleans, Louisiana.

The records of Dr. BROWN contain no additional information inasmuch as the treatment was rendered during World War II and the doctor stated that he was extremely busy and was unable to keep detailed records.

Commission Exhibit No. 1938

on 11/26/63 at New Orleans, Louisiana File # NO 89-69

by SA MERRIMAN D. DIVEN/lrs Date dictated 11/27/63

334

This document contains neither recommendations nor conclusions of the FBI. It is the property of the FBI and is loaned to your agency; it and its contents are not to be distributed outside your agency.

COMMISSION EXHIBIT NO. 1938

FD-302 (Rev. 1-25-60)

FEDERAL BUREAU OF INVESTIGATION

Date November 26, 1963

1

Mr. JOSEPH COLLARA, 15 East Chalmette Circle, St. Bernard, advised that he was the President of the St. Bernard Pistol and Rifle Range Association and that he knew of no member by the name of LEE H. OSWALD and/or A. J. HIDELL or other similar phonetic sounding names.

COLLARA advised that the only other rifle associations in the area of which he knew were the Louisiana State Pistol and Rifle Association and the Crescent Gun Club.

— Commission Exhibit No. 1939 —

On 11/26/63 at New Orleans, La. File # NO 89-69

by SA JOHN WILLIAM MILLER/mh Date dictated 11/26/63

335

COMMISSION EXHIBIT No. 1939

FD-302 (Rev. 1-25-60)

FEDERAL BUREAU OF INVESTIGATION

Date November 26, 1963

Mr. ALFRED A. CLAUDE, JR., 2905 Buffon Street, Chalmette, Louisiana, telephone number 271-3281, was interviewed at his place of employment Chrysler Aerospace Division, National Aeronautics and Space Administration (NASA), Michoud, Louisiana.

Mr. CLAUDE stated that he recalled LEE H. OSWALD in that while he was in the personnel department of the William B. Reily and Company, Inc., 640 Magazine Street, New Orleans, Louisiana, OSWALD answered an advertisement which was run in the local newspaper for maintenance employees. He stated that he could not recall the exact date but it was exactly four weeks prior to the time that he, CLAUDE, resigned his position with the William B. Reily and Company, Inc. which was on July 1, 1963. He stated that he did not have much contact with OSWALD but that he talked to him at the time he filed his application, checked over his application form, and noted that he had stated thereon that he had just recently been discharged from the U.S. Marine Corps. He stated that he was satisfied with the application filled out by OSWALD and his brief conversation with him and recommended that he be hired as an oiler. He stated that OSWALD's job as an oiler was to see that the machines were kept oiled and that he was also responsible for keeping the machines clean.

He stated that OSWALD did not associate with the other employees but seemed to stay by himself most of the time even during the coffee breaks and during the lunch period. He also advised that the only argument he ever had with OSWALD was when he put OSWALD on a late shift so that the machines could be oiled and cleaned after they had been used during the day and that OSWALD complained that he did not like to work on the late shift and he was advised by Mr. CLAUDE that he would see what arrangements could be made to again place him on a regular shift.

Mr. CLAUDE also advised that the work performed by OSWALD was very poor and that he had been on the verge of firing him on several occasions and the only reason he did not fire OSWALD was in view of the fact that the

— Commission Exhibit No. 1940 —

On 11/26/63 at New Orleans, Louisiana File # NO 89-69

by SA G. MYRYWIN ALDERSON :sms Date dictated 11/26/63

336

COMMISSION EXHIBIT No. 1940

NO 89-69/sms
2

maintenance department was short of employees and he decided to keep OSWALD on the job until additional employees could be hired.

He stated he did not know who OSWALD associated with after working hours and also he did not know what his activities were after he left the William B. Reily Company, Inc. each day. He also stated that he had never heard OSWALD discuss owning a gun or contemplating purchasing a gun.

Mr. CLAUDE stated that he never saw OSWALD drive an automobile and believed that he came to work each day on the Magazine bus inasmuch as he resided on Magazine Street and believed that the number was in the 4900 block. He also stated that OSWALD was never visited by his wife and that OSWALD had never made any statements indicating that he had resided in Russia and had married a Russian girl.

337

COMMISSION EXHIBIT No. 1940—Continued

FD-302 (Rev. 1-25-60)

FEDERAL BUREAU OF INVESTIGATION

Date November 27, 1963

Mr. JOHN D. BRANYON, 1316½ Short Street, New Orleans, Louisiana, was interviewed at his place of employment, the Boeing Aircraft Division, National Aeronautics and Space Administration, Michoud, Louisiana.

Mr. BRANYON stated that he was acquainted with LEE H. OSWALD inasmuch as he was then working for the William B. Reily Company, Inc., 640 Magazine Street, New Orleans, Louisiana, when OSWALD was hired in the maintenance department around June 1, 1963.

Mr. BRANYON stated that OSWALD was the "lone wolf" type always staying aloof from the other employees and never associating with them during the coffee breaks or lunch period. He stated that he had very little conversation with OSWALD but recalled that OSWALD told him that he was married, that he was an ex-marine, and that he was living with his folks. He stated that he did not recall if OSWALD furnished any address for his residence.

Mr. BRANYON advised that when OSWALD was hired he was turned over to him for instructions as to what he should do in the maintenance department in connection with his work as an oiler. He stated his job was to insure that the machines were kept oiled at all times and that he was also responsible for cleaning the machines after they had been used during the day. He stated that OSWALD was a poor worker and that he had to criticize him several times in view of the poor work he was doing in keeping the machines clean. He stated that OSWALD was still employed by the William B. Reily Company, Inc. when he, BRANYON, resigned on July 3, 1963, but that he was sure in view of the poor work that OSWALD was doing that he was not employed very long after July 3, 1963. He stated that he would not recommend OSWALD for any employment in view of the poor work that he had done while employed by the William B. Reily Company, Inc.

Mr. BRANYON stated he did not know who OSWALD associated with after working hours and he also did not know what his activities were after he left the William

— Commission Exhibit No. 1941 —

On 11/26/63 at New Orleans, Louisiana File # NO 89-69

by SA G. MYRYWIN ALDERSON :sms Date dictated 11/26/63

348

This document contains neither recommendations nor conclusions of the FBI. It is the property of the FBI and is loaned to your agency; it and its contents are not to be distributed outside your agency.

COMMISSION EXHIBIT No. 1941

NO 89-69/sms
2

B. Reily Company, Inc. each day. He also stated that he had never heard OSWALD discuss owning a gun or contemplating purchasing a gun.

349

COMMISSION EXHIBIT No. 1941—Continued

FD-302 (Rev. 1-25-60)

FEDERAL BUREAU OF INVESTIGATION

[redacted]

— Commission Exhibit No. 1942 — Date November 29, 1963

1

Lieutenant FRANCIS L. MARTELLO, Platoon Commander, First District, New Orleans Police Department, advised that on August 9, 1963 Lieutenant WILLIAM GAILLOT and Patrolmen FRANK HAYWARD and FRANK WILSON arrested LEE HARVEY OSWALD in the 700 block of Canal Street and charged him with violation of the City Ordinance relative to disturbing the peace by creating a scene. Arrested at the same time were CELSO MACARIO HERNANDEZ, CARLOS JOSE BRINGUIER and MIGUEL MARIANO CRUZ.

On the following morning about 10 a.m., August 10, 1963, Lieutenant MARTELLO noted a placard and some handbills which pertained to the Fair Play for Cuba Committee. He determined that it was the property of an arrested subject by the name of OSWALD. He asked the doorman to bring OSWALD in for an interview.

Lieutenant MARTELLO stated that as a result of this interview with OSWALD, he had made some detailed notes, which he still has in his possession, although he had not at any time dictated a report as a result of this interview. Lieutenant MARTELLO furnished the following memorandum concerning his interview of OSWALD on August 10, 1963, which he prepared as a result of a refreshment of his recollection from his original notes. Lieutenant MARTELLO remarked that his interview of OSWALD was merely for his general information and not in the nature of an official interrogation since he had been previously interviewed by the Intelligence Unit of the New Orleans Police Department.

Re Interview of LEE HARVEY OSWALD at First District Station, New Orleans Police Department on August 10, 1963:

"About 10 a.m. on Saturday, August 10, 1963, I observed a placard and handbills which had been placed into evidence against an accused person. This placard contained information concerning the Fair Play for Cuba Committee. I determined that a subject by the name of LEE HARVEY OSWALD was arrested on Friday, August 9, 1963 when he was passing out handbills on Canal Street and was carrying this placard about his person.

On 11/29/63 at New Orleans, Louisiana File # NO 89-69

by SA JOHN L. QUIGLEY /lyc Date dictated 11/29/63

364

COMMISSION EXHIBIT No. 1942

NO 89-69
2

"Prior to being assigned to the First District, he had worked with the Intelligence Unit for two years and since I was generally familiar with various groups and organizations that demonstrate or picket in the city, I decided I would question this individual to see if I could develop any information which would be of value and to ascertain if all interested parties had been notified.

"I requested the doorman to bring LEE HARVEY OSWALD into the interview room. I then took the material which was to be used as evidence into this room. At the same time I reviewed the arrest record on OSWALD and determined that while he was distributing Fair Play for Cuba literature on the street he became involved in a disturbance with CELSO MACARIO HERNANDEZ, CARLOS JOSE BRINGUIER and MIGUEL MARIANO CRUZ.

"When OSWALD was brought into the office, I introduced myself to him as Lieutenant FRANCIS L. MARTELLO and I was in uniform at the time.

"I asked OSWALD if he had any identification papers. At this time OSWALD produced his wallet. Upon my request, he removed the papers and I examined them. He had in his wallet a number of miscellaneous papers, cards and identification items. The only ones that I felt were of any significance were the following, which I made note of:

"1. Social Security Card bearing #433-54-3937 in the name of LEE HARVEY OSWALD;

"2. Selective Service draft card in the name of LEE HARVEY OSWALD bearing #41-114-395-32, classification - 4A. (I do not know what draft board was registered with.)

"3. Card bearing name LEE HARVEY OSWALD reflecting he was a member of the Fair Play for Cuba Committee; address listed as 799 Broadway, New York 3, New York; telephone #ORegon 4-8295, headquarters for Fair Play for Cuba Committee. Card was signed by V. T. LEE, Executive Secretary; card issued 5/28/63.

365

COMMISSION EXHIBIT No. 1942—Continued

NO 89-69
3

"4. Card for the New Orleans Chapter of the Fair Play for Cuba Committee in name of LEE HARVEY OSWALD signed by A. J. HIDELL, Chapter President, issued June 6, 1963

"The notes of my interview reflect that OSWALD gave his date of birth as October 18, 1938 at New Orleans, Louisiana; that he served three years in the U. S. Marine Corps and stated he was honorably discharged on July 17, 1959 from Santa Ana, California. His wife's name was MARINO PROSSA, a white female, age 21. OSWALD stated he had one daughter, JUNE LEE OSWALD, white female, 17 months of age, and he had been residing at 4907 Magazine Street with his wife and daughter for the past four months. OSWALD said that since 1959 he resided at 4709 Mercedes Street in Fort Worth, Texas and had also lived in Arlington, Texas. OSWALD said his mother's name was MARGARET OSWALD, his father, ROBERT LEE OSWALD, being deceased. He told me he had two brothers, ROBERT OSWALD, living in Fort Worth, Texas, and JOHN OSWALD, Arlington, Texas. He also stated he lived somewhere on Exchange Place in New Orleans but could not remember the address, and that he had attended Beauregard Junior High School and Warren Easton High School, both in New Orleans, and that he attended Riegeala West Elementary School in Fort Worth, Texas. OSWALD told me he had moved to New Orleans from Fort Worth about four months ago.

"When questioned about the Fair Play for Cuba Committee, OSWALD stated that he had been a member for three months. I asked how he had become affiliated with the Fair Play for Cuba Committee and he stated he became interested in that Committee in Los Angeles, California in 1958 while in the U. S. Marine Corps. The facts as to just how he first became interested in the Fair Play for Cuba Committee while in the Marine Corps are vague, however I recall that he said he had obtained some Fair Play for Cuba Committee literature and had gotten into some difficulty in the Marine Corps for having this literature.

"OSWALD was asked how many members of the Fair Play for Cuba Committee were in the New Orleans Chapter and he stated there were 35. I asked him to identify the members of the Fair Play for Cuba Committee in New

366

COMMISSION EXHIBIT No. 1942—Continued

NO 89-69
4

Orleans and he refused to give names of the members or any identifying data regarding them. OSWALD was asked why he refused and he said that this was a minority group holding unpopular views at this time and it would not be beneficial to them if he gave their names. OSWALD was asked approximately how many people attended meetings of the New Orleans Chapter of the Fair Play for Cuba Committee and he said approximately five attended the meetings, which were held once a month. He was asked where and he said at various places in the city. He was asked specifically at what addresses or locations were the meetings held and stated the meetings were held on Pine Street. He was asked at whose residence the meetings were held and he refused to give any further information. It should be noted at this time during prior investigation conducted, while I was a member of the Intelligence Unit, information was developed that Fair Play for Cuba Committee literature was found in the 1000 block of Pine Street, New Orleans, which was near the residence of Dr. LEONARD REISSMAN, a professor at Tulane University. This investigation was conducted by me.

"As I remember, Dr. REISSMAN was reported to be a member of the New Orleans Council of Peaceful Alternatives which is a 'ban the bomb' group recently established in the city and had conducted meetings and two or three demonstrations in the city. Knowing that Dr. REISSMAN was reportedly a member of the New Orleans Council of Peaceful Alternatives I thought there might be a tie between this organization and the Fair Play for Cuba Committee.

"When OSWALD stated that meetings of the Fair Play for Cuba Committee had been held on Pine Street, the name of Dr. REISSMAN came to mind. I asked OSWALD if he knew Dr. REISSMAN or if he held meetings at Dr. REISSMAN's house. OSWALD did not give me a direct answer to this question, however I gathered from the expression on his face and what appeared to be an immediate nervous reactions that there was possibly a connection between Dr. REISSMAN and OSWALD; this, however, is purely an assumption on my own part and I have nothing on which to base this. I also asked OSWALD if he knew a Dr. FORREST E. LA VIOLETTE, a professor at Tulane University.

367

NO 89-69
5

I asked him this question because I remembered that LA VIOLETTE allegedly had possession of Fair Play for Cuba literature during the year 1962. I cannot remember any further details about this nor do I have any information that he is or was connected with the Fair Play for Cuba Committee in New Orleans. OSWALD became very evasive in his answers and would not divulge any information concerning the Fair Play for Cuba Committee, where the group met, or the identities of the members.

OSWALD was then asked what religion he practiced and he stated he was a Lutheran and also that he was presently unemployed but had worked at William B. Reily Coffee Company, New Orleans, about three months, working on heavy machinery and earned $60 per week. He worked from May to July 17, 1963 at that company. He further stated that he worked for Jax Brewery approximately 1½ months ago.

"I asked him again about the members of the Fair Play for Cuba Committee in New Orleans and why the information was such a big secret; that if had nothing to hide, he would give me the information. OSWALD said one of the members of the Fair Play for Cuba Committee in New Orleans was named 'John' and that this individual went to Tulane University. He refused to give any more information concerning the Fair Play for Cuba Committee in New Orleans.

"Since he did not appear to be particularly receptive at this time, the interview was concluded and he was returned to the cell block. Prior to entering the cell block, OSWALD was again allowed to use the telephone.

"Several hours later after OSWALD was interviewed by a Special Agent of the Federal Bureau of Investigation, a white female came to the station and identified herself as Mrs. MURAT, who stated she was a relative of OSWALD and lived on France Street. She stated she wanted

368

to know the charge against OSWALD and I told her, explaining to her the procedure whereby OSWALD could be released. She became very reluctant to become involved in the release of OSWALD as she stated since he was involved with the Fair Play for Cuba Committee, she did not want to get mixed up with it in any way. I spoke to her concerning OSWALD's background and she stated OSWALD had a hard time coming up insofar as his family life was concerned and she felt that this had a direct bearing on his actions and that he had gone to Russia and stayed over there for a few years; he married while in Russia and came back to the United States with his wife. She stated OSWALD did not allow anything but Russian to be spoken in his home. She was asked why he did not allow English to be spoken and she related she had spoken to OSWALD's wife about this and she said this was his desire. She further stated she had asked OSWALD's wife if she liked America and the wife answered 'Yes I do' but said her husband (OSWALD) did not like America. I did not question her any further.

"After Mrs. MURAT left, I decided to further question OSWALD and had him again brought out of the cell to me. I then asked if he had given me all of the needed information about his background and he said he had. I asked him if he lived in Russia and he stated that somebody had told me this. He then admitted he had lived in Russia for 2½years, going there by "slow boat to Europe." I asked him how he got over there and he related he left Fort Worth, Texas, stayed in New Orleans a few days and then took the "slow boat to Europe." He took a tour of Europe and wound up in Russia. He lived in Moscow and Minsk, Russia and told me he lived there from October, 1959 to July, 1962. I asked him if his wife was Russian and he said yes. He said her true name was MARINO PROSSA and that it was an abreviation of her name, MARINO PROSSAKAYA; he said she was an alien M-1. I then asked him if he was a communist and he said he was not. I asked him if he was a socialist and he said 'guilty.' We then spoke at length concerning the philosophies of communism, socialism and America. He said he was in full accord with the book, Das Kapital,

369

which book was written by KARL MARX. I know that this book condemns the American way of government in entirety. I asked him if he thought that the communist way of life was better than the American way of life and he replied there was not true communism in Russia. He said that Marx was a socialist and although communism is attributed to MARX, that MARX was not a communist but a socialist. He stated this was the reason he did not consider himself to be a communist. I asked him what his opinion was of the form of communism in Russia since he had lived there for two years and he replied 'It stunk.' He said they have 'fat stinking politicians over there just like we have over here' and that they do not follow the great concepts of KARL MARX, that the leaders have everything and the people are still poor and depressed. I asked OSWALD why he would not allow members of his family to learn English as this would be required to educate his children and communicate with people. He stated the reason why he did this was because he hated America and he did not want them to become 'Americanized' and that his plans were to go back to Russia. He stated he had already applied to the State Department for a visa to go back by using the excuse that his wife was a Russian. I asked him what he thought about President JOHN F. KENNEDY and NIKITA KHRUSHCHEV. He said he thought they got along very well together. I then asked him if he had to place allegiance or make a decision between Russia or America, which he would choose and he said 'I would place my allegiance at the foot of democracy.' I then asked him if he would consider himself a 'student of the world', explaining that I meant by this a person who attempts to find a Utopia on earth'and that he said he could be classified as such an individual. I asked him if he had any religious convictions and whether he believed in God since KARL MARX did not believe in God. I was trying to find out if he was an atheist. His answer to me was that he was christened as a Lutheran but that he has not followed any religion since youth. I asked him if he was an agnostic and he said he could be classified 'as a Marxist in his beliefs.' I spoke to him about the Fair Play for Cuba Committee again and

370

NO 89-69
8

asked him if he knew that CASTRO had admitted that he was a Marxist-Leninist and he said he did. He was then asked if he truly believed CASTRO was really interested in the welfare of the Cuban people and he replied that he was not going to discuss the merits and demerits of CASTRO but was primarily concerned with the poor people of Cuba and that if this country would have good relations with the poor people of Cuba and quit worrying about CASTRO, that was his main concern; he stated this was the reason he was interested in the Fair Play for Cuba Committee.

"OSWALD was then returned to the cell block.

"I then took my notes, along with several copies of the literature of OSWALD, and placed them in a file folder, in the file cabinet.

"The day after the assassination of President JOHN F. KENNEDY, Mr. ADRIAN G. VIAL, U. S. Secret Service, who had spoken to me earlier at about 3 a.m. Saturday morning, November 23, 1963, wherein he had obtained information regarding my interview with OSWALD, came to the First District Station on Saturday, November 23, 1963 at about 3 p.m. and told me the Secret Service was conducting an official investigation regarding the assassination of the President of the United States. At the outset of the interview I got out the original file folder on LEE HARVEY OSWALD, opened it and gave Mr. VIAL all of the literature I had obtained from OSWALD, which consisted of some pamphlets, leaflets and booklets put out by the Fair Play for Cuba Committee headquarters. Upon going through these pamphlets I discovered a photograph of LEE HARVEY OSWALD which appeared to be a passport photograph, and a small piece of white paper containing handwritten notes on same. This photograph and paper had inadvertently become misplaced with the literature during the interview I had with OSWALD. This piece of paper, which was folded over twice and was about 2" by 3" in size, contained some English writing and some writing which appeared to me to be in a foreign language which I could not identify. Before I gave

3·71

COMMISSION EXHIBIT No. 1942—Continued

NO 89-69
9

this paper to Mr. VIAL, I made a copy of the information, which is as follows:

372

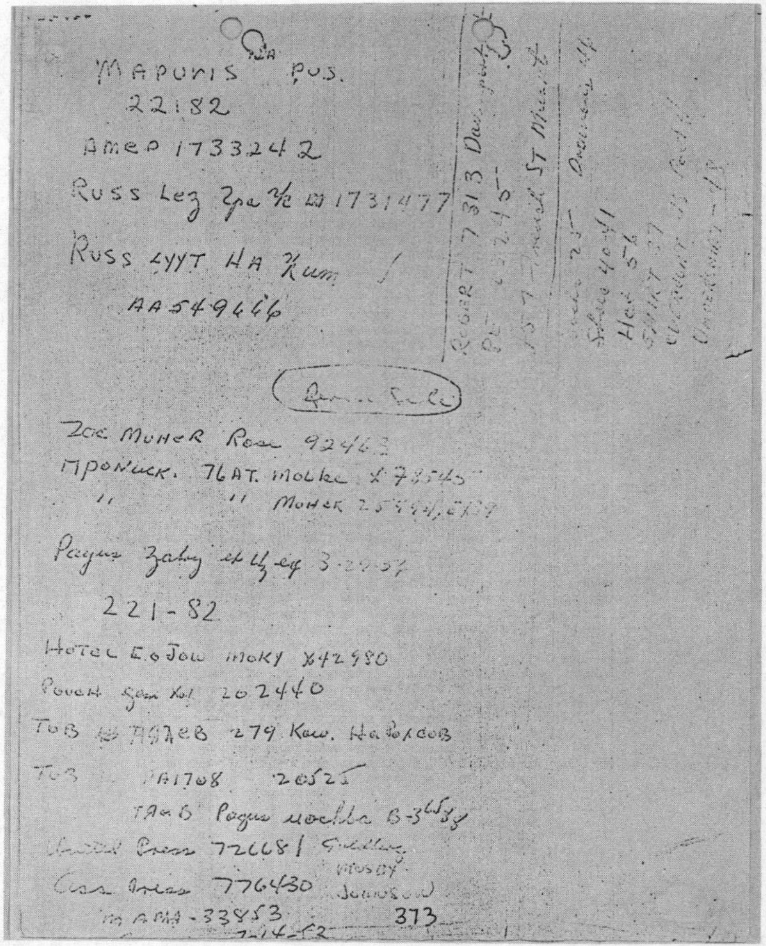
Mapuris pus.
22182
Amep 1733242
Russ Lez 1731477
Russ Hа
AA549446
221-82
Hotel 842980
202440
279
20525
726681
776430
Johnson
33853
373

APPLICATION FOR EMPLOYMENT

Date July 13, 1962

Name (Last Name First) Oswald Age 22 Born: Mo. Oct Day 18 Year 1939

Address 1501 7th St. Telephone PE-23245 Soc. Sec. No. 433 54 [redacted]

How long have you lived at this address? Birthplace? New Orleans Citizen? ✓ yes

Male ✓ Female Weight 150 Height 5 9 Any serious illness? none

Single Married ✓ Other No. Children 1 Ages 5 months

Other Dependents wife Explain

What kind of work are you applying for? sheet metal

What special qualifications do you have? 2½ years experience

What office machines can you operate? none

Who referred you to us? Texas State Em.

Do you have any relatives working for this Company? No

MILITARY SERVICE RECORD

Have you served in the Armed Forces? yes From 1956 To 1959

Branch of Service U S M C Duties sheet metal & mach.

Rank or rating at time of enlistment Pvt. Rating at time of discharge Sgt

Type of discharge Honourable Any disability? No

EDUCATION

SCHOOL	DATE FROM	DATE TO	NAME OF SCHOOL	CITY	COURSE	DID YOU GRADUATE
GRAMMAR	1950	1953	R. Glen West	F. W.	Gen	
HIGH	1953	1956	Jackson S H S	New Orleans	Gen	
COLLEGE						
OTHER						

EXPERIENCE (ENTER LAST JOB FIRST)

NAME AND ADDRESS OF COMPANY	DATE FROM	DATE TO	LIST YOUR DUTIES	STARTING SALARY	FINAL SALARY	REASON FOR LEAVING
Active Duty USMC			machinist and sheet metal worker			

Commission Exhibit No. 1943

REFERENCES (NOT RELATIVES)

NAME	ADDRESS	OCCUPATION
Peter P Gregory	Cont. in. Life Bldg.	Consultant oil Eng
Robert Oswald	Acme Brick Co.	Jun. Ex.

COMMISSION EXHIBIT NO. 1943

PAYROLL INFORMATION RECORD

PLANT: FT. WORTH DATE OF EMPLOYMENT: 7-17-62 RATE: $1.25 hr.

NAME: LEE HARVEY OSWALD S.S.NO.: 433-54-3937 DEPENDENTS: 3

ADDRESS: 1501 WEST 7TH. CITY: FT. WORTH STATE: TEXAS

JOB DESCRIPTION: SHEET METAL HELPER TEMPORARY: ☐ PERMANENT: ☒

ATTACHED TO THIS FORM ARE:

Employee's Withholding Exemption Certificate; FEDERAL (FORM W-4)
" " " GEORGIA

Any other forms which may be required for payroll calc

APPROVED BY: Tommy

— Commission Exhibit No. 1943-A —

FORM W-4 (Rev. June 1959) U. S. Treasury Department Internal Revenue Service

EMPLOYEE'S WITHHOLDING EXEMPTION CERTIFICATE

Print full name: LEE HARVEY OSWALD Social Security No. 435-54-3937

Print home address: 1501 WEST 7th ST. City FORT WORTH Zone TEXAS

EMPLOYEE: File this form with your employer. Otherwise, he must withhold U. S. income tax from your wages without exemption.

EMPLOYER: Keep this certificate with your records. If the employee is believed to have claimed too many exemptions, the District Director should be so advised.

HOW TO CLAIM YOUR WITHHOLDING EXEMPTIONS

1. If SINGLE, and you claim an exemption, write the figure "1" ....
2. If MARRIED, one exemption each for husband and wife if not claimed on another certificate.
   (a) If you claim both of these exemptions, write the figure "2"
   (b) If you claim one of these exemptions, write the figure "1" 2
   (c) If you claim neither of these exemptions, write "0"
3. Exemptions for age and blindness (applicable only to you and your wife but not to dependents):
   (a) If you or your wife will be 65 years of age or older at the end of the year, and you claim this exemption, write "1"; if both will be 65 or older, and you claim both of these exemptions, write "2" ....
   (b) If you or your wife are blind, and you claim this exemption, write the figure "1"; if both are blind, and you claim both of these exemptions, write the figure "2" ....
4. If you claim exemptions for one or more dependents, write the number of such exemptions. (Do not claim exemption for a dependent unless you are qualified under instruction 4 on other side.) 1
5. Add the number of exemptions which you have claimed above and write the total 3
6. Additional withholding per pay period under agreement with employer. See Instruction 1 .... $........

I CERTIFY that the number of withholding exemptions claimed on this certificate does not exceed the number to which I am entitled.

(Date) July 17, 1962 (Signed) Lee H Oswald

COMMISSION EXHIBIT NO. 1943–A

INSTRUCTIONS:

(1) All forms MUST be TYPEWRITTEN except for signature.
(2) Forms must be completed before the employee starts work.
(3) Forms on all new employees must be sent to the Franklin Park plant with the time cards covering the week in which the employee is hired.
(4) All spaces and lines of this form MUST be filled in.
(5) Use LEGAL NAMES only. DO NOT use nicknames or abbreviations.

TERMINATION OF EMPLOYMENT RECORD

PLANT: FT. WORTH DATE HIRED: 7-17-62 DATE TERMINATED: 10-8-62

NAME: LEE OSWALD S.S.NO. 433-54-3937 WOULD YOU REHIRE? YES

ADDRESS: 1501 WEST 7TH. CITY: FT. WORTH STATE: TEXAS

REASON FOR TERMINATION: ACCEPTED BETTER PAYING POSITION.

APPROVED BY: H. L. Conway

NOTE: This report must be TYPEWRITTEN:

— Commission Exhibit No. 1943-B —

405

1. NAME IN FULL — Last / First / Middle	SELECTIVE SERVICE NUMBER
OSWALD Lee Harvey	41 114 39 532
2. PLACE OF RESIDENCE — *Street and Number or RFD Route*: 3124 West 5th St.	3. DATE OF BIRTH: Oct 18, 1939
City, Town, or Village: Fort Worth — *Zone*: 7 — *County*: Tarrant — *State*: Texas	4. PLACE OF BIRTH: New Orleans, La.

5. MAILING ADDRESS (*If different from place of residence*) *Street and Number or RFD Route*

City, Town, or Village *Zone* *County* *State*

6. NAME AND ADDRESS OF PERSON WHO WILL ALWAYS KNOW YOUR ADDRESS

Robert Oswald, 7313 Davenport St., Ft. Worth(Brother)

7. OCCUPATION	8. NATURE OF BUSINESS, SERVICE RENDERED, OR CHIEF PRODUCT
Unemployed	

9. FIRM OR INDIVIDUAL BY WHOM EMPLOYED

10. PLACE OF EMPLOYMENT OR BUSINESS

Form Approved
Budget Bureau No. 33-R099.7.

SELECTIVE SERVICE SYSTEM
REGISTRATION CARD

SSS Form No. 1 (Revised 6-11-58) (over)

COMMISSION EXHIBIT NO. 1944

11. Active duty in the Armed Forces of the United States or a cobelligerent nation since Sept. 16, 1940:

BRANCH OF ARMED FORCES OR COUNTRY	SERVICE NO.	DATE OF ENTRY	DATE OF SEPARATION
USMC	1653230	24 Oct 56	11 Sep 59

12. Present membership in a reserve component of the Armed Forces:

BRANCH OF ARMED FORCES	SERVICE NO.	DATE OF ENTRY	GRADE
USMCR	1653230	11 Sep 59	Pfc

ORGANIZATION MARTC NAS Glenview, Ill

I affirm that I have verified the foregoing answers and that they are true:

Lee H. Oswald
(*Signature of registrant*)

DESCRIPTION OF REGISTRANT

13. Color of eyes Blue Color of hair Brown Complexion Med Height (approx.) 5 ft. 11 in.

Weight (approx.) 150 Other obvious physical characteristics that will aid in identification:

None

I certify that my answers are true; that the person registered has read or has had read to him his own answers; that I have witnessed his signature or mark and that all of his answers of which I have knowledge are true, except as follows:

None to my knowledge

Sep 14, 1959 (*Date of registration*) Lydia T. Sheridan (*Signature of registrar*)

Registrar for Local Board 114 (*Number*) Fort Worth (*City or county*) Texas (*State*)

GPO : 1958 OF—469390

COMMISSION EXHIBIT NO. 1944—Continued

GAN
7010
Date 11/26/63
Justice
7334
Addressograph Room

111-114 114 N R.

LEGEND: Insert N/A to the items below which are not applicable.

PERSONAL DATA

1. LAST NAME - FIRST NAME - MIDDLE NAME: OSWALD, Lee Harvey
2. SERVICE NUMBER: 1653230
3a. GRADE, RATE OR RANK: PFC (E-2)
b. DATE OF RANK (Day, Month, Year): 1Mar59
4. DEPARTMENT, COMPONENT AND BRANCH OR CLASS: USMC
5. PLACE OF BIRTH (City and State or Country): New Orleans, Louisiana
6. DATE OF BIRTH: DAY 18 MONTH Oct YEAR 39
7a. RACE: Caucasian
b. SEX: Male
c. COLOR HAIR: Brown
d. COLOR EYES: Grey
e. HEIGHT: 71"
f. WEIGHT: 150
8. U.S. CITIZEN: X YES ☐ NO
9. MARITAL STATUS: Single
10a. HIGHEST CIVILIAN EDUCATION LEVEL ATTAINED: High School - 1
b. MAJOR COURSE OR FIELD: Academic

TRANSFER OR DISCHARGE DATA

11a. TYPE OF TRANSFER OR DISCHARGE: Transferred to Marine Corps Reserve
b. STATION OR INSTALLATION AT WHICH EFFECTED: MABS, MCAS, El Toro, (Santa Ana), California
c. REASON AND AUTHORITY: 226-Dependency. Par 10273 MARCORMAN & MCO 1900.2B & CG 3dMAW's 5th End of 31Aug59
d. EFFECTIVE DATE: DAY 11 MONTH Sep YEAR 59
12. LAST DUTY ASSIGNMENT AND MAJOR COMMAND: MACS-9, MWHG, 3dMAW, AirFMFPac, MCAS, ElToro(SantaAna)California
13a. CHARACTER OF SERVICE: HONORABLE
b. TYPE OF CERTIFICATE: DD-217-MC

SELECTIVE SERVICE DATA

14. SELECTIVE SERVICE NUMBER: N/A
15. SELECTIVE SERVICE LOCAL BOARD NUMBER, CITY, COUNTY AND STATE: N/A
16. DATE INDUCTED: DAY MONTH N/A YEAR
17. DISTRICT OR AREA COMMAND TO WHICH RESERVIST TRANSFERRED: MARTC NAS, Glenview, Illinois

SERVICE DATA

18. TERMINAL DATE OF RESERVE OBLIGATION: DAY 8 MONTH Dec YEAR 62
19. CURRENT ACTIVE SERVICE OTHER THAN BY INDUCTION
a. SOURCE OF ENTRY: X ENLISTED (First Enlistment) ☐ ENLISTED (Prior Service) ☐ REENLISTED ☐ OTHER:
b. TERM OF SERVICE (Years): 3
c. DATE OF ENTRY: DAY 24 MONTH Oct YEAR 56
20. PRIOR REGULAR ENLISTMENTS: NONE
21. GRADE, RATE OR RANK AT TIME OF ENTRY INTO CURRENT ACTIVE SERVICE: Private
22. PLACE OF ENTRY INTO CURRENT ACTIVE SERVICE (City and State): Dallas, Texas
23. HOME OF RECORD AT TIME OF ENTRY INTO ACTIVE SERVICE (Street, RFD, City, County and State): 4936 Collinwood Street Fort Worth, Tarrant, Texas
25a. SPECIALTY NUMBER AND TITLE: 6741: AvnElectronic Operator
b. RELATED CIVILIAN OCCUPATION AND D. O. T. NUMBER: Radio Operator 0-61.30

24. STATEMENT OF SERVICE		YEARS	MONTHS	DAYS
a. CREDITABLE FOR BASIC PAY PURPOSES	(1) NET SERVICE THIS PERIOD	2	9	3
	(2) OTHER SERVICE	0	0	0
	(3) TOTAL (Line (1) + line (2))	2	9	3
b. TOTAL ACTIVE SERVICE		2	9	3
c. FOREIGN AND/OR SEA SERVICE		1	2	24

26. DECORATIONS, MEDALS, BADGES, COMMENDATIONS, CITATIONS AND CAMPAIGN RIBBONS AWARDED OR AUTHORIZED: NONE
27. WOUNDS RECEIVED AS A RESULT OF ACTION WITH ENEMY FORCES (Place and date, if known): NONE

Texas Local Board No. 114
Selective Service System
OCT 12 1959
300 W. Vickery, Room 2227
Fort Worth 4, Texas

28. SERVICE SCHOOLS OR COLLEGES, COLLEGE TRAINING, COURSES AND/OR POST-GRADUATE COURSES SUCCESSFULLY COMPLETED

SCHOOL OR COURSE a	DATES (From - To) b	MAJOR COURSES c
Jacksonville, Florida	18Mar57-3May57	AvnFundamentalCl "A" Scol
Biloxi, Mississippi	6May57-19Jun57	ACAWOperCrse

29. OTHER SERVICE TRAINING COURSES SUCCESSFULLY COMPLETED: USAFI GED HSLevel

VA DATA

30a. GOVERNMENT LIFE INSURANCE IN FORCE: ☐ YES X NO
b. AMOUNT OF ALLOTMENT: N/A
c. MONTH ALLOTMENT DISCONTINUED: N/A
31a. VA BENEFITS PREVIOUSLY APPLIED FOR (Specify type): NONE
b. VA CLAIM NUMBER: C- N/A

AUTHENTICATION

32. REMARKS

Lump sum leave settlement due but not settled.
Mileage paid: $91.56
Recommended for Reenlistment.
Time lost current active duty: Forty-five (45) days
Periods in a non-pay status: From 29Jun58 to 12Aug58
Good Conduct Medal period commences 27Jun58 (1st Award)
Total payment on separation: $132.30 (9/11/59)

33. PERMANENT ADDRESS FOR MAILING PURPOSES AFTER TRANSFER OR DISCHARGE (Street, RFD, City, County and State): 3124 W. 5th Street, Fort Worth, Tarrant, Texas
34. SIGNATURE OF PERSON BEING TRANSFERRED OR DISCHARGED: Lee Harvey Oswald
35a. TYPED NAME, GRADE AND TITLE OF AUTHORIZING OFFICER: A.G.AYERS Jr, 1stLt USMCR Ass't OIC SepSec
b. SIGNATURE OF OFFICER AUTHORIZED TO SIGN: AGAyers Jr.

DD FORM 1 NOV 55 214 REPLACES EDITION OF 1 JUL 52 WHICH IS OBSOLETE
ARMED FORCES OF THE UNITED STATES REPORT OF TRANSFER OR DISCHARGE
5

COMMISSION EXHIBIT No. 1944—Continued

GOLDRING'S — Date ______

APPLICATION FOR EMPLOYMENT

NAME LEE (First) HARVEY (Middle or Maiden) Oswald (Last) 433-54-3937 (Social Security Number)

ADDRESS 757 FRENCH ST. PHONE HU-84326

Date of Birth Oct 18, 1939 Birthplace NEW ORLEANS In New Orleans Since CONT. in

Female ______	Own Home ______	Number of dependents 2	Color cau
Male ✓	Rent ______	Ages of children 14 mon.	Height 5 9 Weight 150
Single ______	Board ______	Adult dependents 1	Eyes Grey Hair br
Married ✓	Live (Relatives ✓ with (Parents	Relatives Employed Here none	
Widowed ______	Purchasing Home ______		
Divorced ______			
Separated ______			

PHYSICAL CHARACTERISTICS

none (State Any Physical Defect) — none (Describe Any Serious Illness in Past Five Years)

If special position applied for, what? Shoe salesman Minimum starting salary $1.35 Hr.

Otherwise, what type of work? ______

Permanent ✓ Temporary ______ Full Time ✓ Part Time ______

IN CASE OF ACCIDENT SEND WORD TO

NAME Oswald Relationship parents

ADDRESS 757 French Phone HU-84326

EDUCATION

Circle Years Completed in Each School Attended	Name and Location of School	Major Subjects Studied	Date Completed
Elementary 1 2 3 4 5 6 7 8			
High 1 2 3 (4)	warren Easton	Gen. math Drawing ect.	1957
College 1 2 3 4			
Business or Vocational 1 2 3 4			
Night or Correspondence 1 2			

Give Details of Any Other Educational Training technical military

Commission Exhibit No. 1945

COMMISSION EXHIBIT NO. 1945

Referred to GOLDRING'S by: ______

EMPLOYMENT RECORD

1. My last employer was active Duty From Mo. ___ Yr. ___ To Mo. ___ Yr. ___
Address U S M C Kind of Business ______ Phone ______
My work was ______ Salary ______ Supervisor ______
I left because ______ If married since, give maiden name ______

2. My previous employer was Rhealees From Mo. Feb Yr. 57 To Mo. april Yr. 57
Address 710 canal Kind of Business Shoes (Millinery)
My work was part-time shoe-sales Salary 100 Hr. Supervisor Mr. Goodman
I left because after Easter holidays If married since, give maiden name ______

3. My previous employer was ______ From Mo. ___ Yr. ___ To Mo. ___ Yr. ___
Address ______ Kind of Business ______
My work was ______ Salary ______ Supervisor ______
I left because ______ If married since, give maiden name ______

Give names and addresses of three persons, not relatives who have known you for three years.

NAME	ADDRESS	OCCUPATION
Dutz Murret	720 Germain St.	Shipping checker
alice Barre	carondelet St.	Retired
George Wikell	705 Polk St.	College Student

DO NOT WRITE BELOW THIS LINE

Interviewer's Comments: ______

RATING: Appearance ______ Dress ______ Manner ______
Speech ______ Voice ______ Alertness ______

Employed Date ______ Department ______ Position ______
Starting Salary ______ Supervisor ______ Department Manager ______
Possibility of Advancement ______

Commission Exhibit No. 1945, p. 2

COMMISSION EXHIBIT NO. 1945—Continued

Cosmos Shipping Company, Inc. Date: august 6

Full name LEE H. OSWALD Soc Sec No. 433-54-3937

Address 4907 MAGAZINE Phone No. HU 84326

Age 23 Where born NEW ORLEANS Citizen of U S

Single ______ Married / Dependents /

Present Employer ______

Previous Employer GERARD F. TUJAGUE 442 CANAL

Next Previous Employer Active Duty USMC

Type of position applied for clerk

List office machines you can operate adding machine

mimeograph, TYPE WRITER

Typist ✓ Words per Minute 20

When can you report for work IMM.

Salary desired 1.35 HR. Least salary you would consider $50.

References Duty MURRETT 757 French

CHARLES LABLACE 2905 MAGAZINE

RUTH KOLPHOR 412 Pine ST.

Applicants signature

Lee H. Oswald

Commission Exhibit No. 1946

Date 11/29/63

APPLICATION

Name: LEE H. OSWALD

Address: 757 FRENCH ST.

Phone: HU-84326

Age: 25

Education: H.S. (WARREN EASTON)

Previous Employment: (State length of time employed)

WM. B. REILY CO 3 MONTHS MAY-JULY

640 MAGAZINE ST. AS MAINTANCE MECHANIC

Reason for leaving:

Reduction BY COMPANY OF MAINTANCE CREW

Military status: 3 YRS. U.S.M.C. HONOURABLE DISCHARGE MAY 1960 – MAY 1963

Maritial status: MARRIED, 1 CHILD

References: (Give three)

JOHN MURRETT 811 FLORIDA HU.

CHARLES HARRISON TULANE UN.

WM. OSWALD

501 N JEFF DAVIS

ROOM 201

Commission Exhibit No. 1947

FORM 742 SN   7858

LYKES BROS. STEAMSHIP CO., INC.

"PASSENGER IMMIGRATION QUESTIONNAIRE -- LEAVING UNITED STATES" Ticket Form ______ No. ______

INFORMATION REQUIRED BY U. S. GOVERNMENT

(A separate form is required for each passenger) Date 9/16/59

Port of Embarkation (From) New Orleans Port of Debarkation (To) Le Havre

Steamer Marion LYKES Voyage ______ Sailing Date 9/18/59 (APPROXIMATE) Room ______ Berth ______

(PLEASE PRINT - ALL COPIES MUST BE LEGIBLE)

SECTION "A" FOR ALL PASSENGERS

1. Last or Family Name OSWALD Occupation Shipping Export Agent
2. First Name Lee Middle Harvey
3a. Age 19 3b. Date of Birth 10 (MONTH) 18 (DAY) 39 (YEAR) 3c. Sex: Male [V] Mrs. [ ] Miss [ ]
4. Place of Birth: If in U. S. New Orleans La (CITY AND STATE OR TERRITORY) If outside U. S. — (COUNTRY) Race White
5a. Nationality USA (COUNTRY OF CITIZENSHIP) 5b. Passport Number 1733242
5c. Date and Place Issued 9/10/59 New Orleans La 5d. Valid To (Date) 9/10/61

SECTION "B" FOR U. S. CITIZENS AND NATIONALS ONLY

6. *If naturalized U. S. citizen—show date and place naturalized —
7. Military Permit or Visa Held—Country — Kind — Period — Valid To —
8. Last address in U. S. 3124 W. 5th St. (HOUSE NUMBER AND STREET) Ft. Worth Texas (CITY AND STATE)
9. Length of time passenger intends to remain abroad Two months (IF INDEFINITELY OR PERMANENTLY SO STATE AND NAME COUNTRY)

SECTION "C" FOR ALIENS ONLY

10a. Date and place of last Entry into USA ______
10b. Was such entry as a permanent resident or temporary visitor ______
11. Travel Document (Answer ONE of the following):
(a) Serial number of Form 257a ______ (Non Immigration Visa)
or (b) Serial number of Form I-94a ______ (Visitor's Permit)
or (c) Red serial number of Form I-132a ______ (Re-Entry Permit)
or (d) Form I-424 [ ]

12. Alien Sailing Permit (Income Tax Clearance)
Number ______
Place issued ______
Date ______

SECTION "D" FOR ALL PASSENGERS

13. Address (Temporary or Permanent) at or near U. S. Port of Boarding the Steamer (Embarkation Port) — (HOUSE NUMBER AND STREET) OR Liberty Hotel (HOTEL) New Orleans La (CITY AND STATE) (TELEPHONE NO.)
14. Permanent address (Whether or not in U. S.) 3124 W. 5th (HOUSE NUMBER AND STREET) Ft Worth (CITY) Texas (STATE OR PROVINCE)
15. Foreign Address (Temporary or Permanent) — (HOUSE NUMBER AND STREET) OR (HOTEL) (CITY)
16. Baggage: Trunks ______ Suitcases ONE Other (List) ______ Total ______
17. For the purpose of having accurate information and to prevent anything from being printed against your wishes, please advise. (May be omitted if desired.)
(a) Organization or Company with which connected —
(b) Location of Company —
(c) Nature of Business Pleasure (d) Your title —
18. Purpose of Trip: Business ______ Pleasure Pleasure Other ______

*If passenger is a naturalized U. S. citizen also show U. S. naturalization certificate number preceded by "Certif." If such certificate does not have a number, then show date and place of naturalization only.
Such a Passenger MUST have in his possession at time of re-entry into USA, either his naturalization certificate or a passport, to show evidence of U. S. citizenship.

I hereby certify that to the best of my knowledge and belief, the foregoing statements are true and correct.

x Lee H Oswald
SIGNATURE OF PASSENGER (PARENT MAY SIGN FOR CHILDREN)

DISTRIBUTION—Original and duplicate to Passenger Department at New Orleans La

— Commission Exhibit No. 1948 —

COMMISSION EXHIBIT No. 1948

PLEASE FILL OUT APPLICATION BLANK COMPLETELY............

NAME Oswald Lee H. (LAST NAME FIRST) STREET & NUMBER 2515 W. 5th St. TOWN Irving

PHONE NO BL 31628 SOCIAL SECURITY NO. 433-54-3937 AGE 23 WEIGHT 150 HEIGHT 5'9

PLACE OF BIRTH New Orleans, La HOW LONG LIVED IN DALLAS continuously

FINISHED WHAT GRADE IN SCHOOL 11th NAME SCHOOL Arlington Heights TOWN Ft. Worth, Tex.

DID YOU ATTEND COLLEGE no HOW LONG — NAME COLLEGE —

RACE C MARRIED (V) OR SINGLE ( ) HOW MANY DEPENDENTS 2 dependents

WHERE DID YOU LAST WORK U.S.M.C. (three years) NATURE OF WORK air-Wing

REASON FOR LEAVING LAST JOB Honourable discharge

HOW LONG DID YOU WORK ON YOUR LAST JOB three years

WHERE IS YOUR FATHER EMPLOYED Dead NATURE OF WORK —

IS YOUR MOTHER EMPLOYED yes NATURE OF WORK Practical nurse

MEMBER OF ORGANIZATIONS: — (CHURCH) — (LODGE) — (VETERAN)

HAVE YOU ANY PHYSICAL DEFECTS (ANSWER YES OR NO) IF ANSWER IS YES STATE WHAT THEY ARE:

no

DO YOU ROOM AND BOARD no DO YOU LIVE WITH PARENTS no

SHOULD YOU LIKE TO MENTION SOME OF YOUR SPECIAL ABILITIES YOU WOULD LIKE COMPANY TO KNOW IN CONSIDERING YOUR APPLICATION USE THE THREE LINES BELOW.

Clearical (accounting) work in military service, experienced with Ditto, adding and some typing machine and filing system

DATE OF APPLICATION Oct. 15, 1963

Lee H Oswald
SIGNATURE OF APPLICANT

— Commission Exhibit No. 1949 —

COMMISSION EXHIBIT No. 1949

H S Aiken

11/23/63

Commission Exhibit No. 1949, p.2

COMMISSION EXHIBIT No. 1949—Continued

FORM W-4 (Rev. July 1961)
U. S. Treasury Department
Internal Revenue Service

EMPLOYEE'S WITHHOLDING EXEMPTION CERTIFICATE

Print full name LEE HARVEY OSWALD Social Security Account Number 433-54-3937

Print home address 2515 WEST 5th ST. City IRVING Zone ...... State TEXAS

EMPLOYEE: File this form with your employer. Otherwise, he must withhold U. S. income tax from your wages without exemption.

EMPLOYER: Keep this certificate with your records. If the employee is believed to have claimed too many exemptions, the District Director should be so advised.

DL-25

HOW TO CLAIM YOUR WITHHOLDING EXEMPTIONS

1. If SINGLE, and you claim an exemption, write the figure "1" ....
2. If MARRIED, one exemption each is allowable for husband and wife if not claimed on another certificate.
   (a) If you claim both of these exemptions, write the figure "2"
   (b) If you claim one of these exemptions, write the figure "1"
   (c) If you claim neither of these exemptions, write "0" 2
3. Exemptions for age and blindness (applicable only to you and your wife but not to dependents):
   (a) If you or your wife will be 65 years of age or older at the end of the year, and you claim this exemption, write "1"; if both will be 65 or older, and you claim both of these exemptions, write "2" ....
   (b) If you or your wife are blind, and you claim this exemption, write the figure "1"; if both are blind, and you claim both of these exemptions, write the figure "2" ....
4. If you claim exemptions for one or more dependents, write the number of such exemptions. (Do not claim exemption for a dependent unless you are qualified under instruction 4 on other side.) 2
5. Add the number of exemptions which you have claimed above and write the total 4
6. Additional withholding per pay period under agreement with employer. *See* Instruction 1 .... $........

I CERTIFY that the number of withholding exemptions claimed on this certificate does not exceed the number to which I am entitled.

(Date) Oct 16, 1963   16—75908—2   (Signed) Lee H. Oswald

Commission Exhibit No. 1949, p.3

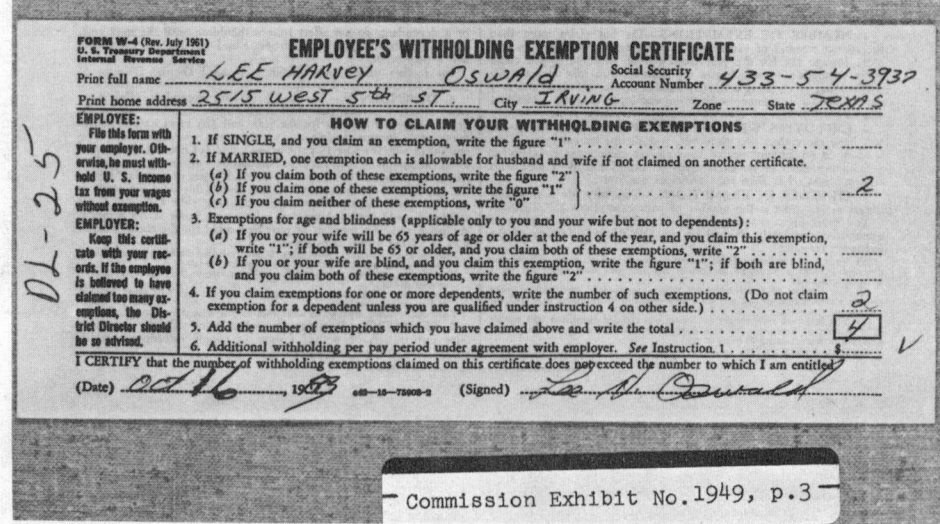

COMMISSION EXHIBIT No. 1949—Continued

NO	DATE OCTOBER 16 TO 31, 1963 EMPLOYEES	M	T	16 W	17 T	18 F	19 S	21 M	22 T	23 W	24 T	25 F	26 S	28 M	29 T	30 W	31 T	F	S
1	W. H. SHELLEY			8	8	3 / 8		8	3 / 8	8	8	3 / 8		8	8	8	8		
2	M. S. AIKEN			8	8	8		8	8	8	8	8		8	8	8	8		
4	JACK DOUGHERTY			8	8	8		8	3 / 8	8	8	8		8	8	8	8		
8	EDWARD SHIELDS			8	8	8		8	8	8	8	8		8	8	8	8		
13	TROY WEST			8	8	8		8	8	8	8	8		8	8	8	8		
5	JAMES JARMAN			8	8	8		8	8	8	8	8		8	8	8	8		
39	EDDIE PIPER			8	8	8		8	8	8	8	8		8	8	8	8		
17	HAROLD NORMAN			8	8	8		8	3 / 8	8	8	8		8	8	8	8		
30	BILLY LOVELADY			8	8	3 / 8		8	3 / 8	8	8	8		8	8	8	8		
29	FRANK KAISER			8	8	3 / 8		8	3 / 8	8	8	8		8	8	8	8		
20	[illegible] MENTER			8	8	8		8	8	8	8	8		8	8	8	8		
47	CARL JONES			8	8	8		8	8	8	8	8		8	8	8	8		
40	GORDON SMITH			8	8	8		8	8	8	8	8		8	8	8	8		
38	ROY EDWARD LEWIS			8	8	3 / 8		8	3 / 8	8	8	8		8	8	8	8		
39	DANIEL ARCE			8	8	8		8	8	8	8	8		8	8	8	8		
45	BONNIE RAY WILLIAMS			8	8	8		8	8	8	8	8		8	8	8	8		
65	TRUETT DON FELTS			[illegible]	[illegible]	[illegible]		[illegible]	[illegible]	[illegible]	[illegible]	[illegible]		8	8	8	8		
48	WESLEY FRAZIER			8	8	8		[illegible]	[illegible]	[illegible]	[illegible]	[illegible]		[illegible]	8	8	8		
13	CHARLES GIVENS			8	8	8		8	8	8	8	8		8	8	8	8		
18	LEE OSWALD			8	8	8		8	8	8	8	8		8	8	8	8		

Commission Exhibit No. 1949, p.4

D-188

Commission Exhibit No. 1949—Continued

SEMIMONTHLY PAYROLL

NO	DATE NOVEMBER 1 TO 15, 1963					1	2	4	5	6	7	8	9	11	12	13	14	15	
	EMPLOYEES	M	T	W	T	F	S	M	T	W	T	F	S	M	T	W	T	F	S
1	[illegible] H. SHELLEY					8		8	8	8	8	8		X	8	8	8	8	
2	H. S. AIKEN					8		8	8	8	8	8		X	8	8	8	8	
6	JACK DOUGHERTY					8		8	8	8	8	8		X	8	8	8	8	
8	EDWARD SHIELDS					8		8	8	8	8	8		X	8	8	8	8	
13	TROY WEST					8		8	8	8	8	8		X	8	8	8	8	
5	JAMES JARMAN					8		8	8	8	8	8		X	8	8	8	8	
39	EDDIE PIPER					8		8	8	8	8	8		X	8	8	8	8	
17	HAROLD NORMAN					8		8	8	8	8	8		X	8	8	8	8	
10	BILLY LOVELADY					8		5	5	5	5	5		X	8	8	8	8	
29	FRANK KAISER					8		8	8	8	8	8		X	8	8	8	8	
28	FRANKLIN WESTER					8		8	8	8	8	8		✓	8	8	8	8	
47	CARL JONES					8		8	8	8	8	8		✓	8	8	8	8	
40	GORDON SMITH					8		8	8	8	8	8		X	8	8	8	8	
58	ROY EDWARD LEWIS					8		8	8	8	8	8		✓	8	8	8	8	
99	DANIEL ARCE					[illegible]		8	8	8	8	8		X	8	8	8	8	
63	BONNIE RAY WILLIAMS					[illegible]		[illegible]	[illegible]	[illegible]	[illegible]	[illegible]		✓	8	8	8	8	
65	[illegible] DON FELTS					8		8	8	8	[illegible]	[illegible]		[illegible]	[illegible]	8	8	8	
68	WESLEY FRAZIER					8		8	8	8	8	8		X	8	8	8	8	
15	CHARLES GIVENS					8		8	8	8	8	8		X	8	8	8	8	
12	LEE OSWALD					8		8	8	8	8	8		✓	8	8	8	8	

Commission Exhibit No. 1949, p.5

COMMISSION EXHIBIT No. 1949—Continued

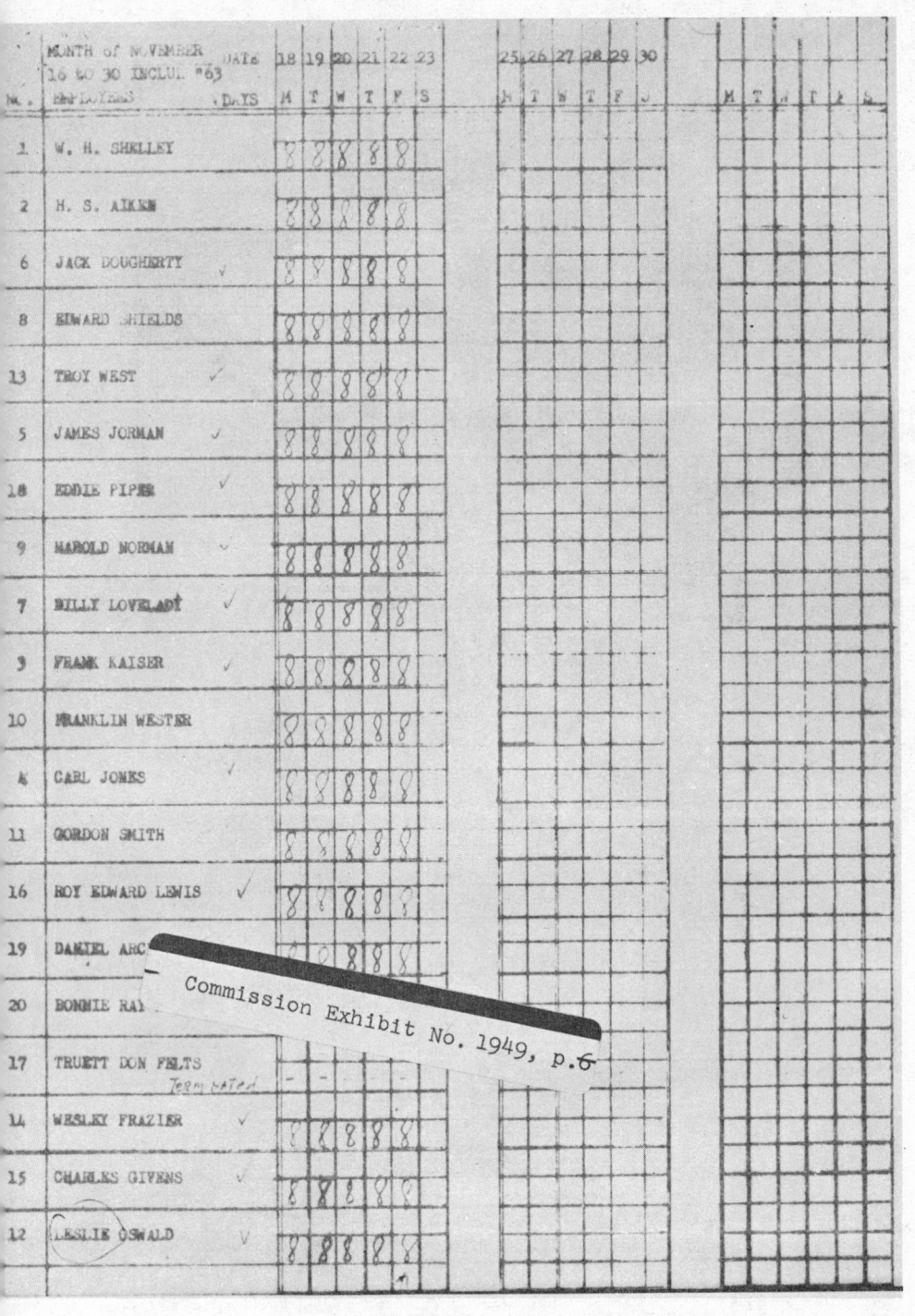

No.	MONTH of NOVEMBER 16 to 30 INCLUL '63 EMPLOYEES	DAYS	18 M	19 T	20 W	21 T	22 F	23 S	25 M	26 T	27 W	28 T	29 F	30 S
1	W. H. SHELLEY		8	8	8	8	8							
2	H. S. AIKEN		8	8	8	8	8							
6	JACK DOUGHERTY	✓	8	8	8	8	8							
8	EDWARD SHIELDS		8	8	8	8	8							
13	TROY WEST	✓	8	8	8	8	8							
5	JAMES JORMAN	✓	8	8	8	8	8							
18	EDDIE PIPER	✓	8	8	8	8	8							
9	HAROLD NORMAN	✓	8	8	8	8	8							
7	BILLY LOVELADY	✓	8	8	8	8	8							
3	FRANK KAISER	✓	8	8	8	8	8							
10	FRANKLIN WESTER		8	8	8	8	8							
4	CARL JONES	✓	8	8	8	8	8							
11	GORDON SMITH		8	8	8	8	8							
16	ROY EDWARD LEWIS	✓	8	8	8	8	8							
19	DANIEL ARC…				8	8	8							
20	BONNIE RAY…													
17	TRUETT DON FELTS Terminated		-	-			-							
14	WESLEY FRAZIER	✓	8	8	8	8	8							
15	CHARLES GIVENS	✓	8	8	8	8	8							
12	LESLIE OSWALD	✓	8	8	8	8	8							

Commission Exhibit No. 1949, p. 6

COMMISSION EXHIBIT NO. 1949—Continued

~~TRGEN~~ TBCH

COTTON PICKIN' APPLICATION

INACTIVE

PRINT NAME ONLY — LAST NAME / FIRST NAME / INITIAL	Oswald / Lee / H.
STREET ADDRESS	2515 W. 5th St.
CITY / P.O. ZONE / STATE	Irving / / Texas
HOME PHONE	BL 31628
BUSINESS PHONE	—
MESSAGE PHONE	—
HUSBAND OR WIFE'S NAME	Marina
WHERE EMPLOYED / HOW LONG / PHONE	unemployed
OCCUPATION	Comm. Photo.
INCOME	150 HR
RENT / OWN HOME / BOARD / PARENTS	Rent X
YOUR AGE	23
BIRTH DATE	Oct 18 39
HEIGHT	5 9
WEIGHT	140
NO. CHILDREN AGES	1 - 20 months
WHO CARES FOR CHILDREN	wife
AUTOMOBILE — OWN (YES / NO) / YEAR / AVAILABLE (YES / NO) / MAKE	OWN: NO (circled)
HOW LONG IN THIS AREA	15 yrs.
SINGLE / MARRIED / ENGAGED / DIVORCED	Married (marked)
HOW LONG	2 yrs
U. S. VETERAN (YES / NO)	YES (circled)
FROM / TO	Oct. 1959 / Oct. 1962
BRANCH OF SERVICE	USMC
RATING	SGT.
DRAFT CLASSIFICATION	IV-3
NATIONALITY	U.S.
CHURCH AFFILIATION	Luth.
REFERRED TO US BY: 1. NEWSPAPER / 2. FRIEND / 3. EMPLOYER	1. A
POSITION DESIRED	Printing Co.
1.	Comm. Photographer — 53-121
2.	Clerk — DATE 10-4-63
3.	Mail Clerk
MONTHLY SALARY EXPECTED	278.00
MINIMUM MONTHLY SALARY	250.00
EVER BEEN BONDED (YES / NO)	NO (circled)
BONDABLE NOW (YES / NO)	
CONSIDER BUSINESS INVESTMENT (YES / NO) / HOW MUCH	NO (circled)
WILL YOU RE-LOCATE (YES / NO)	NO (circled)
WILL YOU TRAVEL (YES / NO)	NO (circled)
ANY PHYSICAL DEFECTS (YES / NO) / IF SO DESCRIBE	NO (circled) —
HOBBIES	1. 2. 3.

EDUCATION	NAME OF SCHOOL CITY AND STATE	COURSE	YEARS	YEAR GRAD.			DESCRIPTION
GRADE SCHOOL	Ridgleighwest	General	—		NIGHT SCHOOL		
HIGH SCHOOL	Arlington Heights	General	4	1956	TECHNICAL OR TRADE SCHOOLS	Radar Oper.	
COLLEGE OR UNIVERSITY	None			DEGREE	OTHER:		

JOB EXPERIENCE — STARTING WITH PRESENT OR MOST RECENT POSITION

FROM / TO	FIRM NAME / ADDRESS	POSITION HELD / SUPERVISOR	MO. SALARY REC'D	REASON FOR LEAVING / KIND OF BUSINESS	THEIR PHONE NUMBER
From May 63 To Sept 63	Louv-R-Pak Co. / 210 N E Valcer St. Ft. Worth	Clerk / Tom Lopez	1.35	Seasonal work	2
From Oct 62 To May 63	Jaggers-Chiles-Stovall / 522 Browder St. Dallas	Photographer / John Graciues	150 HR	Cut in work force / Typography	2
From Mo. Yr. To Mo. Yr.	U.S.M.C.				
From Mo. Yr. To Mo. Yr.					

(Margin notations: 5 mo.; 7 mo.)

DESIGNATE FIELDS OR SKILLS IN WHICH YOU HAVE EXPERIENCE OR TRAINING

☐ OFFICE: ☐ MANUAL ☐ ELECTRIC TYPE SPEED ☐ SHORTHAND ☐ SPEEDWRITING ☐ DICTAPHONE ☐ TELETYPE ☐ KEY PUNCH ☐ TWX ☐ PBX ☐ PLUG ☐ KEY NO. LINES ☑ ADDING MACHINE ☑ MIMEO-GRAPH ☐ ADDRESS-O-GRAPH ☑ FILE CLERK ☐ CASH REGISTER ☐ KARD-EX ☐ OTHER

☐ BOOK-KEEPING: ☐ FULL CHARGE ☐ ASSISTANT ☐ PAY-ROLL ☐ MACHINE ☐ COMPTOMETER ☐ N.C.R. # ☐ CALCULATOR ☐ BILLING MACHINE ☐ IBM # ☐ ACCOUNTING ☐ CERTIFIED ☐ SENIOR ☐ JUNIOR ☐ COST ☐ TAX

☐ ENGINEERING: ☐ MECH ☐ ELECT. ☐ CHEM ☐ CIVIL ☐ SAFETY ☐ STAT ☐ INDUSTRIAL ☐ OTHER ☐ DRAFTSMAN ☐ MECH. STRUCTURAL ☐ ARCH. ☐ CHEMIST ☐ ADVERTISING ☐ COPYWRITER ☐ ARTIST ☐ PRODUCTION ☑ LAYOUT ☐ SALES

A. B. (circled) C. — Photo Art Layout Exp. Darkroom Exp. Commerical Dev.

A. B. (circled) C. — 1.35 hr

Commission Exhibit No. 1950

COMMISSION EXHIBIT NO. 1950

10/10	1:30 pm	DEVILBISS CO.	Ro.

COUNSELOR

COMPANY

ADDRESS

POSITION — SALARY

DATE HIRED — STARTING DATE

PAY SCHEDULE — FIRST CHECK

SCHEDULE — FEE

1.

2.

3.

4.

X

Ardmore Print Co.

JOBCO

612 ADOLPHUS TOWER
DALLAS 2, TEXAS

RIverside 8-7604

Licensed and Bonded

NO OBLIGATION — FEES EFFECTIVE ONLY UPON ACCEPTANCE OF EMPLOYMENT OFFERED

AGREEMENT

I hereby acknowledge the filing of my application with JOBCO to assist me in securing a position and agree that providing I accept a position through JOBCO either directly or indirectly, any time within one (1) year from the execution of this contract, to pay JOBCO an amount equal to forty per cent (40%) of the first month's salary, draw, commissions, or gross earnings, whichever sum is larger. It is understood that all fees are figured on thirty (30) calendar days, on the basis of four and one-third weeks to the month.

I further agree to pay the total fee within thirty (30) days of commencing employment. I understand that the total fee may either be paid cash in full upon acceptance of a position, or payable as I am paid, whether weekly, bi-weekly, monthly, or semi-monthly. However, a cash fee must be paid if the position accepted requires relocation outside the City of Dallas.

It is further understood that all positions are to be considered permanent and that the same fee schedule shall apply to any position accepted by applicant. It is understood that the duration of employment in no way shall effect the amount of the fee.

I promise and agree to keep all information obtained from JOBCO concerning employment strictly confidential and for my exclusive use. I also promise and agree to immediately report to JOBCO any and all results from interviews with employers.

I have read the foregoing agreement carefully and I fully understand all the terms contained therein, and I promise and agree to be bound thereby.

Dated: Oct. 4, 1963 Signed: Lee H Oswald

Social Security No. 433-54-3937

Accepted By JOBCO: Signed: [signature]

BPD 12-12-63

CHARACTER REFERENCE: Elena Hall

ADDRESS: 4760 Trail Lane Dr.

PHONE NUMBER: WA 6-3741

CLOSEST FRIEND: George DeMorenschildt

ADDRESS: 6628 Dickens

PHONE NUMBER: EN 3-1365

BANK

SAVINGS ACCOUNT — CHECKING ACCOUNT

DRIVERS LICENSE

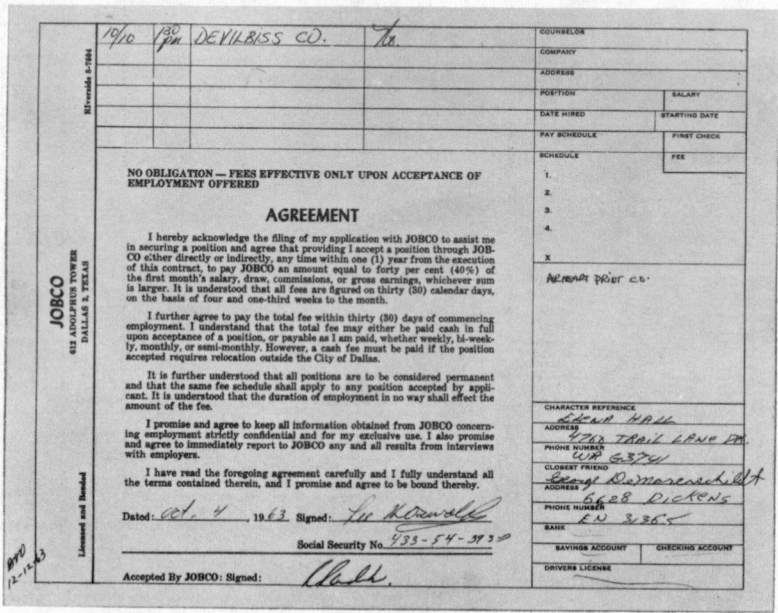

COMMISSION EXHIBIT NO. 1950—Continued

Present or Last Position	From To	JAGGERS-CHILES-STOVAl	DALLAS- 522 Browder St.	John Grieves	TYPOGRAPHY	PHOTOGRAPH	135	LAID OF BECAUSE OF CUT IN NIGHT SHIFT
Next Previous	From To							
" "	From To							
" "	From To							
" "	From To							
" "	From To							
" "	From To							
" "	From To							
" "	From To							
" "	From To							
" "	From To							
" "	From To							

Personal References

Name Dutz MURRETT	Address 757 French St.	Phone No. HU 84326
Name W.S. OSWALD	Address 136 ELMEER METRIE	Phone No. ?

(Please use ink)

Name (Last, First, Middle) OSWAld LEE HARVEY	Home Phone HU 84326 Office Phone	Single / Married / Separated / Divorced / Widow	No. of Children / Age 1 year	Height 5' 9 Weight 150	Color of Eyes GREY
Address 757 FRENCH ST.	Date of Birth 10/18/39 Place NEW ORLEANS	Age 23	Nationality AMERICAN Relocate? NO	Color of Hair BR.	Religion PROT.
Previous Address	Position Desired TELLER TRAINEE			Social Security No. 433-54-3937	Salary? Least Considered $135 MO.

EDUCATION

		Yr. Graduated	Major	Military Service	Do not write in this space
High School	ARLINGTON HEIGHTS S.H.S.	1959	GEN.	3 YRS.-USMC	A- ✓
Business School				How long in New Orleans CONTIN.	P- ✓
College or University				Referred by Ad.	R-

Length of Experience in or on following:

Advertising	Claim Adj.	Accounting	Bookkeeping	Type	Teletype	Filing	Technician	Med. Detailist	Shipping Clk.	Other Skills
Automobile	Investment	CPA	Full Chg.	Speed 25 Manual ✓	Dictaphone	Adding Mch.	Kind	Engineers	Receiving Clk.	PHOTOGRAPHY
Banking	Lumber	Senior	Ass't.	Elec.	Ediphone	Calculator	Chemist	Kind	Warehousemen	Cam.
Credit Collections	Machinery	Junior	A/c Rec.	Shorthand	Other Dict. Mch.	Kind	Pharmacist	Architect	Mechanic	
Credit Mgr.	Med. Tech.	Cost	A/c Pay.	Speed	Billing Mch.	Comptometer	Sales	Drafting	Helper	
Finance	Oil	Tax	Bkpg. Mach.	Typewriter Billing	Kind	Office Mgr.	Kind	Construction	Kind	
Insurance	Oil Well Sup.	Payroll	Kind	Statistical Typist	Mimeograph	Comptroller	Sales Mgr.	Electricians	Guards	
Kind	PBX	Cashier	Post. Mch.	Tab. Mch.	Multigraph	Personnel	Sales Eng.	Plumbing	Welders	
Rate Clerk	Tel. Sol.	Timekeeper	Kind	Key Punch	Addressograph	Purchasing	Trainee	Truck Drivers	Route Sales	

COMMISSION EXHIBIT No. 1951

Mutual Understanding is the Foundation of Pleasant Business Relations. This is your Agreement with us — Read it Carefully Before You Sign It!

AGREEMENT

1. This agreement entered into this date between A-1 EMPLOYMENT SERVICE hereinafter referred to as the agency and hereinafter referred to as applicant, in which the applicant agrees to pay and the agency agrees to receive in full payment for each employment procured a fee based on the following schedule, for permanent employment:

Up to \$149.99—30%; \$150.00 thru \$249.99—35%; \$250.00 thru \$349.99—40%; \$350.00 up 45% of applicant's first full month's wages received in cash from any salary, drawing account or commission. Where applicant is paid at a weekly rate, a month's wages shall be computed at 4 and ⅓ times the weekly rate, as authorized by the Commissioner of Labor.

For temporary employment 10% of applicant's wages received in cash from any salary, drawing account, or commission.

2. It is agreed by the parties hereto that permanent employment is procured employment lasting three or more consecutive and continuous calendar months; and that temporary employment is procured employment terminated in less than three calendar months by the employer.

3. It is further agreed that applicant shall at all times have the right to refuse any employment tendered without being required to give reasons for such refusal; and the Service charge of the agency is earned when applicant accepts employment and is payable as salary is received.

4. If the charge made herein is for permanent employment which in fact becomes temporary, then applicant shall be entitled to a refund of the unearned differences of the service charge. If a temporary placement becomes permanent a full permanent fee shall be due.

5. Should applicant accept a sales position involving a training period then the agency shall have the right at its option to determine a month's wages received by taking an average of the first three months wages received as a basis for the fee due the agency. When this is done, applicant agrees to pay the agency 10% of all earnings received for the first three months, at the end of which period the final fee will be computed and any balance due paid.

6. Should applicant voluntarily leave a position that applicant has accepted, applicant agrees to pay the whole fee agreed upon, except that in no case will the fee amount to more than 45% of the total wage that applicant has received.

7. Should applicant accept a position through the agency and subsequently applicant's present employer offers better employment as a direct result of applicant's having accepted a better outside job through the agency, applicant agrees that such offer shall constitute a bona fide order to the agency authorizing referral and that acceptance of such offer from the present employer shall be considered as a placement for which applicant agrees to pay a fee in accordance with the schedule shown herein for permanent work.

8. The agency agrees that it will not under any interpretation of this contract make more than one service charge for any one referral.

9. It is agreed that acceptance of an introduction card by the applicant from the agency takes precedence over any previous application the applicant may have filed with an employer to which the introduction card is addressed.

10. Applicant hereby stipulates and agrees to a penalty of fifteen (15%) per cent as attorney's fee, on the earned charges and remuneration due the agency should it become necessary for the agency to obtain counsel or collection service, or resort to court action to collect same.

11. Applicant hereby permits investigation of business and personal references as given on registration card, and any information secured by such investigation shall be held confidential between the agency and the prospective employer.

12. It is agreed and understood that transportation to and from interviews will be borne by the job applicant.

13. Should applicant fail to pay the service charge as heretofore agreed, applicant may by mutual agreement with the employer authorize the employer with whom placed by the agency to deduct from any salary, drawing account or commissions the amount due the agency and to pay same to the agency.

14. I have read the above agreement, and I fully understand and will abide by its contents

(Signature of applicant) (Date) 19 63

A-1 EMPLOYMENT SERVICE, 1409 National Bank of Commerce Bldg.

COMMISSION DUE AND PAYABLE DURING 1st MONTH OF EMPLOYMENT

Have you been Bonded? no	Do you have a checking or saving a/c? What Bank? no	Do you own a car? Make? no	Can you buy one? Model
Do you live with Parents? Rent? Own Home? yes (relatives)	Name, Address Phone No. of Parents		
	Occupation of Father Decesed	Occupation of Mother Retired	
Does your Husband (Wife) work? no	Occupation of Husband (Wife)	Name of Company	
Social Activities Clubs		Hobbies	
Physical Handicaps none		Date of last Physical Examination 1962	

Do not write below this line. Referred to:

1 5/15 - Weber Photo	7
2	8
3	9
4	10
5	11

1951, p. 2

COMMISSION EXHIBIT No. 1951—Continued

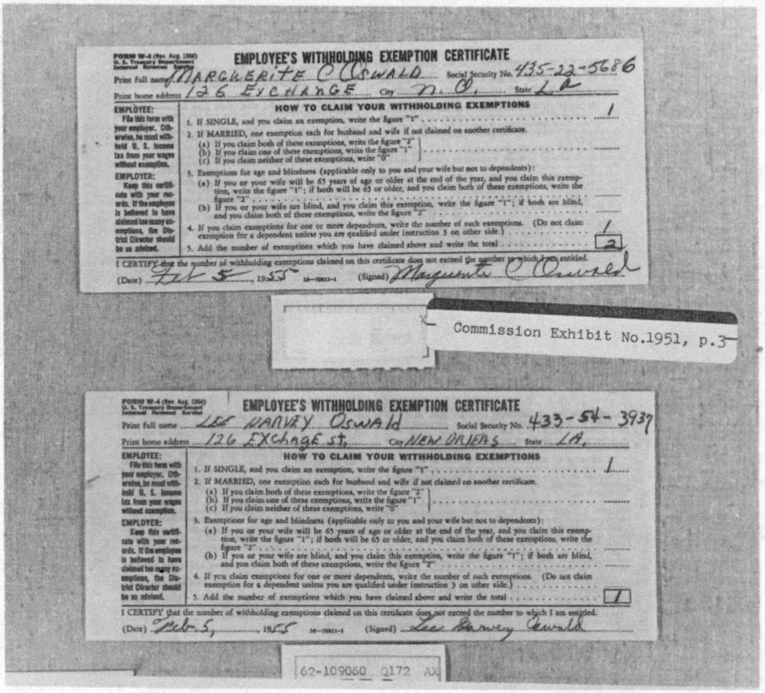

FORM W-4 (Rev. Aug. 1954)
U. S. Treasury Department
Internal Revenue Service

EMPLOYEE'S WITHHOLDING EXEMPTION CERTIFICATE

Print full name MARGUERITE C OSWALD Social Security No. 435-22-5686
Print home address 126 EXCHANGE City N. O. State LA

EMPLOYEE: File this form with your employer. Otherwise, he must withhold U. S. income tax from your wages without exemption.

EMPLOYER: Keep this certificate with your records. If the employee is believed to have claimed too many exemptions, the District Director should be so advised.

HOW TO CLAIM YOUR WITHHOLDING EXEMPTIONS

1. If SINGLE, and you claim an exemption, write the figure "1" 1
2. If MARRIED, one exemption each for husband and wife if not claimed on another certificate.
   (a) If you claim both of these exemptions, write the figure "2"
   (b) If you claim one of these exemptions, write the figure "1"
   (c) If you claim neither of these exemptions, write "0"
3. Exemptions for age and blindness (applicable only to you and your wife but not to dependents):
   (a) If you or your wife will be 65 years of age or older at the end of the year, and you claim this exemption, write the figure "1"; if both will be 65 or older, and you claim both of these exemptions, write the figure "2"
   (b) If you or your wife are blind, and you claim this exemption, write the figure "1"; if both are blind, and you claim both of these exemptions, write the figure "2"
4. If you claim exemptions for one or more dependents, write the number of such exemptions. (Do not claim exemption for a dependent unless you are qualified under instruction 3 on other side.) 1
5. Add the number of exemptions which you have claimed above and write the total 2

I CERTIFY that the number of withholding exemptions claimed on this certificate does not exceed the number to which I am entitled.

(Date) Feb 5, 1955 16—70611-1 (Signed) Marguerite C Oswald

Commission Exhibit No.1951, p.3

FORM W-4 (Rev. Aug. 1954)
U. S. Treasury Department
Internal Revenue Service

EMPLOYEE'S WITHHOLDING EXEMPTION CERTIFICATE

Print full name LEE HARVEY OSWALD Social Security No. 433-54-3937
Print home address 126 EXCHAGE St. City NEW ORLEANS State LA.

EMPLOYEE: File this form with your employer. Otherwise, he must withhold U. S. income tax from your wages without exemption.

EMPLOYER: Keep this certificate with your records. If the employee is believed to have claimed too many exemptions, the District Director should be so advised.

HOW TO CLAIM YOUR WITHHOLDING EXEMPTIONS

1. If SINGLE, and you claim an exemption, write the figure "1" 1
2. If MARRIED, one exemption each for husband and wife if not claimed on another certificate.
   (a) If you claim both of these exemptions, write the figure "2"
   (b) If you claim one of these exemptions, write the figure "1"
   (c) If you claim neither of these exemptions, write "0"
3. Exemptions for age and blindness (applicable only to you and your wife but not to dependents):
   (a) If you or your wife will be 65 years of age or older at the end of the year, and you claim this exemption, write the figure "1"; if both will be 65 or older, and you claim both of these exemptions, write the figure "2"
   (b) If you or your wife are blind, and you claim this exemption, write the figure "1"; if both are blind, and you claim both of these exemptions, write the figure "2"
4. If you claim exemptions for one or more dependents, write the number of such exemptions. (Do not claim exemption for a dependent unless you are qualified under instruction 3 on other side.)
5. Add the number of exemptions which you have claimed above and write the total 1

I CERTIFY that the number of withholding exemptions claimed on this certificate does not exceed the number to which I am entitled.

(Date) Feb. 5, 1955 16—70611-1 (Signed) Lee Harvey Oswald

62-109060 Q172 AX

COMMISSION EXHIBIT No. 1951—Continued

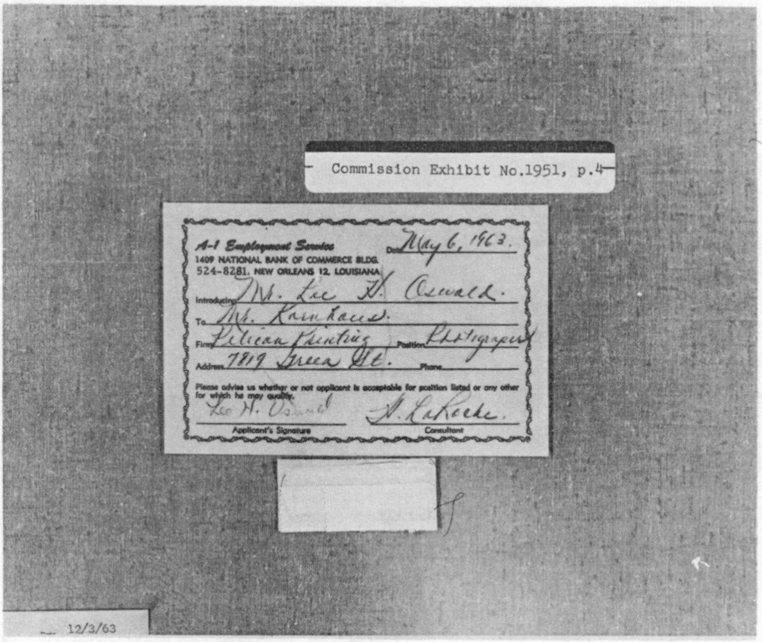

Commission Exhibit No.1951, p.4

A-1 Employment Service
1409 NATIONAL BANK OF COMMERCE BLDG.
524-8281, NEW ORLEANS 12, LOUISIANA

Date May 6, 1963.

Introducing Mr. Lee H. Oswald.
To Mr. Rainhaus.
Firm Pelican Printing Position Photographer
Address 7819 Green St. Phone

Please advise us whether or not applicant is acceptable for position listed or any other for which he may qualify.

Lee H. Oswald — Applicant's Signature
A. LaRoche — Consultant

12/3/63

COMMISSION EXHIBIT No. 1951—Continued

IDENTIFICATION BUREAU
CRIME SCENE SEARCH SECTION
POLICE DEPARTMENT DALLAS, TEXAS

DATE SUBMITTED 3-15-64 TIME 9:45 a CSS# ____________

OFFICER Howlett OF USSS SUBMITTED TO THE CSS OF THE IDENTIFICATION BUREAU THE FOLLOWING:

2 Curtain Rods — white enamel
(4 pcs) marked 275 + 276

EXAMINATION REQUESTED: check for prints.

LOCATION WHERE COMMITTED ____________

NATURE OF OFFENSE ____________ DATE ____________ OFFENSE# ____________

COMPLAINANT ____________

SUSPECT ____________ RACE ____ SEX ____ AGE ____ ID# ____________

____________ RACE ____ SEX ____ AGE ____ ID# ____________

SIGNATURE OF PERSON SUBMITTING SPECIMEN John Joe Howlett ID# ____________

SIGNATURE OF PERSON RECEIVING SPECIMEN J C Day ID# ____________

SPECIMEN RELEASED TO ____________

DATE 3-26-64 TIME 7:50 a BY J C Day

RESULTS:

1 legible print — does not belong to Oswald
Day

COMMISSION EXHIBIT No. 1952

UNITED STATES DEPARTMENT OF JUSTICE

FEDERAL BUREAU OF INVESTIGATION

In Reply, Please Refer to File No.

Dallas, Texas

June 10, 1964

LEE HARVEY OSWALD

The President's Commission, by letter dated May 20, 1964, requested additional investigation in connection with the attempted assassination of Major General EDWIN A. WALKER, at Dallas, Texas, on April 10, 1963.

On May 28, 1964, B. G. BROWN, Police Officer assigned to the Crime Scene Search Section (CSSS), Dallas, Texas, Police Department, advised that on the night of April 10, 1963, he was dispatched to 4011 Turtle Creek Boulevard, Dallas, to conduct a crime scene search in connection with a shooting at that residence. BROWN identified the residence as that of Major General EDWIN A. WALKER, United States Army (Retired).

After his arrival at the residence, Patrolman B. G. NORVELL handed BROWN a bullet, which NORVELL stated he had found among some papers and literature in the room next to the room where General WALKER had been sitting at the time of the shooting. BROWN stated the bullet apparently had come through the wall between the two rooms, as there was a hole in this wall. BROWN stated he marked the bullet and took it back to the CSSS at the Dallas Police Department, where he kept it for safekeeping.

BROWN made available copies of the below-listed Dallas Police Department reports concerning investigation conducted by that agency in connection with the shooting at WALKER's residence:

1. General Offense Report dated April 10, 1963, by Officers D. P. TUCKER and B. G. NORVELL.

2. Supplementary Offense Report dated April 10, 1963, by Police Department Detectives I. F. VAN CLEAVE and D. E. McELROY.

COMMISSION EXHIBIT No. 1953

3. Supplementary Offense Report dated April 11, 1963, by Police Department Detectives C. R. DELLINGER and F. M. ROSE.

4. Supplementary Offense Report dated April 7, 1964, by Police Department Detective C. R. DELLINGER.

These copies are being maintained in the files of the Dallas Office of the Federal Bureau of Investigation.

On May 28, 1964, DON E. McELROY, Detective, Burglary and Theft Squad, Dallas, Texas, Police Department, advised that on the night of April 10, 1963, he was dispatched to 4011 Turtle Creek Boulevard to investigate a shooting. This address is the residence of Major General EDWIN A. WALKER, United States Army (Retired).

McELROY, a police officer for thirteen years, advised it appeared the bullet had entered through a window in the back of the house and gone through a wall next to which General WALKER had been sitting at the time. In the room next to where General WALKER had been sitting, Mr. McELROY stated he found a spent bullet among some papers and literature. There was a hole in the wall through which the bullet had apparently entered. Mr. McELROY stated he picked up the bullet and later gave it to Officer B. G. BROWN, of the Crime Scene Search Section, Dallas Police Department.

On June 2, 1964, D. P. TUCKER, Patrolman, Dallas, Texas, Police Department, residence, 2632 Lakeland Drive, Dallas, Texas, advised that on the night of April 10, 1963, he and his partner, Patrolman B. G. NORVELL, were sent by the Dallas Police Department radio dispatcher to 4011 Turtle Creek Boulevard, Dallas, concerning a shooting. Officer TUCKER stated this is the residence of Major General EDWIN A. WALKER.

COMMISSION EXHIBIT No. 1953—Continued

Re: LEE HARVEY OSWALD

At the residence while investigating the shooting, which included interviews of General WALKER and other persons at the residence and conducting a search of the area, Officer NORVELL found a bullet in a battered condition which apparently had been the bullet fired through the window which barely missed General WALKER. Officer TUCKER stated Officer NORVELL found this bullet in the room adjoining the room where General WALKER was sitting at the time the shot was fired. There was a hole in the wall near where General WALKER had been sitting. In the adjacent room, NORVELL found the bullet among some papers and literature and later gave this bullet to Detective D. E. McELROY. McELROY advised NORVELL and TUCKER that he, McELROY, would give the bullet to the Dallas Police Department Crime Laboratory. Officer TUCKER stated he did not know whether or not NORVELL had marked the bullet for identification and when NORVELL gave it to McELROY this was the last that TUCKER ever saw of the bullet.

On June 1, 1964, Sergeant H. H. SPRINGER, Personnel Bureau, Dallas, Texas, Police Department, advised that Officer B. G. NORVELL resigned from the Police Department on May 4, 1963. At that time, NORVELL resided at 4829 Live Oak Street, Dallas, Texas.

On June 3, 1964, BILLY GENE NORVELL, Apartment 147, 1603 Darr Street, Irving, Texas, advised he was employed as a Patrolman by the Dallas, Texas, Police Department from December 1, 1962 to May 4, 1963.

On the night of April 10, 1963, at about 9:00 PM, while working with Patrolman D. P. TUCKER, NORVELL and TUCKER received radio instructions to "meet the complainant" at 4011 Turtle Creek Boulevard. NORVELL stated he and his partner proceeded immediately to this address, arriving about five minutes after receiving the radio instructions. Upon arrival, they were met at the front door by Major General EDWIN A. WALKER, who told them he wanted to "show" them something. General WALKER led the

Re: LEE HARVEY OSWALD

officers to a study in the back of the house, where he showed them a hole in the wall, and stated this had been caused by a shot which had entered through a window at the back of the house and went through the wall about three inches above WALKER's head. NORVELL stated he and his partner inspected the window where the bullet entered and then called the Burglary and Theft Squad of the Dallas Police Department, requesting that detectives be sent out to handle the investigation. NORVELL advised that he and TUCKER then went to the room adjoining the study between which was the wall that the bullet had passed through. In this adjoining room, the officers found numerous bundles of literature and papers stacked against this common wall. Upon removing same, they found a mushroomed bullet lying on one of the stacks of literature near the hole in the wall. NORVELL stated he then picked up the bullet and scratched his initials "B. N." or his initial "N" on the base of it. NORVELL stated that later he gave this bullet to Detective McELROY, of the Burglary and Theft Squad, and McELROY advised that he would take the bullet to the Dallas Police Department Crime Laboratory for examination. NORVELL stated he did not observe McELROY mark the bullet for identification while in NORVELL's presence. NORVELL advised this was the last time he had seen this bullet. He stated the bullet was mutilated and mushroomed from impact, except for the base and a fraction of an inch from the base.

On May 28, 1964, Lieutenant J. C. DAY, Officer in Charge of the Crime Scene Search Section (CSSS), Dallas, Texas, Police Department, advised that on April 25, 1963, he took a bullet from the CSSS, marked it for identification, and then personally took it to the City - County Criminal Investigation Laboratory, Parkland Memorial Hospital, where he gave it to F. T. ALEXANDER and LOUIE L. ANDERSON. The bullet was turned over to these men with a request from Lieutenant DAY for examination to identify the gun which had fired the bullet. Within a few days, Lieutenant DAY received an oral report from the City - County Criminal Investigation Laboratory that the Laboratory could not identify the gun which fired the bullet because of the battered condition of the bullet.

Lieutenant DAY stated the bullet remained in the custody of the City - County Criminal Investigation Laboratory until December 2, 1963, when Lieutenant DAY personally went to Parkland Memorial Hospital, picked up the bullet, and returned it to the Dallas Police Department CSSS.

Lieutenant DAY stated his records show that at 4:10 PM, on December 2, 1963, he personally turned over this bullet to Federal Bureau of Investigation Agent BARDWELL D. ODUM.

On June 1, 1964, FLOYD T. ALEXANDER, City - County Criminal Investigation Laboratory, Parkland Memorial Hospital, Dallas, Texas, advised his records show that on April 25, 1963, he received a bullet in damaged condition, which had apparently been fired, from Lieutenant J. C. DAY, of the Crime Scene Search Section, Dallas Police Department. The receipt for this bullet was signed by ALEXANDER and his assistant, LOUIE L. ANDERSON, as this is their usual procedure on receipt of any possible evidence.

ALEXANDER had been requested by Lieutenant DAY only to determine, if possible, the type of gun which fired the bullet in question. Upon examination, ALEXANDER was only able to ascertain the types of guns from which the bullet could have been fired but that this was speculation on his part. He explained this was due to the fact he did not have any weapon with which to make a comparison.

ALEXANDER stated he subsequently, date unrecalled, made an oral report to Lieutenant DAY that he had been unable to definitely determine what type of gun fired the bullet and advised Lieutenant DAY the types of guns which could have possibly fired the bullet. He stated the oral report was made as there was nothing on which to base a written report other than the above speculation.

ALEXANDER stated his records show the bullet was maintained in his custody at the Laboratory in Parkland Memorial

Hospital from April 25, 1963, until December 2, 1963, when it was released to Lieutenant DAY.

Files of the Dallas Office of the Federal Bureau of Investigation show that Special Agent BARDWELL D. ODUM transmitted by registered mail a bullet to the Federal Bureau of Investigation Laboratory on December 2, 1963. This bullet had been obtained by Special Agent ODUM from Lieutenant J. C. DAY, Crime Scene Search Section, Dallas, Texas, Police Department, on December 2, 1963. This bullet was subsequently designated by the Federal Bureau of Investigation Laboratory as Specimen No. Q-188. This bullet is Item No. C-148.

Item No. C-148 was delivered to the President's Commission on March 21, 1964. It was returned to the Federal Bureau of Investigation Laboratory by the President's Commission on May 1, 1964, where it is now retained.

On June 3, 1964, Lieutenant J. C. DAY, Crime Scene Search Section, Dallas, Texas, Police Department, furnished copies of seven photographs taken April 10, 1963, in or near the residence of Major General EDWIN A. WALKER, 4011 Turtle Creek Boulevard, Dallas, Texas, by Officer B. G. BROWN, who is assigned to the Crime Scene Search Section. These photographs are described as follows:

1. Scene depicting the entry of a shot through WALKER's residence near the upper portion of the window frame. This photograph was taken from inside looking out.

2. Photograph depicting a scene showing the entry of a bullet through the screen and window of WALKER's residence. This photograph was taken from the outside of the residence looking in.

Re: LEE HARVEY OSWALD

3. Photograph depicting a scene taken inside WALKER's residence and of the wall which was to WALKER's left at the time of the shot. This photograph depicts the hole in the wall made by the bullet which, according to General WALKER, was about 3" above his head.

4. Photograph taken in the adjoining room to the room where WALKER was sitting at the time of the shot. It depicts a scene showing a bullet hole in the wall near some packages and just below a painting. This was where the bullet entered the adjoining room and the area where the bullet was found by the police.

5. Photograph taken outside of the residence of General WALKER near the alley and depicts what appears to be part of a tire track and a roller. The significance of this picture is unknown, other than it was taken for possible future use as evidence.

6. Photograph taken from the alley behind WALKER's residence looking towards a wooden fence. It was believed that it was in this area that the would-be assassin stood when he fired the shot at General WALKER.

7. Photograph taken from where officers believed the assailant stood at the time he fired the shot into WALKER's residence. Photograph depicts part of the back of WALKER's residence, the window through which the bullet entered, and the chair where WALKER was sitting at the time of the shooting.

-7-

COMMISSION EXHIBIT No. 1953—Continued

Re: LEE HARVEY OSWALD

On June 3, 1964, ROBERT A. SURREY, residence, 3506 Lindenwood, Highland Park, business, 2700 Haskell Avenue, Dallas, Texas, furnished the following information:

On Monday night, April 8, 1963, at about 9:00 to 9:30 p.m., SURREY arrived in the area of the residence of General EDWIN A. WALKER, 4011 Turtle Creek Boulevard. SURREY was proceeding up Avondale Street in order to turn into the alley and enter the WALKER residence by the alley entrance. Prior to turning into the alley, he observed a 1963 dark brown or maroon, four-door Ford, parked on Avondale with two men sitting in it. Rather than turn into the alley, SURREY proceeded around the block and entered the Mormon Church Parking Lot, located on the property adjoining the WALKER residence to the north, and parked his car in this lot. He then went to a position in one of the neighboring yards where he could observe the two men. He observed them get out of the car, walk up the alley and onto the WALKER property and look into windows of the WALKER house. At about this point, SURREY went to their automobile, where he checked the rear of the car, and observed there was no license plate on the rear. He then opened the door and looked into the car and opened the glove compartment. He observed nothing in the car or glove compartment which would help identify the occupants. He then went back to his car and drove to a position where he could observe the 1963 Ford leave.

About a half hour after SURREY first observed this car, the two men returned to it and drove off down Turtle Creek Boulevard, then south to Pacific Street. At this point, SURREY stated he was unable to continue following this automobile.

SURREY stated he had never seen either of these two men before or since this incident, and was of the opinion that neither of these two men was identical with LEE HARVEY OSWALD. He described one of the men as a white male, in his 30's, about 5' 10" to 6' tall, and weighing about 190 pounds. SURREY described the second individual as a white male, in his 30's, about 5' 10" to 6' tall, and weighing about 160 pounds. He stated both men were well dressed in suits, dress shirts and ties.

-8-

COMMISSION EXHIBIT No. 1953—Continued

Mr. SURREY stated he is not certain he could identify either man if he ever observed them again.

On the night of April 10, 1963, SURREY stated he was not at WALKER's residence, but received a call from General WALKER shortly after the shooting incident, or shortly after 9:00 PM. He stated he proceeded from his residence directly to WALKER's residence, arriving there at about the same time as did the first police car. SURREY stated he observed one of these uniformed police officers find a mushroomed bullet in the room adjoining that where General WALKER had been sitting when the shot was fired through the window.

SURREY was shown a photograph, which is Commission Exhibit No. 5, Federal Bureau of Investigation Inventory No. 369, and which depicts the rear of General WALKER's residence and a 1957 Chevrolet.

It appears that this photograph was mutilated, in that the area on the back of the Chevrolet where the license plate would normally be found has been torn out.

SURREY stated this car appears identical to one owned and operated by CHARLIE KLIHR, a frequent visitor to General WALKER's residence. SURREY stated KLIHR resides in Irving, Texas, and is employed by Texas Instruments.

On June 3, 1964, WALTER KIRK COLEMAN, 4338 Newton Street, Dallas, Texas, age 15, furnished the following information:

On April 10, 1963, sometime between 9:00 and 10:00 PM, COLEMAN, along with his godfather, RONALD ANDRIES, was building some shelves in COLEMAN's bedroom. At the time, COLEMAN was standing in the doorway which leads from his bedroom to the outside of the house on the north side of his residence. COLEMAN heard a blast and his first impression was that it was a car backfire. COLEMAN ran immediately to the fence which separates the property

where he resides and that of the Mormon Church Parking Lot. COLEMAN stepped up on a bicycle, which was leaning against the fence, and which put him in a position to look into the Mormon Church Parking Lot and the back of the church property.

Upon looking into this parking lot, COLEMAN observed two men, hereinafter referred to as No. 1 and No. 2. No. 1 was at the back of a white or beige 1950 Ford and was hurrying towards the driver's side of this car. COLEMAN observed no other person in the car. The car was parked headed towards Turtle Creek Boulevard (or away from COLEMAN) with the motor running and the headlights on. No. 2 was about ten yards behind No. 1 at a point about twenty-five feet inside the church property, or parking lot, from the alley entrance to this parking lot. No. 1 was almost directly in front of COLEMAN and No. 2 was to COLEMAN's right. No. 2 was walking in a direction away from the alley entrance and towards a 1958 black over white, two-door Chevrolet sedan. This Chevrolet was parked in the second parking slot to the east of the alley entrance headed in towards a fence which separates the church property and that of General EDWIN A. WALKER. A Renault automobile belonging to the church caretaker was parked in the first parking slot.

COLEMAN stated his immediate attention was directed toward No. 1. No. 1 got into the 1950 Ford and, as he did so, glanced back in the direction of COLEMAN. This man got into the car and drove off at a normal rate of speed towards the exit from the church parking lot onto Turtle Creek Boulevard. COLEMAN stated he did not notice if No. 1 was carrying anything in his hands. He stated No. 1 was wearing khaki pants, a sport shirt with figures in it, and was a white male, about 19 or 20 years of age, about 5'10" tall, and weighing about 130 pounds. He stated this man had dark, bushy hair, a thin face with a large nose, and was "real skinny."

COLEMAN stated he was able to observe this even though it was nighttime, as the church has a floodlight which was on at the time, and which lights up the parking lot.

COLEMAN then looked back towards No. 2 and observed that he was, by this time, at the driver's side of the Chevrolet. He had the door open and the front seat pushed forward. He was leaning through the car door and into the back seat area of this car. COLEMAN then returned to his residence and did not observe how or when No. 2 left the parking lot. About an hour later, while being questioned by a police officer, COLEMAN noticed that the Chevrolet was gone, as were all other cars that had been in the parking lot when he first observed the two men, with the exception of the caretaker's Renault. COLEMAN advised that, when he first observed these two men, along with the 1950 Ford and the 1958 Chevrolet, there were about six other cars parked in the parking lot.

COLEMAN described No. 2 as a white male, about 6'1", about 200 pounds, wearing a dark, long-sleeve shirt, and dark pants. COLEMAN advised he never saw No. 2's face and could not furnish any information as to his age. He also stated he did not recall anything about No. 2's hair. He advised that when he first observed No. 2 he did not notice if he was carrying anything, although this was possible, as his attention was mainly directed towards No. 1 at that time.

COLEMAN advised he had never seen either man or either car at any time before or after this incident.

COLEMAN stated he has seen numerous photographs of LEE HARVEY OSWALD and he was shown a photograph of OSWALD among several other photographs. He stated that neither man resembled OSWALD and that he had never seen anyone in or around the WALKER residence or the church before or after April 10, 1963, who resembled LEE HARVEY OSWALD.

COLEMAN explained that, from where he was standing looking over the fence, he could not see down the alley behind WALKER's residence, as there is a stockade fence around some

garbage cans in the southwest corner of the church parking lot, and this blocked his view down the alley.

It was personally observed on June 3, 1964, by Special Agents of the Federal Bureau of Investigation that the distance from the door in the residence of WALTER KIRK COLEMAN, 4338 Newton Street, Dallas, Texas, to the place at the stockade fence where he observed incidents on the night of April 10, 1963, in the church parking lot at about 9:00 PM, is approximately fourteen feet.

COLEMAN was requested to re-enact his actions upon hearing the blast of what he first thought was a backfire on the night of April 10, 1963. It was personally observed by Special Agents of the Federal Bureau of Investigation that it required COLEMAN two seconds to go from where he was standing in a doorway to the stockade fence, a distance of about fourteen feet.

It was personally observed by Special Agents of the Federal Bureau of Investigation, based on information furnished by WALTER KIRK COLEMAN on June 3, 1964, that from the point where COLEMAN states he observed a man walking towards a 1950 Ford to the alley entrance of the church parking lot it is approximately forty-five feet. It was also personally observed that the distance from where COLEMAN states he first saw a man walking towards a 1958 Chevrolet is twenty-one feet to the alley entrance of the church parking lot.

It was personally observed by Special Agents of the Federal Bureau of Investigation that it is approximately thirty-five feet from the alley entrance of the WALKER property (4011 Turtle Creek Boulevard) to the alley entrance of the church parking lot.

On June 4, 1964, WALTER KIRK COLEMAN, 4338 Newton Street, Dallas, Texas, was reinterviewed in connection with the information he had previously furnished Federal Bureau of Investigation Agents on June 3, 1964, in connection with incidents he observed on the night of April 10, 1963, in the parking lot of the Mormon Church. This church parking lot is located adjacent to the property of Major General EDWIN A. WALKER, United States Army (Retired), 4011 Turtle Creek Boulevard, Dallas, Texas.

COLEMAN stated he was able to observe what he had seen because the lights in the church and the floodlight, which is attached to the church building and lights up the church parking lot, were on at the time.

Concerning the foreign-made car he had observed parked next to the 1958 black and white Chevrolet, COLEMAN stated he believes this was a Renault, but it could have been some other make of automobile, as he does not know what a Renault looks like.

He stated at the time there were about six other cars observed by him in the lot other than the 1950 white or light beige Ford and the 1958 Chevrolet. He added, however, there could have been some other cars parked to his left as he looked into the lot as he did not look in that direction.

He stated the reason he ran to the fence and looked into the church parking lot was that he became curious after hearing what he thought was a backfire of an automobile as it is unusual to hear such noises in this neighborhood. He returned to the house because he did not think that a shot had been fired, and there was no other reason for him to continue observing the man near the 1958 black and white Chevrolet.

On June 3, 1964, H. M. HART, Detective, Criminal Intelligence Section, Dallas, Texas, Police Department, advised that during the past month he has compiled a list of automobiles observed in and around the residence of General EDWIN A. WALKER, 4011 Turtle Creek Boulevard, Dallas. These cars had been observed by HART on various occasions during this period of time.

Upon checking this list, HART stated he had no information that a 1950 white or beige Ford or a 1958 black over white Chevrolet, two-door sedan, had ever been observed by him. HART explained that some of the cars he had observed had been parked in the church parking lot, which adjoins General WALKER's property to the north.

HART reviewed information compiled by the Intelligence Section since December, 1962, concerning activities in and around the residence of General WALKER and of General WALKER and his associates. This review failed to show any knowledge by the Intelligence Section of a 1950 white or beige Ford or a 1958 black over white Chevrolet.

On June 4, 1964, Mr. E. OWEN HANSEN, 3328 Leahy Drive, Dallas, Texas, advised that he is presently a Bishop of the Church of Jesus Christ of Latter Day Saints, Ward Number One, located at 4027 Turtle Creek Boulevard, Dallas, Texas. He advised that as of April, 1963, he had the title of a Counselor for the above church.

HANSEN related that, in regard to church services scheduled, he does not hold services on the first Sunday evening of each month and, after reviewing a calendar, advised that they did not have services at the church on April 7, 1963. He advised they have Wednesday evening services at the church on every Wednesday except during the month of August. HANSEN stated the Wednesday evening services were scheduled from 7:30 PM until 9:00 PM, and that usually everyone had departed the church by 9:15 PM to 9:20 PM.

HANSEN stated he does not recall whether he was in attendance at the church on the evening of April 10, 1963, and has not heard anyone make comments concerning his attendance the night that someone had taken a shot at Major General EDWIN A. WALKER. HANSEN also advised he does not recall seeing a 1950 beige or white Ford or a 1958 black over white Chevrolet parked in the parking lot at the church, nor does he know of any of the church members who own automobiles described as above.

HANSEN related that during the day there are usually cars parked along the fence next to the WALKER residence which do not belong to church members. He advised they are probably friends of WALKER or other people residing in the area of the church.

HANSEN related that insofar as attendance at the church on the night of April 10, 1963, Mr. CARL SPRECKLESON, of 1317 Belaire Street, Richardson, Texas (telephone number AD 5-1642), would have this information as he is presently in charge of the records of the church. He also advised that Mr. ED HEATH, who is a detective with the Dallas, Texas, Police Department, is a part-time custodian at the church and may have been on duty the night of April 10, 1963.

HANSEN stated that the dress on Wednesday evening for the young people is usually classified as being casual, in that they wear sport shirts and slacks, and that the adults usually wear shirts, ties and suits to the services.

HANSEN estimated that the parking lot is usually one-half to two-thirds full for the Wednesday night services.

On June 4, 1964, SCOTT HANSEN, age 15, 3328 Leahy Drive, Dallas, Texas, advised that he is the son of E. OWEN HANSEN, and that he is a member of the Church of Jesus Christ of Latter Day Saints, located at 4027 Turtle Creek Boulevard, Dallas.

He advised that he was present at the church on the night of April 10, 1963, attending a Scout meeting and, to the best of his recollection, he arrived at approximately 7:15 PM and left at approximately 9:30 PM. He advised that he was inside the church from the time of his arrival until the time of his departure.

HANSEN stated that he recalls observing a 1958 black over white Chevrolet parked along the fence next to Major General EDWIN A. WALKER's property on the night of April 10, 1963. He stated that he recalls seeing the same automobile parked along this fence on a previous Wednesday, but has not seen the car in the church lot since April 10, 1963. He stated that he was talking to another Boy Scout by the name of DAVID CLEMENS concerning the appearance of the automobile and remarked he thought that it was a "pretty good-looking car."

HANSEN also advised that he does not recall observing a 1949 or 1950 white or beigb-colored Ford in the parking lot.

HANSEN stated that a church member by the name of JOE ST. JOHN, who is presently a student at Southern Methodist University, drives a Karmann Ghia and usually parks in the parking lot near the fence dividing the church property from that of Major General WALKER. He stated ST. JOHN might possibly recall seeing the 1958 Chevrolet parked in that area.

HANSEN stated that Scoutmaster HAROLD RAY CLUTS would have a knowledge of the Boy Scouts present for the meeting on the night of April 10, 1963.

On June 4, 1964, EDWIN D. HEATH, JR., 1102 Dearborn Circle, Richardson, Texas, advised he is a Detective on the Dallas, Texas, Police Department, and works as a part-time custodian at the Church of Jesus Christ of Latter Day Saints, located at 4027 Turtle Creek Boulevard, Dallas. HEATH stated he is also a member of this church.

HEATH related he spends approximately fifteen hours each week at the church in taking care of the property; however, on the night of April 10, 1963, he was working the evening shift at the Police Department and was not present for the Wednesday evening services.

He advised that, knowing the Police Department was interested in the shooting, he had made inquiry of various members for any possible information they may have concerning the shooting; however, his efforts met with negative results.

HEATH stated he has never observed a 1958 black over white Chevrolet parked in the parking lot, nor does he know of any member who has owned a 1958 black over white Chevrolet. He also advised he has never observed, nor does he know of any member who has owned, a 1949 or 1950 white or beige Ford automobile.

HEATH stated that church member JOE ST. JOHN has a foreign-made car and usually parks near the fence located next to WALKER's property.

HEATH related that the parking lot is poorly lighted, due to the fact the neighbors had previously complained to the church concerning the bright lights. HEATH related he believed that enough light would be present on the lot for an individual to obtain a description of a person standing in the lot, as well as to identify various automobiles. He stated he believes the colors of the automobiles could be distinguished by the light in the church parking lot.

On June 4, 1964, photographs were taken of the parking lot area of the Church of Jesus Christ of Latter Day Saints, 4027 Turtle Creek Boulevard, Dallas, Texas. It is noted this parking lot is located adjacent to and just north of the residence of Major General EDWIN A. WALKER (Retired), at 4011 Turtle Creek Boulevard, Dallas.

Photograph designated as DL-53 (1) is a view of the parking lot looking south toward the entrance to the alley. The alley, just beyond the entrance to the parking lot, runs directly behind the residence of Major General WALKER.

DL-53 (2) and (3) are views of the church parking lot looking east toward the parking lot entrance at Turtle Creek Boulevard. The wooden fence on the right-hand side of the photograph divides the property of the church from that of the residence of General WALKER.

These photographs were taken from the same location that WALTER KIRK COLEMAN, of 4338 Newton Street, stated he was standing immediately after he heard the loud noise the night of April 10, 1963.

The above photographs were taken with a Bureau-owned 4X5 Speed Graphic Camera.

In connection with the copies of Police Department reports furnished by Officer B. G. BROWN, Dallas, Texas, Police Department, on May 28, 1964, concerning investigation by that agency of the shooting at the residence of Major General WALKER on April 10, 1963, the following discrepancies as determined through this investigation should be noted:

1. The report of Officers D. P. TUCKER and B. G. NORVELL states, "Officer B. G. NORVELL found the bullet..." and it "was given to Det. G. B. BROWN, Crime Laboratory Division." On May 28, 1964, Detective DON E. McELROY advised he found the bullet and turned it over to Officer BROWN. On the same date, Officer BROWN stated he obtained the bullet from Officer NORVELL. Officer TUCKER, on June 2, 1964, and former Officer NORVELL, on June 3, 1964, both stated NORVELL found the bullet and he, in turn, gave it to McELROY, who said he would take it or give it to the Dallas Police Department Crime Laboratory.

Re: LEE HARVEY OSWALD

2. The report of Officers TUCKER and NORVELL states, "A witness by ear, Kirk Coleman, w/m/14, 4338 Newton, LA 8 7059, states he was sitting in the back room of his home, and heard what sounded like a shot from a shotgun, and he ran outside and pulled himself up over the stockade fence in the rear yard, and as he looked onto the church parking lot he saw some unk/w/m/ speed down the driveway towards Turtle Crkke, in either 49 or 50 Ford, light green. He then noticed what appeared to be a w/m with the door open on a 58 Chev., blk with white stripe down side, states this person had the seat pushed up and was leaning over as if he was putting something into the floorboards. This person got inside the Chev. and sped away from the lot. (There was a meetting of some sort in the church, and the lot was full of car, but at the time the time the witness looked out there these were the only people on the lot)." On June 3, 1964, WALTER KIRK COLEMAN, 4338 Newton Street, Dallas, Texas, furnished Special Agents of the Federal Bureau of Investigation the following noted discrepancies in connection with the above report:

(a) COLEMAN was standing at an outside door at the time of the shot, not "sitting in the back room."

(b) The shot sounded to COLEMAN like a car backfire, not a "shot from a shotgun."

(c) COLEMAN observed one unknown white male hurrying towards a 1950 white or beige Ford (not light green) and, after getting in behind the steering wheel, this person drove away at a normal rate of speed. He did not "speed down the driveway."

-19-

Re: LEE HARVEY OSWALD

(d) COLEMAN observed a second unknown white male at a point about twenty-five feet inside the church property, from the alley entrance or exit. When COLEMAN next observed this individual, this person was at the driver's side of a 1958 black over white Chevrolet, two-door sedan, not a "58 Chev. blk with white stripe down side."

(e) COLEMAN stated this second individual was observed by him leaning front of the car into the back seat area of the Chevrolet and COLEMAN could not tell what this man was doing, nor did COLEMAN watch what this man was doing because, at this point, COLEMAN returned to his residence.

(f) The TUCKER - NORVELL report states COLEMAN advised the lot was "full of cars." COLEMAN advised the Special Agents there were about six other cars in addition to the Ford and Chevrolet in the lot at the time.

(g) The TUCKER - NORVELL report reflects interview of "Robert Suwrey" (correct spelling SURREY) concerning two men in a dark 1963 Ford seen by SURREY on Monday, April 8, 1963, in the alley behind WALKER's residence. The report of Detectives McELROY and VAN CLEAVE, dated April 10, 1963, states SURREY saw the 1963 Ford and two men, no other description, on April 6, 1963 (Saturday), parked at the rear of WALKER's residence. The report of Officers DELLINGER and ROSE, dated April 11, 1963, contains an interview of SURREY concerning the incident about seeing the 1963 Ford and two men, but does not state when SURREY saw this car or the men and the report gives the impression it occurred on April 10, 1963.

-20-

(h) On June 3, 1964, ROBERT A. SURREY advised Special Agents of the Federal Bureau of Investigation he observed the 1963 dark brown or maroon Ford parked on Avondale Street near the alley entrance, which alley runs behind WALKER's residence. SURREY stated this incident took place on April 8, 1963 (Monday), and he described the individuals as one being a white male in his 30's, 5'10" to 6' tall, 160 pounds, and the second as a white male, in his 30's, 5'10" to 6' tall, weighing 190 pounds. He stated both men were well-dressed in suits, shirts and ties.

On June 1, 1964, Mrs. ROSS BOUVE, 4001 Turtle Creek Boulevard, Dallas, Texas, Business Manager for the Jackson Clinic, 3929 Fairmount, advised she has resided at the residence of Doctor RUTH JACKSON, 4001 Turtle Creek Boulevard, for about six years. She stated the wing in which she resides in the house overlooks the entire property belonging to Major General EDWIN A. WALKER, 4011 Turtle Creek Boulevard. Mrs. BOUVE advised that Doctor RUTH JACKSON resides in the wing on the opposite side of the house and on the night of April 10, 1963, Doctor JACKSON was not in a position to hear or see anything which occurred at the WALKER residence. She further advised that Doctor JACKSON does not own a dog.

Mrs. BOUVE stated she owns a "border collie" named "Toby" which she usually keeps in the fenced back yard, which area is directly next to the back yard area of the WALKER residence. She advised that "Toby" will bark loud at anyone or anything in the alley area at the rear of their residence, or at anyone or anything on the WALKER property. On April 10, 1963, "Toby" was placed in the laundry room by Mrs. BOUVE sometime after dark, as "Toby" had been barking loud and long earlier in the evening at the numerous people coming and going from the

WALKER residence, and at the numerous people coming and going to church services at the Mormon Church located on the other side of the WALKER residence. Mrs. BOUVE stated her other dog, "Two-Bit," is a Yorkshire terrier who usually remains inside the house and who does not bark while in the house.

Prior to the shooting incident on April 10, 1963, at the WALKER residence, Mrs. BOUVE stated she heard "Toby" growling and barking in the laundry room, but she took no notice of this because this was his usual behavior and especially on Wednesday nights when church services are held at the Mormon Church. She, therefore, did not make any check to ascertain why the dog was barking. Upon hearing what she thought was a backfire, Mrs. BOUVE stated she thought nothing of it. She explained there is heavy traffic on Turtle Creek Boulevard and numerous cars also drive through the alley at the rear of the house en route to the Mormon Church. Her first impression was that the noise was a backfire and she, therefore, did nothing about it. She stated she did not look out her window at the WALKER residence until much later when she heard police cars arrive.

She advised that, immediately after hearing what she thought was a backfire, she could not recall having heard anyone run from the area or any car driving away. She further stated that on the Sunday previous to the shooting, April 7, 1963, she noticed nothing unusual in or about the WALKER residence, other than there had been a large crowd at the Mormon Church on Sunday night.

She advised her dog "Toby" became very sick on April 11 and 12, 1963. She stated she was of the opinion someone had given him something to quiet him or drug him or poison him, because he did become sick and vomited extensively on April 11 and 12, 1963. She did not take him to a veterinarian. She stated she based her belief that the dog had been given something because of the shooting incident and the dog's habit of barking at anyone or anything in the alley area. She stated she had no other basis for this belief or any proof whatsoever, and this was only opinion on her part.

Mrs. BOUVE was shown a photograph of LEE HARVEY OSWALD and advised she had never seen anyone resembling OSWALD at or near the WALKER residence at any time.

On June 1, 1964, by personal observation, Special Agents of the Federal Bureau of Investigation determined that the railroad tracks located nearest to the residence of Major General EDWIN A. WALKER, United States Army (Retired), 4011 Turtle Creek Boulevard, Dallas, Texas, are those of the Missouri, Kansas, and Texas (MKT) Railroad. These tracks are approximately 0.3 of a mile southeast from WALKER's residence and are almost parallel to Turtle Creek Boulevard in this area.

It was also determined, through personal observation, that directly across the street (Turtle Creek Boulevard) from WALKER's residence there is a park area, which extends approximately 0.6 of a mile to the northeast from WALKER's residence and approximately 1.8 miles to the southwest from WALKER's residence. This park area parallels Turtle Creek Boulevard and the MKT railroad tracks and, in most places, adjoins the property of the railroad. This park and the railroad property, in numerous places, is comprised of heavily wooded areas and thick underbrush, affording innumerable places where an object the size of a rifle could be easily hidden, buried, or otherwise secreted. It was also personally observed that along the railroad right-of-way there are many paths and trails leading from the park area through the woods and underbrush up to the railroad tracks.

No "open fields" were observed adjoining the railroad tracks in this area.

By walking directly to the east or southeast from the rear of the WALKER residence, a person has immediate access to the wooded brushy area and the railroad tracks.

It should be noted that Photograph No. 5 of Item No. 6 has been previously identified by personal observation by Special Agents of the Federal Bureau of Investigation as a scene depicting

a section of the MKT railroad tracks located approximately 0.7 of a mile southeast of WALKER's residence and near the Dallas Theatre Center.

On June 4, 1964, personal observation of the Missouri, Kansas and Texas (MKT) railroad tracks in the area of Major General EDWIN A. WALKER's residence, 4011 Turtle Creek Boulevard, Dallas, Texas, by Special Agents of the Federal Bureau of Investigation determined that Photograph No. 1 in Item No. 70, depicting a view of the railroad tracks, was taken approximately 109 yards northeast of the MKT railroad overpass at Blackburn Street. At the point where the photograph was taken, it was noted that there is a footpath leading down the railroad embankment to Turtle Creek Drive. At the point where the photograph was taken, the railroad tracks are approximately twenty-five to thirty feet above street level, and it is approximately ninety feet from the tracks to the curb line of Turtle Creek Drive. The area from the railroad tracks to the curb line is a heavily-wooded area with two or three large piles of brush, which have evidently been stacked in this area for a considerable length of time. Near the path and located between Turtle Creek Drive and the railroad embankment, it was noted that a drainage sewer, approximately six feet tall and four or five feet wide, ran underneath the railroad and Turtle Creek Boulevard.

It was personally observed by Special Agents of the Federal Bureau of Investigation that from the point where the path enters Turtle Creek Drive to the rear of Major General EDWIN A. WALKER's residence, via the most direct traffic route, it is .45 mile. The route traveled to record the mileage was via Turtle Creek Drive to the intersection of Stonebridge Drive and northeast on Turtle Creek Boulevard to Irving Street, west on Irving Street to the alley, and then northeast in the alley to the rear of Major General EDWIN A. WALKER's residence.

It was also noted that Photograph No. 1 in Item No. 70 was taken approximately .25 mile north by northeast of the point where Photograph No. 5 of Item No. 6 was taken. Both photographs depict a view of the MKT railroad tracks.

Re: LEE HARVEY OSWALD

Personal observation of the MKT railroad tracks at the point where Photograph No. 1 of Item No. 70 was taken by Special Agents of the Federal Bureau of Investigation revealed the following identical reference points as depicted in the photograph:

The tenth railroad tie from the bottom of the picture is extended approximately four or five inches out of line with the rest of the ties. It was noted the extended railroad tie is three ties above a connection on the right-hand railroad track.

The metal utility tower, as depicted in the center of the photograph, was observed in the same location in reference to the extended railroad tie.

The railroad signal device located to the right of the tracks and at a point where it appears to disappear at the top of photograph was observed in the same location.

To the right of the railroad signal device a telephone post can be observed leaning at a 45-degree angle and used as a brace against another telephone post. In the photograph, it is the fourth telephone post from the right-hand edge of the picture.

On the left side of the photograph, a portion of a house can be observed. From personal observation of the area, it is believed this house is the rear of the duplex at 3338-40 Blackburn Street.

On June 3, 1964, aerial photographs of the area in and around the residence of Major General EDWIN A. WALKER, United States Army (Retired), 4011 Turtle Creek Boulevard, were taken by Special Agents of the Federal Bureau of Investigation from a Bell Aircraft Company helicopter piloted by WAYNE SPILKER.

These photographs bearing the below-listed identification designations are described as follows:

-25-

COMMISSION EXHIBIT No. 1953—Continued

Re: LEE HARVEY OSWALD

PHOTO DESIGNATION	DESCRIPTION
DL 52(1)	Photograph taken looking northeast with Missouri, Kansas, and Texas (MKT) railroad tracks running from the bottom of the photograph through the right center to the upper-right center of the photograph and Turtle Creek Boulevard to the left of these railroad tracks running from the bottom left of the photograph up through the left-hand side of the photograph. This street is a six-lane road. North Central Expressway is depicted in the upper-right corner of the photograph.
DL 52(2)	Photograph looking southeast with the downtown area of Dallas in the upper-right center of the photograph, North Central Expressway running from the left-hand side of the photograph through the upper center of the photograph toward the downtown area, and Preston Road in the bottom center of the photograph.
DL 52(3)	Photograph looking northeast depicting North Central Expressway in the lower front of the photograph, Fitzhugh Street in the lower right of the photograph, and Love Field in the upper-right corner of the photograph.
DL 52(4)	Photograph looking southeast depicts the residence of Major General EDWIN A. WALKER in the lower center of the photograph, Turtle Creek Boulevard running from the lower left-hand corner

-26-

COMMISSION EXHIBIT No. 1953—Continued

PHOTO DESIGNATION	DESCRIPTION
DL 52(4) (cont'd)	diagonally toward the upper-right center of the photograph, and North Central Expressway at the upper portion of the photograph running from left to right.
DL 52(5)	Photograph looking southwest with the MKT railroad tracks running from the lower left-hand corner of the photograph through the left center of the photograph. The downtown area of Dallas is in the upper left-hand corner of the photograph.
DL 52(6)	Photograph looking southwest, the residence of Major General EDWIN A. WALKER in the lower center of the photograph, Oaklawn Avenue running from the right center of the photograph through the middle of the photograph and then turning toward the upper left-hand corner of the photograph. Turtle Creek Boulevard is shown from the lower-left center of the photograph across the photograph to the lower-right corner.

On June 3, 1964, Mr. V. C. SNIDER, Schedule Engineer, Schedule Department, Dallas Transit Company, Dallas, Texas, furnished the following information concerning buses available to passengers inbound towards the downtown area of Dallas, Texas, from the general area in and around 4011 Turtle Creek Boulevard, Dallas, Texas:

BUS RUN NUMBER	BUS RUN DESIGNATION	ROUTE
52	Singleton	Via Lemmon Avenue to Central Expressway, south to Pacific Street, west to Lamar Street, north to McKinney Avenue, then west out Singleton Boulevard to the area of town known as "West Dallas"
36	Preston Hollow Express	Via Oaklawn Avenue to Blackburn, east to Central Expressway, south to Elm Street, west to Lamar Street, north to Ross Avenue, then return via Central Expressway and the above route (in reverse) to the area of Dallas known as "Preston Hollow"
4	Bishop	From the SMU Campus south on Hillcrest and Abbott Streets to Knox Street, east to Cole Street, south to Blackburn, then east to Central Expressway, south to Elm Street, west to Houston Street, then via Houston Street viaduct to Marsalis Avenue, south to Colorado Street, west to Bishop Street, south to Davis Street, then west to Llewellyn Street, from where it returns via the the same route to the SMU Campus. This bus crosses Neely Street in the 400 block west
54	Beverly Hills	Departs from Love Field, Dallas, south on Cedar Springs Avenue to Bowen, then west via McKinney to St. Paul Street, then south to Main Street, then west via Main Street, West Commerce Street and the Fort Worth Cutoff to Plymouth Street, then south to Colorado, then west via Westmount and Davis Street to Gilpin Street, from where it returns via the same route to Love Field

BUS RUN NUMBER	BUS RUN DESIGNATION	ROUTE
37	Urbandale	Starts at Lovers Lane and Denton Road, then via Thurston and Maple Street south to Oaklawn, then to Fairmount, south to McKinney, west to Lamar, then east via Main Street to an area in East Dallas known as "Urbandale"
232	Ervay	Starts at the Greenway Park area on Loma Alta Street and proceeds to the downtown area via Loma Alta, Fairway, Gilbert, Oaklawn, Maple and Cedar Springs to Akard Streets, then to Ervay and south through the downtown area via Ervay to an area of Dallas known as "South Dallas"
38	Lisbon	Starts at Lovers Lane and Harry Hines Boulevard and proceeds southeast on Harry Hines Boulevard to Akard Street, then south to Corinth Street, where it crosses into the Oak Cliff area of Dallas to Illinois Avenue, then via Illinois, Kiest and Sunnyvale Streets to Overton Street, from where it returns via the same route

Mr. SNIDER advised that it would be impossible to state when a particular bus would pass through a general area without knowing an exact intersection or bus stop. If such were known, it could be determined within five or ten minutes when a particular bus would be at that particular bus stop.

Mr. SNIDER further stated that any passenger, after paying his fare on any bus, can obtain a transfer coupon which entitles him to board any other bus in the downtown area. He

stated this person could board the second bus at any one of a number of transfer points in the downtown area.

It should be noted that the scene depicted in Photograph No. 5, Item No. 6, has been identified through previous investigation on May 18, 1964, as reported on pages 258 and 259, of the report of Special Agent ROBERT P. GEMBERLING, dated May 28, 1964, at Dallas. In this photograph, there is depicted a railroad curving to the left with a metal utility pole on the left and a building in the left center of the photograph.

It should be noted that the scene depicted in Photograph No. 2, Item No. 7, has been identified through previous investigation on May 20, 1964, as reported on pages 260, 261 and 262, of the report of Special Agent ROBERT P. GEMBERLING, dated May 28, 1964, at Dallas. In this photograph, there is depicted an alley in the center, a two-story house on the right, a multi-story building under construction in the background, and some trees and a wooden fence on the left.

It should be noted that information concerning buses available to anyone in the downtown area of Dallas who desires transportation to the Oak Cliff area of Dallas was previously obtained on March 10, 1964, and reported on pages 176 - 183, of the report of Special Agent ROBERT P. GEMBERLING, dated April 15, 1964, at Dallas. On any bus traveling to the downtown area of Dallas from the general area near the residence of Major General EDWIN A. WALKER, United States Army (Retired), 4011 Turtle Creek Boulevard, Dallas, a passenger, after paying his fare, can obtain a transfer coupon, which entitles him to board any bus destined for the Oak Cliff area at any of the many transfer points in the downtown area. This would be necessary only if the original bus was not destined for a desired destination point in the Oak Cliff area.

As of April 10, 1963, LEE HARVEY OSWALD and his wife, MARINA, were residing at 214 West Neely Street, which is located in the Oak Cliff area and which is near the bus route

Re: LEE HARVEY OSWALD

of the bus designated as "Bishop," Bus Run No. 4. (See interview of V. C. SNIDER, Dallas Transit Company, June 3, 1964.)

On June 4, 1964, MARINA OSWALD was interviewed at her residence, 629 Belt Line Road, Richardson, Texas.

She was questioned further concerning conversations she had had with LEE HARVEY OSWALD about his visits to the house of General EDWIN A. WALKER, Dallas, Texas.

She said she had asked OSWALD how he had arrived at the WALKER home on the night he had attempted to kill WALKER by shooting him. OSWALD replied that he had walked up to the house. MARINA said she later learned OSWALD had taken a bus to the vicinity of the WALKER home and she presumes that he had gotten off the bus a distance from the WALKER home and had traversed the remaining distance on foot. She said OSWALD had said also he had returned to their home by bus after the attempted assassination. MARINA advised she was not aware of what buses OSWALD took to arrive in the vicinity of the WALKER home or to leave the vicinity of the WALKER home en route back to their home.

MARINA said she remembers OSWALD telling her he had run away from the WALKER house after the attempted assassination and that he could run very fast. She said she does not recall that OSWALD told her how far he ran or what bus he boarded or where he boarded the bus.

She does remember OSWALD told her he came home on the bus after the attempted assassination.

MARINA said she does not recall OSWALD telling her what he did with his rifle after he made the first trip to the WALKER home for the purpose of assassinating General WALKER. She said he did not bring the rifle into their home upon his return to her knowledge. She said she did not ask him what he had done with the rifle on this first visit of OSWALD to the

Re: LEE HARVEY OSWALD

WALKER home for the purpose of assassinating WALKER. She does recall she had asked OSWALD when he returned home and confessed he had attempted to assassinate General WALKER that night what he had done with the rifle because she was afraid the rifle might be found and traced to OSWALD. In answer to her query, OSWALD told her he had buried the rifle in the ground or in the bushes far away from the actual spot of the shooting. She recalls OSWALD mentioned a field and also a railroad track and she has the impression OSWALD might have meant he hid the rifle in a field near a railroad track.

MARINA said she recalled OSWALD showing her photographs he had taken of the General WALKER home. She also recalled OSWALD had shown her some photographs he had taken which depicted a railroad track. It is her recollection that these railroad tracks were near the WALKER house. She said she recalls seeing an automobile in one of the photographs of the WALKER house, but did not recall what type of an automobile it was or whether or not it had a license plate on it.

MARINA was asked if OSWALD had mentioned being associated with any other person in connection with the attempted assassination of WALKER. She said OSWALD had never mentioned another person in this connection. She said she was sure in her own mind he had planned and attempted the assassination completely alone. She said it was not like OSWALD to be associated with anybody else in such an endeavor.

MARINA said she did not know that OSWALD had known or associated with anyone in April, 1963, who owned a 1963 Ford automobile or a 1949 or a 1950 Ford automobile or a 1958 Chevrolet. She said he had never mentioned a large collie dog or any other type dog which had been near the WALKER residence. She does recall OSWALD mentioned on one occasion, when they were discussing the WALKER incident, a gathering at a church near the WALKER house. He told her he had postponed his assassination attempt until the evening of the gathering at this church.

COMMISSION EXHIBIT No. 1953-A

COMMISSION EXHIBIT No. 1953-B

In connection with the interviews of WALTER KIRK COLEMAN, 4338 Newton, Dallas, on 6/3 and 4/64, symbols on photograph identified as follows:

"A" - is place where 1950 white or beige Ford first observed by COLEMAN;
"B" - is place where 1958 black over white, tudor Chevrolet first observed by COLEMAN;
" C"- is alley entrance into Mormon Church parking lot, and which alley is directly behind property of Major General EDWIN A. WALKER, U. S. Army (retired), 4011 Turtle Creek Blvd.
"1" - is place where unknown white male, No. 1, first observed by COLEMAN.
"2" - is place where unknown white male, No.2, first observed by COLEMAN.
"3" - is COLEMAN's position for observing incidents of 4/10/63, from behind stockade fence.

COMMISSION EXHIBIT No. 1953-B—Continued

COMMISSION EXHIBIT No. 1953-C

In connection with the interviews of WALTER KIRK COLEMAN, 4338 Newton, Dallas, on 6/3 and 4/64, symbols on photograph identified as follows:

"A" - is place where 1950 white or beige Ford first observed by COLEMAN;

"B" - is place where 1958 black over white, tudor Chevrolet first observed by COLEMAN;

"C" - is alley entrance into Mormon Church parking lot, and which alley entrance is obscured from COLEMAN's vision due to stockade fence around garbage cans.

"1" - is place whereunknown white male, No. 1, first observed by COLEMAN.

"2" - is pååce where unknown white male, No. 2, first observed by COLEMAN.

"3" - is COLEMAN's position for observing incidents of 4/10/63, from behind stockade fence.

1017

DL-53 (2)
Taken 6-4-64
by SA Ivan D Lee
Dallas FBI

DL # 100-10461

COMMISSION EXHIBIT No. 1953-C—Continued

COMMISSION EXHIBIT No. 1953-D

In connection with the interviews of WALTER KIRK COLEMAN, 4338 Newton, Dallas, on 6/3 and 4/64, symbols on photograph identified as follows:
"B" - is place where 1958 black over white, tudor Chevrolet first observed by COLEMAN;
"C" - is alley entrance into Mormon Church parking lot, and which alley enhrance is obscured from COLEMAN's vision due to stockade fence around garbage cans.
"2" - is place where unknown white male, No. 2, first observed by COLEMAN. (Note-photo taken from COLEMAN's position, as of 4/10/63.)

997

DL - 53 (3)
Taken 6-4-64
by SA Ivan D Lee
Dallas FBI
DL 100-10461

COMMISSION EXHIBIT No. 1953-D—Continued

2515 W. 5th St.
Irving, Texas
April 2, 1964

Mr. Albert Jenner
President's Commission on the Assassination
of President Kennedy
200 Maryland Ave, N. E.
Washington, D. C. 20002

Dear Mr. Jenner:

Herewith the letter I read to you over the phone which my mother found at her home and sent to me after each of us had returned home from Washington, D. C.. You are welcome to include it in my testimony if you feel it useful.

It is a letter written and dispatched by me to my mother. By the postmark on the envolope I judge it left my home (the postman picks up mail as well as delivers it) the morning of the date on the postmark, Dec. 7, 1963.

The letter is in exactly the same condition now as when I dispatched it, with the exception that my mother has written the date received on the front of the envolope. The two arrows from the line "from newsmen I've learned" go respectively to the two following sentences, as I think is clear when you look at the letter. The two following sentences being: (That shot was taken Apr. 10th. He got the Rifle Mar. 20th.)

I would appreciate it if you return this letter to my mother at the following address:

Mrs. William Hyde
4400 Glenmawr Ave.
Columbus, Ohio 43224

Sincerely,

Ruth Paine

Ruth Paine

COMMISSION EXHIBIT NO. 1954

COMMISSION EXHIBIT NO. 1955

Dear Mom,

Signal's off on the Look Magazine article. Other editors opposed the ~~ess~~ editor that had worked with me, ~~&~~ saying the story had already been sufficiently told by newspaper coverage. Will you tell Rose you've mentioned the matter to? ~~Merrill D. wrote knowing It's~~ likely I won't get to write →

COMMISSION EXHIBIT No. 1956

2

him. I guess I'll try to write him.

I'm very depressed by the news just on the radio: Marina O. says Lee bragged to her he had shot at Gen. Walker. (That shot was taken from newsmen I've learned Apr 10th. He got the rifle Mar. 20th.) Would I'd had more awareness of what manner of man this was. How I grieve at the loss of the president.

Love, Ruth.

COMMISSION EXHIBIT No. 1956—Continued

OFFICE OF THE DIRECTOR

UNITED STATES DEPARTMENT OF JUSTICE
FEDERAL BUREAU OF INVESTIGATION
WASHINGTON, D.C. 20535

June 15, 1964

BY COURIER SERVICE

Honorable J. Lee Rankin
General Counsel
The President's Commission
200 Maryland Avenue, N. E.
Washington, D. C.

Dear Mr. Rankin:

Reference is made to your letter of June 2, 1964, requesting that this Bureau obtain for the Commission a copy of the baptismal certificate of June Lee Oswald.

Enclosed for the Commission is a copy of a certification by Reverend Dmitri R. Royster, Rector, St. Seraphim Eastern Orthodox Church, Dallas, Texas, of the baptism of June Oswald on October 16, 1962. There is also enclosed a certification by Reverend Royster of the baptism of Rachel Oswald on April 9, 1964.

For the information of the Commission, Reverend Royster advised that the Baptismal Record Book of St. Seraphim Eastern Orthodox Church is divided into three parts, separated by two vertical perforations. One part consists of a stub containing the record of baptism and is forwarded to the Metropolitan Council, 105 East Houston Street, New York, New York. The second part is the baptismal certificate which is forwarded to the parents of the baptized child. The third part is a stub which remains in the permanent Baptismal Record Book maintained by the St. Seraphim Eastern Orthodox Church. Reverend Royster advised that the enclosed baptism certifications of June Oswald and Rachel Oswald were made by him from the Baptismal Record Book and he further advised that duplicates of the baptismal certificates for the Oswald children are not available in Church records.

Sincerely yours,

J. Edgar Hoover

Enclosures (2)

COMMISSION EXHIBIT NO. 1957

St. Seraphim Eastern Orthodox Church
4203 NEWTON AVENUE
DALLAS 19, TEXAS
LA8-3741 DA 1-0620

June 8, 1964

To Whom It May Concern:

The following is an exact copy of entry no. 32122 in the Baptismal Record Book of St. Seraphim Eastern Orthodox Church:

"Parish Record

Name of Child June Oswald

Name of Parents Lee Harvey Oswald
(Father's Name)
and Marina Nicholaevna Oswald
(Mother's Name)

Address 4760 Trail Lake Dr. Ft. Worth, Tx
(Number and Street, City, State)

Date of Birth Feb. 15, 1962

Date of Baptism and Confirmation Oct. 16, 1962

At. St. Seraphim Church

Place of Birth Minsk Soviet Union
(City) (State)

God Parents Elena Hall

Sacraments Performed By Rev. Dmitri Royster"

Dmitri R. Royster
Dmitri R. Royster, Rector
St. Seraphim Eastern Orthodox Church

COMMISSION EXHIBIT NO. 1957–A

St. Seraphim Eastern Orthodox Church

4203 NEWTON AVENUE

DALLAS 19, TEXAS

LA8-3741 DA 1-0620

June 8, 1964

Whom It May Concern:

The following is an exact copy of entry no. 32145 the Baptismal Record Book of St. Seraphim Eastern thodox Church:

"Parish Record

me of Child Rachel Oswald

me of Parents Lee Harvey Oswald
(Father's Name)
and Marina Nikolaevna Oswald
(Mother's Name)

dress 629 Belt Line Rd. Richardson, Tex.
(Number and Street, City, State)

te of Birth Oct. 20, 1963

te of Baptism and Confirmation April 9, 1964

St. Seraphim's Church

ace of Birth Dallas, Tex.
(City) (State)

d Parents Katherine Ford

craments Performed by Rev. Dmitri Royster"

(Rev.) Dmitri R. Royster

Dmitri R. Royster, Rector
St. Seraphim Eastern Orthodox Church

COMMISSION EXHIBIT NO. 1957–B

JUDGMENT

Mrs.Marguerite Claverie Pic,Jr, No.202306

vs Civil District Court

Edward J.Pic,Jr, Division."D"

-------ooOoo------

On motion of Raoul Serre,Jr,attorney for plaintiff,and on producing to the Court due proof in support of plaintiff's demand,and the Court considering the law and evidence to be in favor of plaintiff,for the reasons orally assigned.

It is ordered,adjudged and decreed,that the default herein entered on June 15th 1933,be now confirmed and made final,and,accordingly,there be Judgment in favor of plaintiff,Mrs.Marguerite Claverie Pic,Jr,and against defendant,Edward J.Pic,Jr,her husband,decreeing an absolute divorce between them,and granting plaintiff the right to resume her maiden name,and for all costs.

Judgment rendered and read in open Court June 22nd 1933,

Judgment read and signed in open Court June 23rd 1933,

Walter ... Judge,

Commission Exhibit No. 1958

A TRUE COPY
DEPUTY CLERK, CIVIL DISTRICT COURT
PARISH OF ORLEANS
STATE OF LA.

COMMISSION EXHIBIT NO. 1958

JUDGMENT

Margaret Keating,wife of Robert E.Lee Oswald, No.188845

vs Civil District Court

Robert E.Lee Oswald, Division."D"

-----ooOoo------

On motion of Rolla A.Tichenor,Sr,attorney for plaintiff,and on producing to the Court due proof in support of plaintiff's demand,and the Court considering the law and evidence to be in favor of plaintiff,for the reasons orally assigned.

It is ordered,adjudged and decreed,that the default herein entered on December 27th 1932,be now confirmed and made final,and,accordingly,there be Judgment in favor of plaintiff,Mrs.Margaret Keating,wife of Robert E.Lee Oswald, and against defendant,Robert E.Lee Oswald,her husband,decreeing an absolute divorce between thema,and for all costs.

It is further ordered,adjudged and decreed,that there be Judgment ordering and condemning Robert E.Lee Oswald to pay alimony to Mrs.Margaret Keating Oswald, at the rate of $12.50 per week,same to start from date of this Judgment,and to continue until the further orders of this Court.

Judgment rendered and read in open Court January 3rd 1933,

Judgment read and signed in open Court January 10th 1933,

Judge

Commission Exhibit No. 1959

A TRUE COPY
DEPUTY CLERK, CIVIL DISTRICT COURT
PARISH OF ORLEANS
STATE OF LA.

CO-2-34,030

U. S. SECRET SERVICE

June 10, 1964.

AIC McDermott, Boston

AIC Sorrels, Dallas

President's Commission on Assassination of President Kennedy.

On June 9, 1964, l. d. phone call was received from Mr. John Ely of the President's Commission on Assassination of President Kennedy requesting that the records of Tarrant (Ft.Worth) and Dallas (Dallas) county clerks' offices be checked for record of a divorce granted to Edwin A. Ekdahl and Jasmine Ekdahl, and if such a record should be found that a certified copy of the decree be obtained and forwarded to the Commission (through Inspector Kelley). No such record was found.

Edwin A. Ekdahl was formerly married to Marguerite C. Oswald, mother of Lee Harvey Oswald. A record of the divorce granted to Ekdahl from Marguerite C. Ekdahl was found and certified copy of the papers in this case have been obtained. This divorce was granted June 24, 1948.

Today I talked to Robert Oswald, son of Mrs. Marguerite Oswald, and he stated that Edwin A. Ekdahl came from Boston, Mass., and that no doubt he got his other divorce there.

It is requested that search of the records be made in Boston and if record is found that certified copy of the decree (and other papers if deemed advisable) be obtained and forwarded to Inspector Kelley.

S

Airmail

cc: Chief - Attn. Inspr. Kelley

COMMISSION EXHIBIT No. 1960

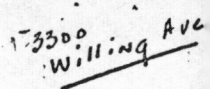

WALLACE AND KORTH
ATTORNEYS AT LAW
FORT WORTH, TEXAS

1-3300 Willing Ave

NO. 15537-D

EDWIN A. EKDAHL	|	IN THE DISTRICT COURT
vs.	|	OF TARRANT COUNTY, TEXAS,
MARGUERITE C. EKDAHL	|	____ JUDICIAL DISTRICT.

TO THE HONORABLE JUDGE OF SAID COURT:

Comes now EDWIN A. EKDAHL, hereinafter called plaintiff, complaining of MARGUERITE C. EKDAHL, hereinafter called defendant, and for cause of action would respectfully show the Court as follows:

1.

Plaintiff is now and has been for more than twelve months preceding the filing of this petition an actual bona fide resident of the State of Texas, and has resided in Tarrant County, Texas, for more than six months immediately preceding the filing of this petition. Defendant is a resident of Tarrant County, Texas.

2.

Plaintiff and defendant were duly and legally married to each other on or about May 5, 1945, at Rockwall, Texas, and have lived together as husband and wife for the majority of the time from said date until on or about January 10, 1948, at which time they were permanently separated, and have not since that date lived together as man and wife.

3.

Plaintiff has at all times conducted himself with propriety, doing his duty as a husband while married to the defendant, and has treated the defendant at all times with kindness and forbearance and has been guilty of no act or acts bringing

COMMISSION EXHIBIT NO. 1960-A

about or causing the hereinafter described acts, omissions and conditions on defendant's part.

4.

The defendant, disregarding the solemnity of her marriage vow and her obligation to treat plaintiff with kindness, forbearance and attention, shortly after the first of February, 1947, commenced a course of harsh and cruel treatment toward this plaintiff which has continued with very slight interruptions until the date of the filing of this petition.

On diverse occasions while said parties lived together as man and wife, defendant was guilty of excesses, harsh and cruel treatment and outrages toward this plaintiff of such a nature as to render their further living together as husband and wife wholly insupportable, and that as a consequence of all of said harsh and cruel treatment, some of which is hereinafter detailed, of which defendant was guilty toward this plaintiff, plaintiff and defendant were finally, on January 10, 1948, separated and have not since said date lived together as husband and wife nor cohabited since that date.

Plaintiff would show to the Court that, as examples of the harsh and cruel treatment of which defendant was guilty which began shortly after February 1, 1947, the defendant would constantly nag at plaintiff and argue with reference to money matters and, in a violent outburst of temper on or about the 25th day of February, 1947, accused plaintiff of infidelity, and with the intention of doing him bodily harm, threw a bottle at plaintiff which barely missed his head. That on or about March 17, 1947, defendant scratched plaintiff severely on his left arm, and struck him a number of times on the chest. That subsequently during the early part of April, 1947, and on or about April 3, 1947, in another outburst of uncontrollable temper, defendant threw a cookie jar at plaintiff, such act on defendant's part being with the intent of doing serious bodily injury. That on or about May 9, 1947, the defendant again in an outburst of anger and uncontrollable temper, and with the intention of doing the plaintiff bodily harm, aimed a glass at plaintiff, which narrowly missed striking him in the head and causing such violent exertion on his part to avoid being struck that he became partially paralyzed in his right arm. That on or about January 10, 1948, the defendant again in an outburst of anger and uncontrollable temper informed the plaintiff that she had consulted with the District Attorney of Tarrant County, Texas, or one of his assistants, and had determined that she could legally order plaintiff out of the home, and she forthwith directed the said plaintiff to leave the home immediately and never to return, and plaintiff being highly nervous and afflicted with a heart ailment was fearful of subjecting himself to such further outbursts, and therefore complied with defendant's order.

That plaintiff is ill and has been for a period of several years suffering from a heart ailment, which condition requires him to be under the care of a physician. That at the time of the marriage of plaintiff and defendant, defendant was fully advised of plaintiff's physical condition, and all of her ill treatment of plaintiff was with the full knowledge of plaintiff's condition and the likely serious results of her actions.

That plaintiff has been a dutiful and kind husband, and has amply provided for the defendant during the marriage, and most recently doing his duty as a husband cared and provided for defendant when she became ill and of necessity had to undergo a minor surgical operation, from which operation she has now fully recovered.

That prior to plaintiff being ordered out of his home by defendant, defendant purloined a diary kept by the plaintiff covering the year 1944, which was long prior to the date that plaintiff and the defendant were married, and has likewise purloined and kept from plaintiff certain other private papers, and that plaintiff has often requested the return of his diary and other papers, but in each instance the defendant has refused to return that which is rightfully his.

That as a consequence of all of the above and foregoing acts of harsh and cruel treatment, and the fact that plaintiff has no way of knowing when the defendant will fly into a rage and exhibit an outburst of uncontrollable temper, plaintiff has become highly nervous and his heart ailment has become aggravated to such an extent that a continuation thereof and of the marital relationship would result in a serious impairment of plaintiff's health.

5.

That no children have been born to plaintiff and defendant as a result of their said marriage.

6.

That there has been no community property accumulated by plaintiff and defendant, or either of them, during the period of the marital relationship with the exception of a few items of personal belongings and furniture, to which articles plaintiff hereby waives any right, title or interest.

7.

That plaintiff hereby acknowledges his responsibility to support the defendant during the pendency of this suit, and hereby agrees to make payment of the sum of $150.00 per month for such support.

-4-

COMMISSION EXHIBIT No. 1960-A—Continued

WHEREFORE, Premises considered, plaintiff prays that defendant be cited to appear and answer herein; that on final hearing hereof plaintiff have judgment dissolving the marriage now existing between plaintiff and defendant, that defendant be ordered to return plaintiff's 1944 diary and other private papers, for all court costs, and for such other and further relief, both special and general, at law or in equity, to which plaintiff may show himself justly entitled.

A CERTIFIED COPY.
ATTEST: 6-9- 1964
GEORGE JOHNSON
District Clerk, Tarrant County, Texas
By Roy Leonard
Deputy

WALLACE & KORTH
by Fred Korth
Attorneys for Plaintiff,
812 Neil P. Anderson Building,
Fort Worth, Texas.

COMMISSION EXHIBIT No. 1960-A—Continued

NO. 15537-B

IN THE 17th DISTRICT COURT
OF TARRANT COUNTY, TEXAS.

EDWIN A. EKDAHL

VS.

MARGUERITE C. EKDAHL

PLAINTIFF'S ORIGINAL PETITION

FIL
TARRANT
23 12
LEWIS D.

COMMISSION EXHIBIT No. 1960-A—Continued

McLEAN & McLEAN
ATTORNEYS AT LAW
8TH FLOOR BURK BURNETT BLDG.
DIAL 2-4114

[redacted]

Commission Exhibit No. 1960-B

NO.

EDWIN A. EKDAHL	:	IN THE 17TH DISTRICT COURT
VS.	:	
MARGUERITE C. EKDAHL	:	TARRANT COUNTY, T E X A S.

TO THE HONORABLE JUDGE OF SAID COURT:

Now comes the defendant, Marguerite C. Ekdahl, in the above numbered and entitled cause, and files this, her original answer to plaintiff's original petition, and would show to the Court:

I.

Defendant denies each and every allegation in plaintiff's petition contained, and demands strict proof thereof, and of this she puts herself upon the country.

II.

For further answer herein, if same be necessary, defendant would respectfully show to the Court that if there be any misconduct upon the part of defendant, that same was brought about and caused solely by the acts and misconduct of plaintiff.

III.

Plaintiff further states that because of the action of the plaintiff it became necessary and is necessary to employ counsel to represent her in this suit, and defendant has employed the firm of McLean & McLean and has agreed to pay them a reasonable Attorneys fee.

WHEREFORE, premises considered, defendant prays that plaintiff take nothing by reason hereof, and that she go hence without day with her costs, and that she recover from defendant reasonable attorneys' fee.

McLean & McLean
By John E. McLean
Attorneys for Defendant

A CERTIFIED COPY.
ATTEST: 6-9-1964
GEORGE JOHNSON
District Clerk, Tarrant County, Texas
By Roy [illegible]
Deputy

COMMISSION EXHIBIT No. 1960-B

NO. 155 37-D

EDWIN A. EKDAHL

VS

MARGUERITE C. EKDAHL

- - - - - - - - - - - - - - - - - -

ORIGINAL ANSWER OF DEFENDANT

- - - - - - - - - - - - - - - - - -

FILED
TARRANT COUNTY
JUN 15 9 57 AM 194[illegible]
LEWIS D. [illegible]LL JR.
DIST. CLERK

McLEAN & McLEAN
ATTORNEYS AT LAW
8TH FLOOR BURK BURNETT BLDG.
DIAL 2-4114

COMMISSION EXHIBIT No. 1960-B—Continued

WALLACE AND KORTH
ATTORNEYS AT LAW
FORT WORTH, TEXAS

NO. 15537-D

EDWIN A. EKDAHL		IN THE DISTRICT COURT
vs.		OF TARRANT COUNTY, TEXAS,
MARGUERITE C. EKDAHL		17TH JUDICIAL DISTRICT

JUDGMENT

On the 15th day of June, 1948, came on to be heard the above entitled and numbered cause, wherein EDWIN A. EKDAHL is plaintiff, and MARGUERITE C. EKDAHL is defendant, and the plaintiff and the defendant having through their attorneys of record announced ready for trial, and came a jury of twelve good and lawful men, who being duly impanelled and sworn and having heard the pleadings, the evidence and the argument of counsel on their oaths do for their verdict, in response to the following special issues, definitions and instructions submitted to them by the Court on the 16th day of June, 1948, make the following respective findings:

No. 15,537-D

Edwin A. Ekdahl,		In the District Court of
vs.		Tarrant County, Texas,
Marguerite C. Ekdahl.		17th Judicial District.

COURT'S CHARGE

Gentlemen of the Jury:

This case is submitted to you upon special issues, and you will, from the evidence introduced before you, answer the following questions:

COMMISSION EXHIBIT No. 1960-C

Special Issue No. 1:

Question: Do you find from the preponderance of the evidence that the defendant, Mrs. Ekdahl, is guilty of excesses, cruel treatment, or outrages toward the plaintiff, Edwin A. Ekdahl, of such a nature as to render their living together insupportable? Answer "yes" or "no."

Answer: Yes.

You are instructed that the term "excesses, cruel treatment or outrages" as used in this charge means physical violence; and also includes conduct, demeanor and language of one party toward the other of such a cruel nature as to affect the mind or sensibilities of the other to such a degree as to affect the physical welfare of the person subjected to such conduct.

Special Issue No. 2:

If you have answered the preceding question "no," you need not answer this question, but if you have answered the same "yes," then answer:

Question: Do you find from the preponderance of the evidence that such excesses, cruel treatment, or outrages, if any, were not provoked by the conduct of the plaintiff toward the defendant? Answer: "They were not provoked" or "they were provoked."

Answer: They were not provoked.

Special Issue No. 3:

Question: What do you find from the preponderance of the evidence is a reasonable attorney fee to be allowed to the defendant for representation in this case? Answer by giving amount of money.

Answer: $250.00.

By the term "preponderance of the evidence" is meant the greater weight of the credible testimony.

YOU ARE THE EXCLUSIVE JUDGES of the credibility of the witnesses, of the weight to be given to their testimony, and of the facts proved, but the law you will receive from the Court as given to you herein and be governed thereby.

(Signed) Frank Culver, Jr.
Judge Presiding.

We, the jury, return our answers to the above and foregoing questions as our verdict in this case.

(Signed) J. J. Hardin
Foreman.

-2-

COMMISSION EXHIBIT No. 1960-C—Continued

The said findings were received by the Court and were filed and entered of record on the minutes of such Court.

The Court having been advised by the parties that an agreement had been entered into with respect to the disposition of any community property owned by plaintiff and defendant, and the Court having further been advised that with reference to such agreement and settlement, the plaintiff, Edwin A. Ekdahl, has agreed to make payment of the sum of $1,500.00 in cash to the said Marguerite C. Ekdahl in full and final settlement of any and all rights which she might have or may assert or hereafter assert in the community property of the said Edwin A. Ekdahl and Marguerite C. Ekdahl, and the Court having found that such agreement is fair and reasonable and should be approved, and the Court having been further advised that the said Edwin A. Ekdahl releases and quitclaims any interest which he may have in and to any and all jewelry, rings, wearing apparel and personal ornaments in possession of Marguerite C. Ekdahl, and likewise releases and quitclaims any interest in and to any silverware, dishes, glassware, linens, drapes, furniture and furnishings in possession of the said Marguerite C. Ekdahl, and further releases any and all claim to any money or bank accounts standing in the name of Marguerite C. Ekdahl, all of said property by such agreement being the separate property of the said Marguerite C. Ekdahl, and the Court having been further advised that the said Marguerite C. Ekdahl releases and quitclaims any interest which she may have by virtue of such marriage to Edwin A. Ekdahl or otherwise to any and all property of every kind and character wheresoever situated, including all money and bank accounts, but not limited thereto, now standing in the name of Edwin A. Ekdahl, either in his individual name or in joint accounts with others, and likewise including, but not limited to, all personal earnings and salaries of the said Edwin A. Ekdahl:

Whereupon, the plaintiff having made and the Court having duly heard and considered his motion for judgment, and such additional considerations and findings as were authorized by law having been had and made, including but not limited to the finding that plaintiff is and has been an actual bona fide resident of the State of Texas for more than twelve months and has resided in Tarrant County for more than six months; likewise including but not limited to the finding that there have been no children born as a result of said marriage; likewise including but not limited to the finding that defendant, Marguerite C. Ekdahl, desires the restoration of her former name, Marguerite C. Oswald; and the Court having heard and approved the agreement hereinabove set out, the Court is of the opinion that judgment should be rendered as follows for the plaintiff:

IT IS THEREFORE CONSIDERED, ORDERED, ADJUDGED AND DECREED By the Court, on this the 24th day of June, 1948, that the bonds of matrimony heretofore existing between plaintiff, Edwin A. Ekdahl, and the defendant, Marguerite C. Ekdahl, be and they are hereby dissolved, and that said plaintiff be and he is hereby granted a decree of divorce from the defendant based upon the above and foregoing jury finding, and the finding of the Court, that the defendant has been guilty of excesses, cruel treatment and outrages against the plaintiff of such a nature as to render their further living together wholly insupportable.

IT IS FURTHER ORDERED By the Court that the agreement heretofore entered into between plaintiff and defendant as above detailed with reference to the disposition of community property is hereby approved by the Court.

-4-

COMMISSION EXHIBIT No. 1960-C—Continued

IT IS FURTHER ORDERED By the Court that defendant's former name, Marguerite C. Oswald, be restored to her.

IT IS THE FURTHER ORDER Of the Court that the sum of $250.00 be paid to the firm of McLean & McLean, attorneys for the defendant, as a reasonable attorneys' fee for their representation of the defendant herein; that all court costs herein expended be assessed against the defendant, for all of which execution may issue. Rendered and entered this 24th June 1948

Frank Culver Jr.
Judge.

Approved as to Form:

WALLACE & KORTH
by Fred Korth
Attorneys for Plaintiff,
Edwin A. Ekdahl.

McLEAN & McLEAN
by
Attorneys for Defendant,
Marguerite C. Ekdahl.

A CERTIFIED COPY,
ATTEST: 6-9-1964
GEORGE JOHNSON
District Clerk, Tarrant County, Texas
By Roy Howard
Deputy

-5-

COMMISSION EXHIBIT No. 1960-C—Continued

NO. 15537-D

IN THE 17TH DISTRICT COURT
OF TARRANT COUNTY, TEXAS

EDWIN A. EKDAHL

vs.

MARGUERITE C. EKDAHL

JUDGMENT

Recorded

Book - A46

Page — 804

COMMISSION EXHIBIT No. 1960-C—Continued

MEMORANDUM FOR THE ASSISTANT GENERAL COUNSEL (MANPOWER)
DEPARTMENT OF DEFENSE

Subj: Information for President"s Commission on the assassination of President Kennedy; your request for

Encl: (1) Mr. J. Lee Rankin's ltr of 19 May 1964 addressed to HQMC re subj

1. In accordance with the request contained in your memorandum of 7 May 1964, the following is provided for your information concerning Lee Harvey OSWALD, relating to his service, while a member of the Marine Corps. In addition, this information is provided with a view toward your advising the President's Commission that it is also in response to Mr. J. Lee Rankin's letter of 19 May 1964 (enclosure (1)).

a. Description of Advanced or Formal Training which OSWALD received while a Member of the Marine Corps

(1) OSWALD attended an Aviation Fundamental School, Naval Air Technical Training Center, Naval Air Station, Jacksonville, Florida from 18 March 1957 to 3 May 1957. During this period, his course of instruction consisted essentially of the following:

(a) Security of Classified Matter

(b) USMC Organizations, Missions and Systems

(c) Navy Plotting Symbols and Lectures

(d) Practical Application of (c) above

(e) Basic Radar Theory

(f) Equipments and Safety Measures

(g) Communications

(h) Search and Rescue Procedures

(i) Air Traffic Control Procedures

COMMISSION EXHIBIT No. 1961

(j) Map Reading

(k) Weather

(l) Aircraft Recognition

(m) Combat Information Centrals

(2) From 4 May 1957 to 17 June 1957, OSWALD attended the Aircraft Control and Warning Operator Course at Keesler Air Force Base, Mississippi. His course of instruction at the aforementioned command consisted of the following:

(a) Radar Familiarization

(b) Operation of Radar Indicators

(c) Aircraft Warning Indicators

(d) Aircraft Control and Warning Systems

(e) Operation of Aircraft Warning Installations

(f) Electronic Countermeasures

(g) Familiarization Courses in Organization of Marine Aviation, Marine Air Support and Air Control Systems, Communication Nets and Usage and Naval Plotting Symbols and Procedures

b. Type of Work which OSWALD did while a Member of the Marine Corps

(1) OSWALD performed duties in the Marine Corps as an Aviation Electronics Operator, except for a short period during October 1958 when he was given general duty assignments. From 4 September 1959 to 11 September 1959, during a period when OSWALD was awaiting release to inactive duty, OSWALD performed no duties.

c. Information Relating to OSWALD's Security Clearance while Member of the Marine Corps and Description of Classified Information which may have been available to OSWALD

(1) OSWALD was granted a final clearance on 3 May 1957

2

COMMISSION EXHIBIT No. 1961—Continued

to handle confidential matter. Such action, following a careful records check, was required in connection with OSWALD's assignment to the Aviation Fundamental School, Naval Air Technical Training Center and the Aircraft Control and Warning Cperations Course at Keesler Air Force Base. As far as can be determined at this time, OSWALD in all probability, had access to confidential matter while a student at the aforementioned commands during courses of instruction relating to Radar Jamming and Identification - "Friend or Foe" procedures. Because of his grade and lack of experience, he would not normally have had access to classified matter in the performance of his duties as an Aviation Electronics Cperator following completion of his training heretofore described. There is no evidence contained in the personnel file that OSWALD's security clearance was ever terminated, nor is there evidence that he was granted access to any information of higher than confidential characterization. It was, however, the practice of the Marine Corps, that on occasions where assignments, similar to OSWALD's, required a higher clearance than confidential in order to perform specific, classified electronic duties, personnel with clearances commensurate with the duties to be performed were assigned thereto.

d. <u>Stations and Units to which OSWALD was assigned after his Enlistment into the Marine Corps on 24 October 1956 at Dallas, Texas, and Dates Assigned</u>

26 Oct 1956 - 18 Jan 1957	2d Recruit Training Battalion, Marine Corps Recruit Depot, San Diego, California
20 Jan 1957 - 26 Feb 1957	"A" Company, 1st Battalio 2nd Infantry Training Regiment, Marine Corps Base, Camp Pendleton, California
18 Mar 1957 - 3 May 1957	Marine Aviation Detachment Naval Air Technical Training Command, Jacksonville, Florida

4 May 1957 - 19 Jun 1957	Keesler Air Force Base, Biloxi, Mississippi
9 Jul 1957 - 21 Aug 1957	4th Replacement Battalion, MAT&RC, Marine Corps Air Station, El Toro (Santa Ana), California
22 Aug 1957 - 12 Sep 1957	Enroute from San Diego, California to Yokosuka, Japan aboard the USS BEXAR
12 Sep 1957 - 27 Oct 1957	MACS-1, MAG-11, 1st Marine Aircraft Wing, FMF, Atsugu, Japan
27 Oct 1957 - 15 Nov 1957	U. S. Naval Hospital, Yokosuka, Japan
16 Nov 1957 - 20 Nov 1957	MACS-1, MAG-11, 1st Marine Aircraft Wing, FMF, Atsugi, Japan
20 Nov 1957 - 6 Mar 1958	Embarked aboard Terrell County, LST 1157 with MACS-1 MAG-11, 1st Marine Aircraft Wing at Yokosuka, Japan on 20 November 1957 for maneuvers. Arrived in Philippine Islands area 20 November 1957
7 Mar 1958 - 18 Mar 1958	Sailed from Corregidor, P. I. with MACS-1, MAG-11, 1st Marine Aircraft Wing on 7 March 1958 aboard the USS WEXFORD COUNTY, LST 1168. Arrived at Atsugi, Japan 18 March 1958
18 Mar 1958 - 13 Sep 1958	MACS-1, MAG-11, 1st Marine Aircraft Wing, Atsugi, Japan

DK-atv

14 Sep 1958 - 6 Oct 1958	Embarked aboard AKA 105 with MACS-1, MAG-11, 1st Marine Aircraft Wing and sailed from Yokosuka, Japan on 14 September 1958 for South China Sea area. Was at Ping Tung, North Taiwan on 30 September 1958; returned to Atsugi, Japan on 5 October 1958
6 Oct 1958 - 1 Nov 1958	On duty with Sub-Unit 1, H&MS-11, MAG-11, 1st Marine Aircraft Wing at Atsugi, Japan. (Sick at Atsugi Station Hospital from 7 October 1958 to 13 October 1958).
2 Nov 1958 - 15 Nov 1958	Departed Yokosuka, Japan on 2 November 1958 aboard USNS BARRETT, arriving in San Francisco, California on 15 November 1958
16 Nov 1958 - 21 Dec 1958	Casual Company, Department of the Pacific, Marine Barracks, U. S. Naval Station, Treasure Island, San Francisco, California, processing for leave and proceed time
22 Dec 1958 - 10 Sep 1959	MACS-9, MWHG, 3rd Marine Aircraft Wing, Marine Corps Air Station, El Toro (Santa Ana), California

2. As indicated above, the units to which OSWALD was attached did not change their geographical location except as indicated.

COMMISSION EXHIBIT No. 1961—Continued

FD-302 (Rev. 1-25-60)

FEDERAL BUREAU OF INVESTIGATION

Date June 26, 1964

1

ALLEN R. FELDE, 3307 North 22nd Street, advised that he had enlisted in the United States Marine Corps at Milwaukee, Wisconsin in October, 1956 and had met LEE HARVEY OSWALD as a United States Marine Corps recruit about October 23, 1956, while both of them were assigned to Platoon 2060, 2nd Battalion, M.C.R.D., San Diego, California. Both men were stationed at San Diego until January, 1957, at which time FELDE stated that they were transferred to Camp Pendleton for combat training. This combat training lasted until May, 1957 and during this time FELDE was assigned to the same squad of eight men, all of whom shared the same tent. During May, 1957, OSWALD and FELDE were transferred to the A & P School at Jacksonville, Florida and in approximately July, 1957 they were both sent to Aviation Electronics School in Memphis, Tennessee. During September, 1957 FELDE transferred to the Marine Corps Air Station at Opa Locka, Florida and did not see OSWALD after this date.

During his association with OSWALD, FELDE recalled that OSWALD continually discussed politics in which topic none of the young Marines had any interest. OSWALD was an argumentative type of person and would frequently take the opposite side of an argument just for the sake of a debate. OSWALD was not popular with the other recruits, and his company was avoided if possible.

According to FELDE, OSWALD continually wrote to United States Senators about certain issues in which OSWALD believed strongly but which were not known to FELDE. One senator in particular who was in receipt of a number of OSWALD's letters was Senator THURMAN. FELDE remembered that OSWALD had expressed a dislike for people of wealth and that he championed the cause of the working man. On frequent occasions OSWALD found fault with EISENHOWER and TRUMAN and had been against the United States participation in the Korean War since OSWALD stated that one million men were killed in this war and nothing was accomplished. OSWALD had condemned EISENHOWER because of EISENHOWER's poor tactics in the utilization of a tank unit at the time of the invasion of Europe. FELDE had the impression at the time of his

On 6/25/64 at MILWAUKEE, WISCONSIN File # MI 62-1178

by SA ROBERT E. SCHOENECKER/sve Date dictated 6/26/64

COMMISSION EXHIBIT No. 1962

MI 62-1178
- 2 -

association with OSWALD that OSWALD was "left winged."

According to FELDE, at the time that the eight-man squad was assigned to Camp Pendleton and was permitted to take their first weekend leave, the entire group took a taxi cab to Tiajuana, Mexico, at which point OSWALD left the squad and was seen again only when the squad returned to Camp Pendleton. FEDLE said this was also true of at least four weekend leaves that the men took in Los Angeles. OSWALD would ride with the group to Los Angeles in a bus but would leave the rest of the men at the bus depot and would not be observed again until the squad returned to Camp Pendleton.

FELDE recalled that OSWALD spent much of his time reading in Marine base libraries as well as in his quarters. During the time that he was at Camp Pendleton and also Jacksonville, Florida as well as Memphis, Tennessee, OSWALD was observed with a brown leatherette covered book with gold, Old English type letters about 250 pages thick, and a small blue book about 100 pages. FELDE did not know the exact nature of these books. FELDE stated that although he had been on the rifle range with OSWALD, he could not recall if he was a good shot or not. FELDE described OSWALD as being a good talker and having an excellent vocabularly.

COMMISSION EXHIBIT NO. 1962—Continued

1
DL 89-43
HJO:mvs

The following is a schedule showing known addresses of LEE HARVEY OSWALD from the time of his birth:

Dates	Address	Source Information Obtained From
10-18-39	Born New Orleans, La.	Bureau of Vital Statistics, New Orleans
About 1939 to 1941	Alvar St., New Orleans, La.	Mrs. CHARLES F. MURRET, 757 French St., New Orleans, La.
10-14-41	1010 Bartholomew St., New Orleans, La.	Dr. CUTHBERT J. BROWN, 1110 Maison, Blanche Building, New Orleans
8-17-42	2136 Broadway, New Orleans, La.	"
9-10-42	227 Atlantic Avenue, Algiers, La.	"
About 1945 to 1946	4801 Victor, Dallas, Texas	ROYDON SCHULTZ, 4726 Victor, Dallas, Texas
4-18-45	4801 Victor, Dallas, Texas	C. J. PRICE, Administrator, Parkland Memorial Hospital, Dallas, Texas
2-8-46	Grandburg Road, Route 45, Benbrook, Texas	MARY LOU LAUTENSLAGER, Harris Hospital, Fort Worth, Texas
About 1946	600 West 24th Street, Covington, La.	Mrs. BENNIE COMMENGE, 111 West 25th St., Covington, La.
About 1946	311 Vermont Street, Covington, La.	Mrs. A. LOGAN MAGRUDER, 321 Vermont Street, Covington, La.

COMMISSION EXHIBIT NO. 1963

2
DL 89-43
HJO:mvs

Dates	Address	Source Information Obtained From
9-19-46	311 Vermont Street, Covington, La.	Mrs. BEVERLY RICHARDSON, Covington, La.
1-27-47	1505 8th Avenue, Fort Worth, Texas	Mrs. LUELLA MERRETT, Ridglea West Elementary School, Fort Worth, Texas
1947	1505 8th Avenue, Fort Worth, Texas	Operator 47, Retail Merchants Association, Fort Worth, Texas
1948	3300 Willing Street, Fort Worth, Texas	Operator 47, Retail Merchants Association, Fort Worth, Texas
2-10-49	7408 Ewing, Fort Worth, Texas	PATRICIA AARONS, Personnel Clerk, Lerner's Shops, New York City
December, 1949 to 1952	7408 Ewing, Fort Worth, Texas	HERMAN CONWAY, 7420 Ewing, Fort Worth, Texas
1949 to 1952	7408 Ewing, Fort Worth, Texas	THOMAS W. TURNER, 7417 Ewing, Fort Worth, Texas
July and August, 1952	325 East 92nd Street, New York, New York	JOHN EDWARD PIC, U. S. Air Force, Lackland Air Force Base, Texas
August, 1952 to January, 1954	1455 Sheridan Avenue, and 825 East 179th St., Bronx, New York	Family Court File of City of New York, made available by Judge FLORENCE KELLY

544

COMMISSION EXHIBIT No. 1963—Continued

3
DL 89-43
HJO:mvs

Dates	Address	Source Information Obtained From
May or June, 1954 to about February, 1955	1454 St. Mary Street, New Orleans, La.	MYRTLE EVANS, 1910 Prytania St., New Orleans, La.
February, 1955 to about April, 1955	1452 St. Mary Street, New Orleans, La.	"
1955 to Spring, 1956	126 Exchange Place, New Orleans, La.	Mrs. MILDRED SAWYER, 126 Exchange Place, New Orleans, La.
11-10-55 to January, 1956	126 Exchange Place, New Orleans, La.	GERALD F. TUJAGUE, 442 Canal Street, New Orleans, La.
1-17-56	126 Exchange Place, New Orleans, La.	NICK MAZZA, J. R. Michels, Inc., New Orleans, La.
7-1-56 until joined U. S. Marine Corps	4936 Collingwood, Fort Worth, Texas	Mrs. JAMES TAYLOR, 4936 Collingwood, Fort Worth, Texas
10-26-56 to 1-20-57	U. S. Marine Corps, Recruit Depot, San Diego, California	WILLIAM EARL ODOM, Department of Defense, Pentagon Building
1-20-57 to 2-26-57	M.C.B., Camp Pendleton, California	"
3-18-57 to 5-3-57	M.A.D., NATTC, Jacksonville, Florida	"
5-4-57 to 6-19-57	Detached Duty, Kessler Air Force Base, Mississippi	"
7-9-57	M.C.A.S., El Toro, California	"
9-12-57 to 12-22-58	Fleet Marines, Pacific Area	"

545

COMMISSION EXHIBIT No. 1963—Continued

4
DL 89-43
HJO:mvs

Dates	Address	Source Information Obtained From
12-22-58, to 9-11-59	M.C.A.S., El Toro, California	WILLIAM EARL ODOM, Department of Defense, Pentagon Building

It should be noted that Mr. L. M. McCRACKEN, 3830 West 6th Street, Fort Worth, Texas, advised that OSWALD in about 1957 was on leave for two weeks and spent this time with his mother at 3830 West 6th Street, Fort Worth, Texas.

It also should be noted that Mrs. CHARLES F. MURRET, 757 French Street, New Orleans, Louisiana, advised that while OSWALD was assigned to Mississippi, he visited one Saturday with her and her family.

Dates	Address	Source Information Obtained From
1959 for few days after discharge from U.S.M.C.	3124 West 5th Street, Fort Worth, Texas	Mrs. GRACE CRAMER, 3124 West 5th Street, Fort Worth, Texas
9-14-59	3124 West 5th Street, Fort Worth, Texas	DIXIE L. WILSON, Selective Service Local Boards 111-114, Fort Worth, Texas
9-16-59	Completed immigration questionnaire at New Orleans and gave temporary address, Liberty Hotel, New Orleans, La.	CHARLES G. STOKES, Lykes Brothers SS Company, New Orleans, La.
9-19-59	Embarked New Orleans on SS Marion Lykes	ROBERT S. RADER, Lykes Brothers SS Company, New Orleans, La.
9-20-59	SS Marion Lykes departed New Orleans, La.	Mrs. RUTH SCOGGIN, Lykes Brothers SS Company, Houston, Texas

546

COMMISSION EXHIBIT No. 1963—Continued

5
DL 89-43
HJO:mvs

Dates	Address	Source Information Obtained From
10-8-59	SS Marion Lykes arrived Le Havre, France	ROBERT F. RADER, Lykes Brothers SS Co., New Orleans, La.
10-15-59	Entered Russia from Helsinki, Finland	ONI Files, 8th Naval District, Algiers, La.
10-16-59 to 1-4-60	Berlin and Metropole Hotels, Moscow, Russia	Personal papers of OSWALD
1-5-60 to July, 1962	Minsk, Russia	Personal papers of OSWALD
June, 1961 and June, 1962	Visited Moscow	Personal papers of OSWALD
10-19-61	Apartment 24, #4 Kalinin, Minsk, Russia	L. A. MACK, Immigration and Naturalization Service, Dallas, Texas
1-17-62	Apartment 24, Kalinin Street, Minsk, Russia	EUGENE URBAN, Immigration and Naturalization Service, New Orleans, La.
2-22-62	Kalinin Street, 4-27 Minsk, Russia	R. McC. THOMPKINS, Brigadier General, U. S. Marine Corps

It should be noted that Kalinin Street was later changed to Communist Street.

Dates	Address	Source Information Obtained From
5-20-62 to 5-30-62	Hotels Ostankino and Berlin, Moscow, Russia	MARINA OSWALD
5-30-62	Departed Moscow by train and traveled through Poland, Germany and Holland and boarded ship for U. S.	"

547

COMMISSION EXHIBIT No. 1963—Continued

Dates	Address	Source Information Obtained From
6-4-62 to 6-13-62	Aboard SS Maasdam from Holland to U. S.	LEE HARVEY OSWALD
6-13-62	SS Maasdam docked at Hoboken, New Jersey	Inspector CARL JOHNSON, Immigration and Naturalization Service, New York
6-14-62	Flew to Dallas, Texas	LEE HARVEY OSWALD
June, 1962	7313 Davenport, Fort Worth, Texas	Mrs. PENNY PEARSON, 7317 Davenport, Fort Worth, Texas
6-26-62	7313 Davenport, Fort Worth, Texas	LEE HARVEY OSWALD
7-13-62	1501 7th Street, Fort Worth, Texas	HIRAM L. CONWAY, 200 East North Vacek Street, Fort Worth, Texas
8-16-62	2703 Mercedes St., Fort Worth, Texas	LEE HARVEY OSWALD
9-6-62	2703 Mercedes St., Fort Worth, Texas	Correspondence with Russian Embassy
9-22-62	2703 Mercedes St., Fort Worth, Texas	Mr. E. L. CARTER, Jr., Credit Manager, Montgomery Ward, Fort Worth, Texas
Summer and Fall, about three months, 1962	2703 Mercedes St., Fort Worth, Texas	CHESTER ALLEN RIGGS, Jr., 250 Carroll, Fort Worth, Texas
Possibly October-November, 1962	1501 7th Street, Apt. 101, Fort Worth, Texas, with mother	Mr. and Mrs. L. R. HUFFMAN, 1516 South Harrison Street, San Angelo, Texas

COMMISSION EXHIBIT No. 1963—Continued

Dates	Address	Source Information Obtained From
10-10-62	Changed address from 2703 Mercedes, Fort Worth, Texas, to Post Office Box 2915, Dallas, Texas	Confidential Informant Dallas T-7
10-15/19-62	Room 415, YMCA, North Ervay, Dallas, Texas	JOE McREE, Resident Manager, YMCA, Dallas, Texas

It should be noted that OSWALD in October, 1962, also gave the address, 3519 Fairmount, Dallas, Texas; however, Mrs. RICHARD S. BURDICK, 3829 Normandy, Highland Park, Texas, advised OSWALD never did reside at this address. His wife, however, did stay at this address for a short time in October, 1962. MARINA OSWALD also in October and first of November, 1962, resided in the homes of Mrs. FRANK HENRY RAY, 4524 Alta Vista Lane, Dallas, Texas; Mrs. JOHN R. HALL, 4760 Trail Lake Drive, Fort Worth, Texas; and from November 11 to 17, 1962, she resided with Mrs. KATHERINE FORD, 14057 Brookcust, Dallas, Texas.

Dates	Address	Source Information Obtained From
11-3-62 to 3-2-63	Apartment 2, 604 Elsbeth, Dallas, Texas	Mrs. M. F. TOBIAS, 602 Elsbeth, Dallas, Texas
3-2-63 to 5-1-63	214 West Neeley Street, Dallas, Texas	Mr. W. GEORGE, 6769 Inverness, Dallas, Texas
4-12-63	214 West Neeley Street, Dallas, Texas	Confidential Informant Dallas T-8
4-24-63	OSWALD taken to bus station by Mrs. RUTH PAINE, 2515 West 5th St., Irving, Texas, to leave for New Orleans, La., and MARINA moved to PAINE residence	Mrs. RUTH PAINE, 2515 West 5th St., Irving, Texas

COMMISSION EXHIBIT No. 1963—Continued

8
DL 89-43
HJO:mvs/gmf

Dates	Address	Source Information Obtained From
Last of April, 1963, until rented apartment at 4905 Magazine St., New Orleans	757 French Street, New Orleans, La.	Mrs. CHARLES MURRET, 757 French Street, New Orleans, La.
4-29-63	757 France Street, New Orleans, La.	Confidential Informant Dallas T-9
5-3-63	757 French Street, New Orleans, La.	Mrs. LILLIAN DESLATTE, A-1 Employment Agency, New Orleans, La.
5-6-63	757 France Street, New Orleans, La.	Confidential Informant Dallas T-8
5-9-63	757 French Street, New Orleans, La.	WILLIAM I. MONAGHAN, 640 Magazine St. New Orleans, La.
5-9-63 to September, 1963	4905 Magazine Street, New Orleans, La.	Mrs. BLAINE GREGORY, 414 Emerald Street, New Orleans, La.
5-10/11-63	Mrs. PAINE drove MARINA to New Orleans	Mrs. RUTH PAINE
5-9-63 to 9-23-63	4905 Magazine Street, New Orleans, La.	Mrs. JESSE JAMES GARNER, 4911 Magazine St., New Orleans, La.
5-12-63	Change of address from P. O. Box 2914 to 4907 Magazine St., New Orleans, La.	Confidential Informant Dallas T-10
6-3-63 to 9-24-63	Post Office Box 30061, New Orleans, La.	Confidential Informant Dallas T-11
July or August, 1963	Spent one night in motel at Mobile, Ala. with wife and Mr. and Mrs. CHARLES F. MURRET	Mrs. CHARLES F. MURRET

9
DL 89-43
HJO:mvs

Dates	Address	Source Information Obtained From
9-23-63	Mrs. PAINE left New Orleans with MARINA	Mrs. RUTH PAINE
9-24-63	PAINE and MARINA arrived Irving, Texas	"
9-26-63	OSWALD entered Mexico at Nuevo Laredo	HARVEY CASH, American Consul, Nuevo Laredo
10-3-63	OSWALD left Mexico at Nuevo Laredo	"
10-3-63	YMCA, Room 601, Dallas, Texas	JOE McREE, Manager, YMCA, Dallas, Texas
10-4-63	OSWALD arrived at PAINE residence, Irving, Texas	Mrs. RUTH PAINE
10-5/6-63	2515 West 5th St., Irving, Texas	"
10-7-63	PAINE took OSWALD to bus station at Irving, Texas	"
10-7/14-63	621 North Marsalis, Drive, Dallas, Texas	Mrs. MARY BLEDSOE, 621 North Marsalis Drive, Dallas, Texas
10-12-63	Spent night at 2515 West 5th St., Irving, Texas	Mrs. RUTH PAINE

10
DL 89-43
HJO:mvs/gmf

Dates	Address	Source Information Obtained From
10-13-63	Spent day and night, 2515 West 5th St., Irving, Texas	Mrs. RUTH PAINE
10-14-63	OSWALD taken to Irving bus stop	"
10-14-63 to 11-22-63	1026 North Beckley, Dallas, Texas, in name of O. H. LEE	Mrs. GLADYS JOHNSON, 1026 North Beckley
10-18-63	Arrived at 2515 West 5th St., Irving, Texas	Mrs. RUTH PAINE
10-19/20-63	At 2515 West 5th St., Irving, Texas	"
10-21-63	Left for work but returned to 2515 West 5th St. for night	"
10-22-63	Left 2515 West 5th St., Irving, Texas for work	"
10-25-63	After work, went to 2515 West 5th St., Irving, Texas	"
10-26/27-63	At 2515 West 5th St., Irving, Texas	"
10-28-63	Left 2515 West 5th St., Irving, Texas for work	"
11-1-63	Post Office Box 6225 Terminal Annex, Dallas, Texas	Confidential Informant Dallas T-10
11-1-63	After work, went to 2515 West 5th St., Irving, Texas	Mrs. RUTH PAINE

552

COMMISSION EXHIBIT No. 1963—Continued

11
DL 89-43
HJO:mvs

Dates	Address	Source Information Obtained From
11-2 and 3-63	Day and night, 2515 West 5th St., Irving, Texas	Mrs. RUTH PAINE
11-4-63	Left 2515 West 5th St., Irving, Texas for work	"
11-8-63	Went to 2515 West 5th St., Irving, Texas after work	"
11-9,10,11-63	At 2515 West 5th St., Irving, Texas	"
11-12-63	Left 2515 West 5th St., Irving, Texas for work	"
11-21-63	Arrived at 2515 West 5th Street, Irving, Texas, about 5:15 P.M.	"
11-22-63	OSWALD had left 2515 West 5th Street, Irving, Texas when Mrs. PAINE got up about 7:30 A.M.	"

553

COMMISSION EXHIBIT No. 1963—Continued

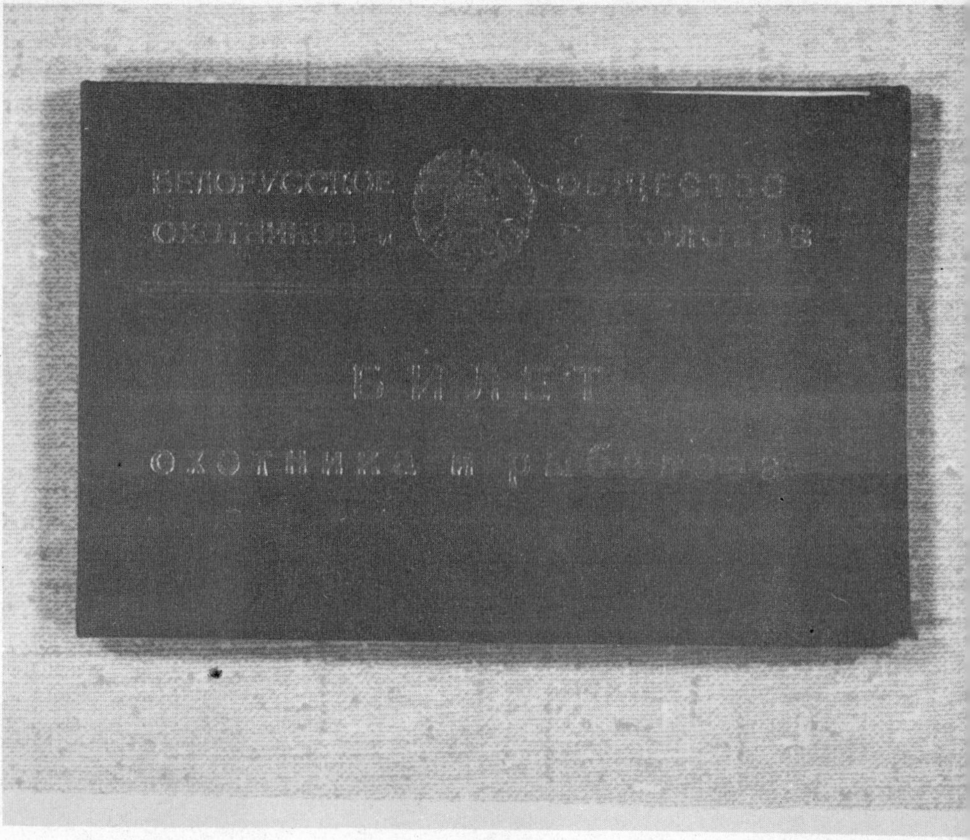

COMMISSION EXHIBIT No. 1964

TRANSLATION FROM RUSSIAN

Photograph #1:

BELORUSSIAN (WHITE RUSSIAN) SOCIETY
OF HUNTERS AND FISHERMEN

CERTIFICATE
of a
HUNTER AND FISHERMAN

COMMISSION EXHIBIT No. 1964—Continued

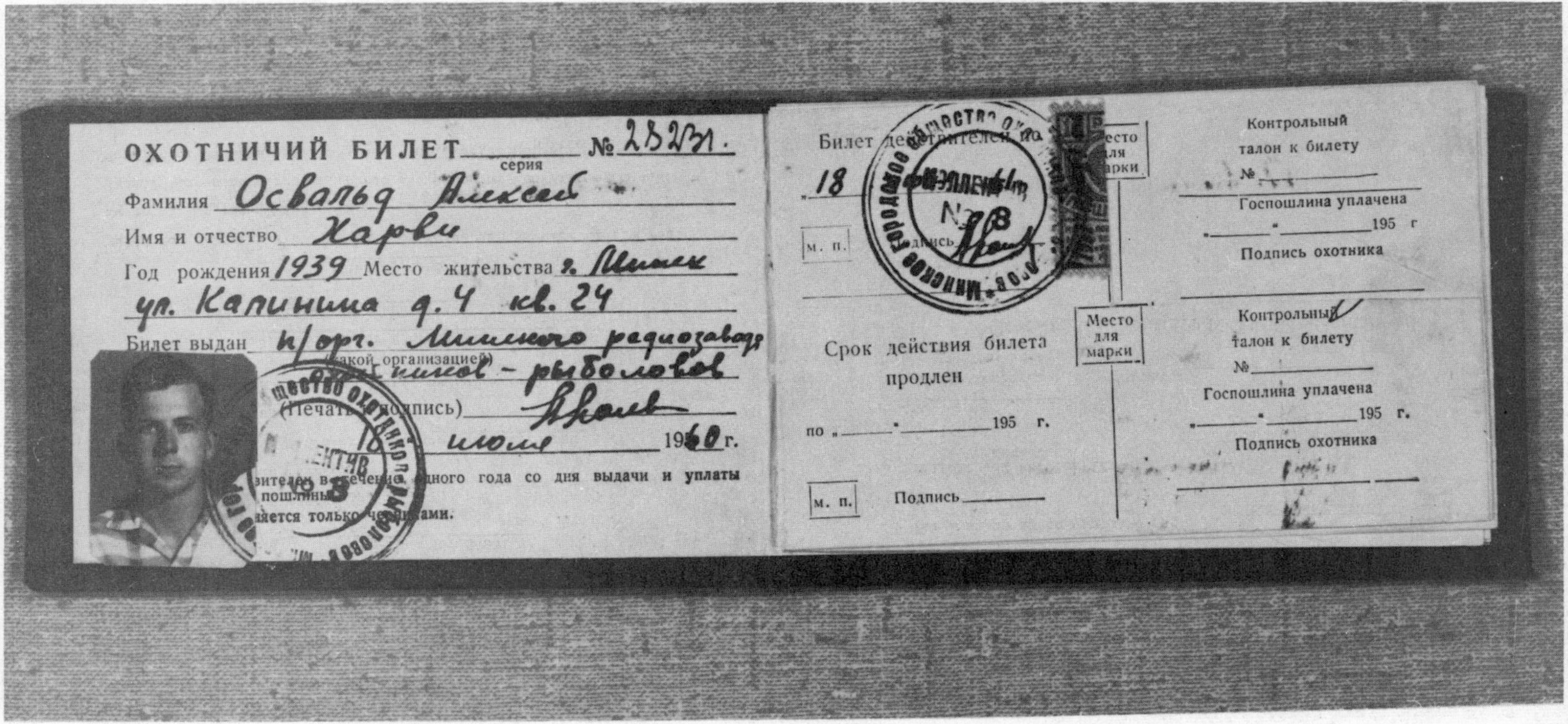
ОХОТНИЧИЙ БИЛЕТ ______ серия № 28231.
Фамилия Освальд Алексей
Имя и отчество Харви
Год рождения 1939 Место жительства г. Минск
ул. Калинина д. 4 кв. 24
Билет выдан п/орг. Минского радиозавода
(какой организацией) охотников - рыболовов
(Печать и подпись)
18 июня 1960 г.
пошлины
вителен в течение одного года со дня выдачи и уплаты
яется только членами.

Билет действителен по
18
м. п.
Подпись
Место для марки
Срок действия билета продлен
по „ ___ " ______ 195 г.
м. п. Подпись ______
Место для марки

Контрольный талон к билету
№ ______
Госпошлина уплачена
„ ___ " ______ 195 г
Подпись охотника

Контрольный талон к билету
№ ______
Госпошлина уплачена
„ ___ " ______ 195 г.
Подпись охотника

Commission Exhibit No. 1964—Continued

TRANSLATION FROM RUSSIAN

Photograph #2

(Left page)

HUNTING CERTIFICATE ____ series No. 28231.

Surname: Oswald, Aleksey (sic)

Name and patronymic Harvey

Year of birth 1939 Place of residence city of Minsk

ul. Kalinina, house 4, apartment 24

Certificate issued by p/org. (party organization?) of the Minsk (organization)

Radio Factory of Hunters and Fishermen

(Stamp and signature) P. Palev (?)

July 18, 1960

Valid for one year from the date of issue and payment of the fee.

To be filled out in ink only.

(Lower left-hand corner): photo and stamp of the City of Minsk Society of Hunters and Fishermen, Collective No. 3.

* * * * * * * * * * *

COMMISSION EXHIBIT No. 1964—Continued

(Right page)

Certificate is valid to July 18, 1961 — Place for stamp — Control Coupon for Certificate

m. p. (place for stamp) — Signature P. Palev (?) — No.________

State fee paid

(same stamp as on opposite page) — Hunter's signature ________ 195__

Validity of the certificate extended — (the same text as above repeated)

to______________ 195_

(place for stamp) Signature____________________

COMMISSION EXHIBIT No. 1964—Continued

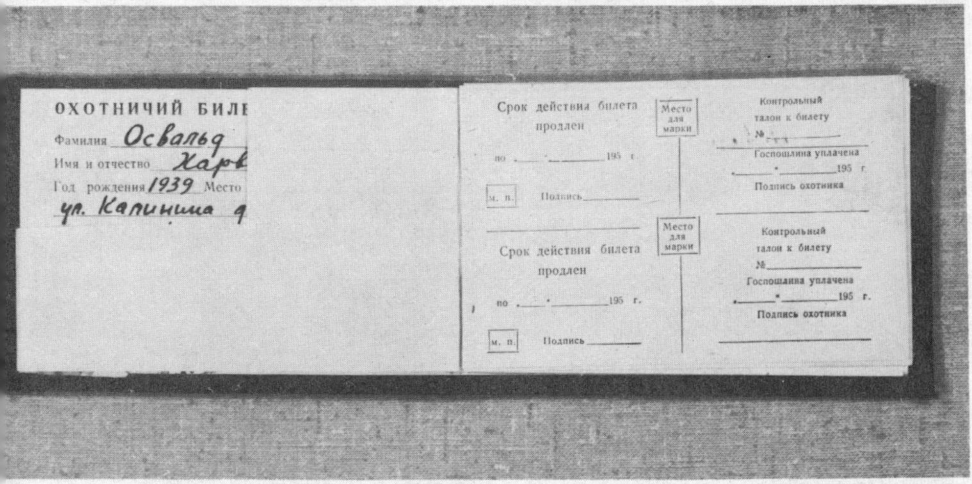

COMMISSION EXHIBIT No. 1964—Continued

TRANSLATION FROM RUSSIAN

Photograph #3

(Left page, a portion showing where the next page was cut out)

HUNTING CERTIFICATE

Surname Oswald

Name and patronymic Harv(ey)

Year of birth 1939 Place (of residence)

ul. Kalinina, h(ouse)

* * * * *

(Right page)

Translator's Note: This page was not filled out and has the same printed text as the right page on Photograph #2.

COMMISSION EXHIBIT No. 1964—Continued

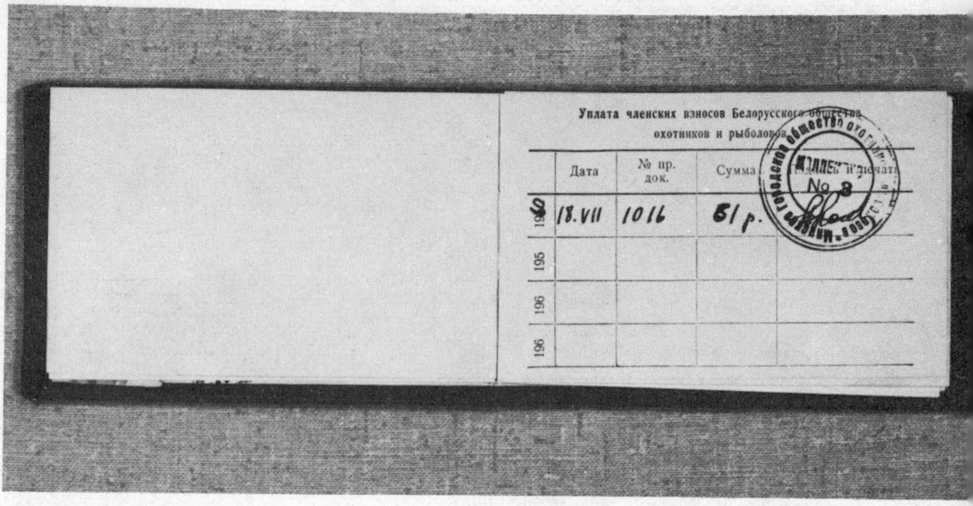

COMMISSION EXHIBIT No. 1964—Continued

TRANSLATION FROM RUSSIAN

Photograph #4

(Left page is blank)

* * * * *

(Right page)

PAYMENT OF MEMBERSHIP FEES OF THE BELORUSSIAN SOCIETY OF HUNTERS AND FISHERMEN

	Date	No. of pr. (?) document	Amount	Signature and stamp
1960	7/18	1016	61 rubles	(Stamp of the City of Minsk Society of Hunters and Fishermen, Collective No. 3.) (Signature: P. Palev)

COMMISSION EXHIBIT No. 1964—Continued

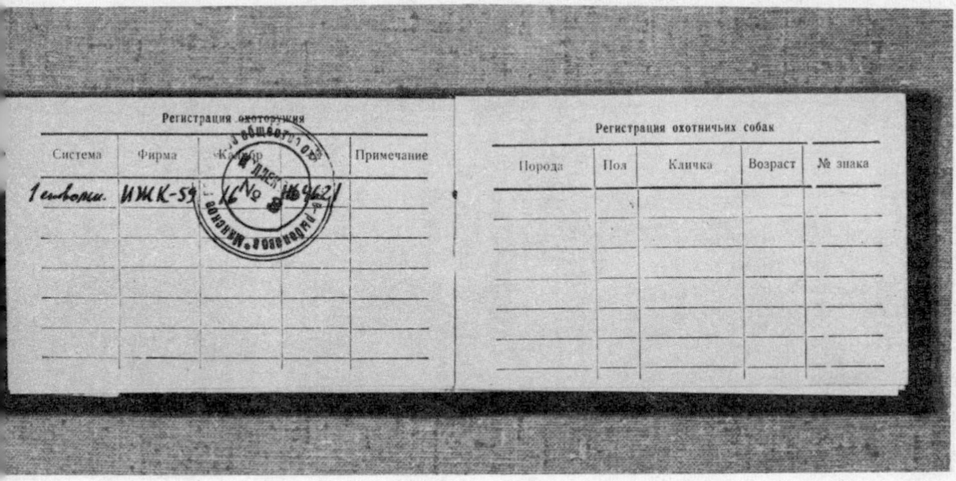

Регистрация охоторужия

Система	Фирма	Калибр	№	Примечание
1 ствол.	ИЖК-59	16	№ 64621	

Регистрация охотничьих собак

Порода	Пол	Кличка	Возраст	№ знака

COMMISSION EXHIBIT No. 1964—Continued

TRANSLATION FROM RUSSIAN

Photograph #5

(Left page)

Registration of Hunting Weapons

System	Firm (manufacturer)	Caliber (gauge)	No.	Remarks
Single-barrelled	IZhK-59 (Izhevsk K-59?)	16	N 64621	

(Stamp of the City of Minsk Society of Hunters and Fishermen, Collective No. 3)

COMMISSION EXHIBIT No. 1964—Continued

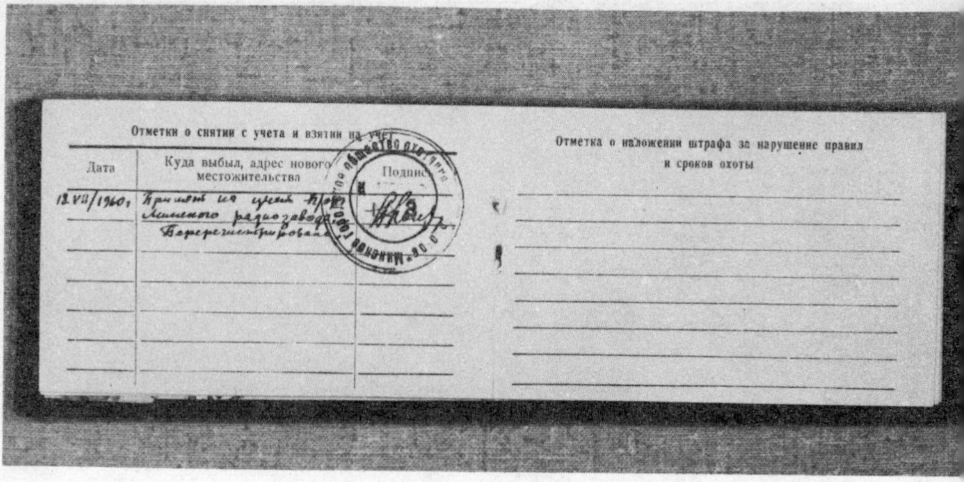

Отметки о снятии с учета и взятии на учет

Дата	Куда выбыл, адрес нового местожительства	Подпись

Отметка о наложении штрафа за нарушение правил и сроков охоты

Commission Exhibit No. 1964—Continued

TRANSLATION FROM RUSSIAN

Photograph #6

(Left page)

Entries on Striking off the Register and Registration

Date	To where departed, address of new place of residence	Signature
7/18/1960	Registered, p/org. of the Minsk Radio Factory Reregistered	(Stamp of the City of Minsk Society of Hunters and Fishermen and signature: P. Palev)

* * * * *

(Right page)

Entry on Imposition of Fine for Violation of the Rules and Periods of Hunting

(No entries on this page)

Commission Exhibit No. 1964—Continued

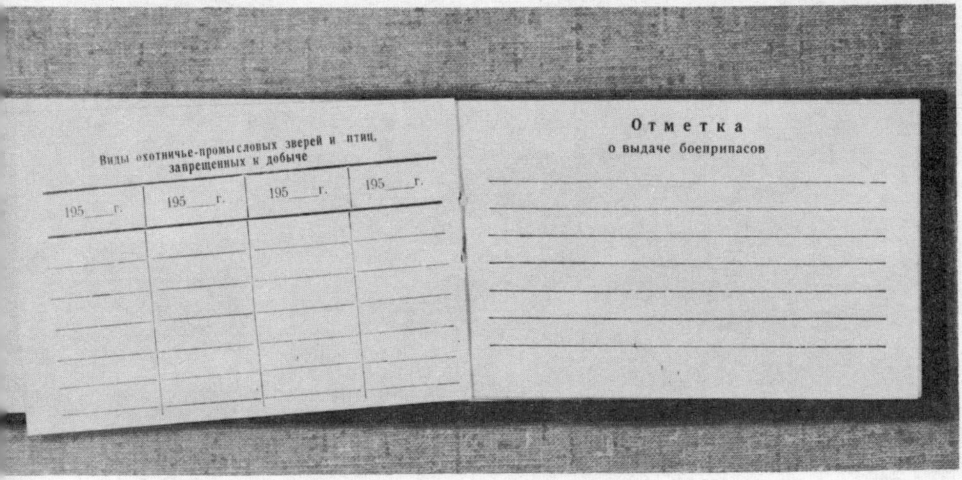

COMMISSION EXHIBIT No. 1964—Continued

TRANSLATION FROM RUSSIAN

Photograph #7

(Left page)

Types of Game Animals and Birds

Prohibited for Hunting

195--	195--	195--	195--

(This page is blank)

* * * *

(Right page)

Entry on Issue of
Ammunition

(This page is blank)

COMMISSION EXHIBIT No. 1964—Continued

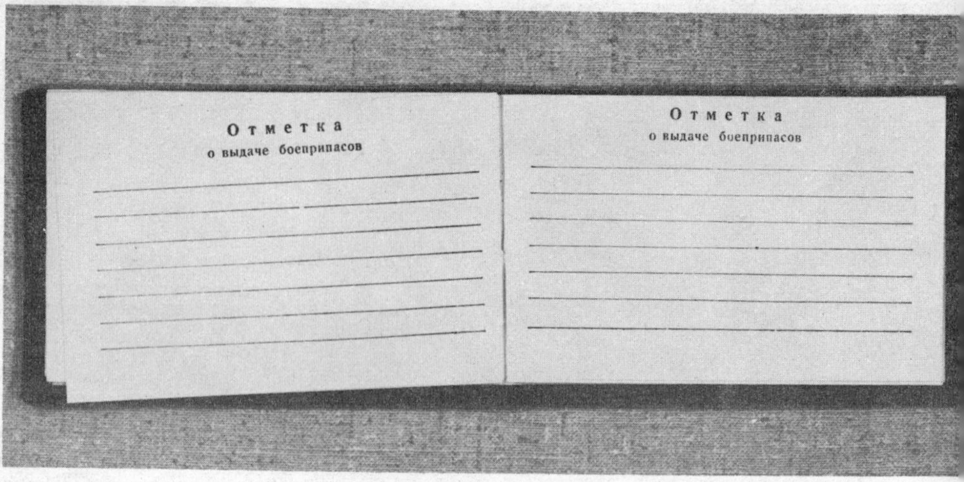

COMMISSION EXHIBIT No. 1964—Continued

TRANSLATION FROM RUSSIAN

Photograph #3

Heading of the left and right pages: "Entry on Issue of Ammunition." Both pages are left blank.

COMMISSION EXHIBIT No. 1964—Continued

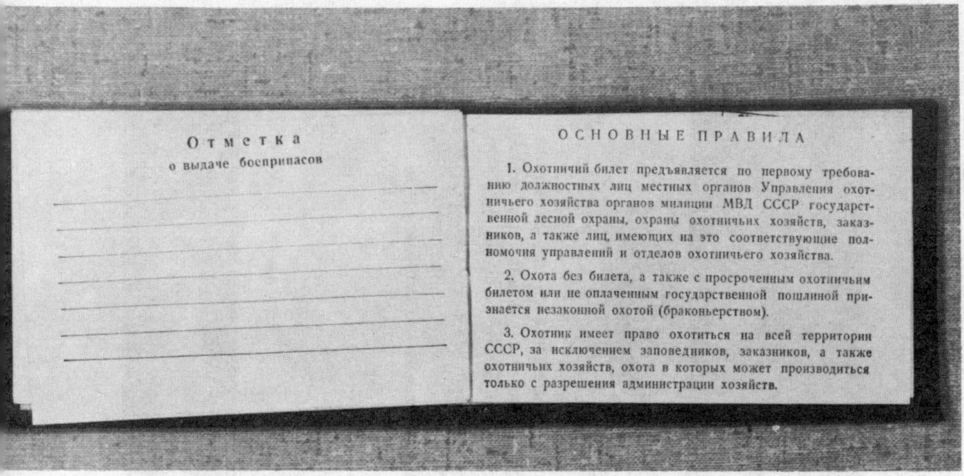

Отметка
о выдаче боеприпасов

ОСНОВНЫЕ ПРАВИЛА

1. Охотничий билет предъявляется по первому требованию должностных лиц местных органов Управления охотничьего хозяйства органов милиции МВД СССР государственной лесной охраны, охраны охотничьих хозяйств, заказников, а также лиц, имеющих на это соответствующие полномочия управлений и отделов охотничьего хозяйства.

2. Охота без билета, а также с просроченным охотничьим билетом или не оплаченным государственной пошлиной признается незаконной охотой (браконьерством).

3. Охотник имеет право охотиться на всей территории СССР, за исключением заповедников, заказников, а также охотничьих хозяйств, охота в которых может производиться только с разрешения администрации хозяйств.

COMMISSION EXHIBIT No. 1964—Continued

TRANSLATION FROM RUSSIAN

Photograph #9

(Left page)

Entry on Issue of Ammunition

(No entries on this page)

* * * * * * *

(Right page)

BASIC REGULATIONS

1. Hunting certificate should be shown on the first demand of officials of local organs of the Administration of Hunting Grounds, organs of militia of the Ministry of Internal Affairs of the USSR, state forest guards, guards of hunting grounds and preserves, as well as persons properly authorized by the administrations and sections of hunting economy.

2. Hunting without certificate, or with the one which has lapsed, or on which the state fee was not paid, is considered the illegal hunting (poaching).

3. A hunter has the right to hunt upon the entire territory of the USSR, with the exception of special sanctuaries or preserves, as well as hunting grounds, where hunting can be engaged in only with permission of the administration of the grounds.

COMMISSION EXHIBIT No. 1964—Continued

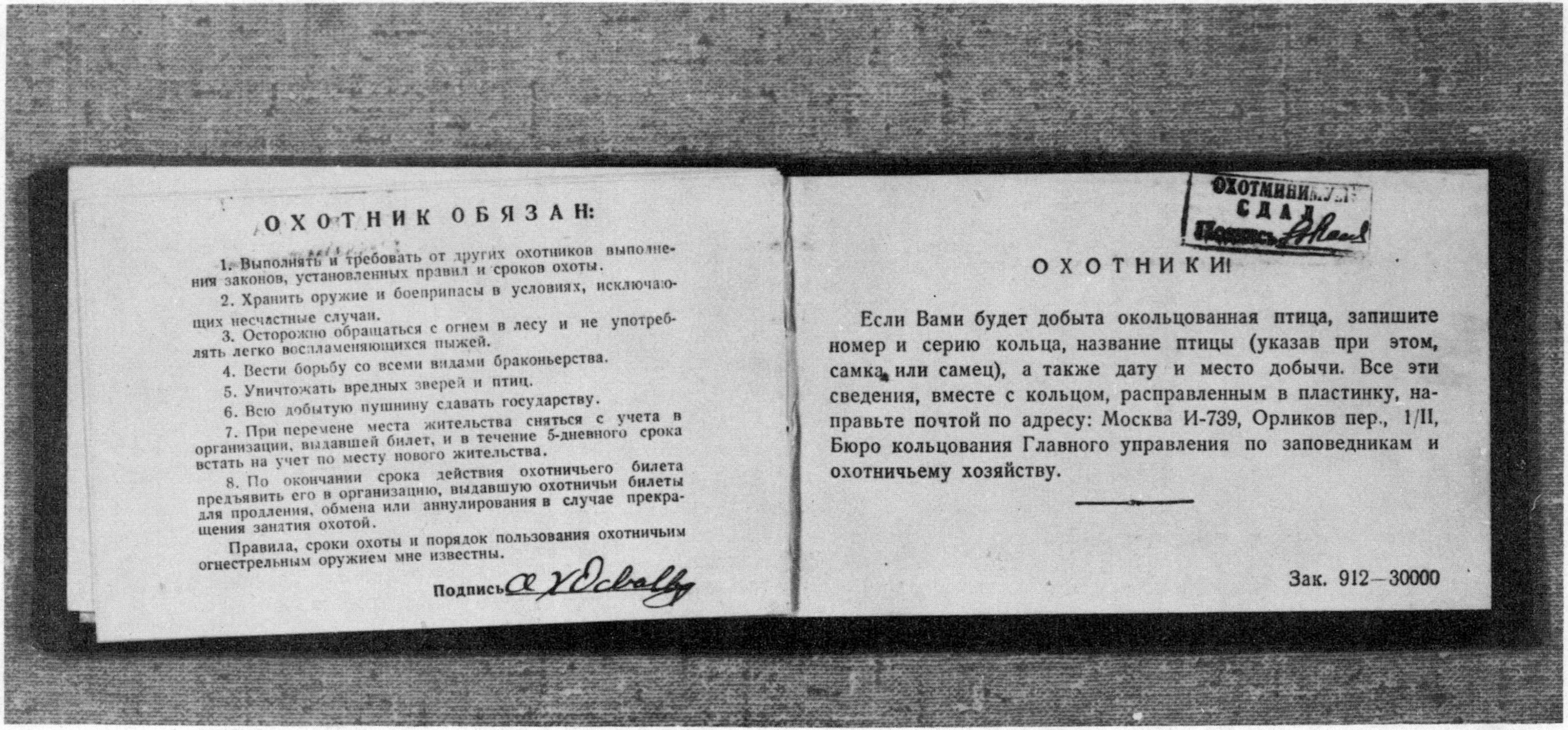

ОХОТНИК ОБЯЗАН:

1. Выполнять и требовать от других охотников выполнения законов, установленных правил и сроков охоты.
2. Хранить оружие и боеприпасы в условиях, исключающих несчастные случаи.
3. Осторожно обращаться с огнем в лесу и не употреблять легко воспламеняющихся пыжей.
4. Вести борьбу со всеми видами браконьерства.
5. Уничтожать вредных зверей и птиц.
6. Всю добытую пушнину сдавать государству.
7. При перемене места жительства сняться с учета в организации, выдавшей билет, и в течение 5-дневного срока встать на учет по месту нового жительства.
8. По окончании срока действия охотничьего билета предъявить его в организацию, выдавшую охотничьи билеты для продления, обмена или аннулирования в случае прекращения занятия охотой.

Правила, сроки охоты и порядок пользования охотничьим огнестрельным оружием мне известны.

Подпись

ОХОТНИКИ!

Если Вами будет добыта окольцованная птица, запишите номер и серию кольца, название птицы (указав при этом, самка или самец), а также дату и место добычи. Все эти сведения, вместе с кольцом, расправленным в пластинку, направьте почтой по адресу: Москва И-739, Орликов пер., 1/II, Бюро кольцования Главного управления по заповедникам и охотничьему хозяйству.

Зак. 912—30000

COMMISSION EXHIBIT No. 1964—Continued

TRANSLATION FROM RUSSIAN

Photograph #10

(Left page)

A HUNTER MUST

1. Observe and demand from other hunters the observance of laws, established regulations and hunting seasons.

2. Keep weapons and ammunition in conditions which exclude accidents.

3. Be careful in handling shooting in the forest and not use easily-inflammable wads.

4. Carry on struggle against any type of poaching.

5. Destroy harmful beasts and birds (vermin).

6. Deliver to the state all the furs obtained.

7. In changing residence, have his name taken off the register in the organization issuing the certificate and register within 5 days at the place of new residence.

8. On the lapsing of validity of the hunting certificate, present it at the organization which issued the hunting certificates (sic) for extention, exchange, or cancellation in case of discontinuance of hunting activities.

I am familiar with regulations, hunting seasons and the way of using hunting firearms.

Signature: A. H. Oswald

COMMISSION EXHIBIT No. 1964—Continued

Photograph #10

(Right page)

HUNTERS!

If you obtain a banded bird, take down the number and series of the band, the name of the bird (indicating whether male or female), as well as the date and place where obtained. Mail all this information, together with the flattened-out band, to the following address: Banding Bureau of the Chief Administration of Preserves and Hunting Grounds, Orlikov per. 1/11, Moscow I-739.

Order 912-30,000

Stamp in the upper right-hand corner:

Delivered Hunting Minimum
Signature: P. Palev.

COMMISSION EXHIBIT No. 1964—Continued

FD-302 (Rev. 3-3-59) FEDERAL BUREAU OF IN[redacted] Commission Exhibit No. 1965

Date 3/26/64

1

Mr. O. V. CAMPBELL, Vice President, Texas School Book Depository, 411 Elm Street, Dallas, Texas, furnished a Photocopy of Invoice No. 6410, reflecting a shipment on March 19, 1963, of fifty-eight rolls of 24", 60 lb., Kraft Wrapping Paper from the Texas Paper Company in Dallas. CAMPBELL advised this shipment of paper lasted until January, 1964, when a reorder became necessary.

CAMPBELL advised that, if OSWALD had obtained Kraft paper from the Depository Building during the time he was employed there, it would have come from this shipment.

CAMPBELL advised that the last shipment of gummed 3" tape ordered by his company prior to the employment of OSWALD was a shipment of fifty cartons of 3", 60-lb., safety-sealed gummed paper tape received by his firm, 3/29/63, from Weaver Tape & Specialties Company, 9236 Church Road, Dallas, Texas, under Invoice No. 1585. CAMPBELL advised that any 3" gummed tape on the premises during OSWALD's employment at the Texas School Book Depository would have come from this shipment.

on 3/25/64 at Dallas, Texas 131 File # 100-10461

by Special Agents EUGENE F. PETRAKIS & A. RAYMOND SWITZER/eah Date dictated 3/26/64

COMMISSION EXHIBIT No. 1965

FD-302 (Rev. 3-3-59) FEDERAL BUREAU OF INVESTIGATION

1

Date 3/12/64

Mr. FRANKLIN KAISER advised he is an order clerk and truck driver for the Texas School Book Depository, Inc. (TSBD) at 411 Elm Street in Dallas, Texas. He said he has been employed in that capacity for about one year. Mr. KAISER produced a "home-made" clip board which measures 9¼" by 11¼". It is constructed of corrugated cardboard covered with 3" Kraft paper shipping tape and has a 2" metal "LEB" binder clip. KAISER said that he gave this board to LEE HARVEY OSWALD so that OSWALD could clip his orders to it when he was filling the orders as an employee of TSBD. He said that he believed OSWALD used this board on November 22, 1963, prior to the assassination of President KENNEDY and he, KAISER, located the board on the sixth floor in the northwest corner of the TSBD building east of the stairwell wall between two rows of stacked boxed books a few days after the assassination of President JOHN F. KENNEDY.

The clip board was identified by Special Agent ARTHUR E. CARTER writing "100-10461", "3/10/64" and the initials "AEC".

Mr. KAISER advised he resides in a trailer park located at 5230 Ledbetter Drive in Dallas, Texas.

on 3/10/64 at Dallas, Texas 170 File # DL 100-10461

by Special Agent ARTHUR E. CARTER/gs Date dictated 3/11/64

COMMISSION EXHIBIT No. 1966

FD-302 (Rev. 3-3-59) **FEDERAL BUREAU OF INVESTIGATION**

1

Date 11/23/63

ROGER CRAIG, 7711 Piedmont, Apartment B, phone EVergreen 1-4851, employed as a Deputy Sheriff, Dallas County Sheriff's Department, advised that he was standing in front of the Dallas Sheriff's Office, 505 Main Street, at the time the motorcade of President JOHN F. KENNEDY was approaching the triple underpass. He stated that he heard a shot and ran around the corner onto Houston Street and went through the parking area and briefly searched area on Elm Street. Shortly after this, approximately 3 or 4 minutes, came back across Elm Street and observed an individual run down the grass area from the direction of the Texas School Book Depository. He heard this individual whistle and a white Rambler station wagon, driven by a Negro male, pulled over to the curb and said individual got in and the car headed toward the Dallas-Fort Worth Turnpike.

CRAIG stated that at 5:18 PM, November 22, 1963, he was given an opportunity to observe LEE HARVEY OSWALD in the office of Captain J. W. FRITZ in the Homicide and Robbery Bureau, Dallas Police Department, and that he is positive that OSWALD is identical with the same individual he observed getting into the Rambler station wagon as mentioned above.

on 11/22/63 at Dallas, Texas File # DL 89-43

by Special Agent JAMES W. BOOKHOUT/cah Date dictated 11/23/63

69

COMMISSION EXHIBIT No. 1967

LOCATION OF EYEWITNESSES TO THE MOVEMENTS OF LEE HARVEY OSWALD IN THE VICINITY OF THE TIPPIT KILLING

COMMISSION EXHIBIT No. 1968

COMMISSION EXHIBIT NO. 1969

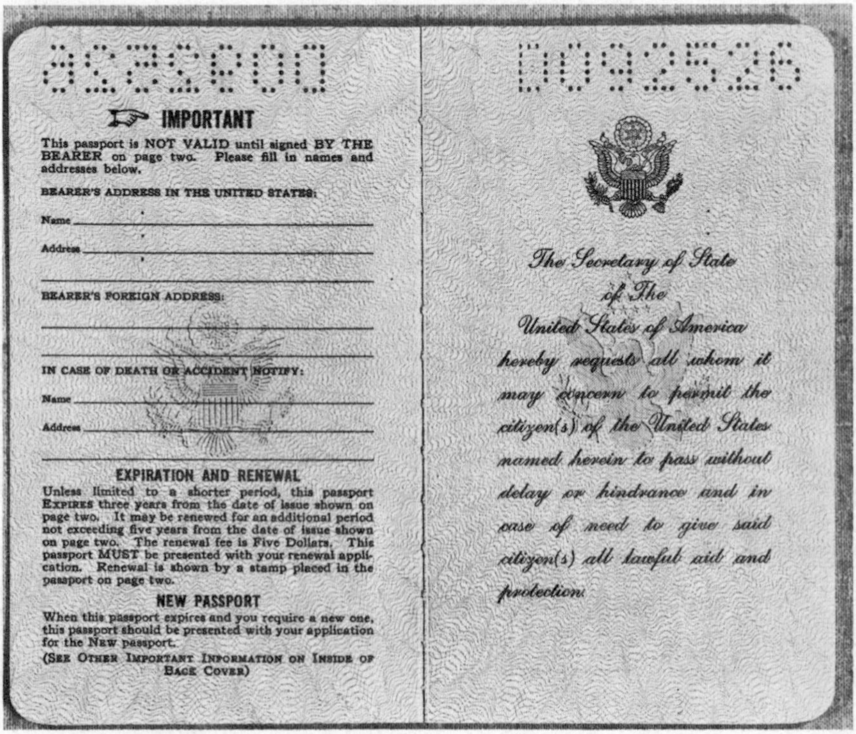

D092526

IMPORTANT

This passport is NOT VALID until signed BY THE BEARER on page two. Please fill in names and addresses below.

BEARER'S ADDRESS IN THE UNITED STATES:

Name ______

Address ______

______

BEARER'S FOREIGN ADDRESS:

______

______

IN CASE OF DEATH OR ACCIDENT NOTIFY:

Name ______

Address ______

______

EXPIRATION AND RENEWAL

Unless limited to a shorter period, this passport EXPIRES three years from the date of issue shown on page two. It may be renewed for an additional period not exceeding five years from the date of issue shown on page two. The renewal fee is Five Dollars. This passport MUST be presented with your renewal application. Renewal is shown by a stamp placed in the passport on page two.

NEW PASSPORT

When this passport expires and you require a new one, this passport should be presented with your application for the NEW passport.

(SEE OTHER IMPORTANT INFORMATION ON INSIDE OF BACK COVER)

D092526

The Secretary of State of The United States of America hereby requests all whom it may concern to permit the citizen(s) of the United States named herein to pass without delay or hindrance and in case of need to give said citizen(s) all lawful aid and protection.

COMMISSION EXHIBIT NO. 1969—Continued

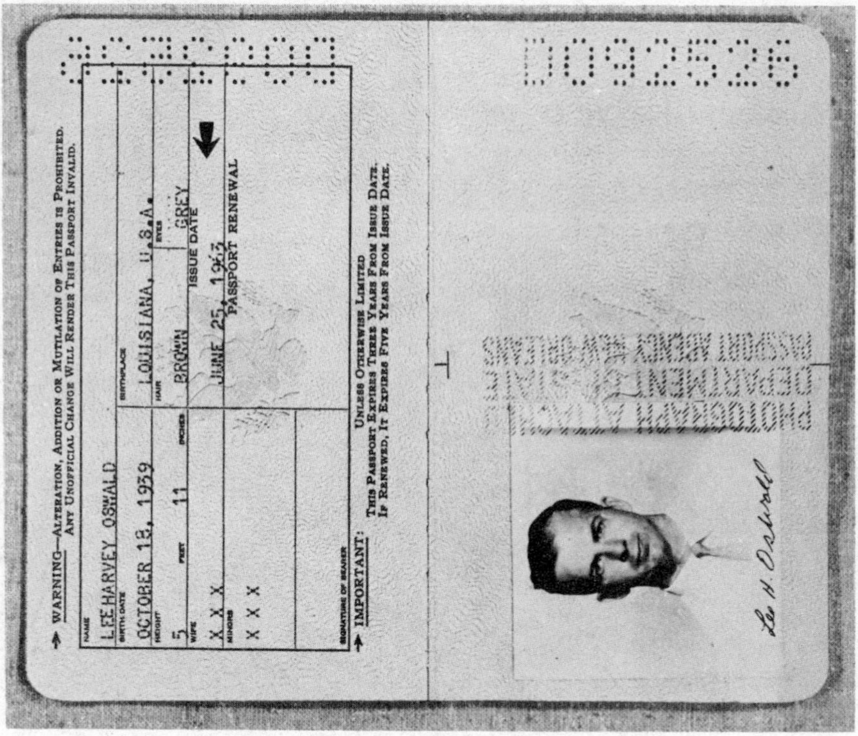
D092526

WARNING—ALTERATION, ADDITION OR MUTILATION OF ENTRIES IS PROHIBITED.
ANY UNOFFICIAL CHANGE WILL RENDER THIS PASSPORT INVALID.

NAME: LEE HARVEY OSWALD
BIRTH DATE: OCTOBER 18, 1939
BIRTHPLACE: LOUISIANA, U.S.A.
HEIGHT: 5 FEET 11 INCHES
HAIR: BROWN
EYES: GREY
WIFE: X X X
ISSUE DATE: JUNE 25, 1963
MINORS: X X X
PASSPORT RENEWAL

SIGNATURE OF BEARER

IMPORTANT: UNLESS OTHERWISE LIMITED
THIS PASSPORT EXPIRES THREE YEARS FROM ISSUE DATE.
IF RENEWED, IT EXPIRES FIVE YEARS FROM ISSUE DATE.

PHOTOGRAPH ATTACHED
DEPARTMENT OF STATE
PASSPORT AGENCY NEW ORLEANS

Lee H. Oswald

COMMISSION EXHIBIT No. 1969—Continued

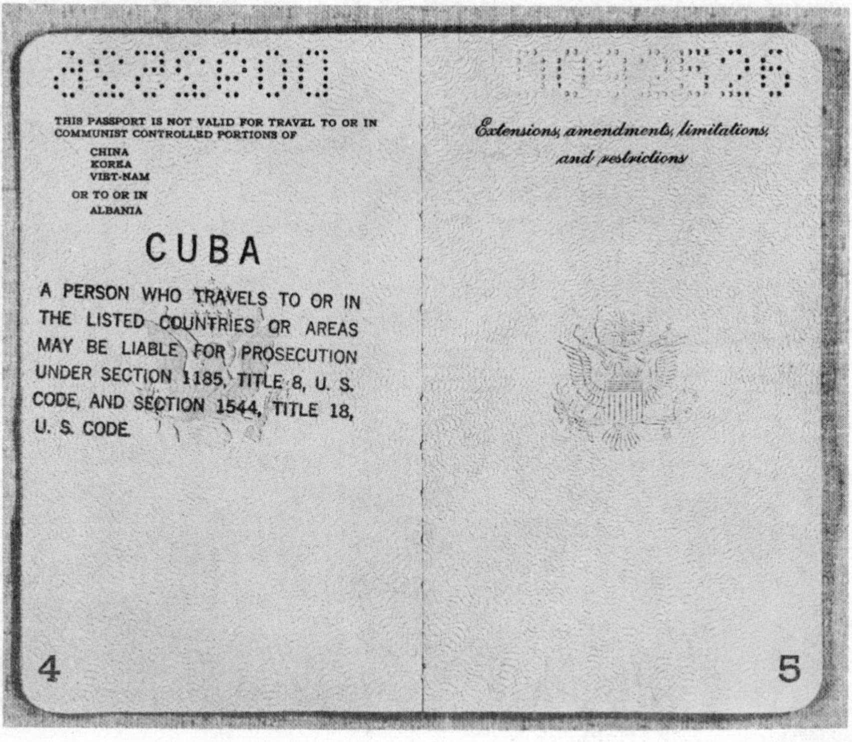
D092526

THIS PASSPORT IS NOT VALID FOR TRAVEL TO OR IN COMMUNIST CONTROLLED PORTIONS OF

CHINA
KOREA
VIET-NAM

OR TO OR IN

ALBANIA

CUBA

A PERSON WHO TRAVELS TO OR IN THE LISTED COUNTRIES OR AREAS MAY BE LIABLE FOR PROSECUTION UNDER SECTION 1185, TITLE 8, U. S. CODE, AND SECTION 1544, TITLE 18, U. S. CODE.

4

D092526

Extensions, amendments, limitations, and restrictions

5

COMMISSION EXHIBIT No. 1969—Continued

Visas
IT IS THE RESPONSIBILITY OF THE PASSPORT BEARER
TO OBTAIN NECESSARY VISAS
6
Visas
7

COMMISSION EXHIBIT No. 1969—Continued

COMMISSION EXHIBIT No. 1969—Continued

COMMISSION EXHIBIT No. 1969—Continued

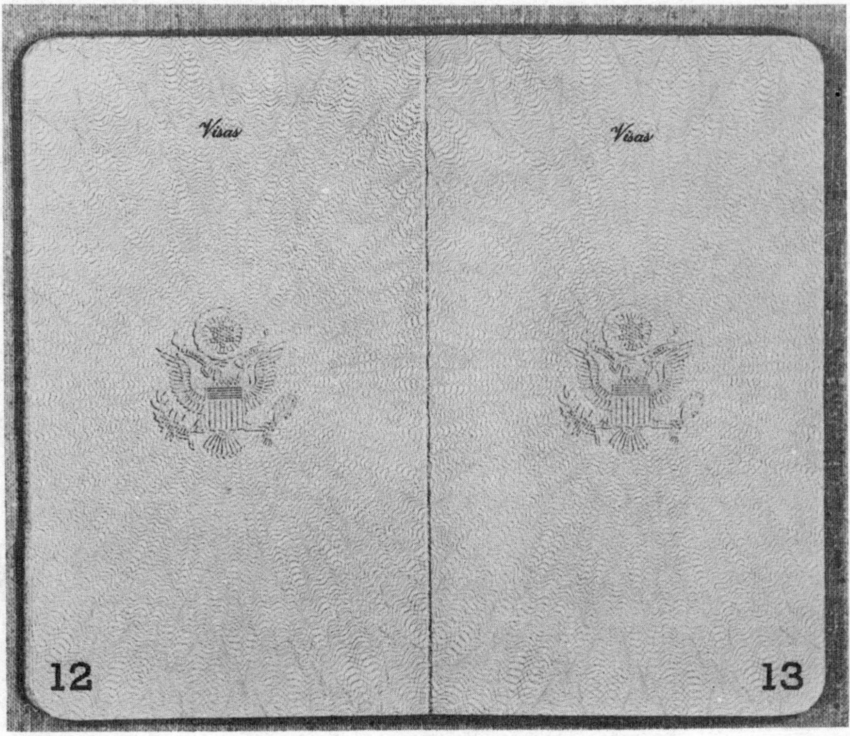

COMMISSION EXHIBIT No. 1969—Continued

COMMISSION EXHIBIT No. 1969—Continued

COMMISSION EXHIBIT No. 1969—Continued

COMMISSION EXHIBIT No. 1969—Continued

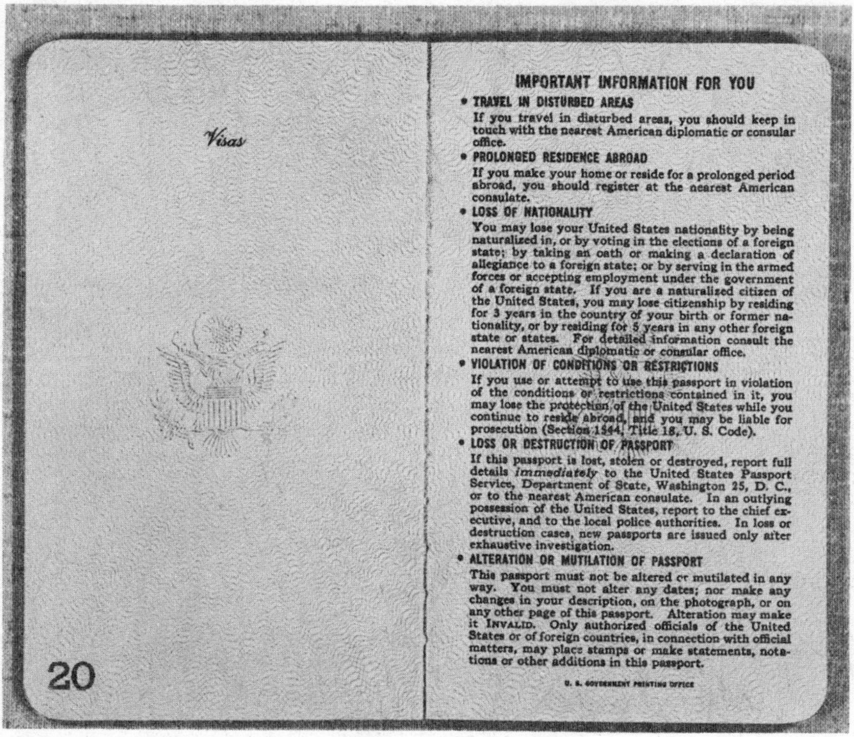

IMPORTANT INFORMATION FOR YOU

- TRAVEL IN DISTURBED AREAS

If you travel in disturbed areas, you should keep in touch with the nearest American diplomatic or consular office.

- PROLONGED RESIDENCE ABROAD

If you make your home or reside for a prolonged period abroad, you should register at the nearest American consulate.

- LOSS OF NATIONALITY

You may lose your United States nationality by being naturalized in, or by voting in the elections of a foreign state; by taking an oath or making a declaration of allegiance to a foreign state; or by serving in the armed forces or accepting employment under the government of a foreign state. If you are a naturalized citizen of the United States, you may lose citizenship by residing for 3 years in the country of your birth or former nationality, or by residing for 5 years in any other foreign state or states. For detailed information consult the nearest American diplomatic or consular office.

- VIOLATION OF CONDITIONS OR RESTRICTIONS

If you use or attempt to use this passport in violation of the conditions or restrictions contained in it, you may lose the protection of the United States while you continue to reside abroad, and you may be liable for prosecution (Section 1544, Title 18, U. S. Code).

- LOSS OR DESTRUCTION OF PASSPORT

If this passport is lost, stolen or destroyed, report full details *immediately* to the United States Passport Service, Department of State, Washington 25, D. C., or to the nearest American consulate. In an outlying possession of the United States, report to the chief executive, and to the local police authorities. In loss or destruction cases, new passports are issued only after exhaustive investigation.

- ALTERATION OR MUTILATION OF PASSPORT

This passport must not be altered or mutilated in any way. You must not alter any dates; nor make any changes in your description, on the photograph, or on any other page of this passport. Alteration may make it INVALID. Only authorized officials of the United States or of foreign countries, in connection with official matters, may place stamps or make statements, notations or other additions in this passport.

U. S. GOVERNMENT PRINTING OFFICE

COMMISSION EXHIBIT No. 1969—Continued

FD-302 (Rev. 3-3-59)

FEDERAL BUREAU OF INVESTIGATION

1

Date 7/17/64

O. V. CAMPBELL, Vice-President of the Texas School Book Depository, Dallas, advised that JOE MOLINA had been under his direct supervision when employed as Credit Manager of this company. CAMPBELL said that their business had boomed tremendously in the past year, that in the Fall of 1963, they were swamped with orders and it was obvious they were going to have to go into automation in order to operate efficiently.

In November 1963, the company hired one JOHN L. PRIMM, an independent efficiency expert, to make a survey of their operations. PRIMM conducted this survey on five separate dates from November 1963, to about February 15, 1964. CAMPBELL was not satisfied with PRIMM's work, principally because he spoke in generalities rather than specifics, and his services were discontinued.

At about the same time, the company also had experts in from the Frieden Company, 2905 Swiss Avenue, specifically, one ROBERT BEAZLEY of that firm, a representative from the Burroughs Company, and from Management Data Service, to conduct similar surveys and to make recommendations as to how to make the company's operations more efficient. The company finally decided to use the services and machines sold by the Frieden Company.

Throughout these surveys, it became apparent that the firm would be top-heavy at the level of JOE MOLINA's job, if they went to automation, and that either the job of OTIS WILLIAMS, in charge of the Bookkeeping Department, or of JOE MOLINA, the Credit Manager, would have to be abolished, and the accounting operation put under the supervision of one of these two men.

He said both MOLINA and WILLIAMS had been with the company about the same length of time. Both were completely capable and efficient. He felt that WILLIAMS perhaps had a little more over-all knowledge of the operations of the

on 7/14/64 at Dallas, Texas File # DL 100-9847

by Special Agent W. JAMES WOOD/ds Date dictated 7/15/64

- 35 -

COMMISSION EXHIBIT No. 1970

2

DL 100-9847

Accounting Department than did MOLINA. In addition, about once a year it was necessary for CAMPBELL to call MOLINA "on the carpet," for various reasons, principally, because MOLINA found it difficult, at times, to take orders and suggestions, and because of MOLINA's inclination to be a bit too independent in his job. For these reasons alone, CAMPBELL decided to retain WILLIAMS and let MOLINA go.

CAMPBELL pointed out that in none of the surveys was there any recommendation made as to what jobs should be abolished or who should be discharged, but that such studies made it obvious one of the two jobs held by WILLIAMS and MOLINA would have to be abolished, and the choice was made by CAMPBELL.

The company had planned to have the Accounting Department automated by May 1, 1964. Actually, automation did not take effect until July 1, 1964. However, because it was obvious that MOLINA's job would be abolished, the company felt it their duty to notify him as soon as possible so he could seek other work, and to make a generous settlement with him because of his sixteen years of service with them.

CAMPBELL said he heard reports over television and the radio, shortly following the assassination of President KENNEDY, that MOLINA might have a subversive background, but that he had received no substantiating information to prove this, and that such allegations were not a factor in the discharge of MOLINA.

MOLINA was given notice of termination, and was offered a contract to receive a salary for a period after his separation, and termination pay. Mr. CAMPBELL stated MOLINA consulted with his attorney before signing this contract.

CAMPBELL exhibited the contract signed by MOLINA, which stated his employment was being terminated as of the date of the contract, December 12, 1963, and the following severance pay would be given him:

- 36 -

COMMISSION EXHIBIT No. 1970—Continued

1. Full salary for December 1963.
2. Christmas present of $150.
3. Severance pay in the amount equal to full monthly salary for January, February and March 1964.
4. Additional severance of one-half of his full monthly salary for April, May and June 1964.
5. If the company paid a bonus to its employees for their fiscal year ending April 30, 1964, the company would pay to MOLINA the amount of the bonus for his eight months service from May through December 1963.

The last paragraph of this contract reads as follows:

"The said JOE R. MOLINA approves the foregoing and agrees that payment of the amounts above specified shall operate to release and discharge all claims of every kind that the said JOE R. MOLINA has or may have against the Texas School Depository."

The company also wrote a letter for MOLINA dated December 30, 1963, "to whom it may concern," giving him an excellent recommendation as a good and faithful employee, and stating he was being let go because the company was going to install a system of automation for the Accounting Department, and many positions would either be consolidated or eliminated. The letter stated that since they were not too sure of the future possibility for him at that time, they felt the fair thing would be to advise MOLINA of the intended change so he could seek employment elsewhere.

CAMPBELL said that in January 1964, the employment manager of the Neuhoff Packing Company in Dallas called him and questioned him about MOLINA's past employment, saying

there was an opening in the credit union of that company. He said he gave MOLINA an excellent recommendation. He said MOLINA had done some work for a credit union in connection with his church work, and should be excellent for the job. He later heard MOLINA went to work for the Neuhoff Company, but he did not know the date of such employment.

Mr. CAMPBELL said MOLINA had been an excellent employee throughout the period of his affiliation with the Texas School Book Depository, that there had never been any reason to question his loyalty or his affiliations throughout this period, and that although CAMPBELL found the allegations against MOLINA disturbing, he did not place much stock in them, and such allegations were not a factor in the discharging of MOLINA.

FD-302 (Rev. 3-3-59)

FEDERAL BUREAU OF INVESTIGATION

Date August 19, 1964

1

O. V. CAMPBELL, Vice President, Texas School Book Depository, Dallas, was interviewed at his residence at 7120 Twin Creek Lane, Dallas. He was reinterviewed for the purpose of clarifying information he had previously given in view of information furnished by JOE R. MOLINA. He was advised that JOE R. MOLINA has claimed that about ten days after publicity concerning his interrogation by Police, he (MOLINA) was told that he could no longer sign outgoing letters at his (MOLINA'S) place of employment; and shortly thereafter, all letterheads which bore his name were taken from him; that, thereafter, he had contacted Mr. O. V. CAMPBELL who had told him that allegations made about his loyalty would have to be cleared up; that the company had received crank calls and several customers said they would not buy books from the company as long as it had a subversive working for it.

Mr. CAMPBELL stated the adverse publicity received by JOE R. MOLINA was not the reason for MOLINA's termination from employment at the Texas School Book Depository. Mr. CAMPBELL advised that the officials of his company, prior to the date of the assassination of President KENNEDY, had already made up their minds to let MOLINA go because the department in which he was employed had become overloaded due to automation. He stated the fact that MOLINA, immediately following the day of President KENNEDY's assassination, received adverse publicity to the effect that he might have some subversive affiliation was not the reason why MOLINA's employment by that firm was terminated. The officials believed it would be unjust to keep him on in only a Clerk position, automation having taken over much of MOLINA's duties. Mr. CAMPBELL explained that all accounting at the present time at that firm is done by automation. He stated, however, that if the officials had not already made up their minds to let MOLINA go, they would have considered the

on 8/18/64 at Dallas, Texas File # DL 100-9847

by Special Agent EDWIN D. KUYKENDALL/itf Date dictated 8/18/64

-38a-

This document contains neither recommendations nor conclusions of the FBI. It is the property of the FBI and is loaned to your agency; it and its contents are not to be distributed outside your agency.

DL 100-9847
2

adverse publicity against MOLINA as a possible reason for letting him go, but before using that as such a reason, they would have tried to find out more concerning the allegations against MOLINA. He said they would have employed some investigative agency to help them determine if there was any foundation to those allegations before using same as a reason for terminating him.

Mr. CAMPBELL stated his firm acts as agents and distributors for about forty different book publishers and that his firm is constantly interested in being certain that none of the books would be of such nature they should not be utilized by school students. He stated the Texas Educational Agency, Austin, Texas, is constantly checking into school books to be certain there is no subversive aspect about any of the books used in public schools. He stated that State Agency is constantly pressured by various individuals in that regard in order to be certain that no books teaching communism or other subversive activities would fall into the hands of public school students.

Mr. CAMPBELL stated that immediately following President KENNEDY'S assassination and the adverse publicity received by JOE R. MOLINA, his firm, as a strictly precautionary measure, decided to have no more letters sent out over MOLINA'S signature. He and other officials of his firm had heard allegations over radio and television concerning the possibility that MOLINA might have some subversive affiliation or background, but they had no information that would establish such allegations as being true. He stated the letterhead stationery of that firm did not carry MOLINA'S name, and the only forms that bore MOLINA'S name were "offset" letters which contained MOLINA'S name as signer. He explained that "offset" letters were form letters that had been prepared previously and numerous copies had been run off through a photographic process for later use by MOLINA. These form letters were used by the firm as collection letters, and MOLINA had been

-38b-

DL 100-9847
3

sending them out to various customers merely filling in blanks on that letter as would be appropriate. Mr. CAMPBELL stated he had his secretaries, BONNIE RITCHEY and CAROLYN ARNOLD, gather up the unused copies of those "offset" letters that con[illegible]d MOLINA'S name. He said there were two different kinds of those form letters, and there may have been three, all of which reflected JOE MOLINA'S name as the signer and identified MOLINA as Credit Manager. Mr. CAMPBELL stated SARAH STANTON is an employee at that firm, but she had not assisted in collecting those forms bearing MOLINA'S name.

Mr. CAMPBELL stated those form letters were taken up as a precautionary measure done solely toward not losing customers. He stated that within a few days after the day of President KENNEDY'S assassination, possibly during the first week thereafter, he discussed this matter very briefly with MOLINA telling him that at least for the present time until the adverse publicity concerning MOLINA had been cleared up, it was believed that no letters should be sent out over MOLINA'S signature. Mr. CAMPBELL said at that time, all [illegible] and other officials of his firm knew about the allegations concerning MOLINA was what they had heard on radio and television. Mr. CAMPBELL stated he did not tell MOLINA that he had received any crank telephone calls or that several customers had written in stating they would not buy books from the company as long as it had a subversive working for it. He stated he does not recall that the firm ever received any crank telephone calls of that nature and, as of that date, no letters had been received of that nature. He stated he recalls that only about three uncomplimentary letters had been received by the firm subsequent to the assassination and none of those had been received as of the time CAMPBELL engaged in that conversation with MOLINA. He said one such uncomplimentary letter was received later in December, 1963, one about the first of January, 1964, and one about February, 1964.

-38c-

COMMISSION EXHIBIT No. 1970—Continued

UNITED STATES DEPARTMENT OF JUSTICE

FEDERAL BUREAU OF INVESTIGATION

In Reply, Please Refer to File No.

Dallas, Texas
February 20, 1964

RE: LEE HARVEY OSWALD

Exhibit D-74 is a book entitled, "Book of Useful Advice" in the Russian language containing 865 pages, the first 18 pages of which are missing. This is a book on cooking and other useful information with green and blue binding in which book was found the letter written by LEE HARVEY OSWALD concerning his attempted shooting of General EDWIN A. WALKER at Dallas, Texas on April 10, 1963.

This book was obtained from Inspector TOM KELLEY, U. S. Secret Service, Dallas, Texas on December 3, 1963.

The results of investigation pertaining to this exhibit are reflected on page 710 of the report of SA ROBERT P. GEMBERLING dated December 23, 1963 at Dallas, Texas; on page 51 of the report of SA ROBERT P. GEMBERLING dated January 22, 1964 at Dallas, Texas; and on page 59 of the report of SA ROBERT P. GEMBERLING dated February 11, 1964 at Dallas, Texas.

COMMISSION EXHIBIT No. 1971

КНИГА
СОВЕТОВ

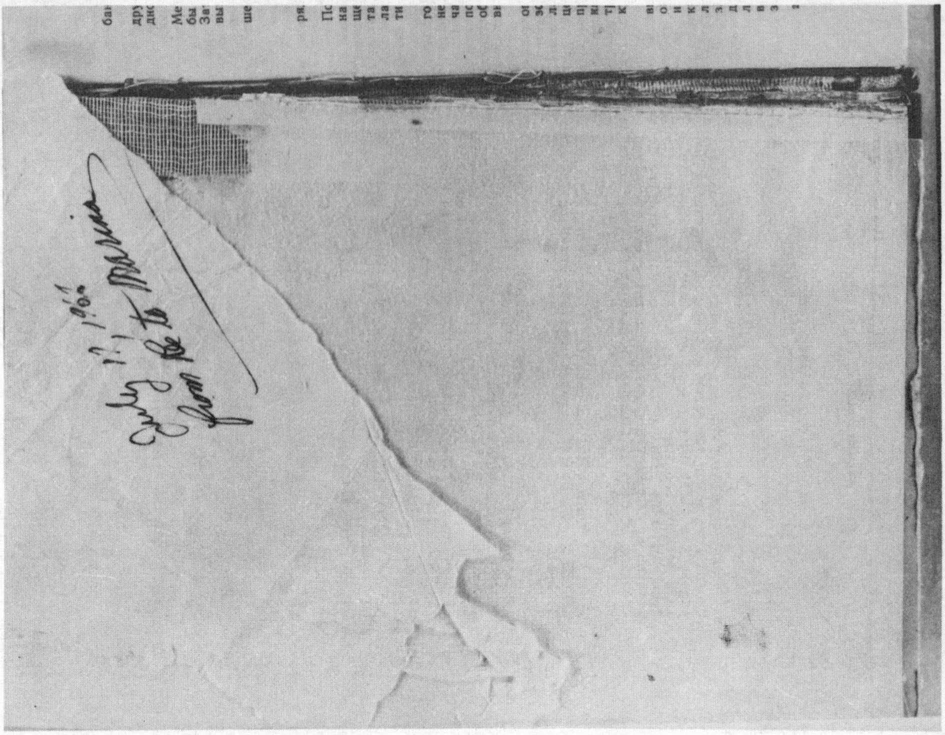

ВОДЯНАЯ БАНЯ

Кулинарная обработка требует иногда варки продукта на водяной бане или на пару.

Для устройства водяной бани нужны две кастрюли, одна меньше другой, чтобы меньшую можно было поставить внутрь большой, на ее дно, на две щепочки или на две проволоки.

В маленькую кастрюлю кладут продукты, которые надо сварить. Между стенками обеих кастрюль наливают воду с таким расчетом, чтобы вода не доходила до края меньшей кастрюли сантиметров на пять. Затем обе кастрюли закрывают крышкой и ставят на огонь. По мере выкипания воду нужно доливать. Так варят продукты до готовности.

Чаще всего на такой водяной бане варят каши и всякого рода тушеные блюда.

ОФОРМЛЕНИЕ ПРАЗДНИЧНЫХ БЛЮД

Каждой хозяйке хочется, чтобы ее праздничный стол выглядел нарядно. Сервировка стола во многом зависит от умения и вкуса хозяйки.

Самое лучшее украшение стола — умело приготовленные кушанья. Постарайтесь сделать их не только вкусными, но и привлекательными на вид. Начнем с такой распространенной закуски, как сельдь. Очищенную и нарезанную селедку укладывают на селедочницу или тарелку так, чтобы она имела вид целой рыбы. К голове селедки можно приделать «усики» из зеленого или репчатого лука, а вокруг разложить ломтики вареного картофеля, свеклы, огурцов.

Хорошие украшения для многих кушаний получаются из сливочного масла. Проще всего сделать из него «гвоздички». Для этого возьмите не очень твердый брикет масла и, придерживая левой рукой его нижнюю часть, завернутую в бумагу, ножом, который вы держите в правой руке, поскребите 12—15 раз верх брикета по направлению к себе. На ноже образуется веерообразная масса. Снимите ее с ножа и соедините концы внизу. Края готовой «гвоздички» слегка посыпьте красным перцем.

При помощи чайной ложки, которую время от времени следует опускать в горячую воду, можно сделать из масла «ромашку» или «розочку». Придайте маслу форму усеченного конуса, затем начните делать «лепестки»: вдавите ложку в середину конуса и, наклонив ее от центра к себе, рывком выньте из масла. Овальная поверхность ложки придает маслу форму лепестка. Чтобы получить «розочку», в промежутках между лепестками первого ряда, но чуть ниже, делайте второй и третий ряды. Цветами из масла хорошо украсить икру, паштет и другие кушанья.

Для украшения винегрета подходят вырезанные из вареной моркови или свеклы звездочки, кружочки и красиво уложенные ломтики овощей. Готовя салат, хозяйка думает о том, как его украсить сверху, и обычно отбирает для этого самые крепкие огурчики, самые аккуратные кружочки нарезанного яйца, ровные ломтики мяса, отставляет одну — две ложки зеленого горошка. Уложив салат пирамидой или иначе (это будет зависеть от формы посуды), полейте его майонезом или сметаной, тогда украшения будут резче выделяться. По краям посуды с салатом разложите зеленый горошек и огурцы, нарезанные кусочками или в виде веера, подрезая тонко огурец поперек почти до самого края, который закрепляет дольки, чтобы они не разошлись.

2* 19

Переплет, суперобложка, форзац
А. САПЕТКО
Рисунки на шмуцтитулах
Ю. ПУЧИНСКОГО
Титул, заставки, концовки, инициалы и художественное редактирование
В. ХОРЕВСКОГО

Редакторы М. Бруневская и О. Гутковская
Технические редакторы А. Труханова и Н. Степанова
Корректоры А. Федорова, А. Ткачева, И. Мещанинова

Подп. к печати с матриц 10/VIII 1960 г. Тираж 200 000 (1—100 000) экз. Формат 70×100 1/16. Физ. печ. л. 54,75. Усл. печ. л. 75. Уч.-изд. л. 66,6. Цена 21 руб. С 1/1 1961 г.— 2 руб. 10 коп. Зак. 1065.

Полиграфкомбинат им. Я. Коласа, г. Минск, Красная, 23.

COMMISSION EXHIBIT No. 1971—Continued

COMMISSION EXHIBIT No. 1971—Continued

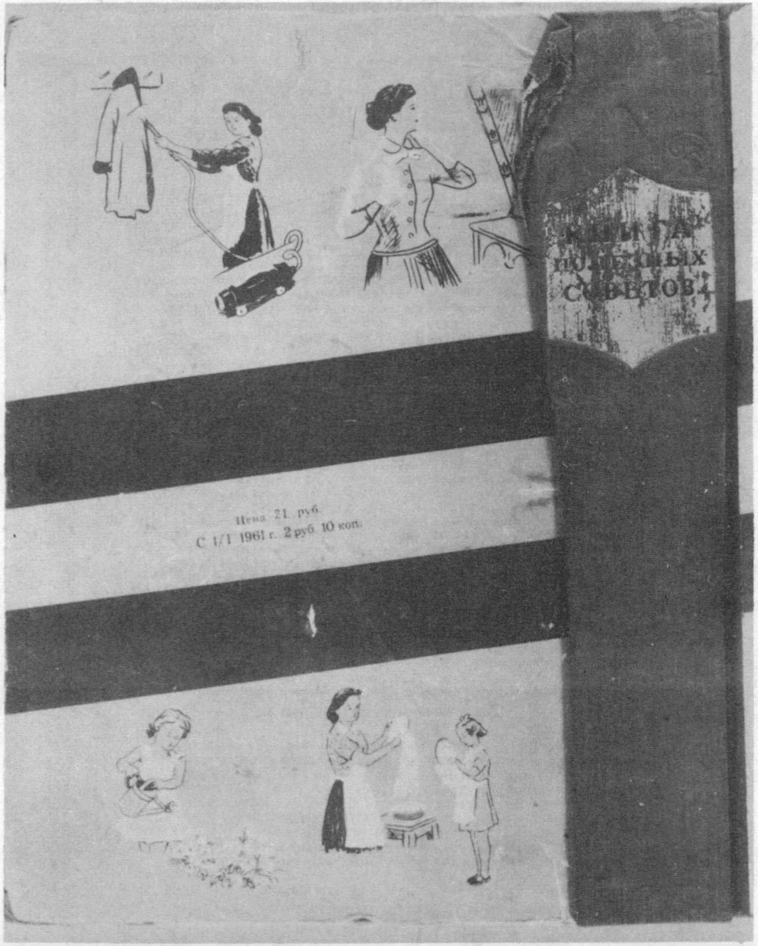

UNITED STATES DEPARTMENT OF JUSTICE

FEDERAL BUREAU OF INVESTIGATION

In Reply, Please Refer to File No.

Dallas, Texas
June 1, 1964

LEE HARVEY OSWALD

On May 25, 26 and 27, 1964, microfilm copies of all editions of the "Dallas Times Herald" and the "Dallas Morning News," daily newspapers published at Dallas, Texas, for the period March 16 through May 16, 1963, were reviewed at the Dallas Public Library, Dallas, Texas, by Special Agents of the Federal Bureau of Investigation.

The April 18, 21, 23 and 24, 1963, editions of the "Dallas Times Herald" contain articles concerning the visit of the Vice President, LYNDON B. JOHNSON, to Dallas, Texas, for the second Annual NASA Manned Space Flight Conference. The Vice President delivered the major address at this Conference on April 23, 1963. According to the articles, Mr. JOHNSON arrived in Dallas before Noon on April 23, 1963, and departed Dallas later that same day.

The April 24, 1963, edition of the "Dallas Times Herald" is headlined, "LBJ Sees Kennedy Dallas Visit - One-Day Texas Tour Eyed." This article reflects that "President KENNEDY may visit Dallas and other major Texas cities this summer, Vice President LYNDON B. JOHNSON said during his whirlwind visit here. The Vice President said he hopes President KENNEDY's schedule will permit him to attend a breakfast in Ft. Worth, a luncheon in Dallas, an afternoon tea in San Antonio and a dinner in Houston on a one-day visit to Texas in the near future. Mr. JOHNSON mentioned the possibility of the presidential visit during an hour-long session with executives of the Times Herald and KRLD-AM-FM and TV Tuesday afternoon."

The April 3, 18, 21, 23 and 24, 1963, editions of the "Dallas Morning News" also contain articles concerning the visit of Vice President JOHNSON to Dallas for the second Annual NASA Manned Space Flight Conference.

COMMISSION EXHIBIT NO. 1972

Re: LEE HARVEY OSWALD

With the exception of the above-mentioned articles dealing with Mr. JOHNSON's visit to Dallas, no mention was found in the newspapers reviewed of any visit or proposed visit of any other political leader of the approximate stature of former Vice President of the United States, RICHARD M. NIXON.

- 2 -

COMMISSION EXHIBIT No. 1972—Continued

On February 28, 1964, the Honorable RICHARD M. NIXON, former Vice-President of the U. S., was contacted by Assistant Director in Charge of the New York Office, JOHN F. MALONE, and furnished the following information:

Mr. NIXON advised that the only time he was in Dallas, Texas during 1963 was two days prior to the assassination of President JOHN F. KENNEDY. He vaguely thought there

was some invitation extended during the early part of 1963, probably in April, for him to come to Dallas, but that it never materialized, nor did he give any consideration to going there. Mr. NIXON could not even recall the circumstances surrounding the invitation, but did observe that conceivably there could have been some publicity indicating that he had been invited to come to Dallas. Mr. NIXON said that if anything more concrete comes to his mind or after his secretary checks his records which would indicate the circumstances surrounding this, he would immediately notify the Federal Bureau of Investigation (FBI). He did say positively that he had no intention of visiting Dallas during April, 1963.

COMMISSION EXHIBIT No. 1973

UNITED STATES DEPARTMENT OF JUSTICE

FEDERAL BUREAU OF INVESTIGATION

In Reply, Please Refer to
File No.

Dallas, Texas
August 11, 1964

ASSASSINATION OF PRESIDENT JOHN FITZGERALD KENNEDY, NOVEMBER 22, 1963, DALLAS, TEXAS

By letter dated July 16, 1964, the President's Commission referred to a memorandum captioned "Dallas, Texas, March 23, 1964." This memorandum contained the transcripts of all radio transmissions from Channel 1 and Channel 2 of the Dallas Police Department radio station covering the period from 10:00 A.M., November 22, 1963, to 6:00 P.M., November 24, 1963, as they relate to the assassination of President KENNEDY, the murder of Dallas Police Officer J. D. TIPPIT, investigations of said assassination and murder, and the security and movement of LEE HARVEY OSWALD to the Dallas County Jail.

The President's Commission letter advised that in view of the importance of these transcripts, it was desired that the Federal Bureau of Investigation obtain the original tapes of the radio broadcasts and a new transcript be prepared from these tapes for the period 10:00 A.M. to 3:00 P.M. on Friday, November 22, 1963, and from 10:00 A.M. to 2:00 P.M. on Sunday, November 24, 1963. The President's Commission letter requested that the name of the reporting police officer be listed alongside each message.

On July 21, 1964, Chief of Police JESSE E. CURRY, Dallas Police Department, Dallas, Texas, made available to a Special Agent of the Federal Bureau of Investigation the original recordings reflecting the radio transmissions of Channel 1 and Channel 2 of Dallas Police Department Radio Station KKB 364 for the above-described period, and these recordings were reviewed by a Special Agent of the Federal Bureau of Investigation on July 21, 22, 23 and 24, 1964, at the Dallas Police Department.

COMMISSION EXHIBIT No. 1974

Re: ASSASSINATION OF PRESIDENT JOHN FITZGERALD KENNEDY, NOVEMBER 22, 1963, DALLAS, TEXAS

The radio transmissions for the period 10:00 A.M. to 3:00 P.M. on November 22, 1963, and 10:00 A.M. to 2:00 P.M. on November 24, 1963, on Channel 1 of Dallas Police Radio Station KKB 364 were recorded on dictabelts using "Dictaphones" purchased by the Dallas Police Department in 1957. These dictabelts are badly worn from being played and, in many places, the dictabelt skips and some of the messages are garbled.

The radio transmissions for the period 10:00 A.M. to 3:00 P.M. on November 22, 1963, on Channel 2 of Dallas Police Radio Station KKB 364 were recorded on a "Gray Audograph" recorder using 8½" flexible Celluloid discs. This equipment was purchased by the Dallas Police Department in the early 1950's. It was noted that these discs are badly worn from being played. In many places, the discs skip and portions of the messages are garbled.

On July 21, 1964, Lieutenant D.H. GASSETT, Platoon Commander, Dallas Police Department, advised that on November 22, 1963, between the hours of 10:00 A.M. and 3:00 P.M., three radio dispatchers were on duty at the Dallas Police Department at the same time. He stated that two dispatchers handled Channel 1, each working an opposite side of the radio console which separated one dispatcher from the sight of the other. On this radio console, above each dispatcher, are a series of knobs with a unit number assigned to each knob. The purpose of the knobs is to indicate which units are "in service" and which units are "out of service." Upon being contacted by any of the units the dispatcher, in addition to replying to the unit calling, adjusts the knob relating to the unit calling, to either the "in service" or "out of service" position.

The third radio dispatcher's position is located at one end of the radio console. This position is for the Channel 2 dispatcher. Channel 2 is usually used only when a special situation is anticipated, as was the case on November 22, 1963, during the Presidential motorcade. This relieves the volume of

COMMISSION EXHIBIT No. 1974—Continued

radio traffic on Channel 1 and permits those dispatchers to handle other traffic with greater ease.

Lieutenant GASSETT advised that each dispatcher has a time stamp clock before him and pointed out these clocks are not synchronized. He demonstrated by simultaneously time stamping a blank piece of paper, using two of the clocks. It was noted that one clock stamped the time as 11:16 A.M. and that the other clock stamped the time as 11:17 A.M. He stated this would explain a time element variation between Channel 1 and Channel 2. He further pointed out that the position of the hands on the clock appear different, depending on the angle of sight from which one is looking at the clock. He stated a short person would have a different angle of sight than a tall person. Lieutenant GASSETT stated this quite probably could explain the time element variation of the shooting of Officer J. D. TIPPIT with the Channel 1 entry indicating the approximate time as 1:16 P.M. and the Channel 2 entry indicating the approximate time as 1:18 P.M.

Lieutenant GASSETT also pointed out that the information relating to the shooting of Officer TIPPIT was broadcast to the Dallas Police Department on Channel 1 by a citizen using Officer TIPPIT's police car radio, which is a different radio frequency than Channel 2. He stated that this same information was then rebroadcast on Channel 2, which could also explain the time element variation between 1:16 P.M. and 1:18 P.M.

The following is a transcript of the radio transmissions from Channel 1 and Channel 2 of the Dallas Police Radio Station KKB 364 for the periods 10:00 A.M. to 3:00 P.M. on November 22, 1963, and 10:00 A.M. to 2:00 P.M. on November 24, 1963, it being noted that Channel 2 was not operating during the period 10:00 A.M. to 2:00 P.M. on November 24, 1963, as they relate to the assassination of President KENNEDY, murder of Dallas Police Officer J. D. TIPPIT, investigations of said assassination and murder, and the security and movement of LEE HARVEY OSWALD to the Dallas County Jail:

COMMISSION EXHIBIT No. 1974—Continued

Channel 1, 10:00 A.M. - 3:00 P.M., November 22, 1963

Caller	Conversation
Dispatcher (J. A. MC DANIEL and B. D. HUFFSTUTLER	10:00 A.M., KKB-364
Dispatcher (MC DANIEL and HUFFSTUTLER)	39 (Patrolmen J. F. BUTCHER and C. W. COMER)
39 (Patrolmen BUTCHER and COMER)	39 (Patrolmen BUTCHER and COMER)
Dispatcher (MC DANIEL and HUFFSTUTLER)	Channel 2 (10:06)
285 (Patrolman J. Y. ALVIS)	285 (Patrolman J. Y. ALVIS)
Dispatcher (MC DANIEL and HUFFSTUTLER	285 (Patrolman ALVIS)
285 (Patrolman ALVIS)	Out Love Field assignment.
Dispatcher (MC DANIEL and HUFFSTUTLER)	10-4, 10:08.
260 (Sergeant D. V. HARKNESS)	260 (Sergeant HARKNESS)
Dispatcher (MC DANIEL and HUFFSTUTLER)	260 (Sergeant HARKNESS)
260 (HARKNESS)	Let me talk to 290 (Sergeant E. B. HOWARD), please.
Dispatcher (MC DANIEL and HUFFSTUTLER)	290 (HOWARD).
290 (HOWARD)	290 (HOWARD).

COMMISSION EXHIBIT No. 1974—Continued

Re: A SASSINATION OF PRESIDENT
JOHN FITZGERALD KENNEDY,
NOVEMBER 22, 1963, DALLAS, TEXAS

Caller	Conversation
260 (HARKNESS)	290 (HOWARD), this is 260 (HARKNESS). They have removed those signs down on Houston between Main and Elm. Do you know anything about it?
290 (HOWARD)	On the east or west side?
260 (HARKNESS)	East.
290 (HOWARD)	290 (HOWARD) to 260 (HARKNESS).
260 (HARKNESS)	260 (HARKNESS).
Dispatcher (MC DANIEL and HUFFSTUTLER)	Advised on east side.
290 (HOWARD)	There's not supposed to be "no park" on east side.
260 (HARKNESS)	10-4. (10:10)
(End of Belt One)	
272 (Patrolman R. F. CALE)	272 (CALE).
Dispatcher (MC DANIEL and HUFFSTUTLER)	272 (CALE).
272 (CALE)	Would you check with 260 (HARKNESS) for me, please, sir, and see if they're going to allow these people to park out here on Cedar Springs. We've had a number of people to ask

COMMISSION EXHIBIT No. 1974—Continued

Re: ASSASSINATION OF PRESIDENT
JOHN FITZGERALD KENNEDY,
NOVEMBER 22, 1963, DALLAS, TEXAS

Caller	Conversation
	us -- I mean on Turtle Creek out here -- We've had a number of people to ask us if they could park along the curb out here.
Dispatcher (MC DANIEL and HUFFSTUTLER)	125 (Captain P. W. LAWRENCE) (10:21)
Dispatcher (MC DANIEL and HUFFSTUTLER)	30 (Sergeant R. C. CHILDERS), call Operator 2. (One of telephone positions in radio room.)
30 (Sergeant R. C. CHILDERS)	10-4. (10:21)
Dispatcher (MC DANIEL and HUFFSTUTLER)	260 (HARKNESS) or 270 (HOWARD)
260 (HARKNESS)	260 (HARKNESS).
Dispatcher (MC DANIEL and HUFFSTUTLER)	How about that parking on Turtle Creek? Are they going to be allowed to park on the side of the street out there?
260 (HARKNESS)	Contact 125 (LAWRENCE) on Channel 2.
Dispatcher (MC DANIEL and HUFFSTUTLER)	10-4. (10:23)
Dispatcher (MC DANIEL and HUFFSTUTLER)	272 (CALE).

COMMISSION EXHIBIT No. 1974—Continued

Re: ASSASSINATION OF PRESIDENT
JOHN FITZGERALD KENNEDY,
NOVEMBER 22, 1963, DALLAS, TEXAS

Caller	Conversation
272 (CALE)	272 (CALE).
Dispatcher (MC DANIEL and HUFFSTUTLER)	Yes, let them park.
272 (CALE)	10-4, thank you.
Dispatcher (MC DANIEL and HUFFSTUTLER)	39 (Patrolmen J. F. BUTCHER and C. W. COMER)...(10:24)
Dispatcher (MC DANIEL and HUFFSTUTLER	20 (Sergeant S. W. BURKHART) (10:39)
1 (Chief JESSE E. CURRY)	1 (CURRY)
Dispatcher (MC DANIEL and HUFFSTUTLER)	1 (CURRY)
1 (CURRY)	Tell them they need a man to work traffic at Mockingbird and Cedar Springs at the entrance to Love Field. It's very heavy.
Dispatcher (MC DANIEL and HUFFSTUTLER)	10-4. (10:43)
260 (HARKNESS)	260 (HARKNESS).
Dispatcher (MC DANIEL and HUFFSTUTLER).	260 (HARKNESS).
260 (HARKNESS)	Will be out at the Sheriff's Office a few minutes.

- 7 -

COMMISSION EXHIBIT No. 1974—Continued

Re: ASSASSINATION OF PRESIDENT
JOHN FITZGERALD KENNEDY,
NOVEMBER 22, 1963, DALLAS, TEXAS

Caller	Conversation
Dispatcher (MC DANIEL and HUFFSTUTLER)	10-4. (10:44)
581 (Unknown)	581 (Unknown) out at the Trade Mart.
Dispatcher (MC DANIEL and HUFFSTUTLER)	10-4, 581 (Unknown). (10:49)
(End of Belt Two)	
21 (Patrolmen D. P. TUCKER and C. R. GRAHAM)	21 (TUCKER and GRAHAM)
Dispatcher (MC DANIEL and HUFFSTUTLER)	32 (Patrolmen J. T. SMITH and W. L. HACKNEY).
32 (SMITH and HACKNEY)	32 (SMITH and HACKNEY).
Dispatcher (MC DANIEL and HUFFSTUTLER)	Report to 20 (BURKHART) at the old Love Field for your assignments, 10:54, on a mark out.
21 (TUCKER and GRAHAM)	10-4.
32 (SMITH and HACKNEY)	10-4.
4 (Chief N. T. FISHER)	4 (FISHER).
Dispatcher (MC DANIEL and HUFFSTUTLER)	4 (FISHER).
4 (FISHER)	Let me talk to 39 (BUTCHER and COMER).
Dispatcher (MC DANIEL and HUFFSTUTLER)	39 (BUTCHER and COMER).

- 8 -

COMMISSION EXHIBIT No. 1974—Continued

Re: ASSASSINATION OF PRESIDENT
JOHN FITZGERALD KENNEDY,
NOVEMBER 22, 1963, DALLAS, TEXAS

Caller	Conversation
4 (FISHER)	4 (FISHER) to 39 (BUTCHER and COMER), the landing will be southeast, won't it?
Dispatcher (MC DANIEL and HUFFSTUTLER)	He's on Channel 2, 4 (FISHER).
4 (FISHER)	10-4. (10:55)
260 (HARKNESS)	260 (HARKNESS).
Dispatcher (MC DANIEL and HUFFSTUTLER)	260 (HARKNESS).
260 (HARKNESS)	Clear from Sheriff's Office, switching to Channel 2.
Dispatcher (MC DANIEL and HUFFSTUTLER)	10-4, 10:58.
2 (Chief CHARLES BATCHELOR)	2 (BATCHELOR)
Dispatcher (MC DANIEL and HUFFSTUTLER)	2 (BATCHELOR)
2 (BATCHELOR)	Tell 1 (CURRY) I'm sending the pins he wanted by motorcycle officer. Should be there in a few minutes.
Dispatcher (MC DANIEL and HUFFSTUTLER)	10-4. (11:07)
271 (Patrolman J. MURPHY)	271 (MURPHY).
Dispatcher (MC DANIEL and HUFFSTUTLER)	271 (MURPHY).

COMMISSION EXHIBIT No. 1974—Continued

Re: ASSASSINATION OF PRESIDENT
JOHN FITZGERALD KENNEDY,
NOVEMBER 22, 1963, DALLAS, TEXAS

Caller	Conversation
271 (MURPHY)	Could you send a City wrecker to the Triple Underpass; just west of the underpass on Elm to clear a stalled truck from the route of the escort?
Dispatcher (MC DANIEL and HUFFSTUTLER)	10-4. (11:07)
118 (Patrolman R. B. COUNTS)	118 (COUNTS).
Dispatcher (MC DANIEL and HUFFSTUTLER)	118 (COUNTS).
118 (COUNTS)	Could you disregard me on that call? I've got an Air Force truck here that has the President's Seal and Flags in it and he's got to get to the Dallas Trade Mart before the President does -- in about ten or fifteen minutes. I'll escort him out there about Code 2. (Urgent -- siren and red lights as needed at intersection).
Dispatcher (MC DANIEL and HUFFSTUTLER)	Disregard the call. (11:08)
118 (COUNTS)	118 (COUNTS).
Dispatcher (MC DANIEL and HUFFSTUTLER)	118 (COUNTS).
118 (COUNTS)	What hundred block of Stemmons does that Trade Mart run off of?

COMMISSION EXHIBIT No. 1974—Continued

Re: ASSASSINATION OF PRESIDENT
JOHN FITZGERALD KENNEDY,
NOVEMBER 22, 1963, DALLAS, TEXAS

Caller	Conversation
Dispatcher (MC DANIEL and HUFFSTUTLER)	Right at Industrial. (11:09)
118 (COUNTS)	10-4.
271 (Patrolman J. MURPHY)	271 (MURPHY).
Dispatcher (MC DANIEL and HUFFSTUTLER)	271 (MURPHY).
271 (MURPHY)	Disregard the wrecker at the Triple Underpass. We got a truck to push him out of there.
Dispatcher (MC DANIEL and HUFFSTUTLER)	10-4. (11:16)
	Considerable interference. No pertinent transmissions discernible.
(End of Belt Three)	
118 (COUNTS)	118 (COUNTS) clear and en route back to the district.
Dispatcher (MC DANIEL and HUFFSTUTLER)	118 (COUNTS) clear, 11:38.
2 (BATCHELOR)	9 (Inspector J. H. SAWYER)
Dispatcher (MC DANIEL and HUFFSTUTLER)	9 (SAWYER)
2 (BATCHELOR)	This is 2 (BATCHELOR) calling 9 (SAWYER).

- 11 -

COMMISSION EXHIBIT No. 1974—Continued

Re: ASSASSINATION OF PRESIDENT
JOHN FITZGERALD KENNEDY,
NOVEMBER 22, 1963, DALLAS, TEXAS

Caller	Conversation
Dispatcher (MC DANIEL and HUFFSTUTLER)	Stand by, 2 (BATCHELOR).
9 (SAWYER)	9 (SAWYER) to 2 (BATCHELOR).
2 (BATCHELOR)	Go ahead, 9 (SAWYER).
9 (SAWYER)	Crowds along Harwood are quite light. I was just wondering if we could pick up two or three of these officers along here. I think we could do without them and take them down on Main Street.
2 (BATCHELOR)	Are they on intersections?
9 (SAWYER)	No, they are in the middle.
2 (BATCHELOR)	Yeah. If that's the situation, go ahead and pick them up and move them in there.
9 (SAWYER)	10-4. (11:43)
280 (Sergeant W. C. CAMPBELL)	280 (CAMPBELL).
Dispatcher (MC DANIEL and HUFFSTUTLER)	280 (CAMPBELL).
280 (CAMPBELL)	See if you can contact 9 (SAWYER). Will you try him on Channel 1 and 2 both? We need him bad at Main and Ervay. (Garbled.)

- 12 -

COMMISSION EXHIBIT No. 1974—Continued

Re: ASSASSINATION OF PRESIDENT
JOHN FITZGERALD KENNEDY,
NOVEMBER 22, 1963, DALLAS, TEXAS

Caller	Conversation
Dispatcher (MC DANIEL and HUFFSTUTLER)	9 (SAWYER).
280 (CAMPBELL)	280 (CAMPBELL) to 9 (SAWYER)... (11:45)
Dispatcher (MC DANIEL and HUFFSTUTLER)	9 (SAWYER)... (11:46)
280 (CAMPBELL)	280 (CAMPBELL).
Dispatcher (MC DANIEL and HUFFSTUTLER)	280 (CAMPBELL).
280 (CAMPBELL)	Were you able to contact him?
Dispatcher (MC DANIEL and HUFFSTUTLER)	No, he hasn't answered yet, 280 (CAMPBELL).
280 (CAMPBELL)	Try him on Channel 2.
Dispatcher (MC DANIEL and HUFFSTUTLER)	We're trying both places.
Dispatcher (MC DANIEL and HUFFSTUTLER)	Channel 2, 280 (CAMPBELL). (11:48)
104 (Patrolman J. M. VALENTINE)	104 (VALENTINE).
Dispatcher (MC DANIEL and HUFFSTUTLER)	104 (VALENTINE).
104 (VALENTINE)	Is the President going to come down Ervay?
Dispatcher (MC DANIEL and HUFFSTUTLER)	Down Main, across Ervay. (11:51)

(End of Belt Four)

COMMISSION EXHIBIT No. 1974—Continued

Re: ASSASSINATION OF PRESIDENT
JOHN FITZGERALD KENNEDY,
NOVEMBER 22, 1963, DALLAS, TEXAS

Caller	Conversation
Dispatcher (MC DANIEL and HUFFSTUTLER)	104 (VALENTINE), you will have to come in on Main, make a left turn into basement.
104 (VALENTINE)	10-4.
24 (Patrolman D. L. PATE)	24 (PATE).
Dispatcher (MC DANIEL and HUFFSTUTLER)	24 (PATE).
24 (PATE)	You might notify anything running on emergency out here in North Dallas that Mockingbird, Lemmon, Cedar Springs and Denton Drive is all jammed.
Dispatcher (MC DANIEL and HUFFSTUTLER)	10-4.
260 (HARKNESS)	260 (HARKNESS).
Dispatcher (MC DANIEL and HUFFSTUTLER)	260 (HARKNESS).
260 (HARKNESS)	Is 6 (Deputy Chief RAY LUNDAY) on Channel 2?
Dispatcher (MC DANIEL and HUFFSTUTLER)	He is at Main and Harwood on the street.
157 (Patrolman J. W. WILLIAMS)	157 (WILLIAMS) to 159... (Unknown)
289 (Not assigned, believe it was 260 - HARKNESS)	289 (Not assigned).

COMMISSION EXHIBIT No. 1974—Continued

Re: ASSASSINATION OF PRESIDENT
JOHN FITZGERALD KENNEDY,
NOVEMBER 22, 1963, DALLAS, TEXAS

Caller	Conversation
Dispatcher (MC DANIEL and HUFFSTUTLER)	289 (Not assigned).
289 (Not assigned)	Give us an ambulance, 100 N. Houston Street - epileptic seizure.
Dispatcher (MC DANIEL and HUFFSTUTLER)	10-4.
289 (Not assigned)	Make it Code 3. (Emergency -- red lights and sirens.)
Dispatcher (MC DANIEL and HUFFSTUTLER)	Be a white? (12:19)
289 (Not assigned)	289 (Not assigned).
Dispatcher (MC DANIEL and HUFFSTUTLER)	289 (Not assigned).
289 (Not assigned)	Make that ambulance Code 3. (Emergency -- red lights and sirens.) Can you give me the direction he will be coming in?
Dispatcher (MC DANIEL and HUFFSTUTLER)	606 (Ambulance)
606 (Ambulance)	606 (Ambulance).
Dispatcher (MC DANIEL and HUFFSTUTLER)	What's your location?
606 (Ambulance)	About Harwood and Cedar Springs now.

- 15 -

COMMISSION EXHIBIT No. 1974—Continued

Re: ASSASSINATION OF PRESIDENT
JOHN FITZGERALD KENNEDY,
NOVEMBER 22, 1963, DALLAS, TEXAS

Caller	Conversation
Dispatcher (MC DANIEL and HUFFSTUTLER)	10-4. Code 3 (Emergency -- red lights and sirens) on a signal 28 (emergency sick call), 100 N. Houston, 12:20.
Dispatcher (MC DANIEL and HUFFSTUTLER)	Harwood and Cedar Springs, 289 (Not assigned).
289 (Not assigned)	10-4.
Dispatcher (MC DANIEL and HUFFSTUTLER)	289 (Not assigned).
289 (Not assigned)	289 (Not assigned).
Dispatcher (MC DANIEL and HUFFSTUTLER)	Go ahead and start your set up.
289 (Not assigned)	10-4.
111 (Patrolman J. G. POLLARD)	111 (POLLARD).
Dispatcher (MC DANIEL and HUFFSTUTLER)	111 (POLLARD).
111 (POLLARD)	We are going to have to take this prisoner to Parkland. Is Harwood Street blocked all the way?
Dispatcher (MC DANIEL and HUFFSTUTLER)	Yes, all the way, 111 (POLLARD).
111 (POLLARD)	10-4.

- 16 -

COMMISSION EXHIBIT No. 1974—Continued

Re: ASSASSINATION OF PRESIDENT
JOHN FITZGERALD KENNEDY,
NOVEMBER 22, 1963, DALLAS, TEXAS

Caller	Conversation
606 (Ambulance)	606 (Ambulance) out.
Dispatcher (MC DANIEL and HUFFSTUTLER)	10-4, 606 (Ambulance), 12:24.
606 (Ambulance)	606 (Ambulance).
Dispatcher (MC DANIEL and HUFFSTUTLER	606 (Ambulance)
606 (Ambulance)	We are en route Parkland (garbled). This is a signal 16. (Investigation injured person.)
Dispatcher (MC DANIEL and HUFFSTUTLER)	En route whére, 606 (Ambulance)?
606 (Ambulance)	En route Parkland.
Dispatcher (MC DANIEL and HUFFSTUTLER)	10-4. You need a squad to meet you there?
606 (Ambulance)	10-4.
252 (Patrolman F. T. CHANCE)	252 (CHANCE).
Dispatcher (MC DANIEL and HUFFSTUTLER)	252 (CHANCE).
252 (CHANCE)	Out here at the intersection of Fairmount and Cedar Springs there is a "V" shape piece of land out here with no improvements on it. Someone during the parade backed over a water faucet out here and it is

COMMISSION EXHIBIT No. 1974—Continued

Re: ASSASSINATION OF PRESIDENT
JOHN FITZGERALD KENNEDY,
NOVEMBER 22, 1963, DALLAS, TEXAS

Caller	Conversation
	shooting water into the air. Wonder if you can contact the Water Department and have them come out here and turn it off.
Dispatcher (MC DANIEL and HUFFSTUTLER)	10-4, 12:25.
252 (CHANCE)	252 (CHANCE), I'm clear.
Dispatcher (MC DANIEL and HUFFSTUTLER)	10-4, 12:25.
258 (Patrolman R. A. DAVENPORT)	258 (DAVENPORT) Clear.
Dispatcher (MC DANIEL and HUFFSTUTLER)	258 (DAVENPORT clear, 12:26.
38 (Patrolman F. G. WOODROW)	38 (WOODROW).
Dispatcher (C. E. HULSE and M. J. JACKSON)	38 (WOODROW).
38 (WOODROW)	Might tell some of those people involved handling this deal at the Market Hall these people are walking across Southbound Stemmons in front of the Marriott Hotel and all the way down south.
Dispatcher (HULSE and JACKSON)	10-4, 38 (WOODROW). (Transmitter stuck on one of the mobile units; nothing readable for some time after 38's (WOODROW) last transmission. Sirens audible. Garbled transmissions.)(12:34)

COMMISSION EXHIBIT No. 1974—Continued

Re: ASSASSINATION OF PRESIDENT
JOHN FITZGERALD KENNEDY,
NOVEMBER 22, 1963, DALLAS, TEXAS

Caller	Conversation
Dispatcher (HULSE and JACKSON)	24 (Patrolman D. L. PATE.)
24 (PATE)	24 (PATE).
Dispatcher (HULSE and JACKSON)	Report to Inwood and Stemmons, cut all traffic for the ambulance going to Parkland Code 3. (Emergency -- red lights and sirens)
24 (PATE)	Inwood and Stemmons?
Dispatcher (HULSE and JACKSON)	Inwood and Stemmons where they come off of Stemmons going to Parkland.
24 (PATE)	10-4.
Dispatcher (HULSE and JACKSON)	Make your assignment Code 3 (Emergency -- red lights and sirens), 24 (PATE).
24 (PATE)	10-4. (12:35)
Dispatcher (HULSE and JACKSON)	21 (Patrolmen D. P. TUCKER and C. R. GRAHAM)
21 (TUCKER and GRAHAM)	21 (TUCKER and GRAHAM).
Dispatcher (HULSE and JACKSON)	Code 3 (Emergency -- red lights and sirens) Stemmons and Inwood, cut traffic.
21 (TUCKER and GRAHAM)	10-4.
Dispatcher (HULSE and JACKSON)	4 (Deputy Chief N. T. FISHER), did you call? (Garbled transmission)

- 19 -

COMMISSION EXHIBIT No. 1974—Continued

Re: ASSASSINATION OF PRESIDENT
JOHN FITZGERALD KENNEDY,
NOVEMBER 22, 1963, DALLAS, TEXAS

Caller	Conversation
Dispatcher (HULSE and JACKSON)	4 (FISHER), we have a mike button stuck open. We can't hear anything. (Garbled transmission)
Dispatcher (HULSE and JACKSON)	Attention all emergency equipment - attention all emergency equipment; do not use Industrial Boulevard; do not use Industrial Boulevard, 12:36.
Dispatcher (HULSE and JACKSON)	35 (Patrolman J. M. LEWIS), did you receive?
35 (LEWIS)	I've got it. (12:37)
Dispatcher (HULSE and JACKSON)	(Garbled.)
Dispatcher (HULSE and JACKSON)	Inwood and Stemmons and assist 24 (PATE); 21 (TUCKER and GRAHAM), go on up there to Hines and cut that service road off there where the ambulance can go on to Parkland.
(Garbled) (24, PATE?)	10-4.
Dispatcher (HULSE and JACKSON)	4 (Deputy Chief N. T. FISHER), did you call?
4 (FISHER)	Yes. I don't know what happened to the officer assigned to Cedar Springs and Mockingbird, but they're not there and the traffic is really snafued.
32 (Patrolmen J. T. SMITH and W. L. HACKNEY)	32 (SMITH and HACKNEY) clear.

- 20 -

COMMISSION EXHIBIT No. 1974—Continued

Re: ASSASSINATION OF PRESIDENT
JOHN FITZGERALD KENNEDY,
NOVEMBER 22, 1963, DALLAS, TEXAS

Caller	Conversation
Dispatcher (HULSE and JACKSON)	32 (SMITH and HACKNEY) on mark out report to Cedar Springs and Mockingbird.
32 (SMITH and HACKNEY)	10-4.
24 (PATE)	24 (PATE).
Dispatcher (HULSE and JACKSON)	24 (PATE).
24 (PATE)	These ambulance must have already passed Stemmons and Inwood.
Dispatcher (HULSE and JACKSON)	10-4.
24 (PATE)	Was APB (Accident Prevention Bureau) car supposed to be following the ambulance?
Dispatcher (HULSE and JACKSON)	Unknown, 24 (PATE).
21 (Patrolmen D. P. TUCKER and C. R. GRAHAM)	21 (TUCKER and GRAHAM).
Dispatcher (HULSE and JACKSON)	21 (TUCKER and GRAHAM).
21 (TUCKER and GRAHAM)	What do you want us to do here at the service road on Hines?
Dispatcher (HULSE and JACKSON)	Has the ambulance gone through already?
21 (TUCKER and GRAHAM)	We just arrived.
Dispatcher (HULSE and JACKSON)	Stand by there until we notify you.

COMMISSION EXHIBIT No. 1974—Continued

Re: ASSASSINATION OF PRESIDENT
JOHN FITZGERALD KENNEDY,
NOVEMBER 22, 1963, DALLAS, TEXAS

Caller	Conversation
21 (TUCKER and GRAHAM)	10-4.
20 (Sergeant SAMUEL BURKHART)	20 (BURKHART).
Dispatcher (HULSE and JACKSON)	20 (BURKHART).
20 (BURKHART)	I'm on Hines in front of Parkland. What is this emergency on this ambulance?
Dispatcher (HULSE and JACKSON)	20 (BURKHART), there's been a shooting in downtown area involving the President.
20 (BURKHART)	10-4.
269 (Patrolman L. E. BEILHARZ)	269 (BEILHARZ).
Dispatcher (HULSE and JACKSON)	269 (BEILHARZ).
269 (BEILHARZ)	Will you check with my supervisor and see where he wants me to go. I am through with my second assignment.
	(12:40)
(End Belt Five)	
Dispatcher (HULSE and JACKSON)	260 (Sergeant D. V. HARKNESS)
Dispatcher (HULSE and JACKSON)	260...260 (HARKNESS)
4 (FISHER)	4 (FISHER)
Dispatcher (HULSE and JACKSON)	4 (FISHER)

COMMISSION EXHIBIT No. 1974—Continued

Caller	Conversation
4 (FISHER)	Is 32 (SMITH and HACKNEY) one-man or two-man?
Dispatcher (HULSE and JACKSON)	He's 2-man.
4 (FISHER)	10-4. It's going to take at least two men.
Dispatcher (HULSE and JACKSON)	32 (SMITH and HACKNEY), have you arrived?
32 (SMITH and HACKNEY)	No, we are in North Dallas on this call. We are at Webb Chapel and Royal Lane right now.
20 (BURKHART)	20 (BURKHART)
Dispatcher (HULSE and JACKSON)	20 (BURKHART)
20 (BURKHART)	That ambulance hasn't arrived at Parkland. Do you have any other information on it?
Dispatcher (HULSE and JACKSON)	601 (Ambulance)
(Garbled)	(Garbled)
Dispatcher (HULSE and JACKSON)	101 (Patrolman B. L. BASS).
101 (BASS)	101 (BASS).
Dispatcher (HULSE and JACKSON)	Elm and Houston.
601 (Ambulance)	601 (Ambulance).
Dispatcher (HULSE and JACKSON)	What's your location, 601 (Ambulance)?

Caller	Conversation
601 (Ambulance)	Here at the market.
Dispatcher (HULSE and JACKSON)	Repeat.
601 (Ambulance)	I'm here at the market.
Dispatcher (HULSE and JACKSON)	Disregard.
Unknown	We are at Parkland.
2 (BATCHELOR)	2 (BATCHELOR).
Dispatcher (HULSE and JACKSON)	Attention all squads, report to downtown area, Code 3 (Emergency - red lights and sirens) to Elm and Houston, with caution.
233 (Patrolman J. T. FORSTON)	233 (FORSTON).
Dispatcher (HULSE and JACKSON)	233 (FORSTON).
233 (FORSTON)	I'm at Elm and Houston.
Dispatcher (HULSE and JACKSON)	10-4. (Numerous squads checking out - many garbled messages.)
Dispatcher (Sergeant G. D. HENSLEE)	Attention all squads - Attention all squads. At Elm and Houston reported to be an unknown white male, approximately 30, slender build, height 5 feet 10 inches, weight 165 pounds, reported to be armed with what is believed to be a .30 caliber rifle. Attention, all squads, the

Re: ASSASSINATION OF PRESIDENT
JOHN FITZGERALD KENNEDY,
NOVEMBER 22, 1963, DALLAS, TEXAS

Caller	Conversation
	suspect is believed to be a white male, 30, 5 feet 10 inches, slender build, 165 pounds, armed with what is thought to be a 30-30 rifle. No further description or information at this time.
Dispatcher (HENSLEE)	12:45 KKB-364, Dallas.
Unknown	What is he wanted for?
Dispatcher (HULSE and JACKSON)	Signal 19 (shooting), involving the President.
233 (Patrolman J. T. FORSTON)	233 (FORSTON).
Dispatcher (HULSE and JACKSON)	233 (FORSTON).
233 (FORSTON)	He is thought to be in this Texas School Book Depository here on Northwest corner Elm and Houston.
102 (Patrolmen B. L. JONES and M. D. HALL)	Out this location.
Dispatcher (HULSE and JACKSON)	10-4. 102 (JONES and HALL) and 233 (FORSTON).
81 (Patrolman J. L. ANGELL)	81 (ANGELL).
Dispatcher (HULSE and JACKSON)	81 (ANGELL).
81 (ANGELL)	I'll be going north on Industrial from Corinth.

Re: ASSASSINATION OF PRESIDENT
JOHN FITZGERALD KENNEDY,
NOVEMBER 22, 1963, DALLAS, TEXAS

Caller	Conversation
Dispatcher (HULSE and JACKSON)	10-4, 81 (ANGELL).
Dispatcher (HULSE and JACKSON)	87 (Patrolman R. C. NELSON) - 78 (Patrolman J. D. TIPPIT), move into Central Oak Cliff area.
78 (Patrolman J. D. TIPPIT)	I'm at Kiest and Bonnieview.
87 (Patrolman R. C. NELSON)	I's going north of Marsalis on R. L. Thornton.
605 (Ambulance)	605 (Ambulance), Code 5 (en route) VA (Veterans Administration Hospital).
93 (Patrolman H. M. ASHCRAFT)	93 (ASHCRAFT) to 531 (telephone extension of Dispatcher HENSLEE). I'm clear, where do you want me to go?
Dispatcher (HENSLEE)	Report to old School Book Depository, Elm and Houston area.
Dispatcher (HULSE and JACKSON)	Unit clearing?
95 (Patrolmen M. N. MC DONALD and T. R. GREGORY)	95 (MC DONALD and GREGORY), clear.
Dispatcher (HULSE and JACKSON)	95 (MC DONALD and GREGORY), clear, 12:46. (Garbled transmission.)
Dispatcher (HULSE and JACKSON)	Elm and Houston 77 (Patrolman W. E. SMITH) at School Book Depository.

Re: ASSASSINATION OF PRESIDENT
JOHN FITZGERALD KENNEDY,
NOVEMBER 22, 1963, DALLAS, TEXAS

Caller	Conversation
77 (Patrolman W. E. SMITH)	10-4. (Numerous squads checked out at School Book Depository, all call numbers not discernible.)
116 (Patrolman R. J. ROSS)	116 (ROSS), clear.
Dispatcher (HULSE and JACKSON)	116 (ROSS), clear, report to Triple Underpass.
116 (ROSS)	10-4.
24 (Patrolman D. L. PATE)	24 (PATE).
Dispatcher (HULSE and JACKSON)	24 (PATE).
24 (PATE)	I'll be out at Triple Underpass.
Dispatcher (HULSE and JACKSON)	10-4.
Dispatcher (HULSE and JACKSON)	19 (Sergeant OWENS), report to Elm and Houston.
19 (Sergeant OWENS)	10-4. Code 3? (Emergency, red lights and sirens.)
Dispatcher (HULSE and JACKSON)	Yes.
95 (MC DONALD and GREGORY)	95 (MC DONALD and GREGORY).
Dispatcher (HULSE and M. J. MC DONALD)	95 (M. N. MC DONALD and GREGORY).
95 (M. N. MC DONALD and GREGORY)	What's going on?

COMMISSION EXHIBIT No. 1974—Continued

Re: ASSASSINATION OF PRESIDENT
JOHN FITZGERALD KENNEDY,
NOVEMBER 22, 1963, DALLAS, TEXAS

Caller	Conversation
Dispatcher (HULSE and JACKSON)	Signal 19 (shooting) involving the President - suspect white male, 30, slender build, 5 feet 10 inches, 165 pounds, believed to have used a .30 caliber rifle, believed to be in School Book Depository Building, Elm and Houston at this time. 12:48.
550/2 (Sergeant G. L. HILL)	550/2 (HILL).
Dispatcher (HULSE and JACKSON)	Go ahead, 550/2 (HILL).
550/2 (Sergeant G. L. HILL)	550/2 (HILL) and 104 (Patrolman J.M. VALENTINE en route Elm and Houston, Code 3. (Emergency - red lights and sirens.)
Dispatcher (HULSE and JACKSON)	10-4.
174 (Patrolman J. W. BROOKS)	174 (BROOKS) is en route.
Dispatcher (HULSE and JACKSON)	10-4.
212 (Patrolman L. W. SPRADLIN)	212 (SPRADLIN) is en route.
Dispatcher (HULSE and JACKSON)	212's (SPRADLIN) out.
40 (Sergeant D. F. FLUSCHE)	40 (FLUSCHE).
Dispatcher (HULSE and JACKSON)	40 (FLUSCHE).
40 (FLUSCHE)	Clear. I'll head down that way from out here on Skillman.
Dispatcher (HULSE and JACKSON)	10-4, 40 (FLUSCHE).

COMMISSION EXHIBIT No. 1974—Continued

Re: ASSASSINATION OF PRESIDENT
JOHN FITZGERALD KENNEDY,
NOVEMBER 22, 1963, DALLAS, TEXAS

Caller	Conversation
22 (Patrolman L. L. HILL)	22 (HILL).
Dispatcher (HULSE and JACKSON)	23 (Dispatcher answered 23 in error.)
22 (Patrolman L. L. HILL)	22 (HILL).
Dispatcher (HULSE and JACKSON)	22 (HILL).
22 (Patrolman L. L. HILL)	I'm at Industrial and Continental. Where do you want me?
Dispatcher (HULSE and JACKSON)	Report to the vicinity of the Triple Underpass, Elm and Houston.
22 (Patrolman L. L. HILL)	10-4.
87 (Patrolman R. C. NELSON)	87 (NELSON).
101 (Patrolman B. L. BASS)	101's (BASS) on south end of the Houston Street viaduct.
Dispatcher (HULSE and JACKSON)	10-4.
116 (Patrolman R. J. ROSS)	116 (ROSS).
Dispatcher (HULSE and JACKSON)	116 (ROSS).
116 (ROSS)	Any code on it?
Dispatcher (HULSE and JACKSON)	3. (Emergency - red lights and sirens.)
116 (ROSS)	10-4.
81 (Patrolman J. L. ANGELL)	81 (ANGELL).

COMMISSION EXHIBIT No. 1974—Continued

Re: ASSASSINATION OF PRESIDENT
JOHN FITZGERALD KENNEDY,
NOVEMBER 22, 1963, DALLAS, TEXAS

Caller	Conversation
Dispatcher (HULSE and JACKSON)	81 (ANGELL).
81 (ANGELL)	Out.
Dispatcher (HULSE and JACKSON)	10-4.
4 (Chief FISHER)	4 (FISHER).
Dispatcher (HULSE and JACKSON)	(Unknown unit) call Station 7. (Civil Section, Dallas County Sheriff's Office.) (Followed by unreadable conversation.)
Dispatcher (HULSE and JACKSON)	Repeat, 4 (FISHER).
4 (Chief FISHER)	Who's in charge down there at that area?
Dispatcher (HULSE and JACKSON)	(Unknown) is en route. He'll be in charge.
4 (Chief FISHER)	10-4.
Dispatcher (HULSE and JACKSON)	100 or 60 (Sergeant J. A. PUTNAM).
60 (Sergeant J. A. PUTNAM)	60 (PUTNAM).
Dispatcher (HULSE and JACKSON)	Have you arrived?
60 (PUTNAM)	Yes, I've just arrived Elm and Houston now.
Dispatcher (HULSE and JACKSON)	10-4. 212 (Patrolman L. W. SPRADLIN) report to the downtown area, 12:49.
15 (Captain C. E. TALBERT)	15 (TALBERT).

COMMISSION EXHIBIT No. 1974—Continued

Re: ASSASSINATION OF PRESIDENT
JOHN FITZGERALD KENNEDY,
NOVEMBER 22, 1963, DALLAS, TEXAS

Caller	Conversation
115 (Patrolman G. D. BENNINGFIELD)	115 (BENNINGFIELD) is out downtown, also.
223 (Patrolman C. E. LEWIS)	223 (LEWIS) is out downtown.
15 (Captain C. E. TALBERT)	15's (TALBERT) at the scene. The building is the old Purse Company on the east side of Houston. Have that cut off on the backside, willyou? Make sure nobody leaves there.
Dispatcher (HULSE and JACKSON)	10-4, 15 (TALBERT).
15 (TALBERT)	15 (TALBERT) is in charge down here - correction, 5's (Deputy Chief GEORGE L. LUMPKIN) in charge down here.
Dispatcher (HULSE and JACKSON)	10-4. Did you receive, 4 (Chief N. T. FISHER)?
4 (FISHER)	Yes, I did. Thank you.
Unknown	Any clothing description?
Dispatcher (HULSE and JACKSON)	No clothing description. A white male approximately 30, slender build, 5'10", weight 165.
605 (Ambulance)	605 (Ambulance).
Dispatcher (HULSE and JACKSON)	605 (Ambulance).
605 (Ambulance)	This call on Crockett is going to be a drunk. You don't have a downtown squad clear, do you?

Commission Exhibit No. 1974—Continued

Re: ASSASSINATION OF PRESIDENT
JOHN FITZGERALD KENNEDY,
NOVEMBER 22, 1963, DALLAS, TEXAS

Caller	Conversation
Dispatcher (HULSE and JACKSON)	No, disregard and return to service.
Unknown	We're clear.
212 (Patrolman L. W. SPRADLIN)	212 (SPRADLIN).
Dispatcher (HULSE and JACKSON)	605 (Ambulance), let that drunk go.
605 (Ambulance)	10-4.
212 (Pacrolman L. W. SPRADLIN)	212 (SPRADLIN).
Dispatcher (HULSE and JACKSON)	212 (SPRADLIN).
212 (SPRADLIN)	I'll report to the rear of that building.
Dispatcher (HULSE and JACKSON)	10-4.
252(Patrolman F. T. CHANCE)	252's (CHANCE) out Elm and Houston.
Dispatcher (HULSE and JACKSON)	10-4.
45 (Patrolman N. L. STANGLIN)	45's (STANGLIN) clear.
Dispatcher (HULSE and JACKSON)	45 (STANGLIN) clear 12:51.
C.I.D. (Criminal Investigation Division) (unknown) 396	396 (C.I.D., Criminal Investigation Division)
Dispatcher	396 (C.I.D., Criminal Investigation Division)
396 (C.I.D., Criminal Investigation Division)	Which hospital is he?

Commission Exhibit No. 1974—Continued

Re: ASSASSINATION OF PRESIDENT
JOHN FITZGERALD KENNEDY,
NOVEMBER 22, 1963, DALLAS, TEXAS

Caller	Conversation
Dispatcher (HULSE and JACKSON)	Parkland.
396 (C.I.D., Criminal Investigation Division)	10-4.
601 (Ambulance)	601 (Ambulance).
Dispatcher (HULSE and JACKSON)	601 (Ambulance).
601 (Ambulance)	We'll stand by at Parkland.
Dispatcher (HULSE and JACKSON)	10-4. (12:51)
Dispatcher (HULSE and JACKSON)	Are you en route to Parkland, 601 (Ambulance)?
601 (Ambulance)	I'm standing by here at Parkland.
24 (Patrolman D. L. PATE)	24 (PATE).
Dispatcher (HULSE and JACKSON)	24 (PATE).
24 (PATE)	We're clear. What do you want us to do?
Dispatcher (HULSE and JACKSON)	Do you have a description on the suspect, 24 (PATE)?
24 (PATE)	10-4.
Dispatcher (HULSE and JACKSON)	Remain in that vicinity.
24 (PATE)	10-4.
79 (Patrolman B. W. ANGLIN)	79 (ANGLIN).

Re: ASSASSINATION OF PRESIDENT
JOHN FITZGERALD KENNEDY,
NOVEMBER 22, 1963, DALLAS, TEXAS

Caller	Conversation
Dispatcher (HULSE and JACKSON)	79 (ANGLIN).
79 (ANGLIN)	Going to be out at the Triple Underpass.
Dispatcher (HULSE and JACKSON)	Received. (12:52)
87 (Patrolman R. C. NELSON)	87 (NELSON).
Dispatcher (HULSE and JACKSON)	87 (NELSON).
87 (NELSON)	Out down here.
Dispatcher (HULSE and JACKSON)	10-4.
49 (Patrolman C. R. GILBREATH)	49 (GILBREATH).
Dispatcher (HULSE and JACKSON)	49 (GILBREATH).
49 (GILBREATH)	I'm going to be in the downtown area.
Dispatcher (HULSE and JACKSON)	10-4.
35 (Patrolman J. M. LEWIS)	35 (LEWIS).
Dispatcher (HULSE and JACKSON)	35 (LEWIS).
35 (LEWIS)	I'm going down that way, down Stemmons.
Dispatcher (HULSE and JACKSON)	10-4, 35 (LEWIS).
252 (Patrolman F. T. CHANCE)	252 (CHANCE).
Dispatcher (HULSE and JACKSON)	252 (CHANCE).

Re: ASSASSINATION OF PRESIDENT
JOHN FITZGERALD KENNEDY,
NOVEMBER 22, 1963, DALLAS, TEXAS

Caller	Conversation
252 (Patrolman F. T. CHANCE)	Is this the place where it has Texas School Book Depository on it?
Dispatcher (HULSE and JACKSON)	Yes. (12:53)
49 (Patrolman C. R. GILBREATH)	49 (GILBREATH).
Dispatcher (HULSE and JACKSON)	49 (GILBREATH).
49 (GILBREATH)	Code 6 (out at destination), Triple Underpass.
Dispatcher (HULSE and JACKSON)	Repeat.
49 (GI'BREATH)	Code 6 (out at destination), Triple Underpass.
Dispatcher (HULSE and JACKSON)	10-4.
174 (Patrolman J. W. BROOKS)	174 (BROOKS).
Dispatcher (HULSE and JACKSON)	174 (BROOKS).
174 (BROOKS)	Be out along the tracks just west of the building.
Dispatcher (HULSE and JACKSON)	10-4.
263 (Patrolman W. C. BRASHER)	263 (BRASHER).
Dispatcher (HULSE and JACKSON)	263 (BRASHER).
263 (BRASHER)	I have two radio patrolmen myself. Do they want us to go down there or stay out here with our after talk assignments?

- 35 -

COMMISSION EXHIBIT No. 1974—Continued

Re: ASSASSINATION OF PRESIDENT
JOHN FITZGERALD KENNEDY,
NOVEMBER 22, 1963, DALLAS, TEXAS

Caller	Conversation
Dispatcher (HULSE and JACKSON)	Who's with you?
263 (BRASHER)	Moore and Murdock, Radio Patrolmen.
Dispatcher (HULSE and JACKSON)	263 (BRASHER), disregard any other assignment you might have had and remain at that location.
232/2 (Patrolman A. E. GARRISON)	232/2 (GARRISON).
Dispatcher (HULSE and JACKSON)	232/2 (GARRISON).
232/2 (GARRISON)	I'm boxed in at Parkland. It's going to be a while before I can get back in service.
Dispatcner (HULSE and JACKSON)	10-4.
263 (Patrolman W. C. BRASHER)	263 (BRASHER).
Dispatcher (HULSE and JACKSON)	263 (BRASHER).
263 (BRASHER)	We're out on Harry Hines Boulevard. Do they want us to go down there around where the shooting occurred?
Dispatcher (HULSE and JACKSON)	10-4.
263 (BRASHER)	10-4. (12:54)
Dispatcher (JACKSON and HULSE)	78 (Patrolman J. D. TIPPIT).
78 (TIPPIT)	78 (TIPPIT).
Dispatcher (JACKSON and HULSE)	You are in the Oak Cliff area, are you not?

- 36 -

COMMISSION EXHIBIT No. 1974—Continued

Re: ASSASSINATION OF PRESIDENT
JOHN FITZGERALD KENNEDY,
NOVEMBER 22, 1963, DALLAS, TEXAS

Caller	Conversation
78 (TIPPIT)	Lancaster and 8th.
Dispatcher (JACKSON and HULSE)	You will be at large for any emergency that comes in.
78 (TIPPIT)	10-4.
21 (Patrolmen D. P. TUCKER and C. R. GRAHAM)	24...correction, 21 (TUCKER and GRAHAM)
Dispatcher (HULSE and JACKSON)	21 (TUCKER and GRAHAM).
21 (TUCKER and GRAHAM)	We're still out here on Hines. Do you want us to go in the downtown area?
Dispatcher (HULSE and JACKSON)	Yes, 21 (TUCKER and GRAHAM).
21 (TUCKER and GRAHAM)	10-4. (12:55)
49 (Patrolman C. R. GILBREATH)	49 (GILBREATH).
Dispatcher (HULSE and JACKSON)	49 (GILBREATH).
49 (GILBREATH)	Do you have any clothing description?
Dispatcher (HULSE and JACKSON)	No. A white male, approximately 30, slender build, height 5'10", weight 165 is all the information.
49 (GILBREATH)	10-4.
21 (TUCKER and GRAHAM)	21 (TUCKER and GRAHAM).
Dispatcher (HULSE and JACKSON)	21 (TUCKER and GRAHAM).

Re: ASSASSINATION OF PRESIDENT
JOHN FITZGERALD KENNEDY,
NOVEMBER 22, 1963, DALLAS, TEXAS

Caller	Conversation
21 (TUCKER and GRAHAM)	Is this routine or Code 3? (Emergency - red lights and sirens.)
Dispatcher (HULSE and JACKSON)	Code 3 (Emergency - red lights and sirens.)
Unknown Traffic Officer	Traffic Officer to Dispatcher...
Dispatcher (HULSE and JACKSON)	Go ahead.
Unknown Traffic Officer	I have an eye witness over here who saw the President get hit. The witness is over here at the T&P Railway Overpass at the Stemmons Service Road.
Dispatcher (HULSE and JACKSON)	15 (Captain C. E. TALBERT)
Dispatcher (HULSE and JACKSON)	What radio are you using, Traffic Officer?
Unknown Traffic Officer	I'm using a three wheeler radio.
Dispatcher (HULSE and JACKSON)	10-4. 5 (Deputy Chief GEORGE L. LUMPKIN)...
107 (Patrolman C. F. GOODSON)	He's in the building down here, I think.
Dispatcher (HULSE and JACKSON)	10-4. 60 (Sergeant J. A. PUTNAM) or 100 (Sergeant W.G. JENNINGS)
107 (GOODSON)	15 (Captain C. E. TALBERT) started around the building when he heard this over the speaker.

Re: ASSASSINATION OF PRESIDENT
JOHN FITZGERALD KENNEDY,
NOVEMBER 22, 1963, DALLAS, TEXAS

Caller	Conversation
Dispatcher (HULSE and JACKSON)	10-4. Did he receive the information?
107 (GOODSON)	Apparently so. He turned and started the other way. He can hear the radios down here.
Dispatcher (HULSE and JACKSON)	10-4.
Garbled transmission.	Garbled transmission.
12 (Captain G. D. KING)	15 (Captain C. E. TALBERT).
Dispatcher (HULSE and JACKSON)	312 (Homicide)(Detectives L.D. MONTGOMERY, L.C. GRAVES and MARVIN JOHNSON)
312 (Homicide)(Detectives MONTGOMERY, GRAVES and JOHNSON)	312 (Homicide). (Detectives MONTGOMERY, GRAVES and JOHNSON)
Dispatcher (HULSE and JACKSON)	Did you receive that information, 312 (Homicide)? (Detectives (MONTGOMERY, GRAVES and JOHNSON)
312 (Homicide)(Detectives MONTGOMERY, GRAVES and JOHNSON)	Repeat.
Dispatcher (HULSE and JACKSON)	The three wheel unit that has the eye witness of the shooting on the T&P Railroad Overpass at Stemmons, just beyond the Triple Underpass.
Unknown	Stemmons Freeway....the Service Road.
Dispatcher (HULSE and JACKSON)	Hold on to him.
19 (Sergeant C. B. OWENS)	19 (OWENS), I'm at this location; at the Triple Underpass. Where do you want me?

COMMISSION EXHIBIT No. 1974—Continued

Re: ASSASSINATION OF PRESIDENT
JOHN FITZGERALD KENNEDY,
NOVEMBER 22, 1963, DALLAS, TEXAS

Caller	Conversation
Dispatcher (HULSE and JACKSON)	A three wheel unit has an eye witness that saw the shooting, 19 (OWENS). He's on the overpass of the T&P Railroad at Stemmons.
19 (Sergeant C. B. OWENS)	I see him over there. I'll go over there.
Dispatcher (HULSE and JACKSON)	10-4.
15 (Captain C. E. TALBERT)	15 (TALBERT).
Dispatcher (HULSE and JACKSON)	15 (TALBERT).
15 (TALBERT)	100 (Sgt. JENNINGS) has got about six men checking out that railroad yard, back toward that direction. If you get any information on the shooting...(garbled transmission).
Dispatcher (HULSE and JACKSON)	10-4.
312 (Homicide) (Detectives MONTGOMERY, GRAVES and JOHNSON)	312 (Homicide). (Detectives MONTGOMERY, GRAVES and JOHNSON)
Dispatcher (HULSE and JACKSON)	312 (Homicide). (Detectives MONTGOMERY, GRAVES and JOHNSON)
312 (Homicide) (Detectives MONTGOMERY, GRAVES and JOHNSON)	Where's the Command Post?
Dispatcher (HULSE and JACKSON)	At Elm and Houston.
312 (Homicide) (Detectives MONTGOMERY, GRAVES and JOHNSON)	10-4.
15 (Captain C. E. TALBERT)	15 (TALBERT).
Dispatcher (HULSE and JACKSON)	15 (TALBERT).

COMMISSION EXHIBIT No. 1974—Continued

Re: ASSASSINATION OF PRESIDENT
JOHN FITZGERALD KENNEDY,
NOVEMBER 22, 1963, DALLAS, TEXAS

Caller	Conversation
15 (Captain C. E. TALBERT)	Call those Canine Units back in; Norman's dog and the Sergeant's dog. Call them back in, if you will.
Dispatcher (HULSE and JACKSON)	10-4.
260 (Sergeant D. V. HARKNESS)	260 (HARKNESS).
Dispatcher (HULSE and JACKSON)	260 (HARKNESS).
260 (HARKNESS)	Give us 508 (Crime Laboratory station wagon, W. E. BARNES) down to the Texas School Book Depository.
Dispatcher (HULSE and JACKSON)	10-4.
Dispatcher (HULSE and JACKSON)	15 (Captain C. E. TALBERT).
15 (TALBERT)	15 (TALBERT).
Dispatcher (HULSE and JACKSON)	Where do you want them to report to - Elm and Houston?
15 (TALBERT)	10-4. It's the School Book Depository Building. It will be a hard one to search out thoroughly without those dogs.
Dispatcher (HULSE and JACKSON)	10-4.
Dispatcher (HULSE and JACKSON)	508 (Crime Laboratory station wagon, W. E. BARNES) is en route.
40/2 (Unknown)	40/2...40/2 (Unknown)

Re: ASSASSINATION OF PRESIDENT
JOHN FITZGERALD KENNEDY,
NOVEMBER 22, 1963, DALLAS, TEXAS

Caller	Conversation
Dispatcher (HULSE and JACKSON)	40/2 (Unknown).
40/2 (Unknown)	We'll need two more cars to report to the President's plane out here for escort service, please, sir.
19 (Sergeant C. B. OWENS)	19 (OWENS).
Dispatcher (HULSE and JACKSON)	19 (OWENS).
19 (OWENS)	I have the one that saw the President get hit in my car. I'm on the Elm Street side of the Triple Underpass just before you go up on Stemmons.
Dispatcher (HULSE and JACKSON)	Received.
492 (Criminal Investigation Division)	492 (Criminal Investigation Division).
Dispatcher (HULSE and JACKSON)	492 (Criminal Investigation Divsion).
492 (Criminal Investigation Division)	We've been instructed to go to the scene. What code?
Dispatcher (HULSE and JACKSON)	Code 3. (Emergency - red lights and sirens.)
Dispatcher (HULSE and JACKSON)	5 (Deputy Chief GEORGE L. LUMPKIN).
15 (Captain C. E. TALBERT)	15 (TALBERT).
Dispatcher (HULSE and JACKSON)	15 (TALBERT).

Re: ASSASSINATION OF PRESIDENT
JOHN FITZGERALD KENNEDY,
NOVEMBER 22, 1963, DALLAS, TEXAS

Caller	Conversation
15 (Captain C. E. TALBERT)	I think 5 (Deputy Chief GEORGE L. LUMPKIN) and 9 (Inspector J. H. SAWYER) both are in the building.
Dispatcher (HULSE and JACKSON)	10-4. Did you receive 19's (Sergeant C. B. OWENS) transmission?
15 (Captain C. E. TALBERT)	No, I didn't.
Dispatcher (HULSE and JACKSON)	He has the person that saw the shooting in his car. He's returning to the location.
15 (Captain C. E. TALBERT)	10-4.
15 (TALBERT)	Have you got condition yet?
Dispatcher (HULSE and JACKSON)	No.
19 (Sergeant C. B. OWENS)	19 (OWENS).
Dispatcher (HULSE and JACKSON)	19 (OWENS).
19 (OWENS)	He didn't see the shooting. He saw the President get hit.
Dispatcher (HULSE and JACKSON)	10-4.
Dispatcher (HULSE and JACKSON)	Any unit...
Dispatcher (HULSE and JACKSON)	45. (Patrolman N. L. STANGLIN)
Dispatcher (HULSE and JACKSON)	78 (TIPPIT) location...

COMMISSION EXHIBIT No. 1974—Continued

Re: ASSASSINATION OF PRESIDENT
JOHN FITZGERALD KENNEDY,
NOVEMBER 22, 1963, DALLAS, TEXAS

Caller	Conversation
Dispatcher (HULSE and JACKSON)	45 (Patrolman N. L. STANGLIN) or 47 (Patrolman W. F. MORRIS)
45 (Patrolman N. L. STANGLIN)	45 (STANGLIN).
Dispatcher	What's your location?
45 (STANGLIN)	Gaston and Abrams. (This was followed by intermodulation similar, according to Dallas Police Department, to that most often originating from the Dallas Power and Light Company radio.)
48 (Patrolman A. D. DUNCAN)	48 (DUNCAN)
Dispatcher (HULSE and JACKSON)	48 (DUNCAN) (Followed by more interference)
Dispatcher (HULSE and JACKSON)	Repeat, 48 (DUNCAN).
48 (DUNCAN)	Was that Park Lane and Greenville?
Dispatcher (HULSE and JACKSON)	Stand by.
Dispatcher (HULSE and JACKSON)	Any unit near the 2000 block Commerce...
508 (Crime Laboratory station wagon, W. E. BARNES)	508's (W. E. BARNES) 2000 Commerce.
Dispatcher (HULSE and JACKSON)	Disregard, 508 (W. E. BARNES), return to the scene.
241 (Patrolman J. P. HOLLINGSWORTH)	241 (HOLLINGSWORTH).

COMMISSION EXHIBIT No. 1974—Continued

Re: ASSASSINATION OF PRESIDENT
JOHN FITZGERALD KENNEDY,
NOVEMBER 22, 1963, DALLAS, TEXAS

Caller	Conversation
Dispatcher (HULSE and JACKSON)	241 (HOLLINGSWORTH), your location?
241 (HOLLINGSWORTH)	Live Oak and Central.
Dispatcher (HULSE and JACKSON)	Code 3, (Emergency - red lights and sirens) the Blood Bank, 2000 Commerce, take to Parkland.
241 (HOLLINGSWORTH)	En route.
607 (Ambulance)	607 (Ambulance, Code 5 (en route).
Dispatcher (HULSE and JACKSON)	10-4, 607 (Ambulance). Will be 2109, 241 (HOLLINGSWORTH).
16 (Sergeant R. D. SHIPLEY)	16 (SHIPLEY)
241 (HOLLINGSWORTH)	10-4, front or rear?
16 (SHIPLEY)	I'm at Akard and Main if you want me to make that.
Dispatcher (HULSE and JACKSON)	10-4. 241 (HOLLINGSWORTH)
241 (HOLLINGSWORTH)	Go ahead.
Dispatcher (HULSE and JACKSON)	Code 4 (disregard), 16's (SHIPLEY) going to make it.
241 (HOLLINGSWORTH)	10-4.
Dispatcher (HULSE and JACKSON)	Will be the front door, 16 (SHIPLEY).
16 (SHIPLEY)	10-4.

COMMISSION EXHIBIT No. 1974—Continued

Re: ASSASSINATION OF PRESIDENT
JOHN FITZGERALD KENNEDY,
NOVEMBER 22, 1963, DALLAS, TEXAS

Caller	Conversation
309 (Patrolman W. W. TIPPETT)	309 (TIPPETT).
Dispatcher (HULSE and JACKSON)	309 (TIPPETT).
309 (TIPPETT)	Have you heard from 300 (Captain J. W. FRITZ)?
Dispatcher (HULSE and JACKSON)	Negative (1:04 p.m.)
309 (Patrolman W. W. TIPPETT)	309 (TIPPETT), what squad has that subject that's supposed to have seen the shooting?
Dispatcher (HULSE)	He didn't see the shooting, 309 Patrolman W. W. TIPPETT). He saw the President get hit. That is 19 (Sergeant C. B. OWENS). He has the person in his car.
309 (Patrolman W. W. TIPPETT)	10-4. Do you have the information that this came from the Book Depository down there?
Dispatcher (HULSE and JACKSON)	Yes.
309 (Patrolman W. W. TIPPETT)	10-4. It's well covered off here.
241 (Patrolman J. P. HOLLINGSWORTH)	241 (HOLLINGSWORTH).
Dispatcher (HULSE and JACKSON)	241 (HOLLINGSWORTH).
241 (HOLLINGSWORTH)	I'm Code 5 (en route) at the Blood Bank.
Dispatcher (HULSE and JACKSON)	10-4. 16 (Sergeant R. D. SHIPLEY).

COMMISSION EXHIBIT No. 1974—Continued

Re: ASSASSINATION OF PRESIDENT
JOHN FITZGERALD KENNEDY,
NOVEMBER 22, 1963, DALLAS, TEXAS

Caller	Conversation
16 (Sergeant R. D. SHIPLEY)	16 (SHIPLEY).
Dispatcher (HULSE and JACKSON)	Code 4, (disregard), 241's (Patrolman J. P. HOLLINGSWORTH) there. He's going to take it.
16 (SHIPLEY)	10-4.
241 (Patrolman J. P. HOLLINGS-WORTH)	241's (HOLLINGSWORTH) got it and gone.
4 (Chief N. T. FISHER)	4 (FISHER) to 15 (Captain C. E. TALBERT).
4 (FISHER)	4 (FISHER).
Dispatcher (HULSE and JACKSON)	4 (FISHER).
4 (FISHER)	See if you can raise 15 (Captain C. E. TALBERT).
Dispatcher (HULSE and JACKSON)	15 (TALBERT)
15 (TALBERT)	15 (TALBERT), did you call?
4 (Chief N. T. FISHER)	If you can contact 15 (TALBERT), see if he thinks it advisable to send some of the people from out here, down there to relieve some of the squads that are on duty.
Dispatcher (HULSE and JACKSON)	Did you receive, 15 (TALBERT)?
15 (TALBERT)	10-4, 4 (FISHER) (1:07)
15 (TALBERT)	15 (TALBERT) to 4 (FISHER).

Re: ASSASSINATION OF PRESIDENT
JOHN FITZGERALD KENNEDY,
NOVEMBER 22, 1963, DALLAS, TEXAS

Caller	Conversation
4 (Chief N. T. FISHER)	Go ahead.
15 (Captain C. E. TALBERT)	Is 4 (FISHER) at the Market Hall?
4 (FISHER)	No, I'm at Love Field.
15 (TALBERT)	Do you have radio contact with anyone at Market Hall?
4 (FISHER)	15/2's (Captain J. M. SOUTER) on the air.
58	(Garbled).
15 (Captain C. E. TALBERT)	15/2 (Captain J. M. SOUTER)
Dispatcher (HULSE and JACKSON)	15/2 (SOUTER).
488	488 (Garbled) (1:08)
261 (Patrolman C. M. BARNHART)	261 (BARNHART).
Dispatcher (HULSE and JACKSON)	261 (BARNHART).
261 (BARNHART)	Do you have any clothing description yet?
Dispatcher (HULSE and JACKSON)	All we have is a white male 30, slender build, 5'10", 165 pounds, armed with a .30 caliber rifle.
15 (Captain C. E. TALBERT)	15 (TALBERT).
261 (Patrolman C. M. BARNHART)	I have a subject that fits that description in size. He's drunk, down at the north end of Laws Street. Do you want to have

Re: ASSASSINATION OF PRESIDENT
JOHN ""TZGERALD KENNEDY,
NOVEM R 22, 1963, DALLAS, TEXAS

Caller	Conversation
	Someone to check him?
Dispatcher (HULSE and JACKSON)	15 (Captain C. E. TALBERT).
15 (TALBERT)	15 (TALBERT).
Dispatcher (HULSE and JACKSON)	Can you get to him?
Dispatcher (HULSE and JACKSON)	261 (Patrolman C. M. BARNHART), are you near that person?
261 (BARNHART)	I've got him on my motor.
Dispatcher (HULSE and JACKSON)	Be at the north end of Laws at the dead-end?
261 (Patrolman C. M. BARNHART)	10-4.
388 (Criminal Investigation Divsion, Dallas Police Department, occupant of unit unknown)	388 (Criminal Investigation Division)
Dispatcher (HULSE and JACKSON)	388 (Criminal Investigation Division)
388 (Criminal Investigation Division)	---members of the CID (Criminal Investigation Division) en route to Elm and Houston as ordered.
Dispatcher (HULSE and JACKSON)	Have 312 (Detectives MONTGOMERY, GRAVES and JOHNSON), 305 (Detectives J.R. LEAVELLE, E.R. BECK, G. R. BOYCE), 386 (Patrolman P.R. PEACE), 380...correction, 492 (Special Service Bureau) and 309 (Detectives H.H. BLESSING and C.N. DHORITY and Patrolman C.W. BROWN).

Re: ASSASSINATION OF PRESIDENT
JOHN FITZGERALD KENNEDY,
NOVEMBER 22, 1963, DALLAS, TEXAS

Caller	Conversation
388 (Criminal Identification Division)	We're en route that location to await orders there. I don't know.....do.
Dispatcher (HULSE and JACKSON)	10-4. 15 (Captain C. E. TALBERT)
260 (Sergeant D. V. HARKNESS)	260 (HARKNESS).
Dispatcher (HULSE and JACKSON)	260 (HARKNESS).
260 (HARKNESS)	Inform the squads that anyone that gets any information regarding this incident down here, to bring it to 9 (Inspector J. H. SAWYER) at Elm and Houston; bring the person to 9 (SAWYER) at Elm and Houston.
Dispatcher (HULSE and JACKSON)	Did you receive, 261 (Patrolman C. M. BARNHART)?
15 (Captain C. E. TALBERT)	15 (TALBERT).
Dispatcher (HULSE and JACKSON)	15 (TALBERT).
15 (TALBERT)	If you can get 15/2 (Captain J. M. SOUTER), would you get him to put some personnel on those railroad tracks near Market Hall and proceed back toward this location to check out the tracks in this immediate vicinity.
Dispatcher (HULSE and JACKSON)	10-4. 15/2 (Captain J. M. SOUTER).
Dispatcher (HULSE and JACKSON)	10-4, 15 (Captain C. E. TALBERT). He's on Channel 2. He has the information.

Re: ASSASSINATION OF PRESIDENT
JOHN FITZGERALD KENNEDY,
NOVEMBER 22, 1963, DALLAS, TEXAS

Caller	Conversation
Dispatcher (HULSE and JACKSON)	15 (Captain C. E. TALBERT).
15 (TALBERT)	15 (TALBERT).
Dispatcher (HULSE and JACKSON)	Do you have anyone you can send to the dead-end of Laws Street? 261 (Patrolman C. M. BARNHART) has a suspect on the back of his motor.
15 (Captain C. E. TALBERT)	10-4. (1:11)
(End of Belt Six)	
212 (Patrolman L. W. SPRADLIN)	212 (SPRADLIN).
Dispatcher (HULSE and JACKSON)	212 (SPRADLIN).
212 (SPRADLIN)	Have you got another squad that can meet that unit at the dead-end of Laws? I'm blocked in over here and can't get out.
Dispatcher (HULSE and JACKSON)	Yes, disregard. I have someone there now.
212 (SPRADLIN)	10-4.
261 (Patrolman C. M. BARNHART)	261 (BARNHART).
Dispatcher (HULSE and JACKSON)	261 (BARNHART).
261 (BARNHART)	I'm going to stay on these rail-road tracks at the dead-end of Laws.
Dispatcher (HULSE and JACKSON)	10-4. (1:15 p.m.)

COMMISSION EXHIBIT No. 1974—Continued

Re: ASSASSINATION OF PRESIDENT
JOHN FITZGERALD KENNEDY,
NOVEMBER 22, 1963, DALLAS, TEXAS

Caller	Conversation
120 (Sergeant G. B. RICHCREEK)	120 (RICHCREEK).
Dispatcher (HULSE and JACKSON)	120 (RICHCREEK).
120 (RICHCREEK)	29 (Patrolman J. M. WILLIAMS) and 99 (Patrolman S. E. NORMAN) are en route to their respective homes to pick up a car and a dog and then will clear on Channel 1. You advise them where to go.
Dispatcher (HULSE and JACKSON)	10-4. 15 (Captain C. E. TALBERT), did you receive?
15 (TALBERT)	10-4.
Dispatcher (HULSE and JACKSON)	Attention all squads - any telephone truck en route to Parkland, Code 3 (Emergency - red lights and sirens), give him the way in, 1:16.
Unknown	(Sounded like 6.)
Dispatcher (HULSE and JACKSON)	Unit ending in 6....
Citizen	Hello, police operator....
Dispatcher (HULSE and JACKSON)	Go ahead....Go ahead, citizen using the police (citizen cut in).
Citizen	We've had a shooting out here.
Dispatcher (HULSE and JACKSON)	Where's it at?

COMMISSION EXHIBIT No. 1974—Continued

Re: ASSASSINATION OF PRESIDENT
JOHN FITZGERALD KENNEDY,
NOVEMBER 22, 1963, DALLAS, TEXAS

Caller	Conversation
Dispatcher (HULSE and JACKSON)	The citizen using police radio....(Citizen cut in)
Citizen	On 10th Street.
Dispatcher (HULSE and JACKSON)	What location on 10th Street?
Citizen	Between Marsalis and Beckley. It's a police officer. Somebody shot him....what's this?... 404 10th Street.
Dispatcher (JACKSON)	78 (Patrolman J. D. TIPPIT).
Citizen	....you got that? It's in a police car number 10.
Dispatcher (JACKSON and HULSE)	78 (Patrolman J. D. TIPPIT).
Citizen	Hello, police operator, did you get that? A police officer, 510 East Jefferson.
Dispatcher (JACKSON)	Signal 19 (shooting) involving a police officer, 510 East Jefferson.
Citizen	Thank you.
35 (Patrolman J. M. LEWIS)	35 (LEWIS).
Dispatcher (HULSE and JACKSON)	The citizen using the police radio remain off the air now.
Dispatcher (HULSE and JACKSON)	91 (Patrolman W. D. MENTZEL)...

COMMISSION EXHIBIT No. 1974—Continued

Re: ASSASSINATION OF PRESIDENT
JOHN FITZGERALD KENNEDY,
NOVEMBER 22, 1963, DALLAS, TEXAS

Caller	Conversation
69 (Patrolman A. R. BROCK)	69's (BROCK) going out there.
Dispatcher (HULSE and JACKSON)	10-4, 69 (BROCK), Code 3 (Emergency - red lights and sirens.)
602 (Ambulance)	602 (Ambulance) Code 5 (en route).
211 (Patrolmen RAY HAWKINS and E. R. BAGGETT)	211 (HAWKINS and BAGGETT).
Dispatcher (HULSE and JACKSON)	211 (HAWKINS and BAGGETT).
211 (HAWKINS and BAGGETT)	We're clear at Industrial and Stemmons. Will go on out there.
Dispatcher (HULSE and JACKSON)	10-4, 211 (HAWKINS and BAGGETT).
15 (Captain C. E. TALBERT)	15 (TALBERT).
603 (Ambulance)	603 (Ambulance, Code 5 (en route) Baylor.
602 (Ambulance)	Code 6 (out at destination).
Dispatcher (HULSE and JACKSON)	10-4, 603 (Ambulance) and 602 (Ambulance), 1:19.
602 (Ambulance)	What's that address on Jefferson?
Dispatcher (HULSE and JACKSON)	501 East 10th.
85 (Patrolman R. W. WALKER)	85 (WALKER) out.
19 (Sergeant C. B. OWENS)	19 (OWENS).
Dispatcher (HULSE and JACKSON)	19 (OWENS).

COMMISSION EXHIBIT No. 1974—Continued

Re: ASSASSINATION OF PRESIDENT
JOHN FITZGERALD KENNEDY,
NOVEMBER 22, 1963, DALLAS, TEXAS

Caller	Conversation
19 (Sergeant C. B. OWENS)	Give me the correct address on the shooting.
Dispatcher (HULSE and JACKSON)	501 East 10th.
105 (Patrolmen J. M. POE and L. E. JEZ)	105 (POE and JEZ)
602 (Ambulance)	602 (Ambulance) Code 6 (out at destination.
105 (Patrolmen J. M. POE and L. E. JEZ)	Was 519 East Jefferson correct?
Dispatcher (HULSE and JACKSON)	We have two locations, 501 East Jefferson and 501 East 10th. 19 (Sergeant C. B. OWENS), are you en route?
105 (POE and JEZ)	This is an officer.
19 (Sergeant C. B. OWENS)	10-4.
19 (OWENS)	19 (OWENS) is en route.
Dispatcher (HULSE and JACKSON)	10-4, 19 (OWENS).
605 (Ambulance)	605 (Ambulance), Code 5 (en route).
Dispatcher (HULSE and JACKSON)	10-4, 605 (Ambulance), 1:19.
Dispatcher (HULSE and JACKSON)	85, (Patrolman R. W. WALKER).
602 (Ambulance)	602 (Ambulance).
Dispatcher (HULSE and JACKSON	85 (Patrolman R. W. WALKER).

COMMISSION EXHIBIT No. 1974—Continued

Re: ASSASSINATION OF PRESIDENT
JOHN FITZGERALD KENNEDY,
NOVEMBER 22, 1963, DALLAS, TEXAS

Caller	Conversation
85 (Patrolman R. W. WALKER)	85 (WALKER).
Dispatcher (HULSE and JACKSON)	The subject's running west on Jefferson from the location.
85 (Patrolman R. W. WALKER)	10-4.
Dispatcher (HULSE and JACKSON)	No physical description.
Citizen	Hello, hello, hello....
602 (Ambulance)	602 (Ambulance)
Citizen	---from out here on 10th Street, 500 block. This police officer's just shot, I think he's dead.
Dispatcher (HULSE and JACKSON)	10-4, we have the information. The citizen using the radio, remain off the radio now.
Dispatcher (HULSE and JACKSON)	15 (Captain C. E. TALBERT).
15 (Captain C. E. TALBERT)	15 (TALBERT).
Dispatcher (HULSE and JACKSON)	Channel 2.
15 (TALBERT)	I'm using a three wheeler motor. I'll have to go to another radio.
Dispatcher (HULSE and JACKSON)	15 (TALBERT), did you receive the information on the police officer shot?
15 (Captain C. E. TALBERT)	10-4, but didn't that citizen say first he was on Jefferson, then on 10th and then Chesapeake?

COMMISSION EXHIBIT No. 1974—Continued

Re: ASSASSINATION OF PRESIDENT
JOHN FITZGERALD KENNEDY,
NOVEMBER 22, 1963, DALLAS, TEXAS

Caller	Conversation
Dispatcher (HULSE and JACKSON)	Yes.
15 (Captain C. E. TALBERT)	Do they relate?
Dispatcher (HULSE and JACKSON)	Yes, at Denver.
15 (Captain C. E. TALBERT)	19 (Sergeant C. B. OWENS) will be en route shortly.
Dispatcher (HULSE and JACKSON)	10-4.
91 (Patrolman W. D. MENTZEL)	91 (MENTZEL) will be clear.
Dispatcher (HULSE and JACKSON)	91 (MENTZEL), have a signal 19 (shooting) involving police officer 400 East 10th. Suspect last seen running west on Jefferson. No description at this time.
Dispatcher (HULSE and JACKSON)	Suspect just passed 401 East Jefferson.
91 (Patrolman W. D. MENTZEL)	10-4.
85 (Patrolman R. W. WALKER)	85 (WALKER).
Dispatcher (HULSE and JACKSON)	85 (WALKER).
85 (WALKER)	(Garbled transmission.)
Dispatcher (HULSE and JACKSON)	Give us the correct location on it, 85 (Patrolman R. W. WALKER). We have three different locations.
85 (WALKER)	I haven't seen anything on Jefferson yet.

Re: ASSASSINATION OF PRESIDENT
JOHN FITZGERALD KENNEDY,
NOVEMBER 22, 1963, DALLAS, TEXAS

Caller	Conversation
Dispatcher (HULSE)	10-4. Check 501 East 10th at Denver.
85 (Patrolman R. W. WALKER)	10-4.
Dispatcher (HULSE and JACKSON)	91 (Patrolman W. D. MENTZEL).
91 (MENTZEL)	91 (MENTZEL).
Dispatcher (HULSE and JACKSON)	Subject just passed 401 East Jefferson.
91 (Patrolman W. D. MENTZEL)	10-4.
Unknown	Where did he just pass?
Dispatcher (HULSE and JACKSON)	401 East Jefferson.
87 (Patrolman R. C. NELSON)	87 (NELSON).
Dispatcher (HULSE and JACKSON)	87 (NELSON).
87 (NELSON)	I'm in my car here at Elm and Houston. Do you want me to go over there?
Dispatcher (HULSE and JACKSON)	87 (Patrolman R. C. NELSON), report to 4340 West Davis at the service station for information regarding suspect on this signal 19 (shooting) of the President.
87 (Patrolman R. C. NELSON)	4340.
Dispatcher (HULSE and JACKSON)	Code 3 (Emergency - red lights and sirens) (1:22)

Re: ASSASSINATION OF PRESIDENT
JOHN FITZGERALD KENNEDY,
NOVEMBER 22, 1963, DALLAS, TEXAS

Caller	Conversation
85 (Patrolman R. W. WALKER)	85 (WALKER).
Dispatcher (HULSE and JACKSON)	85 (WALKER).
85 (WALKER)	We have a description on this suspect over here on Jefferson. Last seen about the 300 East Jefferson. He's a white male, about 30, 5'8", black hair, slender, wearing a white jacket, white shirt and dark slacks.
Dispatcher (HULSE and JACKSON)	Armed with what?
85 (WALKER)	Unknown.
105 (Patrolman J. M. POE and L. E. JEZ)	105 (POE and JEZ)
Dispatcher (HULSE and JACKSON)	105 (POE and JEZ)
105 (POE and JEZ)	We're at the location now.
Dispatcher (HULSE and JACKSON)	10-4.
19 (Sergeant C. B. OWENS)	19's (OWENS) Code 6 (out at destination).
Dispatcher (HULSE and JACKSON)	10-4, 19 (OWENS).
Dispatcher (HULSE and JACKSON)	85 (Patrolman R. W. WALKER).
85 (Patrolman R. W. WALKER)	85 (WALKER).
Dispatcher (HULSE and JACKSON)	Repeat his clothing description.

- 59 -

COMMISSION EXHIBIT No. 1974—Continued

Re: ASSASSINATION OF PRESIDENT
JOHN FITZGERALD KENNEDY,
NOVEMBER 22, 1963, DALLAS, TEXAS

Caller	Conversation
85 (Patrolman R. W. WALKER)	Wearing a white jacket, believed to be a white shirt and dark slacks.
Dispatcher (HULSE and JACKSON)	10-4.
603 (Ambulance)	603 (Ambulance) out Baylor.
Dispatcher (HULSE and JACKSON)	10-4, 603 (Ambulance), 1:23.
Unknown	What was his direction of travel on Jefferson?
Dispatcher (HULSE and JACKSON)	Traveling west on Jefferson, 400 block. Last seen 401 West Jefferson, correction, it will be east.
Dispatcher (HULSE and JACKSON)	Wanted for investigation of assault to murder of a police officer, a white male, approximately 30, 5'8", slender build, has black hair, a white jacket, a white shirt and dark trousers. The suspect last seen running west on Jefferson from 400 East Jefferson, 1:24.
Dispatcher (JACKSON)	Does anybody know the condition of the officer?
Dispatcher (HULSE and JACKSON)	602 (Ambulance)
87 (Patrolman R. C. NELSON)	87 (NELSON).
Dispatcher (HULSE and JACKSON)	87 (NELSON).

- 60 -

COMMISSION EXHIBIT No. 1974—Continued

Re: ASSASSINATION OF PRESIDENT
JOHN FITZGERALD KENNEDY,
NOVEMBER 22, 1963, DALLAS, TEXAS

Caller	Conversation
87 (Patrolman R. C. NELSON)	Is that 4340 West Davis?
Dispatcher (HULSE and JACKSON)	Yes.
87 (NELSON)	10-4.
Dispatcher (HULSE and JACKSON)	Said he pulled in there and bought some gas. Driving a white Pontiac, '61 or '62 station wagon with a prefix "Pecos" "Ellis". He had a rifle laying in the seat.
87 (Patrolman R. C. NELSON)	10-4.
Dispatcher (HULSE and JACKSON)	We have a citizen following this car at this time - unknown direction. (1:25)
Dispatcher (HULSE and JACKSON)	Any unit near Gaston...3600 Gaston, at the Blood Bank...
257 (Patrolman C. E. WHITMAN)	257's (WHITMAN) downtown.
Dispatcher (HULSE and JACKSON)	Can you escort some blood?
257 (WHITMAN)	Which way's he going?
75 (Patrolman E. G. SEBASTIAN)	75's (SEBASTIAN) at Forest and Central.
Dispatcher (HULSE and JACKSON)	10-4.
257 (WHITMAN)	I'm Central and Pacific right now; 257 (WHITMAN)

Re: ASSASSINATION OF PRESIDENT
JOHN FITZGERALD KENNEDY,
NOVEMBER 22, 1963, DALLAS, TEXAS

Caller	Conversation
279 (Unknown)	279...279 (Unknown).
Dispatcher (HULSE and JACKSON)	279 (Unknown).
279 (Unknown)	We believe we've got that suspect on shooting this officer out here. Got his white jacket. Believe he dumped it on this parking lot behind this service station at 400 block East Jefferson, across from Dudley-Hughes, and he had a white jacket on. We believe this is it.
Dispatcher (HULSE and JACKSON)	10-4, you do not have the suspect, is that correct?
279 (Unknown)	No, just the jacket laying on the ground.
Dispatcher (HULSE and JACKSON)	What unit is going to take that blood to Parkland, Code 3 (Emergency - red lights and sirens)?
257 (Patrolman C. E. WHITMAN)	Where is it?
Dispatcher (HULSE and JACKSON)	3600 Gaston, Wadley Blood Center.
257 (WHITMAN)	I got it.
91 (Patrolman W. D. MENTZEL)	91 (MENTZEL).
Dispatcher (HULSE and JACKSON)	91 (MENTZEL).

Re: ASSASSINATION OF PRESIDENT
JOHN FITZGERALD KENNEDY,
NOVEMBER 22, 1963, DALLAS, TEXAS

Caller	Conversation
91 (Patrolman W. D. MENTZEL)	What was the description beside the white jacket?
Dispatcher (HULSE and JACKSON)	White male, 30, 5'8", black hair, slender build, white shirt, white jacket, black trousers, going west on Jefferson from the 300 block.
550/2 (Sergeant GERALD L. HILL)	550/2 (HILL).
Dispatcher (HULSE and JACKSON)	Go ahead.
550/2 (Sergeant GERALD L. HILL)	I'm at 12th and Beckley now - have a man in the car with me that can identify the suspect if anybody gets him, the one.
Dispatcher (HULSE and JACKSON)	10-4.
Dispatcher (HULSE and JACKSON)	Return to service, 599, (Cockrell Hill Squad)
599 (Cockrell Hill Squad)	10-4.
Dispatcher (HULSE and JACKSON)	550/2 (Sergeant GERALD L. HILL).
550/2 (Sergeant GERALD L. HILL)	550/2 (HILL).
Dispatcher (HULSE and JACKSON)	Have you been to the scene?
550/2 (Sergeant GERALD L. HILL)	10-4. The officers were already gone when I got there. He was driving car # 10.
Dispatcher (HULSE and JACKSON)	Do you know what ambulance took him? We had three going.

COMMISSION EXHIBIT No. 1974—Continued

Re: ASSASSINATION OF PRESIDENT
JOHN FITZGERALD KENNEDY,
NOVEMBER 22, 1963, DALLAS, TEXAS

Caller	Conversation
550/2 (Sergeant GERALD L. HILL)	No, DUDLEY HUGHES passed in front of me going to Beckley - looked like he might have had him.
Dispatcher (HULSE and JACKSON)	602 (Ambulance)
85 (Patrolman R. W. WALKER)	Did someone find a jacket?
Dispatcher (HULSE and JACKSON)	Unknown, 85 (WALKER).
19 (Sergeant C. B. OWENS)	19 (OWENS).
Dispatcher (HULSE and JACKSON)	19 (OWENS).
19 (Sergeant C. B. OWENS)	One of the men here at the service station that saw him seems to think he is in this block of 400 East Jefferson, behind this service station. Will you get me some more squads over here?
79 (Patrolman B. W. ANGLIN)	En route.
412 (Criminal Investigation Division)	En route. (Garbled transmission, sounded like other squads also en route.)
Dispatcher (HULSE and JACKSON)	10-4, 412 (Criminal Investigation Division). 75 (Patrolman E. G. SEBASTIAN).
75 (Patrolman E. G. SEBASTIAN)	Go ahead.
Dispatcher (HULSE and JACKSON)	400 East Jefferson.

COMMISSION EXHIBIT No. 1974—Continued

Re: ASSASSINATION OF PRESIDENT
JOHN FITZGERALD KENNEDY,
NOVEMBER 22, 1963, DALLAS, TEXAS

Caller	Conversation
75 (Patrolman E. G. SEBASTIAN)	We're almost there.
Dispatcher (HULSE and JACKSON)	19 (Sergeant C. B. OWENS), where did the officer go?
550/2 (Sergeant GERALD L. HILL)	550/2 (HILL).
19 (Sergeant C. B. OWENS)	I saw some squads towards Methodist real fast -- I'll bet that's where he is.
75 (Patrolman E. G. SEBASTIAN)	75 (SEBASTIAN).
Dispatcher (HULSE and JACKSON)	400 East Jefferson, report in that vicinity.
75 (Patrolman E. G. SEBASTIAN)	Code 2 (urgent, red lights and sirens as needed.)
Dispatcher (HULSE and JACKSON)	Yes.
76 (Patrolman H. H. HORN)	76 (HORN)
Dispatcher (HULSE and JACKSON)	76 (HORN)
76 (Patrolman H. H. HORN)	I'm en route over there.
Dispatcher (HULSE and JACKSON)	10-4.
16 (Sergeant R. D. SHIPLEY)	I'll be out on East Jefferson.
Dispatcher (HULSE and JACKSON)	10-4, 16 (SHIPLEY).
77 (Patrolman W. E. SMITH)	77 (SMITH).
Dispatcher (HULSE and JACKSON)	77 (SMITH).

COMMISSION EXHIBIT No. 1974—Continued

Re: ASSASSINATION OF PRESIDENT
JOHN FITZGERALD KENNEDY,
NOVEMBER 22, 1963, DALLAS, TEXAS

Caller	Conversation
77 (Patrolman W. E. SMITH)	Going back over on about 400 East Jefferson.
Dispatcher (HULSE and JACKSON)	Yes.
93 (Patrolman H. M. ASHCRAFT)	En route 400 East Jefferson.
Dispatcher (HULSE and JACKSON)	10-4.
29 (Patrolman J. M. WILLIAMS)	Out 400 West Jefferson.
Dispatcher (HULSE and JACKSON)	10-4.
Dispatcher (HULSE and JACKSON)	79 (Patrolman B. W. ANGLIN).
79 (Patrolman B. W. ANGLIN)	You calling 79 (ANGLIN)?
Dispatcher (HULSE and JACKSON)	Are you en route 300 East Jefferson?
79 (Patrolman B. W. ANGLIN)	10-4.
95 (Patrolmen M. M. MC DONALD and T. R. GREGORY)	95 (MC DONALD and GREGORY) is en route.
Dispatcher (HULSE and JACKSON)	10-4, 95 (MC DONALD and GREGORY).
93 (Patrolman H. M. ASHCRAFT)	Is en route.
Dispatcher (HULSE and JACKSON)	10-4, 93 (ASHCRAFT).
221 (Patrolman H. W. SUMMERS)	Is down here.
Dispatcher (HULSE and JACKSON)	10-4, 221 (SUMMERS).
223 (Patrolman C. T. WALKER)	223 (Patrolman C. T. WALKER) is there.

COMMISSION EXHIBIT No. 1974—Continued

Re: ASSASSINATION OF PRESIDENT
JOHN FITZGERALD KENNEDY,
NOVEMBER 22, 1963, DALLAS, TEXAS

Caller	Conversation
Dispatcher (HULSE and JACKSON)	10-4.
Dispatcher (HULSE and JACKSON)	19. (Sergeant C. B. OWENS)
19 (Sergeant C. B. OWENS)	19 (OWENS)
Dispatcher (HULSE and JACKSON)	Do you have the information?
19 (Sergeant C. B. OWENS)	No, what?
Dispatcher (HULSE and JACKSON)	On 2. (Instructed to go to Channel 2.)
75 (Patrolman E. G. SEBASTIAN)	75 (SEBASTIAN)
Dispatcher (HULSE and JACKSON)	75 (SEBASTIAN)
75 (Patrolman E. G. SEBASTIAN)	National Broadcasting Company is reporting DOA (Dead on Arrival).
Dispatcher (HULSE and JACKSON)	That's correct.
Unknown	Is that the officer?
Dispatcher (HULSE and JACKSON)	Yes. (Garbled transmission.)
Dispatcher (HULSE and JACKSON)	No, that's not correct 75 (Patrolman E. G. SEBASTIAN), 19 (Sergeant C. B. OWENS).
Unknown	What officer was it?
Dispatcher (JACKSON and HULSE)	J. D. TIPPIT.
87 (Patrolman R. C. NELSON)	87 (NELSON).

COMMISSION EXHIBIT No. 1974—Continued

Re: ASSASSINATION OF PRESIDENT
JOHN FITZGERALD KENNEDY,
NOVEMBER 22, 1963, DALLAS, TEXAS

Caller	Conversation
Dispatcher (HULSE and JACKSON)	87 (Patrolman R. C. NELSON).
87 (NELSON)	A white station wagon believed to be PE3435, unknown make and model, late model, occupied by two white males left this fellow's station going east on Davis and believed to have a shotgun or rifle laying in back seat.
Dispatcher (HULSE and JACKSON)	Received, 87 (Patrolman R. C. NELSON).
87 (Patrolman R. C. NELSON)	87 (NELSON) will be en route down there on Jefferson.
Dispatcher (HULSE and JACKSON)	87 (NELSON), when you get down there see if you can find that car at the scene.
87 (NELSON)	10-4. Code 2 (urgent - red lights and siren as needed).
Dispatcher (HULSE and JACKSON)	Code 3 (Emergency - red lights and sirens).
87 (NELSON)	10-4.
Dispatcher (HULSE and JACKSON)	19 (Sergeant C. B. OWENS).
Dispatcher (HULSE and JACKSON)	1 (Chief of Police JESSE E. CURRY)
111 (Patrolman J. G. POLLARD)	111 (POLLARD)
Dispatcher (HULSE and JACKSON	111 (POLLARD)
111 (POLLARD)	They say he is running west in the alley between Jefferson and Tenth.

COMMISSION EXHIBIT No. 1974—Continued

Re: ASSASSINATION OF PRESIDENT
JOHN FITZGERALD KENNEDY,
NOVEMBER 22, 1963, DALLAS, TEXAS

Caller	Conversation
Dispatcher (HULSE and JACKSON)	85 (Patrolman R. W. WALKER)
85 (Patrolman R. W. WALKER)	85 (Patrolman R. W. WALKER)
Dispatcher (HULSE and JACKSON)	West in the alley between Jefferson and Tenth.
85 (Patrolman R. W. WALKER)	10-4.
87 (Patrolman R. C. NELSON)	87 (NELSON), 10-4.
75 (Patrolman E. G. SEBASTIAN)	75 (SEBASTIAN) received.
599 (Cockrell Hill Squad)	599 (Cockrell Hill Squad) is in service.
Dispatcher (HULSE and J. A. MC DANIEL)	599 (Cockrell Hill Squad) clear 1:32.
Dispatcher (MC DANIEL)	Escorts going north on Hines. Cut your sirens. Escorts going north on Hines. Cut your sirens.
Dispatcher (HULSE)	10-4, 605 (Ambulance), 1:33
Unknown	Clothing the description on that suspect.
Dispatcher (HULSE and MC DANIEL)	White male, 30, 5'8", very slender build, black hair, a white jacket, white shirt and dark slacks, 1:33.
19 (Sergeant C. B. OWENS)	19 (OWENS).
Dispatcher (HULSE and MC DANIEL)	19 (OWENS).

COMMISSION EXHIBIT No. 1974—Continued

Re: ASSASSINATION OF PRESIDENT
JOHN FITZGERALD KENNEDY,
NOVEMBER 22, 1963, DALLAS, TEXAS

Caller	Conversation
19 (Sergeant C. B. OWENS)	Do you know what kind of a call he was on?
Dispatcher (HULSE and MC DANIEL)	What kind of what?
19 (OWENS)	Was he on a call or anything?
Dispatcher (HULSE and MC DANIEL)	No.
19 (OWENS)	10-4.
Dispatcher (HULSE and MC DANIEL)	Do you have any information for us, 19 (Sergeant C. B. OWENS)?
19 (OWENS)	No, we are shaking down these old houses in the 400 block East Jefferson right now.
95 (Patrolman M. N. MC DONALD)	95 (MC DONALD)
Dispatcher (HULSE and MC DANIEL)	Go ahead.
95 (MC DONALD)	Send me a squad over here at Tenth and Crawford to check out this church basement.
Dispatcher (HULSE and MC DANIEL)	Any squad Tenth and Crawford?
66 (Patrolman F. S. WILLIAMS)	66 (WILLIAMS) is en route.
Dispatcher (HULSE and MC DANIEL)	10-4.
Unknown	Was that Crawford and Jefferson?
Dispatcher (HULSE and MC DANIEL)	Tenth and Jefferson.

COMMISSION EXHIBIT No. 1974—Continued

Re: ASSASSINATION OF PRESIDENT
JOHN FITZGERALD KENNEDY,
NOVEMBER 22, 1963, DALLAS, TEXAS

Caller	Conversation
Unknown	10-4.
Dispatcher (HULSE and MC DANIEL)	87 (Patrolman R. C. NELSON).
87 (Patrolman R. C. NELSON)	87 (NELSON).
Dispatcher (HULSE and MC DANIEL)	PE3435 (garbled address) story, 1961 Falcon, 4-door.
87 (Patrolman R. C. NELSON)	He wasn't sure of license number.
Dispatcher (HULSE and MC DANIEL)	10-4.
16 (Sergeant R. D. SHIPLEY)	16 (SHIPLEY)
Dispatcher (HULSE and MC DANIEL)	16 (SHIPLEY)
16 (SHIPLEY)	Prefix and color on that car again.
223 (Patrolman C. T. WALKER)	223 (WALKER)
Dispatcher (HULSE and MC DANIEL)	Go ahead, 223 (WALKER).
223 (Patrolman C. T. WALKER)	He is in the library, Jefferson, East 500 block, Marsalis and Jefferson. (Several squads talking at one time, unable to read).
Dispatcher (HULSE and MC DANIEL)	What location, 223 (Patrolman C. T. WALKER)?
223 (Patrolman C. T. WALKER)	Library Jefferson and Marsalis. I'm going around back.

COMMISSION EXHIBIT No. 1974—Continued

Re: ASSASSINATION OF PRESIDENT
JOHN FITZGERALD KENNEDY,
NOVEMBER 22, 1963, DALLAS, TEXAS

Caller	Conversation
223 (Patrolman C. T. WALKER)	Get them here fast.
Dispatcher (HULSE and MC DANIEL)	Any unit near Marsalis and Jefferson. (Several squads talking again -- unable to read.)
85 (Patrolman R. W. WALKER)	En route.
Dispatcher (HULSE and MC DANIEL)	10-4, 85 (Patrolman R. W. WALKER).
Unknown	Called.
Dispatcher (HULSE and MC DANIEL)	Go ahead.
Unknown	En route.
Dispatcher (HULSE and MC DANIEL)	10-4.
29 (Patrolman J. WILLIAMS)	29 (Patrolman J. WILLIAMS).
Dispatcher (HULSE and MC DANIEL)	29 (Patrolman J. WILLIAMS).
29 (Patrolman J. WILLIAMS)	Clear, I'll be in the downtown area any place you can use me.
Dispatcher (HULSE and MC DANIEL)	Jefferson and Marsalis, 29 (Patrolman J. WILLIAMS).
29 (Patrolman J. WILLIAMS)	En route.
22 (Patrolman L. L. HILL)	22 (Patrolman L. L. HILL).
Dispatcher (HULSE and MC DANIEL)	22 (Patrolman L. L. HILL).

COMMISSION EXHIBIT No. 1974—Continued

Re: ASSASSINATION OF PRESIDENT
JOHN FITZGERALD KENNEDY,
NOVEMBER 22, 1963, DALLAS, TEXAS

Caller	Conversation
22 (Patrolman L. L. HILL)	They got him hemmed up - looks like in this building over here at the corner.
Unknown	Where you be?
85 (Patrolman R. W. WALKER)	Is at library.
Dispatcher (HULSE and MC DANIEL)	10-4.
211 (Patrolmen R. HAWKINS and E. R. BAGGETT)	Is out at location.
Dispatcher (HULSE and MC DANIEL)	10-4.
19 (Sergeant C. B. OWENS)	19 (OWENS)
Dispatcher (HULSE and MC DANIEL)	19 (OWENS)
19 (OWENS)	We are all at the library.
Dispatcher (HULSE and MC DANIEL)	10-4. 223 (Patrolman C. T. WALKER) is supposed to be there.
19 (OWENS)	We are at the side of the building now.
Dispatcher (HULSE and MC DANIEL)	10-4.
Unknown	Where is it?
Dispatcher (HULSE and MC DANIEL)	Marsalis and Jefferson.
Unknown	What and Jefferson?
Dispatcher (HULSE and MC DANIEL)	Marsalis.

COMMISSION EXHIBIT No. 1974—Continued

Re: ASSASSINATION OF PRESIDENT
JOHN FITZGERALD KENNEDY,
NOVEMBER 22, 1963, DALLAS, TEXAS

Caller	Conversation
221 (Patrolman H. W. SUMMERS)	221 (SUMMERS)
Dispatcher (HULSE and MC DANIEL)	221 (SUMMERS)
221 (SUMMERS)	Might can give you some additional information. I got an eyeball witness to the get-away man; that suspect in this shooting. He is a white male, 27, 5'11", 165, black wavy hair, fair complected, wearing light gray Eisenhower-type jacket, dark trousers and a white shirt and but last seen running on the north side of the street from Patton on Jefferson; on East Jefferson, and was apparently armed with a .32, dark finish, automatic pistol which he had in his right hand.
Dispatcher (HULSE and MC DANIEL)	10-4. For you information, 221 (Patrolman H. W. SUMMERS), they have the suspect cornered in the library Marsalis and Jefferson.
221 (Patrolman H. W. SUMMERS)	10-4. This man can positively identify him if they need him.
Dispatcher (HULSE and MC DANIEL)	Well, they do have the suspect under arrest now.
Unknown	221 (Patrolman H. W. SUMMERS), hang on to your witness.

COMMISSION EXHIBIT No. 1974—Continued

Re: ASSASSINATION OF PRESIDENT
JOHN FITZGERALD KENNEDY,
NOVEMBER 22, 1963, DALLAS, TEXAS

Caller	Conversation
Dispatcher (HULSE)	Well, hold on to him.
19 (Sergeant C. B. OWENS)	19 (OWENS).
Dispatcher (HULSE and MC DANIEL)	19 (OWENS).
19 (Sergeant C. B. OWENS)	It was the wrong man.
Dispatcher (HULSE and MC DANIEL)	10-4. Disregard all the information on the suspect arrested. It was the wrong man.
Dispatcher (HULSE and MC DANIEL)	221 (Patrolman H. W. SUMMERS).
221 (Patrolman H. W. SUMMERS)	Yes.
Dispatcher (HULSE and MC DANIEL)	Stand by....19..
19 (Sergeant C. B. OWENS)	19 (OWENS)
Dispatcher (HULSE and MC DANIEL)	221 (Patrolman H. W. SUMMERS) has an eye witness to the shooting. You want him to hold onto him?
19 (Sergeant C. B. OWENS)	What did you say?
Dispatcher (HULSE and MC DANIEL)	You want him to keep the eye witness at the scene?
19 (Sergeant C. B. OWENS)	Yes.
Dispatcher (HULSE and MC DANIEL)	10-4.
221 (Patrolman H. W. SUMMERS)	I'm in front of 404 West - East 10th right now. I got two witnesses - the one that talked to the officer and one that observed the man.

COMMISSION EXHIBIT No. 1974—Continued

Re: ASSASSINATION OF PRESIDENT
JOHN FITZGERALD KENNEDY,
NOVEMBER 22, 1963, DALLAS, TEXAS

Caller	Conversation
Dispatcher (HULSE and MC DANIEL)	242 (Patrolman B. T. THORNHILL), location?
242 (Patrolman B. T. THORNHILL)	242 (THORNHILL), R. L. Thornton and Marsalis.
Dispatcher (HULSE and MC DANIEL)	243 (Patrolman B. L. APPLE)
550 (Captain W. R. WESTBROOK)	550 (WESTBROOK)
Dispatcher (HULSE and MC DANIEL)	550 (WESTBROOK).
550 (Captain W. R. WESTBROOK)	What officer have you got commanding this area over here where the officer was shot?
Dispatcher (HULSE and MC DANIEL)	19 (Sergeant C. B. OWENS).
550 (Captain W. R. WESTBROOK)	Repeat.
Dispatcher (HULSE and MC DANIEL)	19 (Sergeant C. B. OWENS).
550 (Captain W. R. WESTBROOK)	19 (Sergeant C. B. OWENS).
19 (Sergeant C. B. OWENS)	19 (Sergeant C. B. OWENS).
550 (Captain W. R. WESTBROOK)	19 (OWENS), what is your location?
19 (Sergeant C. B. OWENS)	I'm at Marsalis and Jefferson right now.
550 (Captain W. R. WESTBROOK)	There's nothing to this Marsalis here. Let's get back up to Jefferson (followed by some interference, sounded like work... to North Jefferson) (transmission

COMMISSION EXHIBIT No. 1974—Continued

Re: ASSASSINATION OF PRESIDENT
JOHN FITZGERALD KENNEDY,
NOVEMBER 22, 1963, DALLAS, TEXAS

Caller	Conversation
	interrupted by 223. (Patrolman C. T. WALKER.)
223 (Patrolman C. T. WALKER)	223 (Patrolman C. T. WALKER).
550 (Captain W. R. WESTBROOK)	We got a witness that saw him go up North Jefferson and he shed his jacket -- let's check that vicinity, towards Tyler.
Dispatcher (HULSE and MC DANIEL)	223 (Patrolman C. T. WALKER).
223 (Patrolman C. T. WALKER)	That was just a boy running to tell them what happened. He works there.
Dispatcher (HULSE and MC DANIEL)	243, location?
241 (Patrolman J. P. HOLLINGS-WORTH)	241 (HOLLINGSWORTH), is 1000 North Central.
Dispatcher (HULSE and MC DANIEL)	10-4. Report to third floor of the Sheraton - contact the officer there for an escort to Parkland, 1:40.
87 (Patrolman R. C. NELSON)	87 (NELSON).
49 (Patrolman C. R. GILBREATH)	49 (GILBREATH).
Dispatcher (HULSE and MC DANIEL)	49 (GILBREATH).
49 (Patrolman C. R. GILBREATH)	I'm back in the car, where do you want me?
Dispatcher (HULSE and MC DANIEL)	Remain in downtown area.

- 77 -

COMMISSION EXHIBIT No. 1974—Continued

Re: ASSASSINATION OF PRESIDENT
JOHN FITZGERALD KENNEDY,
NOVEMBER 22, 1963, DALLAS, TEXAS

Caller	Conversation
Dispatcher (HULSE and MC DANIEL)	You receive, 241 (Patrolman J. P. HOLLINGSWORTH)?
241 (Patrolman J. P. HOLLINGS-WORTH)	10-4. Whereabouts on third floor?
550/2 (Sergeant G. HILL)	550/2 (HILL).
Dispatcher (HULSE and MC DANIEL)	Go ahead, 550/2 (HILL).
550/2 (Sergeant G. HILL)	The sholl at the scene indicates that the suspect is armed with an automatic .38 rather than a pistol.
Dispatcher (HULSE and MC DANIEL)	10-4.
492 (Special Service Bureau, Dallas Police Department, occupant unknown)	492 (Special Service Bureau, Dallas Police Department)
Dispatcher (HULSE and MC DANIEL)	19 (Sergeant C. B. OWENS)
19 (Sergeant C. B. OWENS)	19 (Sergeant C. B. OWENS)
Dispatcher (HULSE and MC DANIEL)	19 (OWENS), are you en route to 404 East 10th where 221 (Patrolman H. W. SUMMERS) has the eye witness.
19 (Sergeant C. B. OWENS)	Yes.
Dispatcher (HULSE and MC DANIEL)	10-4.
492 (Special Service Bureau)	492 (Special Service Bureau).

- 78 -

COMMISSION EXHIBIT No. 1974—Continued

Re: ASSASSINATION OF PRESIDENT
JOHN FITZGERALD KENNEDY,
NOVEMBER 22, 1963, DALLAS, TEXAS

Caller	Conversation
Dispatcher (HULSE and MC DANIEL)	492 (Special Service Bureau)
492 (Special Service Bureau)	We have been instructed to report to the Oak Cliff scene. What location and what code?
Dispatcher (HULSE and MC DANIEL)	300 East Jefferson.
492 (Special Service Bureau)	Code?
Dispatcher (HULSE and MC DANIEL)	Code 2. (Urgent - red lights and siren as needed.)
19 (Sergeant C. B. OWENS)	19 (OWENS).
Dispatcher (HULSE and MC DANIEL)	19 (Sergeant C. B. OWENS).
19 (Sergeant C. B. OWENS)	Is 80 Sergeant H. F. DANS in service?
Dispatcher (HULSE and MC DANIEL)	80, (Sergeant H. F. DANS).
19 (Sergeant C. B. OWENS)	I think he was sent down to Elm and Central. We need somebody to notify that Officer's wife.
Dispatcher (HULSE and MC DANIEL)	80, (Sergeant H. F. DANS).
Dispatcher (HULSE and MC DANIEL)	241 (Patrolman J. P. HOLLINGSWORTH).
210 (Sergeant J. M. YOUNG)	210 (Sergeant J. M. YOUNG).
Dispatcher (HULSE and MC DANIEL)	210 (Sergeant J. M. YOUNG).
210 (Sergeant J. M. YOUNG)	I'm at Hines and Wolfe. Does 19 (Sergeant C. B. OWENS) want me out in Oak Cliff?

COMMISSION EXHIBIT No. 1974—Continued

Re: ASSASSINATION OF PRESIDENT
JOHN FITZGERALD KENNEDY,
NOVEMBER 22, 1963, DALLAS, TEXAS

Caller	Conversation
Dispatcher (HULSE and MC DANIEL)	19 (Sergeant C. B. OWENS).
210 (Sergeant J. M. YOUNG)	I'll head that way.
Dispatcher (HULSE and MC DANIEL)	10-4.
19 (Sergeant C. B. OWENS)	19 (OWENS).
Dispatcher (HULSE and MC DANIEL)	19 (OWENS), can you use 210 (Sergeant J. M. YOUNG) over there?
Dispatcher (HULSE and MC DANIEL)	241 (Patrolman J. P. HOLLINGS-WORTH).
410 (Criminal Investigation Division)	410 (Criminal Investigation Division)
Dispatcher (HULSE and MC DANIEL)	410 (Criminal Investigation Division)
410 (Criminal Investigation Division)	410 (Criminal Investigation Division) en route from Trade Mart with three detectives to City Hall unless otherwise directed.
Dispatcher (HULSE and MC DANIEL)	10-4, 410 (Criminal Investigation Division), 1:43.
Dispatcher (HULSE and MC DANIEL)	241 (Patrolman J. P. HOLLINGS-WORTH).
87 (Patrolman R. C. NELSON)	87 (NELSON).
Dispatcher (HULSE and MC DANIEL)	87 (NELSON).

COMMISSION EXHIBIT No. 1974—Continued

Re: ASSASSINATION OF PRESIDENT
JOHN FITZGERALD KENNEDY,
NOVEMBER 22, 1963, DALLAS, TEXAS

Caller	Conversation
Dispatcher (HULSE and MC DANIEL)	87 (Patrolman R. C. NELSON), was that a Pontiac or a Falcon?
87 (Patrolman R. C. NELSON)	He didn't say what kind of a car it would be. He said it was a white car with a luggage rack on top. He wasn't sure of the model, talked like it was a big car, though.
Dispatcher (HULSE and MC DANIEL)	10-4.
392 (Criminal Investigation Division)	392 (Criminal Investigation Division).
Dispatcher (HULSE and MC DANIEL)	392 (Criminal Investigation Division).
392 (Criminal Investigation Division)	392 (Criminal Investigation Division) and 362 (Criminal Investigation Division) in service from Fed Mart; from the -
Dispatcher (HULSE and MC DANIEL)	10-4.
392 (Criminal Investigation Division)	Ready for assignment.
(End of Belt Seven)	
Dispatcher (HULSE and MC DANIEL)	10-4 (1:44)
87 (Patrolman R. C. NELSON)	What was the last location anybody had on the suspect over here in Oak Cliff?

COMMISSION EXHIBIT No. 1974—Continued

Re: ASSASSINATION OF PRESIDENT
JOHN FITZGERALD KENNEDY,
NOVEMBER 22, 1963, DALLAS, TEXAS

Caller	Conversation
Dispatcher (HULSE and MC DANIEL)	Running north on Patton.
222 (Patrolman V. R. NOLAN)	222 (NOLAN), clear.
Dispatcher (HULSE and MC DANIEL)	222 (NOLAN), clear, 1:45.
Dispatcher (MC DANIEL)	252
252	Would you check through Austin and get registration, please, on (belt skipping) H Henry, S Sam, 1877, down here at this shooting which took place in regards to the President.
Dispatcher (HULSE and MC DANIEL)	19 (Sergeant C. B. OWENS)
Dispatcher (HULSE and MC DANIEL)	19 (Sergeant C. B. OWENS)
252	252
Dispatcher (HULSE and MC DANIEL)	252
252	Did you receive the license number?
Dispatcher (HULSE and MC DANIEL)	No, give it to us again.
252	H Henry, S Sam, 1877, Texas 1963.
Dispatcher (HULSE and MC DANIEL)	10-4.
79 (Patrolman B. W. ANGLIN)	79 (ANGLIN)

COMMISSION EXHIBIT No. 1974—Continued

Caller	Conversation
Dispatcher (HULSE and MC DANIEL)	79 (Patrolman B. W. ANGLIN).
79 (ANGLIN)	(Garbled transmission.)
Dispatcher (HULSE and MC DANIEL)	Have information a suspect just went in the Texas Theatre on West Jefferson.
79 (Patrolman B. W. ANGLIN)	10-4.
Dispatcher (HULSE and MC DANIEL)	10-4. Supposed to be hiding in the balcony.
85 (Patrolman R. W. WALKER)	85 (Patrolman R. W. WALKER), en route.
Dispatcher (HULSE and MC DANIEL)	65 (Patrolman W. A. EVERETT) clear, 1:46.
111 (Patrolman J. G. POLLARD)	111 (POLLARD), en route.
Dispatcher (HULSE and MC DANIEL)	10-4, 111 (POLLARD).
76 (Patrolman H. H. HORN)	76 (HORN), Code 5 (en route).
Dispatcher (HULSE and MC DANIEL)	10-4.
9 (Inspector J. H. SAWYER)	9 (SAWYER).
Dispatcher (HULSE and MC DANIEL)	9 (SAWYER).
9 (Inspector J. H. SAWYER)	We have a man that we would like to have you pass this on to CID (Criminal Investigation Division) to see if we can pick this man up. CHARLES DOUGLAS GIVENS,

COMMISSION EXHIBIT No. 1974—Continued

Caller	Conversation
	G-I-V-E-N-S. He is a colored male, 37, 6'3", 165 pounds, I.D.# Sheriff Department 37954. He is a porter that worked on this floor up here. He has a police record and he left.
Dispatcher (HULSE and MC DANIEL)	10-4.
550/2 (Sergeant G. HILL)	550/2 (Sergeant G. HILL)
Dispatcher (HULSE and MC DANIEL)	550/2 (Sergeant G. HILL)
550/2 (Sergeant G. HILL)	Do you have any additional information on this Oak Cliff suspect?
492 (Special Service Bureau)	492 (Special Service Bureau) out at Texas Theatre.
Dispatcher (HULSE and MC DANIEL)	10-4.
Dispatcher (HULSE and MC DANIEL)	They think he is at the Texas Theatre, 550/2 (Sergeant G. HILL).
550/2 (Sergeant G. HILL)	10-4.
Dispatcher (HULSE and MC DANIEL)	In the balcony.
Dispatcher (HULSE and MC DANIEL)	241 (Patrolman J. G. HOLLINGSWORTH)
241 (Patrolman J. G. HOLLINGSWORTH)	Go ahead.
Dispatcher (HULSE and MC DANIEL)	You make pickup at the Sheraton?
241 (Patrolman J. G. HOLLINGSWORTH)	No, I couldn't find him. He is not in the front, he's not on the side and he is not on the third floor.

COMMISSION EXHIBIT No. 1974—Continued

Re: ASSASSINATION OF PRESIDENT
JOHN FITZGERALD KENNEDY,
NOVEMBER 22, 1963, DALLAS, TEXAS

Caller	Conversation
108	108
Dispatcher (HULSE and MC DANIEL)	Wait right there, 108
08	I run 'em on out here myself. I'm at Parkland now going back to communications center.
Dispatcher (HULSE and MC DANIEL)	10-4, 241 (Patrolman J. G. HOLLINGSWORTH), you are clear, 1:47.
508 (W. E. BARNES)	508 (BARNES)
Dispatcher (HULSE and MC DANIEL)	508 (BARNES).
508 (BARNES)	Notify our office to send us four slides and need additional metallic kit. Extra metallic kit. Bring to the sixth floor down here at Houston and Elm.
Dispatcher (HULSE and MC DANIEL)	That extra metallic, what was that?
508 (BARNES)	A metallic kit.
Dispatcher (HULSE and MC DANIEL)	10-4.
Dispatcher (HULSE and MC DANIEL)	Have some squad cover off the rear of theater fire escape.
211 (Patrolman R. HAWKINS)	211 (HAWKINS).

Re: ASSASSINATION OF PRESIDENT
JOHN FITZGERALD KENNEDY,
NOVEMBER 22, 1963, DALLAS, TEXAS

Caller	Conversation
Dispatcher (HULSE and MC DANIEL)	211 (Patrolman R. HAWKINS)
211 (HAWKINS)	There's about five squads back here with me now.
Dispatcher (HULSE and MC DANIEL)	10-4. (1:48)
99 (Patrolman S. E.NORMAN)	99 (NORMAN)
Dispatcher (HULSE and MC DANIEL)	99 (NORMAN).
99 (NORMAN)	I am in my car. Where do you want me to go?
Dispatcher (HULSE and MC DANIEL)	Stand by, 99 (NORMAN).
Dispatcher (HULSE and MC DANIEL)	15 (Captain C. E. TALBERT)
15 (Captain C. E. TALBERT)	15 (TALBERT).
Dispatcher (HULSE and MC DANIEL)	Where do you want 99 (Patrolman S. E. NORMAN)?
15 (TALBERT)	Send him to the Texas Theatre as they don't need him down at the book bindery.
Dispatcher (HULSE and MC DANIEL)	10-4. Texas Theatre on West Jefferson, 99 (NORMAN).
29 (Patrolman J. WILLIAMS)	29 (WILLIAMS).
Dispatcher (HULSE and MC DANIEL)	29 (WILLIAMS).
29 (WILLIAMS)	About two blocks away.

Caller	Conversation
Dispatcher (HULSE and MC DANIEL)	10-4. Handle assignment. 99 (Patrolman S. E. NORMAN) report to the Book Depository Elm and Houston.
99 (NORMAN)	10-4.
19 (Sergeant C. B. OWENS)	19 (OWENS).
Dispatcher (HULSE and MC DANIEL)	19 (OWENS).
19 (OWENS)	15 (Captain C. E. TALBERT) and some squads are going to the Texas Theatre. I remain here at the scene.
Dispatcher (HULSE and MC DANIEL)	10-4, 1:49.
19 (Sergeant C. B. OWENS)	19 (OWENS).
Dispatcher (HULSE and MC DANIEL)	19 (OWENS).
19 (OWENS)	Did you get anybody to go by the officer's house?
Dispatcher (HULSE and MC DANIEL)	19 (OWENS), we are going to have 210 (Sergeant J. M. YOUNG) contact you there. Would you give him the information? He said he would handle it.
19 (Sergeant C. B. OWENS)	10-4.
26 (Patrolman G. W. HAMMER)	26 (HAMMER).
Dispatcher (HULSE and MC DANIEL)	26 (HAMMER).

COMMISSION EXHIBIT No. 1974—Continued

Caller	Conversation
26 (Patrolman G. W. HAMMER)	We remain out to Homicide Bureau with a witness on this officer's shooting.
Dispatcher (HULSE and MC DANIEL)	10-4. (1:51)
550/2 (Sergeant G. HILL)	550/2 (HILL)
Dispatcher (HULSE and MC DANIEL)	550/2 (HILL).
550/2 (Sergeant G. HILL)	Suspect on shooting of police officer is apprehended and en route to the station.
Dispatcher (HULSE and MC DANIEL)	10-4. At the Texas Theatre?
550/2 (Sergeant G. HILL)	Caught him in the lower floor of the Texas Theatre after a fight.
Dispatcher (HULSE and MC DANIEL)	10-4.
3 (Deputy Chief M. W. STEVEN-SON)	3 (STEVENSON).
Dispatcher (HULSE and MC DANIEL)	3 (STEVENSON).
3 (STEVENSON)	2 (Assistant Chief of Police CHARLES BATCHELOR) and 3 (STEVENSON) are on the air. We are en route to Parkland Hospital now. Will be en route back to the station in a few moments. What do you have working at the Texas Theatre?

COMMISSION EXHIBIT No. 1974—Continued

Re: ASSASSINATION OF PRESIDENT
JOHN FITZGERALD KENNEDY,
NOVEMBER 22, 1963, DALLAS, TEXAS

Caller	Conversation
Dispatcher (HULSE and MC DANIEL)	We have a shooting of a police officer which was DOA (Dead On Arrival) at Methodist. The suspect has been apprehended at the Texas Theatre - en route to the station.
3 (Deputy Chief M. W. STEVENSON)	10-4. Thank you.
91 (Patrolman W. D. MENTZEL)	91 (MENTZEL) clear.
Dispatcher (HULSE and MC DANIEL)	91 (MENTZEL) clear, 1:53.
242 (Patrolman B. T. THORNHILL)	242 (THORNHILL).
Dispatcher (HULSE and MC DANIEL)	242 (THORNHILL).
242 (THORNHILL)	The suspect was arrested?
Dispatcher (HULSE and MC DANIEL)	Yes.
305 (Homicide)	305 (Homicide).
Dispatcher (HULSE and MC DANIEL)	305 (Homicide).
305 (Homicide)	Tell that squad to stand by there for me with that man.
Dispatcher (HULSE and MC DANIEL)	550/2 (Sergeant G. HILL).
550/2 (Sergeant G. HILL)	223 (Patrolman C. T. WALKER) is in the car with us. Have someone pick his car up at the rear of the Texas Theatre and take it to the station. It's got the keys in it.

Re: ASSASSINATION OF PRESIDENT
JOHN FITZGERALD KENNEDY,
NOVEMBER 22, 1963, DALLAS, TEXAS

Caller	Conversation
Dispatcher (HULSE and MC DANIEL)	10-4.
Dispatcher (HULSE and MC DANIEL)	91 (Patrolman W. D. MENTZEL).
91 (Patrolman W. D. MENTZEL)	91 (MENTZEL).
Dispatcher (HULSE and MC DANIEL)	Report back to the Texas Theatre - Get 223's (Patrolman C. T. WALKER) car or his keys and lock it up.
91 (MENTZEL)	10-4.
221 (Patrolman H. W. SUMMERS)	221 (SUMMERS).
Dispatcher (HULSE and MC DANIEL)	221 (SUMMERS).
221 (SUMMERS)	509 (Crime Laboratory, Dallas Police Department) said he would be out 400 block East 10th a few minutes.
Dispatcher (HULSE and MC DANIEL)	10-4, 221 (SUMMERS) 22 (Patrolman L. L. HILL)
22 (Patrolman L. L. HILL)	210's (Sergeant J. M. YOUNG) here. Did you say you had him? Or somebody had him?
Dispatcher (HULSE and MC DANIEL)	The suspect has been arrested at the Texas Theatre.
Unknown	Where is he? Who's got him?
Dispatcher (HULSE and MC DANIEL)	550/2 (Sergeant G. HILL) and 223 (Patrolman C. T. WALKER).

Caller	Conversation
550/2 (Sergeant G. HILL)	550/2 (Sergeant G. HILL).
Dispatcher (HULSE and MC DANIEL)	Go ahead.
550/2 (Sergeant G. HILL)	Special Service Unit is with us, also; we are in his car; 492 (Special Service Bureau).
Dispatcher (HULSE and MC DANIEL)	10-4.
15 (Captain C. E. TALBERT)	15 (TALBERT) to 550/2 (Sergeant G. HILL).
305 (Homicide)	305 (Homicide) to 550/2 (Sergeant G. HILL).
15 (Captain C. E. TALBERT)	What's your location?
550/2 (Sergeant G. HILL)	Go ahead to 550/2 (Sergeant G. HILL).
15 (Captain C. E. TALBERT)	15 (TALBERT) to 550/2 (Sergeant G. HILL). Your location?
550/2 (Sergeant G. HILL)	Zangs and Colorado.
15 (Captain C. E. TALBERT)	You do have the suspect arrested in the Texas Theatre?
550/2 (Sergeant G. HILL)	Yes, sir, him and the gun.
15 (Captain C. E. TALBERT)	10-4, (1:55).
91 (Patrolman W. D. MENTZEL)	91 (MENTZEL).
Dispatcher (HULSE and MC DANIEL)	91 (MENTZEL).

COMMISSION EXHIBIT No. 1974—Continued

Caller	Conversation
91 (Patrolman W. D. MENTZEL)	What do you want me to do with the keys after I lock that car up?
Dispatcher (HULSE and MC DANIEL)	Just keep them until you contact 223 (Patrolman C. T. WALKER).
91 (MENTZEL)	10-4.
211 (Patrolman R. HAWKINS)	211 (HAWKINS).
Dispatcher (HULSE and MC DANIEL)	211 (HAWKINS).
211 (HAWKINS)	Captain Westbrook wants a photographer up here at the Texas Theatre.
Dispatcher (HULSE and MC DANIEL)	509 (Crime Laboratory) is supposed to be en route.
211 (HAWKINS)	Message received.
221 (Patrolman H. W. SUMMERS)	509 (Crime Laboratory) is 400 block East 10th. He's out down there, he said.
Dispatcher (HULSE and MC DANIEL)	10-4. Send him on up to the Texas Theatre, 221 (Patrolman H. W. SUMMERS).
221 (Patrolman H. W. SUMMERS)	He's got his speaker on. I've already left there. I guess he'll come on up.
Dispatcher (HULSE and MC DANIEL)	Go back by and contact him. 49 (Patrolman C. R. GILBREATH).

COMMISSION EXHIBIT No. 1974—Continued

Re: ASSASSINATION OF PRESIDENT
JOHN FITZGERALD KENNEDY,
NOVEMBER 22, 1963, DALLAS, TEXAS

Caller	Conversation
49 (Patrolman C. R. GILBREATH)	49 (GILBREATH).
Dispatcher (HULSE and MC DANIEL)	Report to the City Hall Identification Bureau, pick up some equipment, take down to the scene of the earlier shooting on Houston.
49 (Patrolman C. R. GILBREATH)	10-4. (1:56)
Dispatcher (HULSE and MC DANIEL)	32 (Patrolmen J. T. SMITH and W. L. HACKNEY)
32 (Patrolmen J. T. SMITH and W. L. HACKNEY)	32 (SMITH and HACKNEY)
Dispatcher (HULSE and MC DANIEL)	On Shorecrest at the end of the North-South runway, report to that location, 1:57 p.m.
32 (SMITH and HACKNEY)	10-4.
Dispatcher (HULSE and MC DANIEL)	32 (SMITH and HACKNEY)
32 (SMITH and HACKNEY)	32 (SMITH and HACKNEY)
Dispatcher (HULSE and MC DANIEL)	Keep everyone moved out of that area, when you arrive.
32 (SMITH and HACKNEY)	10-4.
61 (Patrolmen G. W. TEMPLE and R. E. VAUGHN)	61 (TEMPLE and VAUGHN)
Dispatcher (HULSE and MC DANIEL)	61 (TEMPLE and VAUGHN)

COMMISSION EXHIBIT No. 1974—Continued

Re: ASSASSINATION OF PRESIDENT
JOHN FITZGERALD KENNEDY,
NOVEMBER 22, 1963, DALLAS, TEXAS

Caller	Conversation
61 (Patrolmen G. W. TEMPLE and R. E. VAUGHN)	We have information from the agent out here at T&P. Said that the train is stopped on the overpass, the triple overpass; that there was a person jumping at the ninth boxcar from the front engine. Said he is hiding in a car.
Dispatcher (HULSE and MC DANIEL)	Is the train stopped there now?
61 (TEMPLE and VAUGHN)	I'm in behind the Texas School Depository. He has the train stopped. He said it is the ninth car from the engine. Gondola-type car; said he is hunkered down inside.
Dispatcher (HULSE and MC DANIEL)	Any squad Elm and Houston...
392 (Criminal Investigation Division)	392 (Criminal Investigation Division)
Dispatcher (HULSE and MC DANIEL)	392 (Criminal Investigation Division), did you receive that information?
392 (Criminal Investigation Division)	10-4. En route.
Dispatcher (HULSE and MC DANIEL)	10-4.
241 (Patrolman J. P. HOLLINGSWORTH)	241 (HOLLINGSWORTH) en route.
361 (Criminal Investigation Division)	361 (Criminal Investigation Division) en route.

COMMISSION EXHIBIT No. 1974—Continued

Re: ASSASSINATION OF PRESIDENT
JOHN FITZGERALD KENNEDY,
NOVEMBER 22, 1963, DALLAS, TEXAS

Caller	Conversation
498 (Patrolman D. A. GREEN)	498 (Patrolman D.A. GREEN) is going back.
Dispatcher (HULSE and MC DANIEL)	10-4, 498 (Patrolman D. A. GREEN) out, 1:59.
224 (Patrolman R. D. WILSON)	224's (WILSON) en route.
375 (Criminal Investigation Division)	375's (Criminal Investigation Division) en route.
505 (Crime Laboratory)	505 (Crime Laboratory)
Dispatcher (HULSE and MC DANIEL)	505 (Crime Laboratory.
505 (Crime Laboratory)	Do you need a photographer at the theatre?
Dispatcher (HULSE and MC DANIEL)	Repeat.
505 (Crime Laboratory)	Do you need a photographer at the theatre?
Dispatcher (HULSE and MC DANIEL)	Yes, at the theatre.
505 (Crime Laboratory)	We're at 10th and Patton now - be through here just a few minutes; will be en route.
Dispatcher (HULSE and MC DANIEL)	10-4, 505 (Crime Laboratory), 1:59 p.m. 433 (Lieutenant C. C. WALLACE)
311 (Homicide)	311 (Homicide) received, we're standing by.

- 95 -

COMMISSION EXHIBIT No. 1974—Continued

Re: ASSASSINATION OF PRESIDENT
JOHN FITZGERALD KENNEDY,
NOVEMBER 22, 1963, DALLAS, TEXAS

Caller	Conversation
26 (Patrolman G. W. HAMMER)	26 (HAMMER).
Dispatcher (HULSE and MC DANIEL)	26 (HAMMER).
26 (Patrolman G. W. HAMMER)	See if you can raise somebody over there at TIPPIT's car.
221 (Patrolman H. W. SUMMERS)	221 (SUMMERS) just left there, what do you want to know?
26 (Patrolman G. W. HAMMER)	Go back and get this witness's shoes she left on the hood of the car and we'll be in Homicide Bureau.
221 (Patrolman H. W. SUMMERS)	Captain DOUGHTY has got them.
26 (Patrolman G. W. HAMMER)	10-4.
16 (Patrolman R. D. SHIPLEY)	16 (SHIPLEY).
Dispatcher (HULSE and MC DANIEL)	16 (SHIPLEY).
16 (Patrolman R. D. SHIPLEY)	Clear on East Jefferson; will be headed to East Dallas unless you need me somewhere.
Dispat her (HULSE and MC DANIEL)	10-4, 2:00 p.m. KKB 364 (Microphone stuck open now - very noisy signals)
91 (Patrolman W. D. MENTZEL)	91 (MENTZEL).
Dispatcher (HULSE and MC DANIEL)	91 (MENTZEL).
91 (MENTZEL)	Which one of these Accident Prevention Bureau cars is 223 (Patrolman C. T. WALKER)?

- 96 -

COMMISSION EXHIBIT No. 1974—Continued

Re: ASSASSINATION OF PRESIDENT
JOHN FITZGERALD KENNEDY,
NOVEMBER 22, 1963, DALLAS, TEXAS

Caller	Conversation
Dispatcher (HULSE and MC DANIEL)	The one around at the back door.
91 (Patrolman W. D. MENTZEL)	There' two around back here. One of them running and one with the keys in it.
Unknown	Number 81.
66 (Patrolman F. S. WILLIAMS)	66 (WILLIAMS)
Dispatcher (HULSE and MC DANIEL)	66 (WILLIAMS)
66 (WILLIAMS)	See if you can contact 79 Patrolman B. W. ANGLIN) and have him return up here to 400 East Jefferson.
Dispatcher (HULSE and MC DANIEL)	79 (Patrolman B. W. ANGLIN).
22 (Patrolman L. L. HILL)	22 (Patrolman L. L. HILL).
Dispatcher (HULSE and MC DANIEL)	22 (Patrolman L. L. HILL).
22 (Patrolman L. L. HILL)	In case (unable to read) regarding Officer TIPPIT's pistol, I gave it to Sergeant OWENS.
Dispatcher (HULSE and MC DANIEL)	10-4.
581 (Unknown)	581 (Unknown) out at Parkland.
95 (Patrolman M. N. MC DONALD)	95 (MC DONALD)
Dispatcher (HULSE and MC DANIEL)	95 (MC DONALD)
95 (MC DONALD)	I'm en route downtown to make a statement.

- 97 -

COMMISSION EXHIBIT No. 1974—Continued

Re: ASSASSINATION OF PRESIDENT
JOHN FITZGERALD KENNEDY,
NOVEMBER 22, 1963, DALLAS, TEXAS

Caller	Conversation
Dispatcher (HULSE and MC DANIEL)	10-4, 2:01.
305 (Homicide)	305 (Homicide).
Dispatcher (HULSE and MC DANIEL)	305 (Homicide).
305 (Homicide)	See if you can ascertain what squad has the lady witness to this shooting in Oak Cliff.
26 (Patrolman G. W. HAMMER)	26 (HAMMER) does.
305 (Homicide)	Where are you?
26 (HAMMER)	I'm at the City Hall fixing to go in the basement.
305 (Homicide)	10-4. I'll meet you there.
Dispatcher (HULSE and MC DANIEL)	300
29 (Patrolman J. WILLIAMS)	29 (WILLIAMS)
Dispatcher (HULSE and MC DANIEL)	29 (WILLIAMS).
29 (WILLIAMS)	Clear from the Texas Theatre. Do you want me to report downton now?
Dispatcher (HULSE and MC DANIEL)	Yes, 29 (WILLIAMS).
Dispatcher (HULSE and MC DANIEL)	19 (Sergeant C. B. OWENS)
19 (Sergeant C. B. OWENS)	19 (OWENS).
Dispatcher (HULSE and MC DANIEL)	Are you en route Methodist now?

- 98 -

COMMISSION EXHIBIT No. 1974—Continued

Re: ASSASSINATION OF PRESIDENT
JOHN FITZGERALD KENNEDY,
NOVEMBER 22, 1963, DALLAS, TEXAS

Caller	Conversation
19 (Sergeant C. B. OWENS)	Yes.
Dispatcher (HULSE and MC DANIEL)	10-4. 2:02.
91 (Patrolmen W. D. MENTZEL and J. W. COURSON)	91 (MENTZEL and COURSON), I locked up one car but the other one's still running back there.
211 (Patrolman R. HAWKINS)	211 (HAWKINS).
Dispatcher (HULSE and MC DANIEL)	211 (HAWKINS).
211 (Patrolman R. HAWKINS)	That's mine. We're getting in it now. We're going to head for City Hall; they've got my handcuffs.
Dispatcher (HULSE and MC DANIEL)	10-4.
Unknown	Are they checking that train?
Dispatcher (MC DANIEL)	Yes, (garbled) other units got it.
474A (Special Service Bureau)	474A (Special Service Bureau)
Dispatcher (HULSE and MC DANIEL)	474A (Special Service Bureau)
474A (Special Service Bureau)	We need one wrecker on the parking lot just west of Cobb Stadium for suspect's car.
Dispatcher (HULSE and MC DANIEL)	10-4, 474A (Special Service Bureau), 2:04.

- 99 -

COMMISSION EXHIBIT No. 1974—Continued

Re: ASSASSINATION OF PRESIDENT
JOHN FITZGERALD KENNEDY,
NOVEMBER 22, 1963, DALLAS, TEXAS

Caller	Conversation
Dispatcher (HULSE and MC DANIEL)	29 (Patrolman J. WILLIAMS).
29 (Patrolman J. WILLIAMS)	Go ahead.
Dispatcher (HULSE and MC DANIEL)	Report to Parkland, entrance to Parkland, Code 2 (Urgent - red lights and siren as needed.)
29 (Patrolman J. WILLIAMS)	To Parkland, Code 2 (Urgent - red lights and siren as needed.)
Dispatcher (HULSE and MC DANIEL)	99 (Patrolman S. E. NORMAN).
99 (Patrolman S. E. NORMAN)	99 (NORMAN).
Dispatcher (HULSE and MC DANIEL)	Report to Parkland entrance, Code 2 (Urgent - red lights and siren as needed.)
99 (Patrolman S. E. NORMAN)	10-4.
509 (Crime Laboratory)	509 (Crime Laboratory).
Dispatcher (HULSE and MC DANIEL)	509 (Crime Laboratory).
509 (Crime Laboratory)	I'm clear here from Patton and 10th, I'm Code 5 (en route) at the Texas Theatre.
Dispatcher (HULSE and MC DANIEL)	505 (Crime Laboratory) went to the Texas Theatre, 509 (Crime Laboratory), just go ahead and clear. 2:04.
75 (Patrolman E. G. SEBASTIAN)	75 (SEBASTIAN).
Dispatcher (HULSE and MC DANIEL)	75 (SEBASTIAN).

- 100 -

COMMISSION EXHIBIT No. 1974—Continued

Re: ASSASSINATION OF PRESIDENT
JOHN FITZGERALD KENNEDY,
NOVEMBER 22, 1963, DALLAS, TEXAS

Caller	Conversation
75 (Patrolman E. G. SEBASTIAN)	I'm still in front of the theatre if anybody wants anybody over here.
Dispatcher (HULSE)	10-4.
49 (Patrolman C. R. GILBREATH)	49 (GILBREATH).
Dispatcher (HULSE and MC DANIEL)	49 (GILBREATH).
49 (GILBREATH)	I'm Code 5 (en route) to Elm and Houston from the City Hall.
Dispatcher (HULSE and MC DANIEL)	10-4.
447 (Special Service Bureau)	447 (Special Service Bureau).
Dispatcher (HULSE and MC DANIEL)	447 (Special Service Bureau).
447 (Special Service Bureau)	See if 3 (Deputy Chief M. W. STEVENSON) is back on the air.
Dispatcher (HULSE and MC DANIEL)	3 (STEVENSON)... (2:08 p.m.)
Dispatcher (HULSE and MC DANIEL)	3 (STEVENSON)
606 (Ambulance)	606 (Ambulance).
Dispatcher (HULSE and MC DANIEL)	606 (Ambulance).
606 (Ambulance)	We're instructed here at Parkland to clear through you to get us cleared through Love Field Area. We have a coach for the casket.
2 (Assistant Chief CHARLES BATCHELOR)	2 (BATCHELOR).

COMMISSION EXHIBIT No. 1974—Continued

Re: ASSASSINATION OF PRESIDENT
JOHN FITZGERALD KENNEDY,
NOVEMBER 22, 1963, DALLAS, TEXAS

Caller	Conversation
Dispatcher (HULSE and MC DANIEL)	2 (Assistant Chief CHARLES BATCHELOR).
2 (BATCHELOR)	Notify the escort that's clear of the convoy on Hines Boulevard to drop back and pick up the bus.
Dispatcher (HULSE and MC DANIEL)	Which....
153 (Patrolman J. W. COURSON)	153 (COURSON), I'm the last motorcycle. What did you want?
Dispatcher (HULSE and MC DANIEL)	Wants you to drop back and pick up the bus.
153 (Patrolman J. W. COURSON)	10-4.
153 (Patrolman J. W. COURSON)	Has that bus left yet or is it still at Parkland?
Dispatcher (HULSE and MC DANIEL)	2 (Assistant Chief CHARLES BATCHELOR).
2 (BATCHELOR)	It's still at Parkland. Go back and get it.
53 (Patrolman J. W. COURSON)	10-4. (2:10 p.m.)
305 (Homicide)	305 (Homicide).
Dispatcher (HULSE and MC DANIEL)	305 (Homicide).
305 (Homicide)	Check with my office and see if they need me now or want me to go back to Elm and Houston.

COMMISSION EXHIBIT No. 1974—Continued

Re: ASSASSINATION OF PRESIDENT
JOHN FITZGERALD KENNEDY,
NOVEMBER 22, 1963, DALLAS, TEXAS

Caller	Conversation
Dispatcher (HULSE)	10-4, 305 (Homicide).
447 (Special Service Bureau)	447 (Special Service Bureau).
Dispatcher (HULSE and MC DANIEL)	447 (Special Service Bureau).
447 (Special Service Bureau)	See if any squad on the air knows whereabouts of Lieutenant WALLACE, if they took him to the Trade Mart building.
Dispatcher (HULSE and MC DANIEL)	443 (Lieutenant WALLACE).
Dispatcher (HULSE and MC DANIEL)	447 (Special Service Bureau).
447 (Special Service Bureau)	All right.
Dispatcher (HULSE and MC DANIEL)	447 (Special Service Bureau), repeat your transmission.
447 (Special Service Bureau)	I would like to contact any squad that took Lieutenant WALLACE from the Trade Mart building.
Dispatcher (HULSE and MC DANIEL)	305 (Homicide).(Detectives J.R. LEAVELLE, E.R. BECK and J.R. BOYCE)
305 (Homicide)(Detectives LEAVELLE, BECK and BOYCE)	305 (Homicide). (Detectives LEAVELLE, BECK and BOYCE)
Dispatcher (HULSE and MC DANIEL)	305 (Homicide), return to your office. Any squad knowing 443's (Lieutenant WALLACE) whereabouts, acknowledge.
Unknown	Who is 443 (Lieutenant WALLACE)?
Dispatcher (HULSE and MC DANIEL)	Lieutenant WALLACE.

- 103 -

COMMISSION EXHIBIT No. 1974—Continued

Re: ASSASSINATION OF PRESIDENT
JOHN FITZGERALD KENNEDY,
NOVEMBER 22, 1963, DALLAS, TEXAS

Caller	Conversation
Unknown	He's out at the theatre.
153 (Patrolman J. W. COURSON)	153 (COURSON).
Dispatcher (HULSE and MC DANIEL)	153 (COURSON).
153 (COURSON)	Is 2 (Assistant Chief CHARLES BATCHELOR) on the air?
2 (Assistant Chief CHARLES BATCHELOR)	2 (BATCHELOR).
153 (Patrolman J. W. COURSON)	This bus is empty here behind Parkland at the emergency entrance. He said he didn't have anyone to go out there.
384 (Unknown)	384 (Unknown)
Dispatcher (HULSE and MC DANIEL)	384 (Unknown).
384 (Unknown)	Lieutenant WALLACE is at the Sheriff's Office.
Dispatcher (HULSE and MC DANIEL)	10-4, 447 (Special Service Bureau), 443's (Lieutenant WALLACE) is at the Sheriff's Office.
447 (Special Service Bureau)	All right; that's 433 (Lieutenant WALLACE).
Dispatcher (HULSE and MC DANIEL)	2 (Assistant Chief CHARLES BATCHELOR).
2 (Assistant Chief CHARLES BATCHELOR)	The motorcycle officer at Parkland - tell him to stay with that bus until he's ready to go.

- 104 -

COMMISSION EXHIBIT No. 1974—Continued

Re: ASSASSINATION OF PRESIDENT
JOHN FITZGERALD KENNEDY,
NOVEMBER 22, 1963, DALLAS, TEXAS

Caller	Conversation
153 (Patrolman J. W. COURSON)	10-4. (2:13 p.m.)
606 (Ambulance)	606 (Ambulance).
Dispatcher (MC DANIEL)	606 (Ambulance).
606 (Ambulance)	Do you have any idea where this casket coach is that we're supposed to get.
Dispatcher (MC DANIEL)	606 (Ambulance).
606 (Ambulance)	606 (Ambulance).
Dispatcher (MC DANIEL)	Was it supposed to be at Love Field?
606 (Ambulance)	10-4. We're approaching Air Cargo now. An officer out at Parkland told us to contact you and have 39 (BUTCHER and COMER) meet us.
Dispatcher (MC DANIEL)	10-4, stand by.
Dispatcher (HULSE and MC DANIEL)	509 (Crime Laboratory) or 507 (Crime Laboratory)
Dispatcher (HULSE and MC DANIEL)	505 (Captain G. M. DOUGHTY)
15 (Captain C. E. TALBERT)	15 (TALBERT) is out at Methodist.
Dispatcher (HULSE and MC DANIEL)	Received 15 (TALBERT), 2:16.
Dispatcher (HULSE and MC DANIEL)	509 (Crime Laboratory) or 507 (Crime Laboratory)

Re: ASSASSINATION OF PRESIDENT
JOHN FITZGERALD KENNEDY,
NOVEMBER 22, 1963, DALLAS, TEXAS

Caller	Conversation
Dispatcher (HULSE and MC DANIEL)	469 (Special Service Bureau), call your office.
153 (Patrolman J. W. COURSON)	153 (COURSON).
Dispatcher (HULSE and MC DANIEL)	153 (COURSON).
(End of Belt Eight)	
153 (Patrolman J. W. COURSON)	On this bus I am staying with there is a lot of equipment; typewriter, suitcases and such on this bus - in case they want to get it to the airplane.
Dispatcher (HULSE and MC DANIEL)	41 (Patrolman T. R. BURTON) and 45 (Patrolman N. L. STANGLIN), report to 5818 Belmont - have information that person just out of a car with a rifle at this location, 2:19.
41 (Patrolman T. R. BURTON)	10-4.
45 (Patrolman N. L. STANGLIN)	10-4.
47 (Patrolman W. F. MORRIS)	What is the address, I'll go over there, too?
Dispatcher (HULSE and MC DANIEL)	5818 Belmont.
47 (Patrolman W. F. MORRIS)	10-4.
41 (Patrolman T. R. BURTON)	41 (BURTON).
Dispatcher (HULSE and MC DANIEL)	41 (BURTON).

Re: ASSASSINATION OF PRESIDENT
JOHN FITZGERALD KENNEDY,
NOVEMBER 22, 1963, DALLAS, TEXAS

Caller	Conversation
41 (Patrolman T. R. BURTON)	I am down town - do you want 47 (Patrolman W. F. MORRIS) to handle my end?
Dispatcher (HULSE and MC DANIEL)	Yes, continue in that direction.
320 (Auto Theft)	320 (Auto Theft).
Dispatcher (HULSE and MC DANIEL)	320 (Auto Theft).
320 (Auto Theft)	The subject in this car on Field, what is he supposed to have?
Dispatcher (HULSE and MC DANIEL)	Unknown, 320 (Auto Theft), just a white male, 20, signal 32 (suspicious person).
320 (Auto Theft)	10-4.
Dispatcher (HULSE and MC DANIEL)	45 (Patrolman N. L. STANGLIN) and 47 (Patrolman W. F. MORRIS) for your information; reported to have gotten out of a light green, two-tone car and went into 5818 Belmont, this apartment house.
45 (Patrolman N. L. STANGLIN)	Received.
47 (Patrolman W. F. MORRIS)	Received.
Dispatcher (HULSE and MC DANIEL)	474A (Special Service Bureau).
474A (Special Service Bureau)	474A (Special Service Bureau).

- 107 -

COMMISSION EXHIBIT No. 1974—Continued

Re: ASSASSINATION OF PRESIDENT
JOHN FITZGERALD KENNEDY,
NOVEMBER 22, 1963, DALLAS, TEXAS

Caller	Conversation
Dispatcher (HULSE and MC DANIEL)	474A (Special Service Bureau), there is a subject on this overpass carrying a rifle; railroad tracks, Cobb Stadium. Can you see him?
474A (Special Service Bureau)	No, we can't see from here, but we'll go over and get him.
Dispatcher (HULSE and MC DANIEL)	10-4.
113 (Patrolman C. R. OSBURN)	113 (OSBURN).
Dispatcher (HULSE and MC DANIEL)	113 (OSBURN).
113 (Patrolman C. R. OSBURN)	I have Third Platoon Officer, JOE B. JONES, with me. We are to remain out on special assignment from Elm and Houston to "The Dallas Morning News" with Mr. SORRELS of the Secret Service.
Dispatcher (HULSE and MC DANIEL)	10-4, 113 (Patrolman C. R. OSBURN). 2:21.
320 (Auto Theft)	320 (Auto Theft).
Dispatcher (HULSE and MC DANIEL)	320 (Auto Theft).
320 (Auto Theft)	All clear 100 North Field.
Dispatcher (HULSE and MC DANIEL)	10-4. 105 (Patrolmen J. M. POE and L. E. JEZ), disregard.
48 (Patrolman A. D. DUNCAN)	48 (DUNCAN) clear.

- 108 -

COMMISSION EXHIBIT No. 1974—Continued

Re: ASSASSINATION OF PRESIDENT
JOHN FITZGERALD KENNEDY,
NOVEMBER 22, 1963, DALLAS, TEXAS

Caller	Conversation
Dispatcher (HULSE and MC DANIEL)	48 (Patrolman A. D. DUNCAN) clear, 2:23.
Dispatcher (HULSE and MC DANIEL)	22 (Patrolman L. L. HILL).
22 (Patrolman L. L. HILL)	22 (HILL).
Dispatcher (HULSE and MC DANIEL)	22 (HILL), go out toward Cobb Stadium on the railroad track overpass. There is a white male carrying a rifle. Meet 474A (Special Service Bureau) at that location.
22 (HILL)	10-4.
105 (Patrolmen J. M. POE and L. E. JEZ)	Clear 2:24 p.m.
16 (Sergeant R. D. SHIPLEY)	16 (SHIPLEY).
Dispatcher (HULSE and MC DANIEL)	16 (SHIPLEY).
16 (SHIPLEY)	Will be out 5818 Belmont. For your information, the light green car, License Number RB8950, and a light colored Falcon NX3171 is sitting at the location.
Dispatcher (HULSE and MC DANIEL)	10-4.
Dispatcher (HULSE and MC DANIEL)	Any unit at the Texas Theatre.
75 (Patrolman E. G. SEBASTIAN)	75 (SEBASTIAN) just left.

- 109 -

COMMISSION EXHIBIT No. 1974—Continued

Re: ASSASSINATION OF PRESIDENT
JOHN FITZGERALD KENNEDY,
NOVEMBER 22, 1963, DALLAS, TEXAS

Caller	Conversation
Dispatcher (HULSE and MC DANIEL)	75 (Patrolman E. G. SEBASTIAN) and 69 (Patrolman A. R. BROCK), return back to the location. They want the theatre shaken down good for two hulls. Believe the subject reloaded his pistol in the theatre. We need the two hulls, 2:26.
75 (Patrolman E. G. SEBASTIAN)	10-4.
105 (Patrolmen J. M. POE and L. E. JEZ)	105 (POE and JEZ).
Dispatcher (HULSE and MC DANIEL)	105 (POE and JEZ).
105 (POE and JEZ)	105 (POE and JEZ), I have recovered two hulls at the scene and they were turned over to the Crime Lab to PETE BARNES.
Dispatcher (HULSE and MC DANIEL)	Received.
79 (Patrolman B. W. ANGLIN)	79 (ANGLIN).
Dispatcher (HULSE and MC DANIEL)	79 (ANGLIN).
79 (Patrolman B. W. ANGLIN)	Do you still need the theatre shook down?
Dispatcher (HULSE and MC DANIEL)	Disregard at this time. 2:26.
41 (Patrolman T. R. BURTON)	41 (BURTON) out at 5818 Belmont.
Dispatcher (HULSE and MC DANIEL)	2:26.

- 110 -

COMMISSION EXHIBIT No. 1974—Continued

Re: ASSASSINATION OF PRESIDENT
JOHN FITZGERALD KENNEDY,
NOVEMBER 22, 1963, DALLAS, TEXAS

Caller	Conversation
562 (Wrecker)	562 (Wrecker).
Dispatcher (HULSE and MC DANIEL)	562 (Wrecker).
562 (Wrecker)	I'll be down here at Cobb Stadium Parking Lot for that suspect's car.
Dispatcher (HULSE and MC DANIEL)	Stand by there, 562 (Wrecker). 474A (Special Service Bureau) will be back in a minute.
562 (Wrecker)	10-4, thank you.
Dispatcher (HULSE and MC DANIEL)	75 (Patrolman E. G. SEBASTIAN) and 69 (A. R. BROCK) disregard, return to service. 2:27.
75 (SEBASTIAN)	Clear.
69 (BROCK)	Clear.
52 (Unknown)	52 (Unknown).
Dispatcher (HULSE and MC DANIEL)	52 (Unknown).
52 (Unknown)	In regard to suspect, the T. C. Cobb Stadium; was it the Hines Overpass, the railroad overpass or the freeway overpass?
Dispatcher (HULSE and MC DANIEL)	He is walking on the (someone cut in, unable to read).
52 (Unknown)	10-4. Was that north or southbound, or do you know?

- 111 -

COMMISSION EXHIBIT No. 1974—Continued

Re: ASSASSINATION OF PRESIDENT
JOHN FITZGERALD KENNEDY,
NOVEMBER 22, 1963, DALLAS, TEXAS

Caller	Conversation
Dispatcher (HULSE and MC DANIEL)	Unknown.
52 (Unknown)	10-4.
607 (Ambulance)	607 (Ambulance) Code 5 (en route) Baylor.
Dispatcher (HULSE and MC DANIEL)	10-4, 2:28.
Dispatcher (HULSE and MC DANIEL)	474A (Special Service Bureau).
474A (Special Service Bureau)	474A (Special Service Bureau).
Dispatcher (HULSE and MC DANIEL)	That wrecker's down there on the Cobb Stadium parking lot.
474A (Special Service Bureau)	We will meet him there.
22 (Patrolman L. L. HILL)	22 (Patrolman L. L. HILL).
Dispatcher (HULSE and MC DANIEL)	22 (Patrolman L. L. HILL).
22 (Patrolman L. L. HILL)	I am here with him looking at the car.
Dispatcher (HULSE and MC DANIEL)	474A (Special Service Bureau), 22 (Patrolman L. L. HILL) is with the wrecker at this time.
474A (Special Service Bureau)	The car that we want picked up is on the parking lot in front of the Merchandise Mart just north of Cobb Stadium. Will meet him there and take him to it.
22 (Patrolman L. L. HILL)	Is it a 1964 Falcon?

- 112 -

COMMISSION EXHIBIT No. 1974—Continued

Re: ASSASSINATION OF PRESIDENT
JOHN FITZGERALD KENNEDY,
NOVEMBER 22, 1963, DALLAS, TEXAS

Caller	Conversation
474A (Special Service Bureau)	No, it is a red panel truck with writing on the side.
79 (Patrolman B. W. ANGLIN)	79 (ANGLIN).
Dispatcher (HULSE and MC DANIEL)	79 (ANGLIN), Code 4 (disregard) - your call; Code 3 (Emergency - red lights and sirens) - to the officer's house that was shot, 2:29.
79 (Patrolman B. W. ANGLIN)	10-4.
Dispatcher (HULSE and MC DANIEL)	474A (Special Service Bureau)
474A (Special Service Bureau)	474A (Special Service Bureau)
Dispatcher (HULSE and MC DANIEL)	The license number on the car you are picking up?
474A (Special Service Bureau)	Stand by.
474A (Special Service Bureau)	474A (Special Service Bureau)
Dispatcher (HULSE and MC DANIEL)	Go ahead.
474A (Special Service Bureau)	The license is 3E9087.
Dispatcher (HULSE and MC DANIEL)	10-4.
Dispatcher (HULSE and MC DANIEL)	Attention all squads in the Oak Cliff area - pick up for investigation of a CCW (carrying a concealed weapon), the occupants of a 1957 Chevrolet sedan bearing License

COMMISSION EXHIBIT No. 1974—Continued

Re: ASSASSINATION OF PRESIDENT
JOHN FITZGERALD KENNEDY,
NOVEMBER 22, 1963, DALLAS, TEXAS

Caller	Conversation
	Number NA4445 last seen in vicinity Tenth and Jefferson, 2:33. (Repeats message.)
Dispatcher (HULSE and MC DANIEL)	Any unit near the Texas Theatre?
75 (Patrolman E. G. SEBASTIAN)	75's (SEBASTIAN) at Young and Houston.
Dispatcher (HULSE and MC DANIEL)	75 (SEBASTIAN), report back to the Texas Theatre and call Operator 10 on a mark out, 2:33.
75 (Patrolman E. G. SEBASTIAN)	10-4.
599 (Cockrell Hill Squad)	599 (Cockrell Hill Squad).
Dispatcher (HULSE and MC DANIEL)	599 (Cockrell Hill Squad).
599 (Cockrell Hill Squad)	599 (Cockrell Hill Squad), was that a 1957 Chevrolet converti-ble?
Dispatcher (HULSE and MC DANIEL)	Unknown.
599 (Cockrell Hill Squad)	10-4.
79 (P trolman B. W. ANGLIN)	79 (ANGLIN).
Dispatcher (HULSE and MC DANIEL)	79 (ANGLIN).
79 (Patrolman B. W. ANGLIN)	Any further instructions at the location of the officer's house?
Dispatcher (HULSE and MC DANIEL)	No, 79 (ANGLIN), just go on out, and we have another officer's wife en route.

COMMISSION EXHIBIT No. 1974—Continued

Re: ASSASSINATION OF PRESIDENT
JOHN FITZGERALD KENNEDY,
NOVEMBER 22, 1963, DALLAS, TEXAS

Caller	Conversation
79 (Patrolman B. W. ANGLIN)	10-4.
111/2 (Unknown)	111/2 (Unknown).
Dispatcher (HULSE and MC DANIEL)	111/2 (Unknown).
111/2 (Unknown)	This is the officer assigned from 511 working communications center from the White House at the Sheraton. I have an escort going to Love Field and need 39 (BUTCHER and COMER) to pick me up at the entrance and escort me to the Presidential plane.
Dispatcher (HULSE and MC DANIEL)	Any unit at Love Field...
111/2 (Unknown)	111/2 (Unknown).
Dispatcher (HULSE and MC DANIEL)	111/2 (Unknown).
111/2 (Unknown)	Did you get me some help out there?
Dispatcher (HULSE and MC DANIEL)	Stand by 111/2.
111/2 (Unknown)	I'll be using this car for emergency runs possibly throughout the rest of the evening. Shall I use that call number?
Dispatcher (HULSE and MC DANIEL)	111/2 they are standing by for your arrival.

COMMISSION EXHIBIT No. 1974—Continued

Re: ASSASSINATION OF PRESIDENT
JOHN FITZGERALD KENNEDY,
NOVEMBER 22, 1963, DALLAS, TEXAS

Caller	Conversation
	(Garbled transmission.) (2:48)
(End of Belt Nine)	
9 (Inspector J. H. SAWYER)	9 (SAWYER)
Dispatcher (HULSE and MC DANIEL)	Go ahead, 9 (SAWYER).
9 (Inspector J. H. SAWYER)	We've got about forty men down here and most of them got off between 1:00, 2:00 and 3:00. I am wondering if we are going to be able to get relief for some of these men or whether we're going to have to work them on through overtime. Can you check for me?
	(No other pertinent transmissions through 3:00 P.M.)

Channel 1, 10:00 A.M. - 2:00 P.M., Sunday, November 24, 1963

Caller	Conversation
128 (Lieutenant W. F. SOUTHARD)	128 (SOUTHARD).
Dispatcher (B. R. GRAMMER)	128 (SOUTHARD).
128 (SOUTHARD)	Contact Sergeant YOUNG on 515 (telephone extension in Police Department); advise him to contact all the three wheelers and all the point control men that are due on at 2:00 p.m. and

COMMISSION EXHIBIT No. 1974—Continued

Re: ASSASSINATION OF PRESIDENT
JOHN FITZGERALD KENNEDY,
NOVEMBER 22, 1963, DALLAS, TEXAS

Caller	Conversation
	have them to report to Elm and Houston at noon.
Dispatcher (GRAMMER)	10-4. (10:00 a.m.)
125 (Captain P. W. LAWRENCE)	125 (LAWRENCE).
Dispatcher (GRAMMER)	125 (LAWRENCE).
125 (LAWRENCE)	Contact the assembly room and ask them to send out about five more reserves to the Command Post at Elm and Houston.
Dispatcher (GRAMMER)	Message received, 10:02 A.M.
Dispatcher (GRAMMER)	103 (Patrolman J. M. VALENTINE)
103 (Patrolman J. M. VALENTINE)	Go ahead.
Dispatcher (GRAMMER)	Report to the basement to transport reserves to Elm and Houston Command Post.
103 (VALENTINE)	10-4. (10:03 a.m.)
103 (VALENTINE)	103 (VALENTINE) clear.
Dispatcher (GRAMMER)	103 (VALENTINE) clear, 10:13.
111 (Patrolman G. K. SPRINGER)	111 (SPRINGER).
111 (SPRINGER)	Did you know there is additional messages going to the TIPPITS or did he want me to go back there after I deliver these?

- 117 -

COMMISSION EXHIBIT No. 1974—Continued

Re: ASSASSINATION OF PRESIDENT
JOHN FITZGERALD KENNEDY,
NOVEMBER 22, 1963, DALLAS, TEXAS

Caller	Conversation
Dispatcher (M. J. JACKSON and C. E. HULSE)	Go back to the office now.
111 (Patrolman G. K. SPRINGER)	Now?
Dispatcher (JACKSON and HULSE)	Yes.
111 (SPRINGER)	10-4. (10:29 a.m.)
39 (Patrolmen C. W. COMER and J. F. BUTCHER)	39 (COMER and BUTCHER) out at the terminal.
Dispatcher (JACKSON and HULSE)	39 (COMER and BUTCHER) out at 10:30 a.m. KKB 364.
	(Various units check in and out - routine messages.)
(End of Belt One) (10:36 a.m.)	
602 (Ambulance)	602 (Ambulance) clear, 11:19.
Dispatcher (JACKSON and HULSE)	(Garbled transmission) report to the Basement Code 3 (Emergency - red lights and sirens). 108 (Patrolman R. J. ROSS) is en route.
Dispatcher (JACKSON and HULSE)	10-4, 108 (Patrolman R. J. ROSS). 118 (Patrolman V. O'DELL).
Dispatcher (JACKSON and HULSE)	118 (Patrolman V. O'DELL).
118 (Patrolman V. O'DELL)	118 (O'DELL).

- 118 -

COMMISSION EXHIBIT No. 1974—Continued

Re: ASSASSINATION OF PRESIDENT
JOHN FITZGERALD KENNEDY,
NOVEMBER 22, 1963, DALLAS, TEXAS

Caller	Conversation
Dispatcher (JACKSON and HULSE)	Code 3 (Emergency - red lights and sirens) report to basement.
118 (Patrolman V. O'DELL)	10-4.
Dispatcher (JACKSON and HULSE)	95 (Patrolman C. W. HARRISON), Code 3 (Emergency - red lights and sirens) to basement.
95 (Patrolman C. W. HARRISON)	En route.
Dispatcher (JACKSON and HULSE)	605 (Ambulance).
605 (Ambulance)	605 (Ambulance).
Dispatcher (JACKSON and HULSE)	Code 3 (Emergency - red lights and sirens) report to basement, City Hall.
605 (Ambulance)	10-4.
126 (Captain THOMPSON)	Anybody else?
Dispatcher (JACKSON and HULSE)	No, that's all.
61 (Patrolman G. W. TEMPLE)	61 (TEMPLE) clear.
Dispatcher (JACKSON and HULSE)	61 (TEMPLE) clear, 11:21.
Dispatcher (JACKSON and HULSE)	(Unknown) - clear, remain on air, do not check out on traffic or any other violations unless it's an emergency, 11:22 a.m.
Unknown	Need anybody else down in the basement?

- 119 -

COMMISSION EXHIBIT No. 1974—Continued

Re: ASSASSINATION OF PRESIDENT
JOHN FITZGERALD KENNEDY,
NOVEMBER 22, 1963, DALLAS, TEXAS

Caller	Conversation
Dispatcher (JACKSON and HULSE)	No.
Unknown	All right.
115 (Patrolman J. G. POLLARD)	115 (POLLARD).
Dispatcher (JACKSON and HULSE)	115 (POLLARD).
115 (POLLARD)	I'm clear. What was that message?
Dispatcher (JACKSON and HULSE)	Do not check out on traffic; just stay in service.
115 (POLLARD)	10-4.
Dispatcher (JACKSON and HULSE)	Unless it is an emergency.
Unknown	What is the nature.
Dispatcher (JACKSON and HULSE)	It's a shooting.
Unknown	Is anybody on 2?
Dispatcher (JACKSON and HULSE)	Go ahead.
Dispatcher (JACKSON and HULSE)	607 (Ambulance) (11:24)
Dispatcher (JACKSON and HULSE)	607 (Ambulance)
605 (Ambulance)	605 (Ambulance)
Dispatcher (JACKSON and HULSE)	Location?
605 (Ambulance)	(Sounded like) Ross and Field now. (Siren very loud.)

- 120 -

COMMISSION EXHIBIT No. 1974—Continued

Re: ASSASSINATION OF PRESIDENT
JOHN FITZGERALD KENNEDY,
NOVEMBER 22, 1963, DALLAS, TEXAS

Caller	Conversation
607 (Ambulance)	607 (Ambulance), Code 5 (en route).
Dispatcher (JACKSON and HULSE)	10-4, 607 (Ambulance), what is your destination?
607 (Ambulance)	(Sounded like City Jail.)
Dispatcher (JACKSON and HULSE)	Code 4 (disregard), 605 (Ambulance) is at location.
Dispatcher (JACKSON and HULSE)	108 (Patrolman R. J. ROSS) 118 (Patrolman V. O'DELL) or 95 (Patrolman C. W. HARRISON)
Unknown	Go ahead.
Dispatcher (JACKSON and HULSE)	108 (Patrolman R. J. ROSS) 118 (Patrolman V. O'DELL) or 95 (Patrolman C. W. HARRISON); the first squad to arrive - stand by your radio so we will have radio contact with the basement.
Unknown	10-4, out City Hall. (Sounds like 95, Patrolman C. W. HARRISON).
63 (Patrolman C. F. BENTLEY)	63 (BENTLEY).
Dispatcher (JACKSON and HULSE)	63 (BENTLEY).
63 (BENTLEY)	I'm Code 6. (Out at destination.) What do you need?
Dispatcher (JACKSON and HULSE)	Remain by your radio, 63 (BENTLEY), so we will have radio contact.

COMMISSION EXHIBIT No. 1974—Continued

Re: ASSASSINATION OF PRESIDENT
JOHN FITZGERALD KENNEDY,
NOVEMBER 22, 1963, DALLAS, TEXAS

Caller	Conversation
63 (Patrolman C. F. BENTLEY)	10-4.
83 (Patrolman R. L. CROSS)	83 (CROSS).
Dispatcher (JACKSON and HULSE)	83 (CROSS).
83 (CROSS)	Do you have suspect or do you have description?
Dispatcher (JACKSON and HULSE)	unknown, 83 (CROSS).
118 (Patrolman V. O'DELL)	118 (O'DELL).
Dispatcher (JACKSON and HULSE)	118 (O'DELL).
118 (O'DELL)	I'm right behind the ambulance. do you want me to follow him out?
Dispatcher (JACKSON and HULSE)	Is there anybody in the ambulance with him?
118 (O'DELL)	What's that?
Dispatcher (JACKSON and HULSE)	Is there anyone in the ambulance with him?
118 (O'DELL)	I'm sure they are. There is a crowd in front of me.
Dispatcher (JACKSON and HULSE)	No. Disregard. Remain around the City Hall.
118 (O'DELL)	10-4. (11:26 a.m.)
118 (O'DELL)	118 (O'DELL).

COMMISSION EXHIBIT No. 1974—Continued

Re: ASSASSINATION OF PRESIDENT
JOHN FITZGERALD KENNEDY,
NOVEMBER 22, 1963, DALLAS, TEXAS

Caller	Conversation
Dispatcher (JACKSON and HULSE)	118 (Patrolman V. O'DELL).
118 (O'DELL)	They pushed me out of the basement behind the ambulance.
Dispatcher (JACKSON and HULSE)	118 (O'DELL), 10-4.
118 (O'DELL)	I'll be with it.
Dispatcher (JACKSON and HULSE)	10-4.
43 (Patrolman W. E. HIBBS)	43 (HIBBS).
Dispatcher (JACKSON and HULSE)	43 (HIBBS).
43 (HIBBS) —	What are these patrolmen supposed to be working, this traffic on Main or on Elm rather?
Dispatcher (JACKSON and HULSE)	No instructions at this time, 43 (HIBBS).
43 (HIBBS)	10-4. (11:26 a.m.)
63 (Patrolman C. F. BENTLEY)	63 (BENTLEY).
Dispatcher (JACKSON and HULSE)	68 (meant 63, Patrolman C. F. BENTLEY).
63 (Patrolman C. F. BENTLEY)	63 (BENTLEY).
Dispatcher (JACKSON and HULSE)	63 (BENTLEY).
63 (BENTLEY)	Is that one man squad with that ambulance?

COMMISSION EXHIBIT No. 1974—Continued

Re: ASSASSINATION OF PRESIDENT
JOHN FITZGERALD KENNEDY,
NOVEMBER 22, 1963, DALLAS, TEXAS

Caller	Conversation
Dispatcher (JACKSON and HULSE)	Yes.
63 (Patrolman C. F. BENTLEY)	10-4. I'm gonna be code 5 (en route); I'm out.
Dispatcher (JACKSON and HULSE)	10-4.
20 (Patrolman S. W. BURKHART)	Where they going?
Dispatcher (JACKSON and HULSE)	Parkland.
20 (BURKHART)	I'll be out there.
Dispatcher (JACKSON and HULSE)	10-4, 20 (BURKHART), 11:27.
231 (Patrolman R. D. WILSON)	231 (WILSON).
Dispatcher (JACKSON and HULSE)	231 (WILSON).
231 (Patrolman R. D. WILSON)	We are in bad need of a traffic officer Commerce and Harwood. I'll be out.
Dispatcher (JACKSON and HULSE)	10-4.
18 (Lieutenant R. S. PIERCE)	18 (PIERCE).
Dispatcher (JACKSON and HULSE)	18 (PIERCE).
18 (PIERCE)	We will be Code 5 (en route) Parkland.
Dispatcher (JACKSON and HULSE)	10-4, 18 (PIERCE).
113 (Patrolman C. R. ORSBURN)	Clear.

COMMISSION EXHIBIT No. 1974—Continued

Re: ASSASSINATION OF PRESIDENT
JOHN FITZGERALD KENNEDY,
NOVEMBER 22, 1963, DALLAS, TEXAS

Caller	Conversation
Dispatcher (JACKSON and HULSE)	113 (Patrolman C. R. ORSBURN) clear, 11:27.
23 (Patrolman K. K. ANDERSON)	23 (ANDERSON).
Dispatcher (JACKSON and HULSE)	23 (ANDERSON).
23 (ANDERSON)	See if you can find out if we are supposed to be on our stations on Elm Street.
Dispatcher (JACKSON and HULSE)	Yes, until further notified.
108 (Patrolman R. J. ROSS)	108 (ROSS).
Dispatcher (JACKSON and HULSE)	108 (ROSS).
108 (ROSS)	I'm down here in the basement. I can't get through into the garage down here for all these newsmen and everything so I'm just going to block the driveway.
Dispatcher (JACKSON and HULSE)	10-4.
211 (Patrolman R. C. SEIDMEYER)	Clear.
Dispatcher (JACKSON and HULSE)	211 (SEIDMEYER) clear, 11:28.
Unknown	Did they get the suspect?
Dispatcher (JACKSON and HULSE)	Unknown.
232 (Patrolman J. W. LOVING)	232 (LOVING) clear.

COMMISSION EXHIBIT No. 1974—Continued

Re: ASSASSINATION OF PRESIDENT
JOHN FITZGERALD KENNEDY,
NOVEMBER 22, 1963, DALLAS, TEXAS

Caller	Conversation
Dispatcher (JACKSON and HULSE)	232 (Patrolman J. W. LOVING).
232 (LOVING)	Disregard my Signal 5 (Mark out, coffee or to eat).
Dispatcher (JACKSON and HULSE)	10-4, 11:28 a.m.
19 (Patrolman D. F. STEELE)	19 (STEELE).
Dispatcher (JACKSON and HULSE)	19 (STEELE).
19 (STEELE)	Does 15 (Captain C. E. TALBERT) want me to report to Parkland?
Dispatcher (JACKSON and HULSE)	Stand by, we will notify you. 20 (Sergeant G. H. REED) is going to be at location. We will notify you.
(End of Belt Two) (11:30 a.m.)	
41 (Patrolman B. J. MC DONALD)	41 (MC DONALD).
Dispatcher (JACKSON and HULSE)	41 (MC DONALD).
41 (MC DONALD)	I have stopped a man out here on a traffic violation. He is the head X-ray technician. They give him an emergency call to report to Parkland. I'm going to escort him there, Code 3 (Emergency - red lights and sirens.)
Dispatcher (JACKSON and HULSE)	10-4.

COMMISSION EXHIBIT No. 1974—Continued

Re: ASSASSINATION OF PRESIDENT
JOHN FITZGERALD KENNEDY,
NOVEMBER 22, 1963, DALLAS, TEXAS

Caller	Conversation
605 (Ambulance)	Out Parkland. (11:31 a.m.)
48 (Patrolmen T. R. BURTON and D. K. ERWIN)	48 (BURTON and ERWIN).
Dispatcher (JACKSON and HULSE)	48 (BURTON and ERWIN).
48 (BURTON and ERWIN)	I 'm on a traffic assignment down here at Elm and Houston.
Dispatcher (JACKSON and HULSE)	Remain on your assignment until further notified, 48 (BURTON and ERWIN).
48 (BURTON and ERWIN)	10-4.
18 (Lieutenant R. S. PIERCE)	18 (PIERCE) to 19 (Patrolman D. F. STEELE)
19 (Patrolman D. F. STEELE)	Go ahead.
18 (PIERCE)	Send me two squads to Parkland; a total of four men.
19 (STEELE)	10-4.
19 (STEELE)	19 (STEELE) to 93 (Patrolman H. M. ASHCRAFT)
Dispatcher (JACKSON and HULSE)	He is on 511 (telephone extension in Police Department).
115 (Patrolman J. G. POLLARD)	115 (POLLARD) is close to Parkland.
Dispatcher (JACKSON and HULSE)	10-4.

COMMISSION EXHIBIT No. 1974—Continued

Re: ASSASSINATION OF PRESIDENT
JOHN FITZGERALD KENNEDY,
NOVEMBER 22, 1963, DALLAS, TEXAS

Caller	Conversation
19 (Patrolman D. F. STEELE)	Two-man, 115 (Patrolman J. G. POLLARD)?
115 (Patrolman J. G. POLLARD)	I'm close to Parkland. I'll be out here.
Dispatcher (JACKSON and HULSE)	24 (Patrolman T. E. LUNA).
24 (Patrolman T. E. LUNA)	10-4.
Dispatcher (JACKSON and HULSE)	24 (LUNA).
24 (LUNA)	Did you say go to Parkland?
Dispatcher (JACKSON and HULSE)	Yes, 24 (LUNA).
24 (LUNA)	I can't hear you. You are talking too low.
Dispatcher (JACKSON and HULSE)	53 (Patrolmen G. L. TOLBERT and M. E. FERRIS).
53 (Patrolmen G. L. TOLBERT and M. E. FERRIS)	53 (TOLBERT and FERRIS).
Dispatcher (JACKSON and HULSE)	You two-man, 53 (TOLBERT and FERRIS)?
53 (TOLBERT and FERRIS)	Yes, my partner Lamar and Elm.
Dispatcher (JACKSON and HULSE)	Pick him up and report to Parkland.
53 (TOLBERT and FERRIS)	10-4.
53 (TOLBERT and FERRIS)	53 (TOLBERT and FERRIS).

COMMISSION EXHIBIT No. 1974—Continued

Re: ASSASSINATION OF PRESIDENT
JOHN FITZGERALD KENNEDY,
NOVEMBER 22, 1963, DALLAS, TEXAS

Caller	Conversation
Dispatcher (FARR and B. D. HUFFSTUTLER)	53 (Patrolmen G. L. TOLBERT and M. E. FERRIS).
53 (TOLBERT and FERRIS)	What code?
Dispatcher (FARR and HUFFSTUTLER)	Code 3 (Emergency - red lights and sirens.)
53 (TOLBERT and FERRIS)	10-4.
17 (Lieutenant H. T. WOODALL)	17 (WOODALL).
Dispatcher (FARR and HUFFSTUTLER)	17 (WOODALL).
17 (WOODALL)	Out at Parkland.
Dispatcher (FARR and HUFFSTUTLER)	10-4.
Dispatcher (FARR and HUFFSTUTLER)	Attention all officers working the Elm Street assignment, all officers working the Elm Street assignment, leave your corners and report Code 2 (Urgent - red lights and siren as needed.) to Parkland Emergency and check out with the dispatcher, 11:36.
21 (Patrolman J. RAZ)	21 (RAZ) is en route.
Dispatcher (JACKSON and HULSE)	10-4, 21 (RAZ).
103 (Patrolman J. M. VALENTINE)	Clear. Where do you want me to go?
Dispatcher (JACKSON and HULSE)	Remain in service, 103 (VALENTINE).

COMMISSION EXHIBIT No. 1974—Continued

Re: ASSASSINATION OF PRESIDENT
JOHN FITZGERALD KENNEDY,
NOVEMBER 22, 1963, DALLAS, TEXAS

Caller	Conversation
97 (Patrolman L. L. FOX)	97 (FOX).
Dispatcher (JACKSON and HULSE)	97 (FOX).
97 (FOX)	Will be en route Parkland Emergency.
Dispatcher (JACKSON and HULSE)	10-4.
17 (Lieutenant H. T. WOODALL)	17 (WOODALL).
Dispatcher (FARR and HUFFSTUTLER)	17 (WOODALL).
17 (WOODALL)	Have a squad stop at the entrance to Parkland; there where you turn in; and cut traffic.
Dispatcher (FARR and HUFFSTUTLER)	Attention all squads reporting to Parkland, remain at the entrance to Parkland and cut the traffic. No traffic will be allowed in the emergency room unless it is an emergency. 11:37.
53 (Patrolmen G. L. TOLBERT and M. E. FERRIS)	53 (TOLBERT and FERRIS) en route.
Dispatcher (FARR and HUFFSTUTLER)	10-4, 53 (TOLBERT and FERRIS).
Dispatcher (FARR and HUFFSTUTLER)	Attention all officers working the Elm Street assignment, all officers working the Elm Street assignment,

COMMISSION EXHIBIT No. 1974—Continued

Re: ASSASSINATION OF PRESIDENT
JOHN FITZGERALD KENNEDY,
NOVEMBER 22, 1963, DALLAS, TEXAS

Caller	Conversation
	report to Parkland Emergency and cut the traffic at the emergency entrance, Code 2 (Urgent - red lights and siren as needed) 11:39.
53 (Patrolman G. L. TOBERT and M. E. FERRIS)	53 (TOLBERT and FERRIS) is out and got it out.
Dispatcher (FARR and HUFFSTUTLER)	10-4.
Dispatcher (FARR and HUFFSTUTLER)	Try to take charge there and get on Channel 2.
136 (Patrolman B. W. HARGIS)	136 (HARGIS).
Dispatcher (FARR and HUFFSTUTLER)	136 (HARGIS).
136 (HARGIS)	I'm here at Elm and Market. What did you say about people assigned to Elm?
Dispatcher (FARR and HUFFSTUTLER	Are you....Stand by, 136 (HARGIS). Are you on that assignment on Elm Street?
136 (HARGIS)	Elm and Market.
Dispatcher (FARR and HUFFSTUTLER)	You on your motor?
381 (Criminal Investigation Division)	381 (Criminal Investigation Division), Code 2 (Urgent - red lights and siren as needed) to Parkland.

- 131 -

COMMISSION EXHIBIT No. 1974—Continued

Re: ASSASSINATION OF PRESIDENT
JOHN FITZGERALD KENNEDY,
NOVEMBER 22, 1963, DALLAS, TEXAS

Caller	Conversation
Dispatcher (FARR and HUFFSTUTLER)	10-4, 381 (Criminal Investigation Division)
Dispatcher (FARR and HUFFSTUTLER)	136 (Patrolman B. W. HARGIS), report to Parkland.
136 (Patrolman B. W. HARGIS)	10-4. Emergency?
Dispatcher (FARR and HUFFSTUTLER)	Yes, to Parkland Emergency, at the entrance. (Garbled.)
23 (Patrolman K. K. ANDERSON)	23 (ANDERSON).
Dispatcher (FARR and HUFFSTUTLER)	23 (ANDERSON)
23 (ANDERSON)	Hines and Lofland cutting traffic.
Dispatcher (FARR and HUFFSTUTLER)	10-4, 11:40.
48 (Patrolmen T. R. BURTON and D. K. ERWIN)	48 (BURTON and ERWIN)
Dispatcher (FARR and HUFFSTUTLER)	Unit calling?
48 (Patrolmen T. R. BURTON and D. K. ERWIN)	48 (BURTON and ERWIN) is out at Parkland.
Dispatcher (FARR and HUFFSTUTLER)	113 (Patrolman C. R. ORSBURN).
113 (Patrolman C. R. ORSBURN)	113 (ORSBURN).

- 132 -

COMMISSION EXHIBIT No. 1974—Continued

Re: ASSASSINATION OF PRESIDENT JOHN FITZGERALD KENNEDY, NOVEMBER 22, 1963, DALLAS, TEXAS

Caller	Conversation
Dispatcher (FARR and HUFFSTUTLER)	Code 3 (Emergency - red lights and sirens) to Wadley, pick up blood, take to Parkland.
113 (Patrolman C. R. ORSBURN)	On Gaston?
Dispatcher (HUFFSTUTLER and FARR)	Yes.
113 (ORSBURN)	10-4.
40 (Patrolman D. F. FLUSCHE)	40 (FLUSCHE).
Dispatcher (FARR and HUFFSTUTLER)	40 (FLUSCHE).
40 (FLUSCHE)	Do we have any more people en route out here? We need some more help with the pedestrian traffic. It's drifting out around the grounds.
Dispatcher (FARR and HUFFSTUTLER)	31 (Patrolman E. N. STANSELL).
31 (Patrolman E. N. STANSELL)	31 (STANSELL).
Dispatcher (FARR and HUFFSTUTLER)	Report to Parkland.
111 (Patrolman SPRINGER)	Show 111 (SPRINGER) in service.
Dispatcher (FARR and HUFFSTUTLER)	32 (Patrolman J. T. SMITH), report to Parkland.
32 (Patrolman J. T. SMITH)	32 (J. T. SMITH), 10-4.

COMMISSION EXHIBIT No. 1974—Continued

Re: ASSASSINATION OF PRESIDENT JOHN FITZGERALD KENNEDY, NOVEMBER 22, 1963, DALLAS, TEXAS

Caller	Conversation
Dispatcher (FARR and HUFFSTUTLER)	Will two additional squads be enough, 40 (Patrolman D. F. FLUSCHE)?
32 (Patrolman J. T. SMITH)	Any code on this?
Dispatcher (FARR and HUFFSTUTLER)	Code 2 (Urgent - red lights and siren as needed).
111 (Patrolman SPRINGER)	Is in front of Wadley if you want me to go.
Dispatcher (FARR and HUFFSTUTLER)	10-4, pick it up, 111 (SPRINGER).
Dispatcher (FARR and HUFFSTUTLER)	113 (Patrolman C. R. ORSBURN).
113 (Patrolman C. R. ORSBURN)	113 (ORSBURN).
Dispatcher (FARR and HUFFSTUTLER)	Code 4 (disregard), 111 (SPRINGER) is out there.
113 (Patrolman C. R. ORSBURN)	10-4. (11:50)
113 (ORSBURN)	Put me out with 111 (SPRINGER).
Dispatcher (FARR and HUFFSTUTLER)	10-4.
605 (Ambulance)	605 (Ambulance) clear from Parkland.
Dispatcher (FARR and HUFFSTUTLER)	10-4, 605 (Ambulance), 11:51.

COMMISSION EXHIBIT No. 1974—Continued

Re: ASSASSINATION OF PRESIDENT
JOHN FITZGERALD KENNEDY,
NOVEMBER 22, 1963, DALLAS, TEXAS

Caller	Conversation
Dispatcher (FARR and HUFFSTUTLER)	Any CID (Criminal Investigation Division) Officer at Parkland Emergency....any CID (Criminal Investigation Division) Officer at Parkland...
18 (Lieutenant R. S. PIERCE)	18 (PIERCE)
Dispatcher (FARR and HUFFSTUTLER)	18 (PIERCE)
18 (Lieutenant R. S. PIERCE)	If you can get 17 (Lieutenant H. T. WOODALL) at the Command Post, he probably can get you a CID (Criminal Investigation Division) Officer. I saw a number of them out there a minute ago.
Dispatcher (FARR and HUFFSTUTLER)	Any officer near....disregard, 11:53 a.m.
113 (Patrolman C. R. ORSBURN)	113 (ORSBURN).
Dispatcher (FARR and HUFFSTUTLER)	113 (ORSBURN).
113 (Patrolman C. R. ORSBURN)	111 (Patrolman SPRINGER) has got it and en route and I am clear.
Dispatcher (FARR and HUFFSTUTLER)	11:54.
108 (Patrolman R. J. ROSS)	108 (ROSS).
Dispatcher (FARR and HUFFSTUTLER)	108 (ROSS).

- 135 -

COMMISSION EXHIBIT No. 1974—Continued

Re: ASSASSINATION OF PRESIDENT
JOHN FITZGERALD KENNEDY,
NOVEMBER 22, 1963, DALLAS, TEXAS

Caller	Conversation
108 (Patrolman R. J. ROSS)	Any further assignment for me? I'm still in the basement.
Dispatcher (FARR and HUFFSTUTLER)	10-4. (11:54).
Dispatcher (FARR and HUFFSTUTLER)	108 (ROSS) are you needed in the basement?
108 (ROSS)	I don't believe so. They have about cleared out.
Dispatcher (FARR and HUFFSTUTLER)	Return to service.
108 (Patrolman R. J. ROSS)	10-4. (11:55 a.m.)
Dispatcher (FARR and HUFFSTUTLER)	101 (Patrolman N. P. DORAN).
101 (Patrolman N. P. DORAN)	101 (DORAN).
Dispatcher (FARR and HUFFSTUTLER)	On a mark out report to Main and Harwood, transfer all reserve officers to Parkland Hospital, 11:59.
101 (Patrolman N. P. DORAN)	10-4.
701 (Mr. C. D. WEST, Civil Defense Coordinator)	701 (Mr. C. D. WEST, Civil Defense Coordinator)
Dispatcher (FARR and HUFFSTUTLER)	701 (Mr. C. D. WEST)

- 136 -

COMMISSION EXHIBIT No. 1974—Continued

Re: ASSASSINATION OF PRESIDENT
JOHN FITZGERALD KENNEDY,
NOVEMBER 22, 1963, DALLAS, TEXAS

Caller	Conversation
701 (Mr. C. D. WEST)	If you need a command post inside Parkland or another building, I have that A. C. Equipment transmitting and receiving on Channel 1 only.
Dispatcher (FARR and HUFFSTUTLER)	10-4, 701 (Mr. C. D. WEST). We will notify you. (12:01)
101 (Patrolman N. P. DORAN)	101 (DORAN) en route to Parkland from the basement.
Dispatcher (FARR and HUFFSTUTLER)	Received 101 (DORAN), 12:05 p.m.
101 (Patrolman N. P. DORAN)	101 (DORAN).
Dispatcher (FARR and HUFFSTUTLER)	101 (DORAN).
101 (DORAN)	Any code on this transfer?
Dispatcher (FARR and HUFFSTUTLER)	Code 2 (Urgent - red lights and siren as needed), 101 (DORAN).
101 (DORAN)	10-4.
Dispatcher (FARR and HUFFSTUTLER)	Use caution, 101 (DORAN); there is other emergency equipment running in that area.
(End of Belt Three)	
101 (DORAN)	10-4. (12:15 p.m.)
101 (DORAN)	101 (DORAN).

COMMISSION EXHIBIT No. 1974—Continued

Re: ASSASSINATION OF PRESIDENT
JOHN FITZGERALD KENNEDY,
NOVEMBER 22, 1963, DALLAS, TEXAS

Caller	Conversation
Dispatcher (FARR and HUFFSTUTLER)	101 (Patrolman N. P. DORAN)
101 (Patrolman N. P. DORAN)	Leaving Parkland now, en route to basement now to get another load. Would you call down there and have one of the reserve supervisors round up about six; have them ready in the basement?
Dispatcher (FARR and HUFFSTUTLER)	12:16 p.m.
99 (Patrolman S. E. NORMAN)	99 (NORMAN), Code 5 (en route) to Parkland.
Dispatcher (FARR and HUFFSTUTLER)	10-4, 99 (NORMAN), 12:17.
29 (Patrolman J. M. WILLIAMS)	29 (WILLIAMS).
Dispatcher (FARR and HUFFSTUTLER)	29 (WILLIAMS).
29 (Patrolman J. M. WILLIAMS)	Code 5 (en route), PMH (Parkland Memorial Hospital).
Dispatcher (FARR and HUFFSTUTLER)	10-4. 12:17.
Dispatcher (FARR and HUFFSTUTLER)	101 (Patrolman N. P. DORAN)
101 (Patrolman N. P. DORAN)	101 (DORAN)

COMMISSION EXHIBIT No. 1974—Continued

Re: ASSASSINATION OF PRESIDENT
JOHN FITZGERALD KENNEDY,
NOVEMBER 22, 1963, DALLAS, TEXAS

Caller	Conversation
Dispatcher (FARR and HUFFSTUTLER)	Report to Conference Room, Room 324, to pick up the police reserves.
101 (Patrolman N. P. DORAN)	Report where?
Dispatcher (FARR and HUFFSTUTLER)	The Conference Room - Room 324.
101 (DORAN)	10-4. (12:18 p.m.)
262 (Patrolman T. W. YETTS)	262 (YETTS).
Dispatcher (FARR and HUFFSTUTLER)	262 (YETTS).
262 (Patrolman T. W. YETTS)	Myself and five other three wheelers en route to Parkland.
Dispatcher (FARR and HUFFSTUTLER)	12:18.
120 (Sergeant G. B. RICHCREEK)	120 (RICHCREEK).
Dispatcher (FARR and HUFFSTUTLER)	120 (RICHCREEK).
120 (Sergeant G. B. RICHCREEK)	I'll be en route to rear of Parkland Hospital. Did you contact 29 (Patrolman J. M. WILLIAMS) and 99 (Patrolman S. E. NORMAN)?
Dispatcher (FARR and HUFFSTUTLER)	They are en route at this time.

Re: ASSASSINATION OF PRESIDENT
JOHN FITZGERALD KENNEDY,
NOVEMBER 22, 1963, DALLAS, TEXAS

Caller	Conversation
120 (Sergeant G. B. RICHCREEK)	10-4. I don't know what the crowd situation is out there but the Fire Department left the rope at the Trade Mart at Stemmons and Industrial. Have a squad go by there and pick up all that rope and report to Parkland with it.
Dispatcher (FARR and HUFFSTUTLER)	113 (Patrolman C. R. ORSBURN).
113 (Patrolman C. R. ORSBURN)	Stemmons and Industrial. Any code?
120 (Sergeant G. B. RICHCREEK)	What is the crowd situation at Parkland?
Dispatcher (FARR and HUFFSTUTLER)	Channel 2, 120 (Sergeant G. B. RICHCREEK). Code 1 (Routine), 113 (Patrolman C. R. ORSBURN).
113 (Patrolman C. R. ORSBURN)	10-4.
120 (Sergeant G. B. RICHCREEK)	120 (RICHCREEK).
Dispatcher (FARR and HUFFSTUTLER)	120 (RICHCREEK).
120 (Sergeant G. B. RICHCREEK)	I'm going to switch to Channel 2 just a moment. (12:25 p.m.)
29 (Patrolman J. M. WILLIAMS)	Code 6. (Out at destination).
Dispatcher (FARR and HUFFSTUTLER)	10-4, 29 (Patrolman J. M. WILLIAMS, 12:26 p.m. 103 (Patrolman J. M. VALENTINE), code 4 (disregard).

Re: ASSASSINATION OF PRESIDENT
JOHN FITZGERALD KENNEDY,
NOVEMBER 22, 1963, DALLAS, TEXAS

Caller	Conversation
Dispatcher (HULSE and JACKSON)	61 (Patrolman G. W. TEMPLE), your location?
61 (Patrolman G. W. TEMPLE)	Fair Park.
Dispatcher (HULSE and JACKSON)	Code 3 (Emergency - red lights and sirens), report to Wadley Blood Bank, transfer blood to Parkland.
61 (Patrolman G. W. TEMPLE)	10-4.
99 (Patrolman S. E. NORMAN)	Code 6 (out at destination) Parkland.
Dispatcher (HULSE and JACKSON)	10-4, 99 (Patrolman S. E. NORMAN), 12:33 p.m.
101 (Patrolman N. P. DORAN)	Clear.
Dispatcher (HULSE and JACKSON)	101 (DORAN) clear, 12:34 p.m.
48 (Patrolman T. R. BURTON and D. K. ERWIN)	48 (BURTON and ERWIN)
Dispatcher (HULSE and JACKSON)	48 (BURTON and ERWIN)
48 (BURTON and ERWIN)	We are clear at Parkland assignment, en route to radio station; mike trouble.
Dispatcher (HULSE and JACKSON)	10-4, 12:37 p.m.
43 (Patrolman W. E. HIBBS)	43 (HIBBS).
Dispatcher (HULSE and JACKSON)	43 (HIBBS).

COMMISSION EXHIBIT No. 1974—Continued

Re: ASSASSINATION OF PRESIDENT
JOHN FITZGERALD KENNEDY,
NOVEMBER 22, 1963, DALLAS, TEXAS

Caller	Conversation
43 (Patrolman W. E. HIBBS)	Clear at Parkland en route to our...back to our district.
Dispatcher (HULSE and JACKSON)	Clear, 12:37 p.m.
120 (Sergeant G. B. RICHCREEK)	120 (RICHCREEK)
Dispatcher (HULSE and JACKSON)	120 (RICHCREEK)
120 (Sergeant G. B. RICHCREEK)	What have you heard from 113 (Patrolman C. R. ORSBURN) on the rope?
Dispatcher (HULSE and JACKSON)	113 (ORSBURN) or 103 (Patrolman J. M. VALENTINE).
103 (Patrolman J. M. VALENTINE)	I'm not out there yet. I'm at Industrial and Oak Lawn at this time.
Dispatcher (HULSE and JACKSON)	Let us know something as soon as you get there.
103 (Patrolman J. M. VALENTINE)	All right.
120 (Sergeant G. B. RICHCREEK)	I'm going to switch to Channel 2 just a minute.
Dispatcher (HULSE and JACKSON)	10-4.
113 (Patrolman C. R. ORSBURN)	113 (ORSBURN).
Dispatcher (HULSE and JACKSON)	113 (ORSBURN).
113 (Patrolman C. R. ORSBURN)	I've got the rope en route to Parkland.

COMMISSION EXHIBIT No. 1974—Continued

Re: ASSASSINATION OF PRESIDENT
JOHN FITZGERALD KENNEDY,
NOVEMBER 22, 1963, DALLAS, TEXAS

Caller	Conversation
Dispatcher (HULSE and JACKSON)	10-4. 120 (Sergeant G. B. RICHCREEK).
120 (Sergeant G. B. RICHCREEK)	10-4. Tell him to report to the rear of Parkland with it, no code.
Dispatcher (HULSE and JACKSON)	Code 1 (routine) to the rear, 113 (Patrolman C. R. ORSBURN).
113 (Patrolman C. R. ORSBURN)	10-4. (12:39 p.m.)
Dispatcher (HULSE and JACKSON)	Any unit at Parkland...any unit at Parkland?
Dispatcher (HULSE and JACKSON)	40 (Patrolman D. F. FLUSCHE), you at Parkland?
40 (Patrolman D. F. FLUSCHE)	Yes, I am at the front entrance.
Dispatcher (HULSE and JACKSON)	Disregard. We have unit on Channel 2 now.
40 (Patrolman D. F. FLUSCHE)	10-4.
61 (Patrolman G. W. TEMPLE)	61 (TEMPLE) en route to Parkland.
Dispatcher (HULSE and JACKSON)	10-4, 61 (TEMPLE), 12:47.
113 (Patrolman C. R. ORSBURN)	Clear at Parkland.
Dispatcher (HULSE and JACKSON)	113 (ORSBURN) clear, 12:48 p.m.
101 (Patrolman N. P. DORAN)	101 (DORAN)

COMMISSION EXHIBIT No. 1974—Continued

Re: ASSASSINATION OF PRESIDENT
JOHN FITZGERALD KENNEDY,
NOVEMBER 22, 1963, DALLAS, TEXAS

Caller	Conversation
Dispatcher (HULSE and JACKSON)	101 (Patrolman N. P. DORAN)
101 (Patrolman N. P. DORAN)	Elm Street is impassable from St. Paul on down.
Dispatcher (HULSE and JACKSON)	10-4, 12:57 p.m.
Dispatcher (HULSE and JACKSON)	Attention any unit on emergency call, do not use Elm Street. Any unit on emergency call, do not use Elm Street.
118 (Patrolman V. O'DELL)	118 (O'DELL).
Dispatcher (HULSE and JACKSON)	118 (O'DELL).
118 (O'DELL)	I'm clear at Parkland.
Dispatcher (HULSE and JACKSON)	Clear, 12:58.
61 (Patrolman G. W. TEMPLE)	Clear at Parkland.
Dispatcher (HULSE and JACKSON)	61 (TEMPLE) clear, 12:59 p.m.
Dispatcher (HULSE and JACKSON)	101 (Patrolman N. P. DORAN), your location?
101 (Patrolman N. P. DORAN)	Young and Field.
(End of Belt Four)	
103 (Patrolman J. M. VALENTINE)	103 (VALENTINE)
Dispatcher (HULSE and JACKSON)	103 (VALENTINE)

COMMISSION EXHIBIT No. 1974—Continued

Re: ASSASSINATION OF PRESIDENT
JOHN FITZGERALD KENNEDY,
NOVEMBER 22, 1963, DALLAS, TEXAS

Caller	Conversation
103 (Patrolman J. M. VALENTINE)	103 (VALENTINE) En route to Parkland.
Dispatcher (HULSE and JACKSON)	101 (Patrolman N. P. DORAN), your location?
101 (Patrolman N. P. DORAN)	Harwood and Ross.
Dispatcher (HULSE and JACKSON)	Code 3 (Emergency - red lights and sirens) Wadley Blood Bank; transfer blood to Parkland.
101 (Patrolman N. P. DORAN)	10-4.
103 (Patrolman J. M. VALENTINE)	103 (VALENTINE).
Dispatcher (HULSE and JACKSON)	103 (VALENTINE).
103 (Patrolman J. M. VALENTINE)	I'm going out there anyway if you want me to go by there.
Dispatcher (HULSE and JACKSON)	10-4, you might as well. 101 (Patrolman N. P. DORAN), Code 4 (disregard), 103 (Patrolman J. M. VALENTINE) will get it.
97 (Patrolman L. L. FOX)	Clear Parkland Hospital.
Dispatcher (HULSE and JACKSON)	10-4, 1:12 p.m.
Dispatcher (HULSE and JACKSON)	101 (Patrolman N. P. DORAN).
101 (Patrolman N. P. DORAN)	101 (DORAN).
Dispatcher (HULSE and JACKSON)	101 (DORAN), report to basement. Transfer reserve to Elm and Houston, 1:25 p.m.

COMMISSION EXHIBIT No. 1974—Continued

Re: ASSASSINATION OF PRESIDENT
JOHN FITZGERALD KENNEDY,
NOVEMBER 22, 1963, DALLAS, TEXAS

Caller	Conversation
101 (Patrolman N. P. DORAN)	10-4.
Unknown	Can we get into basement yet?
Dispatcher (HULSE and JACKSON)	As far as we know, it's all clear, 1:32 p.m.
Dispatcher (HULSE and JACKSON)	430 (Captain F. M. MARTIN).
Dispatcher (HULSE and JACKSON)	430 (Captain F. M. MARTIN).
430 (Captain F. M. MARTIN)	430 (Captain F. M. MARTIN).
Dispatcher (HULSE and JACKSON)	430 (MARTIN), disregard you present assignment. Call 3 (Deputy Chief M. W. STEVENSON) on 622 (telephone extension at Police Department) as soon as possible, 1:34 p.m.
430 (Captain F. M. MARTIN)	10-4.
232 (Patrolman J. W. LOVING)	232 (LOVING).
Dispatcher (HULSE and JACKSON)	232 (LOVING).
232 (Patrolman J. W. LOVING)	Can you get into City Hall now?
Dispatcher (HULSE and JACKSON)	Unknown, 232 (LOVING).
232 (Patrolman J. W. LOVING)	I got a DWI (driving while intoxicated). I was wondering if was still crowded and if you could get in or not.
Unknown	Yeah, you can get in down there.

(End of Belt Five)

COMMISSION EXHIBIT No. 1974—Continued

Re: ASSASSINATION OF PRESIDENT
JOHN FITZGERALD KENNEDY,
NOVEMBER 22, 1963, DALLAS, TEXAS

Caller	Conversation
Dispatcher (HULSE and JACKSON)	105 (Patrolman R. E. VAUGHN)
Dispatcher (HULSE and JACKSON)	105 (Patrolman R. E. VAUGHN)
105 (Patrolman R. E. VAUGHN)	105 (VAUGHN).
Dispatcher (HULSE and JACKSON)	105 (VAUGHN)
105 (Patrolman R. E. VAUGHN)	105 (VAUGHN), you call?
Dispatcher (HULSE and JACKSON)	Stand by 105 (VAUGHN).
Dispatcher (HULSE and JACKSON)	105 (VAUGHN), call 15 (Captain C. E. TALBERT) on 401 (telephone extension at Parkland) at Parkland, 1:49.
105 (Patrolman R. E. VAUGHN)	All right.
63 (Patrolman C. F. BENTLEY)	63 (BENTLEY).
Dispatcher (HULSE and JACKSON)	63 (BENTLEY).
63 (Patrolman C. F. BENTLEY)	I'm going to be clear at Parkland, en route to garage, get another battery on this car.
Dispatcher (HULSE and JACKSON)	10-4.
Dispatcher (HULSE and JACKSON)	Any homicide unit have Judge MC BRIDE in their unit with them?
136 (Patrolman B. W. HARGIS)	136 (HARGIS), I believe Judge MC BRIDE is at Parkland Hospital.
Dispatcher (HULSE and JACKSON)	10-4, 2:18 p.m.

COMMISSION EXHIBIT No. 1974—Continued

Re: ASSASSINATION OF PRESIDENT
JOHN FITZGERALD KENNEDY,
NOVEMBER 22, 1963, DALLAS, TEXAS

Channel 2, 10:00 AM - 3:00 PM, November 22, 1963

Caller	Conversation
Dispatcher (Sergeant H. D. HENSLEE)	39 (Patrolmen J. F. BUTCHER and C. W. COMER), would you stay on Channel 2. We have another alert 2 (standby for a potential airplane crash problem at Love Field), did you know it?
39 (Patrolmen J. F. BUTCHER and C. W. COMER)	No.
5 (Deputy Chief of Police GEORGE L. LUMPKIN)	What was it?
Dispatcher (HENSLEE)	An alert 2 (standby for a potential airplane crash problem at Love Field).
Dispatcher (HENSLEE)	5 (Deputy Chief of Police GEORGE L. LUMPKIN), it has been tapped out - the plane is down. 10:15 a.m. KKB-364
24 (Patrolman D. L. PATE)	Is there an ambulance en route out here, 39? (Patrolmen J. F. BUTCHER and C. W. COMER)
39 (Patrolmen J. F. BUTCHER and C. W. COMER)	Yeah.
24 (Patrolman D. L. PATE)	Well, tell him to come on around here to the Fire Station, that's where he's supposed to be.

COMMISSION EXHIBIT No. 1974—Continued

Re: ASSASSINATION OF PRESIDENT
JOHN FITZGERALD KENNEDY,
NOVEMBER 22, 1963, DALLAS, TEXAS

Caller	Conversation
39 (Patrolman J. F. BUTCHER and C. W. COMER)	All right.
Dispatcher (HENSLEE)	30 (Sergeant R. C. CHILDERS)
30 (Sergeant R. C. CHILDERS)	Go ahead.
Dispatcher (HENSLEE)	Any information as to the estimation of the crowd out there now?
30 (Sergeant R. C. CHILDERS)	About 500.
Dispatcher (HENSLEE)	10:30 a.m. KKB-364.
30 (Sergeant R. C. CHILDERS)	When the planes make their landing approach, I'm going to use 21 (Patrolmen D. P. TUCKER and C. R. GRAHAM) and 32 (Patrolmen J. T. SMITH and W. L. HACKNEY), (they're both 2-man) to cut traffic. How about holding them off anything they might get tied up on for the next few minutes - then we'll have them meet me at the old Love Field Terminal.
Dispatcher (HENSLEE)	About what time?
30 (Sergeant R. C. CHILDERS)	Well, you'd better have them meet me no later than 11:00 a.m.
1 (Chief of Police JESSE E. CURRY)	I want to advise we need someone to work traffic Mockingbird and Cedar Springs.

Re: ASSASSINATION OF PRESIDENT
JOHN FITZGERALD KENNEDY,
NOVEMBER 22, 1963, DALLAS, TEXAS

Caller	Conversation
257 (Patrolman C. E. WHITMAN)	We have four men here.
1 (Chief of Police JESSE E. CURRY)	DECKER and I went through Mockingbird and Cedar Springs and didn't see anyone working. Have them form two lanes and help them make left turns that are backing up about two blocks.
Dispatcher (HENSLEE)	10:45 a.m. KKB-364.
125 (Captain P. W. LAWRENCE)	I am approaching Mockingbird and Cedar Springs. I'll get the men working.
Dispatcher (HENSLEE)	10-4. I'll advise 4 (Deputy Chief of Police N. T. FISHER) to disregard contact at the Trade Mart.
1 (Chief of Police JESSE E. CURRY)	Some of the detectives out here don't have the proper identification. Ask him if he has anymore down there.
Dispatcher (HENSLEE)	15/2 (Captain J. M. SOUTER), can you notify 3 (Deputy Chief of Police M. W. STEVENSON) that some of his detectives are at Love Field and do not have the proper identification. 1 (Chief of Police JESSE E. CURRY) is standing by for the information.
4 (Deputy Chief of Police N. T. FISHER)	39 (Patrolmen J. F. BUTCHER and C. W. COMER), landing will be at Southeast, won't it?
39 (Patrolmen J. F. BUTCHER and C. W. COMER)	Yes, sir.
4 (Deputy Chief of Police N. T. FISHER)	We want to be sure that you get your squads alerted so that they cut the traffic on Northwest Highway just prior to the President's plans coming over Love Field.

Re: ASSASSINATION OF PRESIDENT
JOHN FITZGERALD KENNEDY,
NOVEMBER 22, 1963, DALLAS, TEXAS

Caller	Conversation
Dispatcher (HENSLEE)	4 (Deputy Chief of Police N. T. FISHER), we sent 21 (Patrolmen D. P. TUCKER and C. R. GRAHAM) and 32 (Patrolmen J. T. SMITH and W. L. HACKNEY) to the old Love Field Terminal to meet 20 (Sergeant S. W. BURKHART).
4 (Deputy Chief of Police N. T. FISHER)	10-4.
Dispatcher (HENSLEE)	30 (Sergeant R. C. CHILDERS), when you start receiving information from the tower on that plane, advise 531 (Radio Dispatcher's telephone extension).
30 (Sergeant R. C. CHILDERS)	10-4. Will be on Channel 2.
Dispatcher (HENSLEE)	4 (Deputy Chief of Police N. T. FISHER), will you advise as to the crowd estimate and weather condition at this time? 11:00 a.m. KKB-364.
4 (Deputy Chief of Police N. T. FISHER)	10-4. It's not raining now and we have an estimate of a crowd of 1100 people.
2 (Assistant Chief of Police CHARLES BATCHELOR)	What is 1's (Chief of Police JESSE E. CURRY) location at love Field? (11:02)
1 (Chief of Police JESSE E. CURRY)	Right at the Love Field where the plane will unload.
Dispatcher (HENSLEE)	2 (Assistant Chief of Police CHARLES BATCHELOR), he is at Love Field where the planes are to unload.

COMMISSION EXHIBIT No. 1974—Continued

Re: ASSASSINATION OF PRESIDENT
JOHN FITZGERALD KENNEDY,
NOVEMBER 22, 1963, DALLAS, TEXAS

Caller	Conversation
Dispatcher (HENSLEE)	1 (Chief of Police JESSE E. CURRY), 2 (Assistant Chief of Police CHARLES BATCHELOR) advises he is sending the identification to your location by motorcycle officer.
1 (Chief of Police JESSE E. CURRY)	10-4. (11:15 a.m.)
Dispatcher (HENSLEE)	39 (Patrolmen J. F. BUTCHER and C. W. COMER), do you have any information yet?
39 (Patrolmen J. F. BUTCHER and C. W. COMER)	No.
4 (Deputy Chief of Police N. T. FISHER)	39 (Patrolmen J. F. BUTCHER and C. W. COMER), they changed landing directions on us, did you know that?
39 (Patrolmen J. F, BUTCHER and C. W. COMER)	Yes, sir.
4 (Deputy Chief of Police N. T. FISHER)	10-4. We will have to set up at Mockingbird there.
9 (Inspector J. H. SAWYER)	2 (Assistant Chief of Police CHARLES BATCHELOR), are we going to have any more men on Main Street than what we have now assigned? The crowds are getting large and we have very few officers.
2 (Assistant Chief of Police CHARLES BATCHELOR)	The only ones we have are assigned on the corners. There should be reserves assigned along the route.

COMMISSION EXHIBIT No. 1974—Continued

Re: ASSASSINATION OF PRESIDENT
JOHN FITZGERALD KENNEDY,
NOVEMBER 22, 1963, DALLAS, TEXAS

Caller	Conversation
9 (Inspector J. H. SAWYER)	The route on Harwood is not so bad. If we had some of those men we could certainly use them.
30 (Sergeant R. C. CHILDERS)	21 (Patrolmen D. P. TUCKER and C. R. GRAHAM) and 32 (Patrolmen J. T. SMITH and W. L. HACKNEY), cut traffic.
21 (Patrolmen D. P. TUCKER and C. R. GRAHAM) & 32 (Patrolmen J. T. SMITH and W. L. HACKNEY)	10-4.
2 (Assistant Chief of Police CHARLES BATCHELOR)	9 (Inspector J. H. SAWYER), have you received information that his arrival is about 20 minutes late?
9 (Inspector J. H. SAWYER)	I have not received the information.
Dispatcher (HENSLEE)	2 (Assistant Chief of Police CHARLES BATCHELOR), Air Force 1 is on final approach now.
30 (Sergeant R. C. CHILDERS)	One plane is down, second plane is coming in and Air Force 1 will be right behind it.
Dispatcher (HENSLEE)	10-4. 11:34 a.m.
2 (Assistant Chief of Police CHARLES BATCHELOR)	9 (Inspector J. H. SAWYER), we have some 15 solo motorcycle officers that are assigned with the convoy. These can probably help in controlling crowd - as to approach, there are five in front of the convoy plus those on the side. I think they will be able to move back the crowd.

COMMISSION EXHIBIT No. 1974—Continued

Re: ASSASSINATION OF PRESIDENT
JOHN FITZGERALD KENNEDY,
NOVEMBER 22, 1963, DALLAS, TEXAS

Caller	Conversation
9 (Inspector J. H. SAWYER)	10-4. Message received.
Dispatcher (HENSLEE)	39 (Patrolmen J. F. BUTCHER and C. W. COMER), is Air Force 1 down?
39 (Patrolmen J. F. BUTCHER and C. W. COMER)	No, he is just coming in.
Unknown	He's down.
Dispatcher (HENSLEE)	21 (Patrolmen D. P. TUCKER and C. R. GRAHAM) & 32 (Patrolmen J. T. SMITH and W. L. HACKNEY), all clear, 11:35 a.m.
30 (Sergeant R. C. CHILDERS)	Air Force 1 is not on the ground yet.
531 (Sergeant G. D. HENSLEE)	21 (Patrolmen D. P. TUCKER and C. R. GRAHAM) & 32 (Patrolmen J. T. SMITH and W. L. HACKNEY), remain on your assignment.
21 (Patrolmen D. P. TUCKER and C. R. GRAHAM) & 32 (Patrolmen J. T. SMITH and W. L. HACKNEY)	10-4.
30 (Sergeant R. C. CHILDERS)	He is on the ground. (11:37 a.m.)
Dispatcher (HENSLEE)	30 (Sergeant R. C. CHILDERS), weather and crowd estimate.
30 (Sergeant R. C. CHILDERS)	Weather is good.

COMMISSION EXHIBIT No. 1974—Continued

Re: ASSASSINATION OF PRESIDENT
JOHN FITZGERALD KENNEDY,
NOVEMBER 22, 1963, DALLAS, TEXAS

Caller	Conversation
540 (Patrolmen A. B. HAMMETT)	Will remain clear the rest of the day. Temperature probably stay about the same.
20 (Sergeant S. W. BURKHART)	There is quite a crowd all along Mockingbird Lane and around the Coca-Cola Bottling Plant. There is quite a crowd.
250 (Sergeant W. H. SIMPSON)	Ask 125 (Captain P. W. LAWRENCE) if he wants a man assigned to Herschel and Lemmon and at the signal light.
125 (Captain P. W. LAWRENCE)	Yes, have one of the men from Loma Alto and Lemmon go there.
5 (Deputy Chief of Police GEORGE L. LUMPKIN)	5 (Deputy Chief of Police GEORGE L. LUMPKIN) to 1 (Chief of Police JESSE E. CURRY) out at communications - I'm at the front gate out here.
1 (Chief of Police JESSE E. CURRY)	Loud and clear.
280 (Sergeant GEORGE W. C. CAMPBELL)	9 (Inspector J. SAWYER), Ervay Street is completely blocked with pedestrians and is completely out of control. I have 2 3-wheels with me and we still can't get the pedestrians off of Ervay so Ervay is completely closed.
9 (Inspector J. H. SAWYER)	10-4. I am on my way there.

COMMISSION EXHIBIT No. 1974—Continued

Re: ASSASSINATION OF PRESIDENT
JOHN FITZGERALD KENNEDY,
NOVEMBER 22, 1963, DALLAS, TEXAS

Caller	Conversation
15/2 (Captain J. M. SOUTER)	Progress report, please.
5 (Deputy Chief of Police GEORGE L. LUMPKIN)	Moving out very slow.
15/2 (Captain J. M. SOUTER)	10-4.
1 (Chief of Police JESSE E. CURRY)	5 (Deputy Chief of Police GEORGE L. LUMPKIN), that traffic up and around Mockingbird - try to get them over to one side. (11:50 a.m.)
1 (Chief of Police JESSE E. CURRY)	1 (Chief of Police JESSE E. CURRY) to Motorcycle Escort - send 2 men to Mockingbird and Cedar Springs to help clear the traffic.
Unknown	What is the location now?
1 (Chief of Police JESSE E. CURRY)	Just made the turn out of Love Field onto Cedar Springs now.
Dispatcher (HENSLEE)	15/2 (Captain J. M. SOUTER), they are just leaving the field now on Cedar Springs at 15 mph.
5 (Deputy Chief of Police GEORGE L. LUMPKIN)	5 (Deputy Chief of Police GEORGE L. LUMPKIN) to 1 (Chief of Police JESSE E. CURRY), might need a motorcycle at Lemmon and Manor Way. Quite a few people on Lemmon on the median strip and on the curbs. Location now?
1 (Chief of Police JESSE E. CURRY)	At Airdrome and Mockingbird Lane.

COMMISSION EXHIBIT No. 1974—Continued

Re: ASSASSINATION OF PRESIDENT
JOHN FITZGERALD KENNEDY,
NOVEMBER 22, 1963, DALLAS, TEXAS

Caller	Conversation
Dispatcher (HENSLEE)	9 (Inspector J. H. SAWYER), Airdrome and Mockingbird Lane - proceeding approximately 15 mph.
Dispatcher (HENSLEE)	12:00 Noon KKB-364.
1 (Chief of Police JESSE E. CURRY)	At Lemmon, approaching Inwood at approximately 12 to 15 mph. (12:01 p.m.)
3 (Deputy Chief M. W. STEVENSON)	The ambulance is standing by?
Dispatcher (HENSLEE)	Standing by at Love Field and when they complete that assignment, they will report to your location.
1 (Chief of Police JESSE E. CURRY)	1 (Chief of Police JESSE E. CURRY) to motorcycle leading - drop back closer - hold up about 50 feet ahead of us.
Unknown	15/2 (Captain J. M. SOUTER), this greeting committee has turned South on Hines from Mockingbird. (12:03 p.m.)
(End of Record #1)	
5 (Deputy Chief of Police GEORGE L. LUMPKIN)	1 (Chief of Police JESSE E. CURRY), what is your location now?
1 (Chief of Police JESSE E. CURRY)	We are approaching underpass - Cotton Belt - near Loma Alto.
Dispatcher (HENSLEE)	15/2 (Captain J. M. SOUTER), now on Lemmon near Loma Alto (12:05 p.m.)
1 (Chief of Police JESSE E. CURRY)	1 (Chief of Police JESSE E. CURRY) to Motorcycle Escort - 3 or 4 miles faster.

COMMISSION EXHIBIT No. 1974—Continued

Re: ASSASSINATION OF PRESIDENT
JOHN FITZGERALD KENNEDY,
NOVEMBER 22, 1963, DALLAS, TEXAS

Caller	Conversation
1 (Chief of Police JESSE E. CURRY)	1 (Chief of Police JESSE E. CURRY) to escort - pull those cars off the street
1 (Chief of Police JESSE E. CURRY)	Cut traffic at Oak Lawn.
5 (Deputy Chief of Police GEORGE L. LUMPKIN)	We have got a pretty good crowd of people down here at Turtle Creek.
1 (Chief of Police JESSE E. CURRY)	5 (Deputy Chief of Police GEORGE L. LUMPKIN), get the traffic off of it.
Dispatcher (HENSLEE)	Are you approaching Oak Lawn?
1 (Chief of Police JESSE E. CURRY)	About a block away at Knight Street.
Dispatcher (HENSLEE)	15/2 (Captain J. M. SOUTER), on Lemmon now.
1 (Chief of Police JESSE E. CURRY)	Crossing Oak Lawn.
15/2 (Captain J. M. SOUTER)	Advise 3 (Deputy Chief M. W. STEVENSON) that the ambulances have arrived and are standing by.
Dispatcher (HENSLEE)	3 (Deputy Chief M. W. STEVENSON), the ambulances have arrived and are standing by, 12:11 p.m.
1 (Chief of Police JESSE E. CURRY)	Just turning off Turtle Creek.

COMMISSION EXHIBIT No. 1974—Continued

Re: ASSASSINATION OF PRESIDENT
JOHN FITZGERALD KENNEDY,
NOVEMBER 22, 1963, DALLAS, TEXAS

Caller	Conversation
Dispatcher (HENSLEE)	Just turning off onto Turtle Creek off Lemmon.
1 (Chief of Police JESSE E. CURRY)	12 mph.
1 (Chief of Police JESSE E. CURRY)	At the MK&T Underpass at Turtle Creek.
Dispatcher (HENSLEE)	10-4, 12:14 p.m.
1 (Chief of Police JESSE E. CURRY)	1 (Chief of Police JESSE E. CURRY) to Motorcycle Escort - 3 or 4 miles faster, let's try it.
Dispatcher (HENSLEE)	12:15 p.m. KKB - 364 Dallas.
Dispatcher (HENSLEE)	9 (Inspector J. H. SAWYER), now turning onto Cedar Springs Road off Turtle Creek; Cedar Springs and Fairmount. (12:16 p.m.)
139 (Patrolman L. H. MARSHALL)	For your information, have cars lined up on both shoulders of Lemmon north from (garbled) to Oak Lawn.
5 (Deputy Chief of Police GEORGE L. LUMPKIN)	1 (Chief of Police JESSE E. CURRY), going to be a pretty good crowd from Ross on, on Harwood Street.
3 (Deputy Chief M. W. STEVENSON)	1 (Chief of Police JESSE E. CURRY), everything in good shape at Market Hall - traffic's moving well, not any crowd on side of street - good crowd along the barricades.

- 159 -

COMMISSION EXHIBIT No. 1974—Continued

Re: ASSASSINATION OF PRESIDENT
JOHN FITZGERALD KENNEDY,
NOVEMBER 22, 1963, DALLAS, TEXAS

Caller	Conversation
Dispatcher (HENSLEE)	1 (Chief of Police JESSE E. CURRY), for your information, Stemmons is pretty well crowded from Continental on to the Trade Mart.
1 (Chief of Police JESSE E. CURRY)	5 (Deputy Chief of Police GEORGE L. LUMPKIN), have an officer keep the crowd over to Harwood and Ross. They are out of the street here.
5 (Deputy Chief of Police GEORGE L. LUMPKIN)	We got them.
Dispatcher (HENSLEE)	1 (Chief of Police JESSE E. CURRY, are you approaching Ross?
1 (Chief of Police JESSE E. CURRY)	10-4. Just approaching at this time.
Dispatcher (HENSLEE)	10-4. 12:20 p.m.
Dispatcher (HENSLEE)	15/2 (Captain J. M. SOUTER), are you reading all right now?
15/2 (Captain J. M. SOUTER)	10-4.
212 (Patrolman L. W. SPRADLIN)	Telephone crew wants to know what time the president will be back through here so they can clear out.
Dispatcher (HENSLEE)	What location?

- 160 -

COMMISSION EXHIBIT No. 1974—Continued

Re: ASSASSINATION OF PRESIDENT
JOHN FITZGERALD KENNEDY,
NOVEMBER 22, 1963, DALLAS, TEXAS

Caller	Conversation
212 (Patrolman L. W. SPRADLIN)	On Mockingbird near Denton.
Dispatcher (HENSLEE)	It will probably be after 2:30 p.m.
5 (Deputy Chief of Police GEORGE L. LUMPKIN)	1 (Chief of Police JESSE E. CURRY), crowd on Main Street in real good shape. They have them back off of the curb.
1 (Chief of Police JESSE E. CURRY)	Good shape, we are just about to cross Live Oak.
Dispatcher (HENSLEE)	12:22 p.m.
1 (Chief of Police)	1 (Chief of Police JESSE E. CURRY) to escort - drop back. We will have to go at a real slow speed here on now.
1 (Chief of Police)	1 (Chief of Police JESSE E. CURRY) to motorcycle - hold up escort. O.K. move along.
1 (Chief of Police JESSE E. CURRY)	Check and see if we have everything in sight. Check with the rear car.
Dispatcher (HENSLEE)	1 (Chief of Police JESSE E. CURRY), who is in the rear car?
158 (Patrolman L. S. DAVENPORT)	Everything is O.K.
Dispatcher (HENSLEE)	1 (Chief of Police JESSE E. CURRY), 158 (Patrolman L. S. DAVENPORT) advise O.K., 12:26 p.m.
1 (Chief of Police JESSE E. CURRY)	Crossing Lamar Street.

COMMISSION EXHIBIT No. 1974—Continued

Re: ASSASSINATION OF PRESIDENT
JOHN FITZGERALD KENNEDY,
NOVEMBER 22, 1963, DALLAS, TEXAS

Caller	Conversation
Dispatcher (HENSLEE)	10-4. Pretty good crowd there, 12:28 p.m.
1 (Chief of Police JESSE E. CURRY)	Big crowd, yes.
5 (Deputy Chief of Police GEORGE L. LUMPKIN)	Notify Captain Souter of the location of the convoy now.
Dispatcher (HENSLEE)	15/2 (Captain J. M. SOUTER), now on Main, probably just past Lamar.
1 (Chief of Police JESSE E. CURRY)	Just crossing Market Street (12:28 p.m.)
4 (Deputy Chief of Police N. T. FISHER)	125 (Captain P. W. LAWRENCE), what traffic personnel do you have on Mockingbird?
125 (Captain P. W. LAWRENCE)	"On Mockingbird at Cedar Springs," is the question?
4 (Deputy Chief of Police N. T. FISHER)	10-4. It's moving out of this lot very slow.
125 (Captain P. W. LAWRENCE)	I am at the Trade Mart now headed out that way.
4 (Deputy Chief of Police N. T. FISHER)	That is all right - I'll check it.
1 (Chief of Police JESSE E. CURRY)	Approaching Triple Underpass.

COMMISSION EXHIBIT No. 1974—Continued

Caller	Conversation
Dispatcher (HENSLEE)	12:30 p.m. KKB 364.
1 (Chief of Police JESSE E. CURRY)	Go to the hospital - Parkland Hospital. Have them stand by.
1 (Chief of Police JESSE E. CURRY)	Get a man on top of that triple underpass and see what happened up there.
1 (Chief of Police JESSE E. CURRY)	Have Parkland stand by.
Dallas 1 (Sheriff J. E. "BILL" DECKER)	I am sure it's going to take some time to get your man in there. Pull every one of my men in there.
Dispatcher (HENSLEE)	Dallas 1 (Sheriff J. E. "BILL" DECKER), repeat, I didn't get all of it. I didn't quite understand all of it.
Dallas 1 (Sheriff J. E. "BILL" DECKER)	Have my office move all available man out of my office into the railroad yard to try to determine what happened in there and hold everything secure until Homicide and other investigators should get there.
Dispatcher(HENSLEE)	10-4. Dallas 1 (Sheriff J. E. "BILL" DECKER) - Station 5 (Dallas County Sheriff Dispatcher) will be notified.
Dispatcher (HENSLEE)	1 (Chief of Police JESSE E. CURRY), any information whatsoever?

COMMISSION EXHIBIT No. 1974—Continued

Caller	Conversation
1 (Chief of Police JESSE E. CURRY)	Looks like the President has been hit. Have Parkland stand by.
Dispatcher (HENSLEE)	10-4. They (Parkland) have been notified.
4 (Deputy Chief of Police N. T. FISHER)	We have those canine units in that vicinity, don't we?
1 (Chief of Police JESSE E. CURRY)	Headed to Parkland. Something's wrong with Channel 1.
5 (Deputy Chief of Police GEORGE L. LUMPKIN)	1 (Chief of Police JESSE E. CURRY), what do you want with these men out here with me?
1 (Chief of Police JESSE E. CURRY)	Just go on to Parkland Hospital with me.
83 (Patrolman R. L. GROSS)	Dispatcher on Channel 1 seems to have his mike stuck.
1 (Chief of Police JESSE E. CURRY)	Get these trucks out of the way. Hold everything. Get out of the way.
Dispatcher (HENSLEE)	Unknown motorcycle - up on Stemmons with his mike stuck open on Channel 1. Could you send someone up there to tell him to shut it off? (12:34 p.m.)
190 (Sergeant S. Q. BELLAH)	Do you still want me to hold this traffic on Stemmons until we find out something?

COMMISSION EXHIBIT No. 1974—Continued

Re: ASSASSINATION OF PRESIDENT
JOHN FITZGERALD KENNEDY,
NOVEMBER 22, 1963, DALLAS, TEXAS

Caller	Conversation
1 (Chief of Police JESSE E. CURRY)	Keep everything out of this emergency entrance.
Dispatcher (HENSLEE)	Did you get all that information, 136 (Patrolman B. W. HARGIS)
136 (Patrolman B. W. HARGIS)	10-4.
142 (Patrolman C. A. HAYGOOD)	I just talked to a guy up here who was standing close to it and the best he could tell it came from the Texas School Book Depository Building here with that Hertz Renting sign on top.
Dispatcher (HENSLEE)	10-4. Get his name, address, telephone number there - all the information that you can from him. 12:35 p.m.
15/2 (Captain J. M. SOUTER)	Captain advises have all emergency equipment - have 283 (Patrolman C. R. HAMILTON) cut the traffic at Hines and Industrial. Have all emergency units on South Industrial.
531 (Sergeant G. D. HENSLEE)	283 (Patrolman C. R. HAMILTON), cut traffic Hines and Industrial.
Dispatcher (HENSLEE)	Attention, do not use Industrial Blvd. (12:36 p.m.)
260 (Sergeant D. V. HARKNESS)	I have a witness that says that it came from the 5th floor of the Texas Book Depository Store.

COMMISSION EXHIBIT No. 1974—Continued

Re: ASSASSINATION OF PRESIDENT
JOHN FITZGERALD KENNEDY,
NOVEMBER 22, 1963, DALLAS, TEXAS

Caller	Conversation
Dispatcher (HENSLEE)	220 (Sergeant W. R. RUSSELL), keep all emergency equipment off the entrance to Parkland and all of the emergency equipment there off of Industrial Boulevard.
Unknown	We have the emergency entrance secured. (12:37 p.m.)
125 (Captain P. W. LAWRENCE)	We have the emergency entrance to Parkland secured.
22 (Patrolman L. L. HILL)	Get some men up here to cover this school depository building. It's believed the shot came from, as you see it on Elm Street, looking toward the building, it would be upper right hand corner, second window from the end.
Dispatcher (HENSLEE)	10-4. How many do you have there?
22 (Patrolman L. L. HILL)	I have one guy that was possibly hit by a richochet from the bullet off the concrete and another one saw the President slump.
Dispatcher (HENSLEE)	10-4.
137 (Patrolman E. D. BREWER)	We have a man here who says he saw him pull the weapon back through the window from the southeast corner of that depository building.

COMMISSION EXHIBIT No. 1974—Continued

Re: ASSASSINATION OF PRESIDENT
JOHN FITZGERALD KENNEDY,
NOVEMBER 22, 1963, DALLAS, TEXAS

Caller	Conversation
Dispatcher (HENSLEE)	All right, do you have the building covered off?
137 (Patrolman E.D. BREWER)	No, about 3/4 of a block away from there.
Dispatcher (HENSLEE)	All right, pull on down there.
137 (Patrolman E.D. BREWER)	10-4. I'll leave these witnesses here.
257 (Patrolman C.E. WHIT-MAN)	Do you want us to go back to Mocking-bird and Cedar Springs?
Dispatcher (HENSLEE)	10-4.
290 (Sergeant E.B. HOWARD)	See if you can contact 125 (Captain P.W. LAWRENCE).
125 (Captain P.W. LAWRENCE)	290 (Sergeant E.B. HOWARD), I am at Parkland.
290 (Sergeant E.B. HOWARD)	125 (Captain P.W. LAWRENCE), do you want us to stay on Industrial or where do you want us to go?
125 (Captain P.W. LAWRENCE)	At your location right now.
2 (Assistant Chief of Police CHARLES BATCHELOR)	Can you give us any information as to what happened for these people out here, evidently they had - seriousness of it - the President involved - 1 (Chief of Police JESSE E. CURRY) is at Parkland, along with Dallas 1 (Sheriff J. E. "BILL" DECKER). We have word it is unknown - Texas Depository Store. corner of Elm and Field - officers are now surrounding and searching the building. (Garbled)

- 167 -

COMMISSION EXHIBIT No. 1974—Continued

Re: ASSASSINATION OF PRESIDENT
JOHN FITZGERALD KENNEDY,
NOVEMBER 22, 1963, DALLAS, TEXAS

Caller	Conversation
2 (Assistant Chief of Police CHARLES BATCHELOR)	Where did this happen - at Field and Main?
Dispatcher (HENSLEE)	At Stemmons and the Triple Underpass - 12:40 p.m.
Dispatcher (HENSLEE)	2 (Assistant Chief of Police CHARLES BATCHELOR), there's a possibility that 6 or 7 more people may have been shot.
295 (Patrolman WILLIAM PRICE)	I believe the Presidents head was practically blown off.
303 (Detectives R. M. SIMS & E. L. BOYD)	What hospital did the President go to?
Dispatcher (HENSLEE)	Parkland Hospital.
Dispatcher (HENSLEE)	303 (Detectives R. M. SIMS & E. L. BOYD), where are you?
303 (Detectives R. M. SIMS & E. L. BOYD)	Parkland Hospital.
300 (Captain JOHN WILL FRITZ)	300 (Captain JOHN WILL FRITZ) en route.
Dispatcher (HENSLEE)	300 (Captain JOHN WILL FRITZ), are you en route to Elm and Houston to that store?
300 (Captain JOHN WILL FRITZ)	En route to the hospital.

- 168 -

COMMISSION EXHIBIT No. 1974—Continued

Re: ASSASSINATION OF PRESIDENT
JOHN FITZGERALD KENNEDY,
NOVEMBER 22, 1963, DALLAS, TEXAS

Caller	Conversation
Dispatcher (HENSLEE)	295 (Patrolman WILLIAM PRICE), do you know the extent of the injury?
295 (Patrolman WILLIAM PRICE)	It's not for me to say, I can't say. (12:41 p.m.)
5 (Deputy Chief of Police GEORGE L. LUMPKIN)	Give me a squad to Elm and Houston.
15/2 (Captain J. M. SOUTER)	Did they advise they have the suspect?
Dispatcher (HENSLEE)	No, they do not have the suspect.
9 (Inspector J. H. SAWYER)	We need some more men down at the Texas School Book Depository. We should have some on Main if we could get someone to pick up and bring them down here.
250 (Sergeant W. A. SIMPSON)	I will start down Elm Street and pick up as many as I can on the way (12:43 p.m.).
190 (Sergeant S. Q. BELLAH)	We can release this traffic here? We can go down there or stay here and hold it.
Dispatcher (HENSLEE)	Release the traffic and report Code 3 (Emergency-red lights and sirens) to Elm and Houston, 12:43 p.m.
15 (Captain C. E. TALBERT)	Are you having them contain that block or 2 block area?

COMMISSION EXHIBIT No. 1974—Continued

Re: ASSASSINATION OF PRESIDENT
JOHN FITZGERALD KENNEDY,
NOVEMBER 22, 1963, DALLAS, TEXAS

Caller	Conversation
Dispatcher (HENSLEE)	Yes, we are trying to seal off that building until it can be searched.
15 (Captain C. E. TALBERT)	More than that building. Extend out from that building so it can be searched.
267 (Patrolman J. H. CALDWELL)	Do you want me to head south?
Dispatcher (HENSLEE)	Yes, 12:44 p.m.
9 (Inspector J. H. SAWYER)	The type of weapon looked like a 30-30 rifle or some type of Winchester.
Dispatcher (HENSLEE)	9 (Inspector J. H. SAWYER), it was a rifle?
9 (Inspector J. H. Sawyer)	A rifle, yes
Dispatcher (HENSLEE)	9 (Inspector J. H. SAWYER), any clothing description?
9 (Inspector J. H. SAWYER)	About 30, 5'10", 165 pounds
Dispatcher (HENSLEE)	Attention all squads, the suspect in the shooting at Elm and Houston is supposed to be an unknown white male, approximately 30, 165 pounds, slender build, armed with what is thought to be a 30-30 rifle. - repeat, unknown white male, approximately 30, 165 pounds, slender build. No further description at this time or information, 12:45 p.m.

COMMISSION EXHIBIT No. 1974—Continued

Re: ASSASSINATION OF PRESIDENT
JOHN FITZGERALD KENNEDY,
NOVEMBER 22, 1963, DALLAS, TEXAS

Caller	Conversation
15 (Captain C. E. TALBERT)	Could 9 (Inspector J. H. SAWYER) determine whether man was supposed to have been still in the building or was he supposed to have left?
Dispatcher (HENSLEE)	I didn't know for sure and the witnesses didn't have the description, but we have got that building saturated by now and we should know something before long
9 (Inspector J. H. SAWYER)	On this building, it's unknown whether he is still in the building or not known if he was there in the first place.
531 (Sergeant G. D. HENSLEE)	Well, all the information we have received, 9 (Inspector J. H. SAWYER), indicates that it did come from about the 5th or 4th floor of that building.
5 (Deputy Chief of Police GEORGE L. LUMPKIN)	What building?
Dispatcher (HENSLEE)	The Texas School Book and Depository Building, 5 (Deputy Chief of Police GEORGE L. LUMPKIN), at Elm and Houston.
(End of Record #2)	

COMMISSION EXHIBIT No. 1974—Continued

Re: ASSASSINATION OF PRESIDENT
JOHN FITZGERALD KENNEDY,
NOVEMBER 22, 1963, DALLAS, TEXAS

Caller	Conversation
260 (Sergeant D. V. HARKNESS)	We have an epileptic before this. The person went to Parkland Hospital. Send a squad there to get all the information you can. (12:48 p.m.)
Dispatcher (HENSLEE)	125 (Captain P. W. LAWRENCE), do you have any information that the governor also was hit?
125 (Captain P. W. LAWRENCE)	Not yet, I'll check in just a minute.
157 (Patrolman J. W. WILLIAMS)	Have you notified a DPS (Texas Department of Public Safety) on this suspect yet?
Dispatcher (HENSLEE)	Haven't had time yet but we will.
15/2 (Captain J. M. SOUTER)	2 (Assistant Chief of Police CHARLES BATCHELOR), advises to contact 401 (phone extension at Parkland Hospital) at Parkland and see if I can (garbled)
Dispatcher (HENSLEE)	Stand by.
2 (Assistant Chief of Police CHARLES BATCHELOR)	Contact the Parkland Hospital and see whether the President will be able to appear out here or not. We have all these people and we want to know what to announce out here.
Dispatcher (HENSLEE)	Yes, as soon as we can obtain that information.

COMMISSION EXHIBIT No. 1974—Continued

Re: ASSASSINATION OF PRESIDENT
JOHN FITZGERALD KENNEDY,
NOVEMBER 22, 1963, DALLAS, TEXAS

Caller	Conversation
211 (Patrolmen R. HAWKINS and E. R. BAGGETT)	Numerous people asking us what happened. Can you give us any information about it at this time?
Dispatcher (HENSLEE)	Wounded the President or the extent of it at this time. 12:51 p.m.
211 (Patrolmen R. HAWKINS and E. R. BAGGETT)	Was he shot or do you know?
Dispatcher (HENSLEE)	I understand he was involved in it, yes.
211 (Patrolmen R. HAWKINS and E. R. BAGGETT)	10-4. Thank you.
125 (Captain P. W. LAWRENCE)	The governr was also shot.
Dispatcher (HENSLEE)	10-4.
Dispatcher (HENSLEE)	125 (Captain P. W. LAWRENCE), can you obtain from 1 (Chief of Police JESSE E. CURRY) if the President is going to appear at the Trade Mart?
1 (Chief of Police JESSE E. CURRY)	It's very doubtful.
2 (Assistant Chief of Police CHARLES BATCHELOR)	(garbled) whether or not what his condition is so we can know what to tell people (garbled).

COMMISSION EXHIBIT No. 1974—Continued

Re: ASSASSINATION OF PRESIDENT
JOHN FITZGERALD KENNEDY,
NOVEMBER 22, 1963, DALLAS, TEXAS

Caller	Conversation
2 (Assistant Chief of Police CHARLES BATCHELOR)	Are there any definite arrangements being made as to whether he will or will not appear?
1 (Chief of Police JESSE E. CURRY)	Not at this time that I know of. I don't know but I feel reasonably sure that he will not.
190 (Sergeant S. Q. BELLAH)	We need some ropes here at Main and Houston. We are getting a terrific crowd.
Dispatcher (HENSLEE)	What else do you need?
190 (Sergeant S. Q. BELLAH)	Just a lot of rope.
Dispatcher (HENSLEE)	We are going to send a Fire Department Rescue Unit with a lot of rope to that location, 12:54 p.m.
31 (Patrolman J. E. CHISM)	Have a squad go to Community Blood Bank and pick up some blood and bring to Parkland, Code 3 (Urgent. Red lights and siren as needed.)
Dispatcher (HENSLEE)	Have they been notified?
31 (Patrolman J. E. CHISM)	10-4. Parkland has notified them.
15/2 (Captain J. M. SOUTER)	2 (Assistant Chief of Police CHARLES BATCHELOR) requests information the condition of the President and also if the governor was hit.

COMMISSION EXHIBIT No. 1974—Continued

Re: ASSASSINATION OF PRESIDENT
JOHN FITZGERALD KENNEDY,
NOVEMBER 22, 1963, DALLAS, TEXAS

Caller	Conversation
Dispatcher (HENSLEE)	Have information that the governor was hit, 1:03 p.m.
15/2 (Captain J. M. SOUTER)	4 (Deputy Chief of Police N. T. FISHER), there was some statement made concerning the outer perimeter - he stated (This conversation was covered by other squads and unable to read it from the recorder).
39 (Patrolmen J. F. BUTCHER and C. W. COMER)	Clear me on Code 2 (Urgent. Red lights and sirens as needed at intersections) assignment and 30's (Sergeant R. C. CHILDERS) station wagon, the Secret Service agents downtown. (1:09 p.m.)
139 (Patrolman L. H. MARSHALL)	Have 39 (Patrolmen J. F. BUTCHER and C. W. COMER) meet me at the entrance to Love Field. I have the 2 Presidential cars en route out there.
Dispatcher (HENSLEE)	139 (Patrolman L. H. MARSHALL), you will have to take them on yourself because he is coming downtown.
139 (Patrolman L. H. MARSHALL)	See if you can find out where they are supposed to go out here.
39 (Patrolmen J. F. BUTCHER and C. W. COMER)	I am in sergeant's car and other half of 39 is still at the field in the Love Field car.

COMMISSION EXHIBIT No. 1974—Continued

Re: ASSASSINATION OF PRESIDENT
JOHN FITZGERALD KENNEDY,
NOVEMBER 22, 1963, DALLAS, TEXAS

Caller	Conversation
Dispatcher (HENSLEE)	15/2 (Captain J. M. SOUTER), do you have 29 (Patrolman J. M. WILLIAMS) and 99 (Patrolman S. E. NORMAN) there?
Dispatcher (HENSLEE)	That is the 2 dog men that are supposed to be working it without the dogs. We can use them if you can release them.
2 (Assistant Chief of Police CHARLES BATCHELOR)	Find out any further information at Parkland about the condition of the President, whether he can be there or not. Mr. Crull is standing by here and needs to know immediately if you can find out so we can do something to these people out here.
Dispatcher (HENSLEE)	10-4. 1:11 p.m.
9 (Inspector J. H. SAWYER)	On the 3rd floor of this book company down here, we found empty rifle hulls and it looked like the man had been here for some time. We are checking it out now.
Dispatcher (HENSLEE)	10-4. 1:12 p.m.
158 (Patrolman L. S. DEBENPORT)	Notify 170 (Sergeant R. SMART) I am taking prisoner to the downtown jail and that I'll report back to him down to Parkland as soon as I can.
243 (Patrolman B. L. APPLE)	I am down here with this 3-wheeler at the dead end. He has a loud colored jacket on. He is pretty drunk. Do you want me to take him up there or what do you want me to do with him?

COMMISSION EXHIBIT No. 1974—Continued

Re: ASSASSINATION OF PRESIDENT
JOHN FITZGERALD KENNEDY,
NOVEMBER 22, 1963, DALLAS, TEXAS

Caller	Conversation
Dispatcher (HENSLEE)	Take him back up there to 505 Main and contact 9 (Inspector J. H. SAWYER) at Elm and Houston.
243 (Patrolman B. L. APPLE)	10-4.
39 (Patrolman L. H. MARSHALL)	I have 2 Presidential vehicles and I am trying to get across the field.
Dispatcher (HENSLEE)	10-4. If I can contact 39 (Patrolmen J. F. BUTCHER and C. W. COMER), I'll try to.
Dispatcher (HENSLEE)	4 (Deputy Chief of Police N. T. FISHER) call 504 (Patrolman E. E. TAYLOR) immediately. Do you have 39 (Patrolmen J. F. BUTCHER and C. W. COMER) there with you? 139 (Patrolman L. H. MARSHALL) needs clearance across the field with those cars.
Dispatcher (HENSLEE)	4 (Deputy Chief of Police N. T. FISHER), do we hold all that is on duty now?
4 (Deputy Chief of Police N. T. FISHER)	10-4. That is right.
Dispatcher (HENSLEE)	General Broadcast - All squads, we have a report that an officer has been involved in a shooting in the 400 E. 10th. 1:18 p.m.

COMMISSION EXHIBIT No. 1974—Continued

Re: ASSASSINATION OF PRESIDENT
JOHN FITZGERALD KENNEDY,
NOVEMBER 22, 1963, DALLAS, TEXAS

Caller	Conversation
280 (Sergeant GEORGE W. C. CAMPBELL)	Do we have a Command post set up anywhere for extra squads. We need additional men to work traffic around Parkland Hospital.
Dispatcher (HENSLEE)	Well, about everything I have got tied up now is down at Elm and Houston. 1:19 p.m.
Dispatcher (HENSLEE)	Notify 1 (Chief of Police JESSE E. CURRY) that we have an officer involved in a shooting at 10th and Patton. We don't know the extent of it yet.
2 (Assistant Chief of Police CHARLES BATCHELOR)	We got some officers that we could release. Do you need them anywhere?
Dispatcher (HENSLEE)	Yes, we could use some at Parkland Emergency and the traffic on Hines is terrific.
39 (Patrolmen J. F. BUTCHER and C. W. COMER)	I am at the Sheraton with the Secret Service men. Do you have anyone to carry back?
Dispatcher (HENSLEE)	No, not right now.
251 (Patrolman J. E. JENNINGS)	I was en route back to 2's (Assistant Chief of Police CHARLES BATCHELOR) location but if he doesn't need me there, I am right here at Parkland Hospital.

COMMISSION EXHIBIT No. 1974—Continued

Caller	Conversation
Dispatcher (HENSLEE)	10-4. Check out there and help with the traffic.
Dispatcher (HENSLEE)	Go ahead, 19 (Sergeant C. B. OWENS). Are you en route? Yes. It's in the 400 or 500 block of E. 10th, I believe.
19 (Sergeant C. B. OWENS)	10-4. We are almost Code 6 (Out at destination).
Dispatcher (HENSLEE)	10-4. 1:21 p.m.
170 (Sergeant R. SMART)	Any manpower that you can spare have them to meet 170 (Sergeant R. SMART) or 280 (Sergeant GEORGE W. C. CAMPBELL) at the entrance out here (Parkland Hospital) on Hines.
251 (Patrolman J. E. JENNINGS)	I am right here at the entrance now if you want me to check out.
Dispatcher (HENSLEE)	Yes, go ahead.
10 (Inspector H. J. PUTNAM, JR.)	By orders of #1 (Chief of Police JESSE E. CURRY), get us 20 more uniformed officers out here to the entrance of Parkland Emergency entrance immediately.
Dispatcher (HENSLEE)	251 (Patrolman J. E. JENNINGS), are you there at Parkland Emergency entrance?
251 (Patrolman J. E. JENNINGS)	Yes.

COMMISSION EXHIBIT No. 1974—Continued

Re: ASSASSINATION OF PRESIDENT
JOHN FITZGERALD KENNEDY,
NOVEMBER 22, 1963, DALLAS, TEXAS

Caller	Conversation
Dispatcher (HENSLEE)	10-4.
	(Garbled)
10 (Inspector J. B. JONES)	At this time it was a precautionary move.
Dispatcher (HENSLEE)	Wants 20 men Parkland at this time. 1:25 p.m.
15/2 (Captain J. M. SOUTER)	I'm en route.
254 (Patrolman J. B. JONES)	Can I help you?
Dispatcher (HENSLEE)	Yes, report to Hines in the 5200 block.
254 (Patrolman J. B. JONES)	What code?
Dispatcher (HENSLEE)	Code 1 (Routine).
10 (Inspector J. B. JONES)	Bring him around to the emergency entrance.
Dispatcher (HENSLEE)	Do you want him, Code 2? (Urgent. Red lights and sirens as needed at intersections)
10 (Inspector J. B. JONES)	Yes.
Dispatcher (HENSLEE)	All squads en route to Parkland Code 2 (Urgent. Red lights and sirens as needed at intersections).
254 (Patrolman J. B. JONES)	I am en route.

COMMISSION EXHIBIT No. 1974—Continued

Re: ASSASSINATION OF PRESIDENT
JOHN FITZGERALD KENNEDY,
NOVEMBER 22, 1963, DALLAS, TEXAS

Caller	Conversation
Dispatcher (HENSLEE)	10 (Inspector J. B. JONES), would it be possible to establish a Command Post there with a radio to man a car with a Channel 2 and get somebody to man it?
10 (Inspector J. B. JONES)	Yes, it will be done immediately. (1:26 p.m.)
4 (Deputy Chief of Police N. T. FISHER)	Do you have any condition of the officer on 10th?
Dispatcher (HENSLEE)	Stand by. Notify 1 (Chief of Police JESSE E. CURRY) that officer involved in this shooting, Officer J. D. TIPPIT, we believe, was pronounced DOA (Dead On Arrival) at Methodist 1:28 p.m.
4 (Deputy Chief of Police N. T. FISHER)	Is there any indication that it has any connection with this other shooting?
Dispatcher (HENSLEE)	Well, the descriptions on the suspect are similar and it is possible.
4 (Deputy Chief of Police N. T. FISHER)	Thank you.
Dispatcher (HENSLEE)	10-4. 1:29 p.m.
15 (Captain C. E. TALBERT)	If you get ahold of 15/2 (Captain J. M. SOUTER) to send some of his people to relieve people at the scene on this book building, we will meet back in service.

COMMISSION EXHIBIT No. 1974—Continued

Re: ASSASSINATION OF PRESIDENT
JOHN FITZGERALD KENNEDY,
NOVEMBER 22, 1963, DALLAS, TEXAS

Caller	Conversation
Dispatcher (HENSLEE)	15 (Captain C. E. TALBERT), you received the information on TIPPIT, didn't you?
15 (Captain C. E. TALBERT)	10-4. En route to Oak Cliff now.
Dispatcher (HENSLEE)	15 (Captain C. E. TALBERT), do you want 4 (Deputy Chief of Police N. T. FISHER) to relieve some of those people on the building?
15 (Captain C. E. TALBERT)	He has some people at Love Field I think I can send down here.
Dispatcher (HENSLEE)	I think he is going to have to leave them, Captain, because they are going to have to move back out. They are not going to allow anybody on that field.
15 (Captain C. E. TALBERT)	Check with 15/2 (Captain J. M. SOUTER) and see if he has any he can spare.
Dispatcher (HENSLEE)	Well, I have got 20 from him and I had to send them out to Parkland and block it off.
15 (Captain C. E. TALBERT)	We will leave it like it is.
Dispatcher (HENSLEE)	Clear. 1:30 p.m.

COMMISSION EXHIBIT No. 1974—Continued

Re: ASSASSINATION OF PRESIDENT
JOHN FITZGERALD KENNEDY,
NOVEMBER 22, 1963, DALLAS, TEXAS

Caller	Conversation
211 (Patrolmen R. HAWKINS and E. R. BAGGETT)	Can you give Captain WESTBROOK any information as to where he was shot?
Dispatcher (HENSLEE)	Repeat.
211 (Patrolmen R. HAWKINS and E. R. BAGGETT)	Can you give Captain WESTBROOK any information as to where this happened?
Dispatcher (HENSLEE)	It was in the 400 block of East 10th near Patton.
15 (Captain C. E. TALBERT)	Did you say he was DOA (Dead On Arrival) at Methodist?
Dispatcher (HENSLEE)	Yes.
15 (Captain C. E. TALBERT)	Have they released any condition on the President?
Dispatcher (HENSLEE)	We understand he is DOA (Dead On Arrival), too.
Unknown	Was the governor hit?
Dispatcher (HENSLEE)	Unknown.
15 (Captain C. E. TALBERT)	Was 19 (Sergeant C. B. OWENS) asking for a squad to cover that area?
531 (Sergeant G. D. HENSLEE)	Yes, we have 10 squads over there now.
15 (Captain C. E. TALBERT)	Do you think you have a suspect?

- 183 -

COMMISSION EXHIBIT No. 1974—Continued

Re: ASSASSINATION OF PRESIDENT
JOHN FITZGERALD KENNEDY,
NOVEMBER 22, 1963, DALLAS, TEXAS

Caller	Conversation
Dispatcher (HENSLEE)	800 E. Jefferson, 15 (Captain C. E. TALBERT).
15 (Captain C. E. TALBERT)	10-4. Have you run a make on that license number yet?
Dispatcher (HENSLEE)	Yes, we are running a (garbled) on it now.
234 (Patrolman J. B. JONES)	Do you want us at the emergency entrance or at the front?
Dispatcher (HENSLEE)	They are going to set up a Command Post at the entrance at Hines on Lofland Drive and don't let any traffic in there whatsoever unless its an emergency.
9 (Inspector J. H. SAWYER)	Have the escorts cut their sirens.
Dispatcher (HENSLEE)	Cut the sirens, escorts. Cut the sirens.
10 (Inspector J. B. JONES)	Notify the escorts on North Hines to cut their sirens.
Dispatcher (HENSLEE)	Attention escorts going north on Hines - cut your sirens.
Dispatcher (HENSLEE)	Notify 9 (Inspector J. H. SAWYER) that we have information that the ladder that runs up to the roof on this building there is concealed space under a sheet metal plate, sheet metal has to be raised and there is some concealed space under that sheet metal. 1:33 p.m.

- 184 -

COMMISSION EXHIBIT No. 1974—Continued

Re: ASSASSINATION OF PRESIDENT
JOHN FITZGERALD KENNEDY,
NOVEMBER 22, 1963, DALLAS, TEXAS

Caller	Conversation
Dispatcher (HENSLEE)	Lead escort motorcycles escort - cut your sirens. 1:33 p.m. Continue broadcasting for the escorts to cut their sirens. Attention escort, 1 (Chief of Police JESSE E. CURRY) now going north on Hines cut your siren. 1:34 p.m.
1 (Chief of Police JESSE E. CURRY)	With as little attention as possible, get up and break traffic ahead of the cars.
10 (Inspector J. B. JONES)	He said notify those jockeys to attract as little attention as possible, barely crack the intersection, get up and break traffic ahead of the cars.
Dispatcher (HENSLEE)	Attention: motorcycle escort with 1 (Chief of Police JESSE E. CURRY) - attract as little attention as possible, continue advising the escort to cut the siren. 1:35 p.m.
9 (Inspector J. H. SAWYER)	I have been out of the car. Have you been trying to contact me?
Dispatcher (HENSLEE)	Did you get that information. Did the motor jockey give you the information about the building?
9 (Inspector J. H. SAWYER)	It's being secured now.

Re: ASSASSINATION OF PRESIDENT
JOHN FITZGERALD KENNEDY,
NOVEMBER 22, 1963, DALLAS, TEXAS

Caller	Conversation
Dispatcher (HENSLEE)	1 (Chief of Police JESSE E. CURRY) or Dallas 1 (Sheriff J. E. "BILL" DECKER) when we get to the Main entrance (garbled) Are you en route to Love Field?
1 (Chief of Police JESSE E. CURRY)	Yes, but don't put it on the air. (1:37 p.m.)
39 (Patrolmen J. F. BUTCHER and C. W. COMER)	I got a State Unit going Southwest Airmotive to pick up (garbled)
2 (Assistant Chief of Police CHARLES BATCHELOR)	We have information that someone to pick the governor's wife up.
1 (Chief of Police JESSE E. CURRY)	Don't let any cars follow us into the field.
Dispatcher (HENSLEE)	10-4.
2 (Assistant Chief of Police CHARLES BATCHELOR)	Mrs. CONNALLY (Governor's mother) is being flown in here from Austin. She will arrive at Love Field. A State car will be standing by but it will probably be an hour before she gets here. Notify the Command Post at Parkland to get her through when she arrives. (Garbled)
Dispatcher (HENSLEE)	10-4.

Re: ASSASSINATION OF PRESIDENT
JOHN FITZGERALD KENNEDY,
NOVEMBER 22, 1963, DALLAS, TEXAS

Caller	Conversation
Dispatcher (HENSLEE)	Dispatcher (HENSLEE) to Parkland Command Post - Mrs. CONNALLY will arrive in about an hour. Be sure to let her through.
Parkland Command Post	10-4.
Dispatcher (HENSLEE)	1 (Chief of Police JESSE E. CURRY), Dallas 1 (Sheriff J. E. "BILL" DECKER) is standing by at Sta. 5, his office.
1 (Chief of Police JESSE E. CURRY)	10-4.
Dispatcher (HENSLEE)	1:40 p.m.
Dispatcher (HENSLEE)	Surgeon being flown in from Galveston to Dallas Love Field. Looking for someone stand by and escort him to Parkland. He should be by in about 30 minutes.
550/2 (Sergeant GERALD L. HILL)	A witness reports that he last was seen in the Abundant Life Temple about the 400 block. We are fixing to go in and shake it down.
Dispatcher (HENSLEE)	Is that the one that was involved in the shooting of the officer?
550/2 (Sergeant GERALD L. HILL)	Yes.

- 187 -

COMMISSION EXHIBIT No. 1974—Continued

Re: ASSASSINATION OF PRESIDENT
JOHN FITZGERALD KENNEDY,
NOVEMBER 22, 1963, DALLAS, TEXAS

Caller	Conversation
Dispatcher (HENSLEE)	They already have him.
550/2 (Sergeant GERALD L. HILL)	No, that wasn't the right one. (1:44 p.m.)
Dispatcher (HENSLEE)	Anybody at Elm and Houston?
297 (Three-wheel motorcycle, operator unknown)	10-4.
Dispatcher (HENSLEE)	297 (Patrolman C. E. WHITMAN), contact 9 (Inspector J. H. SAWYER) and notify him they are holding up a north-bound freight train there in the yard and they want to shake it down before they let it go. Do you want to send some officers over there to shake it down?
297 (Three-wheel motorcycle, operator unknown)	10-4.
551 (Sergeant H. H. STRINGER)	The jacket the suspect was wearing over here on Jefferson bears a laundry tag with the letter B 9738. See if there is any way you can check this laundry tag.
138 (Patrolman D. L. JACKSON)	We need a Justice of the Peace at Parkland Hospital, Code 3 (Emergency. Red lights and sirens).
Dispatcher (HENSLEE)	10-4.
	(Garbled)

- 188 -

COMMISSION EXHIBIT No. 1974—Continued

Re: ASSASSINATION OF PRESIDENT
JOHN FITZGERALD KENNEDY,
NOVEMBER 22, 1963, DALLAS, TEXAS

Caller	Conversation
550/2 (Sergeant GERALD L. HILL)	Advise someone to get in the alley and behind that building at the fire escape.
(End of Record #3)	
Dispatcher (HENSLEE)	5 (Deputy Chief GEORGE L. LUMPKIN), an aide to the Vice President by the name of Mansport will arrive at Southwest Airmotive at 2:05 and will you also advise Secret Service.
5 (Deputy Chief GEORGE L. LUMPKIN)	All right.
39 (In Sergeant's car)	39 A half. (One occupant in this unit at this time).
Dispatcher (HENSLEE)	Go ahead.
39 (A half. One occupant in this unit at this time)	39 is in front of me stationed right across the airstrip from me right in front of Southwest Airmotive. What have you got? (garbled)
Dispatcher (HENSLEE)	We need an escort there at Southwest Airmotive at 2:05 p.m. 1:50 p.m.
210 (Sergeant J. M. YOUNG)	Has anybody made arrangements or picked TIPPIT's wife up?
Dispatcher (HENSLEE)	I am not sure, 210 (Sergeant J. M. YOUNG).

COMMISSION EXHIBIT No. 1974—Continued

Re: ASSASSINATION OF PRESIDENT
JOHN FITZGERALD KENNEDY,
NOVEMBER 22, 1963, DALLAS, TEXAS

Caller	Conversation
210 (Sergeant J. M. YOUNG)	If you give me the address, I will go up there and pick her up.
Dispatcher (HENSLEE)	Yes, you go pick her up. I do not have anybody to send right now.
210 (Sergeant J. M. YOUNG)	I'll call 505 (telephone extension at Dallas Police Department which has the home addresses for Dallas police officers) for the address.
39 (Other half. One occupant in this unit at this time)	I am going back to the Southwest Airmotive. 39 has the State unit.
Dispatcher (HENSLEE)	10-4, 39. 1:51 p.m.
410 (Captain O. A. JONES)	Ask 15/2 (Captain J. M. SOUTER) if he has any extra officers there to help hold back the crowd on the south side of Parkland Hospital.
1 (Chief of Police JESSE E. CURRY)	What are the circumstances of J. D. TIPPIT?
Dispatcher (HENSLEE)	We do not have it all clear yet, 1 (Chief of Police JESSE E. CURRY). He was involved in a shooting and was DOA (Dead On Arrival) at Methodist and I am sorry that is all I have right now.
1 (Chief of Police JESSE E. CURRY)	Did they get the suspects?

COMMISSION EXHIBIT No. 1974—Continued

Re: ASSASSINATION OF PRESIDENT
JOHN FITZGERALD KENNEDY,
NOVEMBER 22, 1963, DALLAS, TEXAS

Caller	Conversation
Dispatcher (HENSLEE)	We believe we have him in the Texas Theater now.
1 (Chief of Police JESSE E. CURRY)	10-4.
39 (A half. One occupant in this unit at this time)	Is he to arrive at 2:05?
Dispatcher (HENSLEE)	Yes.
39 (A half. One occupant in this unit at this time)	I'll stand by.
4 (Deputy Chief N. T. FISHER)	The latest information is they are supposed to stop them over in the vicinity where we are now. (Garbled) Would you check with the tower and see if this is correct?
39 (A half. One occupant in this unit at this time)	I'm in the sergeant's car and 39 has the tower radio.
4 (Deputy Chief N. T. FISHER)	Well, where is he?
39 (In Sergeant's car)	He has gone with the State unit to pick up the governor's wife.
Dispatcher (HENSLEE)	We have apprehended a suspect in the shooting at the Texas Theater.
1 (Chief of Police JESSE E. CURRY)	10-4.

- 191 -

COMMISSION EXHIBIT No. 1974—Continued

Re: ASSASSINATION OF PRESIDENT
JOHN FITZGERALD KENNEDY,
NOVEMBER 22, 1963, DALLAS, TEXAS

Caller	Conversation
Dispatcher (HENSLEE)	Repeat, 1 (Chief of Police JESSE E. CURRY).
1 (Chief of Police JESSE E. CURRY)	I'm at Love Field (1:54 p.m.)
11 (Inspector CHRISTOPHER KOCKAS)	You say the officer is DOA (Dead On Arrival)?
Dispatcher (HENSLEE)	Yes, 11 (Inspector CHRISTOPHER KOCKAS).
11 (Inspector CHRISTOPHER KOCKAS)	10-4.
4 (Deputy Chief N. T. FISHER)	We need a squad standing by on Mockingbird at the end of runway 13. Also need one at the north end of that same runway at Shorecrest there.
Dispatcher (HENSLEE)	10-4. I'll see if I can find you one.
Dispatcher (HENSLEE)	Is there any officer near Love Field?
Dispatcher (HENSLEE)	161 (Patrolman B. J. DALE), we need you on Mockingbird at the end of Runway 13, Love Field, between Airdrome and Cedar Springs.
161 (Patrolman B. J. DALE)	On or off the field? (Garbled)
Unknown	Off the field, 161 (Patrolman B. J. DALE).

- 192 -

COMMISSION EXHIBIT No. 1974—Continued

Re: ASSASSINATION OF PRESIDENT
JOHN FITZGERALD KENNEDY,
NOVEMBER 22, 1963, DALLAS, TEXAS

Caller	Conversation
210 (Sergeant J. M. YOUNG)	I'm downtown, J. D. TIPPIT lives 7500 So. Beckley. I'm running Code 2 (Urgent. Red lights and sirens as needed at intersections) to his wife's house.
Dispatcher (HENSLEE)	Yes, go ahead. 1:56 p.m.
Dispatcher (HENSLEE)	4 (Deputy Chief N. T. FISHER), I've got 32 (Patrolman J. T. SMITH and W. L. HACKNEY) going down on Shorecrest. What do you want him to do?
4 (Deputy Chief N. T. FISHER)	I want them to stand by at the end of that runway and be sure that everyone moved out.
550 (Captain W. R. WESTBROOK)	You probably know that they are en route from the Texas Theater with that suspect. They are bringing him straight to City Hall.
39 (In Sergeant's car)	See if you can get the Regular 39 car and have them ask the tower the place the aide is coming in.
257 (Patrolman C. E. WHITMAN)	You need me out at Love Field?
Dispatcher (HENSLEE)	No, where are you now?
257 (Patrolman C. E. WHITMAN)	I'm on Hall Street at Oak Lawn.
Dispatcher (HENSLEE)	I need you back out there to Parkland about Code 2 (Urgent. Red lights and sirens as needed at intersections).

Re: ASSASSINATION OF PRESIDENT
JOHN FITZGERALD KENNEDY,
NOVEMBER 22, 1963, DALLAS, TEXAS

Caller	Conversation
257 (Patrolman C. E. WHITMAN)	10-4. I'm en route. Any particular place?
Dispatcher (HENSLEE)	No, just grab you a handful of corner. There's a Command Post set up there at Parkland, 257 (Patrolman C. E. WHITMAN).
39 (In Sergeant's car)	I've been advised by Southwest Airmotive the aides are arriving at Southwest Airmotive and will park here in 5 minutes.
Dispatcher (HENSLEE)	10-4. I can't raise your partner.
39 (In Sergeant's car)	10-4. He's taking care of Gov. CONNALLY's wife, I believe.
Dispatcher (HENSLEE)	2:00 p.m. KKB 364 Dallas.
253 (Patrolman W. M. HUGGINS)	I've got back to my car at Cedar Springs and Mockingbird - which way you want me to go?
Dispatcher (HENSLEE)	Parkland Hospital, Code 2 (Urgent. Red lights and sirens as needed at intersections).
253 (Patrolman W. M. HUGGINS)	En route.
Dispatcher (HENSLEE)	2:01 p.m.

Re: ASSASSINATION OF PRESIDENT
JOHN FITZGERALD KENNEDY,
NOVEMBER 22, 1963, DALLAS, TEXAS

Caller	Conversation
Dispatcher (HENSLEE)	Go down to Elm and Houston. Contact Capt. FRITZ. Tell him to contact his office.
Unknown	Captain FRITZ just left about a minute ago. He's in his car.
(Garbled)	
85 (Patrolman R. W. WALKER)	Any report on condition on the President or Governor?
Dispatcher (HENSLEE)	I understand the President is DOA (Dead On Arrival). I don't know about him (the governor).
Dispatcher (HENSLEE)	4 (Deputy Chief N. T. FISHER), do you know where Air Force 1 is?
4 (Deputy Chief N. T. FISHER)	Yes, it's out here at the air cargo entrance on the field.
Dispatcher (HENSLEE)	10-4.
4 (Deputy Chief N. T. FISHER)	If you can contact 39 out at Southwest Airmotive, that the airplane is going to be taxied to this area, not there.
Dispatcher (HENSLEE)	39, did you receive?

- 195 -

COMMISSION EXHIBIT No. 1974—Continued

Re: ASSASSINATION OF PRESIDENT
JOHN FITZGERALD KENNEDY,
NOVEMBER 22, 1963, DALLAS, TEXAS

Caller	Conversation
39	Yes, I haven't seen the governor's aide. I'll take the Presidential aide. We're heading for Gate 26 where the plane is supposed to come in.
Dispatcher (HENSLEE)	39, did you receive information on Air Force 1?
39	Repeat.
Dispatcher (HENSLEE)	1, it's parked over there by air cargo freight entrance.
550 (Captain W. R. WESTBROOK)	Notify my office, I'm en route, will you?
Dispatcher (HENSLEE)	10-4. 2:03 p.m.)
Dispatcher (HENSLEE)	Command Post at Parkland?
Dispatcher (HENSLEE)	170 (Sergeant R. SMART), how many officers do you have now, do you know?
170 (Sergeant R. SMART)	I'm at the entrance here on Hines. I'm not at the Command Post in the rear.
Dispatcher (HENSLEE)	10-4. What's your traffic situation there?
170 (Sergeant R. SMART)	Heavy.
Dispatcher (HENSLEE)	170 (Sergeant R. SMART), I can't raise anyone back there. I'm sending 2 dog officers, Code 2 (Urgent. Red lights and sirens as needed at intersections), just in case they're needed.

- 196 -

COMMISSION EXHIBIT No. 1974—Continued

Re: ASSASSINATION OF PRESIDENT
JOHN FITZGERALD KENNEDY,
NOVEMBER 22, 1963, DALLAS, TEXAS

Caller	Conversation
170 (Sergeant R. SMART)	10-4. It's possible we'll need them.
Dispatcher (HENSLEE)	2:04 p.m.
(Garbled)	
Dispatcher (HENSLEE)	Yes, to your location.
139 (Patrolman L. H. MARSHALL)	Know the location of that plane?
Dispatcher (HENSLEE)	Yes. If you'll get hold of 4 (Deputy Chief N. T. FISHER) there at the air cargo freight entrance, he'll direct you to it.
139 (Patrolman L. H. MARSHALL)	10-4.
4 (Deputy Chief N. T. FISHER)	139 (Patrolman L. H. MARSHALL), come in Cedar Springs past the Ramada Inn and I'll be waiting for you at the first cut-off off Cedar Springs to your right.
138 (Patrolman D. L. JACKSON)	10-4.
139 (Patrolman L. H. MARSHALL)	10-4.
Dispatcher (HENSLEE)	170 (Sergeant R. SMART), do you know if 3 (Deputy Chief M. W. STEVENSON) has come through there?

COMMISSION EXHIBIT No. 1974—Continued

Re: ASSASSINATION OF PRESIDENT
JOHN FITZGERALD KENNEDY,
NOVEMBER 22, 1963, DALLAS, TEXAS

Caller	Conversation
(Garbled)	
Dispatcher (HENSLEE)	Someone relay for 3 (Deputy Chief M. W. STEVENSON). I'm not receiving.
4 (Deputy Chief N. T. FISHER)	4 (Deputy Chief N. T. FISHER), to the unit on the Parkland escort to Love Field.
39 (Patrolmen J. F. BUTCHER and C. W. COMER)	This is 39 (Patrolman J. F. BUTCHER and C. W. COMER) with the Presidential aide and governor's aide.
4 (Deputy Chief N. T. FISHER)	4 (Deputy Chief N. T. FISHER), to the unit escorting people from Parkland to Love Field.
4 (Deputy Chief N. T. FISHER)	138 (Patrolman D. L. JACKSON), did you get my message awhile ago? I'll be waiting for you here at the cut-off.
138 (Patrolman D. L. JACKSON)	10-4.
39 (Patrolmen J. F. BUTCHER and C. W. COMER)	Would you notify some unit at Parkland to kind of help us get through when we get there?
Dispatcher (HENSLEE)	Yes. It is policed.
170 (Sergeant R. SMART)	The crowd is dispersing out here now.
Dispatcher (HENSLEE)	10-4. 2:10 p.m.

COMMISSION EXHIBIT No. 1974—Continued

Re: ASSASSINATION OF PRESIDENT
JOHN FITZGERALD KENNEDY,
NOVEMBER 22, 1963, DALLAS, TEXAS

Caller	Conversation
138 (Patrolman D. L. JACKSON)	4 (Deputy Chief N. T. FISHER), approaching Mockingbird on Cedar Springs.
4 (Deputy Chief N. T. FISHER)	All right. Come right on in.
83 (Patrolman P. L. GROSS)	I'm going to be out at the City Hall with 550 (Captain W. R. WESTBROOK).
Dispatcher (HENSLEE)	10-4.
251 (Patrolman J. E. JENNINGS)	Could you contact someone out there at the airport and have them advise Mr. KILDOFF, he's in the White House Staff, and tell him the poolmen he's concerned about are en route; that I'm bringing them to the plane?
Dispatcher (HENSLEE)	4 (Deputy Chief N. T. FISHER), did you receive?
4 (Deputy Chief N. T. FISHER)	The poolmen he's concerned with are what?
Dispatcher (HENSLEE)	Are en route to that location.
4 (Deputy Chief N. T. FISHER)	10-4.
Dispatcher (HENSLEE)	2:15 p.m. KKB 364.
251 (Patrolman J. E. JENNINGS)	This gentleman in this White House Staff wanted to know if you got that message to Mr. KILDOFF out there at the airport.

COMMISSION EXHIBIT No. 1974—Continued

Re: ASSASSINATION OF PRESIDENT
JOHN FITZGERALD KENNEDY,
NOVEMBER 22, 1963, DALLAS, TEXAS

Caller	Conversation
Dispatcher (HENSLEE)	Yes, that's 10-4. It has been delivered. 4 (Deputy Chief N. T. FISHER) is standing by and has notified them.
251 (Patrolman J. E. JENNINGS)	10-4, and these gentlemen also wish to know if it would be possible for your office to make a collect call to Washington to deliver a message for them.
Dispatcher (HENSLEE)	I'm sorry my phones are all tied up.
170 (Sergeant R. SMART)	Have any word whether the 7-3 traffic will hold over?
Dispatcher (HENSLEE)	The word I have right now is everyone that is on duty now will remain on duty until further notice (Garbled).
170 (Sergeant R. SMART)	10-4.
251 (Patrolman J. E. JENNINGS)	Do you know where 39 (Patrolmen J. F. BUTCHER and C. W. COMER) is now standing by. I'm on Denton just north of Mockingbird.
Dispatcher (HENSLEE)	(Garbled) Well, I got one going to Parkland and the other one is on the field somewhere.
251 (Patrolman J. E. JENNINGS)	10-4. Do you know where I can take these men to get them to the plane?
Dispatcher (HENSLEE)	4 (Deputy Chief N. T. FISHER) is sitting up there in his car.

COMMISSION EXHIBIT No. 1974—Continued

Re: ASSASSINATION OF PRESIDENT
JOHN FITZGERALD KENNEDY,
NOVEMBER 22, 1963, DALLAS, TEXAS

Caller	Conversation
251 (Patrolman J. E. JENNINGS)	That's up Cedar Springs?
Dispatcher (HENSLEE)	That's right. Past the Ramada & Hertz Rent-A-Car and turn right.
4 (Deputy Chief N. T. FISHER)	Who's that calling for me?
Dispatcher (HENSLEE)	That's 139 (Patrolman L. H. MARSHALL). He has those aides en route out there.
4 (Deputy Chief N. T. FISHER)	10-4.
Unknown	No, that's 39.
257 (Patrolman C. E. WHITMAN)	I'm clear from Parkland. They said they don't need me. I'm going to start toward Love Field if you need me out there somewhere.
Dispatcher (HENSLEE)	Yes, you might go. You probably are.
138 (Patrolman D. L. JACKSON)	(Garbled) 138 (Patrolman D. L. JACKSON) to 130 (Sergeant R. L. STRIEGEL), 123 (Captain P. W. LAWRENCE) is getting in his car now.
130 (Sergeant R. L. STRIEGEL)	125 (Captain P. W. LAWRENCE), we have several men out here at Parkland which we don't need. You want to release some of these men?

Re: ASSASSINATON OF PRESIDENT
JOHN FITZGERALD KENNEDY,
NOVEMBER 22, 1963, DALLAS, TEXAS

Caller	Conversation
125 (Captain P. W. LAWRENCE)	(Garbled) I don't want to release any of them yet. Hold them right now.
Dispatcher (HENSLEE)	2:24 p.m.
Disptacher (HENSLEE)	Any officer near the City Hall that's in a car....
15/2 (Captain J. M. SOUTER)	Would you have someone call 511 (Telephone extension of the Dallas Police Department Crime) and advise the Third Platoon supervisor that will be coming on that the senior sergeant is tied up at Parkland Hospital and will be unable to get there. I'm tied up at the Trade Mart and will be unable to get there for the senior officer present to put the detail to work from Central Station and also is 4 (Deputy Chief N. T. FISHER) on the air?
Dispatcher (HENSLEE)	4 (Deputy Chief N. T. FISHER) is on the air.
18 (Sergeant R. E. DUGGER)	(Garbled) I can leave Parkland right now. I'm afraid I'd better make it about 3:00 p.m.
Dispatcher (HENSLEE)	4 (Deputy Chief N. T. FISHER), 15 (Captain C. E. TALBERT) wants to talk to you, but I have some information I need to give to you right now. A Mr. BILL MOYERS is on his way in to swear in Mr. JOHNSON as President and he will need an escort, but we don't know when he is going to get there.

Re: ASSASSINATION OF PRESIDENT
JOHN FITZGERALD KENNEDY,
NOVEMBER 22, 1963, DALLAS, TEXAS

Caller	Conversation
4 (Deputy Chief N.T. FISHER)	All right. We'll be standing by here.
Dispatcher (HENSLEE)	15/2 (Captain J. M. SOUTER), can you read 4 (Deputy Chief N.T. FISHER)?
4 (Deputy Chief N.T. FISHER)	Stand by. There is a train going by.
107 (Patrolman C.F. GOODSON)	Any better location on that deal down here at Cobb Stadium?
Dispatcher (HENSLEE)	No, that's all we had on it.
107 (Patrolman C.F. GOODSON)	(Garbled) 10-4. There're about 15 or 20 officers out here covering this. Nobody can find anything.
18 (Sergeant R.E. DUGGER)	15/2 (Captain J.M. SOUTER), we have approximately 6 to 8 jockeys out here and 15 officers standing by out here. We have no actual need for except about 2. Can you advise?
15/2 (Captain J.M. SOUTER)	Release all you don't need out there.
170 (Sergeant R. SMART)	18 (Sergeant R.E. DUGGER), have the motorcycle officers report to 170 (Sergeant R. SMART) here at the entrance.
(Garbled)	
Dispatcher (HENSLEE)	4 (Deputy Chief N.T. FISHER), President JOHNSON's bags are the 2 blue hanging bags and 2 handbags are on that plane. They are initialed with his initials and they want them brought to him at Parkland.
4 (Deputy Chief N.T. FISHER)	2 blue handbags and 2 hanging bags?

COMMISSION EXHIBIT No. 1974—Continued

Re: ASSASSINATION OF PRESIDENT
JOHN FITZGERALD KENNEDY,
NOVEMBER 22, 1963, DALLAS, TEXAS

Caller	Conversation
Dispatcher (HENSLEE)	No, 2 blue hanging bags and 2 handbags with his initials on them.
4 (Deputy Chief N. T. FISHER)	10-4. We'll get them.
125 (Captain P. W. LAWRENCE)	I need 1 solo supervisor and half of those men at Parkland out here.
Dispatcher (HENSLEE)	170 (Sergeant R. SMART), 125 (Captain P. W. LAWRENCE) wants you and half......
15/2 (Captain J. M. SOUTER)	4 (Deputy Chief N. T. FISHER), the building people at the Trade Mart request we leave some men inside the building. Will you tell 4 (Deputy Chief N. T. FISHER) I'll have 6 or 7 6 to 2 officers here and 2 service division officers that I'll hold until they are no longer required?
Dispatcher (HENSLEE)	You 10-4 on that 4 (Deputy Chief N. T. FISHER)?
4 (Deputy Chief N. T. FISHER)	Yes.
170 (Sergeant R. SMART)	Notify 125 (Captain P. W. LAWRENCE) I'm en route with 5 (officers). (2:32 p.m.)
162 (Patrolman J. W. WILLIAMS)	Can you get ahold of 39 (Patrolman J. F. BUTCHER and C. W. COMER) - ask him to switch to Channel 2. I need him in a hurry.

COMMISSION EXHIBIT No. 1974—Continued

Re: ASSASSINATION OF PRESIDENT
JOHN FITZGERALD KENNEDY,
NOVEMBER 22, 1963, DALLAS, TEXAS

Caller	Conversation
162 (Patrolman J. W. WILLIAMS)	39 (Patrolmen J. F. BUTCHER and C. W. COMER), we are over here at Southwest Airmotive. We need to come across the field. Can you come over and help us?
Dispatcher (HENSLEE)	162 (Patrolman J. W. WILLIAMS), I still haven't been able to contact 39 that's on the field. All I can suggest is go ahead and take that perimeter road and go on across. We don't have any contact with the tower.
162 (Patrolman J. W. WILLIAMS)	10-4. We're going.
4 (Deputy Chief N. T. FISHER)	Where did you get that information about those 2 blue hanging bags and the 2 handbags?
Dispatcher (HENSLEE)	One of the telephone clerks brought it in here and said they talked to them at Parkland.
70 (Sergeant S. E. VARNER)	I called that information in from Parkland. We got it from the 2nd floor. It should be Governor CONNALLY's bags. They were on the Presidential plane. They didn't know if they had been taken off or left on the plane.
Dispatcher (HENSLEE)	170, are they CONNALLY's or JOHNSON's?

Re: ASSASSINATION OF PRESIDENT
JOHN FITZGERALD KENNEDY,
NOVEMBER 22, 1963, DALLAS, TEXAS

Caller	Conversation
70 (Sergeant S. E. VARNER)	It's my understanding they were Governor CONNALLY's.
Dispatcher (HENSLEE)	10-4. We got it as Johnson's. Did you receive 4 (Deputy Chief N. T. FISHER)?
39 (Patrolmen J. F. BUTCHER and C. W. COMER)	You call us?
Dispatcher (HENSLEE)	39 (Patrolmen J. F. BUTCHER and C. W. COMER), are you on the field?
39 (Patrolmen J. F. BUTCHER and C. W. COMER)	Yes.
Dispatcher (HENSLEE)	We need tower clearance for that jockey, that's going across the field.
39 (Patrolmen J. F. BUTCHER and C. W. COMER)	Go ahead.
(Garbled)	
Dispatcher (HENSLEE)	4 (Deputy Chief N. T. FISHER), we have information now that Judge SARAH HUGHES is leaving Parkland en route to Love Field to swear President JOHNSON in. What are you going to need out there? Are you in pretty good shape?
4 (Deputy Chief N. T. FISHER)	Yes.

Re: ASSASSINATION OF PRESIDENT
JOHN FITZGERALD KENNEDY,
NOVEMBER 22, 1963, DALLAS, TEXAS

Caller	Conversation
Dispatcher (HENSLEE)	10-4. 2:35 p.m.
Dispatcher (HENSLEE)	4 (Deputy Chief N. T. FISHER), I don't know how she's going. I guess someone may be escorting her.
(Garbled)	
4 (Deputy Chief N. T. FISHER)	Is that Mrs. CONNALLY wanting those bags or Governor CONNALLY?
Dispatcher (HENSLEE)	70 (Sergeant S. E. VARNER) was the one that was supposed to have called it in and I guess it was the Governor.
4 (Deputy Chief N. T. FISHER)	Would you have them double check it?
Dispatcher (HENSLEE)	10-4. Also we have another escort coming in out there wanting the .... stand by a minute. Wanting 39 (Patrolman J. F. BUTCHER and C. W. COMER) to meet them at the entrance to Love Field. It's some more of those VIP's.
4 (Deputy Chief N. T. FISHER)	10-4. You know who they are, or where they're coming from?
Dispatcher (HENSLEE)	They're coming from the Sheraton, 4 (Deputy Chief N. T. FISHER)
(Garbled)	

COMMISSION EXHIBIT No. 1974—Continued

Re: ASSASSINATION OF PRESIDENT
JOHN FITZGERALD KENNEDY,
NOVEMBER 22, 1963, DALLAS, TEXAS

Caller	Conversation
170 (Sergeant R. SMART)	125 (Captain P. W. LAWRENCE), your location?
125 (Captain P. W. LAWRENCE)	Love Field.
18 (Sergeant R. E. DUGGER)	Transportation for 3 of us back from the Trade Mart please.
174 (Patrolman J. W. BROOKS)	I've got some people going to Parkland. I'll pick them up and bring them back.
Dispatcher (HENSLEE)	10-4. 2:38 p.m.
(End of Record #4)	
Dispatcher (HENSLEE)	Did you receive 4 (should be 174 - Patrolman J. W. BROOKS)?
174 (Patrolman J. W. BROOKS)	No, I didn't - which field is he talking about?
Dispatcher (HENSLEE)	He's talking about Love Field.
174 (Patrolman J. W. BROOKS)	Yes, sir, we're going to Parkland.
Dispatcher (HENSLEE)	10-4.
18 (Sergeant R. E. DUGGER)	I have Judge JOHNSTON here with me at Parkland. Was there just one fatality from the shooting with the President's party?

COMMISSION EXHIBIT No. 1974—Continued

Re: ASSASSINATION OF PRESIDENT
JOHN FITZGERALD KENNEDY,
NOVEMBER 22, 1963, DALLAS, TEXAS

Caller	Conversation
Dispatcher (HENSLEE)	That's the latest I had on it, 18 (Sergeant R. E. DUGGER).
Dispatcher (HENSLEE)	18 (Sergeant R. E. DUGGER), there were some more injured but I don't know who they were or how severe.
18 (Sergeant R. E. DUGGER)	I didn't read you. You know anything about an injured Secret Service Agent?
Dispatcher (HENSLEE)	No, I do not. There were some more injured but I don't know who they were.
174 (Patrolman J. W. BROOKS)	One of the Secret Service men on the field -- Elm and Houston; said that it came over his teletype that one of the Secret Service men had been killed.
Dispatcher (HENSLEE)	Well, 10-4. I don't have that information.
18 (Sergeant R. E. DUGGER)	I believe this is going to be incorrect. He's not at Parkland. Can you have someone canvass the major hospitals please?
	(Garbled)
139 (Patrolman L. H. MARSHALL)	I have a man out here that doesn't know anything about that.
Dispatcher (HENSLEE)	10-4.

COMMISSION EXHIBIT No. 1974—Continued

Re: ASSASSINATION OF PRESIDENT
JOHN FITZGERALD KENNEDY,
NOVEMBER 22, 1963, DALLAS, TEXAS

Caller	Conversation
Dispatcher (HENSLEE)	Att. all Criminal Intelligence Units - report to your office immediately. 12:41 p.m.
16 (Sergeant R. D. SHIPLEY)	Was that rifle recovered that was used in the shooting?
Dispatcher (HENSLEE)	Not that I know of. All we found were some empty hulls.
16 (Sergeant R. D. SHIPLEY)	Do you know what kind it was?
Dispatcher (HENSLEE)	I'm not sure. 300 (Captain JOHN WILL FRITZ) was down there, that's Captain FRITZ there. Can you call him?
16 (Sergeant R. D. SHIPLEY)	10-4. I'll try to find a telephone and would you check and see if 40's (Sergeant D. F. FLUCHE) at the sub-station? He may have to hold detail for the 3rd Platoon.
Dispatcher (HENSLEE)	I haven't got a phone I can call out there on.
16 (Sergeant R. D. SHIPLEY)	10-4.
Dispatcher (HENSLEE)	4 (Deputy Chief N. T. FISHER), do you know anything about a Dr. SHOWERS that is supposed to be out there?

COMMISSION EXHIBIT No. 1974—Continued

Re: ASSASSINATION OF PRESIDENT
JOHN FITZGERALD KENNEDY,
NOVEMBER 22, 1963, DALLAS, TEXAS

Caller	Conversation
4 (Deputy Chief N. T. FISHER)	No, I sure don't.
Dispatcher (HENSLEE)	Well, I've got a note here says have the escort for Dr. SHOWERS at Love Field contact the tower when he gets there.
4 (Deputy Chief N. T. FISHER)	Is it the one coming out of Galveston?
Dispatcher (HENSLEE)	Yeah, that's the one. I guess that's him.
4 (Deputy Chief N. T. FISHER)	That was 1 (Chief of Police JESSE E. CURRY) that called me, didn't have any concrete information. We're ready for him when he comes in.
Dispatcher (HENSLEE)	O.K. 10-4.
113 (Patrolman C. R. OSBORN)	Mr. SORRELS asked that you contact Station 5 (Dallas County Sheriff's Dispatcher) and notify Mr. ALLEN SWEAT - be sure that he broadcasts the information on the witness that saw a truck, to his men.
Dispatcher (HENSLEE)	10-4.
Dispatcher (HENSLEE)	9 (Inspector J. H. SAWYER), I talked to 6 (Deputy Chief RAY LUNDAY) and he advised if you need them, keep them. If you don't, let them go.
9 (Inspector J. H. SAWYER)	10-4.

Re: ASSASSINATION OF PRESIDENT
JOHN FITZGERALD KENNEDY,
NOVEMBER 22, 1963, DALLAS, TEXAS

Caller	Conversation
Dispatcher (HENSLEE)	2:45 p.m. KKB 364.
161 (Patrolman B. J. DALE)	4 (Deputy Chief N. T. FISHER), you did say awhile ago no press allowed on the field?
4 (Deputy Chief N. T. FISHER)	Right. No press.
161 (Patrolman B. J. DALE)	10-4. There's a press car just come around me. He's coming around. They're entering off Lemmon Avenue on that side.
4 (Deputy Chief N. T. FISHER)	Coming around where?
161 (Patrolman B. J. DALE)	Should up about the commercial entrance around behind Continental Hangar 1.
4 (Deputy Chief N. T. FISHER)	The plane taxiing out is the Air Force 1. If you think it's necessary you might head over that way and keep them back from that runway. (Garbled)
174 (Patrolman J. W. BROOKS)	Where's the people that want a ride?
Dispatcher (HENSLEE)	I didn't hear you.
174 (Patrolman J. W. BROOKS)	I was supposed to pick up some people here at Parkland - take them back to the Trade Mart.

Re: ASSASSINATION OF PRESIDENT
JOHN FITZGERALD KENNEDY,
NOVEMBER 22, 1963, DALLAS, TEXAS

Caller	Conversation
Dispatcher (HENSLEE)	That was Sgt. DUGGER, I believe.
18 (Sergeant R. E. DUGGER)	Go ahead to 18.
Dispatcher (HENSLEE)	174 (Patrolman J. W. BROOKS) is waiting to take you back over there, Sergeant DUGGER.
(Garbled)	
1 (Chief of Police JESSE E. CURRY)	Air Force 1 is airborne. (2:47 p.m.)
Dispatcher (HENSLEE)	1 (Chief of Police JESSE E. CURRY), do you want us to hold everyone on duty until further notice?
1 (Chief of Police JESSE E. CURRY)	Yes, Chief BATCHELOR and Chief STEVENSON will be back in the office in a minute. I'll be there shortly.
Dispatcher (HENSLEE)	10-4. 2:47 p.m.
280 (Sergeant GEORGE W. C. CAMPBELL)	He says release the men or hold them?
Dispatcher (HENSLEE)	All officers are to remain on duty until further notice, 280 (Sergeant GEORGE W. C. CAMPBELL).

COMMISSION EXHIBIT No. 1974—Continued

Re: ASSASSINATION OF PRESIDENT
JOHN FITZGERALD KENNEDY,
NOVEMBER 22, 1963, DALLAS, TEXAS

Caller	Conversation
280 (Sergeant GEORGE W. C. CAMPBELL)	We got more than we need out here at Parkland. Where you want to put them?
Dispatcher (HENSLEE)	4 (Deputy Chief N. T. FISHER), you need some men at Love Field?
4 (Deputy Chief N. T. FISHER)	No, we're in good shape.
Dispatcher (HENSLEE)	I guess just stand by and hold them. Wait, just a minute. He's out of the car, 280 (Sergeant GEORGE W. C. CAMPBELL) - just stand by and hold them. Wait, just a minute. He's out of the car, 280 - just stand by and we'll notify you.
280 (Sergeant GEORGE W. C. CAMPBELL)	10-4.
161 (Patrolman B. J. DALE)	4 (Deputy Chief N. T. FISHER), there's a man here in a car with the White House Press. You have any information?
4 (Deputy Chief N. T. FISHER)	White House press?
(Garbled)	
161 (Patrolman B. J. DALE)	Yes, he's wanting to get in the press plane.
4 (Deputy Chief N. T. FISHER)	All right, he can come on down to the air freight cargo building and walk from there.

COMMISSION EXHIBIT No. 1974—Continued

Caller	Conversation
1 (Patrolman B. J. DALE)	10-4.
0 (Patrolman D. L. CKSON)	130 (Patrolman D. L. JACKSON) to 174 (Patrolman J. W. BROOKS) - You are to remain on duty.
4 (Patrolman J. W. OOKS)	Yes sir, I heard him. I'm at Parkland.
spatcher (HENSLEE)	2:52 p.m.
spatcher (HENSLEE)	225 (Accident Prevention Bureau) call your home immediately.
4 (Patrolman R. D. LSON)	111 (Patrolman J. G. POLLARD) and I are together in the downtown area. My car is over on Swiss. We had a prisoner earlier in the day. What do you recommend we do?
spatcher (HENSLEE)	Go get your car and get in service.
(Deputy Chief N. T. SHER)	Say, if you get any inquiry, I did get those bags of Governor CONNALLY's off the airplane. Also got BILL STINSON's bags on the governor's staff. I'll get someone to carry them to Parkland.
spatcher (HENSLEE)	10-4. 2:57 p.m.
5 (Patrolman W. E. RKER)	What's the ambulance got over on West Jefferson at Dudley Hughes.
spatcher (HENSLEE)	Wait a minute. That's an injured person, 175 (Patrolman W. E. BARKER). 3:00 p.m. KKB 364.

COMMISSION EXHIBIT No. 1974—Continued

Re: ASSASSINATION OF PRESIDENT
JOHN FITZGERALD KENNEDY,
NOVEMBER 22, 1963, DALLAS, TEXAS

Caller	Conversation
161 (Patrolman B. J. DALE)	10-4.
130 (Patrolman D. L. JACKSON)	130 (Patrolman D. L. JACKSON) to 174 (Patrolman J. W. BROOKS) - You are to remain on duty.
174 (Patrolman J. W. BROOKS)	Yes sir, I heard him. I'm at Parkland.
Dispatcher (HENSLEE)	2:52 p.m.
Dispatcher (HENSLEE)	225 (Accident Prevention Bureau) call your home immediately.
224 (Patrolman R. D. WILSON)	111 (Patrolman J. G. POLLARD) and I are together in the downtown area. My car is over on Swiss. We had a prisoner earlier in the day. What do you recommend we do?
Dispatcher (HENSLEE)	Go get your car and get in service.
4 (Deputy Chief N. T. FISHER)	Say, if you get any inquiry, I did get those bags of Governor CONNALLY's off the airplane. Also got BILL STINSON's bags on the governor's staff. I'll get someone to carry them to Parkland.
Dispatcher (HENSLEE)	10-4. 2:57 p.m.
175 (Patrolman W. E. BARKER)	What's the ambulance got over on West Jefferson at Dudley Hughes.
Dispatcher (HENSLEE)	Wait a minute. That's an injured person, 175 (Patrolman W. E. BARKER). 3:00 p.m. KKB 364.

- 216 -

COMMISSION EXHIBIT No. 1974—Continued

OFFICE OF THE DIRECTOR

UNITED STATES DEPARTMENT OF JUSTICE
FEDERAL BUREAU OF INVESTIGATION

WASHINGTON 25, D.C.

June 29, 1964

BY COURIER SERVICE

Honorable J. Lee Rankin
General Counsel
The President's Commission
200 Maryland Avenue, N. E.
Washington, D. C.

Dear Mr. Rankin:

Reference is made to our letter dated June 23, 1964, advising that we were checking the Dallas newspapers from October 1, 1963, to November 22, 1963, to ascertain if there was an article in a Dallas newspaper which indicated that Mr. Richard M. Nixon planned a trip to Dallas during such period.

We have determined that the "Dallas Times-Herald" for November 21, 1963, and the "Dallas Morning News" for November 22, 1963, both carried articles indicating Mr. Nixon was in Dallas on November 21, 1963, for business reasons. Two copies of each of these articles are enclosed for the information of the Commission.

We have now reviewed all the Dallas newspapers for the period January 1, 1963, to November 22, 1963, except for the period May 15, 1963, to October 1, 1963, when Oswald was not a resident of the Dallas area. We have located no articles indicating Mr. Nixon planned a trip to Dallas during the afore-mentioned period except for the two articles mentioned above.

This concludes our inquiries in this particular matter.

Sincerely yours,

J. Edgar Hoover

Enclosures (4)

COMMISSION EXHIBIT No. 1975

FD-350 (Rev. 7-16-63)

(Mount Clipping in Space Below)

Nixon Here Before JFK on 'Business'

By BEN STEVENS
Staff Writer

Former Vice President Richard M. Nixon said Thursday President Kennedy's "non-political" trip proves Texas is a major battleground in the 1964 presidential election.

Mr. Nixon was in Dallas on a "quick business trip" as an attorney for the soft drink firm his New York law partnership represents.

The man President Kennedy narrowly defeated in the 1960 elections said there was no change in his position not to make another try for the nation's top office, but he added:

"That doesn't mean I don't expect not to do everything I possibly can to the extent my private responsibilities allow to work for the election of the party's nominees."

The former vice president said he would be "right in the thick of the fight" lending his support to the man chosen to lead the party.

While sharply criticizing President Kennedy—"His public relations are brilliant, but his performance is poor."—he urged a courteous reception for President Kennedy and Vice President Johnson Friday.

"Heckling is not an unusual occurrence in the United States," said Mr. Nixon, adding he had had it "much rougher" than U.N. Ambassador Adlai Stevenson received at his Dallas U.N. Day speech.

He called the treatment of Ambassador Stevenson "deplorable." "Overenthusiastic opponents," he said, "really harm their own cause and help their opponents by showing discourtesy."

Mr. Nixon added that "on the other hand, peaceful picketing is in the American tradition."

GOP PROSPECTS

The former vice president said Republican prospects for 1964 are increasing.

"The reason that interest in the GOP continues going up is because Kennedy's stock has been steadily going down," Mr. Nixon said.

Mr. Nixon said the President's "failure to handle Congress where he has a 2-1 majority" is one of his greatest weaknesses.

"It shows his lack of leadership much better than anything else," he said.

Mr. Nixon said he had no favorite for his party's nomination.

"It's too early to make a choice," he said. "I want to hear what they say and see how they conduct themselves during the campaign. You can tell a lot about a man by how he conducts his campaign.

PARTY SQUABBLES

The former vice president appeared concerned over squabbles between factions within the Republican party, and between candidates and potential candidates.

"My advice to them is to fight each other less and start fighting Kennedy more," Mr. Nixon said.

The former vice president arrived in Dallas Wednesday night

(Indicate page, name of newspaper, city and state.)

1 "The Dallas Times-Herald" Dallas, Texas

Date: November 21, 1963
Edition:
Author:
Editor: Felix R. McKnight
Title:

Character:
or
Classification:
Submitting Office: Dallas

☐ Being Investigated

COMMISSION EXHIBIT No. 1975—Continued

NIXON TODAY . . . JFK TOMORROW

Former Vice President Richard M. Nixon, left, found himself in Dallas on a "quick business trip" Thursday on the eve of President Kennedy's visit to the city. With Mr. Nixon is Don Kendall, president of Pepsi Cola Bottling Co. Mr. Nixon's New York law partnership represents the soft drink company.

to attend a board meeting of t Pepsi-Cola Co., which is rep sented by his New York law pa nership. He plans to leave Dall Friday morning, a few hours fore the arrival of President Ke nedy.

Mr. Nixon said that although planned to talk by telephone several Dallas Republican leade he had no plans for a form meeting with them.

Commission Exhibit No. 1975—Continued

Nixon Predicts JFK May Drop Johnson

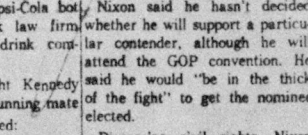

By CARL FREUND

Former Vice-President Richard M. Nixon predicted here Thursday that President Kennedy will drop Lyndon Johnson from the No. 2 spot on the Democratic ticket if a close race appears likely next year.

Nixon said Johnson is becoming a "political liability" to the Democratic party.

Nixon, who was defeated by President Kennedy in a close race in 1960, flew to Dallas Thursday for a meeting of Pepsi-Cola bottlers. His New York law firm represents the soft drink company.

Asked if he thought Kennedy would choose a new running mate next year, Nixon replied:

"President Kennedy has stated he intends to keep Lyndon as the vice-presidential nominee. The fact they are coming to Texas together, I believe, indicates the President means what he said.

"But we must remember that President Kennedy and his advisers are practical politicians. I believe that, if they think the race is a shoo-in, they will keep Lyndon. Otherwise, I think, they will choose someone who can help the Democratic ticket.

"Lyndon was chosen in 1960 because he could help the ticket in the South. Now he is becoming a political liability in the South, just as he is in the North."

Nixon appeared relaxed as he answered questions and jabbed at the Kennedy administration during an informal press coference in his Baker Hotel suite.

Nixon repeated his statements that he is not seeking the Republican presidential nomination, but sidestepped a question about whether he would accept the nomination if the GOP national convention offered it to him.

"I cannot conceive of circumstances under which that would happen," he said.

The former vice-president said Barry Goldwater is the front-runner now for the Republican nomination, but Gov. Nelson Rockefeller "is a good hand shaker" and could move up quickly.

"Rockefeller will go to New Hampshire and shake every hand there before its residents vote," Nixon said. "If Goldwater doesn't go there and shake some hands, he could lose some of his lead."

Nixon said he sees little chance of a Goldwater-Rockefeller convention deadlock which would throw the nomination to someone who isn't seeking it.

Nixon said he hasn't decided whether he will support a particular contender, although he will attend the GOP convention. He said he would "be in the thick of the fight" to get the nominee elected.

Discussing civil rights, Nixon said the Kennedy administration must share the blame for racial demonstrations.

"Kennedy promised more than he could deliver," Nixon said. "I don't think we should try to outpromise the Democrats. It would be a serious mistake."

Nixon said he would not go as far as Gov. Rockefeller in the civil rights field. On the other hand, Nixon continued, he could not agree with views attributed to Goldwater that the federal governmetnt should leave civil rights to the states.

Nixon, who will leave Love Field two hours before President Kennedy arrives, also said:

1. The two-party system has now become a reality in the South and Republicans appear likely to make more gains.

2. The reputation of the U.S. Senate is at stake in the investigation of Bobby Baker, former secretary to the Democratic majority.

3. The Republican nominee should launch an all-out attack on the administration's record in handling foreign relations and unemployment, but should avoid a "personality contest" with Kennedy.

—Dallas News Staff Photo by Tom Dillard

Richard Nixon . . . He sees Barry ahead in GOP, LBJ out as No. 2 Demo.

DALLAS MORNING NEWS
Early City Edition
Sec. 4 Page 1
Nov. 22, 1963

Commission Exhibit No. 1975—Continued